The New Sabin

Cumulative Index to Volumes I - X

Entries 1-25946

The New Sabin;

Books Described by Joseph Sabin and His

Successors, Now Described Again on the

Basis of Examination of Originals,

and Fully Indexed by Title, Subject,

Joint Authors, and Institutions and Agencies

by

Lawrence S. Thompson

Cumulative Index to Volumes I - X

Entries 1-25946

The Whitston Publishing Company
Troy, New York
1986

Library of Congress Catalog Number 73-85960

ISBN 0-87875-330-3

Printed in the United States of America

IN MEMORIAM

Lawrence Sidney Thompson, the redoubtable scholar, collector, and bibliographer who conceived and carried out these *ten* volumes of *The New Sabin*, died on 19 April 1986 at Lexington, Kentucky. It will remain for other hands to complete the task which he began with the publication of the first volume in 1974.

The New Sabin, like the old, is bold and formidable in both its scope and scale. Yet it represents but one among many gargantuan projects which Prof. Thompson addressed over some forty years as an active researcher and interpreter of literary culture. *The New Sabin* presages a massive bibliographical record with full texts reproduced separately in microform, and it comprises the kind of project which might be the major undertaking of a large association or institution. To Dr. Thompson it was almost a diversion, for he had similarly approached reproducing in microform the great bibliography of Western Americana, *The Plains and the Rockies*, as well as Thomas D. Clark's *Travels in the Old South*. He prepared, moreover, microform editions of French Revolutionary pamphlets, Black literature, and a large Kentucky culture series. There were other comprehensive series, as well. Dr. Thompson thought in architectonic terms and savored a project all the more for its thoroughness.

Although he was, as *The New Sabin* testifies, a dedicated bibliographer, his interests were manifold. Following academic preparation at universities in Chapel Hill, Chicago, Ann Arbor, and Uppsala, he served as an FBI agent in South America during World War II. From 1948 to 1963 he was Director of Libraries and thereafter Professor of Classical Languages and Literature at the University of Kentucky. He was a linguist, a folklorist, an editor, a publisher, a reviewer. He stood, on the one hand, a regionalist with a love for the American South and its culture; on the other, a cosmopolitan as much at ease in Uppsala, Ankara, Lisbon, Montreal or Havana as in his native North Carolina. The eminent bibliographer Ralph Shaw (half of the famed "Shaw and Shoemaker") observed wittily:

There once was a fellow named Larry,
Whose knowledge of all things was scarey,
He speaks Latin and Greek
—and Arabic this week—
And he'll do it all night, so be wary.

Though Shaw here celebrates the agile linguist, it was the remarkable versatility in "all things" that so clearly set Lawrence
Thompson apart in the academic world. He explored the
folklore of brooms and tobacco, of sparrows and buzzards, and of
hogs in the Ohio Valley. He spoke about and published essays
on printing history and on modern fine printing as well as on
the history of book binding. He was drawn to Tibetan xylographs
and wrote on such topics as anthropodermic bibliopegy and
bibliokleptomania. Not only an author of articles and mono-
graphs, he served as book review editor for the *Papers of the
Bibliographical Society of America* and *The American Book
Collector*; he was associate editor of *Imprimatur* and of *Kentucky
Folklore Record*; he was also the publisher of *American Notes &
Queries*, of *Germanic Notes*, and of *Appalachian Notes*. In
addition, he conducted for many years the Southern and the Mid-
western Books Competitions.

    Not at all a reclusive scholar, Dr. Thompson was a social
and gregarious man. He regularly attended the annual New
York meetings of the Bibliographical Society of America. He was
a member of the Grolier Club of the City of New York, having
been proposed by Frederic W. Goudy. (He once brought the
Grolier Club to Lexington where member Sir Frank Francis,
Director of the British Museum, was made a Kentucky Colonel.)
He was a member also of the Caxton Club, the Rowfant Club, the
Pittsburgh Bibliophiles, The Filson Club, the Private Libraries
Association, the Kentucky Civil War Round Table, the Society of
the Cincinnati, and other organizations civic, fraternal, and
bibliographical. He was a corresponding member of the
Historical Committee of the Boersenverein des Deutschen
Buchhandels in Frankfurt am Main, a Life Governor of the
Antiquarian and Numismatic Society of Montreal, and was
affiliated with the Sociedad de Bibliofilos de Argentina (Buenos
Aires) and the Gutenberg-Gesellschaft (Mainz). His activities
were many, and included a year as president of the Rare Book
and Manuscript Section of the Association of College and Research Libraries.

    An ardent collector, Dr. Thompson assembled an exten-
sive library in bibliography and Kentuckiana. He also made
significant gifts of materials to Auburn University, Berea
College, and to his *alma mater*, the University of North
Carolina. At the University of Kentucky he established the

library's Algernon Dickson Thompson Fund in memory of his wife, who died in 1962, and he eagerly pursued materials to add to the collections.

Lawrence Thompson was a gifted and learned man whose love for scholarship and libaries was paramount. Among many constructive achievements are his contributions to building the research collections at the University of Kentucky, his published essays, his microform publishing projects, and his extensive bibliographies. *The New Sabin*, even as a fragment, is a tribute to the energy and vision of a man dedicated to enhancing the research opportunities of his colleagues and his heirs in the world of learning.

James D. Birchfield

ABC do espiritismo, 19814
Aa, Pieter van der, 1659-1733, 2
Aabye, Karen, 2485
Aanteekeningen op eene reis door de Vereinigde
   Staten van Nord Amerika en Canada, 6844
Aaron (slave), 24861
Ab-sa-ra-ka, home of the Crows, 16153
Aba, B., pseud., 4915
Abad, Diego José, 1727-1779, 5803-5805
Abad, José Ramón, 17946
Aballi, Angel Arturo, 17947
Abalos, Jorge W., 17948
Abarca y Valda, José Ignacio de, 5807
Abarca y Valda, José Mariano de, b.1720,
   5806, 5807
Abascal, Valentin, 5808
The abasement of the Northmores, 10016
Abbad y Lasierra, Iñigo, 1745-1813, 3
Abbay, Thomas, 5204
The abbaye des vigerons, 9131
L'abbé, 11408
Abbeville, Claude d', fl. 1614, 5809
Abbey, James, 2486
The abbey garden, 10919
Abbot, Abiel, 1765-1859, 6, 7
Abbot, Abiel, 1770-1828, 4, 5, 8, 5810
Abbot, Allen O., 2487
Abbot, Ephraim, 1779-1870, 6
Abbot, Gordham Dummer, 17949
Abbot, Henry Larcom, 1831-1927, 22600
Abbot, Jacob, 1803-1879, 9, 10
Abbot, John, 1750-1840?, 5202
Abbot, Willis John, 1863-1934, 5811
Abbot family (Arthur Abbot, of Ipswich,
   Mass., d.167-), 6; (George Abbot, of
   Andover, Mass., d.1681), 6; (George Abbot,
   of Norwalk, Conn., d.1689?), 6; (George
   Abbot, of Rowley, Mass., d.1647), 6;
   (Robert Abbot, of Branford, Conn., d.
   1658), 6; (Thomas Abbot, of Rowley,
   Mass. d.1695), 6
Abbott, Abijah, 23567
Abbott, Carlisle Stewart, b.1828, 15804
Abbott, John Stevens Cabot, 1805-1877, 11-14,
   15805
Abbott, Joseph Carter, 1825-1882, 2439
Abbott, Lyman, 1835-1922, 8425
Abbott, Simon C., 1826-1858, 15
Abbring, Hermanus Johannes, 1787-1874, 16
Abby Forbes, 9675
Abdy, Edward Strutt, 1791-1846, 17, 18
Abeille, J., 19
Abel, Annie Heloise, 1873-, 23829
Aben, Athar J., 17950
Abenteuer in Mexiko, 6614
Abercrombie, James, 1758-1841, 20

Abernethy, George, 15806
Abernethy, Thomas Perkins, 13514, 14725
Abert, James William, 2488, 5533
Abert, John James, 1788-1863, 21
Abingdon, Willoughby Bertie, 4th earl of,
   1740-1799, 22
Abingdon, Willoughby Bertle, 4th earl of,
   1740-1799. Thoughts on Mr. Burke's Letter
   to the sheriffs of Bristol, 13389
Abington, Mass., Geneal., 22509; Hist.,
   12816, 22509
Abipones, 6602
Abismos humanos, 21720
Abnaki Indians, 972, 12657; Fiction, 9986;
   Missions, 1288, 1289, 1290
Abner, Daryl, 14866
Abney, A. H., 15807
Abo, N. M., 2915
Aboal Amaro, José Alberto, 17951
A abolição (esboção histórico) 1831-1888,
   24328
La abolición de la esclavitud en las
   Antillas españolas, 24747
La abolición de la esclavitud en países
   de colonización europea, 23852
La abolición de la esclavitud y el proyecto
   del señor Moret, 23830
Abolition a sedition, 23832
Abolition, and the relation of races, 977
The abolition conspiracy to destroy the
   union, 23833
Abolition fanaticism in New York, 24310
Abolition is national death, 23834
Abolition Society of Paint Valley, 3131,
   3132
Abolitionism exposed, corrected, 23835
An abolitionist, 24396
L'Abolitioniste français, 23836
Abolitionists, 1043, 23835, 24005, 24006,
   24016, 24108, 24111, 24148, 24167,
   24177, 24422, 24593, 24637, 24680,
   24711, 24918, 24992, 24993, 25000,
   25001, 25034, 25105, 25265, 25332,
   25416, 25523, 25590, 25701, 25808,
   25874
Aborigines' Protection Society, London,
   5182, 5813
Abortion, Legal aspects, 14676
Abouhamad H., Jeannette, 17952, 17953
Abrahall, Chandos Hoskyns, 23
Abraham Lincoln, 5640, 5814
Abraham Lincoln Association, Springfield,
   Ill., 5815, 5816, 5821
Abraham Lincoln Book Shop, Chicago, 6586,
   6667
Abraham Lincoln Centre and All Souls Church,

Chicago, 5817
Abraham Lincoln Foundation, New York, 5818
Abraham Lincoln, his life in Illinois, 6004
Abraham Lincoln in Great Britain, 7073
Abraham Lincoln Memorial.Garden, Springfield,
  Ill., 5819
Abraham Lincoln Memorial Highway Association,
  5820
Abraham Lincoln quarterly, 5821
Abraham Lincoln sees Peoria, 6653
Abraham Lincoln traveled this way, 3907
Abraham Lincoln University, 5818, 5822
Abraham Lincoln's character, 11544
Abraham Lincoln's last case in Chicago, 5823
Abraham Page, esq., 9907
Abrahams, Roger D., 17954, 17955, 17956
Abrego, Leopoldo, 17957
Abreu, Adilson Avansi, 17958
Abreu, Casimiro de, 17959
Abreu, Cid T., 17960
Abreu, Florencio de, 17961
Abreu, Jayme, 17962
Abreu, Modesto de, 17963
Abreu, Nelson de, 17964
Abreu, Oldemar Cardim, 17965
Abreu de Galindo, Juan de, 24
Abreu Gómez, Ermilo, 17966, 17967
The absent Lord of Rochefort, 5616
Abusada-Salah, Roberto, 17968
El abuso del derecho como limitación al
  ejercicio de los derechos subjetivos, 20085
O abutre e outras estórias, 19693
Acacia, 2563
Acacia negra, Rio Grande do Sul, 18919
Academia Brasileira de Letras, Rio de
  Janeiro, 20630
Academia Campinense de Letras, 17969
Academia Colombiana, Bogotá, 20405
Academia Colombiana de Historia, 17970
Academia Costarricense de la Historia, 17971
Academia de Ciencias de Cuba. Instituto de
  Geología, 17972-3, 4
Academia de Ciencias de Cuba. Instituto de
  Suelos, 17975
Academia de la Historia, Madrid, 7657
Academia Española, 17976
Academia Nacional de Agronomía y Veterinaria,
  Buenos Aires, Actas, 18922
Academia Nacional de Ciencias, 20470
Academia Nacional de la Historia, Buenos
  Aires, 17977
Academia Nacional de la Historia, Caracas,
  6956, 17978, 17979, 17980, 17981, 17982,
  19783, 17984, 17985, 17986, 17987, 17988,
  19289, 19621, 19635
Academia Nacional de San Carlos, México, 7401,
  17989
Academia Paulista de Letras, Biblioteca,
  19529
Academia Pernambucana de Letras, Recife,
  19111
Academia Real das sciencias, Lisbon,
  11525
Academia Venezolana de la Lengua, Colección
  clásicos venezolanos, 19110
Académie d'agriculture de France, Paris,
  11983
Academy of Natural Sciences, Philadelphia,
  23426, 23427
Academy of Natural Sciences of Philadelphia.
  Conchological section, 259
Acadia, 6487, 6575, 6951, 7268, 7865,
  8045, 8984; see also Nova Scotia
Acadian geology, 22053
Acadians, 3597, 7865, 8045
L'Acadie, 147
Acapulco, los lunes, 19757
Acarina, 20667
Acasubi, Hilario, 1807-1875, 18931
Acasuso, Rubén, 17990
La accesión en el derecho agrario, 20053
Accession (law), Mexico, 20053
Accidents, Colombia, 20345
Accioli, Roberto, 17991
Accioly, Marcus, 17992
Acción del estado en la agricultura nacional
  hasta el año 1959, 20518
La acción escrita, 19815
Acción para el desarrollo, Lima, 17993
Acción Popular (Peru). Secretaría Nacional
  de Propaganda, 17994
Accolon of Gaul, 2948
Acedo, Pedro Perdomo, 17995
Acereto, Albino, 5825
Acevedo, Edberto Oscar, 17996, 17997
Acevedo Escobedo, Antonio, 1909-, ed., 6273
Achates, pseud., 25278
Achenbach, Hermann, 27
Achenwall, Gottfried, 1719-1772, 28
Achtung, ¡Peligro! 17990
Achury Valenzuela, Darío, 17998, 19941
El ácido sórbico y su aplicación en
  enología, 18457
Acioli, J., 17999
Ackermann, Fritz, 18000
Ackley, Richard Thomas, 1832-1881, 18509
The Acme Haversack's Lincoln memoranda, 5826
Acme publishing co., Chicago, pub., 7760
Acosta, Aledia de, 19746
Acosta, Cecilio, 18001
Acosta, Joaquín, 1799-1852, 29
Acosta, José de, 1539(ca)-1600, 5827

Acosta, Ricardo, 18002
Acosta Hermoso, Eduardo, 18003
Acosta Hoyos, Luis Eduardo, 18004, 18005
Acosta Saignes, Miguel, 18006-18009
Acosta y Lara, Eduardo F., 18010
Acqua, Amadeo dell', 18001
Acquaviva, Edelmira Duarte de, 18012-18014
The acquisition of Oregon Territory, 17568
Acre, Brazil, Descr. & trav., 19928;
    Econ. cond., 18744, 20554
Acrelius, Israel, 1714-1800, 30
Acrostics, 6093
An act to block up the harbour of Boston!
    21754
Acta amazonica, 18015
Acta in Commitijs Provincialibus Angelo-
    politanae Sancti Michaelis, 5828
Acta Provincialis, S. Michaelis Archãg and
    SS. Angelorum Provinciae Ordinis
    Praedicatorum, 5829
Actaeon, 9314
Actas y antecedentes, 20415
Actinides, 19065, 20446-20449
L'actio de peculio annalis contro gli eredi,
    25559
Actions and defenses (Roman law), 25559
Active service, 9209, 24100
Acton, Me., Hist., 2360
Actors, Correspondence, reminiscencss, etc.,
    5211, 5212, 5560, 11251, 16615
The actress of Padua, 10815
The acts of Dr. Bray's visitation, 1448
Acts of the anti-slavery apostles, 25273
Actualizacion del léxico español, 18255
Acuerdo de Cartagena, 20283
Acuña B., Olda María, 18016
Acuña, Cristóbal de, b.1597, 31
Acuña de Figueroa, Francisco Esteban, 18017
Acuña Galé, Julián, 18018
Adair, James, trader with the Indians, 32
Adair, John, 1759-1840, 13666
Adair Co.Ky., Churches, 13899
Adalaska, 1248
Adam, Félix, 18019
Adam, Floyd, 10163
Adam, George, 2700, 15810
Adam, Paul Auguste Marie, 1862-1920, 2489
Adam, William, b.1799, 33
Adam family (John Adam, 1714-1802), 33
Adam Johnstone's son, 9219
Adam W. Snyder and his period in Illinois
    history, 5225
Adami, João Spadari, 18020
Adamo y Arriaga, José, d.1698, 5830
Adams, Abigail (Smith) 1744-1818, 62
Adams, Alice Dana, 1864-, 23837

Adams, Amos, 1728-1775, 34, 35
Adams, Charles Baker, 1814-1853, 36, 37,
    12354
Adams, Charles Francis, 1807-1886, 38, 39,
    40, 41, 42, 62, 63
Adams, Charles Francis, 1835-1915, 5831
Adams, Daniel, 1773-1864, 43, 23420
Adams, David Phineas, ed., 23447
Adams, Eliphalet, 1677-1753, 44
Adams, Mrs. Emma Hildreth, 15811
Adams, Ephraim, 1818-, 15812
Adams, Ephraim D., 15813
Adams, Ephraim Douglass, 1865- ed., 16630
Adams, Francis Colburn, 45, 46, 47, 48
Adams, George Everett, 1840-, 5832, 5833
Adams, George Washington, d.1829, 49, 2221
Adams, Hannah, 1755-1831, 50, 51, 52, 53, 54
Adams, Herbert Baxter, 1850-1901, 2490
Adams, Horace, 5834
Adams, James Capen, 2491, 3888
Adams, James Taylor, 1892-, 15641
Adams, Joachim, tr., 17345
Adams, John, 1704-1740, 55
Adams, John, pres. U.S., 1735-1826, 56, 57,
    58, 59, 60, 61, 62, 63, 1808, 6393,
    11480, 12179, 12197, 12207, 12601,
    13615, 21944, 21986, 21997, 22736, 23820
Adams, John, 1750?-1814, 64
Adams, John, 1760?-1829, 10698
Adams, John Greenleaf, 1810-1887, 65
Adams, John Gregory Bishop, 1841-1900, 2492
Adams, John Merriman, 1834-, 5835
Adams, John Quincy, pres. U.S., 1767-1848,
    66, 67, 68, 69, 70, 71, 72, 73, 74, 75,
    76, 77, 78, 79, 80, 81, 12115, 12401,
    12527, 15814, 22372, 23516, 23838, 25574
Adams, Oscar Fay, 10283
Adams, Owen M., 14968
Adams, Randolph Greenfield, 1892-, 5836,
    13515
Adams, Richard Newbold, 18021-18024
Adams, Robert, sailor, 23839
Adams, Samuel, 1722-1803, 60, 11385
Adams, Seth, dependant, 1912
Adams, W.L., 5837
Adams, William Bridges, 1797-1872, 25097
Adams, William Edwin, 1832-, 2494
Adams, William Henry Davenport, 1828-1891,
    tr., 4935
Adams, William L., 15815, 15816
Adams, Zabdiel, 1739-1801, 2101
Adams Co., Idaho, Hist., 16705
Adams Co., Pa., Hist., Fiction, 8715
Adams family (Henry Adams, d.1646), 6836;
    (Stephen Olney Adams), 1620-1718), 5835;
    (William Adams, of Ipswich, Mass., d.1661),

418
Adamson, Archibald R., 1839-, 15817
Adamson, Augustus Pitt, 1844-, 2494
Adamson, John, 1787-1855, 82
Adamson, Sydney, illustr., 13824
Adamson, Thomas, 83
Adán ciego, 19902
Adán y Arriaga, José, see Adamo y Arriaga, José
Adato Green, Victoria, 18025
The adder's den, 2149
Addey, Markinfield, 84, 85
Addition, Lucia H. Faxon, 15818
Addoms, Jonas Smith, fl.1792, 86
Addums, Moses, pseud. of George William Bagby, 2590, 2591
Adeler, Max, pseud., 9006
Adelman, David C., 5840
Adelung, Friedrich von, 1768-1843, 97
Adelung, Johann Christoph, 1732-1806, 97, 1589
Adem, J., 18026
Ades, Michael L., 15802, 15803
Adet, Pierre-Auguste, 1763-1834, 5841, 6774
Adet, Walter, 18027
Adger, John Bailey, 1810-1899, 98
Los adioses, 20086
The Adirondack; or Life in the woods, 22380
Adirondack iron and steel company, New York, 99
Adirondack mountains, 10398, 12630, 22380;
    Descr. & trav., 22381
Adlam, Samuel, 1798-1880, 100
Adlard, George, 101
Adler, John Hans, 18028
Administração sindical, 19866
La administración de los programas de desarrollo de la comunidad en América Latina, 20029
La administración financiera del Estado, 18337
Administration dissected, 102
The administration of John Adams, 23820
Administrative and political divisions, California, 16126
Administrative law, Brazil, 19349; Cambodia, 23803; Chile, 19853; France, 952; Venezuela, 19480
Administrative procedure, Mexico, 19888
The administratrix, 9286
Admiralty, 9918
Adney, Edwin Tappan, 1868-1950, 15819
Adolescence, 18012, 19776
Adolescencia e identidad, 18012
Os adolescentes de hoje e de amanha, 18617
Adolphus, John, 1768-1845, 103
Adonais, Isa, 19394, 18029
Adorno Benitez, Felix, 18030
Adrain, Garnett Bowditch, 1816-1878, 23848
Adrian, 10009
Adrift in Dixie, 3553

Adrift on an ice-pan, 6899
Adrift with a vengeance, 9172
Adsit, Mrs. C.D., 15820
Adsonville, 8481
Adult education, Brazil, 19368, 19369; Latin America, 19368
Adultery, 23767
Advance and retreat, 3922
Advance in the Antilles, 6907
Advancing education in Kentucky, 14553
Adventure and adventurers, 1450, 2616, 2987, 3786, 3890, 9007, 12562
The adventure of the missing briefs, 6006
An adventure on a frozen lake, 9972
The adventurer, 8669
The adventurer of the northern wilds, 9432
Adventures amidst the equatorial forests and rivers of South America, 5315
Adventures in California and Nicaragua, 17885; Mexico and the Rocky Mountains, 5053; rebeldom, 3387; search of a living in Spanish America, 8289; Texas, 4334
Adventures in the Apache country, 2837; Comanche country, 5651, 1115; far west, 2680, 2683, 15904; gold region, 10501; path of empire, 17699; wilderness, 10398; wilds of the U.S. and British America provinces, 4215, 7240
Adventures of a consul abroad, 7523
The adventures of a forty-niner, 16961; French captain, 3618; Georgian, 11031; New Bedford boy on sea and land, 12562; night, 9294; wanderer, 10503; widow, 9499
Adventures of Alf. Wilson, 5737
The adventures of an enthusiast, 10330
The adventures of Audubon, 15129; Big-Foot Wallace, 3330
Adventures of Bill Longley, 17050; Col. Gracchus Vanderbomb, 4109
The adventures of Daniel Boone, 14289
Adventures of Elder Triptolemus Tub, 10659
The adventures of Harry Franco, 8845; Hector Wigler, 11222; Isaac P. Rose, 17136; James Sharan, 5128; Miles Wallingford, 9127; my cousin Smooth, 8456
Adventures of pioneer children, 13889
The adventures of Search for Life, 10313; Sir Lyon Bouse, 11144
Adventures of the first settlers on the Oregon or Columbia river, 5017
The adventures of three Southerns, 2924; Uncle Sam, 9507
Adventures on the Columbia River, 16285; Mosquito shore, 8008, 13496

4

Adventures with Indians and game, 15838
Adversity, 14094
Advice and guide to emigrants, 4643
Advice of a father to a son engaging in the
  work of the Evangelical ministry, 22181
An advice to the churches of the faithful,
  23495
Advice to the officers of the British army,
  12460
Aenolamia Fennah, 20213
Aenone, 10142
Aengemerckte voorvallen op de vredens
  articulen met Portugael, 104
Aeronautics, Colombia, 19201; Commercial,
  19862; Commercial, Kentucky, 14549;
  Flights, 7362; History, Kentucky, 14943;
  Private, Laws and regulations, Chile,
  19235
Afoot and alone; a walk from sea to sea by
  the southern route, 23506
The affair at King's Mountain, 7th October,
  1780, 13997
Affaires de l'Angleterre et de l'Amérique,
  105
The affectionate address of women of
  Great Britain, 25630
Affleck, I.D., ed., 17561
Afinidades entre el Paraguay y la Banda
  Oriental en 1811, 19783
Afalo, Frederick George, 1870-1918, 2495
Afloat and ashore, 9127
Afoot and alone, 4843
Africa, 24563; Colonization, Negroes,
  12783; Commerce, Portugal, 25031;
  Descr. & trav., 4853, 5073, 13335,
  17854, 23964, 24126; Disc. & explor.,
  1081; Entomology, 4684; Hist., 11589,
  18983; native races, 24563; Politics,
  25710; North, Descr. & trav., 25394;
  South, Descr. & trav., 8106; West, 24565;
  West, Descr. & trav., 12147, 22434, 24565;
  West, Maps, 25943
Africa and the American flag, 12147
Africa, biografía del colonialismo, 18983
Africa: slave or free?, 24563
Africa's redemption, 24434
African colonization society, 24537
African colonization unveiled, 5039
The African in America, 25891
The African servant; an authentic narrative,
  25388
African servitude, 106
African slave trade in Jamaica, and comparative
  treatment of slaves, 25494
African slavery in America, 24647
African society, Boston, 24266

The African squadron, 2265
The Afro-American press and its editors,
  25220
Afro-Asia, 18698
Afro-Brazilian culture, 19874
Afro-Cuban poetry, 24969
Afrograptidae - Brazil, 19779
After Dinner Club, Moline, Ill., 5842, 5843
After freedom, 4839
After half-century, Big Red still races in
  realm of legend, 15054
After his kind, 10472
After many days, 5417
After the storm, 5174
After the war, 4927
Aftermath, 8511
Against human nature, 10539
Against the world, 11058
Agassiz, George Russell, 1862-, ed., 4321
Agassiz, Louis, 1807-1873, 107, 108, 109,
  1404
Agatha Webb, 10661
Agave, Therapeutic use, 726
The Age, a southern monthly eclectic
  magazine, 23849
Age and youth, 13565
Agee, George W., 15821
Agency (law), Austria, 25633
Agency (Roman law) 25457, 25633, 25851
Agency for International Development.
  Regional Technical Aids Center, 18031
Agente de ligação, 18225
Ager, Carolus, jt. author, 9509
Aggavvam in America, 23744
Aging, Kentucky, 15722, 15789
Aging, Area agency handbook on, 13608
Aging patterns in a rural and an urban
  area of Kentucky, 15789
The agitation of slavery, 23850
Agli State Uniti, il pericolo americano,
  4385
Agnes, 8555, 10525
Agnes Farriday, 9011
Agnes Goodmaid, 10713
Agnes Hilton, 9881
Agnes Stanhope, 10607
Agnes Wentworth, 10470
Agnew, J.L., joint author, 24810
Agnew, John Holmes, 1804-1865, 110
The agnostic, 4792
Agonía y muerte del Caravaggio, 18002
Agor, Weston H., 18032
Agostini, Victor, 18033
Agostino, María Marta d', 19025, 19026
Agrarian law, Colombia, 20322
Agrarian reform and politics, 20079

Agrarianism, 24596
Agrarno-kresti'īanskiĭ vopros na sovremennom
  etape natsional'no-osvobodietel'nogo
  dvizheniīa v stranakh Azii, 18077
Agraz García de Alba, Gabriel, 18034
Agreda y Sánchez, José María de, 1837-1916,
  tr., 6835
Agresti, Antonio, 1866-1927, 5844
Agricola, 3370, 23296
Agricultura em Brasilia, 19419
Agricultura en el desierto, 19142
A agricultura subdesenvolvida, 18035
Agricultural chemistry, 13234, 13307,
  15145
Agricultural colonies, Chile, 20127
Agricultural colonies, Colombia, Putumayo
  (Comisaria), 20306
Agricultural colonies, Mexico, 18965
Agricultural courts and procedure, Mexico,
  18855
Agricultural credit, Bolivia, 18649
Agricultural credit, Mexico, 18106
Agricultural editors association, 7584
Agricultural education, Mexico, 19644
Agricultural engineering, Bibl., 19145
Agricultural exhibitions, Kentucky, 14738
Agricultural extension work, Colombia, 19835
Agricultural laborers, Bolivia, 18333;
  Brazil, 19621; Costa Rica, 20461; Mexico,
  19148, 20535; Uruguay, 20050
Agricultural laws and legislation, 18640;
  Mexico, 20053
Agricultural prices, Venezuela, 19113
Agricultural production, Brazil, 19310
Agricultural productivity in Colombia, 18618
Agricultural society of St. John's Collecton,
  S.C., 25469
Agricultural tour in the United States and
  Upper Canada, 2506
Agriculture, 1657, 4704, 21805
Agriculture, Addresses, essays, lectures,
  1253, 12296, 12962, 13124, 13265, 22711,
  22832, 23269, 23116, 23179
Agriculture, Argentine Republic, 18424,
  18427, 18792, 18793, 18794; Bahama
  Islands, 19522; Barbados, 20214;
  Belgium, 12735; Bermuda, 19522;
  Bibliography, Catálogo, 18451; Bolivia,
  Bibliography, 19788; Brazil, 18603, 18777,
  18979, 19399, 19408, 19416, 19419,
  19453, 19682; Brazil, Statistics, 19425;
  Brazil, Northeastern, 18788; British
  Columbia, 6177; British Honduras, 19494,
  19522; California, 16107; Canada, 2506,
  4078, 5271, 12552, Chile, 10010, 00116,
  20117, Cochabamba, Bolivia, 19126;

Colombia, 18618, 18619, 18988, 20269,
  20274, 20282, 20288, 20337; Colombia,
  Statistics, 20271; Cuba, 613; Dictionaries,
  11957, 13234; Economic aspects, 17788;
  Dominican Republic, 19523; Economic
  aspects, 19361, 19856, 19873, 20116;
  Economic aspects, Argentine Republic,
  Collections, 18754; Economic aspects,
  Bibliography, 18267; Economic aspects,
  Brazil, 19310, 19866; Economic aspects,
  Brazil, Addresses, essays, lectures, 18035;
  Economic aspects, Chile, 20518; Economic
  aspects, Chile, Bibliography, 18265;
  Economic aspects, Colombia, 18618, 20308,
  20322; Economic aspects, Colombia, Boyaca
  (Dept.), 19971; Economic aspects, Colombia,
  Cesar, 20336; Economic aspects, Colombia,
  Valle de Cauca, 20491; Economic aspects,
  Costa Rica, 18575, 20461; Economic aspects,
  Cuba, 20695; Economic aspects, Mexico,
  18106, 19644, 20535; Economic aspects
  Mexico, Bibliography, 18266; Economic
  aspects, Mexico, Yucatan, 20083;
  Economic aspects, Peru, 18545; Economic
  aspects, Peru, Bibliography, 20704;
  Economic aspects, El Salvador, 20642;
  Economic aspects, Societies, 20308;
  Economic aspects, Venezuela, 20429;
  Ecuador, 18899; England, 12735; France,
  12735; French Guiana, 1202, 1831; Georgia,
  13307; Greece, Modern, 19142; Guatemala,
  18594; Guatemala, Bibliography, 18753;
  Guianas, 19522; Handbooks, manuals, etc.,
  23682; Honduras, 20641; Israel, 19142;
  Jamaica, 1035, 23957; Kentucky, 14433, 14511,
  14723, 15307; Kentucky, Sources, 14023;
  Law, Colombia, 20327; Laws and regulations,
  20337; Louisiana, 3231; Maryland, 23386;
  Massachusetts, 1538, 23289; Mexico, 7262,
  19847; Mexico, Yucatan, 20083; Missouri,
  4698; Nebraska, 17259; New Brunswick, 13274;
  North America, 5049; North Carolina, 5040;
  North Dakota, 17531; Oruro, Bolivia, 19127;
  Pennsylvania, 23348; Period., Indexes,
  19788; Peru, 20028; Santa Catarina, Brazil,
  19420, 19469; Santa Cruz, Bolivia, 19128;
  São Thomé e Principe, 25935; Social aspects,
  20043; Societies, 1538; Societies,
  Dominican Republic, 18241; South Carolina,
  13265, 23643; Southern states, 11368;
  Study and teaching, 15274; Study and
  teaching, Kentucky, 14660, 15392;
  Tripolitania, 19142; Tropics, 20096,
  11368; U.S., 2506, 3039, 4078, 17090,
  22291, 23753, 23754; Venezuela, 20093;
  Virginia, 21825; The West, 16729; West

6

Indies, 576, 1080
Agriculture, Cooperative, 18603, 18973, 20289;
  Colombia, 19835; Laws and regulations,
  Brazil, 19356; Panama, 19087; Uruguay,
  18675
Agriculture, Prehistoric, Utah, 17636
Agriculture and state, Bolivia, 18649; Chile,
  20518; Colombia, 18640, 20287, 20322;
  Spanish America, 19027
Agriculture and technology, Brazil, 19315
Agriculture and trade of El Salvador, 20640
A agro-industria do caju no Nordeste, 18779
Aguado, Pedro de, 18036
Aguado-Andreut, Salvador, 18037
Aguas termales de Cartago, Costa Rica, 5845
Aguayo, Carlos Guillermo, 18038
Agudo Freites, Raúl, 18039
El aguila y la serpiente, 19967
Agüero, Pedro de, 1821-, 111
Aguero y Sota, Baltasar de, 5846
Aguiar, Luis Crestovão Dias de, 18040
Aguilar, Antonio, 18041
Aguilar, Carlos H., 18042
Aguilar, Esperanza, 18043
Aguilar, Federico Cornelio, 1834-1887, 5847
Aguilar, Luis A., 18044
Aguilar, Santiago, 18045
Aguilar Arevalo, Roberto, 1901-1966, 15822
Aguilar Arroyo, Mario Roberto, 18046
Aguilar Barroso, Francisco, 18047
Aguilar Bulgrelli, Oscar, 18048
Aguilar Chavez, M., 18049
Aguilar Gorrondona, José Luis, 18050, 18051
Aguilar Merlo, Carlos de, 18052
Aguilar Villa, Mario Alberto, 18053
Aguilera, Francisco, 18054
Aguilera, Francisco Vicente, 1821-1877,
  23851
Aguilera, Julio Fausto, 18055
Aguilera Ripoll, Ana Margarita, 18051
Aguinsky de Iribarne, Esther, 18057
Aguirre, Angel M., 18058
Aguirre, J. M., 18059, 18060
Aguirre, José M., 5848
Aguirre, Juan Francisco, d.1811, 5849
Aguirre, Manuel J., 18061
Aguirre, Nataniel, 18062
Aguirre Beltran,Gonzalo, 18063, 18064
Aguirre Gamio, Hernando, 18065
Aguirre Godoy, Mario, 18066, 18067
Aguirre Prieto, Javier, 18068
Agulla, Juan Carlos, 18069, 20473
Agustini, Delmira, 18070, 18071
Ahandagbe, André, 18363
Ahumada, Juan Antonio, 18072
Ahumada, B. J., 18073

Ahumada y Centurión, José de, 23852
Ahumada y Villalón, Agustín de, marqués de
  las Amarillas, viceroy of Mexico, d.1760,
  5807; Poetry, 5806
Ai; a social vision, 9324
The aid-de-camp, 4329
Aiken, Charles S., comp., 15823
Aiken, John, 112
Aiken, Peter Freeland, 113
Aiken, Solomon, 1758-1833, 114
Aikin, John, 1747-1822, 115
Aikman, William, 1824-1909, 116, 117
Aimard, Gustave, 1818-1883, 2496, 15824-
  15827
Aimée's marriage, 9190
Aimes, Hubert Hillary Suffern, 23853, 23854
Ainslie, Hew, 1792-1878, 2497, 13517
Ainsworth, Danforth Hurlburt, 1828-, 15828
Ainsworth, William Harrison, 1805-1882, 118
Air pilots, Correspondence, reminiscences,
  etc., 19201
Air pollution, Venezuela, 19639
Aires de Menezes, Durval, 18074
Aislabie, John, 1670-1742, 119
Ajofrín, Francisco de, 18075
Akademiiā nauk SSSR. Institut Latinskoĭ
  Ameriki, 18076
Akademiiā nauk SSSR. Institut mirovoĭ
  ekonomiki i mezhdunarodnykh otnosheniĭ,
  18077
Aked, Charles Frederic, 1864-, 5850
Akins, Thomas B., ed., 7599
Akron, O., Hist., 16976
Alabama (Confederate cruiser)
  5123, 12003, 13405, 23593
Alabama. Agricultural Experiment Station,
  18078
Alabama, Antiquities, 15681; Bibliography,
  15140; Biography, 3576; Description &
  travel, 3171, 3595, 3650, 4173, 4791, 5034,
  5706, 5717, 14749, 15527; Description,
  Guide-books, 13544; Economic condition,
  15611; Fiction, 3926; Finance, 17580;
  History, 13456, 25550, 25936, 25937; Laws,
  statutes, etc., 21756, 24506; Pub. govt.,
  24722; Social condition, 15611; Social
  life & customs, 707
The Alabama and Kearsarge, 12003
Alabama infantry. 1st regt., 1861-1865, 4369
Alabama infantry. 60th regt., 1862-1865,
  5130
Alabidocarpus Ewing, 20667
Alachua Co., Florida, Descr. & trav., 5647
Alagoas. Universidade Federal, 18658
Alamán, Lucas, 1792-1853, defendant, 120,
  18079

Alamance, 11164
Alameda, Co., Cal., Biog., 16770; Hist.,
  16669, 16770
Alamo, 17704
Alamo, Siege, 1836, 16537
Alamo, Story of the, 16511
Alarco, Luis Felipe, 18080
Alarcón, José C., 18081
Alarcón de Folgar, Romelia, 18082
Alarío di Filippo, Mario, 18083
The alarm bell, 121
Alas y garras, 6610
Alaska, 11941, 16076; Annexation, 16498;
  Antiq., 2231; Bound., Canada, 6053, 6054
  6181; Descr. & trav., 4750, 5915, 6162,
  6192, 6237, 6422, 7369, 7982, 8410, 16001,
  16046, 16050, 16076, 16289, 16390, 16417,
  16508, 16556, 16647, 16958, 17040, 17064,
  17217, 17390, 17849; Descr. & trav., Guide-
  books, 5978, 5979; Econ. cond., 15858; Hist.,
  15972, 16008, 16362; Gold mining company,
  17104; Yukon game-lands, 7369
Alayo Delmau, Pastor, 18084-18086
Alayo Soto, Rafael, 18087
Alayón García, Giraldo, 18088-18090
Alayotityus manus, Cuba, 18533
Alazragui Alonso, Jaime A., 18091
Alba, Raphael de, 7837
Alba, Victor, 18092
Alban, 9974
Albano, José, 18093
Albany, Ky., 13813
Albany, N.Y., Biog., 11829; Hist., 857, 858;
  Hist., Civil war, 11829; Dudley observatory,
  12331, 12332
Albany congress, 1754, 12898
Albear, Jesús Francisco de, 18094
Albemarle Sound, 3358
Albenino, Nicolas de, 1514?-, 122
Alberdi, Juan Bautista, 1810-1884, 123, 18095
Alberdi-Sarmiento lecture series, 19718
Alberini, Coroliano, 18096, 18097
Alberione, Santiago, 18098
Alberta, Descr. & trav., 6226, 7392, 7656,
  8007, 8074, 8126, 8383
Albertario, Emilio, 1885-, 23855
Albertazzi Avendaño, José, 18099
Alberti, Giorgio, 18100
Alberti, Leandro, 1479-1552, 124
Alberti, Rafael, 18101
Albertus Magnus, bp. of Ratisbon, 126
The Albertyoe Company, 16049
Albiol Estapé, Enrique, 18102
Albism, 111 , Hist , 2258 16528
Albornoz, Orlando, 18103, 18104
Albornoz, Víctor Manuel, 18105

Albornoz de la Escosura, Alvaro de, 18106
Albright, Philip, 8037
Albro, John Adams, 1799-1866, 127
The album, 10197
Album de México monumental, 6865
Album del Ferrocarril mexicano, 6815
Album gráfico de la República Mexicana,
  6691
Album mexicano, 5851
Album of Louisville, 13518
Album of the Mexican railway, 6815
Albuquerque, Byron Wilson Pereira de,
  18107-18113
Albuquerque, Carlos Roberto Abreu de,
  jt. author, 20555
Albuquerque, Francisco Uchoa de, 18114
Albuquerque, Isolda Rocha e Silva, 18115,
  18116
Albuquerque, Olavo A., 18117
Albuquerque, Sérgio Moacir de, 18118
Albuquerque, Tereza Tenório de, 18119
Alcala, Valeria Ortiz (Batson) 1914-, 19789
Alcalá Galiano, Dionisio de, 1760-1805,
  5852, 16477
Alcalá González, María Guadaleupe, 18120
Alcalá y Henke, Agustín, 23856
Un alcalde bajo los álamos, 18052
Alcántara, José Salvador, 18121
Alcaraz, Juan Miguel de, 23623
Alcaraz Gomes, Flávio, 18122
Alcaraz Vieco, Hernán, 18123
Alcázar, Moises, 18504
Alcázar y Zúñiga, Andrés del, conde de la
  Marquina, 5853, 5854
Alcedo, Antonio de, 1736-1812, 128, 18124
Alcedo y Herrera, Dionisio de, 1690-1777,
  5855
The alchemist, 9486
Alchemy, Fiction, 8937
Alcira, Altavista, Ana, 18125
Alckmin, José Geraldo Rodrigues de, 18126
Alcocer, Ignacio, 7932
Alcocer y Sasinana, Baltasar de, 5856
Alcoforado, Francisco, 129
Alcohol, 18350, 19216
Alcoholism, 20172
Alcorta, Jorge Alberto, 18127
Alcott, Louisa May, 1832-1888, 130, 131,
  10163
Alcover y Beltrán, Antonio Miguel, 1875-,
  5857
Aldao, Carlos A., 1860-, 5858
Aldarondo Galván, Etiony, 18128
Alday, Francisco, 18129
Aldeane, 9837
Alden, Ebenezer, 1788-1881, 132

8

Alden, John, d.1687, 23623
Alden, Joseph, 1807-1885, 133
Alden, Timothy, 1771-1839, 134, 135, 136, 137, 138
Alden family (Isaac Alden, 1755-1822), 16512
Alderbrook, 10082
Alderson, Math W., 15829
Aldrey, Fausto Teodoro de, 18130
Aldrich, Julia Carter, 5859
Aldrich, Lewis Cass, 5860
Aldrich, Lorenzo D., 2398
Aldrich, Thomas Bailey, 1836-1907, jt. author, 10447
Aldrich, Vernice M., 15830
Aldridge, Reginald, 15831
Aldridge, William, 1737-1797, 4396, 23143
Aldunate Philips, Arturo, 1902-, 2499
Alduvin, Ricardo D., 7451
Aleck and Pete, 8504
Alegre, Francisco Javier, 1729-1788, 139
Alegre, Rodolfo, 18131
Alegría, Alfredo, 18132
Alegría, Ciro, 18133
Alegría, Paula, 18134
Aleixo, Pedro, 18135
Alem do silencio, 19995
Alemães e descendentes do Rio Grande do Sul na guerra do Paraguai, 18937
Alemán, Mateo, 1547-1614?, 5861, 5862
Alemán Alemán, Eloisa, 18136
Alemann, Juan Ernesto, 18137
Alencar, Hunald de, 18138
Alencar, João Bezerra de, ed., 19357
Alencar, Joaquim Eduarde de, 18139
Alencar, José Martiniano de, 18140, 18141
Ales, Manuel, 18142
Alessio Robles, Vito, 1879-, ed., 7536, 7878
Alexander (ship), 7912
Alexander, Alexander, fl. 1825, 140
Alexander, Ann (Tuke), 1767-1849, 21757, 23857
Alexander, Arabal Wilbur, 13519
Alexander, Archibald, 1772-1851, 141, 142, 148, 23858, 24935
Alexander, Caleb, 1755-1828, 143
Alexander, Charles A., 144
Alexander, Charles W., Philadelphia, pub., 8553, 10932
Alexander, Charles Wesley, 1837-1927, 2500, 2501
Alexander, G.W., 2048
Alexander, George William, 1802-1890, 145, 146
Alexander, Sir James Edward, 1803-1885, 147, 1331, 2502, 5863
Alexander, James Waddell, 1804-1859, 148, 2503

Alexander, John, 13520-13522, 13833
Alexander, John H., 13523, 13927
Alexander, John Henry, 1812-1867, 149, 150
Alexander, Oaula, 13524
Alexander, Sue, 14739
Alexander, William, 1726-1783, 21758
Alexander, William T., 23859
Alexander family, 757, 13013
Alexandria,Va., 4966; Citizens, 151; Hist., 151; Soc. life & cust., 9761
Alexia, 8450
Alfaro, Francisco de, 16th cent., 5864
Alfaro, Gustavo A., 18143
Alfaro González, Anastasio, 18144
Alfaro Monroy, Graciela, 18145
Alfaro R., José F., 18146
Alfaro y Acevedo, José Jorge, 6160
Alfieri, Vittorio, 1749-1803, 152
Alfonso, Pedro Antonio, 153
Alfonso V, el Magnánimo, king of Aragon, d.1458-, Poetry, 6118
Alford, Julius C., 23860
Alford and Selina, 10673
Alfred, 9709
Algar, W.H., 2504
Algebra, Abstract, 19824
Alger, William Rounseville, 1822-1905, 154-157, 238, 23861
Algeria - Descr. & trav., 7858, 8877, 11036, 11811, 24419, 25242; Hist. 1516-1830, 24752, 24753; Soc. life & cust., 24102
The Algerine captive, 11036
The Algerine slaves, 23862
The Algerine spy in Pennsylvania, 10317
Algiers, Battle of, 1816, 12481
Algiers (City), Descr., 1425
Algonquian language, Dictionaries, English, 7224; French, 13143; Glossaries, vocabularies, etc., 7223
Alguiar Derpick, Juan, 18147
The Alhambra, 9993, 16228
Aliança Renovadora nacional, Comissão Coordenadora de Estudos do Nordeste, 18148
La Alianza para el progreso y el desarrollo social en América Latina, 20040
Alice (yacht), 3950
Alice Brand, 10617
Alice Gordon, 8490
Alice Mannering, 8541
Alice Murray, 9882
Alice of old Vincennes, 10961
Alice Singleton, 10816
Alice Tracy, 9282
Alice Waters, 9863

Alida, 2006, 9086
Alien Americans, 5102
Alien and sedition laws, 1798, 4400, 13500, 15650, 21986
The alienigenae of the United States, 1308
The aliens, 4400
Aliens, Illegal, 24224
Alif-Laila, 9678
Alimentación con suplemento proteico en terneros destetados temprano, 18403
Alina Derlay, 10195
Alisky, Marvin, 18149-18152
Allan, Dorothy Carter, 1896-, 5865
Allan-Olney, Mary, 2505
Allan, William, 1837-1889, 12924
Allard, Paul, 1841-1916, 23863, 23864
Allardice, Robert Barclay, 1779-1854, 2506
Allegheny College, Meadville, Pa., 159
Allegheny Co., Pa., Biog., 7455
The Allegheny magazine, 158
Allegheny mountains, 4217, 4694, 23674
Allegheny river, Descr., 2561
Allegheny Roughs, 3493
Allegiance, 12480
Allegories of life, 8464
Allemagne, d', 2507
Allen, Miss A.J., comp., 2508, 15832
Allen, Albert Henry, jt. comp., 14925, 14926
Allen, Andrew, 1740-1825, 160; Claims vs. U.S., 160
Allen, B. F., 15841
Allen, Bird, d.1841, 7917
Allen, Ethan, 1738-1789, 161-171, 5866
Allen, George, 1792-1883, 172, 173, 15833, 15834
Allen, George, 1808-1876, ed., 22267
Allen, George W., ed., 21928
Allen, Harrison, 1841-1897, 174
Allen, Ira, 1751-1814, 175-178
Allen, J.A.., 14595
Allen, James, 1739-1808, 179
Allen, James, 1809-1837, 180
Allen, James, ed., 13931
Allen, James Lane, 1849-1925, 2509, 7385, 8219, 8221, 8222, 13535-13533, 14298, 14763, 14894, 15575, 15576
Allen, Joel Asaph, 1838-1921, 15835
Allen, John, fl.1764, supposed author, 181
Allen, John, 1763-1812, 182
Allen, John, of Hackney, ed., 1721
Allen, John Rowan, 14079
Allen, John Taylor, 15836
Allen, Joseph, 1772-1806, 183
Allen, Joseph, 1790-1873, 184, 22590
Allen, Joseph, 1810?-1864, 185, 186

Allen, Joseph Henry, 1820-1898, 187, 188, 23865, 23866
Allen, Lewis Leonidas, 189, 190
Allen, Lyman Whitney, 1854-1930, 5867, 5868, 5869
Allen, Myron Oliver, 191
Allen, Obridge, 2510
Allen, Paul, 1775-1826, 192, 193, 194, 4272, 13385, 17030
Allen, Richard, bp., 1760-1831, 13284
Allen, Richard L., 1808-1873, 195
Allen, Robert, late of Peru, 196
Allen, Solomon Metcalf, 1789-1817, 12570
Allen, Stephen Merrill, 1819-1894, 23867
Allen, Thomas Newton, 1839-, 23868
Allen, W. W., 15837
Allen, Wilkes, 1775-1845, 197
Allen, William, 1780-1873, 198
Allen, William, 1784-1868, 199, 200, 201, 202, 203, 204
Allen, William, 1803-1879, 205
Allen, William Alonzo, 1848-, 15838, 15839
Allen, William G., 206
Allen, William Henry, 1808-1882, 207, 208
Allen, William Joshua, 1828-1901, 209
Allen, William M., 15840
Allen, William Pitt, d.1802, 23229
Allen, William Ray, 13534
Allen Co., Ky., 13610, 13613; Maps, 14562
Allende Arrau, Jorge de, 18153
Allende-Lezama, Luciano Pedro, 18154
Allender, Phoebe Jo, 13535
Allevi, Aquiles, 18155
Alley, John Bassett, 1817-1896, 210
Allgemeine histoire der reisen zu wasser und lande, 211
Alliance for Progress, 19578, 20040
Alliance for Progress weekly newsletter, 18156
Allibone, Samuel Austin, 1816-1889, 212
Allie in Beulah land, 14302
Alliende, Felipe, 18157
The allies and the late ministry defended against France, and the present friends of France, 22299
Allin, John, 1596-1671, 213
Alling, Jeremiah, 214
Allinson, William J., ed., 25147
Allison, Esther Margarita, 18158
Allison, John, 1812-1878, 23869
Allison, Joseph, 1819-1896, 215
Allison, Patrick, 1740-1802, 216
Allison, Young Ewing, 1853-1932, 13536-13538, 15304; The dead men's song, 14332; The curious legende of Louis Phillippe in Kentucky, 13537

Alloza, Juan de, 1598-1666, 5870
Allsop, Robert, ed., 217
Allsop, Thomas, 1795-1880, 217
Allsopp, Fred W., 15842
Allston, Robert Francis Withers, 1801-1864, 218, 5871, 23643
Allston, Washington, 1779-1843, 2511-2514, 3469
Alltag in USA, 5661
An alluring little footpath and other Kentucky poems, 14258
Allworth abbey, 10829
Allyn, John, 1767-1823, 219, **220**
Almada, José de, 23870
Almairac, S., jt. author, 21741
Almanach intéressant dans les circonstances présentes, 2804
Almanach royal d'Haiti, 18159
Almanacs, American, 239, 326, 1876, 13539, 13547, 13815, 13816, 14067-14069, 14464, 14711-14720, 14727-14732, 15689, 15690, 15776, 24849, 25114, 25746; Cherokee, 16183; French - Haiti, 18159; Kentucky, 13539, 14067-14069, 14464, 14711-14720, 14727-14732, 15689-15691, 15776; Nova Scotia, 5872, 5873; Spanish, 8436
Almanaque Brasileiro Garnier, Anno 1-11, 18160
Almanaque de Juarez, 19758
Almazán, José Pascual, 1813-1895, 19968
Almazán, José Pascual. Un héreje y un musulmán, 19968
Almbert, Alfred d', 1813-1887, 221
Almeida, Abílio Perura de, 18161
Almeida, Aluisio de, 18162
Almuda, Antonio da Rocha, 18163
Almeida, Dayl de, 18164
Almeida, Elpidio de, 18165
Almeida, Fernando Flavio Marques de, 18166
Almeida, Fernando Henrique Mendes de, ed., 19287
Almeida, Fernando Mendes de, 18167
Almeida, Haroldo Ubirajara de, 18168
Almeida, Liberalino Pires de, ed., 19357
Almeida, Mauro Lauria de, 18169
Almeida, Nelly Alves de, 18170
Almeida, Nicholas, illustr., 18138
Almeida, Paulo Mendes de, 18171
Almeida, Pires de, 18172
Almeida, Renato, 18173-18175
Almeida, Theodoro Figueira de, 18176
Almeida Portugal, Luis de, 5° Conde de Avintes, 2° Marquês do Lavradio, 18177
Almenar de Ochoa, Elena, 18178
Almon, John, 1737-1805, 222, 223, 224, 225,

226, 11748
Almost a priest, 11210
Almost persuaded, 3773
The alms-house, 10760
Almshouses, New England, 9475
Alnomuc, 8533
Alnwick castle, 12585
Alonso, Isidoro, 18179, 18180
Alonso, Juan Bautista, b.1821, 25555
Alonso, María Rosa, 18181, 18182
Alonso, Rodolfo, 18183
Alonso Avila, Antonio, 18184
Alonso de San Juan, 5874, 18185
Alonso Novo, Manuel, 18186
Alonso y Sanjurjo, Eugenio, 23871
Alor Leal, Angel Luis, 18187
Al'perovich, Moseĭ Samoĭlovich, 18188
Alphabet, 2351, 16377
Alphonsine, 10197
Alpine Club of Canada, 6317
Alpizar Caire, Ramón, 5875
Alrededor de la jaula, 20444
Alsinet, José, 227
Alsographia americana, 15216
Alsop, George, 1638-, 2515
Alsop, Richard, 1761-1815, 228, 229, 22713, 22714
Alstead, N.H., History, 479
Alsterlund, B., 13540
Alston, R.A., 15029
Alston, William Jeffreys, 1800-1876, 23872
Altamira, Juan Rodríguez de Albuerne, marqués de, 5876
Altamirano, Carlos Luis, 18189
Altamirano, Diego, 5877
Altars of sacrifice, 11185
Altbabylonische Rechtsurkunden aus der Zeit der Hammurabi-dynastie, 24248
Altbreisach, Germany, History, 22234
Alter, J. Cecil, 1879-, 15844-15847, 17813, 17821
Alter und verbesserter schreib-kalender, 5427
Alternativas para el desarrollo urbano de Bogotá, 19100
Alternative programs for suspended and expelled children, 15636
Altes und neues aus der Neuen Welt, 4280
Altezor, Carlos, 18190
Althea Vernon, 10194
Alton, Illinois, Riot, 1051, 1837, 25725
Alton trials of Winthrop vs. Gilman, who was indicted, 25725
Altowan, 5278
Altsheler, Joseph Alexander, 1862-1919, 2516-2522, 13541

El aluvión de Huaraz, 20459
Alva y Astorga, Pedro de, d.1667, 5878, 5879
Alvar, Carlos, ed., 18245
Alvar, Elena, 18191, 18193
Alvar López, Manuel, 18192-18194
Alvarado, Arcilio, 18195
Alvarado, Hermógenes, 23873
Alvarado, Rafael, 18196
Alvarado Arellano, Carlos Raúl, 18197
Alvarado de Ricord, Elsie, 18198
Alvarado Garaicoa, Teodoro, 18199-18201
Alvarado Pinto, Carlos Román, 5880
Alvarado Tezozomoc, Fernando, fl.1598, 5881, 18202
Alvarenga, Delamar, 18203
Alvarenga, Luis de Melo, 18204
Álvares, Walter T., 18205, 18206
Álvares de Azevedo, Manoel Antonio, 18207
Álvarez, Alonzo, pseud., 25861
Álvarez, Francisco, Asturian, 230
Álvarez, Ignacio, 18208
Álvarez, J., 18209
Álvarez, José Justo, 1821-1897, 5884
Álvarez, José María, 1777-1820, 231
Álvarez, José Rogelio, 18210
Álvarez, Martins d', 18211
Álvarez, Ticul, 18212
Álvarez Cáceres, Carlos, 18213
Álvarez Conde, José, 18214
Álvarez de Cienfuegos y Campos, José Alberto, 18215
Álvarez de Peralta, José Antonio, 24291
Álvarez de Prado, Simón, 6851
Álvarez de Vega, Nicolás, 6381
Álvarez de Velasco, Gabriel, fl.1650, 5882, 5883
Álvarez del Castillo, Miguel, 18216
Álvarez Diaz, José R., 18217
Álvarez Nazario, Manuel, 18218
Álvarez O., Federico, 18219
Álvarez Sosa, Arturo, 18220
Álvarez Tabío, Fernando, 18221
Álvarez Vásquez, Mario, 18222
Alvear Acevedo, Carlos, 18223, 18224
Alvear y Ponce de León, Diego de, 1740-1830. Diario de la segunda partida demarcadora de limites en la América meridional, 18940
Alves, Albérico Barroso, 18225
Alves, Gorgônio Barbosa, 18226
Alves, José Brito, 18227
Alves, María Helena X., 18228
Alves, Maricta, 18229
Alves, Rodrigues, 18230

Alves Roçadas, José Augusto, 23874
Alvim, Agostinho Neves de Arruda, ed., 19338
Alvim, Decio Ferraz, 18231
Alvin, Juan, 5885
Alvord, Benjamin, 1813-1884, 232
Alvord, Clarence Walworth, 1868, ed., 2523, 23875
Alvord, James C., d.1839, 24990, 24991
Alvord, John Watson, 1807-1880, 233
Alvord family (Alexander Alvord, 1620?-1683), 1426
El alzamiento, 19922
Al alzamiento del 9 de octubre en Macaca, 20548
Alzamora Valdez, Mario, 18232
Alzate y Ramírez, José Antonio, 1738-1845, 6400, 6401
Amabel, 10167
Amado, Jorge, 18233
Amador de los Rios, José, 1818-1878, ed., 7657
Aman-Jean, François, 18234
Amanda, 8849
Amanda and love, 9575
Amanda Willson, 8891
O amante de minha mulher, 21736
Amapa, Brazil, Economic condition, 18744
Amaral, A., 18235
Amaral, Antonio Barreto do, 18236
Amaral, Rubens do, 18237
Amaral Filho, Zebino Pacheco do, jt. author, 20555
Amaru, Severino, pseud., 7516
Amat y Junient, Manuel de, viceroy of Peru, 18th cent., 5886
Amati, Giacinto, 1778-1850, 234
Amato, Antonio, 18450
The Amazon, and the Atlantic Slopes of South America, 23373
Amazon region, Brazil, 19304, 19323, 19441, 19449; Bibliography, 19439, 19457; Description, 19436, 19443; Economic conditions, 19433, 19434, 19437, 19438, 19443, 19444, 19447, 19448, 19450, 19451; Economic policy, 19454; Maps, 19446, 19452; Maps, Bibliography, 19463; Research, 19442
Amazon river, 31, 577, 1670, 5939, 7218, 11259, 23373; Description, 19322, 23566; Discovery & exploration, 20652; Fiction, 23527; History, 19317
Amazon Valley, 961; Economic condition, 18742, 19435, 20457; Economic policy, 18742, 18743; Maps, Bibliography, 18029; Population, 19045; Social condition, 19045,

19435;
Amazonas, Brazil, Economic condition, 20554
Amazônia, 18741, 18742, 19433-19435
Amazônia brasileira, 19449
A Amazônia é o novo Brazil, 19436
Amazônia is the new Brazil, 19436
Amazônia legal, 19437
The Amazonian republic, 10707
L'Amazonie est le nouveau Brésil, 19436
The ambassador in spite of himself, 10298
The ambassadors, 7115
Amberglow of Abraham Lincoln and Joshua
  Speed, 6831
The ambiguities, 10347
An ambitious man, 11163
The ambitious wasp, 10046
An ambitious woman, 9500
Ambriano, John, 18238
Ambrose, Daniel Leib, 2524
Ambrose, Paul, pseud., 24710
Ambrosetti, Juan B., 1865-1917, 19610
Ambrosio de Letinez, 9597
Amburgey family, 14225
Amcham guide to Mexico, 8101
L'âme américaine, 4587
Amedeus, father, 1872, 13543
Amelia, pseud., 5669
Amelia Sherwood, 8527
America, 235, 236, 1974, 4363, 6200, 12105,
  16526; Antiquities, 249, 1081, 1100, 1443,
  11498, 13298, 15221, 22390, 22473;
  Bibliography, 2476, 18124, 22088;
  Bibliography, Catalogs, 23200, 23273,
  23274, 23275, 23530, 24544, 23687;
  Biography, 1238; Climate, 23804;
  Commerce, France, 11711; Description
  & travel, 321, 971, 1557, 1852, 2857,
  3653, 4392, 4507, 4900, 5316, 5319,
  5793, 6674, 7040, 7629, 8124, 11408,
  11586, 11615, 12994, 16020, 16553,
  22279, 22283, 22564, 23575; Description
  & travel, Gazetteers, 128, 251;
  Description & travel, Maps, 22696,
  23138; Discovery & exploration, 311, 582,
  765, 1081, 1101, 1261, 1598, 2484, 2857,
  6623, 6832, 7034, 7035, 7209, 7221, 7657,
  8083, 8160, 8169, 8401, 11523, 11615,
  12112, 17852, 20065, 21782, 22285, 22895,
  23072, 23541, 23692, 25110; Discovery &
  exploration, Basque, 7567; Discovery &
  exploration, Bibliography, 20195, 22311,
  22312; Discovery & exploration, English,
  1479, 6925, 23043; Discovery & exploration
  - French, 1827, 4144, 6396, 7268, 11715;
  Discovery & exploration, German, 22195;
  Discovery & exploration, Irish, 1005;

Discovery & exploration, Norse, 1005,
  1026, 1322, 22071; Discovery & exploration
  - Phenician, 13298; Discovery & exploration
  - Poetry, 13293; Discovery & exploration,
  Portuguese, 22231; Discovery &
  exploration, Pre-Columbian, 610, 4035,
  23336; Discovery & exploration, Spanish,
  26, 3547, 4631, 6430, 7393, 7567, 7649,
  11708, 12448, 13109, 16640; Discovery
  & exploration, Spanish, Poetry, 794;
  Discovery & exploration, Welsh, 1692,
  22421; Early accounts to 1600, 29, 373,
  374, 375, 376, 406, 407, 794, 1186, 1187,
  4631, 5827, 5909, 5920, 8168, 1600, 18299,
  18994, 21783, 22195, 23652; Early works to
  1600, 7657; Geography, 6125; History, 1112,
  1598, 2420, 5793, 11589, 15232; History,
  Period., 321; History, Poetry, 809, 819;
  History, Sources, 19632; Industrial,
  history, 24085; Maps, 128; Maps, Early,
  23575; Politics, 12105
America after sixty years, 4858
America and American Methodism 4061
America and Europe, 3721
America and her army, 22932
America and other poems, 5236
America, and the American church, 2943
America and the American people, 4898
America and the Americans, 2645, 3109, 6104
America and the Americans from a French point
  of view, 3053
America as I found it, 3319
America at home, 4307
America by river and rail, 3434
America compared with England, 2525
America dissected, being a full and true
  account of all the American colonies, 22996
America during and after thw ear, 3433
América (estudios históricos y filológicos),
  7305
The America I saw in 1916-1918, 5230
America in 1876, 4251
America, its realities and resources, 5782
América latina en su música, 19820
América Latina, 18239
L'America libera, 152
America, past, present and prospective, 22605
America revisited, 4376, 5063
L'America, ricerca della felicità, 5070
America saved, 1550
L'America vittoriosa, 4642
America yesterday and to-day, 24334
America's appeal to the impartial world, 237
America's misfortune, 23876
America's remembrances, 12725
American, 1262, 7116, 24834

American academy of arts and science,
Boston, 238
The American alarm, 181
The American almanac and repository of useful
knowledge, 239
American and foreign Anti-slavery reporter,
23877
American and Foreign Anti-slavery Society,
23877-23880, 24848, 24849, 24850, 24851,
25842
The American annual, 3334
The American annual encyclopaedia and
register of important events, 240
The American annual register, 241
American Antiquarian Society, Worcester,
Mass., 242, 243, 244, 12748, 13204, 24267
American Anti-slavery Society, 1339, 8181,
13184, 23835, 23881-23888, 24016, 24019,
24121, 24141, 24382, 24577, 24836, 24976,
25244, 25336, 25377, 25842, 25869
American archives, 11844
American association for the advancement
of science, 245
American Atlantic and Pacific Ship Canal
Company, 1897
American Autograph Shop, Merion Station,
Pa., 5887
American Automobile Association, 13544
American ballads and songs, 302, 12250
American Castile, 23178
The American bee, 246
American biblical repository, 23518
An American biographical and historical
dictionary, 201, 202, 203
American biographical notes, 22570
American biographical publishing company,
pub., 8260
American biography and genealogy, 16089
The American bird-keeper's manual, 23093
American board of commissioners for foreign
missions, 23535, 23889, 24486, 24625,
25866
The American Board of Missions and Slavery.
A reprint of the correspondence in the
"nonconformist" newspaper, 24625
American book collector, 13545
The American boy's life of Washington,
13057
American bureau of mines, New York, 247
The American captives in Havana, being
Ferdinand Clark's reply to Nicholas P.
Frest, consul at that place, 21937
The American cardinal, 10175
The American church and the American
union, 11694
The American churches, 2718

An American citizen, 411, 11774
The American citizen's manual of reference,
12520
The American claimant, 9024
The American coast pilot, 2526, 2527
American coin, 8528
American colonization society, 639, 1699,
5254, 6429, 11563, 11565, 12618, 12692,
12827, 13184, 22980, 24074, 24232, 24422,
24536, 24719, 24773, 24846, 24949, 25053,
24211
The American common-place book of prose, a
collection of eloquent and interesting
extracts from writings of American authors
21900
The American commonwealth, 1630
The American conflict, 24522
American Continental Congress, 5 September,
1774, 21759
American cottage library, 2315
The American cotton industry, 5792
American Council of Learned Societies,
13546
American criminal trials, 11719
The American crisis, 4763
The American cruiser, 10223
The American cyclops, the hero of New
Orleans, and spoiler of silver spoons,
22957
American debate; a history of political and
economic controversy in the United States,
25050
The American debater, 22858
American destiny, 248
American education, 4739, 23099
American Education Society, 289
American Education Society. Quarterly
register, 289
American Education Society. Quarterly
register and journal, 289
The American Egypt, 5932
American encyclopedia of printing, 23537
American enterprise, 2528
American entomology, 5079
American essays, 13513, 13626
American estates and gardens, 3435
American Ethnological Society, 249
American evening entertainments, 8934
American family antiquity, 8365
An American family in Germany, 8877
The American family Robinson, 2664
The American farmer's almanac, 13547
American female guardian society and
Home for the friendless, New York, 22293
The American female poets, 4424
American fiction, 15530; Bibliography, 1513

(Collections), 10122, 10675
American Friends Service Committee, 24722
The American flag, 22157
American Fur Company, 17404, 17859
The American fur trade of the far West, 16195
American gardener's calendar, 22971
The American gazette, 250
The American gazetteer, 251
The American genealogist, 15047
American genealogy, 12847
American geographical society of New York, 22435
The American geography, 4539
The American gift book, 252
An American girl abroad, 10157
An American girl in Mexico, 7364
An American grove of new or revised trees and shrubs..., 15216
American hazard, 4884
The American hero, 11688
American herpetology, 12683
American highways, 5127
American Historical Association, 25662
The American historical magazine, 254
American historical society, Washington, D.C., 255
The American idea, and what grows out of it, 11729
American Imprints Inventory (Kentucky), 14925, 14926, 15574
The American in Algiers, 256
The American Indian, 630
The American Indian as slave holder and secessionist, 23829
American institute of instruction, 257
American Institute of Mining, Metallurgical, and Petroleum Engineers, 5888
American International Association, 18240
American international relief committee, for the suffering operatives of Great Britain, 258
The American Italy, 16692
American journal of conchology, 259
The American journal of education, 260
The American journal of education and college review, 261
The American journal of improvements in the useful arts, 262
The American kalendar, 263
The American keepsake, 264
The American laborer, 11226
The American lady, 21823
American Legion. Kentucky Department, 13548
American life, 5028
American life at home, 8950

American literary gazette and publishers' circular, 265
American literature (Collections) 3699, 10154, 15345; (Selections, extracts, etc.) 8626, 9517, 9616, 11605, 13483; Addresses, essays, lectures, 4433; Bibliography, 212, 21859; Bibliography, Early, 11697; Bibliography, Period., 265; California, 17192; History & criticism, 3332, 3803, 5165, 11759, 14764, 15517, 21879, 25438; Kentucky, 5446, 15533; Maryland, 3077, 5264; 19th century, 8612; Ohio Valley, 5566; Periodicals, 277, 3857, 5678, 5679; Southern states, 2632, 3183, 3536, 4408, 5346, 10357, 15345, 15413; Virginia, 22308; The West, 1984, 3043, 3563;
The American lounger, 3996
American loyalists, 160, 2383, 3336, 3418, 11689, 11923, 11967, 12190, 12602, 12799; Pennsylvania, 1370; South Carolina, 11614
American lyrics, 13293
The American magazine, 266
The American magazine and monthly chronicle for the British Colonies, 267
The American magazine of wit, 268
American manual of the grape vines and the art of making wine, 15217
The American mariners, 3188
American mechanics' magazine, 269
American medical botany, 1267
The American medical review, and journal of original and selected papers in medicine and surgery, 21760
The American melodies, 11886
The American military pocket atlas, 5082
American mind, 1461
The American mineralogical journal, 270
American minstrel, consisting of poetical essays on various subjects, 23409
The American mission in the Sandwich islands, 22174
American missionary memorial, 4794
American missions to the heathen, 22496
The American monthly magazine and critical review, 271
The American monthly review, 272, 1935
The American museum, 273
The American musical miscellany, 274
The American nation, 15219, 24576
American national song-book, 22792
American naval battles, 275, 276
American naval biography, 656
The American negotiator, 23824
American negro slavery, 25254
American neutrality, 1141, 12668

American news company, New York, 23478
American newspapers, History, 1640; New
  Hampshire, 137
American nights' entertainments, 9658
An American nobleman, 8547
American notes, 5325
American notes and pictures from Italy,
  6588, 6589
American notes and queries, 277, 5889
American notes for general circulation,
  3243
American numismatic society, 278
American orations, 279, 7005, 11671
American oratory, 279
American party, 2194, 5083, 11677, 24219
American peace society, 1815, 11370
American periodicals, History, 1640
American Pharmaceutical Association, 281
American philosophical society, Philadelphia,
  282, 283, 284, 285, 286, 13084
American photographs, 5485
An American physician, 11042
The American pioneer, 287
American poetry, (Collections) 3258, 3701,
  4294, 4424, 5264; Early 19th century,
  History & criticism, 10560; History and
  criticism, 2788; Kentucky, 3245; Periodicals,
  15257; Southern states, 15073; The West,
  2376
American poets, Ohio, 15644
The American planter, 22734
The American political tradition, 14650
An American politician, 6491
American politics, 12649
American posts, 17008
The American prejudice against color, 206
American principles, 69
The American privateer, 9040
American prose literature, 3702, 3802, 21900
The American quarterly observer, 288
The American quarterly register, 289
The American querist, 11721
The American question, 290, 291, 2483
American railway guide, 292, 3035
American Reform Tract and Book Society,
  Cincinnati, pub., 23925
The American register, 293, 294
American rejected addresses, 1268
The American remembrancer, 295, 12673
American Republic society of Philadelphia,
  13767
American republics, 7482; Foreign relations,
  league of nations, 8270
American resistance indefensible, 206
American resorts, 4039
The American review, 297, 317

American revolution society, Charleston,
  S.C., 11448, 12391, 12445, 12611, 22784
American Royalists, 23782
American satire, 2800, 5475
The American scene, 4040
American scenery, 5729
American scenes and Christian slavery, 3185
An American selection of lessons in reading
  and speaking, 23761
American sketches, 298
The American slave-trade, 25579, 25712
American slavery, 23890-92, 24880
American society, 5443
American society for promoting national
  unity, 299
American society for the encouragement of
  domestic manufactures, 300
An American soldier, pseud., 10601
The American spectator, 301
The American spelling book, 15683
The American spy, 10765
The American star, 302
The American statesman, 763
American statistical association, 303, 304,
  305
An American story-book, 9187
American summer resorts, 4620
American Sunday-school Union, 12583, 25670
The American system, 2453
The American telegraph and signal book,
  1207
American telegraph magazine, 306
American temperance society, 307, 668
American temperance union, 307
American Thanksgiving dinner, 308
American tract society, 460, 24673, 22850;
  Boston, 309, 25863; New York, 25629
An American tradition, 11187
The American traveller, 310, 3032, 3861,
  6434
The American tropics, 6471
The American union, 11303
American union commission, 312, 313
American Union for the Relief and Improvement
  of the Colored Race, 23893
American Unitarian Association, 22286
The American universal magazine, 314
American University, Washington, D.C.,
  20398
The American wanderer, 315
The American war, 7537, 12580, 25293
The American weekly messenger, 316
The American Whig review, 317
American wit and humor, 268, 318, 2600,
  3731, 3863, 5412, 6114, 8116, 6042,
  8493, 8616, 8642, 8684, 8917, 9009,

16

9248, 10253, 10488, 10714, 10817, 13859,
14562, 14767, 14834, 14938, 15088,
15103, 15312, 15393, 15394; Georgia, 3492
American wives and English husbands, 8591
American womanhood: its pecularities and
necessities, 22649
The American's guide, 253
The American's own book, 280
Americana, 4206
Americana in a state university library,
13832
Americanism in literature, 4433
Americanisms, Dictionaries, 907
The Americans, 4551
Americans against liberty, 23595
The Americans as they are, 5112
The Americans at home, 4377
Americans in Canada, Legal status, laws,
etc., 7967
Americans in France, 1917
Americans in Rome, 10191
The Americans in their moral, social and
political relations, 3710, 12477
Americans of gentle birth and their
ancestors, 7753
Americanus examined, 319
Americanus, pseud., 11879
Americas as they are, 15344
Americus, pseud., 320, 23894
Amerika! Amerika! 2584
Amerika, dargestellt durch sich selbst, 321
Amerika heute und morgen, 3900
Amerika i vor tid, 2938
Amerika, in alle zyne byzonderheden
beschouwd, 2529
Amerika in bildern und text, 4607
Amerika in wort und bild, 3832
Amerika noch nicht am Ziele! 5551
Amerika, seet fra et landbostandpunkt, 2539
Amerika slår till, 5574
Amerika, Wanderungen eines Deutschen, 5703
Amerika wie es ist, 4184
Amerikaansche voyagien, 1193
Amerikanische Jagd- und Reiseabenteuer aus
meinem Leben in den westlichen Indianerge-
bieten, 5306
Amerikanische lebensbilder, 4190
Amerikanische reisebilder mit besonderer
berücksichtigung der dermaligen religiösen,
4766
Amerikanische streiflichter, 2659
Das amerikanische volk, 5172
Amerikanisches, 4182
Amerikanisches magazin, 322
Amerikanisches wanderbuch, 6074
Amerikas wichtigste charakteristik nach land

und leuten, 11586
L'Amérique angloise, ou Description des
isles et terres du roi d'Angleterre,
dans l'Amérique, 21789
L'Amérique au XXe siècle, 4279
L'Amérique en plusieurs cartes nouvelles,
et exactes, et at en divers traitez de
geographie et d'histoire, 23575
L'Amérique protestante, 4937
Ames, Fisher, 1758-1808, 69, 323, 324,
5890
Ames, Glenn C., 18241
Ames, John H., 15849
Ames, Julius Rubens, 1801-1850, 325,
15859, 17017
Ames, Mrs. Mary (Clemmer) Hudson, 1839-
1884, 2530-2532, 2931
Ames, Nathaniel, 1708-1764, 326
Ames, Pelham Warren, 1839-, ed., 5890
Ames, Samuel, 1806-1865, plaintiff, 1399
Ames González, Edmundo, 18242
Amezquita de Almeida, Josefina, 18243
Amherst, Mass., Geneal., 21800
Amherst College, 327, 328, 329, 8667;
History, 22506; Library, 330; Registers,
329
Amherst, Jeffrey Amherst, 1st baron,
1717-1797, 331
Amherst's expedition against Ticonderoga
and Crown Point, 331, 1759
Amicus republicae, pseud., 332
Amidon, Charles Fremont, 1856-1937, 17448
O amigo, 19696
Los amigos de la patria y de la juventud,
1815-1816, 18244
Amis et fortune, 3217
Amis y Amiles; cantar de gesta francés
del siglo XIII, 18245
Amish in Kentucky, 15434
Amistad (Schooner), 70. 789, 24789
The amnesty again, 8146
Amnesty question, 8147
El amor, 19584
Amor patriae, 24177, 25519
Amor real, 20565
Amora, Antonio Soares, 18246
Os amores de Gabriela, 18953
Amorim, Alaide Sardá de, 18247
Amorim, Eduardo Guedes de, 18248
Amorim, Enrique, 18249
Amory, Charles Bean, 1841-, 2533
Amory, Thomas Coffin, 1812-1889, 333
Amos, Andrew, 1791-1860, ed., 334
Amparo (Writ), Mexico, 20705
Ampère, Jean Jacques Antoine, 1800-1864,
335, 336, 5891

Amphibians, Kentucky, 13706
Amphlett, William, 337
Ampzing, Samuel, 1591?-1632, 338
Amster, Mauricio, 18250
Amsterdams dam-praetje, 339
Amsterdams tafel-praetje, 340
The amulet, 341
Amunátegui, Gregorio Victor, 1830-1899,
    jt. author, 5893
Amunátegui, Miguel Luis, 1828-1888,
    5892, 5893, 18251, 18252
Amusement for a winter's evening, 23596
Amusing and thrilling adventures of a
    California artist, 4118
Amy Denbrook, 11122
Ana, Marcos, pseud., 18253
Anabalón Ramírez, Carlos, 18254
Anaconda, 13964
Anahuac, 8159, 8251
Anais da Sociedade Botânica do Brasil,
    20423
The Analectic magazine, 342
Analfabetismo en la Argentina, 18421
Anania, Giovanni Lorenzo d', 343
Ananias, 9745
Anastasi, Atilio, 18255
Anastasio's revenge, 9254
Anastrepha suspensa Loew, 20076
Anatomia patológica das afecções
    hepáticas, 18879
Anaya Espinasse, José Maria, 18256 to
    18260
Anaya Monroy, Fernando, 18261
Anburey, Thomas, 344, 345, 346, 347, 5894,
    5895
The ancestors of Peter Atherly, 9793
Anchieta, José de, 1534-1579, 1189, 18262,
    18644
Anchorage, Ky., High School. Genealogical
    Society, 13549
Anchorage, Ky. St. Lucke's Church, 14895
The anchoret reclaimed, 10983
Les anciennes villes du Nouveau monde, 6406
Ancient Arabic order of the nobles of the
    mystic shrine, 17613
The ancient cities of the new world, 6407
Ancient history, 4881
The ancient landmark, 15666
Ancient life in Kentucky, 14151
The ancient monuments of North and South
    America, 15221
The ancient right of the English nation to
    the American fishery, 11331
Ancilla Demontes, 9017
Ancona, Eligio, 1035 1893. El filibustero,
    19968

Ancona, Eligio, 1835-1893. Los mártires
    del Anahuac, 19968
Ancona, Eligio, 1835-1893. Memorias de
    un alférez, 19968
The Andalusian rope-dancer, 10434
Andele, 17186
Anderde discovrs by forma van messieve,
    348
Anderson, A. W., 18263
Anderson, Adam, 1692?-1765, 23076, 22986
Anderson, Alexander, 1775-1870, illustr.,
    12851
Anderson, Alexander Caulfield, 5896,
    5897, 5898, 5899, 5900
Anderson, Alexander Dwight, 15850
Anderson, Barbara, 5901
Anderson, Bernice Gibbs, 15851
Anderson, Charles, 15852
Anderson, Charles, 1814-1895, 2534, 2535,
    13550
Anderson, Charles Palmerston, bp., 1863-
    1930, 5902
Anderson, Charles W., 18264
Anderson, David, 2536, 5903, 5904
Anderson, Edward Lovell, 1842-, 13551
Anderson, Ephraim McDowell, 2537
Anderson, Homer, 5905
Anderson, Hugh, d.1748, 5335
Anderson, J. J., 15853
Anderson, James Blythe, 13552
Anderson, James S., 2538
Anderson, John, b.1831?, 25740
Anderson, John, fl. 1859, 24175
Anderson, John T., 5906
Anderson, Mrs. Mabel Washbourne, 15854
Anderson, Margaret Steele, 1875-, 13553
Anderson, Meg W., 14496
Anderson, Melville Best, 1851-, tr.,
    16994, 16995
Anderson, Richard C., 13883
Anderson, Robert Clough, 1750-1826, 15801
Anderson, T. J., 23927
Anderson, Teresa J., 18265-18267
Anderson, eatman, 20195
Anderson family, 15801
Andersonville, Ga. Military prison,
    3432, 3649, 3956, 4145, 4278, 4293,
    4322, 4350, 4476, 4543, 4617, 4676,
    4896, 4970, 5046, 5047, 12621,
    23928
Andersonville, Ga. National Cemetery,
    23928
Andersonville violets, 9073
Andersson, Theodore, 18268
Andery, Paulo Adib, 18869
Andes, 1431; Description & travel, 22540;

18

Venezuelan, History, 18536
Andover, Mass., History, 7
Andover and Danville, 13554
Andover Theological Seminary, 634, 22105;
    Library, 349, 350
Andrada, Auro moura, 18270
Andrada e Silva, José Bonifácio de, 18271,
    18272
Andrade, Alonso de, 1590-1672, 5907
Andrade, Antônio Ferreira de, 18273
Andrade, Carlos Américo Morato de, 18274
Andrade, Carlos Drummond de, 20074
Andrade, Federico Alberto de, 18275
Andrade, Gilberto Osório de Oliveira, 18276,
    18277
Andrade, illustr., 7955
Andrade, Jaime, 18276
Andrade, Jorge, 18279, 18280
Andrade, José Bonifácio Lafayette de, 18271
Andrade, Leonhilda Litran M., 19220
Andrade, Luís Antônio de, 18126
Andrade, Manuel Correia de, 18281, 18282
Andrade, Mário de, 1893-1945, 18167, 20091,
    20233
Andrade, Oswaldo de, 18283, 20091
Andrade Barrientos, Néstor, 18284
Andrade e Silva, José Bonifacio de, 1763-1838,
    24012
Andrade-Lima, Dardano de, 18285
Andrade Moscoso, Carlos, 18286
Andrade y Cordero, César, 18287
André, Mme, Henriette Joséphine (Walther)
    1807-1886, 23910
André, John, 1751-1780, 351-355, 1175-1177,
    8526, 23576, 23599, 23628; Fiction, 8785,
    8967
Andrea, 19584
Andreana, 355
Andreasen, H., 2539
Andreazza, Mario David, 18288, 18289
Andree, Karl Theodor, 1808-1875, 2540, 2541
Andreoli, Arturo, 18290
Andreoni, João Antonio, 18291
Andreozzi, Maria Rosa, 18292
Andrés, Affredo, 18293
Andres, (Mrs.) Amelia Ann, 2543
Andrés, de Guadalupe, father, 1602-1668, 6820
Andrés Octavio, José, 18294
Andrew, Abram Piatt, 1843-, 2542
Andrew, James O., 14995
Andrew, James Osgood, Bp., 1794-1871, 948, 2543
Andrew, John, illustr., 4403, 17687
Andrew Bentley, 8882
Andrews, Charles, 356
Andrews, Charles C., 357
Andrews, Charles McLean, ed., 5087

Andrews, Charles Wesley, 1807-1875, 358
Andrews, David H., 18295
Andrews, Eliza Frances, 1840-, 2544
Andrews, Ethan Allen, 1787-1858, 2545
Andrews, Evangeline Walter, ed., 5087
Andrews, George, 5908
Andrews, Israel Ward, 13555
Andrews, Joseph, 359
Andrews, Mrs. Mary Raymond (Shipman)
    d.1936, 2546, 2547
Andrews, Rufus F., 360
Andrews, Sidney, 361
Andrews, W. S., 362
Andrews family, 5908
Andrews' illustrations of the West Indies,
    362
Andriani, Jácome Francisco, 8272
Andromeda, 9526
Andros, Sir Edmund, 1637-1714, as governor
    of England, 1688 and 1689; character in
    M.A. Denison, The lover's trials, 9389
Andros, Thomas, 1759-1845, 363, 364
Andueza, José Maria de, 365
Andy M'Gee's chorus girl, 9363
Anecdotes, American, 3731, 5411, 5412
Anecdotes, Gt. Brit., 13450; U.S., 13450
Anecdotes américaines, ou Histoire abrégée
    des principaux événements arrivés dans
    le nouveau monde, 22564
Anecdotes of the life of the Right Hon.
    William Pitt, 222
Anecdotes secrètes sur la révolution du 18
    fructidor, 366
Anent the North American continent, 367
Anent the United States and Confederate
    States of North America, 368
Angarita Arvelo, Rafael, 18296
Angel, Myron, 15855, 15856, 16774
The angel and the demon, 8556
The angel child, 9216
Angela Meriel, Saint, 1474-1540, 22749
Angeles Caballero, César Augusto, 18297
Angelescu, Victor, 18298
Angelis, Pedro de, 1784-1859, 369-372, 432,
    18940, 21761
Angell, Homer Daniel, 17790
Angelo, C. Aubrey, 2548
Angels, 13049; Art, 11108
Angelus studio, Portland, Or., 16769
Anghiera, Pietro Martire d', 1455-1526,
    373-376, 5909, 5920, 18299
Angier, Joseph, 377
Angina maligna, 2119
Angle, Paul McClelland, 1900-1975, 5910,
    5911, 7280, 7282
An angler's reminiscences, 3758

Anglesey, Richard Annesley, 6th earl of, 1694-1761, defendant, 23896
Anglo-American literature and manners, 11759
Anglo-Californian, pseud., 378
Anglo-Chilean tribunal of arbitration, 1894-1896, 20108
Anglo-Dutch war, 1780-1784, 13281
Anglo-French war, 1755-1763, 650, 22136, 23560, 23606. 24830
Anglo-French war, 1778-1783, 13281
Anglo-Norman dialect - Dictionaries, 11425
Anglo-Saxon race, 2534
The Anglo-Saxons historic and romantic America, 6463
Anglo-Saxons, onward!, 9332
Anglo-Spanish war, 1718-1720, 1221
Anglo-Spanish war, 1779-1783, 13281
The anglomaniacs, 9758
Angola, 18369
Angola , Description & travel, 25113; Economic condition, 23874; Relations (general) with Brazil, 18369
Anguiano, Mateo de, 1649-1726, 19855
Angular distribution of photo fission fragments from uranium, 19867
Angulo V., Jorge, 18300
Angulos de México, 7400
Aniba duckei Kostermans, 18351
Un animal de Deus, 18643
Animal lore, 15529
Animal magnetism, 1406
Animal personalities, 15457
Animals, Habits and Behavior of, 14156, 16164
Animals, Legends and Stories of, 24562
Anjos, Nelson da Franca Ribeiro dos, 18301
Ann Ellsworth, 9702
Ann Rutledge, 5912
Anna Clayton, 9401
Annaes marítimos e coloniaes, 379
The annals of administration, 380
Annals of Dedham, 23086
Annals of historical and natural science..., 15227
The annals of Jamaica, 1499
Annals of nature, 15222
Annals of Pennsylvania, from the discovery of the Delaware, 22376
The annals of Salem, 2243
Annals of the aristocracy, 11168
Annals of the City of Kansas, 5233
Annals of the fifty seventh regiment Indiana volunteers, 4164
Annals of the Nineteenth Ohio battery, 15587

Annals of the town of Keene, 2455
Annals of the town of Providence, 23653
Annals of the wars of the nineteenth century, 22011
Annals of the West, 4752
Annapolis, 12652; History, 169, 23170; St. Ann's parish, 169
Anne, 9355
Anne, queen consort of Louis XIII, king of France, 1601-1666, Fiction, 10931
Anneke, Fritz, 381
Anner' Lizer's stumblin' block, by P.L. Dunbar, 24319
Annesley, James, 1715-1760, fiction, drama, poetry, etc., 23896
Annetta, 9965
Annette, 11057
The annexation of Russian America to the United States, 16498
Annexation of Texas, 16211
Annie Grayson, 10166
Annie Kilburn, 9938
Annie Reilly, 10271
Annie Tousey's little game, 9916
Annina, 11198
Annuities, Private, 14669
Annuttaliga Hammock, Fla., 3486
Un anónimo poema gauchesco de 1835 sobre la guerra de la Independencia, 18302
An anonymous letter, 9358
Anschauungen und erfahrungen in Nordamerika, 2767
Ansermo of the crag, 8847
Der ansiedler im Missouri-staate, 970
Anson, George Anson, baron, 1697-1762, 885
Anspach, Frederick Rinehart, 1815-1867, 382
Anspach, Lewis Amadeus, 383, 384, 385
Ansted, David Thomas, 1814-1880, 386, 387, 15857
Antartic regions, 4678, 13200, 19724, 22322; Description, 20121; Maps, 20121, 20135
Ante bellum, 9103
Antecedentes agrarios del municipio de Atlacomulco, 20246
Antecedentes do homem, 18664
Antecedentes para la documentación legislativa, 18411, 18413, 18414, 18416, 18417
Antelope Co., Neb., History, 17005
Anteprojeto de lei agraria, 19861
Anthoine de Saint-Joseph, Arthur, baron, b.1829, ed., 388
Anthoine de Saint-Joseph, Fortuné, 1794-1853, 388
Anthology society, Boston, 23447
Anthon, George Christian, 1820-1877, 300
Anthon, Henry, 1795-1861, 390, 391

Anthon, John, 1784-1863, 392
Anthony, free Negro, d.1798, 24765
Anthony, A.V.S., illustr., 17336
Anthony, Elliott, 1827-1898, 393
Anthracite coal, Pennsylvania, 8376
Anthropogeography, 19131
Anthropogeography, U.S., 8003
Anthropology, 18023, 20364; Addresses,
  essays, lectures, 25510; Periodicals,
  19751
Anthropometry, Mexico, Bibliography, 20361
An anti-abolitionist, 13168
Anti-communist movements, 20404
Anti-duelling association of New York, 1063
Anti-fanaticism: a tale of the South, 24068
Anti-Fugitive slave law meeting, 24311
Anti-Jackson Convention, Richmond, Va.,
  5913
Anti-masonic convention, Middleburg, Vt.,
  780, 1830
Antimasonic Party, 173, 458, 780, 10384,
  11257, 11562, 12166, 12181, 12203, 12399,
  12587, 24645
Anti-rent troubles, New York, 1839-1846,
  12334; Fiction, 9129, 9149
Anti-slavery addresses of 1844 and 1845,
  24151
Anti-slavery before Garrison, 23930
The anti-slavery bugle, 24007
The anti-slavery cause in America and its
  martyrs, 15714
Anti-Slavery Conference, Paris, 1867, 23897
Anti-Slavery Convention of American Women,
  1st, New York, 1837, 23898-99; 2nd,
  Philadelphia, 1838, 23900; 3d, Philadelphia,
  1839, 23901-02
Anti-slavery crises, 23903
The anti-slavery crusade; a chronicle of the
  gathering storm, 25012
Anti-slavery days, 24138
Anti-slavery hymns, designed to aid the cause
  of human rights, 25586
Anti-slavery in Virginia: extracts from Thomas
  Jefferson, General Washington and others,
  24223
Anti-slavery melodies: for the friends of
  freedom, 23867
Anti-slavery memoranda, 25384
The anti-slavery movement in Kentucky prior
  to 1850..., 14960
Anti-slavery nominations, 23904
The anti-slavery papers of James Russell
  Lowell, 23901
Anti-slavery Party, 24152
The anti-slavery picknick; a collection of
  speeches, poems, dialogues and songs, 24166

Anti-slavery record, 23905
The anti-slavery reform, its principle and
  method, 24000
Anti-slavery Society, London, 23906
Anti-slavery Society of Salem and Vicinity,
  Salem, Mass., 23907
The anti-slavery struggle, 23908
The antislavery struggle and triumph in the
  Methodist Episcopal Church, 25012
Anti-Van Buren members of the General
  Assembly of Virginia, 5914
Anticipation continued, 394
Anticipation of marginal notes on the
  declaration of government, 395
Anticosti Island, 6511, 6512
An antidote against Toryism, 23782
An antidote to John Wood's poison, 11768
An antidote to mormonism, 22796
Antidote to the merino-mania now progressing
  through the United States, 396
Antigua and the Antiguans, 397
Antigua, Description & travel, 397, 5808,
  8181; History, 397, 5808, 12172
La antigüedad clásica en el pensamiento
  historiográfico español del siglo XIX,
  16038
Antigüedad del hombre en México y Centro-
  américa, 18634
Antigüedades americanas, 610
Antilles, Lesser, Description & travel,
  4998, 5569, 7204, 22107
Antinucci, Alfonso Eduardo, 18303
Antioch Christian Church, Fayette County,
  Ky., 14200
Antioch College, Yellow Springs, O., 23084
Antioquía, Colombia (State), Economic
  condition, 18340; Politics & government,
  18305; Statistics, 18304, 18305
Antioquía, Tierra de trabajo y progreso,
  18306
Antiquarian researches, 12970
Antiques, Catalogs, 15684
Antiquities of America explained, 22473
Antiquities of the Mesa Verde national
  park, 16506
Antiquities of the southern Indians, 4104
Antiquities of the West, 3002
Antofagasta, History, 20681
Antoine, Antoine, de Saint-Gervais, 1776-
  1836, 398
Antología arcaica, 19530
Antología de la poesía gauchesca, 18931
Antología de costumbristas venezolanos
  del siglo XIX, 18307
Antología de poetas cearenses contemporâneos,
  18308

Uma antologia do conto cearense, 18309
La antropología física en México, 20361
Antologia nacional, 6692
Antologia poética do movimento antroponautica, 18310
Anton, George F., 18311
L'Antoniade, 5024
Antonio, Nicolás, 1617-1684, 399, 400
Antonio de Ciudad Real, supposed joint author, 5874
Antonioletti, Rodrigo, 18312
Antonita, the female contrabandista, 10251
Antony Brade, 10247
Antrobus, Benjamin, d.1715, 401
Ants, Cuba, 18085; North Dakota, 17868
Antunes, Clóvis, 18313
Antúnez y Acevedo, Rafael, 402
The Anvil Press of Lexington, Kentucky, 15523
Anville, Jean Baptiste Bourgignon d', 1697-1789, 2549
Anza, Juan Bautista de, 16533, 16534
... The Anza expedition of 1775-1776, 16533
Anzalaz, Fermín Alfredo, ed., 18318
Anzola Gómez, Gabriel, 18319
Año espiritual, 7666
An Apache campaign in the Sierra Madre, 16022
Apache country, 2837
Apache Indians, 5299, 15863, 16287, 16297, 16449, 16816; Fiction, 16466; Wars, 1883-1886, 16022, 16816; Wars, 1883-1886, Fiction, 16467
Apalachicola land company, 1413
Aparicio, Luis, 18320
Aparicio, Laurencio, Angel, 18321
Aparicio, Sebastian de, 1502-1600, 6384
Aperçus sur les institutions et les moeurs des Américains, 4478
Apes, William, b.1798, 403, 404, 405
Apgaua, Paulo, 18322
Aphorisms and apothegms, 18169
Aphorisms and reflections, 5237
Apianus, Petrus, 1495-1552, 406, 407
La apicultura en su aspecto económico, 19899
Aplicación práctica de la proyección mercator transversal universal, 19936
Aplicaciones del algebra moderna a la inferencia estadística, 19824
O apocalípse ou O capeta de caruaru, 20427
The apocatastasis; or, Progress backwards, 23166
Apolla, Arnaldo, 1879-, 5915
Apollinaire, Guillaume, 18323
Apollonius, levinus, 16th cent., 408
Apología de la intolerancia religiosa, Segunda parte, 19780
An apology, 358

An apology for the times, 409
An apology for the true Christian divinity, 21768
The apology of patriots, 566
Aportes para realizar trabajos de investigació acerca de historia rural, 18592
Der apostel von Ohio, 14254
An apostle of the wilderness, 16800
Apostolic succession, 12156, 21890, 21891
Apostólicos afanes de la compañía de Jesus, 23480
Appalachia, 15138, 15475, 15611; Bibliography, 14051, 15139, 15415, 15416, 15455, 15664; Description, 13558, 15645; Economic conditions, 13649, 13691, 14491, 14657; Fiction, 3366, 4561, 4563, 4567, 8758, 9867, 10592, 13619, 31732, 13745, 13781, 14351; Fiction, Bibliography, 13654, 15135; Kentuckiana, 15416; Poetry, 14924; Population, 14491; Social condition, 13649, 13691, 14657; Social life and customs, 13715
Appalachian coal miners want decent working conditions, 13556
Appalachian Kentucky Health Manpower Service, 13557
Appalachian literature, 15136
Appalachian Mountain club, Boston, 16174
Appalachian region, Description & travel, 2997, 3261, 3626, 4559, 5789; Social conditions, 3769; Social life & customs, 3522
Appalshop, Inc., Whitesburg, Ky., 13558
The apparition, 9702
"Appasionata", 19879
Appelbaum, Richard P., 18324
Apple Blossoms, 11191
Applegate, Jesse A., 1835-1919, 15861
Appler, Augustus C., 15862
Appleton, E.H., 8597
Appleton, James, 1785-1862, 23911
Appleton, Jesse, 1772-1819, 414-417
Appleton, John, 1809-1869, 23275
Appleton, Nathan, 1779-1861, 754, 25194
Appleton, William Sumner, 1840-1902, 418
Appleton family (Samuel Appleton, 1586-1670), 13222
Appleton, firm, publishers, New York, 6318
Appleton's general guide to the U.S. & Canada, 2550, 2551
Appleton's guide to Mexico, 6454, 6455
Appleton's handbook of American travel, 2552, 5916, 5917
Appleton's illustrated handbook of American travel, 5910
Appleton's new and complete U.S. guide-book

for travellers, 8388
Appleton's railroad and steamboat companion, 5724, 8389
Appleton's southern and western travellers' guide, 5725
Appomattox, pseud., 23912
Appomattox campaign, 1865, 22256
Apprentices, 23113; West Indies, British, 23903
Apprenticeship, 23972
Appun, Karl Ferdinand, 18325
Apra y el colonialismo neoliberal, 18065
Aprenda analise, 19497
Aprendizaje y psicagogía de atrasados mentales, 18639
April hopes, 9939
April's sowing, 8883
Aprista (Partido), Perú, 19895
Aprovietamento dos finos de carvão vegetal, 19506
Apthorp, East, 1732 or 3-1816, 419; Considerations on the institution and conduct of the Society for the propagation of the gospel, 23397
An aquatic expedition from Gilbraltar to Barcelona, 10916
Aquidneck, 1575
O ar que nos envolve, 19033
Ara, Guillermo, 18326, 18327
The Arab wife, 8542
Arabesques, 9660
Arabs, History, 18691
Arabs in Spain, Bio-bibliography, 400
Aracati, Brazil, 19462
Arachnida - Cuba, 18088, 18525, 18526; Uropygi, 18530
Arago, Dominique François Jean, 1786-1853, 423
Arago, Jacques Étienne Victor, 1790-1855, 420-423
Arai, Alberto T., 18328
Aramayo Alzérreca, Oscar, 18329
Aramburu de la Cuesta, Juan B., 18330
Arana, V. M., 18331
Arana Sánchez, Jorge, 18332
Aranda Alvarez, Guillermo, 18333
Aranda Sánchez, Francisco, 18334
Araneda Bravo, Fidel, 18335, 18336
Araneda Dörr, Hugo, 18337
Arango Cano, Jesús, 18338, 18339
Arango R., Mariano, 18340
Arango y Nuñez del Castillo, José de, 1765-1851, 424, 612; Independencia de la isla de Cuba, 424
Aránquiz Donoso, Horacio, 18341
Aránguiz Lezaeta, Eliana, 18342

Aranha, Graca, 18343
Aranibar, Carlos, 20194
Araoz de la Madrid, Gregorio, 1795-1857, 5919
The Arapahoe half breed, 4972
Arapahoe County, Colorado, History, 16782
Araquistain, Luis, 18344
Arator, 23682
Aratu, Brazil, Description, 18844
La Araucana, 6677-6688
Araucania, History, Poetry, 6680-6686, 6688
Araucanian Indians, 8291, 10574, 18997; Religion and mythology, 19889; Rites and ceremonies, 19889; Wars, 8309
Araucho, Manuel de, 1803-1842, 18931
Arauco, Chile (Province), Description & travel, 2108
Araújo, Acrísio Tôrres, 18345
Araújo, Aloyr Queiroz de, 18346
Araújo, Delio Moreira de, 18347
Araújo, Helton Carlos de, 18348
Araújo, Iaperi, 18349
Araújo, José de Sousa Azevedo Pizarro e, 1753-1830, 19298
Araújo, Nancy de Queiroz, 18340
Araújo, Vivaldo Campbell de, 18351
Araujo e Silva, Domingos de, 1834-, 425
Araujo Filho, José Ribeiro de, 18352
Araújo Sánchez, Francisco, 18353
Araújo Villegas, Arturo, 18354
Aravena Arredondo, Leonardo, 18355
Arawak language, 23517
Araya, Carlomagno, 18356
Araya, Guillermo, 18357
Araya, José Francisco, 18358
Die Arbeits-verfassung der englischen Kolonien in Nord-amerika, 25442
Arbeláez, Fernando, comp., 18359
Arbeláez Camacho, Carlos, 18360
Arbeláez Lema, Federico, 18361
Arbella (ship), 6810
Arber, Edward, 1836-1912, ed., 5920
Arbitrary arrests in the South, 5372
Arbitration and award, Chile, 18355
Arbitration, International, 8270
Arboleda, José Rafael, 18362, 18363
Arc measures, 11403
The Arcade hotel guide, for the use of strangers visiting Philadelphia, 21820
Arce, Francisco de, 5921
Arce, José, 18364, 18365
Arce, Luis A., 18366
Arce de Vásquez, Margot, 18367
Archaeologiae americanae telluris collectanea

et specimina, 928
Archaeological excavations in Mesa Verde
National Park, 16971
Archaeological researches in Kentucky
and Indiana, 15210
Archaeological sites in Mexico, 6715
Archangelsky, Sergio, 18368
The archbishop, 8770
The archbishop's unguarded moment and
other stories, 8473
Archdale, John, 1642?-1717, 426, 2553
Archelaus, philosopher, fl.5th century
B.C., 19734
Archenholz, Johann Wilhelm von, 1743-
1812, 427, 428
Archer, Armstrong, 429
Archer, Maria, 18369
Archer, William Segar, 1789-1855, 430,
431
Archery, 5400
Archibald, A., 6315
Archila, Ricarda, 1909-, 16550, 18370,
18371
Architecture, Brazil, 20632; Conservation
and restoration, 19748; Colombian, 20507;
Colonial, Colombia, 18360, 20508;
Domestric, 15097; Domestic, Kentucky,
13901, 14766, 14787, 14951, 14968, 16720;
Domestic, Lexington, Ky., 14118, 14966;
Domestic, Louisville, Ky., 14072, 15293;
Domestic, U.S., 3435; European, 21735;
History, 19136; Latin American, Addresses,
essays, lectures, 18360; Latin American,
Colonial period, 19749; Mexico, 7711;
Theory of, 20632: Venezuelan, 19749
Archiveros de Argentina, Jornadas, 2nd,
Córdoba, 1969, 18372
Archives, 18256, 18260; Argentine Republic,
18257-18259, 18372, 18592; Brazil, 19245;
California, 16125; Chile, 20166; Colorado,
17896; Kentucky, 14626; Latin America,
18372; Maryland, 149; Nebraska, 17597;
Oregon, 17309; U.S., 919; Venezuela,
19484
Archivo americano y espíritu de la prensa
del mundo, 432
Archivos, historia e información, 18256
Archivos de ciencias de la educación
(Indexes), 19553
Archivos de pedagogía y ciencias afines
(Indexes), 19553
Arcila Farías, Eduardo, 18373
Arciniegas, Germán, 18374, 18375
Arcos, Juan, 18376
Arctic (steamship), 6303
Arctic enterprise, 23

The Arctic expedition, 1910, 6303
Arctic miscellanies, 433
The Arctic prairies, 8007
Arctic races, 22322
Arctic regions, 433, 614, 615, 883, 1066,
1067, 1116, 1117, 2213, 2428, 2585, 3528,
3529, 4678, 5169, 6048, 6058, 6303, 6449,
6623, 6870, 7591, 7652, 7695, 7696, 8050,
8123, 8134, 11238, 11582, 12560, 13428,
22322, 22366, 22846, 23405; Description
& exploration, 4175, 4880; Maps, 7109;
Poetry, 23, 1376
The Arctic regions and Hudson's Bay route,
17439
Arctic rewards and their claimants, 434
Arctic rovings, 12562
An arctic voyage to Baffin's bay, 6870
Arcturus, 435; Selections from, 10326
Ardao, Arturo, 18377, 18378
The ardent desire and sincere cry, or a
true believer in Jesus Christ, 21762
Ardery, Julia Spencer,("Mrs. William
Breckinridge Ardery"), 13560-13562,
13695, 13833, 14018, 15142
Ardery, W.B., 13560-13562, 13833
Ardiuni, Juvenal, 18382
Ardón, Víctor M., 18379-18381
Arduz Caballero, Walter, 18383
Areão, João Steudel, 18384
Arébalo, Nicolás de, 6754
Arellano, Jesús, 18386
Arellano Jiménez, Guillermo, 18387
Arellano Moreno, Antonio, 18388, 18389
Arena, Andrés R., 18922
Arenales, José Alvarez de, 1798-1862, 369,
436, 437
Arenales, Juan Antonio Alvarez de, b.1770,
369, 436
Arenas, Antonio Vicente, 18390
Ares Somoza, Paulino, 18391
Arcta, Carlos Manuel, 18519-18520
Aretza de Ramón y Rivera, Isabel, 18392
Aretz-Thiele, Isabel, 18393
Arévalo Martínez, Rafael, 18394
Arey, Henry W., 438
Areytos, 5155
Arfwedson, Carl David, 439, 440, 441
La Argentina, 794
La Argentina ante los problemas mundiales,
18498
Argentine essays, 20221
Argentine literature (Selections, extracts,
etc.), 19798; History & criticism, 18327,
19798; 19th century, Addresses, essays,
lectures, 10704; Periodicals, 5961, 6244
Argentine periodicals, 17977, 18244

Argentine philosophy, 18096, 18097
Argentine poetry (collections), 18931
Argentine Republic, 1719; Archivo General,
18397; Bibliography, 20470; Biblioteca.
Servicio de Referencia, 18415-18417;
Biography, 19764, 12510; Boundaries, 372,
19724; Boundaries, Bolivia, 7953;
Boundaries, Chile, 18900; Caja Nacional
de Ahorro Postal, 18398, 18399; Census,
1960, 18445, 18447, 18448; Centro de
Documentación Científica, 18400; Centro
Nacional de Documentación e Información
Educativa, 18401; Comisión de Integración
Eléctrica, 18402; Comisión Nacional de
Administración del Fondo de Apoyo al
Desarrollo Económico, 18403-18405; Comisión
Nacional de Energía Atómica, 18406;
Comisión de Energía Atómica. Departamento
de Metalurgía, 18407; Comisión Nacional
Ejecutiva del 150. Aniversario de la
Revolución de Mayo, 17977, 18244; Comisión
Nacional Ejecutiva de Homenaje, 18408;
Commerce, Laws and regulations, 18464;
Congreso. Biblioteca, 18409; Congreso.
Biblioteca. Bibliografía sobre la
vivienda, 18410; Congreso. Biblioteca.
Departamento de Legislación Comparada,
18414; Congreso. Biblioteca. Immigración,
18411; Congreso. Biblioteca. Ley de control
de precios..., 18412; Congreso. Biblioteca.
Vivienda, 18413; Congreso. Cámara de
senadores, 7953, 18418, 18419; Consejo de
Investigaciones Científicas Reuniones a
realizares en la República Argentina en
1970, 18420; Consejo Federal de Inversiones,
18421-18429; Consejo Nacional de Desarrollo,
18430; Consejo Nacional de Desarrollo. Junta
Nacional de Carnes, 18431; Consejo Nacional
de Desarrollo. Secretaría. Serie C, 18432;
Consejo Nacional de Desarrollo. Sector
Educacion, 18433; Consejo Nacional de
Investigaciones Cientificas y Técnicas,
18434-18436, 18400; Constitution, 18095,
18365, 18437, 18438; Constitutional history,
18095, 18364; Constitutional law, 123, 18365;
Departamento de Estadística, 18439;
Departamento de Estudios Históricos Navales.
Serie B: Historia naval argentina, 18671;
Departamento de Estudios Históricos Navales.
Serie C: Biografías navales argentinas,
18670; Description & travel, 359, 592, 1023,
1028, 1380, 1431, 7977, 11964, 12249, 12497,
12498, 12519, 12529, 13054, 18957, 22629,
22788, 23046; Dirección General de
Investigaciones Agrícolas, 18440; Dirección
General de Parques Nacionales, 18441, 18442;

Dirección Nacional de Energía y
Combustibles, 18443; Dirección Nacional
de Estadística y Censos, 18444-18448;
Dirección Nacional de Fiscalización y
Comercialización Ganadera, 18449;
Dirección Nacional de Geología y Minería,
18450; Economic conditions, 697, 12519,
13054, 18404, 18405, 18410, 18412, 18425,
18433, 18496, 18502, 18729, 18792, 18793,
18794, 19796, 19799, 19146, 20396; Economic
policy, 18155, 18430; Emigration &
immigration, 437; Estación Experimental
Agropecuaria Anguil, 18451; Foreign
relations, 18498; Foreign relations,
Brazil, 19382; Foreign relations, France,
21761; Foreign relations, Mexico, 7792;
Foreign relations, Uruguay, 1764; Fuerza
Aerea Argentina, 18452; History, 1588,
12249, 18689; History, 1535-1617,
Poetry, 794; History, 1776-1810, 596;
History, To 1810, 592, 594; History,
1810-, 7708; History, 1817-1860, 432,
1023, 1764, 7943, 19676, 21761, 22788;
History, 1930-60, 18395; History,
Colonial period, 17997; History, Periodicals,
6244; History, Revolution of May, 18398;
History, Sources, 370; History, War of
Independence, 1810-1817, Bibliography,
19613; History, War of Independence,
1810-1817, 7708, 7762, 7943; History,
War of Independence, 1810-1817, Naval
operations, 18671; History, War of
Independence, 1810-1817, Sources, 1662,
17977, 18244; History, Military, 19676;
Imprints, 19548; Industries, 18427,
18446, 20004; Instituto de Biología
Marina, 18453; Instituto Experimental
del Mogólico, 18454; Instituto Geográfico
Militar, 18455; Instituto Nacional de
Previsión Social, 18456; Instituto
Nacional de Tecnología Agropecuaria.
Colección científica, 19571; Instituto
Nacional de Vitivinicultura, 18457,
18458, 18459; Junta Nacional de Carnes,
19618; Laws, statutes, etc., 18560-18473;
Lotería de Beneficencia Nacional y Casinos,
manual oficial descriptivo (una institución
al servicio del país), 18396; Maps, 18455;
Ministerio de Agricultura y Ganadería,
18474; Ministerio de Asistencia Social y
Salud Pública, 18475; Ministerio de
Cultura y Educación. Departamento de
Estadística Educativa, 18476-18490;
Ministerio de Educación y Justicia, 18491;
Ministerio de Educación y Justica.
Departamento de Documentacíon e Información

Educativa, 18492; Ministerio de obras y Servicios Públicos. Subsecretaría de Energía, 18493; Ministerio de Trabajo y Seguridad Social, 18494; Museo Colonial e Histórico "Enrique Udaondo", 18259; Navy, 19585; Periodicals, 5961; Policía Federal. Museo, 18495; Politics & government, 123, 18011, 18416, 18417, 18437, 18438, Politics & government, 123, 18011, 18416, 18417, 18437, 18438, 18501, 19765, 20232; Politics & government, 1810-1817, 7943, 8026; Politics & government, 1817-1860, 7943, 8026, 23076; Population, 18448, 19677, 20360; Presidencia de la nación, 18496; Presidencia de la nación. Secretaría General, 18497; Presidente, 1958-(Frondizi), 18498; Secretaría de Agricultura y Ganadería, 18499; Secretaría de Estado de Cultura y Educación, 18700; Secretaría de Estado de Vivienda, 18500; Secretaría de Estado de Vivienda. Banco Hipotecario Nacional, 18501; Secretaría de Prensa, 18502; Servicio de Hidrografía naval. Departamento de Meteorología, 18503; Social conditions, 18433, 18689, 19146; Social life & customs, 7977; Statistics, 18444, 19677; Subsecretaria de Mineria. Estudios de geologia y mineria económica. Serie argentina, 19981
Argonauts of California, 16715
The Argonauts of North Liberty, 9776
Argow, Wendelin Waldemar Wieland, 1891-, 5922
Arguedas, Alcides, 1879-1946, 5923, 7752, 18504, 18505
Argueta, Manlio, 18506
Arguin, 24622
Argyll, John George Edward Henry Douglas Sutherland Campbell, 9th duke of, 1845-1914, 5924-5929, 7970
Arias, Abelardo, 18507-18511
Arias, Hermes Duarte, 18512
Arias B., Jorge 18513
Arias Ramírez, Javier, 18514
Arias Robalino, Augusto, 18515
Arid regions, 7468
Arikara and Cheyenne earth lodge sites in North and South Dakota, 17686
Arikara ceremonials, 17889
The Arikara Indian fight, 2554
Arikara Indians, 2554, 4942, 17458, 17710, 17000, 17801
Arín Urmazábal, Ángel de, 18516
Arinos, Afonso, 18517
Aristides, pseud., 12652, 12653

Aristocracy, 807, 808, 11169, 11232
Aristocracy in America, 3711
The aristocrat, 8799
L'aristocratie en Amérique, 3558
Aristodemus, pseud., 1516
Aristóteles, Política, 18518
Arithmetic, before 1800, 22638
Ariza S., Alberto E., 18521, 18522
Arizona, 4341, 4545, 14896, 17239, 17508; Biography, 16334, 16771, 17883; Commerce, 14056; Description & travel, 2575, 2837, 3113, 4341, 4544, 4922, 5539, 6087, 6088, 6139, 6165, 14749, 15527, 15811, 15867, 16158, 16287; Directories, 16243; History, 3113, 16334, 16771, 16874, 17230, 24304; Politics & government, 4545; Public lands, 17669
Arizona's yesterday, 16119
Ark (sailing vessel), 7374
Arkansas, 5100, 15893; Archives, 17479; Bibliography, 15864; Biography, 1350, 17604, 21785; Constitution, 16266; Description & travel, 2739, 3304, 3425, 3479, 3594, 3790, 4173, 4411, 4480, 4632, 4799, 4973, 5062, 5098, 16204, 16588, 16739, 16808, 17209, 17212, 17574, 17837; Description & travel, Views, 15871; Fiction, 4902; Finance, 17580; History, 4825, 15842, 15864, 15865, 15866, 15871, 15980, 15981, 15982, 16672, 16737, 17137, 17478, 17604; History, Civil war, 1350, 1351, 11244, 16451, 17219, 17774, 21785; History Commission, 16743; Poetry, 14404; Politics & government, Civil war, 4800
Arkansas Co. Ark., History, 16670
Arkansas history commission and its work, 16743
Arkansas military institute, Tulip, Arkansas, 17388
An Arkansas planter, 4902
Arkansas River, 4632
Arkwright, Sir Richard, 1732-1792, 12483
Arlach, H. de T. d', 442
Arlt, Mirta, 18523
Arlt, Roberto, 1900-1942, 19906
The arm-chair of Tustenuggee, 10783
Armand, pseud., 5306
Las armas secretas, 20529
Armas, Luis F. de, 18524-18533
Armas Chitty, José Antonio de, 18534-18541
Armas Lara, Marcial, 18542
Armas y Céspedes, José de, 1834 1900, 23914
Armellada, Cesáreo de, 10543
Armendariz, José de, see Castelfuerto, José

26

de Armendáriz, marqués de, Viceroy of Peru.
Armenta C., Santiago, 18544
Armes, Elizabeth Marie, 5930
Armes, George Augustus, 1844-1919, 15868
Armestar V., Miguel A., 18545
Armesto, Alejandro, 18546
Armijo, Antonio, 2555
Armijo, Roberto, 18547, 18548
Armistead, Wilson, 1819?-1868, 443-445, 496, 23915, 23916
Armistead family, 6812
Armitage, Jacob, 24412
Armitage, John, 1807-1856, 446
Armitage, Thomas, 1819-1896, 447
Armor-plate, 1219
Armony, Miguel, 20449
Armored vessels, 1219
Armour, 8534
Armroyd, George, 448
Arms and the man, 3928
Arms of Amsterdam (Ship), 25168
Armstrong, A. N., 15869
Armstrong, Sir Alexander, 1818-1899, 449
Armstrong, Benjamin G., 1820-, 15870
Armstrong, Edward, 450, 1651
Armstrong, George Dodd, 1813-1899, 451, 452
Armstrong, John, 1758-1843, 455, 1917, 2364, 13100, 22923
Armstrong, John J., 453, 454
Armstrong, Kosciuszko, 455
Armstrong, Kosciuszko, 455; review of Thomas L. McKenney's Narrative (1847), 22923
Armstrong, Lebbeus, 1775-1860, 456, 457, 458
Armstrong, Mrs. Louise (Van Voorhis) 1889-, 5931
Armstrong, Moses Kimball, 13563
Armstrong, Robert, 459
Armstrong, Robert G., 460
Armstrong, William, 461
Army and Navy chronicle, 11228
The Army and Navy chronicle and scientific repository, 462
The Army & navy official gazette, 463
The army chaplain's manual, 12628
The army hymn book, 464
Army letters, 4622
Army letters from an officer's wife, 5004
Army life, 3592, 4399
Army life in a black regiment, 3864
Army life of an Illinois solider, 5732
The Army of the Cumberland, 13827
The army ration, 12907
Army regulations adopted for use of the

Army of the Confederate States, 2067
An army wife, 10109
Arnau Macías, Manuel, 18550
Arnaud, Achille, 1826-, 465
Arnaud, Expedito, 18551-18555
Arnedo Álvarez, Gerónimo, 18556
Arnett, Maralea, 13564
Arnold, Benedict,1741-1801, 354, 355, 466, 467, 23618; Fiction, 8785, 8967, 10510, 10513
Arnold, Channing, 5932
Arnold, Charles Henry, 468
Arnold, George, 1834-1865, 8597
Arnold, Isaac Newton, 1815-1884, 469, 470, 471, 472, 473, 5933, 5934, 5935, 6415, 7279
Arnold, James G., 14713, 14714
Arnold, Josias Lyndon, 1768-1796, 474
Arnold, Matthew, 1822-1888, 2556
Arnold, Samuel, 1622-1693, 23814
Arnold, Samuel, 1838(ca.)-1906, defendant, 1305
Arnold, Samuel George, 1806-1891, 475, 476
Arnold, Samuel Green, 1821-1880, 477, 478
Arnold, Seth S., 479
Arnold, W.E. A history of Methodism in Kentucky, 15701
Arnold, W.P., 13565
Arnold, William E., comp., 2557
Arnold at Saratoga, 10510
Arnot, Andrew, 1722-1803, 22264
Arnott, George Arnott Walker, 1799-1868,.. jt., 12883
Arnould, Ambroise Marie, 1750?-1812, 480
Arocho Rivera, Minerva, 18557
Aromita, 19687
Aroostook, The lady of the, 9946
Aroostook River and Valley, Description and travel, 12868
Arosemena, Justo, 1817-1896, 18976
Arózqueta Rojano, Sadot, 18558
Arqueología, 20482
Arqueología peruana, 19141
La arquitectura de Bonampak, 18328
Arraes, Miguel, 18559
Arraes, Raymundo de Monte, 18560
Arrangoiz y Berzábal, Francisco de Paula de, 18561
Arras, Mario S., 18562, 18563
Arrate y Acosta, José Martín Félix de, 18569
Arreaza Calatrava, José Tadeo, 18565
Arredondo, Antonio de, 2558
Arredondo, Oscar, 18566
Arredondo Andrade, Patricio, 18567
Arredondo Fernández, Jaime, 18568
Arredondo y Miranda, Francisco de, 18569

Arredondo's historical proof of Spain's
  title to Georgia, 2558
Arrendamientos y aparcerías rurales,
  18460
Arreola, Juan José, 18570
Arriaga, Eduardo, 18571
Arriaga, Miguel, 5936
Arriaga, Noël de, 18572
Arriaga, Pablo José de, 1564-, 5937, 18473
Arriaga Paz, Rafael, 18574
Arricivita, Juan Domingo, 2559
Arrieta Chavarría, Omar, 18575
Arrington, Alfred W., 1810-1867, 481
Arriola, Juan de, b.1698, 5938
L'arrivée des pères capucins, 1899
Arrom, José Juan, 18576
Arróniz, Marcos, d.1858 or 9, 482, 483
The arrows of love, 9315
Arrowsmith, Aaron, 1750-1823, 128
Arroyo, Leonardo, 18577
Arroyo de Colón, María, 18578
Arroyo Llano, Rodolfo, 18579
Arroyo Soto, Victor Manuel, 18580
Arrufat, Antón, 18581
Arsenals, U.S., 25775
Art, 825; Addresses, essays, lectures,
  2511; American (pre-Columbian), 18328,
  19588, 19939; Ancient, Catalogs, 22429;
  Aneedotes, facatiae, satire, etc.., 10186;
  Brazilian, 18812, 18961, Byzantine, 727;
  Colonial, Venezuela, 18737; Etruscan,
  19640; Exhibitions, Catalogs, 19665;
  Germany, 22675; Greco-Roman, 19640;
  History, 22683; History, Brazil, 18812;
  Indian, 19588, 20509; Italy, 22675; Mayan,
  18328; Mexico, 6940, 17989; Pre-Columbian,
  18328, 19588, 19939,; Private collections,
  22429; São Paulo (city), 18171; Spanish-
  American, 18633; Study and teaching,
  Curricula, 20585; U.S., 1227, 2135, 22683;
  U.S., History, 2135; Venezuelan, 18737,
  19739
Art and industry, 12373
Art and morals, 825, 5388
Art criticism, 13978
Art culture, 825
L'art de l'Amérique précolombienne, 19588
The art-idea: sculpture, painting, and
  architecture in America, 22683
Art industries and trade, Mexico, 18584
The art of living, 9637
The art of mettals, 773
The art of war, 2015
Art work of Louisville, 13568
Artaud, Antonín, 18582
Arte, sociedade e região, 19708

Arte de construcción, 7436
Arte de el idioma maya, 1136
Da arte de falar mal, 20456
Arte de grammatica da lengua brasilica da
  naçam kiriri, 23062
Arte de la lengua mexicana, 583
Arte menor, 18975
Arte popular de México, 18584
Arte popular del Ecuador, 18278
El arte popular en la América Latina, 18633
Artecona de Thompson, Marialuisa, 18583
Artemesia longinaris Bate, 19188
Artemus Ward, 8874
Artemus Ward in London, 8875
Artemus Ward on his visit to Abe Lincoln,
  6201
Artemus Ward's panorama, 8876
Artes de México, 18584
Artese, Edla Monteiro, 18585
Artesian wells, 23339
Arthur, Alexander Alan, 13955
Arthur, Sir George, bart., 1784-1854,
  24020
Arthur, Richard, 5939
Arthur, Samuel John, 5940
Arthur, Timothy Shay, 1809-1885, 484-487,
  11673
Arthur Bonnicastle, 9886
Arthur Woodleigh, 9649
Arthus, Gotthard, 1570-1630?, 488
Articles of agreement, 489
Artie, 8475
Artigas, José Gervasio, 1764-1850, 18850,
  20620
Artigue, Jean d', 5941
Artillery, Coast, 837
Artist-life in Italy, 9659
The artist of the beautiful, 9823
The artist's bride, 2670
The artist's dream, 11047
The artist's love, 10830
An artist's tour, 4196
An artistic necessity, 10283
Artists, American, 2135; Correspondence,
  reminiscences, etc., 14297, 14301;
  Fiction, 10301; Kentucky, 13963
Artrip, Fullen, 5942
Artrip, Louise, 5942
Arts Club, Louisville, Ky., 13567
Arts of design in the United States, 2135
Aruana, 18248
Asamblea Interuniversitaria de Filología
  y Literaturas Hispánicas, 18586
Asanh, 9123
Asbury, Francis, 1745-1816, 490, 3302,
  14944, 15388

Asbury, Henry, 1810-1896, 15873
Ascanio, Osvaldo, 18587
Asceticism, Catholic church, 7673
Aschmann, Hermann P., 18588
Ascoli, Carlos A. de, 18589
Ascutney street, 11151
Asenjo, Conrado, 18590
El asfalto de los infiernos, 18002
Asfixiologia forense, 21738
Asfura Prado, Jorge, 18591
Asgill, Sir Charles, 1762-1823, 13008
Ashburn, George W., d.1868, 25339
Ashe, E. M., illustr., 2546
Ashe, Samuel A'Court, 1840-1938, 5943
Ashe, Thomas, fl. 1682, 491, 2560
Ashe, Thomas, 1770-1835, 492-494, 2561
Asher, Adolf, 1800-1853, 495
Asher, Jeremiah, b.1812, 496
Ashes and incense, 2609
The ashes of southern homes, 4736
Ashland (home of Henry Clay in
  Lexington, Ky.), 13603, 14780
Ashland, Ky. Centennial Committee,
  13568; History, 13568; Unity Baptist
  Church, 15555
The Ashland march, 13741
The Ashland melodies, 13569
Ashland Oil and Refining Company, 13675
Ashley, Chester, 1790-1848, 497
Ashley, David H., 13570
Ashley, James Monroe,1824-1896, 498, 499,
  5944-5946, 23917
Ashley, John, d.1751, 500, 501
Ashley, William Henry, 2554, 4942
Ashmead, A. S., 5947
Ashmore, John D., 1819-, 23918
Ashmun, George, 1804-1870, 502, 23919
Ashmun, Jehudi, 1794-1828, 503, 12508,
  25943
Ashworth, Henry, 1794-1880, 2562
Así es México, 7485
Asia, Description & travel, 4853;
  History, 11589
The Asiatic cholera in Winchester in 1833,
  14102
Asido al viento, 18562
Asiento treaty, 1713, 25077
Asinari, Amanda, 18592
Askaros Kassis, 9380
Asleep, 9667
Asmodeus, 8889
Asociación Colombiana de Bibliotecarios.
  Boletín, 19106
Asociación Colombiana de Facultades de
  Medicina, 20345-20348, 18593
Asociación de Amigos del País, Guatemala,

Asociación de Bibliotecarios Graduados de
  la República Argentina, 18595
Asociación Demográfica Costarricense, 18596
Asociación Interamericana de Bibliotecarios
  y Documentalistas Agrícolas, 18597
Asociación mexicana automovílistica, 7990
Asociación mexicana de turismo, 5948, 5949,
  7485
Asociación Nacional de Industriales, Bogotá,
  20275, 20326, 18598, 18599
Asociacion Obrera Minera Argentina, 18600
Asociación Venezolana de Facultades
  (Escuelas) de Medicina, 18601
Aspendale, 10565
The Aspern papers, 7117
Asphalt rock, 14038
Asphodel, 9515
Aspidosperma, 18107, 18108
Aspillaga H., Gonzalo, 18602
Aspinall, Sir Algernon Edward, 1871-, 5950,
  5951
Aspinwall, Thomas, 1786-1876, 505
Asplund, John, d.1807, 506
Assall, Friedrich, Wilhelm, 507
The assassination and history of the
  conspiracy, 508
Assassination of President Lincoln and
  the capture of John Wilkes Booth...,
  13869
The assay office and the proposed mint
  at New Westminster, 7822
Assaying, Tables, calculations, etc., 6702
L'Assemblée des noirs, 5952
Assiniboia (District) 1836-1870, Council,
  7641
Assiniboine river, 3878
Assistance (Ship), 433, 6058
Associação Brasileira de Credito e
  assistencia rural, 18603
Associação central da agricultura portugueza,
  24966
Associação dos Advogados de São Paulo.
  Departamento de Cultura, 18126
Associação maritima e colonial, Lisbon, 379
Associates of Doctor Thomas Bray for founding
  clerical libraries and supporting negro
  schools, 958, 1006, 1610, 11260, 11635,
  12161, 22329, 23635, 23752
Association of American geologists and
  naturalists, 509
Association of Caribbean Universities and
  Research Institutes, 18604
Association of Franklin medal scholars,
  Boston, 510
Association of Friends for Promoting the
  Abolition of Slavery, and Improving the

Condition of the Free People of Color, 23920, 24927
Association of Friends for the diffusion of religious and useful knowledge, 1158
Association of masters of the Boston public schools. Rejoinder to the "Reply" of the Hon. Horace Mann, 23082; Remarks on the Seventh annual report of the Hon. Horace Mann, 23089
Associations, Kentucky, 13622
Assollant, Alfred, i.e. Jean Baptiste Alfred, 1827-1886, 2563
Assumpçao, Rosely Maria Viegas, 18605
Assunção, Fernando O., 18606
Assyro-Babylonian language - Texts, 24248
Asters and disasters of society, 10419
Astey V., Luis, 18920, 19051, 18607, 18608
Asti, Felice, 511
Asti Vera, Armando, 18609
Astié, Jean Frédéric, 1822-1894, 512
Astley, Thomas, 211
Aston, Anthony, 2564
"Astonished at America," 5799
The astonishing adventure of James Botello, 10338
Astor, John Jacob, 1763-1848, 5017, 17404
Astor library, New York, 513-518
Astoria, 3971, 4026
Astoria, Or., 4026, 5017
Astounding disclosures!, 13018
Astrada, Carlos, 18610
The astrologer of the nineteenth century, 10693
Astrology, 6480, 7418, 7419
The astronomical diary, 326
Astronomy, 15224; Addresses, essays, lectures, 81; Early works to 1800, 6728; History, 23037; Observations, 993, 7092
Astudillo, Rubén, 18611
Astudillo Espinosa, Carlos J., 18612
Astudillo Sandoval, Homero, 18613
Asuntos económicos, 18415
Atala, 5026, 20087
Atanasiú, Andrés Homero, 18614
Atcher, Charles L., 13571
Atcheson, Nathaniel, 1771-1825, 519, 520
Atchinson, Kansas, Directories, 2566
Atchinson city directory, 2566
Atchison, David Rice, 1807-1886, 521
Atcon, Rudolph P., 18615
Aten, Henry J., 1841-, 2567
Atenção, signos, graus de informação, 18660
Ateneo de Costa Rica, 5064
Ateneo de Honduras, 5555
Ateneo de la Juventud, 18616
El Ateneo de Lima, 5956

Athabasca and Peace River treaty exhibition, 1899, 7392
Athaliah, 9655
Athalie, 3272
Athanasio, I. Emilio, 18617
Athar Neto, Aben, see Aben Athar, J., 1914-.
Athenaeum association, New York, 5957
Athens, Ky., Fiction, 13599
Atherton, Mrs. Gertrude Franklin (Horn) 1857-1948, 15874
Atherton, William, 15875
Athol, Mass. First church, 11848; History, 11848
Atkins, John, 1685-1757, 522
Atkins, John, d.1834, 1411
Atkins, Smith Dykins, 1836-1913, 5958, 23922
Atkins, Thomas Astley, 1839-1916, 21763
Atkinson, Archibald, 1792-1872, 523
Atkinson, C.F., 4301
Atkinson, Christopher William, 524
Atkinson, Edward, 1827-1905, 525, 526
Atkinson, Mrs. Eleanor (Stackhouse) 1863-, 5959, 5960
Atkinson, George Henry, 1819-1889, 15876, 15877
Atkinson, John, 527
Atkinson, L. Jay, 18618, 18619
Atkinson, Mrs. Nancy (Bates), 15877
Atkinson-O'Fallen, Expedition, 17460
Atkinson, William King, 528
Atlacomulco, Mexico, History, 20246
Atlanta campaign, 1864, 2945, 3075, 3830, 4077, 4749, 16397
Atlantic City - History, 11666
The Atlantic club-book, 529
Atlantic coast, Description & travel, 27, 2724, 4620, 12852, 22730; Guidebooks, 12567; History, 23541
The Atlantic navigator, 530
Atlantic states, Description & travel, 1992, 2506, 2944, 3446, 3449, 3553, 3632, 3734, 3975, 4022, 4040, 4137, 4197, 4263, 4410, 4574, 4584, 5151, 5341, 5405, 5634, 6104, 6547, 6548, 7172, 7345, 7346, 7347, 7549, 11948, 17286, 22993; Guide-books, 8388, 14003
Atlantic telegraph company, London, 531, 532
Atlántico, 50 [i.e., cincuenta años] (1910-1960), 18620
Atlántico, Colombia (Department), History, 18620; Industrial, 18620
Atlántida, 5961, 18632
Atlantis, 533, 1443, 5157
Atlantis arisen, 17825
Atlas censitario industrial do Brasil, 10404
Atlas de Economía Colombiana, 18759

Atlas do Brasil, 19278
Atlas lingüístico-etnográfico del sur de Chile, 18357
Atlas metódico para la enseñanza de la geografía de la República Mexicana, 6816
Atlas of Bourbon, Clark, Fayette, Jessamine and Woodford Counties, Ky., 13646
Atlas of Muskingum Co., Ohio, 1068
Atlases, 1111, 20357, 23678; Brazilian, 19278
Atlee, Benjamin Champneys, 1872-, 23923
Atlee, Edwin Pitt, 1799-1836, 534
Atlee, Washington Lemuel, 1808-1878, 535
Atomic bomb, Testing, 19028
Atomic energy and meteorology, 18073
Atomic energy research, Bogotá, 18073
Atonement, 2896; Early works to 1800, 21955
Atrocious judges, 24080
Atson, William, 536
Attack and defense (military science), 23031
Attakapas district, La., Hist., 15911
Atterbury, John Guest, 1811-1887, 538
The attitude of Thaddeus Stevens toward the conduct of the civil war, 25918
Attleborough, Mass., Hist., 11936
Attmore, William, 2568
Attorneys, 554
The attractions of New Haven, Connecticut, 12030
Attraverso gli Stati Uniti, 4427
Attucks, Crispus, d.1770, 23477
Atwater, Caleb, 1778-1867, 507, 539-542, 2569, 11229
Atwater, Jesse, 543
Atwell, H. Wallace, 16631
Atwood, A., 15878
Atwood, Edward Summer, 1833-1888, 544
Atwood, Thomas, d.1793, 545
Atwood, William, d.1705?, 546
Atzerodt, George A., 1835-1865, defendant, 1305
Aub, Max, 1908, 18621
Aubert, Georges, 5964
Aubert du Bayet, Jean Baptiste Annibal, 1759-1797, Fiction, 3582
Aubertin, John James, 1818-1900, 2570, 5965
Aubin, Joseph Marius Alexis, b.1802, 6105
Aubin, Nicolas, b.ca. 1655, 1435
Auburn, N.Y., History, 22289
Aucaigne, Félix, d.1914, 547
Auchinleck, Gilbert, 548
Audio-visual education, 19565
Audouard, Olympe, 2571
Audré, John, 1751-1780, Fiction, 10513
Audrin, José M., 18622
Audry, François Xavier, d.1854, 3723

Audubon, John James, 1785-1851, 549, 2572-2574, 4924, 8217, 13572, 14824, 15129, 15879, 17670, 21764
Audubon, John Woodhouse, 1812-1862, 2575, 2576, 5966, 21764
Audubon, Maria Rebecca, 1843-, 15879
Audubon and his journals, 15879
Audubon's western journal, 2575
Auerbach, Herbert Samuel, 1882-1945, 15880-15882, 17821
Die Aufstände der unfreien Arbeiter 143-129 v. Chr., 24051
Aufenthalt und reisen in Mexico in den jahren 1825 bis 1834, 6254
Aufricht, Hans, 18623
Auger, Edouard, 550, 15883
Aughey, John Hill, b.1828, 551, 23924
Aughey, Samuel, 15884, 15885
Augusta, Ga., History, 4105
Augusta, Wis., 15848
Augusta Co., Va., History, 14027
Auguste, Carlet R., 18624
Augustinians, 7843
Augustinians in Chile, 8056
Augustinians in Venezuela, History, 19688
Aulnay-Charnisay, Charles de Menou, sieur d', 1605-1650, Fiction, 8953, 8984
Aunt Becky's army-life, 4693
Aunt Caroline's present, 9676
Aunt Charlotte, 10669
Aunt Cynthia Dallett, 10042
Aunt Eliza and her slaves, 25664
Aunt Jane of Kentucky, 15090A
Aunt Jane's hero, 10561
Aunt Leanna, 5003
Aunt Mandy's investment, 24319
Aunt Mary, 10904
Aunt Patty's scrap-bag, 3840
Aunt Phebe, Uncle Tom and others, 25014
Aunt Phillie's cabin, 9457
Aunt Randy, 10790
Aunt Sally, 23925
Aurand, Ammon Monroe, 1895-, 7412, 14480
Aureola, 10289
Aurifodina, 10501
Aurora and Pennsylvania gazette, Philadelphia, 12080
Aurora de Chile, 5967
La aurora en Copacabana, 6274
Aurora y el mestizo, 18052
The auroraphone, 9069
Ausencias y retornos, 19017
Aussichten für gebildete Deutsche in Nordamerika, 4289
Austin, Arthur Williams, 1807-1884, 552
Austin, Benjamin, 1752-1820, 553, 554

Austin, David, 1760-1831, 555, 556
Austin, Sir Horatio Thomas, 1800 or 1-
  1865, 433
Austin, Ivers James, 1808-1889, 557-559
Austin, J.P., 2577
Austin, James Trecothick, 1784-1870.
  Remarks on Dr. Channing's "Slavery",
  25301, 25504
Austin, James Trecothick, 1784-1870,
  560-563, 23926
Austin, Mrs. Jane (Goodwin) 1831-1894,
  10283
Austin, Mrs. Mary Hunter, 1868-1934,
  15886, 15887
Austin, Moses, 1761-1821, 564
Austin, Samuel, 1760-1830, 565-567
Austin, Stephen Fuller, 1793-1836, 568,
  5968, 15888, 15915, 17866
Austin, Thomas R., 13573
Austin, William, 1778-1841, 569
Austin, Texas, Social condition, 16680
The Austin dam, 17711
Austral, Antonio G., 18626
Australia, Description & travel, 3977,
  3991, 4636, 7556, 16501, 16520, 17854
Austria, José de, 18627
Austrian succession, War of, 1740-1748,
  11265
Des auswanderers handbuch, 5020
Das Auswanderungsbuch, 2705
Auszüge aus briefen aus Nord-Amerika, 2578
The author turned critic, 11978
Authors, American, 22549; Autographs,
  8612; California, 17192; New York
  (State), 1904; Portraits, 10154;
  Venezuelan, 18966
Authors and publishers, 22144
An author's reading and its consequences,
  9762
Authorship, 10406
Auto de Vicente Anes Joeira, 18628
Auto representado na festa de São
  Lourenço, 18262, 18644
Autobiographical sketches and
  recollections, 3006
An autobiography, 9427
The autobiography and ministerial life
  of the Rev. John Johnston, D.D., 13275
Autobiography and reminiscences of Rev.
  John Graham, 22264
Autobiography, correspondence, etc., of
  Lyman Beecher, 1059
Autobiography of a female slave, 24040
The autobiography of a married woman, 8613
The autobiography of a New England farm-
  house, 8962

Autobiography of a pioneer, 5791, 23497
Autobiography of a Shaker, 12093
Autobiography of an actress, 4965
The autobiography of an adventurer, 16316
The autobiography of an artist's daughter,
  11048
Autobiography of an English soldier in the
  United States army, 2605
Autobiography of James Silk Buckingham, 11600
Autobiography of John G. Fee, 3427
Autobiography of Rev. Francis Frederick, 3532
Autographs, Collections, 11546; Facsimiles,
  22105; United States - Facsimiles, 23927
Autographs for freedom, 9666
Autographs of prominent men of the southern
  confederacy and historical documents, 23927
Automatic Bridget, 9909
Automation, 18676
Automobiles, Road guides, 7677, 7990;
  Guatemala, 6909
Automobile industry and trade, Argentine
  Republic, 19690; Brazil, 19378
Automovil Club de Chile, 18629, 18630
Autopista Bogotá-Medellin y sistema vial
  afluente, 20487
L'autre monde, 3660
An autumn holiday in the United States and
  Canada, 7199
Autumn leaves, 8444
An autumn tour in the United States and
  Canada, 4022, 4432
Autumnal leaves, 8989
Auxier, George Washington, 18631
Auyias-Turenne, Raymond, 1861-, 15889
Auza, Néstor Tomás, 18632
Avaliação financeira do sistema de incentivos
  fiscais no Nordeste, 20558
Avalle, habitant cultivateur de Saint-
  Dominique, 576
Avalos, Ansieta, Benigno, 18633
Avalos, Odilón, 18210
Avalos Guzman, Gustavo, 5969
Avary, Mrs. Myrta (Lockett) 2579, 10448
Ave-Lallemant, Robert Christian Berthold,
  1812-1884, 577, 578
Aveleyra Arroyo de Anda, Luis, 18634, 18635
Avellaneda, Manuel O., 18636
Avenel, Georges d', vicomte, 1855-1939, 2580
The avenger, 10528
La aventura de México, 18646
An average American army officer, 16078
An average man, 9638
Averill, Charles E., 2581
Averill, James R., 23928
Avery, David, 1746-1818, 579
Avery, Ephraim K., d.1869, 11170, 12688, 22158

Avery, Mrs. R. J., 2582
Avery, Ralph Emmett, 5970
Avery Glibun, 10417
Aves, Thomas, defendant, 580
Aves islands, Venezuela, 11514
Aveson, Robert, 16485
Avezac-Macaya, Armand d', 1800-1875,
   581, 582
Aviaries, 17666
The avifauna of northern Latin America,
   19525
Avila, Esteban de, 1549-1601, 5971
Avila, Federico, 18637
Avila, Fernando Bastos de, 18638
Avila, Francisco de, Franciscan, 583
Avila, Francisco J., 18639
Avila, Pedro Arias de, known as Pedrarias
   Dávila, d.1530, 7567
Avila Camacho, Manuel, pres. Mexico, 1896-,
   7482
Avila Franco, Julio César, 18640
Avila Garron, José, 18641
Avis aux habitans des colonies,
   particulièrement à ceux de l'isle
   S. Dominique, 22747
Avis aux ordres privilegres, 808
Avisos pastorales, 6275
Avity, Pierre d', sieur de Montmartin,
   1573-1635, 584
Avolio, 3820
Awad, Mohamed, 23929
The awakened South, 4459
An awakening, 11191
The awakening of a nation, 7342
The awakening of the desert, 15987
Away in the wilderness, 585
Awes, Addison, jr., 15890
Awful calamities, 586
Axes, 14232
Axon, James R., 13574
Ayacucho, Battle of, 1824, 19176
Ayala, Francisco, 18642
Ayala, Manuel José de, 1726-1805, 5972
Ayala, Walmir, 18262, 18643-18645; O galo
   de Belém, 18977
Ayala Anguiano, Armando, 18646
Ayala-Castañares, Agustín, 18647, 19016
Ayala Echavarri, Rafael, 18648
Ayala Mercado, Manuel, 18649
Ayala Queirolo, Victor, 18650
Ayars, Mrs. James S., 13795
Ayer, Anna, d.1821, 2218
Ayer, Benjamin Franklin, 1825-1903, 1874
Ayer, I. Winslow, 15891
Ayers, Elisha, 587
Ayers, Nathaniel Monroe, 1846-, 15892

Ayeta, Francisco de, 5973, 7918
Ayllon, Nicolas de Dios, d.1677, 6385
Aylwin, Mariana, 18341
Ayon de Messner, Digna E., 18651
Ayres, Lula Cardoso, 18652
Ayres, Philip, 1683-1712, ed., 21765
Ayres and Givens, firm, Louisville, Ky.,
   13575
Ayres de Casal, Manuel, b.1754?, 11230
Ayscough, Samuel, 1745-1804, 588
Ayub M., Alejandro R., 18653
Azara, Agustín de, marqués de Nibbiano,
   592, 596
Azerbaijan, Relations (general) with Cuba,
   7189
Azevedo, Antonio Carlos Thyse de, 18654
Azevedo, Aroldo de, 18655
Azevedo, Arthur, 18656
Azevedo, Helio Carvalho Antunes de, 18657
Azevedo, João Ferreira de, 18658
Azevedo, Manoel Antônio Alvares de, 18659
Azevedo, Marcello Casado d', 18660-18662
Azevedo, Murillo Nunes de, 18663
Azevedo, Sanzio de, 18862
Azevedo, Thales de, 18664-18665
Azevedo, Vicente de, 18659
Azevedo, Victor de, 18666
Azevedo do Amaral, Ignacio M., 18667
Azeves, Angel Hector, 18668
Azlor, Joseph de, Marqués de San Miguel de
   Azuayo, 4742
Azofeifa, Isaac Felipe, 18669
Azopardo, Juan Bautista, 1772-1848, 18670
Azopardo, Mercedes G., 18670, 18671
Azores, 7017; Description & travel,
   4571, 6961
Aztec land, 5991
Aztec language, 583
Aztec language, Dialects, Tetelcingo,
   19479; Dictionaries, Spanish, 19479;
   Texts, 2011, 7932
Aztecs, 12366, 7932
Azara, Felix de, 1746-1821, 589-598
Azarian, 10853
Azile, 9250
Azuela, Mariano, 19736; Los caciques,
   19967; Los de abajo, 19967; Las
   moscas, 19967
Aztlan, 17494

Baa, Enid M., 18672
Babbidge, Charles, 599
Babbitt, Benjamin B., 600
Babbitt, Elijah, 1796-1887, 601, 602

Babcock, Mrs. Bernie (Smade) 1868-,
5974, 15893
Babcock, George R., d.1876, 603
Babcock, Jan Victor, 13576
Babcock, Rufus, 1798-1875, 4728
Babcock, Samuel Brazer, 1807-1873, 604
Babson, John James, 1809-1886, 605
Babylon's fall in Maryland, 5305
Baca, Eleuterio, 17451
Bach, Moriz, 606
Bacha, Magdala Lisboa, 18673
Bache, Alexander Dallas, 1806-1867, 607
Bache, Franklin, 1792-1864, 608
Bache, René, illustr., 10253
Bache, William, 1811-, 609
Bache Halsey Stuart, Inc., New York,
18674
Bachelder, John Badger, 1825-1894, 2583
Bachelor Ben, 10681
A bachelor maid, 9759
The bachelor's Christmas, 9639, 10770
The bachelor's elysium, 14242
A bachelor's story, 8893
The bachelor's ward, 8935
Bachelors and butterflies, 8552
Bachiller y Morales, Antonio, 1812-1889,
610-613
Bachini, Epimenio, 18675
Bachmann, Ida, 2584
Bachmann, John, 1790-1874, 21764
Bachofen, Johann Jacob, 13577
Bacigalupo Bottazzi, Virgilio, 18676
Back, Sir George, 1796-1878, 614, 615, 2585
The backbone of Nebraska, 17165
Backman, Daniel And., 11231
The backslider, 10183
Backus, Azel, 1765-1817, 616
Backus, Isaac, 1724-1806, 617-622, 22575
Backus, Joseph, b.1667, 623
Backus, Simon, 624
Backwoods and prairies, 4919
The backwoods of Canada, 8225
The backwoodsman, 4720, 5772, 15777, 17687
Back-yard grangers, 10792
Bacon, Alvin Q., d.1863, 2586
Bacon, Anthony, 625
Bacon, Delia Salter, 1811-1859
Bacon, Edward, 1830-1901, 2587
Bacon, Mrs. Eliza Ann (Munroe), 626
Bacon, George Washington, 1830-1921, 627-
629, 5975
Bacon, Henry, 1813-1856, 626
Bacon, James, fl.1795, 630
Bacon, John, 1738-1820, 631, 632
Bacon, Leonard, 1802-1881, 633-642, 25184
Bacon, Leonard Woolsey, 1830-1907, 643, 23930

Bacon, Mrs. Lydia B. (Stetson), 1786-1853,
644
Bacon, Oliver N., 645
Bacon, Thomas, 1700 (ca.)-1768, 646, 23931
The Bacon College story: 1836-1865..., 15439
Bacon's rebellion, 1676, 3662, 5297;
Fiction, 8784, 9592, 10885, 5478
Bacourt, Adolphe Fourier de, 1801-1865, 2588
Bacqueville de la Potherie, Claude Charles
Le Roy, 1668-1738, 647
Bacteriology, Agricultural, 20281
The bad wife's looking glass, 23766
Badano, Ariel H., 18677
Baddeck, 8343
Bade, William Frederic, 1871-, 17245
Baden, Mrs. Francis (Henshaw) d.1911, 10830,
10834, 10844
Badger, George Edmund, 1795-1866, 648, 22266
Badger, Henry Clay, 1832-1894, 5976
Badger, Joseph, 1757-1846, 15894
Badger, Joseph, 1792-1852, 22525
Badger, William Whittlesey, 649
Badia, Marco Antonio, 650
Badillo, Luisa Bernardi de, 5977
Badin, Stephen Theodore, 1768-1853, 651
Baena, Antônio Ladislau Monteiro, 18678
Baedeker, Karl, firm, publishers, Leipzig,
5978-5981
Baegert, Jakob, 1717-1772, 15895
Baer, Werner, 18679
Baerresen, Donald W., 18680
Baers, Johannes, d.1653, 652, 653, 18681
Baethgen, Raúl E., 18682
Báez, Buenaventura, 18683
Báez, Jorge, 18982
Báez Ortiz, Bolivar, 18684
Baeza Flores, Alberto, 1914, 18685
Baeza Gajardo, Mario, 18686
Baeza González, Oliva, 18687
Baffin's Bay, 7912, 8134; Description, 7930
Baffled schemes, 8637
Bagby, George William, 1828-1883, 2589-2591
Bagg, Lyman Hotchkiss, 1846-1911, 2592
Bagnasco, Hector Horacio, 18798
Bagot, Lewis, bp. of St. Asaph, 1740-1802,
654
Bagú, Sergio, 18688, 18689
Bahamas, Description & travel, 5101, 9774,
22940; History, 25932
Bahamonde N., Nebaldo, 18690
Bahia, Brazil (State), Administrative and
political divisions, 18694; Arquivo
Público, 18691; Comissão de Planejamento
Fconômico, 18692; Departamento de Estradas
de Rodagem, 18693; Departamento Estadual de
Estatistica, 18694; Description & travel, 577;

34

Secretaria das Minas e Energia, 18695, 18696; Secretaria do Trabalho e Bem Estar Social, 18697
Bahia, Brazil. Universidade Federal, 18698; Centro de Estudos Afro-Orientais, 18691
Bahía Blanca, Argentine Republic. Universidad Nacional del Sur, 18699, 186700; Bibliography, 18699; Centro de Documentación Bibliotecológica, 18701
Bahía, Juarez, 18702
Bahía Tongoy, 20129
Bahr, Max, 1863-, 2593
Baides, Marqués de, 8291
Baigts Romani, Luis, 18703
El baile de los cautivos, 18002
Bailes Pastoris, 18977
Bailey, Alexander Hamilton, 1817-1874, 23932
Bailey, Clay Wade, 13578
Bailey, Florence Augusta (Merriam) "Mrs. Vernon Bailey", 15896
Bailey, G. S., 13579
Bailey, Gamaliel, 1807-1859, 24371
Bailey, Goldsmith F., 1823-1862, 655
Bailey, Isaac, d.1824, 656
Bailey, Jacob, 1731-1808, 923
Bailey, John J., 657, 18704
Bailey, John W., 658
Bailey, Joseph Weidon, 1863-1929, 16220
Bailey, Mary F., 16164
Bailey, Mrs. Nellie C. (Benthusen) b.1862, 16873
Bailey, Philip James, 1916-1902, 659
Bailey, Robert, b.1773, 660
Bailey, Rufus William, 1793-1863, 23933
Bailey, Silas, 1809-1874, 661
Bailey, Washington, 1831-, 15897
Bailey, Wilfred Ormrod, 5982
Bailey, William, 662
Baillie-Grohman, Mrs. Florence (Nickalls), 5983
Baillie-Grohman, William Adolph, 1851-, 5983
Baillie, Hugh, 663
Baily, Francis, 1774-1844, 2594
Baily, John, fl.1811-1850, 664, 13342, 23203
Bain, Read, 15466
Bainbridge, William, 1774-1833, 12711
Baines, Edward, 1774-1848, 665
Baines, Thomas F. O'M., 15898
Baird, Henry Carey, 1825-1912, 666, 23934
Baird, Robert, 1798-1863, 667-673, 2595, 13580; A letter to Lord Brougham, on the subject of American slavery, 12344
Baird, Samuel John, 1817-1893, 674
Baird, Sarah Elizabeth (Pentland) 1878-, 15899

Baird, Spencer Fullerton, 1823-1887, 675-679, 5255
Baird, Thomas H., 23935
Baisre, Juan, 18705
Baja California, Bibliography, 18238; History, 21953
Bajarlía, Juan Jacobo, 18706
Bajon, fl. 1763, 680
A bake-pan for dough-faces. By one of them, 24973
The baked head, 8647
Baked meats of the funeral, 9713
Baker, Charles S., 15900
Baker, Charles T., 5984
Baker, Chile, 18312
Baker, Daniel, fl. 1650-1660, 681
Baker, Daniel, 1791-1857, 2599
Baker, David Charles, 5985
Baker, DeWitt Clinton, 1832-1881, 2596, 15901
Baker, Edward Dickinson, 1811-1861, 682, 16936
Baker, Frank Collins, 1867-, 5986
Baker, George E., 683
Baker, George Melville, 1832-1890, 684
Baker, Henry Felt, 1797-1857, 685
Baker, Hozial H., 2597
Baker, James, d.1854, 686
Baker, James Loring, 687-689
Baker, John Freeman, 690
Baker, John Martin, 691, 692
Baker, LaFayette Charles, 1826-1868, 693, 2598
Baker, Lindsey, 1868-1949, 13581
Baker, Louis, 692
Baker, Nathanael, 1706-1733, 22169
Baker, Rachel, 61794, 23041
Baker, Ray Stannard, 1870-1946, 5987
Baker, Robert J., 18707
Baker, William Deal, 1812-1876, 694
Baker, William Mumford, 1825-1883, 2599
Baker family, 15438
Baker-Howard feud, 13744
Baker-Hunt Foundation, 15438
Balaam and his master, 9745
Balada del saxofonista que perdió el tren de la frontera, 18293
Balada do terror e 8 variações, 19154
The Balance (Albany, 1808), 695
Balance of payments, 19813 ; Spanish America, 20032
Balance of trade, 687
Balances económicos de Chile, 20162
O balanço da dynastia, 19191
Balanzat, Manuel, 18708
Balassa, Bela A., 18709

Balbi, Adriano, 1782-1848, 696
Balbuena, Bernardo de, see Valbuena, Bernardo de.
Balcarce, Mariano, b.1808, 697
Balch, Thomas, 1821-1877, 698
Balderrama Hugues, Alejandro, 18710
Baldridge, Samuel Coulter, 1829-1898, 699, 15902
Baldwin, Abraham Chittenden, 1804-1887, 24856
Baldwin, Charles N., 700
Baldwin, Ebenezer, d.1837, 701-703
Baldwin, Frank, 5988
Baldwin, George Rumford, 1798-1888, 704
Baldwin, Henry, 1780-1844, 705
Baldwin, James Fowle, 1782-1862, 23251
Baldwin, John Denison, 1809-1883, 706
Baldwin, Joseph Glover, 1815-1864, 707-708
Baldwin, Loammi, 1780-1838, 709, 710, 1906
Baldwin, Oliver P., 2600-2601
Baldwin, Roger Sherman, 1793-1863, 23936
Baldwin, Samuel, 1731-1784, 711
Baldwin, Thomas, 1753-1825, 712-714, 1851, 13582
Bale, Ida L., 5989
Balech, Enrique, 18711-18714
Balestier, Joseph Nerée, 716, 717, 17477
Balestier, Wolcott, 10146
Balke, Judith, 18716
Ball, Benjamin Lincoln, 718
Ball, Charles, 719
Ball, Jacqueline Page, 13583, 13790
Ball, John, 2602
Ball, Nicholas, 15903
Ball's Bluff, Va., Battle of, 1861, 2085, 16936
Ballad, Robert E., 2603
The ballad of Black Bess, 13584
The ballad singer, 15053
Ballads, American, 14400, 15491, 15515; Bibliography,15134
Ballads, Appalachian, Bibliography, 15134
Ballads for little folks, 2928
Ballads, lyrics, and hymns, 2929
Ballads of the war, 22432
Ballagh, James Curtis, 15413, 23937, 23938
Ballantyne, Robert Michael, 1825-1894, 2604, 5990, 15904
Ballard, William, 1780-1827, 720
Ballentine, George, 1812?, 2605
Ballescá, Santiago, 8025
Ballesteros Gaibrois, Manuel, 18717
Ballew, Stephen Morris, 16130
Ballingall, Neal, 13505
Ballinger, H. R., illustr., 15091

Ballivian Calderón, René, 18718
The ballot box, 801
Ballot box and battle field, 25927
Ballou, Adin, 1803-1890, 721, 23939
Ballou, Hosea, 1771-1852, 723
Ballou, John, 722
Ballou, Maturin Murray, 1820-1895, 723-724, 5991-5992
Ballston, N.Y., 23414
Balme, Joshua Rhodes, 724, 2606
Balmis, Francisco Xavier de, 726
Balogh, Thomas, 18719
Balseiro, José Augustin, 18720
Balta y Montero, José Toribio, pres. Peru, 1814-1872, 18926
Balseiro, Aliomar, 18715
Baltimore, 11596; Battle of, 1814, 22448, 22777; Battle of 1814, Poetry, 2196; Board of school commissioners, 22900; Citizens, 23217; Colonization Convention, 1841, 23980; Description, Guide-books, 5666; Directories, 1756; History, Revolution, 2423, 11560, 21917; Police, 23217; Riot, 1812, 22014; Wars, 23219
Baltimore and Ohio railroad company, 2771, 4174, 4694, 4695, 5993, 23218
Baltra Cortés, Alberto, 18721
Bambuk, Description & travel, 344
Bame, H.D., illustr., 8630
Banahan, J.E., 14668
Banana, 20469, 21723
Banana Festival, Fulton, Ky., 14382
Banani: the transition from slavery to freedom in Zanzibar and Pemba, 25137
Banchero, Giuseppe, 727
Banco Agrícola y Pecuario, Caracas, 18722
Banco Argentino del Atlántico, 18723
Banco Central de Costa Rica, 18725
Banco Central de Honduras, 18726
Banco Central de la República Argentina, Buenos Aires, 18415, 18727-18729
Banco Central de Nicaragua, 18730
Banco Central de Reserva de El Salvador, San Salvador, 18731
Banco Central de Reserva del Perú, 18732, 18733
Banco Central de Venezuela, 18734-18737, 20646
Banco Centroamericano de Integración Económica, 18738, 18739, 18740
Banco da Amazônia, 18741-18744
Banco das cismas, 20651
Banco de Crédito del Perú, Lima, 18841, 18745
Banco de Desenvolvimento de Espírito Santo, 18746, 18747
Banco de Desenvolvimento de Minas Gerais,

Belo Horizonte, 18748-18750;
Departamento de Desenvolvimento
Mineral, 18751; Estudos regionais,
18749
Banco de Desenvolvimento do Estado de
Pernambuco, 18752; Carteira de Crédito
Industrial, 18752
Banco de Guatemala. Departamento de
Investigaciones Agropecuarias e
Industriales, 18753
Banco de la Provincia de Río Negro.
Departamento de Promoción, Crédito
Agrario, Cooperativismo y Colonización,
18754
Banco de la República, Bogotá, 18755-18758;
Departamento de Investigaciones
Económicas, 18759-18760; Museo de Oro,
18761
Banco de la República Oriental del Paraguay,
18762
Banco de México, 18763; Biblioteca, 18764-
18766; Biblioteca. Serie de bibliografías
especiales, 18765-18766; Departamento de
Estudios Económicos, 18767; Departamento
de Investigaciones Industriales, 18768-
18771; Departamento de Investigaciones
Industriales, Bibliography, 18769;
Departamento de Investigaciones
Industriales. Estudio de los recursos
humanos de México, 18984; Subdirección
de Investigación Económica y Bancaria,
18772
Banco de Previsión Social, Mendoza, Argentina
Republic, 18773
Banco de Previsión Social, Montevideo, 18774
Banco del Caribe, Caracas, 18775
Banco di San Giorgio, Genoa, 22146
Banco do Estado de São Paulo, 18776
Banco do Nordeste do Brazil, Fortaleza,
18777-18778, 20558-20559, 20562, 20564;
Departamento de Estudos Econômicos do
Nordeste, 18779-18784; Departamento
Industrial e de Investimentos, 18785;
Divisão de Agricultura, 18786-18787;
Escritorio Técnico de Estudos Econômicos
do Nordeste, 18788-18789; Publicações,
18780-18784, 18786, 18787
Banco Econômico da Bahia, 18790
Banco Español del Río de la Plata, Buenos
Aires, 18791
Banco Ganadero Argentino, Buenos Aires.
Servicio de Investigaciones Económicas,
18792-18794
Banco Industrial de Jalisco, 18795, 20099
Banco Industrial de la República Argentina,
18797; Dirección de Promoción y

Desarrollo Industrial, 18091; Departamento
de Economía, 18798; Dirección Promoción y
Desarrollo Industrial, 18799-18800;
División Económica, 18801-18802
Banco Nacional de Comercio Exterior, S.A.,
Mexico, 18803-18806
Banco Nacional de Costa Rica, San José, 18807
Banco Nacional de México, 5994
Banco Obrero, Caracas, 18808-18810
Banco Regional de Brasília, 18832
Bancos centrales, 18415
Bancos de rescate, 19719
Bancroft, A. C., 13586
Bancroft, Aaron, 1755-1839, 728-732
Bancroft, Edward, 1744-1821, 733-734
Bancroft, Edward Nathaniel, 1772-1842, 735
Bancroft, George, 1800-1891, 736-744, 5995,
11917, 22607, 25574; History of the United
States v.9., 12395
Bancroft, Hubert Howe, 1832-1918, 5996,
15905-15909, 18811
Bandanna ballads, 5659
Bandeira, Antônio Rangel, 18812
Bandeira, Manuel, 18813
Bandelier, Adolphe Francis Alphonse, 1840-
1914, 4631
Bandelier, Mrs. Fanny R., 4631
El bandido chileno Joaquín Murieta en
California, 16841
The bandit of Austria, 11183
The bandit of the ocean, 8698
The bandits of the Osage, 2671
The banditti of the prairies, 16014
The banditti of the Rocky Mountains, 2607
Bandung. Institut Teknologi, 15699
Bangor, Me. Ordinances, etc., 745
Bangou, Henri, 18414
Bangs, Edward, 1756-1818, 746-747
Bangs, Edward Dillingham, 1790-1838, 748
Bangs, Nathan, 1778-1862, 749-750
Bangs, S. K., 13587
Banister, Thomas, fl. 1715, 751-752
Banister, William Bostwick, 1773-1853, 753
Bank bills or paper currency, 754
The Bank dinner, 13588
Bank-notes, 12886
Bank of Maryland, Baltimore, 13256
Bank of North America, Philadelphia, 11843
Bank of the United States, 1791-1811, 543,
11843, 13488, 14468
Bank of the United States, 1816-1836, 11843,
12133, 12270, 22922; Speeches in Congress,
1315, 22586, 22856, 22998, 23240, 23633
Bank of Virginia, 756
Bank robbers and the detectives, 10526
Banking law, Brazil, 18227; New York (State),

21956; South Carolina, 11877
The Bankrupt law of the United States, 1867, 22666
Bankruptcy, 14665; Massachusetts, 11926; U.S., 11797, 22666
Banks, Henry, fl. 1781-1826, 755, 756, 13589
Banks, John, d.1784, 755, 13589
Banks, Mrs. Nancy Huston, 1850-, 2608, 13590, 13591
Banks, Nathaniel Prentice, 1816-1894, 1328
Banks, Thomas Christopher, 1765-1854, 757-758
Banks and banking, 2001, 14665; Argentine Republic, 18728; Brazil, 18778, 20379, 20383; Canada, 6309; Costa Rica, Statistics, 18725; Central, Law and legislation, 18623; Central, Law and legislation, Argentine Republic, 18415; Central America, 18739; Chile, 18676, 20173; Colombia, 20280; Costa Rica, 20616; Cuba, 20693; Directories, 11804; History, 2422, 22463; Kentucky, 13698, 13833, 14070, 14071, 14957, 15347, 15768; Laws and regulations, Costa Rica, 20592; Lexington, Ky., 15081; Massachusetts, 754; Mexico, Bibliography, 18763; New York (State), 21956; Peru, 19719, 19966; El Salvador, 18731; U.S., 543, 685, 1900, 2378, 2379, 2422, 12326, 12682, 21814, 22463, 22464; U.S., History, 11843, 12327; Virginia, 756
The banners of a free people set up in the name of their God, 22717
Bannister, Saxe, 1790-1877, 759-761
Bannockburn for sale, 13592
Un baño en el arroyo, 20648
Banquet in honor of the Honorable H. Church Ford, 13593
Banta, Richard Elwell, 3693, 13594
Banvard, John, 1815-1891, 762
Banvard, Joseph, 1810-1887, 763-769
Banville, Théodore de, 7544
El BAP y su gente, 18722
Baptism, 13779, 14196, 15268; Early works to 1800, 11979; mode and design, 14196
Baptist, Leona, 13595
Baptist church, Kentucky, 15242, 15730
The Baptist denomination, 12758
Baptista, Priscilla, 18815
Baptista Filho, Olavo, 18816
Baptista Quevedo, Alfredo, 18817
Baptiste, Quebec, 22022
Baptists, 506, 1406, 4728, 12758, 14144; Biography, 15430; Doctrinal and controversial works, 619; History, 1146, 15503; History, Kentucky, 15430;

Missions, 4344; New England, 621, 767, 17756; New Hampshire, 11899; Ohio, Miami association, 2137; Oregon, 16517; Rhode Island, 100; South Carolina, 10446
The Baptists and slavery, 1840-1845, 25327
Baptists in Kentucky, 13783, 13891, 13912, 13943, 14485, 14722, 14791, 14853, 14855, 14887, 14892, 14981, 15110, 15198, 15207, 15302, 15360, 15373, 15555, 15694, 15721, 15730, 15780, 24524; Bibliography, 15583; Fiction, 14009
Baptists in Texas, 17838
Baptists in the Southern states, 15417
Baqueiro, Serapio, 1838-1900, 21766
Bar Association of the City of Boston, 5997
Bar Harbor days, 9760
Bar Harbor tales, 9773
The bar-rooms at Brantley, 8557
Baraboo, Wis., 15848
Baraga, Friedrich, bp., 1797-1868, 770-771, 21767
Baralt, Rafael María, 1810-1860, 772, 18818
Baranyai, Leopoldo, 18819
Barata, Manoel, 18820
Baratta, María de, 18821
Baraya, José María, 18822
Barba, Alvaro Alonso, b.1569, 773, 5998
Barba de Coronado, Juan, 5999
Barbadiana, 18825
Barbados, Appropriations and expenditures, 18824; Bibliography, 18825; Commerce, 18827; Commissioner of Police, 18823; Description & travel, 8181, 21943, 25276; Economic condition, 18824, 18884; Elections, 18828; History, 11876, 18825, 23940, 24261; Legislature. House of Assembly, 23940; Politics & government, 774, 18828, 18885; Prime Minister, 18824; Public Library, Bridgetown, 18825; Register of births, etc., 18826; Registration Office, 18826; Statistical Service, 18827; Supervisor of Elections, 18828; vital statistics, 18826
The Barbados packet, 774
La bárbara memoria, 19952
Barbaroux, Charles Ogé, 1792-1867, 775
Barbary states, Description & travel, 25217, 25395; History, 1516-1830, 24476; Social life & customs, 24102, 24408
Barbe, Waitman, 1864-1924, 2609, 2610
Barbé-Marbois, François, marquis de, 1745-1837, 776-778, 1831, 7938, 7939, 7941
Barbee, David Rankin, 1874-, 6000
Barber, Daniel, 1756-1834, 779
Barber, Edward Downing, 1806-1855, 780
Barber, Elizabeth C, 786
Barber, Harold, 13919

Barber, John Warner, 1798-1885, 781-792
Barber, Lucius W., 1839-1872, 2611
Barberena, Santiago Ignacio, 18829
Barberis, Luis A., 18465
Barbesieu, 14758
Barbeu-Dubourg, Jacques, 1709-1779, 793
Barbieri, Vicente, 18830, 18831
Barbosa, Dom Marcos. Um menino nos foi
    dado, 18977
Barbosa, Francisco de Assis, 19498
Barbosa, Frederico Lopes Meira, 19293
Barbosa, José Expedicto, 18832
Barbosa, Joseph, 6001
Barbosa, Maria Dorothéa, 18833
Barbosa, Ruy, 1849-1923, 18834, 24328
Barbosa, Waldemar de Almeida, 18835
Barbosa da Silva, Luiz, 1840-1875, 23941
Barbour, George M., 2612
Barbour, James, 1775-1842, 6002, 23942
Barbour, Ralph Henry, 1870-, 8797
Barbour, Roger, 1919-, 13629
Barboza, Onédia Célia de Carvalho, 18836
Barboza de la Torre, Pedro A., 18837
Barceló Sifontes, Lyll, 18838
Barcelona. Biblioteca Central, 18839;
    Cámara Oficial de Comercio y
    Navegación, 18840
Barclay, James W., 15910
Barclay, Peter. A persuasive to the people
    of Scotland, 12156
Barclay, Robert, 1648-1690, 21768
Barclay Compton, 10196
The Barclays of Boston, 10456
Barco Centenera, Martin del, b.1535,
    794
Bard, Samuel, 1742-1821, 23000
Bard, Samuel A., pseud., 13485
Bard, William, 1777-1853, 795
Barde, Alexandre, 15911
Bardella, Granfranco, 18841
Bardem, Juan Antonio, 18842, 18843
Bardstown, Ky. Christian Church, 14099;
    History, 14912, 15045; Hotels, inns,
    etc., 15098; Woman's Club, 13596
Barère de Vieuzac, Bertrand, 1755-1841,
    6003
Barham, William, 796
Barhydt, David Parish, d.1908, 797
Baril, V.L. comte de la Hure, 798
Barinetti, Carlo, 799
Barite, 14117
Barker, Charles Albro, 1904-, 20660
Barker, David, 1797-1834, 800
Barker, Elihu, 13597
Barker, Eugene Campbell, 1874-, 15916-
    15912, 16892

Barker, George Payson, 1807-1848, 1620
Barker, Harry Ellsworth, 1862-, 6004
Barker, Henry Stites, 1850-1928, 13598
Barker, James Nelson, 1784-1858. The Indian
    princess, 1447
Barker, Jacob, 1779-1871, 801, 802
Barker, Joseph, 1751-1815, 803, 804
Barker, Robert, b.1729, 805
Barker, T. F., 13599
Barker, W. M., 13600
Barker, William, 13885
Barker's luck, 6971
Barkley, Alben William, 1877-1956, 13602-
    13604, 14211, 14249, 14649, 15043, 15621
Barkley, Archibald Henry, 1872-1956, 13605
Barksdale, William, 1821-1863, 23943
Barley Wood, 10474
Barlow, Edward, 1639-1719, 806
Barlow, Joel, 1754-1812, 807-819, 6005, 11232;
    The Columbiad, 12419
Barnard, Daniel Dewey, 1797-1861, 820-824
Barnard, Frederick Augustus Porter, 1809-
    1889, 825-827
Barnard, George N., 828
Barnard, Henry, 1811-1900, 260, 261, 829-831
Barnard, John, 1681-1770, 832
Barnard, John Augustine, b.1661?, 21796
Barnard, John Gross, 1815-1882, 833-839
Barnard, Thomas, 1716-1776, 841, 843
Barnard, Thomas, 1748-1814, 840, 842
Barnave, Antoine-Pierre-Joseph-Marie, 1761-
    1793, 7507
Barneby, William Henry, 1843-, 15917
Barnes, Albert, 1798-1870, 844-850, 13357
Barnes, Ben, 18844
Barnes, Charles Merritt, 15918
Barnes, David, 1731-1811, 851
Barnes, David M., 852
Barnes, Demas, 1827-1888, 15919
Barnes, George Owen, 1827-, 4860
Barnes, Isaac O., 853
Barnes, James C., 13606
Barnes, Joseph, 854-855
Barnes, Thomas, 1749-1816, 856
Barnes, William, 1824-1913, 857, 858
Barnes, William Croft, 1858-1936, 15920
Barnes, William Horatio, 859, 11233
Barnet, James, 860
Barnett, Mrs. Evelyn Scott (Snead) 2613-2614
Barnett, Francis, b.1785, 861
Barney, C., 2615
Barney, Nathaniel, 24420
Barnola, Pedro Pablo, 18845-18846
Barnstable Bay, 23261
Barnum, E.M., 862
Barnum, George Henry, 21769

39

Barnum, H. L., 863
Barnum, James Harvey, 2616
Barnum, Phineas Taylor, 1810-1891, 864,
  11234
Barnum's Parnassus, 1773
Barnwell, Stephen Elliott, 6632
Baron, G., 18936
Barón Castro, Rodolfo, 18847
Baron Montez of Panama and Paris, 9672
The Baron of Cherubusco, 10675
Barondess, Benjamin, 1891-, 6006
Baronia anglica concentrata, 758
Barr, James, 2617
Barr, John, 4589
Barr, Knut August, 1871-1929, 2618
Barr, Lockwood Anderson, 1883-, 13214
Barr, Stephen A., 13607
Barr, Thomas Hughes, 1807-1877, 865
Barr family, 13607
Barra, Ezekiel I., 15921
Barra da solidão, 18074
Barra do Corda, Brazil, 21732
Barracchini, Hugo, 18190
Barraclough, Solon, 18848
Barrage, Joseph Perrin, 1842-1863, 1791
Barral e da Pedra Branca, Luisa Margarida
  Portugal de Barros, condessa de, 18849
Barrán, José Pedro, 18850
Barrande, Joachim, 1799-1883, 866
Barranquilla, Colombia, 18620
Barrantes Ferrero, Mario, 18851, 18852
Barras, Louis, comte de, d.1788, 13473
Barre, W.L., 868, 869, 4401
Barre Academy, Barre, Vt., 867
Barré de Saint-Venant, Jean, 1737-1810,
  11235
Barreda, Francisco de, 6007
Barreda, Pedro F., 18853
Barreda, Roque de la, 8272
Barreda Avila, Rubén, 18854
Barreda Fernández, Salvador, 18855
Barreda y Laos, Felipe, 18856
Barreiro, Antonio, 15922, 17392
Barrell, Joseph, d.1804, 13341
Barren County, Ky., 13610, 13613; Maps,
  14596
The barren ground of northern Canada,
  17389
Barren River, 14220
Barren River Area Development District,
  Bowling Green, Ky., 13608-13613, 13862
Barrenechea, Juan de, 6008
Barrera, Manuel, 18857
Barrera Oviedo, Jorge, 18858
Barrera M., Pedro Nel, 20351, 20352
Barrera Parra, Jaime, 18859

Barrera Sánchez, Ramón, 18860
Barrère, Pierre, 1690-1755, 870
Barreto, Abilio, 18861
Barreto, Carlos Eduardo, 19284
Barreto, Livio, 18862
Barreto, Luiz Muniz, 18863
Barreto, Paulo, 18864
Barreto de Menezes, Tobras, 18865
Barreto Soulier, Jorge, 18866
Barrett, Benjamin Fiske, 1808-1892, 871
Barrett, Frank William Zelotes, 1867-, 6009
Barrett, Jay Amos, 1865-, 15923, 17260
Barrett, Jonathan Fay, 1817-1885, 21770
Barrett, Joseph Hartwell, 1824-1910, 872,
  873, 874
Barrette, J.E.T., 6010
Barretto, Fernando de Castro Paes, see
  Castro Paes Barretto, Fernando
Barretto, Vicente, 18867
Barría Serón, Jorge, 18868
Barrientos, Felipe Santiago, 6011
Barrientos O., René, 18869
Barrientos Restrepo, Samuel, 18870, 18871
Barriga Vallalba, Antonio M., 18872
Barrillon, François Guillaume, 875
Barringer, Daniel Moreau, 1806-1873, 876
Barrington, Daines, 1727-1800, 877, 878,
  23461
Barrington, Shute, bp. of Durham, 1734-1826,
  11236
Barrington, William Wildman Barrington, 2d
  viscount, 1717-1793, 11236
Barrio, Paulino del, 879
Barrios, Gilberto, 18873
Barrios, Juan de, fl. 1590-1610, 6012
Barrios, Justo Rufino, 1835-1885, 19572
Barroco, 18874
Barron, James, 1769-1851, 880, 22069
Barron, Samuel Benton, 1834-1912, 2619
Barrón Angeles, Pablo, 18875
Barros, André de, 881
Barros, Edgar de Vasconcelos, 19864
Barros, Ivan de Queiroz, 18876
Barros, João de, 1496-1570, 882
Barros, Leandro Gomes de, 1865-1918,
  Bibliography, 18911
Barros, Maria Nazareth M.M. de, 18877
Barros, Raquel, 18878
Barros Arana, Diego, 1830-1907, 8112
Barros Coelho, Raimundo de, 18879
Barroso, Gustavo, 18880
Barroso, Jorge Alberto, 18881
Barroso, Maria Alice, 18882
Barrow, Asa C., 13614
Barrow, Errol Walton, 18883-18885
Barrow, Sir John, bart., 1764-1848, 883 ###,

11237, 11238
Barrow, John, 1808-1898, 1924
Barrow, Robert, 3247
Barrow, Washington, 1817-1866, 887
Barrow Straits, 8134
Barrows, Elijah Porter, 1807-1888, 888
Barrows, Willard, 1806-1868, 15924
Barrows, William, 1815-1891, 889, 15924-15926
Barruel-Beauvert, Philippe Auguste de, 890
Barrutia, Salvador, 18917
Barry, Charles, 6013
Barry, Etheldred B., illustr., 2613
Barry, Henry, 1750-1822, 11239
Barry, Henry W., d.1875, 23944
Barry, John Stetson, 1819-1872, 891, 892, 21771
Barry, Patrick, 893
Barry, Theodore Augustus, 1825-1881, 15927
Barry, Thomas, 2620
Barry, William Farquhar, 1818-1879, 839
Barry, William Taylor, 1785-1835, 894, 13615, 15577
Barstow, Benjamin, 895-896
Barstow, George, 1812-1883, 897-898
Bart Ridgeley, 10618
Barter, Brazil, 19338
A bartered birthright, 10304
Barthe, Joseph Guillaume, 1818-, 899
Barthelmess, Richard, 900
Bartholow, Otho F., 6014-6015
Bartleby, 10346
Bartletson, John, 2621, 16296
Bartlett, David Vandewater Golden, 1828-1912, 901-902
Bartlett, Elisha, 1804-1855, 903-905, 2622, 2623, 7093, 13616, 13617
Bartlett, Ichabod S., 15928
Bartlett, John Russell, 1805-1886, 906-909, 2624, 23945
Bartlett, John Sherren, 1790-1863, 910
Bartlett, Joseph, 1686-1754, 1972
Bartlett, Joseph, 1763-1827, 911
Bartlett, Josiah, 1759-1820, 912-916
Bartlett, Josiah, 1768-1838, 917
Bartlett, Josiah, 1803-1853, 917
Bartlett, Montgomery Robert, 918
Bartlett, Napier, 1836-1877, 2625
Bartlett, Richard, 1794-1837, 919
Bartlett, Samuel Ripley, 1837-, 920
Bartlett, Washington Allen, 1820-1871, 921
Bartlett, William Francis, 1840-1876, 4683
Bartlett, William Henry, 1809-1854, 922, 5729, 21772
Bartlett, William Stoodley, 1809-1883, 923

Bartley, James Avis, 1830-, 924
Bartol, Cyrus Augustus, 1813-1900, 925
Bartolozzi, Francesco, 1727-1815, 21787
Barton, Andrew, pseud., 926
Barton, Benjamin Smith, 927-933, 23498
Barton, Charles Crillon, d.1851, 934
Barton, Cyrus, d.1855, 935-936
Barton, David, 1783-1837, 937, 11240
Barton, Edward H., d.1859, 938
Barton, Harry Scott, 1862-, 2626
Barton, Ira Moore, 1796-1867, 636
Barton, James L., d.1869, 939-940
Barton, Mary, 6016
Barton, O.S., 22829
Barton, Robert S., 6017-6019
Barton, Seth, 1795-1850, 23946
Barton, Thomas H., 1828-, 2627
Barton, Wayne, 18887
Barton, William, 1754-1817, 941, 21773
Barton, William Eleazar, 1861-1930, 2628-2630, 6020-6023, 13618-13619, 23947
Barton, William Paul Crillon, 1786-1856, 942-944, 11241, 21774
Barton, William Sumner, 1824-1899, 945
Bartos, Robert E., 18888
Bartram, John, 1699-1777, 5291, 11242
Bartram, William, 1739-1823, 946, 2631
Baruchelli, Paolo, 23948
Barufaldi, Rogelio, 1932-, 19925
Barus, Vlastimil, 18889-18893
O BASA e o desenvolvimento da Amazônia, 18743
Basadre, Jorge, 18894
Basalenque, Diego, 1577-1651, 947
Basava Fernández del Valle, Augustín, 18895-18896
Bascom, H.B., 14995
Bascom, Henry Bidleman, bp., 1796-1850, 948, 3835; Methodism and slavery, 25213
Bascom, Jonathan, 949
Bascom family (Thomas Bascom, d.1682), 12701
Bascón Carvajal, Federico, 18897
Bascuñán, Carlos, 18341
Bascuñán Valdés, Antonio, 18898
Bashford, James Whitford, bp., 1849-, 15929
Basile, David Giovanni, 18899
Basílico, Ernesto, 18900
Basire, James, 1769-1822, engr., 21787
Baskervill, William Malone, 1850-1899, 2632
Basket, Katheryn, 13564
Basketball, 15310; Kentucky. University, 15788; Rules, 20393, 20394
Baskett, James Newton, 1849-, 2633
Baskin, O.L. & co., Chicago pub., 16782
Baskin, Robert Newton, 1835-, 15930-15932
Basque language, 97
Bassells Batalla, Angel, 7408, 18901

41

Bassett, John Spencer, 23949
Bassett, Samuel Clay, 1844-, 15933
The bastard, 9546
Basterot, Florimond Jacques, comte de, 950
Bastida, Aguirre Jacinto, 18902
Bastide, Roger, 1898-1974, 18698, 18903,
   18904
The bastiles of the North, 2479
Bastos, Carlos Alberto de Miranda, 18301
Bastos, Jairo Martins, 18905
Bastrop Co., Texas, Biography, 16780
Basurto, Jorge, 18906
Basurto Escalera, Francisco, 18907
Batalha, Wilson de Souza Campas, 18908
Batalla de Yanacocha, 951
Batalla del Pantano de Vargas, 1819,
   18909
Batbie, Anselme Polycarpe, 1828-1887, 952
Batch, Donald L., 13706-13707
Batch, Thomas, 1821-1877, 2731
Batchelder, Eugene, 1822-1878, 953-954
Batchelder, George Alexander, 15934
Batchelder, John Putnam, 1784-1868, 955
Batchelder, Samuel, 1784-1879, 956
Batchelder, Samuel, 1830-1888, 957
Batcheller family, 21999
Batcheller, Tyler, 1793-1862, 21999
Bateman, Charlotte, 13620
Bateman, Edmund, 958
Bateman, Newton, 1822-1897, 6024
Bates, Barnabas, 1785-1853, 959
Bates, David Homer, 1843-1926, 6025
Bates, Edmond Franklin, 1851-, 15936
Bates, Edward, 1793-1869, 960
Bates, Elisha, 1779 or 80-1861, 2636-2638
Bates, Emily Katharine, 2639
Bates, Finis Langdon, 6026
Bates, Henry Walter, 1825-1892, 961
Bates, Isaac Chapman, 1780-1845, 962
Bates, James Hale, 1826-1901, 6027
Bates, Joshua, 1776-1854, 963-964
Bates, Katharine Lee, 1859-1929?, 8969
Bates, Lindon Wallace, jr., 1883-, 6028
Bates, Marcus W., 15937
Bates, Mary, 965
Bates, Mrs. D.B., 15935, 21775
Bates, Myron, 15257
Bath, William Pulteney, earl of, 1684-
   1764, 21776
Bath Co., Ky., Bibliography, 14413
Baths, 1089
Bathurst, Henry Bathurst, 3rd earl of,
   1762-1834, 6029, 13512
Batis Muñuz, Agustín Huberto, 18910
Batista, Hugolino de Sena, 18911
Batista, Sebastião Nunes, 18911

Batista Ballesteros, Isaias, 18912
Batista Villareal, Teresita, 18913
Batista y Zaldívar, Fulgencio, pres. Cuba,
   1901-, 20701
Baton Rouge, La., History, Civil war, 3199
Batres, Leopoldo, 7490, 7491
Batres de Zea, Dolores, 18914
Batres y Montúfar, José de, 18915-18917
Bats, 174; Cuba, 20667; Middle America, 18707;
   Parasites, 20672, 20674, 20675
Battaile, Elizabeth Kinkead, 1887-, 13621
Batten, John Mullin, 1837-1916, 2640
Battey, Thomas C., 15938
Battistella, Ernesto H., 19157
Battistessa, Angel J., 18918
Battle, J.H., 15143
Battle, Kemp Plummer, 1831-1919, ed., 4486
The battle cry, 13731
Battle echoes, 13063
Battle field and prison pen, 5555
The battle-fields of the republic, 12715
Battle-fields of the South, 968
The battlefields of our fathers, 11006
The battle-fields of Virginia, 12924
The battle forest, 5745
The battle of Bunker Hill, 3382, 11481
The battle of Chancellorsville and the
   Eleventh army corps, 966
The battle of Coney Island, 8652
The battle of Fort Sumter and first victory
   of the southern troops, 11243
The battle of freedom, 3503
Battle of King's Mountain, 15357
Battle of Lake Erie monument association, 967
The battle of Lexington, 10670
The battle of Monmouth, 10921
The battle of Monterey, 4407
The battle of New Orleans, 15402, 15770
The battle of principles, 24609
The battle of the books, recorded by an
   unknown writer for the use of authors and
   publishers, 22144
The battle of Tippecanoe, 5603
The battle of the Blue Licks, 14509
The battle of the Thanes, 15790
Battle-pieces and aspects of the war, 25027
Battles, U.S., 12715, 22050
Battles of the British navy, 185
Battles of the United States, by sea and land,
   22050
Batty, Joseph, 15940
Batwell, Daniel, 969
Baucke, Oswaldo, 18919
Baudelaire, Charles, 1821-1867, 18920, 18921,
   19194
Baudissin, Adelbert Heinrich, graf von, 1820-

1871, 970, 23950
Baudou, Alejandro C., 18922
Baudry des Lozières, Louis Narcisse, 1761-1841, 2641
Bauerle, Charles, illustr., 4283
Baugher, Ruby Dell, 13623-13625
Baughman, the Oklahoma scout, 15941
Baughman, Theodore, 1845-, 15941
Baumann, Felix, 1868-, 2642
Baumann, Ludwig Adolph, 1734?-1802, 971
Baumbach, Ludwig Carl Wilhelm von, 1799-1883, 2643
Baumgardt, B.R. & co., 16877
Baumgartner, Andreas, 1844-1936, 2644
Baure Indians, Bolivia, Language, 18815
Bausman, Lottie M., 23951
Baxley, Henry Willis, 1803-1876, 15942
Baxter, James Phinney, 1831-1921, 6030, 6031, 24959
Baxter, Joseph, 1676-1745, 972
Baxter, Perceval P., 6031
Baxter, Sylvester, 1850-, 6032
Baxter, U.J., 3537
Baxter, William, 11244
Baxter, William Edward, 1825-1890, 2645
Bay, Jens Christian, 1871-, 13626, 13627, 15304
Bay, William Van Ness, 1818-1894, 23952
The Bay-path; a tale of New England colonial life, 22527
Bayard, Ferdinand Marie, 1768-, 2646
Bayard, James, 973
Bayard, James Asheton, 1767-1815, 974-978, 12244
Bayard, James Asheton, 1799-1880, 977, 978
Bayard, Lewis Pintard, 1791-1840, 979
Bayard, Nicholas, 1644?-1707, 546, 980, 981
Bayard, Samuel, 1767-1840, 982
Bayard, William, 1764?-1826, 983
Bayard, William, 1814-1907, 24174
Bayardo Bengoa, Fernando, La tutela penal del secreto, 18923
Bayfield, Wisconsin, 984
Bayley, Daniel, d.1792, 985
Bayley, Frederic William Naylor, 1808-1853, 986
Bayley, James, 1650-1706/7, 23471
Bayley, James Roosevelt, abp., 1814-1877, 987
Bayley, Richard, 1745-1801, 988
Baylies, Francis, 1783-1852, 989-992, 2647
Baylor, Orval W., 6033-6035, 13628
Bayliss, Lilian, illustr., 13824
Bayly, William, 1737-1810, 993
Bayman, Mrs. A. Phelps, 994
Bayne, Charles Joseph, 1870-, 2648

Bayne, David R., 18924
Bayne, Peter, 1830-1896, 995
Bayona Posada, Nicolás, 18925
Baz, Gustavo Adolfo, 1852-1904, 6036, 6037
Bazán, F. Mario, 18926
Bazán, Rogelio, 18927
Bazancourt, César Lecat, baron de, 1810-1865, 996
Bazant, Jan, 18928
Bazile, L., 997
Bazin, René, 1853-1932, 2649
Bazzanella, Waldemiro, 18929
Beach, David, 998
Beach, Lewis, 1835-1886, 999
Beach, Samuel B., 1000
Beach, Thomas Miller, 1841-1894, 6038
Beaconsfield, Benjamin Disraeli, 1st earl of, 1804-1881, 23612, 23613
Beadle, Charles, 2650
Beadle, Delos White, 1001
Beadle, Erastus, 1821-1894, 15534
Beadle, John Hanson, 1840-1897, 2651, 16751
The beads of Tasmer, 8720
Beagle Channel, Chile, 18900
Beagle expedition, 1831-1836, 22041
Beal, John Yates, 1835-1865, 4311
Beale, Charles T., 3122
Beale, Edward Fitzgerald, 1822-1893, 2652, 2653, 3826, 16015
Beale, George William, 1842-, 2654
Beale, Joseph H., 2655
Beale, Richard Lee Tuberville, 1819-1893, 2656
Beall, John Bramblett, 1833-1917, 15943
Beall, John Yates, 1835-1865, 1002, 7410
Beals, James, 1844?-, 3076
Beaman, Fernando C., 1814-1882, 1003, 1004
Beamish, North Ludlow, 1797-1872, 1005
Bean, Dottie, 13629
Bean, Robert, 3111
Beanlands, Arthur John, 1857-1918, 6178
Beans, 18777
Bear, John W., 1800-, 13630
Bear flag battalion, 16844
Bear flag party, 16845
Bear Lake Co., Id., 17762
Bearcroft, Philip, 1697-1761, 1006, 1007
Beard, Daniel Carter, 1850-1941, illustr., 13618
Beard, James A., 13631
Beard, Mrs. Joseph, 14635
Beard, Oliver Thomas, 1832-, 23953
Beard, Richard, 1799-1880, 13632, 13633
Beard, W.L., 10448
Beardslee, George W., 1008
Beardsley, Eben Edwards, 1808-1891, 1009, 1010

43

Beardsley, Frank Grenville, 1870-, 13634
Beardsley, Levi, 1785-1857, 1011
Beardsley family (William Beardsley, 1605?-1661), 1010
The bearer of dispatches, 14242
Bearing arms in the twenty-seventh Massachusetts regiment of volunteers infantry during the Civil War, 3235
Bearse, Austin, 23954
Beating back, 16888
Beatrix Randolph, 9805
Beatson, Robert, 1742-1818, 1012
Beatty, Bessie, 1886-, 15944, 17882
Beatty, Charles, 1715?-1772, 1013, 1014
Beatty, John, 1828-1914, 2657
Beattyville and Lee County, 15382
Beauchamp, Alphonse de, 1767-1832, 1015-1017, 21777
Beauchamp, Jereboam O., 1801-1826, 13635, 13636, 13870, 13907
Beauchamp, William Martin, 1890-1925, 21906
The Beauchamp-Sharp tragedy, 13870
The Beauchamp tragedy in Kentucky, 13635
Beauchampe, 10766
The Beauforts, 8794
Beaufoy, Mark, 1764-1827, 878, 1018
Beaugrand, Honoré, 1849-1906, 6039, 15945
Beauharnais family - Fiction, 9532
Beaujon, Oscar, 18930, 20019
Beaujour, Louis Auguste Felix, baron de, 1763-1836, 1019, 1020
Beaumarchais, Pierre Augustin Caron de, 1732-1799, 1868
Beaumont, Arthur J., 1021, 1022
Beaumont, Augustus Hardin, 23955
Beaumont, J.A.B., 1023
Beaumont, Pablo de la Purísima Concepcion, 6040
Beaumont, William, 1785-1855, 15946
Beaumont College, Harrodsburg, Ky., 13637
Beaumont de La Bonnière, Gustave Auguste de, 1802-1866, 2658, 23956
Beaumont Inn, Harrodsburg, Kentucky, 13637, 14197
Beauregard, George, 6041
Beauregard, Pierre Gustave Toutant, 1818-1893, 2037
Beauseincourt, The romance of, 5618
Beautés de l'histoire du Canada, 11760
The beauties and celebrities of the nation, 12020
Beauties of California, 16650
The beauties of the Hon. Henry Clay, 13840
The beauties of Washington Irving, 9994
The beautiful Jewess Rachel Mendoza, 8703
The beautiful star, 2994

The beautiful widow, 8558
The beauty of a well cultivated heart, 9486
Beauvais, Anne, de, 1586-1620, 22749
Beauvallet, Léon, 1829-1885, 1024
Beauvois, Eugène. 1835-, 1026
Beaven, James, 1025
Beaver (steamship), 17076
Beaverhead Co., Mont., History, 17291
Beccaria, C., 18936
Becco, Horacio Jorge, 1924-, 18931-18933
Becerra, Ricardo, 1836-1905, 6042
Becerra F., Jesús María, 18934
Becerra López, José Luis, 18935
Becher, Carl Christian, 6043-6045
Becher, Henry C.R., 6046
Bechtel, Johannes, 1690-1777, ed., 1027
Beck, Carl, 1856-1911, 2659
Beck, James Burnie, 1822-1890, 15616
Beck, John Brodhead, 1794-1851, 1029
Beck, Lewis Caleb, 1798-1853, 1030-1032, 11245, 21778
Beck, Paul, 1760?-1844, 1033
Beck, Richard, 17737
Beck, Theodoric Romeyn, 1791-1855, 12608
Beck-Bernard, Mme. Lina (Bernard), 1028
Becker, F., 18936
Becker, George Ferdinand, 15947
Becker, John H., 2660
Becker, Klaus, 18937
Becker, Maxwell E., 18938
Becket, John J. à, 10283
Beckett, Sylvester Breakmore, 1812-1882, 1034
Beckford, William, d.1799, 1035, 23957
Beckham, John Crepps Wickliffe, 1860-1940, 15254
Beckham vs. Taylor, 15254
Beckley, Hosea, 1036
Beckman, Ernst, 1850-1924, 2661
Beckner, Lucien, 13638-13642; Indian burial ground, Fullerton, Ky., 15686
Beckner, Marie Warren, 13643
Beckner, W.M., 13644, 13645
Beckwith, Edward Griffin, 5519, 5523
Beckwith, Frank, 15948, 15949
Beckwith, George Cone, 1800-1870, 1037, 11370
Bécquer, Gustavo Adolfo, 1836-1870, 18939
Becu, Teodoro, 1890-, 18940
Bed-time stories (More), 10392
Bedford, Cornelia E., illustr., 9268
Bedford, Gunning S., 1038, 1039
Bedford, Hilory S., 15950
Bedford, John Russell, 4th duke of, 1710-1771, 1040
Bedford, Kentucky, 15273
Bedford, N.M., History, 853
Bedford, N.Y. St. Matthew's Church, 13177, 24672

Bedford Springs, Pa., 21921
Bedinger, Daniel, 1041
Bedregal, Guillermo, 1926-, 18941-18946
Bedrnik, Petr., 18947
Bee culture, U.S., 13436
The bee hunter, 5412, 9140
Beebe, Gilbert J., 23958
Beebe, Henry S., 15951
Beech Bluff, 11092
Beechen brook, 4854
The beechen tree, 5378
Beecher, Catherine Esther, 1800-1878, 1042-1047, 1052
Beecher, Charles, 1815-1900, 1048-1050, 1059
Beecher, Edward, 1803-1895, 1051
Beecher, Eunice White (Bullard), 2662
Beecher, George, 1809-1843, 1052
Beecher, Henry Ward, 1813-1887, 1053-1058, 6047, 7039, 24937; Norwood, 11773, 11949
Beecher, Lyman, 1775-1863, 1059-1065, 11246, 11247, 12469
Beechey, Frederick William, 1796-1856, 1066, 1067, 6048, 12883
Beede, Aaron McGaffey, 15952
Beef Argentine Republic, 18431
Beeler, Elizabeth, 14050
Beers, D.G., 13646
Beers, Mrs. Fannie A., 2663, 21779
Beers, Frederick W., 1068
Beers, Howard W., 13647, 13648
Beers, William Pitt, 1766-1810, 1069
Bees, 1081, 9046, 12733, 13436, 19899; Cuba, 11343
Beesly, Edward Spencer, 1831-, 13104
Beeson, John, b.1803, 1070, 15953
Beeston, William, b.1636, 21765
Beethoven, Ludwig van, 1770-1827, 19879, 20468
Beetles, Mexico, 1871
Beets and beet sugar, France, 11970
Die Befreiung durch Census, 24271
Begbie, Matthew Baille, 6183
Begg, Alexander, 1839-1897, 6049-6056, 7384
The beggar on horseback, 10705
A beggar's story, 14974
Beginnings of literary culture in the Ohio Valley, 5566
The beginnings of the Cincinnati southern railway, 13701
Begley, Michael J., 13649
Begonias, Therapeutic use, 726
Behaim, Martin, 1459?-1506, 1081, 22146
Die Behandlung der Arbeit im Privatrecht, 24355
Behavior modification, 15636
Behemoth, 10322, 10326

Behen, John, 14050
Behnke, Julius Camillus, 1859-, comp. and tr., 17007
A beira do corpo, 18645
Beira rio, beira vida, 19218
Beiting, Ralph, 14739
Beker, Ana, 6057
Beknopte en zakelyke beschryving der voornaamste engelsche volkplantingen, 1071
'Bel of Prairie Eden, 10211
A bela Madame Vargas, 18864
Belaúnde, Victor Andres, 1883-, 7464
Belaúnde Giunassi, César, 18948
Belaúnde Terry, Fernando, 17994
Belcher, Edward, 6058, 6059
Belcher, Jonathan, 1681-1757, 1780
Belcher, Jonathan, 1710-1776, 1780
Belcher, Joseph, 1669-1723, 1072, 1073
Belcher, Joseph, 1794-1859, 1074, 1075
Belcher, Mrs. Mary (Partridge) 1685-1736, 1780
Belchertown, Massachusetts. Congregational church, 22155; Genealogy, 22155
Belcourt, George Antoine, 1803-1874, 11353, 15954
Belden, David, 1832-, 6060
Belden, Elizur, 1763-1786, 12812
Belden, Ezekiel Porter, 1823-1911, 1076, 1077
Belden, George P., 15955, 15956
Belden, Josiah, 16926
Belém, History, 20665
Beleña, Eusebio Buenaventura, 1736-1794, 1078
Belew, Pascal Perry, 1894-, 6061, 13650
Belfast, Ireland, 11248
Belfiore, Carlos J., 18949
Belgians in Virginia, 2242
Die belgische neutralität, 1079
Belgium Neutrality, 1079
Belgrano, Manuel, 1770-1820, 7708
Belgrove, William, 1080
Belhaven tales, 9761
Belice, tierra nuestra, 6803
Belinfante, George, 1837-, 23959
Belisario Peña Gómez, José María, 1834-1906, 20717
Belisle, David W., 2664
Belize, 18950; Foreign relations, Guatemala, 18950; Foreign relations, Mexico, 18950
Belknap, Jeremy, 1744-1798, 1081-1084, 21780
Bell, Agrippa Nelson, 1820-1911, 1085, 23960
Bell, Andrew, of Southampton, fl.1838-1866, 1086
Bell, Benjamin, 1752-1836, 11249
Bell, Charles Napier, 6062, 6225
Bell, Colen W., 24722
Bell, Earl H., 15957
Bell, Eleanora May, 1901?-, 13651

Bell, Hiram, 1808-1855, 1087
Bell, Horace, 15958
Bell, James Stanislaus, ed., 8164
Bell, John, 1796-1872, 1088, 1089
Bell, John, 1797-1869, 1091, 1091, 11250
Bell, John Calhoun, 1851-, 15959
Bell, John Thomas, 1842-, 2665, 15960
Bell, Joshua Fry, 1811-1870, 1092
Bell, Landon C., 6063
Bell, Louis, 1837-1865, 11415
Bell, Luther Vose, 1806-1862, 1093, 12054
Bell, Marcus A., 23961
Bell, Orelia Key, 1864-, 2666
Bell, Robert, fl. 1570, 1094
Bell, Ulric, 13548
Bell, Rev. William, 1095
Bell, William Abraham, 15961
Bell Escalona, Eduardo, 18951, 20147
Bell Martin, 8559
The bell-ringer of Angel's, 6963
Bell Smith abroad, 10520
The bell-tower, 10346
Bella, 8796
"Bella Vista," Agua Caliente, Costa
    Rica, 5845
Bellamy, B.W., 9769
Bellamy, George Anne, 1731?-1788, 11251
Bellamy, Joseph, 1719-1790, 1096-1098,
    23332
Bellardi, Luigi, 1818-1889, 1099
The belle and the bleu, 9702
Belle Boyd in camp and prison, 11455
Belle Brittan on a tour, 2357
The belle of Bayou Luie, 9579
A belle of Canada City, 6969
The belle of the Bluegrass Country, 15168
Belle Scott, 10055
Bellecombe, André Ursule Casse de, 1822-
    1897, 1100
Bellegarde, Dantes, 1877-, 6064, 18952
Bellegarde, Jean Baptiste Morvan de,
    1648-1734, 1101
Bellegarrigue, A., 1102
Bellemare, Gabriel de, 1846-, 1104
Bellemare, Louis i.e. Eugene Louis Gabriel
    de, 1809-1852, 1103-1108, 6065
Bellers, John, 1654-1725, 8165
Belleville, Ill., 16754
Belleza, Newton, 18953, 18954
Belligerency, 1142, 12668, 12669
Bellin, Jacques Nicolas, 1703-1772, 1109-
    1111, 2667
Bellisio, Norberto Bernardo, 18955
Bello, Andrés, 1781-1865, 18219, 18252,
    18956, 19176
Bello, Luis Mario, 18957

Bello Hernández, Ernest, 18958
Belloc, Hippolyte, 1112
Bellolio, Walter, 18959
Bellomont, Charles Coote, earl of, 1738?-1800,
    1113
Bellon de Saint Quentin, J., 1114
Bellorin, José Francisco, illustr., 19952
Belloro, Tommaso, 1741-1821, 1115
Bellot, Joseph René, 1826-1853, 1116, 1117
Bellows, Henry Whitney, 1814-1882, 1118-1122
Bellows family (Benjamin Bellows, 1712-1777),
    1119
Belloy, Auguste, marquis de, 1815-1871, 1123
Belly, Félix, 1816-1886, 1124, 1125
Belmar, Francisco, 1859-, 6066
Belmont, Mass. - History, 558
Belmonte, Benjamin Elie Colaço, 1126, 1127
Belmonte Román, Lucía, 18960
Belo Horizonte, Brazil, 18861; Universidade
    de Minas Gerais. Instituto de Pesquisas
    Radioativas. Publicação, 19703
Belo Horizonte (prefetura) Museo de Arte,
    18961
Belot, Charles, 1128
Belot, Gustave de, 1129
Below, Ernst, 1845-1910, 6067
Below the salt, 4983
Belsham, Jacobus, 1130
Belsham, Thomas, 1750-1829, 11252
Belsham, W.J., 1131
Belsham, William, 1752-1827, 21781
Belt, Edward W., 1132
Beltrami, Giacomo Constantino, 1779-1855,
    1133-1135, 6068
Beltrán, Enrique, 18962
Beltrán, Pedro, fl. 1742, 1136
Beltrán Avila, Marcos, 18963
Beltrán de Beltrán y Barnuevo, Luis, 6160
Beltrán Farrera, Carolina Elda, 18964
Beltrán Farrera, María Elena, 18965
Beltrán Guerrero, Luis, 1914-, 18966
Beltrán Heredia, B. Augusto, 18967
Beman, Nathan Sidney Smith, 1785-1871, 1137,
    1138
Bembo, Pietro, cardinal, 1470-1547, 1139, 1140
Bemis, George, 1816-1878, 1141-1143
Bemis, Katharine Isabel, 16807
Bemis, Samuel Flagg, 1891-, 18968
Benaím Pinto, Henrique, 18969
Benasso, Eve, 18970
Benatti, Felicio Padula, 18971
Benavente, Diego José, 1789-1867, 1144
Benavides, Alonso de, fl. 1630, 1145
Benavides Lazo, Persio A., 18972
Benavides Pinho, Diva, 18973
Benavides Ramírez, María Eva, 18974

46

Benavides y de la Cueva, Diego de, 6069
Ben-Bear, 8801
The bench and bar of Georgia, 13434
The bench and bar of Texas, 17074
Bench marks shown on maps of the upper
  Big Sandy valley, 14589
Bender family, 16883
The Benders in Kansas, 16883
Bendezú, Francisco, 18975
Bendfeldt Rojas, Lourdes, 19627
Benedetti, Adolfo Alberto, 18976
Benedetti, Lucia. Sigamos a estrela, 18977
Benedict, David, 1779-1874, 1146, 1147
Benedict, Erastus Cornelius, 1800-1880,
  1148
Benedict, George Grenville, 1826-1907,
  1149
Benedict, George Wyllys, 1796-1871, 23962
Benedict, Harry Yandell, 1869-, 15962
Benedict, Jennie C., 13652, 13653
Benedict, Kirby, 1810-1874, 1150
Benedict, Lewis, 1785-1862, 12576
Benedict, Mrs. Susan (Stafford), 1790-
  1869, 12576
Benedict, William B.? ed., 10315
The Benedictines, 9132
Benedictines, Bibliography, 14696
Benetti, Heloisa Domingues, 18978
Benevides Pinho, Diva, 18979
Benezet, Anthony, 1713-1784, 1151-1158,
  23963, 23964, 24290
Benger, Elizabeth Ogilvy, 1778-1827. A
  poem occasioned by the abolition of the
  slave trade, in 1806, 1809, 25285
Bengoa,Juan León, 1895-, 18980
Benham, Asahel, 1159
Benítez, Jose R., 6070, 18981
Benítez, Luis G., 18982
Benítez Zenteno, Raúl, 18984
Benito, Miguel, 18985
Benito Cereno, 10346
Benjamin, Harold Raymond Wayne, 1893-,
  18986
Benjamin, Israel Joseph, 1818-1864, 2668
Benjamin, Judah Philip, 1811-1884, 1160-
  1166
Benjamin, L.N., 1167
Benjamin, Marcus, 1857-1932, 15963
Benjamin, Samuel Greene Wheeler, 1837-
  1914, 1168
El Benjamin de la ss.^ma trinidad, 5853
Benjamin Sherwood Hedrick, 24548
Benko, François, 18987
Benners, Alfred H., 23965
Bennet, Isaac, 1803?-1856, 15902
Bennett, Andrew J., b.1841 or 2, 2669

Bennett, Daniel K., 1830-1897, 1169
Bennett, Edmund Hatch, 1824-1898, 1378
Bennett, Emerson, 1822-1905, 1170, 2670-2685
Bennett, Emily Thacher B., 1171
Bennett, Frederick Debell, 1172
Bennett, G.J., 22796
Bennett, Gae A., 18988
Bennett, James, 1812 or 3-1869, 15964
Bennett, John C., 15965
Bennett, William P., 15966
Bennett, William Wallace, 1821-1887, 2686
Bennie Ben Cree, 9082
Bennington, Vt. First Church, 13206; History,
  13206; Battle of, 1777, 22656
Bennion, Israel, 15967
Benny, 4165
Benoist, Pierre Vincent, comte, 1758-1834, 946
Bensley: a story of to-day, 8894
Benson, Alfred G., 1173
Benson, Egbert, 1746-1833, 1174-1177
Benson, Henry Clark, b.1815, 1178
Benson, Nettie Lee, 18989-18991
The Benson family, 8550
Benson family (William Benson, 1718-1755),
  2412
Bent, St. Vrain, & co., 5503
Bentham, Edward, 1707-1776, 1179
Bentham, Jeremy, 1748-1832, 1180, 1181, 11253
Bentley, William, 1759-1819, 1182
Bentley, William H., 2687
Bento, Claudio Moreira, 18992, 18993
Bentom, Clark, 11254
Benton, Jesse, 15968
Benton, Joseph Augustine, 15969
Benton, Nathaniel Soley, 1183
Benton, Thomas Hart, 1782-1858, 1184, 1185,
  2688-2690, 5508, 11255, 15970, 16554,
  23966, 23967
Benton's policy of selling and developing the
  mineral lands, 2079
Bent's Fort   Fiction, 2672
Benwell, J., 2691
Benzoni, Girolamo, b.1519, 1186, 1187, 18994,
  21782
Bera Cerxcada, Antonio, 6071
Berard, Augusta Blanche, 1824-1901, 1188
Berard's history of the United States, 1188
Berardinelli, Cleonice, ed., 18628
The Berber, 10336
Berbers, 10336
Berbice (Colony), Description & travel,
  22739, 24735
Berbice Commission, 25817
Berbice river, 1193
Berchmans, Jean, Saint, 1599-1621, 1189
Berckenhagen, Ernesto, 18995

Berdan's United States sharpshooters in the Army of the Potomac, 5267
Berdiales, Germán, 18996
Berdichewsky, Bernardo, 18997
Berea, Ky., 15686; Economic condition, 14536
Berea College, Berea, Ky., 3427, 13715, 14257, 14536, 15078, 15130, 15609, 15654; History, 15131; Library, 13654, 15134, 15135, 15137, 15389
Berenice, 9386
Berenstein, C.A., 18998
Berettari, Sebastiano, 1543-1622, 1189
Berg, George H., 18999
Berg, Joseph Frederick, 1812-1871, 1190
Bergamín, José, 1895-, 19000
Bergel Olivares, Reynaldo, 19001
Berger, Carlos Roberto, 19002
Berger, Friedrich Ludwig von, 1701-1735, 1191
Berger, Martin Luther, 1839-1906, 6655
Berger, W.M., illustr., 15265
Bergés Chupani, Manuel D., 19003
Bergh, Henry, 1811-1888, 1192
Berghaus, Erwin, 1894-, 2692
Berghaus, Heinrich Karl Wilhelm, 1797-1884, 1836
Berghes, Carlos de, 2186
Berghoff, Stephan, 1891-, 2693
Berghold, Alexander, 15971
Bergmann, Gregorio, 1894-, 19011
Bergoeing Guida, Jean Pierre, 19004-19010
Bergstrom, Bill, 13655
The Bering sea arbitration, 15972
Bering Strait, 7209
Berkel, Adriaan van, 1193
Berkeley, George, bp. of Cloyne, 1685-1753, 1194-1196, 11256
Berkeley, George Charles Grantley Fitz-hardinge, 1800-1881, 1197
Berkeley, Sir William, 1608?-1677, 1198
Berkeley Co., S.C., 4023
The Berkeleys and their neighbors, 5114
Berkshire association of Congregational ministers, Berkshire co., Mass., 2251
Berkshire Co., Mass., 2251, 12279; History, 2251
Berlandier, Luis, d.1851, 7480; Bibliography, 8049
Bermann, Gregorio, 1894-, 19011
Bermuda islands, 2426, 4947, 19012; Census, 1960, 19012; Description & travel, 1110, 12680, 21943, 23150; Fiction, 3998; Guide-books, 7616, 7617, 8102, Religious and ecclesiastical institutions, 1195
Bermúdez, Federico, 19013
Bermúdez, José Manuel, 1764-1830, 1199

Bermúdez, Oscar, 19014
Bermúdez, Pedro Joaquín, 1905-, 19015, 19016
Bermúdez de Belloso, Mercedes, 19017
Bermúdez Lemón, C., 19018
The Bermudian, 13491
Bernal, Calixto, 1804-1886, 19034
Bernal, Ignacio, 19019, 19020
Bernal, José María, 19021
Bernal Guardia, Targidio A., 19022
Bernal Maya, Nazario, 19023
Bernal Zapata, Rebeca, 20290
Bernáldez, Andrés, d.1513?, 1200
Bernard, Mrs. Bayle, 2695
Bernard, David, 1798-1876, 11257
Bernard, Sir Francis, bart., 1712?-1779, 1125
Bernard, Francis, 21784, 23703
Bernard, Jean Frédéric, d.1752, 1201, 2694
Bernard, John, 1756-1828, 2695
Bernard, Louis, b.1781, 1202, 1203
Bernard, Mountague, 1820-1882, 1204, 1205
Bernard, Pierre, 1895-, 23968
Bernard, Thalès, 1821-1878, ed. Translation of Handwörterbuch der griechischen und römischen mythologie, 22658
Bernard, Sir Thomas, bart., 1750-1818, 686
Bernard Lile, 9020
Bernardo de Quirós, Alvaro, 7644
Bernard's American journal of education, 260
Bernaschina González, Mario, 19024
Bernasconi, Irene, 19025, 19026
Bernath, Ursula, 7440-7442
Bernedo, Vicente, 1562-1619, 7453
Bernhard, Guillermo, 19027
Bernhard, Karl, duke of Saxe-Weimar-Eisenach, 1792-1862, 2696, 23969
Bernicia, 8721
Bernier, Joseph Elzear, 6303
Bernstorff, J.H. von, Graf, 4607
Berquin-Duvallon, 1206
Berredo, Bernardo Pereira de, d.1748, 11259
Berrera V., Humberto, 19028
Berrettini, Célia, 19029
Berrian, Richard, 1207
Berrian, Samuel, 1208
Berrian, William, 1787-1862, 1209-1211
Berriman, William, 11260
Berrios, Héctor H., 1922-, 7747
Berry, C.B., 1812-1900, 2697
Berry, Carrie Williams, 13656
Berry, Charles R., 18989
Berry, Harrison, b.1816, 1212
Berry, Henry, 1213
Berry, Philip, 1214, 1215
Berry, Robert Taylor, 1812-1877, 1216
Berry, Thomas Franklin, 1832-, 2698
Derry, Wendell, 1934-, 13657

erryer, Pierre Antoine, 1790-1868, 1217
ertha, 10760
ertha and her baptism, 8470
ertha the beauty, 11156
ertha's engagement, 10865
erthet, Luiz Arthaud, 19030
erthoud, Edward L., 15974
erthoud, James, 15500
ertram, Gordon W., 19031
ertrand, André, 1913-, 19032
erutti, María José, 19033
esançon's annual register of the state of
  Mississippi, 2699
eschke, William, 1218, 1219, 3700, 15810
eschreibung des Brittischen Amerika zur
  ersparung der englischen karten, 4248
eschreibung einer reise durch die
  Vereinigten Staaten von Nord-Amerika
  in den jahren 1838 bis 1840, 3595
eschryving der colonien van Groot-
  Britanje in Noord-Amerika, 2701
essau, Oscar, illustr., 4215
essie Wilmerton, 11125
essie's fortune, 9891
est, Edna Hunter, 13658, 13659
est, Robert, 13660
este, John Richard Digby, 1806-1885, 1220
estiario, 20529
ta Theta Pi Fraternity, History, 15400
tagh, William, 1221
tancès, Ramón Emeterio, 25334
tancourt, José Ramón de, 1823-1890, 19034
tancourt, Rómulo, Pres. Venezuela, 1908-,
  19035-19043
tancourt Díaz, Jesús, 19044
tencourt, José de Souza, 19045
e betrothed. A nation's vow, 24255
thune, George Washington, 1805-1862,
  1222-1227
thune, Mrs. Joanna (Graham) 1770-1849,
  1225, 22262
tker, John P., 23970
e betrayed, 10580
ttarello, Italo, 19046
ttendorf, João Filippe, b.1626?, 1228
ttle, Edward, 23971
ttridge, William Craddock, 1791-1879, 1229
tts, Alexander Davis, 1832-, 2702
tts, Craven Langstroth, 9460
tts, Louis, illustr., 13704
tts, Mary Eliza Wilson, 1824-1854, 15577
tts, William Archibald, 2702
tty, 11167
tty Alden: the first born daughter of the
  Pilgrims, 8600
uchat Ruchardt, Cecilia, 1947-, 19047

Beukma, K. Jz., 1230
Bevan, William, 23972
Bevens, W.E., 2703
Beverages, Carbonated   Brazil, 20504
Beveraggi Allende, Walter Manuel, 19048
Beveridge, Albert Jeremiah, 1892-1927, 6000
Beverley, Robert, ca.1673-ca.1722, 1231, 1232
Beverly, 11061
The Beverly family, 8968
Bevins, Ann, 13661, 15423
Bewick, Thomas, 1753-1828, illustr., 82
The bewildered querists and other nonsense,
  9248
Beyer, Edward, 1820?-1865, 2704
Beyer, Moritz, 1807-1854, 1233, 1234, 2705
Bianchi, Alberto G., 2706
Bianchi, Andrés, 18239
Bianchi Gundián, Manuel, 1895-, 19049
Bianco, Enrico, illustr., 20073
Bianconi, F., 1840-, 6072
Biart, Lucien, 1828-1897, 1235, 1236, 6073,
  6074, 11261, 19050
Bibaud, Maximilien, 1824-, 1237-1240
Bibaud, Michel, 1782-1857, 1241, 1242
Bibb, Henry, b.1815, 1243
Bibb lettuce, 13631
Bible, N.T. Acts. Manduruku, 19053; N.T.
  Gospels, Meditations, 18226; N.T. Mark.
  Portuguese. Negromonte, 1967, 19052;
  N.T. Mark. Munduruku, 1967, 19052; N.T.
  Matthew V-VII, Sermons, 1384; N.T.
  Revelation, Prophecies, 12093; O.T.
  Criticism, interpretation, etc., 15226,
  15556; O.T. Daniel, XII, 3, 2790; O.T.
  Esther, Drama, 15068; O.T. Psalms,
  Commentaries, 7030, 19051; Prophecies, 556;
  Publication and distribution, Societies,
  22510; Study and teaching, 13606
The Bible against slavery, 24301
The Bible in the public schools, 13439
Bible in the schools, 13043, 13439
Bible inspiration, 3110
Bible servitude, 1722
The Bible view of slavery reconsidered, 25138
The Biblical argument on slavery, 25914
Biblicus, pseud., 25138
Bibliografía basileira de documentação, 19305
Bibliografía cartográfica do Nordeste, 19463
Bibliografía de Daniel Valcárcel, 19054
Bibliografía de la novela venezolana, 19741
Bibliografía florestal brasileira, 20239
Bibliografía geográfica de Mexico, 7488
Bibliografía gonçalvina, centenário de Antônio
  Gonçalves Dias, 1864-1964, 19055
Bibliografía hidrogeologica de la República
  Mexicana, 19085

49

Bibliografía industrial de México, 18771
Bibliographical Society of America, 13662
Bibliographie des plans de developpement, 19791
Bibliography, 517, 8186, 20184; Best books, 12491; Early printed books, 22486; Kentuckyana library...., 13663; Paperback editions, 18295; Period, 265; Rare books, 2476; Rare books   Catalogs,19057; National - Brazilian, 19504
Bibliography of development plans, 19791
A bibliography of the state of Ohio, 5407
The Bibliophile Society, 6075
Biblioteca de escritores caldenses, 19195
Biblioteca de la Academia Nacional de la Historia, 17980, 17982-17984, 17986-17988, 18036, 18389, 18627, 18994, 19527, 19688, 19737, 19738, 19855, 19864, 19905, 19921, 19996, 20251
Biblioteca de la Universidad del Valle, 19858
Biblioteca de psiquiatría, psicopatología y psicosomática. Serie menor, 19011
Biblioteca de textos filosoficos, 19735
Biblioteca del estudiante universitario, 18202
La biblioteca en Colombia, 20267
Biblioteca Lincoln, Buenos Aires, 19056
Biblioteca Municipal Mário de Andrade, Sao Paulo, 19057
El bibliotecario universitario, 18837
Bibliotecas especializadas brasileiras, 19307
Bibliotheca americana, 2476
Bibliotheca americana vetustissima, 22311
Bibliotheca hispana vetus, 400
Bibliothèque américaine, 1244
Bibliothèque de la Faculté de philosophie & lettres de l'université de Liège, fasc. 1, 24543
Bibliothèque linguistique américaine, 6076
Bibra, Ernst, freiherr von, 1806-1878, 1245
The bicentennial polka, 14392
Bickel, Karl August, 2707
Bickell, Richard, 1246
Bickford, Eli, 1754-1856, 1753
Bickford, James, 1247
Bickford, Mrs. Mary Ann (Dunn) 1824-1845, 1247
Bickley, George, 18968
Bickley, George W.L., 1248, 1249
Bicknell, George W., 2709
Bicknell, John, fl.1774, 24264
A bicycle of Cathay, 10886
Bidart Campos, German Jose, 19058
Biddle, Charles, 1250

Biddle, Charles John, 1819-1873, 1251, 1252
Biddle, Clement Cornell, 1784-1855, ed., 23578
Biddle, Craig, 1823-1910, 1253
Biddle, Mrs. Ellen (McGowan) 1841-, 2710
Biddle, George Washington, 1818-1897, 1254
Biddle, James Cornell, 1795-1838, 1255, 1256
Biddle, Nicholas, 1786-1844, 1257-1259, 4272, 12276, 17030
Biddle, Richard, 1796-1847, 1260-1262, 11262
Bidwell, Barnabas, 1763-1833, 6873
Bidwell, John, 1819-1900, 2711, 15963, 15975, 15976, 16926, 17533
Biempica y Sotomayor, Salvador, bp., 1730-186 6077-6079
Bienal Armando Reverón, 19739
La Bienaventurada Rosa Pervana de S. Maria, 7694
Los bienes de la Iglesia en México, 18928
Bienkowski, A., pub., 6983
Bierce, Lucius Verus, 1801-1876, 1263
Bierstadt, Albert, illustr., 5584
Biesanz, John, 19059
Biesanz, Mavis, 19059
Big Abel, and the little Manhattan, 10323
The big bear of Arkansas, 4832
Big Bend Country, 17032
Big Dick, the king of the negroes, 10068
Big Hole Valley, Mont., 17291
Big Horn expedition, 17197
Big Horn mountains, 17871
Big Horn region, 17683
Big river to cross, 2860
Big Sandy River, 14751, 15469; Maps, 15626
The Big Sandy Valley, 14059, 14589; Bibliography, 14419; Description, 13935; Maps, 14593
The big strike on Heavy Tree Hill, 6967
Big Wichita River, 5532
Bigatti, Alfredo, 19520
Bigelow, Abijah, 1264
Bigelow, Alpheus, 25029
Bigelow, Burton, 6080
Bigelow, Erastus Brigham, 1814-1879, 1265, 12
Bigelow, Jacob, 1787-1879, 1267-1271
Bigelow, John, 1817-1911, 1272, 1273, 2712, 6081, 11263
Bigelow, John Flavel, 1818-1884, 11264
Bigelow, John Reynolds, 1274
Bigelow, Timothy, 1739-1790, 22426
Bigelow, Timothy, 1767-1821, 1275, 1276
Bigelow, Tyler, 1277
Biggs, James, 1278, 1279
Biggs, William, 11265
Bigland, John, 1750-1832, 1280, 11266
Bigler, Henry William, 1815-, 15977

50

Bigler, John, 2891
Bigler, William, 1814-1880, 1281, 1282
Biglow, H., ed., 271
Biglow, William, 1773-1844, 1283-1286
The Biglow papers, 23902
Bigney, Mark Frederick, 1817-1886, 1287
Bigodes, 21752
Bigot, Jacques, 1644-1711, 1288-1290
Bigotry exposed, 23973
Bigsby, John Jeremiah, 1291
Bijdrage tot de kennis der kolonie Suriname, 24767
Bijdragen tot de kennis der nederlandsche en vreemde koloniën, 23974
Bilak, León, 1903-, 19060
Bilder aus dem gesellschaftlichen leben der Nord-Amerikaner, 2713
Bilharinho, José Soares, 19061
Bilingual schooling, 18268
Bill, Fred A., 15978
Bill, Ledyard, 1836-1907, 1292, 2714, 11267
Bill Arp, so called, 5186, 25529
Bill Arp's peace papers, 5187
Bill drafting manual for the Kentucky General Assembly..., 14606
Bill Drock's investment, 8975
Bill family (John Bill, d.1638), 1292
Bill Jones of Paradise Valley, Oklahoma, 16134
Billardon de Sauvigny, Edmé Louis, 1293
Billaud-Varenne, Jacques Nicolas, 1756-1819, 1294
Billecocq, Jean Baptiste Louis Joseph, 1765-1829, 5423, 13397
Billerica, Mass., 11268; First Congregational church, 11892; History, 11268
The billiard table, 14242
Billinghurst, Charles, 1818-1865, 23975
Billings, Mrs. Eliza (Allen) b.1826, 1295
Billings, John Davis, 1842-, 2715
Billington's valentine, 10465
Bills of exchange, U.S., 22999
Billtry, 9318
Billy Buck's visit, with his master, to England, 10861
Billy LeRoy, the Colorado bandit, 16320
Billy the kid, 3575
Biloxi, Description, 3597
Bimbalhada e sarabandas, 20197
Bimbi, Gerardo A., 19062
Bimetalism, 22956
Bingham, Helen, 15979
Bingham, Hiram, 1789-1869, 1296, 1297
Bingham, Joel Foote, 1827-1914, 1298-1301
Bingham, John Armor, 1815-1900, 1302-1305, 11269

Bingham, J.C., 1306
Bingham, Kinsley Scott, 1808-1861, 1307, 23976
Bingley, William, 1774-1823, 2716
Binkerd, Adam D., 13664
Binney, Horace, 1780-1875, 1308-1315, 6082, 11270, 11271; An eulogium upon the Hon. William Tilghman, 12296; The privilege of the writ of habeas corpus under the Constitution, 1676, 11272, 12461, 13134, 25067
Binney, William, 1316, 7783
Binney, William Greene, 1833-, 1317, 1318
Binns, John, 1772-1860, 1319, 1320
Binns, William, 1321
Bio-bibliography, 18124
Biografías militares, 18822
Biographia americana, 12171
Biographical and historical memoirs of the early pioneer settlers in Ohio, 3868
The biographical annual, 12455
A biographical dictionary, 1397, 12007
The biographical encyclopaedia of Kentucky of the dead and living men of the nineteenth century, 13665
Biographical, literary, and political anecdotes, of several of the most eminent persons of the present age, 223
A biographical notice of Com. Jesse D. Elliott, 22687
A biographical notice of Daniel Drake, M.D., of Cincinnati, 14984
The biographical remains of Rev. George Beecher, 1052
A biographical romance, 8800
Biographical sketch of General John Adair, 13666
Biographical sketch of Hon. Charles Fenton Mercer, 6826
Biographical sketch of the Hon. John L. Helm, 14577
Biographical sketch of the Hon. Lazarus W. Powell, 14578
A biographical sketch of the life of the late Capt. Michael Cresap, 13138
A biographical sketch of the life of William B. Ide, 16844
Biographical sketch of Thomas Singularity, 10434
Biographical sketches, 2905
Biographical sketches of General Nathaniel Massie, General Duncan McArthur, Captain William Wells, and General Simon Kenton, 4347
Biography, 1525, 12296, 12890, 15604, 21942; Dictionaries, 700, 1397, 23187; Juvenile literature, 1954

Biography of Christopher Merkley, 17183
The biography of Elder David Purviance,
    4866
Biography of General Lewis Cass, 22447
Biological investigations in Mexico, 6862
Biondelli, Bernardino, 1804-1886, 1322
Bionne, Henri, d.1881, 1323
Biot, Jean Baptiste, 1774-1862, 1324
Bioy Casares, Adolfo, 19164
Birch, Edmund Pendleton, 1824-1883, 1325
Birch, James H., 1804-1878, 11273
Birch, Thomas E., 13667
Birch, Thomas Ledlie, d.1808, 1326
Birch Nest Farm, Fayette County, Ky.,
    15361
Bird, Francis William, 1809-1894, 1327,
    1328, 11274, 11275
Bird, Henry Merttins, 1329
Bird, Horace A., 15986
Bird, Isaac, 1793-1876, 1330
Bird, James, 1788-1839, 1331
Bird, Mark Baker, 1807-1880, 6083, 19063
Bird, Robert Montgomery, 1806-1854,
    1332, 1333, 2717; Nick of the woods,
    14983
Bird, William A., 1796-1878, 1334
Bird family, 1330
Bird lore, Kentucky, 15541
Bird-song, 5398
Birds, 15879; Arctic regions, 6302;
    Argentine Republic, 589; California,
    17869; Classification, 549; Cuba, 18889-
    18891; Eggs and nests, 1486; Europe,
    11349; Geographical distribution, 11349;
    Jamaica, 12324; Kentucky, 14090;
    Massachusetts, 23401; Minnesota, 4664;
    New Hampshire, 6111; North America, 549,
    675, 676, 1486, 11349, 13572; Nova Scotia,
    6111; Oregon, 17751; Paraguay, 589, 598;
    Pennsylvania, 931; Pictorial works, 5735;
    Rocky Mountains, 5524; South America,
    19525; U.S., 5735, 16279; Wisconsin,
    4664
The birds of America, 13572
Birds of prey, Argentine Republic, 20450
Birds of the Northwest, 16279
Birdseye, George W., 1844-, 11276
Birge, Edward B., 14127
Birge, Julius Charles, 1839-1923, 14987
Birkbeck, Morris, 1764-1825, 1335-1337, 3487,
    15988, 15989, 16528; Bibliography, 15989;
    Letters from Illinois, 3039, 3424, 13233,
    24379; Notes on a journey in America, 3039,
    3424
Birkinbine, Henry E., 6084
Birkinbine, John, 1844-, 6084

Birkinshaw, Maria Louisa, 1338
Birney, James Gillespie, 1792-1857, 1339-1342
    2718-2720, 23977
Birney, William, 1819-1907, 23977
Biron, Armand Louis de Gontaut, duc de Lauzun
    1747-1793, 2721
Birová, A., 19064
The birth and death of nations, 22910
Birth control Religious aspects, 19706
Birth rate, Peru, 19207
The birthday gifts, 8807
A birthday present for Lincoln, 5865
The birth-mark, 9823
Bisbie, D.T., 1343
Bisch, P.M., 19065-19067
Bischoff, Efraín U., 19068
Biscuits, Beaten, 14010
Bishop, Abraham, 1763-1844, 1344-1349
Bishop, Albert Webb, 1832-1901, 1350, 1351
    21785
Bishop, Mrs. Anna (Rivière) 1814-1884, 6085,
    8230
Bishop, Ella, d.1926, 13742, 14201
Bishop, Mrs. Harriet E., 1817-1883, 1352,
    21786
Bishop, Isabella Lucy (Bird) "Mrs. J.E. Bisho
    1831-1904, 2722, 6086
Bishop, Joel Prentiss, 1814-1901, 1353-1355
Bishop, John Leander, 1820-1868, 1356
Bishop, John Soast, 1834-1915, 11277
Bishop, Joseph, b.1770, 3668
Bishop, Judson Wade, 1831-1917, 11278, 13668
Bishop, Levi, 1815-1881, 23978
Bishop, Matthew, fl.1701-1744, 1357
Bishop, Nathaniel Holmes, 1837-1902, 2723, 27
Bishop, Putnam P., 1358
Bishop, Robert Hamilton, 1777-1855, 1359,
    13669-13671
Bishop, Samuel G., 11279
Bishop, Will C., 17640
Bishop, William Henry, 6087, 6088
Bishop, William W., 17011
The bishop and Nannette, 9668
The bishop's conversion, 10333
The bishop's ghost and the printer's baby,
    10896
The bishop's son, 8946
Bishops, U.S., 14255
Bison, 14595; American, 15835, 16900
Bisset, George, d.1788, 1360
Bisset, Robert, 1759-1805, 1361-1363
Bissette, Cyrille Charles Auguste, 1795-1858,
    23979, 23980
Bitar letayf, Marcelo, 19069
Biting tales of rattlesnakes and men, 14333
A bitola métrica no sistema ferroviario

brasileiro, 18347
Bits of blarney, 10291
Bits of family history..., 13838
Bittencourt, Benour C., 19178
Bittencourt, Edgard de Moura, 19070
Bitter harvest, 14202
Bitter Root mountains, 16760
Bivins, Viola (Cobb) 1863-, 15990
The bivouac, 14219
The bivouac and the battlefield, 4630
The bivouac of the dead and its author
   ..., 15239
Bixby, O.H., 2725
Le bizco, 1235
Björck, Tobias Er., 1364
Black, Chauncey Forward, d.1904, 22753
Black, Jeremiah Sullivan, 1810-1883,
   1367-1369, 15991
Black, Robert, 6089
Black, William Harman, 1868-, 6090, 6091
Black and white, 4221
Black bass, 14311
Black blood and white, 10787
The black book, 5033
The black brigade of Cincinnati, 11836
Black code, 25178
The black crook, 8808
The black cross, 10668
The black devils and other poems, 14982
Black diamonds, 10198
Black diamonds gathered in the darkey homes
   of the South, 4813
Black farm operators and rural-farm
   population in Kentucky, 1900-1970, 24161
The black gauntlet, 10715, 25455
Black Hawk, Sauk Chief, 1767-1838, 1365,
   1366, 3282
Black Hawk, Colorado, 17514
Black Hawk Army, 13672
Black Hawk War, 1832, 1366, 3081, 5596,
   9585, 12148, 16214
Black Hawk's last raid, 1866, 16590
Black Hills, 16261, 16887, 17683, 17871;
   South Dakota, Description & travel,
   16309, 16400, 17122, 17123; South
   Dakota, Fiction, 3373; South Dakota,
   History, 5201, 17525
Black Hills Expedition of 1874, 17858
The Black Hills gold rush, 16042, 16992
The Black hills of South Dakota, 17525
The black hood, 24295
Black ice, 10988
Black list, 1370
The black man, or Haytian independence, 19063
Black masters: a side-light on slavery, 25902
The black plume rifles, 9936

Black Ralph, the forest fiend!, 4990
The Black Republican, 25613
Black Republican imposture exposed!, 1371
The Black Riders of Congarie, 10775
Black River Falls, Wis., 15848
The black sheep, 10289
Black spirits and white, 9204
The black wolf's breed, 9400
Blackbeard, 8699
Blackberry Creek, Ky. - Maps, 14592
Blackburn, Colin Blackburn, baron, 1813-1896,
   2199
Blackburn, James Knox Polk, 1837-1923, 2726
Blackburn, John F., 14263
Blackburn, William Maxwell, 1828-1898, 1372
Blackburne, Francis, 1705-1787, 21787
Blackford, Charles Minor, 1833-1903, 2727
Blackford, Dominique de, 1373
Blackford, Mrs. Susan Leigh (Colston) 1835-
   1903, 2727
Blackie, Walter Graham, 1816-1906, 1374
Blackley, Frederick Rogers, 1375
Blackmar, Frank Wilson, 1854-1931, 15992
Blackmore, Richard Doddridge, 1825-1900, 1376
Blackmore, William, d.1878, 15993, 16401
Blacknall, O.W., 6092
Blackstone, Sir William, 1723-1780.
   Commentaries, 1181
The Blackwater chronicle, 4157
Blackwell, Robert, 6093
Blackwell, Robert S., 1823-1863, 1377, 1378
Blackwell, Sarah Ellen, 1828-, 6094
Bladensburg, Battle of, 1814 - Poetry, 1379
The Bladensburg races, 1379
Blades o' bluegrass, 3245
Bladh, Carl Edvard, 1790-1851, 1380
Blagden, George Washington, 1802-1884, 1381
Blahutiak, Alojz, 19071, 19072
Blaine, James Gillespie, 1830-1893, 1382, 8261
Blaine Co., Mont. - History, 17290
Blair, Francis Preston, 1791-1876, 6095
Blair, Francis Preston, 1821-1875, 1383, 2728,
   22779, 23981-23983
Blair, George E., 15994
Blair, James, 1656-1743, 1384, 3805
Blair, James, 15567, 15995
Blair, John Durbarrow, 1759-1823, 1385
Blair, Montgomery, 1813-1883, 1386, 6096,
   6097, 11280, 23843
Blair, Samuel, 1741-1818, 1387, 1388
Blairet, Louis, 19073
Blake, Dominick T., d.1839, 1389
Blake, Francis, 1774-1817, 1390, 11281
Blake, George, 1768?-1841, 1391, 1392, 12681
Blake, Harrison Gray, 1818-1876, 1393, 6098
Blake, Henry Nichols, 1838-, 1394

Blake, J.A., pub., 16686
Blake, James, 1688-1753, 1395
Blake, John Lauris, 1788-1857, 1396-1398
Blake, Joseph M., 1809-1879, 1399
Blake, Mrs. Mary Elizabeth, 1840-1907,
  6099, 15996
Blake, Mortimer, 1813-1884, 1400
Blake, Robert, 1599-1657, 22132
Blake, Samuel, 1797-1867, 1401
Blake, Thaddeus C., 13673
Blake, William J., 1402
Blake, William O., 1403
Blake, William Phipps, 1826-, 1404, 11282,
  11283
Blake family (Samuel Blake, 1715-1754),
  1401
Blake family (William Blake, 1594-1663),
  1401
Blake's Hand-book of Colorado, 16686
Blakeslee, Bernard F., 2729
Blakiston, Thomas Wright, 1832-1891, 2730,
  15997
Blakeman, Learner, 1781?-1815, 2818
Blakslee, Solomon, 1762-1835, 1405
Blanc, Hippolyte, b.1820, 1406
Blanch y Blanco, Celestino, 19074
Blanchard, Amos, of Cincinnati, 1407, 1408
Blanchard, Calvin, 1409
Blanchard, Charles, 1410
Blanchard, Claude, 1742-1802, 2731
Blanchard, Ira Henry Thomas, d.1845, 1411
Blanchard, Jonathan, 1811-1892, 23984
Blanchard, Joshua Pollard, 1782-1868, 1412
Blanchard, P., 2732
Blanchard, Rufus, 1821-1904, 15998
Blanche Gilroy, 9926
Blanche of Brandywine, 10212
Blanche Talbot, 3997
Blanchelande, royal lieutenant in Haiti,
  7828
Blanchet, Francis Norbert, 15999
Blanco, Andrés Eloy, 1898-1955, 19075,
  19076
Blanco, Eduardo, 1839-1912, 19077
Blanco,Enrique José, 19078
Blanco, José Félix, 1782-1872, 19079
Blanco, Ricardo Román, 19080
Blanco-Fombona, Rufino, 1874-, 6109, 6814,
  7245, 7635, 7637, 8009, 8267
Blanco Moreno, Roberto, 19081
Blanco Segura, Ricardo, 19082
Bland, Theodorick, 1777-1846, 23221
Bland, Thomas, 1809-1885, 1318
Bland, Thomas Augustus, 1830-, 10888
Blandford, Mass. - History, 12230
Blanding, Stephen F., 2733

Blandon H., Aldemar, 19083
Blane, William Newnham, 1800-1825, 2734
Blankstein, Charles S., 19084
Blanton, Alice Rogers Clay, 13674
Blanton, Lindsay Hughes, 8192, 15545
Blaschke, Eduardo, 16001
Blásquez López, Luis, 1900-, 19085
Blatchford, Eliphalet Wickes, 1826-1914, 22417
Blatchford, John, 1762(ca.)-1794(ca.), 11284
Blatchford, Richard M., 1413
Blatchford, Samuel, 1767-1828, 1414, 24765
Blatchford, Thomas Windeatt, 1794-1866, 1415
Blattidae, 18115
Blaug, Mark, 19086
Blauvelt, 1416
Blauvelt, Charles Clare, 6100
Blayer, Paul G., 13675
Bledsoe, A.J., 6101
Bledsoe, Albert Taylor, 1809-1877, 2735, 2736
Bledsoe, Anthony Jennings, 1858-, 16002
Bledsoe, Jesse, 13676
Bleecker, Anthony, 1770-1827, 25394
Bleeker, Leonard, 1417
The Blemmertons, 10423
Blennerhassett, Harman, 1764?-1831, 15314
The blessed bees, 9046
Blessing of the hounds, 14977, 15309
Blessington, Joseph P., 2737
Bletzer, Keith V., 19087
Blevins, Billy, 13677
Bleznick, Donald W., 19088
Blichfeldt, Emil Harry, 1874-, 6102
Blind, 11443; Education, 7181; Education,
  Brazil, 19364
Blind, Books for the, 14387, 19364
Blind fish, 15111
Blind leaders of the blind, 9054
The blind sisters, 11173
The blindman's offering, 11443
The blindman's world, 8773
Bliss, Charles R., 16003
Bliss, Edward, 1822-1877, 2738
Bliss, George, 1764-1830, 1418
Bliss, George, 1793-1873, 1419, 1420
Bliss, George, 1813-, 23985
Bliss, Henry, 1797?-1873, 1421
Bliss, Leonard, 1811-1842, 11285
Bliss, Philemon, 1814-1889, 1422
Bliss, Robert S., 1805-, 16004
Bliss, Stephen, 1787-1847, 15902
Bliss, Sylvester, 11286, 21788
Bliss Institute, Belize, British Honduras,
  19089
The Blithedale romance, 9818
Blixen, Hyalmar, 19090
Blocher, W.D., 2739

Blocher's Arkansas land-guide, 2739
Block, Ben A., 16005
Block, Pedro, 1914-, 19091, 19092
Blockade, 12222
A blockaded family, 3728
The blockheads, 1423
Blockley and Merion agricultural society, Pa., 1455
Blodget, Lorin, 1823-1901, 1424, 11287
Blodget, Samuel, 1757, 1814, 11288
Blois, John T., 11289
Blom, Frans Ferdinand, 1893-, 8212
Blome, Richard, d.1705, 1425, 21789
Blondel, Georges, 1856-, 2740
Blood, Henry Ames, 1838-1901? 11290
Blood, Henry M., 16006
Blood, William, 11291
Blood, Circulation, 535
Blood-horse, 13678
The blood of Rachel, 15068
The blood of the Mohawk!, 10158
Bloodgood, Simeon DeWitt, 1799-1866, 11292, 11293
Bloody Brook, Battle of, 1675, 12110
A bloody butchery by the British Troops: or The runaway fight of the regulars, 21790
The bloody chasm, 9369
The bloody junto, 3134
Bloody Knife (Sioux-Arikara Indian), 17705
The bloody week, 11294
Bloomfield, Conn., History, 23664
Bloomfield, Me., History, 12657
Bloomington, Ill., History, 16100
Bloomington, Ind., Social life & customs, 9705
Blooms of the berry, 2949
Bloor, Alfred Janson, d.1917, 11295
Blossom (Ship), 1066, 6048, 12883
Blouet, Guillaume Abel, 1795-1853, 3229
Blouët, Paul, i.e. Léon Paul, 1848-1903, 2741
Blount, William, 1749-1800, defendant, 11296
The blovdy tenent, 23799
Blow, Henry Taylor, 1817-1875, 11297
Blowe, Daniel, 2742, 21791
The Bloxhams, 10196
Blue, Daniel, 2743
The blue and the gray, 2577
The blue cotton umbrella, 10194
Bluegrass, 14723
The blue grass and environs, 14710
Bluegrass and laurel, 14762
Blue-grass and rhododendron, 3522
Blue grass ballads and other verse, 15652
The bluegrass country, 14080
The bluegrass of Kentucky, 14024, 14766

A blue grass Penelope, 9788
The blue-grass region of Kentucky, 2509, 5432
The blue-grass region of Kentucky and other Kentucky articles, 13525
The blue grass region of Kentucky, geography of the, 13979
A blue-grass thoroughbred, 14217
The Blue guide to Cuba, 6103
The blue handkerchief, 14961
Blue Licks, Battle of the, 7376, 13860, 14031, 14509, 14510, 14641, 14788, 15739, 15794
Blue Licks Battle - Field monument, 14510
Blue Licks Battlefield State Park, 14642, 14788
The blue ribbon cook book, 13652
Blue ribbons, 10200
Blue Ridge Mountains - Fiction, 8758
Blumenthal, Ida (Gawell) 1869-, 2744
Blundell, Bezer, 11298
Blundeville, Thomas, fl.1561, 21792
Blunt, Joseph, 1792-1860, 241, 11299, 21793, 21794
Blunt, Stanhope English, 1850-1926, 17776
Blutstein, Howard, 19093
Blyth, Joseph, 11300
Board of agents for the American loyalists, 12190
Board of aid to land ownership, Boston, 2745
Board of Trade Resources of Colorado, 16364
The boarding school, 9548
The boarding school of Mary Todd Lincoln, 15586
Boarding-school scenes, 10953
Boardman, George Dana, 1828-1903, 11301
Boardman, George Nye, 1825-1915, 11302
Boardman, Henry Augustus, 1808-1880, 11303-11313
Boardman, James, 6104
Boardman, John, 1824-1883, 16007
Boards of trade, 12788
The boarwolf, 10693
Boats and boating - Kentucky, 14559
Bob Rutherford and his wife, 10372
Bobadella G., Patricio A., 19094
Boban, Eugène, 6105
"Bobbie", 8821
Bobbio, Norberto, 1909-, 19691
The bobolink minstrel, 1677
Bocage, Manuel Maria de Barbosa du, 1765-, 20233
Bock, Carl Heinz, 19095
Bockett, Elias, 11314
Bocock, John Holmes, 1813-1872, 2746
Boddily, John, 1755-1802, 11315
Bodenstedt, Friedrich Martin von, 1819-1892, 2747

Bodley, Edith Fosdick, 13679
Bodley, Temple, 13680, 13681, 14836
Bodley, Thomas, 14129
Boesnier, 11316
Bogardus, Carl R., 13682, 13683
Bogart, David Schuyler, 1770-1839, 11317, 22101
Bogart, Willian Henry, 1810-1888, 2749, 11318
Bogen, Frederich W., 11319
Boggs, Edward Brenton, 1821-1895, 13177
Boggs, Robert, 175-?-1827, 13791
Boggs, Samuel S., 2749
Boggs, William Robertson, 1829-1911, 2750
Boggs family, 13791
Bogle, Robert, 1258
Bogotá. Biblioteca Nacional. Archivo Histórico, 20255; Description, 19100; Escuela Superior de Administración Pública, 19096; Universidad de los Andes. Centro de Estudios sobre Desarrollo Económico, 19077, 19078; Universidad de Los Andes. Departamento de Historia, 20255; Universidad Javeriana, 19099; Universidad Nacional. Centro de Bibliografía y Documentación, 18960; Universidad Nacional de Colombia. Centro de Investigaciones para el Desarrollo, 19100, 19101; Universidad Nacional de Colombia. Facultad de Ingeniería e Ingeniería Química. Biblioteca, 19102; Universidad Nacional. Facultad de Medicina, 18960; Universidad Nacional. Facultad de Sociología. Serie latino-americana, 19503; Universidad Nacional de Colombia. Instituto de Ciencias Naturales, 19103; Universidad Nacional de Colombia. Oficina de Planeación, 19104
Bogrand, Ricardo, 1930-, 19105
Bohemia invaded, 9533
The Bohemian, 11320
Bohemian days in San Francisco, 6978
The Bohemian girl, 9740
Bohn, Henry George, 1796-1844, 13004, 21795
Bohorquez C., José Ignacio, 19106
Bohun, Edmund, 1645-1699, 11321, 21796
Bohun family, 11321
Boies, Andrew J., 2751
The boiler explosion of the Martin boiler on board the U.S. "double-ender" Chenango, 11322
Boillot, Leon, 16008
Boimare, A.L., 11323
The Bois Brûlé, 10827
Boisgilbert, Edmund, pseud., 9412
Boislecomte, André Olivier Ernest Sain de, b.1799, 11324

Boissonnade, Prosper, 1862-1935, 19107
Boiteux, Lucas Alexandre, 19108
Bokee, David A., 1805-1860, 21797
Boker, George Henry, 1823-1890, 11325, 11326
Bokum, Hermann, 1807-1878, 2752, 11327-11329
Bolanyo, 10593
"Bolbodimyia" Bigot, 20543
Bold works at the bridge, 10042
Boldori, Rosa, 19109
Bolduc, Jean-Baptiste-Zacharie, 2753, 6106
Bolet Peraza, Nicanor, 1838-1906, 19110
Boletim técnico de sericicultura, 17965, 19171, 19172
Boletin bibliografico pernambucano, 19111
Boletín de geologia, Bucaramanga, 19112
Boletín de precios de productos agropecuarios. Caracas, 19113
Boletín del Museo del Mar, 18866
Boletín hidrológico, Valle del Cauca, 20492
Boletín histórico de Puerto Rico, 6107
Bolin, Daniel Lynn, 13684, 13685
Bolívar, Fernando S., 2754
Bolívar, Rafael, 19114
Bolívar, Simón, 1783-1830, 6028, 6108-6110, 6250, 6476, 6794, 6866, 7015, 7053, 7243, 7245, 7625-7637, 7761, 8026, 18199, 18845, 18930, 18963, 19115, 19487, 19761, 20655
Bolívar, Simón, 1783-1830 - Poetry, 18583, 20467
Bolívar en el Perú, 6250
Bolivia, 13272
Bolivia, Bound., Argentine republic, 7953; Census, 19120; Comisión Nacional de Estudio de la Caña y del Azucar, 19116; Comité Nacional de Inversiones, 19117; Constitution, 12513, 19118; Description & travel, 11964, 18637, 21853; Dirección Nacional de Estadística y Censos, 19119, 19120; Dirección Nacional de Informaciones, 19121, 19122; Economic conditions, 18943, 18945, 19122, 20209-20211, 20432; Economic policy, 18943, 18944, 18945, 19117; Foreign relations - Chile, 20156; History, 1825-, 7752, 18030, 18946, 19121; History, Fiction, 18062; History, Revolution, 1964, 18869; History, Wars of independence, 1809-1825, 5923, 7752; Laws, statutes, etc., 19117, 19123, 19124; Ministerio de Educación y Bellas Artes, 18815; Ministerio de Relaciones Exteriores, 19125; Politics & government, 18869, 18963, 23130; Population, 19120; Rural condition, 18333; Servicio Agrícola Interamericano, 19126-19129; Social conditions, 19122, 19576, 20210; Statistics, 19119
Bolivian Gulf Oil Company, 19725

Bollaert, William, 1807-1876, 11330
Bollan, William, d.1776, 11331-11336, 21798
Boller, Henry A., 16009
Bolles, Frank, 1856-1894, 6111
Bolles, James Aaron, 1810-1894, 11337
Bolles, John Augustus, 1809-1878, 11338, 11339
Bolles, Lucius, 1779-1884, 11340
Bolles family (Joseph Bolles, 1608-1678), 11338
Bolling, Phillip A., 23986
Bollmann, Erich, 1769-1821, 11341, 11342
Bollo, Sarah, 19130
Boloix, Pablo, 11343
Bolsi, Alfredo S., 19131
Bolton, Charles Edward, 1841-1901, 2755
Bolton, Edward Chichester, 11344
Bolton, Herbert Eugene, 1870-, 16010, 16011, 16488, 16951
Bolton, Robert, 1814-1877, 11345, 11346
Bolton, William, 21799
Bolton, Eng. (Lancashire) Mechanics' institution, 2562
Boltovsky, Esteban, 19132-19135
Boltshauser, Joao, 19136
Boltwood, Lucius Manlius, 1825-1905, 21800
Bolzius, Reverend, 4908
Bombal, Susana, 19137
Bombardement de Valparaiso, 11347
Bombardement et entière destruction de Grey-town, 890
Bombino Matienzo, Juan P., 19138
Bomfim, Paulo, 19139
Bon Harbor, Kentucky, Description, 15600
Bona, Felix de, 1821?-1889, 11348
Bonafina Dorrego, Andrés, 19140
Bonampak, Mexico, 18328
Bonavia, Duccio B., 19141
Bonanya mines, New, 16384
Bonaparte, Charles Lucien Jules Laurent, prince de Canino, 1803-1857, 11349
Bonaparte, Roland Napoleon, prince, 1858-1924, 7494
Bonar, Lewis J., 6112
Bonazzi, Augusto, 19142
Bonazzi, M.V., 19142
Bond, Alvan, 1793-1882, 11350, 11351
Bond, Beverly Waugh, 1882-, 5229
Bond, Christiana, 6113
Bond, Henry, 1790-1859, 21801
Bond, J. Harman, 16012
Bond, John Wesley, 1825-1903, 11352, 11353, 16013
Bond, Mrs. Lydia Kennedy, 13686
Bond, Samuel R., 5535

Bond, Samuel Start, 19143
Bond, William Cranch, 1789-1859, 11354
Bond, William Key, d.1864, 11355, 11356
Bondage a moral institution, 11357
Bondage of midnight, 14385
Bonds, Puerto Rico, 18674
Bonduel, Florimond J., 11358
Bondurant, Jacke, 15455
Bone, John Herbert A., 1830-1906, 2756, 11359
A bone to gnaw, 1931, 1932
Boner, John Henry, 1845-1903, 2757
Bonet, Federico, 1906-, 19599
Bonet de Sotillo, Dolores, 19144
Bonfanti, Celestino, 19145, 19746
Bonfanti, Enrique, 19146
Bonfield, 3998
Bonifacio, José (O moço), 19147
Bonifacius. An essay upon the good,..., 23299
Bonifaz Ezeta, Angel, 19148
Bonifaz Nuño, Alberto, 19149
Bonilha, Nivaldo Alves, 17965
Bonilla, Policarpo, pres. Honduras, 1858-1926, 7451
Bonilla, Sonia, 19150
Bonilla Echeverri, Oscar, 19151
Bonilla Gómez, Hermenegildo, 19152
Bonneau, Alexandre, 1820-, 11360
Bonnefaux, L., 11361
Bonnefoy, Antoine, 2758
Bonnell, George William, 2759
Bonnell, Joseph Gatch, 5215
Bonner, John, 1828-1899, 11362
Bonner, Sherwood, pseud., 14899
Bonnet, Edmond, 1848-, 19153
Bonnet, Guy Joseph, 1773-1843, 19153
Bonnet, J. Esprit, 21802
Bonnet, Stede, d.1718, 11363
Bonneville, Benjamin Louis Eulalie de, ca. 1795-1878, 4028
Bonneville, Zacharie de Pazzi de, 11364
Bonney, Edward, 16014
Bonney, William H., 1859-1881, 3575, 7755
Bonnie Belmont, 16219
Bonny Kate, 5418
Bonnycastle, Sir Richard Henry, 1791-1847, 11365-11367
Bonomi, Maria, 19154, 19155
Bonpland, Aimé Jacques Alexandre Goujaud, called, 1773-1858, 7092
Bonrepos, Chevalier de, 2760
Bonsal, Stephen, 1863-, 16015
Bonynge, Francis, 11368
Bonzon, Alfred, 19156
The Book and slavery irreconcilable, 23995
Book collecting, 8186, 15740; U.S., 7001
A book for an hour, 9025

A book for Massachusetts children, in familiar letters from a father, 22460
Book industries and trade, Exhibitions, Brazil, 19289-19291
The book of American negro spirituals, 24678
Book of anecdotes, 6114
The book of bubbles, 11369
The book of four and twenty chapters, 9477
A book of gold, 4771
A book of martyrs, 9084
The book of my lady, 10767
The book of peace, 11370
The book of religions, 22370
The book of Saint Nicholas, 10480
The book of Texas, 15962
The book of the colonies, 12173
The book of the continuation of foreign passages, 11371
A book of the heart, 10362
A book of the Hudson, 9995
The book of the navy, 12174
Book of the prophet, Stephen, son of Douglas, 6115
The book of the signers, 1590
Book verse, 684
A book without a title, 11035
Bookbinding, 8186; U.S., 8188
Booker, Anton S., 13687
Bookplates, 14854
Books and reading, Congresses, 20398
Books and reading for children, 19897
Books in human development, 20398
Booksellers and bookselling, Kentucky, Bibliography, 13662; U.S., 7001
Bookstaver, James N., 13688
Bookwalter, John Wesley, 16016
Boole, George, 1815-1864, 18609, 19157
Boole, William H., 11372
The boom in the "Calaveras Clarion," 6972
The boom of a western city, 9124
The booming of Acre Hill, 8674
Boone County, Kentucky, 14738; History, 14869
Boone, Daniel, 1734-1820, 2748, 3445, 12730, 13199, 13689, 13742, 13961, 14091, 14113, 14235, 14236, 14265, 14289, 14350, 14423, 14532, 14823, 14922, 14993, 15374; Drama, 13595; Fiction, 4621, 13961; Poetry, 2844
Boone, H.H., 22302
Boone, Nathan, 1782-1857?, 17062
Boone, Samuel, 14022
The Boone family and Kentucky Baptists, 13943
Boone Island, Me., 2089
Boone's Creek Baptist association of Kentucky, 13912

Boone's Creek Baptist Church, Athens, Ky., 13783
Boonesborough, Ky., 13641, 14942, 15240; History, 13742, 14335, 15240
Boorjes de Oropesa, Ambrosio, 8275
Boorn, Jesse, 12761
The Boot on the other leg, 11373
Booth, Benjamin F., 1837?-, 2761
Booth, George Wilson, 1844-1914, 2762
Booth, John Wilkes, 1838-1865, 5987, 6026, 6116, 6293, 6580, 6827, 7163, 8218, 13869, 22282; Fiction, 3134
Booth, Mary Louise, 1831-1889, 2413, 11374, 12199, 16580, 21803
Booth, Mrs. Charles, 13690
Booth, Richard M., 13691
Booth, Robert Russell, 11375
Booth, Sherman M., 11376, 25911
Bootlegging, 13655
"Boots and saddles," 16317
Boott, John Wright, 1788 or 9-1845, 1577, 21815
Booty, James Horatio, 2763
Booz, Allen and Hamilton, 13692
Boquady, Jesus Barros, 19158
Borax, 17648
Borba, Hermilo, 19159
Borba Filho, Hermilo, 1917-, 19161, 19162
Borcke, Heros von, 1835-1895, 2764
Bordeaux, Albert François Joseph, 1865-, 6117
Borden, Nathaniel B., 1801-1865, 11377
Borden, William, 1689-1748, 2765
Border adventures, 953
Border and bastille, 4230
The border and the buffalo, 16271
The border bandits, 16079
Border beagles, 10768
Border fights and fighters, 13704
The border outlaws, 16079
Border reminiscences, 17127
The border rover, 2672
The border ruffian, 9202
The border ruffian code in Kansas, 11378
A border shepherdess, 8722
The border states, 4154
Border states of Mexico, 6942, 6943
Border war, 4110
Border wars of the American revolution, 15449
Bordertown institute, Bordertown, N.J., 21804
Bordley, John Beale, 1727-1804, 21805
Bordón, F. Arturo, 19163
Boreas, Breckenridge and the Blue, 17733
Boreostracon corondanus, 19918
Borges, Jorge Luis, 1899-, 19137, 19164
Borges, José Carlos Cavaleanti, 19165, 19166
Borges, Pedro, 19167

58

Borges, Wilson Alvarenga, 19168
Borges R., Julio César, 19169
Borqia, Cesare, 1476?-1507, Fiction, 8590
Borgo Derpich, José Luis, 19170
Borgonovi, Arnaldo, 19171, 19172
Borja, Francisco de, príncipe de
  Esquilache, 1582-1658, 6118-6120
Borja y Borja, Ramiro, 19173, 19174
Borjas Sánchez, José A., 19175
Borland, Solon, 1808-1864, 11379
Borragán, Maria Teresa, 6121, 6122
Borrero Moscoso, Alfonso María, 1866-1926,
  19176, 19177
Borrett, George Tuthill, 11380, 16017
Borthwick, J.D., 16018
Borthwick, Peter, 1804-1852, 23987, 25685
Bortoluzzi, Carlos Alfredo, 19178
Bory de Saint-Vincent, Jean Baptiste
  Geneviève Marcellin, baron, 1778-1846,
  2213, 11381
Bosbyshell, Oliver Christian, 1839-, 2766
Boscán F., Luís A., 19179
Bosch, Carlos, 19180
Bosch, Gerardus-Balthasar, 1794-1839, 11382
Bosch, Jorge, 19181
Bosch, Juan, Pres. Dominican Republic,
  1909-, 19182-19184
Bosch, Leonard Eduard, 1792-1865, 11382
Bosch, Lidia P., 19565
Bosch Garcia, Carlos, 19185
Bosch-Spencer, Guillaume Henri, 1802-1873,
  11383
Boschi, Enrique E., 19186-19188
Bosi, Alfredo, 18272, 19046, 19147
The bosom serpent, 3848
Boson, Gerson de Britto Mello, 18189, 18190
Boss, Henry Rush, 1835-, 16019
Bosshard, Heinrich, 2767
Bossi, Bartolomi, 1812-1891, 11384
Bossu, Jean Barnard, 1720-1792, 2768
Boston, Ambrose, 13833
Boston, 12009, 23988; Back Bay district,
  23252; Board of trade, 526; Channing
  home, 10978; Citizens, 23989; City
  Council, 6123, 6124, 12330, 23088;
  Committee, 22086; Committee of Vigilance,
  25199; Common council, 12242;
  Constitutional Meeting, 1850, 23991;
  Description, 2092, 12542, 22543;
  Description, Guide-books, 11442, 13427;
  Directories, 1756; Emancipation statute,
  23988; Fiction, 5037; Fire, 1711, 23321;
  Fire, 1760, 23396; Fire, 1872, 2345;
  First church, 2306, 12060, 22912; First
  church, Jamaica Plain, 12363; Garrison
  Meeting, 1846, 23992; Genealogy, 1505,
1506; Harbor, 12330, 23252; History, 2092,
  11683, 22066, 22543; History, Anti-slavery
  movement, 1830-1863, 23954, 23989; History,
  Colonial period, Fiction, 8994; History,
  Chronology, 11442; History, Fiction, 9980;
  History, Revolution, Fiction, 9136, 9137,
  10632, 10633; King's chapel, 2266, 12415;
  King's Chapel burial ground, 1505; Mercantile
  library association, 684, 1383; Municipal
  court, 1951, 11607; National peace jubilee
  and musical festival, 1869, 12267; New
  North church, 2358; Police, 333, 22466;
  Politics & goverment, Colonial period,
  1596; Politics & goverment, Revolution,
  11385; Public works, 12338; Riots, 24531;
  St. Paul's church, 13170; Sanit.aff., 11921;
  Siege, 1775-1776, 698; Social life & customs,
  10151, 10205, 12538; Tremont house, 12011;
  Washingtonian home, 22313; Water supply, 710,
  2177, 2179; Water supply, Mystic lakes,
  12908; Wharves, 11436
Boston and Providence railroad, 11935, 23250,
  23251
Boston and Worcester railroad, 12494
Boston before the revolution, 8994
The Boston conspiracy, 10632
Boston daily times, 1951
Boston dispensary, 1970
Boston Franklin association, 1693
Boston massacre, 1770, 179, 11790, 13373,
  11571, 21753, 22443, 22736, 23690, 23748;
  Poetry, 23592, 23477, 23502
Boston neighbors in town and out, 10546
Boston notions; being an authentic and
  concise account of "that village," from
  1630 to 1847, 22066
The Boston spy, 10205
Boston Tea Party, 21754, 21806, 23683
Boston two hundred years ago, 8822,
  10179
Boston water-power company, 23252
Boston weekly report of public sales and
  arrivals, 22079, 22080
The Bostonian prophet, 11386
Bostowicz, Richard, 20457
Bostrom, Rob, 13693
Bostwick, David, 1721-1763, 11387
Bostwick, Henry, 1787-1836 or 7, 11388
Boswell, Ira Matthews, 13694
Bosworth, Newton, d.1848, 21807
Botafogo, A.J.S., 19191
Botany, 15225, 22230; Amazon region, 18110-
  18112; Antarctic regions, 22555; Arctic
  regions, 6302; Argentine Republic, 19857;
  Barbados, 23393; Barren County, Ky., 14369;
  Brazil, 20423, 23201; California, San

Diego, 17554; Colombia, 19103; Congresses, 20423; Cuba, 18018; Dictionaries, 22163; Ecology, Brazil, 18285; District of Columbia, 1480; Economic, 4827, 14598, 18186; Edmonson County, Ky., 14369; Georgia, 12041; Kentucky, 13576, 14339, 15348; Mackenzie district, 8252; Massachusetts, 12807, 22502, 23265; Mexico, 7019, 7969, 12883; Minnesota, 4664; Missouri Valley, 2784; Morphology, 13004; New Jersey, 21774; New York (State), 1911; North America, 942, 15222, 15231, 16416, 22163; Oceania, 12883; Pennsylvania, 21774; Rocky Mountains, 5524; Sicily, 15223; Santa Catarina, Brazil, 20685; South America, 7092, 12883; South Carolina, 12041; Southern states, 4827, 17245; Southwest, New, 5513; U.S., 1031, 1267, 2462, 2940, 11245, 11620, 11803, 12355, 22268; Virginia, 930, 3703; West Indies, 11620; Wisconsin, 4664
Botany, Medical, 1267, 4827, 11803, 19998; Brazil, 23201
Botany Bay, 10790
Botany of the northern and middle states, 11245
Boteler, Alexander Robinson, 1815-1892, 11389
Botelho, Pero de, 19192
Botelho de Oliveira, Manuel, 1636-1711, 19193
Botello de Flores, Conselo, 19194
Botero, Ebel, 1928-, 19195
Botero, Giovanni, 1540-1617, 6125, 21808
Botero M., Rodrigo, 20489
Botero Ramos, Enulio, 19196
Botero Salazar, Julio, 1904-, 19197
Botocudo Indians, Language, 13282
Botta, Anne Charlotte (Lynch) 1815-1891, 6902
Botta, Carlo Giuseppe Guglielmo, 1766-1837, 11390, 15973
Botta, Paul Émile, 1804?-1870, 15973
Bottineau County, N.D., 16104; History, 16103
Bottling machinery, 17332
Botts, John Minor, 1802-1869, 11391, 23993
Botume, Elizabeth Hyde, 2769
Boturini Benaducci, Lorenyo, 1702-1751, 11392
Boucard, Adolphe, 16020
Boucarut, Alcide, b.1825, 11393
Bouchacourt, Charles, 11394
Boucher, Chauncy Samuel, 1886-, 23994
Boucher, Jonathan, 1738-1804, 11395, 23618
Boucher, Pierre, sieur de Boucherville, 1620?-1717, 0120
Boucher de la Bruère, fils, 11396
Bouchette, Joseph, 1774-1841, 6127, 6128

Bouchot, Auguste, 11397
Boudinot, Elias, 1740-1821, 11400-11402
Boudinot, Elias, d.1839, 11398, 11399
Bougnot, J., 21740
Bouguer, Pierre, 1698-1758, 11403
Bouillé, René, marquis de, 1802-1882, 11404
Bouillé, François Claude Amour, marquis de, 1739-1800, 11404
Bouis, Amedée Théodore, 11405, 16021
Boulanger, Nicolas Antoine, 1722-1759, 11406
Boulder, Colorado, Description, 17514
Boulet, Abbé, 24753
Boulter, Hugh, abp. of Armagh, 1672-1742, 11407
Boulton, Alfredo, 19198
Boulton, Charles Arkoll, b.1841, 6129
Bound down, 9519
Bound labor interest in the U.S., 22734
Bounded sets of holomorphic mappings, 18881
Bounties, Military, U.S., 12131
Bounty (Ship), 884, 10698, 12609
Bouquet's expedition, 1764, 23639
Bourbon County, Ky., Biography, 13559; Bourbon County 175th Birthday Celebration, Inc., 13695; History, 13695, 14602, 14886, 15142, 15549; Maps, 13646, 13674
Bourbon whiskey, 15096, 15395, 15543
Bourdon, Louis Gabriel, 1741-1795, 11408
Bourgeois, Léon Victor Auguste, 1851-1925, 7494
Les bourgeois de la Compagnie du Nord-Ouest, 17148
Bourget, Paul-Charles-Joseph, 1852-1935, 2770
Bourgois, François, 19199
Bourinot, Sir John George, 1837-1902, 6130-6133
Bourke, John Gregory, 1843-1896, 16022-16025
Bourne, Benjamin Franklin, 11409
Bourne, Edward Emerson, 11410
Bourne, Edward Gaylord, 1860-1908, 17140
Bourne, George, 1780-1845, 11411, 13483, 23995, 23996
Bourne, Henry Richard Fox, 1837-1909, 11412
Bourne, William Oland, 11413
Bouroncle Carreón, Alfonso, 19200
Boutelle, John Alonzo, 1426
Bouton, Jacques, 1592-1658, 11414
Bouton, John Bell, 1830-1902, 11415
Bouton, Nathaniel, 1799-1878, 11416-11420, 21809
Bouturine-Benaduci, Lorenzo, ca.1702-1750, 6105
Boutwell, George Sewall, 1818-1905, 6134, 11421, 11422, 11647, 21810, 23997, 23998
Boutwell, W.T., 16026
Bouve, Mrs. Pauline Carrington (Rust) 23999
Bouvet de Cressé, Auguste Jean Baptiste,

1772-1839, 11423, 11424
Bouvier, John, 1787-1851, 11425
Boves, José Tomás, 1782-1814, 19839
Bowden, Clyde N., 13825
Bowden, Darlene, 13833
Bowditch, Charles Pickering, 1842-1921, 6135
Bowditch, Henry Ingersoll, 1808-1892, 11426-11430
Bowditch, Nathaniel, 1773-1838, 11431, 11434
Bowditch, Nathaniel, 1839-1863, 11430
Bowditch, Nathaniel Ingersoll, 1805-1861, 11432-11436
Bowditch, William Ingersoll, 1819-1909, 2400, 11437-11439,
Bowdler, Thomas, 1754-1825, 11440
Bowdoin, James, 1752-1811, 1644, 22708
Bowdoin College, 414, 6136, 11441, 22708
Bowdoin port-folio, 11441
The bowels of a battle-ship, 10608
Bowen, Abel, 1790-1850, 11442
Bowen, Alfred D., 16027
Bowen, B.F., Logansport, Ind., publ., 6559
Bowen, Benjamin B., 1819-1905, 11443
Bowen, Christopher Columbus, 1832-, 22937
Bowen, Eli, 1824-, 2771, 11444, 21811
Bowen, Francis, 1811-1890, 239, 11445, 11446
Bowen, Henry L., 1810-1865, 11447
Bowen, Nathaniel, 1779-1839, 11448, 24001
Bowen, Noel Hill, d.1872, 11449
Bower, William Clayton, illustr., 13696, 15447
Bowers, A. Herbert, 8596
Bowers, Claude Gernade, 1878-1958, 6137
Bowker, J., 11450
Bowles, Charles S.P., 11451
Bowles, Leonard C., Boston pub., 3098
Bowles, Samuel, 1826-1878, 2772, 16028-16030
Bowling, William King, 1808-1885, 11452, 11453
Bowling Green, Ky., 13613, 14220; Description, 13697
Bowling Green and Warren County. Immigration Society, Bowling Green, Ky., 13697
Bowlsby, Alice Augusta, d.1871, 9648
Bowman, John Bryan, 1824-1891, 15274
Bowman, Joseph, 21938
Bowman, Samuel Millard, 1815-1885, 11454
Bowman family, 15678
Bowmar, Daniel M., 13698
Bownas, Samuel, 1676-1753, 2773, 12655
Bowyer, Robert, 1758-1834, 25285
Box, Henry W., 6138
Box, Michael James, 6139

Boy, Herbert, 19201
The boy in the cloth cap, 10808
The boy inventor, 1669
Boy life on the prairies, 16574
The boy of Mount Rhigi, 10722
The boy orator of Zepata City, 9358
The boy spy, 4163
The boy travellers in Mexico, 7202
Boyacá, Colombia (Dept.), Economic condition, 20351
Boyanov, I., 19202
Boyce, J.R., 6140
Boyce, Neith, 1872-, 8969
Boyce, William Dickson, 1848-1929, 6141, 16031
Boyce family, 7433
Boyd, Andrew, 6142
Boyd, Belle, 1844-1900, 11455
Boyd, Daniel French, 1834-, 6915
Boyd, Hugh, 1746-1794, 11456
Boyd, John, 11457
Boyd, John Parker, 1764-1830, 11458
Boyd, Linn, 1800-1859, 14582
Boyd, Mrs. Lucinda Joan Rogers, 1840-, 13700
Boyd, Samuel Stillman, 1807-1867, 11459, 24002
Boyd, William, d.1800, 11460
Boyd, William Kenneth, 1879-, 2750
Boyd-Bowman, Peter, 19203, 19204
Boyd County, Ky., History, 13568; Homemaker's Club, 13699; Maps, 14590
Boyde, Henry, 24753
Boyden, Ebenezer, 1803-1891, 24003
Boyden, Henry Paine, 13701
Boykin, Edward M., 21812
Boyle, Frederick, b.1841, 11461
Boyle, Henry, 11462
Boyle, Robert, 1527-1691, 11463
Boyle, Mrs. Virginia (Frazer) 1863-, 2774, 2775
Boyle Co., Ky., 4812; History, 14065; Maps, 13962, 14277
Boylston, Peter, pseud., 9268
Boylston, Thomas, 1720-1798, 11464
Boylston, Ward Nicholas, 1749-1828, 11464
Boylston, Zabdiel, 1679-1766, 11465
Boynton, Charles Brandon, 1806-1883, 2776, 11466-11469
Boynton, Edward Carlisle, 1824-1893, 11470, 23727
The boys and girls stories of the war..., 11471
The boys in blue, 12835
The boys in blue of 1861-1865, 4255
The boys in white, 3537
Boys, stay at home, 3651
Boze family, 14363
Bozeman, 15829

Bozman, John Leeds, 1757-1823, 11472
Brabant, Augustin Joseph, 1845-1912, 6143
Brace, Charles Loring, 1826-1890, 11473, 16032
A brace of boys, 10250
Bracebridge Hall, 9996
Bracho Valle, Felipe, 19205, 19206
Bracht, Victor, 1819-1886, 2777
Brackenridge, Henry Marie, 1786-1871, 2778, 2779, 11474-11480
Brackenridge, Hugh Henry, 1748-1871, 2780-2782, 11481-11484
Brackett, Albert Gallatin, 1829-1896, 2783, 6144
Brackett, Edward Augustus, 1818-1908, 11485
Brackett, Jeffrey Richardson, 1860-, 24668
Brackett, Joseph Warren, 1775-1826, 11486
Brackmann, Richard, 19811
Bradburn, Mrs. Frances H., 24004
Bradburn, George, 1806-1880, 11487, 24004, 24989
Bradbury, Charles, 1798-1864, 11488
Bradbury, James Ware, 1802-1901, 11489, 11490
Bradbury, John, fl.1809, 2784
Braddock's campaign, 1755, 3404, 5072, 16658, 23456, 23457, 23493, 23524
Bradford, Alden, 1765-1843, 11491-11497, 21813
Bradford, Alexander Warfield, 1815-1867, 11498, 11499
Bradford, Annie Chambers, pseud., 10098
Bradford, Arthur Bullus, 1810-1899, 24005
Bradford, Benjamin Chambers, d.1867, 4165
Bradford, Ebenezer, 1746-1801, 11500, 11501
Bradford, Ephraim Putnam, 1776-1845, 11502
Bradford, Gamaliel, 1795-1839, 24006
Bradford, George W., 1796-1883, 11503
Bradford, James Morgan, d.1837, 7885
Bradford, John, 1749-1830, 6445, 7885, 13833, 13855, 14718, 14719, 15746
Bradford, Mary F., 6145
Bradford, Moses, 1765-1838, 11504
Bradford, Samuel Dexter, 11505
Bradford, Samuel Fisher, 1776-1837, 1427, 21884
Bradford, Thomas Gamaliel, 1867
Bradford, Ward, b.1809, 16033
Bradford, William John Alden, 1791-1858, 11506, 16861
Bradley, Arthur Granville, 1850-1943, 2785, 2786, 6146-6149
Bradley, Daniel, 13702
Bradley, E.R., 13562
Bradley, George S., 2787

Bradley, John C., 6150
Bradley, Robert M., 13703
Bradley, Thomas H., 6151
Bradley family, 6150
Bradshaw, Benjamin Spencer, 19207
Bradshaw, Sidney Ernest, 1869-, 2788
Bradstreet, John, 1711-1774, 22571
Brady, Cyrus Townsend, 1861-1920, 13704, **16034,** 16035
Brady, Eugene A., 19208, 19209
Brady, Samuel, 1756-1785, 22316
Brady, William, 2789
Braga, Virginia Rayol, 1950-, 19210
Bragg, Braxton, 1817-1876, 2039
Brainerd, C.N., 11507
Brainerd, Cephas, 1831-1910, 7283
Brainerd, David, 1718-1747, 6152
Braines, 10394
Braintree, Mass., History, 39
Brake, Hezekiah, b.1814, 16036
Braman, D.E.E., 16037
Bramantip, Bocardo, pseud, 6243
Bramlette, Thomas Elliott, 1817-, 13705
Branagan, Thomas, b.1774, 1428, 1429, 1941
A branch of May, 5916
A branch road, 9606
Branch, William, jr., 1430
Branco, José Moreira Brandão Castello, see Castello Branco, José Moreira Brandao.
Brand, Charles, 1431
Brand-Hollis, Thomas, 1719?-1804, 22124
Branda, Adolfo, 19211
Brandao, Ademar Torres, 19212
Brandao, Ambrosio Fernandes, fl.1585-1613, 19213
The branded hand, 10270, 24007
Brandegee, Augustus, 1828-, 1432
Brandeis, Fanny, 13567
Brandeis, Louis Dembitz, 1856-1941, 14111
Brandes, Karl, 1433
Brandin, Abel Victorino, 1434
Brandon, 10977
Brandt, Geeraert, 1626-1685, 1435
Brandywine, Battle of, 1777, Fiction, 10212
Braniff, Oscar, 19214
Brannan, John, 1436
Brannan, William Penn, 1825-1866, 1437
Brannon de Samayoa, Carmen, 1899-, 19215
Branson, Branley A., 13706, 13707
Brant, Joseph, Mohawk chief, 1742-1807, 23671; Fiction, 10396
Brantly, William Theophilus, 1787-1845, 1438
Brashears, Noah, 1439
Brasil, Assis, 19218
Brasil, Maria Avaliadora de Souza, 13213
Brasil, a terra e o homem, 18655

Brasil/açucar, 19216
Brasil ano 2.000, 19217
Brasil: bibliografia do ensino superior, 19248
O Brasil em números, 19276
Brasil, fronteira da Africa, 18369
O Brasil na II Grande Guerra, 19929
Brasilia. O desenvolvimento da comunidade en Brasilia; uma estrategia de participação social, 19220
Brasilia, 19220, 19393; Bibliography, 19257; History, 18176; Maps, 19301, 19401
Brasilia. Universidade, 19221-19223; Biblioteca Central, 19224; Faculdade de Arquitetura e Urbanismo, 19225, 19226; Instituto Central de Artes, 19225, 19226
Brasilia e o problema da federação brasileira, 19806
Brasseur de Bourbourg, Charles Étienne, 1814-1874, 1440-1444, 6153
Brassey, Annie (Allnutt) baroness, 1839-1887, 6154
Brattle family (Thomas Brattle, 1624?-1683), 12700
Brau, Salvador, 19227
Braun, Kurt, 19228, 19229
Braun L., Juan, 19230
Brauns, Frederick William, 1830-1895, 1445
The brave and happy soldier, 23151
The brave boy hunters of Kentucky, 15704
Brave hearts, 10591
A brave little Quakeress, 10653
Bravo, Abel, 1861-1934, 20017
Bravo, Nicolás, 7407
Bravo, Pedro, 19231
Bravo Arauz, Bolivar, 19232
Bravo B., José María, 19233
Bravo Covarrubias, Hipólito, 19234
Bravo Echeverria, Pablo R., 19235
Bravo G., Luis R., 19236
Bravo Garzón, Roberto, 19237
Bravo Lira, Bernardino, 19238
The bravo, 9128
Bravo en 1812, 7407
The bravo's daughter, 9433
Brawley, Benjamin Griffith, 1882-1939, 24009
Braxton, Carter M., 1446, 24484
Braxton's bar, 9307
Bray, John, 1782-1822, 1447
Bray, Thomas, 1656-1730, 1448, 1449, 2790
Bray, Warwick, 19803
Brayman, James O., 1815-1887, 1450

Brayton, Matthew, 2756
Brazen gates, 10805
Brazer, John, 1787-1846, 1451, 22542
Brazer, Samuel, 1785-1823, 1452
Brazer, Samuel, jr., 1453
Brazil, 798, 2138, 3401, 6881, 18160, 19213, 22307, 23021, 24440; Agencia Nacional, 19239; Antiquities, 19324, 19325; Armed forces, 19402; Army, 24965; Arquivo Nacional, 19240-19244, 19376; Arquivo Nacional. Serviço de Registro e Assistência, 19245; Bibliography, 11636, 19240, 19258, 19289-19291, 19327, 19390, 19457, 19504, 19819, 19237, 19259, 19260; Boundaries, Paraguay, 591, 596; Campanha Nacional de Alimentação Escolar, 19246; Campanha Nacional de Educação dos Cegos, 19364; Campanha Nacional de Merenda Escolar, 19247; Capital, 18176; Census, 1872, 1890, 19299, 19300, 19312, 19397, 19426; Centro Brasileiro de Pesquisas Educacionais, 19248, 19249; Civilization, 19500, 19812; Climate, 19314; Commerce, 19418, 19430, 19431, 23390; Commerce, History, 1526; Commerce, U.S., 691; Commercial policy, 23372; Comissão de coordenação e Implementação de Técnicas Financeiras, 19250, 19251; Comissão Encarregada de conservação dos Portos e das Obras Publicas Geraes da Provincia de Pernambuco, 19251; Comissão Nacional de Energia Nuclear, 19252; Comissão Oceanográfica, 19296; Companhia do Desenvolvimento do Plantalto Central, 19253; Confederação Nacional da Industria, 19254; Congresso, 19255, 19256; Congresso. Câmara dos deputados,19257, 24009; Congresso. Câmara dos Deputados. Biblioteca, 19258-19262; Congresso. Câmara dos deputados. Comissão de Ciência e Tecnologia, 19263; Congresso. Câmara dos Deputados. Comissão de Educação e Cultura, 19264; Congresso. Câmara dos Deputados.Comissão de Relações Exteriores, 19265; Congresso. Câmara dos Deputados. Comissão especial do estatuto da mulher, 19266; Congresso. Câmara dos Deputados. Comissão Especial sobre Poluição Ambiental, 19267; Congresso. Camara dos Deputados. Diretoria Legislativa, 19268; Congresso. Câmara dos Deputados. Documentos parlamentares, 19256; Congresso. Câmara dos Deputados. Secretaria Geral da Presidência, 19269; Congresso. Diretoria de Informação Legislativa, 19270; Congresso Salaries, pensions, etc., 19339; Congresso. Senado, 19339; Conselho do Desenvolvimento, 19271-19273; Conselho do Desenvolvimento. Programa

de metas, 19413; Conselho de
Desenvolvimento de Pernambuco, 19274;
Conselho de estado, 25503; Conselho
Nacional de Economia, 19275; Conselho
Nacional de Estatistica, 19276, 19277;
Conselho Nacional de Geografia, 19278-
19281; Conselho Nacional de Pesquisas,
19324, 19325; Conselho Tecnico de
Economia e Finanças, 19282; Constitution,
19255, 19283-19287; Constitutional law,
19270; Departamento Administrativo do
Serviço Publico, 19288; Departamento de
Cooperativismo e Extensão Rural. Divisão
de Cooperativismo, 19356; Departamento de
Imprensa Nacional, 19289-19291;
Departamento Nacional da Produção Mineral,
19292; Departamento Nacional da Produçao
Mineral. 4o. Distrito Nordeste, 19293;
Departamento Nacional de Estradas de
Rodagem, 19294; Description & travel, 31,
492, 578, 798, 1720, 3401, 4389, 5454,
5849, 7218, 7339, 7757, 8024, 11230,
11636, 11811, 12518, 12519, 12906, 18247,
18248, 18282, 18655, 19281, 19472, 20231,
20234, 23380, 23652, 24737, 24738, 24965,
25884; Diplomatic and consular service,
Registers, 19392; Diretoria de Hidro-
grafia e Navegação, 19295, 19296; Diretoria
do Dominio da União, 19297; Diretoria do
Patrimônio Histórico e Artístico Nacional,
19298; Diretoria Geral de Estatistica,
19299, 19300, 24010; Distrito Federal.
Departamento de Turismo, 19301; Economic
conditions, 492, 798, 12518, 12519, 18148,
18282, 18291, 18741, 18744, 18778, 18973,
18979, 19217, 19250, 19253, 19254, 19271,
19361, 19372, 19403, 19407, 19433, 19448,
20072, 20379, 20563, 23580; Economic
conditions, Legislation, 19404; Economic
conditions, Statistics, 19406; Economic
policy, 18560,19239, 19400, 19407, 19408,
19409, 19412, 19413, 19774, 20562; Embassy,
Washington, 19302; Emigration & immigration,
2138, 24965; Exercito. Força Expedicionaria
Brasileira, 1944-1945, 19929; Foreign
relations, 1017, 19383, 19384, 19386,
19388, 19395; Foreign relations, Argentine
Republic, 19382; Foreign relations, Great
Britain, 24125; Foreign relations,
Treaties, 19471; Foreign relations,
U.S.S.R., 19387; Foreign economic
relations, 18559; Fundação Getulio Vargas,
19000, 19200; Governo do Distrito Federal,
20379, 20380-20383; History, 7640, 12648,
18177, 18248, 18271, 18666, 18667, 18880,
19242, 19243, 19244, 19386, 19391, 19605,

19874, 21739; History, 1549-1762, 1543;
History, 1763-1821, 446; History, To 1821,
1016, 1542, 1551, 6881, 11259, 11530, 21777,
22407; History, To 1821, Sources, 18397;
History, 1822-1889, 446, 6640, 18163;
History, 1822-1889, 21777; History, 1822-
1889, Sources, 19191; History, Bibliography,
19160; History, Colonial period, 19376,
19681; History, Conselheiro Insurrection,
1897, 18343; History, Dutch conquest, 1624-
1654, 104, 339, 340, 653, 1526, 1542, 8323,
18681; History, Dutch conquest, 1624-1654 -
Fiction, 22083; History, Periodicals, 18874;
History, Sources, 19318, 19375, 19381;
History, Sources, Bibliography, 19245;
History, Naval, 20553; Immigration and
emigration, 19242; Industries, 18785, 19254,
19429, 19432, 19774, 20004, 20378; Industries
- Maps, 19424; Instituto Brasileiro de
Bibliografia e Documentação, 19305-19308;
Instituto Brasileiro de Directo Financeiro,
19309; Instituto Brasileiro de Economia,
19310; Instituto Brasileiro de Estatistica,
19311; Instituto Brasileiro de Geografia e
Estatistica, 19312; Instituto de Planejamento
Econômico e Social, 19313, 19314; Instituto
de Planejamento Econômico e Social,
Bibliography, 19313; Instituto de Plane-
jamento Econômico e Social. Instituto de
Planejamento. Setor de Agricultura, 19315;
Instituto do Açucar e do Alcool, 19216,
19316; Instituto Histórico e Geográfico
Brasileiro, 19317, 19318; Instituto Nacional
Colonizaçao e Reforma Agraria, 19319;
Instituto Nacional de Estudos Pedagogicos,
19320, 19321; Instituto Nacional de
Estudios Pedagógicos. Publicações. Série
Estudios e pesquisas, 19709; Instituto
Nacional de Pesquisas da Amazônia, 18015,
19322; Instituto Nacional de Pesquisas da
Amazônia. Botânica, Publicação, 18351;
Instituto Nacional de Pesquisas da
Amazônia. Museo Paraense Emilio Goeldi,
Museo Goeldi, 19323-19325; Instituto
Nacional de Previdência Social, 19326,
19359; Instituto Nacional de Previdência
Social. Departamento de Estatistica, 19326;
Instituto Nacional de Previdência Social.
Mensario estatistico-atuarial, 19326;
Instituto Nacional do Desenvolvimento
Agrario, 19346; Instituto Nacional do Livro,
19327; Laws, statutes, etc., 18322, 18551,
18741, 19255, 19256, 19328-19362, 19367,
19071, 19404, 19877, 23895, 24009-24011,
26603; Learned institutions and societies,
19318; Maps, 19394; Ministerio da

Agricultura, 18919, 19251, 24012, 25503;
Ministerio da Educação e Cultura, 19364,
19365; Ministerio da Educação e Cultura.
Instituto Nacional de Estados Pedagogicos,
19366, 19367; Ministério da Educação e
Cultura. Movimento Brasileiro de
Alfabetezação, 19368, 19369; Ministerio
da Fazenda, 19370, 24011; Ministério da
Fazenda. Comissão de Reforma, 19371;
Ministério da Fazenda. Contadoria geral
da república, 19372; Ministerio da
Fazenda. Secretaria da Receita Federal,
19373, 19397; Ministerio da Guerra.
Biblioteca do Exercito, 19929; Ministerio
da Instrucção, Correios e Telegraphos,
19374; Ministerio da Justiça. Arquivo
Nacional. Publicações históricas, 18849,
19375, 19376; Ministerio da Justiça.
Arquivo Nacional see also Brazil. Arquivo
Nacional; Ministerio da Saúde. Departamento
Nacional de Endemias Purais, 19377;
Ministerio da Viação e obras Publicas,
19378; Ministerio das Minas e Energia
Comissão Nacional de Energia Nuclear,
19379, 19380; Ministerio das Relações
Exteriores, 19381-19389; Ministerio das
Relações Exteriores. Biblioteca, 19390;
Ministerio das Relações Exteriores.
Comissão de estudos dos textos da
Historia do Brasil, 19391; Ministerio
das Relações Exteriores. Departamento
de Administração, 19392; Ministerio das
Relações Exteriores. Divisão Cultural,
19393; Ministerio das Relações Exteriores.
Mapoteca, 19394; Ministerio das Relações
Exteriores. Serviço de Documentação,
19395; Ministerio das Relações Exteriores.
Serviço de Publicações, 19396; Ministerio
de Indústria e do Comercio. Instituto
Brasileiro do Café, 19398, 19399;
Ministerio de Planejamento e Coordenação
Economica, 19400; Ministerio de Viação e
Obras, 19401; Ministerio do Exercito,
19402; Ministerio do Interior, 19403;
Ministerio do Interior. Coordenação de
Comunicação Social, 19404; Ministerio do
Interior. Superintendência da Região Sul,
19405; Ministerio do Planejamento e
Coordenação Economica, 19406; Ministerio
do Planejamento e Coordenação Geral, 19407,
19408; Ministerio Extraordinario para o
Planejamento e Coordenação Economica,
19409; Nationality, 7640; Neutrality,
2051; Nobility, 19956, 21739; Officials
and employees, Salaries, allowances,
etc., 19958; Patrimônio Histórico e

Artístico Nacional, 19325; Policia Criminal
Internacional-Interpol, 19410; Politics &
government, 18270, 18667, 18834, 19250,
19259, 19260, 19268, 19269, 19283, 19284,
19285, 19286, 19287, 19349, 19376, 19411,
19414, 19415, 19806, 20049, 20071, 20072,
24101; Politics & government, 1763-1821,
18867; Politics & government, 1822-1889,
798, 1017, 18867, 19191, 24010, 24125,
25066, 25076; Politics & government, 1954-,
18559, 19800; Population, 19299, 19311,
20560, 24010; Presidência, 19411; Presidência.
Serviço de Documentação, 19413; Presidente,
1961-(Goulart), 19414, 19415; Public lands,
19297; Relações, 25503; Relations (general)
with Angola, 18369; Relations (general) with
the Rio de la Plata region, 18397; Religion,
20402; Serviço de Economia Rural, 19416;
Serviço de Estatística da Educação e Cultura,
19417; Serviço de Estatistica Economica e
Financeira, 19418; Serviço de Informação
Agricola, 19419, 19420; Serviço de Proteção
aos Indios, 18554, 24012; Serviço Nacional
de Aprendizagem Industrial. Departamento
Regional de São Paulo, 19421, 19422;
Serviço Nacional de Aprendizagem Industrial.
Departamento Regional de Espírito Santo,
19423; Serviço Nacional de Recenseamento.
VII Recenseamento geral do Brasil. Serie
especial, 19424-19432; Serviço Nacional de
Recenseamento. VII recenseamento geral do
Brasil. Serie nacional, 19425, 19430, 19431;
Social conditions, 18282, 18697, 19217, 19311,
19723; Social condition, Congresses, 20426;
Social life & customs, 3401, 19669, 19871;
Statistics, 19276, 19311, 19405; Superinten-
dência de Desenvolvimento da Amazônia.
Divisão di Documentação, 19435; Superinten-
dência do Desenvolvimento da Amazônia,
19433, 19434, 19436-19452; Superintendência
do Desenvolvimento do Maranhão, 19453;
Superintendência do Desenvolvimento do
Nordeste, 19454-19461; Superintendência do
Desenvolvimento do Nordeste. Departmento de
Recursos Humanos, 19462; Superintendência do
Desenvolvimento do Nordeste. Departamento de
Recursos Naturais, 19463; Superintendência do
Desenvolvimento do Nordeste. Divisão de
Pesquisas Experimentação Agropecuaria, 19464;
Superintendência do Desenvolvimento da
Região Sul, 19564-19470; Supremo tribunal de
justiça, 25503; Supremo Tribunal Federal,
19363; Treaties, etc., 19471; Tribunal
Superior Eleitoral, 19330
Brazil, Northeast, 18148, 18560, 19302, 19801;
Economic condition, 19458, 19460, 19461,

20559, 20562, 20564; Economic policy, 19273, 19305, 19454, 19455, 19456, 19458, 19459, 19461; Maps, Bibliography, 19463
Brazil and the river Plate in 1868, 12519
Brazil-Japan Emulsion Collaboration, 20025
Brazil nut, 18275
Brazil 71, Cultural aspects, 19472
Brazil, the home for southerners, 2138
Brazil, the river Plate, and the Falkland Islands, 12518
Brazilian army, Medals, badges, decorations, etc., 19402
Brazilian essays, 18343, 18812, 20644
The Brazilian income tax regulations, 19332
Brazilian literature, 19874; Bibliography, 19111, 19818, 20421; Campinas, 17969; Collections, 19926, 20451; History & criticism, 18246, 18658, 19708, 19930, 20056, 20091, 20516, 20629; Magnetic recordings, 18054; São Paulo (State), 19931; Societies, 19926; 20th century, 17969; 20th century, Addresses, essays, lectures, 18577; Translations into foreign languages , Bibliography, 19390
Brazilian music, 20091
The Brazilian Northeast, 19302, 19456
Brazilian periodicals, 19385
Brazilian poetry, 18308, 19710; Brazil, Northeast , History & criticism, 19709
Brazilian slave trade, 1838, 24013
Brazos River, 5532
The bread-winners, 9828, 10424
The breakdown of provincial urban power structure and the rise of peasant movements, 18100
Breakthrough, 19579
Breathitt County, Kentucky, 14336; Board of Education, 15781; Description, 14116, 15781; Maps, 14563
Breaux, Gustav, 13679
Breazeale, J.W.M., 11508
La brecha tecnológica, 18021
Breck, Daniel, 1788-1871
Breck, James Lloyd, 1818-1876, 16800
Breck, Robert L., 1454
Breck, Samuel, 1771-1862, 1455-1458, 13093, 25224
Breckenridge, Mrs. Issa Desha, 13708
Breckinridge, John Bayne, 1913-, 13709
Breckinridge, John Cabell, 1821-1875, 3417, 14381, 11000, 16442, 34014; Speech on executive usurpation, 6351
Breckenridge, Joseph Cabell, 1788-1824,

13669, 13833
Breckinridge, Madeleine McDowell, 1872-1920, 13711
Breckinridge, Robert J., 13710, 14229
Breckinridge, Robert Jefferson, 1800-1871, 1459-1467, 2791-2794, 5698, 15708; Theology, 13554
Breckinridge, Sophonisba Preston, 1866-1948, 13711, 14797, 15612
Breckinridge, William Campbell Preston, 1837-1904, 2795, 13712
Breckinridge Co., Ky., 5953; History, 2795, 13607, 13684, 15398; Views, 15565
Breech-loaders versus muzzle-loaders, 11989
Breed, William Pratt, 1816-1889, 1468-1470
Breen, Henry Hegart, 11509
Breese, Sidney, 1800-1878, 1471, 1472, 16040
Breezing, Belle, ca.1861-1941, 13833, 14164, 15585, 15597
Brehme, Hugo, 6155, 1656
Bremer, Fredrika, 1801-1865, 1473, 6157, 13713
Brenchley, Julius Lucius, 1816-1873, 4931
Brene, José R., 19473
Brenes Mesen, Roberto, 1874-1947, 19474
Brenes Quesada, Luis Guillermo, 19007, 19009, 19475, 19476
Brennand, Deborah, 19477
Brent, Henry Johnson, 1811-1880, 1474
Brent, John Carroll, 1475
Brent, Linda, pseud., 10008
Brenton, Edward Pelham, 1774-1839, 1476, 1477
Brents, John A., 1478
Brereton, John, fl.1603, 1479
Brereton, John A., 1480
Brerewood, Edward, 1565?-1613, 11510
Bresolen, Antônio, 19478
Bressani, Francesco Giuseppe, 1612-1672, 1481, 1482
Bressant, 6992
Brett, William Henry, 1818-1886, 1483, 11511
Breugel, Gaspard Philippe Charles van, 1798-1888, 1484
Breve antologia, 19972
Brevoort, James Carson, 1818-1887, 1485
Brewer, Charles, 6162
Brewer, Forrest, 19479
Brewer, Jean G., 19479
Brewer, Thomas Mayo, 1814-1880, 1486
Brewer, William A., 1487
Brewer Carías, Allan-Randolph, 19480, 19481
Brewer Carías, Charles, 19639
Brewerton, George Douglass, 2796, 11512
Brewing, 22281
Brewster, Charles Warren, 1802-1868, 1488
Brewster, Francis E., 1489, 1490
Brewster, George, 2797

Brewster, Jarvis, 1491
Brewster, Lewis Waterbury, 1830-, 6163
Brewster, Mrs. Martha, fl.1757, 1492
Brewster family (William Brewster, 1566 or 7-1644), 6163
Brezieres, Maurice, 19482
Briano, Giorgio, 1493
Briant, Charles C., 2798
Brice, Angel Francisco, 19483
Brice, James R., 11513
Brice, John, 1494
Brice family, 11513
Briceño, Mariano de, 11514
Briceño Jáuregui, Manuel, 19143
Briceño Perozo, Maria, 1917-, 17443, 19484-19488
Briceño-Picon, Mario, 1928-, 19489
Brick-dust, 10534
Brickell, John, 1710?-1745, 2799, 11515
Bricks, 13942
Bricks without straw, 10989
Bricktop, pseud., 10792-10798
The bridal eve, 10172
The bride and the maiden, 4003
The bride and Buena Vista, 9719
The bride of a ghost, 10962
The bride of Fort Edward, 8631
The bride of Llewellyn, 10831
The bride of the mistletoe, 8512
The bride of the northern wilds, 9292
The bride of the wilderness, 2673
A bridegroom, 10598
Bridel, Jean Louis, 1759-1821, 1495
Bridge, Horatio, 1806-1893, 24015
Bridge, James Howard, 1858-, 2800
Bridge, Josiah, 1739-1801, 11516
Bridge, Thomas, 1657-1715, 1496, 1497
Bridge, William, 1600?-1670, 12300
Bridgeman, Thomas, b.1795, 1503-1506
Bridgeport, Conn., Library association, 1498
Bridger, James, 1804-1881, 17945
Bridger's Pass, 2621, 2845
Bridges, George Wilson, 1499
Bridges, John Henry, 1832-1906, 13104
Bridges, Kentucky, 13938; U.S., 21922
Bridges, Suspension, Kentucky, 14075
Bridgewater, Mass., 1500; History, 1500
Bridgham, Samuel Willard, 1774-1840, 1501, 1502
Bridwell, Margaret Morris, 13714
Bridwell, N.W., 6164
Briet, Philippe, 1601-1668, 1515
The brigand, 2674
Brigands and robbers, 16319, 16626, 22868
Brigdon, Philip, 15055

Briggs, Charles Frederick, 1804-1877, 11520
Briggs, Elinor, 19490
Briggs, George Ware, 1810-1895, 1517, 1518
Briggs, Harold E., 16042-16045
Briggs, Henry, 1561-1630, 5632
Briggs, Horace, 16046
Briggs, John, 1519
Briggs, Lloyd Vernon, 1863-, 6165
Briggs, Nathan M., 12403
Brigham, Amariah, 1798-1849, 12302
Brigham, William, 1806-1869, 1520
Brigham, William F., 1839-1865, 22842
Brigham, William Tufts, 1841-1926, 6166
Brigham Young's record of blood!, 17068
Brigham's destroying angel, 16751
Bright, Jesse David, 1812-1875, 1521, 13231
Bright, John, 1811-1889, 1522, 1946
Bright, Jonathan Brown, 1800-1879, 1523
Bright, William, 5775
Bright days in the old plantation time, 8691
Bright extremes in human life, 11041
Bright family, 1523
Bright family (Henry Bright, bapt. 1602), 1523
The bright side of prison life, 5329
Bright skies and dark shadows, 3441
Brightly's orphan, 11194
Brighton, John George, 1524
Brighton, Mass., Directories, 1566
Brightwell, Cecilia Lucy, 1811-1875, 1525
Bril-gesicht voor de verblinde eyghen baet-suchtige handelaers op Brasil, 1526
Brimblecomb, Nicholas, pseud., 1527
Brine, Lindesay, 1834-1906, 6167
Brininstool, Earl Alonzo, 1870-, 7755
Brink, McCormick, & co., publishers, 6168
Brink (W.R.) and company, 6169
Brinsley, John, fl.1633, 1528
Brinsmade, Thomas Clar, 1802-1868, 22587
Brinson, Lessie Brannen, 6170
Brinton, Daniel Garrison, 1837-1899, 1529, 2802
Brinton, John Hill, 1832-1907, 2803
Brion de la Tour, Louis, 2804
Briones, Guillermo, 19491
Briquets (Friel), 19506
Brisbane, Albert, 1809-1890, 1530
Brisbin, James Sanks, 1837-1892, 1531, 15955, 15956
Brisco, Joseph, d.1657, Poetry, 23807
Briscoe, C.B., 19492
Briscoe, Vera, 13717
Brisée, 8850
Briseño Hermosillo, Rodolfo, 19493
Brissot de Warville, Anacharsis, 6171
Brissot de Warville, Jean Pierre, 1754-1793, 1532, 2805, 6172, 11521, 11522
Bristed, Charles Astor, 1820-1874, 1533-1535

Bristed, John, 1778-1855, 1536, 1537, 2806
Bristling with thorns, 23953
Bristoe Station, Va., Battle of, 1863, 2073
Bristol, Sherlock, 1815-1906, 16047
Bristol, William M., 16048
Bristol, Pa., 609
Bristol academy, Taunton, Mass., 2249
Bristol and Clifton Ladies Anti-slavery
  Society, Bristol, Eng., 24016
Bristol Co. (Mass.) agricultural society,
  1538; church history, 22183
Britain and her colonies, 13040
Britannia, 12368
Britannia major, 1539
Britannia triumphant, 1540
British America, 7367, 12825; Description
  & travel, 1425; Description & travel,
  Guide-books, 5724
British and Foreign Anti-slavery Society,
  London, 23897, 24017-24019, 24214, 25842
British and Foreign Bible Society, 24033
British association for the advancement of
  science, 6551
British colonial episcopate, Centenary of
  the, 23492
British colonization society, 12827
British Columbia, 5837, 6013, 6178, 6198,
  6769, 7363, 16354; Bureau of Mines, 6174;
  Bureau of Provincial Information, 6175;
  Canada's most westerly province, 6176;
  Department of Agriculture, 6177;
  Description & travel, 2730, 2753, 4481,
  5839, 5896, 5897, 5983, 6106, 6173, 6176,
  6179, 6180, 6192, 6198, 6226, 6237, 6555,
  6600, 6890, 7063, 7259, 7324, 7360, 7460,
  7579, 7656, 8074, 8126, 8284, 8285, 8286,
  8372, 8383, 8420, 11662, 15811, 15917,
  16417, 16477, 17119, 23406; Exploring
  expedition, 6179; Forestry, 6182; Gold
  discoveries, 5898, 6173; History, 5839,
  6051, 7539, 12774; Lands and Works
  Department, 6179; Lands Department, 6180;
  Maps, 5593; Northern Interior, 7539;
  Politics & government, 8284-8286;
  Population, 6175; Porcupine District
  Commission, 6181; Public lands, 6180;
  Royal Commission of Inquiry on Timber and
  Forestry, 6182; Royal Commission on
  Acquisition of Texada Island, 6183;
  Its present resources and future
  possibilities, 6178
British Columbia and Vancouver's Island, 6173
British diplomatic correspondence concerning
  the republic of Texas, 1830-1848, 16000
British emigrant society, Susquehanna Co.,
  Pa., 13233

The British emigrants' "hand book", 17268
British Guiana, 12641, 13449, 13475, 18325,
  25697; Description & travel, 2502, 5319,
  12589, 25276; History, 1516, 22739, 24048,
  24735, 24881; Politics & government, 24518
British Honduras, 2353, 6803, 12704, 13485;
  Bibliography, 19089; Boundaries, Guatemala,
  8298; Boundaries, Mexico, 8433; Citizens,
  24020; Department of Agriculture, 19494;
  Description & travel, 7623; Economic
  conditions, 7623; History, 8298, 24020
British Honduras question, 8433
British in Mexico, 7065
The British in Philadelphia, 10066
British in Spain, 7065
British interests and activities in Texas, 15813
The British invasion of Kentucky, 13871
The British mission of the church of the
  Puritans, 24686
British Museum, 19632; Department of Oriental
  Antiquities and Ethnography, 19495
British North America, 1541, 3877
The British sailor's discovery, 11523
British South Africa Company, 24564
British temperance emigration society and
  saving fund, 11524
The British treaty, 21817
The British worthies, 12286
Brito, Amelia, 18094
Brito, Ignacio Machado, 19496
Brito, Otario T., 19497
Brito, Paulo José Miguel de, d.1832, 11525
Brito Broca, 19498
Brito Figueroa, Federico, 19499
Brito Freire, Francisco de, 1542, 1543
Briton (Frigate), 23615
Brittan, Samuel Byron, 12590
Britten, Mrs. Emma (Hardinge) d.1899, 6184
Britto, Jomard Muniz de, 1937-, 19500
Britto, Rubens da Silva, 19501
Britto García, Luis, 19502
Britton, James B., 2807
Britton, John, 1771-1857, 1544
Britton, Wiley, 2808
"Bro," 11207
Broad, Amos, 11526
Broad, Mrs. Demis, 11526
Broad form deed, 14016
Broad River valley, Ga., 12263
Broadbent, Sylvia M., 19503
Broaderick, Cephas, pseud., 9613
The Broadway, 11527
Broadway Methodist Church, Paducah, Ky., 14323
Broadway pneumatic underground railway, 13068
Brock, Charles F., illustr., 11159
Brock, Sir Isaac, 1769-1812, 7613

Brock, R.A., 3662
Brockett, Linus Pierpont, 1820-1893, 1545-
  1548, 11528, 23331
Brocklehurst, Thomas Unett, 6185
Brockley Moor, 10171
Brockway, Diodate, 1776-1849, 1549
Brockway, Thomas, 1745-1807, 1550, 2809,
  12087
Brockwell, Charles, 1551
Brodbeck, Sully, 19504
Brode, Gertrude, 10899
Broderick, David Colbreth, 1820-1859, 17075
Broderick and Gwin, 17306
Brodhead, Mrs. Eva Wilder (McGlasson) 1870-
  1915, 2810-2812
Brodhead, John Romeyn, 1814-1873, 1552, 1553,
  11529
Brodie, Walter, 1554
Brodigan, Thomas, 1555
Broeck, Matheus van den, 11530
Broersma, Gossen. Evolución y tendencia
  de los precios del estaño, 18942
Broide, Julio, 19505
Broke, Hezekiah, 2813
Broke, Horatio George, 16050
Broke, Sir Philip Bowes Vere, 1776-1841,
  1524
Broke family, 1524
The broken engagement, 10832
Broken idols, 10899
A broken looking-glass, 9740
The broken seal, 12399
Brokenburne, 2774
Brokesby, Francis, 1637-1714, 1556
Bromley, Clara Fitzroy (Kelly), 1557
Bromley, George Tisdale, 1817-, 16051
Bromley, Walter, 1558, 1559, 11531
Bromme, Traugott, 1802-1866, 1560-1562,
  2814, 6186, 11532
Bromwell, William, 1563, 21928
Bromwell, William Jeremy, 1834-1874,
  11533
Bronaugh, Warren Carter, b.1839, 16052
Bronner, Milton, 3827
Bronson, Barry, 13833
Bronson, Edgar Beecher, 1856-1917, 16053,
  16054
Bronson, Francis S., 2815
Bronson, Harry, 13718
Bronson, Henry, 1804-1893, 11534, 11535
Bronson's travelers' directory, 2815
The bronze Buddha, 9326
The bronzed beauty of Paris, 10835
Brook, Benjamin, 1776-1848, 11536
Brook, Harry E., 16055
Brooke, Francis Taliaferro, 1763-1851, 11537

Brooke, Henry, 1703?-1783, 1564
Brooke, John T., 11538
Brooke, Rupert, 1887-1915, 6187
Brooker, William H., 16056
Brookes, Iveson L., 24021, 24022
Brookes, Richard, fl.1750, 1565, 2816
Brookfield, Mass., History, 6392
Brookline, Mass., Directories, 1566
Brooklyn, N.Y., 11539, 13262; Charters, 1568,
  1569, 11541; History, 22222; Ordinances,
  etc., 1569, 1570, 11540; Politics &
  government, 11539; Registers, 11541; Water
  committee, 22774; Water-supply, 1571, 1729,
  22774; Water works, 1571
The Brooklyn city and Kings county record:
  a budget of general information..., 11541
Brooklyn city library, 11542
Brooks, Abbie M., 2817
Brooks, Charles, 1795-1872, 1572-1574
Brooks, Charles Timothy, 1813-1883, 1575,
  11543
Brooks, David, 1744-1802, 1576
Brooks, Edward, 1784-1859, 1577, 21815
Brooks, Elizabeth, 16057
Brooks, Erastus, 1815-1886, 24023
Brooks, Geraldine, 1875-, 6188
Brooks, Helen, 16058
Brooks, James, 1810-1873, 6189, 24024
Brooks, John, 1752-1825, 1578
Brooks, John, 1792-, 2818
Brooks, Juanita, 16059
Brooks, Nathan Covington, 1809-1898, 1579,
  1580
Brooks, Noah, 1830-1903, 6190, 6191
Brooks, Phillips, bp., 1835-1893, 1581, 1582
The Brookside strike, 13556, 13719, 14005,
  14269
Brooksmith, 7122
Broom, Jacob, 1808-1864, 1583
Broom, Walter William, 1584, 11544
Broomall, John Martin, 1816-1894, 1585
Broome, Mary Ann (Stewart) Barker, lady, d.
  1911, 2819
Brooms, 15525
Brosch, Carlos Dias, 1920-, 19506-19509
Brosnan, Cornelius James, 1882-, 16060
Bross, Dieter, 20713
Bross, William, 1813-1890, 1586, 1587, 8431,
  16061
Brossard, Alfred de, 1588
Brosses, Charles de, 1709-1777, 1589
Brother Jonathan's welcome to Kossuth, 954
Brother Jonathan's wife, 11545
"Brother McGarvey," 15035
Brother Mason, the circuit rider, 8854
A brother of Christ, 13947

A brother to dragons, 5465
The brother's revenge, 9855
Brotherhead, William, 1590, 1591, 11546
Brotherhood, 9266
The brotherhood of thieves, 24420
Brothers, Thomas, 1592
The brothers, 9841
The brothers in arms, 9842
The brothers' war, 25353
Brotherton, Mrs. Alice (Williams), 2820
Brough, John, 1811-1865, 1593, 7565
Brougham and Vaux, Henry Peter Brougham, 1st baron, 1778-1868, 1594-1597, 11547, 11548
Broughton, Thomas, 11549
Broughton, William Robert, 6192
Brouillet, Jean Baptiste Abraham, 1813-1884, 16062
Brovedani, Bruno, 19510
Browder, Earl Russell, 1891-, 6193
Browder, John Caldwell, 13720
Brower, Arier C., 2881
Brown, Aaron Venable, 1795-1859, 11550, 11551
Brown, Abiel, 21816
Brown, Albert Gallatin, 1813-1880, 11552, 24025, 24026
Brown, Alexander Enos, d.1865, 11553
Brown, Andrew, 1748-1813, 11554
Brown, Augustus Cleveland, 1839-, 2821
Brown, Benjamin Gratz, 1826-1885, 24027-24029
Brown, Charles, 24030
Brown, Charles Brockden, 1771-1810, 293, 297, 11555, 21817
Brown, Charles E., 16063
Brown, David, 1786-1875, 2822
Brown, David L., 2823
Brown, David Paul, 1795-1872, 11556
Brown, Deidamia (Covell), 21818
Brown, Edmund Randolph, 1845-, 2824
Brown, James Henry, 16064
Brown, Francis, 1784-1820, 11557
Brown, Francis Henry, 1835-1917, 12737
Brown, Frederick Thomas, 1822-1893, 11558, 11559
Brown, George Stayley, 6194
Brown, George William, 1812-1891, 11560
Brown, Henry, 1789-1849, 11561, 11562
Brown, Hugh, 1811?-1888, 24031
Brown, Isaac, fugitive slave, 24096
Brown, Isaac Van Arsdale, 1784-1861, 11563-11565, 24032
Brown, J. Words of John Brown, 23990
Brown, J. Robert, 2825
Brown, James, 1766-1835, 15751
Brown, James, 1800-1855, 22488
Brown, James Bryce, 21819
Brown, James D., 21820
Brown, James Stephens, b.1828, 16065, 16066
Brown, John, 1722-1787, 11566
Brown, John, 1757-1837, 7276, 14967
Brown, John, 1771-1850, 24033
Brown, John, 1800-1859, 6417, 13386, 24121, 24303, 24599, 24838, 25128, 25135, 25415, 25416, 25438, 25451, 25690, 25733, 25895
Brown, John, 1800-1859, Fiction, 9960, 10007, 24117
Brown, John, 1843-, 16067
Brown, John, fl.1858, 6195, 24034
Brown, John Henry, 1810-1905, 16068
Brown, John Henry, 1820-1895, 2826-2828
Brown, John Howard, 1840-, 7227
Brown, John Mason, 1837-1890, 2829, 13721
Brown, John Mathias, 1745-1838, 11567
Brown, John Thomas, 1869-, 13722, 13723
Brown, John Walker, 1814-1849, 979
Brown, Jonathan, 11568
Brown, Lawrence, 24678
Brown, Leland A., 13724
Brown, Leonard, 1837-1914, 11569
Brown, Lloyd Arnold, 3205
Brown, Lyle C., 19511
Brown, Marcus Monroe, 1854-, 6196
Brown, Mary Edwards, 1866-1958, 6197, 15508
Brown, Mason, 1799-1867, 13363
Brown, Nathan, 25410
Brown, Orlando, 13452
Brown, Peter, 1784-1863, 11570
Brown, Philip Francis, 1842-, 2830
Brown, R.C. Lundon, 6198
Brown, Rebecca Warren, 11571
Brown, Robert, 1842-1895, 25217
Brown, Robert T., 19512
Brown, Samuel, 1768-1805, 11572
Brown, Samuel Gilman, 1813-1885, 11573
Brown, Samuel R., 1775-18-7, 2831, 11574, 11575
Brown, Sarah Poseg, 1859-, 6199
Brown, Tarleton, 1757-1846, 2832
Brown, Theodore M., 13725
Brown, Thomas, 13726, 13727
Brown, Virginia Stuart, illustr., 5816
Brown, Rev. William, 25594
Brown, William, of Leeds, 6200
Brown, William B., 24035
Brown, William H., 1796-1867, 16069, 24036
Brown, William Lacy, 1913-, 19513
Brown, William Linn, 11109
Brown, William Perry, 10125
Brown, William Wells, b.1814, 2833, 2886, 24037

Brown family, 11554
Brown's political history of Oregon, 16064
Brown's revenge, 10863
Brown's three years in the Kentucky prisons,
  13726
Brown and Williamson Tobacco Company, 15570
Brown Co., Wis., 15848
Brown University, Biography, 2425; Class of
  1802, 12284; History, 12490, 12492; John
  Carter Brown Library, 16534, 19514,
  19515
Browne, Mrs. Alice (Harriman) 1861-1925,
  16070
Browne, Charles Farrar, 1834-1867, 6201
Browne, Dinah (Hope), 25506
Browne, Dunn, pseud., 3457
Browne, Edith A., 1874-, 6202
Browne, Francis Fisher, 1843-1913, 2836
Browne, George Waldo, 1851-1930, 17850
Browne, John Ross, 1821-1875, 2837, 2838,
  11676, 16071-16073, 16124
Browne, Junius Henri, 1833-1902, 2839
Browne, Martha (Griffith), 24040
Browne, Nathaniel Borodaille, 1819-1875,
  11577
Browne, Patrick, 1720?-1790, 11578
Browne, Peter Arrell, 1782-1860, 11579,
  11580
Browne, Sir Thomas, 1605-1682, 11581
Browne, Thomas M., 3044
Browne, William Hand, 4080
Browne, William Henry James, 11583
Brownell, Charles DeWolf, 1822-, 11583
Brownell, Henry Howard, 1820-1872, 1598-
  1600, 11584
Brownell, Thomas, d.1872, 1601
Brownell, Thomas Church, bp., 1779-1865,
  1602
Browning, Charles, b.1765, 1603
Browning, Charles Henry, 6203-6205
Browning, Clyde E., 19516
Browning, Graeme, 13728
Browning, Harley L., 19517
Browning, I.B., 14563, 14564
Browning, John, 19518
Browning, Meshach, b.1781, 11585
Browning, Orville Hickman, 1806-1881,
  7279; 24041, 24042; Addresses, sermons,
  etc., 5934
Browning, Robert, 1812-1889, 7119
Browning, Samuel, 1604
Brownlow, William Gannaway, 1805-1877, 1605,
  2840, 16074, 24043
The Browns of Liberty Hall..., 15204
Brownson, Orestes Augustus, 1803-1876, 1606,
  1606

1607, 16075
Brownstown, Mich., Battle of, August 5, 1812,
  11944
Brubacher, John S., 19519
Bruce, Archibald, 1777-1818, 270
Bruce, Benjamin Gratz, 1827-, 15548
Bruce, E.M., 23927
Bruce, Eli, 1793-1832, 4531
Bruce, George A., 6206
Bruce, Hamilton, 1608
Bruce, Henry Clay, 1836-1902, 24044
Bruce, James C., 1609
Bruce, John Jessie, 2841
Bruce, Lewis, 1610
Bruce, Miner W., 16076
Bruce, Peter Henry, 1692-1757, 1611, 1612
Bruchesi, Jean, 1901, 6207
Brückner, G., 11586
Brüder über dem meer, 3653
Bruges, Roger, graf von, 6208
Brughetti, Romualdo, 19520
Brundle, John, 1882-, 6209, 6210
Bruni Celli, Blas, 19521
Brunson, Alfred, 1793-1882, 1613, 16077
Brunswick, Georgia - Description, 5207
Brunswick canal and railroad company, 709
Brunt, Jonathan, b.1760, 1614
Brush, John C., 1615
Brush, Samuel, 1616
Brussels. Conference, 1889-1890, 24025,
  25832
Brutus, Lucius Junius, pseud., 11587
Bruun, Ellen (Raon) 1892-, 2842
Bruyas, Jacques, 1635-1712, 11588
Bruzen de La Martinière, Antoine Augustin,
  1662-1746, 11589
Bry, Theodor de, 1528-1598, 23555
Bryan, Claude Glennon, 1876-, 7687
Bryan, Daniel, 1795-1866, 1617-1619, 2843,
  2844
Bryan, Edward B., 24046
Bryan, Francis Theodore, 2845, 5547
Bryan, George, 13729
Bryan, George J., 1620
Bryan, Hugh, 1699-1753, 1621
Bryan, James, 1810-1881, 1622, 1623
Bryan, Mrs. Mary (Baird), 1861-, 6211
Bryan, Roger Bates, 1860-, 16078
Bryan, Thomas Barbour, 1828-1906, 11590
Bryan, Wilhelmus Bogart, 24047
Bryan, William Jennings, 1860-1925, 6211, 7263
Bryan, William Smith, 1846-, 7639
Bryan Station, Fayette Co., Ky., 4891;
  Drama, 13958; Siege of, 1782
Bryan Station heroes and heroines, 14356
Bryant, Charles S., 1624

71

Bryant, Edwin, 1805-1869, 2846, 16923
Bryant, George Syng, 1824-1875, 15561
Bryant, James Ray M'Corkle, 1802-1866,
  1625
Bryant, John R., 15349
Bryant, Joseph, 1742-1807, 7429
Bryant, Joshua, 24048
Bryant, Wilbur Franklin, 6212
Bryant, William Cullen, 1794-1878, 1626-
  1629, 6213, 6214, 11591, 11592, 12742,
  21821, 23469
The Bryant homestead-book, 12742
Bryce, George, 1844-1931, 6215-6236,
  17526
Bryce, James Bryce, viscount, 1838-1922,
  1630
Brydges, Harold, pseud., 2800
Brydges, Sir Samuel Egerton, bart., 1762-
  1837, 1631
Bryner, Byron Cloyd, 1849-, 2847
Bryozoa, 15067
Buache, J.N., 6237
Buache, Philippe, 6238, 7109
Bubbles of fiction, 8747
Los bucaneros de las Indias occidentales,
  6956
Bucaramanga. Universidad Industrial de
  Santander. Departamento de Geología,
  19112; Publicaciones científicas, 19112
Bucareli y Urana, Antonio María, 1717-1779,
  23461
The buccaneer, 12552
The buccaneer of King's bridge, 9636
Buccaneers, 427, 428, 1730, 6256, 6956,
  9962, 9963, 10074, 21765, 22035,
  22190, 22280
Buchan, David, b.1780, 1067
Buchan, David Stewart Erskine, 11th earl of,
  1742-1829, 1632
Buchan, Susan (Grosvenor) 1882-, 6239
Buchanan, Archibald, 11593
Buchanan, Claudius, 1766-1815. Christian
  researches in Asia, 24033
Buchanan, George, 1763-1808, 24049
Buchanan, Isaac, 1810-1883, 1633
Buchanan, James, pres. U.S., 1791-1868,
  1634, 2848, 6586, 14838, 22566, 24050
Buchanan, James, British consul at New York,
  11594
Buchanan, James A., of Baltimore, 12133
Buchanan, Joseph, 1785-1829, 13730
Buchanan, Joseph Rodes, 1814-1899, 11595
Buchanan, Thompson, 1877-1937, 2849
Buchanan, William B., 11606
Bücher, Karl, 1847-1930, 24051
Bucher, Walter H. Geology of the Jeptha Knob,

  15512
Buck, Charles Neville, 1879-, 13733
Buck, Edward, 1635
Buck, Edward, of Boston, 11597
Buck, Wilbur Frances, 19522, 19523
Buck, William C., 24052
Buck, William Joseph, 1825-, 1636, 1637
Buckalew, Charles Rollin, 1821-1899, 2076,
  25770
Bucke, Charles, 1781-1846, 11598
Buckholtz, L. von, 1638
Buckingham, Henry A., 1639
Buckingham, James Silk, 1786-1855, 2850,
  11599-11603
Buckingham, John Edward, 1828-1909, 6240
Buckingham, Joseph H., 1806-1880, 11604
Buckingham, Joseph Tinker, 1779-1861, 1640,
  11605-11607, 24994
Buckingham, Samuel Giles, 1641
Buckle, D., 19524
Buckler, Thomas Hepburn, 1812-1901, 1642
Buckley, Kate, 6241, 6242
Buckley, Michael Bernard, 1831-1872, 6241,
  6242
The Buckley Lady, 9578
Buckley Wildlife Sanctuary, Woodford County,
  Kentucky, 14047
Buckminster, Joseph, 1751-1812, 1643, 11608
Buckminster, Joseph Stevens, 1784-1812, 1644-
  1646
Buckminster, Lydia Nelson (Hastings) b.1818,
  11609
Buckner, Aylett, 1828-1864, 1647
Buckner, G.D., 13734
Buckner, Henry F., 1818-1882, 1648
Buckner, Simon Bolivar, 1823-1914, 13735
"Buckra" land, 11174
Bucks co., Pa., Biography, 1636; History,
  1636; History, Revolution, 22049
Buckskin Mose, 10508
Buckwheat, 15145
Budan, A., 1649
Budd, Thomas, d.1698, 1650-1652
Budget, Barbados, 18824; Chile, 20150, 20659;
  Colombia, 20278; Kentucky, 14621; U.S.,
  22662; Venezuela, 19502
Budington, William Ives, 1815-1879, 1653, 1654
Buds and bird-voices, 9823
Buds and blossoms of piety, 401
The buds of beauty, 21882
Buechler, Johann Ulrich, 2851
Buechner, Helmut K., 19525
Buechner, Jimmie H., 19525
Buel, Alexander Woodruff, 1813-1868, 1655
Buel, David, 1784-1860, 1656
Buel, James William, 1849-1920, 16079, 16080

Buel, Jesse, 1778-1839, 1657
Buel, Oliver Prince, 1838-1899, 6243
Buell, Don Carlos, 1818-1898, 1658
Buell, P.L., 1659
Buell, Samuel, 1716-1798, 1660, 1661, 22033
Buell, Samuel, 1771-1787, 1660
Un buen oficio, 19823
Buena Vista, 3149
Buenas Van Severn, J. Picardo, 19526
Buenaventura de Carrocera, Father, 19527
Bueno, Antônio Sylvio Cunha, 19528
Bueno, Francisco de Assis Vieira, 1816-1908, 19529
Bueno, Francisco da Silveira, 1808-, 19530
Bueno, Miguel, 19531
Bueno, Salvador, 19532, 19533
Buenos Aires, 1662; Biblioteca Lincoln, 19534, 19535; Bolsa de Comercio, 18137, 19536; Description, 12518; History, 20506; Junta provisional gubernativa, 1810, 1662; Universidad, 6244, 19140; Universidad Católica Argentina, 19537; Universidad Nacional. Biblioteca, 19543; Universidad Nacional. Departamento de Matemática. Cursos y seminarios de matemática, 20621; Universidad Nacional. Departamento de Orientación Vocacional, 19538; Universidad Nacional. Facultad de Arquitectura y Urbanismo. Biblioteca, 19539; Universidad Nacional. Instituto Bibliotecológico, 19540-19545; Universidad Nacional. Instituto de investigaciones históricas, 24094; Universidad Nacional. Servicio universitario de Salud. Departamento de Estadística, 19546
Buenos Aires (Province) Asesoría General de Gobierno, 19554, 19555; Constitution, 123, 19547; Description & travel, 594; Direccion de Cultura, 19548; Dirección de Vialidad, 19549-19551; Dirección de Vialidad. Biblioteca Técnica, 19552; History, 23096; Instituto Bibliográfico, 19553; Laws, statutes, etc., 18460, 19554, 19555; Politics & government, 19547
Buenos Aires and Argentine gleamings, 13054
Buenos Aires and Chile, Sketches of, 12529
Bufalos de agua, 20286
Buff and blue, 10880
Buffalo, 16095; Chamber of commerce, 1663; Charters, 1664; Commerce, 22333, 22408; Common council, 11610; First Presbyterian church, 11850; Harbor, 11610; History, 11850; Industry, 22408; Manufactures, 23115; Ordinances, etc., 1664
Buffalo Bill, 7712, 16093, 1622?
"Buffalo Bill" from prairie to palace, 16093

Buffalo Bill's life story, 16223
Buffalo Co., Nebraska   Biography, 15933; History, 15933
Buffalo historical society, 1334
The buffalo in trade and commerce, 16095
Buffalo Jones' forty years of adventure, 16900
Buffalo library, Buffalo, N.Y., 24623
Buffalo society of natural sciences, 1911
Buffinton, James, 24053
Buffum, Edward Gould, 16081
Buffum, George Tower, 1846-, 16082, 16083
Bufill, Jose Angel, 19556
Buford, Nick, 19557
Buford, Thomas, 13736
Bugbee, Lester G., 16084, 24054
Buggenhagen, Erich Arnold von, 19558
Buhle echoes, 2836
Buguelsky, Turi Y., 19559-19561
Buble, M., 1665
Buhler Lorca, Gustavo, 19562
Buhoup, Jonathan W., 1666
Buide, Mario S., 19563
Building-tools and implements, 14950
Building a new empire, 15892
Building codes, Brazil, 18654
The building industry in Kentucky, 15451
Building laws, Washington, D.C., 1686
Building on the rock, 10474
Buist, George, 1770-1808, 1667
Buitrago de Santiago, Zayda, 7747
Buley, R. Carlyle, 15155
Bulfinch, Benjamin S., 1668
Bulfinch, Thomas, 1796-1867, 1669, 1670
Bulger's reputation, 6971
Bulhões, Octavio Couvea de, 19564
Bulkeley, Peter, 1583-1659, 1671
Bulkley, Charles Henry Augustus, 1819-1893, 1672, 1673
Bulkley, Edwin Adolphus, 1826-1905, 1674
Bull, Charles Livingston, 14832
Bull, Jacqueline Page, 1911-, 13583, 13737, 13790, 14695, 15269, 15500, 15559
Bull, Jerome Case, 10283
The bull-fight, 10909
Bull Run, 1st battle, 1861, 833, 11640, 12042
Bull Run, 2d battle, 1862, 7325, 8373
Bull-us, Hector, pseud., 10482
Bullard, Frederic Lauriston, 1873-, 6586
Bullard, Henry Adams, 1788-1851, 1675
Bullaude, José, 19565
Bullen, George, 1816-1894, 25631
Buller, Charles, 1806-1848, 6647, 6648
Bullet and shell, 5715
Bullitt, John Christian, 1824-1902, 1676
Bullitt, Thomas Walker, 1838-1910, 24055
Bullitt family, 24055

Bulloch, James Dunwoody, 1823-1901, 16085
Bullock, Alexander Hamilton, 1816-1882, 6245
Bullock, Walter Overton, 13738
Bullock, William, fl.1649, 2852
Bullock, William, fl.1808-1828, 2853, 6246-6248
Bullock House, Lexington, Ky., 14129
Bullrich, Silvina, 19566
Bulnes, Francisco, 1848-, 6249
Bulnes, Gonzalo, 1851-, 6250
Bulnes Cerda, Arturo, 19567
Bülow, Dietrich i.e. Adam Heinrich Dietrich, freiherr von, 1757-1807, 2854
The bulwark of truth, 22205
O bumba-meuboi, 20551
Bumgardner, Helen A., 13739
Bunce, Oliver Bell, 1828-1890, 6214, 11611
Buncombe Co., N.C., Description & travel, 3603; Fiction, 10543
Bungay, George Washington, 1818-1892, 1677-1679, 13050
Bungener, Laurence Louis Felix, 1814-1874, 6251
Bunker Hill, 1707; Battle of 1775, 569, 1882, 2349, 11491, 11839, 12055, 12982, 14470, 21970, 22065, 23758; Drama, 11481; Poetry, 3382
Bunker Hill declaration, 1680
Bunn, Alfred, 1796?-1860, 1681
Bunn, Matthew, b.1772?, 2855
Bunn, Thomas, 24056
Bunnell, David C., b.1793, 1682
Bunnell, Lafayette H., 16087
Bunner, E., 1683
The Bunsby papers, 8856
Bunse, Heinrich A., 19568
Bunsen, Christian Karl Josias, Freiherr von, 1791-1860, 24057
Bunte briefe aus Amerika, 5795
Buntline, Ned, pseud., 10078-10081
Bunyan, Mary, b.1650, Fiction, 3506
Buon, 18159
Burbank, Addison, 1895-, 6252
Burbank, Caleb, 1761-1849, 1684, 1685
Burbano, José Ignacio, 19569
Burbridge, Stephen Gano, 1831-1894, 13318
Burch, George W., 6253
Burch, Samuel, 1686
Burchard, Jedediah, 1687
Burchard, Samuel Dickinson, 1812-1891, 1688
Burchell, Thomas, 1799-1846, 1689
Burchell, William Fitzer, 1689
Burchett, Josiah, 1666?-1746, 1690, 1691
Burcoa, Pedro Anibal, 19570
Burden, Jesse R., 24058

The burden of Christopher, 9096
The burden of the South, 1710
Burder, George, 1752-1832, 1692, 14972
Burdett, Charles, 1815-, 2856
Burdette, Mary G., 16088
Burdette, Robert Jones, 1844-1914, 16089-16091
Burdick, Usher T., 16092
Burdick, William, 1693
Burdon, William, 1764-1818, 12145
Bureau Co., Ill., Description, Maps, 17154; History, 17157
Burford, Robert, 1791-1861, 1694
Burge, William, 1787-1849, 1695
Burges, Bartholomew, 1696
Burges, Tristam, 1770-1853, 1697, 11447
Burgess, Chalon, 18-?-1903, 1698
Burgess, Dyer, 24645
Burgess, Ebenezer, 1790-1870, 1699, 1700
Burgess, George, bp., 1809-1866, 1701
Burgess, John William, 1844-1931, 24059
Burgess, Mrs. Neva Summers, 14781
Burgess family (Thomas Burgess, d.1685), 1700
Burgheim, Max, 13740
Burgheim, Philip, 13741
The burglar who moved paradise, 11080
The burglar's fate and the detectives, 10527
Burgoa, Francisco de, 1605-1681, 1702
Burgoo, 13710, 14010
Burgos, Juan Jacinto, 19571
Burgoyne, Arthur Gordon, 1863-1914, 21822
Burgoyne, John, 1722-1792, 1703-1705, 11519, 11612, 11688, 22410
Burgoyne, Sir John Fox, bart., 1782-1871, 1706
Burgoyne's invasion, 1777, 345-347, 1704, 1705, 4960, 5894, 5895, 11519, 11612, 22410, 23534; Fiction, 2522
Burguess, Paul, 19572
A burial among the mountains, 10747
Buried alive (behind prison walls) for a quarter of a century, 24463
Burk, Ignacio, 19573
Burk, John Daly, d.1808, 1707, 11613, 11658
Burk, John Junius, 1800?-1866, 11658
Burkart, Josef, 1798-1874, 6254
Burke, Aedanus, 1743?-1802?, 11614
Burke, Arthur Meredyth, 6255
Burke, Clyde T., 13742
Burke, Edmund, 1729?-1797, 22830, 22950
Burke, Edmund, 1729?-1797. A letter from Edmund Burke..., 22; A letter... on the affairs of America, 21860; Speech... on American taxation, 23604; Speech... on moving his resolutions for conciliation, 23722
Burke, Edmund, 1809-1882, 24060
Burke, John, d.1873, 1710, 1711

Burke, John M., 16093
Burke, Joseph Henry, 1908-, 19574, 19575
Burke, Melvin, 19576
Burke, William, 1752-1836, 1712, 1714,
  2858, 19577
Burke, William, d.1798, 2857, 11615
Burke, William, fl.1805-1810, 1713
Burke, William. La libertad de cultos,
  19780
Burke, William Alvard, 1811-1887, 1426
Burke, William S., 16094
Burke family (Richard Burke, of Sudbury,
  Mass., 1640?-1693 or 4), 1426
Burkesville and Cumberland County, 14910
Burkett, W. Keith, 13743
Burkitt, Lemuel, 11619
Burks, David D., 19578
Burks Branch Baptist Church, Shelby Co.,
  Ky., 13891
Burleigh, Charles Calistus, 1810-1878,
  24061, 24062, 25602
Burleigh, Joseph Bartlett, 1715
Burleigh, Walter Atwood, 1820-1896, 1716
Burleigh, William Henry, 1812-1871, 1717,
  12590
Burlend, Edward, d.1875, 2859
Burlend, Mrs. Rebecca, 1793-1872, 2859
Burleson Co., Tex., Biography, 16780
Burlingame, Anson, 1820-1870, 1718
Burlingame, Merrill G., 16095
Burlington co., N.J., 8445
Burman, Ben Lucien, 1895-1984, 2860
Burmann, Johannes, 1646-1764, 11620
Burmeister, Hermann, 1807-1892, 1719, 1720,
  24063
Burn, Andrew, 1742-1814, 1721
Burnaby, Andrew, 1734?-1812, 2861, 11621
Burnam, Curtis Field, 1820-1909, 14378
Burnap, George Washington, 1802-1859,
  11622, 11746
Burnap, Uzziah Cicero, 1794-1854, 1722;
  Bible servitude, 25465
A Burne-Jones head, 10669
Burnet, Mrs. Ann, 1754?-1789, 1725
Burnet, Jacob, 1770-1853, 1723, 12084
Burnet, Matthias, 1749-1806, 1724,
  1725
Burnet, William, 1688-1729, 22171
Burnett, Alfred, b.1823 or 4, 1726
Burnett, Henry Clay, 1825-1866, 1727,
  25064
Burnett, Peter Hardeman, 1807-1895, 1728,
  16099
Burnett, Ward B., 1729
Burney, James, 1750-1821, 1730, 6256, 11623,
  11624

Burnham, Benjamin Franklin, 1830-1898, 6257
Burnham, George P., 9453
Burnham, George Pickering, 1814-1902, 1731
Burnham, John Howard, 1834-1917, 16100
Burnham, L. Forbes S., 19579-19582
Burnham, Richard, 1711-1752, 1732
Burning of Havre de Grace, 10310
The burning of the convent, 10070
The burning of the St. Louis theatre, 5863
Burnings bewailed: in a sermon, occasioned
  by the lamentable fire which was in Boston,
  October 2, 1711, 23321
Burns, Anthony, 1834-1862, 24140, 24250, 24600,
  24756, 25201
Burns, Jabez, 1805-1876, 2862
Burns, James Anderson, 13744
Burns, James R., 11625
Burns, Robert, 1759-1796, 1733
Burns, Robert Ferrier, 1826-1896, 23119
Burnside, Ky., 15409
Burnside, Samuel McGregore, 1783-1850, 1734
Burnyeat, John, 1631-1690, 1735
Burpee, Lawrence Johnstone, 1873-, 16989, 17251
Burr, A.G., 16101-16104
Burr, Aaron, 1716-1757, 11626
Burr, Aaron, 1756-1836, 9022, 11627, 11628,
  11770, 12068, 13365, 13497, 16105, 21898,
  21899, 23819; Bibliography, 15564; Fiction,
  14437
Burr, Aril Bond, 13745
Burr, Charles Chauncey, 1817-1883, 1736, 1737
Burr, Fearing, 11629
Burr, Helen M., illustr., 13745
Burr, James E., 25337
Burr, Samuel Jones, 11630
Burr, William, 1738
Burr conspiracy, 1805-1807, 11627, 11628,
  13511, 16490; Fiction, 10929
Burrage, Henry Sweetser, 1837-1926, 24959
Burriel, Andres Marcos, 1719-1762, 17823
Burrill, George Rawson, 1770-1818, 1739, 11631
Burrill, James, 1772-1820, 474
Burrill Coleman, colored, 9081
Burriss, Charles Walker, 1860-, 6258
Burritt, Elihu, 1810-1879, 2863, 11632
Burroughs, Jeremiah, 1599-1646, 12308
Burroughs, Adoniram J., d.1865, 22304
Burroughs, Charles, 1787-1868, 1740, 11633
Burroughs, Stephen, 1765-1840, 11634
Burroughs, Wilbur Greeley, 1886-, 13746,
  15327, 24065; Geology of the Berea region,
  15686
Burrows, E.J., 1741
Burrows, John Lansing, 1814-1893, 1742, 1743
Burrows, John McDowell, 16106
Burrows, Rube, 1854-1890, 15821, 21769

Burrus, Ernesto J., 20006
Burson, William, 1833-, 2864
Bursztyn Dobry, Rosa, 19583
Burt, John S.G., 13081
Burton, 3999
Burton, Elijah P., 2865
Burton, John, 1696-1771, 11635
Burton, Karen Sue, 13747
Burton, Lewis William, bp., 1852-1940, 13748
Burton, Sir Richard Francis, 1821-1890, 1744, 11636
Burton, Warren, 1800-1866, 1746, 11637
Burton, William Evans, 1802-1860, 1747
Burtschi, Joseph Charles, 1874-, 7980
Burtt-Davy, Joseph, 1870-, 16107
Burus, Anthony, 1834-1862, 11438
Burwell, William MacCreary, 1809-1888, 1748, 1749, 11638, 23849
Bury, Viscount, 6259
Burzaco, Raul Horacio, 19584
Burzio, Humberto F., 19585
Busaniche, Jose Luis, 1892-, 19586
Busby, Allie B., 16108
Busch, Moritz, 1821-1899, 2866, 16109
Busche, Jack R., 14048
Buse, Hermann, 19587
Bush, Celeste E., 1188
Bush, George, 1796-1859, 22452
Bush, Isidor, 1822-1898, 24066
Bush, James Mills, 1808-1875, 13605, 15561
Bush, Joseph H., 1794-1865, 15197
Bush, William, 1746-1815, 13908
Bush settlement of pioneer days..., 13911
The bush that burned with fire... (sermon), 22134
Bushnell, Charles Ira, 1826-1883, 1176, 1750-1754, 1966, 2832, 11284, 12753, 23634
Bushnell, G.H.S., 19588
Bushnell, Horace, 1802-1876, 1755, 11640-11642
Bushnell, Simon, 25496
The bushwhackers, 4553
Bushy Run, Battle of, 1763, 23639
Business, 19671; Laws and regulations, Kentucky, 14535
A business advertiser and general directory of the city of Chicago, 21911
Business cycles, 19807
Business directory of the principal southern cities, 1766
Business education, 14654
Business enterprises, Registration and

transfer, Argentine Republic, 20241
Business ethics, 2105
Busk, Hans, 1815-1882, 1757
Bussierre, Marie Theodore Renouard, vicomte de, 1802-1865, 11643
Bustamante, Anastasio, pres. Mexico, 1780-1853, 120
Bustamante, Carlos Calixto, fl.1773, 19852
Bustamante, Carlos María de, 1774-1848, 139, 1758-1763, 19589, 20007
Bustamante, José Luis, 1799-1857, 1764
Bustamante Arellana, Carlos, 19590
Bustamante Muñoz, A., 19591
Busteed, Richard, 1822-1898, 11644, 11645
Bustos, Miguel Angel, 19592
Bustos Cerecedo, Miguel, 1912-, 19593
Busy moments of an idle woman, 8827
A busy time in Mexico, 7758
Butcher, Solomon Devore, 1856-, 16110
Butel-Dumont, Georges Marie, 1725-1788, 2867, 6260, 6261
Buteler, Patricio, 19594
Buthidae, Cuba, 18524, 18531, 18533
Butler, Benjamin Franklin, 1795-1858, 11646, 13412, 22957
Butler, Benjamin Franklin, 1818-1893, 1765, 11647, 12986
Butler, Caleb, 1776-1854, 1766, 1767
Butler, Charles, of Philadelphia, 21823
Butler, Charles Henry, 1859-1940, 19595
Butler, Clement Moore, 1810-1890, 1768, 1769, 11648
Butler, Edward C., 6262
Butler, Eileen, 16113
Butler, George Bernard, 1809-1886, 11649, 11690
Butler, Henry E., 11650
Butler, James, 1755?-1842, 24067
Butler, James Davie, 1815-1905, 1770, 16111, 16112, 16529
Butler, Jay Caldwell, 1844-1885, 2868
Butler, John, bp., 1717-1802, 1771, 11651
Butler, John Wesley, 19596
Butler, Joseph H., 19597
Butler, Mann, 1784-1852, 1772, 2869, 13749-13751
Butler, Ovid, 1801-1881, 25540
Butler, Pierce M., 1807-1867, 25689
Butler, Rector Laphan, 3329
Butler, Watson Hubbard, 1878-, 2868
Butler, William Allen, 1825-1902, 1773-1775
Butler, Sir William Francis, 1838-1910, 6263-6265, 16113
Butler, William Orlando, 1793-1880, 2728
Butler family (John Butler, 1677-1759), 1707
Butler Co., Ky., 13610, 13613, 14220

Butler co., Ohio, Biography, 14883
Butt, Louise E., 19598
Butt, Louise R., 20479
Butt, Martha Haines, b.1834, 24068
Butte St. Paul, Bottineau County, N.D., 16101
Butter, 18474
Butterfield, Carlos, 11652
Butterfield, Consul Willshire, 1824-1899, 11653, 16114, 16115
Butterfield, Horatio Quincy, 1822-1894, 1776
Butterlen, Jacques, 19599
Butterneggs, 10790
Butterworth, Hezekiah, 1839-1905, 2870, 2871
Buttles, J.B., 22863
Büttner, Johann Carl, 1754-, 2872
Büttner, Johann Gottfried, 2873
Button's inn, 10990
The Buttonwoods, 8922
Buttrick, Tilly, b.1783, 1777, 2874
Butts, Charles, 14565, 14596
Butts, J.T., 22808
Buxo, Jose Pascual, 19600, 19601
Buxton, Sir Thomas Powell, 1786-1845, 25180, 25711
Buzeta, Pedro Antonio, 6364
Buzhardt, Beaufort Simpson, 1838-1862, 2875
Buzzards, 15525
Buzzards Bay, 23261
Byam, George, 11654, 11655
Byberry Township, Pa., Genealogy, 23197; History, 23197
Bye paths of biography, 1525
Byerley, Sir John, 6246, 6247
Byerley, Thomas, 1788-1826, 13450
Byers, Samuel Hawkins Marshall, 1838-1933, 2876, 16116
Byers, William Newton, 1831-1903, 2877, 16117
Byfield, Mrs. Sarah (Leverett) 1673-1730, 21886
Byles, Mather, 1707-1788, 1778-1780
Byrd, William, 1674-1744, 2878, 11656
Byrdsall, Fitzwilliam, 1781
Byrne, Bernard M., 1782
Byrne, Lee, 1876-, 24069
Byrne, P.E., 16118
Byrne, Sally, 13549
Byrnes, Thomas F., 1847?-, 9815
The Byrnes of Glengoulah, 10426
Byron, George Gordon Noël Byron, 6th baron, 1788-1824, 18172
Byron, George Gordon Noel Byron, 6th baron, 1788-1824, Critical reception in Brazil, 18836
Bywater, John, 2784

Byxbee, O.F., 6266

Caballero, Francisco Jose, 5803
Caballero, Manuel, 7532
Caballero Deloya, Miguel, 19602
Caballero León, Luis F., 19603
Caballero y Góngora, Antonio, Cardinal, 1723-1796, 8204
Cabañas, Trinidad, pres. Honduras, d.1871, 12877
Cabell, Mrs. Julia (Mayo), 1783
Cabell, Mrs. Margaret Couch (Anthony) 1814-1882, 21824
Cabell, Nathaniel Francis, 1807-1891, 21825
Cabello, Henry, 19639
Cabello de Balboa, Miguel, 16th cent., 21826
Cabin and gondola, 11198
The cabin and parlor, 10509
The cabin book, 10717
The Cabinet, 1784
The cabinet conference, 21827
The cabinet organ, 9581
Cabinet work, Kentucky, 14800
Cable, George Washington, 1844-1925, 3417; The Grandissimes, 5025
Cables, Submarine, Atlantic, 531, 532, 11520
Cabot, James Elliot, 1821-1903, 108, 1785, 6267
Cabot, John, d.1498, 1261, 22285
Cabot, Sebastian, ca.1474-1557, 1261, 22285
Cabral, Eunice de Manso, 19604
Cabral, Leonor Scliar, 20091
Cabral, Octaviano, 19605
Cabral, Plinio, 19606
Cabrera, Luis, 6268
Cabrera, Miguel, 1695-1768, 1786
Cabrera, Pablo Felix, 23538
Cabrera, Pancho, 19607
Cabrera, R., 19202
Cabrera Acevedo, Gustavo, 18984
Cabrera Malo, José Joaquín, 19639
Cabrera y Quintero, Cayetano, d.1775, 1787, 6269
Cacao, 20420, 23519
Cacao, Cuba, 20686
Caccia, Antonio, 1788
Cacciamani, Miguel A., 20547
Cáceres, Esther de, 18070
Cáceres de Díaz, Lyda, 19608
Cáceres Freyre, Julián Bernardo, 19609, 19610
Cachet, 9723
Los caciques, 19967
Cacoethes scribendi, 10730
Caddell, Cecilia Mary, d.1877, 1789
Caddy, Alice, illustr., 2860

77

O cadeado negro, 19477
Cademartori, José, 19611
Cadernos de folclore, 18175, 19810
Cadet days, 10111
Cadet life at West Point, 2481
Cadillac, Antoine de la Mothe, 1656(ca.)-1730?, Fiction, 6520
Cadiz, Diego Jose de, 1743-1801, 6270
Cadiz, Ky., Economic condition, 14537
Cadogan, George, 2879
Cadwalader, John, 1742-1786, 1790
Cadwalader, John, 1805-1879, 24071
Cadwell, Charkes K., 2880
Cady, Daniel Reed, 1813-1879, 1791
Cady, John Henry, 1846-, 16119
Caeiro, Olivio, 19612
Caesar, Caius Julius, 102?-44 B.C., 17991
Caesar's column, 9412
Caffese, Maria Esther, 19613
Caffrey, Andrew, 24072
Cage-birds, 23093
Cagliero, Juan, 1838-1926, 18419
Cahaba, Ala., Military prison, 3812
Cahoone, Sarah S., 1792
Caillet-Bois, J., 19614
Caillot, Severin, 19615
El caiman barbudo, 19616
Cain, Joseph, 2881
Cain against Abel, 2298
Caines, George, 1771-1825, 1793
Caird, Sir James, 1816-1892, 6271
Cairnes, John Elliott, 1823-1875, 1794, 24073
Cairo, Ill., 1795
Cairo city property, Cairo, Ill, 1795
Caius Gracchus, pseud., 24074
Caja de Prevision de la Marina Mercante Nacional, 20145
Caja de Prevision de la Marina Mercante Nacional. Sección Tripulantes de Naves y Operarios Marítimos, 20145
Cajina-Vega, Mario, 1930-, 19617
Cakes and ale at Woodbine, 1975
Calamy, Edmund, 1671-1732, 1796, 23306
Calatayud y Borda, Cipriano Gerónimo, 1735-1814, 1797
Calavar, 1332
Calazar canino, 18139
Calculations on American population, 23792
Caldano, Julio, 19618
Caldas, Celso, 19619
Caldeira, Admardo Terra, 19620
Caldeira, Clovis, 19621
Caldera, Rafael, 19622, 19623
Calderón, Arturo, 19624
Calderón, Félix Antonio, 1890-1923, 19625

Calderón, Fernando, 1809-1845, 19626
Calderón, Fray Francisco Santiago, bp., d.1736, 6275
Calderón, Jacinto, 6276
Calderón, José B., 19627
Calderón, Juan Alonso, 6277
Calderón Amaya, Luis Jesus, 19628
Calderon de la Barca, Frances Erskine (Inglis), 1804-1882, 1798, 6272, 6273
Calderón de la Barca, Pedro, 1600-1681, 6274
Calderón de Muñoz, Alba Rosa, 19629
Calderón de Meto Caballero, Maria, 19630
Calderón Otondo, Fernando, 19631
Calderón Quyano, José Antonio, 19632
Calderón Vega, Luis, 19633
Calderoni, A.V., 19634
The Calderwood secret, 10045
Caldwell, Charles, 1772-1853, 1799, 1800, 2882-2888, 13752-13773
Caldwell, Howard Walter, 1858-, 16120, 17260
Caldwell, James, d.1770, 23477
Caldwell, James Fitz James, 2889
Caldwell, John D., 13826
Caldwell, John Edwards, 1769-1819, 2890
Caldwell, John H., 1820-, 24075
Caldwell, Joseph Blake, d.1811, 1801
Caldwell, Samuel Lunt, 1820-1887, 1802
Caldwell, William, 14276
Caldwell family, 14888
Caldwell, Kansas, History, 16548
Caldwell Co., Ky., Description, 14913, 15085
Caleb Krinkle, 9057
Caleb West, master diver, 5192
Calef, John, 1725-1812, 1803
Calendar, Mayan, 6135, 18887
Calendar, Mexican, 6644, 7932
Calendar of Maryland state-papers, Index to, 149
Calendario manual y guía universal de forasteros en Venezuela para el año 1810, 19635
Calendars, 18163, 19420
Calendrier de Philadelphie, 793
Calero, Orlando, 19636
Calero y Moreira, Jacinto, 7463
Calhoun, John Caldwell, 1782-1850, 499, 965, 3720, 5946, 8232, 12444, 12610, 12626, 22705 24076, 24077, 24554, 24827, 25102, 25769
Calhoun, William Barron, 1796-1865, 23253
Calhoun, Ky., Economic condition, 14541; History, 15024
Cali, Colombia. Universidad del Valle, 19638, 19859; Departamento de Bibliotecas, 19637; Oficina de Planeación Universitaria, 19638
Calico, 11075
Calico, Forrest, 1885-, 14970

California, 2486, 11394, 13261, 15837,
16190, 16303, 16357, 16513, 16535,
16582, 16587, 16706, 17078, 17130,
17505, 17822, 17823; (ship), 6624;
Antiquities, 16741, 17265, 17621,
17622, 17938; Archives, 16460; Bar,
17607; Bibliography, 15905, 17088, 17789;
Biography, 15906, 16089, 16334, 16612,
16653, 16862, 16879, 17354, 17427,
17667, 17693, 17702, 17883; "Boom,"
1886, 17818; Boundaries, 16611, 16865;
Centennial celebrations, etc., 17789;
Climate, 16633, 17471, 17472;
Constitution, 1804, 16124, 17753;
Constitutional history, 16833;
Description & travel, 550, 2132, 2491,
2498, 2555, 2575, 2576, 2597, 2624, 2668,
2711, 2846, 2891, 3018, 3047, 3105, 3117,
3420, 3459, 3515, 3541, 3631, 3730, 3740,
3772, 3955, 4068, 4139, 4213, 4372, 4398,
4715, 4756, 4922, 4931, 5060, 5125, 5145,
5301, 5336, 5351, 5410, 5492, 5588, 6027,
6400, 6401, 7057, 7256, 7371, 7913, 8038,
8157, 8158, 8175, 8406, 8407, 10355,
11834, 15823, 15883, 15886, 15890, 15898,
15899, 15903, 15905, 15935, 15937, 15942,
15958, 15973, 15976, 15996, 16016, 16032,
16048, 16055, 16081, 16122, 16128, 16130,
16131, 16145, 16159, 16161, 16178, 16181,
16182, 16190, 16193, 16199, 16200, 16202,
16206, 16208, 16222, 16228, 16233, 16253,
16259, 16286, 16324, 16359, 16374, 16386,
16432, 16434, 16442, 16454, 16461, 16482,
16488, 16492, 16494, 16495, 16496, 16505,
16518, 16512, 16533, 16540, 16617, 16623,
16657, 16668, 16682, 16711, 16715, 16717,
16735, 16736, 16753, 16791, 16797, 16806,
16809, 16815, 16836, 16837, 16851, 16863,
16870, 16877, 16878, 16896, 16897, 16898,
16899, 16907, 16915, 16934, 16935, 16950,
16954, 16957, 16963, 17007, 17022, 17025,
17026, 17029, 17034, 17054, 17055, 17056,
17067, 17069, 17133, 17134, 17189, 17214,
17215, 17243, 17244, 17245, 17246, 17249,
17250, 17280, 17281, 17305, 17327, 17328,
17369, 17381, 17382, 17383, 17393, 17417,
17419, 17421, 17444, 17472, 17481, 17489,
17503, 17510, 17529, 17537, 17546, 17557,
17559, 17562, 17567, 17572, 17585, 17588,
17589, 17592, 17594, 17618, 17643, 17659,
17662, 17734, 17735, 17742, 17745, 17757,
17758, 17765, 17800, 17803, 17805, 17842,
17844, 17849, 17853, 17854, 17887, 17903,
17913, 17919, 17925, 18886, 20660, 22822,
23562; Description & travel, Guide-books,
3735; Description & travel, Maps, 16534;

Description & travel, Views, 16650, 16712,
17613, 17831; Directories, 17131, 17397,
17398, 17513; Economic conditions, 16254,
16504, 17585, 17702, 17718; Families,
Periodicals, 24853; Fiction, 4499, 16664;
Fruit industry, 16194; Genealogy, 16089;
Genealogy, Societies, 16132; Geology, 17879;
Gold, 17676; Gold discoveries, 550, 2132,
3220, 3730, 3740, 4372, 5078, 5351, 5410,
5758, 8157, 8158, 10501, 11394, 13261,
15808, 15837, 15966, 15976, 16018, 16065,
16086, 16128, 16139, 16149, 16157, 16358,
16359, 16386, 16417, 16435, 16493, 16494,
16501, 16505, 16520, 16525, 16540, 16587,
16673, 16709, 16736, 16790, 16836, 16929,
16954, 16961, 17013, 17069, 17100, 17124,
17133, 17189, 17204, 17246, 17346, 17358,
17359, 17376, 17477, 17505, 17567, 17571,
17594, 17601, 17616, 17662, 17664, 17806,
17830, 17834, 17850, 17872, 17908, 17926,
23562; Gold discoveries, Fiction, 15904,
17833; Golden jubilee, 17296; Governor,
1851-1855 (John Bigler), 2891; History,
5406, 6101, 7842, 15874, 15905, 15906,
15909, 15975, 16127, 16145, 16213, 16217,
16230, 16272, 16311, 16334, 16340, 16360,
16262, 16459, 16472, 16488, 16510, 16559,
16561, 16638, 16639, 16653, 16654, 16655,
16656, 16669, 16683, 16699, 16701, 16717,
16789, 16792, 16844, 16845, 16850, 16862,
16906, 16931, 17027, 17099, 17124, 17177,
17220, 17230, 17282, 17285, 17296, 17344,
17345, 17364, 17423, 17477, 17486, 17503,
17533, 17534, 17549, 17556, 17576, 17615,
17618, 17675, 17693, 17743, 17766, 17798,
17895, 17898, 17927, 24853; History   To
1840, 21953; History, 1840-1850, 22208;
History, To 1846, 3420, 16155, 16176, 16210,
16496, 16595, 16829; History, 1846-1850,
3151, 3962, 11842, 16610, 17073, 17600;
History, 1849-1856, 20660; History,
Bibliography, 16281; History, Civil war,
17377; History, Societies, 16129, 17639;
History, Religious, 17712; Industries and
resources, 16123; Lands, 16423, 16783,
16991, 17689, 17817; Legislature. Senate.
Committee on Internal Improvements, 2892;
Maps, 15947; Militia, 17656; Missions,
16160, 17054, 17206, 17302, 17496, 17827;
Politics & government, 11552, 11692, 12362,
15944, 16039, 16149, 16343, 16559, 16610,
16683, 16750, 16936, 17006, 17075, 17306,
17380, 17523, 17584, 17773, 23879, 23936,
23976, 24106, 24479, 24525, 24721, 24974,
25090, 25215, 25350, 25387, 25417, 25427,
25484, 25822, 25900; Politics & government,

Civil war, 1685, 16015; Social life & customs, 8878, 10501, 12841, 15969, 16018, 16071, 16388, 16521, 16955, 17286, 17336, 17403, 17756, 17908, 17928; State board of agriculture, 11282; State College, San Francisco. Library, 19640; State library, Sacramento. Sutro branch, San Francisco, 6278; State University, San Diego. Library, 18238; Surveys, 3541; University. Advisory Mission. Colombian Higher Education Project, 20294; University. Library. Bancroft collection, 17739; University, Los Angeles. Latin American Center, 19641, 20409
California: an Englishman's impression of the Golden state..., 16899
California and India in romantic aspects, 17336
California and its gold mines, 217, 17505
California and its missions, 16217
California and its resources, 17585
The California and Oregon trail, 4705
California and the Californians, 16907
California as I saw it..., 22822
California as seen by a pioneer, 1850-1900, 17590
California coast trails, 16181
California desert trails, 16182
California genealogical society, 16132
California gold, 16065
California guide book, 17327
California, Gulf of, 2003, 6955
California: her wealth and resources, 17601
California in 1837, 16454
California in 1850, 5301
California in 1867-1868, 16032
California in the years 1843, '44, and '45, 17735
California infantry, 1st regt., 1861-1865, 17377; Company K., 17378
California: its gold and its inhabitants, 16836
California, Lower, 15843, 16073, 17822, 17823; Description & travel, 7174, 15905, 16768, 16951, 23562; History, 15907, 16210, 16217, 16535, 16768, 17549; Indians, 15895; Mines and mining, 17755
California Northwestern Railway vacation 1905, 16131
California notes..., 17765
The California of the padres, 16829
California of the south, 17037
The California overland express, 5336
California pastoral, 15905
California revisited 1858-1897, 16934
California sketches, 3549, 16178, 16521
California, Southern, 16090, 17037, 17271

17644, 17819; Antiquities, 16749; Biography, 16091, 16652, 16653; Description & travel, 6087, 6088, 16692, 17681, 23506; Description & travel, Guide books, 16880; History, 16653; History, Societies, 17645
California. Supreme court, 17380
California, the cornucopia of the world, 16122
California, the land of the sun, 15886
California the wonderful, 17130
California three hundred and fifty years ago, 9068
California today, 15823
California trails, 16668
A California tramp and later footprints, 16935
California under Spain and Mexico, 1535-1847, 17586
California welcomes you, 17613
California's El Dorado yesterday and today, 16890
The Californiacs, 16863
The Californian Crusoe, 4948
Californiana: and sketches of the southwest, 16048
The Californians, 16518
Californians and Mormons, 16374
La Californie et les états du Pacifique, 17026
Californien unmittelbar vor and nach der entdeckung des goldes, 17034
Californiens gegenwart und zukunft, von J. Hoppe, 16815
Calisto y Melibea, amantes cortesanos, 18059
Calkiní, Códice de, 20230
Calkins, Franklin Welles, 1857-, 16133
Call, Richard Ellsworth, 1856-1917, 3949, 13774-13777
Call, Richard Keith, 1791-1862, 21828, 24078
The call of the Cumberlands, 13732, 14053
A call to the unfaithful professors of truth, 12083
Calla-Lilies and Hannah, 9575
Callan, John F., 1805
Callcott, Maria (Dundas) Graham, lady, 1785-1842, 6279
La calle de San Francisco, 6473, 20481
La calle de Valverde, 18621
Calleja, Felix María, conde de Calderón, viceroy of Mexico, b.1750, 1759
Callender, James Thomson, 1758-1803, 1806-1811, 11757, 21878; The history of the United States for 1796, 12604; Political progress of Great Britain, 1932
Callender, John, 1706-1748, 1812
Callender, John, 1772-1833, 1813
Callicot, Theophilus Carey, b.1826, 1814
Callison, John James, 1855-, 16134
A calm observer, 24835

A calm review of the measures employed in
the religious awakening in Boston, in
1842, 22008
Calmon, Pedro, 19642
Calny, Eugenia, 1930-, 19643
Caloca Laurias, Ramiro, 19644
Calonge, Jesús Hidalgo, 19966
Caloya, 10783
The Calumet, 1815
Calvache, Antonio, 19645
Calvento y Machuca, D. Mártires, 19646
Calvert, George Henry, 1803-1889, 1816
Calvert, Henry Murray, 2893
Calvert family, 1603
Calvert of Strathore, 3639
Calviello, Beatriz O., 19647
Calvin, George, 1875-1928, 6461
Calvinism, 11896, 22561
Calvo, A., 19064
Calvo, Joaquín Bernardo, 1857-1915, 6280
Calzada, Bernardo María de la, 20391
Calzada Bolandi, Jorge, 19648
Calzada G., José Jesús, 1950-, 19649
Calzadella, Juan, 19651
Calzadella Núñez, Ramon, 19652
Calzadiaz Barrera, Alberto, 19650
Camacho, Simón, 19653
Camacho Camacho, Hipolito, 19654
Camacho Guizado, Eduardo, 19655
Camacho Henriquez, Guillermo, 19656
Camacho Perea, Miguel, 19657
Camacho Roldán, Salvador, 1827-1900,
2894, 6281
Camacho y Palma, José, 6160
Cámara, Arruda, 19658
Cámara, J. Mattoso, 19659
Cámara, Jaime de Barros, Cardinal, 1894-,
19660
Cámara Cascudo, Luis da, 1899-, 19661,
19662
Cámara Oficial Española de Comercio en lo
Estados Unidos Mexicanos, 18981
Camarero, Antonio, 19663
Camargo, Cándido Procopio, 19664
Camargo, Enaura Maria de Pádua, 19665
Camargo, Jerónimo de, 6282
Camargo, Joracy, 1893-1973, 19666-19668
Camargo, José Francisco de, 19669, 19670
Camargo, Juan, 8008
Camargo, Lenita Correa, 19671
Camargo Piñuela, Sergio, 19672
Camarlinghi Rosas, José, 19673
Los camarones comerciales de la familia
Penaeidae de la costa atlántica de
América del Sur, 19186
Cambreleng, Churchill Caldom, 1786-1862, 1817

Cambridge, Mass., History, 12864
Camden, 4336
The camel hunt, 9488
Camelback mountain, 10052
Cameron, Agnes Deans, 6283
Cameron, Allan, 1818
Cameron, Archibald, 1771-1836, 2895, 2896
Cameron, Mrs. Charlotte (Wales-Almy), 6284
Cameron, Donald Roderick, 1834-, 8148
Cameron, Edward Robert, 1857-, 6285
Cameron, Hugh, 21829
Cameron, Kenneth Walter, 1908-, 6286
Cameron, Rebecca, 5148
Cameron hall, 9269
Camillus, pseud., 12801
Caminha, Pedro Vaz de, 15th cent., 11230
Caminhos brasileiros, 18035
Caminhos da evangelização; para o batismo,
crisma e Eucaristia, 19674
Caminos, 7105
Los caminos de México, 7481
Caminos, Roberto, 19675
Caminos de Artola, Aurora Rosa, 19676
Camisa, Zulma C., 19677
Camison, Rosendo, 6287
Cammarota, Federico, 19678
Camões, Luís de, 1524-1580, 19264
Camões e o Jáo, 17959
Camp, George King, 2897
Camp, Henry Ward, 1839-1864, 5471
Camp, Phineas, 1788-1868, 11657
Camp and field life of the Fifth New York
volunteer infantry, 3177
Camp and prison journal, embracing scenes
in the camp, on the march, and in prisons,
22211
Camp, court and siege, 3895
Camp, field and prison life, 5628
Camp-fire and cotton field, 4192
Camp fires in the Canadian Rockies, 7063
Camp fires of the confederacy, 14777
Camp fires of the red men, 10450
Camp Ford prison, 3684
Camp life in Florida, 3759
Camp-life in the Adirondacks, 10398
Camp, march and battle-field, 5275
Camp Nelson, Ky., 14739
Camp Nelson's long and varied history in
beginning a new chapter, 13778
Camp Pleasant Branch, Franklin County, Ky.,
14430
The camp, the bivouac, and the battlefield,
2567
The campaign in Illinois, 7284, 24727
Campaign literature, 1800, Democratic-
Republican, 1344, 1345; Federalist, 1910

Campaign literature, 1801, Federal, New York (state), 12598
Campaign literature, 1808, Democratic, Republican, 94
Campaign literature, 1824, Adams, 2190; Clay, 96; Jackson, 13455, 23825, 23915
Campaign literature, 1828, Democratic, 935, 24278
Campaign literature, 1829, Republican, Rhode Island, 12798
Campaign literature, 1832, National Republican, 12106
Campaign literature, 1840, Democratic, 24416; Whig, 1680, 22378, 22462, 25589
Campaign literature, 1844, Democratic, 25574; Liberal Party, 24143; Whig, 24122
Campaign literature, 1848, Democratic, 22085, 24276; Free-soil, 13168, 25174; Whig, 23205, 25845
Campaign literature, 1852, Whig, 1087
Campaign literature, 1854, Republican, Massachusetts, 25647
Campaign literature, 1855, Republican, Ohio, 24113
Campaign literature, 1856, Democratic, 1371, 5406, 5559, 11550, 23943, 24571, 25613; Republican, 3024, 6095, 11378, 13176, 24222, 24482, 24818, 25281, 25286, 25326, 25372, 25481, 25841
Campaign literature, 1857, Democratic, Minnesota, 25400
Campaign literature, 1858, Democratic, 24324
Campaign literature, 1859, Democratic (Southern), 12369; Republican, 24863
Campaign literature, 1860, Constitutional union, 13945, 23993; Democratic, 6565, 7818, 7892, 8200, 24336, 24376, 25237, 25895; Democratic (Northern), 410; Democratic (southern), 1163, 22137, 24014, 24242, 24258, 25714; Free constitutionalists, 89; Republican, 210, 499, 1307, 1717, 2477, 6098, 6288, 7043, 7840, 8088, 8430, 24042, 24679, 25307, 25371, 25458, 25652, 25727, 25813, 25906
Campaign literature, 1862, Democratic, 24277; Democratic, New York, 22936
Campaign literature, 1863, Democratic, New York, 21920; Republican, 13203; Republican, Pennsylvania, 25270, 25920
Campaign literature, 1864, Democratic, 1367, 2076, 6566-6572, 7156, 7293, 7355, 7720, 11915, 11981, 22803; Republican, 1533, 1593, 2082, 5838, 6416, 6437, 6957,

7214, 7292, 7497, 7742, 8138, 8329, 12370, 22078
Campaign literature, 1866, Republican, 10230
Campaign literature, 1868, Republican, 11669, 12782, 24787
Campaign literature, 1900, Democratic, 7377; Republican, 7294
The campaign of 1860, 6288
The campaign of the Forty-fifth regiment, Massachusetts volunteer militia, 3958
Campaign sketches of the war with Mexico, 22413
Campaign songs, 1844, Whig, 13392
Campaign songs, 1860, Republican, 1677, 1305
Campaign songs, 1868, Republican, 12782
Campaign songs, 1879, Greenback, 5143
Campaigning against the Sioux, 16908
Campaigning with Crook, 10112
Campaigns in Virginia, Maryland, etc., 1849
The campaigns of Walker's Texas division, 273
Campamento, 19967
Campanella, Tommaso, 1568-1639, 1819
Campanha, Vilma Alves, 19950
A campanha abolicionista (1879-1888), 25076
Campanha integrada de reflorestamento; manual 1966-1968, 19680
Campanha Nacional de Alimentação Escolar, 182
Campanhole, Adriano, 19341
Una Campaña parlamentaria, 24079
Campaña Barrera, Anibal, 19679
Campbell, A.W., 2898
Campbell, Alexander, 1788-1866, 6300, 7378, 7658, 13779, 14207, 15442, 21914
Campbell, Alexander, 1788-1866. Tract for the people of Kentucky, 24021
Campbell, Charles, 1807-1876, 1232, 1820, 11658
Campbell, Dugald Forbes, 1866
Campbell, George, 1719-1796, 1821
Campbell, Sir George, 1824-1892, 2899
Campbell, Hardy, 4215
Campbell, James, 1822
Campbell, John, bookseller, Philadelphia, 182
Campbell, John, paper dealer, New York. Considerations and arguments..., 83
Campbell, John, 1708-1775, 13509, 21830
Campbell, John Archibald, 1811-1889, 2900
Campbell, John Campbell, 1st baron, 1779-1861 24080
Campbell, John Charles, 1867-1919, 2901
Campbell, John Francis, 2902
Campbell, John Kerr, 6289
Campbell, John Lyle, 1818-1886, 2903
Campbell, John Nicholson, 1798-1864, 21831
Campbell, John Poage, 1767-1814, 2904, 13780
Campbell, John Richard, 21832

Campbell, John Wilson, 1782-1833, 2905
Campbell, Laurence Dundas, 11456
Campbell, Lewis Davis, 1811-1882, 24081
Campbell, Patrick, 6290
Campbell, Reau, 6291, 6292
Campbell, Robert, 1808-1894, 6232, 16135
Campbell, Robert J., 1837-1927, 2945
Campbell, Scott, pseud., 9343
Campbell, T.C., 15180
Campbell, Thomas, 1777-1844, 1824
Campbell, W.P., 6293
Campbell, William Carey, 16136
Campbell, William Henry, 1808-1890, 21833
Campbell, William W., 1806-1881, 11778
Campbell Co., Va., 14845
Campe, Joachim Heinrich, 1746-1818, 21834
Campello, Alberto Jose, 19681
The camphene lamp, 9877
Campillo, Gines, 6294
Campina do Monte Alegre, 18162
Campina Grande, Brazil, History, 18165
Campinas, Brazil, Description, 19684;
  History, 19584; Instituto Agronomico
  do Estado de Sao Paulo, 19682, 19683;
  Prefeitura Municipal, 19684
Camping, 16616
Camping and cruising in Florida, 3838
Camping in Colorado, 16616
Camping out in California, 17489
Campino Vidal, José Miguel, 19685
Campion, J.S., 16137
Campisteguy, Juan, Pres. Uruguay, 19686
Campo, Estanislao del, 1834-1880, 18931
Campo, Luis del, 19687
Campo del Pozo, Fernando, 19688
Campo Lacasa, Critina, 19689
Campobello, Nellie. Cartucho, 19967;
  Las manos de mama, 19967
Campos, Alberto L., 19690
Campos, Asterio, 19691
Campos, Dea Regina Bouret, 19692
Campos, Eduardo, 1923-, 19693
Campos, Fernando Arruda, 19694
Campos, Geir, 1924-, 19695, 19696
Campos, Gerardo, 19697
Campos, José Maria Moreira, 1914-, 19698
Campos, Julieta, 19699
Campos, Martin, 19700
Campos, Maximiano, 1941-, 19701, 19702
Campos, Milton, 19703
Campos, Noêmia Simões de, 19704
Campos, P.N., 19705, 19706
Campos, Paulo de Almeida, 19707
Campos, Renato Carneiro, 19708-19710
Campos, Roberto, 19400
Campos, Sabino de, 1893-, 19711

Campos, Theresa Catharina de Goes, 19712
Campos Andapia, Antonio, 19713
Campos Carvalho, M. Vicentina, 19246
Campos Harriet, Fernando, 19714
Campos Jiménez, Carlos María, 19715
Campos Leão, José Joaquim de, 1829-1883,
  19716, 19717
Campos-Menéndez, Enrique, 1914-, 19718
Camprubi Alcazar, Carlos, 19719
Camps and prisons, 3307
Campuzano, Severino, 7752
Camuel, Cynthia H., 14668
Camus, Albert, 1913-1960, 20074
Can abolitionists vote or take office under
  the United States Constitution? 25260
O cana-de-açúcar em Minas Gerais, 20556
Canaan, Me., History, 12657
Canada, 1541, 2385, 4363, 6295, 6147, 6666,
  7923, 11336, 11601, 12372, 12588, 12749,
  12825, 12833, 13005, 22935, 22997, 23072;
  Archives, 6296, 6297; Army, 6129; Auditor-
  general's office, 6298; Bibliography, 2217;
  Biography, 1238, 6532; Boundaries, Alaska,
  6053, 6054, 6181; Boundaries, U.S., 1334;
  Census, 8129; Church history, 5227;
  Civilization, 6735; Climate, 2118; Colonies,
  7979; Commerce, 1633, 12079; Commerce,
  New York (State), 22730; Commerce, U.S.,
  893, 2007, 5534, 12738, 12954; Commercial
  policy, 1633, 12544; Courts, 334; Department
  of Agriculture, 6299, 8240; Department of
  Justice, 6300, 6301; Department of Marine
  and Fisheries, 6302, 6303; Department of
  Militia and Defence, 6304; Department of
  public works, 6748, 6749; Department of the
  Interior, 6305, 6310, 8372; Department of
  the Interior. Natural resources intelligence
  branch, 6306; Description & travel, 25, 147,
  344, 345, 347, 440, 441, 669, 1291, 1738,
  1852, 1992, 2502, 2536, 2549, 2562, 2573,
  2504, 2716, 2722, 2734, 2742, 2763, 2814,
  2862, 2902, 2944, 2964, 3064, 3109, 3176,
  3179, 3253, 3256, 3385, 3396, 3400, 3551,
  3555, 3632, 3641, 3687, 3720, 3734, 3738,
  3761, 3784, 3837, 3881, 3891, 3921, 3952,
  3991, 4047, 4078, 4138, 4202, 4266, 4268,
  4288, 4319, 4357, 4397, 4421, 4432, 4439,
  4496, 4511, 4514, 4522, 4536, 4569, 4574,
  4585, 4644, 4681, 4710, 4722, 4750, 4751,
  4789, 4806, 4807, 4840, 4959, 5051, 5408,
  5456, 5458, 5462, 5464, 5485, 5570, 5571,
  5670, 5671, 5681, 5894, 5895, 5915, 5924,
  5926, 2927, 2928, 2929, 5990, 6039, 6057,
  6074, 6104, 6126, 6127, 6146, 6147, 6186,
  6187, 6200, 6239, 6241, 6242, 6260, 6261,
  6271, 6289, 6290, 6310, 6313, 6317, 6319,

6320, 6321, 6322, 6323, 6324, 6325, 6436, 6440, 6463, 6511, 6512, 6517, 6547, 6548, 6550, 6557, 6576, 6577, 6578, 6588, 6589, 6590, 6591, 6624, 6634, 6639, 6641, 6703, 6704, 6718, 6727, 6748, 6749, 6768, 6780, 6825, 6829, 6843, 6844, 6858, 6880, 6884, 6885, 6911, 6922, 6932, 6945, 6946, 6947, 6998, 7012, 7016, 7017, 7046, 7054, 7081, 7134, 7170, 7171, 7172, 7173, 7199, 7203, 7210, 7222, 7223, 7224, 7225, 7229, 7240, 7243, 7244, 7252, 7254, 7266, 7272, 7314, 7344, 7345, 7346, 7347, 7350, 7367, 7372, 7373, 7413, 7438, 7454, 7549, 7556, 7557, 7558, 7559, 7628, 7638, 7766, 7799, 7808, 7841, 7862, 7899, 7922, 7967, 7970, 8023, 8042, 8114, 8121, 8129, 8149, 8160, 8201, 8225, 8226, 8228, 8229, 8238, 8246, 8259, 8320, 8321, 8325, 8338, 8356, 8359, 8360, 8361, 8362, 8363, 8364, 8370, 8379, 8390, 8410, 8413, 8417, 8418, 11292, 11352, 11365, 11380, 12566, 12854, 13337, 13444, 16212, 16643, 17098, 17440, 21791, 21874, 22697, 22751, 23476, Gazetteers, 7331, Guide-books, 2147, 2550, 2551, 4614, 5726, 5916, 5917, 5918, 5978, 5979, 6090, 6091, 6130, 6308, 6318, 6551, 6675, 7267, 7748, 8388, 8389, 12092, 12846, 12852, 22909, Maps, 6807, 7764, Maps, Bibliography, 6296, 8210, Periodicals, 6307, Views, 3733, 6307, 7597; Economic conditions, 519, 1240, 2195, 3641, 6310, 7078, 7428, 8022; Emigration & immigration, 1095, 1291, 2195, 4847, 6132, 7367, 7979, 8091, 8240, 8370, 11601, 12092, 12350, 12372; Emigration & immigration, History, 7198; Exploring expeditions, 3200, 3878, 4685, 6302, 6303, 6312; Genealogy, Dictionaries, 8153; General Sources, 8129; Geological survey, 6308; History, 1441, 1978, 6130, 6131, 6146, 6231, 6239, 6278, 6825, 6829, 6903, 7062, 7193, 7361, 7367, 7550, 7593, 7808, 7809, 7841, 8023, 8224, 11760, 12826, 22979; History, To 1763 (New France), 25, 647, 1239, 2972, 3597, 3990, 4051, 6126, 6396, 6443, 6599, 6649, 6703, 6735, 6737, 7197, 7222, 7223, 7224, 7692, 7767, 8129, 8197, 8338, 8401, 13046, 22697, 22751; History, To 1763 (New France), Fiction, 1858, 1859, 6520, 6622, 7467, 7688; History -1755-1763, 6148, 6397, 8412, 8413, 8414; History, 1755-1763, Sources, 23222; History, 1763-1867, 1242, 6149, 7613, 8333, 11396; History, 1763-1867, Sources, 6007; History, 1763-1791, Sources, 23222; History, 1841-, 6574; History, 1867-, 7776; History, 19th cent., 6532; History, Addresses, Essays, lectures, 7525; History, Fenian invasions, 1866-1870, 6038; History, Fiction, 6379, 8955, 9972; History, Periodicals, 6307; History, Rebellion, 1837-1838, 2202, 6647, 6996, 6997, 8333, 9972, 10915, 12031, 12784, 17286, 22945; History, Sources, 7149; Intellectual life, 1240, 6133; Laws, statutes, etc., 6309; Mail, 6555; Maps, 14471; National development bureau, 6306; Northern Co-ordination and Research Centre, 7328; Parliament. House of Commons. Select standing committee on banking and commerce, 6309; Parliament. Senate. Select committee on resources of territory between Labrador and the Rocky Mountains, 6310; Parliament. Select committee on Rupert's Land, Red River, and North-west territory, 6311; Politics & government, 1841, 6259, 6647, 8042; Politics & government, 1841-1867, 22879; Politics & government, To 1763, 11882; Politics & government, 1763-1867, 899, 22905; Politics & government, 1763-1791, 23222, 23224; Politics & government, 1775-1783, 2130; Politics & government, 1781-1841, 6648, 6996; Politics & government, 1791-1841; 13512, 23051; Politics & government, 1828-1838, 12031; Politics & government, 1837-1838, 1180, 11807, 12319; Politics & government, 1841-1867, 2386, 6285, 6549, 11344; Politics & government, 1867-, 7776, 8042, 8370; Politics & government, 1867-1914, 13035; Provincial secretary's office, 3200, 3881, 6312, 6313; Railroads, 6320; Royal Canadian mounted police, 6995, 8106; Secretary of State, 6314-6316; Social life & customs, 4397, 6634, 6892, 7046; Statistics, 6127; Surveys, 8372; U.S., 13446
Canada and the Canadian question, 8042
Canada and the twentieth century, 7428
Le Canada français, 6307
Canada in the twentieth century, 6147
Canada: past, present, and future, 8048
Canada: the country, its people, 7350
Canada, the new nation, 8370
Canada west and Hudson's Bay company, 5812
Canada's fertile northland, 6310
The Canadas in 1841, 11365
Canadia, 1130
Canadian Alpine journal, 6317
Canadian ballads, and occasional verses, 22873
The Canadian captive, 9977
The Canadian controversy, 12031
Canadian folk life and folk-lore, 6892
The Canadian guide book, 6318
The Canadian halfbreed rebellions of 1870 and

1885, 16438
Canadian invasion, 1775-1776, 571, 2367,
  11680, 12780; Fiction, 9986
Canadian nights, 6641
The Canadian northwest, 7641
The Canadian Pacific, 6320
The Canadian Pacific Railway Company, 6176,
  6319-6323, 6704, 6748, 6749, 17849;
  Colonization Dept., Calgary, 6323
The Canadian Pacific Rockies, 6324
Canadian pictures, 5926
Canadian poetry (collection), 22095
Canadian Rocky Mountains, 6086
A Canadian tour, 6325
The Canadians of Oregon, 17120
The canal-board, 10904
Canal Concepción y Canal oeste, 20130
Canal Murray, 20131
Canal policy of the state of New York,
  21835
Canale, Michele Giuseppe, b.1808, 727
Canale de Dotto, Isidora, 19720
Canals, Georgia, 709; Indiana, 13081;
  Maryland, 12691, 23221; New York (state),
  21835; Pennsylvania, 21842, 23221; U.S.,
  473, 2471, 5340, 23779; Virginia, 22670
Canals, Interoceanic, 1861, 12454
The canary family, 10730
Canary Islands, 11381; Description &
  travel, 24, 21783; History, 24
Canby, Margaret T., 21836
The cancelled will, 9442
Canchalagua, 16582
Cancino, Luis A., 19721
Canción famosa a un desengaño, 5938
Cancionero, 17992
El cancionero infantil de Hispanoamérica,
  18056
Canciones de viento, 18563
Candace, 9254
Candelas, José B., 19722
Candia, N.H., Genealogy, 12000; History,
  12000
Candidius, Georgius, 12067
Cândido de Mello e Souza, Antônio, 1918-,
  19723
Candidus, pseud., 24833
Candioti, Alberto Maria, 1889-, 19724
Candler, Isaac, 2906
Candler, John, 1787-1869, 24082
The Cane Ridge Meeting House, 14940, 15292
Canedo M., Oscar Justiniano, 19725
Canewood, 14104
Canfield, Chauncey de Leon, 1843-1909, 16139
Canfield, Delos Lincoln, 1903-, 19726
Canga, Pedro, 20055

Canigonet, merchant in Haiti, 6326
Canisius, Theodor, 6327
Cann, Marion Stuart, 13781
Cannabis indica, 10249
Cannabis sativa, 8516
Canning, George, 1770-1827, 2420, 12115, 24083
Cannon, Arthur, reporter, 25897
Cannon, Frank Jenne, 1859-, 16140, 16141
Cannon, J.P., 2907
Cannon, Joseph Gurney, 1836-1926, 7530
Cannon, Mrs. Lucretia P. (Hanly), 10405
Cannon, Miles, 16142
Cano, Juan, 6329
Cano, Juan Sebastien del, 1526, 7567
The canoe and the saddle, 8403
The canoe Aurora, 4583
A canoe voyage up the Minnay Sotor, 2237
Canoes, 1898
Canoes and canoeing, 11636
Canolles: the fortunes of a partisan of '81,
  9104
Canon family, 7435
Canon law, 7732
Canonge, Louis Placide, 1822-1893, 2908
Canons of the Diocese of Lexington, 15203
Canosa Capdeville, Tamandu, 19728
Canot, Capitaine, pseud., 24187
Canova, Andrew P., 2909
Canseco Vincourt, Jorge, 19729
Cansinos Assens, Raphael, 1883-, 7893
Cant, 4275
Cantel, Raymond, 19730
Cantigas que o vento leva, 19711
Canto, Gilberto de Ulhoa, 19309
Canto a la amada viva y muerta, 18099
Canto a la ciudad de los cuatro nombres, 18383
Canto a los hijos, 19076
El canto cuencano, 20476
O canto do cisne negro, 20514
Canto solar a Venezuela, 18534
Canton, Alfredo, of Panama, 19731
Canton, Conn., Genealogy, 21816
Cantonwine, Alexander, 16143
Cantos de Cifar, 20683
Cantos del oriente venezolano, 19833
Cantos del trópico, 18519
Cantos Navideños en el folklore Venezolano,
  18392
Cantrill, James Campbell, 1870-1923, 15619
Canyon and crater, 16016
Canyons of the Colorado, 17422
Cañas y Villacorte, José Simeón, 1767-1838,
  23873
Cañedo, Estanislao, 1825
Cañizales Márquez, Jose, 19727
Cañizares, Jose de, 1676-1750, 6328

Cap and bells, 4730
Cap Polonio, 6939
Cap sheaf, 9872
Caparroso, Carlos Arturo, 19732
Cape, Wilson, 16144
Cape Breton, 11336, 23193; Description
& travel, Maps, 11707
Cape Cod, Description & travel, 2328,
22938
Cape Cod and all along shore, 10427
Cape Cod ship canal, 23261
Cape of Good Hope, Description & travel,
24489
Capela, José das Neves, 20554
Capen, Nahum, 1804-1886, 24084
Capers, Gabriel. Bondage a moral institution,
24407
Capers, Henry Dickson, 1835-1910, 2910
Capers, William (port.), 14995
Capistrán Garza, René, 19733
Capital, 19807, 25797
A capital federal, 18656
Capital punishment, 456, 22150, 23259,
24179, 25925
Capitalism, 18638
Capitalismo, comunismo y libertad, 18338
Capitan, Louis, 1854-1929, 24085
The capitol quick step, 14194
Capitols, 15406
Capoeira (Dance), 19810
Capote F., Fausto, 19179
Cappelletti, Angel J., 19734, 19735
Cappelletti, Mauro, 19736
Capron, Elisha S., 16145
Capron family (Ranfield Capron, 1683-1752),
22522
Capsadell, Lou, pseud., 9726
Captain Blake, 10113
Captain Brand, of the "Centipede", 11195
Captain Close, 10114
Captain Dreams, 10115
Captain Eli's best ear, 10896
Captain Gray's company, 3322
Captain Hall in America, 1260
Capt. James Box's adventures and explorations
in new and old Mexico, 6139
Captain Jeff, 17121
Captain Jim's friend, 6970
Captain Jinks, 10863
Captain John Baptiste Saucier at Fort
Chartres in the Illinois, 5226
Captain Kidd's money, 10909
Captain Kyd, 4000, 9979
Captain Santa Claus, 10113
Captain Tom: a resurrection, 10427
Captain Velasco; and the young lieutenant,

9988
The captain's lady, 14242
The captain's romance, 4903, 10598
The captain's story, 5447, 10338
The captive, 10827
The captive boy in Terra del Fuego, 12637
The captive boys of Rensselaerville, 10570
The captive in Patagonia, 11409
A captive of war, 3983
The captives, 24102
The captivity in Babylon, 1902
The capture, the prison pen, and the escape,
3621
Capture and escape, 4142, 16986
Capture at sea, 12667, 12669, 22342, 23011,
23144, 23145
The capture, death and burial of J. Wilkes
Booth, 5987
Captured by the Indians, 16150
The captured dream, 9580
Captured in escaping, 9251
A captured Santa Claus, 25187
Capturing a locomotive, 4805
The Capuchin, 14243
Capuchins, 5809; Missions, 1899, 18543, 19527
Capuchins in Brazil, 1899
Capuchins in Venezuela, 18543, 19527, 19855
Cara sucia, 19673
Carabantes, José de, 1628-1694, 19855
Carabela, 18377
Carabobo, Battle of, 1821, 19077
Caracas, 18540; Cathedral. Cabildo, 19737,
19738; Description, 19639, 19754; History,
18535, 19485; Museo de Bellas Artes, 19198;
Museo Nacional de Bellas Artes, 19739,
19740; Universidad Central, Bibliography,
19742-19744, 19746; Universidad Central,
Centro de Estudios Literarios, 19741;
Universidad Central. Consejo de Desarrollo
Científico y Humanístico, 19742-19747;
Universidad Central. Escuela de Periodismo.
Cuaderno, 18219; Universidad Central.
Facultad de Arquitectura, 19748; Universidad
Central. Facultad de Arquitectura y
Urbanismo, 19749; Universidad Central.
Facultad de Derecho, 19750; Universidad
Central. Facultad de Derecho. Colección de
estudios jurídicos, v.26, 18051; Universidad
Central. Facultad de Derechos. Colección
Tesis de doctorado, 19480; Universidad
Central. Instituto de Antropología e
Historia, 19751; Universidad Central.
Instituto de Antropología e Historia.
Serie de fuentes históricas, 18388;
Universidad Central. Instituto de
Antropologia e Historia. Serie de historia

18539; Universidad Central. Instituto
de Estudios Políticos, 19752; Universidad
Central. Instituto de Investigaciones
Económicas, 17952, 17953; Universidad
Central. Instituto de Investigaciones de
Prensa, 19753
Caracas à través de los tiempos, 19754
Caraffa, Vincent de, 24691
Caraguatatuba, Brazil, 20677
Caram Mafud, Carlos, 19755
La caraota y otras leguminosas de grano en
Venezuela, 19771
Caratteri di alcuni nuovi generi e nuove
specie di animali e piante della Sicilia,
15223
Caraway, Thaddeus Horatius, 1871-1931, 5834
Carayon, Auguste, 1813-1874, 19756
Carballedo, Emilio, 1925-, 19757-19759
Carballo Hernández, Miguel Angel, 19760
Carbonell, Diego, 1884-1945, 19761
Carbonieri, José Fernando de Mafra, 19762
Carbutt, Mary (Rhodes), Lady, "Mrs. E.H.
Carbutt", 6330
Cárcamo Tercero, Hernán, 19763
Cárcano, Miguel Angel, 1889-, 19764, 19765
The Carcellini emerald, 9762
Carciente, Jacob, 19766
Carden, Allen D., fl.1837, 2911
Cárdenas, Pedro de, 6677-6679, 6687
Cárdenas C., Antonio Luis, 19767
Cárdenas Espinoza, Eliecer, 1950-, 20649
Cárdenas Valdez, Rigoberto, 19768
Cardiel Reyes, Raul, 19769
The cardinal's daughter, 5611
The cardinal's snuff box, 9739
Cardome; a romance of Kentucky, 25055
Cardona, Adalberto de, 6331, 6332
Cardona, Miguel, 1903-1964, 19770
Cardona-Álvarez, Canuto, 1919-, 19771
Cardona Peña, Alfredo, 19772
Cardoso, Eleyson, 19501
Cardoso, Fernando Henrique, 19773, 19774
Cardoso, Lucio, 1913-1968, 19775
Cardoso, Ofélia Boisson, 19776-19778
Cardoso, Roberto N., 19779
Cardot, Carlos Felice, 19780, 19781
Cardoza y Aragón, Luis, 1904-, 19782
Cardozo, Efraim, 1906-, 19783
Cardozo, Flávio José, 19784
Cardozo, Jacob Newton, 11659, 21840
Cardozo, Lubio, 19785-19787
Cardozo Gonzales, Armando, 19788
Care, Henry, 1646-1688, 11660
The care and use of the county archives of
California, 16125
Carew, Bampfylde-Moore, 1693-1758, 2912, 4275

Carey, Charles Henry, 16146
Carey, Eustace, 1791-1855, 21841
Carey, Henry Charles, 1793-1879, 24086
Carey, John L., 24087; Slavery in Maryland,
25614
Carey, Mathew, 1760-1839, 273, 295, 2913,
11373, 11661, 13284, 13496, 21842-21848
Carey, William, 1761-1834, 21841
Carey's American pocket atlas, 2913
Carib Indians, 397, 574, 11414, 23517
Carib Indians in Brazil, 20540
Carib language, Dictionaries, 4998
Caribbean area, Bibliography, 20371;
Economic policy, Bibliography, 19791;
Politics, 19822; Research, 19792; Social
policy, Bibliography, 19791
Caribbean Commission, 6333, 19789
Caribbean Conference on Mental Health, 19790
Caribbean fruit fly, 20076
Caribbean Organization, 19791
Caribbean Scholars' Conference, 10th, 19792
Caribbean sea, 7533, 7917, 18375; Maps, 7995
Caribbean studies, 18604
Caribbean tourist trade, 6333
Caribbeana 1900-1965, 20371
Cariboo, The...gold fields of British Columbia,
11662
Cariboo district, 17113
La caricatura política argentina, 18011
Caricature, Argentine Republic, 18011
Caricatures and cartoons, 7537; U.S., 24819
Carilla, Emilio, 19792-19799
Carillo Sánchez, Jaime, 19602
Caring for no man, 10550
Carita, 4744
Caritat, H., 1244
Carl Werner, 10769
Carlé, Erwin, 1876-1923, 2914
Carles, Rubén Dario, 6334
Carleton, 11175
Carleton, Clifford, illustr., 9581
Carleton, George Washington, pub., 25657
Carleton, James Henry, 1814-1873, 2915, 2916,
6335
Carli, Gileno de, 19800, 19801
Carlier, Auguste, 1803-1890, 1826, 11663
Carlile, John Snyder, 18-7-1878, 25770
Carlile, Thomas, 1792-1824, 11664
Carlin, Thomas, 13288
Carlisle, George William Frederick Howard,
7th earl of, 1802-1864, 2917, 13782
Carlos IV, king of Spain, 1748-1819 - Poetry,
7626
Carlotina and the Sanfedesti, 9497
Carlotta's intended, 5310
Carlton, Ambrose B., 16147

87

Carlton, Robert, pseud., 12554
Carlyle, Thomas, 1795-1881, 11665, 24088, 25690; Latter-day pamphlets, 25925
Carmagnani, Marcello, 19802
Carman, Bliss, 1861-1929, 14466
Carman, Louis Dale, 1860-, 6336-6338
Carmela, 10966
Carmelites, Discalced, 7520
Carmen miserabile, a solemn lacrymatory for the grave of Jonathan Marsh, 21849
Carmen's inheritance, 5419
Carmichael, Mrs. A.C., 6339
Carmichael, Elizabeth, 19803
Carmichael, Sarah E., 6340
Carnahan, David Todd, 1820-1901, 6341
Carnahan, James, 1775-1859, 13275
Carnegie, James, 1827-1905, Earl of Southesk, 6342
Carnegie Institution of Washington. Department of Economics and Sociology, 14284
Carneiro, André, 19804, 20623
Carneiro, Cyro de Athayde, 1899-, 19805
Carneiro, David, 1904-, 19806-19809
Carneiro, Edison, 19810-19812
Carneiro, Eryma, 19309
Carneiro, Levi, 1882-, 20630
Carneiro, Octavio Augusto Dias, 1912-, 19813
Carneiro, Victor Ribas, 19814
Carneiro Campos, Renato. See Campos, Renato Carneiro.
Carneiro Leão, Antonio, 1887-, 2918
Carnero Checa, Genaro, 19815
Carnes, J.E., 24089
Carnesworthe, pseud., 11666
Carnival, Nevis, 17955; Tobago, 17955, 17956
El carnival de Oruro y el proceso ideológico e historia de los grupos folklóricos, 18967
Carnochan, Janet, 6532, 24090
Caro, Miguel Antonio, pres. Colombia, 1843-1909, 19143, 19816, 19817, 20715, 20717, 20718
Carochi, Horacio, d.1662, 7667
Carolana, 3103
Carolina, 491, 2560, 24852; Description & travel, 4629; Proprietors, 24852
Carolina chronicle, 4075
Carolina Constitution, 3860
Carolina described more fully than heretofore, 2919
Carolina sports, 3369
Carolina sports by land and water, 12048

Caroline, 16075
Caroline Nichols, 10310
Caroline Wilhelmina, queen consort of George II, king of Great Britain and Ireland, 1683-1737, 23338
Carolinian, pseud., 25806
Caroni, Italo, 19818
Carpeaux, Otto Maria, 1900-, 19819
Carpenter, Francis Bicknell, 1830-1900, 6343
Carpenter, George W., 1802-1860, 11667
Carpenter, Hugh Smith, 11668
Carpenter, Lewis C., 16148
Carpenter, Matthew Hale, 1824-1881, 11669
Carpenter, Philip Pearsall, 1819-1877, 11670
Carpenter, Sandra, 13783
Carpenter, Stanley B., 13784
Carpenter, Stanley S., 14390
Carpenter, Stephen Cullen, d.ca.1820, 11671
Carpenter, Thomas, 2337
Carpenter, William Henry, 1813-1899, 484-486, 11672, 11673
Carpenter, William W., 6344
Carpentier, Alejo, 19820
The carpetbagger, 4904
Carpio, Adolfo P., 19821
Carpio Castillo, Ruben, 19822
Carr, Clark Ezra, 1836-1919, 6345, 6346
Carr, Ellwood J., 14047
Carr, John, 11674, 16149
Carr, Julian Shakespeare, 1845-1924, 6347
Carr, Patrick, d.1770, 23477
Carr, Spencer, 1811-1880, 11675
Carranza, Luján, 19823
Carranza, Roque G., 19824
Carranza, Venustiano, pres. Mexico, 1859-1920, 6268
Carrasco, 25555
Carrasco, Pedro, 19825
Carrasco Puente, Rafael, 1902-, 19826, 19827
Carrasquera, Susana Noemi, 19828
Carrasquilla, Tomas, 19829, 19830
Carrazedo, Renato Octavio, 19831
Carreira, Antonio, 24091, 24092
Carreño, Alberto María, 1875-, 6835, 19832
Carreño, F., 19833
Carreño, Teresa, 8292
Carreño Latorre, Hector, 19834
Carreño Luengas, Alfredo, 19835
Carrera, Daniel P., 19836
Carrera Andrade, Jorge, 1903-, 19837
Carrera Bascuñán, Helena, 19838
Carrera Damas, German, 19747, 19839-19842
Carrera Stampa, Manuel, 19843
Carretera panamericana, 18629, 19001
Carriage friends, 9802
The carriage-lamps, 9216

Carried by storm, 9523
Carrier, A.H., 13785
Carrigan, Mrs. Wilhelmina (Buce), 16150
Carril, Bonifacio del, 19844
Carrillo, Alonso, 6348
Carrillo, Crescencio, 7836
Carrillo, José, 6349
Carrillo, Mariano, 6350
Carrillo Batalla, Tomas Enrique, 19845,
   19846
Carrillo Blanco, Fidencio, 19847
Carrillo de Córdoba, Fernando, 6011
Carrillo de Córdoba, Hernan, 6011
Carrillo E., Francisco Eduardo del,
   19848, 19849
Carrillo Flores, Antonio, 19850
Carrillo Laso de la Vega, Alonso, 1582-
   1647, 5998
Carrillo y Gabriel, Abelardo, 19851
Carrington, Frances (Courtney), 16151
Carrington, Henry Beebee, 1824-1912,
   16152
Carrington, John W., 11676
Carrington, Mrs. Margaret Irvin (Sullivant),
   1831-1870, 16153
Carrio de la Vandera, Alonso,b.ca.1706,
   19852
Carrión, Alonso, 6354
Carrión, Antonio, 8441
Carrizo Inostroza, Mireya, 19853
Carro, José Manuel, 20528
Carro Carro, Mario César, 19854
Carrocera, Buenaventura de, 19855
Carroll, Anna Ella, 1815-1894, 6094, 6351,
   11677-11679
Carroll, Charles, 1737-1832, 5030, 11680
Carroll, Chuck, 13786
Carroll, George Ryerson, 1831-1895, 16154
Carroll, Joseph Cephas, 24093
Carroll, Mary Puis, 16155
Carroll, Thomas F., 19856
Carroll O'Donoghue, 9491
Carson, Andrew Carlisle, 16156
Carson, Christopher, 1809-1868, 2581,
   2796, 2856, 2920, 4759, 14350, 15805,
   17379, 17545
Carson, James H., d.1853, 16157
Carson, Thomas, 16158
Carstarphon, James E., 16159
Cartagena, Colombia, History, Sources,
   20018; Siege, 1741, 573, 13334
Cartaginese, Martha S., 19857
Cartago, Costa Rica, 5845
Carter, Abdiel, 3747
Carter, Charles Franklin, 16160, 16161
Carter, Clarence Edwin, 2523

Carter, Howell, 2921
Carter, James Gordon, 1795-1849, 23263
Carter, Joseph Coleman, 1808-1875, 15561
Carter, Robert, pub., New York, 2212
Carter, Robert T., 15400
Carter, Roland, 15766
Carter, Tom, 13787, 13788
Carter, William Giles Harding, 1851-1929,
   16162, 16163
Carter Cave, Ky., 14914
Carter County, Ky., Maps, 14590
Carter Quarterman, 8653
Carthage, Colonies, 13425; History, 23570
Cartier, Jacques, 1827
Cartier to Frontenac, 8401
Cartilla electoral, 19024
Cartilla patriótica, 19489
A cartografia da região amazônica, 18029
La cartographie de Mammonth Cave (Kentucky),
   13774
Cartucho, 19967
Cartwright, David W., 16164
Cartwright, Peter, 1785-1872, 2922, 13789,
   23479, 23554
Caruthers, William Alexander, 1802-1846,
   2923-2925
Carvajal, Mario, 1896-, 19858, 19859
Carvajal de Arocha, Mercedes, 19860
Carvalhal, Tânis Franco, 20091
Carvalho, Afranio de, 19861
Carvalho, Alfredo de, 18681
Carvalho, Benedito de, 19863
Carvalho, Cônego José Geraldo V. de, 19864
Carvalho, Doris de Queiroz, 19865
Carvalho, Elias Pessoa de, 19866
Carvalho, Eloisa de, 19281
Carvalho, Hervasio Guimarães de, 19867-19869
Carvalho, José Augusto, 19870
Carvalho, Marceleno de, 19871
Carvalho, Maria do Ceu, and Agostinho Dias
   Carneiro, 19872
Carvalho, Mercedes Cardozo Pessoa de, 19873
Carvalho, Rodrigues de, 1905-, 19874, 19875
Carvalho, S.N., 2926
Carvalho, Tito, 19876
Carvalho, Vicente Augusto de, 1866-1924, 20233
Carvalho, Arp Procopio de, 19862
Carvalho de Mendonça, José Xavier, 19877
Carvalho e Silva, Maximiano de, 19878
Carvalho Lopez, Octacileo de, 19879, 19880
Carvalho Neto, Paulo de, 1923-, 19881-19885
Carvallo Concha, Adolfo, 19886
Carvallo Hederra, Sergio, 19887, 20146
Carvallo Salazar, José Leonardo, 19888
Carver, Hartwell, 16165
Carver, Jonathan, 1710-1780, 2927, 11681,

89

11682
Carver, Robin, 11683
Carver, William F., 1840-, 6353
Cary, Alice, 1820-1871, 2531, 2928-2932
Cary, Lott, 1780-1828, 12508
Cary, Phoebe, 1824-1871, 2531, 2928, 2931, 2933
Cary, Richard Leander, 1854-1918, 14746
Cary, Thomas Greaves, 1791-1859, 11684-11686
Casa Braccio, 6492
Casa Calderón, Angel Ventura Calderón, marqués de, 8277
Casa de Rui Barbosa, Rio de Janeiro, 19878
Casahonda, Jorge, 7320
Casalbon y Geli, Rafael, 1729-1787, 399
Casamiquela, Rodolfo M., 19889-19891
Casanate, Luis de, 6354
Casanova, Eduardo, 19639
Casares, Manuel José, 6160
Casas, Bartolomé de las, bp. of Chiapa, 1476-1566, 6355-6363, 19892-19894, 22401, 24094, 24095
Casas, Felipe de las, d.1732, 6378
Casas Grieve, Luis Felipe de las, 19895
Casas Mota y Flores, Lucas de las, 6364
Casasanta, Tereza, 19897
Casasús de Sierra, Margarita, 19898
Cascade Cave, Ky., 14914
Cascade range, 16972
Cascavel (Ceará), Economic policy, 20013
Cascia, Adolfo, 19899
Casco Bay, Me., 6030, 21973
Cascudo, Luis de Câmara, 1899-, 19900
Case, Alden Buell, 1851-1932, 19901
Case, Charles, b.1817, 11687
Case, Francis M., 3255
Case, J.I., threshing machine co., Racine, Wis., 9078
Case, Wheeler, d.1793, 11688
Casement, Gray, 1870-, 6724
Casey, Alfredo, 19902
Casey, Charles, 2934
Casey, Joseph, 1814-1879, 11692
Cashew nut industry - Brazil, Northeast, 18779
Casimir Leautaud, Jean, 19903
Casket of reminiscences, 3496
Caskoden, Edwin, pseud., 10309
Casler, John Overton, 1838-, 2935
Casler, Melyer, 2936
Caso, Antonio, 1883-1946, 16577, 18616
Caspipina s letters, 11990
Cass, Lewis, 1782-1866, 5693, 6450, 21850, 22447, 24098, 24946, 25484

Cass, Norma, 13790
Cass County, Mich., History, 23547
Cassani, Jorge Luis, 19904
Cassani, Joseph, 1673-1750, 19905
Cassani, Juan Emilio, 20203
Cassas, Luis Augusto, 1953-, 18310
Casseday, Benjamin, 2937
Cassegrain, Arthur, 21851
Cassell, John, 1817-, 2938
La cassette verte de monsieur de Sartine, 23701
Cassidy, Samuel M., 13791
Cassidy family, 13791
Cassin, John, 1813-1869, 675
Cassini, Jean Dominique, comte de, 1748-1845, 6400, 6401
Cassiodorus, Flavius Magnus Aurelius, Senator, ca. 487-ca. 583, 13792
Cassius Marcellus Clay, 2898
Cast adrift, 8560
Castagnino, Raul H., 19906, 19907
Castaigne, A., illustr., 6492
Castaneyra, Isidro Alphonso de, 6365
Castanha do Pará, 18275, 19440
Castañé Recoud, Carlos, 19908
Castañeda, Francisco, 19909
Castañeda, Francisco de Paula, 1776-1832 - Drama, 18980
Castañeda, Gabriel Angel, 19910
Castañeda Alarcón, José A., 19911
Castaño, Luis, 19912
Castaño, Emilio, 17993
Castaño Rodriguez, Jesús, 19913
Casteel, J. Doyle, 19914
Castelar y Ripoll, Emilio, 1832-1899, 7794, 24099
Castelfuerte, José de Armendáriz, marqués de, viceroy of Peru, 6366-6368
Castell, William, d.1645, 21852
Castellano, Enrique, 19915
Castellanos, Alfredo, 19916-19919
Castellanos, Diego Luis, 19920
Castellanos, Juan de, 1522-1607, Language, 18192, 19921
Castellanos, Luis, 19922
Castellanos, Zulma J.A. de, 19923, 19924
Castellanos de Losada, Basilio Sebastian, 1807-1891, 592, 596
Castellanos García, Gerardo, 1879-, 6369
Castelli, Eugenio, 19925
Castello, Jose Aderaldo, 19926
Castello, Lucia, 19927
Castello Branco, José Moreira Brandão, 19928
Castello Branco, Manoel Ihomaz, 19929

Castelman, Richard, 2986, 21910
Castelnau, Francis, comte de, 1812-1880, 2939, 11693, 21853
Castelo, Jose Aderaldo, 19930, 19931
Castera, Jean Henri, b.ca. 1755, 13411
Castiglioni, Luigi, conte, 1756 or 1757-1832, 2940
Castilla Rosa Pérez, Elías, 19932
Castillero, Andres, 1166
Castillero Pimentel, Ernesto, 1912-, 19933, 19934
Castillero Reyes, Ernesto de Jesús, 1889-, 19935
Castillo, Benjamin E. del, 2941
Castillo, Carlos José del, 19936
Castillo, Domingo B., 19937
Castillo, Eduardo, 1889-, 19938
Castillo, Eladio A. del, 1867-1960, 19781
Castillo, F., 6371, 6372
Castillo, Martin del, d.1680, 6373, 6374
Castillo, Pedro del, 17th century, 6276
Castillo de Herrera, Alonso de, 6370
Castillo F., Victor M., 19939
Castillo Ruiz, Rafael de, 19940
Castillo y Guevara, Francisca Josefa de, 19941
Castillo y Piña, José, 6375
Castine, 8632
Castiñeira de Dios, José Maria, 19942
Castiñeiras, Pedro F., 19943
The casting away of Mrs. Lecks and Mrs. Aleshine, 10887
Castle Dismal, 10770
Castle Nowhere, 11205
Castle Thunder (Confederate prison), 2048
Castleman, Alfred Lewis, 1809-1877, 21854
Castleman, John Breckinridge, 1841-1918, 24100
Castler Crosier, 8843
Castles in the air, 9059, 10554
Castles near Spain, 9740
Casto, William T., 1824-1862, 13872
The Casto-Metcalfe duel, 13872
Castonnet des Fosses, Henri Louis, 1840-1898, 19944
Castorena, José de Jesús, 19945
Castorena y Ursúa, Juan Ignacio de, 1668-1733, 6754
Castrillo, Hernando, 1586-1667, 6376
Castrillón Muñoz, Aurelio, 19946
Castro, Américo, 1885-, 19947
Castro, Carlo Antonio, 19948
Castro, Casimiro, 6815
Castro, Claudio de, 19949, 19950
Castro, Dolores, 19951
Castro, Henry, 1786-1865, 2942

Castro, Ida María Groen Caiado de, 19983
Castro, José Antonio, 19952-19954
Castro, José Félix, 19955
Castro, Lorenzo, 6377
Castro, Luis de, 6378
Castro, M. Vianna de, 19956
Castro, Manuel de, 1898-, 19957
Castro, Mauro Cunha Campos de Moraes e, 19958
Castro Aguirre, Constancio de, 19959
Castro Alves, Antonio de, 1847-1871, 19960-19962
Castro Bastos, Leonidas, 19963-19965
Castro Contreras, Jaime, 19966
Castro Leal, Antonio, 7891, 19967, 19968
Castro Najera, Miguel Antonio, 19969
Castro Paes Barretto, Fernando de, 24101
Castro Pineda, Lucio, 19970
Castro Romero, Jorge, 19971
Castro Saavedra, Carlos, 19972, 19973
Castro Viana, Djalma, 1900-, 19974
Castro y Bachiller, Raymundo de, 19975
Casudo, Luis da Câmara, 19976
Caswall, Henry, 1810-1870, 2943, 2944, 11694, 11695
Caswell, Alexis, 1799-1877, 11696
The cat who lives at Ashland, 15370
The cat-fight; a mock heroic poem, 22901
Catá, Alvaro, d.1908, 19977
Catalán, Hilda, 19978
Catalani, Wally R., 19979
Catalano, Edmundo Fernando, 19980
Catalano, Luciano R., 19981
Cataldi D., Alberto, 19982
Catalogaçao simplificada usada na Biblioteca Publica do Estado, 19983
Cataloging, 19983
Cataloging of lantern slides, 19539
Catalogs, Booksellers, 21855; U.S., 11697
Catalogs, Library, 12727
Catalogs, Publishers', U.S., 21859
Catamarca, Argentina, Social life and customs, 19131
The catastrophe, 8951
Catcott, Alexander, 11698
Cate, Wirt Armistead, 1900-, 2945
Catechism of the Diocese of Lexington with a map of the Diocese, 13748
Catecismo de geografía de la República Mexicana, 5977
Catesby, Mark, 1683-1749, 1828, 2946
Catfish catching squirrels, 10310
Catharine, 8471
Cathcart, Almira, d.1869? 8553
Cathcart, James Leander, 1767-1843, 24102
Cathcart, John, 1829
A cathedral courtship, 11157

Catherwood, Frederick, 1830
Catherwood, Mary (Hartwell) 1847-1902, 6379
The Catholic chapter in the history of the
  U.S., 12990
Catholic church. Archdiocese of Belo
  Horizonte, Directories, 19984; Biography,
  7770; Clergy, 7993; Collected works,
  7733; Conferencia Episcopal de Colombia,
  19985; Congregatio sacrorum rituum, 6380;
  Dictionaries, 5870; Doctrinal and
  controversial works, Catholic authors,
  5870; Education, 19197; Education, U.S.,
  2000; Liturgy and ritual, 7863; Liturgy
  and ritual, Mercedarian, 6365; Liturgy
  and ritual. Ritual, 6381; Mexico. Archbishop, 6382; Missions, 651, 2366, 5227,
  6796, 6799, 7718, 8171, 17167, 17302,
  17347, 17496, 17704; Pastoral letters and
  charges, 7326, 7327, 7895, 7948; Pope,
  1644-1655, 6383; Pope, 1644-1655 (Innocentius
  X) Cum sicuti accepimus (14 May 1648), 7669;
  Pope, 1740-1758 (Benedictus XIV), 7013;
  Prayer-books and devotions, Spanish,
  7668, 8279; Sacra Rituum Congregatio, 6384,
  6385; Sermons, 1797, 7031, 20534; Society
  of Jesus, 19986
Catholic Church in Bolivia, Statistics,
  18180
Catholic Church in Brasilia, 20422
Catholic Church in Brazil, Directories,
  19984
Catholic Church in Canada, 1441, 16552,
  23029, 23224
Catholic Church in Chile, 18336, 19989;
  Comite Permanente de los obispos de Chile,
  19987; Secretariado General del Episcopado
  de Chile, 19988, 19989
Catholic Church in Colombia, 19858;
  Congresses, 19985
Catholic Church in Cuba, 18321
Catholic Church in Iowa, History, 16932
Catholic Church in Ireland, 11256, 19780
Catholic Church in Kentucky, 14357, 14873,
  15317, 15318, 15450, 15680; Missions,
  5250
Catholic Church in Latin America, 18179
Catholic Church in Louisville, Ky., 15171
Catholic Church in Mexico, 5973, 6275,
  12480, 19825, 20203
Catholic Church in Missouri, 17297
Catholic Church in Montana, 17333
Catholic Church in Nebraska, 17547
Catholic Church in New York (City), History,
  987
Catholic Church in Canadian Northwest, 16552
Catholic Church in Oregon, 15999

Catholic Church in Peru, 7770; Statistics,
  18180
Catholic Church in Puerto Rico, 19689
Catholic Church in South America, 2373
Catholic Church in Spain, 7731
Catholic Church in Spanish America, 6432, 8443
Catholic Church in the U.S., 5067, 7351, 10579
  11677, 11679, 17167
Catholic Church in Utah, 16708
Catholic Church in Venezuela, 19780, 19996;
  History, Sources, 19738
Catholic Committee of Appalachia, 13649
The Catholic emigrants, 9416
The Catholic history of North America, 22874
The Catholic Iroquois, 10730
Catholic literature, 10675
The Catholic man, 11027
Catholic missions and missionaries among the
  Indians of Dakota, 17287
The Catholic question, 14240
Catholic University of America, 5235
Catholics in Maryland, 170, 2088
Catholics in New York (City), 987, 12991
Catholics in North America, 22874
Catholics in Spanish America, 7674
Catholics in Texas, 5368
Catholics in the U.S., 121, 12990, 14240
Catineau-Laroche, Pierre Marie Sebastien,
  1772-1828, 1831
Catlin, George, 1796-1872, 1832-1838, 16166-
  16168
El catolicismo popular de los tarascos, 19825
Caton, John Dean, 1812-1895, 1410
Catskill, N.Y., 1839
Catskill association, 1839
Cattaraugus Co., N.Y., 23080; Biography, 23080
Cattaraugus County agricultural and horti-
  cultural society, 23080
Cattermole, E.G., 16169
Cattle, 4704; Argentine Republic, 18431;
  Brazil, 18750, 19408; Canada, 16288;
  North Dakota, 17674; Rio Grande do Sul,
  Brazil, Statistics, 19470; Santa Catarina,
  Brazil, Statistics, 19466
Cattle industry, Texas, 5942
Cattle ranching in McKenzie County, 17586
Cattle trade, Southwest, Old, 17086; Texas,
  16716; The West, 16835
Catto, William T., 1840
Caturelli, Alberto, 19991-19994
Cauca Valley, Climate, 20492-20494; Economic
  conditions, 19657; Social condition, 19657
Cauchon, Joseph, 1841
Caucuses of 1860, 6030
Caudevilla y Escudero, Joaquin, 6396
Caudill, Rebecca ("Mrs. James S. Ayars"), 137

Cauduro, Milia, 19995
Caughnawaga Indians, 5199
Caught in an Apache raid, 16465
Caught on the ebb-tide, 10653
Caulin, Antonio, b.1719, 19996
Caulkins, Frances Manwaring, 1795-1869, 1842, 1843
Cause and contrast, 13414
Cause and cure, 24670
The cause of it, 9330
Causten, James H., 1844
A caution to sinners against abusing the patience of God, 2259
Cautla Morclos, 7313
Cauvin, R.S., 6730
Cavada, Frederick Fernandez, 1832-1871, 1845
Cavalcante, José Candido Marques, 19997
Cavalcante, Paulo B., 19998, 19999
Cavalcanti, Clóves de Vasconcelos, 20000
Cavalcanti, Cordelia Robalinho, 20001
Cavalcanti, Emiliano di, 1897-, illustr., 18233, 20002
Cavalcanti, Pericles de Souza, 20003
Cavalcanti, Waldemiro, 18862
The cavaliers of England, 9842
The cavaliers of the Cross, 9543
The cavaliers of Virginia, 2923
Cavallin, Albano, 19674
Cavallón, Juan de, 16th cent., 17971
Cavarozzi, Marcelo, 20004
Cavazos Garza, Israel, 20005
Cave, Sally Bullock, 1865-1958, 13796
Cave-In Rock, 15686
Cave life, 15111
A caveat against unreasonable and unscriptural separations, 11699
Cavelier, Jean, 1846
Cavender, Curtis H., 1847
Caverly, Abiel Moore, 1817-1879, 11700
Caverly, Robert Boodey, 1806-1887, 11701
The Cavern of death, 10693
Caves, 15243, 15490; Kentucky, 13857, 14595, 15117, 15200
Cavling, Henrik, 1859-, 2947
Cavo, Andres, 1739-1803, 20006, 20007
Cawein, Madison Julius, 1865-1914, 2948-2956, 13798-13805, 13929, 15303, 15577
Cawles, The misses, illustr., 25189
Caxias do Sul, Brazil, History, 18020
Caxton Club, Chicago, 7282
Caxton, Laura, pseud., 9088
Cayce, Edgar, 1877-1945, 14037
Caylus, Ernest, 11703
Los cazadores primitivos en Mesoamerica, 18635

Cazalis, Oche, 20008
Cazeaux, Pierre Euryale, 615
Cazneau, Jane Maria (McManus) 1807-1878, 24103
Cazneau, Mrs. William Leslie, 2957
Cea, José Roberto, 1939-, 20009-20011
Ceará, Brazil (State). Superintendência do Desenvolvimento Econômico e Cultural, 20012, 20014; Superintendência do Desenvolvimento Econômico e Social, 20013; Universidade Federal. Departamento de Educação e Cultura, 20015; Universidade Federal. Instituto de Pesquisas Econômicas, 19462
Cecil Drieme, 11192
Cecil, E., pseud.? 11703
Cecil, Edgar Algernon Robert Gascoyne-Cecil, viscount, 1864-, 24791
Cecio, Valdelino, 1952-, 18310
Cedar, 7693
Cedar Rapids, Ia., Biography, 16154; History, 16154
Cedarholm, Rev. A., 1822-1867, 6387
Cedarholm, Caroline, 6387
Cedeño Cenci, Diógenes F., 20016, 20017
Cedulario de las provincias de Santa Marta y Cartagena de Indias, siglo XVI, 20018
Celebra la muy noble, 7478
The celebrated jumping frog of Calaveras County, 9026
The celebrity, 9002
Celeste, 19823; the pirate's daughter, 9443
The celestial railroad, 9823
Celestial wonders and philosophy, 15224
Celli, Blas Bruni, 20019
Celio, 9544
Cella, Raymond, 14520
Celtic languages, 23048
Cemeteries, East Attleborough, Mass., 11935; Military Kentucky, 13778
Cenas dos evangelhos, 18226
'Cension, 8611
Censo jeneral de la republica de Chile, 20157
Censo nacional de manufacturas [Chile], 20170
Censoria lictoria, 9471
Censoria lictoria of facts and folks, 9472
Censorship, Lexington, Ky., 15532
Censures, Ecclesiastical, 5971
Census of slaves, 1755, 25167
Cent-vingt jours de service actif, 6542
Centellas, Isabel, 20020
El centenario de "El Tradicionista," 19816
The centenary of Abraham Lincoln's birth, 7633
The centenary of Kentucky, 14092
The centenary of Wesleyan Methodism, 22653

A centenary sermon, delivered before the presbytery of Fayetteville, at the Bluff church, the 18th day of October, 1858, 22908
The centennial celebration at Cherry Valley, 11778
A centennial exhibit of education in Kentucky, 14554
The centennial history of Oregon, 1811-1912, 16581
A centennial history of Sayre School, 1854-1954..., 13873
Centennial history of the city of Washington, 6514
Centennial of Presbyterianism in Kentucky [1783-1883], 13806
Centennial preview (University of Kentucky), 14647
Centeola, 10957
Centrais Elétricas de Minas Gerais, S.A. Centro de Documentação, 20021
Central America, 442, 664, 1124, 7521, 7675, 8097, 13484; Antiquities, 1830, 7439, 18316, 18634; Antiquities, Bibliography, 19019; Bibliography, 6166, 18316; Civilization, 20484; Commerce, 18740; Description & travel, 1957, 1958, 2366, 4196, 4213, 4967, 5492, 6057, 6258, 6440, 6545, 6776, 6784, 6796, 6798, 6799, 6800, 6840, 6961, 7228, 7343, 7534, 7541, 7583, 7623, 7751, 7878, 7883, 7913, 7917, 7952, 8168, 8239, 8243, 8336, 11655, 13165, 20022, 23142; Description & travel, Guide-books, 7653; Economic condition, 7623, 18738, 18739, 18740, 20373; Economic policy, 20373; History, 6789, 8281, 13343, 16538, 18024, 18316, 18989, 23449; Politics, 5848; Literature, 20709; Politics & government, 18989; Population, 18513; Relations (general) with Spain, 20484; Statistics, 8336
Central America and its problems, 7675
Central American Bank for Economic Integration, 20022
The Central American delegation to the first constituent congress of Mexico, 18989
Central American transportation study, 20022
Central City, Col., Description, 17514
The central gold region, 3615
Central Pacific Railraod Company, 17327
Central railroad of New Jersey, 12486
Central University, Richmond, Ky., 15545
Central University of Kentucky, Richmond, Ky., 15792

Centre College. Danville, Ky., 13807, 15190, 15545; History, 15400, 20023
Centro Brasileiro de Pesquisas Fisicas, 20023
Centro Brasileiro de Pesquisas Fisicas Chacaltaya emulsion chamber experiment, etc. 20024, 20025
Centro das Industrias das Cidades Industrais de Minas Gerais, 20026
Centro de Desarrollo Industrial del Ecuador, 18278
Centro de Documentación e Información Social Cristiano, La Habana, 20027
Centro de Documentación Económico-Social, Lima, 20028
Centro de Educación Fundamental para el Desarrollo de la Comunidad en América Latina, 20029, 20030
Centro de Estudios Monetarios Latinoamericanos 19564, 20031-20033
Centro de Fomento y Productividad Industrial, Guatemala, 20034
Centro de Historia del Estado Mérida, 20035
Centro Latino Americano de Pesquisas de Ciencias Sociais, 18688, 20036-20029
Centro para el Desarrollo Económico y Social de America Latina, 20040
Centro Regional de Alfabetización Funcional en las Zonas Rurales de América Latina, 20041
Centro Regional de Educación Fundamental para la América Latina, Patzcuaro, Mexico, 18319
Centro Regional de la UNESCO..., 20042
Central Rural Universitário de Treinamento e de Ação Comunitária, 20043
Century association, New York, 11704
The century in southwest Texas, 17617
A century of caste, 25838
Century of progress, 1846-1946, 14994
Century's record of Winchester's post office, 13808
Cepeda Ulloa, Fernando, 20044
Cerámica de la luna en los Andes venezolanos, 18007
Cerámica popular do nordeste, 19161
Cerda Catalan, Alfonso, 20045
Cerda G., Enrique, 20046
Cerda G., Hugo, 20046
Cerda Silva, Roberto de la, 20047
Cereceda, Raul, 20048
Cerisier, Antoine Marie, d.1828, 11705
Cerna, Ismael, 1856-1901, 19910; La penitenciaria de Guatemala, 19901
Cerqueira Filho, Gisalio, 20049
Cerro Mercado, Mexico, 6708
Cerruti Aicardi, Hector J., 20050

Cervantes de Salazar, Francisco, ca.1514-
1575, 6388, 6389, 20051
Cervantes Saavedra, Miguel de, 1547-1616,
20052; Don Quixote, 20679
Cervantes Tapia, Onesimo, 20053
Cervantes Villarreal, Jose Rafael, 1946-,
20054
César, Guilhermino, 20055-20058
Cesnola, Luigi Palma di, 1832-1904, 11706
Céspedes, Augusto, 20059
Céspedes, Carlos Manuel de, 1871-1939,
20060
Céspedes, Ramón, 23851
Céspedes Ponce, Gicela, 1927-, 20061
Céspedes y del Castillo, Carlos Manuel de,
1819-1874, 20062
Céspedes y Quesada, Carlos Manuel de,
1871-1939, 20062
Ceuleneer, Adolphe de, 16171
Cevallos, Miguel Angel, 1887-, 20063
Cevallos Arízaga, Benjamin, 20064
Cevallos García, Gabriel, 20065
Ceylon, Description & travel, 11456
Chabert de Cogolin, Joseph Bernard,
marquis de, 1724-1805, 11707
Chabrand, Emile, 6390
Chacaltaya emulsion chamber experiment,
20024
Chace, Elizabeth (Buffum), 1806-1899,
24104
Chacel, Rosa, 1898-, 20066
Chaclan Toc, Patrocinio Francisco,
20067
Chaco, El Gran, 437, 595
Chaco Austral, Argentine republic, 13144
Chaco War, 1932-1935, 18030, 19908;
Fiction, 20059
Chacon, Dulce, 20068
Chacón y Rumbea, Luis Roberto, 20069
Chadbourne, Paul Ansel, 1823-1883,
21856
Chadwick, John White, 1804-1904, 24620
Chafee, Calvin C., b.1811, 21857
Chafee, George D., 6391
Chaffin, William Ladd, 1837-1922, 2958,
21858
Chagas, José, 20070
Chagas, Paulo Pinheiro, 20071-20073
Chagas, Wilson, 20074, 20075
Chahtima, pseud. of Adrien Emmanuel
Rouquette
The chainbearer, 9129
The chained mother, 3782
Chains and freedom: or, The life and
adventures of Peter Wheeler, a colored
man yet living, 2482?

The chairman chastised, 12468
Chaix, Paul Georges Gabriel, 1808-1901, 11708
Chalbaud Zerpa, Reinaldo, 20075
Chalk marks of overland travel Pike's Peak-
wards, 4712
Chalkley, Lyman, 13809
Chalkley, Thomas, 1675-1741, 2959
Challen, Howard, 21859
Challenger (Ship), 2108
Chalmers, George, 1742-1825, 11709, 21860-
21863
Chalmers, Lionel, 1715-1777, 2960
Chalmers, Thomas, 1780-1847, 24486
Chamberlain, Daniel Henry, 1835-190-? 6392
Chamberlain, Joseph Perkins, 1873-, 25832
Chamberlain, Leander Trowbridge, 1837-1913,
6392
Chamberlain, Leo Martin, 1896-1968, 13810
Chamberlain, Mellen, 1821-1900, 6393
Chamberlain, Nathan Henry, 6394
Chamberlaine, William W., 1836?-, 2961
Chamberlayne, Churchill Gibson, 1876-, 2962
Chamberlayne, John Hampden, 1838-1882, 2962
Chambers, D. L., 20076
Chambers, Ernest John, 1862-1925, 6310
Chambers, James, d.1801, 13886
Chambers, John, 1780-1852, 16172
Chambers, Julius, 1850-1920, 16173
Chambers, T. Bell, 13811
Chambers, William, 1800-1883, 2963, 2964,
11710
Chambers family, 16576
Chambersburg, Pa., History, 2410, 16576
Chambon, fl. 1775, 11711
Chambon, Ludovic, 6395
The Chameleon, 8967
Chamerovzow, Louis Alexis, 24034
Chamfort, Sebastien Roch Nicolas, called,
1740?-1794, 23435
Chamie, Mario, 20077
Chamier, Frederick, 1796-1870, 22674
Chamorro Rodriguez, Luis Emilio, 20078
Champ d'Asile, Tex., 5032, 17033
Champagny, Jean Baptiste Nompère de, duc de
Cadore, 1756-1834, 11712
Champigny, Jean, chevalier de, 1717-1787?,
2965, 2966
Champion, Richard, 1743-1791, 11713
The champions of freedom, 11204
Champlain, Samuel de, 1567-1635, 6396, 6443,
6599, 11714, 11715
Champlain, N.Y., 12724
Champlain, Lake , Description & travel, 22128
Champlin, James, 1821-, 2967
Champney, E. W., 10163
Champney, J. Wells, illustr., 4173, 14749

Champneys, John, fl.1775-1778, 21864
Chance compositions, 18203
A chance shot, 10669
Chancellor, Richard, d.1556, 12192
Chancellorsville, Battle of, 1863, 966, 2034, 4335, 12924
Chandler, Adoniram, 11716
Chandler, Albert Benjamin, 1898-, 14211, 15769
Chandler, Charles Frederick, 1836-1925, 11717
Chandler, Daniel, 409
Chandler, Elizabeth Margaret, 1807-1834, 2968, 2969
Chandler, James, 1706-1789, 11718
Chandler, Rev. Joseph, 24105
Chandler, Joseph Ripley, 1792-1880, 12276, 24106
Chandler, Julian Alvin Carroll, 1872-1934, 15413
Chandler, Peleg Whitman, 1816-1889, 11719, 11720
Chandler, Samuel, 1713-1775, 605, 21865
Chandler, Thomas Bradbury, 1726-1790, 11721, 11722, 13379, 13394
Chandler, Woodruff T., 1852-, 13812
Chandless, William, 2970
Chandley, Juanita K., 13813
Chaney, Elsa, 20079
Change: a poem pronounced at Roxbury, October VIII, MDCCCXXX, 22269
A change of the luck, 9533
The changed brides, 10833
Chanler, John Winthrop, 1826-1877, 21866
Channing, Edward Tyrrel, 1790-1856, 11723
Channing, Henry, 1760?-1840, 11724
Channing, Walter, 1786-1876, 11725, 21867
Channing, William Ellery, 1780-1842, 1118, 22529, 24107, 24835, 25692
Channing, William Ellery, 1780-1842. A letter to the Hon. Henry Clay, 23781; Slavery, 563, 23926, 25363
Channing, William Francis, 1820-, 11726
Channing, William Henry, 1810-1884, 11727, 23489
Chanticleer, 10324
Chao, Villar, illustr., 18546
Chap-books, 805; Brazilian, Addresses, essays, lectures, 19730
Chapais, Thomas, 1858-1946, 6397
The chapel of St. Mary, 10955
The chaperone, 7126
Chapin, Alonzo Bowen, 1808-1858, 11728
Chapin, Edwin Hubbell, 1814-1880, 11729, 21868, 24475
Chapin, Frederick Hastings, 16174

Chapin, Orange, b.1790, 11730
Chapin, Stephen, 1778-1845, 11731
Chapin, William, 1802-1888, 21869
Chapin family (Samuel Chapin, d.1675), 11730, 11732
The Chapin gathering, 11732
A chaplain's campaign with Gen. Butler, 12986
The chaplains and clergy of the revolution, 12775
Chapleau, Joseph Adolphe, 6398, 6399, 8231
Chaplin, Charles, 1889-, 6562
Chaplin, Jeremiah, 1776-1841, 21841
Chaplin, William Edwards, 16175
Chaplin, William Laurence, b.ca.1798, 24097
Chapman, Anne MacKaye, 1922-, 20080
Chapman, Charles Edward, 1880-1941, 16176, 16442
Chapman, Frederick William, 1806-1876, 21870
Chapman, George Thomas, 13814
Chapman, Henry Samuel, 1803-1881, 11733
Chapman, Isaac A., 11734
Chapman, J. Linton, illustr., 11196
Chapman, John Gadsby, 1808-1889, 11735
Chapman, John Jay, 1862-1933, 24108
Chapman, Mrs. Maria (Weston) 1806-1885, 11736, 11737
Chapman, Nathaniel, 1780-1853, 11671
Chapman, Robert D., 1839-, 2971
Chapman, Samuel, 1859-1943, 20081
Chapman, Samuel D., 16177
Chapman, Silas, 11738
Chapman, Virgil Munday, 1895-1951, 15620
Chapman publishing company, Chicago, pub., 17413-17415
Chappaqua, N.Y., 9036
Chappe d'Auteroche, Jean, 1728-1769, 6400, 6401
Chappell, Edward, 1792-1861, 21871, 21872
Chappelsmith, John, 11739
Chappert, Jacques, 20082
The character of Abraham Lincoln, 7702
The character of Rev. John Eliot, D.D., 12168
A character of the province of Maryland, 2515
Characteristics, 10366
Characters, 11741
Characters versus farmers, 15459
Charcoal, 19506
Charcoal sketches, 10414
Chard, Thomas S., 16178
Chardon, Daniel Marc Antoine, 1730-1795?, 11742
Chardon, Roland Emanuel Paul, 20083
Charette, 10691
A chariot of fire, 25023
Charitable societies, 21070
Charity, 1990, Addresses, essays, lectures, 11340

The charity "boom", 9056
Charity Green, 9795
Charity's reward, 9844
Charlecote, 11183
Charles, Cecil, 6402
Charles Elwood, 8886
Charles Hess, 10827
Charles Hopewell, 4713
Charless, Joseph, 1772-1834, 7380
Charless' Kentucky, Tennessee, and Ohio
    almanac, 13815, 13816
Charleston, Max, 13817
Charleston, S.C., 8237, 24109, 24110;
    Census, 1848, 11744; Citizens, 24111;
    City Council, 11744, 24111; City
    Council. Committee on ways and means,
    11745; Description, 4146, 4178;
    Description, Guide-books, 4428;
    Directory, 1756; Fire, 1861, 12959;
    History, 3530, 21840, 24995; History,
    Revolution, Fiction, 10774; Magnolia
    cemetery, 5158; Meeting on Religious
    Instruction of Negroes, 24112; Siege,
    1780, 5493, 12932; Siege, 1863, 2037,
    4650, 25039; Slave insurrection, 1822,
    25278; Unitarian church, 11746
Charleston, Mass., City council, 704;
    First church, 1653, 1654; History, 914,
    2350; McLean asylum for the insane, 2359;
    Ursuline convent, 9586, 10070; Water
    supply, 704
Charlevoix, Pierre François Xavier de,
    1682-1761, 25, 2972, 6403, 6404, 20084,
    21873, 21874
Charley Reynolds, 17474
Charlie Whittler's Christmas party, 10465
Charlotte Temple, 10676
Charlotte's daughter, 10677
Charlton, Edwin Azro, 1828-1896, 11747
Charlton, William Henry, 2973
Charlton de Rivero Palacio, Frances, 1904-,
    19015
Charmingfare, 12000
Charnay, Désiré, 1828-1915, 6405-6409
Charpenne, Pierre, 6410
Charria Angulo, Pedro Manuel, 20085
Charrney, Theodore S., 6411
Charrúa Indians, 18010
Charry Lara, Fernando, 20086
Charter and by-laws of the Polytechnic
    society of Kentucky, 13818
The charter of the corporation of Trinity
    church defended, 12817
The charter of the rector and inhabitants
    of the city of New York, 12817
The chartered millions; Rhodesia and the

challenge to the British commonwealth, 24564
The chartered rag light, 14468
Charteris, 10341
The Charters of the British colonies in
    America, 11748
Charton, Édouard Thomas, 1807-1890, 11749
The chase, 9134
Chase, C. Thurston, b.1819, 11750, 21876
Chase, Charles Monroe, 16180
Chase, Ezra B., 11751
Chase, Francis, 11752
Chase, Franklin Henry, 1864-, 25584
Chase, George Wingate, 1826-1867, 11753, 12943
Chase, Henry, 11754
Chase, Henry B., 2218
Chase, Horace, 1788-1875, 11755
Chase, Joseph Smeaton, 1864-, 16181, 16182
Chase, Loring, 10197
Chase, Lucien Bonaparte, 1817-1864, 2974,
    21875
Chase, Mary M., 1822-1852, 21876
Chase, Moses, 1797-1878, 25856
Chase, Philander, bp., 1775-1852, 2975-2977
Chase, Pliny Earle, 1820-1886, 11756
Chase, Salmon Portland, 1808-1873, 2978,
    6698, 21877, 24113, 24114, 24151, 25171,
    25391, 25532
Chase, Samuel, 1741-1811, defendant, 11757,
    21878
Chase, Simeon B., 25223
Chase, Thomas, 1827-1892, 6412
Chase, Warren, 1813-1891, 11758
Chasles, Philarète, 1798-1878, 11759, 11760,
    21879
Chastellux, François Jean, marquis de, 1734-
    1788. Voyage dans l'Amérique Septentrionale,
    2979, 11521, 13009, 21880, 23618
Château d'Or, 9892
Chateaubriand, François René, vicomte de,
    1768-1848, 20087, 21881
Chateaugay region, 12630
The chatelaine of Burnt Ridge, 6973
The chatelaine of La Trinite, 9590
Chatham (ship), 8283
Chattanooga, 10056; Battle of, 1863, 23429
Chattanooga railroad expedition, 1862, 3417,
    4805, 5737
Chatterjee, Sudhananda, 1912-, 6413
Chatterton, Augustus, 21882
Chaudron, Mrs. Adelaide de Vendel, 11761,
    21883
Chaudron, Jean Simon, 21884
Chaudron's spelling book, 11761
Chaumonot, Pierre Joseph Marie, 1611-1693,
    11762
Chauncey, Charles, 1777-1849, 1314, 11307, 21885

Chauncey, Nathaniel, 1789-1865, 2294
Chauncy, Charles, 1705-1787, 11763, 11764, 13098, 21886-21888, 23775
Chautard, Léon, 11765
Chauveau, Pierre Joseph Olivier, 1820-1890, 6414, 21889
Chauveton, Urbain, 16th cent., 1187, 21783
Chauvin, dit Joyeuse, 2758
Chavarría, Agustin Bernardo de, 6694, 6695
Chavarría Flores, Manuel, 20088
Chavarría Olivares, Daniel, 20089
Chavero, Alfredo, 1841-1906, 7873
Chaverri Benavides, Guillermo, 20090
Chaverri Rodríguez, Gil, 20090
Chaves, Flavio Loureiro, 20091, 20657
Chaves, João Gabriel, 20092
Chaves, Luis Fernando, 20093
Chaves, Mario M., 20094
Chaves, Miguel Martins, 19315
Chaves, Nelson, 20095, 20096
Chaves, Ronald, 20097
Chaves, Sylla M., 20098
Chávez, Nabor, 8209
Chávez Hayhoe, Arturo, 20099
Chávez Suarez, Socrates, 20100
Chazelle, Marie-Christine, 18363
Chazotte, Peter Stephen, ca.1770-ca. 1849, 11766, 11767
Che! wah! wah! 8122
Cheadle, Walter Butler, 1835-1910, 4481
Cheap cotton by free labor, 525
Cheap, healthy and happy homes in West Virginia, 3104
A cheap trip to the great Salt Lake City, 16546
A checkered life, 14483
Checkley, John, 1680-1754, 21890-21893
Checkley, Samuel, 1696-1769, 21894, 21895
Chee-ho-Carte, 3919
Cheek, Dolores S., 14962
Cheek, Philip, 1841-, 2980
Cheek, Thomas A., 24115
Cheerful yesterdays, 24599
Cheese, 18474, 18801
Cheetham, James, 1772-1810, 11768-11771, 13497, 21896-21899, 23819
Cheever, Ezekiel, 1614-1708, 829, 23704
Cheever, George Barrell, 1807-1890, 11772, 21900-21902, 23890, 24116, 24686
Cheever, Henry Theodore, 1814-1897, ed., 2074, 21903
Cheever, Samuel, 1639-1724, 21904
Chelmsford, Mass., History, 197
Chelonia, 107
Cheltnam, Charles Smith, 12397
Chemical analyses, 15145

Chemical elements, 13660
Chemical examination of the urinary calculi..., 15146
Chemical engineering libraries, Catalogs, 19102
Chemical industries, Brazil, 18605
Chemical plants, Pilot plants, 18605
Chemical report of the coals, clays, mineral waters, etc. of Kentucky..., 15147
Le chemin de la croix, 20218
Chemistry, History, 22255; Textbooks, 20090
Chemung Valley, History, 21905
Chen, Ari, 20101
Chen, Chi-Yi, 20102
Chenango Co., N.Y., History, 11813
Chenango (Gunboat), 11322
Chenault, Robert, 13819
Chenery, Hollis B., 20103
Cheney, J., illustr., 2513
Cheney, S.W., illustr., 2513
Cheney, Theseus Apoleon, 1830-1878, 21905
Cheney, Timothy Collingwood, 1808-1871, 21906
Cher, Henry W.B., pseud., 11773
Cherault, Mrs. Inez Bateman, 1886-, 7182
Cheraw Indians, 12416
Les chercheurs d'or au Mexique, 6755
The Cherokee embassage, 10769
Cherokee Hills, Stories of the, 5397
Cherokee Indians, 1090, 2237, 3342, 4217, 4396 5423, 5723, 11398, 11775, 11776, 12263, 13448, 16184, 16185, 16187, 23143, 23728; Government relations, 11399, 11774, 21907, 23811; History, Civil war, 21907; Land transfers, 23715, 23625; Treaties, 12104, 21978, 23811; Wars, 1759-1761, Fiction, 4565
Cherokee language, Texts, 11777, 16183, 16184, 23045, 23532
Cherokee nation, 11774, 11775, 21907; Constitution, 11776; Laws, statutes, etc., 11776; Treaties, 1861, 21978
Cherokee primer, 11777
Cherry, Henry Hardin, 13820
Cherry, Thomas Crittenden, 13821
Cherry Valley, N.Y., 11778; History, 11778
Cherrycote, 9764
Chertudi, Susand, 20104
Chervin, Nicolas, 1783-1843, 11779
Chesapeake and Delware canal, 12271
Chesapeake and Ohio canal company, 11780, 21908, 21909, 23218
Chesapeake Bay, 4136
Chesapeake-Leopard affair, 1807, 413, 880
Chesebro', Caroline, 1825-1873, 8597, 9769
Cheshire Co., N.H., Biography, 7094; History, 7094

Cheshire library association, Cheshire, Mass., 1848
Cheshire school, Cheshire, Conn., 1009
Chesney, Charles Cornwallis, 1826-1876, 1849, 1850
Chesnutt, Charles Waddell, 1858-1932, 2981, 2982
Chess, 13693
Chess pie, 14010
Chessman, Daniel, 1787-1839, 1851
Chest-diseases, 6466
Chester, Albert Tracy, 1812-1892, 11850
Chester, Anson G., 4140
Chester, Anthony, 2983
Chester, Charles Anderson, d.1849, 10204
Chester, Clarence Lyon, 1877-, 5928
Chester, Greville John, 1830-1892, 1852
Chester, John, 1749-1809, 23159
Chester, John, 1785-1829, 1853
Chester, John, 1832-1910, 1854
Chester, Joseph Lemuel, 1821-1882, 1855-1857
The Chester family, 9584
Chesterman, William Dallas, 1845-1904, 2984, 2985
Chestnuts, Pará, Brazil, 19440
Chetlain, Augustus Louis, 1824-1914, 16188
Chetwood, William Rufus, d.1766, 2986, 2987, 21910
Chevalier, Henri Emile, 1828-1879, 1858, 1859, 24117
Chevalier, Michel, 1806-1879, 1860-1867, 2988
The Chevalier Saint Agar, 11018
Chevallie, P.J., 1868
Cheves, Mrs. Elizabeth Washington (Foote), 1869
Cheves, Langdon, 1776-1857, 1870, 24118, 24119
Chevrolat, Auguste, 1871
Chew, John H., 1872
Cheyenne, Wyo., Biography, 17881
Cheyenne earth lodge sites in North and South Dakota, 17686
Cheyenne Indians, 3398, 5776; Wars, 1876, 16023
Chi Delta Phi. Xi Chapter, University of Kentucky, 15634
Chiabrera, Gabriello, 1552-1638, 1873
Chiapas, Mexico, Antiquities, 1830; Description & travel, 7996; History, 20105
Chibcha Indians, 19503
Chibougamou, Quebec, Description, 8393
Chicago, 1874; Board of education, 1875; Council, 12512, 16061; Common Council,

24964; Description, 3894, 4696; Description, Guide-books, 12484; Description, Views, 1877; Directory, 1876, 21911; Douglas monument, 2109; Emancipation meeting, Sept. 7, 1862, 25205; Fire, 1871, 16828; Fire, 1871, Fiction, 10643; History, 716, 1878, 8431, 10141, 16061, 16188; Manufactures, 12512; Massacre, 1812, 16952; Mechanics' institute, 1878; World's Columbian exposition, 1893, California, 17192; World's Columbian exposition, 1893, Jamaica, 7114
The Chicago almanac and advertiser, 1876
Chicago bar association, 6415
The Chicago Copperhead Convention, 6416
Chicago city directory and business advertiser, 21911
Chicago Historical Society, 16069, 24036, 24160, 24950, 25835
Chicago illustrated, 1877
Chicago magazine, 1878
Chicago Tribune, 6417
Chicago's first great lawsuit, 25322
Chicanery (Law), 20085; Colombia, 20085
Chickamauga, Battle of, 1863, 2039, 5483; The price of Chattanooga, 24399
Chickasaw Indians, Wars, 1730-1740, 22728
Chickering, Arthur Merton, 20106
Chickering, Jesse, 1797-1855, 1879, 24120
Chico, Irmão, 20107
Chicora, 3671
Chicora and other regions of the conquerors and the conquered, 11996
Chidlaw, Benjamin Williams, 1811-1892, 1880, 16192
The chief, 5218
The chieftain of Churubusco, 9716
Chihuahua, Mexico (State), Description & travel, 2624, 7837, 8122, 16476, 17469, 18886
Child, Andrew, 2989
Child, David Lee, 1794-1874, 1881-1885, 25029
Child, John, 1886
Child, Mrs. Lydia Maria (Francis) 1802-1880, 1887-1895, 10008, 24121, 25029; Looking toward sunset, 24664
Child, Robert, 1613-1654, 12735
The child and the man, 12590
The child captives, 12922
Child custody, Kentucky, 14667
Child guidance centers, 19524
Child guidance clinics, 19524
The child of the bay, 9050
The child of the islands, 9650
Child study, 19778
Child welfare, Kentucky, 14623
Childbirth, 17278

Children, 10910, 19778; Biography, 13159; Care and hygiene, 19246; Caribbean area, 19790; Charities, protection, etc., 11473, 22293; Employment, Brazil, 19421; Employment, South Carolina, 5562, 5563; Kentucky, 14623; Nutrition, 19246, 20312, 20313
Children of destiny, 5115
The children of light, 8985
The children of the border, 4992
The children of the king, 6493
The children out-of-doors, 4772
Children of the Caribbean, 19790
Children's aid society, New York, 11473
Children's literature, Confederate States of America, 11471; Brazilian, History & criticism, 18577
Children's plays, 18977; Brazilian, 20539
Children's songs, Spanish American, History & criticism, 18056
Childs, David Lee, 24122
Childs, Henry Halsey, 1783-1868, 1896
Childs, John Wesley, 1800-1850, 14046
Childs, Orville Whitmore, 1803-1870, 1897
The child's funeral, 10747
A child's history of the United States, 11362
The child's mother, 9376
Chile, Antiquites, 11330, 18997; Archivo Nacional, 20166; Bibliography, Periodicals, 7846; Boundary, Argentine Republic, 18900; Census, 20157-20159, 20168; Colonization, 20127; Comisión de Estudios de la Seguridad Social, 20109; Comisión de Planeamiento Integral de la Educación, 20110; Congreso. Biblioteca, 20111, 20112; Congreso. Cámara de Diputados, Rules and practice, 20113, 20114; Congreso. Redactor de las sesiones, 7275; Congreso. Redactor extraordinario, 7275; Congreso. Senado, 18032; Conserjeria Nacional de Promoción Popular, 20115; Constitution, 20113, 20114; Corporación de la Reforma Agraria, 20116; Corte Suprema, 18951; Departamento de Economía Agraria, 20117, 20118; Departamento de Estudios Financieros, 20119; Departamento de Navegación e Hidrografía, 20120, 20121; Description & travel, 420, 6279, 6929, 6930, 7050, 8319, 10574, 11654, 12529, 13277, 18630; Description & travel, Views, 20181; Dirección de Abastecemiento de Petroleo, 20122; Dirección de Bibliotecas, Archivos y Museos, 20123, 20124; Dirección de Contabilidad, 20125; Dirección de Estadistica y Censos. Estadística chilena, 20126; Dirección General de Estadística. Estadística chilena, 20126; Dirección General de Talleres Fiscales de Prisiones, 20166; Economic conditions, 7651, 18725, 19611, 19802, 20162-20164, 20496; Economic policy, 20165; Emigration & immigration, 20127; Financial statistics, 20150; Foreign relation, Bolivia, 20156; History, 6734, 8291, 19238; History, Bibliography, 18341; History, Colonial period, 18153; History, Periodicals, 7848, 7851, 7852; History, Revolution, 1891, Claims, 20108; History, Sources, 20166; History, War of independence 1810-1824, 1144, 5892, 5893, 5967, 6279, 6640, 7631, 12841, 13277, 20519; History, War with Spain, 1865-1866, 11347, 18251; Housing, 20168; Industries, 20004; Informe del ajente de Chile ante el Tribunal Arbitral Anglo-Chileno, 20108; Inspección Jeneral de Tierras i Colonización, 20127; Instituto Geográfico Militar, 20128; Instituto Hidrográfico de la Armada de Chile, 20129-20136; Laws, statutes, etc., 19887, 20137-20147, 20167; Laws, statutes, etc. Ley de elecciones, 19024; Maps, 20120, 20121, 20129-20132, 20134, 20136; Ministerio de Educación 20148, 20149; Ministerio de Hacienda, 879, 20150-20153; Ministerio de Instruccion Pública, 20154; Ministerio de Marina, 20155; Ministerio de Relaciones Exteriores, 20156; Ministerio de Salud Pública y Prevision Social, Appropriations and expenditures, 20119; Oficina Central de Estadística, 20157 20160; Oficina de Estudios Tributarios, 20161; Oficina de Planificación Nacional. ODEPLAN, ser.4, 20162; Oficina de Planificación Nacional, 20162-20165; Politics & government, 5967, 7651, 19886, 20114, 20137, 20151, 20152; Politics & government, Addresses, essays, lectures, 19718; Politics & government, Periodicals, 7275, 20522; Population, 20169; Public lands, 20127; Public works, 20164; Religion, 19987; Rural conditions, 19988; Servicio de Seguridad Social, 20167; Servicio Nacional de Estadística, 20168-20170; Servicio Nacional de Estadística y Censos. Estadística chilena 20126; Servicio Nacional de Salud, 20171, 20172; Social conditions, 7651, 19230; Social conditions, Bibliography, 20180; Social life & customs, 1245; Statistics, 20117, 20126, 20160, 20169; Superintendencia de Bancos, 20173; Superintendencia de Educación, 20174-20176; Superintendencia de Educación. Direccion de Educación Secundaria, 20177, Superintendencia de Educación. Oficina de Planeamiento, 20178, 20179; Superintendencia de Seguridad Social, 20180; Suprema Junta

Interior Gubernativa. Registro oficial, 20522
Chile (Colony) Real Audiencia Archivo, 20166
Chile al día, 20181
Chile Chico (Province), 18312
Chilean fiction, 20389
Chilean literature, Bibliography, 20123; Periodical, 7851
Chilean periodicals, 7275, 20522
Chiles, J.B., 16926
Chillicothe, Ohio, History, 14096
Chillicothe Association for Promoting Morality and Good Order, 2990
Chiloe, Chile (Province), 2436; Economic condition, 18284; Social condition, 18284
Chilton, Edward, fl.1710-1727, 3805
Chim: his Washington winter, 9308
"Chimmie Fadden", 10997
The chimney-corner, 10902
China, Constitutional history, 24538; Description & travel, 22252, 23692; Foreign relation, 7913; Politics & government, 1900-, 24538
Chinard, Gilbert, 1881-, 7222
Chinchilla V., Eduardo, 20182
Chinese in British Guiana, 22702
Chinese in California, 16957, 24332
Chinese in the U.S., 24159, 25271
Chinese slave trade-coolyism, 24159
Chiniquy, Charles Paschal Telesphore, 1809-1899, 6418
Chinook, In the land of, 17290
Chinook jargon, 5307; Dictionaries, 5898; Glossaries, vocabularies, etc., 4690, 5017, 7360, 8403, 12233; Texts, 16456
The chip boy of the dry dock, 8938
Chipeta, queen of Ute Indians, 17452
Chipman, Daniel, 1765-1850, 21912, 21913
Chipman, Nathaniel, 1752-1843, 11781, 21913
Chipman, Norton P., 16193, 16194
Chippewa Falls, Wis., 15848
Chippewa Indians, 5343, 8428, 13313, 13314, 13360, 15870, 25498; Legends, 17036; Missions, 16800
Chippewa language, 12967; Dictionaries, English, 770; Glossaries, vocabularies, etc., 17048; Grammar, 771; Texts, 2375, 2381, 13312
Chips from the workshop, 13115
Chips of cedar, 13623
Chips of the old block, 16358

Chira Island, Costa Rica, 19004
Chirino, Oton, 20183
Chirinos, Victor Manuel, 20184
Chisholm, Daniel Fare, 1866-, 5942
Chisholm Trail, 5942
Chita, 9832
Chittenden, Hiram Martin, 1858-1917, 16195
Chittenden, W.B., 22745
The chivalric sailor, 10730
Chivers, Thomas Holley, 1809-1858, 2991-2994, 15577
Chivington, John Milton, 2995
Chivington massacre of the Cheyenne Indians, 5776
Choateville Christian Church. Franklin County, Ky., 13968
Chocolate, 6480
Choctaw Indians, 1178
A choice, 10283
The choice of Paris, 8783
The choir invisible, 8513
Choirs (Music), 9620
Choisy, 10901
Cholenec, Pierre, 1641-1723, 16956
Cholera, 13919; Asiatic, 14102; Asiatic, Baltimore, 1849, 1642; Asiatic, New York (City) 1832, 23570; Asiatic, U.S., 156
The cholera at Quebec, 11173
Cholera epidemic, Kentucky, 14889; Lexington, Ky., 1833, 13833; Winchester, Ky., 1833, 14102
Cholera in Lexington, 14290
A chorographical and statistical description of the District of Columbia, 23745
Chorpenning, George, 16196; Claims vs. U.S., 16196
Choses d'Amérique, 4234
Chouteau, Auguste, 16197
Chovel, Rafael, 7480
Christ Church, Louisville, Ky., 13822
Christ Episcopal Church, Lexington, Ky., 13934
Christ in the camp, 4119
Christ rejected, 9858
Christ the resurrection and the life, 22101
Christian art and symbolism, 11108
The Christian Baptist... Ed. by Alexander Campbell, 21914
Christian biography, 1732, 11566, 22205, 22370
Christian citizenship and honest legislation, 13031
Christian communion with slave holders: Will the Alliance sanction it? 25928
Christian County, Kentucky, Description, 14193; History, 14380, 15141
Christian ethics, 22542

The Christian Indian, 8999
Christian Journal, 24123
Christian life, 995, 9119, 11081, 13159,
  14972, 23296, 23299, 23302; Catholic
  authors, 7032, 7033, 20634
Christian memorials of the war, 12516
A Christian merchant, 1742
Christian patriotism, 12179
The Christian register, and moral and
  theological review, 21915
The Christian retrospect and register,
  667
The Christian review, 24022
The Christian spectator, 23518
The Christian, the student, and pastor,
  exemplified, 11566
The Christian traveller, 4913
The Christian's companion, 23785
The Christian's duty to render to Caesar
  the things that are Caesar's,
  considered, 21916
Christiana, Pa., Riot 1851, 24613
Christianity, 20107; Apologetic works ,
  19th century, 8886
Christianity and economics, Addresses,
  essays, lectures, 19021
Christianity and the civil laws, 24920
Christianity versus treason and slavery,
  24124
Christiansen, Haraldo E., 18453
Christiansen, John R., 13823, 13867
Christie, James, jr. fl. 1774-1775, 21917
Christie, Robert, 1788-1856, 11782, 21918
Christie, Thomas, 2996
Christie, William Dougal, 1816-1874,
  24125
Christine, 10311
Christmas, 10910
The Christmas banquet, 9823
Christmas carillons, 4166
The Christmas club, 9463
A Christmas dream, 8839
Christmas eve in war times, 10653
Christmas eve on Lonesome, 9553
A Christmas-eve suit, 10653
Christmas evening legends, 10841
Christmas gift, 14759
Christmas greetings, 6419
The Christmas guest, 10278, 10834
The Christmas holly, 10936
A Christmas in the West Indies, 7194, 7195
Christmas Jenny, 9575
The Christmas mummers, 9916
Christmas music, 10552
Christmas plays, Medieval, 18607
Christmas stories, 3910, 6589, 11101

A Christmas story, 9559
A Christmas surprise, 9254
Christopher, 8723
Christy, David, b.1802, 11783, 11784, 23961,
  24126, 24127
Christy, Howard Chandler, illustr., 3639,
  9360
Chromosomes, 18186
Chronander, Gustav, 11785
Chronological account of remarkable occurrences,
  11786
Chronology, Historical, 6431, 8436, 11562;
  Mexican, 7231
Chu Chu, 6963, 6971
Chubut, Argentine Republic. Dirección General
  de Estadística y Censos, 20185; Statistics,
  20185
Chuck, 10863
Chumacero, Ali, 20186
Chumillas, Julian, d.1696. Memorial jurídico y
  legal, 5885
Chunn, Ida F., 2997
Church, 14144
Church, Benjamin, 1639-1718, 11787-11790
Church, Frederick C., illustr., 24562
Church, George Earl, 1835-1910, 11791
Church, Jeremiah, 2998
Church, John Hubbard, 1772-1840, 11792
Church, R. S. H., 11793
Church, Samuel, 1785-1854, 21919
Church, Sanford Elias, 1815-1880, 21920
Church, Thomas, 1674-1746, 11787
Church, William, 21921
Church and education, 13139, 13890
Church and education in the U.S., 2024
Church and social problems Catholic church,
  18934
Church and state, 622, 624, 13043, 19780
Church and state in Cuba, 18321
Church and state in Massachusetts, 12052
Church and state in Mexico, 12480, 19733,
  20223
Church and state in New England, 1349
Church and state in the U.S., 2000, 25541
Church and state in Virginia, 23015
The church and the slave power, 25786
Church Anti-slavery Society, 24128
Church architecture, São João del Rei,
  Brazil, 18204
The church as it is: or, The forlorn hope
  of slavery, 25274
Church dedication sermons, 5803, 8311, 11746,
  22134
Church discipline, 4120
Church history, 24780, 18th century, 23305;
  19th century, 667, Primitive and early

church, 23863, 24720; Primitive and
early church, Fiction, 10138
Church lands, Mexico, 18928
A church mouse, 9575
Church music, 14374; New England, 12879;
U.S., 12336
Church of England, Sermons, 654, 1007,
1196, 11407, 11651, 13391, 22425, 22630,
23134, 23710
Church of England in America, 1449, 2790;
Government, 1556; Sermons, 1384
Church of England in Canada, 2436
Church of England in Maryland, 1448;
Fiction, 10859
Church of England in New Jersey, 21941,
23397
Church of England in the West Indies, 2790
Church of Jesus Christ of Latter-Day Saints,
2999, 3000, 4846, 8044
Church of Scotland, Government, 23560
Church polity, 23560
Church union, Boston, 600
Churcher, C. S., 1928-, 20187
Churches, Bowling Green, Ky., 15191;
Lexington, Ky., 15184, 15185
The churches and sects of the United States,
12320
Churches of Christ, 13723
Churchill, Charles, 11794
Churchill, Franklin Hunter, 1823-, 16201
Churchill, Sylvester, 1783-1862, 16201
Churchill, Winston, 1871-1947, 6420,
13824
Churchill Downs, Ky., 15308
Churchill Weavers, Berea Ky., 13715
Churchman, John, 1705-1775, 3001
Chydenius, Anders, 1898
Cibola, 8293, 8294, 11474
Ciccotti, Ettore, 1863-1939, 24129
Cicero, Marcus Tullius, 106-43 B.C.,
24421; De republica, 20549, 20188;
Princeps, 20549
Cicloeconomía, 19807
El Cid Campeador, 20189
Cidade de Arapiraca; consumo de produtos
industriais, 18780
Cidade de Mossoró; consumo de produtos
industriais, 18782
A cidade e o campo, 19669
Ciechomski, Juana D. de, 20190-20192
Un ciego de barro, 19990
Cien años de la novela chilena, 20389
Las cien mejores poesías peruanas contem-
poráneas, 19848
Ciencia, tecnología e desenvolvimento, 19263
Ciencia jurídico-penal contemporánea, 19152

Ciencia y sociedad, 20643
Las ciencias médicas en la filatelía cubana,
18958
Las ciencias sociales en Colombia, 18362
Las ciencias sociales en Costa Rica, 19715
Cieza de León, Pedro de, 1518?-1560, 20193,
20194
Cifras provisorias para la Provincia del censo
número, 20472
Cifuentes, Domingo de, fl.1673, 6421
A cigarette from Carcinto, 10125
A cigarette-marker's romance, 9220
Cinchona, 511, 23133
Cincinnati, 3284; Black brigade, 11826;
Board of Education, et al., defendants,
13439; Chamber of Commerce and merchant's
exchange, 21922, 21923; Citizens, 21924;
Committee on the explosion of the Moselle,
21925; Description, 3289, 3290, 11795,
13825, 21932; Fiction, 9495; Fire Dept.,
21926; Great western sanitary fair, 1863,
11468; History, 4384, 13740, 13825, 14330,
16576, 21932; House of refuge, 21927;
Ordinances, etc., 21928, 21929; Politics
& government, 21929; Public Library, 13825;
Public Library. Rare Book Dept., 20195;
Superior Court, 13439; University.
Observatory, 81
Cincinnati colonization society, 21930
The Cincinnati excursion to California, 16202
The Cincinnati miscellany, 3002
The Cincinnati pioneer, 13826
Cincinnati Southern Railway, 3798, 13701
Cincinnatian unique: Daniel Drake, 14347
Cincinnatus, L. Quincius, pseud., 21931
Cinderella, 9356
Cinta Guzmán, Alberto, 20196
Cintra, Alarico, 20197
Cintra de Camargo, Maria Lourdes Sampaio,
20198
Cintrón, José Facundo, 24291
Ciocchini, Hector E., 20199-20201
Cipher, 8601
Cipolla, Arnaldo, 1879-, 6422
Cipriani, Giovanni Battista, d.1785, engr.,
21787
A circle in the sand, 10073
Circle left, 15377
The circle of a century, 9763
Circle-Dot, 16412
Circled by fire, 11211
Circuit court case activity in Kentucky
1950-1960, 15656
Circuit court redistricting, 14793
The circuit rider, 9462
A circuit rider in early Indiana, 6423

Circumstantial evidence, 8696
Cirigliano, Gustavo F. J., 20202, 20203
Cist, Charles, 1792-1868, 3002, 11795, 21932
Cist, Henry M., 13827
Cistercian contemplatives, 13828
Cistercians, 13828
The Cistern, 15460
Cités et ruines américaines, 6408
Cities and towns, 12009; Argentine Republic, 21746; Brazil, 19220, 20379, 20563; Canada, 6858; Colombia, 19100; Kentucky, 14636, 14948; Maps, Bibliography, 14704; Latin America, 19749, 20029, 20030; Planning, Brasilia, 18176; Planning, Girardot, Colombia, 20305; Planning, Quixada, Brazil, 20014; Ruined, extinct, etc., 6408, 6715; U.S., 6858
A citizen, 21837
A citizen of Georgia, 25366
A citizen of Maryland, 4888, 13003
A citizen of Massachusetts, 11917
A citizen of New York, 96, 1784
A citizen of Ohio, 11229
A citizen of Philadelphia, 13101
A citizen of the United States, 12105, 24915
The citizen-soldier, 2657
The citizen soldiers at North Point and Fort McHenry, September 12 & 13, 1814, 22448
Citizens' Advisory Committee on Environmental Quality, 19441
Citizens of Washington Territory, 16970
Citizenship, 1955, 1999, 11920; U.S., 960
Citrus fruits, Argentina, 18949; Marketing, 18949; Mexico, 19574
The citrus industry of Mexico, 19574
City and country life, 10987
City churches, 19197
The City of Endeavor, 9345
The city of Louisville and a glimpse of Kentucky, 13536
The city of the Mormons, 11695
The City of the saints, 1744
The city of the silent, 5158
City pension system, Locally administered, 15716
City planning, Bogotá, 19100; Brazil, 19462
The city urchin and the chaste villagers, 9216
Ciudad Real, Antonio de, 1551 1667, 10106
La ciudad y el viento, 19961
Civeira Taboada, Miguel, 20205

Civics, Study and teaching, 19727
Civil engineering, 15828
Civil government, 25638
Civil government an ordinance of God, 11922, 12050
Civil law, 388; Brazil, 19354; Cambodia, 24804; Ecuador, History, 20064; France, 388; Quebec (Province), 22828; Venezuela, 18050
Civil procedure, 20706; Argentine Republic, 18461-18563, 18468; Brazil, 19335, 19863; Chile, 20141; Colombia, 20316; Dictionaries - Spanish, 20636; New York (State), 12065; Panama, 19022; Uruguay, Dictionaries, 20636; Venezuela, 20706
Civil prudence, 11796
A civil record of Major General Winfield S. Hancock, 24130
Civil rights, 18338, 24722; Cuba, 18184; Dominican Republic, 19049; Guatemala, 18197
A civil servant, 9678
Civil service, Brazil, 19348, 19349; Brazil, Statistics, 19428; Colombia, 20334; Gt. Britain, Examinations, 2013; Labor relations, 14688; U.S., 12530; U.S., Speeches in Congress, 11356
Civil service in the departments, 9038
Civil trial advocacy, Kentucky, 14664
The civil war & slavery in the United States, 24131
Civil War battlefields, 1861-65, 13829
Civil War engagements, skirmishes, etc., in Kentucky, 1861-1865, 13853
The Civil War in Kentucky, 14512
Civil war letters and documents, 4740
Civilization, 21933, 23026; Christian, 13151; Greco-Roman, 25355; History, 22441, 22943, 22944
Civilization in the United States, 2556
Civilization of the Indian natives, 13125
Civilized America, 3663
Civis, pseud., 11797
Civis anglicus, pseud., 21934
Claas Schlaschenschlinger, 10480
Claggett, William, 1790-1870, 11798
Claiborne the rebel, 8942
Claiborne, John Francis Hamtramck, 1809-1854 3003, 3004
La clairière du bois des Hogues, 1108
Clairvoyance, 14037
Clallam language, Glossaries, vocabularies, etc., 12232
El clamor del desterrado, 18854
Clampitt, John Wesley, 1839- , 16205
The clan of No-name, 9217
The clandestine marriage, 9444

The clansman; an historical romance of
  the Ku Klux Klan, 24296
Clap, Thomas, 1703-1767, 11800-11802,
  22025
Clapp, Asahel, 11803
Clapp, Charles B., 11804
Clapp, Henry Austin, 1841-1904, ed., 11203
Clapp, John T., 3005
Clapp, Theodore, 1792-1866, 3006, 21935,
  24132
Clappe, Mrs. Louise Amelia Knapp Smith,
  16206
Clara Moreland, 1170
Clare, Mrs. Josephine, 3007
Claremont, 9005
Clarence, 6964, 10723
Claretie, Jules, 1840-1913, 7494
Clarice, pseud., 20206
Clarière, Etienne, 1735-1793, 2805
Clarimonde: a tale of New Orleans life,
  8752
Clarissimo Johanni Adair, 15594
Clark, Aaron, 11805
Clark, Alonso Howard, 1850-1918, 8076
Clark, Barrett H., 13981
Clark, Benjamin Franklin, 1808-1879,
  11806
Clark, Billy C., 13830, 14455
Clark, Champ, 1850-1921, 14249
Clark, Charles, d.1881, 11807, 11808,
  11809
Clark, Charles Eugene, 6424, 13831
Clark, Charles M., 1834-, 3008
Clark, Christopher, 3009
Clark, D.W., 3452
Clark, Daniel, 1809-1891, 6425, 24133,
  24134
Clark, Daniel Atkinson, 1779-1840, 328,
  11810
Clark, Edward L., 21936
Clark, Ferdinand, 21937
Clark, Francis D., 16207
Clark, George, 1841-, 3010
Clark, George Rogers, 1752-1818, 3017,
  3386, 15391, 15551, 21938
Clark, George Washington, b.1812, 24135
Clark, Hamlet, 1823-1867, 11811
Clark, Henry, 1829-1899, 11812
Clark, Henry Scott, pseud., 13932
Clark, Hiram C., 11813
Clark, Horace Francis, 1815-1873, 11814
Clark, Sir James, bart., 1788-1870, 11815
Clark, James H., 1842-, 3011, 20207
Clark, James Samuel, 1841-, 3012
Clark, Joel W., 11816
Clark, John, 1745-1809?, 13183

Clark, John, 1758-1833, 23487
Clark, John, 1797-1854, 16665
Clark, John Alonso, 1801-, 3013
Clark, Jonas, 1730-1805, 11817
Clark, Jonathan, 11818
Clark, Joseph, 1751-1813, 11819
Clark, Joseph A., 11820
Clark, Joseph Sylvester, 1800-1861, 11821,
  21939
Clark, Joshua Victor Hopkins, 1803-1869,
  11822
Clark, Lawrence, 20208
Clark, Lewis Garrard, 1812-1897, 3014
Clark, Lewis Gaylord, 1808-1873, 9012, 10154
Clark, Lincoln, 1800-1886, 11823
Clark, Margaret Buckner, 14218
Clark, Mary, 1792?-1841, 11824
Clark, Mary, of Washington Co., Va., 2045
Clark, Milton, 1817?-1901, 3014, 24651
Clark, Peter, 1694-1768, 11825
Clark, Peter H., 1826
Clark, Ronald James, 20209-20211
Clark, Rufus Wheelwright, 1813-1886, 11827-
  11830, 21940, 24136
Clark, Susie Champney, 1856-, 16208
Clark, Thomas, 1787-1860, 11381
Clark, Thomas Dionysius, 13832-13834, 14834,
  14897, 14936, 24137
Clark, Thomas March, bp., 1812-1903, 3015,
  11832
Clark, Thomas S., 2587
Clark, Walter Appleton, illustr., 25579
Clark, Wayne E., 20212
Clark, William, 3017
Clark, William, 1770-1838, 4272, 5457, 13385,
  17030
Clark, William Adolphus, 1825-1906, 11833
Clark, William Jared, 1854?-1922, 6426
Clark, Willis Gaylord, 1808-1841, 9012
Clark family, 3386
Clark family (Thomas Clarke, 1599?-1697),
  21947
Clark's expedition against Detroit, 1781, 3386
Clark's expedition to the Illinois, 1778-1779,
  3386, 3760, 21938
Clark's grant, 3386
Clark County, Ky., 15760; Bibliography, 14414;
  Cities and towns, 15488; Description, 13644;
  History, 13614, 13639, 13645, 13909, 14104-
  14107, 14199, 14829, 15030; History,
  Revolutionary War, 14877, 15215; History,
  War of 1812, 15212; Maps, 13646, 13911;
  Meteorites, 14103; Methodism, 15677;
  Mortality, 14635; Wills, 14107
Clark Co., Wis., 15848
Clark County and the battle of the Thames,

105

15212
Clark County in the Texan Revolution,
13639
Clarke, A.B. of Westfield, Mass., 11834
Clarke, A.S., 10448
Clarke, A. St E., 20214
Clarke, Abraham Lynsen, 1768?-1810, 11835
Clarke, Arthur Charles, 1917-, 20213
Clarke, Asa Bement, 3018
Clarke, Edward, 1810-1891, 11836
Clarke, Sir Edward George, 1841-, 11837
Clarke, Edward Hammond, 1820-1877, 11845
Clarke, Frank Wigglesworth, 1847-, 11838
Clarke, George, 1676-1760, 3019
Clarke, James Freeman, 1810-1888, 23891,
24138-24140
Clarke, John, Lieutenant of marines, 11839
Clarke, John, of Philadelphia, 11840
Clarke, John, 1755-1798, -1841
Clarke, John Hopkins, 1789-1870, 11842
Clarke, L.H., reporter, 22450
Clarke, Lewis Garrard, 1815-1897, 24651
Clarke, M., 20214
Clarke, Mrs. Mary Jones (Stimson) 1785-
1866, 11845
Clarke, Mary Washington ("Mrs. Kenneth
Clarke"), 13545
Clarke, Matthew St. Clair, 11843, 11844
Clarke, Pitt, 1763-1835, 11845
Clarke, Robin, 1937-, 20215
Clarke, S.A., 1827-, 16209
Clarke, S.J., publishing company, Chicago,
Ill., 16941
Clarke, Samuel, 1599-1682, 11846, 21942,
21943
Clarke, Samuel, 1791-1859, 21944
Clarke, Samuel Clarke, b.1806, 11847,
21945-21947
Clarke, Samuel Fulton, 1818-1861, 11848
Clarke, Sidney, 1831-1909, 21949
Clarke, Thomas Curtis, 1827-1901, 11849
Clarke, Walter, 1812-1871, 11850, 24141
Clarke, William, M.D. fl.1755, 21950
Clarke school for the deaf, Northampton,
Mass., 21948
Clarkson, James S., 16698
Clarkson, Matthew, 3020
Clarkson, Thomas, 1760-1846, 11851-11855,
12625, 21951, 24142, 24555
Clarkson, Thomas Streatfield, 11856
Claro, María Elena, 20216
Claro, Samuel, 20217
Clary, Dexter, 11857
Clary, Timothy Ferrer, 1817-1912, 11858
Clason, Isaac Starr, 1789?-1834, 11859
Class distinction, Argentine Republic,

Bibliography, 18688
Classical antiquities, Catalogs, 22429
Classical education, 2400
A classificação de Colon, 18978
A classificação de documentos na CEMIG, 20021
Classification , Books , Electric engineering,
20021; Books , Hydrology, 20021
Classification, Colon, 18978
Claude d'Abbeville, father, d.1632, 1899
Claude Melnotte as a detective, 10528
Claudel, Paul, 1868-1955, 20218, 20219
Claudia Hyde, 8759
Claudy, Carl Harry, 1879-, 17198
Claussen, Pierre, chevalier, 1818
Clausson, L.J., 21952
Claver, Pedro, Saint, 1580(ca.)-1654, 6725
Clavijero, Francisco Javier, 1731-1787, 6427,
16210, 16768, 21953
Clavière, Étienne, 1735-1793, 25556
Clavo en la voz, 18121
Clay, Cassius Marcellus, 1810-1903, 2898,
3021-3026, 3884, 13715, 13742, 13833, 17454,
25280, 24143-24146
Clay, Cassius Marcellus, 1846-1913, 13835
Clay, Clement Claiborne, 1819-1882, 24147
Clay, Henrietta, 13838
Clay, Henry, 1777-1852, 382, 708, 1605, 2284,
3720, 5426, 6428, 6429, 7900, 12146, 13550,
13569, 13603, 13741, 13782, 13785, 13833,
13839-13846, 13880, 13898, 14194, 14249,
14309, 14318, 14465, 14780, 14907, 15175,
15183, 15370, 15378, 15403, 15425, 15487,
15668, 15697, 15742, 15801, 16211, 22701,
24144, 24148, 25367, 25846; Exhibitions,
14700; Letter of emancipation, 24021;
Monuments, 14251; Portraits, 15202; Speech..
on the subject of abolition petitions, 1839,
24429
Clay, Jehu Curtis, 1792-1863, 21954
Clay, John, 1851-, 16212
Clay, Mrs. John M., 13847
Clay, Laura, 1849-1941, 14202
Clay, Mrs. Mary Rogers, 15403
Clay, Maurice A., 13848
Clay, William Marion, 13849
Clay family, 13838, 14165, 14780, 15370, 15403
Clay industries, Brazil, 19161; Kentucky,
13942, 14115, 14173, 15147
The Clay minstrel, 13392
Clay sculpture, Brazil, 20509
Clay's quick step, from a favorite French air,
15697
Clays in several parts of Kentucky, 14173
Clayton, William, 1814-1879, 3027
The clean face, 10197
Cleaveland, John, 1722-1799, 21955, 21956

106

Cleaveland, Nehemiah, 1796-1877, 21957, 21958
Cleaves, Peter S., 20220
Cleland, Robert Glass, 16213
Cleland, Thomas, 1778-1858, 3028, 13850
Clemens, Jeremiah, 1814-1865, 21959
Clemens, Orion, 1825-1897, 16214
Clemens, Samuel Langhorne, 1835-1910, 3029
Clemens, Sherrard, 1826-, 24149
Clement Falconer, 10567
Clement, J., 13851
Clemente, Claudio, 1594?-1642 or 3, 6430, 6431, 6432
Clemente, José Edmundo de, 20221
Clements, James I., 16215
Cleopatra's daughter, 8548
Clephane, James Ogilvie, 1842-1910, 22304
Clephane, Walter Collins, 1867-, 24150
Clergy, 11980; Brazil, 24409; Great Britain, 13450; Maryland, 167; Massachusetts, 21964; Massachusetts, Taunton, 22183; New Hampshire, 11416; U.S., 23455
Clergy in Maryland of the Protestant Episcopal church, 167
Clericus, Esculapius, and Scepticus, vs. Col. M. Jewett, and his chemical preparations, 3854
Clerke, Charles, 1741-1779, 23533
Clerkships in Washington, 21960
Clermont, N.Y., 11856
Cleugh, James, 6057
Cleveland, Charles Dexter, 1802-1869, 24151
Cleveland, Edward, 1804-1886, 21961
Cleveland, Mrs. Emeline H., 21962
Cleveland, Grover, pres. U.S., 1837-1908, 6433, 6869
Cleveland, Henry, 3030
Cleveland, John F., 6888
Cleveland, Richard Jeffry, 1773-1860, 21963
The Cleveland family, 10803
Cleymans, Jean, 20222
Clibborn, Edward, 1900
The Cliff Dwellers, 6921
Cliff-dwellings, Colorado, 17279
Clifford, Jeronimy, d.1737, 2026
Clifford Troup, 11127
The Clifford family, 11860
Cliffton, William, 1772-1799, 1901
Clift, Garrett Glenn, 1909-1970, 13751, 13852-13855
Clifton, Ky., 15769
The Clifton picture, 9178

Climate of Kentucky, 14324
The climate of the United States and its endemic influence, 12149
Climatology, Medical, 1434, 11578, 11815, 12791
Climatology of Florida, 4161
Climbs & exploration in the Canadian Rockies, 8126
Clinch, Bryan J., 16217
Clinch, Joseph Hart, d.1884, 1902
Cline, A.J., 11861
Clinedinst, V. West, illustr. 9637, 25191
Clingman, Thomas Lanier, 1812-1897, 1903, 24152, 24153
Clinkscales, John George, 1855-, 24154
Clinton, Charles A., 3031
Clinton, DeWitt, 1769-1828, 1904-1910, 2078, 11862, 13023, 22567
Clinton, George, 1739-1812, 94
Clinton, George William, 1807-1885, 1911
Clinton, Sir Henry, 1738?-1795, 13473
Clinton, Henry Lauren, 1820-1889, 1912
Clinton Bradshaw, 5379
Clinton, Ky., History, 14321; Public Library, 13813
Clinton County, Pa., History, 23425
Clipperton, John, 1221
Clippings from the California press, 1913
Clock and watch making, 11374; Kentucky, 14800; U.S., 11374, 13214
Clocks and watches, 6401
Clopper, Jonas, 1914
The close of the late rebellion, in Rhode-Island, 13220
Closson, H.W., 10122
Clotelle, 2833, 24037
Clothier, Caleb, 23921
Cloud, William, 20223
'A cloud of witness' against slavery and oppression, 443
A cloud on the mountain, 9529
Cloud pictures, 5495
The cloud with a golden border, 9830
The clouds of the mind, 10009
Clough, Simon, 1915
Cloutier, Philip, 14708
Clover and blue grass..., 15091
Cloverport, Ky., History, 15313, 15398; Looking back..., 15398
Cloverly, 9862
Clovernook, 2930, 8947
Club of Odd Volumes, Boston, 2573, 2574
Clubb, Henry Stephen, b.1827, 1916
Clubb, Stephen, b.1762, 1917
Clubs, 24689

Cluny, Alexander, 3032, 6434, 6435
Cluseret, Gustave Paul, 1823-1900, 1918
Clutter, William, 13856
Clutterbuck, Walter J., 7259
The Clyde, 10172
Clyde Wardleigh's promise, 10635
Clymer, George, d.1881, 1919
Clyne, Patricia Edwards, 13857
Coahuila, Mexico, 16911; Description,
    4314, 7219, 7837; History, 7219
Coal, 11444, 13263, 13935, 13936, 13939,
    13941, 14116, 14193, 14336, 14337,
    14565, 15004, 15147, 15686; Brazil,
    Santa Catarina, 19178; Kentucky, 14482,
    15297, 15607; Rhode Island, 12066; U.S.,
    13264
Coal and coal oil, 11444
The coal industry in Kentucky, 14421, 14422
Coal mines and mining, 13936, 13941, 14116,
    14336, 14337, 14447, 15004, 15686; Chile,
    Coronel, 879; Chile, Lota, 879; Harlan
    County, Ky., 13719; Illinois, 22200;
    Kentucky, 13556, 14005, 14016, 14220,
    14269, 14421, 14422, 15645; Pennsylvania,
    8376
Coal-tar products, 12075, 12223
Coal trade, 13263; Kentucky, 14564
Coal's future in Kentucky, 14482
Coale, Charles B., 3033, 16218
Coals of the Licking Valley region and some
    of the contiguous territory, 13936
Coals of the North Fork of Kentucky River
    in Breathitt and Perry Counties, 14336
Coals of the Nortonville quadrangle, 13941
Coann, Pearl Clement, 10425
Coartación: a Spanish institution for the
    advancement of slaves into freedom, 23853
Coast defenses, 837
The Coast of Bohemia, 9940
The Coast survey, 1920
Coasts, Cuba, 8438
Coates, Benjamin, 1921
Coates, Benjamin Hornor, 1922
Coates, Reynell, 1802-1886, 1923
Coats, William, 1924
Coatzacualcos, Mexico, Description, 6410
Cobb, Alfred, 3034
Cobb, Alvan, 1925
Cobb, Ann, 13858
Cobb, Charles, 292, 3035
Cobb, Darius, 1834-1919, 9049
Cobb, Howell, 1815-1868, 1926
Cobb, Irvin Shrewsbury, 1876-1944, 7155,
    13821, 13859, 14384, 15000, 15158
Cobb, Joseph Beckham, 1819-1858, 3036, 3037
Cobb, Lyman, 1800-1864, 1927

Cobb, Sylvanus, 1798-1866, 1928
Cobb, Sylvanus, 1823-1887, 1928
Cobb, Thomas Read Rootes, 1823-1862, 3038
Cobb family, 8103, 15990; (Henry Cobb, d.
    1679), 1928
Cobbe, Frances Power, 1822-1904, 1929
Cobbett, Griffith Owen, 6436
Cobbett, James Paul, 1803-1881, 1930, 21966
Cobbett, John Morgan, 1800-1877, 21966
Cobbett, William, 1763-1835, 1427, 1931-1945,
    2478, 3039, 3965, 11863, 21847, 21964-21966,
    22931, 24155; The life and adventures of
    Peter Porcupine, 1427; The scare-crow, 1427
Cobden, Richard, 1804-1865, 1865, 1946-1949
Cobleigh, Nelson E., 1950
Cobo, Mario, 20224, 20225
Cobos y Luna, Manuel de los, marqués de
    Camarasa, 7920
Coburn, Edward Otis, b.1830, 1951
Coburn, John, 13689
Cobus Yerks, 10480
Coccidae, Cuba, 18087
Coccidiostatics, 18947
Cochabamba, Bolivia (Dept.) Corte Superior,
    20226
Cochin, Augustin, 1823-1872, 2414
Cochran, Andrew McConnell January, 1854-1934,
    13860
Cochran, Clara C., d.1853, 10089
Cochran, John Salisbury, 1841-, 16219
Cochran, Louis, 1899-, 13861
Cochran, William Cox, 1848-, 24156
Cochrane, Clark Betton, 1815-1867, 1952
Cochrane, John, 1813-1898, 1953
Cochrane, John McDowell, 1849-1904, 16102
La cocina moderna, 19720
El cocinero presidencial, 21726
Cock, S., ed., 23839
Cock Mincapié, Olga, 20227
Cock Robin, 10434
Cockayne, M.S., 1954
Cockburn, Sir Alexander James Edmund, 1802-
    1880, 1955
Cockburn, G.F., 1956
Cockburn, John, 1957, 1958, 8303
Cocke, Richard Ivanhoe, 1959
Cocke, William Alexander, 1874-, 16220
Cocke, William Archer, 1960
Cocke, Zitella, 1848?, 3040
Cockrel, Clement, 15257
Cockrell, Thomas J., 7477
Cockrill, W. Willard, 13862
Cockrum, William Munroe, 1837-, 24157
Coelenterata, U.S., 107
Cocoa, 20001
Cocos Island, Description & travel, 8303

Cod-fisheries, 6401, 6575
Codazzi Aguirre, Juan Andrés, 20228
Codding, Milo Defonz, 1961
Coddington, David Smith, 1823-1865, 1962, 6437
Code des noirs, 8053
Code noir, 13147, 24426, 25178
The code of laws for the government of the negro slaves in the island of Jamaica, 13147
Codex Chimalpopocatl, 1442
Codex Cortesianus, 20229
Codex Fejerváry-Mayer, 6438
Codex Gondra, 1442
Codex "Troano", 20229
Códice de Calkiní, 20230
Códice diplomatico colombo-americano, 727
Códice liberado, 20009
Códice Per Abat, 20189
Código da propriedade industrial, 19334
Código de comercio, 18464
Código de minería, 19123
Código procesal civil y comercial de la Nación, 18568
Codman, John, 1782-1847, 1963
Codman, John, 1814-1900, 16221, 16222, 20231, 21967, 21968
Codovilla, Victorio, 20232
Cody, John Sherwin, 8425
Cody, Sherwin, 1868-, 6439
Cody, William Frederick, 1845-1917, 7712, 16223-16225, 16093, 16854, 17118
Coe, David Benton, 1814-1895, 1964
Coe, Escar Olin, 1899-, 13863
Coe, Fanny E., 6440
Coe, Joseph, 21969
Coe family (Robert Coe, b.1596), 1964
Coelho, Nelly Novaes, 20233
Coelho, Paulo Japyassú, 20234, 20235
Coelho Netto, Henrique Maximiniano, 1864-1934, 20236, 20237
Coelho Netto, Zita, 20237
Coerr, Wymberley DeR., 20238
Coffee, Brazil, 20425; Diseases, 17957 Pests, 17957; Statistics, 19398
Coffee and repartee, 8675
Coffeen, Henry Asa, 1841-1913, 16226
Coffeetree, 13784
Coffey, W.A., 1965
Coffin, Alexander, 1765?-1836, 1966
Coffin, Alfred Oscar, 6441
Coffin, Charles, 1779-1851, 21970, 21971
Coffin, Charles Carleton, 1823-1896, 1967, 3041, 11864, 16227
Coffin, Ebenezer, 1769-1816, 1968
Coffin, Frederick M., illustr., 10476

Coffin, George, 16228
Coffin, James Henry, 1806-1873, 1969
Coffin, John Gorham, 1770-1829, 1970
Coffin, Joshua, 1792-1864, 1971-1973
Coffin, Mrs. Kezia (Folger), 1723-1798, 9775
Coffin, Levi, 1798-1877, 3042, 24158
Coffin, Nathaniel Wheeler, 1815-1869, 1974
Coffin, Robert Barry, 1826-1886, 1975
Coffin, Robert Stevenson, 1797-1827, 1617, 1976, 1977
Coffin, Thomas Edward, 1838-, 12637
Coffin, William Foster, 1808-1878, 1978
Coffman, Edward, 1890-, 13864, 13865
Coggeshall, George, 1784-1861, 1979-1981
Coggeshall, William Turner, 1824-1867, 1982-1985, 3043
Coggins, James Caswell, 1865-, 6442
Coghill, Howard, 1858-, 8931
Coghlan, John M., 1835-1879, 24159
Coghlan, Mrs. Margaret (Moncrieffe), 1986
Cogley, Thomas Sydenham, 1840-, 3044
Cognitur, Nochmals zur Zivilität der, 24343
Cogswell, Elliott Colby, 1814-1887, 1987, 1988
Cogswell, Joseph Green, 1786-1871, 514-516
Cogswell, Nathaniel, 1773-1813, 1989
Cohen, Bernard, 21972
Cohen, Ernest Julius, 1869-, 3045
Cohen, Myer M., 1990, 3046
Cohen, Murray, 15257
Cohn, Alfons Fedor, 1878-, 7191
Cohoes, N.Y. Charters, 1991; Ordinances, etc., 1991
A Cohutta Valley shooting match, 10125
Coimbra Filho, Adelmar Faria, 20239
Coinage, Colombia, 18872; Peru, 8312; U.S., 22445
Coinage, International, 150
Coins, 2173, 23190; Argentine Republic, 18727
Coit, Thomas Winthrop, 1803-1885, 11865
Coke, Edward Thomas, 1807-1888, 1992
Coke, Henry John, 1827-1916, 3047
Coke, Thomas, bp., 1747-1814, 1993-1995, 3048, 11866
Colborn, Edward F., 16227
Colby, Charles William, 1867-, 6443
Colby, John, 1787-1817, 3049
Colcha de retalhos, 19974
Colcord Winery, Paris, Kentucky, 15771
Cole, 4727
Cole, Arthur Charles, 1886-, 24160
Cole, Cornelius, 1822-1924, 16230
Cole, E.C., 16868
Cole, George E., 16231
Cole, Gilbert L., 16232
Cole, Jacob Henry, 1847-, 3050
Cole, Thomas, 1801-1848, 1627

Colegio de Economistas de Venezuela, 20240
Colegio de Escribanos de la Provincia de
Buenos Aires. Publicaciones, 20241, 20415
Colegio de Ingenieros de Venezuela, 18373
Colegio Máximo de las Academias de Colombia,
20242
Coleman, Amoss Lee, 1913-, 12823, 13866,
13867, 24141
Coleman, Ann Mary Butler (Crittenden) "Mrs.
Chapman Coleman," 1813-1891, 3051
Coleman, John, 1758?-1816, 22682
Coleman, John Winston, 1898-, 13677, 13742,
13868-13888, 13901, 14040, 15325, 15775,
24162, 24163
Coleman, Laurence, 14646
Coleman, William, 1766-1829, 412, 11587
Coleman, William Macon, 1838-, 6447
Colemodio, José María, 20245
Colen, Mario, 20246, 20247
Colena. José de la, 20248
Coleraine, George Hanger, 4th baron, 1751?-
1824, 3052
Colerick, E. Fenwick, 13889
Coleridge, Samuel Taylor, 1772-1834, 20243
Coles, Edward, 1786-1868, 23875, 25835
Colesworthy, Daniel Clement, 1810-1893,
21973
Colette, Sidonie Gabrielle, 1873-1954,
20244
Colfax, Schuyler, 1823-1885, 1531, 2772
Colhoun, James Edward, 13360
Coll, Pedro Emilio, 20249
Coll Cuchi, Cayetano, 20250
Coll y Prat, Narciso, 20251
Coll y Toste, Cayetano, 1850-1930, 6107
Collaboration, 10020
Collado de la Garza, Gloria, 1940-, 20252
Collamore, Anthony, d.1693, 22754
Collazo, Enrique, 1848-1921, 20253
The collected wisdom of ages, 23685
Collecting of accounts, 14665
Collections, Prejudgment and post-
judgement, 14687
Collective bargaining, 18868; Public
sector, 14688
College of Physicians of Philadelphia, 535
College of the Bible, Lexington, Ky.,
14909, 15035, 15176, 15440, 15556
College of William and Mary, Williamsburg,
Va., 3805
The college, the market, and the court,
11939
College horse, Dartmouth, 9734
Colleges and universities, Finance, 14302;
Kentucky, 13807, 14039, 14600, 14624,
14962, 15112, 15315, 15592, 15802; New

York, 12619; Ohio Valley, 14233; U.S.,
14274
Collell Núñez, José, 20254
Collie, John Norman, 1859-, 8126
Collier, Price, 1860-1913, 3053, 13551
Collier, Robert Lee, 1933-1960, 13890
Collier, Robert R., 24164
Collin, John Francis, 1802-1889, 24165
Collings, Lindon W., 13891
Collins, Clarissa W., 6448
Collins, Dennis, 16234
Collins, Elizabeth, 3054
Collins, Emma (Gowdy) "Mrs. William Leslie
Collins", 3055
Collins, Floyd, 13857
Collins, John, jr., 13288
Collins, John A., 24166, 24167, 25068
Collins, John Sloan, 1839-, 16235
Collins, Lewis, 1797-1870, 13892, 13893;
History of Kentucky, 13894
Collins, R. M., 3056
Collins, Richard H., 1824-1889, 13892-13894
Collins, S.H., 3057
Collins, Stephen Foster, 1826-1864, 7365,
13895, 14122, 15385
Collins, William H., 17565
Collins steamship line, 648
Collinson, Peter, 1694-1768, 22114
Collinson, Richard, 6449
Collinson, T.B., 6449
Collot, Georges Henri Victor, 1752-, 13896
Collyer, Isaac J.P., 24168
Collyer, Joseph, d.1776, 3429
Collyer, Robert H., 3058
Colman, Mrs. Lucy Newhall (Danforth), 1817-
1906, 24169
Colman, Samuel, pub., 4743
Colmenares, Germán, 20255
Colmer, J.G., 8106
Coloane, Francisco A., 20256
Colombia, Administrative and political
divisions, 20272; Anthropology, 18363;
Antiquities, 11330, 18761, 19748; Banco
de la República, 18872; Bibliography, 18314,
18755, 20276, 20292; Biography, 18822;
Caja de Credito Agrario, Industrial y
Minero, 20257; Cámara de Cuentas, 20258;
Casa de Moneda, 18872; Climate, 20492-20494;
Comisión de Estudios del Plan Decenal para
el fomento del Departamento del Chocó,
20259; Comité Nacional de Planeación, 20260;
Commerce, 18988, 20283; Commerce, Congresses,
20412; Consejo Nacional de Política
Económica y Planeación, 20261, 20262;
Departamento Administrativo. Punto Central
de Información, 20270; Departamento

Administrativo de Planeación y Servicios Técnicos, 20259, 20261, 20262, 20266; Departamento Administrativo del Servicio Civil, 20334; Departamento Administrativo Nacional de Estadística, 20267-20269, 20271-20276; Departamento de Prisiones, 20277; Description & travel, 7264, 7583, 8168, 8319, 12569, 13451, 22540; Dirección del Presupuesto, 20278; Dirección Nacional de Estadistica. División político-administrativa, 20272; Directories, 20275; División de Atención Médica, 20279; División de Extensión Agricola, 19835; División de Medicina del Trabajo y Seguridad Industrial, 20325; Economic conditions, 18698, 18757-18760, 18988, 19101, 20257, 20260, 20266, 20274; Economic conditions, Bibliography, 19097; Economic conditions, Maps, 18759; Economic policy, 20261, 20262, 20443, 20488, 20489; Ejército. Biblioteca del Ejército, V, 18822; Ejército. Sección de Historia y Publicaciones, 18909; Fondo Nacional de Ahorro para el Desarrollo Económico y Social, 20280; Foreign relations - U.S., 7859, 12716; History, 18306, 18756, 18872; History,To 1810, 29; History, 1822-1832, 7761, 8267; History, 1832-1886, 7761; History, Bibliography, 18191; History, Periodicals, 7545, 7847, 7956; History, War of independence, 1810-1822, 7322, 7762, 7897, 8009, 8267, 8268, 18822; Industries, 18599, 20275; Instituto Caro y Cuervo. Archivo epistolar colombiano, 20711-20718; Instituto Caro y Cuervo. Publicaciones, 18192, 18193, 19726, 20227; Instituto Colombiano Agropecuario, 20281-20282; Instituto Colombiano de Comercio Exterior, 20283; Instituto Colombiano de Emergia Eléctrica, 20284; Instituto Colombiano de Especialización Técnica en el Exterior, 20285; Instituto Colombiano de la Reforma Agraria. 20286, 20287; Instituto Colombiano de la Reforma Agraria. Comité de Estudios Técnicos, 20288; Instituto Colombiano de la Reforma Agraria. Sección de Cooperativas y Mercadeo, 20289; Instituto Colombiano de Pedagogía, 20290, 20291; Instituto Colombiano para el Fomento de la Educación Superior, 20292-20298; Instituto de Investigaciones Tecnológicas, Bogotá, 20299, 20300; Instituto Geográfico Agustín Codazzi. Departamento Agrológico, 20301-20307; Instituto Nacional de Abastecimientos, 18332, 20308; Instituto Nacional de Fomento Municipal, 20309; Instituto Nacional de Fomento Tabacalero, 20310; Instituto

Nacional de Nutrición de Colombia, 20311-20313; Instituto Nacional de Nutrición de Colombia. Sección de Epidemiología, 20314, 20315; Laws, statutes, etc., 19151, 20278, 20316-20334, 20336, 20342, 20343; Maps, 18759; Ministerio de Agricultura, 18618, 18619, 20327, 20335-20337; Ministerio de Agricultura. Estudios regionales, 20336; Ministerio de Agricultura. Oficina de Planeamento, Coordinación y Evaluación, 20336; Ministerio de Agricultura. Servicio Técnico Agricola Colombiano Americano, 20337; Ministerio de Educación Nacional, 20353; Ministerio de Educación Nacional. Oficina de Planeamiento, Coordinación y Evaluación, 20338, 20339; Ministerio de Educación Nacional. Sección de Orientación Pedagógica, 20340; Ministerio de Educación Nacional. Sección de Orientación Psicopedagógica, 20341; Ministerio de Gobierno, 20333; Ministerio de Minas y Petróleos, 20342; Ministerio de Minas y Petróleos. Empresa Colombiana de Minas, 20343; Ministerio de Obras Públicas, 20344; Minsterio de Salud Publica. Estudio de recursos humanos para la salud y educación médica en Colombia, 20345-20348; Ministerio de Trabajo, 20349; Periodicals, 7683; Policies & government, 18306, 20263-20265; Public lands, 18243; Registraduría Nacional del Estado Civil, 20350; Relations (general) with France, 20242; Servicio Nacional de Aprendizaje, 20351, 20352; Statistics, 18757; Statistics, Medical, 20345-20348; Colombia-U.S. Workshop on Science and Technology, Fusagasuga, 1968, 20353
Colombia: its present state, in respect of climate, soil, 12569
Colombian arquitecture, 20508
Colombian literature, Bibliography, 18191; History & criticisms, 19655, 20717; Periodicals, 7545, 7847
Colombian periodicals, 20276
Colombian poetry (collections), 18359; History & criticisms, 19195, 19732
Colombo, Cristoforo, 1451-1506, 13, 234, 311, 727, 1081, 1123, 1544, 6331, 7305, 7567, 8083, 20356, 22146, 22400; Bibliography, 22312; Codice diplomatio colombo-americano, 727; Drama, 1493; Iconography, 8083; Poetry, 809, 819
Colombo, Haydée, 20354
Colombo family, 1115
Colomina de Rivera, Marta, 20355
Colón, Fernando, 1488-1539, Bibliography, 20356

Colón (Panamá), Description, 6334;
History, 19935
Colón de Córdova Bocanegra y Pacheco
Carlos, 5877
Colón de Córdova y Bocanegra, Francisco,
marqués de Villa mayor, 6850
Colón de Portugal, Alvaro, 5877; Ana
Francisca, 6850; Pedro, 6850
Colón de Toledo, Alvaro, 5877
Colón de Toledo y Larreatigui, Diego,
6850
Colón family, 7567
The colonel, 3038
Colonel Carter of Cartersville, 10807
Col. Chipsham's calendar, 9677
Colonel Dunwoddie, millionaire, 8654
Colonel Eph's shoe-buckles, 10909
Colonel Floyd's wards, 5358, 10940
Colonel Hungerford's daughter, 8466
Col. Judson of Alabama, 8762
Colonel Starbottle's client, 6965
The colonel's awakening, 24319
The colonel's Christmas dinner, 10116
The Colonel's daughter, 10117
The colonel's diary, 4036
Colonels, Kentucky, 15648
Coloniae anglicanae illustratae, 11332
Colonial Dames of America, 13897
Colonial Dames of America in the
Commonwealth of Kentucky, 14821
Colonial families of the U.S.A., 7374
The colonial history of Vincennes, 4229
Colonial records of Spanish Florida, 3066
Colonial Society of Pennsylvania, 23631
A colonial wooing, 8445
Colonies, 11809, 23059, 24327, 25663;
Law, 25492; Slavery, 24733
Les colonies anglaises de 1574 à 1660,
2242
Colonies étrangères et Haiti, résultats
de l'émancipation anglaise, 25454
La colonización de Puerto Rico, 19227
Colonization, 23783; History, 22396;
Period., 379
Colonization and abolition contrasted,
24171
Colonization and Christianity, 12965
Colonization Society, Maine, 24170
The color-guard, 3944
Color in man, 1081
Color studies, 10225
Colorado, 14896, 16156, 16171, 16191,
17301, 17640, 17749; Antiquities,
16300, 16307, 16371, 17200; Bibliography
- Catalogs, 17792; Biography, 16006,
16117, 16755, 17413, 17679, 17881;

Biography, Pictorial works, 17532;
Constitution, 16267; Description & travel,
2738, 2743, 2877, 3008, 3063, 3551, 3677,
3715, 3717, 3987, 4529, 4549, 4707, 5000,
5421, 5455, 5695, 7868, 11134, 15831, 15986,
15993, 16005, 16030, 16096, 16148, 16171,
16174, 16180, 16191, 16222, 16237, 16238,
16239, 16242, 16244-16248, 16251, 16302,
16348, 16364-16371, 16499, 16539, 16544,
16545, 16571, 16586, 16603, 16616, 16621,
16622, 16632, 16686, 16702, 16721, 16725,
16730, 16852, 17016, 17199, 17200, 17362,
17464, 17476, 17511, 17512, 17514, 17515,
17518, 17530, 17536, 17652, 17660, 17661,
17714, 17733, 17752, 17801, 17862, 17863,
17864, 17877, 17878, 17897, 17918, 17920;
Description & travel, Gazetteers, 16302;
Description & travel, Guide-books, 3735;
Directories, 16243; Economic conditions,
17862; Geology, 17651; Gold discoveries,
3616, 3717, 4594, 4707, 4708, 5421; Gold
mines, 5573; History, 2995, 3398, 16117,
16241, 16250, 16382, 16435, 16549, 16659,
16666, 16755, 16756, 16782, 16987, 17357,
17363, 17447, 17630, 17635, 17664, 17679,
17690, 17841; History, Bibliography, 17896;
History, Civil War, 17874; History, Civil-
War, Unionist side, 17627; Maps, 3255,
16721; Militia, 16236; Parks, 17355; Politics
& government, 16391, 17038, 17635, 17888;
Public lands, 17669
Colorado and Utah Rockies, 17801
Colorado cavalry, 2d regt., 1861-1865, 17900
A Colorado colonel, 16136
Colorado gazetteer for 1871, 17514
Colorado in the United States of America,
17878
Colorado: its agriculture, its horticulture,
16247; its mineral and agricultural
resources, 5000; its resources, its men,
16005
Colorado pioneers in picture and story, 16755
Colorado River, 4996, 5517, 5524, 17422,
17736; Description & travel, Views, 16712
Colorado River gold, 16788
Colorado River, Water-rights, 19768
Colorado: some pictures and a few facts, 16365
Colorado the magnificent, 17660
Colorado, the Rocky Mountain gem, 16499
Colorado, The school lands of, 16642
Coloratlas, Kapelusz, 20357
A colored man's reminiscences of James
Madison, 13209
Colossal Cavern, Ky., 14860, 15490
The colossus, 10594
Colt, Mrs. Miriam (Davis) b.1817, 3059

Colton, Calvin, 1789-1857, 13898, 24171
Colton, George Hooker, 1818-1847, ed., 317
Colton, Joseph Hutchins, 1800-1893, 3060, 16252
Colton, Walter, 1797-1851, 16253
Colton's traveler and tourist guide book, 3060
Coltrinari, Lylian, 20358
The Columbia, 16972
Columbia, Ky. Columbia Christian Church, 13899
Columbia, S.C., 17579; Asylum prison, 5058; Burning of, 1865, 5163; Camp Sorghum, 2876
Columbia River, 1670, 3100, 3578, 3971, 4272, 5017, 5526, 15995, 16972, 17030, 17335, 22233
The Columbia River Historical Expedition, 15830
Columbia River valley, 17824
Columbia University, 13174, 22688, 23521; Library, 22724
Columbia's wreath, 1439
The Columbiad, 809
Columbian association, New York, 248
The Columbian naval songster, 12250
The Columbian traveller, and statistical register, 12763
Columbus, pseud., 17323, 24172
Columbus, N.M., History, 19650
Columbus, O. State house, 23339
Colusa Co., California, 17517
Colver, Nathaniel, 1794-1870, 24173
Colvil, Edward, pseud., 10581
Colvin, John B., 1996
Colvin, Russell, 12761
Colvocoresses, George Musalas, 1816-1872, 11867
Colwell, Stephen, 1800-1871, 1997-2001
Colyar, Arthur St. Clair, 1818-1907, 2047
Colyer, Vincent, 1825-1888, 2002
Comadran Ruiz, Jorge, 20359, 20360
Comanche Indians, 3945, 4577, 5533, 12698, 16380, 16449, 17349; Fiction, 5651, 10081
The Comanche's dream, 10081
Comas Camps, Juan, 1900-, 20361-20368
Comayagua, Honduras, Description, Poetry, 18520
Combats and conquests of immortal heroes, 15918
Combe, George, 1788-1858, 3061
Combe, William, 1741-1823, 3052, 4362, 17168
Combier, Cyprien, b.1805, 2003

Combs, Leslie, 1793-1881, 2004, 13900
Combs, Sidney Sayre, 13901, 13902
Combs, Thomas Asbury, 13904
Come forth!, 11069
A comedy of elopement, 10967
The Comet, 21974
Comets, 1696
Comercialización del banano ecuatoriano, 21723
Comercio exterior de México, 1943-1967, 18764
Comettant, Jean Pierre Oscar, 1819-1898, 2005
Comfield, Mrs. Amelia Stratton, 2006
Comfort, Benjamin Freeman, 6450
The comic history of the United States, 10753
Comision de Integración Eléctrica Regional. Subcomité de Sistemas Electricos, 20369; Montevideo, 20370
Comitas, Lambros, 20371
Comitatus, Zedekiah, pseud., 11868
Comité colonial, Paris, 6326
Comité Nacional de Guatemala para el año Geofísico Internacional, 20372
Comité permanente de obispos de Chile, 19987
Commencement, 1283
Commerce (Brig), 25394, 25397
Commerce, 893, 2001, 7913, 19813, 21963, 21988; Addresses, essays, lectures, 12878; Brazil, 20379; History, 480, 1979, 22986; Terminology, 19418
Commerce of the American States, 13477
Commercial associations, 12788
Commercial convention, Detroit, 1865, 2007
Commercial Cuba, 6426
Commercial directory, 2008
Commercial law, 22882; Bolivia, 19124; Brazil, 19355; Kentucky, 14665; Newfoundland, 385; Spain, 402; U.S., 1001, 1494, 1793
Commercial products, Asia, 13154; Spanish America, 11383
A commercial rip-snorter, 10598
Commercial statistics, 22882
Commercial treaties, 18819
A commercial view, and geographical sketch, of the Brasils in South America, 492
Commissão Interestadual da Bacia Paraná-Uruguay, 19683
Commissary Wilson's orderly book, 331
Commissioner Hume, 8697
Committee for Economic Development, 20373
Committee for Kentucky, 13648, 13903, 14246, 14905, 14963
Committee on the coal trade and iron interests of Kentucky, 14584
Commodity exchanges, Buenos Aires, 19536
A common apologie of the chvrch of England: against the vniust challenges of the over iust sect, commonly called Brownists, 22291

Common market, 18770
Common-place book of prose, 21900
Common sense, 24175
Common sense addresses, to the citizens
  of the southern states, 3d ed., enl.,
  and improved, 21843
Commons, Mexico, 19847
The Commonwealth, Boston, 11740
Communication, 18660, 18662; Brazil,
  20379, 20383
Communication and traffic, 22872
Communication in management, 18832
Communion sermons, 11746
Communipaw, 9995
Communism, 1530, 5050, 15501, 18391,
  20027; Argentine Republic, 18556,
  19140, 20232; Cuba, 18888; Latin
  America, 20388; Mexico, 6001; Spanish
  America, 20404; U.S., 6193
Communities, Bibliography, 20036
Community and school, 20483
Community action, 19220
The community colleges, 15031
Commuting patterns of Kentucky counties,
  14533
Compagnie de Saint-Domingue, 24425
Compagnie des colons de la Guyane
  française, Paris, 24176
Compagnie des Indes, 24425
Compagnie des Indes dans les Pais-Bas
  autrichiens, 1191
Compagnie des Indes Orientales, 1201
Le compagnon du père Tom, 24602
Companhia de Desenvolvimento do Estado
  de Goiás, 20375, 20376
Companhia de Industrialização da Paraíba,
  20377, 20378
Companhia do Desenvolvimento do Planalto
  Central, 20379-20383
The companion, 11869
"Co. Aytch", Maury Grays, 5635
Compañia Barrera, Aníbal, 20374
Compañia Colombiana de Seguros, 20384
Compañia de Acero del Pacífico. Santiago,
  Chile, 18213, 20385
Compañia de Seguros El Comercio de
  Córdoba, 20386
Comparative essay on indentured labour
  at St. Thomé and Principe, 23870
Comparative government, 19032
Comparative law, 388
A comparison between the British sugar
  colonies and New England, 2009
A comparison of five mortals' trip to
  Hades, 15364
A comparison of slavery with abolitionism,

24177
Compayré, Gabriel, i.e. Jules Gabriel, 1843-
  1913, 20387
Compendio de la historia de los Estados Unidos
  de America, 2010
Compendio de legislación agropecuaria y
  organismos agrícolas de Colombia, 18640
Compendio del confesionario en mexicano y
  castellano, 2011
Compendio della guerra nata per confini in
  America tra la Francia e l'Inghilterra, 650
Compendio elemental de geografía y estadística
  de la República majicana, 7018
Compendio histórico del descubrimiento y
  colonización de la Nueva Granada, 29
A compendious description of the thirteen
  colonies, 3062
Competition, 19620
Compilation of the laws in force in the
  District of Columbia, April 1, 1868, 22127
The complaint of Mexico, 15834
A complaint to the _____ of _____ against
  a pamphlet, 2012
Complimentary dinner tendered to the Hon.
  Thomas Asbury Combs, 13904
Composers, Kentucky, 14658
A compressed view of the points to be
  discussed, 520
Compromise of 1850, 1091, 1655, 1903, 3672,
  8331, 11692, 14465, 16039, 17584, 22991,
  23709, 23936, 23976, 24026, 24106, 24119,
  24260, 24308, 24313, 24675, 24754, 24935,
  25090, 25095, 25215, 25288, 25387, 25417,
  25427, 25484, 25720, 25744, 25754, 25793,
  25844, 25847, 25900
La computadora en apoyo técnico, 19550
Computer-stored information, 14616
Computers, 19550
Comstock, Samuel, 1802-1824, 9090
Comstock, Theodore Bryant, 1849-1915, 17776
The Comstock club, 16613
Comstock lode, Nev., 17934, 17935
Comunicaciones, entre el señor Carlos Biddle,
  1250
El Comunismo en la América Hispana, 20388
Comunismo en la Universidad de Buenos Aires?
  19140
Conant, Abigail (Huntington) Frink, 1731-1759,
  2016
Conant, Gaius, 1776-1862, 2014
Conant, Helen Peters (Stevens) 1839-1899, 6407
Conant, Sylvanus, 1720-1777, 2015, 2016
Conant, William C., 21975
Concealed weapons, 9916
Concentração de apatita do carbonatito de
  Jacupiranga, Estado de São Paulo, 18269

Concepción, Chile (Province), Industries, 19597; Universidad, 20389, 20390
Conceptos y métodos de la programación por zonas para el desarrollo de la comunidad, 20030
Concerts, Kentucky, 15052
La concesión de servicio público electrico, 18602
Concessions and compromises, 24393
Concessions to America the bane of Britain, 23147
Conciliator, pseud., 2017
A concise answer, to the general inquiry, who, or what are the Shakers, 4373
A concise description of the English and French possessions in North America, 4682
A concise historical account of all the British colonies in North America, 2018
A concise narrative of Gen. Jackson's first invasion of Florida, 23732
Concklin, Seth, 1802-1851, 10521
Conclin, George, 13905
Conclin's new river guide, 13905
Conclusiones in repetitione agitandae, 5846
Concolorcorvo, pseud., 19852
Concord, Mass., 25438;
Concord, N.H., 22626; Geneal.,11417; History, 11417
Concord, Battle of, 1775, 11817, 13418; Poetry, 920
Concord fight, 920
Concordance entre les codes civils etrangers et le Code Napoléon, 388
Concubinage, Brazil, 19070
Conde y Oquendo, Francisco Xavier, 1733-1799, 6451
Condemnatio cum deductione, 25560
Condemnation, Kentucky, 14683, 15334
Conder, John, 1714-1781, 1621
Conder, Josiah, 1789-1855, 2019, 3064, 6452, 13906
Condiciones comunes de las contratas celebradas con los cosecheros de tabaco, 6481
Condict, Ira, 1764-1811, 2020
Condie, David Francis, 1796-1875, 2021
Condie, Thomas, 1775?-1814, 2022
Condillac, Étienne Bonnot de, 1714-1780, 19735, 20391
Condit, Jonathan Bailey, 1808-1876, 2023, 2024
Condition juridique des affranchis, 24689
El Condor de Aconcagua, 20465
Condorcet, Marie Jean Antoine Nicolas

Caritat, marquis de, 1743-1794, 2025, 22089
Condra, George Evert, 16258
La conducción estatal argentina, 18155
The conduct of General Washington, 13008
Conduct of life, 1224, 1489, 5237, 10986, 12892, 13348, 22542
The conduct of Major Gen. Shirley, 21758
The conduct of the administration, 12106
The conduct of the Dutch relating to their breach of treaties with England, 2026
The conduct of the French, with regard to Nova Scotia, 13191
The conduct of the ministry impartially examined, 2027
The conduct of the two bars vindicated, 2028
Conductor Generalis, //Or//....., 21976
La conduite des François justifiée, ou Observations sur un écrit anglois, 22750
Condy, Jeremiah, d.1768, 2029
Cone, Andrew, 2030
Cone, David D., 2031, 2032
Cone, Edward Winfield, 1814-1871, 11870
Cone, Mary, 16259
Cone, Spencer Houghton, 1785-1855, 11870
Cone, Spencer Wallace, 1819-1888, 11870
Conejo Guevara, Adena, 1930-, 20392
Conestoga Indians, 2317
Confederação Brasileira de Basketball, 20393, 20394
Confederação Brasileira de Desportes, 20395
A confederação dos Tampoyos; poema, 23020
Confederação Nacional de Agricultura, 20420
Confederación General Económica de la República Argentina, 20396, 20397
Confederación mundial de organizaciones de profesionales de la enseñanza, 19608
The confederacy of Judah with Assyria, 24105
The Confederate flag on the ocean, 4733
Confederate General Ben Hardin Helm, 7381
A Confederate girl's diary, 3199
Confederate hand-book, 5759
A Confederate idyl, 10163
The Confederate invasion of Kentucky, 1862, 15498
Confederate Power Works, Augusta, Ga., 4885
The Confederate spy, 13952
Confederate States of America, 3140, 3222, 3539, 3617, 3934, 4869, 5759, 15259, 17453, 23559, 25295; Army, 2686; Army Artillery, 2961; Army. Dept. of Mississippi and East Louisiana, 2033; Army. Dept. of Northern Virginia, 2034-2036; Army. Dept. of South Carolina, Georgia and Florida, 2037; Army. Dept. of Southwestern Virginia, 2038; Army. Dept. of Tennessee, 2039; Army-Guard duty, 23030; Army Negro troops, 12223; Army

115

Recruiting, enlistment, etc., 2044, 2053; Army, Registers, 24687; Army, Regulations, 2067; Army. Trans-Mississippi dept., 2040; Army, Transportation, 2059; Biography, 16483, 23927; Bureau of exchange, 2041; Bureau of printing, 2054; Claims, 2045; Congress, 2042, 2043, 2069, 2070; Congress. Conference committees, 2044; Congress. House of representatives. Committee on claims, 2045; Congress. House of representatives. Committee on Quartermaster and commissary departments, 2046; Congress. House of representatives. Committee on ways and means, 2047; Congress. House of representatives. Committee to enquire into the treatment of prisoners at Castle Thunder, 2048; Congress. House of representatives. Roanoke island investigation committee, 2049; Congress. House of representatives. Special committee on the recent military disasters, 2050; Congress. Senate. Committee on finance, 11871; Congress. Senate. Committee on foreign relations, 2051; Congress. Senate. Committee on the judiciary, 2052; Congress. Senate. Select committee on a portion of the message of the president of the 13th instant [March, 1865], 2053; Constitution, 2063, 11872, 12212; Department of justice, 2054, 2055, 24184; District courts. Alabama, 2056; Economic conditions, 22889; Executive departments, 2052; Foreign relations, 16085, 23569, 25432; Foreign relations France, 2712; Foreign relations Great Britain, 4763, 12231; History, 2900, 3202, 3301, 16483, 25290; History , Periodicals, 23849, 24755, 25352; History Sources, 4814; History, Military, 2035, 2036, 2040, 2050, 2068, 2069, 2070, 2071, 3195, 3828, 4610, 11875; Laws, statutes, etc., 2057-2064, 11872, 24178-24180; Memorials, 15009; Navy, 2065, 2712, 5085, 5123, 11950, 16085, 21977; Navy Regulations, 21977; Navy, History, 4035; Navy. Office of ordnance and hydrography, 2066; Navy ordnance and ordnance stores, 21977; Navy, Registers, 2065; Officials and employees, 2052; Officials and employees, Salaries, allowances, etc., 2058; Poetry, 14990; Politics & government, 2042, 3187, 4817, 5344, 6063, 9876, 11874, 12264; Politics & government, Civil War, 22560, 25422; Post-office Dept., 11873; President, 3065, 11874; President (Davis), 24181; Secret

service, 7410, 11455; Social conditions, 8656; Social life & customs, 2544, 3610, 4523, 8634, 23559; Treasury dept., 2060; Treaties, etc., 2063, 21978; War dept., 2034, 2037, 2046, 2067-2073, 11875, 24182-24184
Conference on Antarctica, Washington, D.C., 1959. Tratado antártico, 19724
Conference on the Role of Books in Human Development, Airlie House, 1964, 20398
Conferencia de Facultades (Escuelas) de Derecho (Ciencias Jurídicas, Políticas y Sociales) Latinoamericanas, ed., Santiago de Chile and Valparaíso, 1963, 20399
Conferencia Interamericana de Seguridad Social, 20400
Conferencia Latinoamericana de Ciencias Políticas y Sociales, 20401
Conferência Nacional dos Bispos do Brasil. Secretariado Regional Leste 1, 20402
Conferencia sobre los Problemas de la Urbanización en Guatemala. 1st, Guatemala, 1965, 20403
Conferências interamericanas de educação, 19320
Confession, 2011, 6357
Confession of Michael Martin, or Captain Lightfoot, 23191
The confession of a house-breaker, 10040
The confession of Jereboam Beauchamp, 13636, 13907
Confessions, trials, and biographical sketches of the most cold-blooded murderers..., 21979
The confessions of a bank officer, 8474
The confessions of a frivolous girl, 9640
The confessions of a husband, 4207
The confessions of a magdalen, 8820
The confessions of a minister, 10192
Confessions of a poet, 10451
The confessions of a society man, 9160
The confessions of Emilia Harrington, 11184
Confessions of Richard H. Shuck, 15366
The confessors of Connaught, 10339
Confidence, 10010
The confidence-man, 10343
Confidencias de dos inmigrantes, 19927
A confident tomorrow, 10327
Confidential communications, Lawyers, 19838; Lawyers Chile, 19838
Confinanciera, Bogotá. Public Relations Dept., 20498
Conflict of laws, Great Britain, 20254; U.S., 20254
Conflictos del trabajo, 18494
Conqar, Obadiah, 1768-1848, 2074
Congdon, Charles Taber, 1821-1891, 2075

Conger, Omer T., 23497
A congratulatory letter from a gentleman
   in the West, 12819
Congregational association of Oregon and
   Washington, 16455
Congregational board of publication, 11821,
   13064, 24856
Congregational churches, Catechisms and
   creeds, 22511; Catechisms and creeds,
   Polyglot, 23297; Collected works, 1098;
   Discipline, 631; Doctrinal and
   controversial works, 11801; Government,
   12469, 23333, 23560, 23561; Sermons,
   1725, 13384, 22548, 23334
Congregational churches in Connecticut,
   Saybrook synod, 1708, 22511
Congregational churches in Illinois. General
   association. Rights of Congregationalists
   in Knox college, 658
Congregational churches in Massachusetts,
   11821; Clergy, 1400; General
   Association, 24185
Congregational churches in New England,
   22355, 23813
Congregational churches in New Hampshire,
   Clergy, 11416
Congregational churches in Wisconsin, 11857
Congregational conference and missionary
   society of Maine, 12375
Congregational home missionary society, 845,
   11857, 23230
Congregational publishing society, 22494
Congregational Sunday-school and publishing
   society, 17416
Congregationalism, 11900, 22362, 23333;
   Bibliography, 22105; History, 22105
The congregationalism of the last three
   hundred years, as seen in its literature,
   22105
Congrès international antiesclavagiste,
   2d, Paris, 1900, 24186
Congreso Continental Anticomunista, 4th,
   Antigua, Guatemala, 1958, 20404
Congreso de Academias de la Lengua
   Española, 3d., Bogotá, 1960, 20405
Congreso de Indios de Venezuela, 2d, 14-17
   April, 1972, 20406
Congreso de Instituciones Hispánicas, 1st,
   Madrid, 1963, 20407
Congreso Hispanoamericano de Historia.
   3d., Cartagena, 1961, 20408
Congreso Internacional de Literatura Ibero-
   Americana, 13th, Los Angeles and Caracas,
   1967-1968, 20409
Congreso Jurídico Guatemalteco, 1st.,
   Guatemala, 1960, 20410

Congreso Nacional de Ediles, 5th, Paysandú,
   Uruguay, 1970, 20411
Congreso Nacional de Exportadores, 2d,
   Bogotá, 1968, 20412
Congreso Nacional de Filosofía, Córdoba,
   Argentina, 1971, 20413, 20414
Congreso nacional de geografía, 6453
Congreso notarial Argentino, 1st, Buenos
   Aires, 1917, 20415
Congreso Panamericano de Ferrocarriles, 20416
Congreso Sindical. 1st, Madrid, 1961, 20417
Congreso Venezolano de Petroleo. 1st, Caracas,
   1962, 20418
Congreso Venezolano de Salud Pública. Caracas,
   1961, 20419
Congress (Frigate), 16253
The Congress canvassed, 23586
Congresses and conventions - Argentine
   Republic, 18420
Congresses, International, 19396
Congressional address, 2076
Congressional total abstinence society,
   Washington, D.C., 2077
Os congressistas e a previdência social,
   19339
The congressman's Christmas dream, 9704
Congresso Brasileiro do Cacua, I, Itabuna,
   28-30 July 1967, 20420
Congresso Brasileiro de Critica e Historia
   Literaria, 1.°, Recife   7 a 14 de agôsto
   de 1960, 20421
Congresso Eucarístico Nacional, 8th, Brasília,
   1970, 20422
Congresso Nacional de Botânica, 25th, Mossoró,
   1974, 20423
Congresso Nacional de Policia, 2d, Rio de
   Janeiro, 1967, 20424
Congresso Nacional do Café, 3°, 8 a 11 de
   abril de 1970, moços de Caladas, M.G.
   Anais, 20425
Congresso Nacional dos Institutos de
   Providência Estaduais, 2d.   Recife, 1968,
   20426
Congreve, Richard, 1818-1899, 13104
Conjuntura da castanha do Pará, 18275
The conjured kitchen, 9582
The conjured woman, 2981
Conkling, Alfred, 1789-1874, 2078, 21980
Conkling, Alfred Ronald, 1850-1917, 6454
Conkling, Edgar, 2079, 2080
Conkling, Frederick Augustus, 1816-1891, 2081
Conkling, Henry, 2082
Conkling, Howard, 6456
Conkling, James Cook, 1816-1899, 6415
Conkling, Mrs. Jerusha (Buell) 1749-1782, 1660
Conkling, Margaret Cockburn, "Mrs. Albert

Steele," 1814-1890, 2082
Conkling, Roscoe, 1829-1888, 2084, 2085
Conkwright, Bessie Taul, 13908-13910
Conkwright, S. J., 13911, 13912
Conn, William, 16261, 17122
Conneau, Théophile, 24187
A connected view of the whole internal
  navigation of the United States, 448
Connecticut, Bound., Massachusetts,
  13051; Charters, 11748; Church history,
  642, 23714; Constitutional history,
  634, 13346; Description & travel, 10761;
  Fiction, 10359; Geneal., 2448, 12795;
  General Assembly, 1602; General Assembly.
  Committee on the petition of Sarah M.
  Jarvis, 13171; Governor, 1858-1866
  (W.A. Buckingham), 2086; History, 11641;
  History, Colonial period, 233, 23714;
  History, Colonial period, Sources, 22493;
  History, Revolution, Fiction, 10881;
  Politics & government, 1348; Politics &
  government, 1775-1865, 12844, 12947;
  Politics & government, Civil war, 2086;
  Politics & government, Colonial period,
  635, 12183; Social life & customs, 10761
Connecticut (colony) Governor, 22493
Connecticut historical society, Hartford, 635
Connecticut infantry, 6th regt., 1861-1865,
  2880
Connecticut infantry, 14th regt., 1862-1865,
  3457
Connecticut infantry, 16th regt., 1862-1865,
  2729
Connecticut infantry, 27th regt., 1862-1863,
  5135
Connecticut republicanism, 1344, 1345
Connecticut Society for the Promotion of
  Freedom and the Belief of Persons Unlawfully
  Holden in Bondage, 25232, 25661
Connell, Mrs. Mary, 12834
Connelly, Emma M., 13913
Connelly, William Elsey, 1855-1930, 16262,
  16263, 17260, 17522
Connellsville, Pa., Citizens, 24188
Conner, Eugene H., 13914
Connolly, Alonzo P., 16264
Connor, Charlotte Reeve, 6457
Connor, Mrs. Jeannette M. (Thurber),ed. & tr.,
  3066, 5228
Connor, Selden, 1839-, 6458
Conover, Charlotte Reeve, 6459, 13915
Conover, James F., 3067
Conner, James Hamilton, 1794-1866, 22514
Conquered, 9265
Conquering the wilderness, 5460
The conquerors, 15878

The conquerors of the New World and their
  bondsmen, 24585
The conquest of America, and minor poems,
  22340
The conquest of California and New Mexico,
  3151
The conquest of Canada, 8338
The conquest of Constantinople, 9279
The conquest of Kansas, 17386
The conquest of New Mexico and California,
  16272
The conquest of our great Northwest, 16671
The conquest of Quebec, 12771, 12948
The conquest of Santa Fé and subjugation of
  New Mexico, 3068
The conquest of the old southwest, 14303
The conquest of the Sioux, 16515
Los conquistadores espirituales de América,
  19167
Conrad, David Holmes, 7386
Conrad, Harrison, 1869-, 3069, 3070
Conrad, John, 316
Conrad, Robert Taylor, 1810-1858, 22215
Conrad, Timothy Abbot, 1803-1877, 1404
Conrad Weickhoff, 10769
Conrado, Aldomar, 20427
Conrotte, Manuel, 6460
Conroy, Kitty, 6461
Consalvi, Simon Alberto, 20428
Conscientious objectors, U.S., 7967
A conscript's Christmas, 9745
The conscription act vindicated, 12794
Le conseil des colons de Saint-Domingue, 997
Consejo de Bienestar Rural, Caracas, 20429;
  Oficina de Estudio's Especiales, 19771
Consejo Episcopal Latinoamericano, 20430
Consejo Nacional de la Universidad Peruana,
  20431
Consejo Superior de las Cámaras Oficiales de
  Comercio, Industria y Navegación de Espana,
  20432
Consejo Superior Universitario Centro-
  americano, 20433-20438; Comisión Centro-
  americana en pro de los Estudios Generales,
  20439; Proyecto de Recursos Humanos en C.A.,
  20440
Consent (Law), Mexico, 19969
El consentimiento del interesado, 19969
Conser, Solomon L.M., 1812-, 3071
Conservation of natural resources, 18441
Considerant, Victor Prosper, 1808-1893, 3072,
  16265
Consiglio, Dulce Damasceno de Brito, 20441
A consolation for our grammar schooles, 1528
The consolation prize, 25023
Consortium of Universities of the Metropolitan

Area, 20442
The conspiracy in the North case, 10371
The conspiracy of kings, 810
The conspiracy of Mrs. Bunker, 9791
The conspiracy unveiled, 3969
The conspirators, 8963
Constables, 21976
Constance Allerton, 10197
Constance and Calbot's rival, 9806
Constance Beverly, 9563
Constantinople, Siege, 1453, Fiction, 9279
Constantius and Pulchera, 9878
La Constitución argentina en la teoría y en la práctica, 18365
Constitución quiteña de 1812, 19173
La Constitución y el derecho administrativo mexicanos en relación con la planeación económica, 18964
The constituents of climate with special reference ot the climate of Florida, 4253
Constitution (Frigate), 2136, 22687
Constitution and address of the Committee of vigilance of San Francisco, 17555
The constitution and laws of the Cherokee nation, 11776
Constitution, articles of a faith, standing rules, and general principles of church polity..., 16260
Constitution of a society for abolishing the slave-trade, 25321
Constitution of the Anti-slavery Society, 24191
Constitution of the state of Deseret, 16376
The Constitution of the United States, 24192
The constitution of the United Societies, of Believers, 13916
The constitution, or form of government for the state of Kentucky, 14521
The constitution shown to be consistent with a new election, 3534, 14140
The constitution upheld and maintained, 6957
Constitutional conventions, 22676
Constitutional history, 4946, 22082
Constitutional law, 19058; Great Britain, 25492
Constitutional republicanism, 553
The constitutional rights of the states, 24239
Constitutional union party, 25906
A constitutionalist, 121, 23973
Constitutions, 18976; Latin American, 19118; State, 253, 1274, 12190

Construction, Kentucky, 15451
Construyendo México, 1910-1946, 7315
Consuegra, José, 20443
Consultécnica, San José, Costa Rica, 20022
Consumers, Salvador, Brazil, 18692
Consumption (Economics), 19371; Arapiraca, Brazil, 18780; Argentine Republica, 18425; Fortaleza, Brazil, 18781; Mossoro, Brazil, 18782; New England, 11428; Propria, Brazil, 18783
Contagion and contagious diseases, 13770; Chile, 20170; Prevention, 12757, 14290
Contaminación salina del lago de Maracaibo, 19179
Contemporáneos, 6462
Contempt of court, 1256; U.S., 24080
The contest between Christianity and political Romanism, 11677
The contest between three Indians and one white man, 10570
The contest for California in 1861, 16936
The contest in America, 25048
The contest in America between Great Britain and France, with its consequences and importance, 23438
Conti, Haroldo, 1925-, 20444
Conti, José Bueno, 20445
The Continent, 3073
The continental dragoon, 10877
Continental shelf, 18201, 20044
Continental system of Napoleon, 13113
Continentino, M.A., 19065, 20446-20449
Contino, Francisco, 20450
A Continuation of the state of New-England, 11876
Continued corruption, 11333
Continuous voyages (International law), 12667
Contos Maranhenses, 20451
Contostavlos, Alexander. A narrative of the material facts in relation to the building of the two Greek frigates, 983
Contra Costa Co., Calif., 16772
Contraband of war, 12222
Contrabands and vagrants, 25472
Contract labor, 24198, 24567, 24652, 24790, 24792, 24794; Africa, Portuguese West, 24438; Congresses, 24197, 24199; São Thomé e Principe, 23870, 24967, 25935; São Thomé Island (West Africa), 24966, 25968
Contracts (Roman law), 25561, 25851
Contradições do homen brasileiro, 19500
La contrarrevolución agraria en México, 18574
The contrast, 10184
The contrast: a tale of acts, 14009
The contrast: or William Henry Harrison versus Martin van Buren, 22462

119

Contrasted lives, 10553
O contratador dos diamantes, 18517
Contrato individual de trabajo, 18053
Contratos, 19536
Contreras R., J. Daniel, 20452
Contreras, Raúl, 20453
Contreras Cervantes, Rubén, 20454
Contreras Niño, Victor, 20455
El control obrero en la empresa, 19631
La controversía sobre el Canal Beagle,
  18900
Controversy between Caius Gracchus and
  Opimius [pseud.], 24074
The controversy between Great Britain
  and her colonies reviewed..., 22738
The controversy touching the old stone
  mill, in... Newport, Rhode Island,
  11543
The convalescence of Jack Hamlin, 6977
La convención de Ginebra sobre la
  plataforma continental, 20044
El convenio internacional del estaño,
  18942
The convent and the manse, 8972
The convent's doom, 9586
Convention of banks of the city of
  Charleston, 1841, 11877
Convention between the United States and
  other powers. Slavery. Signed at
  Geneva, September 25, 1926, 24655
Convention for the Improvement of the
  Free People of Color, 24193
Convention of Abolitionists, West
  Bloomfield, N.Y., 1847, 24194
Convention of the Friends of Freedom in
  the Eastern and Middle States, Boston,
  1845, 24195
Convention on the Abolition of Slavery,
  the Slave Trade, and Institutions and
  Practices Similar to Slavery, 24196
Convention relative à l'esclavage,
  Geneve, le 25 septembre, 1926, 24197-
  24199
The convention vindicated from the
  misrepresentations of the enemies of
  our peace, 13505
Convents and nunneries, Peru, 8296
A conversational tour in America, 8356
Conversations around the camp fire, 4924
Conversations on slavery, 10059
Converse, John Kendrick, 1801-1880, 24200
Conversion, 13779, 21975, 23304
A convert of the mission, 6971
Conveyancing, Kentucky, 24715; West
  Indies, 22013
Convict labor, 4934

Conway, Cornelius, 3074
Conway, George Robert Graham, 1873-, 7064
Conway, Moncure Daniel, 1832-1907, 8327,
  22108, 24201, 24202
Cony, Carlos Hector, 20456
Conyngham, Dane, pseud., 9278
Conyngham, David Power, 1840-1883, 3075
Conyngham Foxe and the charity ball, 10122
Cook, Ann, 1786-1826, 13870
Cook, Benjamin F., b.1835 or 6, 3076
Cook, Daniel Pope, 1795-1827, 16069
Cook, Darius B., 16268
Cook, David J., 1840-1907, 16269, 16270
Cook, Daniel Pope, 1795-1827, 24203
Cook, Ebenezer, fl.1708-1732, 3077; The
  sot-weed factor, 5264; Sot-weed redivivus,
  5264
Cook, George Cram, 1873-1924, 8690
Cook, James, 1728-1779, 993, 23533
Cook, Joel, 1842-1910, 3078, 6463
Cook, John R., 1844-1917, 16271
Cook, John W., 16270
Cook, Marlow W., 13917, 15624
Cook, May Estelle, 14797
Cookbooks, 15096
Cooke, Mrs. Grace (MacGowan) 1863-, 10274
Cooke, John, fl.1794, 6464
Cooke, John Esten, 13918-13920
Cooke, John Henry, 1791-1884, 3079
Cooke, Mary Frances, 13921
Cooke, Philip Pendleton, 1816-1850, 3080
Cooke, Philip St. George, 1809-1895, 3081,
  16272, 16273
Cooke, R. T., 10163
Cooke, Mrs. Rose (Terry) 1827-1892, 8597
Cookery (Seafood), 19630
Cookery, Argentine, 19720
Cookery, Indian, 17070
Cookery, Kentucky, 13596, 13621, 13652,
  13653, 13699, 13710, 13972, 14010, 14063,
  14197, 14294, 14295, 14705, 15804, 15813,
  14819, 14821, 14842, 14850, 14851, 15846,
  15049, 15065, 15118, 15122, 15161, 15408,
  15444, 15494, 15550, 15610, 15700
Cookery for institutions, etc., 18228
Cookman, George Grimston, 1800-1841, 1619
Cookson, Sir Charles Alfred, 1829-1906, 13104
Cooley, Henry Scofield, 24204
Cooley, William Desborough, d.1883, 23404
Coolidge, Calvin, pres. U.S., 1872-1933, 8353
Coolidge, Louis Arthur, 1861-1925, 16274
The coolie, his rights and wrongs, 22702
The coon dog, 10042
Cooper, Alonzo, 3082
Cooper, Blair, 20457
Cooper, Colin Campbell, jr., 10737

Cooper, David, 24205, 24206
Cooper, H. H. A., 20458
Cooper, Isaac, 4504
Cooper, James Fenimore, 1789-1851, 863,
  3083, 21981, 22929
Cooper, James M., 21982
Cooper, John E., 15433
Cooper, John Sherman, 1901-, 15124,
  15400, 15614
Cooper, Joseph, 1800-1881, 24207
Cooper, Myers Young, 1873-, 6465
Cooper, Peter, 1791-1883, 24208-24210
Cooper, Samuel, 1725-1783, 11841, 21983,
  21984, 21992
Cooper, Samuel, 1772-1798, 13759
Cooper, Samuel Williams, 1860-, 10737
Cooper, Susan Fenimore, 1813-1894, 21985
Cooper, Thomas, 1759-1839, 3084, 10051,
  11878, 11879, 21986-21989
Cooper, Thomas, 1791 or 2-1880, 24211
Cooper, W. L., 13922
Cooper, William, 1720-1809, 11385
Cooper river, South Carolina, 4023
Cooper union for the advancement of
  science and art, New York, 11880
Cooperación financiera en América
  Latina, 20032
Cooperation, Bibliography, 18973;
  Colombia, 18934
Cooperativas agrícolas, 19835
Cooperative societies, 20115; Argentine
  Republic, 19062; Brazil, 19319;
  Colombia, 18934, 19835; Río Negro,
  Argentine Republic (Province), 19062
Cooperativismo no Brasil, 19319
Cooperativos de producción, 20115
The Coopers, 9800
Coordinación monetaria regional, 20033
Copeland, John, 23466
Copeland, Lewis C., 13923
Copias a la letra, 1078
Copley, John M., 3085
Copp, Elbridge J., 1844-, 3086
Copp's hill burial ground, Boston, 1503
Coppellatti, Angel J., 20188
Copper-distilled, 10863
The Copperhead, 6931, 9567
Copperhead Convention (The Chicago), 6416
Copper industry and trade, U.S., 23188
Copyright, Colombia, 20333; International,
  83, 23343
Copyrights, 4946
The coquette, 9549, 9550
Coquille, Jean Baptiste Victor, 1820-1891,
  6710
Cora Glencoe, 8840

Cora O'Kane, 11190
The coral lady, 10835
Coral Miranda, Reynoldo, 20459
Coral reefs and islands, 12909
Coranna, 9340
Corbella y Fondebila, Antonio, 6466
The Corbet chronicles, 9671
Corbett, Griffith Owen, 6467
Corbin, William Francis, 1833-1863, 13994
Corby, William, 1833-1897, 3087
Corcoran, Michael, 1827-1863, 3088
Corcuera, Arturo, 20460
Cordeiro, Copérnico de Arruda, 1914-, 20461
Cordeiro Álvarez, Ernesto, 20462
Cordeiro Pincheiro Furtado, Antonio Candido,
  1775-1862, 21777
Cordero, Héctor Adolfo, 20563
Cordero Dávila, Gonzalo, 20464
Cordero y León, Ramona María, 20465-20467
Cordero y León, Rigoberto, 20069, 20464,
  20466, 20468
Córdoba, Argentine Republic. Academia
  Nacional de Ciencias, 20470; Cabildo,
  20471; Dirección General de Estadística,
  Censos e Investigaciones, 20472; Economic
  policy, Addresses, essays, lectures, 20474;
  History, Sources, 20471; Industries, 20472;
  Politics & government, 20471; Social
  policy Addresses, essays, lectures, 20474;
  Statistics, 20472; Universidad nacional.
  Dirección General de Publicidad, 20473;
  Universidad nacional. Facultad de
  Arquitectura y Urbanismo, 20474; Universidad
  Nacional. Instituto de Matemática,
  Astronomía y Física, 20475
Córdoba y Salinas, Diego de, 6468-6470
Córdova, Carlos J., 20476
Córdova-Bello, Eleazar, 20477
Cordua, Carla, 20478
Corinne, Utah, History, 15851
Coriolanus, an historical dramina, 16075
Coriolanus, Cn. Marcius, Drama, 16075
Corleone, a tale of Sicily, 9221
Corlett, William Thomas, 1854-, 6471
Corley, Daniel B., 24212
Cormier, Gerald H., 20479
Corn, James Franklin, 6472
Corn Argentine Republic, 20544; Diseases
  and pests, 19071
Corn-laws, Great Britain, 23707
Corn pudding, 14010
Corndeau, 9254
Cornejo Acosta, Maria, 20480
Cornejo Franco, Jose, 6473, 20481
Cornelison, J. H., illustr., 13715
Cornelius, Elias, 1794-1832, 3089, 3342

Cornell, Sarah Maria, 1802-1832, 11170, 12688, 22158
Corner, William, 16275
Corning, Howard, 1867-, 2573, 2574
Cornish, Louis Craig, 6474
Cornish, Louis Henry, 1855-1918, comp., 8076
Cornoa Núñez, J., 20482
Cornwall, Bruce, 16276
Cornwall, Pierre Barlow, 1821-1904, 16276
Cornwall, Vt., Genealogy, 23354; History, 23354
Cornwallis, Charles Cornwallis, 1st marquis, 1738-1805, 13473
Cornwallis, Kinahan, 1839-1917, 3090
Corografia brazilica, 11230
Corona mexicana, 7546
Corona Morfin, Enrique, 20483
Corona of the Nantahalas, 4745
Coronado, Francisco Vasquez de, ca. 1510-1554, 17564
Coronado, Martin, 1850-1919, 19907
Coronado, Nicolas, 6478
Coronado Aguilar, Manuel, 20484
Coronado Padella, Ricardo, 20485
Coronado's expedition to Quivira, 17564
The coronal, 8990
Coronel Urtecho, Jose, 20486
Coroners, 21976
Corporación Autónoma Regional de la Sabana de Bogotá y de los Valles de Ubate y Chiquinguira, 20487
Corporación Autónoma Regional de los Valles del Magdalena y del Sinú, 20488-20490
Corporación Autónoma Regional del Cauca, 20491; Departamento de Aguas, 20492-20494; División de Planeacion Regional, 20495
Corporación de Fomento de la Produccion, 20496
Corporación Financiera Colombiana, 20497
Corporación Financiera Colombiana de Desarrollo Industrial, 20498
Corporación Venezolana de Fomento, 20499, 20500, 20501; Departamento de Estudios y Planificación, 20502; Departamento de Relaciones Públicas, 20503; Division de Estudios Generales, 20504; Sub-gerencia de Servicios Técnicos, 20505
Corporal, pseud., 3729
Corporal punishment, 1927
The corporal's trousers, 9460
Corporation for promoting and propagating the gospel of Jesus Christ in New England, London, 12006, 23790

Corporation law, Argentine Republic, 20245; Argentine Republic, Forms, 20245; New Hampshire, 22414; U.S., 14673
Corporations, Argentine Republic, 18469; Laws and regulations, Colombia, 20317, 20318; Religious, 15349
The corps of observation, 10682
Corradi, Hugo, 20506
Corradine Angulo, Alberto, 20507, 20508
Corrêa, Conceição Gentil, 20509
Corrêa, Lia, 20510-20512
Corrêa, Luis, 1884-1940, 6476, 20513
Corrêa, Nereu, 20514-20516
Corrêa, Pancho, 20517
Corrêa, Virgilio, 1887-, 6475
Correa Reyes, Sergio, 20518
Correas, Edmundo, 1901-, 20519
Correção de textos para examens e concursos, 17963
A correct and authentic narrative of the Indian war in Florida, 2617
A correct narrative of the celebrated Mammoth Cave of Kentucky, 14481
Corrected proofs, 11116
Corredor, Berta, 20520
Corredor, R. C., 20521
Correia, Manoel Francisco, 1831-, 24010
Correio da Manhã, Rio de Janeiro, 20456
Correll, Hal, 16277
Correo de Arauco, 20522
Correo del Orinoco, 6476, 20523
Corresponsal en La Habana, 6745
Corrientes, Argentine Republic. Universidad Nacional del Nordeste. Escuela de Derecho, 20524
Corrientes River, Argentine Republic, 19916
Corro, Guillermo del, 20525-20527
The corrupt judges of the supreme court of the state of California, 17380
Corsan, W. C., 3091
Corsicans in the Barbary States, 24691
Cortado de Kohan, Nuria, 20528
Cortambert, Louis Richard, 1808?-1881, 3092
Cortázar, Julio, 20529, 20530
Corte Real, José Alberto Homem da Cunha, 1832-1885, 24214
The Cortelyou feud, 9538
Cortés, Carlos E., 20531
Cortés, Hernando, 1485-1547, 11, 1544, 6478, 6863, 6864, 7387, 7774, 7775, 16278, 20532, 21834, 22212, 23508; Drama, 6328
Cortés, Jesus M., 20503
Cortés, José Domingo, 1839-1884, 6479
Cortés Lee, Carlos, 1859-1928, 20534
Cortés López, Idulio, 20535

Cortés Pinto, Raúl, 20536
Cortés Santos, Rodulfo, 20537
Cortés Vargas, Carlos, 1883-, 18909
Cortez, Irlemar Chiampi, 20538
Cortez, Nati, 1914-, 20539
Cortez, Roberto, 20540, 20541
Cortijo Herrajz, Tomás, 6480
Cortina, José Antonio, 1852-1884, 7849
Cortland Co., N.Y., History, 12307
Cortland county and the border wars of
  New York, 12307
Corvalán, Juan M. M., 20542
Corwin, Gabriel Smith, b.1802, 24215
Corwin, Thomas, 1794-1865, 3093, 13924,
  24216
Cory, Charles Barney, 3094, 3095
Cory, Charles Estabrook, 1852-, 24217
Corylé, Mary, pseud. See Corders y León,
  Ramona María.
Cos, Poetry, 3820
Cosa, Juan de la, d.1510, 8083
Las cosas más considerables, vista en la
  Nueva España, 6835
Coscarón, Sixto, 20543
Coscia, Adolfo A., 20544-20547
Cosio, Pedro Antonio de, 6481, 6482
Cosmography, 406, 407
Cosmopolite, 3277; pseud., 10172
Cossio Esturo, Adolfino, 20548
Cost and standard of living, 9637, 10786,
  18410; Arapiraca, Brazil, 18780; Chile,
  19802; Fortaleza, Brazil, 18781;
  Kentucky, 14911; Maracaibo, Venezuela,
  18808; Mossoró, Brazil, 18782; Propriá,
  Brazil, 18783; Venezuela, 18735
A cost-benefit approach to educational
  planning in developing countries, 19086
Costa, Aida, 20549
Costa, Cassio, 20550
Costa, Dias da, 20551
Costa, Didio Iratyn Affonso da, 1881-,
  20552, 20553
Costa, José Marcelino Monteiro da, 20554
Costa, Manoel Fernandes da, 20555
Costa, Miguel, 20556
Costa, Newton C. A. da, 20557
Costa, Rubens Vaz da, 20558-20564
Costa, Zeferino da, 20565
Costa e Silva, Arthur, 1902-, 20566
Costa Pôrto, José da, 1909-, 20567
Costa Rica, 6280, 7795, 19059; Census,
  20573-20575, 20580, 20581, 20614;
  Commerce, 20577, 20582; Constitution,
  20568, 20569; Description & travel,
  5845, 7517, 7620, 8303, 8324, 11461,
  18851, 18852, 19093, 20586; Description

& travel, Bibliography, 20588; Dirección
de Extensión Agrícola, 21744; Dirección
General de Estadística y Censos, 20570-
20584; Economic conditions, 18048, 19093,
20575, 20610, 20615; History, 6723, 17971,
18048, 18807, 19093; History, Periodicals,
5954; Industries, 20578, 20583, 20584;
Instituto de Educación Política, 20585;
Instituto Geográfico Nacional, 20586-20588;
Instituto Nacional de Aprendizaje, 20589;
Labor policy, 20589; Laws, statutes, etc.,
20590-20592; Laws, statutes, etc. Código
electoral, 20591; Maps, Bibliography, 20588;
Ministerio de Educación Pública, 20593-
20607; Ministerio de Educación Pública.
Dirección General de Desarrollo Educativo,
20608; Ministerio de Educación Pública.
Dirección General de Planeamiento Educativo,
20609; Ministerio de Hacienda, 20610;
Ministerio de Obras Públicas, 20611;
Ministerio de Trabajo y Bienestar Social,
20612, 20613; Oficina Nacional del Censo,
20614; Oficina de Planificación, 20615;
Politics & government, 20569, 20585, 21749;
Population, 18596, 20614; Registro Central
del Estado Civil, 20591; Secretaría de
Gobernación, 20568; Statistics, 20570, 20577,
20579; Superintendencia de Bancos, 20616;
Tribunal Supremo de Elecciones, 20591;
Universidad, 18316; Universidad Escuela de
Ciencias Económicas, 20617; Universidad
Nacional, San José. Serie histórica y
geográfica, 20080
Costa Rican literature, 18580; History, 18048;
  Periodicals, 5954
Costales Samaniego, Alfredo, 20618
Costanzo, G. A., 20619
Coste d'Arnobat, Charles Pierre, b.1732, 344
Costumbres yankees, 5068
Costume, New England, 2244
Côté, Cyrille Hector Octave, 1809-1850, 22022
Côté, Margaret Y., 1807-1851, 22022
Cotelo, Julio César, 20620
Cotlar, Mischa, 20621
Cotmier, Gerald H., 20622
Cotrim Garaude, Lupe, 20623
Cotta de Varela, Laura B., 20624
The cottage by the sea, 9048
The cottage on the cliff, 9102
Cottage piety exemplified, 9177
Cottages, 11750
Cotter, Joseph Seamon, 1861-, 3096, 7165,
  15580
Cotterill, Robert Spenser, 1884-, 13925, 13926
Cotton, Catherine B., d.1853, 10089
Cotton, John, 1585-1652, 21990, 22812, 23799

Cotton, Nancy Jo, 13927
Cotton, Nathaniel, 1697-1729, 1072
Cotton, 23143, 23053; Colombia, 18146,
  21743; Irrigation, 18146; Soils,
  18146
Cotton culture and the south considered
  with reference to emigration, 4301
Cotton famine, 1861-1864, 258
Cotton growing and manufacture, 13149,
  22070; Africa, 1921; Gt. Britain, 12483;
  Louisiana, 4192; Lowell, Mass., 11686;
  South Carolina, 12418; Southern states,
  4301, 21843, 23058; U.S., 525, 526, 5792,
  22888
Cotton is king, 3361
Cotton machinery, 12202
Cotton manufacture, 12202; U.S., 956
Cotton planters' convention of Georgia,
  13307
The cotton states in the spring and summer
  of 1875, 4612
Cotton stealing, 3097
Cotton trade, 22889; Colombia, 19083
Coues, Elliott, 1842-1899, 6813, 7009,
  15879, 16279, 16990
Couffon, Claude, 20625
Coughenour, C. Milton, 13823
Coulter, Ellis Merton, 1890-, 6483, 13928
Couma (Apocynaceae), 18109
Council for New England, 12747
Counsel, 9802
The counsel of Caiaphas: a sermon, 24523
Counseling, 18013
The counterfeiters, 10434, 10957
Counterfeits and counterfeiting, 13585
The Countess Ida, 9504
Counties, Kentucky, 13787
The country cousin, 10730
A country doctor, 10034
A country girl, 9170
Country life, 5720, 10671, 24421; Argentine
  Republic, 18592; Brazil, 19669, 20291;
  Colombia, 20290; Texas, 7140
Country lodgings, 10197
Country margins and rambles of a journalist,
  9727
The country neighborhood, 9445
The country of the pointed firs, 10035
The country v. the company, 8140
County archives of California, 16125
County government, Kentucky, 14293, 14866;
  Utah, Yearbooks, 17810
Coup d'oeil historique et statistique sur le
  Texas, 0000
Coup d'ocil sur la situation agricole de la
  Guiane française, 1202

Coupon bonds, 11015
Coups d'état, 19965
Cournand, Antonine de, abbé, 1747-1814, 6484
The court circles of the republic, 12020
Court day, Kentucky, 13528
Court-martialled, 9460
Court records, 12890
Court rules, U.S., 21980
Courthouse buildings, Kentucky, 14175
The courting of Sister Wisby, 10037
Courtly love, 18059
Courts, Colombia, 20329; Confederate States
  of America, 2054, 2055, 24809; Kentucky,14085,
  14344, 14556, 14612, 14613, 14793, 15656,
  15741, 15743; Martial,and courts of inquiry
  Brazil, 19358; Martial, and courts of inquiry
  - U.S., 354, 13253, 22824, 22825; Mexico,
  18334; Pennsylvania, 22786; Texas, 12939;
  U.S., 976, 11305, 12244, 21980
Courtship and marriage, 3841
The courtship of Raccoon John Smith, 13861
Cousin Franck's household, 10496
Cousin Lucy and the village teacher, 14242
Cousin William, 10904
The cousins' journey, 3098
Cousseau, Maria Berta, 20626
Cousseau, Maria del, 18298, 18453
Coutin Correa, Donis Pablo, 20627, 20628
Coutinho, Afrânio, 20629, 20630
Coutinho, Aluizio Bezerra, 20631
Coutinho, Evaldo, 20632, 20633
Couto, Diogo do, 1542-1616, continuator, 882
Couto, Gabriel P. Bueno, 20634
Couture, Eduardo J., 1906-1956, 20635, 20636
Couture, Thomas, 14297
Cova, Arabia Teresa, 19746
Cova-García, Pablo, 20637
Covadonga (Schooner), 18251
Covarrubias, Miguel, 1902-1957, 20638
Covell, Alanson L., 1804-1837, 21818
Covell, Lemuel, 1764-1806, 21818
The covenant of God's free grace most sweetly
  unfolded..., 21990
Covenants (Theology), 1671, 23332
Coventry, Charles B., 1801-1875, 955
Covered bridges, Kentucky, 15553
The covered wagon, 16817
Covering end, 7131
Covi, Madeline, 13929
Covington, Ky. Charters, 13930; History, 14036,
  15438; Politics & government, 13930
The cow chace, 351, 352
Cowan, Alexander M., 24218
Cowan, John F., 3099
Cowan, John W., 13931
Cowan, Robert Ernest, 1862-, 16281, 16282

The coward, 10379
The cowards' convention, 1533
Cowboys, 16818, 17623, 17624, 17680
Cowboys and colonels, 17122
Cowen, Benjamin Rush, 1831-1908, 6485
Cowgill, Brad, 15057
Cowley, capt., fl.1683, 22280
Cowper, Pulaski, 3697
Cox, Earnest Sevier, 6486
Cox, Edward T., 16108, 15109
Cox, Edward Travers, 1821-, 4665
Cox, Isaac Joslin, 1873-, 16283
Cox, James, 23113
Cox, John E., 16284
Cox, Leander M., 24219
Cox, Millard F., 1856-, 13932
Cox, Paul, 20639
Cox, Ross, 1793-1853, 3100, 16285
Cox, Samuel H., 24764
Cox, Samuel Sullivan, 1824-1889, 24220
Cox, Sandford C., 3101, 3102
Cox's Creek Baptist Church, Nelson County,
   Ky., 15780
Coxe, Daniel, 1673-1739, 3103
Coxe, Richard Smith, 1792-1865, 24221
Coxe, Tench, 1755-1824, 3084, 21989
Coy, Owen Cochran, 1884-, 16125, 16126
Coy Otero, Alberto, 18892
Coyle, John, d.1838, 22953
Coyner, David H., 3104, 3105, 16286
Coyner, Mary Susan (Coiner), 20640-20642
Coyotes, 10863
Cozzens, Frederick Swartwout, 1818-1869,
   6487, 11704
Cozzens, Samuel Woodworth, 1834-1878, 16387
Crabb, Alfred Leland, jr., 13933
Crabbe, Pierre, 1928-, 20643
Craddock, Charles Egbert, pseud. of Mary
   Noailles Murfree
The cradle of liberty, 8796
The cradle of the new world, 10492
Cradlebaugh, John, 11881
Craesbeck de Mello, Antonio, d.ca.1687,
   23131
Crafford, John, 3106
Craft, David, 1832-1908, 3107
Crafts, William, 1787-1826, 3108
Crafts, William Augustus, 1819-, 10980
Crafty, illustr., 4381
Crag-nest, 9381
Cragin, Aaron Harrison, 1821-1898, 24222
Craib, Alexander, 3109
Craig, Campbell, 23896
Craig, James, 3110
Craig, Sir James Henry, 1748-1812, 21918
Craig, John Roderick, 1837-, 16288

Craig, Lewis, 15242
Craig, Lulu Alice, 16289
Craig, Neville B., 1787-1863, 23474, 23668
Craig, Wheelock, 1824-1868, 6488
Craighead, James Geddes, 1823-1895, 16290
Craigie, Christopher, 9070
Craik, James, 1730?-1814, 6842, 13934
Crakes, Sylvester, jr., 3112, 16291
Cram, Thomas Jefferson, 1807?-1883, 3113
Crambe, pseud., 4887
Cranch, William, 1769-1855, 11587
Crandall, Albert R., 13935, 13936
Crandall, Reuben, 1805?-1838, 24719
Crane, Alice Rollins, 16292
Crane, Cephas Bennett, 1833-, 6489
Crane, James Campbell, 1803-1856, 1742
Crane, James M., 16293
Crane, William, 1790-1866, 24223
Crane and Gorwick, firm, Detroit, 14646
Cranfill, James Britton, 1858-, 16294
Craniology, Collections, 24427
Crary, Charles, d.1863, 11329
Craveiro, Paulo Fernando, 20644
Craviotto, José A., 20645
Crawford, Charles, 13937
Crawford, Charles Howard, 16295
Crawford, Cora Hayward, 6490
Crawford, Dean, 13938
Crawford, Francis Marion, 1854-1909, 6491-6509
Crawford, George Addison, 1827-1891, 16609
Crawford, George Washington, 1798-1872, 12212
Crawford, J. Marshall, 3114
Crawford, Mrs. James Todd, 1763-1842, 14893
Crawford, John Wallace, 1847-1917, 5201
Crawford, Medorem, d.1891, 5538, 16296
Crawford, Thomas, 1818-1857, 22451
Crawford, Thomas J., 13939
Crawford, William, 1788-1847, 3115
Crawford, William Harris, 1772-1834, 11879
Crawford family, 7992
Crawford's Indian campaign, 1782, 2781
Crayon, Geoffrey, pseud., 9996, 10001, 10002
The Crayon miscellany, 4027
Crazut, Rafael J., 20646
La creación de Bolivia, 7752
The creamery man, 9606
Crease, Henry Pering Pellew, 1823-1905, 6183
Creason, Joe C., 13940
The creation of Manitoba, 6049
Creative writing, 15050
Credit, 2001, 2373; Pernambuco, Brazil (State),
   18752
El crédito agrícola y el plan de desarrollo
   agropecuario de Bolivia, 18649
Cree Indians, 8428; Legends, 17036
Cree language, Dictionaries, English, 21871;

Glossaries, vocabularies, etc., 5457;
Grammar, 12967
Creek Indians, 4104, 4824, 12752, 17051,
17194; Government relations, 12130;
Missions, 17051
Creek language, Texts, 1648
Creek war, 1813-1814, 3004, 13456, 22165
Creek war, 1836, Fiction, 9880
Creelman, James, 1859-1915, 20647
Las creencias demónicas griegas, 19663
Creimer, Diana, 20648
Cremony, John Carey, 1815-1879, 16297
The creole, 3036, 4276
Creole (brig), 22693, 24674
The Creole case, and Mr. Webster's
despatch, 22693, 24674
Creole life, A story of, 8926
The Creole orphans, 10495
Crequy, Charles de Blanchefort, duc de,
1573-1638, 8323
Cresap, Bernard, 6510
Cresap, Michael, 1742-1775, 13138, 14276,
17164
Crescent-shine, 12227
Crespel, Emmanuel, 6511, 6512
Crespel, Louis, 6512
Crespo, María R., 20649
Crespo, Osvaldo Victor, 20650
Crespo, Rodrigues, 20651
Crespo Ordoñez, Roberto, 20652, 20653
Crespo Paniagua, Renato, 20654
Crespo Torol, Remigio, 1860-1939, 20655
Crespo y Martínez, Gilberto, 1853-, 6513
Cresswell, Nicholas, 1750-1804, 3116
Cressy, 6966
Creuzbaur, Robert, 3117
Crevecoeur, Michel Guillaume St. Jean de,
called Saint John de Crevecoeur, 1735-
1813, 588, 3118, 9387, 21991
Crew, Harvey W., 6514
Crewdson, John M., 24224
Cri des colons contre un ouvrage de m.
l'évêque et sénateur Grégoire, ayant
pour titre De la littératures des nègres,
25739
Criança e literatura, 19897
The cricket's friends, 10046
Crider, A.F., 13941, 13942
Crim, (Miss) Matt, 3119, 3120
Crime and criminals, 3764, 3781, 4934,
12300, 13766, 13931, 19152; Brazil,
19080; France, 11765, 13358; Germany,
25038; Gt. Britain, 10861; Identification,
19110; Indian Territory, 16700; Kansas,
16883; Kentucky, 13585, 13586, 13954,
15366; Montana, 16392; New York (State),

1965; North Carolina, 5444; Ohio-Cincinnati,
11963; Oklahoma, 16626; Southwest, Old, 9931;
Texas, 16696; U.S., 2642, 4129, 11719, 15599,
16569; The West, 15862, 16269, 16270, 16819,
17447
Crime and its consequences, 8998
Crime and punishment, 2279
Crime and retribution, 9451, 9498
The crime of Henry Vane, 10884
Crime of the clergy, 25425
Crimean war, 1853-1856, 1706
The crimes committed by our government against
the maroons, 12238
The criminal; the crime; the penalty, 22418
Criminal anthropology, 19721
Criminal law, 18898, 19152; Argentine Republic,
18465-18467, 18471, 20524; Brazil, 19337,
19362; Chile, 20140, 20142; Colombia, 18390,
20319; History, 24671; Kentucky, 14570,
14674; Mexico, 1078, 18025, 19969; Orleans
(Ter.), 16940; Spain, 7242; U.S., 1353,
4129
Criminal liability, Chile, 20078
Criminal procedure: history of the criminal
code, 14607; Argentine Republic, 18465,
18466, 18467; Bolivia, 18354; Buenos Aires
(Province), 18466, 18467; Guatemala, 20067;
Orleans (Ter.), 16940
Criminal trial advocacy, Kentucky, 14666;
U.S., 14666
Criminal trials, 11719, 22680
The criminal's career, 10960
Criminalística médico-legal, 21738
Crimora, 9403
The crimson hand, 4052
"Crippled Fayette," of Rockingham, 22698
El cris celeste de las católicas, 7789
Crisfield, John Woodland, 1808-1897, 6515,
24225
The crisis, 10163, 21844, 21845, 21992, 22020,
24226, 24227, 24606
Crisis americana, 7271
The crisis and the man, 6437
A crisis chapter on government, 1409
The crisis in the United States, 24017
The crisis of emancipation in America, 25476
The crisis of sugar colonies, 25608
Crismon, Leo T., 13943
Crispolte, Francisco Maria, 1834-1887, 20656
Criss-cross journeys, 5409
Critchell, Robert Siderfin, 1844-, 16298
Crítica, Buenos Aires, 19724
Critical dialogue between Aboo and Caboo on a
new book, 5025
The critical moment, 13160
A criticism of Mr. Wm. B. Reed's aspersions,

13245
Critical path analysis, 20542
Crittenden, George Bibb, 1812-1880, 13944
Crittenden, John Jordan, 1787-1863, 3051, 13945, 14465, 15801, 18968, 24228, 24229
Crittenden, William Logan, d.1851, 15214
Crittenden, A Kentucky story of love and war..., 14131
Crittenden, Ky. Crittenden Baptist Church, 14791
Crittenden Co., Kentucky, Description, 14193, 15085
Croce, Benedetto, 1866-1952, 20657
Crocheron, Augusta (Joyce) 1844-, 16299
Crocker, Samuel Leonard, 1804-1883, 6516
Crockett, David, 1786-1836, 3121-3123, 3372, 8206, 14350, 16300
Crockett, G. F. H., 13946
Crockett, Ingram, illustr., 13947, 13948
Crockett, Joseph, 1742-1829, 15196
Croffut, William Augustus, 1835-, 6517, 16786
Crofutt, George A., 12371, 16301, 16302, 16631
Croghan, George, d.1782, 3124
Croghan, John, 3125
Croisières de l'Alabama et du Sumter, 23593
Croix, Carlos Francisco de Croix, marques de, 1699-1786, 6518
Croix, Teodoro de, 1730-1791, 6519
Croizart, León, 18994
Croly, David Goodman, 1829-1889, 24230
Crombach, Hermann, 1598-1680, 22749
Cromwell, 9843
Cromwell, Emma Guy, 13949
Cromwell, John Wesley, 1846-, 24231
Cromwell, Oliver, 1599-1658, 2091, 11523; Fiction, 9843
Cronin, David Edward, 1839-, 3126
Cronise, Titus Fey, 16303
Crook, George, 1828-1890, 16024, 16515, 16947
Crook, John, 1831-, 16304
Crooked Billet, Battle of the, 1778, 22047, 22049
Crooked trails, 17467
Crooks, Ramsay, 2528
Croom, Wendell D., 3127
Croome, William, illustr., 12174
Cropper, Carol, 13833
Cropper, James, 1773-1840, 639, 24232
Crops and climate , Argentine Republic, 19571
Croquevielle Brand, Teodoro, 20659

Croquis de viaje, 8382
Croquis et impressions d'Amérique, 3629
Crosby, Alpheus, 1810-1874, 24233
Crosby, Daniel, 1799-1843, 12392
Crosby, Elisha Oscar, 1818-1895, 20660
Crosby, Enoch, 1750-1835, 863
Crosby, James, d.1834, 13331
Crosby, Margaret, 9769
Crosly, Oliver Martin, 3128
Cross, Elsa, 1946-, 20661
Cross, James Conquest, 13950
Cross, Mrs. Louis (Bernadine Cross), 13963
Cross, Osborne, 1803-1876, 3129, 16305
Cross-examination, 14666
Cross purposes, 9382
The cross road store, 13599
Crossby, Peter Alfred, 1842-, 7331
The crossing..., 13824
Crossing the plains, 17152, 17163
Crossley, William J., 3130
Croswell, Andrew, 1709-1785. A letter to Reverend Alexander Cumming, 11896
Crothers, Samuel, 1783-1856, 3131, 3132
Croton aqueduct, 13215
Crouch, Ron, 13951
Crouse, Charles Stevens, 14447, 15512
The Crow captive, 3908
Crow Indians, 16153, 16989
Crowe, Eyre, 1824-, 3133
Crowfield, Christopher, pseud., 10902
Crowley, Mary Catherine, d.1920, 6520
The crown and the cloister, 9417
Crown cork and seal company, Baltimore, Md., 17332
A crown from the spear, 10022
The crown of duty, 9420
Crown Point expedition, 1755, 21888
Crowther and the thirst, 8723
Crozat, Antoine, marquis du Châtel, 1655-1738, 1201
Crozer, Hiram P., 6521
Crozier, Robert Haskins, 3134, 3145, 13952
Cruchaga Gandarillas, Vicente, 20662
Cruchaga Santa María, Angel, 1893-, 20663
The crucible, 13744
Cruel as the grave, 10836
A cruel revenge, 10203
Cruelty disarmed, 10950
Cruelty to children, Legal aspects, 14676
Cruikshank, George, 1792-1878, illustr., 24595
Cruikshank, Isaac Robert, 1789-1850, illustr., 4806
Cruise of a guineaman, 10916
The cruise of a land yacht, 6032
The cruise of the Kaiserin, 6655

The cruise of the Montauk to Bermuda, 4375
Cruise of the Neptune, 6302
The cruise of the Sea-Slipper, 4001
The cruise of the Tomas Barrera, 7007
The cruiser of the capes, 4014
Cruisings, afloat and ashore, 10078
Crumpton, Hezekiah John, 16306
Crumpton, W.B., 16306
Crusade bulls, 7731
The crusade of the Excelsior, 6967
Crusades, Second, 1147-1149, Fiction,
   9235; Third, 1189-1192, Fiction,
   10285
Crusoe in New York, 9678
Crusoe's island, 8878, 16071
Crustacea, 19187
Crustacea, Fossil, Pará, Brazil, 19496
Crustaceans, Chile, 18690; Kentucky,
   15111
Crutchfield, William, 1775?-1812, 2818
Cruz, Arlette Nogueira da, 20664
Cruz, Ernesto de la, 7631
Cruz, Ernesto Horacio da, 1898-, 20665,
   20666
Cruz, Jorge de la, 20667-20676
Cruz, Olga, 20677
Cruz, Raúl de la, 20678
Cruz Coronado, Guillermo de la, 1921-,
   20679
Cruz Costa, João, 20680
Cruz Larena, Jorge, 20681
Cruz Reyna, Gonzalo de la, 20682
Cruz Sandoval, Fernando, 18324
The cry of the children, 5562
Cryptobranchus, 932
Cryptocellus, Cuba, 18525
Crystalina, 3785
Crystalline, 10746
Cuadra, Pablo Antonio, 1912-, 20683,
   20684
Cuatrecasas, José, 20685
Cuauhtemoc, emperor of Mexico, 1495?-
   1525, 13213
Cuba, 365, 5992, 6524, 6556, 6563, 7176,
   13285, 18217, 19615, 23141, 24956;
   Administración General de Café y Cacao,
   20686; Biography, 611, 19532; Caja
   general de jubilaciones y pensiones
   de empleados de bancos, 20693;
   Civilization, 6563; Climate, 5049;
   Comisión nacional de la UNESCO, 20687,
   20688; Constitución, 1901, 20689;
   Convención Constituyente, 1900-1901,
   20689; Departamento de Asuntos
   Económicos Internacionales, 20090;
   Description & travel, 8, 14, 189, 335

336, 724, 1024, 1473, 1628, 2502, 2562,
   2957, 4221, 4227, 4309, 4569, 4571, 4756,
   4769, 4964, 5006, 5454, 5716, 5747, 5810,
   5891, 6157, 6208, 6213, 6426, 6540, 6556,
   6561, 6563, 6661, 6699, 6745, 6904, 6907,
   7007, 7049, 7083, 7086, 7112, 7137, 7189,
   7191, 7212, 7217, 7264, 7370, 7541, 7557,
   7558, 7589, 7639, 7819, 8043, 8104, 8108,
   8161, 8178, 8302, 8421, 8438, 12226, 12956,
   13041, 19944, 20207, 23292, 25734;
   Description & travel, Guide-books, 6103,
   6912; Description & travel, History, 18214;
   Description & travel, Views, 20700;
   Dirección Nacional de Bibliotecas, 20691;
   Economic conditions, 4961, 6426, 12981,
   18217, 19896, 20696, 23914, 24539; Emigration
   & immigration, 25177; Fiction, 4744; Foreign
   relations, 18856; Geology, 18094; Historical
   geography, 19822; History, 724, 6556, 6563,
   15214, 18217, 20060, 20207, 20548, 20696;
   History,To 1810, 18569; History,1899-, 19977;
   History, 1933-, 18888; History,1959-, 18677,
   19078, 19556, 20687; History,Historiography,
   18214; History, Insurrection, 1849-1851,
   13285; History, Insurrection, 1868-1878,
   18569, 20062, 20204, 23851, 24235; History,
   Insurrection, 1868-1878,Fiction, 8696, 9379;
   History,Revolution, 1895-1898, 6750, 19896,
   20253, 20703; Intendencia de ejército y
   hacienda, 20692; Laws, Statutes, etc.,
   20693, 20694, 20598, 24234; Ministerio de
   agricultura, 20695; Ministerio de Educacion,
   20696; Ministerio de Trabajo, 20698;
   Oficina del censo, 6524; Politics &
   government, 424, 6745, 11348, 18631, 19034,
   19073, 19896, 19977, 20689, 20694, 20699,
   20701, 20702, 23913, 24386, 24441, 24539,
   24657, 24940, 25771, 25787; Politics &
   government, Periodicals, 19616; Provisional
   Governor, 1906-1909 (Charles E. Magoon),
   20699; Relations (general) with Azerbaijan,
   7189; Social conditions, 18677, 20687;
   Social life & customs, 6699; Statistics,
   12981
Cuba and the fight for freedom, 20207
Cuba before the United States, 24235
Cuba contemporánea, 6522, 6523
Cuba en su puesto, discursos pronunciados por
   el Sr. Presidente de la República...[1941],
   20701
Cuba for invalids, 12226
Cuba libre, 19615
Cuba past and present, 8302
Cuba Socialista, la Habana, 20702
Cuba, territorio libre de América, 20700
Cuba y Puerto-Rico. Medios de conservar estas

dos Antillas en su estado de esplendor, 24325
Cuban Anti-slavery Committee, New York, 24236
Cuban literature, Afro-Cuban poetry, 24969; Bibliography, 611; History & criticism, 611, 19533; Periodicals, 7845, 7849, 7850
The Cuban question, 1895-1898,19595, 20703
Cuban question, To 1895,1164, 20703
The Cuban question as reflected in the editorial columns of middle western newspapers, 18631
The Cuban question in the Spanish parliament, 24940
Cuban sketches, 8104
Cubas Alvariño, Ana M., 20704
Cubero Sebastián, Pedro, 1640-ca.1696, 6525-6527
Cubism and atonality, 13978
Cudjo's cave, 25726
Cudworth, James, d.1682, 23466
Cudworth, Warren Handel, d.1883, 3136, 6528
Cue Sarquís, Irma, 20705
Cuéllar, José Tomás de, 1830-1894, 19968
Cuenca en Pichincha, 19177
Cuenca, Humberto, 20706-20708
Cuentistas argentinos, 18932
Cuentistas jóvenes de Centro América y Panamá, 20709
Cuento peruano, 19849
Cuentos, 18570, 20529
Cuentos ticos, 6724
Cuentos folkloricos de la Argentina, 20104
Cuentos folklóricos del Ecuador, 19881
Cuentos indígenas venezolanos, 19786
Cuerpo (La idea del) en las letras españolas, 21750
Cuervo, Angel, 1836-1896, 20710, 20711
Cuervo, Rufino José, 1844-1911, 19817, 20711-20718
Cuesta y Cuesta, Alfonso, 21719
Cueva, Diego Martín de la, 5999
Cueva Tamariz, Augustín, 21720-21722
Cueva Silva, Jaime, 21723
Cuevas, Mariano, 1879-1949, 20006, 21724
Cuevas Herrera, Luis, 21725
Cuevas Paralizábal, Carlos, 21726
Cuffee, Paul, 1759-1818, 12803
Cugnet, François Joseph, 1720-1789, 11882, 11883, 11884
Cuguano, Ottobah, 11885
Cui bono? 23718

Culbertson, Thaddeus Ainsworth, 1823-1850, 3137, 16307
Cull, William H., 13953, 13954
Cullen, Cassius C., 11886
Cullen, Edward, 11887
Cullom, William, 1810-1896, 11888
Cullum, George Washington, 1809-1892, 11889
Culpepper co., Va., Genealogy, 3680
The cultivation of flax, 1818
Cultivo de los trigos en el Ecuador, 18387
Cultos afro-brasileiros, 20402
Cultura e opulencia do Brasil, 18291
Cultura venezolana; revista mensual, 21728
Culture, Addresses, essays, lectures, 21727
Culture du poivrier à la Guiane française, 1203
Cumaná, Venezuela. Universidad de Oriente, 21729
Cumback, William, 1829-, 11890
Cumberland County, Ky., 14910, 14915
Cumberland Falls, Whitley County, Kentucky, 14447
Cumberland Gap, Ky., 13955, 14922, 15380, 15642
Cumberland Lake, Ky., 15409
Cumberland Mountains, 15731
Cumberland Presbyterian Church, 13673
Cumberland Presbyterian church in the U.S. Biography, 13632, 13633
Cumberland River, 14751; Upper, 13863
A Cumberland vendetta and other stories, 9554
Cumberlands, The call of the, 13732
Cumbres y barrancas, 7020
Cuming, Fortescue, 1762-1828, 3138, 13956
Cumings, Henry, 1739-1823, 11891-11894
Cumings, Samuel, 3139, 6529, 11895
Cumming, Alexander, 1726-1763, 11896
Cumming, Hiram, 11897
Cumming, Hooper, 1788-1825, 11898
Cumming, Kate, 1835-, 3140
Cummings, Asa, 1796-1856, 21993
Cummings, Ebenezer Edson, 1800-1886, 11899
Cummings, Edward, 8969
Cummings, Edward Estlin, 1894-, 21730
Cummings, F.G., 3142
Cummings, Preston, 1800-1875, 11900
Cummings, Thomas Seir, 1804-1894, 11901
Cummins, Ebenezer Harlow, 665
Cummins, George David, bp., 1822-1876, 11902, 11903
Cummins, H., 17374
Cummins, Sarah J. (Lemmon) 1828-, 16308
Cundinamarca, Colombia (Dept.), 21731
The cuneiform cyclopedist of Chattanooga, 11114
Cuney, Norris Wright, 16698

Cunha, Alarico José da, 21732
Cunha, Celso Ferreira da, 21733
Cunha, Fernando Whitaker Tavares da, 21734
Cunha, Lygia da Fonseca Fernandes da, 21735
Cunha, Odalea de Queiroz, 1907-, 21736
Cunha, Osvaldo Rodriguez da, 21737
Cunha, Persivo, 21738
Cunha, Rui Vieira da, 1926-, 21739
Cunha, S. F. da, 21740, 21741
Cunningham, J., 11904
Cunningham, J. O., 6530
Cunningham, Letitia, 11905
Cunningham, William, 1767-1823, 11906
Cunningham family, 15640
Cunoniaceas, 20685
Cuny, Phil M., 21994
Cunynghame, Sir Arthur Augustus Thurlow, 1812-1884, 3143
A cup of cold water, 10163
Cupid in shoulder-straps, 9664
Cupid's album, 8545
Curaçao, Description & travel, 16, 11382
Curd, William H., 24237
A cure for the spleen, 23596
Curico (Province), Chile, 20163
Curiosa aus der Neuen welt, 3858
Curiosity visits to southern plantations, 24238
A curious collection of trees and shrubs, 1828
Curious incidents, 10310
The curious legend of Louis Philippe in Kentucky..., 13537
Curitiba, Brazil. Museu Paranaense, Bibliography, 18833; Universidade Federal do Paraná, History, 19808; Universidade Federal do Paraná. Departamento de Historia, 21742
Curley, Edwin A., 16309, 16310
Curran, John Joseph, 16311
Curren, Benjamin, 7599
Currency question, 23934; Brazil, 18834; France, 1865; Gt. Britain, 752, 11341; Latin America, 20033; U.S., 40, 2143, 2378-2380, 11119, 12824, 12886, 13229, 22374; U.S., Speeches in Congress, 2406
Currer Lyle, 10603
Currey, Richard Owen, 11907
Currie, David, 6531
Currie, Mrs. Emma Augusta (Harvey) 1829-1913, 6532
Currie, Lauchlin Bernard, 21743
Currie, William, 1754-1828, 11908-11910

Currituck, N.C., Description, 4137
Curry, Jabes Lamar Monroe, 1825-1903, 2042, 24239, 24240
Curry, William T., 1818-1881, 14987
The curse entailed, 8803
The curse of Canaan rightly interpreted, and kindred topics, 24333
The curse of gold, 10866
The curse of Meroz, 23782
The curse of the drunkard's appetite, 9584
Curt, deputy from Guadeloupe, 6770
Curt, Louis, chevalier de, 1722-1804, 6533
Curtis, Benjamin Robbins, 1809-1874, 6669, 7335, 11913, 11914, 21995, 24729
Curtis, Catherine Parker, b.1801, 11847
Curtis, George Ticknor, 1812-1894, 11915-11919, 16312
Curtis, George William, 1824-1892, 11192, 11920, 16313
Curtis, Jonathan, 1786-1861, 21996
Curtis, John Vaughan, 15057
Curtis, Josiah, 1816-1883, 11921
Curtis, Lucius Quintius, 1812-1901, 11922
Curtis, Newton Martin, 1835-1910, 3144
Curtis, Orson Blair, 1841?-1901, 3145
Curtis, Samuel Ryan, 1805-1866, 23482
Curtis, Thomas D., 1935-, 21745
Curtis, W.J., 14603
Curtis, William Eleroy, 16314
Curtis family (William Curtis, 1592-1672) 11847
Curtiss, Mrs. Abby (Allin), 2087
Curtiss, Daniel S., 13957, 16315
Curtius, pseud., 5355
Curutchet, Marta I., 21746
Curwen, Samuel, 1715-1802, 11923
Cushing, Caleb, 1800-1879, 896, 11924, 21997, 21998, 24241-24243
Cushing, Christopher, 1820-1881, 21999
Cushing, Jacob, 1730-1809, 22000
Cushing, John, 1744-1823, 22001
Cushing, John Pearsons, 1861-, 7345
Cushing, Luther Stearns, 1803-1856, 22002
Cushing, S.W., 1818-, 3146, 16316
Cushman, Austin S., 22003
Cushman, Charlotte Saunders, 1816-1876, 12013
Cushman, Esther Cowles, comp., 7066
Cushman, Frederick E., 1843?, 22004
Cushman, Henry Wyles, 1805-1863, 12381, 22005
Cushman, Robert, 1579?-d.1625, 11925, 22006, 22007
Cushman, Robert Woodward, 1800-1868, 11925, 22008
Cushman family, 11925
Cushman family (Robert Cushman, d.1625), 22005
Cushman monument association, 22005

Cussy, Ferdinand de Cornot, baron de, 1795-1866, 22009, 22010
Cust, Sir Edward, bart., 1794-1878, 22011, 22012
Cust, Sir Reginald John, 1828-1913, 22013
Custer, Elizabeth (Bacon) 1842-1933, 16317
Custer, George Armstrong, 1839-1870, 4170, 16118, 16317, 16318, 16385, 16515, 17858
Custer co., Neb., History, 16110
Custis, George Washington Parke, 1781-1857, 22014, 22015
Customs administration, U.S., 12080
The customs of New England, 2244
Cuthbert, Albert, 1785-1856, 24244
Cutler, Benjamin Clarke, 1798-1863, 12360
Cutler, Elbridge Jefferson, 1831-1870, 22016, 22017
Cutler, Jervis, 1768-1844, 3147
Cutler, Joseph, 1815-1885, 11926
Cutler, Manasseh, 1742-1823, 3148, 11927
Cutler, Rufus King, 11928
Cutler, William Parker, 1812-1889, 24245
Cutter, Benjamin, 1803-1864, 22018
Cutter, Charles William, 11929
Cutter, Edward Francis, 6534
Cutter, George Washington, 1801?-1865, 3149, 3150
Cutter, Orlando Phelps, 22019
Cutter, William, 1801-1867, 11930, 22496
Cutter, William McLellan, b.1836, reporter, 1166
Cutter, William Richard, 1847-1918, 22018
Cutter family (Richard Cutter, 1621?-1693), 22018
Cutting, Francis Brockholst, 1805-1870, 11931
Cutting, H. P., 22020
Cutting, Sewall Sylvester, 1813-1882, 24246
Cutts, James Madison, 3151
Cutts, Lucia Beverly, 1851-, 7389
Cuvier, Georges, i.e. Jean Leopold Nicolas Frédéric, baron, 1769-1832, 7092, 22021
Cuyas y Armongol, Arturo, 1845-1925, 6535
Cuyler, Cornelius C., 1783-1850, 11932
Cuyo; anuario de historia del pensamiento argentino, 21747; Universidad Nacional, 17996
Cuza Male, Belkis, 21748
Cuzán, Alfred G., 21749
Cuzco, Peru, 7411; History, 8291
Cventa de lo qve se ha pagado, por gastos generales, 6536
Cvitanovic, Dinko, 21750, 21751

Cycling, 2592
Cyclopaedia of American literature, 3332, 12456
Cymon, pseud., 10828
The Cymry of '76, 13286
The Cynick, 11933
Cynthia Wakeham's money, 10664
Cypress Boardwalk Nature trail, 14167
Cyr, Narcisse, 1823?-1894, 22022
Cysneiros, Lucia Maria Rosa, 21752
Czeika, pseud., 5594

Da Asia de João de Barros e de Diogo de Couto, 882
Dabadie, F., 11934
Dabney, Richard, 1787?-1825, 3152
Dabney, Robert Lewis, 1820-1898, 3153-3155
Dabney, Virginius, 1835-1894, 3156, 3157, 10125
The Dabney will, 8629
Dacanal, José Hildebrando, 20091
Dactylis caespitosa, 22555
Dacus, Joseph A., 3158, 16319
Dade's battle, 1835, 232
Daggett, David, 1764-1851, 12844
Daggett, Herman, 1766-1832, 22023
Daggett, John, 1805-1885, 11935, 11936
Daggett, Naphtali, 1727-1780, 22024, 22025
Daggett, Oliver Ellsworth, 1810-1880, 6537
Daggett, Thomas F., 16320, 15321
Daggs, Ruel, 24247
Dagnall, John Malone, 1818-1917, 11937
The Dagon of Calvinism, 3159
Dagverhaal van eene reis naar Paramaribo, 1484
Dahcotah, 2163
Dahkotah land and Dahkotah life, 23465
Daiches, Samuel, 1878-, 24248
Daily bread, 9683
Daines, Franklin David, 16322
Daingerfield, Foxhall, 1887-1933, 13958, 13959
Dairy products, Argentine Republic, Statistics, 18449
Dairying, Argentine Republic, 18474, 18801
The dairyman's daughter, 23532
Daisy, 11093
Daisy Dare, and Baby Power, 4053
Daisy Swain, the flower of Shenandoah, 11937
Daisy Thornton and Jessie Graham, 9893
Daisy's necklace: and what came of it, 8497
Dake, Orsamus Charles, 11938
Dakota, 16409; Description & travel, 15834,

16541; Economic conditions, 15934;
History, 15934, 16541, 16802; Politics
& government, 17587
Dakota Co., Minn., History, 23440
The Dakota Indian victory dance, 15952
Dakota Indian War, 13563
Dakota Indians, 2153, 3147, 13360, 15939,
15955, 15956, 16054, 16152, 16691,
16802, 16927, 16986, 17174, 17402, 23465;
Government relations, 17730; Missions,
17401, 17491; Wars, 1862-1865, 1624,
12776, 16150, 16264, 16425, 16908, 16927,
21786; Wars, 1876, 16515; Wars, 1890-
1891, 15971
Dakota land and Dakota life, 17263
Dakota language, Glossaries, vocabularies,
etc., 541; Texts, 23535
Dakota Territory   History, 13563, 16043,
16044, 16045, 16284, 17705, 17710
Dakota war whoop, 21786
Dale, E.I., 6538
Dale, J.S. of, pseud. of Frederic Jesup
Stimson, 9641
Dale, Robert William, 1829-1895, 3160
Dale, Samuel, 1772-1841, 3004
Dale Cemetery, Ossining, N.Y., 22026
Dalhoff, N., 24249
Dall, Caroline [Wells](Healey), "Mrs. C.H.A.
Dall", 1822-1912, 11939, 11940
Dall, William Healey, 1845-1927, 11941
Dallas, Alexander James, 1759-1817, 22028
Dallas, George Mifflin, 1792-1864, 1252,
11942, 22029
Dallas, Robert Charles, 1754-1824, 11943,
22031
Dallas, Tex., 16869
Dallasburg Baptist Church, 15694
Dalliba, James, 11944
Dally, 10540
Dalmas, Antoine, 1757-1830, 22027
Dalrymple,Alexander, 1737-1808, 2476,
11945, 11946
Dalrymple,Sir John, bart., 1726-1810,
11947
Dalton, Benjamin Franklin, 1951
Dalton, John Call, 1795-1864, 12382
Dalton, Kit, 1843-1920, 16323
Dalton, William, of Crackenthorpe,
Westmoreland, 11948
Daly, Augustin, 1838-1899, 11949
Daly, Charles Patrick, 1816-1899, 11950
The Dalys of Dalystown, 10438
Dalzell, James McCormick, 1838-1924,
22032
Dame, William Meade, 1844 or 5-, 3161
Dame Fortune smiled, 8714

Dames and daughters of the young republic,
6188
Damon, David, 1787-1843, 22033
Damon, Samuel Chenery, 1815-1885, 15324,
22034
A damphool in the Kentucky legislature, 14503
Dampier, William, 1652-1715, 22035
Dams, Kentucky, 15123
A damsel errant, 11012
The damsel of Darien, 10771
Dan Briordy's gitaway shadder, 9533
Dan to Beersheba, 11951
Dana, Charles Anderson, 1819-1897, 3162,
6539, 22036
Dana, C. W., 16325
Dana, Daniel, 1771-1859, 22037, 22038
Dana, Edmund, 3163
Dana, Mrs. Eliza A. (Fuller), 22039
Dana, James, 1735-1812, 11952, 11953
Dana, James Dwight, 1813-1895, 11954, 11955
Dana, James Freeman, 1793-1827, 11956
Dana, Richard Henry, 1815-1882, 2511, 5831,
6540, 11723, 16326, 24250, 24251
Dana, Richard Henry, 1851-1931, 24251
Dana, Samuel Luther, 1795-1868, 11956
Danbury, Conn., 8642
Dancing, Africa, 18173; Folk and national
dances, 14691; Latin America, 18173
The dancing feather, 4001
Dandolo, Vincenzo, conte, 1758-1819, 511
Dandridge, Mrs. Danske (Bedinger) 1858-1914,
3164, 3165
Danenhower's Chicago city directory, 21911
Danes in Canada, 7314
Danes in the U.S., 7314
Danforth, Edward F., 1893-1963, 13960
Danforth, John, 1660-1730, 22040
Danger, 8561
Danger in the dark, 10091
The danger of being too thorough, 10465
The danger of desertion, 12882
The dangerous condition of the country, 13254
The dangerous ford, 10310
The dangers and sufferings of Robert Eastburn,
11994
Daniel, Frederick S., 3166
Daniel, John Moncure, 1825-1865, 2589
Daniel Boone, 2748, 13595, 13961, 14236
Daniel Boone bicentennial commission, 14008
Daniel Boone National Forest, Ky., 13917, 15409,
15536, 15628-15630
Daniel Thomas, and company, 24252
Daniell, L. E., 16327
Daniells, I. G., 16123
Danielson, J. A., 6541
Danities, Fiction, 10352

The Danities in the Sierras, 10352
Dannemann, Manuel, 18878
Danon, Jacques, 20082
Danses africaines en Amérique Latine, 18173
Dansville, N.Y., 11816
Dantas, José Lucena, 19220
Dante Alighieri, 1265-1321, Folklore, mythology, 19900
Dante Alighieri e a tradição popular no Brasil, 19900
Dante en Nueva York, 19782
D'Antin, Luis, 7532
Danvers, Mass., History, 12658, 24253
Danvers Historical Society, Danvers, Mass., 24253
Danville, Ky., 13962, 15554; History, 13620, 14065, 15426, 15571; Maps, 14277, 15571, 15663; Theological seminary of the Presbyterian church in the U.S.A., 13516, 15170
Danville, Va. Military prison, 4593, 4867
Danville artist draws praise, 13963
Danville literary and social club, Danville, Ky., 13964
The Danville quarterly review, 3167
Danville's historic McDowell House, 13965
Daoust, Charles R., 6542
The dapper gentleman's story, 10172
Darby, George W., 3168
Darby, John Fletcher, 1803-1882, 16328
Darby, William, 1775-1854, 3169-3174
Darien, 7567, 11887; Description & travel, 12278; Scot's colony, 11887
Darien canal, 11887, 12278
Darío, Rubén, 1867-1916, 18037, 19837; Anniversaries, etc., 1967, 20409
The dark and bloody ground, 2682, 4621, 15103
Dark and terrible deeds of George Lathrop, 9328
Dark days of the rebellion, 2761
A dark lantern, 4984
The dark maid of Illinois, 3754, 14243
Darley, Felix Octavius Carr, 1822-1888, illustr., 1747, 3840, 4832, 4833, 5403, 5405, 5411, 5460, 9453, 10000, 10361, 10964, 11101, 22157
Darley, George Marshall, 1847-, 16329
Darlington, Mary Carson (O'Hara) 1824-1915, 16330
Darlington, William, 1782-1863, 22114, 24254
Darlington, William M., 3620, 4425

Darnell, Ermina Jett, 13966, 13967
Darnell, Jacob C., 13968
Darnell, Mrs. James, 14639, 14640
Darryll Gap, 11007
Dartmoor prison, 356, 11107
Dartmouth College, 2226, 9734, 12535, 22207, 22414, 22815; History, 2134; Society of the alumni, 11573; A vindication of the official conduct of the trustees, 2134
D'Arusmont, Mme. Frances (Wright) 1795-1852, 3175, 22241
D'Arusmont, William E. Guthrie, 6543, 24255
Darwin, Charles Robert, 1809-1882, 22041
Dashed against the rock, 9083
Dashes at life with a free pencil, 11176
Datos históricos e iconografía de la educación en México, 19826
Datt, Johann Philipp, 1654-1722, 24256
Daubeny, Charles Giles Bridle, 1795-1867, 3176
Dauchy, George Kellogg, 1829-1912, 5461
The daughter of a Republican, 8621
The daughter of a stoic, 9085
A daughter of New France, 6520
Daughter's College, Harrodsburg, Ky., 13637
A daughter's trials, 8901
Daughters of charity of St. Vincent de Paul, Emmitsburg, Md., 8896
Daughters of Colonial Wars, Kentucky, 13969
Daughters of the American Revolution, 13970; Kentucky, 13971, 15751; Kentucky. Frankfort Chapter, 13972; Kentucky. Lexington Chapter, 14031
Daughters of the revolution and their times, 9058
Dauzats, Adria, 1804-1868, 2732
Dávalos, Balbino, 7340
Dave Summers, 10598
Dave's wife, 10163
Davenport, Alfred, 3177
Davenport, Bishop, 3178, 22042
Davenport, John, 1597-1670, 21990, 22813
Davenport, Montague, 3179
Davenport, O. M., 14804
Davenport, Ia. 16106; Biography, 23794; History, 23794
Davenport past and present, 23794
David, Michael, 3180
David Aldens' daughter, 8602
David Harum, 11124
David Swan, 9827
David Têtu de les raiders de Saint-Alban, 13973
Davidson, Henry M., d.1900, 3181, 4031
Davidson, James Wood, 1829-1905, 3182, 3183
Davidson, John Nelson, 24257

Davidson, Robert, 1808-1876, 3184, 13974
Daviers, William Watkins, 13975
Davies, Ebenezer, 1808-1882, 3185
Davies, Henry Eugene, 1836-1894, 16331
Davies, John Johnson, 1831-, 16332
Daviess, Joseph Hamilton, 15167
Daviess, Maria Thompson, 1872-, 13976, 13977
Daviess County, Ky., 14220
Davila, Enrico Caterino, 1576-1631. Historia delle guerre civil di Francia, 59
Dávila, Martin, 7397
Dávila, Vicente, 1874-, 6544
Davila Solera, José, 8324
Davila Vazquez, Jorge, 1947-, 20649
Davis, Beverly, 13978
Davis, Carlyle Channing, 16333
Davis, Charles E., b.1842 or 3-1915, 3186
Davis, Connee, 15455
Davis, Daniel, 1762-1835, 22043
Davis, Darrell Haug, 1879-, 13979
Davis, Dick, 1838?-1864, 3044
Davis, Ellis Arthur, 16334
Davis, Emerson, 1798-1866, 22044, 22045
Davis, Garrett, 1801-1872, 15615, 25700
Davis, Garrett Morrow, 1851-, 13980
Davis, George, 1820-1896, 2055, 22046
Davis, George Lynn-Lachlan, 2088
Davis, George Turnbull Moore, b.1810-1888, 16335
Davis, Henry Turner, 16336
Davis, Herman Stearns, 1868-, 16987
Davis, Jefferson, pres. C.S.A., 1808-1889, 2736, 3187, 4817, 6848, 7925, 7926, 8232, 8287, 13586, 15259, 22418, 24181, 24258, 24259, 24260, 24883
Davis, John, 1774-1854, 3188, 3189, 3191
Davis, John, 1788-1878, 6546
Davis, John Francis, 1859-, 16125
Davis, Mrs. Mary Evelyn (Moore) 1852-1909, 3191-3194, 16337
Davis, Nicholas A., 3195
Davis, Nicholas Darnell, 1846-1915, 24261
Davis, Owen, 24262
Davis, R. H., 10163
Davis, Mrs. Rebecca Harding, 1831-, 8597
Davis, Richard Harding, 1864-1916, 6545, 16338
Davis, Samuel Post, 1850-1918, ed., 16339

Davis, Stephen, 3196
Davis, Thomas Osborne, 6310
Davis, William E., 14456
Davis, William Heath, 16340
Davis, William J., ed., 4063
Davis, William Jackson, 1818-1864, 22051
Davis, William Watts Hart, 1820-1910, 3197, 6546, 16341, 16342, 22047-22049
Davis, Winfield J., 16343
Davis Co., Ia., History, 16481
Davis de Clark, Nancy, 20208
Davis mountains, Tex., 17441
Davis Strait, 22843
Davison, Gideon Miner, 1791?-1869, 6547, 6548, 23622
Davy, Joseph Burt, 16344
Dawes, Henry Laurens, 1816-1903, 24263
Dawes, Rufus R., 1838-1899, 3198
Dawley, Thomas Robinson, 1832-1904, pub., 13075
Dawn, 8463
Dawn in darkest Africa, 24565
Daws doings, 10099
Dawson, Aeneas MacDonell, 1810-1894, 6549
Dawson, Charles, 16345
Dawson, Henry Barton, 1821-1889, 12352, 12943, 13178, 22050, 22051, 22692
Dawson, J. L., 11744
Dawson, James Lowes, 1801-1879, 6824
Dawson, John Littleton, 1813-1870, 22052
Dawson, Sir John William, 1820-1899, 22053, 22054
Dawson, Moses, 16346
Dawson, S. J., 7922
Dawson, Samuel Edward, 1833-1916, 6550, 6551
Dawson, Mrs. Sarah (Morgan), 3199
Dawson, Simon James, 3200, 6552
Day, Francis, illustr., 9534
Day, Gershom Bulkley, 1804-1852, 17756
Day, Henry Noble, 1808-1890, 15894
Day, Lewis W., b.1839 or 40, 3201
Day, Luella, 16347
Day, Samuel Phillips, 3202, 3203
Day, Sherman, 2892
Day, Thomas, 1748-1789, 24264, 24265
Day, William W., 3204
A day at Laguerre's and other days, 5193
Day-dreams, 8519
A day in the wilderness, 9565
A day of darkness, 21894
A day of fate, 10644
The day of his youth, 8857
The day of my death, 11075
The day of small things, 184
The day of the cyclone, 9582
A day on Cooper river, 4023

The day-star of American freedom, 2088
A day with the padres, 10863
A day's pleasure, 9606, 9941
Daybreak, 9188
Daylight, 4972, 10628
Days and dreams, 13798
Days and events, 4285
Days and nights in the tropics, 6961
The days before the revolution, 9389
The days of Daniel Boone, 4621
Days of horror, 15971
The days of shoddy, 10380
The days of Tammany, 9969
Days on the road, 16744
The days that are no more, 4073
The days we live in, 8483
Dayton, Ohio, History, 6457, 6459,
  13915
Dazey, Charles T., 13981
Deacon Grubb and Old Nick, 9998
Deacon Pheby's selfish nature, 10790
The deacon's week, 9119, 10163
Deacons, 10399
Dead broke, 10439
A dead issue and the live one, 25797
The dead marquise, 10143
Dead men's shores, 11059
The dead men's song, 14332
The deadly lesson of Sand Cave, 13857
Deaf-Education, 7181
Deaf and dumb, 23082
Deal, Charles, pub., 6085
The dealings of God with our nation,
  22585
Dealings with the dead, 10587
Dealtry, William, 22055
Dean, Gilbert, 1819-1870, 22056
Dean, Isaac, 6627
Dean, John, 6627
Dean, John, 1679-1761, 2089
Dean, John Ward, 1815-1902, 2090, 2091,
  22057, 22058
Dean, Paul, 1789-1860, 24266
Dean, Sidney, 1818-1901, 6553
Dean, Silas, 1815-1906, 22059
Dean family, 6627, 11962
Dean le quarteron, 12237
Deane, Charles, 1813-1889, 5205, 22006,
  22060-22062, 23365, 23275, 24267,
  24268
Deane, James, 1801-1858, 11426
Deane, Samuel, 1733-1814, 11957, 11958
Deane, Samuel, 1784-1834, 22063
Deane, Silas, 1737-1789, 11959, 11960
Deane, William Reed, 1809-1871, 11961,
  11962, 22064

"Dear Miss Bettie," 14073
Dearborn, Henry, 1751-1829, 3205, 21970,
  21971, 22065
Dearborn, Henry Alexander Scammell, 1783-1851,
  16349, 22079, 22080
Dearborn, Nathaniel, 1786-1852, 2092, 22066
Deas, Anne (Izard), 13118
Death, 23004
Death at the court-house, 13876
The death of General Montgomery, 11482
The death of Moses, 7178
Death of President Lincoln, 6554, 6902
Death records, 1852-1862, Clark County,
  Kentucky, 14635
The death shot, 10916
The death trail, 11166
Death Valley, Calif., 17648
Death Valley in '49, 17124
Death's doings, 9530
Death's young, 9330
Deaville, Alfred, 6555
Debajo del sol, 19169
Debar, J. H. Diss, 3206
Debates and debating, 22858
DeBeck, William L., 11963
DeBellis, Frank V., 19640
De Berniere, Henry, 22065
De Boilieu, Lambert, 22067
De Bonelli, L. Hugh, 11964
Debouchel, Victor, 3207
De Brahm, John Gerar William, 1717-c.1799,
  3208
Debray, Xavier Blanchard, 16351
Debrett, John, d.1822, 2476
Debt, Imprisonment for, 9368
The debt to Africa, the hope of Liberia,
  23960
Debtor and creditor, 14665, 24343; Laws
  and regulations, 14682
Debtor relief, Report of workshop on law of,
  14682
Debts, Public, 2373; Great Britain, 12008,
  12076; Maryland, 23212; Mexico, 1217;
  Pennsylvania, 23637; U.S., 2189, 12188,
  12224, 12229, 12824, 21995, 22827, 24574
Una decada de Congresos Internacionales de
  Americanistas, 20363
Decadas del Nuevo Mundo, 5909, 18299
La decadencia del analfabetismo, 19000
Decadencia e redenção do Nordeste, 18560
The decadent, 9205
De Camp, John, 1812-1875, 22068
Decatur, Stephen, 1779-1820, 11965, 22069
Decatur, Mrs. Susan (Wheeler), 11965
Decatur, Neb., 16361
De Charms, Richard, 1796-1864, 24269

The decision of the King of the Netherlands, 13463
The decisional role of the Senate in the Chilean political system, 18032
Decius, pseud., 11966
Deck and port, 16253
The deck of the Crescent City, 22130
Decker's second wife, 11198
Deckert, Emil, 1848-1916, 6556, 6557
La declaración unilateral de voluntad como fuente de obligaciones, 18066
Declaration of American independence. Centennial Anniversary, 4 July 1876, 14296
A Declaration of independence, 11967
Declaration of intention, Guatemala, 18066
Declaration of the anti-slavery convention, 24270
A declaration of the doctrines and practice of the church of Christ, 14028
A declaration of the state of the colony and state of affairs in Virginia, 5632
Declaves, Alonso, pseud., 13982
Decline and fall, 11018
The decline and fall of Samuel Sawbones, 17018
The decline and fall of the Hoosac tunnel, 11275
De Coin, Robert L., 22070
Decoration day, 10041
De Cordova, Jacob, 3209, 16352, 16353
De Costa, Benjamin Franklin, 1831-1904, 2093, 22071, 22072
La découverte des sources du Mississippi, 1133
Découvertes et établissements des français dans l'ouest, 7404
Decretum Oxomen beatificationis, 6558
Dedicating in Dixie, 5137
Dedham, Mass., Directories, 1566; History, 22350, 23086
Dedman, Mrs. T. Curry, 14197
De Dios, y sus atributos, 5804
Dee, Henry Drummond, ed., 8420
Deedes, Henry, 3210
Deeds, New York (City), 12442; New York (County), 12442
Deep waters, 9255
Deephaven, 10036
Deer hunting, 8007
Deerfield, Mass., History, 25493; History, Colonial period, 23802, 23892
Deering, Richard, 22073
The deerslayer, 9130
The defeat of Amos Wickliff, 9581

A defence of a book...entitled a modest proof of the order and government settled by Christ and his apostles, 21890
Defence of Baltimore, 2196
Defence of Kenyon College, 2976
Defence of Maj. Gen. Caleb Burbank, 1684
The defence of Petersburg, 4331
A defence of the character and principles of Mr. Jefferson, 12107
A defence of the constitution of England against the libels that have been lately published on it..., 22074
A defence of the doctrine of grace, 2895
A defence of the legislature of Massachusetts, or The rights of New England vindicated, 22075
A defence of the measures of the administration of Thomas Jefferson, 5355
A defence of the resolutions and address of the American Congress, 11968
A defence of the Rockingham party, 11969
A defence of Virginia, 3153
The defence of Warner Mifflin against aspersions cast on him..., 25042
The defenders of the country and its enemies, 1593
Defensa canonica por las Provincias de la compañia de Jesus, 7994
Defensor, pseud., 25682
Deficiencies in our history, 1770
A definition of parties, 13487
Defoe, Daniel, 1661?-1731, supposed author, 2986, 21910, 22076
De Fontaine, Felix Gregory, 1832-1896, 2094
De Forest, Bartholomew S., 3211
De Forest, T. R., 22077
Defrees, John Dougherty, b.1810 or 11-1882, 22078
Degenkolb, Heinrich, 1832-1909, 24271
Degollado, Santos, 1813-1861, 1825
Degoulet, Urbain, 3633
Degrand, Peter Paul Francis, d.1855, 22079, 22080
DeGrott, Alfred Thomas, 1903-, 13983
De Groot, Henry, 3212, 16354
De Hass, Wills, 1818?-1910, 3213
Dehay, Timothée, 1794-1851, 11970
Deiler, John Hanno, 1849-1909, 3214, 3215
Deitz family, 11513
DeJarnette, Daniel C., 1822-1881, 24272, 24273
Dejligt at Amerika ikke ligger langt herfra, 2485
De Jong, Gordon F., 13984, 13985
De Kay, James Ellsworth, 1792-1851, 11373
Deković Torres, José, 18670
De Kroyft, Mrs. Helen (Aldrich) 1818-1915,

22081
Delacroix, Jacques Vincent, 1743-
  1832, 11974, 22082
Delafaye-Bréhier, Mme. Julie, 22083
Delafield, Edward, 1794-1875, 11975
Delafield, John, 1812-1865 or 6, 3216,
  11976
De la Houssaye, Mme. S., 3217, 3218
DeLand, Charles Victor, 1826-, 6559
De Lancey, William Heathcote, bp., 1797-
  1865, 11977
Deland, Clyde O., illustr., 2982,
  6520
Deland, Mrs. Margaret Wade (Campbell)
  1857-, 3219
Delaney, Matilda J. (Sager) 1839-,
  16355
Delano, Alonzo, 1806-1874, 3220,
  16356-16358
Delaplaine, 11062
Delaplaine, Edward Schley, 1893-, 6560
Delaplaine, Joseph, 1777-1824, 11978
De Lara, 3842
Delavan, James, 16359
Delaware, Boundaries, 23733; Description
  & travel, 3490, 5147, 14749; Governor,
  1863-1865 (Cannon), 24274; History,
  2264; History, Colonial period, 3221,
  21954, 22376; Politics & government,
  24274
Delaware breakwater, 13322
Delaware co., N.Y., History, 12334
Delaware Indians, 12804, 23503, 23697;
  Fiction, 9840; Legends, 6153; Missions,
  22391
Delaware language, 13169
Delaware river, 13321
De La Warr, Thomas West, 3d lord, 1577-
  1618, 3221
De Leon, Thomas Cooper, 1839-1914, 3222-
  3227, 24275
El delfin de Corubili, 18144
Delfino, Luiz, 1834-1910, 20514
Delgado, José María, 6561
Delgado, José Matías, 1767-1832, 18847
Delia's doctors, 9239
The deliberation of Mr. Dunkin, 24319
The delight makers, 8673
El delito de abusos dishonestos, 18898
El delito de ataques a las vías de
  comunicación, 18860
El delito de difamación, 18591
El delito de portación de arma de fuego
  sin licencias, 18687
El delito de rapto, 18342
Delius, Eduard, 3228

Dell, William, d.1664, 11979, 11980
Dellenbaugh, Frederick Samuel, 16360
Delluc, Louis, 1890-1924, 6562
Del Mar, Alexander, 1836-, 11981
Del Norte co., Calif., History, 16002
Delta Kappa Gamma, 13986
Delta Sigma Theta, 13987
Deluge, 11698, 22188
Delusion; or, The witch of New England, 22084
Demagny, René, 1930-, 6563
Demarest, James, 1832-, 11982
Demerara (Colony), History, 1516
Demersay, Alfred, d.1891, 11983, 11984
Demetz, Frédéric-Auguste, 1796-1873, 3229
Demeunier, Jean Nicolas, 1741-1814, 11985
De Milt, Alonzo Pierre, 1831-, 16361, 16520
Deming, Henry Champion, 1815-1872, 6564
Democracia y parlamento, 20071
Democracy, 5050, 5429, 8465, 11622, 11665,
  12304, 12443, 15744
Democracy unveiled, 12143
Democrat and Republican. Slavery and Freedom.
  Past and present crises, 23867
Demócrates segundo, 8004
Democratic Association of Pennsylvania, 24058
Democratic party, 553, 1160, 1781, 2076,
  12253, 13325, 23841, 23922, 24242, 25016;
  Fayette county, Ky., 14489; Georgia.
  Convention, 1856, 25612; History, 1307;
  Kentucky, 13988, 13989, 15372; Louisiana,
  25318; Massachusetts. 2d Congressional
  district, 25343; Massachusetts, Waltham,
  24545; National committee, 1848-1852,
  22085, 24276; National committee, 1852-1856,
  3230; National committee, 1860-1864, 6565;
  National committee, 1864-1868, 6566-6572,
  22803; New England, 895; New Jersey, 24277;
  New York (State), 11931; Pennsylvania.
  Philadelphia, 24278; Pennsylvania.
  Philadelphia. Committee of correspondence,
  2211
Democratic Society of Kentucky, 13990-13992
Democratic Woman's Club of Kentucky, 13993
The Democratic woman's journal, 13993
Democratus, pseud., 24279
Demographic explosion in the world and in
  Brazil, 20560
Demographic growth and environmental
  pollution, 20561
De Molai: the last of the military grand
  masters of the order of Templar knights,
  3466
Demonology, 13049
Demonology, 19000
Demonstración legal en defensa de d. Joseph
  del Pozo y Honesto, 7768

De Morgan, Augustus, 1806-1871, ed., 2594
De Moss, John C., 13994
Dempter, John, 25205
Demund, Isaac S., 1803-1888, 24280
The demurrer: or, Proofs of error in the decision of the Supreme court of the state of New York, 22427
Denbo, Bruce F., 13584
Denegri Luna, Félix, 6794
Dengo de Vargas, María Eugenia, 1926-, 19474
Denis, Ferdinand, 1798-1890, 16362, 23060
Denmark, Description & travel, 7223, 7224, 22751
Dennett, Daniel, 3231
The Dennings and their beaux, 10195
Denny, Arthur Armstrong, 1822-1899, 16363
Denny, Ebenezer, 1761-1822, 3232
Denominational colleges, U.S., 2024
De Normandie, James, 1836-1924, 6573
Denron, Jesse, 13995
Denslow, W.W., illustr., 4902
Dent, John Charles, 1841-1888, 6574
Dental public health, Colombia, Statistics, 20348
The dentist, 14242
Denton L., Carlos F., 18016
Denton, Shelby T., 14690
Denton Co., Tex., Biographies, 15936; History, 15936
Denver Biographies, 16782, 17413; Description, 17514; History, 16782, 16987; Northwestern and Pacific railway, 17862
Denys, Nicolas, 1598-1688, 6575
Depew, Chauncey Mitchell, 1834-1928, 16373
De Peyster, John Watts, 1821-1907, 13997
Depositions in videotape, 14664
Deppen, U.L., haberdasher, Louisville, Ky., 13996
Depredations and massacre by the Snake River Indians, 5509
Derby, Elias Hasket, 1803-1880, 22086, 22087
Derby, James Cephas, 1818-1892, 3234
Derby, William P., 3235
The Derby dictionary, 15312
Derleth, August, 1909-1971, 15472
Derecho bolivariano, 18199
Derecho colombiano de familia, 20324
El derecho del señor, 19149
El derecho mercantil en la América Latina, 18858
Derecho penal colombiano, 18390
El derecho procesal agrario como uno de los medios para realizar major la reforma agraria, 18855
Derecho procesal civil, 20706
Derechos de la América del Sur y México, 19577
Los derechos humanos en el derecho constitucional guatemalteco, 18197
Derechos reales no comprendidos en el código civil, 18875
De Ros, John Frederick Fitzgerald, 1804-1861, 6576, 6577
Derprich, Juan, 18147
Derrotero de la costa de Chile, 20121
Derrotero de la expedición en la provincia de los Texas, 4742
Derry, Joseph Tyrone, 1841-, 3236
Derry, N.H., History, 22904
De Rupert, A. E. D., 16374
The dervise of Alfouran, 10693
Desaché, Gaetán, 6578
Desarrollo educacional, 19714
Desarrollo larval de dos especies de crustáceos decapodos en el laboratorio, 19187
De Saussure, Henry William, 1763-1839, 11744, 12695
De Saussure family (Henry de Saussure, fl. 1631), 12695
Desbandada, 19967
Desborough connections, 6975
Descendants of Richard Gardner, of Woburn, 12412
Descobrimento das terras da região acreana, 19928
Descourtilz, Michel-Étienne, 1775-1835, 3237
Descubrimiento (fiction), 20648
Descubrimiento y conquista de Venezuela, 17980
Desengaños sobre las preocupaciones del dia, 6579
Deseret. Constitutional convention, 1849, 16376; General assembly, 16376; The State of, 17230
The Deseret alphabet, 16377
Desert flora, 16182
The deserter, 9565, 10118, 10670
The deserter's daughter, 9856
Deserts, 3266, 16182, 16406; Colombia, 18243; Latin America, 20650
Des Essarts, Alfred Stanislas Langlois, 1811-1893, 2095
Desha, Joseph, 1833-1902, 13877
Desha, Mary, 13708
The Desha-Kimbrough duel, 13877
De Shields, James T., 1861-, 16379, 16380
Deshler & Deshler, 10088

Desjardins, Ernest Emile Antoine, 1823-1886, 22088
La desocupación en el campo y la reforma agraria, 20535
Os despojados, 19831
The despot of Broomsedge Cove, 4554
Despotic doctrines declared by the United States Senate exposed, 12947
Despotism, 11406
The despotism of freedom, 1881
Dessaulles, Louis Antoine, 1819-1895, 24282
Destiny, 10397
The destiny of the races of this continent, 1383
Destruction and reconstruction: personal experiences of the late war, 25673
The destruction of the union is emancipation, 24951
Destructive consequences of dissipation, 10245
Destutt de Tracy, Antonio Louis Claude, comte, 1754-1836, 22089
Desultoria, 9394
Desultory remarks on the question of extending slavery into Missouri, 24254
La desviación del Río Lauca, 19125
A detection of the proceedings and practices of the directors of the Royal African company of England, 2097
Detective stories, 10529
Detectives, 16569; Fiction, 10530
The dethroned heiress, 9446
Detroit, Directories, 22780; History, 22780; History, Fiction, 6520; Public library, 2098; Siege, 1763, 22571, 22823; Surrender to the British, 1812, 12741, 12998-13000, 13504, 22594
Detroit young men's society. Library, 2099, 2100
Deus The pague, 19666
Deuschle, Kurt W., 14290
Deutsch-Amerikanischer Hecker Denkmal-Verein, Cincinnati, 13998
Das deutsche Element in den Vereinigten Staaten von Nordamerika, 1818-1843, 14773
Der deutsche lausbub in Amerika, 2914
Der deutsche Pionier, 3233
Deutschland am Mississippi, 4187
Les deux Amériques, 3406
Deux ans au Mexique, 6710
Deux-Ponts, Guillaume, comte de, 1745-, 3239
De Vane, 9875, 24608
Developing countries, 18709, 19263

Development alternatives for Latin America, 20103
Development banks, Pernambuco, Brazil (State), 18752
Developments in library service in Kentucky, 15276
Devens, Samuel Adams, 2101
De Veny, William, 1852-, 16381
DeVere, Paul, 6580
Devers, Samuel, 13999
Devèze, Jean, 1753-1829, 22091
The devil and Tom Walker, 9998
The devil in America, 24750
The devil in Mexico, 7540
Devil's ditties, 15515
Devil's Ford, 9786
Devil's Lake, Wis., 15848
The devil's visit to "Old Abe", 1325
De Vinne, Daniel, 1793-1883, 24283
Devinny, V., 16382
Devlin, John S., 22092
Devol, George H., 1829-, 3240
Devot, 12289
The devoted, 10827
Devotion, Ebenezer, 1714-1771, 22093
The devotion of Enriquez, 6971
Devotional literature, 7666, 7668, 7670-7672
Dew, Thomas Roderick, 1802-1846, 2103, 22094
Dewart, Edward Hartley, 1826-1903, 22095
Dewees, Mrs. Samuel ("Mrs. Mary Coburn Dewees"), fl.1787, 14000
Dewees, William B., 3241
Dewey, Chester, 1784-1867, 2251, 22096
Dewey, Dellon Marcus, 11986
Dewey, John, 1859-1952, 6581
Dewey, Loring Daniel, 1791-1867, 24284
Dewey, Orville, 16383, 22097-22100, 24511
Dewey, Squire Pierce, 1818-, 16384
The De Willoughby claim, 8905
De Witt, Francis, 23267
De Witt, Robert M., 13386
De Witt, Thomas, 1791-1874, 22101, 22102
De Witt, William Radcliffe, 1792-1867, 22103
De Wolff, J. H., 16385
Dewsberry, William, 1621-1688, 22104
Dexter, A. Hensey, 16386
Dexter, Flavius Lucius, fl.395, 400
Dexter, Franklin, 1793-1857, 2104
Dexter, Henry Martyn, 1821-1890, 6582, 11787, 22105, 22106
Dexter, John Haven, 1791-1876, 2105
Dexter, Orrando Perry, 1854-1903, 7971
Dexter, W. W., 16387
Dey, Peter A., 3255
Deye, Thomas Cockey, 13417
Dez dias em contacto com as selvas brasiluras,

20234
Dhormoys, Paul, 1829-, 6583, 22107
Diagnóstico da economia mineira, 18748
Diagnóstico de la economía venezolana, 20240
The Dial: a monthly magazine for literature, 22108
Dialect tales, 14899
The diamond cross, 10519
Diamond leaves from the lives of the Dimond family, 8761
Diamond mines and mining, Brazil, 11636, 23380
The diamond necklace, 9864
The diamond ring vs. the gold ring, 10267
Diana transfigurada, 19130
Diana Victrix, 9097
Diaries on the road to Santa Fe, 7080
El Diario, Mexico, 6585
Diario de campaña, 1868-1871, 18569
El diario de la Covadonga, 18251
Diario de la navegación y reconocimiento del río Tebicuari, 593
Diario de sesiones de la Convención constituyente de la isla de Cuba, 20689
Diario del viaje que hicimos a México fray Francisco de Ajofrín y fray Fermin de Olite, 18075
Diario que formo yo el ciudadano Antonio Armijo, 2555
Diario y derrotero de lo caminado, visto y observado en el discurso de la visita general de precidios, 4967
Diary of a journey from the Mississippi to the coasts of the Pacific with a United States government expedition, 17218
The diary of a man of fifty, 10011
Diary of a march from El Paso to San Antonio, 17876
The diary of a milliner, 11202
The diary of a pawnbroker, 9397
The diary of a public man, 6586
Diary of a southern refugee, 4354
Diary of a tour in America, 6241, 6242
Diary of a visit to the U.S.A. in the year 1883, 5045
The diary of Barton Griffith, 3693
Diary of E. P. Burton, 2865
The diary of Orville Heckman Browning, 24041
Diary of the great rebellion, 22111
Diary of the Navy Boatswain Opticic, 10701
Diary of the Washburn expedition to the Yellowstone and Firehole rivers in the year 1870, 16979
A diary of the wreck of His Majesty's ship Challenger, 2108
Diary west of the Alleghanies, 3020
Dias, Antonio Gonçalves, 1823-1864, 18000; Bibliography, 19055
Días sin luz, 18970
Los días y (antes), 19834
Díaz, Porfirio. Pres. Mexico, 1830-1915, 20647
Díaz, Ramón, 772
Díaz de Guytián, José, 6536, 7929
Díaz de León, Francisco, 1837-1903, 7834
Díaz de Ortega, Felipe, 7535
Díaz del Castillo, Bernal, 1492-1581?, 22112
Díaz Molina, Iván M., 20462
Díaz Pimienta, Francisco, 8291
Díaz Rodríguez, Manuel, 1871-1927, 19953
Díaz Sánchez, Ramón, 1903-, 19144
Díaz y Díaz, Jesús, 6587
Diccionario biográfico de historia antigua de Mejico, 6821
Diccionario de la legislación peruana, 22228
Diccionario de modismos y regionalismos centroamericanos, 20618
Diccionario de regionalismo de la Provincia de La Rioja, 19609
Diccionario historico e geographico da provincia de S. Pedro, 425
Dicey, Edward, 1832-1911, 3242
Dicionário de lingua portuguêsa. Textos e vocabulários, 18628
Dicionário inglês-português para economistas, 19997
Dick Boyle's business card, 6977
Dick Sands, convict, 10808
Dick Spindler's family Christmas, 6972
Dickens, Charles, 1812-1870, 2623, 3243, 6588-6591; American notes, 11685
Dickenson, Mrs. Luella, 16388
Dickerson, Philip Jackson, 16389
Dickert, Carol Feist, 20371
Dickert, D. Augustus, 3244
Dickey, Mrs. Fannie Porter, 3245
Dickey, Frank Graves, 14650
Dickey, Robert, illustr., 25075
Dickinson, Daniel Stevens, 1800-1866, 6592, 24285
Dickinson, James, 1659-1741, 3246
Dickinson, John, 1732-1808, 13509
Dickinson, John R., 6592
Dickinson, Jonathan, 1663-1722, 3247
Dickinson, Jonathan, 1688-1747. A defence of Presbyterian ordination, 21090
Dickinson, Lydia (Knapp) "Mrs. D.S. Dickinson", 6592

Dickinson, Noadiah Smith, 1815-1876, 24286
Dickson, John, 1783-1852, 24287
Dickson, Moses, 24288
Dickson, Robert, 1768?-1823, 17747
Dickson, Samuel Henry, 1798-1872, 24289
La dictadura de O'Higgins, 5892
A dictionary of all officers, 2402
A dictionary of all religions and religious denominations, 50
A dictionary of Congregational usages and principles, 11900
Dictionary of the Sioux language, 16842
Dictionnaire de linguistique et de philologie comparée, 22699
Dictioptera, 18116
Did he take the prince to ride? 9683
Did the Louisiana purchase extend to the Pacific ocean? 15853
Didática da matematica, 20092
The diddler, 10736
Didimus, H., pseud., 3327
Diego, José de, 18367
Diehl, Louis, 3248
Diener, Frau Mietze (Glanz), 6593
Diet, Argentina, Buenos Aires, 18432; Colombia, El Trébol (Caldas), 20311; Colombia, San Bernardo (Valle del Cauca), 20314; Colombia, San Jacinto, 20315
Dietz, Arthur Arnold, 16390
Diez de La Calle, Juan, fl. 1646, 6594
Diez poemas fieles, 18055
A difference in clay, 10283
Diffusion and solubility of Zn in GaSb, 21740
Digby: chess professor, 8716
A digest of the laws of Maryland, 22428
A digest of the laws of the State of Alabama, 21756
A digest of tropical Mexico, 7823
Digestion, 15946
Digging gold among the Rockies, 16853
Dilke, Sir Charles Wentworth, bart., 1843-1911, 3249
Dill, R. G., 16391
Dillard, Ruth, illustr., 14167
Dillaway, Charles Knapp, 1804-1889, 22113
Dillingham, Richard, 24158
Dillingham, William Henry, 1790-1854, 22114
Dillion, Williams, 14668
Dillon, Arthur, abbé, 8054
Dillon, Peter, 1785-1847
Dillwyn, William, 1743-1824, 24290
Dimitrios and Irene, 9279
Dimitry, Charles Patton, 1837-1910, 3250

Dimmick, Mrs. Catharine Mather (Marvin) 1793-1844, 22116
Dimmick, Luther Fraseur, 1790-1860, 22116
Dimock, Anthony Weston, 1842-1918, 3251
Dimsdale, Thomas Josiah, d.1866, 16392
Dingley, Amasa, 22117
Dining at the crossroads, 14001
Dinmore, Richard, 1765-1811, 22118
The dinner horn, 3316
A dinner in proverty flat, 9533
Dinner speaking, 9683
Dinoflagellata, Argentine Republic, 18711
Dinsmoor, Robert, 1757-1836, 22119
Dinsmore, Arthur, b.1794, 22120
Dinsmore, John of Winslow, 22120
Dinsmore family, 22119
Dinsmore family (John Dinsmore, fl.1719) 22120
Dinwiddie, William, 1867-1934, 6595
Diocese of Lexington (Kentucky) Woman's Auxiliary, 14002
Diogenes of Apollonia, fl. 440 or 330 B.C., 19734
Diomed, 11196
Diomedi, Alexander, 1843-, 16393
Dionysius the weaver's heart's dearest, 10947
El dios de miedo, 19678
Diphtheria, Boston, 1735-1736, 2119
A diplomat's diary, 9257
Diplomatic and consular service, 22010, 23746
Diplomatic code of the United States of America, 12027
Diplomatic memoirs, 6766
Diptera, Cuba, 20676; Mexico, 1099
Los Diputados americanos en las Cortes españolas, 24291
Directions of literary criticism in the seventies, 19088
Directorio de establecimientos de educación oficiales y privados, 20338
Directorio de universidades colombianas, 20295
A directory, business mirror, and historical sketches of Randolph county, 23444
Directory of institutes and centers devoted to research in the Caribbean, 18604
O direito da familia, 19658
Dirksen, Everett M., 14649
The disappearance syndicate and Senator Stanley's story, 9238
The disappointed caterpillar, 10046
Disappointed love, 10089
The disappointment, 926
The discarded wife, 9447
The Disciples in Kentucky..., 14120
Disciples of Christ, 3977, 5288, 7378, 13694,

14909; Bibliography, 13983, 15158;
Biographies, 15179; Fiction, 13722;
History, 13723, 14940; Kentucky, 4866,
13833, 13899, 13966, 13968, 14099,
14120, 14134, 14200, 14325, 14803,
14846, 15035, 15158, 15447, 15556;
Periodicals, 21914
Disciplina Cristá, 20107
Discipline of earth and time for freedom
and immortality, 24292
Disclosures and confessions of Frank A.
Wilmot, 15727
Discordia, Difesa della, 25578
Discothyrea testacea, Cuba, 18085
A discovered pearl, 9575
Discoveries (in geography), 1081, 1979,
7657, 11332, 22740, 23042, 23378;
French, 12082; Portuguese, 882, 23199;
Russian, 11623
The discoveries of America to the year
1525, 17852
The discoveries of John Lederer, 4236
Discovery (ship), 8283
Discovery and exploration, 6431
Discovery and settlement of the valley of
the Mississippi, 4502
The discovery of gold in California,
16435
Discovery of the sources of the
Mississippi, 1135
Discovery of the Yosemite, 16087
Diseases, Causes and theories of
causation, 13768
Disenthralled, 9455
A disillusioned occultist, 8717
Disney, Daniel, 6596
Disney, John, 1746-1816, 22124
Dispharynx nasuta - Cuba, 19064
The dispute with America, 22125
Dissection, 2081
Dissertations, Academic, 18672;
Bibliographies, 14051; Colombia,
18960; Geography, 19516; Universidad
de Buenos Aires, Bibliographies, 19544,
19545
Distances, Tables, etc., 4491
Distillation, 15521
Distillers and distilling, 15125
District of Colombia, 12028, 23835, 23745;
Area, 151; Citizens, 24293; Description
& travel, 14749; Laws, statutes, etc.,
22127; Politics & government, 1802,
23021; Slavery code of the, 25776;
Supreme court, 22304
District of Colombia cavalry. 1st regt.,
1863-1864, 4458

District of Colombia infantry, 1845-1848,
13294
The district school as it was, 11637
El Distrito Federal y territorios de la
República Mexicana, 5936
Distritos industriais da Paraiba, 20377
Disturnell, John, 1801-1877, 3252, 7748,
14003, 22128
Disturnell's guide through the middle,
northern, and eastern states, 14003
The disunionist: a Gulf Treatise upon the
evils of the union between the north and
the south, 24389
Dittenhoefer, Abram Jesse, 1836-, 6597
The diverting history of John Bull and
Brother Jonathan, 10482
The divine goodness displayed, in the
American revolution, 23545
Divine judgments upon tyrants: and compassion
to the oppressed, 22000
The divine mission of Jesus Christ evident
from his life, 13384
Divisão territorial da Bahia, 18694
Divisiones políticas de México, 20089
Divorce, 22271; Kentucky, 14667
Divorced, 9309
Dix, Dorothea Lynde, 1802-1887, 11988
Dix, Dorothy, pseud., 6857
Dix, Edwin Asa, 1860-1911, 6599
Dix, John, 1800?-1865, 3254
Dix, John A., 3255
Dix, John Adams, 1798-1879, 2109, 24294
Dix, John Ross, 4118
Dix, Morgan, 1827-1908, 22129
Dix, Timothy Browne, 2441
Dix, William Giles, d.1898, ?110, 22130
Dix ans sur la côte du Pacifique par un
missionnaire canadien, 6598
Dix dam and Herrington lake, 14741
Dix river, Kentucky, 14114
Dixie, 4886
Dixie after the war, 2579
Dixon, Benjamin Homer, b.1819, 22131
Dixon, E. Toney, 19641
Dixon, George, 6600
Dixon, James, 1788-1871, 3256
Dixon, James, 1814-1873, 2111, 12947
Dixon, Joseph, 3257
Dixon, Samuel Houston, 1855-1941, 3258, 14004
Dixon, Thomas, 1864-1946, 24295-24300
Dixon, William Hepworth, 1821-1879, 3259,
3260, 22132
Dixwell, John, 1607?-1689, 23663
Djakarta. Universitas - Indonesia, 13810,
15699
Doak, Henry Melvil, 1841-, 3261

Doane, George Washington, bp., 1799-1859, 1309, 22133, 22134, 22135
Dobbins, J.B., 24301
Dobbs, Arthur, 1689-1765, 2112, 6601, 16394
Dobrizhoffer, Martin, 1717-1791, 6602
Dobson, John, fl. 1760, 22136
Doc Horne: a story of the streets and town, 8476
Doce mil kilómetros a través de los sistemas de riego en México, 6121
Dock, Herman, 6603
Dr. Abraham Lincoln, 6337
Doctor Breen's practice, 9942
Dr. Bushwhacker, The sayings of, 9197
Doctor Cavallo, 8664
Doctor Claudius, 9222
Dr. Dale, 10937
Doctor Gray's quest, 5496
Doctor Hathern's daughters, 9894
Dr. Heldegger's experiment, 9827
Dr. Huger's intentions, 10899
Doctor Izard, 10665
Doctor Johns, 10359
Doctor Judas, 9052
Dr. Latimer, 8913
Dr. Le Baron and his daughters, 8604
Dr. North and his friends, 10367
Dr. Rigby's papers on Florida, 4962
Dr. Sevier, 8925
Doctor Vandyke, 9105
Doctor Warrick's daughters, 9351
The doctor's Christmas eve, 13526
The doctor's wife, 9355
Doctrina social católica, 18516
The doctrine of sovereign grace opened and vindicated, 619
The doctrines and policy of the Republican party, 22137
The doctrines of Friends, 2636
Documentação administrativa, 19288
Documentação amazônica, 19439
Documentación, Bibliotecológica, 18701
Documentary history of slavery in the United States, 24302
Documentation, 20184; Addresses, essays, lectures, 19288; Bibliography, Brazil, 19305
Dodd, Charles Harold, 1884-1973, Bibliography, 14209
Dodd, Ephraim Shelby, d.1864, 16396
Dodd, Stephen, 11688
Dodd, Stephen, 1777-1856, 22139
Dodd family (Daniel Dodd, d.1664 or 5), 22139
Doddridge, Joseph, 1769-1826, 22140, 22141

Dodds, James 6605
Dodge, Allen Washington, 1804-1878, 22142
Dodge, Fred A., 1858-, jt. author, 17179
Dodge, Grenville Mellen, 1831-1916, 5686, 16397-16399
Dodge, Henry, 1782-1867, 17552
Dodge, Jacob Richards, 1823-1902, 2113
Dodge, Joshua, 22143
Dodge, Mary Abigail, 1833-1896, 2114, 3262, 8597, 22144
Dodge, Paul, 1777-1808, 22145
Dodge, Paul Hunter, 7287
Dodge, Richard Irving, 1827-1895, 16400, 16401
Dodge, Robert, 1820-1899, 2115, 22146
Dodge, William, 1811-1875, 2397
Dodge, William Castle, 1827-1914, 11989
Dodge, William Earl, 1805-1883, 2116, 22147
Dodge, William Sumner, 3263
Dodge City, Kans., 17933
Doesticks, K. Philander, pseud., 11038
Dog and gun, 3924
Doggett, David Seth, 1810-1880, 22148
Dogs, 15657; Legends and stories, 11196
Döhla, Johann Conrad, 1750-1820, 3264
Doheny, Michael, 1805-1862, 22149
Doing Mexico with James, 7047
Doings in Maryland, 10258
Dois ensaios sôbre economia internacional, 19813
Dole, Benjamin, 22150
Dolentes, 18862
Dollard, Robert, 16402
Dollars and cents, 11085
Dollars for Duke Power, 14005
Dollero, Adolfo, 6606
The Dolly dialogues, 9804
Dolly Dillenbeck, 9534
Dolomite   Kentucky, 14552
Dolores, 10193, 10631
Dolph, Eliza, 2221
Dolph Heyliger, 9995
Dolwig, Jacob, 16403
Dolwig, Richard J., 16403
Dom Camurro, 19165
Domenech, Emmanuel Henri Dieudonné, 1826-1886, 3265, 3266, 6607-6609, 16404-16406
The domestic and professional life of Ann Preston, 9331
Domestic committee, 3267
Domestic economy, 9617, 10786
Domestic explosives and other sixth column fancies, 8492
Domestic manners of the Americans, 5463
Domestic relations (Mohammedan law),25399; (Roman law), 24271
Domestic relations   Brazil, 19658; Colombia,

20324; Mexico, 18558; Report of a
seminar on, 14667
Domestic service illustrated, 10726
Domestic sketches, 8624
Domingo de Guzman, Saint, 1170-1221, 7271
Domingo, Marcelino, 1884-, 6610
Domínguez, Francisco Atanasio, 15846
Domínguez, Josefina, 6611
Dominica, 545
Dominican Republic, Commerce, 19523;
Description & travel, 2201, 6583, 6726,
9489; Economic conditions, 6726, 18214;
History, 11348, 19107; Laws, statutes,
etc., 19003; Politics & government,
19049
Dominicans in California, 17549
Dominicans in Leiva, Colombia, 18522
Dominicans in Mexico, 1702, 6276, 7860,
8212
Dominicans in Panama, 18521
Los domínicos y la villa de Leiva, 18522
El dominio del mar, 18201
Dominion government expedition to Hudson
Bay and the Arctic Islands, 6302
The Dominion of Canada with Newfoundland
and an excursion to Alaska, 5979
Don Balasco of Key West, 9673
Don Bullebulle, 6612
Don Miff, 3157
Don Orsino, 6494, 9223
Don Santiago Kirker the Indian fighter,
3268
Don Sebastian, 10338
Doña Xepa, 19091
Doña Andreita y otros retratos, 20684
Donald Marcy, 11070
Donald, Jay, 16407
Donaldson, Mrs. Nanna (Smithwick), comp.,
5223
Donaldson, Sir Stuart Alexander, 1812-
1867, 6613
Donaldson, Thomas, 1815-1877, 2117
Donaldson, William, 22151
Donan, Patrick, 16408-16410
Donavin, Simpson K., 1831-1902, 24303
Donck, Adriaen van der, d.1655, 22152
Donde está el cadáver se reúnen los
buitres, 18321
Doneghy, George W., 3269
Donelson, Fort, Battle of, 1862, 2050
Doniphan, Alexander William, 4957, 4989
Doniphan, Kans., 17473
Doniphan's expedition, 1846-1847, 3068,
3343, 3902, 4303, 5705, 8101
Dovis Coutin, Pablo, 10094
Donkin, Robert, 1727-1821, 22153

Donnant, Denis François, 22154
Donnavan, Corydon, 6614, 6615
Donnel, William M., 16411
Donnelly, Eleanor Cecilia, 1838-1917, 10675
Donner Party, 16820, 16923, 16997, 17096
Donoho, Milford Hill, 1844-, 16412
Donohue, James T., 14006
Donovan, Herman Lee, 13598, 14007
Donovan, Joseph Wesley, 1847-, 16413
Doolittle, James Rood, 1815-1897, 6616, 24304
Doolittle, Mark, d.1855, 22155
The doom of slavery in the union: its safety
out of it, 25714
The doom of the Rebel guard, 11190
The doom of the tory's guard, 9293
The doomed chief, 10958
Door co., Wis., Geneal., 17142; History,
17142
Doorways, candles, and morning, 13624
Dora Norton, 10580
Dora Raymond, 8806
Doran, John, 1807-1878, 22156
Dorchester, Mass., History, 1395
Doré, Gustave, 1832-1883, illustr., 7396
A Doric reed, 3040
Dorn, Georgette Magassy, 18054
Dörnberg, Karl Ludwig, freiherr von, 1749-
1819, 3270
Dornblaser, Thomas Franklin, 1841-, 3271
Dorothea (Ship), 1067
Dorothy, 10163
Dorr, J. C. R., 10163
Dorr, James Augustus, 24305
Dorr rebellion, 1842, 11917, 13220
Dorris, Jonathan Truman, 1883-, 14008
Dorsey, Mrs. Anna Hanson (McKenney), 1815-1896,
10675
Dorsey, Ella Loraine, 1853-1935, 10675
Dorsey, John Larkin, 24302, 24306
Dorsey, Mrs. Sarah Anne (Ellis), 1829-1879,
3272-3274
Doryopteris, Argentine Republic, 19857
Dos Américas, 2941
Los dos baldíos, 19823
Dos ciclos de lirismo colombiano, 19732
Dos microcéfalos "aztecas", 20364
Dos viajes, 18033
Dosch, Henry Ernest, 1841-, 16414
Dostal, M.A., 18998
Dottings by the wayside, 10423
Dottings on the roadside, 7750
Doty, James Duane, 1799-1865, 23421
The double suicide, 9419
The double veil, 10298
A double wedding, 5612
Doubleday, Charles William, 1829-, 16415

Dougall, Allan H., 6617
Dougherty, John, 5503
Dougherty, Michael, 3275
Dougherty, Peter, 1805-1894, 2375
Douglas, Dan, of Georgia, 5335
Douglas, David, 3923
Douglas, David, 1799-1834, 16416
Douglas, James, 5839
Douglas, John, surgeon in British army,
  2118
Douglas, Stephen, pseud., 6115
Douglas, Stephen Arnold, 1813-1861, 2109,
  5933, 5935, 6021, 6115, 6346, 6738,
  7036, 7175, 7284, 7383, 7416, 11590,
  22766, 24258, 24307-24309, 24417, 24769,
  25371, 25727; Popular sovereignty in
  the territories, 1368, 11916
Douglas Camp, Ill., 3085
Douglas family, 22719
Douglass, Adam, supposed author, 9991
Douglass, Frederick, 1817-1895, 6618,
  24310-24312, 24880
Douglass, William, 1691-1752, 2119, 3276
Dove, David James. The Quaker unmask'd-
  1764, 23514
Dove (sailing vessel), 7374
Dovercoat, 9873
Dow, Lorenzo, 1777-1834, 2120, 3277
Dow, Neal, 1804-1897, 1916
Dow, Mrs. Peggy (Holcombe) 1780-1820,
  3278
Dowdell, James Ferguson, 1818-1871, 2121
Dowden, Darnall, 14009
Dowling, Enos Everett, 1905-, 13983
Dowling, Joseph A., 12834
Dowling, Morgan E., 3279
Down among the Crackers, 8997
Down by the sea, 10899
The Down-easters, 10407
Down-home cooking, 14010
Down in Tennessee, 3611
Down in west Kentucky and other poems,
  14128
Down memory's lane, 6199
Down north on the Labrador, 6900
Down our way, 15397
Down South, 3202, 3779
Down South before the war, 25801
Down the great river, 3622
Down the ravine, 4555
Down the river, 9910
The down-trodden, 10787
Down with the black flag of confiscation;
  up with the union jack, 21866
Downey, Edgar, 6619, 6620
Downie, William, 1819-1894, 16417

Downing, Andrew Jackson, 1815-1852, 2122,
  11990
Downing, Clement, 2123
Downing, Jack, pseud., 10818-10822
Downs, Solomon Weathersbee, 1801-1854, 16418,
  24313
Dowse, Thomas, 1772-1856, 6621, 12114, 16419,
  23276
Dox, Peter Myndert, 1813-1891, 2124
Doy, John, 16420
Doyle, Sir Arthur Conan, 1859-1930, 6622
Doyle, George Fergison, 1878-, 13614, 13639,
  13645, 13808, 13909, 14102-14108, 15120,
  15211, 15215, 15488, 15489
Doyle, John Thomas, 1819-1906, 16421
Doyle, William, 6623
Dozier, Orion Theophilus, 1848-1925, 3280
Draft, riot, 1863, 117, 852, 2347, 11294
Drage, Theodore Swaine, 6624
Dragoon campaigns to the Rocky Mountains, 3867
Dragoon expedition, 3281
Dragut, the corsair, 10338
Drainage, 14447
Drake, Benjamin, 1794-1841, 3282-3284
Drake, Charles Daniel, 1811-1892, 24314
Drake, Daniel, 1785-1852, 3285-3293, 3706,
  13626, 14011-14014, 14347-14349, 14486,
  14949, 14984, 15209, 15245
Drake, Eugene B., 16423
Drake, Sir Francis, 1540?-1596, 23491, 23401
Drake, James Madison, 1837-1913, 3294
Drake, Joseph Rodman, 1795-1820, 22157
Drake, Leah Bodine, 14015
Drake, Richard B., 14016
Drake, Samuel Adams, 1833-1905, 3295-3297
Drake, Samuel Gardner, 1798-1875, 991, 2125,
  11279, 11991, 14017, 23325
Drake, Mrs. William Preston, 14018
Drakesboro quadrangle, Kentucky, 13941
Drama, 18523; History and criticism, 18125,
  19159; Popular, Nevis, 17955; Popular,
  Tobago, 17955, 17956
The drama in Pokerville, 9514
The drama of an evening, 10135
Dramas latinos medievales del ciclo de
  Navidad, 18607
Dramatic persons and moods, 4780
Dramatic sketch, 10172
Une drame esclavagiste; prologue de la
  secession américaine, 24117
Drane, Maude, Johnston, 14019
Dranna, William F., 1832-1913,
  16424
Draper, John William, 1811-1882, 2126
Draper, Lyman Copeland, 1815-1891, 2127,
  3509, 5754, 14020-14022

145

Draper mss., Wisconsin historical society, 13729
Drascomb, Alfred Brooks, 1837-1894, 6625
Drax, Henry, 1080
Draxy Miller's dowry, 10006
Drayton, 5149
Drayton, John, 1766-1822, 3298
The dreadful sufferings and thrilling adventures of an overland party of emigrants to California, 2700, 15810
Dream life, 10360
The dream of a loafer, 9486
The dreamers, 8676
Dreams, 24330
Dreams and realities in the life of a pastor and teacher, 9474
Dred, 10903
Dred Scott case, 25197, 25374, 25522
Dredging, 19272
Dreer, Ferdinand Julius, 1812-, 11546
Drees, Ada M. C., 6626
Drees, Charles William, 6626
Drei Jahre in Amerika, 2668
Drescher, Emil, 5773
Dressed to death, 10672
Dreveton, Theodore, 24315
Drew, C.S., 3299
Drewry, William Sidney, 1870-, 24316
Dreyfus, J.G., 14696
A drift from Redwood Camp, 9789
Drift from two shores, 9779
The drift of the war, 11597
"Drifting about", 10321
Driggs, George W., 3300
Dring, Thomas, 1758-1825, 2128
Drinkwater, D.F., 2129
Drinkwater, John, 1882-1937, 5995
Drips, Joseph H., b.1828?, 16425
Drisler, Henry, 1818-1897, 24317
Driven from the path, 10799
Driver licensing, Kentucky, 14282
Le droit des neutres sur mer, 12222
Droop Mountain, W.Va., Battle of, Nov.6, 1863, 2038
Droppings from the heart, 22919
Droulers, Charles, 16426
Drown, Simeon De Witt, 16427, 16428
Drowne's wooden image, 9823
Drugs, Laws and legislation, 18475
Drugstores, Louisville, Ky., 14997
Drumm, Mark, 16429
Drummond, Sir Gordon, 1772-1854, 11782
Drummond, Josiah H., 3592, 6627
The drunkard, 10492
Drury, Luke, 22158
The dual revolutions, 24458

Duane, James, 1733-1797, 13316
Duane, Richard Bache, 1824?-1875, 6628
Duane, W. N., 11657
Duane, William, 1760-1835, 22453
Duane, William, 1807-1882, 2130, 2731, 23169
Duarte Level, Lino, 6629
Du Barry, Edmund L., 7767
Dubitsky, A.M., 20668
Du Bois, Coert, 1881-, 6333
Dubois, Marcel, i.e. Edmond Marcel, 1856-, 7736
Du Bois, William Edward Burghardt, 1868-1963, 24318
Du Bois, William Ewing, 1801-1881, 2173
Du Bose, John Witherspoon, 1836-1918, 3301
Dubuque, History, 16982; Ia. (Archdiocese), History, 16932
Du Chaillu, Paul Belloni, ca.1831-1903, 15157
Duché, Jacob, 1737-1798, 11992
The duchess and Sancho, 10197
The Duchess of Baden, 9532
Du Chilleau, Marie-Charles, marquis, 7941
Duclos-Salinas, Adolfo, 6630
Ducoff, Louis J., 13823
Duden, Gottfried, 3302
Dudley, Benjamin Winslow, 1785-1870, 13605, 13738, 15209
Dudley, Ethelbert, 1818-1862, 7737
Dudley, John, 1805-1898, 2131
Dudley, John H., 16430
Dudley, John Langdon, 1812-1894, 6631
Dudley, Thomas Underwood, 6632
Dudley family (Thomas Dudley, 1576-1653), 101
Dudley, Mass., History, 963
Dudley's defeat, 1813, 2004
The due right of presbyteries, 23560
Due south, 5992
Dueling, 1063, 2807, 9910, 24898; Bracken Co., Ky., 13872; Kentucky, 13524, 14462; Lexington, Ky., 13833; Nelson County, Ky., 13886; Scott Co., Ky., 13877
Dueñas Bolante, Fernando de, 6633
Dueñas y Pinto, Joaquín L., 1859-1910, 17947
Duer, Douglas, illustr., 13731, 13732
Duff, Jeffrey M., 14023
Duff, Louis Blake, 1878-, Portage Road, 8201
Duffels, 9463
Dufferin and Ava, Hariot Georgina (Hamilton), 6634
Duffield, George, 17116
Duffield, George, 1794-1868, 3303, 3304
Duffield, George Crawford, 16431
Duffield, R. Bethune, 17116
Duflot de Mofras, Eugene, 1810-1884, 16432
Dufour, Auguste Henri, 1798-1865, 7396

Dufur, A. J., company, 16433
Dufur, Simon Miltimore, 1843-, 3305
Dugan, Frances L. Smith, 14024, 14025, 15048, 15269, 15500
Dugan, James, 3306
Duganne, Augustine Joseph Hickey, 1823-1884, 3307, 11993
Dugard, Marie, 1862-, 3308
Dugas, George, 1833-, 6635
Dugue, Charles Oscar, 1821-, 3309-3311
Du Halde, Jean Baptiste, 1674-1743, 2466
Duhart, Carmen Gloria, 18341
Duke, Basil Wilson, 1838-1916, 3312, 3417, 14026
Duke, John K., 1844-, 3313
The Duke of Stockbridge, 8774
Duke Power Company, 13556, 14005, 14269
The duke's chase, 10267
Dukes co., Mass., History-Sources, 12931
Dulac, George, pseud., 10507
Dulieu, Marie Henri Joseph, 1815-, 3314
Dull Knife, Cheyenne Chief, d.1879, 16234
Duluth, Minn., 4191, 14768; Description, 14767
La dulzada, 20710
Dumas, Alex T., 3122
Dumas, Alexandre, 1802-1870, 2132; Le comte de Monte-Cristo (sequels), 3467
Dumas, Mathieu, comte, 1753-1807, 3315
Dumas, William Thomas, 1858-, 3316
The dumb girl, 10492
Dumbell, Kate Ethel Mary, 1868-, 16434
Dummer, Fort, 13051
Dumont de Montiguy,Lieutenant, 3317
Dumont, Mary Wolfe, 4941
Dunant, Jean Henri, 1828-, 2133
Dunbar, Edward E., 6636, 16435
Dunbar, John, 3318
Dunbar, M., 6637
Dunbar, Paul Laurence, 1872-1906, 24319
Dunbar, Samuel, 1704-1783, 22346
Dunbar, Seymour, 6638, 17325
Dunbar family, 6637
Duncan Adair, 9251
Duncan, Elizabeth F. (Mrs. Frank L. Duncan), 15445
Duncan, J.W., 13564
Duncan, James, 24320
Duncan, Lew Wallace, 1861-, comp., 16436
Duncan, Mrs. Mary (Grey) Lundie, 3319
Duncan, John Morison, 6639
Duncan, Thomas D., 3320
Dunckel, Johann Daniel, 8037
Dundass, Samuel Rutherford, 3321
Dundonald, Thomas Cochrane, 10th earl of, 1775-1860, 6640, 8112

Dunham, Josiah, 1769-1844, 2134
Duniway, Mrs. Abigail (Scott) 1834-1915, 3322, 16434
Duniway, Clyde Augustus, 1866-, 24321
Dunkley & Woodman, New York, pub., 1756
Dunlap, Boutwell, 14027
Dunlap, William, 1766-1839, 2135, 2136
Dunlavy, John, 1769-, 14028
Dunlevy, A. H., 2137
Dunlevy, Ursula, Sister, 16438
Dunmor quadrangle, Kentucky, 13941
Dunn, Ballard S., 1829-1897, 2138
Dunn, C. Frank, 15586
Dunn, J. E., 16439
Dunn, Jacob Piatt, 1855-1924, 16440, 24322, 24323
Dunn, John, 3323
Dunn, Keller, 15257
Dunn, Thomas, 1761?-1833, 2139
Dunn, William Edward, 1888-, 16441
Dunn co., Wis., 15848
Dunne, Henry C., 24324
A Dunnet shepherdess, 10042
Dunning, Homer N., 1827-, 2140
Dunraven, Windham Thomas Wyndham-Quin, 4th earl of, 1841-1926, 6641
Dunshee, Henry Webb, 2141
Dunsmore's expedition, 1774, 23493
Dunstable, Mass., History, 2297
Dunton, Larkin, 1828-1899, 6440
Dupanloup, Félix Antoine Philibert, bp. of Orléans, 1802-1878, 25615
Dupage Co., Ill., History, 23531
Dupierris, Martial, 24325
Dupin de Sainte-André, 1840-1921, 6642
Du Poisson, Paul, 1692-1729, 16956
Du Ponceau, Peter Stephen, 1760-1844. Eulogium in commemoration of the Honourable William Tilghman, 12296
Dupont, Chevalier de, 8320, 8321
Du Pont, Henry Algernon, 1838-1926, 3324
Du Pont, Samuel Francis, 2142
Dupré, Huntley, 14030
Dupré, Joseph, 1742-1823, 6643
Dupuy, Eliza Ann, 1814?-1881, 24326
Du Puynode, Michel Gustave Partounau, b.1817, 24327
Duque-Estrada, Osorio, 1870-1927, 24328
Duquesne, Fort, History, Fiction, 10293, 10443
Durán, Diego, d.1588?, 6644
Durán, Narciso, 1776-1846, 16442
Durán, Rafael, 5884
Durand, of Dauphine, 3325
Durand, John, 1822-1908, 6645
Durand, Luz María, 6646

147

Durand, René L.-F., 17995
Durango, Luis, 18921
Dureau, Baptiste, 1820-, 3326
Durell, Edward Henry, 1810-, 3327
Durfee, Job, 1790-1847, 22373
Durham, John George Lambton, 1st earl
  of, 1792-, 1840, 6647, 6648
The Durket sperret, 3363
Du Roi, August Wilhelm, 3328
Durrett, Reuben Thomas, 1824-1913,
  14031-14035, 14425
Durrie, Daniel Steele, 1819-1892,
  16443
Du Ru, Paul, 1666-1741, 3329
Duryée's brigade, 1862, 12926
Dussieux, Louis Étienne, 1815-1894, 6649
Dust, 9807
The Dutch dominie of the Catskills, 10396
Dutch East Indies, Economic conditions,
  22884
Dutch Guiana, Bibliography, 25675;
  Description & travel, 1193, 1484,
  5319, 11382, 23517, 24385, 25603,
  25604, 25675; Economic conditions,
  24385, 24583, 24862, 25811;
  Gouverneur, 1755-1759 (C.P. Schimpf),
  25811; History, To 1803, 24601, 25603,
  25604; Politics & government, 24862,
  25435; Sanitary affairs, 24741
Dutch in Brazil, 339
Dutch in Indiana, 1230
Dutch in Iowa, 16801
Dutch in New York (City), Poetry,
  12904
Dutch in the U.S., 1234, 11327
The Dutch pilgrim fathers, 12904
Dutcher, Salem, 4105
Dutchess Co., N.Y., History, 1402
The Dutchman's fireside, 10483, 10484,
  23486
The duties and dignities of American
  freemen, 24660
Dutrône la Couture, Jacques-François,
  6650
Dutton, George, 2143
Duty, 22591
The duty of American women to their
  country, 1042
The duty of living for the good of
  posterity, 11731
Duval, John Crittenden, 1816-1897, 3330,
  16444
Duvergier de Hauranne, Ernest, i.e. Louis
  Pragraw Ernest, 1843 , 3331
Duyckinck, Evert Augustus, 1816-1878, 435,
  3332; Cyclopaedia of American literature,

12456
Duyckinck, George L., 3332
Dwars door het land van Roosevelt, 4189
Dwellers in Gotham, 10053
Dwight, Edward Strong, 1820-1890, 2144
Dwight, Henry O., 24329
Dwight, Theodore, 1764-1846, 229, 2145-2147
Dwight, Theodore, jr., 3173
Dwight, Timothy, 1752-1817, 2148, 22159
Dwight, William, 1831-1888, 2587
Dwinelle, John Whipple, 1816-1881, 16281,
  16445
Dyar, C. W., jt. author, 10371
Dye, Mrs. Eva (Emery), 16446, 16447, 17943
Dye, John Smith, 2149, 22160
Dyer, Mrs. D. B., 16448
Dyer, David, 2150
Dyer, George, 1755-1841, 13489
Dyer, John Percy, 6651
Dyer, John Will, 3333
Dyer, Olive, 3657
The dying confession of Joseph Hare, 3781
The dying legacy of an aged minister of the
  everlasting gospel, to the United States
  of North-America, 23337
Dymock, Gressy, 12735
Dymond, Jonathan, 1796-1828, 2151
Dyson, Howard F., 6652
Dyspepsy, 10492
Dzhalagoniia, Valerii Pavlovich, 7189

The eagle of the Mohawks, 10744
Eagle Pass, Tex., 8958
The eagle's heart, 9603
Earhart, Will, 14127
Eardley-Wilmot, John, 1750-1815, 22161
Earl, J.C., illustr., 8516
Earl Rupert, 10403
Earle, Pliny, 1809-1892, 2152
Earlington and Hopkins County [Kentucky], 15195
Early, Jubal Anderson, 1816-1894, 2153, 24330
Early, Ruth Hairston, 24330
The early abolitionists of Lancaster County,
  25874
Early American orations, 7005
Early and authentic history of Omaha, 1857-
  1870, 16663
Early biography, travels and adventures of
  Rev. James Champlin, 2967
Early California, historical highlights,
  1540-1848, 16595
Early day stories, 17004
The early days and men of California, 17693
Early days in Arkansas, 4825

Early days in California, 16386
Early days in Kansas, 16634
Early days in old Oregon, 16909
Early days in Texas, 17101
The early days of California, 16495
The early days of my episcopate, 16955
Early days of the Yukon, 7630
Early days on the western slope of
Colorado and campfire chats with Otto
Mears, 16891
The early empire builders of the great
west, 13563
Early history of Covington, 14036
The early history of Illinois, 16040
The early history of Michigan, 23609
The early history of the southern states,
12754
Early history of Warren County...
McMinnville, Tenn., 14237
Early life among the Indians, 15870
The early lodge, 17458
Early Maryland poetry, 3077, 5264
Early military history of Kentucky, 13602
Early narratives of the Northwest, 4144
Early poems, 1940-42, 14991
The early sentiment for the annexation
of California, 15213
The early settlement of Kentucky, 13831
Early settlers and Indian fighters of
Southwest Texas, 17647
Early times in Southern California, 15958
Early times in Texas, 16444
Early times in the Massachusetts, 10724
Early times in Meade County, Kentucky,
15275
Early travels in the Tennessee country,
5723
Early years in the far west, 12559
An earnest address to such of the people
called Quakers, 2154
Earth changes: past, present, future,
14037
Earth's holocaust, 9823
Earthly care, a heavenly discipline, 10910
Earthquakes, 2303, 6008, 12800; Chile,
20164; Costa Rica (23 December 1972),
20097; Jamaica, 12208; New England, 2303,
23395, 22398; Nicaragua (23 December
1972), 20097; The West, 4793; Venezuela,
2396
East, Ernest Edward, 1885-, 6653
East, Melville A., 7715
East and west, 5380, 10032
The east coast of Florida, 3813
East (Far East), Description & travel,
6413; History, 882

East Hampton, N.Y., Church history, 1660;
Description, 2395; Genealogy, 22394;
History, 1064, 2395, 22394
East Haven, Conn. Congregational church, 2155
East Indies, Description & travel, 488, 4900,
23199
East Kentucky rock asphalt co., inc., 14038
East of Eden, 13567
East Tennessee relief association of Knoxville,
2156
East Windsor, Conn., History, 23664
Eastburn, James Wallis, 1797-1819, 2157
Eastburn, Joseph, 1748-1828, 12377
Eastburn, Robert, 1710-1778, 2158, 11994
An Easter king, 9330
The Easter of La Mercedes, 10448
Eastern Kentucky, a field for profitable
investment, 13575
Eastern Kentucky State Teachers College,
Richmond, 14039, 14574
Eastern Kentucky University, 14544
Eastern question (Balkan), 11466, 11467
Eastern question (Far East), 7913
Eastern states, Description & travel, 2101
Eastford, 10255
Eastman, Charles Garnage, 1816-1860, 1687
Eastman, Edwin, 16449
Eastman, Francis Smith, 1803-1846 or 7, 11995
Eastman, Hubbard, d.1891, 2159
Eastman, John Robie, 1836-1913, 2160
Eastman, Lucius Root, 1809-1892, 2161
Eastman, Mary F., 6654
Eastman, Mrs. Mary (Henderson) 1818-, 2162,
2163, 3334, 11996
Eastman, Samuel Coffin, 2164
Eastman, Seth, 1808-1875, illustr., 2163, 11996
Eastman family (Roger Eastman, 1611-1694),
2161
Easton, Hosea, 2165
Easton, James, 2166
Easton, John, 1617-1705, 2167
Easton, William, 22103
Easton, Mass., History, 2958
Easton, Pa. Library company, 11997
Eastover Mining Company, 13556, 14005, 14269
Eastwick, Edward Backhouse, 1814-1883, 22162
Easy Warren and his contemporaries, 9063
Eat not thy heart, 9258
Eaton, Amos, 1776-1842, 2168, 22163
Eaton, Arthur Wentworth, 4074
Eaton, Asahel K., 1571
Eaton, B. A., 11998
Eaton, Clement, 1898-, 14040, 24331
Eaton, Cyrus, 1784-1875, 22164
Eaton, Edward Byron, 11999
Eaton, Emily, 22164

Eaton, Francis Brown, 1825-1904, 12000
Eaton, H.M., illustr., 5392
Eaton, Horace, 1810-1883, 12001
Eaton, Jacob, 2169
Eaton, John Henry, 1790-1856, 4996, 12002, 22165
Eaton, Rebecca, 2170
Eaton, Samuel John Mills, 1820-1889, 2171
Eaton, Thomas Treadwell, 1845-1907, 6655, 14855
Eaton, William, 1764-1811, 2172
Eau Claire, Wis., 15848
Eaves, Catherine, pseud., 6656
Eaves, Lucile, 1869-, 24332
Ebb-tide, 10968
Ebeling, Christoph Daniel, 1741-1817, 322
Eben Holden, 8627
Ebenezer Associate Reformed Presbyterian Church, Jessamine Co., Ky., 15323
Eberhard, Carl A., 14041
Eberhardt, Charles Christopher, 1871-, 25772
Eberhardt, Frederick William, 1864-1971, 14042
Eberhart, F.W., 15721
Eberle, John, 1787-1838, 21760
Ebrio al límite del tiempo, 19624
Eby, Henry Harrison, 1841-, 3335
Ecce femina, 10498, 10499
An eccentric egocentric, 14152
Eccentric characters, 10291, 10310
Ecclesiastical history of Utah, 16189
Ecclesiastical law, Massachusetts, 856, 1635
Ecclesiastical reminiscences of the U.S., 5643
Echave y Roxas, Pedro Antonio de, 6368
Echeverría, Carlos Francisco, 19059
Echeverría, Esteban, 1805-1851, 18931
Echezárraga, Juan de, 6657
An echo, 9916
Echo Park Dam, 17840
Echo's aus den Urwäldern, 7272
Echoes from Dartmouth, 9734
Echoes from the backwoods, 4266
Echoes from the Rocky mountains, 16205
Echoes from the south, 4814
Echoes of a belle, 10740
Echoes of the past, 4355, 15976
Echols, John, 2038
Eckdahl, Andrew, 14043, 14044
Eckenrode, Hamilton James, 1881-, 15651
Eckfeldt, Jacob Reese, 1803-1872, 2173
Eckley, Joseph, 1750-1811, 2174
Eckman, James, 6658
Eckstein, Peter, 20103

The eclipse, 2175
A ecologia do grupo afro-brasileiro, 18230
Ecología y distribución de los foraminíferos recientes de la Laguna Madre Tamaulipas, 18647
Ecology, Brazil, 18285
La economía chilena, 19611
Economía cristiana, 19021
La economía del comercio internacional de Venezuela, 19845
A economia do Nordeste e o desenvolvimento nacional, 20562
Economic assistance, American, Argentine Republic, 18404
Economic assistance, Domestic, Colombia, 20261
The economic cost of slave holding in the cotton belt, 25255
Economic development, 18719, 18987, 19670
Economic development of Central America, 20373
Economic history, 22944
Economic policy, 19670
Economics, 11446, 18719, 22839, 23426, 23578; Dictionaries, Portuguese, 19997; History, Cuba, 18217; Mathematical models, 19030
L'économique n'est qu'un aspect du social, 18624
Ecuador, Antiquities, 6868, 11330, 19803; Boundaries, Peru, 18196, 20652; Constitution, 19174; Constitutional history, 19173; Corte Suprema de Justicia, 18612; Description & travel, 7946, 8168, 8299, 22335; Economic conditions, 19084; Foreign relations, Treaties, Indexes, 19591; History, 6370, 6868, 19176, 19177; History, To 1809, 23734; History, 1830-1895, 20658; History, Wars of independence, 1809-1830, 7322, 20658; Instituto Nacional de Pesca del Ecuador, 19199; Instituto Nacional de Pesca. Boletín científico y técnico, 20224, 20225; Laws, statutes, etc., 18612, 20064; Politics & government, 18353, 19174; Politics & government, To 1809, 7946
Ecuadorean essays, 15822, 20653
Ecuadorean literature, Collections, 20649
Ecuadorean poetry (Collections), 19569
La edad incierta, 19927
Eddis, William, 1745?-, 3336
Eddowes, Ralph, 1751-1833, 2176
Eddy, Caleb, 2177
Eddy, Daniel Clarke, 1823-1896, 2178
Eddy, Richard, 1828-1906, 3337, 6659
Eddy, Robert Henry, 1812-1887, 2179
Eddy, Thomas, 1758-1827, 2180
An edelweiss of the Sierras, 9764

Eden, John, 2181
Eden, Richard, 1521?-1576, 373, 5920
Eden, Robert C., d.1907, 3338
The Eden of the South, 5647
Edes, Richard Sullivan, 1810-1877, 4425
Edgar, Cornelius Henry, 1811-1884, 24333
Edgar, J., 25342
Edgar Co., Ill., 6660
Edgar County Historical Society. Paris,
  Illinois, 6660
Edgar Huntly, 8859
Edge, Frederick Milnes, 12003, 24334,
  24335
Edge-hill, 9836
Edgerton, A.P., 2978
Edgerton, Joseph Ketchum, 1818-1893, 24336
Edgerton, Walter, b.1806, 24337
Edinburgh Emancipation Society, 24338,
  24528
Edinburgh review, 24834
Edisto rifles, 4033
Edith, 9339
Edith Lyle, 3911
Edith Moreton, 8892
Edith Vernon, 9451
The editor's run in New Mexico and
  Colorado, 16180
Edmond Dantes, 3467
Edmonds, Francis William, 1806-1863,
  2182
Edmonds, S. Emma E., 3339
Edmonson County, Ky., 13610, 31613, 14220
Edmund Dawn, 8765
Edmunds, A. C. of Lincoln, Neb., 16450
Edmundson, William, 1627-1712, 3340
Edna Browning, 3912, 9895
Educação, sociedade e desenvolvimento,
  17962
Educação, universidade e história da
  primeira universidade do Brasil, 19808
A educação e o ideal democrático, 18986
A educação em Minas Gerais e seus aspectos
  socio-economicos, 19321
Educación, recursos humanos y desarrollo
  económico, 18433
La educación de adultos y los planes de
  desarrollo económico y social en
  Venezuela, 18019
La educación en México antes y después
  de la conquista, 18134
La educación en San Fernando, 20463
La educación industrial en Centro America,
  18381
La educación peruana, 18232
La educación superior en Colombia, 20294
Educación y código cooperativo, 18934

La educación y las ciencias en la sociedad
  de masas, 18069
Education, 2280, 2569, 2797, 5241, 5244,
  5247, 5248, 18320, 20042, 23099; Addresses,
  essays, lectures, 1044, 2249, 2888, 3742,
  5780, 11595, 17388, 22483; Appalachia,
  13715; Argentine Republic, 18069, 18401,
  18408, 18421, 18433, 18491, 20203;
  Argentine Republic, Statistics, 18439,
  18476-18490; Arkansas, History, 17603;
  Bibliography, 19553, 20480; Brazil, 17962,
  18273, 19247, 19366, 19367, 19374, 19500,
  20380, 24010; Brazil, Bibliography, 19248;
  Brazil, Minas Gerais, 19321; California,
  15820; Caribbean area, Bibliography, 19789;
  Chile, 20110, 20148, 20149, 20154, 20174-
  20179, 20480; Chile, History, 19714;
  Colombia, 20273, 20339; Colombia,
  Directories, 20338; Colorado, 16240, 16642;
  Congresses, 13340; Costa Rica, 18048, 20440,
  20589, 20605-20607; Costa Rica, Statistics,
  20593, 20608, 20609; Cuba, 611, 20688;
  Curricula, Argentine Republic, 18401;
  Developing countries, 19086; Economic
  aspects, Canada, Statistics, 19031;
  Economic aspects, Venezuela, 18019;
  Europe, 23090; Finance, Jefferson County,
  Ky., 15057; Guatemala, 20088, 20436;
  Honduras, 20437; Ireland, 1528; Kentucky,
  13523, 13692, 13711, 13820, 13873, 13922,
  13927, 13986, 14192, 14195, 14253, 14499,
  14517, 14531, 14553, 14554, 14575, 14627,
  14726, 14742, 14931, 14998, 14999, 15018,
  15151, 15461; Kentucky, Addresses, essays,
  lectures, 14185; Kentucky, History, 14555;
  Latin America, 19366, 19608, 20435; Latin
  America, Congresses, 19320; Latin America,
  Periodicals, 18156; Laws and regulations,
  Kentucky, 14628; Legislation, Brazil, 19360;
  Louisville, Ky., 14299; Manitoba, Winnipeg,
  6217; Maryland, 8316; Massachusetts,
  Boston, 23083, 23089, 23091; Mexico, 18134,
  18935; Mexico, Addresses, essays, lectures,
  18064; Mexico, History, 19826; Mexico,
  Laws and regulations, 18223; Nebraska,
  History, 16120; New England, 829, 8919,
  11637; New Hampshire, History, 11418; New
  York (State), History, 8697; Nicaragua,
  Statistics, 20438; Ohio, 14082; Ohio,
  Cincinnati, 2267; Pennsylvania, 2319;
  Periodicals, 260, 261, 289; Peru, 18232,
  19932, 20220; Peru, Curricula, 18080;
  Philosophy, 18986, 20202; Poetry, 1618;
  Puerto Rico, 18578, 19608; Rhode Island,
  830; Southern states, 5591; San Fernando,
  Argentina, 20463; Study and teaching, 19519;

151

Texas, 16283, 17015; Texas, History, 16974; U.S., 1042, 4739, 5458, 12346, 12347, 13139, 13226, 14300, 15228, 22044, 23099; Venezuela, 18013, 18014; Virginia, 8316; Wales, 1528
Education, Colonial, Latin America, 20708
Education, Elementary, Brazil, 19417
Education, Higher, 12707, 13340, 19537, 20654; Brazil, 19223; Colombia, 20294, 20297, 20298; Congresses, International, 1961, 20433; Kentucky, 14643, 14648, 15633; Statistics, 19223; Virginia, 23737
Education, Primary, Curricula, 18080
Education, Rural, 18319
Education, Secondary, 20177; Colombia, 20340, 20341
Education and progress of Colombia, 19099
Education and society, 1222
Education and state, 1222
Education at the West, 2024
Education in Nebraska, 16120
Education of adults, 15128
Education of women, 1045, 9548, 11939; Addresses, essays, lectures, 22224; Kentucky, 14736; U.S., 1046
Education, religion and the Kentucky Court of Appeals, 13890
Educational law and legislation, Iowa, 13105
Educational sociology, 20473; Brazil, 17962
Educational television for Kentucky, 15331
Edward, David B., 3341
Edward, George, 1694-1773, 2946
Edward Austin, 4002
Edward Beyer's cyclorama, 2704
Edward Manning, 4003
Edward VII, King of Great Britain, 1841-1910, 3385, 4522, 6414, 8418
Edward Vernon, 8996
Edwards, Bela Bates, 1802-1852, 288, 3342
Edwards, Bryan, 1743-1800, 24339
Edwards, Frank S., 3343
Edwards, Georgie Hortense, 14045
Edwards, Harry Stillwell, 1855-1938, 3344-3347, 24340
Edwards, John Ellis, 1814-, 14046
Edwards, John L., 3348
Edwards, John Newman, 1839-1889, 16451, 16452, 16453
Edwards, Jonathan, 1745-1801, 12004
Edwards, Lawrence, 15766
Edwards, Mrs. Mary Virginia (Plattenbury), 16453

Edwards, Matthew, 1838-1859, 1669
Edwards, Philip Leget, 1812-1869, 3349, 3350, 16454
Edwards, Richard, 3351, 22166
Edwards, Samuel E., 1810-, 3352
Edwards, Sharon, 14047
Edwards, Tryon, 1809-1894, 1098
Edwards, William Seymour, 1856-, 6661
Edwards family, 14045
Edwards co., Ill., 1335, 1336, 1337, 2258, 16528; Bibliographies, 15989; History, 3487, 5765
Edwards' guide to east Florida, 3348
Edwin Brothertoft, 11193
Eells, Myron, 1843-1907, 15877, 16455, 16456; A reply to Professor Bourne's "The Whitman legend", 17140
Eels, William Woodward, 1811-1886. Gratitude for individual and national blessings, 24168
Eenoolovapik, 22843
Efemérides dos principais fatos relacionados com a Campanha, 18163
The effect of secession upon the commercial relations between the North and South, 24888
The effects of good example, 10350
Effects of slavery on morals and industry, 5658
The Effinghams, 10003
Egan, Charles, 1807 or 8-1869, 2183
Egan, Maurice Francis, 1852-1924, 10675
Egan, Michael, 1826?-1888, 3353
Egar, John Hodson, 1882-, 2184
Egerton, H.E., 7899
Egg trade, Maceió, Brazil, 18786
Eggleston, George Cary, 1839-1911, 3354, 3355, 24341
Egleston, Thomas, 1832-1900, 247, 2185
Egloffstein, F. W. von, baron, 2186
Egmont, John Perceval, 2d earl of, 1711-1770, 16457; An examination of the principles... of the two b...rs., 2028
Ego, 9583
Egotisme, 9823
Egypt, Antiquities, 1443; Description & travel, 376, 4507, 5409, 17116; Treaties, etc., 1892-1914 (Abbās II), 24520; Wizārat al-Khārijiyah, 24199
Egypt Ennis, 10825
Ehmann, William D., 14048
Ehrenberg, Hermann, 3356
Ehrmann, Bess Virginia (Hicks), 6662-6665
Eight days with the Confederates, 5003
Eight hundred miles in an ambulance, 16893
Eight months in Illinois, 4648

Eighteen months a prisoner under the Rebel flag, 2749

Eighty years' progress of British North America; showing the wonderful development of its natural resources, 6666

Einhurn, David, 1809-1879, The Rev. Dr. M.J. Raphall's Bible view of slavery reviewed, translated from the February number of "Sinai", 23432

Eirene, 8531

Eisele, Fridolin, 1837-1920, 24343

Eisenberg, Maurice, 8664

Eisenschiml, Otto, 1880-, 6667

Eitrem, Samson, 1872-, 24344

Ekins, Sir Charles, 1768-1855, 2187

El Dorado, 1670, 5351, 8157, 8158, 17590, 17699

El Dorado Co., Cal., Biographies, 17806; History, 16890

El Paso, Texas, 17201

El Paso co., Col., History, 16823

El Salvador, Description & travel, 7974; Periodicals, 7951

Ela, Jacob Hart, 1820-1884, 2188

Elam family, 14049

Elam National Tercentennial Association, 14049

Elder, William, 1806-1885, 2189, 12005

Elder question, Letters on the, 22960

Elder William Brewster and the Brewster family of Portsmouth, New Hampshire, 6163

Elderkin, James D., 1820-, 16458

The elder's wife, 10006

The eldest sister, 10730

Eldredge, Zoeth Skinner, 1846-, 16459, 16460

Eleanor, 9240

Eleanore Cuyler, 9363

The elected mother, 13976

Election (Theology), 619

Election law, Brazil, 19877; Chile, 19024; Costa Rica, 20591; Maryland, 23219; Massachusetts, 1264

The election of president of the United States, 2190

Election sermons, Connecticut, 1097, 1549, 1602, 1724, 12040, 12303, 13033, 22093, 22860, 23160; Massachusetts, 157, 220, 417, 832, 841, 1182, 1963, 2335, 2451, 11516, 11806, 13031, 13407, 21868, 21894, 22033, 22038, 22226, 22347, 22504, 22541, 22916, 23617, 23661, 23667, 23675, 23679, 23717, 23765, 23796; New

Hampshire, 11420, 11502, 11504, 11792, 12050, 12361, 12551, 22581, 22866

Elections, Baltimore, 23217; Bibliography, 14704; Colombia , Statistics, 20350; Kentucky, 15017; Otsego Co., N.Y., 13072; Pennsylvania , Corrupt practices, 13101

Electric power, 20370; Argentine Republic, 18402, 18443, 18493; Brazil, 18290, 20383; Colombia, 20284; Laws and regulations, 18205; Parana, 18290

Electric power distribution, South America, 20369

Electric power-plants, South America, 20369

Electric utilities, Brazil, 19212; Chile, 18602; Venezuela, 20502

Electricity rates, 14776

Electron structure in actinides, 20446

Electronic microscopes, 18512

Electronic structure and electronic correlations in actinides, 20449

Electuaries, 22331

Electuarium novum alexipharmacum, 22331

Elegant Tom Dillar, 10298

Elegiac epistles on the calamities of love and war, 2191

An elegiac ode, 3930

Elegías de varones ilustres de Indias, 19921

An elegy composed on the death of Elder Josiah Shepard, 22167

An elegy occasioned by the melancholy [!] catastrophe which happen'd in the night of the 19th of August, 1774, 22168

An elegy occasioned by the sudden and awful death of Mr. Nathanael Baker [of] Dedham, 22169

An elegy on the late Honorable Titus Hosmer, esq., 811

An elegy on the much lamented death of Nathan Starr, B.A., 22170

An elegy upon His Excellency William Burnet, esq., 22171

Elementa philosophica, 22718

Elemjay, Louise, 3357

An elephant's track, 3191

Elephants, Fossil, 928

L'élévation et la chute de l'empereur Maximilien, 7188

Elfreide of Guldal, 4390

Elgin, Ill., History, 7052

Elias Ortiz, Sergio, 20193

Elinor Fulton, 10185

Eliot, John, 1604-1690, 12006, 13141, 23610, 23790

Eliot, John, 1754-1813, 12007, 12168

Eliot, Jonathan, 1784-1846, 12008

Fliot, Samuel, 1821-1898, 12009

Eliot, Samuel Atkins, 1798-1862, 2104
Eliot, Thomas Dawes, 1808-1870, 12010,
  24345
Eliot, Thomas Stearns, 1898- , 18043
Eliot, William Harvard, 1796-1831, 12011
Eliot el hombre, 18043
Elisabeth, princess of France, 1764-1794,
  11440
Elite (social sciences), 19809
Elite, liderança, e massas, e as nações
  subdesenvolvidas, 19809
Elivas, Knarf, pseud., 10709
The elixir of gold, 5614
The elixir of life, 9825
Eliza et Maria, 24972
Eliza Farnham, 10195
Elizabeth, Christian scientist, 9241
Elizabeth, N.J., History, 22337; Saint
  John's church, 21941, 22314
Elizabethtown, Ky., Biography, 14050;
  History, 14263, 14291; Memorial United
  Methodist Church, 14050
Elizaga, Domingo de, 7910
Elizaga, Lorenzo, 12012
Elizaga, Manuel Cayetano de, 7910
Elizalde, Matias, 8278
Elkanah Brewster's temptation, 10427
Elkins, Hervey. 12013
Elkswatawa, 1775?-1834, 3545, 16346
Ellen, 3782
Ellen Durand, 8711
Ellen Grafton, the lily of Lexington, 8700
Ellen Parry, 8846
Eller, Ronald D., 14051
Ellery, William, 1727-1820, 24601
Ellet, Charles, 1810-1862, 12014-12019
Ellet, Mrs. Elizabeth Fries (Lummis)
  1818-1877, 3358, 3359, 12020-12023
Ellice, Edward, 6668
Ellicott, Andrew, 1754-1820, 3360, 12024
Ellicott, Thomas, 1738-1799, 12100
Ellie, 9106
Ellington, George, pseud., 12025
Ellington, Conn., History, 23664
Elliot, Sir Charles, 1801-1875, 16630
Elliot, Jonathan, 1784-1846, comp.,
  12026-12028, 22172
Elliot, Samuel, 1777-1845, 12029
Elliot, Samuel Atkins, 1798-1862, 25520
Elliot, Samuel Hayes, 1809-1869, 12030
Elliot, Sir Thomas Frederick, 1808-1880,
  12031
Elliot, William, 12032, 12033
Elliot County, Kentucky, Description,
  13936
Elliott, A.B., 16461

Elliott, Benjamin, 1786-1836, 12034
Elliott, Charles, 1792-1869, 12035, 12036,
  14052
Elliott, Charles Wyllys, 1817-1883, 12037
Elliott, E.N., 3361
Elliott, Franklin Reuben, 1817-1878, 12038
Elliott, Harrison, 14053
Elliott, Howard, 16462
Elliott, J.M., 14054
Elliott, Jesse Duncan, 1782-1845, 934, 1697,
  12039, 22687
Elliott, John, 1768-1824, 12040
Elliott, John F., 3362
Elliott, Richard Smith, b.1817, 16463
Elliott, Sarah Barnwell, 1848-1928, 3363-3368
Elliott, Stephen, 1771-1830, 12041
Elliott, Stephen, bp., 1806-1866, 12042-12047
Elliott, Wallace W., & co., pub., 16771, 16773
Elliott, William, 1788-1863, 3369, 3370, 12048
Elliott society of natural history, Charleston,
  S.C., 12049
Ellis, Alexander, 24346
Ellis, Charles Mayo, 1818-1878, 6669
Ellis, Daniel, 1827- , 3371
Ellis, Edward Sylvester, 1840-1916, 3372, 3373,
  16464-16468
Ellis, Elmer E., 16469
Ellis, Ferdinand, 1780-1858, 12050
Ellis, G.A., 12051
Ellis, George Edward, 1814-1894, 12052-12056
Ellis, George W., 12057
Ellis, Henry, 6670
Ellis, Henry, 1731-1806, 12058
Ellis, James Tandy, 1868-1942, 3374, 13710,
  14055
Ellis, John B., 12059
Ellis, Joseph, 14056
Ellis, Mina (Benson) Hubbard, 6671
Ellis, Rufus, 1819-1885, 12060
Ellis, Samuel, 22173
Ellis, Thomas T., 3375
Ellis, William, 1794-1872, 15242, 22174
Ellis, William, captain, 15242
Ellis, William, surgeon, 23533
Ellison, Sherry Sue, 14057
Ellison, Thomas, 1833-1904, 22175,
  24347
Ellsworth, Ephraim Elmer, 7888
Ellsworth, Henry William, 1814-1864, 16470
Ellsworth County, Kansas, History, 16256
The Elm Lick coal bed, 15686
Elmer, Jonathan, 1745-1807, 22176
Elmore, Franklin Harper, 1799-1850, 1339
Elmore, Jamor Buchanan, 1857-1942, 3376, 3377
Elmore, William Lewis, 1856-1942, 15584
Elmwood Inn, 14001, 14058

154

Elocution, 2400
Eloge de M. Franklin, 2025
Elogio de la embriaguez, 19782
Elsie Magoon, 3556
Elsie Venner, 9905
Elsket, 10460
Elson, George, 6671
Elton, Romeo, 1790-1870, 12061
Elvas, Gentleman of, 5469, 7825
Elwyn, Thomas, 2192
Ely, Alfred, 1815-1892, 3378
Ely, Ezra Stiles, 1786-1861, 22177
Ely, Mrs. Mary Harris (Monteith), 1824-
    1849, 12465
Ely, William, 14059
Ely, Zebulon, 1759-1824, 22178
Elze, Karl i.e. Friedrich Karl, 1821-1889,
    533
Ema, Milo y yo, 18222
Emancipate your colonies, 1180
Emancipatie door centralisatie, 24348
Emancipation, 24107, 25908
L'émancipation des esclaves des États-
    Unis d'Amérique, 25064
Emancipation in disguise, 24399
Emancipation in the West Indies, 5385, 8181
Emancipation of the Negro slaves in the
    West Indies colonies considered, 24350
Emancipation proclamation, 2276, 6669,
    7258, 7335, 7466, 7781, 13237, 22056,
    24180, 24683; Bibliography, 5836
El embajador Sarmiento, 19793
The embargo, 1626
Embargo, 1807-1809, 75, 974, 1626, 11281,
    11555, 13088, 23256, 24257, 23656
Embarrassments, 7118, 10012
Embezzlement, Argentine Republic, 19836
Embiotocidae, 109
Emblems, 20199; National, Colombia, 19946
The emblems of fidelity, a comedy in
    letters, 13527
As emboscadas da sorte, 19701
The embroidered handkerchief, 10194
Embry, Jacqueline, 13567
Embryology, Fishes, 20191
O embuçado do Erval, 20055
Emch, Arnold, 1871-, 3379
Emch, Hermann, 3379
Emerson, Charles Noble, 1821-1869, 22179
Emerson, Gouverneur, 1796-1874, 13234,
    22180
Emerson, Frederick Valentine, 1871-, 24351
Emerson, Joseph, 1700-1767, 22181
Emerson, Joseph, 1777-1833, 12203, 22181,
    22182
Emerson, Ralph, 1787-1863, 22182

Emerson, Ralph Waldo, 1803-1882, 6267, 8175
Emerson, William, 1769-1811, 1645, 23447
Emerson, William H., 1833-, 24352
Emery county, Utah, 16776
Emery, Joshua, jr., 1807-1882, 2193
Emery, Samuel Hopkins, 1815-1901, 22183
The emigrant, 5381, 6996, 10921
The emigrant's friend, 4107
The emigrant's and traveler's guide to the
    West, 2595
The emigrant's guide, 1933, 3057, 3169, 3350,
    3380, 4919, 5125, 5345, 5369, 12846, 16541,
    17269, 17270
The emigrant's handbook, and guide to
    Wisconsin, 12169
The emigrant's mother, 8623
Emigranternas land, 4194
Emigration and immigration, 1562, 24814
Emigration and immigration law, 18411;
    Canada, 7967; U.S., 11533
Emigration, emigrants and know-nothings, 2194
Emigration or no emigration, 4789
Emigration. Practical advice to emigrants, 2195
Emigration to Texas, 5365
Emigration to Virginia, 4596
Emigres, 398, 777
Emily Chester, 10732
Emily Mayland, 9194
Eminent domain, 15335; Kentucky, 14683;
    Mexico, 18120, 19234
Emlyn, Thomas, 1663-1741, 14060
Emma Walton, 9448
Emmanuel; the story of the Messiah, 9125
Emmerich-Högen, Ferdinand, 1858-, 6672
Emmerton, James Arthur, 3381
Emmons, Richard, 1788-, 2196, 2197, 3382-3384
Emory, William Hemsley, 1811-1887, 5513, 5516
Emott, James, 1771-1850, 22184
Empey, Jessie K., 16471
Employees' representation in management, 19631;
    Bolivia, 19631
Employment, Kentucky, 14171
Empresa Colombiana de Petroleos, 19096
Empresa editora, s.a., 6673
La empresa y el desarrollo nacional, 18598
Empresário industrial e desenvolvimento
    econômico no Brasil, 19774
Las empresas semifiscales, 18213
The Empress of the ocean, 9721
The empty heart, 10938
Empty pockets, 14242
The empty sleeve, 23407
Emulsion chambers, 20024
En Amérique; de New-York à la Nouvelle-Orléans,
    2975
En camino hacia la democracia, 7682

En courant, le monde, 4751
En deux CV chez les primitifs, 7310
En el corazón de Pascal, 19991
En el sendero gris, 18027
En la rosa de los vientos, 19967
En los Estados Unidos, 4402
En los trópicos, 18325
En México y Cuba, 6513
En resa til Norra America, 7170
En route to the Klondike, 16988
En tierra yankee, 5150
En torno a la axiología de Platón en su tensión perenne ético-religiosa, 19728
En visite chez l'Oncle Sam, 4381
Encalada Vázquez, Oswaldo, 1955-, 20649
The Encantadas, 10346
The enchanged babyhouse, 10046
The enchanted beauty, 9470
An enchanted castle, 4781
The enchanted typewriter, 8677
The enchanted village, 15516
Enciso, Martin Fernández de, 6674
Encroachments of the slave power, 24353
Encuesta alimentaria de la vereda de San Bernardo, 20314
Encuesta de consumo de alimentos en la Capital Federal y gran Buenos Aires, 18432
Encuesta nutricional de El Trébol, 20311
Encuesta nutricional de San Jacinto, 20315
Encyclopaedia of the Presbyterian Church in the United States, 15062
Encyclopedias and dictionaries, 240, 2315
The end of a coil, 11094
The end of earth, 10224
End of the feud and other Kentucky legends, 14396
The end of the irresponsible conflict, 22185, 24354
The end of the vendetta, 9355
The end of the world, 9464
Endangered plants and animals in Kentucky, 13576
Endeavor doin's down to the Corners, 9189
Endemann, Wilhelm, 1825-1899, 24355
Endemias rurais, 19377
The endemic diseases of the United States of America, 13768
Endicott, Charles Moses, 1793-1863, 22186, 22187
An enemy to the king, 10070
Energía hidroeléctrica argentina, 19981
Engel, Samuel, 1702-1784, 22188

Engelhardt, Zephyrin, father, 1851-1934, 16472
Engels, L., 12062
Engineering, Dictionaries, 18995; Study and teaching, 13875; Venezuela, 18373
Engineering libraries, Catalogs, 19102
England, John, bp., 1786-1842, 24356
England, Description & travel, 1832, 1834, 7170, 7207, 11923, 22925
England and America, 12822
England from a back-window, 8641
England, the United States, and the Southern Confederacy, 25440
Der engländischen pflanzstädte in Nord-America, geschichte und handlung, 6260
Englands-exchequer. Or a discourse of the sea and navigation, with some things thereto coincident concerning plantations, 22283
Engleheart, Sir John Gardner Dillman, 1823-1923, 3385
English, Henry, 1803-1855, 12063
English, Mrs. Mary Katharine (Jackson), 16473
English, William Hayden, 1822-1896, 3386, 12064
The English-American, his travail by sea and land, 2366
An English combatant, 968
The English grammar, 14874
English in Illinois, 2258, 16528
The English in the West Indies, 6786
English invasion, 1806-1807, 12249
The English lady, 10310
English language, Dialects, Negro, 3643; Dictionaries, 16842, 19132, 23762; Dictionaries, Algonquian, 7224; Dictionaries, Chippewa, 770; Dictionaries, Cree, 21871; Dictionaries, Maya, 7590; Dictionaries, Portuguese, 19997; Grammar, 14874, 16555; Readers, 23761; Rhetoric, 11723; Study and teaching, 18380; Study and teaching, Curricula, 20603
English liberties, 11660
English literature (Collections), 1631; (Selections: Extracts, etc.), 9517, 9616; Addresses, essays, lectures, 21881; Bibliography, 212; Early modern (to 1700), Bibliography, 1631
English neutrality, 13405
The English orphans, 3913
The English practice, 12065
English satire, 5799
English seamen in the sixteenth century, 24453
English serfdom and American slavery, 3874
The English sportsman in the western prairies, 1197

English West Indian expedition, 1654-1655, 1507, 12368
English West Indian expedition, 1739-1742, 311, 1829, 13339
English West Indian expedition, 1759, 2399
English West Indian expedition, 1795-1796, 12209, 25276
The Englishman deceived, 13474
An Englishman in America, 6922
An Englishman's answer, to the address, from the delegates to the people of Great-Britain, 13388
The Englishman's guide book to the U.S. and Canada, 6675
The Englishman's right: a dialogue between a barrister at law and a juryman, 22360
An Englishman's sketch-book, 11292
The Englishman's story, 9618
An Englishman's travels in America, 2691
An Englishwoman, 25361
The Englishwoman in America, 2722, 4419
An Englishwoman's experience in America, 3447
Engraulis anchoita, 20192
Engraving, Brazilian, Catalogs, 19604
Enlace de gritos, 18189
Ennemoser, Franz Joseph, 14061
Ennis, John W., 3387
Enos, Zimri A., 6676
Enough of war!, 24387
The enquirer after truth, 9401
Enríquez, Edgardo, 20390
Enríquez de Guzmán, Antonio, 7959
El ensayo, 20221
Ensayos filosóficos, 18610
Les enseignements de l'Exposition de Saint-Louis, 2740
Enseñanza audiovisual y comunicación, 19565
O ensino de leitura da 2ª à 6ª série primária, 18673
The entailed hat, 11004
Enterprise (ship), 6449
An entertaining account of all the countries of the known world, 12067
Entertainment for a winter's evening, 12383
Enthusiasm, 12430
Entick, John, 1703-1773?, 3388
An entomological wooing, 9916
Entomology, 18550; Societies, 20485
Entomology, Economic, Central America, 18999
Entre el polvo del camino, 6867
Entre luz y sombra, 19590
Entrecasteaux, Joseph Antoine Bruni, chevalier d', 1739-1793, 11624

The entwined lives of Miss Gabrielle Austin ..., 9246
Enuma Elish, 18608
Environmental pollution, Brazil, 19267; Demographic growth and, 20561
Environmental protection, 19441; Kentucky, 14495; Venezuela, 19639
L'envoi, 10528
The envoy. From free hearts to the free, 24932
Eolah, the white flower of the prairie, 3142
Eolopoesis, 1268
Eonchs of ruby, 2991
Epaminondas, pseud., 12068
An epic trilogy, 5868
Epictetus, 5238
The epidemic of the nineteenth century, 24003
Epidemics, 13770, 13919, 14290, 19377; Maryland, 23184; Mexico, 1787
Episcopacy, 11337, 12156, 21890-21893, 22783
The Episcopal church in the American colonies, 21941
Episcopal Methodism, as it was, and is, 12321
Episcopal tract--no.1, 15454
An episode of West Woodlands, 6971, 9790
Episodes in Van Bibber's life, 9357
Episodes of life in New York, 9632
Episodes of my second life, 3564
Episodes of the everlasting comedy, 3223
An epistle from a young lady to an ensign in the Guards, 12069
An epistle from Edward, an American prisoner in England, to Harriet, in America, 12070
Epistles from the Old Man of the Hills to the people of the valley, 24692
An epistle from William, surnamed Littell, 14833
Epistolario de d. Bernardo O'Higgins, 7631
Epistolario de la Primera República, 17983
Epitaphs, 12071, 23004; Boston, 1503, 1505, 1506; Cambridge, Mass., 12714; Connecticut valley, 1504; Northampton, Mass., 1504; Philadelphia, 21936; U.S., 136; Worcester, Mass., 945
Epitoma de legis hvmane mvndique fictione, 5883
Epping, Charlotte, S.J., 3328
Epsom, N.H., History, 21996
Equal educational opportunity in Kentucky, 15151
Equality, 8775, 11769
Equality of states, 20662
Equations, Convolution, 18998
Equity (law), 15284
Equity pleading and procedure, 11480; Kentucky, 24715; New York (State), 1389
Erasmus, Desiderius, d.1536, 12072
Erato, 3560

Ercilla y Zúñiga, Alonso de, 1533-1594,
6677-6688
Erickson, John, 19803
Erie, Lake, Battle of, 1813, 967, 1682,
1697, 1816, 12039, 22687
Erie canal, 25924
Erie Indians, Poetry, 5692
Erie railroad, 12696
Erinnerungen aus Amerika , 2644
Erinnerungen aus Süd-Amerika, 1245
Erman, Georg Adolf, 1806-1877, 16815
Ermatinger, Charles Oakes Zaccheus,
1851-, 16474
Ermatinger, Edward, 1797-1876, 12073,
12074, 16474
Ernest Carroll, 9659
Ernest Grey, 10334
Ernest Linwood, 9839
Ernest Quest, 3504
Erni, Henry, 12075
Eros, 9316
Eros and Anteros, 8935
An errand to the South in the summer of
1862, 4379
An errant wooing, 9765
Errett, Isaac, 1820-, 14062
Erring, yet noble, 10602
The errors of education, 9890, 14342
Die ersten Amerikaner im Westen, 14774
Erwin, Andrew, 24357
Erwin, Marie H., 16475
Erwin, Milo, 3389
Esbozo de la historia de los primeros
diez años de la revolucion agraria
de México, 7515
Escalala, 1000
Escalante Fontaneda, Hernando d', 3390,
23642
Escalera, Evaristo, 6689
The escape, 11010
The escape of Cowley and Sawyer from
the Indians, 10570
The escape of McKean's scounting party
in Otsego county, 10570
Escapes from Cayenne, 11765
Eschscholtz, Johann Friedrich, 1793-
1831, 22740
L'esclavage... L'évolution de, 24826
L'esclavage à Cuba et la révolution
d'Espagne, 25428
L'esclavage aux Antilles françaises avant
1789, d'après des documents inédits
des archives coloniales, 25240
L'esclavage aux États-Unis, 12237
L'esclavage dans les États Confédérés,
24358

Esclavage et immigration, la question de la
main-d'oeuvre aux Antilles, le décret du
13 février 1852, 24748
L'esclave blanc, 24602
Les esclaves, 2433
Les esclaves des colonies françaises au clergé
français, 23980
Les esclaves publics chez les Romains, 24543
La esclavitud de los negros en la américa
española, 23856
La esclavitud de los negros y la prensa
madrileña, 24359
La esclavitud en Cuba; discurso pronunciado
en la tercera conferencia abolicionista de
1872, 25439
Escobar, Alonso de, 7917
Escobar, Jerónimo de, 8168
Escobar, Manuel de, 6690
Escobedo, Federico, 1874-, 7233, 7234
La escondida, 19967
The escorted lady, 10197
A escravidão nos Estados Unidos, 23956
A escravidão, o clero e o abolicionismo, 24409
O escravo, 19775
Escritor, pseud., 9068
Escritores panameños contemporáneos, 18198
Escritos de ética, 18096
Escudero, José Augustín de, 1801-1862, 16476,
17392
Escudo de armas de Mexico, 1787
Escudo para las Islas Malvinas y adyacencias,
20228
La escuela angloamericana del derecho
internacional privado, 20254
Escuela preparatoria modelo, 20063
La escultura argentina en el siglo xx, 18510
La escultura de Palenque, 6788
Esequibo, La infamia del, 19489
La esfinge mestiza, 7824
Eskimo language, Glossaries, vocabularies,
etc., 8252, 16685
Eskimos, 2464, 6302, 12560, 21871, 22556,
22843
Eskippackithiki, 13909; the last Indian town
in Kentucky, 13640
An Esmeralda of Rocky Cañon, 6972
Esopus Indians, Wars, 1655-1660, 11518
O espaço da arquitetura, 20632
Espeio de la perfecta casada, 7032, 7033
Espelho de três faces, 19210
Esperance, 10169
Esperanza, 9484
Espino Barros, Eugenio, 6691
Espinosa, Antonio, 8433
Espinosa, José D., ed., 7830
Espinosa, José María, b.1796, 7762

Espinosa, Miguel de, 6160
Espinosa y Tello, José, 1763-1815, 16477
Espionage, Fiction, 18225
Espirito Santo, Brazil, Economic conditions, 18746; Rural conditions, 19621
La espuma nace sola, 19105
Espy, Josiah Murdoch, 1771-1847, 3391
Esquema histórico-económico de Venezuela, 18589
Esquisse intéressant du Tableau fidèle des causes qui ont occasioné les révolutions actuelles de l'Amérique Septentrionale, 3392
Esquisse morale et politique des États-Unis et de l'Amérique du Nord, 4552
Essequito (Colony), History, 1516
Essex, Robert Devereux, earl of, 1586-1601, defendant, 22680
Essex (U.S. frigate), 12841
Essex, N.Y., 4726
Essex Co., Mass., 10152; Description & travel, 22546; History, 2246; Politics & government, 24360
Essex County Anti-slavery Convention, Danvers, Mass., 1838, 24360
Essex (Mass.) agricultural society, 12962
Essex Institute, Salem, Mass., 12081, 22186
Esshom, Frank Ellwood, 1865-, 16479
Establishing a newspaper, 6266
The establishment of law and order on western plains, 16381
Estabrooks, Henry L., 3393
Las estaciones, 18927
Estadística aplicada, 20528
Estadística chilena, 20126
Estadística general, 19697
Estado actual y posibilidades del desarrollo agrícola en Venezuela, 20429
El estado-nación y su forma de poder, 18907
El estado y la empresa privada, 20384
Estados para un alba en si, 18072
Los Estados Unidos, 2706, 4292
Los Estados Unidos de América y las repúblicas hispano-americanas de 1810 à 1830, 8269
Estados Unidos, gran aventura del hombre, 2499
Los Estados Unidos y la América del Sur, 4872
Estala, Pedro, 8174
Estampas de México, 7801
Estampas y apologicas, 19858
Estancelin, Louis, 1777-1858, 12082

Estate planning, 14684; Kentucky, 14668, 14669
A estatua, 19696
Estatuetas de cerâmica na cultura Santarem, 20509
Estatuto de la Universidad Nacional del Sur, 18700
O estatuto dos funcionários, 19348
Estatuto jurídico del comercio farmacéutico, 21725
Estaugh, John, 1676-1742, 12083
Este, David Kirkpatrick, 1785-1875, 12084
Estee, Charles Frederick, 12085
Estelle Grant, 9485
Estes Park, Col. , Description, 16174
Estes Rocky Mountain National Park, 16480
Esteva, Adalberto A., 6692, 6693
Estevez y Pombal, Antonio, 6657, 8278
Esteyneffer, Juan de, 1664-1716, 6694, 6695
Esther Wynn's love-letters, 10006
El estilo de vida argentino en Paz, 19764
Estimates on the value of slaves, 1815, 24361
Estournelles de Constant, Paul Henri Benjamin, baron d', 1852-1924, 3394, 7494
Estrada, Genaro, 1887-, 6767
Estratificación y movilidad social en Argentina, 18688
Estván, Bela, b.1827, 3395
Etapas de la vida de un escritor, 18504
Les États Confédérés d'Amérique visités en 1863, 3617
Les États-Unis au xxe siècle, 4260
Les États-Unis contemporains, 4045
Les États-Unis d'Amerique, 3394, 3642
Les États-Unis du Méxique, 7736
Les États-Unis en 1850, 3326
Les États-Unis et la Havane, 4309
Les États-Unis et le Canada, 7413
Les États-Unis et le Méxique, 7396
Les États-Unis, le self-government et le césarisme, 4828
Etchegoyen y Montane, Francisco, 1870-1951, 19603
Etchings of a whaling cruise, 2838
Un été en Amérique, 4235
Eteocles: a tale of Antioch, 8538
The eternal flame, 14831
Ethel Somers, 10826
Ethelind, 8668
Ethell, Henry C., 16481
Etheostoma squamiceps, 15113
Ether, 11432
Etheridge, Kelsic, pseud., 10825
Ethica, 22718
Ethics, 1489, 5883, 10986, 18096, 19531, 22542, 22718, 23113, 25437

The ethics of American slavery, American
  slavery is a crime in substance, 13490
The ethics of literary art, 5388
Ethiopia, Description, 7858
Ethnology, 97, 13228; Addresses, essays,
  lectures, 18665; Africa, West, 24565;
  America, 249; Brazil, 24063;
  Methodology, 20367; Societies, etc.,
  249; South America, 18665, 23566
Ethridge, Willie Snow, 6696
Etidorhpa, 10224
Etiquette, 10147, 19871
Etna Vandemir, 9729
Etourneau, 3396
Étude commerciale-industrielle-économique-
  constitutionnelle, etc. de la grande
  république américaine, 4943
Eudeva language, 12345
Eugene Pickering, 10014
Eulogy on Hugh Swinton Legare, 4856
Eumenes, 12436
Eunice Quince, 9278
Europäische briefe über Amerika von dr.
  Albert Oeri, 4638
Die europäische einwanderung nach den
  Vereinigten Staaten von 1820 bis
  1896, 3214
Europe, 584, 10016, 12108; Commerce, 480;
  Description & travel, 315, 1134, 1628,
  2293, 2755, 3531, 4090, 4153, 6213,
  7105, 9027, 01057, 10226, 10241, 10627,
  12116, 16871, 17116, 22098, 22298,
  22871; Description & travel, Fiction,
  10240; Description & travel, Guide-
  books, 3252; Description & travel
  Views, 21735; Historical geography,
  1515; History, 22396; History, 1648-
  1789, 1611, 1612; History, 1789-1815,
  293, 11786, 28182; History, 1815-1848,
  2420, 12108; History, Bibliography,
  14704; History, Year-books, 293;
  Politics & government, 1819, 11324,
  22396, 23181; Politics & government,
  1648-1789, 480, 22216; Politics &
  government, 1789-1815, 480, 6005,
  12108, 21988; Politics & government
  1815-1848, 22885; Politics & government
  - 1848-1871, 659, 12378; Northern
  Description & travel, 8879; Southern,
  Description & travel, 5073
European delineation of American
  character, 12086
The European stranger in America, 2200
The European traveller in America,
  2809, 12087
European war, 1914-1918, Addresses,

  sermons, etc., 7689
European war, 1914-1918, Deportations from
  Belgium, 23906; Territorial questions,
  24567
The Europeans, 7120
Eustace, John Skey, 1760-1805, 12088
Euthanasia, Legal aspects, 14676
Eustis, William, 1753-1825, 12364
Eva May, the foundling, 9961
Evacuation of Texas, 16514
Evalina's garden, 9578
Evan Dale, 10102
Evangel Wiseman, 9540
Evangelical alliance, 67, 673, 25928
An evangelical ministry, the security of a
  nation, 23230
Evangelical union anti-slavery society of the
  city of New York, 24362
Evangelicus, pseud., 24363
The Evangelist, 25093
The evangelist and other poems, 3101
Evangelistic sermons, 1687
Evangelistic work, 2922, 4469, 14228, 15021,
  22008, 23112
Evans, Albert S., 6697, 16482
Evans, Caleb, 1737-1791, 12089
Evans, Charles, 21878
Evans, Clement Anselm, 16483
Evans, E. Clinton, 2198
Evans, Elwood, 1828-1898, 16484, 16784
Evans, Estwick, 1787-1866, 3397, 12090, 12091
Evans, Francis A., 12092
Evans, Frederick William, 1808-1893, 12093,
  12094
Evans, Sir George DeLacy, 1787-1870, 12095
Evans, Israel, 1747-1807, 12096, 12097
Evans, James, 1801-1846, 13312
Evans, James W., 22458
Evans, John, 1814-1897, 3398, 17109
Evans, John Thomas, see Williams, James, b.1825
Evans, Jonathan, 5077
Evans, Josiah James, 1786-1858, 24364
Evans, Lemuel Dale, 1810-1877, 12098, 24365
Evans, Lewis, 1700?-1756, 3399
Evans, Nancy, 14063
Evans, Nathaniel, 1742-1767, 12099
Evans, Oliver, 1755-1819, 12100
Evans, Thomas, d.1743, 23522
Evans, Thomas Wiltberger, 1823-1897, 12101
Evans, William Jones, M.R.C.S., 12102
Evans, William Julian, 12103
Evans family, Garrard county, Ky., History,
  15522
Evansville, Ind., 14220
Evarts, Jeremiah, 1781-1831, 5452, 12104,
  23728

Evarts, William Maxwell, 1818-1901, 6288, 6698
Evarts family (John Evarts, b.1601), 5835
The eve of the fourth, 9567, 9570
Eveline Neville, 9487
Evelyn, the child of the revolution, 10633
The evening book, 10147
Evening journal, Albany, N.Y., 6288
An evening's adventure, 10163
Evenings at Donaldson manor, 12078
Evenings at Woodlawn 9473
The eventful trip of the Midnight Cry, 11162
Ever forgive, 8765
Everest, Robert, 3400
Everett, Alexander Hill, 1790-1847, 12105-12109
Everett, David, 1770-1813. Essay on the rights and duties of nations, 413
Everett, Edward, 1794-1865, 173, 2156, 7074, 12110-12118, 22189, 22326, 22392
Everett, Edward Franklin, 1840-1899, 12119
Everett, H., 5504
Everett, Horace, 1780-1851, 12120
Everett family (Richard Everett, d. 1682), 12119
Everglades, Florida, 4056, 4633, 5731
Everheart, Lawrence, 1755-1839, 698
Evershaw, Mary, 12121
Every day, 10523
Every man his own guide to the falls of Niagara, 12995
Every man his own letter-writer, 10892
Every man his own property, 24831
Everybody's friend, 10742
Evidence (law), 14664; Confederate States of America, 24178; Guatemala, 18067
Evidence, Hearsay, Chile, 18254
Evidence, Rules of, 14670
The evidence that Abraham Lincoln was not born in lawful wedlock, 6447
Evil, non-resistance to, 2151, 25865
The evil and the good, 9802
The evil tendencies of corporal punishment, 1927
Evils and abuses in the naval and merchant services exposed, 22982
The evils of a dram-shop, 13599
Evolución de la música vocal a través de la historia, 18914
Evolución de la psiquiatría en el Ecuador, 21721

Evolución demográfica argentina durante el período hispano, 20360
Evolución histórica de la estratificacion social en la Argentina, 18689
Evolución legislativa y doctrinaria de la reforma agraria, 20196
La evolución republicana durante la revolución argentina, 7943
Evolución y tendencia de los precios del estaño, 18942
Evolution, History, 23036
The evolution of a life, 3126
The evolution of a state, 5223
Ewart, Frank Carman, 6699
Ewbank, Thomas, 1792-1870, 3401, 12122
Ewell, James, 1773-1832, 12123
Ewell, John D., 3402
Ewer, John, bp. of Bangor, d.1774, 12124, 13098
Ewing, Elbert William Robinson, 1867-, 24366, 24367
Ewing, Thomas, 1789-1871, 12125, 24368
Ewing, Thomas, 1829-1896, 6700, 6701
Ewing, W. Brown, 17846
Excavations (Archaeology), Central America, 18634; Mexico, 18634
The excellencies of lying, 9486
The excellency of a good name, 22024
Excelsior, the crusade of the, 6967
Exchanges, Literary and scientific, 12502
The excise tax law, 12085
Exciting adventures of wild camp life in Leadville, Black Hills and the Gunnison country, 16853
Excommunication, 24788
Excursion appendix, 4020
Excursion d'un touriste au Mexique, 7915
Excursion guide to the Virginia springs and health resorts of western North Carolina and north Georgia, 3403
Excursion through the slave states, 3425, 12139
An excursion to California over the prairie, 4147
Excursion to Montauk, 10912
An excursion to the Mammoth Cave and the barrens of Kentucky, 3184
The execution of Louis Riel, 8185
Execution sermons, 23329, 24765
The executioner of Venice, 4734
Executive power, 11914
Exempla, 11846
L'exemple de l'Amérique, 7432
Exeter Hall, 10268
An exhibit of the losses sustained at the office of discount and deposit, 12133
Exhibitions, 14/40

Las exhortaciones que hacían en México los padres a los hijos, 19892
An exhortation to the inhabitants of the province of South Carolina, 13006
The exile of von Adelstein's soul, 5495
The exiles, 9358
Exiles in Virginia, 3614
The exiles of Florida, 12238
The exiles of Nova Scotia, 11171
Exotic leaves, 4971
The expatriates, 8771
Expatriation, 22363
Expedições militares contra Canudos, 18343
L'expedition militaire de Manitoba, 8128
The expedition of Major General Braddock to Virginia, 3404
Expedition shells, 12328
Expedition to Santa Fé, 3414
Expenditure arising out of trouble in the North-west Territories, 6298
Experiencias y contribuciones para la enseñanza de la lengua oral y escrita, 18492
The experience and travels of Mr. Freeborn Garrettson, 3577
Experience in the war of the great rebellion, 4595
Experience of a Confederate chaplain, 2702
Experience of a Confederate States prisoner, 13507
The experienced farmer's tour in America, 4704
An experienced woodsman, 22615
Experiences from life..., 13650
Experiences in the life of a matrimonial monomaniac, 8448
The experiences of a layman in a country parish, 8449
An experiment in economy, 9363
An experimental study of the east Kentucky mountaineers, 14328
Experimento de fertilidade em solos de tabuleiros, 19464
Experimentos de feijão-mulatinho em tabuleiros, 19464
Expert witnesses, 14664; Medical, 14677
An explanation of the map which delineates that part of the federal lands, 3148
The explanatory charter granted by his majesty King George to the province of Massachusetts-Bay in New England, 23245
Exploration and survey of the Valley of the Great Salt Lake of Utah, 5255
Explorations minéralogique, 6914

Explorers, American, 16733; Spanish, 7393
Export credit, 20032
Expresion de Hispanoamérica, 18720
Express service, U.S., History, 17832
The expressman and the detective, 10529
La expropiación por causa de utilidad pública, 18120
Exquemelin, Alexandre Olivier, 22190
Extenuating circumstances, Chile, 20078
La extirpación de la idolatría en el Peru, 5937
Extra official state papers, 13369
Extradition, 413, 2183, 11837; U.S., 22622
An eye for an eye, 9639
Eye-witness, 11133
Eyes and ears, 1056
Eyma, Louis Xavier, 1816-1876, 3406, 3407
Eyre, Edward John, 1815-1901, 2199, 22595
Eyre, John, 2200, 3408
Eytinge, Sol, illustr., 8156, 11113, 11114

Faber, Kurt, 3409
Fabian, Bentham, 16486
Fables in slang, 8477
Fabre, Hector, 1834-1901, 2202
A fábula da guerra, 20644
Fábula de una verdad, 19215
Fabyan, Robert, d.1513, 22285
A faca, 19696
A face illumined, 10645
The face of Abel, 10283
Face to face with the Mexicans, 7097
Fackler, Calvin Morgan, 14064, 14065
Fackler, Samuel A., 3410
Fact and fiction, 1889, 8991, 10089
Factores políticos en el desarrollo económico de América Latina, 18264
Facts for the people, 2340, 6305, 24371
Factories, 22193
A faded leaf of history, 9355
Fagan, William Long, 1838-, 3411
Fages, Pedro, 16488
Fagoaga, Francisco de, 1679-1736, 6702
Fahnestock, George Wolff, 1823-, 2203
Faillon, Etienne Michel, 1800?-1870, 6703
The failure of David Berry, 10041
A failure of justice, 10608
Faint, yet pursuing, 9282
The fair crusader, 10285
Fair day, 10043
The fair god, 11053
Fair Harvard, 11106
Fair-hope prospect, 9674
Fair Oaks, Battle of, 1862, 16942

The fair Pilgrim, 8632
The fair Puritan, 9849
The fair rebel, 8784
Fairbank, Calvin, 1816-1898, 3412, 24158
Fairbanks, Charles, 1821-, 2204
Fairbanks, George Rainsford, 1820-1906, 2205, 2206
Fairchild, James Harris, 1817-1902, 2207, 24273
Fairfax, Wilson Miles Cary, 12135
Fairfield, Asa Merrill, 1854-, 16489
Fairfield, Genevieve Genevra, 1832-, 11048
Fairfield, Miss Gertrude, 11048
Fairfield, John, 1797-1847, 187
Fairholt, Frederick William, 1814-1866, 2208
Fairhope, the annals of a country church, 14474
Fairs, 14740, 22142; Kentucky, 14738, 15509
Fairy fingers, 10622
Faith, 1497, 5883
Faith and patience, 1468
Faith Campbell, 8588
The faith doctor, 9465
Faith White's letter book, 11149
The faithful governess, 9194
Faithfull, Emily, 1835-1895, 3413
Fajardo, D., 20255
Falck, George Karel, 24374
Falcon, pseud., 15394
Falconbridge, Alexander, d.1792, 2209
Falconer, Richard, 2987
Falconer, Thomas, 1805-1882, 3414, 3415, 16491
Fales, William R., 1820-1850, 2210
Falk, Alfred, 3416
Falkland islands, 371, 12518, 13259, 22941; Description & travel, 21775, 22942
The fall of Aztalan, 144
The fall of Kilman Kon, 9273
The fall of man, 11146
The fall of Mexico, 13213
The fall of the confederacy, 12891
The fall of the Darcys, 9460
The fall of the great republic, 9186
The fall of the Indian, with other poems, 22962
The fall of the mighty lamented, 23338
Fall of the Pequod, 10760
Fall River, 11170
Fall River, Mass. Citizens, 12688, 22158; Politics & government, 11377
The falling flag. Evacuation of Richmond, 21812
Falling of the stars, 14103
Falls of St. Authony, 8991
Falls of Schuylkill, Pa., History, 12525
The falls of Taughannock, 12593
The falls of the Ohio, 14927, 14928
Falmouth reservoir, 15495
Falsehood and forgery detected and exposed, 2211
Fama póstuma del excelentísimo e ilustrísimo señor doctor Juan Domingo Gonzalez de la Riguera, 1199
The fame and glory of England vindicated, 11570
Fame's little day, 10038
Familia de cuentos, 19617
La familia en Costa Rica, 18016
La familia Podolampacea (Dinoflagellata), 18712
A familiar conversational history of the evangelical churches of New York, 2212
Familiar dialogues between Americus and Britannicus, 23189
Familiar letters to Henry Clay, 6919
Das Familien-, Sklaven- und Erbrecht im Qorân, 25399
Family, Brazil, Case studies, 19777; Costa Rica, 18016
Family anecdotes, 9595
The family compact, 8333
The family doctor, 15778
A family feud, 24319
A family flight through Mexico, 6926
Family life education, 19705
Family memorials, 21801
Family memories, 16828
The family of the Fitzroyals, 9836
The family portraits, 10762
Family ties, 25023
Famin, Stanislas Marie César, 1799-1853, 2213
The fanatic, 9494
Fanaticism, and its results, 2214
Fanchette, 9107
Fancies of a whimsical man, 10999
Fancourt, Charles Saint John, 2215
Fancy's show box, 9827
Fanning, David, 1756?-1825, 3418, 12136
Fanning, Edmund, 1769-1841, 12137
Fanning's illustrated gazetteer of the United States, 2216
Fanny Campbell, the female pirate captain, 8670
Fanshawe, 9819
Une fantaisie américaine, 2563
Far from today, 8884
The far West, 3468
Fargo, Frank F., 22191
Faria, Germano Sinval, 19377

163

Farías, José, 19179
Faribault, Georges Barthélemi, 1789-1866, 2217
Farine, Charles, b.1818, 22192
Farley, Harriet, 22193
Farley, Joseph Pearson, 1839-1912, 3419
Farm game habitat evaluation in Kentucky, 15784
Farm life, 9041; Colombia, 20349; Kentucky, 13743
Farm mechanization, Argentine Republic Statistics, 18800
Farm produce, Marketing, 22142
The farm, ranch and range in Oregon, 17255
Farm tenancy, Argentine Republic, 18460; Buenos Aires (Province), 18460; Economic aspects, Texas, 17727; San Vicente, O'Higgins Province, Chile, 20118
A farmacopéia Tiriyó, 19998
Farmer, Daniel Davis, 1793-1822, 2218
Farmer, John, 1789-1838, 1084, 2219, 2220, 7971, 12138, 22194
Farmer, Miles, 2221
A farmer and landholder, of Jessup's Cut, Maryland, 23846
The farmer boy, and how he became commander-in-chief, 22385
The farmer refuted, 12600
The farmer's almanac..., 14067-14069
The farmer's companion, 1657
The farmer's encyclopedia, and dictionary of rural affairs, 13234
Farmers, Kentucky, 24161
Farmers' Bank and Capital Trust Co., Frankfort, Ky., 14070, 14071
Farmhouses, Venezuela, 18009
Farming and ranching in the Canadian North-West, 6704
Farming by inches, 8705
Farming for fun, 10792
Farmington, Louisville, Ky., 14072
Farmington and Locust Grove: two historic Louisville homes, 14072
Farmington's chapter in the Lincoln story, 5901
Farnese, duke of Parma and Piacenza, 1678-1727, 6366
Farnham, Eliza Woodson (Burhans), 16494
Farnham, T.H., 10122
Farnham, Thomas Jefferson, 1804-1848, ??? 3420, 3421, 16495-16497
Farnsley, Alexander Pericles, 1832-1896, 14073
Farnsley, Charles Peaslee, 1907-, 15090

15126
Farnsley, Sally, 1938-, 14073
Farnsworth, John Franklin, 1820-1897, 24375
Farquhar, E.F., 14801
Farquhar, John, 6705
Farragut, David Glasgow, 1801-1870, 1547
Farrar, C.C.S., 2223
Farrar, Eliza Ware (Rotch) "Mrs. John Farrar." 1791-1870, 2224
Farrar, Nathan, 24376
Farrar, Timothy, 1747-1849, 11858
Farrar, Timothy, 1788-1874, 2225, 2226
Farrar, Victor John, 1886-, 16498
Farrar family, 2225
Farrell, Edward P., 14074
Farrell, Ned E., 16499
Farrington, Edmond F., 14075
Farrington, Frank, 1872-, 6706, 6707
Farrington, Oliver Cummings, 1864-, 6708
Farrow, E.A., 16500
Farrow, Henry Pattillo, 2227
A farewell sermon of Mr. Thomas Hooker, 12882
Farewell sermons, 12882, 13243
Farwell, W.B., 2229
The fashion of this world, 8838
The fashion of this world passeth away, 10816
Fashion's analysis, 1416
Fashionable life, 9458
Fashionable watering places, 14242
Fast, Edward Gustavus, 2231
Fast and loose in Dixie, 3294
Fast day sermons, 2230, 22557, 22797, 24377
A fast life on the modern highway, 10930
A fast old widow, 13565
Fasts and feasts, Massachusetts (colony), 21784
The fatal feud, 10590
The fatal gift of beauty, 4985
The fatal letter, 9815
The fatal plot, 10950
The fatal secret, 9498
The fate of a fool, 9287
The fate of blood-thirsty oppressors, 11817
The fate of Franklin, 1376
The fate of Mansfield Humphreys, 11147
The fate of Marcel, 9738
The fate of the Union, 10826
Fate's mysteries, 9037
The father, 10762
Father Boyle, 10747
"Father Clark," or, The pioneer preacher, 23487
Father Drummond and his orphans, 9461
Father Henson's story of his own life, 24551
Father Ignatius in America, 3180
Father Mathew: a biography, 23028

Father Merrill, 8976
Father Rowland, 10531
Father Ryan's poems, 5056
Fathers (Roman law), 24256
The fathers of New England, 1755
The fathers of our republic, 7832
The fathers of the New-Hampshire ministry, 11416
Fauche, Pierre François, 2232
Faucher de Saint-Maurice, Narcisse Henri Edouard, 1844-1897, 6709, 6710
Faulconer, J.B., 14076
Faulhaber, Johanna, 20368
Faulkner, Charles James, 1806-1884, 6711, 22735, 25810
Faulkner, Thomas C., 2233
Fauna boreali-americana, 4956
Fauquier, Francis, 1747-1768, 6712, 11621
Fausett, Thomas, d.1820?, 16658
Faust, Albert Bernhardt, 6713, 6714
Faustino, 19823
Faustino I, emperor of Haiti, 1789?-1867, 6583
Faux, William, 2234, 14077
Favill, Josiah Marshall, 3422
Favor libertatis, 25241
The favored of the gods..., 15383
Favorite recipes, 14856, 15049
Favorite recipes of Logan County Home-makers, 14842
Favorites, Royal, 12802
Fawcett, Benjamin, 1715-1780, 24378
Fawcett, Joseph W., 3423
Fawkes, Guy, 1570-1606 - Fiction, 9463
The fawn of the pale faces, 8835
Fay, Cyrus H., 2235
Fay, George Emory, 1927-, 6715
Fay, Heman Allen, 1779-1865, 2236
Fay, Herbert Wells, 6716
Fay, John D., 1897
Fay, Jonas, 1737-1818, 162
Fay & Davison, Rutland, jt. pub., 23622
Fayette County Bar, Lexington, Ky., 14078, 14079, 14379
Fayette County, Ky., 14080, 14783; History, 13791, 15359, 15547; Maps, 13646, 14787, 14815, 14953, 14954; Politics and government, 14489
Fayetteville, Ark., History, 17137
Fayetteville, N.C. Bluff church, 22908
A fearful responsibility, 9943
Fearon, Henry Bradshaw, b.ca.1770-, 3424, 24379
Fears, Jesse, 15366
The feast of the cranberries, 10298

Featherstonhaugh, George William, 1780-1866, 2237-2239, 3425, 12139
The feats and intrepidity of Colonel Harper, 10570
Federação da Agricultura do Estado da Bahia, 20420
The federal government, 12254
Federal harmony, 1159
Federal Hill, Bardstown, Ky., 13538
The federal judiciary, 11305
Federal jurisdiction in the territories, 15991
Federal law, Quebec, 11883
Federal party, 71, 88, 553, 1349, 12693
Federal rules of evidence, Report of seminar on, 14670
Federal Writers' Project. Kentucky, 14080, 14081
The Federalist, 12140, 13178
The federati of Italy, 9404
Federic, José Luís. 19230
Federmann, Nikolaus, 16th cent., 22195
Federurbian, 12936
Fedric, Francis, 3426
Fee, Burritt, 14082
Fee, John Gregg, 1816-1901, 3427, 14082
The fee system in Kentucky counties..., 15638
Feed-water, 11717
Feeding and feeds, Argentine Republic, 18403; Great Basin, 16646
Feeling (short story), 10904
Feemster, Zenas E., 1813-, 3428
Feet of clay, 8724
The feet of love, 8495
Feindt, Waltraut, 19517
Felch, Alpheus, 1806-1896, 2240
Felice, Guillaume de, 1803-1871, 24380
Felice Cardot, Carlos, 19521
Felipa, 11207
Felipe de Jesus, Saint, d.1597, 23423
Feliú Cruz, Guillermo, 1901-, 24381
Felix, Elisa Rachel, 1821?-1858, 1024
Félix de Jésus María, father, 1706-1772, 6717
Fellow-citizens [of Kentucky], 13990
Fellowes, Gustavus, 9387
Fellows, John, 1759-1844, 2241, 13352
The fellowship of slave holders incompatible with a Christian profession, 24382
The Felmeres, 3364
Felsenhart, Jacques, 1826-, 2242
Felt, Joseph Barlow, 1789-1869, 2243-2247
Feltman, William, 2248
Felton, Cornelius Conway, 1807-1862, 2249
Felton, Franklin Eliot, 2250
Feltus, Henry James, 1775-1828, 13289
Female Anti-slavery Society of Salem, 24038

The female poets of America, 3699
The female prose writers of America, 3802
Female quixotism, 10933
The female rancher, 9295
The female review, 23085
The female spy, 8785
The female volunteer, 1295
Les femmes en Turquie, 25181
Femur fracture, 22798
Fenians (Society), 6038
Fenn, Harry, illustr., 8516, 13704
Fenning, Daniel, 3429
Fenollosa, Mrs. Mary (McNeil), 3430
Fenton, Reuben Eaton, 1819-1885, 24383
Fenwick, Edward Dominic, bp., 1768-1832, 14254
Ferguson, Adam, 1782-1862, 6718
Ferguson, Charles D., 1832 or 3-, 16501
Ferguson, Fergus, 1824-1897, 3431
Ferguson, James, 1710-1776, 22277
Ferguson, James Edward, 1871-1944, 16502
Ferguson, Jesse Babcock, 1819-1870, 24384
Ferguson, Joseph, 3432
Ferguson, Nora Young, 14083
Ferguson, Patrick, 1744-1780, 13515
Ferguson, Robert, 1817-1898, 3433
Ferguson, William, 3434
Ferguson's anecdotical guide to Mexico, 6719
Fergusson, D., 5539
Fermentación y refermentación del cacao cubano, 20061
Fermentation, 18350, 20061
Fermin, Philippe, 1720-1790, 24385
Fern, Fanny, pseud., 10476-10479
Fern leaves from Fanny's port-folio, 10476
Fernández, Enrique, 18102
Fernández, José, 1617-1674, 6725
Fernández, Práxedes, 1886-1936, 18102
Fernández Cabrera, Manuel, 6720
Fernández de Castro, Manuel, 1825-1895, 12141
Fernández de Guzmán, Félix, 6354
Fernández de Liébana, Juan, 6677, 6678
Fernández de Medrano, Sebastian, 1646-1705, 6721, 6722
Fernández de Saravia, Rosa, 7910
Fernández de Velasco, Diego, duque de Frias, 1754-1811, 7959
Fernández del Corral, Francisco, 6806, 7962, 7963
Fernández Duro, Cesáreo, 1830-1908, 16503
Fernández Encarnación, Felipe, 20229
Fernández Golfín y Ferrer, Luis, 1825-1889, 24386

Fernández Guardia, Ricardo, 6723, 6724, 8182
Fernández Mato, Ramón, 6726
Fernández Navarro, A., 7478
Fernández Tuneu, Raul, 19150
Fernando de Lemos, 3583
Fernando III, Saint, king of Castile and Leon, 1199?-1252, 8434
Fernando V el Católico, king of Spain, 1452-1516, 1200
Ferne Fleming, 5613
Fernon, Thomas Sargent, 6727
Fernow, Berthold, 14084
Ferns, Argentine Republic, 19857
Ferrando, Hugo J., 18713
Ferreira Badaro, Roberto, 18774
Ferreira da Silva, Virgolino, known as Lampeão, 1900-1938, 19875
Ferrer, Leonardo, 162301695, 6728
Ferrer de Couto, José, 1820-1877, 24387, 24388, 24593
Ferrill, London, 1789-1854, 13833, 15580
Ferris, Benjamin G., 3436
Ferris, Jacob, 12142
Ferris, John Alexander, 16504
Ferris, Warren Angus, 1810-, 3432, 15847
Ferro Machado, Juan, 6729
Ferrocarril central mexicano, 8211
Ferrocarril mexicano, 6815
Ferrocarriles nacionales de Mexico, 6730
Ferry, Gabriel, pseud., 6065
Ferry, Hippolyte, 16505
The fertile lands of Colorado, 16368
Fertility, Human, 20095
Fertility differences in Peru, 19207
Fertilization of plants, 20521
Fessenden, Mrs. Nathanael, d.1770, 22196
Fessenden, Thomas Green, 1771-1837, 12143
Fessenden, William Pitt, 1806-1869, 24309
Festival-day sermons, 6160, 7789
Festivals   Mexico, 20678
Festoons of fancy, 14834
Fettered for life, 8811
Fetus, circulation in the, 535
Le Feu-follet, 9156
A feudalist, 15423
Feuds, Kentucky, Eastern, 14396, 15261
Feuds and feuding,   Kentucky, 13744, 13745, 14844
Fever, 459, 903, 12102, 13132, 13753
Fewkes, Jesse Walter, 1850-, 16506, 16507
Feyjos de Sosa, Miguel, 6732
Ficklen, John Rose, 1858-1907, 16538
Fiction, theory of, 19184
Fleharty, Stephen F., 3439
Field, Charles D., 3440

Field, David Dudley, 1781-1867, 2251
Field, Henry Martyn, 1822-1907, 3441, 16508
Field, Joseph E., 3442, 16509
Field, M.C., 3443
Field, Maunsell Bradhurst, 1822-1875, 10009, 12502
Field, Stephen Johnson, 1816-1899, 16510
Field, Thomas P., 8385, 14086-14089, 14876
Field, William H., 13567
Field, camp, hospital and prison in the civil war, 3966
Field, forest, and garden botany, 22268
A field manual of Kentucky fishes, 13849
Fielder, E.D., 16511
Fielder, Herbert, 24389
Fielding, Mrs. Harriet Chapin (Root), 1847-, 16512
The fiend's delight, 8802
La fièvre jaune à la Habane, 1128
Fifteen days, 10581
Fifteen minutes around New York, 9545
Fifteen years in Canada, 12749
Fifteen years in the senior order of Shakers, 12013
Fifteen years on the hurricane deck of a Spanish pony, 17624
Fifty Ohio rarities, 1653-1802, 15000
Fifty years a detective, 16569
Fifty years among authors, 3234
Fifty years and over of Akron and Summit county, 16976
Fifty years as a presiding elder, 13789
Fifty years in both hemispheres, 4611
Fifty years in camp and field, 16786
Fifty years in Iowa, 16106
Fifty years in Oregon, 16585
Fifty years of slavery in the USA, 5196
Fifty years' observations of men and events, 16942
Fifty years on the Mississippi, 3654
Figg, Royall W., 3444
Figgins, Jesse Dade, d.1944, 14090
The fight, 9216
The fight for Canada, 8412
The fight for the Union, 2314
The fight in the tree-bridge, 14832
A fight with distances, 2570
The fight with France for North America, 6148
Fighting and drinking were county fair features a century ago, 13528
The fighting Quakers, 11993
Figueiredo, Affonso Celso de Assis, 24011

Figueiredo, Pedro José de, 1762-1826, 21777
Figueroa, Pedro Pablo, 1857-1909, 6734
Figueroa Domenech, J., 6733
Figuras cubanas, 19532
Figuras e fatos da nobreza brasileira, 21739
Figuras y episodios de la historia de Mexico, 18224
The figure in the carpet, 7118, 10012
The figures or types of the Old Testament, 23335
Filcher, Joseph Adams, 16513
El filibustero, 19968
Filisola, Vicente, 16514
The fille de chambre, 10680
Fillmore, Millard, pres. U.S., 1800-1874, 868, 24390, 24656
Fillmore, Fort, N.M., History, Civil war, 17103
Fillmore Co., Minn., Description & travel, 11278; History, 11278
Films and filmstrips, Appalachia, 13558
La filosofía de la historia de Arnold J. Toynbee, 19044
Filosofía del derecho constitucional, 19058
Filosofía dos pára-choques, 18169
La filosofía en Argentina actual, 19992, 19993
Los filósofos modernos en la independencia latinoamericana, 19769
Filson, John, 1747?-1788, 3445, 6446, 14034, 14091, 14424, 15374, 15577, 15745
Filson Club, Louisville, Kentucky, 14092, 14093, 14326, 15301, 15526, 15577
The Filson Club and its activities..., 15299
Filteau, Gérard, 6735
Final de juego, 20529
Finance, 21972; Argentine Republic, 18501, 18797; Brazil, 18322, 18785, 18834, 19370, 19373; Chile, 18724, 20125, 20150, 20153; Confederate States of America, 11659; Great Britain, 1537; Great Britain, History, 13499; Kentucky, 15638, 15639; Latin America, 18715; Massachusetts, 2245, 2269, 22087; Mexico, 1217, 6756, 8423; New York (State), 22898; Peru, 18841; Puerto Rico, 7768; Spain, 5864; U.S., 2379, 7432, 11685, 12229, 13488, 11796, 16504, 23764, 23816, 24877; U.S., History, 1244, 22890; Venezuela, 20646, 22162
Finance, Public, Argentine Republic, 18426; Charleston, S.C., 11745; Chile, 18337, 20119; Dominican Republic, 18684; U.S., To 1789, 12187; U.S., 1789-1800, 12187, 12188
Financiación pública del transporte, 20455
Financial and political affairs of the country, 24165
The financial economy of the United States

Fisher, Thomas Jefferson, 1812-1866, 15431
Fisher, Walter Muirea, 1849-1919, 5996, 16518
Fisher's Landing, Minnesota, 17750
Fisher's river, N.C., 10922
Fisher's river scenes and characters, 10922
Fisheries, 18078; Argentina, 18453, 18798; Canada, 11331; Ecuador, 19199, 20224, 20225; El Salvador, 18924; History, 22986; Kentucky, 13574; Kentucky, Bibliography, 14560; Nova Scotia, 6575; Peru, 19170
The fisher-mans calling, 23301
Fishermen, 23301
Fishery law and legislation, Peru, 18948
Fishes, 2409; Atlantic coast, 12246; Caribbean Sea, 18866; Cuba, 20668; Ecuador, 20225; Florida, 3839; Illinois, 15113; Kentucky, 13849, 14358, 14557, 14559, 15111, 15113, 15375; Kentucky, Bibliography, 14560; New York (State), 1909; North America, 4936, 22420; Ohio river, 4882; Peru, 19170; Reproduction, 20192; Sicily, 15229; Trinidad, 12247
The fishes of west Kentucky, 15375
Fishin' Jimmy, 10790
Fishing, 12257, 16545; Adirondack mountains, 10398, 22380; Florida, 2495, 3094, 3759, 5001; Kentucky, 14311, 14561, 14785; Massachusetts, 22547; New York (State), 12630, 12631; North America, 4216, 4936, 7240, 22420; South Carolina, 3369, 5871, 12048; U.S., 3758, 10571; W. Va., 4157
Fishing and boating in Kentucky, 14559
Fisk, James Liberty, 3455, 3456, 5535
Fisk, John M., 25856
Fisk, Theophilus, 24397
Fisk, Wilbur, 1792-1839, 22524
Fiske, Amos Kidder, 1842-1921, 6739
Fiske, Asa Severance, 3457
Fiske, John, 1842-1901, 6740, 6741
Fiske, Nathan Welby, 1798-1847, 22599
Fiske, Theophilus, 25105
Fitch, Abigail Hetzel, 16519
Fitch, Anna M., 9521
Fitch, Asa, 1809-1878, 11688
Fitch, Charles, 1804-1843, 24398
Fitch, Clyde, i.e. William Clyde, 1865-, 10283
Fitch, Franklyn Y., 16520
Fitch, Graham Newell, 24025
Fitch, John, 1743-1798, 854, 14840

Fitch, John, 24399
Fitch, Joseph B., 14099
Fitch, Thomas, 1700-1774, 22511
Fithian, Philip Vickers, 1747-1776, 3458
Fitoplancton marino, 18713
Fitzgerald, James Edward, 6742
Fitzgerald, Oscar Penn, bp., 1829-1911, 3459, 3460, 16521
Fitzgerald, W.P., 24400
Fitzgerald and Hopkins, 10376
Fitzgibbon, Mary Agnes, 1851-1915, 6743
Fitz-Gubin, 10916
Fitzhugh, George, 1806-1881, 24401
Fitzhugh, Robert H., 6744
Fitzhugh, William Henry, 1792-1830, 24074
Fitz-Hugh St. Clair, the South Carolina rebel boy, 8970
Fitzpatrick, John Clemont, 1876-, ed., 5629
Fitzpatrick, Thomas, 3461-3463
Fitzroy, Robert, 1805-1865, ed. Narrative of surveying voyages of his Majesty's ships Adventure and Beagle, 18900
Fitzwilliam, N.H., History, Civil war, 2419
Fiury, Ed K., 6745
Five acres too much, 10671
Five and twenty years ago, 9874
Five Forks, Va., Battle of, 1865, 23747
Five hundred days in Rebel prisons, 3513
Five hundred dollars, 8971
Five hundred majority, 9969
"Five meals for a dollar," 10808
Five million endowment scheme, 14100
Five months' fine weather in Canada, 6330
Five months in rebeldom, 4455
Five o'clock in the morning, 9779
The five prisoners of Brandt at the massacre of Cherry valley, 10570
The five scalps, 3919
Five years a captive among the Black-Feet Indians, 3112, 16291
Five years a dragoon ('49 to '54) and other adventures on the great plains, 17060
Five years before the mast, 9829
Five years in Pennsylvannia, 12121
Five years in Texas, 4616
Five years in the West, 15840
Fix Zamudio, Héctor. Estudio sobre la juris-dicción constitutional mexicana, 19736
Flack, Captain, 3464, 3465, 16522, 16523
The Flag, 14101
Flagellants and flagellation, 25807
Flaget, Benedict Joseph, bp., 1763-1850, 5251
Flagg, Jared Bradley, 1820-1899, 3469
Flags Colombia, 19946; U.S., 4284, 12615, 22157, 25775
The flame in the wind, 13553

Flameng, Leopold, 1831-, illustr., 1123
Flanagan, James, 1820-1906, 14102-14108
Flandrau, Charles Macomb, 1871-1938,
6746
Flandreau, 9254
Flânerie parisienne aux États-Unis, 221
Flannigan, Mrs., 397
Flash, Henry Lyndon, 3470
Flats in Boston harbor, 23252
Flaubert, Gustave, 1821-1880, 7119
Flax, 1818; Argentine Republic, 20545
Fleeing from fate, 10394
Fleeing to Tarshish, 10250
Fleenor, Creedmore, 14109
Fleming, James T., 14523, 14524
Fleming, Sir Sandford, 1827-1915, 6747-
6749, 7457, 16138
Fleming, Walter Lynwood, 1874-, ed.,
15413
Fleming, William Henry, 1856-, 24402
Flemingsburg, Ky., History, Military,
14101
The Flemmings, 9414
Flesh and spirit, 9179
Fletcher, Charles H., 16524
Fletcher, Daniel Cooledge, 16525
Fletcher, John, 24403
Fletcher, John William, 1729-1785,
12089
Fletcher, Richard, 1788-1869, 2449, 24006
Fletcher, Thomas, 24404
Fletcher, Thomas Clement, 1827-1899,
24405
Fletcher, William Andrew, 1839-, 3471
Fletcher, William S., 1828-, 16765
Fleurs d'été, 5362
Flexner, Anne Crawford, 14110
Flexner, Bernard, 1865-, 14111
The flight of Betsey Lane, 10041
The flight of the shadow, 9317
A flight to Mexico, 5965
A flight to the moon, 9551
Flint, Grover, 1867-1909, 6750
Flint, James, 3472, 14112
Flint, James, 1779-1855, 3479
Flint, Thomas, 1824-1904, 6751
Flint, Timothy, 1780-1840, 3473-3479,
4715, 5677, 14113, 16526
Flinter, George Dawson, d.1838, 2252,
24406, 24922
Flip, 9780
Flippin, John R., 6752
The flirtations of a beauty, 10201
Flirtin' with fashion, 9888
Floods, and ebbs of Lake Ontario,
12239

A flor e o fruto, 19165
Flora de las ciénagas de Cuba, 18018
Flora McDonald, 10172
Flora of the British West Indian islands,
12452
Flora virginica, 3703
Flora's festival, 22437
Florae columbianae prodromus, 1480
Floral home, 1352
Floreana, Paraiso infernal, 19482
El florecimiento de Mexico, 8233
Florence Bardsley's story, 9510
Florence Dalbiac, 11010
Florence de Rohan, 11188
Florence, S.C. Military prison, 3279, 4145,
4476
Florence, the parish orphan, 10178
Florencia, Francisco de, 1619-1695, 6753,
6754
Florerías, 18158
Flores, José Manuel de, 7405, 7406
Flores svmmarvm, 5870
Floriculture, 8706, 8708, 13252
Florida, 1990, 2253, 2270, 2557, 2612, 3172,
3182, 3247, 3295, 3482, 3813, 4962, 5146,
5690, 5718; (C.S.A. steamer), 2051;
Antiquities, 1529; Bibliography, 11323;
Climate, 4161, 4253; Commissioner of lands
and immigration, 2253, 3480-3483;
Constitution, 2254; Convention, 1861-1862,
2254; Description & travel, 2662, 2707, 2714,
2817, 2819, 2841, 2909, 3031, 3094, 3095,
3128, 3138, 3180, 3251, 3348, 3360, 3390,
3480, 3481, 3483, 3484, 3486, 3514, 3579,
3693, 3722, 3759, 3778, 3838, 3876, 3979,
4018, 4038, 4135, 4146, 4173, 4214, 4375,
4580, 4624, 4633, 4656, 4976, 5001, 5012,
5291, 5295, 5353, 5435, 5450, 5572, 5625,
5689, 5747, 5762, 11532, 12024, 15527,
23553, 23798; Description & travel,
Gazetteers, 3814; Description & travel,
Guide-books, 2802, 4239, 4619, 4652, 4889,
4941, 5696; Economic conditions, 3674, 3692;
Fiction, 3656; Finance, 17580; History,
1529, 2206, 5572, 5718; History,
Bibliography, 1529; History, Civil war,
8940; History, Colonial period to 1821,
2205, 3172, 4172; History, Colonial period
to 1821, Sources, 2332; History, Huguenot
colony, 1562-1565, 408, 768, 4226, 7268;
History, Huguenot colony, 1562-1565,
Fiction, 5162; History, Societies, 2255;
History, Spanish colony, 1565-1763, 5228,
20610; History, Spanish colony, 1565-1763,
Sources, 3066; Politics & government,
Civil war, 2254; Social conditions, 3692;

Social life & customs, 3410
Florida Alexander, 10139
Florida as a permanent home, 4038
Florida as it is, 5146
Florida days, 3219
Florida enchantments, 3251
Florida facts both bright and blue, 3128
Florida for tourists, invalids, and
  settlers, 2612
The Florida gazetteer, 3814
Florida historical society, Saint
  Augustine, 2205, 2255
Florida. Its climate, soil and
  productions, 3480-3482, 3484, 3514
Florida: its history, condition, and
  resources, 3295
Florida: its scenery, climate, and
  history, 4214
The Florida of to-day, 3182
The Florida pirate, 2256
The Florida railway and navigation
  company, 3485
The Florida reef, 9135
The Florida settler, 3483
A Florida sketch-book, 5435
Florida state historical society,
  4862
Florida, the Italy of America, 3486
Florilegio medicinal de todas las
  enfermedades, 6694, 6695
Flory, J.S., 16527
Flour, 1032, 1615
Flour-mills, 12100; Kentucky, 14143
The floure of souvence, 10404
Flournoy, John Jacobus, 2257, 12146,
  24407
Flower, Benjamin, 1755-1829, 16528
Flower, George, 1780-1862, 3487
Flower, George Edward, 1847-1884, 14062
Flower, Richard, 1761?-1829, 2258, 3488,
  14364, 16528
Flower de Hundred, 9766
The flower girl of London, 4737
A flower of France, 10687
The flower of Gala Water, 8725
Flower o' the quince, 9740
Flowers, 13252, 23281
Flowers and fruits from the wilderness,
  17233
Flowers from the battle-field, and other
  poems, 21836
The flowers of modern travels, 64
Flowers plucked by a traveller on the
  journey of life, 2075
Floyd, Charles, d.1804, 16529
Floyd, David Bittle, 3489

Floyd County, Ky., Description, 14116
Der Flüchtling, 4497
Fluorspar, 14117, 14173, 15670
Fluorspar deposits of Kentucky, 14117
The flush times of Alabama and Mississippi,
  707
Flute and violin and other Kentucky tales and
  romances..., 13529
Fluvia, Francisco Xavier, 1699-1783, 23480
The Flying Dutchman, 10693
The flying, gray-haired Yank, 3353
The flying regiment, 12351
Flying sparks, 17247
Flynt, Henry, 1675-1760, 2259
Foam of the sea, 8885
Fodere, M., 6755
The foe in the household, 8986
Foerste, August F., 14114, 14115, 14173,
  15037
Foes in ambush, 10119
Fogarty, Kate Hammond, 16530
Foght, Harold Waldstein, 16531
Fohs, F. Julius, 15116, 14117, 14173
Foibles of fancy and rhymes of the times,
  3280
Foiled, 9191
Foley, Daniel, 3490
Foley, Fanny, pseud., 2260
Foley, Thaddeus J., 16532
Folk art Ecuador, 18278; Mexico, 18584
Folk dance music, Brazilian, History and
  criticism, 18175
Folk dancing, Brazil, 18175, 19365;
  Guatemala, 18542
Folk medicine, 15155; Indian, 17342;
  Kentucky, 15525
Folk music, Brazilian, History and criticism,
  18175
Folk songs, 4692; Brazil, 19365; Chile, 18686,
  18878; El Salvador, 18821; French, 2369;
  French Canadian, 2369; Kentucky, 14400,
  14913, 14996, 15132, 15377, 15491, 15515;
  West Indies, 17954; Venezuelan, 18392,
  19833; Venezuelan, History & criticism,
  18392
Folk songs of the Kentucky Mountains, 14913
Folk tales of the Kentucky hills, 14178
Folklore, Argentine Republic, 18318, 20104;
  Brazil, Paraíba, 7685; Brazil, 19365,
  19874, 19900, 19976, 20551; Brazil,
  Theory, methods, etc., 19811; Canada, 6892;
  Ecuador, 19885; El Salvador, Cuzcatlán,
  18821; Kentucky, 14178, 14280, 14769,
  15155, 15513, 15525, 15531, 15535, 15728,
  15729; Mexico, 20364; Ohio Valley, 15525,
  15529; Paraguay, 19882; Study and teaching,

19883; Venezuela, 18006, 18393, 19754;
Venezuela, Addresses, essays,
lectures, 19770
Folklore, Bolivian, 18967
Folklore, Brazilian, 18174
Folklore, Indian, 2163, 17036, 17339
Folklore, Negro, 4106, 8189
Folklore, Venezuelan, 18008
Folklore: love: verse, 14397
Folklore del Paraguay, 19882
Folklore in Brazil, 19811
Folklore y educación, 19883
Folks from Dixie, 24319
Folks next door, 6517
Folkways of the Mammoth Cave region,
15729
Follen, Eliza Lee (Cabot) "Mrs. C.T.C.
Follen," 1787-1860, 2261
Follett, Frederick, 1804-1891, 22198
Follie, b.1761, 24408
"Following the drum"?, 17829
The following lines were occasioned
by the death of Miss Mary Hedges,
22199
Following the flag, 11864
Folsom, George, 1802-1869, 3491
Folsom, James Madison, 1838-, 2262
Folsom, Montgomery M., 1857-, 3492
Folwell, Richard, 1768?-1814, 2022
Fomento a las inversiones: Bolivia, 19117
Fomento industrial, 18414
Fondation d'une colonie française, 5415
Fondo Nacional de Caminos Vecinales de
Colombia, 19233
Fonemas del Baure con atención especial
a la supresión de la vocal, 18815
Fonerden, Clarence A., 3493
Fonseca, Fabian de, d.1813, 6756
Fonseca, Luiz Anselmo da, 1853-, 24409
Font, Pedro, 16533, 16534
Fontaine, Jacques, b.1658, 2263, 3494
Fontaine, W.M., 4418
Fontaine family, 2263
Fontenele, Raimundo, 18310
Food consumption, Argentina, Buenos
Aires, 18432
Food supply, Brazil, 20379; Chile,
20124
A fool of nature, 9808
A fool's errand, by one of the fools,
25713
The fool's opera, 2564
The foolish virgin, 24297
Foot, George, 10002 1967, 3264
Foot, Samuel Augustus, 1780-1846, 11240
Foot family, 2447

Foot's resolution, 1829, 11240, 12479, 23369,
23759
Foote, Andrew Hull, 1806-1863, 2265, 12147
Foote, Henry Stuart, 1804-1880, 2050, 3495-
3498, 24410, 24411
Foote, Henry Wilder, 1838-1889, 2266
Foote, John Parsons, 1783-1865, 2267
Foote, Thomas Moses, 1809-1858, 2268
Foote, William Henry, 1794-1869, 3499, 3500
Foote family (Nathaniel Foote, 1593?-1644),
2447
Footprints, Fossil, 22503
Foot-prints of an itinerant, 3554
Footprints of ancient communism, 16829
Footprints of the pioneers of the Ohio Valley,
5567
"For better, for worse," 10938
For honor's sake, 9275
For the major, 11206
For truth and freedom, 3644
Forage conditions on the northern border of
the Great Basin, 16646
Forage plants, California, 16107
Foraker act, 1900 (Puerto Rico), 20250
Foraminifera, Ecuador, 19135; Tamaulipas,
Mexico, 18647
Foraminifera, Fossil, 19015; Yucatan Peninsula,
19599
Foraminifera, Planctonic, 19133
Foraminíferos calcáreos uniloculares de
profundidades grandes del Atlántico Sur,
19134
Foraminíferos de la zona de manglar de
Guayaquil, 19135
Forbes, A trip to Mexico...,1849-
1850, 6757
Forbes, Abner, 2269
Forbes, Alexander, 1778-1862, 16535
Forbes, Alexander C., 24412
Forbes, Eugene, d.1865, 3501
Forbes, Harrie Rebecca Piper (Smith) "Mrs.
A.S.C. Forbes, 16536
Forbes, James Grant, 2270, 13000
Forbes, Robert Bennet, 1804-1889, 2271
Forbes-Lindsay, Charles Harcourt Ainslie,
1860-, 6758, 6759, 7417
A forbidden marriage, 10202
Force, Peter, 1790-1868, 2272, 2273, 11844
Force, William Quereau, 1820-1880, 462
Forces of change in Latin America, 20238
Ford, Guy Stanton, 16478
Ford, Henry Allen, 2274
Ford, Hiram Church, 1884-, 13593
Ford, Isaac Nelson, 1848-, 6760
Ford, John S., 16537
Ford, Lewis, b.1812, 24413

Ford, Paul Leicester, 1865-1902, 3502
Ford, Thomas, 12148
Ford, Worthington Chauncey, 1858-1941,
  ed., 6761, 6762
Ford, Camp, Texas, 4627
Fore and aft; or, Leaves from the life
  of an old sailor, 23494
The fore-room rug, 11162
A foregone conclusion, 9944
The Foreign enlistment act, 12230
Foreign exchange, 20033; Tables, etc.,
  23824
Foreign trade promotion, Colombia,
  Congresses, 20412
Foreign trade regulation, Chile, 18329
Foreign travellers in the south 1900-
  1950, 15527
Foreman, Anthony, 14118
Forest, Michael, 3508
The forest, 8380, 9975
Forest and prairie, 2675, 2676
Forest and shore, 9977
The forest bride, 10580
Forest conditions in Kentucky, 14244
The forest exiles, 23527
A forest hymn, 11592
Forest life, 10148
Forest life in Acadie, 6954
Forest life in Canada, 7528
The forest pilgrims, 1287
Forest products, 18802
The forest rose, 2677
Forest Retreat, 15153
Forest scenes and incidents, 6998
A forest tragedy, 10221
Forest trees of Kentucky, 14550, 14634
Forester, Fanny, pseud., 10084
The foresters, 1082
Forestier, A., illustr., 10894
Forestiers et voyageurs, 8149
Forests and forestry, Brazil,
  Bibliography, 20239; Chile, 18938;
  Colombia, 20302, 20303; Costa Rica,
  19476; Mexico, 19602; Kentucky,
  14244, 14390, 14550, 14565, 14598,
  14634, 14804, 15627
Forgiven at last, 11060
"The forgiving kiss", 10243
Formação de preços, 19620
Formación histórica de la nacionalidad
  brasileña, 7640
Formación social, moral y cívica, 19727
Las formaciones geológicas de Cuba, 19016
Formaciones vegetales de Colombia, 20303
Forman, Ferris, 1811-1901, 22635
Forman, Jacob Gilbert, 2275, 24414, 25024

Forman, Samuel S., 1765-1862, 3509
The formation of the state of Oklahoma, 16605
Formell Cortina, Francisco, 19559-19561
Forms (Law), Illinois, 13302; Maryland,
  22428; New Hampshire, 11755; Orleans (Ter.),
  16940; U.S., 1001
Forms, Legal, Brazil, 19863
The forms in issuing letters patent by the
  crown of England, 22061
Forney, John Wien, 1817-1881, 3510
Forrest, Archibald Stevenson, illustr, 7006
Forrest House, 3914
Forrest, Michael, 3511
Forrest, Nathan Bedford, 1821-1877, 2698,
  4540, 5778
Forrest, Thomas, 926
Forrest's cavalry corps, C.S.A., 4540
Forrestal; or, The light of the reef, 4004
Forry, Samuel, 1811-1844, 12149
Forster, Georg, 1754-1794, 344
Forster, Johann Reinhold, 1729-1798, 7171,
  7172, 12150
Forster, William Edward, 1818-1886, 2276
Forsyth, J., 7460
Forsyth, John, 1780-1841, 24416
Forsyth, John, 1812-1877, 24417, 24418
Forsyth, Thomas, 25322
Fort Berthold Agency in 1869, 17706
Fort Boonesborough, 14942
Fort Braddock letters, 8841
Fort Buford, 16946
Fort Duquesne, Pa., 16330
Fort Knox, Ky., 15625
Fort Lafayette, 11197
"Fort-La-Fayette life," 2277
Fort Lincoln State Park, 17459
Fort Pitt, Pa., 16330
Fort Pitt and letters from the frontier,
  16330
"Fort Reno," 16448
Fort Scott, Kans., 16609
Fort Sumter, 8237
Ft. Thomas Ky. Highland Methodist Church,
  14119
Fort Totten Trail, 17707
Fortenbaugh, Robert, 1892-, 6763
Fortier, Alcée, 1858-1914, 3512, 16538
Fortieth anniversay of the statehood of
  Oregon, 17311
Fortification, 834, 23121, 23031
A fortnight of folly, 5389
Fortress Monroe, 11194
Fortuna, J., illustr., 18204
The fortunate discovery, 9542
Fortune, Alonzo Willard, 14120
Fortune, William, 1863-, 15304

The fortune of war, 8749
The fortune teller, 10921
The fortune-teller of New Orleans, 4735
Fortune's foot-ball, 24067
The fortunes and misfortunes of an
orphan, 8701
The fortunes of an Irish girl in New
York, 10271
The fortunes of Mr. Mason's successors,
10431
The fortunes of Rachel, 9679
Forty etchings, 3733
'49, the gold-seeker of the Sierras,
10353
Forty-one thieves, 16664
Forty years a fur trader on the upper
Missouri, 16990
Forty years a gambler on the Mississippi,
3240
Forty years among the Indians, 16901
Forty years' familiar letters of James
W. Alexander, 2503
Forty years in Canada, 8106
Forty years of American life, 4603
Forty years of oratory, 5587
Forward, Walter, 2278
Forwood, William H., 17777
Forwood, William Stump, 1830-, 14121
Fosdick, Charles, 3513
Fosgate, Blanchard, 2279
Foss, James H., 3514
Foss, John, 24419
Fossett, Frank, 16539
Fossey, Mathieu de, comte, 1805-, 6764,
6765
Fossil mammals, Argentine Republic,
20527
Fossils, 18209; Argentine Republic, 19918,
20526; Brazil, 19950; Cuba, 18566; Ky.,
14444, 15059, 15067; Pará, Brazil,
19496
Fossils, Marine, South Atlantic, 19134
Fossils in western Utah, 15948
Fossils of the Ordovician time period,
15949
Foster, Benjamin Franklin, 2280
Foster, C., 2281
Foster, Charles, ed., 3515
Foster, Daniel, 2282
Foster, Edmund, 1752-1826, 2283
Foster, Ephraim Hubbard, 1795?-1854,
2284
Foster, Ethan, 2285
Foster, George G., d.1850, 16540
Foster, Henry H., 14667
Foster, James S., 1828-1890, 16541

Foster, John Gray, 1823-1874, 13024
Foster, John Watson, 1836-1917, 6766, 6767
Foster, John Wells, 1815-1873, 12151, 22200
Foster, John Young, 22201
Foster, Lillian, 2286, 22202
Foster, Robert S., 1834-1923, 8040
Foster, Stephen Collins, 1826-1864, 7154,
14123-14127, 13538, 15705
Foster, Stephen Symonds, 1809-1881, 24420,
25275
Foster, William, 1772-1863, 2287
Foster Hall, 14122
Fothergill, 10852
Fothergill, John, 1676-1744, 3516, 12152
Fothergill, John, 1712-1780, 2288
Le fou de Palerme, 4450
Foulke, William Parker, 2289
Found and lost, 10298
Found at Blazing Star, 9780
Found yet lost, 10653
Foundations, 10554
The founder of New France, 6443
The "founders of the republic" on slavery,
11751
Founding (iron), 18512
The founding of Harrodsburg, 14426
The foundling of the Mohawk, 9294
Fountain, Paul, 3517, 6768
The fountain and the bottle, 2290
The four acts of despotism, 23033
The four great powers, 11467
Four Indian kings, 2291
The four kings of Canada, 2291
Four miles up Kentucky River, 14460
Four months among the gold-finders in Alta
California, 17833
Four months in a sneak-box, 2723
Four months in Libby, 4077
Four months in North America, 2973
Four months with Charles Dickens, 4868
Four roads to happiness, 9272
The four silver peaches, 10046
Four weeks in the Rebel army, 4689
Four years among Spanish-Americans, 22335
Four years in a government exploring
expedition, 11867
Four years in rebel capitals, 3222
Four years in the Rockies, 17136
Four years in Secessia, 2839, 4159
Four years in the saddle, 3609
Four years in the Stonewall brigade, 2935
Four years of fighting, 3041
Four years of personal reminiscences of the
war, 4390
Four years on the firing line, 4608
Four years' residence in the West Indies, 986

174

Four years with five armies, 3580
Four years with Morgan and Forrest, 2698
Four years with the Army of the Potomac, 5461
Fourcroy, Bonaventure de, 1610(ca.)-1691, 24421
Fourier, François Marie Charles, 1772-1837, 1530
Fournel, Henri Jérôme Marie, 1799-1876, 2292
Foursin, Pierre, 6769
Fourteen hundred and 91 days in the Confederate army, 3828
Fourteen months in American bastiles, 2463
Fourteen months in southern prisons, 3181
A fourth letter to the people of England, 23606
The fourth of July, 1776, 10218
Fourth of July celebrations, 528, 1876
Fourth of July in Jonesville, 10163
Fourth of July orations, 49, 65, 66, 79, 154, 155, 392, 453, 559, 561, 562, 565, 567, 721, 743, 746, 747, 748, 753, 800, 803, 814, 815, 823, 898, 904, 935, 1208, 1255, 1259, 1319, 1390, 1392, 1453, 1501, 1772, 1800, 1801, 1813, 1822, 1870, 1874, 1989, 2014, 2146, 2250, 2327, 2535, 3478, 11339, 11401, 11558, 11593, 11631, 11644, 11720, 11729, 11798, 11810, 11832, 11929, 11958, 12009, 12107, 12205, 12242, 12270, 12314, 12314, 12356, 12389, 12391, 12411, 12445, 12506, 12579, 12590, 12611, 12632, 12808, 12810, 12870, 13014, 13136, 13137, 13172, 13736, 14317, 15283, 21797, 22001, 22043, 22133, 22159, 22189, 22415, 22537, 22614, 22665, 22669, 22784, 22949, 22973, 23023, 23054, 23065, 23088, 23242, 23383, 23384, 23962, 24105, 24550, 24930, 25054, 25245, 25385, 25621, 25742
Foville, Alfred de, 1842-, 7494
Fowler, Henry, 21876
Fowler, Ila (Earle) 1876-, ed., 13969, 14128
Fowler, Philemon Holsted, 1814-1879, 3518
Fowler, Reginald, 2293
Fowler, Smith W., 1829-1894, 16542
Fowler, William, 1839-1874, 3518
Fowler, William Chauncey, 1793-1881, 2294, 12153
Fowler, William Worthington, 1833-1881, 2295

Fox (steam yacht), 22807
Fox, Charles, 2296
Fox, Charles Barnard, 1833-1895, 12154
Fox, Charles James, 1749-1806, 2307, 11616
Fox, Charles James, 1811-1846, 2297
Fox, Early Lee, 1890-, 24422
Fox, Ebenezer, 1763-1843, 12155
Fox, Elma, 14129
Fox, Frances Barton, 13567
Fox, George, 1624-1691, 2298-2300, 3519
Fox, James D., 3520
Fox, Jesse W., 3521
Fox, John William, 1862-1919, 3522, 13561, 14130, 14131, 14132, 14133, 14216, 15023, 15026, 15104
Fox, Luke, 1586-1635, 2301
Fox, Mrs. Margaret (Askew) Fell, 1614-1702, 3519
Fox, Oliver E., 14133
Fox, Simeon M., 1842-, 3523
Fox, Thomas Bayley, 1808-1876, 2302
Fox, William Henry, 10737
Fox family, 11986
Fox-hunting, 15309, 15657
Fox Indians, 16108, 16634
Fox's martyrs, 2307
Foxcroft, Thomas, 1697-1769, 2303-2306, 12156, 21890
Fra Amerika, 2947
Fracker, George, 2308
Fractures, 13304
Fraga, Clementino, 1881-1971, 19061
A fragment, 9530, 11194
The fragment; or, Letters & poems, 23351
A fragment on government, 1181
Fragments of the history of Bawlfredonia, 1914
The 'fraid cat, 25023
Framingham, Mass., History, 720
Frampton, John, fl. 1577-1596, 23441
Från Förenta Staterna; nitton bref jemte bihang, 3831, 14300
Från Hawaiis ständer till New-Yorks sky-skrapor, 3619
Från nya verlden, 2661
Un Français en Amérique, 5441
France, George W., 16543
France, Lewis B., 1833-1907, 16544, 16545
France, 3229; Chambre des députés, 1814-1848, 25069, 24423; Chambre des pairs, 1814-1848, 25069; Colonies, 1180, 11970, 23919, 24327; Colonies, Administration, 146, 11711, 24425, 25556; Colonies, America, 23059; Colonies Antilles, 6003, 6326, 6533, 6770, 6772, 6896, 6897, 7395, 7815, 8052; Colonies, Antilles, Politics & government, 7395, 7738; Colonies, Antilles, Revolution,

8317; Colonies, Bibliography, 25196;
Colonies. Citoyens de couleur, 6770;
Colonies, Commerce, 6643, 6650;
Colonies, Guiana, 1831, 24176, 24803;
Colonies, Labor and laboring classes,
24428; Colonies, Louisiana, 5229;
Colonies, North America, 4502; Colonies,
Politics & government, 8144; Colonies,
Saint Dominique, 23050; Colonies,
Santo Domingo, 19, 11235; Colonies,
Slavery, 24423, 244234 24428; Colonies,
West Indies, 24803, 25070; Commerce,
6643; Commerce, America, 11711; Commerce
U.S., 2805, 22184, 24784; Commercial
policy, 11711, 11970; Commission
coloniale, 24803; Commission des
affaires coloniales, 24424; Conseil
d'etat, 24425; Conseil général du
commerce, 6771; Constitution, 6778;
Constitutional law, 952; Description
& travel, 1832, 1834, 7207, 11440;
Etat-major de l'armée, 4124; Foreign
relations, 5824, 11466, 11467; Foreign
relations, Argentine Republic, 21761;
Foreign relations, Confederate States
of America, 2712; Foreign relations,
Great Britain, 2183, 22216, 23594,
23701; Foreign relations, South
America, 1588; Foreign relations,
U.S., 1868, 1917, 1934, 2364, 5841,
6773, 6774, 11712, 11927, 12251, 12298,
12801, 13410, 13495, 23459, 23701, 23919;
History, 3079, 6829; History, 1789-1815,
398, 3315, 11786; History, 1789-1815,
Fiction, 11029; History, Carolingian
and early period to 987, 23864; History,
Consulate and empire, 1799-1815, 23182;
History, Louis XIV, 1643-1715, Fiction,
6622, 9400; History, Louis XVI, 1774-1747,
2721; History, Louis Philip, 1830-1848,
2732; History, Medieval period to 1515,
Fiction, 9847; History, Occupation and
evacuation, 1871-1873, 3895; History,
Restoration, 1814-1830, 398; History,
Revolution, 366, 5952, 6003, 6477, 6484,
6533, 8317, 9532, 11522; History,
Revolution 1789-1791, 13441; History,
Revolution, 1789-1793, 11404; History,
Revolution, Causes and character, 11232;
History, Revolution, Fiction, 10365;
History, Revolution, Personal narratives,
777, 1532, 12088; History, Revolution,
Religious history, 6809; History, Second
empire, 1060 1070, 2006, History, Wars
of the Huguenots, 1562-1598, 59; Laws,
statutes, etc., 952, 997, 1201, 24425;

Laws, statutes, etc., 1643-1715 (Louis XIV),
24426; Laws, statutes, etc., 1774-1792
(Louis XVI), 6772; Laws, statutes, etc.
Code civil, 388; Ministère de la marine,
1109, 24428, 24803; Navy, 1949; Navy-lists
of vessels, 1757; Politics & government,
11765; Politics & government, Revolution,
1931, 12207, 23650; Relations (general) with
Colombia, 20242; Treaties, etc., 2183;
Treaties, etc., 1799-1804 (Consulate), 6773;
Tribunat, 6774
France and England in North America, 7692
France and the Confederate navy, 2712
France combattante, 18216
France in America, 8197
Frances Waldeaux, 9352
Francesco d'Assisi, Saint, 1182-1226, 17115
Franchère, Gabriel, 3524
Francis, Convers, 1795-1863, 2309, 12157
Francis, James Bicheno, 1815-1892, 2311
Francis, John Wakefield, 1789-1861, 12158-
12160
Francis, M.C., 10448
Francis, Samuel Ward, 1835-1886, 2312, 2313
Francis, Valentine Mott, 1834-1907, 2314
Francis Abbott, the recluse of Niagara, 1331
Francis & Haley, 2310
Francis Berrian, 3473
The Franciscan missions of California, 17206
Franciscans, 5885, 6775, 17704; Missions,
6468, 6775
Franciscans in Brazil, 22641
Franciscans in California, 16472, 16519,
17115, 17207, 17344, 17345
Franciscans in Chile, 2436, 7100
Franciscans in Mexico, 5828, 5829, 5874, 7096,
7811, 18185, 23420
Franciscans in New Mexico, 1145
Franciscans in Peru, 6468, 6775
Franciscans in Spanish America, 7918
Francisco, by W.L. Beard, 10448
Franck, Harry Alverson, 1881-, 6776, 6777
Francklin, Thomas, 1721-1784, 12161
Franco-German War, 1870-1871, Fiction, 7011
Frank, 24436
Frank, John Peter, 14668
Frank Finlay, 10197
Frank Forester's fish and fishing of the
United States and British provinces of
North America, 22420
Frank Leslie's illustrated newspaper, 6554
The Frank V. DeBellis collection, 19640
Frank Warrington, 9753
Franklin, Newman H., 14222
Frankfort, Ky., 14070, 14967, 15339;
Biography, 14071; Christian Church,

176

13966-14134; Description, 15406;
Description, Guide-books, 14081;
Frankfort Cemetery, 14461; History,
13967, 14071, 14135, 14458; Liberty
Hall, 14436
Frankfort, Paris and Big Sandy railroad,
13836
Frankfort's 175th anniversay, 14135
Franklin, pseud., 3526
Franklin, A.W., 2315
Franklin, Benjamin, 1706-1790, 28, 223,
2025, 2316-2320, 6778, 7511, 7832,
8176, 12162, 12268, 12851, 13223,
21950, 22192, 22204, 22984, 23128,
23701, 23769; Imprints, 12083
Franklin, Benjamin, 1812-1878, 14136
Franklin, Edward, 8815
Franklin, Emlen, 12163
Franklin, Sir John, 1786-1847, 434, 1116,
1117, 1433, 3528, 3529, 4955, 4956,
6058, 6195, 6449, 6870, 7652, 7984,
8050, 8123, 11582, 12560, 13428,
22556, 22846; Fiction, 10735; Poetry,
1376
Franklin, John Benjamin, 16546
Franklin, John Hope, 1915-, 6779
Franklin, Joseph, 1834-, 14136
Franklin, Tenn., Battle of, 1864, 3085
Franklin and Marshall College,
Lancaster, Pa., 2321, 12163
Franklin Baptist Association, Franklin
County, Ky., 15721
Franklin Co., Ky., Churches, 13968;
Description, 14447; History, 14135,
14458
Franklin Co., Mass., 12279
Franklin Co., N.Y., History, 22573
Franklin Co., Ohio, Biography, 23196;
History, 23196
Franklin Co., Vt., History, 5860
Franklin Institute, Philadelphia, 2322,
12268
Frankness, 10904
Fransioli, Joseph, 1817-1890, 12164
Fraser, Charles, 1782-1860, 3530
Fraser, Donald, 1755?-1820, 22205
Fraser, Eliza Anne, 12165
Fraser, Hugh C., 16547
Fraser, John Foster, 1868-1936, 6780, 6781
Fraser, Malcolm, illustr., 4567, 5192
Fraser, Mary (Crawford) d.1922, 16547
Fraser river mines, 7072, 7822
Frases íntimas, 19763
The frauds in Kansas illustrated, 25592
Frazee, George, 1821-1904, 24247
Frazee, Louis Jacob, 1819-1905, 3531

Frazer, Oliver, 1808-1884, 15197
Frazier, Elihu, 24247
Frazier, Thomas Neil, d.1887, 2323
Freaks and kings, 9533
Freaks of fortune, 10062
Fred, and Maria, and me, 10562
Fred Douglass and his mule, 10793
Frederica, the bonnet girl, 9980
Frederick, Francis, 1809?-, 3532
Frederick, Gilbert, b.1841 or 1842, 3533
Frederick de Algeroy, the hero of Camden
Plains, 9612
Frederick Louis, prince of Wales, 1707-1751,
23399
Fredericks, Alfred, illustr., 9805
Fredericksburg, Battle of, 1862, 1446, 22806
Fredericksburg, Va., History, Civil war, 3969
Frédeux, Pierre, 1897-, 6782
Frediani, Luis Maria, 19824
The Fredoniad, 3383
Fredonian insurrection, 1826-1827, 4715
Free and friendly remarks...by Henry Clay,
24429
A free and impartial examination of the
preliminary articles of pacification, 2324
Free at last, 9077
The free-born subject's inheritance, 11660
The free Britons memorial, 11334
Free Church of Scotland. General Assembly,
24430
Free collegiate education, 11595
Free Joe, 9747
The free Negro in Maryland, 1634-1860, 25931
Free negroes and mulattoes, Report,
23258, 24988
Free negroism, 24431
Free ports and zones, Brazil, Manaos, 19342,
19343; Mexico, 18068
Free Produce Association of Friends, of New-
York Yearly meeting, 24432
Free-soil party, 2398, 25174, 25543
Free-soil question, Address on the, 25098
Free Suffrage, pseud., 3534, 14140
Free thoughts, on the proceedings of the
Continental Congress, 23587
Free trade and protection, 2453, 4946;
Free trade, 797, 11505, 11618, 22094,
22368, 23760; Protection, 666, 1266, 2032,
2111, 2278, 11226, 11716, 12975, 15025,
21843, 21845, 21982, 22545, 23100, 23132
Free trade and sailors' rights, 2325
Free Will Baptists, 24433
Free, yet forging their own chains, 10658
The free booter's foe, 8614
The freed boy in Alabama, 25061
Freedley, Edwin Troxell, 1827-1904, 1356

Freedman, Gregory A., 14137, 14138
Freedman, John Joseph, 1835-1921, 12167
Freedmen, 1890, 6582, 24209, 24380, 24431, 24689, 25539, 25758; Ontario, 24758
Freedmen's affairs in Kentucky and Tennessee, 15612
The freedmen's book, 1890
Freedmen in Alabama, 25061
Freedmen in Italy, 25266
Freedmen in Maryland, 25931
Freedmen in Puerto Rico, 25323
Freedmen in Rome, 24632
Freedmen in the District of Colombia, 25781
Freedmen in the Southern States, 25673
Freedmen in Virginia, 25341
Freedmen in the West Indies, British, 24372
Freedom, 22833, 24928
Freedom and slavery, 24731
Freedom and slavery in the United States of America, 25146
The freedom of speech and writing upon public affairs considered, 11335
Freedom of the seas, 941
Freedom or slavery in the United States, being facts and testimonies for the consideration of the British people, 25507
Freedom's early sacrifice, 10765
Freedom's lyre, 24577
Freeman, Edward Augustus, 1823-1892, 3535, 22206
Freeman, Eugene Harrison, 3538
Freeman, Frederick, 1799-1883, 2327, 24434
Freeman, George D., 16548
Freeman, George Washington, bp., 1789-1858, 24435
Freeman, James, 1759-1835, 2328, 12168
Freeman, Mrs. Julia Deane, 3536
Freeman, Mrs. Julia Susan (Wheelock) 1833-1900, 3537
Freeman, Louise Barton, 15282
Freeman, Peyton Randolph, 1775-1868, 22207
Freeman, Samuel, 12169
Freeman, Warren Hapgood, 1844?-, 3538
A Freeman, 12798
Freeman's address to the North Americans, 2326
Freemantle, Sir Arthur James Lyon, 1835-1901, 3539
Free-masonry, 12166
Freemasons, 2241, 7230, 11664, 12181, 12425, 16543, 23175; Addresses, essays, lectures, 912, 1905, 3747, 6336, 12792, 12823, 12923, 13047, 13123; Bibliography, 2415; Biography, 6994; Boston, 12383; Boston. Columbian lodge, 22386; Directories, 13061, 13062; Fiction, 4530, 4533, 10387; Kentucky, 13734; Kentucky. Grand Lodge, 14139; Lexington, Ky., 13883; Louisville, Ky., 14270; Massachusetts. Grand lodge, 1276, 13036; New York (City) Holland lodge, no.8, 717; New York (State), 717; Pennsylvania. Grand lodge, 23022; Period, 23243; Philadelphia. Loge française l'Aménité, no.73, 21884; Poetry, 4532; Rhode Island, 12587, 22372; Rituals, 11257; U.S., Bibliography, 900; U.S., Directories, 13061
Freemen and soldiers of Kentucky, 14599
Freemen awake!, 24436
Freemen's ticket, 24437
Freeport, Andrew, pseud., 6783
Freese, Jacob R., 1826-1885, 2329
Freiberg, Lewis, 14141
Freight and stage lines in Dakota, 16043
Freiheit und sclaverei unter dem Sternenbanner, 3689
Der Freiheitsprozess im klassischen altertum, insbesondere der Prozess um Verginia, 24981
Freinthal, Käte, 8243
Freire de Andrade, Alfredo Augusto, 24438
Der Freischutz, 10693
Die Freistaaten von Nord-Amerika, 4310
Der freistaat von Nordamerika in seinem neuesten zustand, 2854
Freitag, Christina, 14142, 14143
Freitas, José Itamar de, 19217
Freitas de Acosta, Alecia, 16550
Frejes, Francisco, d.1845, 16551
Frelinghuysen, Frederick, 1753-1804, 2330
Frelinghuysen, Theodore, 1787-1862, 2331
Frémont, Donatien, 16552
Frémont, Jessie (Benton) 1824-1902, 12170, 16553, 16554
Frémont, John Charles, 1813-1890, 1273, 1371, 1591, 2926, 3540, 4504, 5406, 5552, 5660, 11842, 16360, 16554, 22208
French, Alice, 1850-1934, 8969
French, Benjamin Franklin, 1799-1877, 2332-2334, 3544, 12171
French, D'Arcy A., 16555
French, Edward, 10125
French, George, 12172, 22209
French, James Strange, 1807-1886, 3545
French, Jonathan, 1740-1809, 2335
French, Justus Clement, 1807
French, Leigh Hill, 1863-, 16556
French, Parker H., 4470

French, Samuel Gibbs, 1818-1910, 3546, 5547, 16557
French and German wine (John E. Madden's Notes on), 14932
French and Indians of Illinois river, 23350
French arrogance, 1934
French Canadians, 6769, 7525, 7841, 8129; Geneal., Dictionaries, 8153
French commerce and manufactures and negro slavery in the United States, 24784
French drama, 19029
French East-India-Company (Company of Mississippi), 3552
French Guiana, 680, 24743; Description & travel, 870, 13358, 23060, 25604; Economic conditions, 870, 1831; Exiles, 366, 11765, 13358
French in Canada, 12350
French in Haiti, 997
French in Illinois, 23350
French in North America, 6737
French in Pennsylvania, 4273
French in Texas, 5032
The French in the heart of America, 6737
French in the Mississippi Valley, 5586, 13501
French in the U.S., 16441
French language, Dictionaries, 19132; Algonquian, 13143; Maya, 7231; Mohawk, 11588; Study and teaching, curricula, 20602
French literature, 18th century, Addresses, essays, lectures, 21881; History & criticism, 19498
The French officer, 10434
French spoliations claims, 1844, 11490, 22820
The French village, 14343
The Frenchman and the bills of exchange, 10528
A Frenchman in America, 2741
The Frenchman's story, 9618
Freneau, Philip Morin, 1752-1832, 474, 4982
Fresadoras, 18117
A fresh catalogue of southern outrages upon northern citizens, 24439
Fresh leaves, 10477
Fresno county, Cal., 17689
Frewen, Moreton, 1853-, 16558
Freycinet, Louis Claude Desaulses de, 1779-1842, 421, 422
Freyre, Gilberto, 1900-, 18652, 19710
Freyreiss, Georg Wilhelm, 1789-1825, 24440

Freytas, Nicolas de, 3547
Frías, Agustín de, 1625-1698, 19855
Frías, Heriberto, 1870-1925, 19968; Leyendas históricas nacionales, 19968
Frias y Jacott, Francisco de, conde de Pozos Dulces, 1809-1877, 24441
Frick, William, 1790-1855, 2336
Fridy, Will, 14342
Friedlander, Julius, 24063
Friedrichsthal, Emanuel R., d.1842, 7917
Friend, Lierena, 1903-, 17909
Friend Barton's "concern", 9529
A friend of Caesar, 9366
Friend Olivia, 8726
A friend to the union, 25368
Friend's meeting, 9683
Friends, Society of, 1151, 1154, 1155, 2637, 3001, 3246, 3340, 3516, 3694, 3905, 3941, 4954, 5077, 5106, 5139, 5293, 5318, 5727, 5744, 5768, 12152, 12434, 21951, 23693, 24661, 25922; Baltimore yearly meeting, 12889; Boston, 10179, 10180; Collected works, 2959, 5769; Doctrinal and controversial works, 681, 1650, 1652, 1735, 2285, 2636, 2773, 12563, 13006, 21768, 23227, 23364, 23365; Epistles, 2299; (Hicksite), 22138; History, 5337, 25849; History, Revolution, 2154, 3614, 12427; Indiana Yearly Meeting, 4659, 24337; Lancaster County, Pennsylvania, 24244; London Yearly Meeting, 24442; Maryland 1650; New England, 2298, 23466; New England Yearly meeting, 4210, 24444; New Jersey, 23515; New York Yearly meeting, 4210, 24443, 24445; Nine Partners monthly meeting, 24451; Northwest, Old, 24868; Pennsylvania, 1448, 1652, 23638; Philadelphia monthly meeting, 5256; Philadelphia Yearly meeting, 2154, 24446-24449; Poetry, 23515; Rhode Island, 24580; Sermons, 22450
Friends and neighbors, 8562
Friends ashore, 10040
Friends of liberty, 24450
Friends of libraries, 14702, 15363
Fries, John, 1764?-1825, defendant, 2337, 11757, 21878
Fries rebellion, 1798-1799, 2337
Friese, Philip C., 2338
Frieze, Jacob, 2339, 2340
The frigate in the offing, 10432
Frignet, Ernest, b.1823, 16559
Frikel, Protásio, 19998
Frisbie, Barnes, 2341
Frisbie, Levi, 1748-1806, 22210
Fritsch, William August, 1841-, 3548
Frizon, Nicolas, d.1737, 1189

Frizzell, Mrs. Lodisa, 16560
Fröbel, Julius, 1805-1893, 3549, 6784
Frobisher, Sir Martin, 1535?-1594, 1201
Frogs, 15525
Froissart ballads, 3080
The frolic, 13861
A frolic among the lawyers, 10953
Fronde, Fiction, 9841, 10312
Frontera junto al mar, 19967
Frontier and pioneer life, 3452, 3731,
3955, 4951, 5412, 5460; Arizona,
15804, 16619, 16620, 16816; Arkansas,
4825; California, 15804, 16149, 17006,
17376, 17850, 17872; Colorado, 16333,
16891, 17493, 17591; Dakota, 16317;
Fiction, 2673, 2675-2678, 2680-2682,
2685, 3744, 3749, 3751, 3834, 4180,
4460, 4498-4990, 4992, 4993, 5061,
10134; Georgia, 10772; Idaho, 16620;
Illinois, 5765, 14314, 16828, 17156,
23528; Illinois, Pike Co., 2859;
Indiana, 9705, 16704; Iowa, 16154,
16431, 16828; Kansas, 12280, 12281,
16381, 16548, 17253, 17933; Kentucky,
3574, 4337, 8789, 13614, 14013, 14372,
15496, 15549; Kentucky, Fiction,
13889; Michigan 16268; Minnesota,
1352, 17401; Mississippi Valley, 2595,
3138, 4069, 12065, 10768, 22219;
Missouri valley, 16990; Montana,
16392, 17290, 17291; Nebraska, 15892,
16110, 16336, 16381; Nevada, 16067;
New Mexico, 16975, 17101; New York
(State), 10569, 11822; North Dakota,
16606, 17531; Northwest, Canadian,
17526; Northwest, Old, 16827; Northwest,
Pacific, 16543; Northwestern states,
16575, 16980, 17325, 17541; Ohio, 3352,
3450, 3954, 4367, 16645; Ohio, Richland
Co., Fiction, 10273; Ohio Valley, 2778,
2922, 3138, 3745, 4469, 5679, 12021,
15199, 15453, 22144; Ontario, 7527, 7528;
Oregon, 15861, 16905, 16937, 17487,
17850; Pacific states, 16033, 17602;
Pennsylvania, 13319; Poetry, 4718; Rocky
mountains, 17136; South Dakota, 17122,
17123; Scioto County, Ohio, 4169;
Southern states, 5558; Southwest, New,
15887, 16271; Southwest, New Fiction,
10863; Southwest, Old, 4726, 4801,
5411, 10964; Tennessee, 3668, 5723;
Texas, 4725, 5223, 7359, 15807, 16067,
16625, 16696, 16835, 16975, 17101,
17121, 17441, 17543, 17623, 17624,
17680; U.S., 4468, 14145, 15715, 16169,
17181; Utah, 16676, 17637, 17682;
Virginia, 22140; Washington (State), 16547;
The West, 2856, 4042, 4759, 5054, 7144,
15926, 15987, 16009, 16036, 16053, 16080,
16083, 16093, 16134, 16137, 16205, 16223,
16224, 16225, 16234, 16345, 16424, 16527,
16594, 16608, 16681, 16684, 16795, 16810,
16818, 16835, 16854, 16893, 16901, 16930,
16987, 16999, 17102, 17114, 17118, 17128,
17224, 17227, 17368, 17469, 17544, 17623,
17680, 17832; Wisconsin, 10141; Wyoming,
16153, 16473, 16997, 17673
The frontier hunter, 3834
Frontier life in Texas, 17121
The frontier missionary, 923
Frontier stories, 9781
Frontignières, fl., 1689, 22190
Frost, Arthur Burdett, 1851-1920, illustr.,
6591, 9006, 9581, 9916, 10895
Frost, Frederick J. Tabor, 5932
Frost, Griffin, 22211
Frost, James Marion, 1849-1916, 14144
Frost, Mrs. Jennett Blakeslee, 22212
Frost, John, 1800-1859, 2342-2344, 6785,
12173-12178, 14145, 14146, 16561, 16562,
22213, 22214
Frost, Joseph H., joint author, 4237
Frost, Mrs. Josephine C., 24451
Frost Argentine Republic, 19571
Frothingham, Frank E., 2345
Frothingham, Nathaniel Langdon, 1793-1870,
2346, 12179, 22912
Frothingham, Octavius Brooks, 1822-1895, 2347,
2348, 24452
Frothingham, Richard, 1812-1880, 2349, 2350
Froude, James Anthony, 1818-1894, 6786,
24453
Fruit, 2122, 12038
Fruit, Culture, Oregon, 16414; Southern
states, 11766; U.S., 2122, 12038
Fruit trade, Ecuador, 21723
Fruits Amazon Valley, 19999
Fruits of Mormonism, 5175
Frutas comestiveis da Amazônia, 19999
Frutos de mi tierra, 19829
Los frutos del tiempo, 18220
Fry, Benjamin St. James, 1824-1892, 12180
Fry, Edmund, 1754-1835, 2351
Fry, Emma V. Sheridan, 10127
Fry, F., 3551
Fry, James Barnet, 1827-1894, 2084, 14147
Fry, Joseph, 1826-1873, 8328
Fry, Joseph Reese, 1811-1865, 22215
Fryd, Norbert, 6787, 20700
Fuente, Beatriz de la, 6788
Fuentes, Bartolomé de, 17th cent., 7109,
16394

Fuentes y Guzmán, Francisco Antonio de, 1643 (ca.)-1699 or 1700, 6789
Fuentes para la historia de América, 18299
Fugate, George W., jr., 14148
Fugette, James Preston, 1825-1899, 24454
Fugitive lines, 5286
The fugitive of the seas, 4016
Fugitive recollections of an army girl of 1899, 16473
The Fugitive slave bill, 25777
Fugitive slave case, 24247
The fugitive slave law in Wisconsin, with reference to nullification sentiment, 24984
Fugitive slave law of 1793, 12366, 24114, 24412, 25770, 25810
Fugitive slave law of 1850, 1048, 1950, 2104, 2735, 22862, 23880, 23946, 23954, 23991, 24136, 24173, 24305, 24308, 24311, 24414, 24477, 24570, 24718, 24724, 24769, 24890, 24897, 24964, 24977, 24984, 25029, 25199, 25200, 25214, 25343, 25385, 25485, 25496, 25646, 25666, 25687, 25744, 25761, 25770, 25911
The fugitive slaves, 9665, 24933, 24977, 25501
Der Führer nach Amerika, 4662
Fullaondo, Jorge R.I., 18800
Fullarton, William, 1754-1808, 2354
Fuller, Arthur Buckminster, 1822-1862, 2358
Fuller, Daniel, 2355
Fuller, Henry Clay, 16563, 17050
Fuller, Henry Weld, 1810-1889, 2356
Fuller, Hiram, 1814?-1880, 2357
Fuller, Mabel Louise, 10283
Fuller, Melville Weston, 1833-1910, 16040
Fuller, Richard, 1804-1876, 22217, 24455-24457, 25538
Fuller, Richard Frederick, 1824-1869, 2358
Fuller, Robert, b.1795?, 2359
Fuller, Samuel, 1767-1842, 22218
Fuller, Samuel, 1802-1895, 22218
Fuller, Stephen, 13147
Fuller, Stuart Jamison, 25772
Fuller, Timothy, 1778-1835, 12181
Fuller family, 13594
Fullerton, A.M., Dr., 9331
Fullerton, T.M., 16564
Fulling mill, 14149
Fullner, G., 1103
Fullonton, Joseph, 2360
Fulmore, Zachary Taylor, 1846-, 16565

Fulton, Alexander R., 1825-1891, 2361, 16566
Fulton, Ambrose Cowperthwaite, 16567, 22219
Fulton, Frances I. Sims, 16568
Fulton, Hugh R., 6790
Fulton, James Alexander, 12182
Fulton, John, 6790
Fulton, John, 1834-1907, 24458
Fulton, Robert, 1765-1815, 2362, 11856, 14840; Fiction, 22341
Fulton family, 6790
Fulton, Ky., 14382, 15280; History, 14150; South Fulton Chamber of Commerce, 14150
Fulton Co., N.Y., 24692
Fun and earnest, 11000
Fun, frigates, and yachting, 10916
Fun-jottings, 11177
La función notarial en muestro medio, 18046
Funcionamiento del Registro Civil en Venezuela, 18178
O funcionário e o mandato eletivo gratuito, 19958
As funções urbanas da zona do mercado central de São Paulo, 17958
Fundação Brasileira para a conservação da natureza, 19441
A fundação de Santos, 19805
Fundación de Antofagasta y su primera decada, 20681
Fundación de estaño en Bolivia, 18943
Fundamentación de la Ley de la propiedad industrial y estudio de los derechos del inventor, 18710
La fundación de la república, 5923
Fundación Eugenio Mendes, 6794
Fundamentalism, 4937; Fiction, 3505
Fundamentos del trabajo con juventudes rurales, 21744
The funding system of the United States and of Great Britain, 12008
A funeral discourse, occasioned by the death of Rev. Andrew Gates, D.D., 21833
A funeral elegy, occasioned by the tragedy at Salem, near Boston, on Thursday afternoon the seventeenth of June, 1773, 22220
A funeral elegy upon the death of that excellent and most worthy gentleman John Winthrop Esq...., 22221
The funeral march of a marionette, 9741
Funeral music, 7058
Funeral music for 22d February, 7058
A funeral oration in memory of Mr. Jonathan Lyman, 702
A funeral oration on the character, life and public services of Henry Clay, 13550
Funeral rites and ceremonies, 15525, 23006; Peru, 6519

A funeral sermon on the death of Governor
Madison, 15387
Funeral sermons, 979, 1645, 1851, 5856,
6378, 6820, 7397, 8005, 8204, 12392,
13034, 13183, 22321, 22346, 22561,
22678
Funes, Gregorio, 1749-1829, 8026, 24095
Fünf wochen im osten der Vereinigten
Staaten und Kanadas, 3553
Fünfzehn jahre in Amerika, 4252
Funkhouser, William Delbert, 1881-1948,
14151-14157
The fur hunters of the far West, 5018
Fur in the hickory, 13830
Fur trade, 5017, 16350; Canada, 4362,
6228, 7886, 8000, 8256, 13397, 13411,
16394, 16989, 17048, 17095, 17251,
22924; Illinois, 16827; Manitoba,
17404; Michigan, 16827; Missouri
valley, 16990; Northwest, Canadian,
17859; Northwest, Pacific, 5018;
Northwestern states, 17541; Oregon,
3323, 4026; Pacific Northwest, 5526;
Rocky Mountains, 2689, 2823, 17136,
17859; Upper Mississippi, 17747;
Utah, 15882; The West, 3105, 4042,
4257, 15847, 16195, 16286; U.S., 5527;
Washington (State) 4641
Furber, George C., 6791
El Fureidis, 9274
Furlong, John James, 1816-1865, 15608
Furlong, Thomas, 1844-, 16569
Furlong Cardiff, Guillermo, 1889-, ed.,
17977, 18244
Furman, Gabriel, 1800-1854, 22222
Furman, Lucy, 1870-, 14158, 14159,
15515
Furman, Richard, 1755-1825, 24459
Furnas, Robert Wilkinson, 1824-1905,
16570, 17260
Furnas co., Neb., 15892
Furness, Henry B., 4031
Furness, William Henry, 1802-1896, 2363,
10521, 24460-24462
Furney, L.A., 5005
The furnished house, 9802
Furniture, New England, 2244
Furtado, André Freire, 20631
Furuna, José Kaoro, 19506, 19508
Fury (ship), 7696, 7697
Fuson, Henry Harvey, 1876-1964, 14160,
14161
Futch, Ladell J., 14162, 14163
Future glory of North America, 8050
Future life, 11100
The future of the country, 6792

Future punishment, 22591

G.A.R. Souvenir sporting guide, 14164
G.S. Isham's guide to California, 4032
Gabaldón Márquez, Joaquín, 17980, 17986,
18817
Gabb, William More, 1839-1878, 2365
El gabinete mexicano durante el segundo
período de la administracion del exmo.
señor presidente d. Anastasio Bustamante,
1760
The gable-roofed house at Snowdon, 9896
Gabriac, Alexis, comte de, 22223
Gabriel Vane, 10246
Gacetas de Caracas, 6793
Gacetas del gobierno del Perú, 6794
Gaddis, Maxwell Pierson, 1811-, 3554
Gadow, Hans Friedrich, 1855-, 6795
Gadsby, John, 1809-1893, 3555
Gadsden, Christopher, 1724-1805, 11448
Gadsden Purchase, 4545
Gage, Emma Abbott, 16571
Gage, Frances Dana (Barker) 1808-1884, 3556
Gage, Moses D., 3557
Gage, Thomas, 1603?-1656, 2366, 6796-6800
Gage, Thomas, 1721-1787, 2367
Gagern, Carlos de, 2368
Gagliardini, Elise Chenault Bennett, 14165
Gagnon, Ernest, 1834-1915, 2369
Gago de Vadillo, Pedro, 6801
Gaillard, Edwin Samuel, 1827-1885, 15786
Gaillardet, Theodore Frédéric, 1808-1882,
3558
Gaines, Edmund Pendleton, 1777-1849, 2370
Gaines, Joe, 14167
Gaines, Thomas S., 24463
Gaines, William H., 14168
'Gainst wind and tide, 14752
Gaither, Burgess Sidney, 1807-1892, 2049
Gaitskill, Laurence R., 14169
A gala dress, 9575
Galbreath, Charles Burleigh, 1858-1934,
24464-24466
Gale, Benjamin, 1715-1790, 2371, 12183,
12819
Gale, George, 1816-1868, 2372, 12184
Gale, Samuel, d.1826, 2373
Gale family, 2372
Gale family (Richard Gale, 1614-1678), 2372
Galena, Ill., History, 16188
Gales, Joseph, 1786-1860, 2374
Galibi Indians, 18555
Galindo y Villa, Jesus, 6802
Gall (Sioux Indian), 17705

Gall, Francis, 6803
Gall, James, 1784?-1874, 2375
Gall, Ludwig, 1791-1863, 3559
Gallagher, William Davis, 1808-1894,
  2376, 3560-3563, 3857
Galland, Isaac, 1790-1858, 12185, 16943
Gallatin, Albert, 1761-1849, 2377, 2378,
  12186-12188, 24467
Gallatin, James, 1796-1876, 2379, 2380
Gallatin County, Ky., History, 13682
Gallaudet, Thomas Hopkins, 1787-1851,
  831, 2381, 22224, 22598
Gallaudet's Picture defining and
  reading book, 2381
Gallegos, Estevan José, d.1787, 6804
Gallenga, Antonio Carlo Napoleone, 1810-
  1895, 3564
Gallinda y Villa, Jesus, 6805
Gallium antimonide, 21741
Gallo, Eduardo L., 6037
Gallo Sopuerta, Francisco, 6806
Gallo Villavicencio, Gertrudiz, 7321
El gallo de San Isidro, 19473
A gallop among American scenery, 5151
Gallotti, Luiz, 20516
Galloway, Joseph, 1731-1803, 2382-2384,
  11722, 12189-12293
Galloway, Juliet, 14170
Galloway, Robert E., 14171
Gallup map & supply co., 6807
The Gallynipper in Yankeeland, 3565
Galpin, Mrs., 10899
Galt, Sir Alexander Tilloch, 1817-1893,
  2385, 2286
Galt, John, 1779-1839, 2387
Galt, John Minson, 1818-1862, 2388,
  12191
The Galt House, Louisville, Kentucky,
  1869-1914, 14172
Galusha, Elon, d.1859, 25632
Galvan Rivera, Mariano, 6808
Galveston, Description, 3927
Galveston, Harrisburg and San Antonio
  Railway, 23927
Galveston Bay and Texas Land Company,
  3566
Gálvez, Juan de, 1750-1807, 6809
Gálvez, Matias de, 1717-1784, 8005
Galvin, J.J., 16796
Gamage, William, 1780-1818, 2389
Gambling, 660, 2882, 3240, 12397,
  15034, 23768; Kentucky, 13560, 14496;
  Unmasked!, 12397
Gamboa, Federico, 1864-, 6036
Game and game animals, Kentucky, 14557
Game and game birds, Kentucky, 14557;

North America, 4935
Game protection, 14557
Game water-birds, 23553
The gamesters, 10949
Gamio, Manuel, 1883-, 7483, 7484, 7486
Gammage, W.L., 3567
Gammell, William, 1812-1889, 12193
La ganadería en el oriente Venezolano y
  Guayana, 20477
Gandía, Enrique de, 1906-, 17977, 18244
Gan-Eden, 13041
Ganem, Mayesse Mahmud, 18322
Ganilh, Anthony, 22225
Gannett, Deborah Sampson, 1760-1827, 23085
Gannett, Ezra Stiles, 1801-1871, 11918,
  12194, 22226, 22227
Gannett, Henry, 1846-1914, 6524, 16572
Gannon, Clell G., 16573, 17460
Gannon, Frederic Augustus, 1881-, 6810
Gano, John, 1727-1804, 3568
Gano, Stephen, 3568
Ganong, William Francis, 1864-, 6290, 6575,
  7253
Gante, Pablo de, 6811
Gap copper mines, 22409
Garat, Aurelia C., 18831
Garay, José de, 1801-1858, 2390
The garb of the pioneer, 14372
Garber, Mrs. Virginia (Armistead), 6812
Garces, Francisco, 15846
Garcés, Francisco Tomás Hermenegildo, 1738-
  1781, 6813
Garces, Henrique, d.1591, 7739
García, José de Jesús Q., 7850
García Avila, Israel, 20676
García Calderón, Francisco, 1834-1905, 22228
García Calderón, Ventura, 1886-, 19852
García Camba, Andrés, 6814
García Carranza, Josefina, 18913
García Chuecos, Héctor, 18627
García Cubas, Antonio, 1832-1912, 6815-6819,
  7018
García de Escañuela, Bartholomé, bp., d.1684,
  6820
García de San Vicente, Nicolas, tr., 21953
García Figueroa, Francisco, 6604
García Gravados, Rafael, 6821
García Icazbalceta, Joaquín, 1825-1894,
  6388, 6389
García Mérou, Martin, 1862-1905, 3569
García Munévar, Alberto, 20336
García y García, Aurelio, 2391
Garcilaso de la Vega, el Inca, 1539-1616,
  12195
Garden, Alexander, 1757-1829, 662, 2392, 2393
The garden of dreams, 2950

183

The garden of the world, 3570, 16325
The gardener's calendar for the states of
  North Carolina, South Carolina, and
  Georgia, 23651
Gardening   Societies, 23282, 23283;
  U.S., 22971
Gardette, Charles Desmarais, 2394
Gardiner, Abraham Sylvester, 6822
Gardiner, Sir Christopher, fl.1630-
  1632, 8468
Gardiner, David, 1784-1844, 2395
Gardiner, George A., 2396
Gardiner, Lion, 1599-1663, 2397
Gardiner, Oliver Cromwell, 2398
Gardiner, Richard, 1723-1781, 2399
Gardiner, Walter Clarke, 12196
Gardiner, William Howard, 1797-1882,
  2400
Gardini, Carlo, 3571
Gardner, Charles Kitchell, 1787-1869,
  2401, 2402
Gardner, Daniel, 2403, 2404
Gardner, Frank Augustine, 1861-, 6823
Gardner, James H., 14173, 14174, 15686
Gardner, James Henry, 6824
Gardner, John, 12197
Gardner, John Lane, 1793-1869, 2405
Gardner, Richard, 1619?-1698, 12412
Gardner, Robert, fl.1845-1866, 17637
Gardner family, 12412
Gardner family (Thomas Gardner, d.1674),
  6823
Gardner, Mass.,   Geneal., 12283; History,
  12283
Garfield, James Abram, pres. U.S., 1831-
  1881, 2406, 2407, 24468; Addresses,
  sermons, etc., 8247
Garfielde, Selucius, 1822-1883, 2408
Garland, Hamlin, 1860-1940, 16574, 16575
Garland, Hugh A., 1805-1854, 3572
Garlick, Theodatus, 1805-1884, 2409
Garman, Allen Don, 1894-, 6923
Garneau, François Xavier, 1809-1866, 6825
Garneau, Hector, 6825
Garnelle, 8798
Garnered sheaves from the writings of
  Albert Deane Richardson, 7867
Garnet, Henry Highland, 1815-1882,
  24469, 25815
Garnett, James Mercer, 1840-1916, 6826,
  12198
Garnett, Muscoe Russell Hunter, 1821-1864,
  24470
Garnsey, John Hendaven, illustr., 9817
Garr, Elizabeth Headley ("Mrs. Amos
  Lawrence"), 14175

Garr, Theressa Ross, 15116
Garrard, Lewis Hector, 1829-1887, 2410, 2411,
  16576
Garrard County, Ky., 14739; Description, 15328;
  Economic conditions, 14540; History, 14970
Garret van Horn, 10705
Garretson, Hans van, pseud., 10714
Garrett, Alexander Charles, bp., 1832-1924,
  3573
Garrett, Betty, 14176
Garrett, Edmund H., illustr., 14466
Garrett, Lewis, 1772-1857, 3574
Garrett, R.B., 6827
Garrett, William, 1809-3576
Garrettson, Freeborn, 1752-1827, 3577, 24471
Garrido, Luis, 16577
Garrison, George P., 16578
Garrison, Joseph Fithian, 1823-1892, 22229
Garrison, Lindley Miller, 1864-, 25782
Garrison, Richard H., 13901
Garrison, Wendell Phillips, 1840-1907, 2412
Garrison, William Lloyd, 1805-1879, 639,
  23930, 23992, 24108, 24531, 24680, 24681,
  25685, 25700
A garrison tangle, 10120
Garstin, Crosbie, 1887-1930, 4146
Garth, 6993
Gartin, Michael, 14177
Garza Mereado, Ario, 16579
Garzo, José, 6828
Gas, Natural, 14442, 14447, 14565; Appalachia,
  14432; Geology, 14338, 14441; Kentucky,
  14428, 14432, 14439, 14566; Lake states,
  14432; Warren County, Ky., 14567
Gasca, Mariano de la, 1776-1839, 22230
Gasche, Charles, illustr., 7886
Gascon, Elvira, illustr., 19898
Un Gascon au Mexique, 6395
Gaskin, E. R., 14178
Gaspar da Madre de Deos (originally Teixera
  de Azevedo) 1715-1800, 22231
Gasparin, Agénor Étienne, comte de, 1810-1871,
  2413, 2414, 12199, 16580, 22232, 24472,
  24473
Gaspé, Philippe Aubert de, 6829
Gaspé district, Quebec,   Description & travel,
  7253, 22757
Gaspey, Thomas W., 7965
Gass, Patrick, 1771-1870, 3578, 22233
Gass family, 14363
Gassett, Henry, 1813-1886, 2415
Gastelum, Bernardo J., 6462
Gaston, Joseph, 1833-, 16581
Gaston, William, 1778-1844, 2416
The gate of the Pacific, 7751
Gates, 22613

Gates, Arnold Francis, 6830, 6831;
 Amberglow, the Lincoln-Rutledge
 booklet, 8369
Gates, Seth M., 24474
Gates, Thomas, 4947
The gates ajar, 11071
The gates between, 11072
The gates open slowly, 14931
Gathered leaves, 22039
Gathered sketches from the early history
 of New Hampshire and Vermont, 11752
El gato y el alambre, 19823
Gaty, Carolyn, 14179
Gaucho (The word), 18606
Gauchos, 18606; Brazil, 19365;
 Poetry, 18931
Gauld, George, 3579
Gause, Isaac, 1843-, 3580
Gaussen, L., 25032
Gautier du Tronchoy, 22234
Gávea, 20550
Gavidia, Francisco, 1865-1955, 18547,
 18548
Gaviões Indians, 18553
Gay, Ebenezer, 1696-1787, 2417, 22235
Gay, Frederick A., 16582
Gay, John, 1685-1732, 12200
Gay, Margaret Cooper ("Mrs. Francis
 Smulders"), 15433
Gay, Mary Ann Harris, 1827-, 3581
Gay, Sydney Howard, 1814-1888, 6833
Gay-Lussac, Joseph Louis, 1778-1850,
 7092
Gay times, 14180
Gayarré, Charles Étienne Arthur, 1805-
 1895, 3582-3584
Gayley, James Fyfe, 1818-1894, 2418
Gaylord, N.M., 24475
Gaylord, William L., 2419
Gazelle, a true tale of the great
 rebellion, 12201
Gazette publications, 2780
A gazetteer of Texas, 16572
A gazetteer of the state of Georgia,
 5138
A gazetteer of the United States,
 12766
A gazetteer of the towns on the western
 waters, 13905
Gazophylacium divinae dilectionis, 7449
Gaztaneta y de Iturribálzga, Antonio,
 1656-1728, 6832
Geary, John White, 1819-1873, 12240
Geary and Kansas, 12240
Geber, a tale of the reign of Harun al
 Raschid, 8792

Gebow, Joseph A., 16584
Geckobia Megnin, 20673
Gee, Joshua, 1654(ca)-1723? 24476
Geer, Curtis Manning, 1864-, 14181
Geer, John James, 1833-, 3585
Geer, Theodore T., 1851-, 16585
The geese of Ganderica, 17169
Geiger, Joseph H., 24477
Geijer, Erik Gustaf, 1783-1847, praeses, 439
Geis, Edna Kirker, 14182
Geist, Margarethe, 3586
Geldard, James, 12202
Gelger, John Lewis, 6834
A gem among the sea-weeds, 9712
The gem of the lake, 11219
Gemälde von Nord-Amerika in allen beziehungen,
 1560
Gemelli Careri, Giovanni Francesco, 1651-1725,
 6835
Gemidos del corazón, 7668
Gemma, Reinerus, Frisius, 1508-1555, 407
Gems of Rocky mountain scenery, 17150
Genealogical and historical notes on Culpeper
 county, Virginia, 3680
Genealogical Forum of Portland Ore., 17778-
 17780
A genealogical memoir of the families of
 Lawrences, 2452
A genealogical register of the first settlers
 of New England, 2219
Genealogical sketch of the Bird family, 1330
Genealogical sketch of the descendants of
 Reinold and Matthew Marvin, who came to
 New England in 1635, 23207
Genealogy, 2294, 13838, 15401; Bibliography,
 15047; Kentucky, 13897, 14721, 15007;
 Periodicals, 14721
Genealogy of the Everett family, 12119
Genealogy of the Henry Adams family, 6836
Genealogy of the Mathes family from about
 1500 to 1847, 23330
Genera of North American Reptilia, 12683
La generación del 18 en la poética
 Venezolana, 19915
The general, 15924
The general, attacked by a subaltern, 11239
General Anti-slavery Convention, London,
 25445
The general character, present and future
 prospects of the people of Ohio, 539
A general circular to all persons of good
 character, 16916
General convention of the Christian church.
 Conferences. Rhode Island and Massachusetts,
 23891; New England, 22338; New York, 22338
General courses and distances G.S.L. City to

185

Fort Limbi, 3521
General Education Board, 14575
General epistle from the council of the
  twelve apostles to the Church of
  Jesus Christ of Latter Day Saints
  abroad, 5790
O general está pintando, 19162
The general gazetteer, 2816
General Harrison, 10310
A general history of the British empire
  in North America, 5781
General Kirby-Smith..., 15077
General Lane's brigade in central Mexico,
  6144
A general map of the new settlement
  called Transilvania, 14183
General practice review, Report of
  seminar on, 14671
The general register of politics and
  literature in Europe and America,
  2420
General Roger W. Hanson, 1827-1863,
  14184
A general survey of the present
  situation of the principal powers,
  12108
A general view of the U.S., 4489
General Washington's marquee, 10310
The general's double, 10121
Generals, U.S., 8263, 22704
Generation, 23368
A generation of destiny, 19718
Genesee consociation, 12203
Genesee region, N.Y., 1495, 3988
Genesee valley, N.Y., 23589
The genesis of California counties,
  16126
Genet, Edmond Charles, 1763-1834,
  12204, 15750
Genética e evolução, 20631
Genetics, 15679, 20631
Geneva. American residents, 12205
Genin, Sylvester, 1822-1850, 12206
Genin, Thomas Hedges, 1796-1868, 3587,
  3588
The genius and posture of America, 154,
  155
Genius and spirit of the Hebrew Bible,
  15226
The genius maker, 9331
Genovés Taragasa, Santiago, 20361
Gente viva, 19661
A gentle bell, 10969
A gentle benefactress, 9070
The gentle boy, 9820, 9827
A gentle ghost, 9575

A gentleman at the bar, 12132
The gentleman from Indiana, 10923
A gentleman from South Carolina, 12289
Gentleman of America, 5229
A gentleman of Japan and a lady, 10238
A gentleman vagabond and some others, 5194
Gentry, Richard, 1788-1837, 6837
Gentry, Thomas Benton, 6837
Gentz, Friedrich Von, 1764-1832, 12207
Geoffroy, William, 22236
Geografía agraria de Venezuela, 20093
Geografía de la República de Guatemala, 7452
Geografía de la República mexicana, 6611,
  7588
Geografía de México, 7320
Geografía de Sergipe, 18345
Geografía do Brasil, 19281
Geografía e historia de correos y tele-
  comunicaciones de Guatemala, 18853
Geografía física de Venezuela, 19767
Geografía nacional de México, 7958
Geografía social y humana de Costa Rica, 7517
Geografía y atlas de la República mexicana,
  8439
Geographic aspects of plantation agriculture
  in Yucatan, 20083
Geographic influences in American slavery,
  24351
A geographical description of the state of
  Louisiana, 3170, 3171
Geographical distribution of animals and
  plants, 5291
Geographical, historical, political,
  philosophical and mechanical essays, 3399
Geographical memoir upon upper California,
  3541
Geographical positions, Cape Breton, 11707;
  Nova Scotia, 11707; Southern states, 3360,
  12024
Geographical society of Baltimore, 25932
A geographical view of the U.S., 3589
Geographie und statistik von Mexiko und
  Central-amerika, 8336
Geographisch-statistische beschreibung von
  Californien, 16711
Geographische gesellschaft (für Thüringen) zu
  Jena, 6841
Geographische wanderungen, 2540
Geography, 584, 1280, 3429, 4466, 5065, 6674,
  7858, 17539, 20587; 21795, 23056, 23498;
  15th-16th cent., 343; 17th-18th cent., 1515,
  3683, 3722, 5066, 6294, 6525, 6526, 6721,
  6722, 8254, 21808, 22277; Bibliography,
  14704, 19516; Congresses, 6453, 26710;
  Dictionaries, 715, 1374, 1505, 2016, 21706,
  22838, 23052; History, 7049, 11332;

Outlines, syllabi, etc., 22495;
Societies, 7654, 20586; Study and
teaching, Brazil, 19279; Textbooks,
7266, 7320, 8440, 19280; Textbooks,
1899-1870, 1396, 14308, 23377;
Textbooks, 1870-, 16258
Geography, Economic, 20000; Historical,
1515; Medieval, 126
A geography of New England, 11286
The geography of South Carolina, 5159
Geography of the Pennyroyal, 15327
Geohistoria del Perú, 19964
Geologic map of Kentucky, 14427
Geologic map of Kentucky and the adjoining
states..., 14428
Geological survey of California, 17879
Geologie pratique de la Louisiane, 5384
Geology, 11954, 12354, 14037, 22021,
22041; Algeria, 387; Allen County,
Ky., 14562; Antarctic regions, 19675;
Arctic regions, 6302; Aratu, Brazil,
18844; Argentine Republic, 1719;
Argentine Republic, Bibliography,
20525; Argentine Republic, Bibliography,
Catalogs, 18450; Arkansas, 2238; Baja
California, Bibliography, 18238;
Barbados, 23393; Barren County, Ky.,
14596; Bath County, Ky., 14413; Big
Sandy River valley, 14419, 14593;
Brazil, 19292, 22320; Brazil,
Amazon region, 19445, 19446;
Breathitt County, Ky., 14563; British
Columbia, 6174; California, 6913,
11283, 17133; Canada, 4685, 6218, 23129;
Canada, Guide-books, 6308; Chira Island,
Costa Rica, 19004; Clark County, Ky.,
14414; Colombia, Collected works,
19112; Colorado, 16721; Connecticut,
23340; Costa Rica, 19008, 19009, 19760,
20586; Cuba, 17972, 17973, 19016,
19559-19561; Cuba, History, 19645;
Cuba, Las Villas, 19202; Cuba, Oriente,
20628; Europe, 387; Henry County, Ky.,
14415; Indiana, 22637; Iowa, 13106;
Jackson Purchase Region, Ky., 15282;
Kentucky, 13939, 14114, 14148, 14174,
14193, 14338, 14369, 14429, 14430,
14441, 14444, 14447, 14448, 14565,
14771, 14902, 14906, 14914-14916,
15005, 15037, 15059, 15086, 15087,
15107-15109, 15330, 15351, 15670;
Kentucky, Bibliography, 14548;
Kentucky, Maps, 14428; Kentucky River
valley, 14420; Knott County, Ky.,
14564; Knox County, Ky., 14416; Louisiana,
5384; Madison County, Ky., 14417;

Massachusetts, 11956, 23265; Menifee
County, Ky., 14418; Mexico, 2186, 6708,
6913; Mexico, Bibliography, 19085; Mexico,
Socorro Island, 18026; Minas Gerais, Brazil,
19292; Minnesota, 13476; Mississippi Valley,
4664, 15698; Missouri, 2238, 4698; Montana,
3817; Nebraska, 247, 3817, 4246, 15884;
Nevada, 6913; New Brunswick, 22053; New
England, 2168; New Mexico, 17775; New York
(State), Putnam Co., 1402; North America,
4386, 7344-7347; North Carolina, 4486;
North Dakota, 16966; Northwest, Canadian,
3878; Nova Scotia, 12221, 22053; Oregon,
2602; Peru, Bibliography, 19963; Prince
Edward Island, 22053; Research, Argentine
Republic, 20525; Research, Kentucky, 14411;
Rocky Mountains, 5524, 16723; São Paulo,
18166, 20358, 20677; Scott County, Ky.,
14591; South Carolina, 12869, 23643;
Southwest, New, 5513; Tennessee, 11907;
U.S., 270, 2239, 3446, 4318, 12574, 14448,
15351, 22817; Utah, 5501, 15948, 15949,
17620, 17786; Uruguay, 19919; Vermont, 23129;
Warren County, Ky., 14567; West Indies,
22819; Wyoming, 17776
Geology, Stratigraphic, 12574; Permian, 23424;
Silurian, 23129; Tertiary, 19919
The geology and mineral resources of Kentucky,
14429
The geology of the earth, 11444
Geomorfologia de Puerto Jiménez, 19005
Geomorphology, 19010
Geonomia de Rio Negro, 19890
Geopolitica do transporte aereo, 19862
George I, king of Great Britain, 1660-1727,
2304
George II, king of Great Britain, 1683-1760,
1388, 2304
George III, king of Great Britain, 1738-1820,
103, 22593, 23016
George, Alfred, 6838
George, Henry, 1839-1897, 6581, 8425
George, Henry, jr., 8425
George, James Zachariah, 1826-1897, 24478
George, Marian M., 6839, 6840
George, Paul, 6841
George Balcombe, 5476
George Cardwell, 10383
George Dennison Prentice, 15676
George Mandeville's husband, 4986
George Mason, the young backwoodsman, 3474
George Melville, 10800
George Washington's last duel, 10460
George Washington's physician, 6842
George Welding, 8998
George, Fort, N.Y., 22072

187

George, Lake, 23206; Battle of, 1755, 21888; History, 2093
George's mother, 9210
Georgetown, Col., Description, 17514
Georgetown, D.C. Ordinances, etc., 12210; St. John's church, 11648
Georgetown [Ky.] quadrangle, 14591
Georgetown, S.C., 4222
Georgetown Baptist Church, Georgetown, Ky., 14485
Georgetown College, Georgetown, Ky., 13793, 14329, 14998, 14999; Fiction, 14009
Georgia, 1668, 3236, 3296; Antiquities, 4102, 13290, 22722; Bibliography, 15140; Biography, 12263, 13434; Boundaries, North Carolina, 22237; Charters, 11748; Commissioners to examine the port and railroad of Brunswick, 709; Constitution, 12211; Convention, 1850, 24479; Convention, 1861, 12212; Description & travel, 2996, 3236, 3425, 3603, 3720, 3722, 3783, 3897, 4173, 4217, 4509, 4588, 4682, 4791, 4950, 5289, 5673, 14749, 15527, 23202; Description & travel, Gazetteers, 5138; Description & travel, Guide-books, 13544; Economic conditions, 3724, 15611, 24081; Fiction, 3773, 3774, 4081-4085, 4087, 4088, 4091, 4295, 4746, 11127, 24340, 25219; Finance, 17580; General Assembly, 22237, 22238; Governor, 1802-1806 (John Milledge), 22237; Governor, 1857-1865 (Joseph E. Brown), 12213; History, 484, 12043, 12263, 13486, 22785; History, Civil war, 2262, 2544, 4523, 24688; History, Colonial period, 958, 1006, 1610, 2558, 3208, 3590, 3860, 4406, 5265, 5266, 5324, 5335, 11260, 11635, 12161, 22329, 23202, 23557, 23635, 23657-23659; History, Revolution, 23670; History, Sources, 12214, 12215; Militia, 2262, 24688; Politics & government, 3872, 11912, 22297, 23811; Politics & government, Civil war, 12212, 22238, 22479; Public lands, 23625; Social conditions, 15611; Social life & customs, 3492, 4086, 4148, 4149, 4247, 12042, 12043
Georgia artillery, Chatham art., 1785?-1865?,4103; Howell's battery, 1863-1865, 3851; Martin's battery, 1862-1863, 3851
Georgia (Colony) Trustees for establishing the colony of Georgia in America, 958, 1006, 1610, 3590, 11260, 11635, 12161, 23202, 23635, 23658, 23752

Georgia historical society, 4650, 12043, 12045, 12214, 12215
Georgia illustrated in a series of views embracing natural scenery and public edifices engraved on steel, 4950
Georgia infantry. 1st regt., 1861-1865, 3851, 4650; 6th regt., 1861-1865, 3127; 10th regt., 1861-1864, Co. K, 12047; 21st regt., 1861-1865, 4608; 61st regt., 1861-1865, 4600; 66th regt., 1863-1865, 4608; Oglethorpe infantry, 1861-1865, 3016
Georgia loyalist, Recollections of a, 4074
Georgia Mississippi company, 1346
Georgia scenes, 10242
A Georgia soldier in the civil war, 2971
Georgia speculation unveiled, 1346
Georgia wit and humor, 5403
Geórgicas mexicanas, 7233, 7234
Geppert, Mrs. Dora Higbee, 3591
Geraldine, 9717
Gerard, Charles Frédéric, 1822-1895, 5255
Gerhart, Emanuel Vogel, 1817-1904, 12163
Germán-Romero, Mario, 20710, 20715
German language, Dialects, 19568; Dictionaries, 18995
German poetry, 14875; Translations into English, 5246
German travellers in the South from the colonial period through 1865, 15528
Germans in Costa Rica, 8324
Germans in Louisville, Ky., 15171
Germans in Mexico, 6917
Germans in Pennsylvania, 12660
Germans in Rio Grande do Sul, Brazil (State), 18937
Germans in Schoharie co., N.Y., 11567
Germans in Texas, 17741
Germans in the U.S., 3233, 4132, 4181, 4290, 4449, 11319, 11327, 14773
Germantown, Pa., 6713
Germantown, Battle of, 1777, 10215
Germantown academy, Germantown, Pa., 12216
Germany, Description & travel, 7806, 8877, 16754, 22675; Emigration & immigration, 1562; History, Henry IV, 1056-1106, Fiction, 10351; Social life & customs, 16754
Germination, 18351
Gerolt, Friedrich Karl Joseph, freiherr von, ca.1798-1789, 2186
Geronimo, Apache chief, 1829- , Fiction, 16465, 16467
Gerontology, 15319
Gerrish, Mary Sewall, 1691-1710, 23472
Gerrish, Theodore, 1846-, 3592
Gerritsen, Carel Victor, 1850-, 3593

188

Gerry, Elbridge, 1744-1814, 560
Gerstäcker, Friedrich Wilhelm Christian, 1816-1872, 3594, 7272, 12217, 16587, 16588
Gerstner, Clara (von Epplen-Härtenstein) von, 3595
Gerstner, Franz Anton, ritter von, 1795-1840, 3595, 3596
Gertrude of Wyoming, 1824
Gervais, Paul, 1816-1879, 21853
Geschichte der englischen kolonien in Nord-Amerika, 6842
Geschichte und handlung der französischen pflanzstädte in Nordamerika, 3597
Geschichte und zustände der Deutschen in Amerika, 4290
Gesner, Abraham, 1797-1864, 12218-12221
Gesner, George Weltden, 12220
Gessner, Ludwig, 1828-1890, 12222
Gethsemani, Abbey of, Nelson County, Kentucky, 13828
Getrouw verhaal van den waren toestant der meest herderloze gemeentens in Pennsylvanien en aangrensende provintien, 5093
Getting under way, 9800
Gettysburg, Battle of, 1863, 1149, 12117, 13140; Poetry, 14990
Gettysburg Address, 6345
Gettysburg College, 1623
Gettysburg national military cemetery, 12117, 14827
Gevers Deynoot, William Theodorus, 6844
Ghent, Treaty of, 1814, 72, 520, 24361
Ghiano, Juan Carlos, 18830
Gholson, Thomas Saunders, 1809-1868, 12223
Gholson, William Yates, 1807-1870, 12224
The ghost, 10480
The ghost coon, 14832
The ghost in the Cap'n Brown house, 10909
The ghost in the mill, 10909
The ghost of law, 11486
The ghost of Redbrook, 9180
A ghost of the Sierras, 9779
Ghost stories, 10693; Kentucky, 14163
Ghostly colloquies, 11001
Ghosts, 1474; Kentucky, 15589
Ghosts I have met and some others, 8678
The ghosts of Stukeley Castle, 6965
The giant and the star, 13799
The giant's coffin, 10783
Gibbes, George M., 12225
Gibbes, Morgan, 25367

Gibbes, Robert Wilson, 1809-1866, 12226, 22239
The gibbet of Regina, 6845
Gibbon, Eduardo A., 6846
Gibbon, John, 1827-1896, 3598
Gibbons, Charles, 1814-1885, 25245
Gibbons, Israel, d.1866, 12227
Gibbons, J.A., 3599
Gibbons, James, 12228
Gibbons, James Joseph, 16589
Gibbons, James Sloan, 1810-1892, 12229
Gibbons, Joseph Kent, 1840-1862, 1659
Gibbons, Thomas, 1720-1785, 1621
Gibbs, Frederick Waymouth, 1821-, 12230, 12231
Gibbs, George, 1815-1873, 12232-12234
Gibbs, Jesse Thomas, 1865-, 24480
Gibbs, Josiah Francis, 1845-, 16590-16593
Gibbs, William, b.1785, 12235
Gibbs, William H., 12236
Gibbs family (Robert Gibbs, 1634?-1674?), 12235
Gibson, Charles Dana, 1867-1944, illustr., 8674, 9361, 9362, 9637
Gibson, J. Watt, b.1829, 16594
Gibson, William, 14185, 14186
Gibson, William, 1788-1868. Reflections on the treatment of fractures of the thigh, 22798
Gibstone, Henry, 12237
Giddings, Joshua Reed, 1795-1864, 12238, 22240, 25358, 25443
Giddins, Edward, 12239
Gifford, Andrew, 1700-1784, 23786
Gifford, John, 1758-1818, 1932
Gifford, Ruth, 16595
Gift, George Washington, b.1833, 16596
Gift-books (Annuals, etc.), 252
Gifts in estate planning, 14669
Giger, Henry Douglas, 6847
Giguet, 366
Gihon, John H., 12240
Gil, Felipe, 1911-, 18762
Un Gil-Blas en Californie, 2132
Gilbert, A., illustr., 4048
Gilbert, Amos, 22241
Gilbert, C.E., 6848
Gilbert, Elizabeth D., 15389
Gilbert, James H., 16597
Gilbert, James Stanley, 1855-1906, 6849
Gilbert, Olive, 24481
Gilbert, William A., 24482
The Gilberts, 9896
Gildersleeve, Benjamin, 15282
Gilead, 10810
Giles, Charles, 1783-1867, 12241
Giles, Howard, illustr., 13704

189

Giles, Joel, 12242
Giles, Leonidas Blanton, 1841-, 3600
Giles, William Branch, 1762-1830,
   12243, 12244, 24483
Giles, William Fell, 1807-1879, 12245
Giles Pretel, Juan de, 6850, 6851
Gilfillan, Lillian, 10125
Gilkes, C.D., 20214
Gill, John, 1841-, 3601
Gill, Theodore Nicholas, 1837-1914,
   12246, 12247
Gilleland, J.C., 12248, 14187
Gillespie, Alexander, 12249
Gillespie, Joseph, 1809-1885, 5933,
   6852, 17035
Gillespy, Edward, 12250
Gillet, Eliphalet, 1768-1848, 12251,
   12252
Gillet, Ransom Hooker, 1800-1876,
   12253, 12254
Gillett, E.H., 21892
Gillette, Abram Dunn, 1807-1882,
   22242, 22243
Gillette, Charles, 12255
Gillette, Daniel Holbrook, 1813-1845,
   22243
Gillette, J.M., 16598-16600
Gillette, Walter Bloomfield, 22243
Gilliam, Albert M., d.1859, 6853, 12256
Gillies, J., 5691
Gillies, John, 1712-1796, 22244
Gilliland, Thaddeus Stephens, 1834-,
   ed., 6854
Gilliman Ogley, 10675
Gillis, Ezra I., 1867-, 13598, 14188
Gillmer, D.R., 24484
Gillmore, Parker, 12257, 16601, 19050
Gillmore, Robert H., 12258
Gillpatrick, Owen Wallace, 6855, 6856
Gilman, Arthur, 1877-1909, 12259
Gilman, Mrs. Caroline (Howard) 1794-
   1888, 2602-2607
Gilman, Daniel Coit, 1831-1908, 12260,
   12261
Gilman, Samuel, 1791-1858, 11746,
   12262, 22245
Gilman family (Edward Gilman, 1587?-
   1681), 12259
Gilmer, Elizabeth (Meriwether) 1861-
   1951, 6857
Gilmer, Francis Walker, 1790-1826, 3068
Gilmer, George Rockingham, 1790-1859,
   12203
Gilmer, John H., 12261, 10066
Gilmor, Harry, 1030 1883, 3609
Gilmore, James Roberts, 1822-1903, 3393,

   3610-3613, 14190
Gilmore, Joseph Henry, 1834-, 12266
Gilmore, Melvin Randolph, 1868-1940, 17890
Gilmore, Patrick Sarsfield, 1829-1892, 12267
Gilpin, Mrs. Eliza, 22246
Gilpin, Henry Dilworth, 1801-1860, 12268-12270,
   22246
Gilpin, Joshua, 12271
Gilpin, Thomas, 1776-1853, 3614, 12272, 12273
Gilpin, William, 1822-1894, 3615, 3616, 16602-
   16604
Giltner, Hellen Fairleight, 14191
Giménez Fernández, Manuel, 19894
Ginés de Sepúlveda, Juan. See Sepúlveda, Juan
   Ginés de.
Giovanna I, queen of Naples, d.1382-Fiction,
   9710
Giovannoli, Harry, 14192
The gypsey of Germantown, 9717
Gipsies, 4275; England, 10517
The gipsy's warning, 9449
Girard, Charles Frédéric, 1822-1895, 677, 3617
Girard, Just [pseud. for Just Jean Etienne Roy]
   1794-1870, 3618
Girard, Stephen, 1750-1831, 438, 12275
Girard College, Philadelphia, 438, 12276
Girardin, Louis Hue, 1771-1825, 11613
Girardot, Colombia - Economic conditions,
   20305; Social conditions, 20305
Girdlestone, Thomas, 1758-1822, 12277
The girl at Cobhurst, 10888
The girl at the halfway house, 9929
A girl of the period, 9762
The girl who died of a broken heart, 6209
Girlhood and womanhood, 9646
Girls, 10655
Girls behind the man from 1905 to 1945,
   14398
Girls of a feather, 8727
The girls' sketching camp, 10163
Girod-Chantranso, Justin, 1750-1841, 4654
Girty, Simon, 1741-1818, 16115; Fiction, 4122,
   8789, 14480
Girty family, 16115
Gisborne, Lionel, 1823-1861, 12278
Gislen, Torsten, 1893-, 3619
Gist, Christopher, c.1706-1759, 3620, 14467
Gist family, 14104
Gittinger, Roy, 16605
The given case, 10016
Glacier national park, 16807
Glaciers, British Columbia, 6890
Gladden, Washington, 1836-1918, 12279
The glades of the Alleghenies, 4694
Gladney, R.S., 24750
Gladston, W.S., 16984

Gladstone, Sir John, bart., 1764-1851, 24485
Gladstone, Thomas H., 12280, 12281
Gladys, 9329 .
Glanmore, a romance of the Revolution, 9043
Glas, George, 1725-1765, 24
Glascott, Cradock, 1743?-1831, 12282
Glasgow Emancipation Society, 24486, 25929
Glasgow Female Anti-Slavery Society, 24487
Glaspell, Mrs. Kate Eldridge, 16606
Glass, Hugh, 2675, 4262
The glass; or, The trials of Helen More, a thrilling temperance tale, 10159
Glass blowing and working, 18210
Glass manufacture, 18796; Guadalajara, Mexico, 18210
The glass window, 14158
Glasscock, Lemuel, b.1801, 22247
Glasses, 7118, 10012
Glassware, Mexico, 18210
Glastonbury, Conn., Geneal, 11728; History, 11728
Glave, E.J., 24488
Glazier, Lewis, 12283
Glazier, Willard, 1841-1905, 3621-2624, 4672, 6858, 16607, 22248
Gleams of light on all sorts of subjects, 12227
Gleanings by the way, 3013
Gleanings from real life, 9609
Gleanings from the portfolio of the "Young'un", 8917
Gleanings from West Lexington Presbytery ..., 15321
Gleanings in Africa, 24489
Gleason, Benjamin, 1777-1847, 12284, 22249
Gleig, George Robert, 1796-1888, 3625
Gleitsmann, William, 1840-1914, 3626
Glen, James, 3627
Glen's Creek, 9896
Glenn, L.C., 14193
Glennair, 9831
The Glenns, 10263
Glezen, Levi. 1774?-1842, 12285
Glisan, Rodney, 1827-1890, 16608
Glittering gold. The true story of the Black Hills, 16309
Globe (Whaling ship), 9090
Gloria Britannorum, 12286
Gloria Mundi, 9566
The glories of the Lord of Hosts, 1778

Glorious news. Boston, Friday 11'clock, 16th May 1766, 22250
Glory, 10238
The glory of America, 137
The glory of the hills, 14431, 14929
Glosario de mareas y corrientes, 20133
A glossary to Say's Entomology, 5081
Glotz, Gustave, 1862-1935, 24490
Gloucester, John, 1776 or 7-1822, 1840
Gloucester, Mass., Geneal., 605; History, 605
Glover, Joshua, fl. 1854, 25911
Glover, Livingston Maturin, 1819-1880, 6859
Glover, Richard, 1712-1785, 12287
Glover, Samuel Taylor, 1813-1884, 12288, 24864
Glover, Thomas, 3628
Gloverson and his silent partners, 10087
Glynn, William C., 14194
Gnaw-wood, 11773
The go-between, 12289
Goadby, Mrs. Robert, 4275
Goats, Santa Catarina, Brazil, Statistics, 19465
Gobat, Albert, 1843-1914, 3629
Gobineau, Joseph Arthur de, 22251
Gobright, Lawrence Augustus, 1816-1879, 12290
God, 5804; Attributes, 11896
God acknowledged, in the nation's bereavement, 22507
God and the soul, 5239
God bless Abraham Lincoln, 24491
God or our country, 11437
God lives in Kentucky, 13690
God rest ye, merry gentlemen, 9217
God ruling the nations for the most glorious end, 13033
God seen above all national calamities, 22242
God sometimes answers his people, 44
God the author of promotion, 22949
God the judge, 2304
God's culture of his vineyard, 1925
God's hand in America, 21902
God's hand in human events, 23231
God's judgments teaching righteousness, 1872
God's protecting providence, 3247
God's ravens, 9606
God's revenge against adultery, 23767
God's revenge against gambling, 23768
God's sovereign government among the nations, 21904
God's ways unsearchable, 13239
Godard-Lange, 12291
Godbey, Edsel T., 14195
Godbey, W.B., 14196
Goddard, Frederick Bartlett, 1834-, 3630,

12292
Goddard, George H., 3631
Goddard, Mrs. Glave, 14197
Goddard, John E., 15648
Goddard, Samuel Aspinwall, 2421
Goddard, Thomas H., 2422
Goddard, William, 1740-1817, 2423, 12293
Goddard, William Giles, 1794-1846, 2424, 2425
Godet, Theodore L., 2426
Godfrey, Edward K., 6860
Godfrey, Thomas, 1736-1763, 2427
Godfrey, William C., 2428
Godin des Odonais, Isabelle de Grandmaison, b.1728?, 23060
Godley, John Robert, 1814-1861, 3632
The godmother's gifts, 10046
Godoy, Juan Gualberto, 1793-1864, 18931
Godoy Alcayaga, Lucila, 1889-, 6861
Godwin, Morgan, fl.1685, 1556, 2429, 12294
Godwin, Parke, 1816-1904, 2430
Godwin, William, 1756-1836, 2431, 2432
Goebel, William, 1845-1900, 14198, 15180, 15181
Goebel-Taylor contest, 1899-1900, 15254
Goebel assassination nearly lead to civil war, 14198
Goedel, C., 12295
Goepp, Charles, 1827-1907, 24492
Goeschen, Otto, 1808-1865, 24493
Goethe, Johann Wolfgang von, 1749-1832. Werther, 21720
Goethe, Mme. Louise, 2433
Goff, Anna Chandler, 13833
Goff, John, 14199
Goffe, William, 1605?-1679, 22574, 23663
Gohier, Urbain Degoulet, called, 1862-, 3633
Goiás (State), Economic conditions, 20375, 20376; see also Goyaz
Going and son, 10370
Going to Shrewsbury, 10043
Going to the Fourth, 15464
Góis, Carlos. Auto de natal, 18977
Gold, A.B., 3515
Gold, 1865, 11684, 17676, 18761, 22712, 22956
Gold diggings on Salmon River, 3521
Gold-dust for the beautifying of lives and homes, 10535
A gold hunter's experience, 16674
The gold hunters of California, 16402
Gold mines and mining, 386, 2575, 5573, 15857, 16008, 16815, 17359, 17830;

Alaska, 16556, 16647; Brazil, 11636, 18291, 23380; British Columbia, 17113; California, 217, 386, 5301, 15857, 16145, 17204, 17315, 17702, 23074; Colorado, 2738, 2877, 3715, 3717, 3987, 4594, 4707, 4708, 5421, 5455, 5695, 16674; Fiction, 5651; Kansas, 2510, 3615, 3715, 3717, 3938, 3987, 4727, 4845; Nebraska, 2510, 3715, 3938, 3987, 4727; North Dakota, 16042, 16992; The Northwest, 862; Nova Scotia, 12777; Oregon, 4249; Texas, 5648; U.S., 16853; Utah, 16788, 17738; Washington, 4249, 4308; Wyoming, 2877
Gold mines of the Gila, 5648
The gold mines of Western Kansas, 4707
The gold mines, scenery and climate of Georgia and the Carolinas, 5289
The gold placers of California, 3515
The gold regions of California, 16540
The gold regions of Kansas and Nebraska, 3938
The gold seekers, 722
Gold standard, 19048
Gold that did not glitter, 3156
Goldberger, Ludwig Max, 3624
Golden, James P., 16430
The golden age, 8959
The golden book of Venice, 11028
The golden bowl, 7121
The golden Christmas, 5160
Golden City, Col., Description, 17514
The golden days of '49, 17246
The golden dream, 15904
Golden dreams and waking realities, 17594
The Golden Eagle, 9051
Golden feather, 9636
The golden fleece, 9809
The golden fleece divided into three parts, 13498
Golden Gate park, 17666
The golden house, 11088
The golden ladder, 11220
The golden legacy, 10374
Golden-mouthed Taylor, 10747
Golden-rod, 9764
The golden rule, 8533, 9256
A golden sorrow, 10541
The golden state, 17078, 17419, 17510
Golden treasures of poetry, romance, and art, 9616
A golden wedding, 3562, 5311, 22120
Golder, John, 12296
Goldie, William Fergusson, 24494, 25894
Goldman, Edward Alphonso, 1873-1946, 6862
Goldsborough, Charles Washington, 1779-1043, 12297
Goldsborough, Louis Malesherbes, 1805-1877,

13202
Goldsborough, William Worthington, 1831-
1901, 3635
Goldsmid, Edmund Marsden, 6925
Goldschmidt, Albert, 5996
Goldschmidt, Levin, 1829-1897, 24495
Goldsmith, Alban, 13620
Goldsmith, Christabel, pseud., 10805,
10806
Goldsmith, Lewis, 1763?-1846, 12298
Goldsmith, Middleton, 1818-1887, 13620
Goldsmith, Oliver, 1794-1861, 2434
Goldsmith family, 12656
Goldsmithing, Brazil, 18229
Golitsyn, Dmitri Dmitrievich, Kniaz,
1770-1840, 22440
Golladay, J.R., 14387, 14388
Golovin, Ivan Gavrilovich, b.1816, 2435
Golpismo, 19965
Gomara, Francisco López de, 1510-1560?,
6863, 6864
Gomery of Montgomery, 11103
Gomes, Alfonso A., 19065-19067, 20446-
20449
Gomes, Eugênio, 19962
Gómez, Antonio. Ensayo político contra
las "Reflexiones" de William Burke,
19780
Gómez, Galo, 20390
Gómez de Avellaneda y Arteaga, Gertrudis,
1814-1873, 12299
Gómez de Parada Fonseca Enríquez, Juan
María, 7321
Gómez P., Francisco, 18340
Gómez Restrepo, Antonio, 20715
Gómez Robledo, Antonio, 1908-, 18518,
18896
Gomot, Hippolyte, 1837-, 7494
Gonçalo Garcia, Saint, 1556-1597, 23017
Goncourt, Edmond Huot de, 1822-1896,
7119
Goncourt, Jules, 1830-1870, 7119
Gondamor, Diego Sarmiento de Acuña,
conde de, 1567-1626, 23583
Gone to Texas, 9680
Góngora, Joannes de, fl.1636, 24496
Góngora y Argote, Luis de, 1561-1627,
19600, 19601, 20199
Gonino, J., 6407
Gonyaulax, Argentine Republic, 18711
Gonzaga ou a revolução de Minas, 19961
González, José, conde de Fuente González,
6657, 8278
González, José Antonio, 6865
González, Juan Vicente, 1810-1866, 6866
González-Blanco, Pedro, 6726

González de Aguëros, Pedro, 2436
González de Argandona, Juana, 8145
González de Mendoza, Juan, bp., 1545-1618,
22252
González de la Llana, Manuel, 6689
González de la Reguera, Juan Domingo, abp. of
Lima, 1720-1805, 1199
González Obregón, Luis, 1865-1938, 19968
González Peña, Carlos, 1885-, 6867
González Suárez, Federico, abp., 1844-1917,
6868
González y Montoya, José, 2437
Gooch, Daniel Wheelwright, 1820-1891, 24497
Good Americans, 9767
The good book, and amenities of nature, 15227
Good company for every day in the year, 9516
Good for the soul, 9374, 9376
Good in all and none all-good, 10279
A good investment, 9522
The good Mr. Bagglethorpe, 10235
The good-natured pendulum, 9683
Good news from a far country, 23666
Good news from Virginia, 5688
The good old way, 23302
Good order established in Pennsylvania and
New Jersey, 1651
Good roads in Southern California, 17055
Good Samaritan, 2029
Good society, 9683
The good time coming, 8563
Good wives, 1891
Goodale, Ebenezer, 2438
Goode, 25412
Goode, William Henry, 1807-1879, 3636
Goode, William O., 1798-1859, 24498
Goodell, William, 1792-1867, 24855
Gooden, Elmer Clayton, 1921-, 14200
Goodenow, John Milton, 1782-1838, 12300
Goodhart, Briscoe, 1845-1927, 3627
Goodhue, Josiah Fletcher, 1791-1863, 12301
Goodlander, Charles W., 16609
Goodloe, Abbe Carter, 1867-, 3638, 3639
Goodloe, Albert Theodore, 3640
Goodloe, Daniel Reaves, b.1814, 2439, 24499,
24500, 25119
Goodloe, Green Clay, 14201
Goodman, Clavia, 14202
Goodman, John Davidson, 1794-1830. Review of
"Fauna Americana", 12686
Goodmane, W.F., 3641
Goodrich, Chauncey Enoch, 1801-1864, 12302
Goodrich, Elizur, 1734-1797, 12303
Goodrich, Frank Boott, 1826-1894, 2440
Goodrich, Frederick Elizur, 1843-1925, 6869
Goodrich, John Z., b.1801, 2441, 7061, 24501
Goodrich, Samuel Griswold, 1793-1860, 2442,

2443, 3642, 12754
Goodricke, Henry, 12304
Goodsir, Robert Anstruther, 6870
Goodwin, Cardinal Leonidas, 1880-, 16610, 16611
Goodwin, Charles Archibald, 1876-, 24476
Goodwin, Charles Carroll, 1832-1917, 16612-16614
Goodwin, Henry Martyn, 1820-1893, 12306
Goodwin, Hermon Camp, 1813-1891, 2444, 12307
Goodwin, Isaac, 2445
Goodwin, Nathaniel, 1782-1855, 2446-2448
Goodwin, Nathaniel Carl, 1857-1919, 16615
Goodwin, Thomas, 1600-1680, 12308
Goodwin, Thomas Shepard, 24502
Gookin, Daniel, 1612?-1687, 12309
Goold, Nathan, 1846-1914, 1803
A goose-chase, 9916
Goranov, G., 19202
Gorden, Thomas Francis, 1787-1860, 12312, 12313
Gordon, Adoniram Judson, 1836-1895, 2449
Gordon, Armistead Churchill, 1855-1931, 3643, 3644
Gordon, Charles, d.1817, 880
Gordon, Donald, 1877-, 3648
Gordon, George Henry, 1825?-1886, 3645
Gordon, H. Panmure, 3646
Gordon, Harry, 3647
Gordon, J.S., illustr., 8252
Gordon, James Bentley, 1750-1819, 12310
Gordon, John, d.1778?, 13503
Gordon, John, d.1845, 12311
Gordon, Julien, pseud., 9257-9265
Gordon, Marquis Lafayette, 1843-1900, 3648
Gordon, S. Anna, 16616
Gordon, Thomas Francis, 1787-1860, 22253, 22254
Gordon, William, 12311
Gordon, William, 1728-1807, 12314
Gordon, William Robert, 1811-1897, 12315, 12316
Gordon-Cumming, Constance Frederica, 1837-, 16617
Gore, Christopher, 1758-1827, 12318, 12414
Gore, Montague, 12319
The gored huntsman, 10693
Gorgas, William Crawford, 1854-1920, 7420
Gorham, John, 1783-1829, 22255
Gorman, John C., 22256
Gorman, Samuel, 6871

Gorman, Willis Arnold, 1816-1876, 24503
Gorrie, Petar Douglass, 1813-1884, 12320, 12321
Gorton, Samuel, 1592-1677, 12322, 22062, 23809
Göschen, Georg Joachim, 1752-1828, 321
Gosnold, Bartholomew, d.1607, 1479
The gospel among the Dakotas, 17491
The gospel-covenant, 1671
Gospel family-order, 2300
The gospel-mystery of sanctification, 14959
Gospel news, 14203
The gospel of slavery: a primer of freedom, 25680
The gospel of typical servitude, 3131
Goss, Ephraim, 12323
Goss, Warren Lee, 1835-1925, 3649
Gosse, Edmund, 1849-1928, 13801
Gosse, Philip Henry, 1810-1888, 3650, 12324, 12325
The gossips of Rivertown, 9801
Gostkowski, G., baron de, 6872
La gota, 20648
Gott, Elizabeth, 7932
Gottfredson, Peter, 16618
Gottheil, Gustav, 8425
Gotthelf, Jeremias, 1797-1854, 19612
Gottsberger, Francis, 6433
Gottschall, Amos H., 1854-, 3651, 3652, 14204
Gouge, William M., 1796-1863, 12326, 12327, 16619
Gough, John Bartholomew, 1817-1886, 22257
Goulart, João, pres. Brazil, 1918-, 19389, 19414, 19415
Gould, Augustus Addison, 1805-1866, 1404, 12328, 12329
Gould, Benjamin Apthorp, 1824-1896, 12330-12332
Gould, Emerson W., b.1811, 3654
Gould, Hannah Flagg, 1789-1865, 12333
Gould, Jay, 1836-1892, 12334
Gould, John Mead, 1839-, 3655
Gould, John W., 1814-1838, 10916, 12335
Gould, Marcus Tullius Cicero, 1793-1860, 22258, 22450
Gould, Nathaniel Duren, 1781-1864, 12336
Goulder, William Armistead, 1821-, 16620
Goulding, Francis Robert, 1810-1881, 3656
Goupil, E. Eugène, 6105
Goupil, René, d.1642, 13227
Gourdin, Robert N., 11745
Gourlay, Robert Fleming, 1778-1863, 6873, 12337, 12330
Gourlie, John Hamilton, 10000
Goussencourt, chevalier de, pseud.? 4654
Gouy-d'Arcy, Louis-Henri-Marthe, marquis de,

1753-1794, 6874
Gove, Aaron, 16240
The governess, 10350
The governing race, 24504
Government, Resistance to, 23939, 24414
Government and liberty described, 620
Government Guides, Inc., Madison,
  Tenn., 14205
Government in Kentucky cities, 14948
The Governor and company of adventurers
  of England, 7978
Governor Dummer academy, South Byfield,
  Mass., 21957
Governors, 15578
The governor's prerogative, 9582
Gowinius, Sven, 2450
Goyaz, Brazil (State), Social life &
  customs, 18622; see also Goias
Graah, Wilhelm August, 1793-1863, 22259
Gracchus, pseud., 14206
Gracchus Vanderlip, Adventures of, 4109
Grace (theology), 2895, 23789; Early
  works to 1800, 12643, 21990
Grace, Henry, b.1730?, 12340
Grace Bartlett, 11187
Grace displayed, 23149
Grace Dudley, 10510
Grace Morton, 10340
Grace Truman, 3505
Grace Weldon, 9980
Gracey, Samuel Levis, 1835-1911, 22260
Gracie's Alabama brigade, 5130
The gracious presence of God, 12040
A graduate of Paris, 5258
Grady, Benjamin Franklin, 1831-, 24505
Grady, Henry Woodfin, 1851-1889, 3657
Graeco-Roman institutions, from anti-
  evolutionist points of view, 25355
Graff, John Franklin, 16621
Graffenried, Edward de, 24506
Gráfica da Un B, 19225
La grafología en la escuela primaria,
  20624
Grafton, Thomas W., 14207
Grafton, Mass., History, 1520
Graham, Albert Alexander, 1860-, 6875
Graham, C.C., 14208
Graham, David, 22261
Graham, Mrs. Ellee D., 22267
Graham, Frederic Ulric, 6876
Graham, Mrs. Isabella (Marshall) 1742-
  1814, 22262
Graham, James, 22263
Graham, James Duncan, 3658, 5546
Graham, James J., ed., 3659
Graham, Jane Hermione, 6876

Graham, John, b.1794, 22264
Graham, John Andrew, 1764-1841, 12341, 12342
Graham, Roscoe William, 14209
Graham, Samuel, 1756-1831, 3659, 22265
Graham, William, 1798-1854, 12343
Graham, William Alexander, 1804-1875, 22266
Graham, William Sloan, 1818-1847, 22267
Graham and I, 11091
Grahame, 10264
Grahame, James, 1765-1811. Africa delivered,
  1809, 25285
Grahame, James, 1790-1842, 12344
Grahame, James John, 22265
Grain, Ecuador, 18387
Grajal, A., 19639
Grammar, Comparative and general, 97
A grammatical sketch of the Heve language,
  12345
La gran experiencia, 20215
Gran Quivira, N.M., 2915
Granada (City) Universidad. Escuela Social.
  Publicaciones, 18215
Granada (Kingdom), History, Spanish conquest,
  1476-1492, 9997; Fiction, 9280
Granary burial ground, Boston, 1506
Granby, Mass., Geneal, 21800
Grand Alliance, War of the, 1689-1697, 1691
Grand Army Hall and Memorial Association of
  Illinois, 6877
Grand army of the republic. Dept. of
  Massachusetts, 22003
Grand canyon, 17422
The grand era of ruin to nations from foreign
  influence, 363
Grand Isle County, Vt., History, 5860
Grand juries, 13089
Grand jury, 14410
Un grand peuple qui se relève, 24473
The grand question, whether war, or no war,
  with Spain, 23740
La grand-tronciade, 21851
Le grand voyage du pays des Hurons, situé en
  l'Amérique vers la mer douce, 23563
A grande festa dos lanceiros, 18993
Las grandes mentiras de nuestra historia, 6249
Grandfather Lickshingle, 9244
Grandfort, Marie (Fontenay) de "Mme. Manoël
  de Grandfort," 3660, 6880; L'autre monde,
  4276
The Grandissimes, 8926
The grandmother of slaves, by her grand-
  daughter, 24664
Grandpapa mouse and his family, 10046
Grandpierre, Jean Henri, 1799-1874, 12346,
  12347
Granger, Amos Phelps, 1789-1866, 24507

195

Granger, Gideon, 1767-1822, 12348, 12349, 22258
Granger, Lewis, 1819-1890, 16623
Granier de Cassagnac, Bernard Adolphe, 1806-1880, 24508, 24509
Granite crags of California, 16617
Grannan, Riley, 1870-1908, 13560, 14493
Grant, Andrew, 6881
Grant, Anne, 14210
Grant, Charles, viscount de Vaux, 12350
Grant, George Monro, 1835-1902, 7384
Grant, Jeannette A., 6882
Grant, Joseph W., 12351
Grant, Philip A., 14211
Grant, Ulysses Simpson, pres. U.S., 1822-1885, 1531, 1547, 3661, 6569, 8374, 22160, 22387, 22584
Grant, William Robertson, 1811-1852, 535
Grantham, Sir Thomas, fl.1673-1711, 3662
Grapes, 15217
Graphology, 20624
Grases, Pedro, 1909-, 6794, 19635
Grasse-Tilly, François Joseph Paul, marquis de, 1722-1788, 4654
Grasses, 14024; California, Northwestern, 16344
Grasses and forage plants, California, 16107
Grassland days and grassland ways, 15359
Grattan, Peachy R., 24510
Grattan, Thomas Colley, 1792-1864, 3663
Gratz family, 13838
Gratz Park, 15643
Grau, Ricardo, illustr., 18975
Graves, George T., 14212
Graves, H.A., 16625
Graves, John Temple, 1856-1925, 3664
Graves, Richard S., 16626
Graves, S.H., 16627
Graves, Thomas Graves, 1st baron, 1725-1802, 12352
Graves, William, 1724?-1801, 12352
Gravier, Gabriel, 1827-1904, 3724, 16628
Gravier, Jacques, 1651-1708, 3665, 3666, 12353
Gravities and gaieties, 9627
Gray, Albert Zabriskie, 1840-1889, 6883
Gray, Alonzo, 1808-1860, 12354
Gray, Andrew, 5370, 5512
Gray, Andrew B., 3667
Gray, Asa, 1810-1888, 12355, 22268
Gray, Barry, pseud., 9060
Gray, Edward, 1764-1810, 12356
Gray, Francis Calley, 1790-1856, 12357, 12358

Gray, Frederick Turell, 1804-1855, 12359
Gray, George, 14260
Gray, Horatio, 1828-1903, 12360
Gray, Hugh, 6884
Gray, John, 1764-1808, 22032
Gray, John Hamilton, b.1814, 6183
Gray, John Thompson, 14213
Gray, John W., 3668
Gray, Robert, 1761-1822, 12361
Gray, Samuel, d.1770, 23477, 23567
Gray, Thomas, 1772-1847, 12362-12364
Gray, Thomas, d.1849, 22269
Gray, Thomas R., 25738
Gray, William Cunningham, 1830-1901, 12365
Gray, William Farley, 3669, 12366
Gray, William M., 16629
The gray and the blue, 10657
The gray champion, 9827
Gray roses, 9740
"Graybeard's" Colorado, 16621
Graydon, Alexander, 1752-1818, 12367
Graydon, William Murray, 10283
Grayling, 10783
Grayson, Andrew J., 3670
Grayson, William John, 1788-1863, 3671, 3672, 24511
Graysons, Memoirs of the, 5474
Gréard, Octave, 1828-1904, 7494
The great American battle, 11677
The great and final experiment, 11164
Great auction sale of slaves, at Savannah, Georgia, March 2d and 3d, 1859, 25689
Great awakening, 11764, 21975
Great Britain, Antiquities, 13225; Army Infantry, Prince of Wales' Leinster regiment (Royal Canadians), 6129; Army, Officers, 12460; Army, Recruiting, enlistment, etc., 12230; Baronetage, 758; Biography, 223, 8177; Biography, bibliography, 212; Church history, 23744; Claims vs. Chile. Martinez de Ferrari, Marcial A., 20108; Colonial Office, 24020, 24512; Colonies, 1514, 2450, 3249, 3388, 4853, 7913, 12825, 13478; Colonies, Administration, 1539, 6786, 13040, 23655, 24518, 24564; Colonies, Africa, 24830; Colonies, Africa, South, 760; Colonies - America, 663, 13070, 13369, 13509, 21789, 22216, 22283, 23570, 23700, 24830; Colonies, America, Commerce, 23654; Colonies, America, Financial questions, 13017; Colonies, Canada, 1180, 12588, 22879, 23051; Colonies, Economic conditions, 4176; Colonies, Education, 1528; Colonies, Jamaica, 23955; Colonies, Law, 11809; Colonies, Native Races, 759, 760; Colonies, North America, 230, 380, 519, 1071, 1709, 2242, 2288, 3737, 4502,

6434, 6435, 6843, 11258, 11656, 12132, 12304, 13040, 23438, 23603, 23655; Colonies, North America, Comm., 6434, 6435; Colonies, North America, Financial questions, 1509, 11617, 13211, 13494, 22758, 23550, 23796, 23604, 23616; Colonies, North America, Financial questions, Pennsylvania, 319; Colonies, Sierra Leone, 24922; Colonies, Tariff, 22624; Colonies, West Indies, 500, 501, 12172, 13327, 22012, 22209, 23147, 24518, 24803, 25608; Comm., 91, 23720; Comm., History, 11904, 21861; Comm., North America, 23594; Comm., Russia, 12192; Comm., South America, 196; Comm., U.S., 1329, 11713, 13477, 21817, 22184, 23147, 23418, 23632, 23656; Comm., West Indies, 2370, 12368; Commercial policy, 751, 752, 1266, 12287, 13478, 21776, 22624, 22768, 22951; Commissioners for sale of incumbered estates in the West Indies, 22013; Commissioners of longitudes, 993; Constitutional history, 22074, 23391; Constitutional history, Sources, 11445; Constitutional law, 11660; Council for Virginia, 23713; Court of King's bench, 2199; Defenses, 1706; Description & travel, 3388, 3564, 3829, 4853, 4954, 5789, 10491, 11157, 11159, 23389; Economic conditions, 112, 1537, 4487, 13113, 21861, 22776; Economic policy, 1539, 23707; Emigration & immigration, 2195, 12337; Emigration & immigration, History, 7158; Fiction, 9641; Foreign Office, 24196, 24513, 24514; Foreign relations, 1947, 6529; Foreign relations, 1760-1789, 13364; Foreign relations, 1837-1901, 11466, 11467; Foreign relations, Brazil, 24125; Foreign relations, Confederate States of America, 4763, 12231; Foreign relations, France, 2183, 22216, 23594, 23701; Foreign relations, Guatemala, 8298; Foreign relations, Netherlands, 2026, 23144, 23145; Foreign relations, South America, 1588, 1713; Foreign relations, Spain, 12129, 12368, 13408, 21776, 23127, 23583, 23594, 23740; Foreign relations, Spanish America, 22769; Foreign relations, Texas, 16630; Foreign relations, Treaties, 11371; Foreign relations, U.S., 295, 519, 520, 1142, 1948, 2183, 2416, 12199, 12231, 12378, 13797, 13405, 21817,

23418, 23443, 25440; Historical geography, 761; History, 15813, 22883, 22986; History, To 449, Sources, 761; History, 1066-1687 Fiction, 9847; History, 1714-1837, 3662; History, 1760-1789, 13499, 22869; History, Addresses, essays, lectures, 23225; History, Charles I, 1625-1649, Pamphlets, 22122; History, Civil war, 1642-1649, Pamphlets, 23743; History, Commonwealth and protectorate, 1649-1660, Fiction, 9843; History, Edward VI and Mary, 1547-1558, Fiction, 10286; History, Elizabeth, 1558-1603, 24453, 22680; History, George I, 1714-1727 Pamphlets, 23608; History, George II, 1727-1760, Pamphlets, 13073, 23605, 23607; History, Geroge III, 1760-1820, 103, 115, 1131, 1362, 21781, 22498, 22593; History, George III, 1760-1820, Pamphlets, 11227, 13431; History, George IV, 1820-1830, 1131; History James I, 1603-1625, 22680; History, Naval, 185, 1540, 1690; History, Naval, 1649-1660, 22132; History, Naval, 18th century, 1012, 1477, 2027; History, Naval, 19th century, 1477, 22674; History, Naval, Stuarts, 1603-1714, 1691; History, Naval, Tudors, 1485-1603, 11412, 24453; History, Norman Conquest, 15157; History, Puritan revolution, 1642-1660 - Fiction, 9842; History, Stuarts, 1603-1714 Fiction, 9463; History, Tudors, 1485-1603, 11412; History, Wars of the Roses, 1455-1485, 4737; India, Office, 24515; Laws, statutes, etc., 23224, 24715, 24914; Laws, statutes, etc., 1485-1509 (Henry VII), 22285; Laws, statutes, etc., 1660-1685 (Charles II), 25419; Laws, statutes, etc., 1689-1694 (William and Mary), 3805; Laws, statutes, etc., 1714-1727 (George I), 23245; Navy, 1949; Navy, Biography, 23177; Navy, History, 2096, 2187; Navy, Lists of vessels, 1757; Neutrality, 1948; Parliament, 6885-6887, 24516, 25557; Parliament, 1768-1774, 22767; Parliament, 1819, 24517; Parliament. House of Lords, 13460; Parliament. Papers by command, cmd., 257, 24196; Parliament. Papers by command, cmd. 2910, 24652; Parliament Reform, 11665; Peerage, 758; Politics & government, 113, 1594, 1597, 2525, 5050, 11456, 11660, 23685; Politics & government, 1642-1649, 23744; Politics & government, 1700-1780, 21827; Politics & government, 1702-1714, Pamphlets, 22299; Politics & government, 1727-1760, 2027, 13408; Politics & government, 1760-1789, 394, 1708, 2307, 11969, 12126, 13258, 13369, 13389, 13395, 13409, 21860, 23223, 23546, 23552, 23700, 23719; Politics &

government, 1760-1820, 22767; Politics & government, 1762-1765, 225; Politics & government, 1775-1783, 22161; Politics & government, 1779, 95, 102; Polotics & government, 1783, 11517; Politics & government, 1784, 11549; Politics & government, 1789-1820, 1932, 11616; Politics & government, 1800-1837, 21966; Politics & government, 1837-1901, 5848; Politics & government, 19th century, 1596; Privy council. Judicial committee, 11809; Public Record Office, 19632; Relations (general) with U.S., 22133; Social life & customs, 8641, 10861, 12785, 12841, 13498; Sovereigns, etc., 22493; Sovereigns, etc., 1649-1658, (Oliver Cromwell), 12368; Treaties, etc., 2183; Treaties, etc., 1760-1820 (George III), 22270; Treaties, etc., 1837-1901, 19095, 24519, 24520
The great Canadian north west, 6050
The great carbuncle, 9827
The great caverns of Kentucky, 13579
The Great central route via Nebraska City to Pike's Peak, 3673
The great condition, 10016
The great conspiracy, 22691
The great country, 5013
The great deliverance and the new career, 2792
The great deserts and forests of North America, 3517
The great diamond hoax and other stirring incidents in the life of Asbury Harpending, 16701
Great distress and loss of the lives of American citizens, 17501
The great divorce case!, 13171
The great fur land, 7886
The great good place, 10016
The great impeachment and trial of Andrew Johnson, 13230
The great issue to be decided in November next!, 12369
Great Lakes, 9619, 12239, 16394; Commerce, 940; Description & travel, 5103, 7454, 22411; Description & travel Guide-books, 22128; Discovery & exploration, 7008, 16995
A great love, 8914
A great man fallen!, 7662
Great opportunities for farmers, business men and investors in Nebraska, 16096
Great orations, 24521
The great plains, 17356
Great plains, Description & travel, 1197

4686, 5060
Great providences toward the loyal part of this nation, 1299
The great question for the people!, 12645
The great rebellion, 11391
Great revival, 14203
Great Revival in Kentucky, 15607
Great Revival of 1801, 4866
The great revolution of 1840, 7594
Great sale of real estate, 14214
Great Salt Lake, 5255, 5604, 16968; Description & travel, 4281
The Great Salt Lake trail, 16854
The great secret, 10083
Great Smoky Mountains, 2997
The great south, 4173
Great southern railway, 3674
The great Southwest, 4598, 15850
The great stone of Sardis, 10889
The great surrender to the rebels in arms, 12370
Great trans-continental tourist's guide, 12371
The great "trunk mystery" of New York city, 9648
The great west, 3570, 3736, 16325, 16722
The greatening of Abraham Lincoln, 7161
Greater Britain, 3249
A greater Kentucky, 13820
Greater Lexington Committee, 14215
Greater Los Angeles and southern California, 16090, 16091
The greatest concern in the world, 23303
"The greatest of these is love," 9331
Greatness in little things, 10584
Greatness the result of goodness, 23777
Greatorex, Eleanor, illustr., 15805
Greatorex, Eliza (Pratt), 16632
Greaves' disappearance, 9817
Grece, Charles Frederick, 12372
Greece, Colonies, 13425, 23570; Economic conditions, 24490; History, 16038; Politics & government, 23570; Social conditions, 25080; Social life & customs, 25944
Greek drama, History & criticism, 18954
Greek language, Grammar, 1500-1800, 6373
Greeley, Horace, 1811-1872, 3026, 3675, 6888, 11226, 11450, 12373, 12374, 22271, 24522
Greeley family, 9036
Greeley, Col., Description, 17514
Greely, A.W. & Glassford, W.A., 16633
Greely, Allen, 1781-1866, 12375
Green, Ashbel, 1762-1848, 12376, 12377, 22272
Green, Beriah, 1795-1874, 24523
Green, Charles Ransley, 1845-1915, 16634
Green, Duff, 1791-1875, 12378

Green, Elisha Winfield, 14825, 24524
Green, Frank William, 6889
Green, George Washington, 1811-1883,
  12393-12395
Green, H.T., 3677
Green, Harold Everett, 14216
Green, Jacob, 1722-1790, 12379
Green, James Stephen, 1817-1870, 16635,
  24525, 24526
Green, Jasper, illustr., 10049
Green, John, 211
Green, John, 1835-1913, 12380
Green, John Bremner, d.1905, 12381
Green, John Orne, 1841-, 12382
Green, John Paterson, 1845-, 3678
Green, Joseph, 1706-1780, 12383
Green, Lewis Warner, 1806-1863, 15591
Green, Mrs. Mary Rowena (Maverick)
  1874-, 17162
Green, Matthew, 1696-1737, 12384
Green, Nelson Winch, 3679
Green, Raleigh Travers, 1872-, 3680
Green, Samuel, d.1822, 12385
Green, Samuel, 1798-1834, 12386
Green, Samuel Abbott, 1530-1818, 3239
Green, Thomas Jefferson, 1801-1863, 3681
Green, Thomas Marshall, 1837-1904, 3682
Green, Warren, 14217
Green, William, 24527
Green, William, 1748-, 3683
Green, William Spotswood, 1847-, 6890
Green family (Thomas Greene, 1606?-
  1667), 12400
Green-back, pseud., 12387
Green Cove Spring, Florida, 5489
The green funeral, 14884
Green mountain annals, 9530
Green peas, picked from the patch of
  Invisible Green, esq., 9242
Green River, 14220, 14751
Greenbacks, 11981, 12387
Greene, Albert Gorton, 1802-1868, 2128
Greene, Asa, 1789-1838, 12388
Greene, Benjamin, 1764-1837, 12389
Greene, Charles S., 12390
Greene, Christopher Rhodes, 1786-1825,
  12391
Greene, David, 1797?-1866, 12392
Greene, J.W., 2269
Greene, Jeremiah Evarts, 1834-1902, 16636
Greene, Jerome B., 12396
Greene, Jesse, 1791-1847, 16637
Greene, John W., 3684
Greene, Jonathan Harrington, b.1812,
  12397
Greene, Mrs. Mary, 16637

Greene, Max, 3685
Greene, Nancy Lewis, 14218, 14766
Greene, Nathaniel, 1742-1786, 12395, 13765
Greene, Richard Henry, 1839-, 12398
Greene, Samuel D., b.1788, 12399
Greene, Samuel Stillman, 1810-1883, 12400
Greene, Talbot, 14219
Greene, W.P., 14220
Greene, William, 1797-1883, 12401
Greene, William Batchelder, 1819-1878, 12402
Greene, William H., 12403
Greene County Colonization Society, 24549
Greenhow, Robert, 1800-1854, 6891, 16638-
  16640, 23541
Greenhow, Rose (O'Neal) 1814-1864, 12404
Greenland, Description & travel, 12459,
  13372, 23069; Poetry, 1375
The Greenland minstrel, 1375
Greenleaf, A.B., 3686
Greenleaf, Benjamin, 1786-1864, 16183
Greenleaf, Jonathan, 1785-1865, 12405, 12406,
  22273
Greenleaf, Lawrence Nichols, b.1838, 12407
Greenleaf, Moses, 1777-1834, 12408, 12409
Greenleaf, Simon, 1783-1853, 12410
Greenleaf family (Edmund Greenleaf, 1574-1671),
  12405
Greenough, William Parker, 1830?-1900, 6892
Greenough, William Whitwell, d.1899, 12411,
  12412
Greenough's directory... of Brookline, 1566
Greenup Association of Baptists, Kentucky,
  15555
Greenup County, Ky., 15481; History, 15471
Greenville, Ky., 14220
Greenwich, Conn., Geneal., 23410; History,
  23410
Greenwood, Andrew, 1776-1816, 12413
Greenwood, Francis William Pitt, 1797-1843,
  12414, 12415
Greenwood, Grace, pseud., 16632
Greenwood, Thomas, 1851-1908, 3687
Greenwood, Thomas Jefferson, 1799-1874,
  22321
Greenwood Cemetery, Brooklyn, 1855, 21958;
  Poetry, 1855
Greenwood leaves, 10222
Greer, Michael, 14221
Gregg, Alexander, bp., 1819-1893, 12255,
  12416
Gregg, Andrew, 1755-1835, 2211
Gregg, Jarvis, 1808-1836, 12417
Gregg, Thomas, b.1808, 16641
Gregg, William, 1800-1867, 12418
Grégoire, Henri-Baptiste, constitutional bp.
  of Blois, 1750-1831, 6484, 6896, 6897, 7622,

12419-12422, 24095, 24534, 25739;
  Observations critiques, 813
Gregory XVI, pope, 1765-1846, 23980,
  24416
Gregory, James F., 17777
Gregory, John, 12423
Gregory, Lair H., 17410
Gregory, Olinthus Gilbert, 1774-1841,
  1721
Gregory, Samuel, 6898
Greifenstein, 6495, 9224
Grenell, Zelotes, 1841-, 17756
Grenfell, Helen L., 16642
Grenfell, Sir William Thomason, 1865-
  1940, 6899-6901
Grenville, George, 1712-1770, 12424,
  13059, 22738
Greswell, William Henry Parri, 1848-1923,
  6903
Greville, Robert Kaye, 1794-1866, 24528
Greville Fane, 7126
Grey, Sir Charles Edward, 1785-1865,
  12426
Grey, Frederick William, 16643
Grey, Isaac, 12427
Greyslaer, 3893
Grez, Vicente, 20158
Grice, Julia, 9331
Grider, George W., 14222
Grider, Henry, 1796-1866, 12428
Gridley, Jackson ex dem. Tuttle vs.,
  22427
Gridley, John, 12429
Gridley, Philo, 1796-1864, 12430
Grier, D.P., 2687
Grier, Thomas Graham, 1865-, 6904
Grierson cavalry raid, 1863, 5321
Griesinger, Theodor, 1809-1884, 3689
Grieve, George, 1748-1809, tr., 2979
Griffin, Augustus, 1767-1866, 12431
Griffin, Bill, 14223
Griffin, Frederick, 12432
Griffin, Gilderoy Wells, 1840-1891, 3690,
  3691
Griffin, John, 1769-1834, 12433
Griffin, Solomon Bulkey, 1852-, 6905
Griffin's journal, 12431
Griffing, B.N., 14224
Griffing, Jane R., 3692
Griffis, Joseph K., 1852-, 16644
Griffis, Robert F., pub., 1877
Griffith, Dorothy Amburgey, 14225, 14226
Griffith, James Barton, 3693
Griffith, John, 1713-1776, 3694, 12434
Griffith, Thomas Waters, 1767-1830,
  12435

Griffith, William, 25122
Griffith, William, 1766-1826, 12436-12438
Griffiths, D., jr., 16645
Griffiths, David, 16646
Grigsby, Hugh Blair, 1806-1881, 12439-12441
Grigsby, Melvin, 1845-, 3695
Grile, Dod, pseud., 8802
Grillparzer, Franz, 1791-1872, 19612
Grim, Charles Frederic, 12442
The grim chieftain of Kansas, 16516
Grimes, Absalom Carlisle, 1834-1911, 3696
Grimes, Bryan, 1828-1880, 3697
Grimes, James Wilson, 1816-1872, 7945, 24529
Grimes, John, 1799-1838, 15197
Grimes, John Bryan, 1868-1923, 11515
Grimes, William, 24530
Grimké, Angelina Emily, 1805-1879, 24531
Grimké, Frederick, 1791-1863, 12443
Grimké, Thomas Smith, 1786-1834, 2151, 12444-
  12446
Grimshaw, William, 1782-1852, 12447, 12448,
  22274
Grimsley, Elizabeth Todd, 7300
Gringo, 3197, 8195
Los gringos, 8406, 8407, 19762
Grinnell, Elizabeth, 1851-, 16647
Grinnell, Joseph, 1877-, 16647
Grinnell, Josiah Bushnell, 1821-1891, 16648,
  16649
Grinnell expedition, 1st, 1850-1851, 13428
Grinnell expedition, 2nd, 1853-1855, 2428,
  13428, 22366
Gripenberg, Alexandra, friherrinna, 1857-
  1913, 3698
Griper (ship), 7695
Griscom, John, 1774-1852, 12450
Griscom, John D., 23920
Griscom, John Hoskins, 1809-1874, 12449-12451
Grisebach, August Heinrich Rudolf, 1814-1879,
  12452
Griset, Ernest, 16401
Griswold, Alexander Viets, bp., 1766-1843,
  12453
Griswold, Mrs. Charlotte A. (Myers), 12457
Griswold, Chauncey D., 12454
Griswold, Hattie Tyng, 10899
Griswold, Norman W., 16650
Griswold, Rufus Wilmot, 1815-1857, 3699-3702,
  12455-12457, 22275
Griswold, Thomas, 14227
Grito en los Andes, 18583
Gritos del capuchino enfermo a todos los
  predicadores del orbe, 8008
The groans of Jamaica, 12458
Groce Camp, Texas, 4627
The grocery man, 10502

Grone, A.C.E. von, 6906
Grone, Carl von, d.1849, 6906
Gronovius, Joannes Fredericus, 1611-1671, 3703; Flora virginica, 930
Groome, W., illustr., 6785
Groot, Jeldert Jansz., 12459
Gros, Jean Baptiste Louis, baron, 1793-1870, 7903
Grose, Francis, 1731?-1791, 12460
Grose, Howard Benjamin, 1851-, 6907
Grose, William, 1812-1900, 3704
Grosó, José L., 7769
Gross, Charles Heebner, 1838-1902, 12461
Gross, Ezra Carter, d.1829, 24532
Gross, Samuel David, 1805-1884, 3705-3708, 12462, 12463
Gross, William, 1796-1823, 12464
Grosscup, Ben S., 5798
Grosvenor, Daniel, 1750-1834, 12466
Grosvenor, David Adams, 1802-1866, 12465
Grosvenor, Ebenezer, 1739-1788, 12466
Grosvenor, Lemuel, 12467
Grotius, pseud, 12468
Groton, Mass. First parish church. Ecclesiastical council 1826, 12469; History, 1766; Public library, 12470
Groton Heights, Battle of, 1781, 22306
The group, 1901
Groups, Theory of, 20621
Groussac, Paul, 1848-1929, 3709, 5849
Grout, Henry Martyn, 12471
Grout, William Wallace, 1836-1902, 12472
Groux, Daniel Edward, 12473
Grove, Joseph, d.1764, 12474
Grover, La Fayette, 1823-1911, 17309
Grover, Martin, 1811-1875, 12475
Groves, Moses, plaintiff in error, 25819
Grow, Galusha Aaron, 1822-1907, 24533
Growler's income tax, 8564
The growth of New York, 12476
Gruff, Growler, pseud., 11933
Gruger, F.R., illustr., 13541, 14159, 14961, 15262
Grund, Francis Joseph, 1805-1863, 3710, 12477, 12478, 16651
Grundy, Felix, 1777-1840, 12479
Grunebaum-Ballin, Paul Frédéric Jean, 1871-, 24534
Grüner, Adelgunde, 3586
La gruta iluminada, 18356
Guadalajara, Mexico. Catedral. Cabildo, 12480; Description, 6472, 7647, 20481; Galleries and museums, 18210; History, 6070, 6846, 7907, 20099; Santuario de Nuestra Señora de San Juan, 6754; Seminario conciliar, 7876; Water-supply, 6364
Guadalajara de Indias, 7663
Guadalupe Hidalgo, Treaty of, 1848, 11942, 16959
Guadalupe, Nuestra Señora de, 1786, 1787, 6160, 6269, 7013, 7789
Guadeloupe, Description & travel, 1649, 4644, 24315; Economic conditions, 25564; History, 2232, 18814
La Guadeloupe pittoresque, 1649
Guadiana, José Guadalupe, illustr., 18562
Guanabara, Brazil, Census, 19427
Guanajuato, Mexico (City), 7422; (State), 7422
Guarani language, Dictionaries, Spanish, 7921
Guapore, hombre y reo, 20100
Guararapes, Battles of, 18992
Guaratinguetá-Aparecida, 20358
Guard, Louis, illustr., 17687
O guarda dos passaros, 18234
Guardian and ward   Venezuela, 18051
The guardian of the flock, 14832
Guasa pura, 19114
Guatemala, 442; Antiquities, 6166, 6167, 6406, 6407, 7551, 19748; Army, 18022; Boundaries, 6803; Boundaries   British Honduras, 8298; Civilization, 6908; Description & travel, 5880, 5921, 6166, 6252, 6452, 6777, 6908, 6984, 7191, 7235, 7236, 7306, 7439, 7452, 7521, 7534, 7551, 7552, 7648, 7655, 7686, 7893, 7917, 7961, 7996, 8075, 8164, 8182, 8183, 8282, 20660; Description & travel   Guide-books, 6455, 6909, 7960; Description & travel   Poetry, 7233, 7234, 7237, 7238; Dirección General de Caminos, 6909; Economic conditions, 7452, 18063; Foreign relations, Belize, 18950; Foreign relations, Gt. Britain, 8298; Foreign relations, Honduras, 12877; History, 6789, 7551, 7686, 20452; History, To 1821, 13342; Industries, 20034; Laws, statutes, etc., 20067; Politics & government 1945-, 20088; Social conditions, 18324; Social life & customs, 6252
Guatemala (City), 5921; Escuela normal central para varones, 6908; Universidad de San Carlos Facultad de Humanidades, Bibliography, 19629; Universidad de San Carlos. Instituto de Investigaciones y Mejoramiento Educativo, 18381; Universidad nacional. Facultad de ciencias jurídicas y sociales. Revista, 8298
Guatemala, ancient and modern, 7551
Guatemala profile, 6252
Guatemala: Mayaland of eternal spring, 7960
Guatimozin, último emperador de Méjico, 12299
Guayaquil. Universidad, 18651
Guadschinsky, Sarah, 19659

Güell y Renté, José, 1819-1884, 12481
Güemes, José Antonio, 19828
Guernsey, Egbert, 1823-1903, 12482
Guerra, Antonio Teixera, 1824-, 19281
Guerra, Eduardo, 6910
Guerra E., Guillermo A., 20335
La guerra de los Charruas en la Banda Oriental, 18010
La guerra de los dioses, 19090
A guerra depois da guerra, 19606
La guerra sagrada, 19729
La guerra separatista de Cuba, 19896
Guerrant, Edward Owings, 1838-1916, 14228
La guerre américaine; son origine et ses vraies causes, 24282
Guerre de la sécession, esquisse des événements militaires et politiques des États-Unis de 1861 à 1865, 24805
La guerre des frères, 2095
Guerren, Charles, 16842
Guerrero, Miguel, illustr., 6754
Guerrero, Raul, 5874
Guerrero, Vicente, pres. Mexico, 1783-1831, 120
Guerrillas, 16263, 22829
The guerrillas of the West, 15862
Guest, Moses, 3713, 6911
Guest, Richard, 12483
Guest, Lady Theodora (Grosvenor) 1840-, 3712
A guest at the Ludlow, 10436
Guests from Bibbet Island, 9995
The guests of Brazil, 13032
The guests of Mrs. Timms, 10038
Gueudeville, Nicolas, 1654(ca.)-1721(ca.), 7222, 7223, 22751
Guggenheimer, Jay Caesar, 24668
Guiana, 7800; Economic conditions, 25564
Guichenot, Alphonse, 21853
Guignard, Philippe, 1820-, 12487
Guild, Calvin, 1808-1897, 12488
Guild, Reuben Aldridge, 1822-1899, 12489-12492
Guild, Samuel Eliot, 1819-1862, 12493
Guild, William, 12494, 12495
Guild family (John Guild, 1616?-1682), 12488
Guillemin-Tarayre, Edmond, 1832-1920, 6913, 6914
Guillermin de Montpinay, Gilbert, 12496
Guillot Castellano, Manuel, 1936-1962, 19556
Guimarães, Carlos da Rocha, 19309
Guimarães, Celso Fout, 1907 , 0716
Guimarães Rosa, João. Grande Sertão: Veredas, 20538

Guinea, Description & travel, 522, 6989, 8320, 8321, 13110
Guinn, James Miller, 1834-, 16652-16656
Guinnard, Auguste, b.1832?, 12497, 12498
Guipon, Leon, illustr., 15266
Guiral Moreno, Mario, 1882-, 6522
Güiraldes, Ricardo, 1886-1927, 18933; Don Segundo sombra, 19925
Guirey, William, 12499
Guitarte, Guillermo L., 20227
Guiteros, Pedro José, 1814-1890, 12500
Guizot, François Pierre Guillaume, 1787-1874, 12501, 12502, 22276
The Gulf and inland waters..., 14939
The Gulf coast, 5710
The Gulf-department in '62, 12781
Gulf Oil, nacionalización de sus bienes, 19725
Gulf states, 4332; Description & travel, 5589, 5710; History, 13456; History, Colonial period., 16441
Gulley, L.C., 15866
Gullion, Carroll Hanks, 14231
Gulliver Joi, 10504
Gulzar, 4923
The gum tree story, 14757
Gun, rod, and saddle, 12257
Gunby, A.L., 6915
Gunn, Alexander, 1784-1829, 12503
Gunn, Benjamin Jesse, 1865-, 6916
Gunn, Mrs. Elizabeth Le Breton, 1811-1906, 16657
Gunn, Lewis Carstairs, 1813-1892, 16657, 25373
Gunn, Otis Berthoude, 1828-1901, 3717
Gunn family (Alexander Gun, 1785-1828), 16657
Gunnar, a tale of Norse life, 8833
Gunnison, John Williams, 1812-1853, 3615, 3616, 3718, 12504, 16591
Gunnison Massacre-1853, 15691
The Gunpowder Plot, 9463, 22680; Fiction, 9463
Gunsaulus, F.W., 17276
Gunston Hall, 7431
Guntersville, Ala., basin-antiquities, 15681
Günther, Erich, 6917
Gupte, Pranay B., 24535
Gurley, Phineas Densmore, 1816-1868, 6918, 12505
Gurley, Ralph Randolph, 1792-1872, 12506-12508, 24536, 24537
Gurney, Alfred, 1845-1898, 3719
Gurney, Joseph, 1744-1815, 23786
Gurney, Joseph John, 1788-1847, 3720, 6919, 24107
Gurowski, Adam, 1805-1866, 3721
Gurrea, Félix, 18251
Guseo, Marco, 24538

Gustavus Vasa, the deliverer of his country, 1564
Gutenberg, Johann, 1397?-1468, 10497
Guthrie, Abelard, 1814-1873, 16262
Guthrie, J.D., 14232
Guthrie, James, 6568
Guthrie, William, 1708-1770, 3722, 22277
Guthrie of the Times, 13541
Gutiérrez, Blas J., 12509
Gutiérrez, Carlos, 8096
Gutiérrez, Juan María, 1809-1878, 7853, 12510, 12511, 18931
Gutiérrez de Quintanilla, José Manuel, 6350
Gutiérrez de la Arena, Diego Martín, 6806, 7962, 7963
Gutiérrez de Lafuente, Antonio, 22278
Gutiérrez del Arroyo, Isabel, 19227
Gutiérrez Nájera, Manuel, 1859-1895, 7844
Gutierrez y Salazar, Pedro, 24539
Gutta-percha, 19002
Guy Rivers, 10772
Guyana, Economic conditions, 19579-19582; Politics & government, 18147, 19579-19581; Another way to socialism, 18147
Guyer, Isaac D., 12512
Guzmán, Antonio Leocádio, 1801-1884, 12513
Guzmán, Juan Joseph, d.1819, 19737
Guzmán, Martín Luis. El aguila y la serpiente, 19967; La sombra del caudillo, 19967
Guzmán Blanco, Antonio, pres. Venezuela, 1829-1899, 18130
Guzmán Cruchaga, Juan, 20453
Guzmán de Alfarache, 5861, 5862
Guzmán Esponda, Eduardo, 20710
Gwin, William McKendree, 1805-1885, 3723
Gyles, John, 1678?-1755, 12514
Gymnocladus dioicus (L.), 13784
Gypsies, 17029
The gypsies of the Danes' dike, 10517

Haas, Elise S., 6920
Haas, J.C., of Philadelphia, 22279
Habeas corpus, 1454, 13089, 13134; Georgia, 22238; U.S., 1676, 6082, 11272, 12461, 13273, 22622, 24080, 25047, 25067
Habersham, Joseph Clay, d.1855, 22514
Habersham, S.E., 3724
L'habitation Saint-Ybars, 4451
El habla de Guanajuato, 19203
Hablar claro, 18183
El habla popular en la literatura costarricense, 18580

Hachard, Marie Madeleine, in religion, Sister Saint Stanislas, 3725
Hacke, William, 22280
Hackelton, Mrs. Marcia W., 12515
Hackensmith, Charles William, 1906-, 14233
Häcker, Ludwig, 22281
Hacker, William, d.1830? 5754
Hacket, Thomas, 1560-1590, 22285
Hackett, Horatio Balch, 1808-1875, 12516
Hackett, James, 12517
Hackett, Karleton, 6921
Hackett, William Henry Young, 1800-1878, 1488
Haco, Dion, pseud., 8133, 22282
Hadden, James, 1845-, 16658
Hadfield, Joseph, 1759-1851, 6922
Hadfield, William, 1806-1887, 12518, 12519
Hadley, John Vestal, 1840-1915, 3726
Hadley, William Hobart, 12520
Hadley, Mass., 12521; Geneal, 21800; History, 12571
Haedens, Kléber, 14234
Haenke, Thaddäus, 1761-1817, 437
Haerne, Désiré Pierre Antonio de, 1804-1890, 24540
Hafen, Le Roy R., 1893-, 16659
Die Haftung für das Verschulden der Angestellten im klassischen römischen Recht, 25457
Hagadorn, Henry J., 1832-1903, 16660
Hagadorn, Wiliam, jr., 12522
Hagar, a story of to-day, 8948
Hagar the martyr, 10876
Hagen, Hermann August, 1817-1893, 12523
Hagen, Hermann Bessel, 1889-, 6923
Hager, Albert David, 1817-1888, 12524
Hager, Heinrich, 3727
Haggard, Henry Rider, 1856-, 7144
Haglee, Henry Morris, 1815-1886, 13024
Hagner, Charles Valerius, 1796-1878, 12525
Hagner, Thomas Holme, 12526
Hagthorpe, John, fl.1627, 22283
Hague, Mrs. Parthenia Antoinette (Vardaman) 1838-, 3728
Hague, William, 1808-1887, 12527, 12528
Haies, Edward, 1479
Haigh, Samuel, 12529
Haight, Henry Huntley, 1825-1878, 24787
Hail Kentucky!, 14383
Hailey, John, 1835-1921, 16661
Haime, Jules, 23153
Hain, Augustus H.F., 12530
Haines, Elijah Middlebrook, 1822-1889, 12531, 12532
Haines, William A., 12533
Haines, Zenas T., 3729
Hair, James T., 22284

The hair-breadth escapes and adventures of "Grizzly Adams," 2491
A hairdresser's experience in high life, 4835
Haiser, Franz, 1871-, 24541
Haiti, 6064, 6924, 7261, 11360, 11974, 22793, 23050, 24703, 24923, 25454; Commerce, 6771, 6874, 7939-7941; Constitution, 7507, 11360; Description & travel, 2768, 6583, 6924, 7143, 8399, 12651, 12704, 19903, 22930, 23114; Economic conditions, 18624; Foreign relations, Spain, 22480; History, 1993, 3237, 3829, 6064, 6477, 7261, 11568, 12704, 22107, 22930, 24339: History, To 1791, 11235; History, 1804, 19063; History, 1804-1844, 12396, 22330; History, Revolution, 1791-1804, 6771, 11423, 11767, 11855, 12861, 19153, 21952, 22027, 22787, 23071, 24751, 25035, 25608, 25739; History, Revolution, 1791-1804 - Claims, 997; History, Revolution, 1791-1804 Fiction, 8599; Politics & government, 6924, 19063, 19903; Politics & government, To 1789, 7269, 7934-7940; Politics & government, 1791-1804, 778, 25556; Politics & government, 1804-1844, 25180; Politics & government, Revolution, 6874, 7507, 7598, 7790, 7828, 7933, 8053; Register, 18159; Social conditions, 18624, 19903
Haiti and Spain: a memorial, by Richard Hill, 22480
Hake, 18298, 18453
Hakluyt, Richard, 1552?-1616, 6925, 22285
Hal Gilman, 3135
Halamar, 9327
Der Halbindianer, 4498
Haldeman, Samuel Stechman, 1812-1880, 5255
Haldeman's Picture of Louisville, 14174
Haldimand, Sir Frederick, 1718-1791, 6297
Hale, Apollos, 21788
Hale, B. E., 12534
Hale, Benjamin, 1797-1863, 12535
Hale, Mrs. C. L., 12536
Hale, Charles, 1831-1882, 12537
Hale, Edward Everett, 1822-1909, 2451, 6926, 8597, 12538, 12539, 16662
Hale, Enoch, 1790-1848, 11725, 12540
Hale, Horace M., 16240
Hale, John, 1800-1852, 3730
Hale, John Parker, 1806-1873, 24542, 25391
Hale, John Peter, 1824-, 14235, 14236
Hale, Lucretia Peabody, 1820-1900, 9507, 9688, 9693
Hale, Sir Matthew, 1609-1676, 21861, 21976

Hale, Mercy, b.1805, 2452
Hale, Nathan, 1755-1776, 7077, 22978; Fiction, 10765
Hale, Nathan, 1784-1863, 2453, 2454, 8804
Hale, Salma, 1787-1866, 2455, 2456, 12541
Hale, Mrs. Sarah Josepha (Buell) 1788-1879, 2457-2459
Hale, Susan, 1833-1910, 6926, 6927
Hale, Will T., 14237
Hale family, 3730
Hales, John Groves, 12542
Haley, Michael Joachim, 1846-, 4676
Haley, Thomas, 12543
The half century, 5330, 22044
A half-century of the Unitarian controversy, 12053
Ett halfår i Nya Verlden, 3698
Een half jaar in Amerika, 4197
Haliburton, Robert Grant, 12544
Haliburton, Thomas Chandler, 1796-1865, 3731, 12545-12548
Haliburton, William, 12549
Halkett, J., 6029
Halkett, John, 1768-1852, 12550
Halkin, Léon, 1872-, 24543
Hall, A. J., 16663
Hall, Aaron, 1751-1814, 12551
Hall, Abraham Oakley, 1826-1898, 3732
Hall, Almira, 15055
Hall, Alfred Bates, 1875-1936, 6928
Hall, Angelo, 1868-, 16664
Hall, Anna Maria (Fielding) "Mrs. S.C. Hall", 1800-1881, 12552
Hall, Arethusa, 1802-1891, 12553
Hall, Barnes M., 1803-1886, 16665
Hall, Basil, 1788-1844, 3733, 3734, 6929, 6930; Travels in North America, 1260, 1262
Hall, Baynard Rush, 12554
Hall, Benjamin Franklin, 1814-1891, 12555-12557
Hall, Benjamin Homer, 1830-1893, 12558, 12559
Hall, Charles Francis, 1821-1871, 12560
Hall, Charles Henry, 1820-1895, 12561
Hall, Clayton Colman, 1847-1916, 2460
Hall, David A., 11843
Hall, Daniel Weston, 1841-, 12562
Hall, David, 1683-1756, 12563
Hall, Edward Brooks, 1800-1866, 12564, 12565, 22286
Hall, Edward Hepple, 1876, 2552, 3735, 3736, 5916, 12566, 12567, 22287
Hall, Edwin, 1802-1877, 12568
Hall, Eliza Calvert, pseud., 15091-15093
Hall, F., 3737
Hall, Fayette, 6931
Hall, Fayr, 22288
Hall, Frances, 15055

Hall, Francis, d.1833, 3738, 6932, 12569
Hall, Frank, 1836-1918, 16666
Hall, Frederic, 1825-1898, 16667
Hall, Frederick, 1780-1843, 3739, 12570, 12571
Hall, Gordon, 1823-1879, 6933, 12572
Hall, Harrison, 1785-1866, 12582
Hall, Henry, 1845-, 22289
Hall, Henry Ware, 1839-1864, 2302
Hall, Hiland, 1795-1885, 22290
Hall, J.B., 3740
Hall, James, of Maryland, 24544
Hall, James, 1744-1826, 3741
Hall, James, 1793-1868, 3742-3754, 5679, 12573, 14240-14243, 16848, 22921; Statistics of the West, 2869
Hall, James, 1811-1878, 5255, 12574
Hall, John, 880, 2503
Hall, John, 1806-1894, 12575
Hall, John Newton, b.1849, 13600
Hall, John Taylor, 12576
Hall, John W., 12577
Hall, Jonathan Prescott, 1796-1862, 12578
Hall, Joseph, bp. of Norwich, 1574-1656, 22291
Hall, Joseph, 1761-1848, 12579
Hall, Marshall, 1790-1857, 3755
Hall, N.A.T., 24415
Hall, Nathan H., 14367
Hall, Nathaniel, 1805-1875, 6934, 24082
Hall, Newman, 1816-1902, 6935, 12580, 12581
Hall, R. Clifford, 14244
Hall, Mrs. Sarah (Ewing) 1761-1830, 12582
Hall, Sydney, illustr., 5926
Hall, Trowbridge, 16668
Hall, Willard, 1780-1875, 12583
Hall, Rev. William A., 12584
Hall, William Henry Bullock, 1837-, 6936
Hall, William Scott, 1905-, 14245, 14246
Hall, Winchester, 1819-, 3756
Hall & co.'s Chicago city directory, 21911
The hall of fantasy, 9823
Halleck, Fitz-Greene, 1790-1867, 12585, 12586
Halleck, Henry Wager, 1815-1872, 22292
Hallen, Albin, 1849-1924, 7494
Haller, Granville Owen, 1820-1897, 3757
Hallett, Benjamin Franklin, 1797-1862, 12587, 24545
Halley, Edmond, 1656-1742, 11945
Halley, William, 16669
Halliburton, Sir Brenton, 1773-1860, 12588, 22470

Halliburton, William Henry, b.1816, 16670
Halliday, Sir Andrew, 1781-1830, 12589
Halliday, Samuel Byram, 1812-1897, 22293
Hallock, Charles, 1834-1917, 3758
Hallock, Gerard, 1800-1866, 12592
Hallock, Leavitt Homan, 1842-, 16671
Hallock, Robert T., 12590
Hallock, William Allen, 1794-1880, 12591
Hallock, William H., 12592
Hallowell, Sarah C., 8587
Hallum, John, 16672
Halpin, Will R., 6937
Halsey, Francis Whiting, 1851-1919, 16673
Halsey, Gaius Leonard, 1819-1891, 16673
Halsey, Lewis, 1843-1914, 12593
Halsey, William, 1765?-1843, 12594
Halstead, Murat, 1829-1908, 6938
A halt at dawn, 11191
Ham, 13631; Country, 14010; Kentucky, 13710
Haman, Sidney Snook, 14280
Hambden, pseud., 12595
Hambleton, Chalkley J., 1829-, 16674
Hambleton, James Pinkney, 12596
Hamblin, Jacob, 1819-, 16675, 16676, 16714, 17043
Hambrecht, George P., 6567
Hamburg-südamerikanische Dampfschifffahrts-gesellschaft, 6939
Hamersly, Lewis Randolph, 1847-1910, 12597
Hamil, Howard Melancthon, 1847-1915, 14247
Hamilton, Alexander, 1757-1804, 708, 1807, 2422, 7311, 7803, 8131, 9022, 12140, 12598-12604, 13496, 22294, 23588, 23708
Hamilton, Alice King. White lilies, 10115
Hamilton, Andrew Jackson, 1815-1875, 12605
Hamilton, Ahne, 14248
Hamilton, Lord Archibald, d.1754, 12606
Hamilton, Lady Augusta, 12607
Hamilton, B.B., 16677
Hamilton, Dorothy, 6940
Hamilton, Frank Hastings, 1813-1886, 12608
Hamilton, Gail, pseud., 3262
Hamilton, George, 12609
Hamilton, H. W., 16678
Hamilton, Henry, pseud., 5236, 5242
Hamilton, Henry, d.1796, 3760
Hamilton, Henry Edward, 16827
Hamilton, Henry S., 1836?-, 16679
Hamilton, Holman, 1910-, 13874, 14249-14251, 14314, 14383, 15238
Hamilton, James, 1786-1857, 12610, 12611
Hamilton, James, 1814-1867, 12612
Hamilton, James Alexander, 1788-1878, 12613, 13178
Hamilton, James Cleland, 1836-, 6941, 24546
Hamilton, John Church, 1792-1882, 24547

Hamilton, Joseph Grégoire de Roulhac, 1878-, 5148, 24548
Hamilton, Leonidas Le Cenci, 6942-6944
Hamilton, Pierce Stevens, 12614
Hamilton, Robert S., 24549
Hamilton, Schuyler, 1822-1903, 12615
Hamilton, Thomas, 1789-1842, 6945-6947, 14252
Hamilton, W. Brooks, 13647
Hamilton, W.H., A strange wound, 10115
Hamilton, Walter, governor of the Leeward islands, 22209
Hamilton, William, 24550
Hamilton, William, 1811-1891, 12616
Hamilton, William B., 16680
Hamilton, William Richard, 1777-1859, 12617
Hamilton, William T., d.1842, 12618
Hamilton, William Thomas, 1796-1884, 24551
Hamilton, William Thomas, 1822-1908, 16681
Hamilton, Wilson, 16682
Hamilton family, 7182, 7803
Hamilton family of Charles county, 7182
Hamilton, Mass., History, 2246
Hamilton College, Clinton, N.Y., 616, 2268, 12619, 12620; Phoenix society, 12430; Union society, 12430
Hamilton County, Ohio, History, 13740, 14330
Hamilton society, New York, 392
Hamilton township, N.J., 8447
The Hamiltons, 8795
Hamlet, James, 23880
Hamlett, Barksdale, 14253
Hamlin, Augustus Choate, 1829-1905, 12621
Hamlin, Hannibal, 1809-1891, 873, 6458, 16683, 22764, 24552
Hamlin, Jabez, 1709-1791, 22621
Hamm, Margherita Arlina, 1871-1907, 6948
Hammer, Bonaventura, 1842-, 14254, 14255
Hammer, Victor Karl, 1882-1967, 8190, 15523, 15542; Bibliography, 14694
Hammett, Samuel Adams, 1816-1865, 3762, 3763
Hammond, Charles, 1813-1878, 12622
Hammond, Isaac B., 16684
Hammond, Jabez Delano, 1778-1855, 12623, 12624, 25026
Hammond, James Henry, 1807-1864, 12625, 12626, 22295, 23643, 24552-24555, 24773
Hammond, John, 3764
Hammond, John, fl. 1655, 12627

Hammond, Jonathan Pinkney, d.1884, 12628
Hammond, Marcus Claudius Marcellus, 1814-1876, 12629
Hammond, Samuel H., 1809-1878, 12630, 12631
Hammond, Wells Stoddard, 12632
Hammond, William Alexander, 1828-1900, 12633
Hammond versus Heamans, 3764
Hamon, Henry, 12634
Hamon, J. Hill, 14256
Hamor, Ralph, the younger, 3765
Hampa afro-cubana, 25179
Hampden, pseud., 12635
Hampshire and Hampden canal company, 1906
Hampshire co., Mass., Description & travel, 2181
Hampton, John, d.ca. 1720, 23044
Hampton, John S., 3766
Hampton, N.H. Congregational church, 415; History, 415
Hampton Heights, 10860
Hampton Roads Peace Conference, 1865, 6347, 7288
Hanaford, Jeremiah Lyford, b.1834, 12636
Hanaford, Mrs. Phebe Ann (Coffin) 1829-1921, 12637, 12538
Hanbury, David T., 16685
Hanckel, Thomas M., 12046, 12639
Hancock, Henry, 16991
Hancock, John, 12640, 12641
Hancock, John, 1671-1752, 12642
Hancock, John, 1702-1744, 12643, 12644, 22296
Hancock, John, 1737-1793, 22454, 22455
Hancock, John, 1824-1893, 12645
Hancock, Richard R., 1841?-1906, 3767
Hancock, William, 12646
Hancock, Winfield Scott, 1824-1886, 24130
Hancock Co., Ill., Biography, 16641; History, 16641
Hand, William M., 12647
The hand but not the heart, 8565
The hand of God in American history, 11264
The hand of God in the great man, 925
The hand of God with the black race, 24939
Handbook for immigrants to the United States, 3768
A handbook of Florida, 4619
Handbook of Iowa, 15998
Hand-book of the state of Mississippi, 4483
Hand-book to Kansas territory, 4910
Handbuch der geographischen wissenschaft, 6923
Hand-clasp of the East and West, 17493
Handelmann, Heinrich, 1827-1891, 12648
A handful of lavender, 1917
Handlin, William Wallace, b.1830, 12649
Handly, James, 16688

The hands, 14257
Hands off, 9681
Hands up, 16269, 16270
Handsaker, Samuel, 16689
Handy, Isaac William Ker, 1815-1878,
  12650
Haney, Lewis Henry, 1882-, 17727
Haney, William Henry, 1882-, 3769
Hanford, Levi, 1759-1854, 1754
Hankey, William Alers, 25370
Hanks, N.C., 6949
Hanley, Mrs. May Carr, 6950
Hanly, Edith Sheldon, 14258
Hanna, Joseph A., 16690
Hanna, Stewart William, d.1851, 12651
Hannaford, Ebenezer, 1840-, 3770
Hannah, 10377
Hannah Thurston, 10926
Hannay, J., 10916
Hannay, James, 1842-1910, 6951
Hannibal, Julius Caesar, pseud., 10198
Hannibal's man, 10144
Hannum, Anna Paschall, 1880-, 17346
Hanover, Mass., Geneal., 892; History,
  892
Hanover, House of, 23608
Hanover College, Hanover, Ind., 22972
Hans, Frederic Malon, 1861-, 16691
Hans, Juan Antonio de, 7108, 7909
Hans Dundermann, 9486
Hansford, 5478
Hanson, Alexander Contee, 1749-1806,
  12652-12654
Hanson, Christian, 12656
Hanson, Mrs. Elizabeth, fl.1703-1741,
  12655
Hanson, John Halloway, 1815-1854, 12656
Hanson, John Wesley, 1823-1901, 3771,
  12657, 12658, 16692
Hanson, Joseph Mills, 1876-, 16693
Hanson, Roger W., 1827-1863, 14184
Hanstaux, Gabriel, 6825
Hanström, Bertil, 1891-, 3772
Hanway, Castner, 1821-1893, 24613
Hanway, Jonas, 1712-1786, 12659
Hapgood, Theodore B., illustr., 15092
The happiness of man the glory of
  God, 1610
Happy-go-lucky, 9754
Happy hearts make happy homes, 10086
Happy home, woman's rights, and divorce,
  9010
Harben, W. H., 10125
Harben, William Nathaniel, 1858-1919,
  3773, 3774, 10125
The Harbinger, 12663

Harbison, Massy (White) "Mrs. J. Harbison,"
  1770, 12664
Harbor and river convention, Chicago, 1847,
  12665
Harbors, Brazil, 19272
Harbough, Henry, 1817-1867, 12660-12662
Harby, Isaac, 1788-1828, 12666
Harby, Mrs. Lee (Cohen), 16694
Harcourt, T. Arundel, d.1884, 5996
Harcourt, Sir William George Granville
  Venables Vernon, 1827-1904, 12667-12669
Hard, Abner, 3775
Hardee, Joseph Gilbert, 14259
Harden, Edward Jenkins, 1813-1873, 12670,
  22297
Harden, Jacob S., 1837-1860, 12671
Harden, Mrs. Louisa (Dorland) d.1859, 12671
Hardenbrook, Mrs. L.E.L., 10448
Hardie, James, 1750?-1826?, 12672-12676
Hardin, Bayless, 14260, 14261
Hardin, Benjamin, 1784-1852, 12677, 34556,
  24873
Hardin, John J., 16695
Hardin, John Wesley, 1853-1895, 16696
Hardin family, 14888
Hardin Co., Ky., 5953; Biography, 6952;
  Fiscal court, 14262; Historical Society,
  6952, 14263; History, 14263, 14873
Harding, Aaron, 24557
Harding, Benjamin, 12678, 14264
Harding, Chester, 14265
Harding, George Canady, 1829-1881, 6953
Harding, Stephen S., 12679
Harding, W. M., 22298
Harding, Warren Gamaliel, pres. U.S., 1865-
  1923, 7079
Hardinge, Sam Walde, 11455
Hardman, William, 1828-1890, 3776
Hardwick, Elizabeth, 14266
Hardwick, Mrs. J.P., 24558
Hardy, Mrs. A., 16232
Hardy, Campbell, 6954
Hardy, Dermont H., 16697
Hardy, Iza Duffus, 3777, 3778
Hardy, John, fl.1670-1671, 12680
Hardy, Mary (McDowell) Duffus, lady, 1825?-
  1891, 3779, 3780
Hardy, Robert William Hale, d.1871, 6955
Hardy, William, 12681
Hare and Hare, City Planners, Landscape
  Architects, Site Planners, Kansas City,
  Missouri, 14267
Hare, Francis, bp. of Chichester, 1671-1740,
  22299
Hare, Joseph Thompson, 3781; Fiction, 9932
Hare, Mrs. Maud (Cuney), 16698

Hare, Robert, 1781-1858, 12682, 22300
Harem, 25181
Harford, John Scandrett, 1785-1866, 22301
Hargis, Thomas Frazier, 1842-1903, 14268
Hargood, Sir William, 1762-1839, 186
Haring, Clarence Henry, 1885-, 6956
Harlan, Edgar Rubey, 1869-, 16431
Harlan, Jacob Wright, 16699
Harlan, James, 1820-1899, 6957
Harlan, Mary B., 3782
Harlan, Richard, 1796-1843, 12683-12686
Harlan Co., Ky., 15021; Pictorial works, 15429
Harlan labor news, 14269
Harland, Marion, pseud. of Mary Virginia (Hawes) Terhune, 1830-1922, 8167, 10163, 10934-10946
The harlot's friend, 9011
Harlow, Louis K., illustr., 3219
Harlow, Samuel R., 22302, 22303
Harman, S.W., 6958, 16700
Harmar, Josiah, 1733-1813, 4096, 12687
Harmar's expedition, 1790, 12687
Harmon, Daniel Williams, 1778-1845, 3784, 6223
Harnden, Harvey, 12688
Harness family, 15640
Harness racing, 13522, 14820
Harney, John Milton, 1789-1825, 3785
Harney, William Shelby, 1800-1889, 12689, 17454
Harney Photogravure Co., Racine, Wis., 15871
Harnisch, Wilhelm, i.e. Christian Wilhelm, 1787-1864, 5660
The harp and the plow, 21839
The harp of Accushnet, 22352
The harp of Sylva, 22723
Harp of the South, 5582
Harp of the West, 15688
Harpe, Micajah, 14460
Harpe, Wiley, 14460
The Harpe's head, 3743, 14241
Harpending, Asbury, 16701
Harper, Francis P., 24559
Harper, Henry Howard, 1871-, 6959
Harper, Robert Goodloe, 1765-1825, 12133, 12690-12694, 24560
Harper, William, 1790-1847, 12695, 24561
Harper, firm, publishers, New York (1864 Harper & brothers), 12486
Harper's Ferry, W. Va., History, 25451: John Brown raid, 1859, 11389, 12779, 13386, 21901, 24116, 24121, 24139, 25128, 25135, 25261, 25451, 25655, 25733, 25895;

John Brown raid, 1859, Fiction, 24117, 25690
Harper's New York and Erie rail-road guide book..., 12696
Harper's weekly, 6554
Harpers' monthly magazine, 318
Harriman, Edward Henry, 1848-1909, 17538
Harrington, Charles, 16702
Harrington, Emilia, The confession of, 11184
Harrington, Leonard E., 1816-1883, 16703
Harrington, Timothy, 1715-1795, 12697
Harriott, John, 1745-1817, 3786
Harris, Alfred W., 14270
Harris, Branson Lewis, b.1817, 16704
Harris, Mrs. Caroline, 4577, 12698
Harris, Charles G., 1869-, 14271
Harris, Charles H., 12699
Harris, Credo Fitch, 1874-, 14272-14273
Harris, Edward Doubleday, 1839-1919, 12700-12702
Harris, Frank, Judge, of Idaho, 16705
Harris, George, of Baltimore, 12703
Harris, George Washington, 1814-1869, 3787, 6960
Harris, Graham H., 1857-, 1875
Harris, J. Dennis, 12704
Harris, James Morrison, 1818-1898, 12705, 16706
Harris, James Sidney, 3788
Harris, Joel Chandler, 1848-1908, 5659, 24562
Harris, Sir John Hoffis, 1874-, 24438, 24563-24567
Harris, Lewis Birdsall, 1816-1893, 3789
Harris, Luther Metcalf, 1789-1865, 12706
Harris, Mary, 22304
Harris, Maude Blanc, 13567
Harris, Miriam (Coles) 1834-1925, 22305
Harris, N. Sayre, 3790
Harris, Nathaniel Edwin, 1846-, 3791
Harris, Norman Dwight, 1870-, 24568
Harris, Raymond. Scriptural researches on the licitness of the slave trade, 25467
Harris, Rufus Carrollton, 14274
Harris, Samuel, 1814-1899, 12707
Harris, Sarah Hollister, 16707
Harris, Thaddeus Mason, 1768-1842, 3792, 12708-12710, 13036, 24569
Harris, Thomas, 1784-1861, 12711
Harris, Thomas L., 1816-1858, 24533, 24570, 24571
Harris, Thomas Mealey, 1817-1906, 23475
Harris, W. A., 12712
Harris, William Charles, 1830-1905, 3793
Harris, William Richard, 1847-1923, 6961, 16708

Harris, William Tell, 3794, 12713
Harris, William Thaddeus, 1826-1854, 12714
Harris, William Wallace, 22306
Harris family (Robert Harris, fl.1650), 12706
Harrisburg, Pa., History, Civil War, 7676
Harrison, Benjamin, pres. U.S., 1833-1901, 3795
Harrison, C. C., 9769
Harrison, Dabney Carr, 1830-1862, 12837
Harrison, David, jr., 22313
Harrison, Ellanetta, 14275
Harrison, Frederic, 1831-1923, 13104
Harrison, Helen Dortch, 22307
Harrison, Henry William, 12715
Harrison, Jesse Burton, 1805-1841, 22308, 24572
Harrison, John P., 13930
Harrison, Mary Ellen, d.1915, 14002
Harrison, Richard Almgill, 1824-1904, 22309, 24573
Harrison, Samuel Alexander, 1822-1890, 3796
Harrison, Walter, 22310
Harrison, William Henry, pres. U.S., 1773-1841, 377, 1223, 3746, 3797, 7594, 11630, 11668, 12716, 22462, 22465, 22597, 22985, 24644, 25342, 25590; Poetry, 5603
Harrison, Z., 3798
Harrison Co., Ky., 14259; Biography, 13559
Harrison's national debt, 24574
Harriss, Julia Mildred, 12717
Harrisse, Henry, 1830-1910, 12718, 22088. 22311, 22312
Harrod, James, 1742-1793, 14276
Harrod's Old fort, 15635
Harrod, Fort, Harrodsburg, Ky., 14425, 15165
Harrodsburg, Ky., 14386; Fiction, 15168; History, 13742, 13817, 13884, 14163, 14781, 15635; Maps, 14277
Harrodsburg, Danville bicentennial map & guide, 14277
Harrold, John, 3799
Harry Burnham, the young Continental, 1639
Harry Henderson's history, 10906
Harsha, David Addison, 1827-1895, 12719
Hart, Adolphus M., 1813-1879, 12720
Hart, Albert Bushnell, 1854-1943, 3800, 24575, 24576, 24933
Hart, Alfred A., 12721

Hart, Birdett, 1821-1906,
Hart, Charles Henry, 1847-1918, 6962, 14278, 14279
Hart, Ephraim J., 3801
Hart, Frederick Weber, 22315
Hart, Henry A., 24686
Hart, Joel Tanner, 1810-1877, 13656, 13708, 14353, 15197
Hart, John Seely, 1810-1877, 3802, 3803
Hart, Joseph C., d.1855, 12722
Hart, Levi, 1738-1808, 12723, 22561
Hart, Lochie, 14280
Hart, Luther, 1783-1834, 12724
Hart, Oliver, 1723-1795, 12725
Hart, Seth, 1763-1832, 12726
Hart family, 15753
Hart family (John Hart, 1651-1714), 22048
Hart and Mapother, Civil Engineers, Louisville, Ky., 14281
Hart County, Ky., 13610, 13613
Harte, Bret, 1836-1902, 6963-6980
Hartford, First church of Christ, 12751; History, 22354; Public library, 12727
Hartford female seminary, Hartford, Conn., 1045, 22224
Hartford hospital, Hartford, 12728
Hartford union mining and trading co., 16709
Harthorn, Cyrus M., 6981
Harthorn's philosophy, 6981
Hartlaub, Gustav, 1814-1900, 589
Hartley, Cecil B., 12729, 12730, 22316
Hartley, David, 1732-1813, 12731, 12732
Hartley, Oliver Cromwell, 1823-1859, 22317
Hartley, Thomas, 1709?-1784, 1157
Hartley, Thomas, 1748-1800, 22318
Hartlib, Samuel, d.1662, 12733-12735
Hartman, illustr., 13947
Hartmann, 16710
Hartmann, Americo, 20370
Hartmann, Carl, 16711
Hartman's historical series, 22198
Hartpence, Alanson, 22319
Hartpence, William Ross, 3804
Hartt, Charles Frederick, 1840-1878, 22320
Hartwell, Abraham, 22321
Hartwell, Henry, 3805
The Hartwell farm, 9088
Hartwig, Georg Ludwig, 1813-1880, 22322, 22323
Harun al Raschid, Fiction, 8792
Harvard College, 24599
Harvard college and its benefactors, 22324
The Harvard register, 22325
Harvard university, 10151, 12357, 12736, 12737, 22324-22327; Biography, 12737, 22194; History, Civil war, 12737; Medical

school, 12872; Museum of comparative
  zoology, 2573; Registers, 12737
Harvest, George, d.1776, 22329
A harvest-day with the Pueblos, 10863
Harvey, Arthur, 1834-, 12738
Harvey, Fred, 16712
Harvey, George, 22323
Harvey, Henry, 12739
Harvey, Prentice A., 14282, 14283
Harvey, William Woodes, 1798-1864,
  22330
Harward, Thomas, 1700-1736, 22331
Harwood, 9181
Harwood, John Edmund, 1771-1806, 22332
Harwood, Thomas, 16713
Hasbrouck, Jacob Louis, 1867-, 6982
The hasheesh eater, 10249
Haskel, Daniel, 1784-1848, 3806
Haskell, Thales H., 1834-1909, 16714
Haskins, C. W., 16715
Haskins, Mrs. Elizabeth (Ladd), 22745
Haskins, William C., 5970, 6983
Haslam, Mrs. Mary (Heywood) 1851-1922,
  14320
Hassam, F. Childe, illustr., 17735
Hassan Assar, caliph of Bagdad, 10693
Hassard, John Rose Greene, 1836-1888,
  22334
Hassaurek, Friedrich, 1832-1885, 22335
Hasse, Adelaide Rosalia, 1868-1953, 14284
Hassel, Johann Georg Heinrich, 1770-1829,
  6984
Hasson, Benjamin F., 3807
Hasted, Frederick, b.1793, 6985
Hastings, Frank Stewart, 16716
Hastings, Hiram P., 22336
Hastings, Lansford Warren, 1819-ca. 1870,
  16717, 16923
Hastings, Mrs. Susannah (Willard)
  Johnson, 1730-1810, 13078
Hastings family (Thomas Hastings, 1605?-
  1685), 11609
The Hastings Cutoff, 16923
Haswell, Anthony, 1756-1816, 4767
Hatboro, Pa., Union library company,
  12740
Hatch, William Stanley, 12741
Hatcher, Mattie Austin, 14285
Hatfield, Edwin Francis, 1807-1883,
  22337, 24577
Hatfield, Julia, 12742
Hatfield family, 14844
Hatfield-McCoy feud, 14844, 15607
Hatfield, Mass., geneal., 21888
Hathaway, Levi, b.1790, 22300
Hathaway, Warren, 1828-1909, 22239

Hatten, Ezra, 13581
Hattersley, John, 22340
Hatton, J. E., 9331
Hatton, Joseph, 1841-1907, 3808, 3809
Hauch, Johannes Carsten, 1790-1872,
The haunted forest, 10693
The haunted school-house at Newburyport,
  Mass., 9799
The haunts of men, 8964
Haupt, Hermann, 1817-1905, 12743
Hauser, Ana, ed., 20712
Die Haussklaverei in Ostafrika, 25850
Haussonville, Gabriel Paul Othemin de Cléron,
  comte d', 1843-1924, 3810
Hautefeuïlle, Laurent Basile, 1805-1875,
  12744, 22342
Havana, Biblioteca Nacional "José Marti",
  Departamento Colección Cubana, 18569
Havana, Description, 799, 4309, 4454,
  4961, 7137, 8282, 12981, 23292; History,
  18569; Ordinances, 24578; Siege, 1762,
  570, 12500, 22918
Havana scheme, 14286, 14287
La Havane, 4454
Haven, Charles Chauncy, 22343, 22344
Haven, Gilbert, bp., 1821-1880, 6986, 6987,
  22345
Haven, Jason, 1733-1803, 22346, 22347
Haven, Joseph, 1816-1874, 12745
Haven, Nathaniel Appleton, 1790-1826, 22348
Haven, Samuel, 1727-1806, 22349
Haven, Samuel Foster, 1806-1881, 12746-12748,
  22350
Havens, Palmer E., b.1818, 6988
Haverhill, 10060
Haverhill, Mass., Church history, 22143;
  Geneal., 11753; History, 11753, 13442
Haviland, Mrs. Laura Smith, 1808-, 14288
Haw, William, 12749
Haw-ho-noo, 4216
Hawaii, 15832; Description & travel, 3047,
  3619, 4196, 5445, 13165, 15942, 15973,
  16016, 16029, 16031, 17281, 17751; History,
  1296, 1297, 22684; Social life & customs,
  10028
Haweis, Hugh Reginald, 1839-1925, 3811
Hawes, Angelica Irene, 1844-1851, 22351
Hawes, Mrs. Angelica H., 22351, 22352
Hawes, Barbara, 12750
Hawes, J. H., 22353
Hawes, Jesse, 1843-1901, 3812
Hawes, Joel, 1789-1867, 12751, 22354, 22355
The Hawk chief, 4024
Hawk's Nest, 9592
Hawker, Peter, 1786-1853, 22356
Hawkesworth, John, 1715?-1773, 11946

Hawkins, Alfred, d.1854, 22357
Hawkins, Armand, pub., 6785
Hawkins, Benjamin, 1754-1816, 12752
Hawkins, Christopher, 1764-1837, 12753
Hawkins, Sir John, 1532-1595, 6989, 6990
Hawkins, John Henry Willis, 1797-1858, 22359
Hawkins, John Parker, 1830-, 16718
Hawkins, Sir Richard, 1562?-1622, 22358
Hawkins, William George, 1823-1909, 22359, 24579
Hawkins family, 16718
The Hawkins zouaves, 5694
Hawks, Francis Lister, 1798-1866, 2263, 12754, 14289, 22294
Hawks, John Milton, 1826-, 3813, 3814
The Hawks of Hawk-Hollow, 1333
Hawkshaw, Sir John, 1811-1891, 12755
Hawles, Sir John, 1645-1716, 22360
Hawley, Bostwick, 1814-1910, 6991
Hawley, J. F., 14290
Hawley, J. R., and company, Cincinnati, pub., 508
Hawley, James Henry, 1847-1929, 16719
Hawley, William Fitz, 1804-1855, 22361
Hawley, Zerah Kent, 1781-1856, 3815, 22362
Hawrecht, Henry, 6614
Hawthorne, Julian, 1846-1934, 6992, 6993, 9092, 10448, 16720
Hawthorne, Nathaniel, 1804-1864, 24015
Hawthorne, Una, 1844-1877, 9825
Hay, George, 1765-1830, 12756, 22362
Hay, John, 1838-1905, 8465
Hay, Thomas Robson, 15717
Hay amigo para amigo, 19193
Haycraft, Samuel, 1795-1878, 14263, 14291
Haycraft's History of Elizabethtown, Kentucky, 14291
Hayden, Mrs. Caroline A., 22364
Hayden, E. V., 16721
Hayden, F. V., 4246
Hayden, Ferdinand Vandeveer, 1829-1887, 3816, 3817, 16722, 16723, 23424
Hayden, Sidney, 6994
Hayden, William, 1785-, 3818
Hayden, William Benjamin, 1816-1893, 22365
Haydon, Arthur Lincoln, 1872-, 6995
Hayes, Alexander L., b.1793, 2321
Hayes, Augustus Allen, 1837-1892, 16724, 16725
Hayes, Isaac Israel, 1832-1881, 22366
Hayes, James, 13917
Hayes, Jeff W., 1853-1917, 16726

Haygarth, John, 1740-1827, 12757
Haygood, Atticus Greene, bp., 1839-1896, 3819
Hayne, M. H. E., 16727
Hayne, Paul Hamilton, 1830-1886, 3820, 3821
Hayne, Robert Young, 1791-1839, 22367-22369, 22852
Hayne, William Hamilton, 1856-1886, 3822
Haynes, Donald, 14292
Haynes, Dudley C., 1809-1888, 12758
Haynes, Edwin Mortimer, 1836-, 3823
Haynes, Gideon, 12759
Haynes, J., 12760
Haynes, John Russell, 6253
Haynes, Lemuel, 1753-1833, 12761
Haynes, Martin A., 1845-, 3824
Haynes, Nathaniel, 14293
Haynes family, 6253
Hayter, Earl W., 16728
Hayward, James, 1786-1866, 12762, 23251
Hayward, John, 1781-1862, 3825, 12763-12768, 22370
Hayward, John Henry, 22371
Hayward, Nicholas, 3325
Hayward's gazetteer of Maine, 12766
Haywood, John, 1762-1826, 12769, 12770
Hazard, Benjamin, 1770-1841, 22372
Hazard, Caroline, 1856-, 24580
Hazard, Charles T., 22377
Hazard, Ebenezer, 1744-1817, 12427
Hazard, Joseph, b.1751?, 12771
Hazard, Rowland Gibson, 1801-1888, 22372-22375
Hazard, Samuel, 1784-1870, 22376
Hazard, Thomas, 1720-1798, 24580
Hazard, Thomas Robinson, 1797-1886, 1399, 22377, 22378
Hazard, Ky., Bowman Memorial Methodist Church, Woman's Society of Christian Service, 14294; Christian Church. Mildred Faulkner Auxiliary, 14295; History, 15162, 15163
Hazard cook book, 14294
A hazard of new fortunes, 9945
Hazel, Harry, pseud., 10068-10071
Hazelrigg, John T., 14296
Hazeltine, Silas Wood, 12773
Hazen, William Babcock, 1830-1887, 16729
Hazlett, William, 1811-1893, 22379
Hazlitt, William Carew, 1834-1913, 12774
He fell in love with his wife, 10647
He knew what was due to the court, 10465
He saw the sun this time, 15466
He would have gotten a lawyer, 10465
Head, Sir Francis Bond, bart., 1793-1875, 6996, 6997
Head, Sir George, 1782-1855, 6998
Head, Jesse, 13884

The head of a hundred, 9630
Headley, Joel Tyler, 1813-1897, 10719, 12775, 22380-22382
Headley, Phineas Camp, 1819-1903, 22383, 22384
The headsman, 9131
Heady, Morrison, 1829-1915, 22385
Heald, Mrs. Jean Sadler, 6999
Healing and salvation for our country, 11306
Health and profit, 3724
Health resorts, watering-places, etc., 4039, 11815; Costa Rica, 5845; Cuba, 12226; Kentucky, 3637, 13882; Virginia, 4605; West Virginia, 4743
Health trip to the tropics, 5730, 15725
Healy, illustr., 10520
Healy, George Peter Alexander, 1813-1894, 14297
Heamans, Roger, 3764
Heap, Gwinn Harris, 3826
A heap o' love, 13830
Heard, Isaac V. D., b.1834, 12776
Heard, John T., 22386
Hearn, Lafcadio, 1850-1904, 3827, 7000, 8205
Hearne, Samuel, 1745-1792, 16731
Heart-histories and life-pictures, 8566
Heart-hungry, 11128
Heart-life in song, 4394
The heart of adamant, 10747
The heart of Mabel Ware, 9834
The heart of Sam Naylor, 8723
The heart of the Alleghanies, 5798
The heart of the Andes, 11194
The heart of the commonwealth, 12966
The heart of the continent, 17063
The heart of the hills, 9555
The heart of the homestead, 9873
The heart of the West, 9835
The heart's highway, 9571
Heartman, Charles Frederick, 7001
Hearts and hands, 10970
Hearts courageous, 15279
The hearts of steel, 10276
Hearts unveiled, 10711
Heartsill, William Williston, 1839-, 3828
Heartt, H. G.. 938
Heath, Herman H., d.1874, 22387
Heath, William, 1737-1814, 21970, 22388
Heath family, 16058
Heathcote, Charles William,1882-, 7002, 24581
Heathcote, George, 22389
The Heathercotes, 3119
Heatherington, Alexander, d.1878, 12777
Heaven, 19164

A heaven-kissing hill, 10301
Heaviside, John T. C., 22390
Hebard, Grace Raymond, 1861-1936, 16732, 16733
Hebbard, William Wallace, 24582
Hebbe, Gustaf Clermens, 1804-1893, 10718
Heck, Earl L. W., 14298
Hecke, J. Valentin, 3829
Hecker, Friedrich Franz Karl, 1811-1881, 13998
Hecker, Thad. C., jt. author, 17893
Heckewelder, John Gottlieb Ernestus, 1743-1823, 22391
Hecla (ship), 7695-7697
Hedge, Frederic Henry, 1805-1890, 22392, 22393
Hedge, Levi, 1766-1844, 12778
Hedged in, 11073
Hedges, 23038
Hedges, Henry Parsons, 1817-1911, 22394
Hedges, Isaac A., 22395
Hedges, Mary, 1749-1768, 22199
Hedley, Fenwick Y., 3830
Hedrick, Benjamin Sherwood, 1827-1886, 24548
Heeckeren, Goddard Philip Cornelis van, 1791-1833, 24583
Heeney, Cornelius, 1754-1848, 7277
Heeren, Arnold Hermann Ludwig, 1760-1842, 22396
Heermans, Forbes, 1856-, 16734
Heermans, J., 22397
Heger, Herbert K., 14299
Hegewisch, Dietrich Hermann, 1746-1812, 322
The heidenmauer, 9132
Heidenreich, Joseph M., 14876
Heights and depths, 9868
Heikel, Karl Felix, 1844-1921, 3831, 14300
Heine, Marie, 22906
Heine, Wilhelm, 1817-1885, 22906
Heinrich XLIV, Count of Reuss, b.1753, 4960
Heinzelmann, Friedrich, 5660
The heir of Charlton, 9524
The heir of the McHulishes, 9790
The heiress, 8559
The heiress of Brandsby, 9618
The heiress of Fall Down castle, 10746
The heiress of Greenhurst, 10867
The heiress of Redstone Hall, 3917
Heitman, Francis Bernard, 1838-1926, 7003
Heizmann, Charles Lawrence, 1846-, 17776
Las heladas en la Argentina, 19571
Helay, George Peter Alexander, 1813-, 14301
Helderberg, Early days of the church in the, 22218
Helen Erskine, 10634
Helen Courtney's wedding day, 10040
Helen Halsey, 10773
Helen Harlow's vow, 11049

Helen Leeson, 9838
Helen Lincoln, 8939
Helena, Ark., Battle of, 1863, 2073
Helena, Mont., 16419
Helfenstein, Ernest, pseud., 10804
Hell, 19164
"Hell fer Sartain," 9553, 9554, 9556
Hell for Harlan County, 14005
Hell on the border, 16700
Heller, Karl Bartholomäus, 1824-1880, 7004
Heller, Louie Regina, 1870-, 7005
Hellman, Florence S., 17797
Hellwald, Friedrich Anton Heller von, 1842-1892, 3832
Helm, Benjamin, 14302
Helm, Benjamin Hardin, 1830-1863, 7381
Helm, John Larne, 1802-1867, 14577
Helm, Lucinda Barbour, 1839-1897, 13519
Helm, Mary (Sherwood) Wightman, 1807-, 3833
Helme, Elizabeth, 21834
Helmer, Charles Downes, 1827-1879, 22398
Helms, Anton Zacharias, 1751-1803, 22399
Helms, Ludvig V., 16735
Heloise, 10640
An help to the language of the natives in New England, 23800
Helper, Hinton Rowan, 1829-1909, 12265, 16736, 23958, 24584, 25751
Helps, Sir Arthur, 1813-1875, 22400, 22401, 24585, 24586
Helps to the study of Presbyterianism, 16074
Helvetius, Claude Adrien, 1715-1771, 22089
Heming, Arthur Henry Howard, 1870-, illustr., 8252
Hemmenway, Moses, 1735-1811, 22402
Hemp, 14737, 15145, 23121; Kentucky, 14433, 15145
Hemp culture in Kentucky, 15145
Hemphill, John, 1803-1862, 22403
Hempstead, Fay, 16737
Henck, Frederic William, 1856-1893, 14492
Henderson, Alexander, of Belize, Central America, 22404
Henderson, Archibald, 1877-1963, 14303-14306, 15750
Henderson, George, 22405
Henderson, George Donald, 1832-1875, 22406
Henderson, George F., 6037, 6815
Henderson, Howard A. M., 14554

Henderson, James, 22407
Henderson, John, 7006, 16738
Henderson, John Brooks, 1870-1920, 7007
Henderson, John J., 22408
Henderson, Joseph F., 3834
Henderson, Richard, 1735-1785, 14306
Henderson, Mrs. S. E., 14307
Henderson, Mrs. Sarah (Fisher) b.1843, 16517
Henderson, Thomas, 13539, 13547, 14308, 14731, 14732
Henderson, Thomas J., 22643
Henderson County, Ky., 14220; History, 13564, 14306, 15436, 15437; Physiography, 14148
Henderson Co., Ill., 16884
Henderson, Ky., 14361; History, 8217, 13564, 14305, 15437
Hendrick, John Thilman, b.1811, 24587
Hendricks, Thomas Andrews, 6869
Hendricks knew it, 10598
Henfrey, Benjamin, 22409
Henkle, Moses Montgomery, 1798-1864, 3835
Henley, David, 1749-1823, 22410
Henneman, John Bell, 1864-1908, 15413
Hennepin, Louis, 1640-1701?, 3836, 7008, 22411; Bibliography, 7008
Hennessy, John, abp., 1823-1900, 16932
Henningsen, Charles Frederick, 1815-1877, 12779
Henrietta Harrison, 10194
Henrique, o navegador, infante of Portugal, 1394-1460, 23042
Henriques, Zaluar de Campos, 20424
Henriquez, Camilo, 1769-1825, ed., 5967
Henry, Alexander, d.1814, 7009
Henry, Alexander, 1739-1824, 3837
Henry, George, 13312
Henry, Gustavus Adolphus, 15202
Henry, Howell Meadoes, 1879-, 24588
Henry, J., illustr., 14351
Henry, Jabez, d.1835, 24589
Henry, James P., 16739
Henry, John Joseph, 1758-1811, 12780
Henry, Joseph, 24590
Henry, Josephine K., 14310
Henry, Patrick, 1736-1799, 5750, 8404, 13347
Henry, Patrick, pseud., 13588
Henry, Robert R., 22412
Henry, William, fl.1851, 25584
Henry, William Seaton, 1816-1851, 22413
Henry, Fort, Battle of, 1862, 2050
Henry Clay's first biographer, 14309
Henry Co., Ia., Biography, 7760; History, 7760
Henry Co., Kentucky, Anecdotes, 14231; History, 14019
Henry Courtland, 9042

Henry Howard, 9981
Henry Irving's impressions of America, 3808
Henry St. John, gentleman, of "Flower of Hundreds," 9108
Henshall, James Alexander, 1844-, 3838, 3839, 14311
Henshaw, David, 1791-1852, 16740, 22414, 22415
Henshaw, Joshua Sidney, 22416
Henshaw, Henry Wetherbee, 1850-, 16741
Henshaw, Mrs. Sarah Edwards (Tyler), b.1822-, 22417
Henson, Josiah, 1789-1883, 24591
Henty, George Alfred, 1832-1902, 7010, 7011
Hentz, Mrs. Caroline Lee (Whiting) 1800-1856, 3840-3849
Hepworth, George Hughes, 1833-1902, 7012, 12781, 22418
A herald of the West, 2517
Heraldry, 23120; Falkland Islands, 20228; Scotland, 22719; U.S., 7437, 7753
The heraldry of the Douglases, 22719
Heras, Antonio, 3850
Herbart, Johann Friedrich, 1776-1846, 20387
Herbert, Charles, 1757-1808, 22419
Herbert, Henry William, 1807-1858, 9803, 22420
Herbert, Sidney, 12782
Herbert, Sir Thomas, 1606-1682, 22421
Herbert Wendall, 9852
Herbermann, Charles George, 5045
Herboso, Pedro, 7013
Here and hereafter, 10524
Here and there in our own country, 3612
Here's to you, Henry Clay!, 14700
Heredia y Mieses, José Francisco, 1776-1820, 7014
Heredity, 14328
Un hereje y un musulmán, 19968
La herencia de Carranza, 6268
Heres, Tomás de, 1795-1842, 7015
Heresy, 11980, 13056
Héricault, Charles Joseph de Ricault, called d', 1823-1899, 22422
Heriot, Georg, 1766-1844, 7016, 7017
The heritage of Dedlow Marsh, 6970
The heritage of the South, 24330
Herkimer Co., N.Y., History, 1183
Herman, 10471
Hermann, Dinger, 10742
Hermann, Isaac, 1838-, 3851
Hermia Suydam, 8593

The hermit, 527
Hermit-crabs, 23692
The hermit in America on a visit to Philadelphia, 11056
The hermit of Holcombe, 8977
The hermit of Nottingham, 8446
Ther hermit of the Chesapeake, 9850
Hermosa, Jesús, 7018
Hernández, Francisco, 1514-1578, 7018
Hernández, José, 1834-1886, 18931; Martín Fierro, 18668, 18991
Hernández, Miguel, 1910-1942, 20625
Hernández, Nerly Lorenzo, 18891
Hernández, Pablo, 1852-1921, 20084
Hernández, Porfirio, 7020
Hernández Arvizu, Juan A., 24592
Hernández de Alba, Guillermo, 1906-, 20714
Hernández Girón, Francisco, 8291
Hernández Gutierrez, Rafael, 1840-1879, 18130
Hernández Iglesias, Fermin, 1833-, 24593
Hernández Luna, Juan, 18616
Hernández y Dávalos, Juan E., 7021
Hernando County, Fla., 3486
Herndon, Dallas T., 16743
Herndon, James, 14312
Herndon, William Henry, 1818-1891, 7022-7029, 14313-14315
Herndon, Robert, illustr., 14897
Herndon, Sarah (Raymond), 16744
Herndon, William Henry, 1818-1891, 15685, 16745
Herne, Peregrine, 3852
Herne the hunter, 10125
A hero in homespun, 8755, 13618
The hero of Kentucky, 13961
The hero of No fiction, 861
Heroes, 13437
Heroes and martyrs of Georgia, 2262
Heroes and patriots of the South, 12729
The heroes of Albany, 11829
Heroes of California, 16879
The heroes of the last lustre, 13437
Heroes of the "rank and file   12835
Heroes of the west, 2685
Heroic women of the West, 14145
The heroine in bronze, 13530
The heroine of faith, 9367
The heroine of Saddle Mountain, 16088
The heroine of Tampico, 9718
The heroine of Tennessee, 10612
The heroine of the Kennebec, 9988
Herold, David E., 1844-1865, 1305
Herr, Franz, Eine kurze Erklärung von dem geschriebenen Haus Cotton, 23227
Herr Regenbogen's concert, 5495
Herrajes, 18737

Herrera C., Rocio, 18340
Herrera Klindt, Bernardo, 19771
Herrera Oria, Enrique, 3853
Herrera Riesco, Juan, 19685
Herrera y Molina, Alonso de, d.1644, 7030-7033
Herrera y Tordesillas, Antonio de, 1559-1625, 7034, 7035
Herrick, Anson, 1812-1868, 22423
Herrick, Jedediah, 1780-1847, 22424
Herrick family (Henerie Hericke, 1604-1671), 22424
Herring, Thomas, abp. of Canterbury, 1693-1757, 22425
Herrington Lake, Ky., 14741; Description, 15328; Maps, 14277
Herrmann, Jesse, 1884-1953, 14316
Herrod, Goliah, 1648
Herschel, Sir John Frederic William bart. 1792-1871, 2594
Hersey, Dr., 14317
Hersey, Charles, 22426
Hersey, John, 1786-1862, 12783
Hersey, Thomas, 3854
Herter, August, 3855
Hertford, Francis Ingram Seymour Conway, 2d marquis of, 1743-1822. Letter to the First Belfast company of volunteers, 1113
Herttel, Thomas, 22427
Herty, Thomas, 22428
Hertz, Bram, 22429
Hertz, Emanuel, 1870-, 7036-7039
Hervey, Frederik, 3429
Hervey, George Washington, 1846-, 16746
Hervey, James, 1714-1758, 1732
Hervey, Nathaniel, 22430
Herz, Henri, 1803-1888, 3856
Herzog, Karl Josef Benjamin, 7040
Hesperia, 5705
The Hesperian, 3857
Hesperos, 3946
Hesperothen, 5051
Hess, John W., 1824-, 16747
Hesselius, Andreas, 1677-1733, 1364
Hesse-Wartegg, Ernst von, 1854-1918, 3858, 3859, 7041
Hester Strong's life work, 10846
Heston, Alfred Miller, 1854-, 24594
Hettler, Max, 1909-1969, 8188
Heurter, Frederick Damien, 7780
Heusken, Henry C.J., 1832-1861, 7701
Heustis, Daniel D., b.1806, 12784
Heustis, Jabez Wiggins, 1784-1841, 22431
Heustis, Louise L., illustr., 10429
Das heutige Mexiko, 8409

Hevia Bolaños, Juan de, 7042
Heward, Robert, 24595
Hewatt, Alexander, 3860
Hewes, George Whitfield, 22432
Hewes, Joseph, 22433
Hewett, Ainslie, 1880-1963, 13567, 14854
Hewett, Daniel, 3861
Hewett, J. F. Napier, 22434
Hewett, John B., 14318
Hewitt, Abram Stevens, 1822-1903, 22435, 22436
Hewitt, Fayette, 14865
Hewitt, Girart, 16748
Hewitt, John Hill, 1801-1890, 22437
Hewitt, Randall Henry, 1840-, 3862
Hewlings, H. A., 9331
Hewson, William, 22438
Hexandria, 9330
Hey, Richard, 1745-1835, 22439
Heyburn, Henry Rueter, 1957-, 24596
Heyden, Thomas, 1798-1870, 22440
Heye, George Gustav, 1874-, 16749
Heylen, Louis, 1828-1863?, 22441
Heyn, Piet, 7274
Heyrick, Elizabeth Coltman, 1769-1831, 24597
Heywood, John Healy, 1818-1880, 11746, 14319
Heywood, Robert, 1786-1868, 14320
Hiatt, Joel W., 4670
Hibbard, Augustine George, 1883-, 22442
Hibbert, Robert, 1770-1849, Facts verified upon oath, 24211
An Hibernian, pseud., 9991
Hibernicus, 3863
Hibiscus moscheutos, 12968
Hichborn, Benjamin, 1746-1817, 22443
Hichborn, Franklin, 16750
Hickcox, John Howard, 1832-1897, 22444, 22445
Hickey, John K., 14683, 14687
Hickey, William, 1787?-1875. 2461
Hickman, Edwin C., 22446
Hickman, George H., 22447
Hickman, John, 1810-1875, 7043
Hickman, Nathaniel, 22448
Hickman, William A., 1815-1877 or 8, 16751
Hickman, Ky., 15280
Hickman Co., Ky. Gazette, 14321; History, 14321
Hickok, James Butler, 1837-1876, 16080
Hickory Hall, 10837
Hicks, Edmund Warne, 1841-, 16752
Hicks, Edward, 1780-1849, 22450
Hicks, Elias, 1748-1830, 22449, 22450
Hicks, Frederick Charles, 14370
Hicks, George, 1835-, 7044
Hicks, Thomas, 1823-1890, 22451
Hidalgo, Bartolomé, 1788-1822, 18931

Hidalgo, Cristobal, 7045
Hidalgo de Cisneras, Diego, 8028, 8274
Hidalgo y Costilla, Miguel, 1753-1811,
   19081
Hidatsa Indians, 17458
Hidden, Samuel, 1760-1837, 1988
The hidden mine, 2518
The hidden path, 10941
Hidden treasure, 11101
Hiebert, Ray Eldon, 20398
Hieronymus, 25806
The Hierophant, 22452
Hiestand-Moore, E. M., 9331
Higbee, D., pseud. of Mrs. Dora Higbee
   Geppert
Higgins, Charles A., 16753
Higgins, Jesse, b.1763, 22453
Higginson, Francis John, 1806-1872,
   24598
Higginson, John, 1616-1708, 23813
Higginson, Stephen, 1743-1828, 22454,
   22455
Higginson, Stephen, 1770-1834, 52
Higginson, Thomas Wentworth, 1823-1911,
   3864, 22456, 24599-24601
High, Edwin W., 1841-, 3865
High Bridge, Ky., 13938
A high civilization the moral duty of
   Georgians, 12043
The high cost of writing, 13795
High-energy-proton fission cross-sections
   of U, Th and Bi, 19868
High etiquette in Harlem, 9533
The "high private", with a full and
   exciting history of the New York
   volunteers, 22457
High Rock Spring, A history of, 22886
Higher Education in Kentucky, 15802
"The higher law," in its application to
   the Fugitive slave bill, 24890
Higher than happiness, 10170
A Highland chronicle, 9407
The Highlanders of the South, 5402
Hight, John J., 1834-1886, 3866
Hightower, Raymond Lee, 14322
Hightower, Ted, 14323
Highway atlas, 6807
Highway law, New York (State), 11293
Highway transport workers, Brazil,
   18169
Highways and byways of the Mississippi
   valley, 4065
Highways and byways of the South, 4066
Higueru, Jerónimo Román de 1n, 1538 1611,
   400
La hija del judío, 19968

Los hijos de Jalisco, 7876
Hildebrand, Samuel S., 1836-1872, 22458
Hildebrand family, 22458
Hildreth, Hosea, 1782-1835, 12785, 22459,
   22460, 22461
Hildreth, James, 1807-1865, 3867
Hildreth, Richard, 1807-1865, 22462-22465,
   24080, 24602
Hildreth, Samuel Prescott, 1783-1863, 3868-
   3870
Hildt, George H., 4353
Hilgard, Theodor Erasmus, 1790-1873, 16754
Hill, Alexander Staveley, 1825-1905, 7046
Hill, Mrs. Alice (Polk) 1854-, 16755, 16756
Hill, Alonzo, 1800-1871, 12786
Hill, Alonzo F., 3871
Hill, Ambrose Powell, 1825-1865, 2073
Hill, Benjamin Harvey, 1823-1882, 2052, 3872
Hill, Benjamin Harvey, jr., 3872
Hill, Clement Hugh, 1836-1898, 22466
Hill, Daniel Harvey, 1821-1889, 24755
Hill, David, d.1810, 13241
Hill, Ebenezer, 1766-1854, 22467, 22477
Hill, Mrs. Elizabeth (Freeman), 22468
Hill, Mrs. Emma Shepard, 7047
Hill, Frederick Trevor, 1866-, 7048
Hill, George Canning, 1825-1898, 22469
Hill, George William, 1824-, 22470, 22471
Hill, Hamilton Andrews, 1827-1895, 12787,
   12788, 22472
Hill, Ira, 22473
Hill, Isaac, 1788-1851, 936, 22474, 22475,
   24603
Hill, Isaac J., 1826-, 3873
Hill, Jerry D., 14324
Hill, John Alexander, 1858-1916, 16757
Hill, John Boynton, 1790-1886, 22476-22478
Hill, Joseph Bancroft, 1796-1864, 22513
Hill, Joseph D., 14325
Hill, Joseph J., 16758
Hill, Luther B., 16759
Hill, Pascoe Grenfell, 1804-1882, 24604
Hill, Paul T., illustr., 3316
Hill, R. T., 17583
Hill, Richard, 1795-1872, 12324, 22480,
   22481, 22793, 24923
Hill, Richard H., 14326
Hill, Robert Homas, 1858-, 7049
Hill, S. S., 7050, 22482
Hill, Sam E., 14507
Hill, Thomas, 1818-1891, 22483
Hill, William, 1769-1852, 22484
Hill, William Henry, b.1816, 22485
Hill, William Henry, 1877-, 22486
Hill family, 15522
Hillard, Elias Brewster, 1825-1895, 12789

Hillard, George Stillman, 1808-1879, tr., 12501, 12790, 22487, 22488
Hillard, Isaac, b.1737, 24605
Hillary, William, d.1763, 12791
Hiller, Joseph, 12792
Hiller, Oliver Prescott, 1814-1870, 22489
Hillery, George A., 13984, 14327
Hillhouse, Augustus Lucas, 1791-1859, 640
Hillhouse, James, 1754-1832, 640, 12793
Hillhouse, James Abraham, 1789-1841, 22491
Hillhouse, Thomas, 1816-1897, 12794
Hillhouse, William, 1757-1833, 22490, 24606, 24607
Hilliard, Henry Washington, 1808-1892, 3874, 3875, 24608
Hillis, Newell Dwight, 1858-1929, 24609
The hills of the Shatemuc, 11095
Hilton, Everett P., 15461
Hilton, Stanley, 15465
Hilton, William, 3876
The Hiltons' holiday, 10038
El Himalaya o la moral de los pájaros, 19592
Himmelwright, Abraham Lincoln Artman, 1865-, 16760
Himself his worst enemy, 8855
Hind, Henry Youle, 1823-1908, 3878-3881, 6666
Hindman, Thomas Carmichael, 1818-1868, 2040
Hindman, Ky., Economic conditions, 14538
Hines, David Theodore, 22492
Hines, Gustavus, 16761-16764
Hines, Harvey K., 1828-1902, 16765, 16766
Hines, Thomas H., 3417
Hinestrosa, Fernando, 20324
Hingham, Mass., History, Colonial period, 6474
Hingham Anti-slavery Society, Hingham, Mass., 24867
Hingston, Edward Peron, ca.1823-1876, 8876
Hinman, Royal Ralph, 1785-1868, 12795, 22493
Hinman, Wilbur F., 3882
Hinton, Richard Josiah, 1830-1901, 4910, 12796
Hintrager, Oscar, 1871-, 3883
Hippon, also called Hipponax, of Samos, fl. 5th cent. B.C., 19734
The hireling and the slave, 3671
Hirsch, Nathaniel David Mitron, 1896-, 14328
Hispanic-American printing, 8187
La Hispano-América del siglo XVI, 7248
Hispanoamérica y su expresión literaria, 19796

Histoire de la catastrophe de Saint-Domingue, 11423
Histoire de la colonie française en Canada, 6703
Histoire de la Louisiane, 3207
Histoire de l'inoculation préservative de la fièvre jaune, 23117
Histoire de l'insurrection des esclaves dans le nord de Saint-Domingue, 25035
Histoire des avanturiers qui se sont signalez dan les Indes, 22190
Histoire et anthropologie du noir en Colombie, 18363
Histoire et commerce des colonies angloises, 2867
Histoire et description générale de la Nouvelle France, 2972
Histoire naturelle du cacao, et du sucre, divisée en deux traités, 23519
L'histoire notable de la Floride, 4226
Histoire véritable et natvrelle des moevrs et prodvctions dv pays de la Novvelle France, 6126
Una historia con alas, 19201
Historia cultural, 18982
Historia de dos curas revolucionarios, 19081
Historia de la cultura en el Paraguay, 18650
Historia de la historiografía venezolana, 19841
Historia de la independencia americana, 7015
Historia de la ingeniería en Venezuela, 18373
Historia de la nación Mexicana, 21724
Historia de la Nueva Andalucia, 19996
Historia de la revolución de México, 24611
Historia de un esfuerzo, 18803
Historia de una ciénaga, 20687
Historia do Brasil desde seu descobrimento em 1500 até 1810, 21777
Historia do espetáculo, 19159
Historia documentada de los agustinos en Venezuela durante la época colonial, 19688
Historia general de las Indias, 6863
Historia general de los hechos de los castellanos en las islas y tierrafirme del mar oceano, 7035
Historia geográfica, civil y política de la isla de S. Juan Bautista de Puerto Rico, 3
Historia gráfica de la Nueva España, 18981
Historia Indiae Occidentalis, 1187
Historia Indiae Orientalis, 488
Historial de las banderas y escudos nacionales, 19946
Historias de cronopios y de fauna, 20529
Historias de uma regiaõ, 19605
Historic facts and fancies, 16127
The historic Lincoln car, 7051

Historic sketches of the cattle trade of the West and Southwest, 17086
Historic sketches of the South, 25406
An historical account of my own life, 1796
An historical account of some memorable actions, particularly in Virginia, 3662
A historical account of the expedition against the Ohio Indians, 23639
An historical account of the rise and progress of the colonies of South Carolina and Georgia, 3860
Historical and biographical tracts. Westminster, 1820, 23583
Historical and descriptive lessons, embracing sketches of the history, character and customs of all nations, 22495
An historical and descriptive narrative of the Mammoth Cave of Kentucky, 14121
Historical and legal examination, 11255
Historical and Philosophical Society of Ohio, 3561
An historical and practical essay on the culture and commerce of tobacco, 5350
Historical and revolutionary incidents of the early settlers of the U.S., 5649
Historical anecdotes, civil and military, 12799
Historical catalogue of Georgetown College, 1829-1917, 14329
Historical collections of Louisiana, 3544
Historical collections of Louisiana and Florida, 2332
Historical collections of Ohio, 3954
Historical collections of the great West, 3955
Historical collections of the state of New York, 785
An historical discourse, delivered in the Central Baptist meeting house, Newport, R.I., January 8th, 1854, 22646
Historical fiction, 15530
A historical narrative and topographical description of Louisiana and West-Florida, 3979
Historical notes on slavery and colonization, 24612
Historical outline of Lower California, 16768
Historical, poetical and pictorial American scenes, 786
The historical reader; containing "The late war between the United States and Great Britain from June, 1010, to February, 1815. In the scriptual style", 22611
Historical Records Survey, American

imprints inventory, 17909; Iowa, 2865; Kentucky 14925, 14926
Historical remarks on the taxation of free states, 13425
Historical sketch of Jersey county, 16677
A historical sketch of Mason County, Kentucky, 14795
A historical sketch of the Congregational Churches in Massachusetts, 11821
A historical sketch of the formation of the confederacy, 11299
Historical sketch of the Middlesex canal, 2177
Historical sketch of the third annual conquest of Florida, 8940
Historical sketch of Tomo-chi-chi, 4104
Historical sketches of North Carolina, 5683
Historical sketches of northern New York and the Adirondack wilderness, 23674
Historical sketches of the old painters, 10186
Historical sketches of the Wabash Valley, 5687
A historical vindication of the abrogation of the plan of union by the Presbyterian Church in the United States of America, 11564
Historicus, pseud., 12668, 12669
The historie of travaile into Virginia Britannia, 5296
Historiography, 19840
History, Addresses, essays, lectures, 877, 11388, 12393, 13116, 21856; Dictionaries, 12673; Methodology, 19904; Outlines, syllabus, etc., 13671, 22495; Philosophy, 20478; Societies, Plains states, 17894; Study and teaching, 11266; Year-books, 241, for 1816, 294
History, ancient, 22188, 24842
History, Modern, Addresses, essays, lectures, 2235
History, Universal, 782, 1280, 1599, 5065, 23367, 23379; Early works to 1800, 584, 4466, 6525, 6526
History and adventure, 1954
The history and adventures of Ned Lorn, 10062
History and its sources, 1485
The history and philosophy of earthquakes, 12800
The history and present state of Virginia, 1231
History and record of the proceedings of the people of Lexington and vicinity, 3884
The history and records of the Elephant club, 11038
The history of a pocket prayer book, 9413
The history of a station, 9348
The history of a very distinguished family, 8462

History of American missions to the heathen, from their commencement to the present time, 22496

A history of American revivals, 13634

The history of an expedition against Fort Du Quesne, 5072

The history of banks, 22463

History of Boston, from 1630 to 1856, 22543

A history of Catholicity in Montana, 17333

History of Cincinnati and Hamilton County, Ohio, 14330

History of Cosmopolite, 3277

History of Cuba, 724

The history of Don Francisco de Miranda's attempt to effect a revolution in South America, 1279

The history of Elgin from 1835 to 1875, 7052

The history of Eliza Wharton, 9549, 9550

A history of emigration from the United Kingdom to North America, 7158

History of Fourteenth Illinois cavalry and the brigades to which it belonged, 15326

History of Franklin County [Ohio], 23196

A history of French influence in the United States, 12801

A history of human life, 9731

History of Indian depredation in Utah, 16618

A history of interesting things found in the rooms of the Kentucky Historical Society, 15237

The history of Jamaica, 24884

The history of James Jaquith, 4047

The history of Jim Crow, 1519

The history of John Bull and Brother Jonathan, 10482

History of Kansas, 22530

History of Lexington, Kentucky, 15241

The history of Magnus Maharba and the Black Dragon, 8866, 8867

History of Montana, 17014

History of Nevada, 15855

A history of New York, 999, 10000

The history of North America, 3885, 8150

The history of North and South America, 5793

A history of Oberlin, 5189

History of Pennsylvania Hall, 25225

The history of Peru, 15951

The history of prime ministers and favorites, in England, 12802

The history of Prince Lee Boo, 12803

The history of Simón Bolívar, 7053

The history of South Carolina, 5161

History of Texas, 2826, 3886

History of Texas from its first settlement in 1685 to its annexation by the U.S. in 1846, 5786

History of the American theatre, 5122

History of the American war, of eighteen hundred and twelve, 22497

History of the backwoods, 4711, 23485

History of the border wars of two centuries, 15606

The history of the British dominions in North America, 7054

The history of the church, 1580

History of the church in Kentucky, 1359

A history of the county of Berkshire, Massachusetts, 2251

History of the Delaware and Iroquois Indians formerly inhabiting the middle states, 12804

History of the early settlement and Indian wars of western Virginia, 3213

History of the establishment and progress of the Christian religion in the islands of the South Sea, 13479

History of the federal government, 11494

History of the First regt. Penn. reserve cavalry, 4286

A history of the haunted caverns of Magdelama, 13272

The history of the hen fever, 1731

History of the Indian tribes of North America, 4359

History of the Indian wars and wars of the revolution of the United States, 15546

A history of the Indian wars with the first settlers of the United States, particularly in New-England, 23571

A history of the ladies' temperance benevolemt societies, 13249

The history of the Lady Betty Stair, 5116

History of the late war in the Plantations, 10099

History of the late war in the western country, 4326

History of the Medical department of the University of Louisville, 15787

History of the mission of the United Brethren among Indians in North America, 13398

A history of the Negro plot, 12911

A history of the New-York Kappa Lambda conspiracy, 12805

A history of the north-western editorial excursion to Arkansas, 4480

History of the Ohio falls cities and their counties, 14331

The history of the Pilgrims, 12806
History of the Presbyterian church in the state of Kentucky, 13974
History of the press in western New-York from the beginning to the middle of the nineteenth, 22198
History of the province of Georgia, 3208
History of the Regulators of northern Indiana, 23460
History of the revolution in Texas, 4592
History of the Second Colorados, 17900
The history of the second ten years of the reign of George the Third, 22498
A history of the separation in Indiana Yearly meeting of Friends, 24337
History of the strange sounds or rappings, heard in Rochester and western New York, 11986
A history of ten Baptist churches, 15503
History of the town of Easton, Mass., 2598
A history of the trial of Castner Hanway and others, 24613
History of the United States, 2456, 12541
The history of the United States for 1796, 1806
History of the United States secret service, 693
A history of the voyages and travels of Capt. Nathaniel Uring, 5556
History of the war between the United States and Mexico, 13196
History of the war between the U.S. and the Sac and Fox nations of Indians, 5596
History of the Wyandott mission, 3451
A history of three of the judges of King Charles I, 23663
The history of Uncle Sam and his boys, 10482
The history of Williamson county, Illinois, 3389
History, romance and philosophy of great American crimes and criminals, 15599
Hitchcock, Benjamin W., 22499
Hitchcock, Champion Ingraham, 14332
Hitchcock, David, 1773-1849, 22500, 22501
Hitchcock, Edward, 1793-1864, 12807, 22502-22506, 24265
Hitchcock, Enos, 1745-1803, 12808-12810
Hitchcock, Ethan Allen, 1798-1870, 16786
Hitchcock, Gad, 1718?-1809, 12811
Hitchcock, Henry, 1829-1902, 3887
Hitchcock, Henry Laurmann, 1813-1873, 22507
Hitchcock, Mary E., 16787

Hitchcock, Oscar Blakeslee, 1828-1897, 13137
Hitchcock, Reuben, 1764-1794, 12812
Hitchcock, Roswell Dwight, 1817-1887, 12813, 12814, 22508
Hite, Cass, 16788
Hither and thither, 2293
Hitherto, 11152
Hits and criticism on the follies of the day, 10536
Hits and dashes, 10828
Hits at the times, 10385
Hittell, John Shertzer, 1825-1901, 12815, 16789-16791
Hittell, Theodore Henry, 1830-, 3888, 16792
The hive of "the bee-hunter", 5412
Hiver caraibe, 7533
Hjelm-Hansen, Paul, 1810-1881, 3889
Ho! for the West! 12566
Hoar, Samuel, 1788-1856, 24995
Hobart, Aaron, 1787-1858, 12816
Hobart, Benjamin, 1781-1877, 22509
Hobart, Charles F., 16793
Hobart, Chauncey, b.1811, 16794
Hobart, Harrison C., 2657
Hobart, John Henry, bp., 1775-1830, 12817, 12818, 13289, 22510
Hobart, Noah, 1706-1773, 12819, 22511
Hobart-Hampden, Hon. Augustus Charles, 1822-1886, 3890
Hobbie, Hannah, 1806-1831, 460
Hobbs, E. D., 14333
Hobbs, George, 1790-, 12820
Hobbs, James, b.1819, 16795
Hobbs family, 12820
Hobby, William, 1707-1765, 12821
Hobby, William J., d.1841, 25366
Hobomok, a tale of early times, 8992
Hochelaga depicta; the early history and present state of the city and island of Montreal, 21807
Hockersmith, Lorenzo Dow, 1833-, 14334
Hocknell, John, 1723?-1799, 12094
Hodge, Charles, 1797-1878, 12822, 22484, 22678
Hodge, Fronya Gail, 14335
Hodge, James M., 14336, 14337
Hodge, Michael, 12823
Hodge, William L., 12824
Hodgen family, 25010
Hodgenville, Ky., 15671; Herald-News, 7055
Hodgepodge, 10736
Hodges, Almon Danforth, 1801-1878, 22512
Hodges, Helen, 14280
Hodges, William R., 24614
Hodges family (William Hodges, d.1654), 22513
Hodgins, John George, 1821-1912, 6666, 12825, 12826

Hodgkin, Frank F., 1846-, 16796
Hodgkin, Thomas, 1798-1866, 12827
Hodgman, Edwin Ruthven, 1819-1900, 22513
Hodgman, Stephen Alexander, 24615
Hodgson, Adam, 3891
Hodgson, Studholme John, 1805-1890, 24616
Hodgson, William Brown, b.1800, 12752, 22514
Hodgsons, William Ballantyne, 1815-1880, 23090
Hoek, Sander van, 1757-1816, 8362
Hoeniger, Nicolaus, fl.1573-1596, 1186
Hoëvell, Wolter Robert, baron van, 1812-1879, 1126
Hofer, Andreas, 1767-1810, 12829
Hoffer family (Matthias Hoffer, 1718?-1803), 12829
Hoffer, Isaac, b.1820, 12829
Hoffer, Jacob R., b.1823, 12829
Hoffman, Charles Fenno, 1806-1884, 3893, 3894
Hoffman, Christian, 12830
Hoffman, Eugene Augustus, 1829-1902, 22515
Hoffman, Francis Suydam, 1828-1886, 466
Hoffman, Frederick Ludwig, 1865-, 7056
Hoffman, Mrs. Virginia Haviside (Hale) 1832-1856, 11902
Hoffman, Wickham, 1821-1900, 3895
Hoffman, William, 22516
Hoffmann, Hermann, 7057, 16797
Hoffmeister, Jonathan M., 12831
Hogan, Edmund, 22517
Hogan, John, 12832
Hogan, John Joseph, bp.1829-1913, 16798
Hogan, John Sheridan, 1815?-1859, 12833
Hogan, William, d.1848, 12834
Hogarth's Sound, 22843
Hoge, Jane Currie (Blaikie) "Mrs. A. H. Hoge", 12835, 22518
Hoge, William James, 1821-1864, 12836, 12837
Hogg, James Stephen, 1851-1906, 16799
Hogs, 15525; Santa Catarina, Brazil - Statistics, 19469
Hogs in Ohio Valley superstition, 15529
The Hohays, 10827
Hoit, C. W., 12838
Hoit, True Worthy, b.1815, 12839
Holanda, Sérgio Buarque de, 19529
Hølaas, Odd, 3896
The Holbey family, 11169
Holbrook, Charles Warren, 1828-1888, 12840
Holbrook, Mrs. Harriott Pinckney, 4804
Holbrook, James, 1812-1864, 22519
Holbrook, Samuel F., b.1793, 12841
Holbrook, Timothy Washington, 22520

Holbrook family (Micah Holbrook, 1732-1817), 12840
Holcombe, Henry, 1762-1824, 3897, 22521
Holcombe, James Philemon, 1820-1873, 3898, 12842, 24617
Holcombe, Theodore Isaac, 1832-, 16800
Holcombe, William Henry, 1825-1893, 12843
The Holcombes, 10299
Holden, Frederic Augustus, 22522
Holden, Horace, b.1810, 22523
Holden, Oliver, 1765-1894, 7058
Holden, Mass. - History, 22034
Holden with the cords, 11201
Hold-fast, Simon, pseud., 12844
Holdich, Joseph, 1804-1893, 12845, 22524
Holditch, Robert, 12846
Holdredge, Sterling M., pub., 3899
Holdsworth, Edward, 1684-1746. Muscipula, 5264
Holgate, Jerome Bonaparte, 12847
Holiday rambles, 5711
Holiday tales, 10400
Holidays at home and abroad, 6838
Holing, J. B., 14338
Holitscher, Arthur, 1869-, 3900
Holladay, Ben, 1819-1887, 3901
Holladay, Harriett MacDonald, 14339, 15370
Holland, Edwind Clifford, 1794-1824, 24618
Holland, Elihu Goodwin, 1817-1878, 22525, 22526
Holland, John, 12848
Holland, Josiah Gilbert, 1819-1881, 7059, 22527, 22528
Holland, Major, 22696
Holland, Mrs. Robert, 22529
Holland, William M., 12849
Holland club, New York, 13008
Hollander, Arie Nicolaas Jan den, 3902
Hollberg, Esaias, 2462
Holley, Frances (Chamberlain), 16802
Holley, Horace, 1781-1827, 2886, 14340, 15580
Holley, Mary Austin, 1784-1846, 3903, 14285
Holley, Myron, 1779-1841, 24619, 25924
Holley, Orville Luther, 1791-1861, 271, 12850-12852
Holley, Sallie, 1818-1893, 24620
Hollick, Frederick, b.1818, 24621
Holliday, Fernandez C., 1814-, 14341
Hollingsworth, Samuel L., 12853-12855
Hollis, Thomas, 1720-1774, 21787
Hollis, N.H., History, 2297
Hollister, Gideon Hiram, 1817-1881, 12856
Hollister, Hiel, 12857
Hollister, Horace, 1822-, 12858
Hollister, Ovanda James, 1834-1892, 3904, 12859, 16803, 17170

Hollister, Uriah S., 1838-, 16804
The hollow of the three hills, 9827
Holloway, Edward, illustr., 8800
Holloway, John N., 22530
Holloway, William, jr., fl.1790-1812, 8969, 22531
Holloway, William Robeson, 1836-1911, 12860
Holly, James Theodore, 1829-, 12861
Holly and pizen, 5312
Hollywood, Calif., 20441
Holloway, nua e crua, 20441
Holman, Frederick V., 16805
Holman, Jesse Lynch, 14342
Holman, Nathan, 1769-1844, 12862
Holman, William Steele, 1822-1897, 12863
Holmden, H. R., 6296
Holme, Benjamin, 1683-1749, 3905
Holmes, A. T., 24954
Holmes, Abiel, 1763-1837, 12864, 12865, 22532, 22533
Holmes, Abraham, 1754-1839, 22534
Holmes, Arthur, 12866
Holmes, Mrs. Charlotte (Steevens), 7060
Holmes, Clay W., 7060
Holmes, Daniel, 3906
Holmes, Daniel Henry, 1851-1908, 14343
Holmes, Elias Bellows, 1810?-1866, 12867
Holmes, Mrs. Elizabeth (Emra) 1804-1843, 22535
Holmes, Ezekiel, 1801-1865, 12868
Holmes, Francis Simmons, 1815-1882, 12869
Holmes, Frederick Lionel, 1883-1946, 3907
Holmes, Hamilton, 3908
Holmes, Isaac, 3909
Holmes, John, 1773-1843, 12870, 12871, 22536
Holmes, Mrs. Mary Jane (Hawes) 1828-1907, 3910-3918, 10163
Holmes, Obadiah, 1606(?)-1682, 7573
Holmes, Oliver Wendell, 1809-1894, 12872, 12663, 22537
Holmes, Reuben, 3919
Holmes, Theophilus Hunter, 1804-1880, 2073
Holomorphic mappings, 18881
"Holster atlas," 5082
Holt, Edwin, 1805-1854, 22538
Holt, Edwin B., 4551
Holt, Joseph, 1807-1894, 12873, 22439
Holton, Edward Dwight, 1815-1892, 16806
Holton, Isaac Farwell, 22540
Holtron, Willem 1750-1936, pub., 1516
Holty, Mathilde Edith, 16807
The holy cross and other tales, 9511

Holy Roman empire, Henry IV, 1056-1106, Fiction, 10351
Holy water, 7957
Holyoake, George Jacob, 1817-1906, 3920, 3921
Holyoke, Edward, 1689-1769, 22541, 22542
Homans, Benjamin, 11228
Homans, Isaac Smith, 1807-1874, 22543
Hombre, mundo, transcendencia, 18154
El hombre de la bandera, 17994
Hombre peregrino, 18685
Los hombres y las ideas, 18871
Home, 10190
Home again, 9696
Home and the world, 10626
A home and where to find one, 5062
Home as found, 9133
Home as I found it, 10003
Home ballads, 2087
The home book of the picturesque, 22544
The home-coming of Jim Wilkes, 6971, 9790
Home economics, Accounting, 18736; Study and teaching, 14632
The home economist, 14813
Home-heroes, saints, and martyrs, 8567
A home in the New World, 3913
Home influence of religion, 8968
Home league, 22545
Home life in Florida, 5625
Home lights and shadows, 487
Home missionary society of Oregon and adjoining territories, 16455
Home nook, 9420
The home of the Badgers, 16648
Home scenes during the rebellion, 10630
Home secrets told by old travellers, 10516
The home side, 9331
Home stories, 9802
Homem-libertação, 18382
O homen e a sua realizacão, 20634
Homenagem a Camões, 19264
Homenaje a la Francia Combatiente, 18216
Homenaje a Rubén Darío, 20409
Homenaje al decano de la Facultad de Humanidades y Educación de la Universidad de los Andes, 21719
Homeopathy, 12884; Addresses, essays, lectures, 22995
Homer, Arthur, 1758-1806, 2476
Homer, James Lloyd, 12874, 22546, 22547
Homer, William Bradford, 1817-1841, 22548
Homes, Henry Augustus, 1812-1887, 12875, 12876
Homes for Boston laborers, 9695
Homes for the people, 3573
The homes of the New World, 1473, 8137, 13713
Homes of American authors, 22549
Homes of American statesmen, 22550

Homespun, 9874
Homestead, 21822
The homestead on the hillside, 3915, 9896
Homestead strike, 1892, 21822
Homeward bound, 9134, 10916
Homeward through America, 3982
Homicide, 14666
Homo, 3310
Homoselle, 10974
Homosexuality, 14180
Hondura, 18394
Honduras, 6402, 8096, 8280, 12877, 12484; Description & travel, 6402, 6777, 7974, 8280, 17233; Description & travel, Guide-books, 7680; Economic conditions, 20469, 20641; Foreign relations, Guatemala, 12877; History, 8281; History, Sources, 12877; Periodicals, 5955; Politics & government, 7451, 20469; Population, 20437; Statistics, 18726
Honduras interoceanic railway, 8096, 13484
Hone, Philip, 1780-1851, 12878
Honest John Vane, 9370
Honey, William, 24622
Honey, Argentine Republic, 19899
Honolulu, Description, 15899, 16253; Social life & customs, 15899
Honor May, 8753
El honor militar, 7719
The honor of the troop, 10608
Honora, Dr., 9331
The Honorable D. Sheffey, 15355
The honorable Peter Sterling and what people thought of him, 9535
Hood, Fred, pseud., 3981
Hood, George, 12879
Hood, John Bell, 1831-1879, 3922
Hood, Samuel, 1800?-1875, 12880
Hood's Texas brigade, 4823
The hoodlum band, 9779
Hoodooed, 15262
Hook, W. E., 16809
Hook, William, 880
Hooke, William, 1601-1678, 12881
Hooker, Edward William, 1794-1875, 22551-22553
Hooker, Joseph, 1814-1879, 7282, 7285
Hooker, Thomas, 1586-1647, 12882, 23561, 22553, 22554
Hooker, William Francis, 1856-, 16810
Hooker, Sir William Jackson, 1785-1865, 3923, 12883, 22555
Hooker, Worthington, 1806-1867, 12884

Hooper, Johnson Jones, 1815-1862, 3924-2926
Hooper, Lucy, 1816-1841, 12885
Hooper, Samuel, 1808-1875, 2380, 2441, 12886
Hooper, William Henry, b.1813, 12887, 16811
Hooper, William Hulme, 1827-1854, 22556
Hoosac tunnel, 1327, 11274, 11275
Hoosatunnuk, Vale of, 204
Hoosier mosaics, 5391
The Hoosier schoolmaster, 9466
Hooton, Charles, 1813?-1847, 3927
Hope, Anthony, pseud., 9804
Hope, James Barron, 1829-1887, 3928-3933, 12888
Hope Leslie, 10724
Hope's anchor, 9914
Hope's fruition, 9601
Hopedale Community, 25586
Hopewell, Menra, 16812
Hopi Indians, 16025
Hopkins, Albert, 1807-1872, 22557
Hopkins, Albert Allis, 1869-, 16813
Hopkins, Daniel, 1734-1814, 22558
Hopkins, Gerrard T., 12889
Hopkins, James Dean, 1773-1840, 12890
Hopkins, Jesse, 22559
Hopkins, John Baker, 1830-1888, 12891
Hopkins, John Castell, 1864-1923, 7062
Hopkins, John Henry, bp.1792-1868, 12892, 24623, 24947; Bible view of slavery, 24301, 24317, 24916, 25019, 25138
Hopkins, Lemuel, 1750-1801, 229
Hopkins, Mark, 1802-1887, 8095, 12893, 22560
Hopkins, Patricia M., 14344
Hopkins, Porter H., 14345
Hopkins, Robert Milton, 1878-1955, 13696, 14346
Hopkins, Samuel, 1693-1755, 12894, 12895
Hopkins, Samuel, 1721-1803, 22561, 24624
Hopkins, Samuel Miles, 1772-1837, 22562
Hopkins, Sarah Winnemucca, 1844?-1891, 16814
Hopkins, Stephen, 1707-1785, 12896-12898
Hopkins, Thomas M., 12899
Hopkins family (Stephen Hopkins, d.1644), 22552
Hopkins County, Ky., 15195; Description, 14193; Economic conditions, 14542
Hopkins grammar school, New Haven, Conn., History, 643
Hopkinson, Francis, 1737-1791, 12900-12902, 22517
Hopkinson, Joseph. 1770-1842, 12903
Hopkinton, Mass., Church history, 22582
Hopkinton, N. Y., 4726
Hopley, Catherine Cooper, 1832 (ca.), 3934
Hopp, Ernest Otto, 1841-1910, 3935
Hoppe, Janus, 16815

Hopper, Charles, 16926
Hooper, Edward, 1816-1888, 12904, 22563
Hooper, Isaac Tatem, 1771-1852, 1892
Hoppin, Augustus, 1828-1896, illustr., 1775, 9289, 9291, 10049
Hoppin, William Jones, 1813-1895, 11704
Hoppner, Richard Belgrave, 22741
Hopson, Peregrine Thomas, 7601
Hopwood, Samuel, 12655
Horace in New York, 11859
Horae svccisivae, 6069
Horce Everett, 10165
Horetzky, Charles, 6748
Horine, Emmet Field, 1885-1964, 14011, 14012, 14347-14349, 14898; Bibliography, 13914
Horine, Robert, 13833
Horn, Hosea B., 3936
Horn, Cape, 22759
Hornaday, William Temple, 1854-1937, 7063
Horne, Henry, 12905
Horner, Gustavus, R. B., 12906
Horner, Hattie, 3937
Horner, Joseph Andrew, ed., 24625
Horner, William B., 3938
Hornet, 12289
Hornot, Antoine, 22564
Horrall, Spillard F., 1829-, 3940
Horrors of slavery, 24712, 25345
Horry, Peter, 23770
Hors d'oeuvres cookbook 1971, 14705
Horse bridges, 15783
Horse racing, 13678, 13716, 14493, 15054, 15066; Kentucky, 14043, 14076, 14496, 15001, 15548; Poetry, 14746; U.S., 2310, 12543, 15001
Horse sense, 15001
Horse Shoe Robinson, 10094
Horse shows, 14740; Lexington, Ky., 14817
A horse story, 13288
The horse thief, 9744
Horseback rides through the Yellowstone national park, 17284
Horsemanship, 13551
Horses, Diseases, 18893; Santa Catarina, Brazil, Statistics, 19467; Trotting, 14250; Walking, 14817
Horsford, Eben Norton, 1818-1893, 12907-12909
Horsford, Jedidiah, 1791-1874, 22565
Horsford, Mrs. Mary (Gardiner) 1824-1855, 12910
Horsmanden, Daniel, 1694-1778, 12911
Horton, H. P., 12912
Horton, Joshua H., 3940
Horton, Rushmore G., b.1826, 12913, 22566

The Hortons, 8950
Hortop, Job, fl.1591, 7064, 7065
Hortus Britanno-Americanus, 1828
Hortus Elginensis, 12916
Horvel Hastings, 10432
Hosack, Alexander, 12914
Hosack, Alexander Eddy, 1805-1871, 12915
Hosack, David, 1769-1835, 12916-12918, 22567
Hosie, John, 8322
Hoskens, Jane Fenn, 1694-, 3941
Hoskin, James, 3942
Hoskins, Nathan, 1795-1869, 3943, 12919
Hosmer, Charlottes, 13424
Hosmer, Hezekiah L., 12920
Hosmer, James Kendall, 1834-1927, 3944
Hosmer, Margaret (Kerr), 1830-1897, 12922
Hosmer, Titus, 1736-1780, 811
Hosmer family (Thomas Hosmer, 1603-1681), 12921
Hosmer, Miss., 4447
Hospital Nuestra Señora del Pilar, 18366
Hospital pencillings, 4841
Hospital sketches, 130
Hospital transports, 13447
Hospitals, 12380; Cuba, 18366; Gt. Brit., 23389; Lexington, Ky., 14811; U.S., 23389
Hospitals, Military, 13304; Mexico, 6482; Naval and marine, 944
Hossack, David, 1769-1835, 11779
Hot and Hot Fish Club, 5871
Hot corn, 10638
Hot plowshares, 10991
Hotchkin, James Harvey, 1781-1851, 22568
Hotchkiss, Frederick William, 1763?-1844, 12923, 22569
Hotchkiss, Jedediah, 1827-1899, 12924
Hotels, motels, etc., Kentucky, 13549, 13637, 14435, 15153, 15603; Louisville, Ky., 14172; Winchester, Ky., 15120
Hotspur, 11063
Hough, Emerson, 1857-1923, 14350, 14351, 16817-16819
Hough, Franklin Benjamin, 1822-1885, 351, 1417, 2167, 12925-12933, 22570-22574
Houghton, Edwin B., 12934
Houghton, Eliza Poor (Donner), 1843-, 16820
Houghton family, 12935
Houghton association, 12935
Houlihan, Ed, 15012
The hour of patriotism, 1300
Hourani, F., 24626
House, E., 3945
The house, 9512
The house at second and Broadway, 14885
A house built upon the sand, 9764
"House divided" speech, 24160

House hunting and moving, 10820
The house in Balfour-street, 3250
The House of Belle Breezing, 14352
The house of Egremont, 10720
The house of the seven gables, 9821
The house of tragedy, 14094
The house on the heath, 10921
The house surgeon and physician, 12647
A house-boat on the Styx, 8679
Houseboating on a colonial waterway, 3978
Household gods, 10394
The household of Bouverie, 5614
The household of McNeil, 8728
Household sketches, 10255
Household tales, 10580
Houser, Martin Luther, 1871-1951, 7066-
7071, 7987
Houses, Bawdy, Kentucky, 15684;
Lexington, Ky., 13833, 14352
Houseworth, Henry, 12936
Housing, Argentine Republic, 18422, 18500;
Argentine Republic, Law and legislation,
18413; Brazil, 19462, 20381; Costa Rica,
Statistics, 20576; Law and legislation,
18413; Lexington, Ky., 14794;
Massachusetts, 9697; New York (City),
12451; Quixada, Brazil, 20014; Venezuela,
18810; Venezuela, Finance, 19138; Zulia,
Venezuela, 18809
Houston, F. W., 14353
Houston, James, b.ca.1690, 12941
Houston, James A., 10057
Houston, James Alexander, 12937
Houston, Mrs. Matilda Charlotte (Jesse)
Fraser, 1815?-1892, 3946, 3947
Houston, Samuel, 1793-1863, 3068, 12938-
12940, 17023, 17024, 17226, 17899
Hovey, Alvah, 1820-1903, 22575
Hovey, Horace Carter, 1833-1914, 3948, 3949,
14354, 22576
Hovey, Ivory, 1714-1803, 12942
Hovey's handbook of the Mammoth cave of
Kentucky, 3948
How, David, 1758-1842, 12943
How, Henry K., 12944, 12945, 24627
How, Samuel Blanchard, 1790-1868, Slave
holding not sinful, 24627, 25792
How, Thomas Tardley, 21915, 22577
Howard, Alice Sturtevant, 3950
Howard, Bezaleel, 1753-1837, 22578
Howard, Edward, d.1841, 12946
Howard, Frank Key, 1826-1872, 2463
Howard, George Elliott, 1849-, 17260
Howard, H. R., 11165
Howard, Helen, 14212
Howard, Henry, 1868-, 3950

Howard, Henry Clay, 14355
Howard, J. H., illustr., 10536, 10538
Howard, John H., 25456
Howard, Katharine, 3950
Howard, McHenry, 3951
Howard, Mark, 1817-1887, 12947
Howard, Middleton, b.1747?, 12948
Howard, Richard L., 3953
Howard, Simeon, 1733-1804, 22579
Howard, Mrs. Virginia Webb, 14356
Howard of Glossop, Winifred (De Lisle), 3952
Howard Pinckney, 10951
The Howards, 8704
Howay, Frederic W., 7072
Howbert, Irving, 1846-, 16823
Howe, Beverly Winslow, 1885-, 7073, 7074
Howe, Daniel Wait, 1839-1920, 24628
Howe, Eber D., b.1798, 12950
Howe, Edgar Watson, 1854-, 7075
Howe, Elias, 1819-1867, 7076
Howe, Elisha P., 12951
Howe, Henry, 1816-1893, 785, 785, 791, 3954,
3955, 7077, 12952, 12953, 22580
Howe, James Blake, d.1844, 22581
Howe, Joseph, 1804-1873, 12954
Howe, Mrs. Julia Ward, 1819-1910, 12955,
12956
Howe, Mark Antony DeWolfe, 1864-, 3887
Howe, Nathanael, 1764-1837, 22582
Howe, Richard Howe, earl, 1726-1799, 886, 2384
Howe, Samuel Gridley, 1801-1876, 12957, 23989,
24629
Howe, Thomas H., 3956
Howe, Timothy Otis, 1816-1883, 12958
Howe, Sir William, 1729-1814, 22031, 23361,
23362
Howe, William Bell White, bp., 1823-1894,
12959
Howe, William Howe, 5th viscount, 1729-1814,
12960, 13421
Howel, Thomas, 344
Howell, E. C., 24230
Howell, George Rogers, 1833-1899, 12961
Howell, John, 1788-1863, 140
Howell, Peter, 1805-, 3957
Howell, Co., Mo., History, 17219
Howells, William Dean, 1837-1920, 4778, 8773
Howes, Frederick, 12962
Howgate grant, 4624
Howison, John, 12963
Howison, Neil M., 16824
Howitt, Emanuel, 12964
Howitt, Mary, 13713
Howitt, Mary (Botham) 1799-1888, 1473, 6157,
11632, 22583
Howitt, William, 1792-1879, 12965

Howland, Edward, 22584
Howland, Henry Jenkins, b.1810, 12966
Howland, John, 1757-1854, 12564
Howlett, Thomas Rosling, 22585
Howlett, William Joseph, 1848-1936, 14357, 16825
Hows, Iohn A., illustr., 11592, 12742
Howse, Joseph, 12967
Howson, Henry, sr., 12968
Hoyne, Thomas, 1817-1883, 6415, 16040
Hoyo, Asturo del, 18133
Hoyt, David Webster, 1833-1921, 12969
Hoyt, Epaphras, 1765-1850, 12970
Hoyt, George Henry, 1837-, 12971
Hoyt, Jesse, 12972, 13412
Hoyt, John W., 16826
Hoyt, Joseph Gibson, 1815-1862, 12973
Hoyt, R. D., 14358
Hoyt family, 12969
Hoyt family (David Hoyt, 1651-1704), 12969
Hoyt family (John Hoyt, d.1687), 12969
Huaraz, Peru, Description, 20459; Earthquake, 1941, 20459
Hubard, Fdmund W., 22586
Hubbard, Charles Eustis, 1842-, 3958
Hubbard, George H., 22587
Hubbard, Gurdon Saltonstall, 1802-1886, 16827
Hubbard, Henry, 1784-1857, 12974, 24630
Hubbard, John Milton, 3959
Hubbard, Leonidas, 1872-1903, 6671
Hubbard, Mrs. Mary Ann (Hubbard) 1820-1909, 16828
Hubbard, Samuel Dickinson, 1799-1855, 12975
Hubbard, William, 1621-1704, 12976, 22588, 23813
Hubbard, William B., 12977
Hubbard family, 16828
Hubbardton, Battle of, 1777, 11812
Hubbell, Seth, 1759-1832, 12978
Hubbell, Stephen, 1802-1884, 12979
Hubbell, William Wheeler, 12980
Hubbell family, 12978
Hubbub, 9281
Huber, illustr., 8458
Huber, B., 12981
Huber, Victor Aimé, 1800-1869, 24631
Hubert, Benjamin F., 6696
Hubert, William Henry, 13041
Hubner, Charles William, 1835-1929, 3960, 3961
Huckleberries gathered from New England hills, 9120
Huddleston, Eugene L., 14359

Huddleston, Walter Dee, 14360, 14361, 15372
Hudibrastic aspects of some editions of the Emancipation Proclamation, 5836
Hudnall, James S., Coals of Martin County [Kentucky], 15686
Hudson, Charles, 1795-1881, 12982, 12983, 22589, 22590, 22591
Hudson, David, 12984
Hudson, Eduard Maco, 12985
Hudson, Henry Norman, 1814-1886, 1765, 12986
Hudson, N. H., History, 2297
The Hudson illustrated with pen and pencil, 12987
Hudson river, 9995, 22610; Description & travel, 12987; Description & travel, Guide-books, 7748
Hudson Strait, 6303
Hudson Bay, 1924, 2604, 4626, 5057, 5990, 6302, 6670, 7808, 12058, 15954, 17439, 21871; Description, 1201, 7809, 7922, 8022
Hudson's Bay a free basin, 6727
The Hudson's Bay and Pacific territories, 7542
Hudson's Bay company, 2604, 4368, 5169, 5812, 5990, 6228, 5298, 6434, 6435, 6605, 6668, 6731, 6742, 6783, 7078, 7575, 7641, 7978, 8140, 8256, 12073, 16394, 16474, 17076, 17231, 17251, 17936, 17943, 23543; History, 17141
The Hudson's Bay company versus Magna Charta and the British people, 6736
The Hudson's Bay company's archives furnish no support to the Whitman saved Oregon story, 17141
The Hudson's Bay territories and Vancouver's island, 7423
Huelsen, Christian Carl Friedrich, 1858-1935, 24632
El huésped alienante, 20355
Huet, Pierre Daniel, bp. 1630-1721, 12988
Huevos y larvas de tres especies de peces marinos, 20191
Huger, Daniel Elliott, 1779-1854, 24112
Hugh Darnaby, 9344, 13980
Hugh Worthington, 3916, 9897
Hughes, Charles Evans, 1862-1948, 7079
Hughes, Mrs. Elizabeth, 16829
Hughes, George Wurtz, 1806-1870, 13294
Hughes, Gerard, 3963
Hughes, Griffith, fl.1750, 22592
Hughes, Henry, 3963
Hughes, Henry, d.1862, 25572
Hughes, James, 1823-1873, 12989
Hughes, Jesse, 13739
Hughes, John, abp. 1797-1864, 12990, 12991, 22334
Hughes, John Starrett, 24633

Hughes, John Taylor, 1817-1862, 3962, 17618
Hughes, Louis, 1832-, 24634
Hughes, Madge, 3963
Hughes, Paul, 14362
Hughes, Thomas, 1822-1896, 3963, 12992
Hughes, Timothy, 3963
Hughes, William, 3963
Hughes, William Edgar, 1840-, 16830
Hughes, William Joseph Leander, 1844-, 14363
The Hughes family and connections, 14363
Hughs, Mrs. Mary (Robson), 12993
Hughston, Jonas A., d.1862, 24635
Hugo, Victor Marie, comte, 1802-1885, 24772, 24836
Hugo Blanc, 9670
The Huguenot, 11188
The Huguenot lovers, 8903
Huguenots, Fiction, 5283
Huguenots in Virginia, 2263, 3325, 3494
Huish, Robert, 1777-1850, 22593
Huit mois en Amérique, 3331
Hulbert, Archer Butler, 1873-1933, 7080
Hulbert, Charles, 1778-1857, 12994
Huldah, the help, 9463
Hule, Laguna de, Costa Rica, 19007
Hulett, T. G., 12995
Hull, Amos Gerald, 1810-1859, 12996
Hull, John Simpson, 3964
Hull, William, 1753-1825, 12998-13000, 13504, 22594
Hull family (Richard Hull, d.1662), 21946
Hull, Mass., Description, 22547
Hulme, Thomas, 3965, 14364
Hulot, Étienne Gabriel Joseph, baron, 1857-1918, 7081
Hulot d'Osery, A. Victor Eugène, vicomte, 21853
Hulsius, Levinus, d.1606. [Collection of voyages], Bibliography, 495
The human comedy, 9106
Human slavery in the Philippines, 25782
Human sunshine, 10669
Humane policy, 760
Humane society of Massachusetts, 2328
Humanitas, pseud., 24636; Cuadernos, 19794; 21853
Humanities, Venezuela, Bibliography, 19744
Humason, William Lawrence, 13001
An humble address and earnest appeal, 23721
The humble address of the publicans of New-England, 13002
An humble enquiry into the Scripture account of Jesus Christ, [with sketch of Thomas Emlyn's life], 14060

Humboldt, Alexander, Freiherr von, 1769-1859, 4500, 4501, 7082-7092, 8111, 13003, 13004, 13107
Humboldt, Wilhelm, freiherr von, 1767-1835, 97
Humboldt Co., Col., Biography, 16149
Humboldt silver mines, 5685
The humbugs of the world, 11234
Hume, Edgar Erskine, 1889-1952, 14365, 14438
Hume, George Henry, 13005
Hume, Hamilton, 22595
Hume, John Ferguson, 1830-, 24637
Hume, Sophia, 1701-1774, 13006
Humes, Thomas William, 1815-1892, 2156
Humfreville, James Lee, 16831
Los humildes, 19013
Humming-birds, 23195
Humor, satire, and sentiment, 10198
The humorists, 9996
The humors of Falconbridge, 10090
Humors of the West, 10621
Humors on the border, 9109
Humphrey, Heman, 1779-1861, 13007, 22596-22599
Humphreys, Andrew Atkinson, 1810-1883, 5514, 5524, 22600
Humphreys, Charles, 14366
Humphreys, Charles Alfred, 1838-, 3966
Humphreys, David, 1680-1740, 22601
Humphreys, David, 1752-1818, 13008-13012, 22602-22604
Humphreys, Edward Rupert, 1820-1893, 22605
Humphrys-Alexander, Alexander, calling himself earl of Stirling, 1783-1859, 757, 13013
Die hundertjährige republik, 2660
Hundley, Daniel Robinson, 1832-1899, 3967, 22606
A hundred battles in the West, 5373
A hundred thousand dollars in gold, 8916
A hundred years ago, 10450, 10977
The hundredth man, 10890
The Hungarian horse dealer, 10693
Hungarians in North Dakota, 16403
The hungry man was fed, 9357, 9363
Hunn, Anthony, 3968
Hunnewell, James Frothingham, 1832-, 5252
Hunnicut, James W., 1814-, 3969
Hunt, 4845
Hunt, Benjamin Faneuil, 1792-1857, 13014
Hunt, Charles Havens, 22607
Hunt, Cornelius E., 22608
Hunt, Daniel, 1806-1869, 13015
Hunt, Edward Bissell, 1822-1863, 13016
Hunt, G. W., 17045
Hunt, Ezra Mundy, 1830-1894, 22609
Hunt, Freeman, 1804-1858, 22610
Hunt, George W., 1831-, 16832

Hunt, Gilbert J., 22611
Hunt, Isaac, 1742?-1809, 13017
Hunt, Harriot Kesia, 1805-1875, 22612
Hunt, James 1833-1869, 13019
Hunt, John Warren, 1826-1859, 13020
Hunt, Richard Morris, 1828-1895, 22613
Hunt, Richard S., 3970
Hunt, Rockwell Dennis, 1868-, 16833
Hunt, Timothy Dwight, 1821-1895, 13021
Hunt, William Gibbes, 1791?-, 1833, 13023, 14367
Hunt, Wilson Price, 3971
Hunt family, 15438, 16832
The hunted chief, 9295
Hunter, Alfred G., 3972
Hunter, David, 1802-1886, 13024, 25615
Hunter, George, 1835-, 16834
Hunter, John, 1728-1793, 3707
Hunter, John Dunn, 1798?-1827, 3973, 3974, 13025
Hunter, John Marvin, 1880-, 16835
Hunter, Joseph, 1783-1861, 13026, 13027
Hunter, Robert Mercer Taliaferro, 1809-1887, 23841, 24638-24640
Hunter, William, 13028
Hunter, William, 1774-1849, 22614
Hunter, William Perceval, 597
The hunter and trapper in North America, 4935
Hunter Ham, 14368
The hunter-naturalist, 5650
A hunter's adventures in the great west, 16601
A hunter's experiences in the southern states of America, 3464, 16522
The hunter's guide, and trapper's companion, 22615
The hunter's vow, 9618
The hunters of Kentucky, 2748, 15770
The hunters of the prairie, 4024
The hunters of the Rocky Mountains, 4993
The hunters' feast, 4924
Hunting, 423, 3852, 5650, 5656, 7063, 12257, 15549, 16164, 16331, 16900, 22615, 23553; Adirondack mountains, 10398, 22380; Alaska, 7369; British Columbia, 8074; Canada, 6641, 6876, 6954, 16685; Central America, 11655; Colorado, 16137; Florida, 3094, 3095, 5001; Great Plains, 4686; Kansas, 16137; Kentucky, 13917, 15657, 15784; Mexico, 18635; Mississippi valley, 3594; New York (State), 12630, 12631, 22381; North America, 4935, 9803, 22390; South Carolina, 12048; Southern states, 3464, 3924, 16522; Texas, 3465, 16523; U.S.,
1197, 5054, 5060, 5983, 11585, 16401, 16601, 16760, 17520, 17521; The West, 3852, 5306, 6641, 15838, 17004, 17185; Yukon Territory, 7369, 8012
Hunting and fishing in Florida, 3094
The hunting flask, 4002
Hunting for gold, 16417
The hunting grounds of the great West, 16401
Hunting in Florida in 1874, 4056
Huntington, Asahel, 1761-1813, 22616
Huntington, Charles S., illustr., 13481, 17641
Huntington, Dan, 1774-1864, 22617
Huntington, Elijah Baldwin, 1816-1877, 22618-22620
Huntington, Elisha, 7093
Huntington, Enoch, 1739-1809, 13029, 13030, 22621
Huntington, Frederic Dan, 1819-1904, 12521, 13031
Huntington, Gurdon, 1818-1875, 13032
Huntington, Jabez, 1733-1782, 22123
Huntington, Jedediah, 1743-1818, 22861
Huntington, Joseph, 1735-1794, 631, 13033
Huntington, Hon. Lucius Seth, 1827-1886, 13035
Huntington, Joshua, 1786-1819, 13034
Huntington, O. B., 16485
Huntington family, 22617
Huntington family (Simon Huntington, 1583-1633), 22618
Huntley, Sir Henry Veel, 1795-1864, 16836
Huntoon, Benjamin, 1792-1864, 13036
Huntt, Henry, 1792-1838, 13037
Hupé, H., 21853
Hurd, Aaron Haynes, 1813-1830, 12845
Hurd, Duane Hamilton, 7094
Hurd, John Codman, 1816-1892, 13038, 24641
Hurd, John R., 13039
Hurd, Rollin Carlos, b.1815, 22622
Hurdis, John L., 13306
Huret, Jules, 1864-1937, 3975
Hurlbert, Jesse Beaufort, 13040
Hurlbert, William Henry, 1827-1895, 4097
Hurlburt family (Samuel Hurlbut, 1748-1816), 22623
Hurlburt family (William Hurlburt, fl.1630), 22623
Hurlbut, Elisha P., 13042, 13043
Hurlbut, Henry Higgins, 1813-1900, 22623
Huron, Lake, Description & travel, 7135
Huron Indians, 23563; Missions, 3451, 23439
Huron language, Glossaries, vocabularies, etc., 7223; Texts, 11762
Hurricanes, 2160
Hurst, John Fletcher, bp 1834-1903, 7764
Hurst, Samuel H., 3976

Hurt, John, 13044
Hurt-Binet, Marc Gabriel, 13045
Hurtado Ruiz-Tagle, Carlos, 19512
Husband and wife, 18145; Mexico, 18145
Huske, John, 1721?-1773, 13046
Huskisson, William, 1770-1830, 22624
Husks, 5358, 10938
Hussey, H., 3977
Hussey, John, 14369
Hussey, Josiah, 13047
Huston, J., 13048
Hutchen, Virginius, 14219
Hutchens, Richard, 14107
Hutchings, James Mason, 1820-1902, 16837, 22625
Hutchings' illustrated California magazine, 17204
Hutchins, Cortelle, 3978
Hutchins, Frank, 3978
Hutchins, John, 1812-1891, 24642
Hutchins, Levi, 1761-1855, 22626
Hutchins, Samuel, 1806-1886, ed., 22626
Hutchins, Stephen C., 1836-1883, 22303
Hutchins, Thomas, 1730-1789, 3979, 3980, 14370
Hutchins family (William Hutchins, fl. 1657), 22626
Hutchinson, Francis, bp. of Down and Connor, 1660-1739, 13049
Hutchinson, John Wallace, 1821-1908, 1677, 13050
Hutchinson, Thomas, 1711-1780, 13051-13053, 22627, 22628; Bibliography, 22060
Hutchinson, Thomas Joseph, b.1820, 13054, 22629
Hutchinson, William, b.1586?, 1856
Hutchinson, William Francis, 1868-1893, 7095
Hutchinson family, 1856
Hutchinson's Republic songster, 13050
Hutchison, John Russell, 1807-1878, 16838
Hutchison, William, 1827-1885, 22213
Huth, Friedrich, 1866-, 3981
Hutson, Mrs. Mary, 1621
The hutted knoll, 9157
Hutton, Daniel Mac-Hir, 14371, 14372
Hutton, Henry Dix, 1824-1907, 13104
Hutton, Lawrence, 1843-1904, 2695
Hutton, Mathew, successively abp. of York and Canterbury, 1693-1758, 22630
Huys in't Bosch (Ship), 24690
Hyatt, H. S., 16839
Hyatt, Thaddeus, 13055, 25655
Hybridization of metals, 19067
Hyde, Alvan, 1768-1833, 13056, 22631
Hyde, Mrs. Anna M., 13057

Hyde, Ezra, 1774-1849, 13058
Hyde, James F. C., 13059
Hyde, John, 1833-1875, 22632
Hyde, John, 1848-1929, 3982
Hyde, S. C., 16840
Hyde, Solon, 3983
Hyde, W. H., illustr., 9637
Hyde, William, 1806-1888, 22633
Hyde, William Lyman, 1819-1896, 13060
Hyde family, 8335
Hyder Ali, pseud. of Cary, Richard Leander, 1854-1918, 14746
Hydraulics, 2311
Hydraulic structures - Argentine Republic, 18423
Hydrology, Feira de Santana, Brazil, 18301
Hyenne, Robert, 16841
Hyer, Joseph Keyes, d.1882, 16842
Hygiene, 22456; Addresses, essays, lectures, 22995; Public, Colombia, 18593; Public, El Trebol, Colombia (Caldas), 20311
Hyland, Peggy, 14373
Hymenoptera, Cuba, 18084
Hymns, Chinook jargon, 16456; Chippewa, 13312; Creek, 1648; English, 464, 985, 2911; Methodist, 15169
Hymns and spirtual songs, 14374
Hyndman, William, b.1842 or 43, 22634
Hyneman Leon, 1805-1879, 13061, 13062
Hyperion, 10240
Hynes family, 14888
The hypnotist, 9581
Hypocrisie unmasked, 23809

I go a-fishing, 10571
"I know you would like him," 10711
I married a soldier, 16975
I remember, 15247
I, thou and the other one, 8729
Ibañez, Diego, Franciscan, 7096
Ibarra, José de, 1688-1756, 6364
Ibarra-Díaz, Gregorio E., 20212
Ibarreta Ribera, Pedro Ignacio, 5803
Iceland, Social conditions, 25893
Icelanders in North Dakota, 17737
Icelandic and Old Norse literature, 25893
Ichikawa, Haruko, 1896-, 3984
Ichthyologia ohiensis, 4882
The ichthyosaurus, 8756
Iconografía policial, 18495
Idaeus, philosopher, 5th cent. B.C., 19734
Idaho, 16773, 17308; Biography, 16719, 17626; Description & travel, 2548, 2903, 3455, 3456, 3551, 4456, 4549, 15876, 16222,

16408, 17408, 17409, 17777; Description
& travel   Guide-books, 3735; History,
2607, 16060, 16661, 16719, 17083;
Legislature, 17083
Idaho: her gold fields, and the routes to
them, 3456
Idaho, Col.   Description, 17514
Ide, George Barton, 1804-1872, 13063
Ide, Jacob, 1785-1880, 13064
Ide, Simeon, 1794-1889, 16844
Ide, William B., 16845
Ide, William Brown, 1796-1852, 16844
La idea colonial de Ponce de León, 18717
La idea del cuerpo eu las letras españolas,
21750
The ideal attained, 9496
Ideal cook book, 14295
Ideologia dos poetas populares do Nordeste,
19709
A ideologia liberal no processo da
independência do Brasil (1789-1824), 18867
Ides, Evert Ysbrandszoon, 12067
The ides of March, 13065
El idioma nacional y las causas de su
degeneración en la Provincia de Bocas del
Toro, 20016
The idiot, 8680
The idiot at home, 8681
Idle hour stories, 15177
Idle songs and idle sonnets, 3069
Idolatry, 9810
Idomen, 8853
Idyllic monologues, 2951
If I were seventeen again, 15468
If Jesus came to Boston, 9682
Iglehart, Fanny (Chambers) Gooch, 1851-,
7097
Iglesia, Cristina, 20243
La Iglesia ante el cambio, 19985
La iglesia católica y la revolución mexicana,
19733
La Iglesia en América Latina, 18179
La Iglesia y el problema del campesinado
chileno, 19988
Iglesia y universidad en América Latina,
20430
Ignatius, Father, 1837-1908, 3180
An ignoble martyr, 9355
Igreja para servir, 19984
La igualdad jurídica de los estados, 20662
Ihrie, George Percy, d.1903, 12689
Ikin, Arthur, 3985
Illegal aliens, seafood and coyotes, 24224
Illex illecebrosus, 19923
Iliff, J. Edgar, 1852-, 14300
Illinois, 13067, 21778; Biography, 860,

8260, 17035; Constitution, 15988;
Constitutional convention, 1862, 393;
Courts, 13302; Description & travel, 1335,
1336, 2234, 2859, 3359, 3424, 3468, 3488,
3597, 3647, 3894, 3943, 4648, 4729, 4919,
5765, 6271, 10141, 12142, 13066, 13283,
13580, 14364, 15988, 17268; Description &
travel, Gazetteers, 21778, 23488;
Directories, 22287; Economic conditions,
13283; Emigration & immigration, 15988;
Fiction, 3754, 9207, 23490; History, 4940,
6676, 6852, 7816, 8431, 11561, 12148,
15084, 16040, 17156, 23440, 23618, 23350;
History, To 1778, Sources, 2523; History
Civil war, 860, 7813; Laws, statutes, etc.,
12531; Negro Emancipation Celebration
Commission, 24643; Politics & government,
16962, 17135, 23875, 24041, 25342; State
Capitol, 7816; Supreme court, 22635;
Western Illinois University, Macomb, 7098
Illinois and the West, 13283
Illinois artillery. 1st regt. Battery A,
1861-1865, 4171
Illinois cavalry. 7th regt., 1861-1865, 3335;
8th regt., 1861-1865, 3775
Illinois Central Railroad, 3986, 13066, 22200
Illinois in 1837, 13067
Illinois Indians, Missions, 12353
Illinois infantry. 2d regt., 1847-1848, 17286;
7th regt., 1861-1865, 2524; 10th regt.,
1861-1865, 16884; 14th regt., 1861-1865,
3306; 15th regt., 1861-1865, 2611; 33d
regt., 1861-1865, 4399; 34th regt., 1861-
1865, 4724; 40th regt., 1861-1865, 3801;
47th regt., 1861-1865, 2847; 59th regt.,
1862-1865, 4223; 61st regt., 1861-1865,
5284; 75th regt., 1862-1865, 3263; 77th
regt., 1862-1865, 2687, 4064; 81st regt.,
1862-1865, 4595; 84th regt., 1862-1865,
5154; 85th regt., 1862-1865, 2567; 86th
regt., 1862-1865, 4179; 88th regt., 1862-
1865, 3525; 102d regt., 1862-1865, 3439;
113th regt., 1862-1965, 4143; 120th regt.,
1862-1865, 4064; 124th regt., 1862-1865,
3953
Illinois reports, 22635
Illiteracy, 19000, 20688; Argentine Republic,
18421; Brazil, 19369; Latin America, 20041;
Mexico, 20041; Venezuela, 18019
Illuminated manuscripts from France, Italy
and Spain (XIVth-XVIII centuries), 13535
Illumination of books and manuscripts, etc.,
6644
Illustrated description of the Broadway
pneumatic underground railway, 13068
The illustrated hand-book, 6206

Illustrated historical sketches of the Indians, 2342
Illustrated history of Nebraska, 17237
An illustrated history of Washington and his times, 22213
The illustrated miners' handbook and guide to Pike's Peak, 3987
Illustrated South America, 6141
Illustrated temperance tales, 8568
Das illustrirte Mississippithal, 4269
I'm a good old rebel, 7804
Im zweiten Waterland, 3855
A imagem autónoma, 20633
La imagen en el espejo, 19699
Imágenes de vivienda, 18500
Imágenes desterradas, 20186
Imaginary wars and battles, 9186
Imitations of the beautiful and poems, 13800
Imlay, Gilbert, fl.1755-1796, 3988, 14375, 15577
Immaculate conception, 5878, 5879, 7478
Immediate emancipation safe and profitable for masters, 25637
The immensity of God, 415
The immigrants' guide to Minnesota in 1856, 13069
Immunity, Ecclesiastical, 24788
Imordes, Inc., Louisville, Ky., 14376
El Imparcial, Guatemala, 19060
Impartial, pseud., 572
Impeachments, U.S., 11269, 11757, 13317, 21878
The imperative nature of duty, 22591
The imperial gazetteer, 1374
El imperio del piojo recuperado, 7516
The importance and advantage of Cape Breton, 11336
The importance of gaining and preserving the friendship of the Indians to the British interest considered, 13361
The importance of moderation in civil rulers, 1963
The importance of religion to the legal profession, 11307
The importance of the British plantations in America to this kingdom, 3737
A importáncia da teoria em educação, 19519
The imposter detected, 1427
Impostors and imposture, 11234
A imprensa brasileira, 18702
Impressions and experiences of the West Indies and North America in 1849, 669
Impressions de voyages et aventures dans le Mexique, 6065
Impressions d'une Française en Amérique,

5570
Impressions of America, 3160, 4840, 5577
Impressions of America and the American churches, 4268
Impressions of Kentucky, 5644
Impressions of Mexico with brush and pen, 6016
Impressions of the West and South, 4178
Impressment, 57, 61, 2416, 23049
Impressment of sailors, Fiction, 24067
Improvements of universities, colleges, and other seats of learning or education in North America, 15228
Impuestos sobre ventas, 19493
Imunidades parlamentares, 18135
Imray, James, and son, pub., 530
Ina, 11104
An inaugural discourse... by Rev. Azel Backus, 616
An inaugural discourse on medical education, 14012
An inaugural discourse on the value of time, and the importance of study to the physician, 13950
Incantations, Portuguese, 20068
The incarnation, 8766
Incas, 7964, 11330, 20194, 21826, 23445, 23509
Inchiquin, the Jesuit's letters, 13087
Income, Kentucky, 13743; Personal, Peru, 19208
Income tax, 18294; Brazil, 19332, 19350, 19351; Colombia, 20332; Kentucky, 14409, 14668; U.S., 14668
Inconsistent formal systems, 20557
Inconstitucionalidad de los capitales constitutivos en la ley mexicana del seguro social, 18613
An increased allowance, 9460
Incumbered estates acts, West Indian, 22013
Indentured servants, 23938
Independence preserved, 3383
Independencia americana, 7625
Independency the object of the Congress in America, 13076
Independent (New York, 1848-1928), 25093, 25288
Independent treasury, 2103, 2848, 13039; Speeches in Congress, 205, 12428
An index finger, 8453
Index of names to History of County of Christian, Kentucky, 14380
Index to the Calendar of Maryland state papers, 149
Index to the map of Kentucky and the Southwest Territory 1794, 14087

India, Description & travel, 5488,
13440, 22421, 23133; History, European
settlements, 1500-1765, 882, 2123,
23199; Social life & customs, 17336
India rubber industry, Peru, 8193,
25772
The India trader's directory in
purchasing the drugs and spices of
Asia and the East Indies, 13154
Indian and Injin, 9148
Indian and white in the Northwest, 17333
Indian atrocities, 2781
Indian battles, captivities, and
adventures, 12177
Indian battles, murders, seiges [!]
and forays in the Southwest, 13077
Indian biography, 23691
Indian burial ground, Fullerton, Ky.,
15686
The Indian captive, 2756
Indian captivity, 5253, 11994
The Indian chamber, 5615
Indian Creek and Jack's Knob coal, salt,
lead, lumber, oil and manufacturing
company, 22636
Indian Creek Christian Church, Harrison
County, Ky., 14846
The Indian detective, 9715
The Indian economic service development
of Guatemala, 18063
Indian Fields, 13645, 14199
Indian fighting parson, 16625
The Indian hater, 3754
The Indian in his wigwam, 5097
Indian legends and other poems, 12910
Indian massacres and tales of the red
skins, 13688
Indian names in Utah geography, 17338
Indian narratives, 13078
Indian nullification of the
unconstitutional laws of Massachusetts,
404
The Indian of the Connecticut, 9164
Indian Old Fields, Clark County, Ky.,
13645, 13909
The Indian princess, 1447
The Indian question, 23739
Indian relations on the Mormon frontier,
16059
Indian remains in southern Georgia, 22722
Indian reminiscence, 15967
The Indian reservation sulphur springs,
13079
Indian reservations in Utah, 17703
Indian rights & our duties, 13007
The Indian scout, 15824

Indian slavery in colonial times within the
present limits of the United States, 24774
The Indian spirit, 4460
Indian Territory, 17433, 23591; Description &
travel, 4863, 15831; History, Civil war,
23829; A pre-Commonwealth, 16439
Indian trade, 17264
Indian traits, 15510
Indian tribes of the lower Mississippi Valley
and adjacent coast of the Gulf of Mexico,
17692
Indian war in Oregon and Washington
territories, 16072
Indian warfare, 23639
Indian wars and pioneers of Texas, 2827
Indian wars and the uprising of 1655 ,
Yonkers depopulated, 21763
Indian wars of the northwest, 6101
Indian wars of the United States, 2343, 17228
Indian wars of the West, 3475
Indian why stories, 17036
The Indian's last fight, 16234
Indiana, 16252, 16470; Biography, 13480;
Constitution, 13080; Description & travel,
1230, 2943, 3314, 3472, 3714, 3739, 3943,
5147, 5375, 12142, 12554, 13580, 14857,
15344; Description & travel, Gazetteers,
23582; History, 6423, 13480, 14084, 24322;
History, Fiction, 10961; Lincoln highway
commission, 7099; Politics & government,
16983; State geologist, 22637; University,
History, 9705
Indiana; a redemption from slavery, 24322
Indiana artillery. 11th battery, 1861-1865,
4663
Indiana canal company, 13081
Indiana cavalry. 7th regt., 1863-1865, 3044
The Indiana gazetteer, or Topographical
dictionary, containing a description of
several counties, towns... etc. in the State
of Indiana, 23582
Indiana grant, 13508
Indiana infantry. 6th regt., 1861-1865, 2798,
3670; 12th regt., 1861-1865, 3557; 21st
regt., 1861-1865, 6953; 27th regt., 1861-
1865, 2824; 36th regt., 1861-1864, 3704;
42d regt., 1861-1865, 3939; 51st regt.,
1861-1865, 3804; 57th regt., 1861-1865,
4164; 58th regt., 1861-1865, 3866; 68th
regt., 1862-1865, 3865; 70th regt., 1862-
1865, 4457; 72d regt., 1862-1865, 4351;
75th regt., 1862-1865, 3489; 81st regt.,
1862-1866, 4528; 82d regt., 1862-1865, 3972;
99th regt., 1862-1865, 4313
Indiana miscellany, 13480
Indiana (Ter.), Governor, 1801-1812

(Harrison), 24644; Description, 12860;
History, 12860
Die Indianer Nord-Amerikas (Catlin), hrsg.
von H. Berghaus, 1836
Indians, 1112, 1838, 7017, 7657, 11364,
11583, 11776, 16166, 16167, 23575;
Antiquities, 3216, 6167, 22473, 22840,
24085; Bibliography, 5996, 20363;
Biography, 2443; History, 2442;
Industrial, 24085; Languages, 7305;
Missions, 13297, 19167; Origin, 32,
311, 1443, 1692, 1922, 11402, 11498,
12964, 13298, 13937, 20366, 22188,
22473, 22840, 22895, 22896, 23178,
23804, 24842; Physical characteristics,
20366; Treatment of, 6355-6363, 8443,
12965, 22401, 24585; Treatment of
Canada, 11531; Treatment of   Latin
America, 19894; Treatment of   Peru,
6828; Treatment of, Spanish America,
19893, 24094, 24095; Treatment of,
U.S., 520, 1070, 1716, 11531, 13007,
15953, 17084, 17085, 21850, 24774,
25789
Indians of Central America, 5996, 7439,
8168, 11461, 18024; Anthropometry,
20362; Bibliography, 19019; Costa
Rica, 8324; Guatemala, 6789, 6908;
Panama, 13502; Religion and mythology,
18042
Indians of Mexico, 1864, 5827, 5881,
5996, 7340, 7341, 7515, 7794, 7802,
8174, 8266, 15895, 18202, 22640, 23828;
Anthropometry, 20362, 20368; Antiquities,
6715, 7932, 11392; Architecture, 7414;
Art, 7192; Bibliography, 19019;
Biography, 6821, 8441; History, 1440,
1442, 7111, 11643; Languages, 6066,
6153; Missions, 23480; Names, 18261;
Religion and mythology, 6644; Rites and
ceremonies, 20678; Social life &
customs, 20678; Southwest, New,
7174
Indians of North America, 9, 405, 1156,
1832-1837, 1898, 2342, 2442, 2541, 3700,
2759, 2799, 2966, 3020, 3100, 3260,
3282, 3318, 3445, 3451, 3463, 3837,
3891, 3892, 4024, 4029, 4360, 4398,
4588, 4631, 4755, 4834, 4863, 5010,
5053, 5097, 5181, 5182, 5234, 5457,
5586, 5609, 5680, 5700, 5752, 6101,
6403, 6404, 7008, 7429, 7766, 7799,
8325, 10827, 11242, 11594, 12184,
12310; 12550, 12994, 13025, 13397,
13476, 13501, 13640, 13688, 14155,
15162, 14204, 15219, 15329, 15489,

15510, 15511, 15810, 15838, 15955, 15956,
16169, 16285, 16405, 16562, 16599, 16901,
17048, 17107, 17128, 17134, 17185, 17193,
17321, 17454, 17615, 17904, 21874, 22895,
22896, 23491, 23571, 23574, 23639, 23731,
24774; Alaska, 2231; Anecdotes, 12750,
15672; Arapahoes, 3462; Arizona, 16500;
Bibliography, 7149, 11323; Biography, 1237,
22921, 23394, 23691; British Columbia, 4641,
7360; California, 17207, 17477, 17865;
California, Fiction, 9068; Canada, 647, 1827,
1836, 2118, 2291, 2604, 3878, 4362, 5812,
5900, 5963, 5990, 6101, 6126, 6396, 6731,
7009, 7135, 7215, 7222, 7223, 7224, 7252,
7550, 7886, 8256, 8338, 11715, 11760, 13411,
16394, 17095, 22751, 22924, 23473; Canada,
Missions, 5227, 5674; Canada, Social life
& customs, 12340; Canada, Treaties, 7392;
Captivities, 1972, 2158, 2620, 2756, 2855,
3112, 3147, 3945, 3973, 3974, 4072, 4096,
4240, 4396, 4577, 5199, 5253, 5299, 5343,
5736, 6353, 8814, 10570, 11513, 11752,
12177, 12340, 12514, 12655, 12664, 12698,
12922, 13077, 13078, 13227, 13582, 14017,
15055, 15396, 16150, 16291, 16380, 16449,
16562, 16927, 16986, 17012, 17186, 17349,
22713, 22714, 22735, 23143, 23556, 23589,
23802; Cheyennes, 3462; Citizenship, 23739;
Civilization of, 11805, 11879; Comanche,
5736; Colorado, 16823; Colorado River valley,
16137; Dakota Territory, 13563, 16728, 17710;
Fiction, 2679, 3545, 3754, 5651, 9163, 10123,
10639, 10784, 10827, 14477; Florida, 1529,
1990, 5718, 23672; Georgia, 4102, 16185,
22722, 23625; Government relations, 1826,
2331, 3065, 5505, 5508, 12104, 12894,
12938, 12940, 13448, 16185, 17085, 17730,
21850, 23739; Gulf States, 5012, 13456;
History, 4359, 11996, 23691; Housing, 17458;
Illinois, 23350; Indian Territory, 4344,
17433, 23591; Iowa, 16566; Kansas, 4025;
Kentucky, 4881, 13645, 13909, 14031, 14199,
14280, 14446, 15549, 15686; Land transfers,
11299, 13508, 23728; Languages, 1827, 3816,
4368, 5307, 5343, 5700, 6797, 7216;
Languages, Collected works, 6076;
Languages, Glossaries, vocabularies, etc.,
2465, 4362, 13360, 17048, Legends, 9619,
16812; Liquor problem, 23307; Maine, 12514;
Maryland, 4929; Massachusetts, 12006, 23880,
23610, 23710; Massachusetts, Martha's
Vineyard, 23394; Maumee Valley, O., 12920;
Medicine, 22727; Michigan, 16268; Minnesota,
11353, 15939, 17263, 17264, 17492, 17836;
Missions, 134, 840, 964, 1014, 1481, 1482,
1556, 2174, 3267, 4037, 4237, 4344, 4546,

5179, 5183, 5597, 5719, 6106, 6152, 6598, 7149, 7718, 12889, 13227, 13314, 13398, 16393, 16455, 16956, 17167, 17302, 17333, 17496, 23520; Missions, Dakota, 17287; Mississippi Valley, 1133, 1134, 2760, 2768, 3147, 4210, 5099; Missouri Valley, 3816, 16307; Montana, 17333; Mortuary customs, 16749; Nebraska, 4025; New England, 12309, 12976, 13141, 22726, 23307, 23325; New Mexico, 1145, 17787; New York, 21763, 22794, 23818; North Carolina, 11515; North Dakota, 15952, 16598, 17000, 17686, 17892, 17893; Northwest, Canadian, 4130, 11353, 16731; Northwest, Old, 23579; Northwest, Pacific, 5017, 5018; Northwestern states, 541, 542, 2784, 7009, 11681, 16009, 16393, 16989, 17272; Nova Scotia, 1558, 1559, 6575, 7268; Ohio Valley, 287, 2113, 3124, 3797, 13296, 14923; Oklahoma, 17331; Ontario, 13314; Oregon, 5183, 17242, 17320, 17685, 17826; Osage, 4924; Pacific coast, 5996, 17168; Pennsylvania, 13125, 13319, 23503; Pennsylvania, Treaties, 23697; Poetry, 5693, 12910; Pottery, 16749; Religion and mythology, 13169; Rhode Island, 2167; Rocky Mountains, 4257, 4701, 5108; Sioux, 13457; Social life & customs, 3334, 3730, 3973, 3974, 4641, 5199, 5343, 11996, 14993, 15870, 16393, 17228; Southern States, 32, 946, 2515, 2631, 2768, 5452, 17194; Southwest, New, 15961, 16297; Southwest, Old, 4632, 16010, 17692; Stone implements, 16741; Tennessee, 11508, 12770, 13077; Texas, 15950, 16379, 17121; Textile industry and fabrics, 16804; Treaties, 1716, 2063, 6450; Utah, 15845, 15967, 16059, 16471, 16500, 16590, 16592, 16618, 17070, 17340, 17341, 17343, 17452, 17470, 17620, 17629, 17703, 17855, 17901; Virginia, 1231, 1232, 1249, 3189, 5204, 5252, 13301; Wars, 2343, 2554, 4942, 9585, 10570, 12177, 13078, 14498, 14993, 15559, 15606, 15860, 16346, 16379, 16424, 16930, 17228; Wars, 1600-1750, 12970, 12976, 23325, 23571; Wars, 1750-1815, 3475, 5754, 12664, 13704, 15546, 16115, 22141, 22735, 23571; Wars, 1775-1783, 12307, 14031, 16440, 22736; Wars, 1781-1795, 3332; Wars, 1790-1791, 22671; Wars, 1815-1875, 1069, 1116, 16440; Wars, 1862-1865, 16399, 17379; Wars, 1866-1895, 16024,

16153, 16234, 16318, 16440, 16947, 17193, 17469, 17653; Wars, Fiction, 4460; Washington (State), 4641; The West, 1836, 1837, 2465, 3081, 3220, 3266, 3688, 4042, 4625, 5145, 5306, 6893, 6894, 6895, 16234, 16401, 16406, 16440, 16681, 16831, 16854, 16990, 17353, 17544, 17847; The West, Juvenile literature, 16133; Wyoming, 16153, 16473

Indians of South America, 592, 596, 598, 8073, 8168, 11330, 13272, 22629, 23566, 25276; Amazon valley, 31; Argentine republic, 7977, 12497, 12498; Brazil, 961, 18313, 18551-18554, 19998, 20540, 20541, 23652, 24012; Brazil Languages, 19659; Brazil, Religion and mythology, 20540; British Guiana, 11291; Chile, 8309, 10574; Colombia, 13350, 13451, 18193, 20255; Dutch Guiana, 23517, 24385; Ecuador, 23734; Guiana, 870, 1483, 25603, 25604; Languages, 18193, 18815; Languages, Collected works, 6076; Legends, 19090; Missions, 7718, 11291, 18543; Names, 19890; Paraguay, 6602; Peru, 25772; Patagonia, 11409; Peru, 5827, 6367, 7167, 18573, 19587, 19893, 20194, 21853, 23535, 23445; Pottery, 18007; Property, 19893; Venezuela, 2473, 18007, 18543, 19627, 20406, 22195; Venezuela, Missions, 19527; Wars, 18010

The Indians of the Pike's Peak region, 16823
Indians of the West Indies, 20356; British, 24339; Legends, 12481
The Indians' revenge, 15971
Indication of sixty-six new genera of plants of North America, 15231
Indice d'ittiologia siciliana ossia catalogo metodico dei nomi latini, 15229
Indice geobiográfico de cuarenta mil pobladores españoles de América en el siglo XVI, 19204
Indices de El Renacimiento, 18910
O indio na consciência urbana, 20541
Os indios Gaviões de oeste, 18553
Indrenius, Andreas Abraham, 2464
Indulgences, 7731
La industria automotriz, 19690
La industria azucarera Argentina, 18091
La industria cerillera en Mexico, 19672
La industria del papel en Colombia, 20495
La industria del vidrio plano, 18796
Industrial arts, Addresses, essays, lectures, 13201; Biography, 12952; Period, 262, 269, 23417; Curricula, 20594
Industrial districts, 20377
Industrial hygiene, law and legislation, Colombia, 20335
Industrial laws and legislation, 18414; Argentine Republic, 18414; Mexico, 18330

Industrial management, 19671
Industrial promotion, 20503
Industrial progress of Mexico, 6084
Industrial property, Brazil, 19334
Industrial protection in developing
  countries, 18709
Industrial relations, Argentine
  Republic, Laws and regulations, 18472
Industrial resources, Kentucky, 14539
Industrial safety, Law and legislation
  Colombia, 20325
Industrial uses for limestone and
  dolomite, 14552
Industrialización del citrus, 18949
Industrialization policies in Peru,
  17968
Industry, Kentucky, 14534, 14535, 14539;
  South Carolina, 5563
Industry and state, Colombia, 20384;
  Latin America, 20004
The inebriate's hut, 10847
Inez, Ky., 14569
La infamia del Esequibo, 19489
Infant baptism, 8470, 9540, 11387, 23332
Infantry drill and tactics, 23470
Infelicia, 4448
Inferences from the pestilence and the
  fast, 156
The infidel converted, 8886
Infidelity unmasked, 24645
The influence of climate and other agents,
  on the human constitution, 459
The influence of the missions on present-
  day California, 16155
Influência das raças sôbre a pureza de sêda
  "grège", 19172
Influencia de algunas capitulaciones en la
  geografía de Venezuela, 18537
Influencia de España en Centro América,
  20484
La influencia de la economía y del estado
  en las huelgas, 18906
Influencia de los estados emotivos, 20078
Influencia del pensamiento de Artigas en
  el Congreso de abril de 1813, 20620
Información turística sobre México, 7337
Information concerning the present state of
  the slave trade, 24646
Information concerning the province of
  North Carolina, 5109
Information for emigrants, 3991
Informe del ajente de Chile ante el
  Tribunal arbitral anglo-chileno, 20108
Informe económico, 20396
Informe en derecho por la defensa de los
  procedimientos de la Real audiencia

de la ciudad de Santiago de Chile,
  7100
Informe sobre la reforma de la seguridad
  social chilena, 20109
Los infortunios de Alonso Ranurez, 19968
Ingalls, Eleazer Stillman, 1820-1879, 3992
Ingalls, Rufus, 3993
An ingenue of the Sierras, 9790
Ingersoll, Charles, 1805-1882, 13082, 13083
Ingersoll, Charles Jared, 1782-1862, 13084-
  13088
Ingersoll, Chester, 1789-1849, 3994
Ingersoll, Edward, 1817-1893, 13089, 13090
Ingersoll, Ernest, 1852-1946, 6318, 16852
Ingersoll, Jared, 1722-1781, 13091
Ingersoll, Jared, 1749-1822, 1312, 11271,
  11789
Ingersoll, Joseph Reed, 1786-1868, 13092-
  13095
Ingersoll, Lurton Dunham, 13096
Ingersoll, Samuel Bridge, 1785-1820, 13097
The Ingham papers, 9683
Ingle, Edward, 3995
Inglis, Charles, bp. of Nova Scotia, 1734-
  1816, 13098
Inglis, James, 1777-1820, 13099
Ingraham, Edward Duncan, 1793-1854, 13100
Ingraham, Joseph Holt, 1809-1860, 3996-4016,
  8967
Ingraham, Prentiss, 1843-1904, 4017, 17118
Ingram, Mrs. Helen K., 4018
Ingram, John Kells, 1823-1907, 24648
The inheritance, 10340
Inheritance and succession (Mohammedan law),
  25399
Inheritance and succession (Roman law), 25452,
  25559
Inheritance and succession, Cambodia, 24804;
  Gt. Britain, 21976; Haiti, 997
Inheritance and transfer tax, Kentucky,
  13819, 14668; U.S., 14668, 14669
An inherited debt, 10283
An initial experience, 10122
Inklings of adventure, 11178
Inkpaduta and sons, 17708
The inland empire, 16378
Inland navigation, 6062, 13825; Congresses,
  12665; Connecticut valley, 1906; Dakota
  Territory, 16045; Kentucky, 15646;
  Pennsylvania, History, 8376; South America,
  23573; U.S., 448, 1860, 3596, 7450, 12665,
  13235, 13446
The inland passage, 17064
Inland Rivers Library, Cincinnati Public
  Library, 13825
The inland sea, 9141

235

Inland voices, 13796
Inland waterway, 4941
Inman, Henry, 1837-1899, 14381, 16854-
16856, 16900
Inman, John, 23367
Inmigración [Argentine Republic], 18411
Die innern communicationen der Vereinigten
Staaten von Nord-amerika, 3596
Innes et al. vs. Roane et al., 7101
Innis, Harry, 14579
Innocent X, Pope, 1575-1655, 6383
Innocent blood crying to God from the
streets of Boston, 13373
An innocent cheat, 3223
An innocent gamester, 9575
The innocents abroad, 9027
Los inolvidables, 18286
Inorganic forces ordained to supersede
human slavery, 12122
An inquiry into the causes and cost of
corrupt state legislation, 13101
Inquiry into the causes which have
retarded the accumulation of wealth and
increase of population in the southern
states, 24500
An inquiry into the effects of putting a
stop to the African slave trade, and of
granting liberty to the slaves in the
British sugar colonies, 25340
An inquiry into the formation of
Washington's Farewell address, 11270
An inquiry into the itinerancy, and
conduct of the Rev. Mr. George
Whitefield, 12821
An inquiry into the nature and results
of the anti-slavery agitation, 24649
An inquiry into the origin of the
antiquities of America, 3216
An inquiry into the present state of the
foreign relations of the Union, 13102
An inquiry into the Scriptural views of
slavery, 846
Inquisition, Colombia, 5999
The inquisitor, 10678
Insane hospitals, 2388
Insanity, U.S., 22686
Insanity as legal defense, 14666
Insausti, Rafael Angel, 20249
Inscriptions, Latin, 727; Rome, 24632
Inscriptions on the grave stones in the
grave yards of Northampton, 1504
Insect control, 18123
Insecticides, 19071
Insects, soil, African, 4680; Catalogs and
collections, 23692; Kentucky, 15111;
North America, 4684, 5079, 22661;

Population density, 19072
Insects, Injurious and beneficial, 18123;
Mexico, 18544
The inseparable trio, 22504
Inside: a chronicle of secession, 8656
Inside Kentucky, 14248
Inside of rebeldom, 2907
Inside out, 1965, 9560
Inside view of slavery, 4706
The insolvent laws of Massachusetts, 11926
The instability of humane greatness, 12644
Installation (Clergy), Anniversary sermons,
22227
Instituciones de derecho real de Castilla y
de Indias, 231
Las instituciones políticas en América Latina,
20048
Instituições de ensino e pesquisa, 20037
Institut d'Afrique, Paris, 24650
Instituto Brasileiro de Geografia e
Estatistica, 18317
Instituto Brasileiro de Reforma Agraria, 19347,
19478
Instituto Brasileiro do Café, 19398
Instituto Colombiano de la Reforma Agraria,
19098; Publicaciones, 20286-20289, 20331
Instituto de Administración Pública (Mexico)
Publicaciones, 19032
Instituto de Asuntos Nucleares, Division de
Radiofisica Sanitaria, 18073
Instituto de Fomento Algodonero, Bogotá,
18146, 19083
Instituto de Investigaciones Tecnológicas,
Bogotá, 20300
Instituto de Pesquisas Tecnológicas, 18605
Instituto de Previdência dos Congressistas,
19339
Instituto Geográfico Agustín Codazzi, Bogotá,
20301-20307
Instituto historico e geografico brasileiro,
Rio de Janeiro, 22641
Instituto Internacional de Literatura
Iberoamericana, 20409
Instituto Lingüistico de Verano, 18815
Instituto Mexicano de Recursos Naturales
Renovables, 7468, 7469
Instituto Nacional de Pesca del Ecuador, 19199
Instituto Nacional do Desenvolvimento Agrario,
19478
Instituto Nacional Indigenista, Mexico, 18584
Instituto Provincial de Investigaciones y
Estudios Toledanos, Publicaciones, Sección
primera: Monografias, 18060
Instrucción fórmula por un facultativo
existente por muchos años en el Perú, 7560
Instructions for the information and benefit

of domestic manufacturers in woolen cloths, 4019
Instructions to the living, from the condition of the dead, 23304
Insubordination, 8569
Insurance, 15332; Automobile, 14663; Automobile, Kentucky, 14678; Fire, U.S., 16298; Inland marine, Chile, 19567; Life, 14617; Life, Addresses, essays, lectures, 10383; Social, 20050; Social, Bolivia, 18333; Social, Brazil, 17950, 19339, 20026; Social, Chile, 18972, 19583, 20109; Social, Chile, Bibliography, 20180; Social, Chile, Law, 20167; Social - Cuba, 20697; Social, Ecuador, 19679, 20374; Social, Kentucky, 13823, 15018; Social, Latin America, 20031; Social, Latin America - Bibliography, 20400; Social Mexico, 18613; Social, Panama, 18972; Social Peru, 19583; Social, Rio de Janeiro (State), 19326; Unemployment, Kentucky, 14520
Insurance agents, Laws and regulations, Kentucky, 14138
The insurgents, 10232
Integración económica en América Latina, 20111
Integrity and religion to be principally regarded, by such as design others to stations of publick trust, 22541
Intellect, 13762, 22718
The intelligence office, 9823
The intemperate, 10762
Inter-American Commission on Human Rights, 19049
Inter-American Development Bank, 19505
Inter-American highway, 7716
Intercolonial railway (Canada), 6747
The Intercourse of nations: being a collection of short, correct and easy rules for reducing thirteen different coins and currencies into each other, 22638
Un interessante testo di Giavoleno, 23855
Interesting detail of the operations of the American fleet, 2172
Interesting history of the Baron de Lovzinski, 13403
Interesting items concerning the journeying of the Latter-Day Saints, 4846
An interesting love story, 9990
Interesting memoirs and documents relating to American slavery, 24651
The interference theory of government, 1534
Internal improvement convention, Baltimore,

1834, 11780
Internal revenue, U.S., 1810
Internal revenue law, U.S., 11422, 12085, 15631, 15632, 22179
Internal security, Argentine Republic, 18416
International American conference. 1st, Washington, D.C., 1889-1890, 4020; 2d, Mexico, 1901-02, 7102
International and Great Northern Railroad, 4021
International Banana Festival links the Americas, 14382
International boundary commission, United States and Mexico, 1849-1853, 5064
International Bureau of the American republics, Washington, D.C., 7103
International commercial convention, Portland, Me., 1868, 13103
International commodity agreements, 18819
International Congress of Americanists, 20363
International Congress of Tropical Agriculture. 3d, London, 1914, 23874, 25935
International Convention with the Object of Securing the Abolition of Slavery and the Slave Trade, 24196, 24652-24655
International copyright, 10326
International economic relations, 18819
International finance, 19048; Bibliography, 19262
International Geophysical Year, 1957-1958, Guatemala, 20372
International law, 2403, 2404, 12026, 18908, 18956, 22292; Periodicals, 19750
International law and relations, 22947; Sources, 23181
International policy, 13104
International sympathies, 25008
International telephone and telegraph corporation, 7104
International Tin Council, 18942
Interpol, 19410
Interpretación de Ruben Darío, 19837
An interrupted finesse, 10283
Intervention, 1205, 11309
The intervention of Peter, 24319
Intima fauna, 19948
The intimate friends, 10207
Into the light, 10441
Into the West, 16277
The intriguers, 8750
Intriguing for a princess, 8786
Introdução à literatura no Brasil, 20629
Introdução aos estudos históricos e sociais, 18877
Introducción a Condillac, 19735
Introducción a la teoría de la representación

237

grupos, 20621
Introducción al simbolismo lógico, 19181
Introduction and early progress of the cotton manufacture in the United States, 956
An introduction to a course of lectures on history, 13671
Introductory address on independence of intellect, 13762
An introductory lecture at the opening of the thirtieth session of the Medical College of Ohio, 3287
An introductory lecture, delivered before the Lexington Mechanic's Institute, 15128
An introductory lecture, on the means of promoting the intellectual improvement of students and physicians, 3288
An introductory lecture, preparatory to a course of instruction on common and statute law, 13676
Intrusive ethnological types in Rupert's Land, 6219
Inventors, 12952
La inversión bursátil, 18137
Inversiones extranjeras en México, 18765, 18766
Invertebrates, Fossil, 2365
Investigación nacional de morbilidad, 20345-23048
Investigator (Ship), 449, 22816
Investment of life insurance funds in Kentucky, 14617
Investment trusts, Mexico, 19713
Investments, 18760, 21972; Argentine Republic, 18470; Brazil, Amazon region, 19437; Brazil, Northest, 20558; Foreign (International law), 19594; Foreign, Argentine Republic, 20397; Foreign, Bolivia, 19117; Foreign, Brazil, 19275; Foreign, Law and legislation, Argentine Republic, 19594; Foreign, Mexico, Bibliography, 18765, 18766
The invisible bond, 14753
The invisible empire, 25713
Invisible rambler, 10678
The invesible route, 17606
Io: a tale of the olden fane, 8754
Iodine, Isotopes, 19703
Ione, 9193
Iowa, 15998, 17269; Board of education, 10100; Boundaries Missouri, 16635; Constitution, 16859; Description & travel, 2361, 4653, 12142, 12185, 16098, 16801, 16858, 17002, 17116,

17268, 17270, 17350, 22755, 23501, 23581; Description & travel, Poetry, 11569; Direct, 17269, 22284; History, Civil war, 5137, 13096; Economic conditions, 16839; History, 16172, 17062, 17289, 17708, 17746; Laws, statutes, etc., 13105; Learned institutions and societies, 13107; Militia, 13096; Politics & government, 7945, 16649, 17288; State Geologist (1866-1870), 13106;
Iowa and the rebellion, 13096
The Iowa band, 15812
Iowa cavalry. 1st regt., 1861-1866, 4303; 5th regt., 1861-1865, 4628; 6th regt., 1863-1865, 16425
Iowa, Colleges, Grinnell, History, 23027
The Iowa handbook, for 1857, 17350
Iowa infantry, 1st regt., 1861, 5610, 17294; 2d regt., 1861-1865, 2665; 5th regt., 1861-1864, 3513, 16116; 22d regt., 1862-1865, 4121
Iowa institute of science and arts, Dubuque, 13107
Iowa language, Grammar, 12616
Iowa state gazetteer, 22284
Iowa: the home for immigrants, 16858
Ipsistos, 10769
Ipswich, Mass., History, 2246
Ira, Vt., History, 17368
Iracema, 18140
Iran Description & travel, 22421
Iredale, Andrew, 4022
Iredell, James, 1751-1799, 22307, 22992
Ireland, John, apb. 1838-1918, 17167
Ireland, John B., 22639
Ireland, Biography, 10291; Comm., 13369; Comm., U.S., 11248; Description & travel, 4954, 5744; History, 7257; History, Fiction, 9491; History, 18th century Fiction, 10276; History, Rebellion of 1798, Fiction, 8544; Poetry, 4781; Politics & government, 1113, 23603; Relations (general) with the U.S., 22874
Irene, 11048
Irigoyen, Ulises, 7105
Irisarri, Antonio José de, 1786-1868, 7106, 19518
Irish, Edwin Marshall, 1848-, 7107
Irish-American wit and humor, 9439
The Irish emigrant, 9991
An Irish garland, 4783
Irish in Canada, 22876
Irish in Kentucky, 15094
Irish in Massachusetts, 9602
Irish in North America, 22875
Irish in Pennsylvania, 12880
Irish in the U.S., 6038, 17295, 22875, 22876

The Irish Ninth in bivouac and battle, 4371
The Irish patriot. Daniel O'Connel's legacy to Irish Americans, 25170
Irish pioneers in Kentucky, 15094
The Irish position in British and in republican North America, 22876
Irish publicists, 10291
The Irish refugee, 10841
Irish Repeal Association of Cincinnati, 24909
Irish riflemen in America, 4242
Irish stories, 10291
Irish Unitarian Christian society, 24656
An Irish wild-flower, 4784
Irish wit and humor, 10291
An Irishman, now in America, 3863
Iron, 18512, 19509; Metallurgy, 12905, 19507
The iron furnace, 551, 23924
Iron Gray, pseud., 25680
The iron horse, 23126
Iron industry and trade, 22435, 22436; Dictionaries, English, 20385; Dictionaries, Spanish, 20385; Gt. Brit., 23654; Kentucky, 14142; New York (State), 99; Ohio, 14792; U.S., 23331, 23103
Iron mines and mining, Mexico, 6708
Iron ores, British Columbia, 6174; New York (State), 99
Iron oxides, 19507
The iron tomb, 8831
The iron trail, 11134
Ironton, O., Board of trade, 14792
Ironwork, 18737
Iroquois Hunt Club, Lexington, Kentucky, 14977
Iroquois Indians, 647, 11242, 11656, 12804, 13361, 21905, 23674; Land transfers, 13508; Treaties, 1775, 3796
Iroquois language, Texts, 23297
Irrigation, Argentine Republic, 18424; Mexico, 6121, 6122
Irrigation canals and flumes, 6122
Irrigation farming, 19142
Irrigation farming in the kingdom of alfalfa, Bow River Valley, 6323
Irvin, Helen Deiss, 14383
Irvin S. Cobb, the man with a cigar, 14389
Irvin, Samuel Mcleary, 1812-, 12616
Irvine, Donald V., 14385
Irvine, Leigh Hadley, 16862
Irvine family, 15888
Irving, Edward, fl.1827, 7883

Irving, Henry, 3808
Irving, John Beaufain, 1800-1881, 4023
Irving, John Treat, 1812-1906, 4024, 4025
Irving, Theodore, 1809-1880, 13108
Irving, Washington, 1783-1859, 342, 656, 4026-4029, 11591, 13109
Irvington, Ky., History, 13684, 13685
Irwin, Mrs. Inez (Haynes), 16863
Irwin, Richard Biddle, 1839-1892, 11454
Irwin, Will H., 9509
Irwin, William Henry, 1873-1948, 16888
Isaacs, Robert, 4030
Isabel, 11020
Isabel Graham, 9844
Isabel I la Catolica, queen of Spain, 1451-1504, 1200, 8083
Isabella (ship), 7912
Isabelle, 8837
Isadore Merton, 10332
Isenberg, James L., 14386
Isequilla Palacio, Juan de la, 7108
Isert, Paul Erdmann, 1757-1789, 13110
Ish-noo-ju-lut-sche, 10744
Isham, Asa Brainerd, 1844-, 4031
Isham, G.S., 4032
Isham, W.P., 17116
Isham, Warren J., 1863, 17116
Isla de Cuba, 24441, 24657
Island bride, 10773
The island neighbors, 8810
The island of Cuba, 189, 7086, 24956
The island of Nantucket, 6860
The island recluse, 9864
An islander, 9769
Islands in the sun, 15469
Islands of the Atlantic, 2213
The islands of the Australasian seas, 13142
Islands of the Pacific, Description & travel, 17594
L'Isle de Cuba et la Havane, 23292
The Isle of Palms, 10416
Isles of spice and palm, 5569
Isnardy, Francisco, 1750-1814, 17986
Isom, Alice Parker, 1848-1924, 16864
Isomeric displacement, 20082
Israel, History, 18611; Politics & government, 18611; Ten lost tribes, 11402
Israel in bondage, 9984
Isrul's bargain, 10465
The issues of the hour, 1961
Istanbul siege, 1453, Fiction, 11054
Isthmian tourists' guide and business directory, 7110
Isthmiana, 8403
An Italian, 799
The Italian bride, 10670

The Italian girl, 11105
Italian language, Dialects, 19568
Italian poetry, History & criticisms, 19046
Italian sights and papal principles, seen through American spectacles, 22685
The Italian sketch book, 11021
Italy, Description & travel, 125, 4507, 6588-6591, 7806, 11021, 21881, 22675, 22685; History, 1492-1559, Fiction, 8589; History, 1815-1870, 12478; Southern, Fiction, 6493
Items from Joe Miller, 10736
Ithaca, N.Y., 2444; Description, 11838
Itinerario para parochos de indios, 7718
Itinerarios y derroteros de la República Mexicana, 5884
Iturbide, Agustín de, emperor of Mexico, 1783-1824, 1761, 6853, 7568, 12256, 13111
Iturri, Francisco, b.1738, 13112
Ivernois, Sir Francis d', 1757-1842, 13113
Ives, Alfred Eaton, 1809-1892, 13114
Ives, Butler, 16865
Ives, Charles, 1815-1880, 13115
Ives, Joseph Christmas, d.1868, 5524
Ives, Levi Silliman, 1797-1867, 13116
Ives, Robert Hale, 1798-1875, 22377
Ivins, Virginia (Wilcox), 16866
Ixmiquilpan, Mexico. San Miguel (Church), 19851
Ixodoidea, 20669-20671
Ixtabucacan, Guatemala, 18324
Ixtlilxochitl, Fernando de Alva, ca.1568-1648, 7111, 7932, 22640
Izard, George, 1777-1828, 13119
Izard, Ralph, 1742-1804, 13117, 13118
Izlar, William Valmore, 4033

Jaboatão, Antonio de Santa Maria, 1695-1764?, 22641, 24017
Jack, Charles James, 1799?-1873, 22642
Jack, Isaac Allen, 24659
Jack, O. G., 16867
A Jack and Jill of the Sierras, 6969
Jack Datchett, the clerk, 9411
Jack Harold, 10960
Jack Hilton's love-affair, 10122
Jack Hopeton, 11031
Jack Horner, 10975
The Ouah Morgan songster, 13120
Jack Tier, 9135
Jack's divorce, 10863

Jackson, A. P., 16868
Jackson, Albert, d.1878, defendant, 22643
Jackson, Andrew, pres. U.S., 1767-1845, 708, 1938, 5599, 5913, 7201, 8824, 10818, 11405, 11823, 13121, 13353, 13839, 13900, 15402, 15738, 17166, 22030, 22165, 22382, 22475, 22644, 22922, 23516, 23554, 23732, 23825, 24357, 25574
Jackson, Andrew, b.1814, 13122
Jackson, Charles, 1775-1855, 13123
Jackson, David Prentice, 1851-, 4036
Jackson, Ebenezer, 13124
Jackson, Francis, 1789-1861, 22645
Jackson, George, 1838-, 16869
Jackson, Halliday, 1771-1835, 13125
Jackson, Helen Marie Hunt, 1831-1885, 7627, 16870-16872
Jackson, Henry, 1798-1863, 13126, 22646
Jackson, Henry Rootes, 1820-1892, 4034, 13127
Jackson, Henry W.R., 4035, 13128
Jackson, Isaac Rand, d.1843, 13129
Jackson, James, 1777-1867, 22647, 22648
Jackson, James, 1810-1834, 22647
Jackson, James Caleb, 1811-1895, 24680, 22649
Jackson, John, d.1855, 13130, 24661
Jackson, John Walker, 22650
Jackson, Jonathan, 1743-1810, 13131
Jackson, Julia Newell, 7112
Jackson, Margaret A., 14389
Jackson, Mary E., 16873
Jackson, Mrs. Pearl (Cashell) 1869-, 16875
Jackson, Oscar Lawrence, 1840-1920, 4036
Jackson, Orick, 16874
Jackson, Robert, 1750-1827, 13132
Jackson, Robert Edmund Scoresby, 1835-1867, 22651
Jackson, Samuel, 1787-1872, 13133
Jackson, Samuel Cram, 1802-1878, 22652
Jackson, Samuel Trevena, 1869-, 7113
Jackson, Tatlow, 13134, 13135
Jackson, Thomas, 1783-1873, 22653, 22654
Jackson, Thomas Jonathan, 1824-1863, 22256, 23621
Jackson, Thomas, 5672
Jackson, Thomas Jonathan, 1824-1863, 85, 3154, 4330, 8034
Jackson, W.E., 14390
Jackson, W.H., 6304
Jackson, William, 1759-1828, 13136
Jackson, William, 1789-1864, 24662
Jackson, William, 1793-1844, 14389
Jackson, William Ayrault, 1832-1861, 13137, 22655
Jackson, William Turrentine, 16876
Jackson, La. Centenary college, 3495
Jackson Co., Michigan, Biography, 6663,

History, 6559
Jackson Co., Ore., Families, 17778-17780
Jackson Democratic association, Washington, D.C., 22085, 24276
Jackson ex dem. Tuttle vs. Gridley, 22427
Jacksonville, Ill., 16847
Jaco, 10310
Jacob, John J., 1758?-1839, 22735
Jacob, John Jeremiah, 1758?-1839, 13138
Jacob, Stephen, 1756-1817, 22656
Jacob, William, 1762?-1851, 22657
Jacob and his sons, or The second part of a conversation between Mary and her mother, 25670
Jacob Brown, 5259
Jacob City, 10448
Jacobi, Eduard Adolf, 1796-1865, 22658
Jacobs, Aletta H., 3593
Jacobs, Bela, 1786-1836, 13139, 22659
Jacobs, Ferdinand, 24663
Jacobs, Harriet Brent, 1817-1896, 24664
Jacobs, Michael, 1808-1871, 13140
Jacobs, Rev. Peter, 4037
Jacobs, Sarah Sprague, b.1813, 13141, 22659
Jacobs, Thomas Jefferson, 13142
Jacobs, W. L., illustr., 25187
Jacquemin, Nicolas, 1736-1819, 13143
Jacquerie, 1358, Fiction, 10507
Jacques, Amédée Florent, 1813-1865, 13144
Jacques, Daniel Harrison, 1825-1877, 4038
Jacquess, James Frazier, 1819-, 3611
Jaeger, Benedict, 22660, 22661
Jagger, William, 22662, 24665
Jahnsenykes, Rev. Williamson, pseud., 10033
Jaime Freyre, Ricardo, 1870-1921, 19799
Jalapa, Mexico, Universidad Veracruzana, Ficcion [series], 18621, 19782, 20066, 20248, 20444
Jalisco, 18795; Constitution, 12480; History, 7876, 23480
Jamaica, 7114, 23495, 24884, 25252; Assembly, 22663; Assembly, 1682, 13145; Commissioner at the World's Columbian exposition, Chicago, 1893, 7114; Description & travel, 1035, 1246, 1272, 1425, 5315, 5492, 6145, 6919, 7264, 7541, 7786, 8181, 8386, 11174, 11578, 23007, 23957, 24082, 24841, 24957, 25011, 25082, 25369, 25478, 25497, 25619, 25620; Economic conditions, 1272, 11578, 25524; Governor, 1682-1684 (Sir Thomas Lynch), 13145; History, 1499, 11371, 22595, 24339, 25369; History, Insurrection, 1865, 2199; History, Maroon war 1795-

1796, 11943; History Slave insurrection, 1831, 25478; History Sources, 12606; Laws, statutes, etc., 13146, 13147, 22664, 24914; Politics & government, 1695, 12458, 13145, 22663, 23955
Jamaica, New York. First Presbyterian church, 22845
Jamaica as it is, 7786
Jamaica, as it was, as it is, and as it may be, 25478
Jamaica at Chicago, 7114
Jamaica in 1850, 1272
The Jamaica magistrate's and vestryman's assistant, 13406
The Jamaica petition for representation in the British House of Commons, or for independence 23955
Jamaica Plain, Mass., Directories, 1566
Jamaica plantership, 22970, 24948
A Jamaica slave plantation, 25256
Jamaica under the apprenticeship system, 25524
James, Alexander MacGregory, 24666
James, Bushrod Washington, 1836-1903, 4039
James, Charles Pinckney, 1818-1899, 13148
James, Charles Tillinghast, 1804-1862, 13149
James, Edwin, 22665
James, Edwin, 1797-1861, 2465, 5343
James, Edwin John, 1812-1882, 22666
James, Frank, 1844-1915, 16079, 16319, 15321
James, George (Haffain Gelastimin), 5597
James, George Payne Rainsford, 1801?-1860, 13150, 22667, 22668
James, George Wharton, 1858-, 16215, 16877-16881, 17344
James, Henry, 1811-1882, 13151, 22669
James, Henry, 1843-1916, 4040, 6187, 7115-7133
James, Horace, 1818-1875, 13152, 24667
James, James, 13153
James, Jessee E., 1875-, 16882
James, Jesse Woodson, 1847-1882, 16079, 16319, 16321, 16407, 16882
James, John Angell, 1785-1859, 25928
James, John Towner, 1851-, 16883
James, Joseph, 13154
James, Joshua, 4041
James, Thomas, 1782-1847, 4042
James, Thomas Horton, 4043, 7134
James, Uriah Pierson, 1811-1889, 4044, 22672
James, William, d.1827, 13155, 13156, 22673, 22674
James, William Dobein, 13157
James River, Va., 3419, 3978, 4136; Description & travel, Guide-books, 2985
James River and Kanawha canal, 1343
James River and Kanawha company, Richmond, 22670

James River company, 22671
James' River guide, 22672
The James River tourist, 2985
James's traveler's companion, 4412
Jameson, Mrs. Anna Brownel (Murphy), 1794-1860, 7135, 7136, 22675
Jameson, John Alexander, 1842-1890, 22676
Jameson, John Franklin, 1859-1937, 24668
Jameson, Robert, 1774-1854, 22021
Jameson, Robert Francis, 7137, 12981
Jameson, Russell Parson, 1878-, 24669
The Jamesons, 9572
Jamestown, Me., 12515
Jamestown, Va., 22677; History, 12888, 22677; History, Fiction, 2923, 3189
Jamestown of Pemaquid, 12515
Jamie Parker, the fugitive, 10522
Jamieson, Milton, 13158
Jamison, Matthew H., 1840-, 16884
Jan Vedder's wife, 8730
Janes, Edmund Storer, bp., 1807-1876, 22679
Janes, Frederic, b.1808, 22679
Janes family (William Janes, 1610?-1690), 22679
Janet Strong, 11008
Janeway, Jacob Jones, 1774-1858, 22678
Janeway, James, 1636?-1674, 13159
Janeway, Thomas Leiper, 1805-1895, 22678
Janice Meredith, a story of the American Revolution, 9536
Jannet, Claudio, 1844-1894, 4045
Jansen, William Hugh, 1914-1979, 14391
Jansenists, 1406
Janson, Charles William, 4046
Janus, pseud., 13160
Janvier, Francis De Haes, 1817-1885, 7138, 13161
Janvier, Thomas Allibone, 7139
Japan   Description & travel, 4751; Fiction, 10238, 12039; Social life & customs, 7610
Japanese in the Hawaiian Islands, 7610
Japanese lady in America, 3984
Japheth, pseud., 24670
Jaques, John Wesley, 13162
Jaques, Mary J., 7140
Jaquith, James, 1781-, 4047
Jardine, David, 1794-1860, 22680
Jardine, L. J., 13163
Jarnagin, Spencer, 1792-1853, 22681
Jarratt, Devereux, 1733-1801, 22002
Jarves, James Jackson, 1820-1888, 13164, 13165, 22683-22685

Jarvis, Abraham, bp., 1739-1813, 13166
Jarvis, Edward, 1803-1884, 22686
Jarvis, Leonard, 1781-1854, 13167
Jarvis, Russell, 1791-1853, 13168, 22687
Jarvis, Samuel Farmar, 1786-1851, 13169-13171
Jarvis, Sarah M'Curdy (Hart), 13171
Jarvis, William Charles, d.1836, 13172, 13173
Jason Edwards, an average man, 9604
Jasper St. Aubyn, 9842
Jastrow, Ignaz, 1856-1937, 24671
Javolenus, Priscus, 23855
Jay, Aimé, d.1881, 4048
Jay, Antoine, 1770-1854, 24738
Jay, Sir James, 1732-1815, 13174, 22688
Jay, John, 1745-1829, 7141, 12140, 13175-13181, 22689, 22694, 23629
Jay, John, 1817-1894, 22690-22692, 24672, 24673, 25732
Jay, John Clarkson, 1808-1891, 13182
Jay, William, 1769-1853, 13183
Jay, William, 1789-1858, 2104, 13184-13187, 22693, 22694, 22510, 24674, 24675, 25732
Jay's treaty, 1794, 295, 323, 324, 1901, 12690, 22270
Jayne, William, 1826-1916, 7142
Jean-Louis, Dulcine, 7143
Jeanne d'Arc, Saint, 1412-1431, Fiction, 9031
Jeannette, 11205
Jeff, John Beveridge Gladwyn, 1841-1893, 7144
Jeff's treasure, 10653
Jefferay, William, 1591-1675, 8610
Jefferds, Charles M., 1837-1863?, 13188
Jefferson, H.E., 16885
Jefferson, T.H., 4049
Jefferson, Thomas, pres. U.S., 1743-1826, 708, 1348, 1910, 2107, 2145, 7145, 7146, 7316, 7832, 8232, 11480, 12068, 12143, 13381, 13393, 13615, 15650, 21997, 22089, 22695, 24466, 24950; Fiction, 9118; Memoir, correspondence, 1829, 13381; Notes on the state of Virginia, 13138, 23451; Personality, 12107; The writings of Thomas Jefferson, 1853-1854, 978
Jefferson, Wade Hampton, 14392
Jefferson against Douglas, 24222
Jefferson College, Washington, Miss., 13189
Jefferson Co., Col., 15974
Jefferson Co., Iowa, History, 16524
Jefferson Co., Ky., 15058; Description, 15569, 15570; History, 14331; Maps, 14927, 14928; Politics & government, 14283; Schools, 15057
Jefferson Co., Neb., 16345; Biography, 16345
Jefferson Co., N.Y., Biography, 22572; History, 22572

The Jefferson-Lemen compact, 24950
Jefferson Medical College, Philadelphia,
  2418, 13190; Registers, 13190
Jefferson Territory, 17363
Jeffersonian democracy, 15744
Jeffersontown, Ky., Baptist Church, 15207
Jeffery, R., 7147
Jefferys, Thomas, d.1771, 4051, 13191,
  13192, 22696, 22697, 22750
Jeffrey, Mrs. Rosa (Vertner) 1828-1894,
  4052-4055
Jeffries, Benjamin Joy, 1833-1915, 11663
Jeffries, John, 1796-1876, 13193
Jeffries, Thomas Fayette, b.1829, 22698
Jehan, Louis François, b.1803, 22699
Jekyll, Nathaniel, 22700
Jelambi, Octavio, 19639
Jelard, 14307
Jemison, Mary, 1743-1833, 23589
Jenckes, Joseph, 1656-1740, Proclamation
  concerning the Rogerene episode in
  Norwich, Conn., in 1725, 623
Jenings, Edmund, 13194, 13374
Jenkins, Charles Jones, 1805-1883, 22701
Jenkins, Edward, 1838-1910, 22702
Jenkins, F. H., 16886
Jenkins, Geoffrey, pseud., 22703
Jenkins, John, b.1614, 7148
Jenkins, John Stilwell, 1818-1852, 13195-
  13200, 22704, 22705, 22706
Jenkins, Joseph, 13201
Jenkins, Robert, 1769-1848, 25585
Jenkins, Samuel, b.1787?, 13286
Jenkins, Samuel B., 7148
Jenkins, Thornton Alexander, 1811-1893,
  13202
Jenkins, Warren, 22707
Jenkins family, 7148
Jenkinson, Isaac, 13203
Jenks, John Whipple Potter, 4056
Jenks, William, 1778-1866, 13204, 22708
Jenney, Walter Proctor, 1849-1921, 16887
Jennings, Alphonso J., 1863-, 16888
Jennings, Dudley S., 13205
Jennings, Isaac, 1816-1887, 13206
Jennings, James, 13207
Jennings, Louis John, 1836-1893, 13208
Jennings, Napoleon Augustus, 1856-1919,
  4057
Jennings, Paul, b.1799, 13209
Jennings, Samuel Kennedy, 1771-1854, 13210
Jennings, Walter Wilson, 14393
Jennings, William, 16889
Jennison, Isaac, 1790-1873, 22958
Jenny Lind in America, 5016
Jensen, Johannes Vilhelm, 1873-1950, 4058

Jenyns, Soame, 1704-1787, 13211
Jermon, J. Wagner, 13212
Jerningham, Edward, 1737-1812, 13213, 22709
Jernegan, Marcus Wilson, 24676
Jerome, Chauncey, 13214
Jerome, a poor man, 9573
Jerrett, Herman Daniel, 1877-, 16890
Jerry, 3366
The Jerry rescue, October 1, 1851, 25584
Jerry's reward, 2613
Jersey (Prison-ship), 364, 1966, 2128
Jersey City, Charters, 22710; Ordinances, etc.,
  22710
Jersey villas, 7126
Jervis, John Bloomfield, 1795-1885, 13215,
  13216
Jessamine, 5359
Jessamine Co., Ky., History, 13778, 15066;
  Maps, 13646
Jessup, William, 1797-1868, 22711
The Jesuit missionary, 10297
The Jesuit relations and allied documents,
  7149
Los jesuitas en el Río de la Plata, 20084
Los Jesuitas quitados y restituidos al mundo,
  17556
Jesuits, 6418, 7150, 7553, 7667, 8086, 12291,
  17556; Bibliography, 19756, 19986;
  Biography, 5907; Fiction, 9497; Letters
  from missions, 2466, 23520; Letters from
  missions (North America), 1288-1290, 3665,
  3666, 7149, 16956; Missions, 1289, 1481,
  1482, 1789, 2466, 3665, 7149, 16956, 23520;
  Provincia de Mexico, 7151
Jesuits in Abyssinia, 7665
Jesuits in Brazil, 19681
Jesuits in California, 17822
Jesuits in Canada, 11762; Fiction, 10297
Jesuits in Lower California, 17822, 17823
Jesuits in México, 139, 6690, 7150, 7669,
  23480; Directories, 7151
Jesuits in Nicaragua, 20656
Jesuits in Paraguay, 20084, 21830, 21873
Jesuits in Peru, 18573
Jesuits in Pimeria Alto, 16951
Jesuits in the United States, 2120
Jesuits in Venezuela, 19905
Jesuits in the West Indies, 11742
Jesus Christ, Biography, 21767; Biography,
  Early life, 8766; Divinity, Early works
  to 1800, 14060; Divinity, Sermons, 13384;
  Fiction, 4008, 9682, 14831; Resurrection,
  9858
Jethro's advice recommended to the inhabitants
  of Boston, 1496
Jets and flashes, 10253

Jett, Ann Searcy, 1843-, 14394
Jevons, William Stanley, 1835-1882, 22712
The Jew of Milan, 9390
Jewell, Frederich Swartz, 1821-1903,
  13217
Jewell, Henry, 4059
Jewell, James William, 1889-, 14395-14408
Jewell, William Ray, ed., 4351
Jewell, Wilson, 1800-1867, 13218
Jewelry, 18761
The jewels, 10310
Jewels of the Third plantation, 10420
Jewels of verse, jungle and limerick,
  14494
Jewert, Russell J., 14409
The Jewess, 10441
Jewett, Charles, 1807-1879, 13219
Jewett, Charles Coffin, 1816-1868, 13220,
  13221
Jewett, Ellen, 1813-1836 - Fiction, 11165
Jewett, Isaac Appleton, 1808-1853, 13222
Jewett, John L., 13223
Jewett, Moses, 3854
Jewett, Paul, 13224
Jewett, Mrs. Susan W., 4060
Jewish criminals, 25038
Jewish Tercentenary Committee, 15133
Jewitt, John Rodgers, 1783-1821, 22713,
  22714
Jewitt, Llewellynn Frederick William,
  1816-1886, 13225
Jews, Antiquities, 13332; History, 13332;
  History, Fiction, 9984, 9989; History,
  To B.C. 586, Fiction, 8454; History,
  To A.D. 70, Fiction, 10058, 10616;
  History, To A.D. 70, Poetry, 1902;
  Legal status, laws, etc., Maryland,
  11480; Social life & customs, 9614
Jews in Georgia, 11912
Jews in Germany, 25038
Jews in Kentucky, Drama, 15133
Jex-Blake, Sophia, 1840-1912, 13226
The Jill Raymond case, 14410
Jillson, Willard Rouse, 1890-1975, 7152-
  7155, 14091, 14411-14452, 14563-14567,
  15243; Bibliography, 15079, 15106
Jim's little woman, 10041
Jiménez, Juan Ramón, 1881-1958, 18058
Jiménez de Asúa, Luis, 18344
Jiménez Escobar, César, 19771
Jiménez Moreno, Wigberto, 7932
Jiménez R., Rogelio, 19006
Jiménez Ramírez, Jaime, 20326
Jiménez Rueda, Julio, 1896-, 6389
Jimeno's and Hartnell's indexes of land
  concessions, 16423

Jimmy's big brother from California, 6978
Jimsella, 24319
Jimty, 9916
Jinny, 9779
Joanna of Naples, 9710, 9711
Job analysis, 18361
Jobson, Frederick James, 1821-1881, 4061
Jocassee, 10783, 19769
Jocknick, Sidney, 1849, 16891
Joe of Lahaina, 10675
Joe's pocket, 10863
Joes abenteuer im wilden Westen, 2693
Joffily, S., 18936
Jogues, Isaac, 1607-1646, 1481, 13227
John, Don D., 14453
John, Eliza, 14453
John and Mary, 9665
John and the demijohn, 11212
John Anderson and I, 9203
John Andross, 9353
John Bradford historical society, Lexington,
  Ky., 15751
John Brent, 5748
John Brown at Harper's Ferry and Charlestown;
  a lecture, 24303
John Bull in America, 10485
John Delavory, 10016
John Doe and Richard Roe, 9632
John Eax and Mamelon, 10992
John Fitzgerald Kennedy, 19261
John Godfrey's fortunes, 10927
John Gray: a Kentucky tale of the olden time,
  8514
John Guilderstring's sin, 10615
John Holden, unionist, 9383, 24275
John Hunter and his pupils, 3707
John L. Stoddard's lectures, 8114
John M. Daniel's latch-key, 2589
John McGovern's poems, 4352
John March, Southerner, 8927
John Merrill's experiment in palmistry, 10448
The John North mystery, 9817
John Norton's vagabond, 10400
John O'Brien, 10642
John Paget, 3367
John Paul's book, 11112
John Randolph, 10310, 10953
John Ship, mariner, 10709
John Smith's funny adventures on a crutch,
  9871
John Smith's letters, 10817
John W. Robertson, 10197
John Ward, preacher, 9375
John Worthington's name, 8777
John's alive, 10962

John's wedding suit, 10465
Johnes, Arthur James, 1809-1871, 13228
Johnny-boy, 6963
Johns, Henry T., b.1827 or 8, 4062
Johns, Jane (Hall) b.1813, 23463
Johns, John, bp., 1796-1876, 22715
Johns, Walter R., 2030
Johns Hopkins University, 4765
Johnson, Adam Rankin, 1834-, 4063
Johnson, Alexander Bryan, 1786-1867,
    7156, 13229, 22716
Johnson, Andrew, pres. U.S., 1808-1875,
    629, 11269, 11868, 13230-13232, 21829,
    22202; Impeachment, 13230
Johnson, Arthur Tysilio, 16899
Johnson, Beverly, 1796-1876, 24815
Johnson, Charles Beneulyn, 1843-1928,
    4064
Johnson, Charles Britten, 1788?-1835,
    13233
Johnson, Clifton, 1865-1940, 4065, 4066
Johnson, Cuthbert William, 1799-1878,
    13234
Johnson, D. Vertner, illustr., 4053
Johnson, Edwin Ferry, 1803-1872, 13235,
    13236
Johnson, Eunice Tolbert, 14454
Johnson, Ezra R., 13237
Johnson, Francis White, 1799-1884,
    16892
Johnson, Frederick H., 13238
Johnson, Gurney, 14455
Johnson, Hannibal Augustus, 1841-, 4067
Johnson, Herrick, 1832-1918, 13239,
    22717
Johnson, Homer Uri, 24677
Johnson, James, 1777-1845, 13240
Johnson, James, 1780-1811, 13241
Johnson, James, 1783-1855, 24875
Johnson, James Weldon, 1871-1938, 24678
Johnson, Jane, b.1820?, 24080, 25103
Johnson, Jeremiah, 1766-1852, 13262
Johnson, John, 24679
Johnson, John Barent, 1769-1803, 13242-
    13244
Johnson, John Graver, 1841-1917, 13245
Johnson, John Rosamond, 1873-, 24678
Johnson, Joseph, 1776-1862, 13246
Johnson, Kenn, 13833, 14456, 14457
Johnson, L. Frank, 1869-1931, 14458
Johnson, Laura (Winthrop) 1825-1889,
    16893
Johnson, Leland R., 14459
Johnson, Lewis Franklin, 1859-1931,
    14460, 14461
Johnson, Lorenzo Dow, 1805-1867,

    13247-13251
Johnson, Louisa, 13252
Johnson, Luther Alexander, 1875-, 17796
Johnson, Madison Conyers, 1807-, 14462
Johnson, Oliver, 1809-1889, 24680, 24681
Johnson, Overton, 4068
Johnson, Parish Barkydt, 1838-, 21906
Johnson, Reverdy, 1796-1876, 6568, 7157,
    13253, 13254, 13255, 13256
Johnson, Richard Mentor, 1781-1850, 13786
Johnson, Richard W., 1827-1897, 4069
Johnson, Robert, fl.1586-1626, 4070, 4071,
    21808
Johnson, Robert Gibbon, 1771-1850, 13257
Johnson, S. M., pseud., 24458
Johnson, Samuel, 1696-1772, 22718
Johnson, Samuel, 1709-1784, 9368, 11968,
    13258-13260, 13462, 14881
Johnson, Samuel Roosevelt, 1802-1873, 13261,
    13262
Johnson, Sidney Smith, 1840-, 16894
Johnson, Sidona V., 16895
Johnson, Stanley Currie, 1878-, 7158
Johnson, Sue, 15455
Johnson, Theodore T., 16896, 16897
Johnson, Thomas, ca.1760-18--(?), 15577
Johnson, Thomas, 14463
Johnson, Mrs. Thomazin Gibson (Blanchard)
    1765-1825, 13250
Johnson, Tom, pseud., 14217
Johnson, Walter Rogers, 1794-1852, 13263,
    13264
Johnson, Sir William, 1715-1774, 7429
Johnson, William, 1771-1834, 13265, 13266,
    13380
Johnson, William Cost, 1806-1860, 13267,
    13268
Johnson, William D., 13269
Johnson, William Melanchthon, 1834-1910, 13270
Johnson & Warner's Kentucky almanac, 14464
Johnson County, Kentucky, Description, 15432;
    History, 15687
Johnson County (Ky.) Historical Society, 15687
Johnson County in his honor, 13786
Johnson's "old woman", 6965
Johnston, Albert Sidney, 1803-1862, Poetry,
    14828
Johnston, Alexander, 14465
Johnston, Annie Fellows, 1863-1931, 14466
Johnston, Charles, 1768-, 4072
Johnston, Charles W., 16898
Johnston, David Claypoole, 1797-1865, illustr.,
    10414, 24682
Johnston, Elias Schellhammer, 1834-1926, 13271
Johnston, Elizabeth Bryant, 1833-1907, 4073,
    24683

Johnston, George Harvey, 1860-1921, 22719
Johnston, Gideon, 1671 (ca.), 4075
Johnston, Sir Harry Hamilton, 1858-1927, 4076
Johnston, Henry Phelps, 1842-1923, 7141
Johnston, Isaac N., 4077
Johnston, James, 13272
Johnston, James F., 13273
Johnston, James Finlay Weir, 1796-1855, 4078, 13274
Johnston, John, 1778-1855, 13275
Johnston, Joseph Eggleston, 1807-1891, 2033, 4079, 5547, 5550
Johnston, Josiah Stoddard, 1784-1833, 13276
Johnston, Josiah Stoddard, 1833-1913, 14467, 24684
Johnston, Margaret, 13426
Johnston, Orramel, 14468
Johnston, Richard Malcolm, 1822-1898, 4080-4091, 6170
Johnston, Samuel Burr, 13277
Johnston, William, 24412
Johnston, William, 1804-1892, 13278
Johnston, William Dawson, 1871-1928, 24685
Johnston, William J., 4092
Johnston, William Preston, 1831-1899, 4093-4095
Johnston family, 4074
Johnstone, Elizabeth, 24686
Johnstone, Walter, 13279
Johnsville in the olden time, 8644
Johonnot, Jackson, 4096
Joining the grangers, 10794
Joint Commission on Kentucky and Tennessee Boundary, 14469
A joint patriotic celebration of the one-hundred and forty-seventh anniversary of the Battle of Bunker Hill by the Kentucky Society [et al.], Sons of the Revolution, 14470
Joint Stock Mutual Merchandising Company, 4975
Joinville, François Ferdinand Philippe Louis Marie d'Orléans, prince de, 1818-1900, 4097
The joke that failed, 9533
Jokes, Dirty, 14391
Joliet, Louis, 1645-1700, 4393, 14471
Jollivet, Adolphe, 1799-1848, 13280
A jolly fellowship, 10891
The jolly Irishman, 15034
Joly de Saint Valier, 13281
Jomard, Edme François, 1777-1862, 13282

Jomini, Henri, baron, 1779-1869. Traité des grandes opérations militaires, 23139
Jonas, E. A., Matthew Harris Jouett, 15747
Jonas, Edward Asher, 1865-, 14472, 14473
Jonathan, pseud., 4098
Jonathan Bull and Mary Bull, by James Madison, 23013
Jonathan Jefferson Whitlaw, 23711
Jonathan Yeadon's justification, 8723
Jonathan's home, 9066
Jonce Smiley, the Yankee boy who had no friends, 11117
Jonckheere, Karel, 1906-, 7159
Jones, Abalom, 13284
Jones, Abner Dumont, 1807-1872, 13283
Jones, Alexander, 1802-1863, 13285, 13286
Jones, Amanda Theodocia, 1835-, 22720
Jones, Anson, 22721
Jones, Arthur Edward, 1838-1918, 7149
Jones, Arthur T., 13288
Jones, Benjamin Washington, 1841-, 4099
Jones, Calvin, 4100
Jones, Cave, 1769-1829, 13289
Jones, Charles A., 1815?-, 4101
Jones, Charles Colcock, 1804-1863, 13292, 24687
Jones, Charles Colcock, jr., 1831-1893, 4102-4106, 13290, 13291, 22722
Jones, Charles Edgeworth, 1867-1931, 24688
Jones, Charles Jesse, 1844-, 16900
Jones, Charles L. S., 13293
Jones, Charles Lee, 13294, 13320
Jones, Daniel Webster, 16901
Jones, David, 1736-1820, 13295, 13296
Jones, David Samuel, 1777-1848, 13324
Jones, E. L., 20214
Jones, Earl, 21744
Jones, Edgar DeWitt, 1876-1956, 7160, 7161
Jones, Edward Conway, 1820-1865, 22723
Jones, Electa Fidelia, b.1806, 13297
Jones, Evan, 16184
Jones, Evan Rowland, 1840-1920, 4107
Jones, George, 1810-1879, 13298, 13299
Jones, George W., 5627
Jones, Henry, 23315
Jones, Horatio Gates, 1822-1893, 13296, 13300
Jones, Hugh, 1669-1760, 4108, 13301
Jones, J. Catron, 14475
Jones, James, 13302
Jones, James Athearn, 1791-1854, 13303
Jones, Janie L., 14476
Jones, John, 1729-1791, 13304
Jones, John Beauchamp, 1810-1866, 4109-4117, 14477
Jones, John G., 13305
Jones, John Matthew, 13306

Jones, John Paul, 1717-1792, 22927, 23612, 23613
Jones, John Paul, 1747-1792, Poetry, 2191
Jones, John Wesley, 4118
Jones, John William, 1836-, 4119
Jones, John Winter, 1805-1881, 22285
Jones, Joseph, 1833-1896, 13307
Jones, Joseph Huntington, 1797-1868, 22272
Jones, Joseph Seawell, 1811?-1855, 13308, 13309
Jones, Kumen, 16902
Jones, Laban, 1796-, 14479
Jones, Lewis Hampton, 7162
Jones, Lot, d.1865, 13310
Jones, Lloyd, 16903
Jones, Morris Charles, 1819-1893, 13311
Jones, Nathaniel Vary, 1822-1863, 16904
Jones, O.V., 15110
Jones, Peter, Chippewa chief, 1802-1856, 13312-13314
Jones, Pleasant, pseud., 10861
Jones, Rebecca M. Burton, 16904
Jones, S.C., 14174
Jones, Samuel, 13315
Jones, Samuel, 1735-1814, 4120
Jones, Samuel, 1819-1887, 2035
Jones, Samuel Calvin, 1828-, 4121
Jones, Samuel W., 13316
Jones, Skelton, 11613
Jones, Thomas, 12310
Jones, Thomas A., 7163
Jones, Thomas ap Thomas, 7162
Jones, Thomas C., 14462
Jones, Thomas D., 1808-1881, 7260
Jones, Thomas Laurens, 1819-1887, 13317
Jones, Thomas Lewis, 1841-, 16905
Jones, Uriah James, 1818-1864, 4122, 13319, 14480
Jones, Walter, 1777-1861, 13320
Jones, William, 1760-1831, 13321, 13322
Jones, William Albert, 1841-1914, 17776
Jones, William Alfred, 1817-1900, 13323, 13324, 22724
Jones, William Basil, 14481
Jones, William C., 16906
Jones, William D., 13325
The Jones family in Ireland, 7257
Jones family (Thomas Jones, d.1713), 13324
Jones's new fin-keel, 9254
Jordan, Cornelia Jane (Matthews) 1830-1898, 13326
Jordan, David S., 16907
Jordan, Ebenezer Stevens, 1819-1890, 7164,

22725
Jordan, Gibbes Walker, 13327
Jordan, James O., 15257
Jordan, Jim, 14482
Jordan, John, fl.1826, 13328
Jordan, Leonard G., 3655
Jordan, Samuel, 13329
Jordan Pando, Roberto, 19122
Jörg, Eduard, 1808-1864, 4123
Jornada Sul-Rio-Grandense de Biblioteconomia e Documentação, 1st, Pôrto Alegre, 1968, 18978, 19504, 19983
Jornado del muerto, 10863
Jorullo, El volcán, 18187
José de Valdivielso y la poesía religiosa tradicional, 18060
José Leite & outros cantos, 18349
Joseph, pseud., 13330
Joseph, Henry, d.1834, 13331
Joseph, Nez Percés chief, d.1904, 16822
Joseph, the Jew, 10047
Joseph and his friend, 10928
Joseph Seaman Cotter, black poet of Kentucky, 7165
Joseph Wheeler, 3224
Josephine Eloise, 9725
Josephus, Flavius, 13332
Josh Billings' encyclopedia and proverbial philosophy of wit and humor, 10742
Josh Billings, hiz sayings, 10743
Josiah Allen as a politician, 9889
Josselyn, John, fl. 1630-1675, 22726, 22727
Jottings from life, 9303
Jottings of a year's sojourn in the South, 5558
Jottrand, Gustave, 1830-1906, 736
Jouet, Alphonse, 1867-, 24689
Jouett, Edward Stockton, 1863-, 14861
Jouett, Matthew Harris, 1787-1827, 14278, 14279, 14472, 15197, 15737, 15747
Jourdanet, D., 7931
Journalism, 6266, 11606; Brazil, 18702; Colorado, 16333; Fiction, 13541
Journalists, 19886
Journalists' letters descriptive of Texas and Mexico, 8180
Joutel, Henri, 1640?-1735, 4126, 22731
Jovita, Maria de Lourdes, 18029
Joy, Benjamin, 13341
Joy, and other poems, 3164
Joy and salvation by Christ; his arm displayed in the Protestant cause, 22349
Joy in tribulation, 1445
Joyce, Isabella, d.1865, 1474
Joyce, John, d.1865, 1474
Joyce, John Alexander, 1842-1915, 14483, 14484

Joyce, Lilian Elwyn (Elliott), 1884-, 13502
The joys and sorrows of American life, 3841
Juan de Austria, 1547-1578, Fiction, 9225
Juan de Castellanos, 18192
Juan de Fuca (Strait), 16477
Juan de la Rosa, 18062
Juan de Santa Maria, brother, d.1622, 7166
Juan Fernandez (Islands), 8878, 16071
Juan y Santacilia, Jorge, 1713-1773, 7167
Juana Inés de la Cruz, Sor, 1651-1695, 7168
Juarez, Benito Pablo, pres. of Mexico, 1806-1872, 8441; Drama, 19758
Juarros, Domingo, 1752-1820, 13342
Jubilee College, Peoria co., Ill., 2975
The jubilee of the Constitution, 74
The Jucklins, 10596
Judd, A. N., 16908
Judd, David Wright, 1838-1888, 13343
Judd, R. D., 14485
Judd, Sylvester, 1789-1860, 22732
Judd, Sylvester, 1813-1853, 12553, 13344
Judd, Thomas, 13345
Judd, William, d.1804, 13346
Judd family (Thomas Judd, 1608?-1688), 22732
Der Jude und sein Sklaventum, 25038
Judge, Jonathan J., 22733
Judge Elbridge, 10597
Judge John Speed and his family, 14319
Judge Longstreet, 3460
The judge's wife, 10394
The judgement of Bolinas Plain, 9793
Judges, Georgia, 13434; Gt. Britain, 12234, 24080; U.S., 11305, 12234
Judgments (Roman law), 25560
The judicial chronicle, 12234
Judicial review, 19736; Cuba, 18821
Judicial review of administrative acts, Mexico, 19882
Judith triumphant, 2849
Judson, Adoniram, 1788-1850, 4128
Judson, Amos M., 4127
Judson, Edward, 1844-, 4128
Judson, Elisha, 1796-1871, 24692
Judson, Katharine Berry, 16909, 16910
Judson, Levi Carroll, 13347, 13348
Juego de dos, 20252
Juettner, Otto, 14486
El juez de columna, 7207
Jug-or-not, 11213
Jugando a la gallina ciega, 18549

Juge, M. A., 22734
Juggernaut, 9468
The juggler, 4560
Juglar, Clément, 1819-1905, 13349
Jugler, Johann Friedrich, 1714-1791, 24693
Juletty, a story of old Kentucky, 14900
"The Julia", 9921
Julia Ormond, 9967
Julian, 11083
Julian, Antonio, b.1722, 13350
Julian George Washington, 1817-1899, 13351, 24694
Julianus, Apostata, emperor of Rome, 331-363, Fiction, 10181
Julien, Denis, 16922, 16925
Juliette, 8649
Julius, Nicolaus Heinrich, 1783-1862, 4129
Junction transistors, 19180
Juniata Valley, Pa., History, 13319
A junior's poems, 3070
Junior League of Lexington, Ky., 14487
Junius, pseud., 12277, 12432, 13352, 14488
Junius, jr., pseud., 13353
Junius redivivus, pseud., 25097
Junkin, David Xavier, 1808-1888, 13354, 13355
Junkin, George, 1790-1868, 13356, 13357, 24695, 25375
Jupiter (Planet), 18863
Jupiter em 1959, 18863
Jurema, Aderbal, 19360
La jurisdicción constitutional de la libertad, 19736
Jurisprudencia tributaria de la Corte Suprema, 18951
Jury, 554, 21976, 22360
Jury selection, 14666
The jury trial of 1900 in the court of public opinion, 7377
"Jus deductionis," 25560
Jusselain, Armand, 13358
Just from Kentucky, 14160
Just in fun, 15785
The just supremacy of Congress over the territories, 11916
Just the little story of Cumberland Gap, 15642
Justice, Martin, illustr., 13977
Justice, 18057; Administration of, Colombia, 20329; Administration of, U.S., 22453
Justice and the judge, 9376
Justice essential to national prosperity, 11376
Justice in the bye-ways, 45
Justice (Early) in Utah, 17258
Justices of the peace, 21976, Kentucky, 24715; Maryland, 22420

Justicia y derecho, 18057
Justification de la resistance des
  colonies américaines aux oppressions
  du gouvernement britannique, 13359
Justina, 10085
Justo Ucundono, prince of Japan, 8816
Jute, 12968
Juvenile courts, 14672
Juvenile delinquency, 14672
Juvenile Emancipation Society, Pawtucket,
  R.I., 24932
Juvenile law and procedure, Report of
  seminar on, 14672
Juvenile poems on various subjects, 2427
Juvenis, pseud., 23862
Juventudes exhaustas, 19731
Jvorova, Irina V., 18094

K. N. Pepper, 10386
Kaam, 4972, 10628
Kaehlig, Theodor, 7169
Kaffee, Zucker und Bananen, 7191
Kaiserin (ship), 6655
Kála-azár, Bibliography, 18139; Brazil,
  18139
Kalm, Pehr, 1715-1779, 1898, 2450, 2462,
  2464, 2484, 7170-7172, 11231, 11785
Kaloolah, 10337
Kamchatka, Description & travel, 16981
The Kanawha Valley, its resources and
  development, 3599
Kanawha Valley, W. Va., Economic
  conditions, 3599
Kane, Elisha Kent, 1820-1857, 2428,
  12005
Kane, John Francis, 1881-, 7173
Kane, John Kentzing, 1795-1858, 25897
Kane, Paul, 1810-1871, 4130
Kane, Thomas Leiper, 1822-1883, 4131,
  16911
Kane County, Utah, History, 17373,
  17582
Kanhoji Angria, d.1731, 2123
Kansas, 3685, 12281; Antiquities, 17473,
  17851; Bibliography, 17793; Centennial
  celebrations, etc., 17793; Description
  & travel, 2129, 2510, 2597, 2776, 3059,
  3063, 3615, 3715, 3717, 3790, 3938,
  3955, 4411, 4495, 4651, 4727, 4803,
  4845, 4910, 4914, 5550, 5646, 5753,
  7772, 8408, 11134, 11512, 12142, 15831,
  16096, 16662, 17147, 17351; Description
  & travel, Guide-books, 3616; Gold
discoveries, 2510, 3717, 4727, 4845;
  History, 3230, 4995, 17386, 17748, 17841,
  24064, 24639, 25119, 25940; History, 1854-
  1861, 5507, 11378, 11512, 12240, 12280,
  12281, 13055, 16263, 16420, 16516, 17143,
  17902, 22530, 24844, 25139, 25357, 25592,
  25803; History, 1854-1861, Fiction,
  11126; History, 1854-1861, Poetry, 24696;
  History, Civil war, 16271; History,
  Fiction, 9202; The Lecompton Constitution,
  24228; Lecompton Resolution, 24307;
  Nebraska bill, 1673, 11888, 12938, 23869,
  23966, 24174, 24724, 24973, 25319; Politics
  & government, 1854-1861, 1054, 1162,
  23983, 25017, 25282, 25904; Politics &
  government, 1854-1861 Speeches in
  Congress, 1161, 1521, 1718, 2121, 11687,
  11814, 21857, 24053, 24133, 24723, 25429,
  25763; Public lands, 12971
Kansas and Missouri, 9202
Kansas cavalry. 7th regt., 1861-1865, 3523
Kansas City, Mo., 17091; Description, 5233,
  16571; History, 17196; Statistics, 5233
Kansas gold region, 4914
Kansas in 1858, 17748
Kansas Indians, 17473
The Kansas-Nebraska struggle, 17828
The Kansas region, 3685
The Kansas war, 24696
Kapp, Friedrich, 1824-1884, 4132, 24697
Kappa Lambda Society, New York, 12805
Kararaô Indians, 18552
Karawanenzüge durch die westlichen prairieen
  und wanderungen in Nord-Mejico, 6893
Kariri language, Grammar, 23062
Kaskaskia, Ill., History, Fiction, 8954
Kaskaskia Indians, Missions, 12353
Kästner, Abraham Gotthelf, 1719-1800, tr.,
  211
Katahdin and the Penobscot, 11194
Kate, Herman Frederick Carel ten, 1858-, 7174
Kate Aylesford, 10511
Kate Clarendon, 2678
Kate Connor, 10919
Kate Felton, 11129
Kate Marstone, 10086
Katharine Lauderdale, 6496
Katharine Walton, 10774
Katie of Birdland, 17666
Katydid's poems, 4366
Kaufman, David Spangler, 1813-1851, 24698
Kaufman, M., 14489
Kaufmann, S., 4039
Kavanaugh, Mrs. Russell, 14490
Kay, Charles Y., 7175
Kaysville, Utah, History, 16006

Kazakova, Liia Samuilovna, 7176
Kearney, Belle, 1863-, 4133
Kearney's expedition, 1846, 3962
Kearns, Thomas, 16913
Kearny, Stephen Watts, 1794-1848, 4134, 16914
Kearsarge (Man-of-war), 12003
Keasbey, Anthony Quinton, 1824-1895, 4135
Keating, William Hypolitus, 1799-1840, 13360
Keatling, Maurice Bagenal St. Leger, d. 1835, tr. 22112
Kechua language, 7411
Keckley, Betsy, pseud., 7177
Keckley, Elizabeth Hobbs, Behind the scenes, 7177
Keef, 9047
Keefer, Thomas Coltrin, 1821-1914, 6666
Keel and saddle, 7842
Keele, William, 1781-1861, 3402
Keeler, Charles Augustus, 16915
Keeling, Larry Dale, 14491
Keeling, Robert James, 1828-1909, 7178
Keen, John S., 14492
Keene, N.H.   History, 2455
Keeneland association, Lexington, Ky., 14493
The Keeneland story, 14076
Keep, Austin Baxter, 24478
Keep cool, 10408
Keese, John, 1805-1856, 12885
Keifer, Joseph Warren, 1836-1936, 24699
Keim, De Benneville Randolph, 1841-1914, 4136, 7179
Keim family, 7179
The Keim and allied families in America and Europe, 7179
Keith, Abraham Wendell, 1835-1897, 22458
Keith, Charles A., 14494
Keith, Elbridge Gerry, 1840-1905, 7180
Keith, George, 1639?-1716, 4137
Keith, Sir William, bart. 1680-1749, 11656, 13494
Keitt, Laurence Massillon, 1824-1864, 23645, 24700
Kelham, Robert, 1717-1808, 11425
Kell, Jeffrey, 14495, 14496
Kelland, Philip, 1808-1879, 4138
Keller, Arthur I., illustr., 5192, 9553, 24296
Keller, George, 4139
Keller, Gottfried, 1819-1890, 19612
Keller, Helen Adams, 1880-1968, 7181
Kelley, Daniel George, 1110
Kelley, Hall Jackson, 1790-1874, 16916-16919

Kelley, Joseph, 16920
Kelley, Julielma M., 14497
Kelley, Mrs. Maria Louisa (Hamilton) 1860-, 7182
Kelley, William Darrah, 1814-1896, 4141, 8257, 16921, 24701-24705
Kelley's Ford, Va., Battle of, 1863, 2034
Kellogg, E.C., 23153
Kellogg, John Azar, 1828-1883, 4142
Kellogg, John Jackson, 1837-, 4143
Kellogg, Louise Phelps, 4144, 14532
Kellogg, Robert H., 4145
Kellom, John H., 2877
Kelly, Charles, 1889-, 16922-16926
Kelly, Fanny (Wiggins) b.1845, 16927
Kelly, Mrs. Florence (Finch) 1858-, 24706
Kelly, J. Wells, 16928
Kelly, Samuel, 1784-, 4146
Kelly, William, 4147, 16929
Kelroy, 10684
Kelsey, D. M., 14498, 16930
Kelsey, Rayner W., 16931
Kelsey, William H., 1812-1879, 24707
Kemble, E.W., illustr., 2741, 3192, 4091, 10896
Kemble, Frances Anne, 1809-1893, 4148, 4149, 7119
Kemp, Janet T., 14499
Kemper, Andrew Carr, 14500
Kemper, George Whitefield, 1870-, 14501
Kemper, James, 1753-1834, 14500
Ken-Tenn-o-rama, 14150
Kenan, Augustus H., 2044
Kendall co., Ill. - History, 16752
Kendall, Amos, 1789-1869, 14502
Kendall, George Wilkins, 1809-1867, 4150, 4151
Kendall, John Jennings, 7183
Kendall, John Smith, 1874-, 7184
Kendall, Reese P., 16933
Kenderdine, Thaddeus S., 16934, 16935
Kendrick, William, 1810-1880, 14985
Kennaway, Sir John Henry, baronet, 1837-1919, 4152
Kennebec river, History, Fiction, 9986
Kennebunkport, Me., Geneal., 11488; History, 11488
Kennedy, Anthony, 1811-1892, 24708
Kennedy, Archibald, 1685?-1763, 13361
Kennedy, Elijah Robinson, 1844-, 16936
Kennedy, George W., 1847-, 16937
Kennedy, H.C., 14503
Kennedy, John, 1813-1900, 24709
Kennedy, John Fitzgerald, Pres. U.S., 1917-1963, Bibliography, 13201
Kennedy, John Pendleton, 1795-1870, 4153-

4156, 7185, 7186, 13362, 24710
Kennedy, Sister Mary Benedicta, 17167
Kennedy, Philip Pendleton, 1795-1870, 4157
Kennedy, William, 1799-1871, 4158, 16630, 16938
Kennedy, William, 1813-1890, 1116, 1117
Kennedy, William Sloane, 1850-, 14504
Kenner, Scipio A., 16939, 17170
Kenney, James, 1780-1849, 10736
Kenney, Lucy, 24711
Kenrick, John, 1755-1833,
Kent, Mrs. E.C., 4159
Kent, Edward E., 6538
Kent, Richard, 6538
Kent, William, 8200
Kent family, 6538
Kenton, Simon, 1755-1836, 7376, 10953, 13742, 14505, 14707, 14920, 22316; Fiction, 5663, 5664
Kentucke Gazette, 13833
The Kentuckian in New York, 2924
The Kentuckians..., 14132
Kentuckians in history and literature, 15577
Kentuckians, to arms!!!, 14506
Kentucky, 14707, 15127, 15566, 15702; Adjutant-general's Office, 14507, 14508; Advisory Committee on Higher Education, 15802; Advisory Committee on the Retirement Systems Study, 13570; Anecdotes, 15039; Antiquities, 14151, 14154, 14446, 14603, 15210, 15681, 15791; Appellant, 14462; Bibliography, 13852, 14248, 14925, 14926, 15140, 15415, 15416, 15455, 15574, 15583; Biography, 1359, 13665, 13681, 13787, 13897, 14658-14660, 14975, 14986, 14989, 15237, 15290, 15296, 15414, 15426, 15519, 15578, 15706, 25551; Biography, Portraits, 15046; Blue Licks Battle-field Monument Commission, 14509, 14510; Boone Bicentennial Commission, 14091, 14532; Boundaries, Tennessee, 14469, 14518; Bureau of Agriculture, Horticulture and Statistics, 14511; Capital and Capitol, 14081, 15588; Caves, 13579; Church history, 1359, 4895, 15514; Civil War Centennial Commission, 13853, 14512, 14513; Claims vs. U.S., 14631; Climate, 14324; Commerce, 14545, 15500; Commission, Louisiana Purchase Exposition, 14514; Commission on Aging, 15722; Commission on Human Rights, 14515, 24713; Commission on Negro Affairs, 14516;

Commission on Public Education, 13692; Commission on Public Education. Curriculum Study Committee, 14517; Commissioners on the Boundary Line, 14518; Committee on Functions and Resources of State Government, 14519; Committee to Study Intermittent Industry, 14520; Constitution, 14140, 14475, 14521-14529, 14619, 14755, 15172, 15353, 15695, 15724, 15732, 15734, 24714; Constitution Revision Committee, 14525, 14526; Constitutional Convention, 1792, 14527; Constitutional Convention, 1799, 14528; Constitutional Convention, 1849-1850, 24714; Constitutional Convention, 1890, 14529; Council of Defense, 14530; Council on Public Higher Education, 13728; Court of Appeals, 13578, 14462, 14583, 24715; Court of Appeals, Officials and employees, Appointments, qualifications, tenure, etc., 14462; Curriculum Study Committee, 14531; Daniel Boone Bicentennial Commission, 14532; Department of Agriculture, 14023; Dept. of Commerce, 14533-14549; Dept. of Conservation, 14550, 14661; Dept. of Conservation, Division of Publicity, 14551; Dept. of Economic Development, 14552; Dept. of Education, 14553-14557, 15636; Dept. of Finance, Division of the Budget, 14558; Dept. of Fish and Wildlife Resources, 13574, 14559-14561; Dept. of Geology and Forestry, 14562-14567; Department of Health, 14772; Dept. of Highways, 14568, 14569; Department of Human Resources, 15636; Dept. of Justice, Bureau of Training, 14570; Department of Library and Archives, Division of Archives and Records, 14023; Dept. of Mines and Minerals, Division of Geology, 14571; Dept. of Public Information, 13923, 14572; Department of Public Instruction, 14661; Dept. of Public Relations, 14573; Description & travel, 1495, 2628, 2771, 2943, 3138, 3424, 3425, 3426, 3472, 3568, 3595, 3714, 3739, 3745, 3750, 3753, 4059, 4173, 4264, 4464, 4640, 4758, 4791, 5147, 5382, 5432, 5601, 5644, 5706, 5730, 6061, 8330, 8349, 13525, 13534, 13558, 13563, 13580, 13647, 13650, 13717, 13790, 13903, 13906, 13923, 13940, 13948, 13956, 14000, 14024, 14077, 14090, 14112, 14133, 14300, 14364, 14365, 14370, 14375, 14429, 14431, 14447, 14452, 14467, 14511, 14545, 14547, 14551, 14571, 14573, 14636, 14638, 14639, 14653, 14661, 14706, 14709, 14710, 14748, 14749, 14766, 14786, 14814, 14845, 14857, 14902, 14905, 14936, 15004, 15020, 15032, 15034, 15087, 15107, 15108, 15109, 15246, 15272,

251

14849, 15008, 15083, 15567, 24715; Legislative Research Commission, 13954, 14495, 14604, 14606-14628, 14867, 14868, 15281, 15451, 15633, 15695, 15734; Legislative Research Commission, Special Advisory Committee on Nuclear Waste Disposal, 14629; Legislative Research Commission, Subcommittee on Long Term Care of the Interim Joint Committee on Health and Welfare, 14630; Legislature, 14611; Legislature, Districting, 14692; Libraries, 13663; Library Commission, 15276; Manners and customs, 14372; Maps, 13597, 14183, 14261, 14427, 14428, 14471, 14512, 14601, 14927, 14928, 15015, 15048, 15311, 15533, 15626; Maps, Bibliography, 14548; Militia, 14507, 14508; Military history, 13602; Names, Geographical, 14087, 14088; Natural history, 14157; Natural resources, 13575; Parks, 14571, 14639, 14640; Penitentiary, Frankfort, 25554; Per., 13790; Physical geography, 13746, 13979, 15327; Physiography, 15330; Pictorial works, 14377; Poetry, 13804, 14212; Politics & government, 3051, 4866, 7155, 13514, 13628, 13721, 13833, 13837, 13844, 13890, 13949, 13989, 13993, 14026, 14044, 14045, 14169, 14198, 14205, 14211, 14293, 14355, 14475, 14502, 14503, 14508, 14519, 14522-14526, 14528, 14529, 14558, 14576, 14585, 14608-14611, 14619, 14621, 14622, 14692, 14733, 14834, 14836, 14867, 14948, 15017, 15033, 15038, 15040, 15064, 15156, 15253, 15258, 15289, 15342, 15372, 15557, 15638, 15639, 15710, 15724, 15726, 15733, 15748, 15773; Politics & government, To 1792, 14835; Politics & government, 1792-1865, 3534, 4264, 4709, 4978, 13588, 13703, 14140, 14206, 14488, 14599, 14822, 14833, 14918, 24145, 24146; Politics & government, 1861-1865, 7187; Politics & government, 1865-, 13318; Politics & government, Bibliography, 14312; Politics & government Civil war, 12873, 13988, 15164; Politics & government, Fiction, 14503; Poor, 14891; Population, 13866, 13867, 13985, 14327, 14491, 14775, 15354, 15504; Provisional government, 1861-1865, 14708; Public Service Commission, 15689; Race relations, 14516; Railroads, 13836, 14782; Registers, 24715;

Religion, 13779, 13833; River, 14739; Senate, Journals, Bibliography, 13852; Sights to see, 14709, 14710; Social conditions, 14328, 15337, 15611; Social life & customs, 2509, 3522, 3745, 4180, 13861, 14760, 15103, 15515, 15531, 15693, 25664; State Agent at Washington, 14631; State Board for Vocational Education, 14632; State Dept. of Health, 14633; State Forest Service, 14634; State Historical Society. Archives Dept., 14635; State Industrial and Commercial Conference, Louisville, 1887, 14636, 14637; State Park Board, 14638; State Park Commission, 14639-14641; State Parks Division, 14642; Statistics, 14546; Unemployment Compensation Commission, 14520; University, 14007, 14267, 14643-14649, 14816, 15105; University, Alumni association, 14644, 14650, 14651; University, Basketball team, 15788; University, Bureau of business research, 13717, 14652; University, Bureau of government research, 13717; University, Bureau of School Service, 14653; University, Centennial Committee, 14654-14656; University, Center for Developmental Change, 14657; University, Center for Public Affairs, 14871; University, College of Adult and Extension Education, 14658, 14659; University, College of Agriculture, 14660; University, College of Agriculture and Home Economics, 14392; University, College of Arts and Sciences, History, 15277; University, College of Commerce, History, 14654; University, College of Education. Bureau of school service, 14661; University, College of Engineering, 14186; University, College of Engineering, History, 13875; University, College of Law, Office of Continuing Legal Education, 14662-14690; University, College of Pharmacy, 14655; University, Department of English language and literature, 14801; University, Dept. of Physical Education, 14691; University, Dept. of Political Science, 14692; University, Dept. of Printing, 14693; University, Dept. of Zoology, 14694; University, History, 14188, 14189, 14383, 14656, 14988, 15421, 15660; University. Institute for Mining and Minerals Research, 13576; University, Library, 13583, 13737, 13832, 14695-14704, 15363, 15524, 15537; University, Library, Manuscripts, 13535; University, Library Associates, 15048; University, Overseas programs, 13810, 15699; University, Policy and organization, 14645; University, Woman's

Club, 14705; Views, 15419
Kentucky administrative regulations,
  15289
Kentucky agricultural school, 15274
The Kentucky Almanac, 14711-14720
Kentucky ancestors, 14721
Kentucky and Bandung, 15699
Kentucky and Tennessee, 4160
Kentucky and Tennessee Skaggs, 14870
Kentucky and the Southwest Territory,
  1794, 14088
Kentucky and the World's fair, St. Louis,
  1904, 14514
Kentucky and Virginia resolutions of
  1798, 13500, 14588, 15650
The Kentucky Appalachian and lake states
  oil and gas fields, 14432
Kentucky Association for Health,
  Physical Education and Recreation,
  13848
The Kentucky ballot, 15017
Kentucky Baptist atlas, 14722
Kentucky Bar Association, 14665-15668,
  14670-14676, 14678-14682, 14690
A Kentucky belle, 13811
Kentucky bluegrass isn't either blue or
  native, 14723
The Kentucky building, 15692
A Kentucky cardinal, 13531-13533
Kentucky cavaliers in Dixie, 4541, 15042
Kentucky cavalry, 1st regt., 1861-1864,
  5348; (Confederate), Partisan rangers,
  1862-1864, 4063
A Kentucky chronicle, 14213
A Kentucky Cinderella, 10808
The Kentucky Civil War Round Table, 14250,
  14724, 15010, 15012
Kentucky coffee tree, 13784
The Kentucky colonel, 13540, 15248
The Kentucky colonels handbook, 15648
Kentucky colonization society, 1459,
  25148
Kentucky (Confederate state), Constitution,
  7187
Kentucky consumer price index, 1969, 14911
Kentucky coon hunt, 15208
Kentucky corrections: the case for reform,
  13953
Kentucky council of teachers of English,
  13933
Kentucky County (Virginia), Convention of
  1784/85, 14725
Kentucky Dam, 15607
Kentucky days, 14399
Kentucky Derby, Churchill Downs, Louisville,
  13716, 15308, 15312

A Kentucky Derby legend -- Col. E.R. Bradley,
  13562
Kentucky Educational Association, 13820,
  14345, 14726
Kentucky environmental and economic
  development policy project, 14495
Kentucky facts, 14573
The Kentucky farmer's almanac, 14727-14732
Kentucky fiction, 15530
Kentucky folks and some others, 9342
Kentucky folk ballads, 15491
Kentucky folk festival dances, 14691
Kentucky forest trees and how to know them,
  14390
Kentucky fossil shells, 15059
Kentucky fried chicken, inc., 15319
Kentucky Futurity, 14820
The "Kentucky Gazette", 15746
The Kentucky gentleman, 14318
A Kentucky girl, 14394
Kentucky Health, Welfare and Salary-limit
  Amendment Committee, 14733
Kentucky hemp, 14433
Kentucky Heritage Commission, 14734
Kentucky historical and genealogical
  magazine, 14735
Kentucky Historical Society, 14934, 15236,
  15577; Genealogical Committee, 14721
The Kentucky Home Schools for Girls, 14736
The Kentucky housewife, 15700
Kentucky in American letters, 5446
Kentucky in fiction, 15534
Kentucky in poetry, 15648
Kentucky in the War of 1812, 15213
Kentucky in Washington, 15290
Kentucky infantry. 1st brigade (C.S.A.) 1861-
  1865, 15799; 6th regt., 1861-1865, 4077;
  22d regt., 1862-1865, 5272; 24th Regt.,
  1861-1865, 14483
Kentucky is my land, 15470
The Kentucky Lake story, 14280
A Kentucky lawyer, 25374
Kentucky Library Association, 15276
Kentucky literature, 13933, 14659, 15050,
  15525, 15538, 15577; Bibliography, 14830;
  Collections, 14897; Periodicals, 15634
Kentucky local planning laws: review and
  analysis, 14868
Kentucky lore, 14769
Kentucky manufacturing, an initial report...,
  14245
Kentucky Marijuana Feasibility Study, Inc.,
  Lexington, Ky., 14737
Kentucky medical association, 15772
Kentucky medical necrology, 15561
The Kentucky Militia in early days, 14105

Kentucky: mother of governors, 15578
Kentucky mountain melodies, 14400
The Kentucky mountains, 15645
Kentucky Normal and Theological Institute, 24524
Kentucky North-Bend Agricultural Society, 14738
The Kentucky novel, 15530
Kentucky of Kentucky, 14761
Kentucky Penal Code, Report of seminar on, 14674
Kentucky periodicals, 15548
Kentucky pioneer women, 15496
Kentucky pioneers and their desendants, 13969
Kentucky Playmakers, 15386
Kentucky poems, 13801
Kentucky poetry, 15073
Kentucky procedure for dissolution of marriage, 14667
Kentucky progress magazine, 13790
A Kentucky protest against slavery, 4945
Kentucky rarities, 13878
Kentucky remembers, 14513
The Kentucky revival, 14930
Kentucky River, 14336, 14337, 14459, 14751, 15607; Description, 14460
The Kentucky River navigation, 15646
Kentucky River scenery, 15393, 15394
Kentucky River soundings, 14739
Kentucky River Valley, Bibliography, 14420
Kentucky Rivers Coalition, 15123
Kentucky sesquicentennial commission, 14783
Kentucky Skaggs, 15647
Kentucky snake superstitions, 15540
Kentucky snakes, 14153
Kentucky Society for the Gradual Relief of the State from Slavery, 25173
Kentucky Society, Sons of the Revolution, 14470
Kentucky State Bar Association, 15758
Kentucky state fair, 14740
Kentucky State Historical Society, 15237
Kentucky state parks, 14434
Kentucky superstition, 15513
Kentucky tavern, 14435
Kentucky tax policy, suggested considerations, 14141
Kentucky, the pioneer state of the west, 13821
Kentucky tourist preferences, 14652
Kentucky tradition, 15531
The Kentucky tragedy, 10766, 13870
Kentucky University, 14501; Harrodsburg Ky., 1858-1865, 15439

Kentucky University alumni book, 14501
Kentucky Utilities Company, Lexington, 14741
Kentucky veterans bonus, 14618
Kentucky's black heritage, 14515, 24713
Kentucky's dissolution of marriage law, 14667
Kentucky's forest resources and industries, 15627
Kentucky's future transportation needs, 14620
Kentucky's ghost, 11075
Kentucky's kindergarten program, 14476
Kentucky's love, 10133
Kentucky's pioneer lithotomists, 13605
Kentucky's resources, 14653, 14661
Kentucky's struggle with its loyalist proprietors, 15368
Kenworthy, Charles James, 4161
Kenyon College, Gambier, O., 2976, 2977, 4776
Kenys, Janet T., 14742
Keokuk, Ia., Description, 16214, 17456; Direct., 17456; History, 16866
Ker, Henry, 4162
Ker, John, 24716
Ker, Leander, 24717
Kératry, Émile, comte de, 1832-1904, 7188
Kercheval, Samuel, 1786-1845?, 22735
Kerbey, Joseph Orton, 1841?-1913, 4163
Kerimov, A., 7189
Kern, Edward M., illustr., 5167
Kerr, Charles, 1863-1950, 14743-14745
Kerr, Hazel Cary, 14746
Kerr, Lewis, 16940
Kershaw, W. L., 16941
Kerwood, Asbury L., 4164
Kessler, Harry Klemens Ulrich, graf von, 1868-, 7190
Ketcham, Edward Hallock, 1835-1863, 11993
Ketcham, John, 1782-1865, 12899
Ketcham, John Townsend, 1838-1863, 11993
Ketchum, Mrs. Annie (Chambers) 1824-1904, 4165-4167, 15369
Kettel, George F., 24718
Key, Francis Scott, 1780-1843, 24719, 25192
Key, Helmer, 1864-, 7191
Key, Thomas Jefferson, 1831-1908, 2945
A key into the language of America, 23800
The key of industrial cooperative government, 8509
Key West, Fiction, 9673
Keyes, Charles M., 4168
Keyes, Erasmus Darwin, 1810-1895, 16942
Keyes, James, 1801-1883, 4169
Keyes, Wade, 2054
A keyhole peep into the past, 14162
Khaled, 6497
Khan-Li, The journal of, 10364
The Kiabab Indians, 16500

Kiana, 10028
A kick for a bite, 1935
Kick him down hill, 10812
Kidd, James Harvey, 1840-, 4170
Kidd, William, c.1645-1701, 4000
Kidder, Daniel Parish, 1815-1891, 4546, 14747
Kidder, Frederic, 1804-1885, 22736
The kidnapped and the ransomed, 10521
A kidnapped colony, 2546
The kidnapping of President Lincoln, 9749
Kidney bean, 19771; Fertilizers and manures, 19464
Kiefer, Bruno, 20091
Kiefl, Franz Xavier, 1869-, 24720
Kiel. Universität, Geographisches Institut, 7979
Kiernan, Brian, 14620
Kiffhaber, Hans, 16th cent., 22195
Kilbourne, David Wells, 1803-1876, 16943
Kilburn, illustr., 10789
Kildhurm's oak, 9811
Killebrew, Joseph Buckner, 14748
Kim, Dong I., 13866, 24161
Kimball, Charles P., 16944
Kimball, Emarette C., 3241
Kimball, Emma Adeline, 1847-, 22737
Kimball, Heber Chase, 1801-1868, 16945
Kimball, Horace, 275, 276
Kimball, James P., 16946
Kimball, Joseph Horace, 1813-1836, 8181
Kimball, Moses, 23260, 23988
Kimball, Richard Burleigh, 1816-1892, ed., 9489
Kimbark, George W., 8429
Kimbell, Charles Bill, 1839-, 4171
Kimber, Edward, 1719-1769, 4172
Kimber, Isaac, 4172
Kimbrough, Alexander, 1839-1921, 13877
Kimbrough, Petrie, 13876
Kincheloe Station, Ky., 15674
Kindergarten, Kentucky, 14476
Kinfolks, 13858
King, C., 10125
King, Charles, 1844-1933, 16947, 16948
King, Clarence, 1842-1901, 8465, 16949
King, Daniel Putnam, 1801-1850, 24721
King, Edward, 14749
King, Edward, 1848-1896, 4173
King, Finlay M., b.1820, 23243
King, Gilbert Hinds, 14025
King, Helen Calvin, 1904-, 14750
King, James, 1750-1784, 993
King, James, 1822-1856, 22191
King, James, d.1841, 21831
King, John T., 4174

King, Martin Luther, 1929-1968, 18195, 24722
King, Preston, 1806-1865, 24723
King, Richard, 4175
King, Thomas Butler, 1804-1864, 5351, 8157, 16950
King, Warren Raymond, 14751
King David, 11207
King George (ship), 6600
King-Kern Divide, 16907
King Noanett, 10885
The king of American highwaymen, 16320
The king of Folly Island and other people, 10037
The king of Honey island, 5392
The king of rivers, 2957, 24103
The king of the northern slope, 14832
The king of the sea, 10079
King Philip's War, 1675-1676, 12, 2125, 2167, 11421, 11787, 11876, 12110, 23319, 23712; Fiction, 9154, 9155, 10885, 10958
King Sham, 12407
King Slavery's council, 25356
King Solomon of Kentucky, 13833
King Tom and the runaways, 25219
The king's jackal, 9359
The king's men, 9641
King's Mountain, N.C., Battle of, 1780, 13515, 13997, 15357, 15424
The king's ship, 11173
Kingdom, William, jr., 4176
Kings Co., Cal., Biography, 17179; History, 17179
Kings Co., N.Y., Registers, 11541
Kingsborough, Edward King, viscount, 1795-1837, 7192
Kingsbury, Gaines Pease, 4177
Kingsbury, Harmon, d.1868, 24724
Kingsbury sketches, 10136
Kingsford, Edward, 24725
Kingsford, William, 1819-1898, 4178, 7193
Kingsley, Charles, 1819-1875, 7194, 7195
Kingsley, F. M., 10448
Kingsley, Henry, 1830-1876, 24726
Kingsley, Rose Georgina, 7196
Kingsley, Vine Wright, 24727
Kingsley, Zaphaniah, 24728
Kinkead, Eleanor Talbot, "Mrs. Thompson Short," 14752-14754
Kinkead, Elizabeth Shelby, 14755
Kinkead, George Blackburn, 14756
Kinne, William Alfred, 14757
Kinnear, John R., 4179
Kinnicutt, Thomas, 1800-1858, 24989
Kino, Eusebio Francisco, 1644-1711, 16951, 23480
Kino's historical memoir of Pimería Alta, 16951

Kinship, 18555
The kinsmen, 10775
Kinzie, John, 1763-1828, 25322
Kinzie, Juliette Augusta (Magill) "Mrs.
John H. Kinzie", 1806-1870, 16952
Kiowa Indians, 15938, 16380, 16644, 17186
Kip, Lawrence, 1836-1899, 16953
Kip, William Ingraham, bp. 1811-1893,
16955, 16956
Kipp, Joseph, 16984
Kippis, Andrew, 1725-1795, 13364
Kirby, Harriet Griswold, 14758, 14759
Kirby, William, 4956
Kirby-Smith, Edmund, 1824-1893, 2035,
15077
Kirchhoff, Theodor, 16957
Kirk, Charles D., 4180, 14760
Kirk, John Foster, 1824-1904, 7774
Kirk, Robert C., 16958
Kirke, Edmund, pseud., 3610-3613, 9621-
9623, 14190
Kirke, Henry, 1842-1925, 7197
Kirker, James, 1793-, 3268
Kirkham, Stanton Davis, 1868-, 7198
Kirland, Caroline Matilda (Stansbury)
1801-1864, 2163
Kirland, Charles Pinckney, 1830-1904,
24729
Kirksey, Elisha J., 25339
Kirkwood, James Pugh, 1807-1877, 1571
Kirkwood, John, 7199
Kirsten, A., 4181
Kirwan, Albert Dennis, 14650
Kisch, Egon Erwin, 1885-1948, 7200
Kismet, 10669
Kist, Leopold, 1824-1902, 4182
Kit Carson, 2581
Kit Carson days, 17545
Kitchel, Harvey Denison, 1812-1895,
24730
Kitchen, Thomas, d.1784, 3388
A kitchen colonel, 9575
Kitchen-middens, California, 17265
Kitchen utensils, 2244
The kite trust, 10660
Kites over Spring Grove, 13625
Kito, 10238
Kittl, Ernest Anton Leopoldo, 1854-,
7654
Kittle, Mrs. Maria, 1721-1779, 8814
Kittle, William, 24731
Kitto, Frank Hugo, 1880-, 6306
Kittredge, Frank Edward, 24732
Kitty Craig, 9892
Klamath Lake Massacre, 2920
Klassmann, Mario, 19568

Klausing, Anton Ernest, 1729-1803, 6843
Kleen, Emil Andreas Gabriel, 1847-, 4183
Kleiber, Joseph, 4184
Klein, Felix, 1862-, 4185
Klein, Julius, 16959
Klein, Roberto M., 20685
Klingberg, Frank J., 4075
Klitgaard, Kaj, 4186
Klondike, 16988
Klondike gold fields, 7630, 15819, 15889,
16008, 16215, 16274, 16292, 16347, 16727,
16787, 16958, 16965, 17334
The Klondike stampede, 15819
Kloppenburg, Fray Buenaventura, 19664
Kloss, Georg Franz Burkhard, 1787-1854, 900
Knapp, Georg Friedrich, 1842-1926, 24733
Knapp, George Leonard, 1872-, 16140
Knapp, J. Augustus, illustr., 10224
Knapp, Jacob, 1779-1874, 23497
Knapp, Samuel Lorenzo, 1783-1838, 13368
Knapsack notes of Gen. Sherman's grand
campaign through the empire state of the
South, 23602
Knaresborough Monthly-meeting, An epistle to
Friends of, 12563
Knauer, Hermann, 4187
The knave of hearts, 9642
Kneedler, H.S., 16960
Knibb, William, 24734
Knickerbocker, Herman W., 13560, 14493
The Knickerbocker, New York, 1833-65, 10154
The Knickerbocker's address to the Stuyvesant
pear tree, 2141
The knife, 9216
Kniffin, G.C., 15143
Kniffin, Thomas Henderson, 14761
Knight, Ann, 14380
Knight, Grant Cochran, 1893-1955, 14762-14765
Knight, Henry Cogswell, 1788-1835, 4188
Knight, Mrs. Sarah (Kemble), 1666-1727, 13366,
13367
Knight, Thomas A., 14766
A knight-errant of the foot-hills, 6970
The knight of Sheppey, 10919
The knight of the golden melice, 8468
A knight of the nets, 8731
The knightly soldier; a biography of Major
Henry Ward' Camp, 5471
Knights of Columbus, Texas state Council,
Historical Commission, 5368
The knights of England, France and Scotland,
9845
Knights of Pythias, 10795
Knights of Tabor, 24288
Knights of the golden circle, 11209, 15173,
18968

257

18697, 19866, 19873, 20479, 20622;
British Guiana, 22702, 23113; Chile,
18868, 19598; Chile, Laws and
regulations, 20143; Colombia, 19228,
19656, 20255; Colorado, 16549; Costa
Rica, 20613; Cuba, 24325; Dwellings,
9695, 9697; Germany, 7806; Gt. Britain,
112, 12522; Greece, 24490, 25080;
Jamaica, 25524; Kentucky, 15598; Latin
America, 18376; Lowell, Mass., 905,
22193; Massachusetts, 9697; Mexico,
20047; New York (City), 12451; Peru,
19491; Rome, 24355, 24894, 25080;
South Carolina, 25259; Statistics,
18697; U.S., 17065, 22833, 22880,
24928, 25797; U.S., Colonial period,
25442; Utah, 17811
Labor contract, Colombia, 18053, 19911;
Mexico, 19945
Labor courts, Colombia, 20320, 20321;
Ecuador, 18612
Labor in Brazil, 20622
Labor in Chile, 19598
Labor in Colombia, 19228
Labor, its history and its prospects,
4666
Labor law, 14675
Labor law and practice in Colombia, 19229
Labor laws and legislation, Argentine
Republic, 18472; Brazil, 19328, 19340,
13941; California, 24332; Colombia,
19229, 20320, 20321, 20328; Costa Rica,
20590; Cuba, 20698; Germany, 24355;
Mexico, 18974, 19945; Peru, 2198;
Puerto Rico, 25577
Labor periodística de don Andrés Bello,
18219
Labor productivity, Argentine Republic,
19980
Labor unions, 22746; Chile, 18857; Utah,
17811
Laboria, 24743
Laboulaye, Édouard René Lefebvre de, 1811-
1883, 512, 2414, 6081, 7214, 24744-24746
Labra y Cadrana, Rafael Maria de, 1843-
1918, 24291, 24747, 25555
Labrador, 384, 6899-6901; Description &
travel, 383, 4368, 6671, 21872, 22067;
History, 383
La Bree, Benjamin, 14777
La Brosse, Jean Baptiste de, 1724-1782,
7215, 7216
Lacarrière, Marguerite, 7217
Lacascade, Pierre, 24748
Lacerda, Pedro Maria de, bp., 1830-1890,
24749

Lacey, John, 1755-1814, 22049
La Chasse, Joseph Pierre de, 1670-1749, 16956
Lachine canal, 1956
Lackawanna Valley, Pa., Description & travel,
12858; History, 12858
Lacon, pseud., 24750
La Condamine, Charles Marie de, 1701-1774,
7218
Lacourcière, Luc, 8149
Lacroix, François Joseph Pamphile, vicomte de,
1774-1842, 24751
Lacroix, Frédéric, d.1864, 2213
Lacroix, Henry, of Montreal, 22742
La Crosse, Wis., History, 11675
La Crosse and Milwaukee Railroad company,
22743
Lacy, B., 22744
The Lacy diamonds, 9182
Ladd, Joseph Brown, 1764-1786, 22745
Ladd, Luther Crawford, 1843-1861, 22765
Ladd, William, 1778-1841, 1815
The ladder of fortune, 8760
Lade, Robert, 4198
Ladies Anti-slavery Society, Providence, R.I.,
24854
The ladies' ball, 10197
Ladies' industrial aid association, of Union
Hall, Boston, 22746
Ladrón de Guevara, Antonio, 7219
Ladrón de Guevara, Baltazar, d.1804, 7220
Ladue, Joseph, 16965
Lady Arabella Johnson, 10760
Lady Betty's governess, 9671
Lady Ernestine, 5616
Lady Jane Grey, 10197
Lady Kildare, 10199
The lady lieutenant, 4199
A lady of Boston, 10920
The lady of Fort St. John, 8953
The lady of Lawford, 11101
The lady of Little Fishing, 11205
The lady of Mount Vernon, 10760
A lady of quality, 8906
The lady of the Aroostook, 9946
The lady of the green and blue, 8941
The lady of the isle, 10838
The lady of the rock, 11187, 11188
The lady of the West, 722
A lady of Warrenton, Va., 10576
The lady, or the tiger? 10892
Lady Ravelgold, 11183
A lady's life in the Rocky Mountains, 6086
A lady's second journey round the world, 13453
Laet, Joannis de, 1593-1649, 7221
Laetrile, 14615
La Fay, the pickpocket, 10310

La Faye, Jean Baptiste de, 24752, 24753
Lafayette, pseud., 14778
Lafayette, Marie Joseph Paul Yves Roch
  Gilbert du Motier, marquis de, 1757-
  1834, 77, 1408, 2346, 4200, 4265, 6428,
  11703, 11924, 12029, 12113, 12417,
  13473, 13879, 14365, 14779, 15202,
  15595, 22383, 22430, 22491, 22902;
  Poetry, 2843
Lafayette, Fort, N.Y., 2277, 2479
La Fayette and the Indian girl of
  Illinois, 10570
Lafayette County, Mo., History, 24633
Lafayette County and the aftermath of
  slavery, 1861-1870, 24633
Lafayette en Amérique en 1824 et 1825,
  4265
Lafayette Female Academy, 14779
Lafayette in Kentucky, 14365
Lafferty, Francis Henry, 1838-, 14784
Lafferty, John Aker, 1833-1905, 14784
Lafferty, L. D., b.1800, 15807
Lafferty, Maude (Ward) "Mrs. W.T.
  Lafferty" 1869-, 14780-14783, 14812
Lafferty, William Thornton, 1856-1923,
  14784
Lafitte, Jean, c.1780-c.1825, 3036;
  Fiction, 4005
Lafitte: the pirate of the Gulf, 4005
Laflin, Bonny Dale, 14785
Lafontaine, Sir Louis Hypolite, bart.,
  1807-1864, 25805
Lafosse, J. F., 22747
Lafragua, José María, 1813-1875, 22748
Lafuente y Alcántara, Miguel, 1817-1850,
  1200
Lagarde, Ernest, 23849
La Grange de Chessieux, Gilbert Arnaud
  François Simon de, 22750
La Grange, Ky., History, 15505
Lagrave, Michel, 7494
Laguna, 6910
La Harpe, Bernard de, 4201
Lahcotah, 16842
Lahontan, Louis Armand de Lom d'Arce,
  baron de, 1666-1715? 4202, 7222-7225,
  15846, 22751
Laicus, 8449
Laicus, Philipp, pseud., 6074
Laird, Wilson M., 16966
Lake commerce, 940
Lake co., Ill., 12532
Lake Forest College, 8431
Lake George, 4624
Lake Metigoshe State Park, 17461
Lake of the Woods, 6220

Lake poets, History and criticisms, 10560
Lakes of Nevada, 17539
Lakewood, 10429
Lalcaca, 7226
Lallemant, Antoine Jean Noel, 22233
Lamar, Lucius Quintus Cincinnatus, 1825-1893,
  4426
Lamar, Mirabeau Buonaparte, 1798-1859, 13371,
  24754
Lamas, Andrés, 1817-1891, 7853
Lamb, John, 1735-1800, 22756
Lamb, Roger, 1756-1830, 4203
Lamb's biographical dictionary of the U.S.,
  7227
Lambert, John, 4204, 7229
Lambert, Will, 16967
Lambert de Sainte-Croix, Alexandre, 1854-,
  4205, 7228
Lambert Lilly, school master [pseud.], 12754
Lamberton, James McCormick, 1856-1915, 7230
Lambourne, Alfred, 16968, 16969
Lame, J. S., 24926
Lamentations upon the never enough bewailed
  death of the Reverend Mr. John Reiner,
  pastor of the Church of Christ at Dover,
  22752
Láminas de signos convencionales, 20128
Lamon, Ward Hill, 1828-1893, 22753
Lampeão, see Ferreira de Silva, Virgolino,
  1900-1938.
Lampejos d'Alma, 19870
Lampert, Carl, 14781
Lampkins, G.W., 14786
Lamprecht, Karl Gotthard, 1856-1915, 4206
Lampton, William James, d.1917, 4207
Lamy, Étienne Marie Victor, 1845-1919, 7525
Lanaghan, Mrs., 397
Lancaster, Clay, Anti-bellum houses
  of the Bluegrass, 14787
Lancaster, James A., 16971
Lancaster, Samuel Christopher, 16972
Lancaster, Ky., Economic conditions, 14540;
  History, Poetry, 4838
Lancaster, Mass., History, 12697; History,
  Colonial period, 2445, 23556
Lancaster co., Neb., Biography, 17411
The lance, cross and canoe, 15002
Land, Taxation, Texas, 17727; Taxation,
  U.S., 25773
Land and fresh water shells of North America,
  1318
A land and its people, 15471
Das land der unbegrenzten möglichkeiten, 3634
Das land der zukunft, 4811
Land-grants, Kentucky, 15339; New England,
  12747; Quebec (Province), 6128; Texas, 12939

Land laws, Brazil, 19346
A land-lover and his land, 5720
The land of contrasts, 4548
The land of enchantment, 17875
The land of gold, 16736
The land of golden grain, 16409
Land of legendary lore, 4017
The land of little rain, 15887
The land of Nome, 17104
Land of sunshine, Southern California, 16055
The land of the almighty dollar, 3646
The land of the Aztecs, 8015
The land of the Montezumas, 6490
The land of the muskeg, 8074
"The land of the sky", 5420
The land of the sum, 8198
The land of Thor, 8879
Land Office records, 15306
Land reform, Bolivia, 20209, 20211; Latin America, 20079
Land reform in the Lake Titicaca region, 19576
Land settlement, Putumayo, Colombia, 20306
Land tenure, 16204, 16906; Africa, 18077; Asia, 18077; Bibliography, 18267, 20112; Bolivia, 19576, 20210; Brazil, 19361; Brazil, Law, 19346, 19347, 19861; Chile, 18848; Chile, Bibliography, 18265; Colombia, 19098; Colombia, Law, 20323, 20330, 20331; Ecuador, 19084; Peru, 20028; Latin America, 18077; Mexico, 18136, 19214, 19644; Mexico, Bibliography, 18266; Mexico, Law, 18574, 18855, 19148, 19234, 20196, 20682; Panama, 19087; Peru, 18100, 18545, 20220; Peru, Bibliography, 20704; Puerto Rico, 21745; Spanish America, 19027, 20520; Uruguay, 18675; U.S., Law, 17159; Venezuela, 20639; Venezuela, History, 19747; Yucatan, 20083
Land tenure and land reform in Latin America, 19856
Land titles, Kentucky, 14016; Lee Co., Ia., 16943; New York (State), Onondaga Co., 12131; San Francisco, 17867
Land und Leute in der Alten und Neuen Welt, 4291
Land-und Seereisen eines St. Gallischen Kantonsbürgers nach Nordamerika und Westindien, 2851
Land use, Kentucky, 14495
Land use at selected interchanges on interstate Highway 75 in north-central

Kentucky, 15602
Land warrants, Kentucky, 15407
The land we love, 24755
Land without chimneys, 6441
Landa, Diego de, 1524-1579, 7231
Landas, K., pseud., 6535
Landasta, Leopoldo, 6956
De landelijke arme blanken in het zuiden der Vereenigde Staten, 3902
Landenberger, Emil, 7232
Lander, Arthur B., 14788, 14789
Lander, Frederick West, 1821-1862, 4208, 16973
Lander, Meta, pseud., 10169
Die länder am untern Rio Bravo del Norte, 8255
Landivar, Rafael, 1731-1793, 7233-7238
Landon, Fred, 24756-24758
A landless farmer, 10040
Landlord and tenant, Brazil, 18126
The landlord at Lion's Head, 9947
Landmarks and other poems, 4773
Landnahme und kolonisation in Canada, 7979
Landolphe, Jean François, 1747-1825, 4209
Landor, William, 11052
Landreise nach Californien, 5086
Landrum, John Morgan, 1815-1861, 24759
Lands of the slave and the free, 7557, 7558
The landscape chamber, 10037
Landscape gardening, 11990
Landscape painting, 7554; U.S., 22544
Lane, Calvin W., 15000
Lane, Henry Smith, 1811-1881, 24763
Lane, James Henry, 1814-1866, 16516, 24760, 24761, 25763
Lane, Job, 1741-1768, 22024
Lane, John J., b.1833, 16974
Lane, Joseph, 1801-1881, 5676, 6144, 15985, 24762
Lane, Lunsford, 24579
Lane, Mrs. Lydia Spencer (Blaney), 16975
Lane, Samuel Alanson, b.1815, 16976
Lane Theological Seminary, Cincinnati, 24764
Lang, Herbert O., 16977
Lang, John Dunmore, 4210, 4211
Lang, William W., 16978
Lang syne, 10814
Langdon, Barnabas, 1008
Langdon, Timothy, 1758-1801, 24765
Lange, Henry, 1821-1893, 2541
Lange, Max, 1832-1899, 7239
Langer, Carl Rudolf, 1893-, 24766
Langford, Nathaniel Pitt, 1832-1911, 16979, 16980
Langsdorff Georg Heinrich, freiherr von, 1774-1852, 16981
Langton, Hugh Hornby, 1862-, 6290

Language, 18660, 18662; Sociological aspects, 18661
Language and languages, 11510, 13228, 22699; Classification, 97
Langworthy, Daniel Avery, 1832-, 4212
Langworthy, Franklin, 1798-ca.1855, 4213
Langworthy, Lucius Hart, 16982
Lanier, James Franklin Doughty, 1800-1881, 16983
Lanier, Sidney, 1842-1881, 4214, 5144; Fiction, 11027
Lanman, Charles, 1819-1895, 3378, 4215-4217, 7240
Lanning, C.M., 16984
Lans, W.H., 24767
Lansdowne, Henry Petty Fitz Maurice, 3d marquis of, 1780-1863, 6246, 6247
Lantern slides, 7578
Laperouse, Jean François de Galaup, comte de, 1741-1788, 11624, 22115
La Peyrere, Isaac de, 1594-1676, 13372
Lapham, Increase Allen, 1811-1875, 16985
Lapham, William Berry, 1828-1894, 4218
La Plata. Universidad Nacional. Departamento de Letras. Monografías y tesis, 19906
Lapse (law), Mexico, 19854
Laramie, 10123
Laranda, Viletta, 24768
Lardizabal y Uribe, Miguel de, 1744-1820, 7241, 7242
Lardner, Dionysius, 1793-1859, 4219
Large, Mary Harriott, 14790
The larger faith, 9184
Larimer, Mrs. Sarah Luse, 16986
Larimer, William, 1809-1875, 16987
Larimer, William Henry Harrison, 1840-1910, 16987
Larned, Edward C., reporter, 12311
Larned, Edwin Channing, 1820-1884, 24769
Larned, Sylvester, 1796-1820, 12507
Laroche, Benjamin, 1797-1852, 24770
La Roche, Frank, 16988
La Rochefoucauld Liancourt, François Alexandre Frédéric, duc de, 1747-1827, 4220, 7243, 7244
Larocque, Francois Antoine, 16989
Larpenteur, Charles, 1803?-1872, 16990
Larrabee, Charles Hathaway, 1820-1883, 16991
Larrazábal, Felipe, 1816-1873, 7245
Lars, Claudia, 19215
Larson, Arthur, 16992, 16993
La Rue family (Abraham La Rue, d.1712) 25010
Larvae, Fishes, 20191, 20192

Lasaga, Juan Lucas de, 7246
La Salle, Nicolas de, 16994
La Salle, Robert Cavelier, Sieur de, 1643-1687, 1846, 4126, 5433, 16491, 16628, 16994, 22731; Bibliography, 16628; Drama, 3311
La señorita, 10863
Lassen co., Cal., History, 16489
Lassepas, Ulises Urbano, 16768
Lastchance Junction, far, far West, 9656
A late and further manifestation of the progress of the gospel amongst the Indians in New England, 12006
The late Mrs. Null, 10893
Later years, 10572
Latham, Allen, 7247
Latham, Henry, 1794-1866, 4221
Latham, Henry Jepson, 16996
Latham, Milton Slocumb, 1827-1882, 378, 24771
Lathers, Richard, 1820-1903, 4222
Lathrop, David, 4223
Lathrop, George, b.1830, 16997
Lathrop, George, d.1848, 9328
Lathrop, Mrs. Jerusha (Talcott) 1717-1805, 10761
Lathrop, John, 1740-1816, 13373
Latimer, George, 25149
The Latimers, 10266
Latin America, 18295, 19511; Antiq., 19748; Bibliography, 19641; Biography, 19921; Colonization, 19204; Commerce, 18770, 18806; Constitutional history, 18095; Description & travel, 8160; Economic conditions, 18264, 18721, 18804, 20103; Economic conditions, 1918-, 18076, 19773, 20038-20040; Economic conditions, 1945, Addresses, essays, lectures, 18239; Economic conditions, 1945, Congresses, 20401; Economic conditions, Period., 18156; Economic integration, 19481; Economic integration, Bibliography, 20111; Economic policy, 18719, 18941, 20619; Historic houses, etc., 19749; History, 18374, 19238, 19487, 19577; History, To 1600, 19204, 19921; History, Bibliography, 19514; History, Congresses, 20408; Industries, 19773; Politics & government, 18076, 18092, 18264, 18704, 18941, 19481, 19577, 19578, 19752, 19850, 20079; Politics & government, Addresses, essays, lectures, 19718; Social conditions, 18076, 19773, 20038-20040, 20388; Social conditions, 1945, Congresses, 20401; Social conditions, Period., 18156; Social life and customs, 19914
Latin American activities and resources, 19641
Latin American library history literature, 18990
Latin American literature, Period., 7835

Latin American periodicals, 18219
Latin American trade patterns, 18680
Latin drama, History & criticism, 18954
Latin drama (comedy), Technique, 25852
Latin drama, Medieval and modern, 18607
Latin language, Grammar, 19817; Gender, 7728; Grammar, 1500-1800, 7436; Tense, 7727, 7728
Latitude, 5852
Latorre, Germán, 7248
Latorre, María Elisa, 20243
Latour, Arsène Lacarrière, 4224
La Tour, Charles Amador de St. Estienne, sieur de, Fiction, 8953, 8984
Latourette, Kenneth Scott, 1884-, 16517
Latourette, Nellie Edith, 16517
Latreille, Pierre Andre, 1762-1833, 7092
Latrobe, Benjamin Henry, 1764-1820, 16998
Latrobe, Charles Joseph, 1801-1875, 4225, 7249
Latrobe, John Hazlehurst Boneval, 1803-1891, 16998, 23592, 24772, 24773
Latta, Robert Ray, 1836-, 16999
A latter day saint, 11132
Latter-day Saints in Utah, 17483
The Latter-Day Saints' emigrants' guide, 3027
Lau, Persy, illustr., 20073
Lauber, Almon Wheeler, 1880-, 4589, 24774
Lauca River, Bolivia, 19125, 20156
Laudonnière, René Goulaine de, 4226
Laugel, Auguste, 1830-1914, 24775
Laughin' in meetin', 10909
Laughs I have taken a pen to, 11177
Launay, Louis de, 1860-1938, 7494
Laura Lovel, 10197
Laura Seymour, 10207
Laurens, Edward R., 24776
Laurens, Henry, 1724-1792, 7250, 13194, 13374, 24777
Laurentius, Saint, Archdeacon of Rome, d. 258, Drama, 18644
Laval, Antoine François, 1664-1728, 4227
Lavallé, Joseph, marquis de Bois-Robert, 1747-1816, 24778, 24779
Lavanha, João Baptista, 1555-1624, 882
Laverdière, Charles Honoré, 1826-1873, 6396
La Verendrye, Pierre Gautier de Varennes, sieur de, 1685-1749, 17000
Laverrenz, Viktor, 1862-, 4228
Lavradio, Marquês do, 18177
Law, John, 1671-1729, 3552; Fiction, 118
Law, John, 1796-1873, 4229, 17001
Law, William, 1686-1761, 1157

Law, Addresses, essays, lectures, 56, 12342, 13676; Anecdotes, facetiae, satire, etc., 707, 5222, 16413; Argentine Republic, 20462; Babylonia, 24248; Bibliography, 14662; Brazil, 17964, 18206; Canada, 11882; Chile, 18898, 20137, 20139; Collected works, 8069, 8072; Colombia, 18870, 19656; Confederate States of America, 2054, 2055; Dictionaries, 11425; Dictionaries, Spanish, 20636; District of Colombia, 1686, 22428; Gt. Britain, History & criticism, 1181; Guatemala, 20410; History & criticism, 11253; Jamaica, 13406; Kentucky, 14671, 14808; Kentucky, Indexes, 24715; Latin America, Congresses, 20399; Maryland, Digests, 22428; Oregon, 4690; Pennsylvania, History & criticisms, 22786; Period., 13338; Peru, Dictionaries, 22228; Philosophy, 18057, 18567, 19691; Research, 20001; Spain, 231; Spain, Collected works, 8072; Spain, Colonies, America, 5972; Spanish America, 231, 7894; Study and teaching, Latin America, Congresses, 20399; Texas, Digests, 22317; U.S., 14671; U.S., History & criticisms, 22453; Uruguay, 20635; Venezuela, 20075
Law, Anglo-Saxon, 24671; Comparative, 952; Germanic, 24671
Law academy of Philadelphia, 22786
Law and medicine, Report of seminar, 14676
The Law and order league, 14074
The law and the testimony concerning slavery, 24780
Law as a profession, 17074
Law Lane, 10037
The law of flats, 11436
The law of God and the statutes of men, 25200
The law of slavery in the United States, 24057
The law, our school-master, 1096
Law reform, 554, 12065
Law reports, digests, etc., Gt. Brit., 12234; Illinois, 22635; Iowa, 16861; Mexico, 1078; U.S., 12234
Lawford hall, 11101
Lawrence, Amos, 1786-1852, 12359, 12893
Lawrence, Amos Adams, 1814-1886, 13149
Lawrence, Catherine S., 24781
Lawrence, Charles, 7602, 7603
Lawrence, George Alfred, 1827-1876, 4230
Lawrence, George Newbold, 1806-1895, 675
Lawrence, Mrs. M.V.T., 16206
Lawrence, Matilda (Slave), 24114
Lawrence, Raymond E., 14791
Lawrence, Sidney, 24782
Lawrence, William, 1819-1899, 24783

Lawrence, William Beach, 1800-1881, 24784
Lawrence County, Ky., Fiction, 15114
Lawrence family, 2452
Lawrence family (John Lawrence, d.1667), 2452
Lawrence, Ia., 16375
Lawrenceburg, Ky., History, 13686
The Lawrences, 11026
The laws of commerce and navigation, 385
The laws of race, as connected with slavery, 24394
Laws of the Cherokee nation, 16187
Laws of the United States, 24785
Laws relating to slavery, A sketch of, 25634
Laws relative to slaves and slave-trade, 25130
Lawson, Albert, 14792
Lawson, Dodate, fl.1693-1698, 22754
Lawson, John, d.1712, 4231, 11515
Lawson, Norman W., 14793
Lawyers, 554, 14078, 14680, 16413, 17607
Lawyers, Biography, 14756, 17074; Brazil, 19345; Brazil, Fees, 19345; Chicago, 6415; Cumberland Co., Me., 12890; Fiction, 5379, 13720; Georgia, 13434; Illinois, 5935, 6415, 17035; Maine, 12890; Massachusetts, 22534; Montgomery County, Ky., 15102; Philadelphia, 1312, 11271, 11556; Tennessee, Direct., 4527; Texas, 17921; U.S., 17091
Lay, Benjamin, 1677-1759, 24786
The lay of gratitude, 2843
Laycock, Craven, 1866-1940, 9734
A layman, 13210
A layman of the Protestant Episcopal church of the Diocese of Connecticut, 25163
Layres, Augustus, 24787
Lays of ancient Virginia, 924
El lazarillo de ciegos caminantes desde Buenos Aires hasta Lima, 19852
Lazell, Frederick John, 17002
The laziest girl in Virginia, 11191
The lazy crow, 10783
Lea, Albert Miller, 1807-1890, 17003, 22755
Lea, Henry Charles, 1825-1909, 24788
Leach, A. J., 17004, 17005
Leach, DeWitt Clinton, 1822-, 24789
Leach, Frank Aleamon, 1846-, 17006
Leach, Josiah Granville, 1842-1922, 7251
Leacock, John, 926
Lead, 11170, 15285; Kentucky, 15005
Lead mines and mining, Missouri, 564, 5100

The leaders of the old bar of Philadelphia, 1312, 11271
Leadership, 19809
League of Kentucky sportsmen, 14557
League of nations, 24514, 24515, 25832; 7th Assembly, 1926, 24791; 8th assembly, 1927, 24792; 9th Assembly, 1928, 24793; 10th Assembly, 1929, 24794; 11th Assembly, 1930, 24795; 12th Assembly, 1931, 24796; 13th Assembly, 1932, 24797; 14th Assembly, 1933, 24798; 15th Assembly, 1934, 24799; 16th Assembly, 1935-1936, 24800; Assembly. Sixth Committee, 24790-24800; Council, 24567
League of the Miami, 2679, 8787
League of Women Voters, Lexington, Ky., 14794
The leaguer of Boston, 9136, 9137
Leah and Rachel, 12627
Leake, Isaac Q., 22756
Leaming, Jeremiah, 1717-1804. A defence of the episcopal government of the church, 23775
Leander, 11017
Leander of Betsy's pride, 9762
A Leander of the East River, 9363
Leandro, 10173
Lear, Tobias, 1762-1816, 4232
Learned, Joseph D., 24801
Learned, William Law, 1821-1904, 13367
Learning and scholarship, 11920
Learning by discovery, 19033
Leases, Brazil, 18126, 19363
Leavell, William Hayne, 1850-, 24478
Leaven for doughfaces, 24919
Leavenworth, Kan., 16094; Board of trade, 16094
Leavenworth, Lawrence and Galveston railroad company, 12971
Leaves, Amazon region, 18111, 18112
Leaves of holly, 15070
Leavitt, Joshua, 1794-1873, 959, 13186
Lebanon, Conn., 22617
Lebanon, Ky., Biography, 14957; History, 14957
Lebanon, N.Y., 23414
Lebas, P.L., 5895
LeBeau, C., 7252
Lebensbilder aus den Vereinigten Staaten von Nordamerika und Texas 5773
LeBlond, Francis Celeste, 1821-1902, 23802
Leboeuf, J. Arthur, 1878-, 8153
Lebovici, S., 19524
Lebrija, Antonio de, 16th cent., 8168
Lecciones de ortodoxía, 19196
Lechevalier, Jules, 1800-1850, 24803
Lechford, Thomas, 1590?-1644?, 13375
Leclerc, Charles Victor Emmanuel, 1772-1802, 3237

Leclerc, Frédéric, 1810-1891, 4233
Leclerc, Max, 1864-, 4234
Leclercq, Chrétien, fl.1641-1695, 7253, 22757
Leclercq, Jules Joseph, 1848-1928, 4235, 7254, 7255
Leclère, Adhémard, 1853-1917, 24804
Lecompton Constitution, 24064
Lecompton Resolution, 24228, 24307
Lecomte, Ferdinand, 1826-1899, 24805, 24806
Lecotabanus Lutz, 20543
Lecouvreur, Frank, 1829-1901, 17007
Lecouvreur, Mrs. Josephine Rosana (Smith), 17007
Lecuna, Vicente, 6110
The Leddy Macmeeken, 13517
Lederer, John, 4236
Ledyard, Addie, illustr., 10392
Ledyard, Edgar M., 17008
Ledyard, Erwin, 9383, 24275
Lee, 24807
Lee, Ann, 1736-1784, 3009, 12094
Lee, Annie Carter, 1839-1862, 3930
Lee, Arthur, 1740-1792, 13376-13378, 22758, 24808
Lee-Boo, d.1784, 12803
Lee, Charles, 3426
Lee, Charles, 1731-1782, 11239, 12277, 13379
Lee, Charles Carter, 1798-1871, 13381
Lee, Charles Henry, 1818-1900, 24809
Lee, Daniel, 1806-1895, 4237
Lee, Mrs. Eleanor Percy, 5615
Lee, F.D., 24810
Lee, Fitzhugh, 1835-1905, 2034
Lee, George, 1778-1802, 13760
Lee, Mrs. Hannah Farnham (Sawyer) 1780-1865, 51
Lee, Henry, 1756-1818, 4238, 4239, 13291, 13380, 13381, 21970
Lee, Henry, 1787-1837, 13380, 13381
Lee, Jason, 1803-1845, 15878, 16766
Lee, John Doyle, 1812-1877, 17009-17011
Lee, L.P., 17012
Lee, Lucy C., 14795
Lee, Nelson, 1807-, 4240
Lee, Richard Henry, 1732-1794, 4241, 13382
Lee, Richard Henry, 1794-1865, 4241
Lee, Robert Edward, 1807-1870, 2034-2036, 4815, 6113, 6744, 7989, 22778; Poetry, 5868
Lee, Mrs. S.M., 7256
Lee, Samuel, d.1807, 998
Lee, William, 22076
Lee, William, 1740-1784, 12094

Lee, William Henry Fitzhugh, 1837-1891, 2034
Lee family (Thomas Lee d.1641), 22485
Lee and his lieutenants, 4815
Lee Co., Ky., 15382
Lee Co., Tex., Biography, 16780
The Lee trial, 17009
Lee's last campaign, with an accurate history of Stonewall Jackson's last wound, 22256
Leech, Arthur Blennerhassett, 4242
Leech, Robert, 7257
The Leech club, 10458
Leeds, Eli R., 24811
Leeds, Samuel Penniman, 1824-1910, 7258
Leeds anti-slavery series, 23915
Leefe, Captain J. G. Buttons, 10115
Leeper, David Rohrer, 17013
Lees, James Arthur, illustr., 7259
Leeson, Michael A., 17014
Leeward islands, Description & travel, 6919; History, 12172, 22209
LéFebure, Roger, 6103
Lefevre, Arthur, 17015
Lefevre, Edwin, 1871-, 8969
Leffingwell, Alfred, 1845-, 24812
Leffingwell, Samuel L., 7260
The left hind foot, 25023
Left out on Lone Star mountain, 9788
Left to herself, 10858
Legal ethics, 11307, 14680; Brazil, 19345
The legal rights, liabilities and duties of women, 23102
Leganés, Diego Felipe de Guzmán, marqués de, 7519
Legard, Allayne Beaumont, 1847-, 17016
Legare, Hugh Swinton, 1797-1843, 4243, 4856
Legare, James Matthews, 1823-1859, 4244
The legend of Black Creek, 3037
A legend of Charlemagne, 10919
The legend of Goodman Poverty, 10298
A legend of Kent, 10172
A legend of "Norwood", 11949
Legend of Oxford, 10762
A legend of Pennsylvania, 10760
The legend of Saint Nicholas, 10480
The legend of Sleepy Hollow, 9995
A legend of the Cape de Verdes, 10338
The legend of the silver band, 15071
A legend of Virginia, 11187
The legendary, 11179
Legends, 10291; Argentine Republic, Neuquen (Province), 19828; England, 9845; France, 9845; Great lakes, 9619; Kentucky, 14178; New England, 10854; Mississippi Valley, 16812; Missouri Valley, 16812; Nova Scotia, 8045; Scotland, 9845
Legends of a log cabin, 9618

Legends of Ireland, 10920
Legends of Mexico, 10213
Legends of New England, 11155
Legends of New York, 8889
Legends of the Ohio Valley, 14923
Legends of the Pine-tree state, 9977
Legends of the sea, 1859
Legends of the West, 3744, 9708
Léger, Jacques Nicolas, 1859-, 7261
Leggett, William, 1802-1839, 21821
Legion, pseud., 24813
The legion of liberty, 15859, 17017
The legionaries, 13932
Legislação sobre os indios do Brasil,
    18551
La legislación antimalárica venezolana,
    20637
Legislación comparada de banca central,
    18623
La legislación pesquera en el Perú,
    18948
Legislation, Brazil, 19268, 19329-19331,
    19353, 19354; Kentucky, 14580, 14604,
    14606, 14608, 15033
Legislative and congressional
    redistricting in Kentucky, 14692
The legislature authority of the British
    Parliament, with respect to North
    America, 23363
Legislative bodies, Brazil, Privileges
    and immunities, 18135; Kentucky, 14606,
    15733; U.S., 22703
A legislative investigation into masonry,
    12587
The legislative process in Kentucky,
    14622
Legislatures, Districting, 14692
LeGobien, Charles, 1653-1708, 2466
Legoyt, Alfred, 1815-1885, 24814
Legrand, John Carroll, 1814-1861, 24815
Legumes, Venezuela, 19771
LeHeureux, Mike, 13862
Lehigh coal and navigation company, 8376
Leib, Charles, 4245
Leidy, Joseph, 1823-1891, 3817, 4246, 4664
Leigh, Benjamin Watkins, 1781-1849, 22867,
    24816
Leigh, Edwin, 24817
Leigh, Sir Egerton, bart., 1733-1788?,
    13383
Leigh, Mrs. Frances (Butler) 1838-1910,
    4247
Leighly, John Barger, 1895-, 15327
Leighton, Rufus, jr., 25200
The Leighton homestead, 3912, 9095
Leisha, J.J., 17018

Leishmaniose canina, 18139
Leiste, Christian, 4248
Leisure moments of an artist, 11485
Leite, Dirceu Cezar, 18844
Leite, Serafim,1890-, 19986
Leiter, Benjamin Franklin, 1813-1866, 24818
Leiva, Colombia, Church history, 18522
Lejeune, Louis, 7262
Leland, Alonzo, 4249, 2450
Leland, Anthony, 8969
Leland, Charles Godfrey, 1824-1903, 17019,
    24819
Leland, Henry Perry, 1828-1868, 24819
Leland, John, 1754-1841, 24820
LeMaire, Jacob, 1585-1616, 22759
LeMaire Strait, 22759
LeMaster, J.R., 14796
Lemen, James, 1760-1823, 24950
Lemer, Jean Baptiste Julien, 1116, 1117
Lemmon, George T., 7263
Lemmon, Jonathan, 25129
Lemmon slave case, 25129
LeMoyne, Auguste, b.1800, 7264
LeMoyne, Francis Julius, 1798-1879, 25234
LeMoyne d'Iberville, Pierre, 1661-1706, 1239
LeMoyne family, 1239
Lemprière, Charles, 1818-1901, 7265
Leng, Sir John, 1828-1906, 4251
Leng, Sir William Christopher, 24821
Lenglet du Fresnoy, Nicolas, 1674-1755, 7266
Lengua y estilo en Sarmiento, 19797
Leni-Leoti, 2680
Lenk, Frau Margarete (Klee) 1841-1917, 4252
Lennox, Mary, pseud., 9103
Lenox, Edward Henry, 1827-, 17020
Lenroot, Katharine Frederica, 1891-, 14797
Lente, Frederick Divoux, 1823-1883, 4253
Leon, Louis, 4254
León, Nicolas, 1859-1929, 7932
Leonard, Albert Charles, 1845-, 4255
Leonard, B.G., 7247
Leonard, Charles C., 22760
Leonard, H.L.W., 4256
Leonard, James Francis, 1834-1862, 15579
Leonard, Zenas, 4257
Leonard family (James Leonard, fl.1650), 22064
Leonardo y Argensola, Bartolomé Juan, 1562-
    1631, 2467, 2468
Leonardos, Stella, Auto de lapinha, 18977
Leoni di Monota, 3931
Leonora of the Yawmish, 9321
The leopard's spots; a romance of the white
    man's burden, 1865-1900, 24298
Lepage, Ennio Silva, 18605
LeFuge du Pluts; Antoine Olmon; J.1776; 1050
Lepidoptera, Cuba, 10652; Georgia, 6202

LePetit, Mathurin, 1693-1729, 16956
LeRaye, Charles, 3147
Lerner, Ira T., 7267
Le Rossignol, James Edward, 1866-, 17021
Leroux, Antoine, 4259
Leroy, 6930
LeRoy, Billy, 16320
Leroy, Julien, 1686-1759, 6401
Leroy-Beaulieu, Paul, 1843-1916, 7494
Leroy-Beaulieu, Pierre, 1871-1915, 4260
Le-Roy y Cassá, Jorge, 1867-1934, 19975
Les Williams, 14800
Lescarbot, Marc, 7268
Lesley, Joseph, 15109
Leslie, Charles, 1650-1722, A short and
    easy method with the deists, 1723, 21893
Leslie, Miriam Florence (Folline) Squier,
    "Mrs. Frank Leslie," d.1914, tr., 7534,
    17022
Leslie Wilmot, 10549
Leslie's retreat, 1775, 22186
Lesquereux, Léo, 1806-1889, 4261, 15108,
    15109
The lesson of the hour, 1854, 8427
The lesson of the master, 7122
Lessons from the war, 13063
Lessons in life, for all who will read
    them, 8570
Lester, Charles Edwards, 1815-1890, 11570,
    17024, 24822, 24823
Lester, John C., 24824
Lester, John Erastus, 17025
Lester, William Stewart, 14798, 14799
Let every man mind his own business, 10904
Let those laugh who win, 10899
Let's talk of Lincoln, 7382
Letcher, John, 1813-1884, 24825
Letcher County, Kentucky, Census, 14226
Lettsom, John Coakley, 1744-1815, 11681
Letourneau, Charles Jean Marie, 1831-1902,
    24826
Leuba, Edmond, 17026
Levant, Description & travel, 344, 8880,
    9027, 22871
Levanto, Leonardo, fl.1741-1776, 7271
Levasnier, Francis E., 24838
Levasseur, Auguste, 4265
Levasseur, Émile, 1828-1911, 7494
Levees, 22438
Levelei Ejszakamerikából, 5783
Leventhal, Ronald S., 14668
Levenworth, 10435
Levering family (Gerhard Levering, fl.
    1685), 13300
Levering family (Wigard Levering, 1648?-
    1745?), 13300

Levett, Christopher, 1586?-1631?, 6030
Levinge, Sir Richard George Augustus, 7th
    bart., 1811-1884, 4266, 7272
Levisa River, Maps, 15626
Lévy, Daniel, 17027
Levy, Kurt L., 19830
The lewd versus the prude, 15532
Lewis, Alfred Henry, 1857-1914, 17028
Lewis, Annie R., 14802
Lewis, Colien Crosby, 14803
Lewis, Sir Charles Edward, 1825-1893, 4267
Lewis, Dio, 1823-1886, 6654, 17029
Lewis, Ella, 14522
Lewis, Enoch, 1776-1856, Review of the causes
    and course of the division in the Yearly
    meeting of Ohio, 2285
Lewis, Evan, 24839-24840
Lewis, George, of Ormiston, 4268
Lewis, Mrs. Helen Cecelia (Clarke), 6654
Lewis, Henry, 1819-1904, 4269
Lewis, Isaac, 1746-1840, 13384
Lewis, John Delaware, 1828-1884, 4270
Lewis, John Henry, 1834-, 4271
Lewis, Matthew Gregory, 1775-1818, 24841
Lewis, Meriwether, 1774-1809, 4272, 5457,
    13385, 17030
Lewis, Oscar, 5995
Lewis, Ralph A., 14804
Lewis, Richard, 5264
Lewis, Robert Benjamin, 24842
Lewis, Tayler, 1802-1877, 110, 24843
Lewis, Thomas P., 14688
Lewis, Tracy Hammond, 17031
Lewis, William, 1745?-1819, 1312, 11271
Lewis, William Stanley, 1876-, 17032
Lewis family, 15640, 23493
Lewis and Clark centennial exposition,
    Portland, Oregon, 1905, 17455
Lewis and Clark expedition, 1670, 3017, 3578,
    4272, 5457, 5529, 5530, 8288, 16529, 16640,
    16997, 17030, 22233
Lewis Co., N.Y., History, 12927
The Lewis publishing company, Chicago, 14989,
    16697, 16849, 17329, 17330, 17931
Lex mercatoria americana, 1793
Lexicon de colombianismos, 18083
The Lexington, 11010
Lexington, Battle of, 1775, 11817, 13418,
    22000
Lexington, Ky., 14080, 14215, 15783; Bar,
    14379; Bibliography, 15159; Biography,
    13698, 13987, 14074; Cemetery, 14179, 14251,
    15009; Central Christian Church. Ladies'
    Aid Society, 14805; Christ Church Cathedral,
    15346; Churches, 13934; Citizens, 14806;
    College of the Bible, 15176; Description,

3424, 13528, 13584, 14030, 14118, 14876, 14966, 15338, 15643; Description, Guide-Books, 13910, 14229; Diocese (of Protestant Episcopal Church in the U.S.A.), 15203; Directories, 14487, 15775; Episcopal Cemetery, 14179; Epworth Methodist Church, 15260; Fiction, 14437; First Methodist Church, 14802; First National Bank and Trust Company, 15347; First Presbyterian Church, 14807; Historic houses, etc., 13902; History, 2258, 3488, 3884, 6457, 6459, 13698, 13788, 13833, 13879, 13881, 13885, 13915, 14025, 14170, 14352, 14410, 14493, 14782, 14809, 14812, 14818, 14848, 14971, 15185, 15202, 15241, 15320, 15410, 15435, 15607, 15754; History, Bibliography, 15116; History, religious, 15560; Laws, statutes, etc., 14808; Lexington-Fayette County Recreation, Tourist and Convention Commission, 14809; Maps, 14267, 14281, 14815, 14952-14956, 15019; Post office, 15658; Public Library, 14810; Riots, 13876; St. Joseph Hospital, 14811; Sesqui-centennial jubilee celebration, 14812; Social conditions, 14794; Social life and customs, 15532, 15597; Woodland Christian Church. Ladies' Aid Society, 14813
Lexington, Mass., Geneal., 22589; History, 22589
Lexington, Mo. Pro-slavery Convention, 1855, 24844
Lexington, S.C., 17579
Lexington (Steamboat), 2352
Lexington and Concord, Battle of, 1775, poetry, 21790
Lexington and Eastern Railway, 14814
Lexington and Ohio railroad, 14782
Lexington and Vicinity Bible Society, 15660
Lexington Chamber of Commerce, 14815
Lexington hydraulic & manufacturing company, Lexington, Kentucky, 14025
Lexington in a nutshell, 14816
Lexington Junior League, 14817
Lexington legacies, 14848
Lexington 1969: Land of horses, tobacco, livestock, college, culture, industry, 14818
Lexington Orphan Society, 15653
Lexington Roller Mills Co., Lexington, Ky., 14819
Lexington Theological Seminary, 14393, 15036, 15440, 15556
Lexington water company, 14025

Lexington trots, 14820
Lexington's slave dealers and their southern trade, 24162
Lexipep cook book, 14819
Leyden. English Dissenters' church, 13026
Leyenda de los ríos Limay y Neuquén, 19828
Leyendas americanas, por Don José Güell y Renté, 12481
Leyendas de las calles de México, 19968
Leyendas históricas nacionales, 19968
Leyva, Antonio de, 7273
Lezay-Marnézia, Claude François Adrien, marquis de, 1735-1800, 4273
Lezes do planalto, 18237
L'Héritier, Louis Francois, 1789-1852, 17033
L'Honoré Naber, Samuel Pierre, 1865-, 7274
The liar, 7123
Libby, Andersonville, Florence, 3799
Libby life, 1845
Libby prison, 1845, 2761, 3417, 4077, 4335, 4867, 4970, 11706
Libel and slander, 23311, 23827; Mexico, 18591
Liber scriptorum, 8612
El Liberal, 7275
Liberalism (Religion), 18378; Brazil, 18867
The Liberator, 23908
Liberator-extra! 24845
Liberia, 2457, 11783, 23960, 24127, 24218, 24544, 24703, 24846, 24913, 25192, 25669; Emigration & immigration, 24773; History, 503, 12147, 12508, 23858, 24008
Liberia, as I found it, in 1858, 24218
Liberia unmasked, 24846
La libertad de cultos, 19780
La libertad religiosa, 19197
Libertad, tierra y amor, 20517
El Libertador enfermo, 18930
Libertas, pseud., 6669, 11570
La liberté aux États-Unis, 1862
Libertomania, 24847
Liberty, 325, 1862, 13038, 13090, 18338, 22439, 22622, 24641
The liberty almanac, 24848-24851
The Liberty and Free Soil Parties in the Northwest, 25543
Liberty and law, 22016
The liberty and property of British subjects asserted, 24852
Liberty and union! Speeches delivered at the Eighteenth ward Republican festival, 25127
The liberty bell, 24853
The liberty cap, 2261
Liberty chimes, 24854
Liberty defended. Fourth of July, 24280
Liberty Hall, 14907
The Liberty Hall cook book, 14821

Liberty Hall, Inc., Louisville, Ky., 7276
Liberty Jones' discovery, 6972
Liberty leaguer, 24855
Liberty of conscience, 12420, 21988, 23790
Liberty of speech, 11335
Liberty of the press, 226, 11335, 12756, 22203, 23122, 23698, 23827; U.S., 11987; Venezuela, 19753
Liberty or slavery, 24856, 25171
Liberty overthrown? 10055
Liberty Party, 25543; Pennsylvania, 24151
The liberty pole, 9977
Liberty, property, and no excise, 22762
Liberty saved, 14822
Liberty Tree, 22762
Liberty's ordeal, 1358
Libra, 8529
The librarian's manual, 12491
Librarians, Directories, 18597
Libraries, 12491; America, 2790; Argentine Republic, 18595, 19535, 20359; Assistants, 18005; Brazil, 19306, 19307, 19865; Colombia, 19106, 20267, 20270; Cuba, 20691; History, 8186; Kentucky, 8186, 14625, 15066, 15276; Kentucky, History, 15276; Latin America, Bibliography, 18990; Mexico, Nuevo León, 16579; Reference service, Argentine Republic, 19535; Resources, 19514; Rhode Island, 19515; U.S., 8186, 13221
Libraries, College and University, 14697, 14698, 15590; Kentucky, 15138; Special, 19307; University, 18837; University, Argentine Republic, 19535; University, Brazil, 19224; University, Colombia, 19637
Library administration, 18005
Library Association of Kentucky, 14286
Library catalogs, Lexington, Ky., 14810; Maine, 23040
Library cooperation, 19307
Library education, Argentine Republic, 18400, 19542; Audio-visual aids, 18292
Library guides, 14697, 14698, 19637
Library rules and regulations, 12470
Library science, 18701, 19056; Bibliography, Catalogs, 19540; Periodicals, Bibliography, Catalogs, 19541
Library service, 18005
Libre albedrío, 19990
Libro de Manuel, 20530
El libro de mis recuerdos, 6819
Libro de oro de la Fuerza Aérea Argentina, 18452
El libro de un chacarero, 20517

El libro rojo del Putumayo, 8193
El libro en España e Hispanoamérica, 18839
Licensed professions, Atlas of Kentucky, 14221
Licht- und schattenbilder republikanischer zustände, 4315
Licking Valley, Kentucky, Description, 13936; Maps, 14594
Liderança de reuniões, 18832
Lidia, 4452
Lieber, Francis, 1800-1872, 24857-24859
Liebknecht, Wilhelm, 1816-1900, 4274
Liebman, Lance M., 15802
Lienhard, Heinrich, 17034
A lieutenant of cavalry in Lee's army, 2654
Lievre, Daniel, La isla del Coco, 8303
Life, a poem in three books, 1430
Life insurance in estate planning, 14669
Liffith Lank, 11113
Liffy Leman, 3034
Lifting the veil, 10294
Ligan, 9431
Ligeret de Chazey, Madame Elénore, 4276
Liggins, Joseph, 24860
Liggon's tobacco warehouse prison, Richmond, 3378, 3793, 4455
Light, 10369
Light, Bianca, 4277
Light, more light, 10091
Light and truth, 24842
The light and truth of slavery, 24861
The light appearing more and more towards the perfect day, 23790
The light dragoon, 10069
The light-keeper, 9977
A light man, 10283
The light of home, 9339
The light of the reef, 4004
Light rising out of obscurity, 23227
A light sovereign, 9741
Lightcap, William Henry, 4278
Lighthall, William Douw, 1857-, 7278
Lighthouses, Brazil, 19295
The lightningrod man, 10346
Lights and lines of Indian character, 11822
Lights and shadows of a life, 9310
Lights and shadows of American life, 3058, 4492
Lights and shadows of domestic life, 10207
The lights and shadows of free masonry, 4530
Lights and shadows of sailor life, 11820
Lights and shadows of southern life, 10495
Lignereux, Saint-André de, 4279
Like a gallant lady, 9019
Lilian, 9662
Lilius, A., 5872, 5873
Lillie, Gordon W., 1860-, 16385

Lily, 8828
The lily and the totem, 5162
Lima, Raul, 18177
Lima, 7050, 7411, 19653; (Archdiocese),
  6828; Universidad de San Marcos,
  19557
Limestone, 14115; Kentucky, 14552
Limitação responsável dos nascimentos,
  19706
Limitation of actions, 19854; Mexico,
  19854
Límite de clase, 18508
The limits of responsibility in reforms,
  25645
Lin, 10420
Linares (Province), Chile, 20163
Linck, F.W.G., 24862
Lincoln, A.W.B., illustr., 9533
Lincoln, Abraham, pres. U.S., 1809-1865,
  465, 470, 627, 872, 873, 874, 1462,
  1545, 3907, 5815, 5816, 5820, 5821,
  5824, 5826, 5833, 5912, 5959, 5960,
  5975, 5982, 6004, 6020, 6075, 6089,
  6092, 6112, 6115, 6191, 6197, 6243,
  6251, 6288, 6327, 6337, 6338, 6343,
  6394, 6411, 6417, 6419, 6439, 6485,
  6486, 6530, 6539, 6560, 6565, 6597,
  6652, 6656, 6660, 6663, 6665, 6676,
  6738, 6779, 6830, 6831, 6848, 6852,
  6878, 6952, 6962, 6982, 6985, 7002,
  7022, 7023, 7025, 7026, 7039, 7044,
  7048, 7067, 7071, 7175, 7239, 7263,
  7279, 7280, 7281, 7282, 7283, 7284-
  7291, 7297, 7298, 7356, 7357, 7366,
  7382, 7402, 7410, 7447, 7450, 7509,
  7565, 7587, 7634, 7660, 7691, 7703,
  7720, 7743, 7746, 7771, 7829, 7839,
  7861, 7889, 7925, 7926, 7927, 7947,
  7980, 7986, 7987, 7991, 8234, 8304,
  8329, 8349, 8352, 8374, 8375, 8381,
  12365, 13869, 14309, 14313, 14315,
  14703, 14770, 14827, 15072, 15506,
  15508, 15562, 15605, 15662, 15671,
  15685, 16724, 16745, 18968, 22528,
  22764, 22766, 23111, 23419, 23554,
  24041, 24249, 24626, 24863-24866,
  26010, 25155, 25307, 25464, 25752,
  25887; Addresses, sermons, etc.,
  168, 544, 604, 690, 699, 736, 742,
  849, 865, 1301, 1316, 1321, 1372,
  1518, 1581, 1674, 1698, 1743, 1854,
  1962, 2184, 5640, 5814, 5832, 5838,
  5850, 5866, 5902, 5905, 5911, 5922,
  5933, 5934, 5944, 5945, 5946, 5960,
  5976, 5995, 6009, 6014, 6015, 6021
  6024, 6047, 6060, 6138, 6184, 6193,

  6245, 6281, 6336, 6341, 6345, 6346, 6391,
  6412, 6420, 6424, 6425, 6465, 6488, 6489,
  6516, 6521, 6528, 6534, 6537, 6543, 6553,
  6564, 6573, 6618, 6625, 6628, 6631, 6659,
  6859, 6871, 6918, 6933, 6935, 6987, 6988,
  6991, 7036, 7037, 7059, 7074, 7107, 7147,
  7160, 7161, 7164, 7178, 7211, 7258, 7295,
  7296, 7307, 7332, 7333, 7352, 7375, 7383,
  7390, 7448, 7503, 7538, 7561, 7563, 7571,
  7582, 7585, 7615, 7662, 7690, 7699, 7700,
  7702, 7713, 7714, 7742, 7744, 7765, 7783,
  7787, 7788, 7805, 7817, 7884, 7890, 7968,
  8031, 8082, 8090, 8093, 8117, 8118, 8125,
  8130, 8135, 8137, 8154, 8184, 8194, 8245,
  8247, 8257, 8432, 11301, 11302, 11375,
  11544, 11650, 12317, 12561, 12622, 12662,
  13065, 13114, 13212, 13239, 13270, 13271,
  21858, 22217, 22229, 22339, 22345, 22365,
  22442, 22507, 22515, 22585, 22725, 22795,
  22808, 22844, 22859, 23171, 23988, 24491,
  25836; Anecdotes, 6025, 6114, 6343, 6439,
  7142, 7336, 7632, 7745, 8348; Anniversaries,
  etc., 5817, 5842, 5843, 5844, 6877, 7329,
  7504, 7505, 7689; Assassination, 508, 1305,
  6009, 6026, 6116, 6240, 6418, 6554, 6580,
  6619, 6658, 6667, 6701, 6705, 7163, 7226,
  7553, 7749, 8132, 8218, 8235, 8262, 8313,
  8354, 8357, 13253, 22282, 23475; Bibliography,
  7330, 8369; Birthplace, 6034, 6035, 6100,
  7055, 8345, 8351; Books and reading, 7066,
  7070; Cartoons, satire, etc., 6201, 8334,
  8866, 8867; Childhood, 6662; Drama, 5220,
  5865, 5931, 5974, 5984, 8214, 13975, 15384;
  Family, 5901, 5953, 6022, 6023, 6442, 6447,
  6620, 6810, 6949, 7024, 7099, 7302, 7573;
  Fiction, 6960, 24299; Funeral and memorial
  services, 7621, 7723, 8385, 8429, 23119;
  Funeral journey to Springfield, 1982, 7051;
  Gettysburg address, 6763; Homes, 7642;
  Journey to Washington, Feb. 1861, 1982, 7676;
  Law practice, 5823, 5887, 5935, 6006, 6018,
  6019, 7614; Medals, 8435; Memorial services,
  5910, 5957, 6123, 6124, 6138, 7645, 8242;
  Monuments, etc., 5818, 5819, 5822, 5993,
  7073, 7301, 7564; Museums, relics, etc.,
  6033, 6034, 6035, 7038; Personality, 7027;
  Poetry, 1168, 1325, 3537, 5393, 5859, 5868,
  5940, 6080, 6083, 6142, 6210, 6340, 6902,
  6916, 7412, 7906, 8039, 8115, 8156, 8419,
  12638, 13050, 13153, 22364; Political career
  before 1861, 6391, 6706, 6707, 7068, 7586,
  7782; Portraits, 7470, 7471, 7633, 25610;
  Relations with Jews, 7409; Relations with
  physicians, 7408; Relics, 8348, Religion,
  5869, 5922, 6014, 6017, 6190, 6931, 7010,
  7029, 7069, 7113, 7445, 7446, 7661, 7721,

7773, 7919, 14314; Songs and music,
7292; Songs and music, Bibliography,
8347; Speech, June 16, 1858, 24160;
Tomb, 6879; Views on slavery, 7352,
8350, 23981, 24160, 25205, 25836; Views
on temperance, 5985, 6541, 7281, 8397
Lincoln, Jairus, 24867
Lincoln, Mary Todd, 1818-1882, 7024, 7300,
15446, 15507, 15508, 15586, 15607,
15662
Lincoln, Nancy (Hanks), 1782-1818, 6210,
6447, 13700
Lincoln, Solomon, 1804-1881, 7302
Lincoln, Solomon, 1828-1907, 5997
Lincoln and his neighbors, 6663
Lincoln and public morality, 6779
Lincoln and Texas, 16724
Lincoln and the convention of 1860, 7782
Lincoln and the mother of Lincoln, 15072
Lincoln as a politician, 7357
Lincoln cabin on Boston Common, 6020
Lincoln campaign songster, 7292
The Lincoln catechism, 7293
Lincoln day addresses, 7142
Lincoln-Douglas debates, 1858, 6021, 6346,
6738, 7026, 7036, 7175, 7390
The Lincoln-Douglas debates and their
application to the present problems,
25672
Lincoln, 1864, McKinley, 1900, 7294
Lincoln family, 6716, 7302
Lincoln Fellowship, Hamilton, Ontario,
7295
Lincoln Fellowship of Southern California,
6004
Lincoln Fellowship of Wisconsin, 7296,
7297
Lincoln Guard of Honor, 7298
Lincoln highway, 8352
Lincoln in Pennsylvania, 7002
Lincoln in Springfield, 5816
Lincoln in the light of his age, 7263
Lincoln in the winter of '60-'61, 7352
Lincoln Marriage Temple, Harrodsburg,
Ky., 13844
Lincoln Memorial, Washington, D.C., 5993,
7299
Lincoln Memorial University, 15458
The Lincoln monument in memory of Scottish-
American soldiers, 7301
Lincoln national life foundation, 8347
Lincoln Pioneer Village, Rockport, Ind.,
6664
Lincoln sheet music, 8347
The Lincoln statue at the University of
Wisconsin, 7296

Lincoln, the man of the people, 7412
Lincoln the poet, 7287
Lincoln Univeristy, Chester Co., Pa., 13269,
25798
Lincoln vs. liquor, 5985
Lincoln's companions on the trip to Antietam,
6560
Lincoln's grave, 5393
Lincoln's "House divided" speech, 24160
Lincoln's Italian volunteers from New York,
7415
Lincoln's legacy, 5940
Lincoln's legacy of inspiration, 7048
Lincoln's love story, 5960
Lincoln's marriage ceremony, 15506
Lincoln's Negro policy, 6486
Lincoln's religion, 14315
Lincoln's Springfield, 7771
The Lincolns in their old Kentucky homes, 6022
Lincoln, Neb., 15849
Lind, John, 1737-1781, 13387, 13388, 13389,
13390, 22767
Lind-Goldschmidt, Jenny Maria, 1820-1887, 5016,
9628
Linda, 3843
Lindau, Martin Bernhard, b.1818, 6893
Lindau, Paul, 1839-1919, 4280
Linden Hill, 9752
Linder, Usher F., 1809-1876, 17035
Linderman, Frank Bird, 1868-1938, 17036
Lindley, Harlow, 1875-, 24868
Lindley, Walter, 1852-, 17037
Lindsay, William, 15406
Lindsay, William Schaw, 1816-1877, 2421
Lindsey, Benjamin Barr, 17038
Lindsey, Maria, 13567
Lindsey, Theophilus, 1723-1808, 11252
Lines, Jorge A., 1891-, 8324
Lines on the death of the Conferate Gen.
Albert Sidney Johnston, 14828
Linforth, James, 4281, 17387
Lingan, James Maccubin, 1752?-1812, 22014
Lingua e verso, 21733
As linguas indigenas brasileiras, 19659
Linguistics, Research, 19659
Links in the golden chain of brotherhood,
13061
Links of friendship, 3096
Linn, John Joseph, 1798-, 4282
Linn, William, 1752-1808. Serious
considerations...1800, 1910
Linn, William Alexander, 1846-1917, 17039
Linn county, Oregon, History, 15841
El lino en su aspecto economico, 20545
Linstant Pradine, S., baron, d.1884, 24869,
24870

Linton, J.F., 7303
Linton, William James, 1812-1897, engr., 12742
The Linton family, 8838
Lintz, Frederick Gustav, 24871
The Linwoods, 10725
The lion and the unicorn, 9360
Lionel Lincoln, 9136, 9137
The lions of the Lord, 17906
Lippe, Joseph Alfred, 1865-, 7304
Lippincott, Horace Mather, 1877-, 12216
Lippincott, James Starr, 1819-1885, 17554
Lippincott, S.J., 10163
Lippincott, Mrs. Sara Jane (Clarke), 1823-1904, 16632
Liquidación histórica del Apra y del colonialismo neoliberal, 18065
Liquor laws, Maine, 1916; Massachusetts, 1275, 11828
Liquor problem, Gt. Britain, 11603; Maine, Fiction, 11044; Massachusetts, 1487, 9879, 11828; New York (City), 23161; U.S., 457
Liquor traffic, Taxation, 13655
Lira, Miguel N. La escondida, 19967
Lirio salvaje, 19625
Lisboa, Alfredo, 1847-1936, 19251
Lisle, Marcus Claiborne, 1862-1894, 15617
Lisle, Samuel, bp., 1683-1749, 13391
Litchfield, Conn., 12724
Litchfield, N.H., History, 2297
Literary and historical miscellanies, 741
Literary and historical society of Quebec, 11449
Literary and philosophical society of New York, 1908
Literary and philosophical society of South-Carolina, Charleston, 13265
A literary courtship under the auspices of Pike's Peak, 9587
Literary forgeries and mystifications, 400
Literary history, Bibliography, 14704
Literary landmarks, U.S., 22549
Literary landmarks of Kentucky, 13933, 14830
Literary life of James K. Paulding, 4721
Literary map of Kentucky, 15533
The literary remains of the late Willis Gaylord Clark, 9012
Literatura argentina, 19798
Literatura nacional y libertad expresiva, 18327
Literature, Collections, 9516; History and criticism, 5338, 18157, 19088,

20201, 20629, 20657, 22245; Comparative, Brazilian and English, 18172; Comparative, English and Brazilian, 18172; Modern, Addresses, essays, lectures, 7119, 19699, 21734; Modern, History and criticism, 4089, Modern, Translations from Portuguese, Bibliography, 19390
Literature on foot, 10862
Lithotomy, 13605
Litsey, Edwin Carlile, 1874-, 14831, 14832
Littell, John Stockton, 1806-1875, 12367, 13392
Littell, William, 1768-1824, 14833-14836, 15401, 24715
Litter, The impact of, 15056
Little, C.F., 10122
Little, Jacob A., 16676
Little, James Alexander, 1831-, 17041
Little, James Amasa, 1822-1908, 17042, 17043
Little, John, 5213
Little, Mrs. Laura Jane (Roys), 24872
Little, Lucius P., 24873
Little Anne's ramble, 9827
Little Bighorn, Battle of, 25 June 1876, 16118, 17272, 17709
The little blind god on rails, 9319
Little Briggs and I, 10250
Little brother, 10250
A little captive maid, 10041
Little Cuba, 8696
The little Dutch sentinel of the Manhadoes, 10480
Little Edward, 10904
A little fool, 10546
Little French Mary, 10038
The little Frenchman and his water lots, 10385
Little Gibraltar, 10394
A little journey to Mexico, 6839
A little journey to Mexico and Central America, 6840
A little journey to the home of Ephraim McDowell, 15041
The little maid at the door, 9578
Little Missouri River, 16573
Little Muddy quadrangle, Kentucky, 13941
A little Norsk, 9605
Little old sod shanty, 13581
A little pilgrimage, 9216
Little pills, 17102
The Little Regiment, 9211
Little Rock, Ark., 15893
Little Rock and Fort Smith Railroad, 8261
Little Rosebud's lovers, 10203
Little sheaves, 16199
The little shepherd of Kingdom Come, 9887
Little Tommy Tucker, 11075

Little tours among history shrines in and about Lexington, 13910
A little traveler, 10040
The little violinist, 8499
Littlejohn, E.G., 17044
Littlepage, Lewis, 1762-1802, 13175
The Littlepage manuscripts, 9129, 9149
Littleton, Edward, b.1626. The groans of the plantations, 22121
Littleton, Mass., History, 2283
Littoral right, Chile, 20138
Liudprandus, bp. of Cremona, d.ca.972, 400
Live or let live, 10726
A live woman in the mines, 16356
The livelies, 10088
Liver, 18879
Livermore, Mrs. Elizabeth D., 4283
Livermore, George, 1809-1865, 12539, 24874, 24875
Livermore, Mrs. Mary Ashton (Rice) 1820-1905, 4284, 14837
Livermore, Thomas Leonard, 1844-1918, 4285
Livermore, Ky., Economic conditions, 14541
Liverpool, Robert Banks Jenkinson, 2d earl of, 1770-1828, 6246, 6247, 22768, 22769
Liverpool. Public Libraries, Museums, and Art gallery, 6438
Liverpool Society for Promoting the Abolition of Slavery, 24876
Livestock, Colombia, 18260; Rio Grande do Sul, Brazil, Statistics, 19470
Livestock expositions, 14740
Living Christianity delineated, 1621
The living female writers of the South, 5346
Living for those we love, 11121
Living in Kentucky, 15720
Living in the country, 9198
Living Kentucky composers, 14658
Living too fast, 8474
The living writers of the South, 3183
Livingston, Edward, 1764-1836, 13393, 22607
Livingston, John Henry, 1746-1825, 12503
Livingston, Phillip, 1716-1778, 13394
Livingston, William, 1723-1790, A letter to...John, lord bishop of Landoff, 13098
Livingston family, 11856, 12503
Livingston County, Kentucky, Description, 15085
Livingstone, Mrs. C.M., 8488
Livret-guide de l'emigrant, 3396
Lizzy Glenn, 8571
El llamado, 19823

Llave del Nuevo Mundo, 18569
Las llaves perdidas, 19898
Lleras Restrepo, Carlos, 20330
Lloréns Torres, Luís, 7305
Llorente, Juan Antonio, 1756-1823, 24095
Llorente Vazquez, Manuel, 7306
Lloyd, Charles, 1735-1773, 13395
Lloyd, Hannibal Evans, 1771-1847, tr., 5701
Lloyd, James T., illustr., 14840
Lloyd, John Uri, 14841
Lloyd, William Penn, 1837-1911, 4286
Lloyd George, David, 1863-1945, 7307
Lloyd's steamboat directory, 14840
Loa, y explicación del arco, 5806
The loaf of peace, 9582
Loaisaga, Manuel de, 7308
Loaysa, García Jofre de, 16th cent., 7567
Lobato, José G., 7309
Lobos de Afuera, 1173
Local government, Connecticut, 12153; Illinois, 12531; Massachusetts, 12153
Local law in Massachusetts and Connecticut, 12153
Lochon, Henri, 7310
Locke, E.W., 13396
Locke, John, 1632-1704, 1614
Lockhart, H., 3884
Lockley, Fred, 17045
Lockwood, James D., 17046
Lockwood, Rufus A., 1811-1857, 17047
Loco-foco, 1781
Locomotive sketches, 1563
Locuções tradicionais no Brasil, 19662
Locust Grove, Louisville, Ky., 14072
Lodge, Henry Cabot, 1850-1924, 7311
Lodwick, Charles, 981
Löehnberg, Alfred, 19085
Loehnis, H., 24877
Loesch, Harold, 20224
The Loftons and Pinkertons, 8578
The lofty and the lowly, 10279
The log cabin, 9618, 13791
Log College, 7070
The log of Commodore Rollingpin, 8944
Logan, 10409
Logan, Benjamin, 1743-1802, 22316
Logan, Mrs. Indiana Washington (Peddicord) 1835-, 4287
Logan, James, advocate, of Edinburgh, 4288
Logan, James, Mingo chief, d.1780, 17164, 22140
Logan, James, 1674-1751, 444
Logan, John A., 14843
Logan, John Alexander, 1826-1886, 7312, 24878
Logan, Stephen Trigg, 1800-1880, 7458
Logan, Walter Seth, 1847-1906, 7313

273

Logan's Crossroads, Wayne County, Kentucky, Battle of, 13944
Logan County, Ky., 13610, 13613, 14149, 14259; Fiction, 13720; History, 13864, 14095; Homemakers, 14842
Logan historical society, 287
Logarithms, Early works to 1800, 1632
Logic, 18609, 19157, 20391; Symbolic and mathematical, 18154, 19181
La lógica, 20391
Logoochie, 10769
The logs of the conquest of Canada, 8413
Loh, Jules, 14844
Löher, Franz von, 1818-1892, 4289
Lok, Michael, 373
Løkken, Thomas Olesen, 1877-, 7314
Loligo brasiliensis Bl., 19924
Lomax, John Avery, 1872-, 15962
Lomax, John Taylor, 1781-1862, 24879
Lombard, Albert, 4292, 22457
Lombardo Toledano, Humberto, 7315
Londeix, Georges, 1932-, 18323
London, John, fl.1678, 22574
London, 7119; Citizens, 24880; Description, 11037, 22925; Small-pox hospital, 23009
A London life, 7123
The London Mathews, 13420
London Missionary Society, 24881, 25370
Londonderry, N.H., History, 22904
The Londonderry celebration, 22904
The lone charge of William B. Perkins, 9217
The lone dove, 10103
The lone house, 8732
The Lone Star, 4991
A Lone Star cowboy, 17623
The Lone Star defenders, 2619
The lonely burial, 10710
The lonely man, 10950
The lonely man of the ocean, 10693
Lonesome Charley, 17709
Long, Alexander, 1816-1886, 24882
Long, Calista Rosser (Cralle), 14845
Long, Carl Littleton, 14846
Long, Daniel Albright, 1844-, 24883
Long, Edward, 1734-1813, 24884
Long, John, Indian trader, 13397, 17048
Long, Lessel, 4293
Long, Orie William, 7316
Long, Stephen Harriman, 1784-1864, 2465, 13360, 17049
Long, Thomas R., 5587
The long ago and the later on, 16051
Long Island, 13323; Battle of, 1776, 13421; Description & travel, 13323

Long Island Historical Society, Brooklyn, 13323
Long Island water works company, 1729
Long, long time ago, 11596
The long run, 9039
Longevity, 2166, 12830
Longfellow, Henry Wadsworth, 1807-1882, 4294, 5840, 7317, 24885; Evangeline, 6882; Song of Hiawatha, Parodies, travesties, etc., 5607
Longfellow, Samuel, 1819-1892, ed., 7317
Longitude, 5852, 11707
Longley, William Preston, 1851-1878, 16563, 17050
Longstreet, Augustus Baldwin, 1790-1870, 3460, 4295, 4296, 24886
Longstreet, James, 1821-1904, 4297
Longworth, Maria Theresa, 1832?, 4298
Lonz Powers, 5662
Look before you leap, 14847
Looking backward in the New South: the rise of agrarianism, 24596
Lookout Mountain, Battle of, 1863, 5352
Loomis, Augustus Ward, 1816-1891, 17051
Loomis, Chester A., 1789-1873, 17052
Loomis, Henry H., 14848
Looney, J.T., 13710
Loose leaves, 10914
Lopes, L.C., 19065
López, Elpidio, 7320
López, Juan Pedro, 1724-1787, 19198
López, Manuel Antonio, b.1803, 7322
López, Narciso, 1798?-1851, 15214
López, P., 19639
López, Vincente Fidel, 1815-1903, 7853
López Cordero, Fr. Antonio, 1678 or 9-1730, 7318
López de Arguleta, José, 7271
López de Avilés, José, 7319
López Herrero, Juan Antonio, 7321
López Montana, Ernesto, 20290
López Valencia, Federico, 4299
López Velarde, Ramón, 1888-1921, 7323
López y Fuentes, Gregorio, 19967
Lorain, John, 4300
Lord, Charles Eliphalet, 1817-1902, 24887
Lord, Daniel, 1795-1868, 24888
Lord, Mrs. Elizabeth (Laughlin), 17053
Lord, George A., 1820-1888, 2469
Lord, J.L., 10899
Lord, John Chase, 1805-1877, 24889, 24890, 24897
Lord, John Keast, 1818-1872, 7324
Lord, Nathan, 1793-1870, 24891, 24892
Lord, Theodore A., 7325
Lord and master, 8811

Lord Hope's choice, 10868
The Lord is to be praised for the
  triumphs of His power, 579
Lord North (Island), 22523
Lord of himself, 5497
Lord's Supper, 13779
Lord's prayer. Polyglot, 97
Lorenzana y Britrón, Francisco Antonio,
  cardinal, 1722-1804, 7326, 7327, 16278
Lorenzo, Ana Maria, 18831
Lorette, 8825
The lorgnette, 10361
Loria, A., 24893
Lorimier, François Marie Thomas Chevalier
  de, 1803-1839, 2202
Lorin, Henri, 1866-, 24085
Lorin Mooruck, 9192
Loring, Edward Greely, 1802-1890, 24250
Loring, Francis William, 4301
Loring, Frederick Wadsworth, 1848-1871,
  9693
Loring, Nathaniel Hall, 1799-1838, 12135
Los Angeles, 17271; Biography, 16090;
  Description & travel, 16090
Los Angeles county, California, 16850
Los Angeles county pioneers of southern
  California, 17645
Los Angeles examiner, 17427
Los de abajo, 19967
Losada, Angel, 8004, 19893
Loskiel, George Henry, 1740-1814, 13398
Lossing, Benson John, 1813-1891, 2481,
  4302, 12901, 13399, 13400
Lost abroad, 11005
Lost amid the fogs, 22835
The lost cause, 25290
The lost cause regained, 4818
The lost child of the Delaware, 10570
The lost children, 10760
The lost continent, 24207
The lost daughter, 3844
The lost heir of Linlithgow, 10839
The lost hunter, 8469
The lost letter of Aaron Burr, 1805, 14437
The lost library, 10506
A lost life, 10373
The lost model, 9911
The lost name, 9311
The lost nationalities of America, 11067
The lost pine mine, 10122
The lost place, 9678
The lost pleiad, 2992
A lost prima donna, 10675
Lost sandstones and lonely skies, 15473
The lost sealers, 9150
The lost ship, 1619

The lost tomb-stone, 10747
The lost trappers, 3105, 16286
The lost treasure found, 4948
The lost wife, 9485
Lotería de Beneficencia Nacional y Casinos,
  18396
Lothrop, Charles Henry, 1831-1890, 4303
Loti, Pierre, pseud. of Viaud, Julien.
Lotos flowers, 4167
Lott, Milton, 17062
Lotteries, 14100, 14387, 14388, 23066;
  Argentine Republic, 18396; Kentucky, 14286,
  14287, 14937, 15112, 15356
The lottery ticket, 10245
Lotus eating: a summer book, 16313
Lotz, James Robert, 7328
Loubat, Joseph Florimond, duc de, 1831-1927,
  6438
Loudoun Co., Va., 22791; History, 3637
Loughborough, John, 17057
Loughborough, Preston S., 14849
Louie's last term at St. Mary's, 22305
Louis, Paul, 1872-, 24894
Louis XIV, king of France, 1638-1715,
  Addresses, sermons, etc., 23313
Louis Philippe, king of the French, 1773-1830,
  13537
Louisa, 9575
Louisa Pallant, 7117
Louisa Williams, 9495
Louisburg, Siege, 1745, 11336, 21887; Fiction,
  9707
Louise Elton, 9854
Louisiana, 1561, 3215, 8907; Bibliography,
  11323; Boundaries, 16491; Bureau of
  immigration, 4304; Citizens, 13401;
  Constitution, 25318; Description & travel,
  1206, 2549, 2578, 2641, 2694, 2768, 2975,
  3117, 3170, 3171, 3215, 3231, 3425, 3476,
  3479, 3595, 3597, 3979, 4173, 4227, 4304,
  4305, 4586, 4657, 4682, 4755, 4758, 4791,
  5287, 5557, 7970, 8320, 8321, 13143, 14749,
  15344, 15527, 22697; Description & travel,
  Guide-books, 13544; Discovery & exploration,
  3329, 3826; Fiction, 3274, 4994, 8926,
  8928, 9000, 24326; Finance, 17580; Geneal.,
  Dictionaries, 8153; General assembly,
  13402; History, 776, 1675, 1683, 2966,
  3207, 3512, 5287, 5840, 23185, 23510;
  History, Civil war, 2587, 3199, 3895,
  4964; History, Colonial period, 2965,
  3317, 3584, 3665, 3725, 4201, 4258, 5229,
  16040, 22731; History, Colonial period,
  Sources, 2332, 3544, 7404, 16010, 17129;
  Politics & government, 13401, 16490;
  Politics & government, Civil war, 801,

9876; Public lands, 22315; Sanit.
affairs, 938; Social life & customs,
3512; Statistics, Vital, 938
Louisiana artillery, Washington artillery,
1840-, 2625, 4671
Louisiana as it is, 3231
Louisiana cavalry (Confederate) 1st regt.,
1861-1864, 2921
Louisiana historical society, New
Orleans, 1675
Louisiana infantry. 1st regt. (U.S.A.),
5195; 2d regt.,Native guard (Colored)
1862-1863, 11326; 3d regt., 1861-1865,
5482; 26th regt., 1862-1865, 3756
Louisiana literature, 3512
Louisiana lottery, 6545
Louisiana militia, 1860-1862, 2625
Louisiana purchase, 776, 1452, 1996, 5287,
5479, 14181, 16640, 16742
Louisiana Purchase Exposition, 4932
Louisiana state immigration association,
4305
Louisiana state medical society, 938
Louisiana State University, 6915
Louisiana studies, 3512
Louisiana (U.S. gunboat), 2733
Louisianais [pseud.] of Alfred Mercier
La Louisiane ensanglantée, 2965
Louisiane , Mexique, Canada, 7970
Louisville, Ky., 15298, 15327, 15441;
Architecture, 13725; Beechmont Younger
Woman's Club, 14850; Biography, 24684;
Calvary Episcopal Church, 14851;
Congregation Adath Israel, 7329;
Churches, 14855; Description, 3755,
14252, 15293, 15569, 15570, 22073;
Description, Views, 13566; Directories,
14862, 15051, 15497; Fiction, 15286;
First Evangelical Lutheran Church,
14041; First Presbyterian Church, 15669;
First Unitarian Church, 13679; Floods,
14863; Free Public Library, 14100,
23895; History, 2937, 4370, 13742,
13921, 14032, 14057, 14376, 14864,
14997, 15125, 15171, 15174, 22073,
24684; Manners and customs, 14073; Maps,
14333, 14863, 14927, 14928; Mission of
Walnut Street Baptist Church, 14853;
Politics & government, 15090;
Presbyterian Theological Seminary of
Kentucky, 15324; Public library of
Kentucky, 15205; Second Presbyterian
Church, 14852; Southern Baptist
Theological Seminary 15418; Twenty-
second and Walnut Baptist Church, 14853;
Twenty-third and Broadway Baptist Church,

14853; University, 14111; University, J.B.
Speed memorial museum, 7330; University,
Library, 14854; University, Medical Dept.,
15787; Views, 13518, 15255; Walnut Street
Baptist Church, 14855; Woman's club, 14856
Louisville and Cincinnati Packet Company,
14857
Louisville and Nashville Railroad, 14006,
14782, 14858-14861
The Louisville directory, 14862, 15497
Louisville flood map showing flooded area of
Louisville, Kentucky, January 1937, 14863
The Louisville Foundation..., 15298
Louisville history "on the air", 14864
Louisville Hotel, Louisville, Ky., 14865
Louisville in 1873, a reminiscence, 14376
Lounsbury, Thomas, 24896
Lounsberry, Clement Augustus, 1843-1926, 17058
Loup River, 16531
Loureiro, Maria Regina Couto, 20555
Louvet de Couvral, Jean Baptiste, 1760-1797,
13403
Love, Horace Thomas, 1807-1895, 24897
Love, Nat, 1854-, 17059
Love, Reid, 13917
Love a victor, 10580
The love affairs of Abraham Lincoln, 7660
The love affairs of an old maid, 8772
Love afloat, 10752
Love among the mistletoe, 3376
Love and loyalty, 10851
Love and principle, 3505
Love and science, 8707
Love and secession, 11197
Love and skates, 11194
Love before breakfast, 10896
Love in a cottage, 9454
Love in idleness, 9226
Love in old clothes, 8897
Love in the nineteenth century, 10566
Love is a spirit, 9812
Love me, love my dog, 9357, 9363
The love of a lifetime, 9285
The love of country, 847
The love of Landry, 9437
Love, or a name, 9813
Love perpetuated: the story of a dagger,
15361
The love scrapes of a lifetime, 8923
The love story of Charles Brandon and Mary
Tudor, 10309
Love the light of life, 10686
Love versus law, 10904
Love with a handsome spendthrift, 10202
Love's cross, 9403
Love's progress, 3602

Lovejoy, Elijah Parish, 1802-1837, 1051, 25725
Lovejoy, Joseph Cammet, 1805-1871, 24898-24900
Lovejoy, Owen, 1811-1864, 24899
Lovell, John, pub., 7331
Lovell, Joseph, 1788-1836, 13360
Lovell's folly, 3845
Lovell's gazetteer of British North America, 7331
The lovely maid of Louisiana, 4994
Loveman, Robert, 1864-1923, 4306
The lover and the tell-tale, 9216
A lover in Cuba, 3377
A lover of his country, 23639
A lover of his king and country, 21916
A lover of truth, 11138
A lover of truth and decency, 13098
The lover's leap, 10827, 10919
The lover's trails, 9389
Lovers and thinkers, 9013
The loves of the gorillas, 11146
The loves of the Lady Arabella, 5117
Lovey Mary, 15263
Lovie, Henry, illustr., 4283
Low, Alfred Maurice, 1860-1929, 4307
Low, Albert Peter, 1861-, 6302
Low, Seth, 1850-1916, 7332
Low incomes of rural people, 13743
The low value set upon human life in the United States, 11308
Lowe, Charles, 1828-1874, 7333
Lowe, Nicholas, 5264
Lowe, Percival Green, 1828-, 17060
Lowell, Daniel W., & co., 4308
Lowell, James Russell, 1819-1891, 7119, 24901, 24902, 24959
Lowell, John, 1769-1840, 13404
Lowell, John Amory, 1798-1881, 1577, 21815
Lowell, Orson, illustr., 4087, 10886
Lowell, Percival, 1571-1665, 22770
Lowell, Robert Traill Spence, 1816-1891, 8597
Lowell, Mass., Sanit. off., 11921
The Lowell factory girl, 8539
Lowell hydraulic experiments, 2311
Lowell Institute lectures, 1868-69, 12052, 12747, 23277
Löwenstern, Isidor, 1815-1858, 4309, 7334, 7917
Ludwig, Gustav, 4310
Lowrey, Grosvenor Porter, 7335, 13405
Lowry, James, 1817-1876, 15561
Lowry, Thomas, 1843-1909, 7336
Loyal League of Union Citizens, 24903

Loyal Legion of the U.S., Directories, 7500
Loyal meeting of the people of New York, 24903
Loyal National League of the State of New York, 2414, 24904-24908
Loyal National Repeal Association of Ireland, 24909
The Loyalist's ammunition, 24910
The loyalists and slavery in New Brunswick, 24659
Loyalty, 1190, 11173, 24911
Loyalty a Christian obligation, 1190
The loyalty for the times, 24912
Loyalty on the frontier, 1350, 21785
Loyola, Martin Ignacio de, fl.1585-1612, 22252
Lozada, Jesús Rodolfo, 1892-, 7337
Lubbock, Francis Richard, 17061
Lubbock, Percy, 7128
Lucas, Corydon L., 1838-, 17062
Lucas, C. P., 7899
Lucas, Sir Charles Prestwood, 1853-1931, 6647
Lucas, Daniel Bedinger, 1836-1909, 4311, 4312, 7338
Lucas, Daniel R., 4313
Lucas, Pierre Hippolyte, 1815?-1899, 21853
Lucas de Ayllon, 10783
Lucas de Montigny, Gabriel, b.1782, 13441
Luccock, John, 7339
La lucha con la pantera, 20248
Lucha y dolor del Paraguay, 19607
Lucia, 9421
Lucia Dare, 3273
Lucinda, 10316
The luck of Roaring Camp, 9784
The luck of the Bogans, 10043
Lucretia and her father, 10248
Lucy Arlyn, 11016
Lucy Howard's journal, 10759
Lucy in the city, 11043
Lucy Maria, 9398
Ludecus, Eduard, 4314
Luden, Heinrich, 2696
Lüders, Charles Henry, 1858-1891, 10737
Ludlow, Fitz Hugh, 1836-1870, 10899, 17063
Ludlow family, 12996, 16576
Ludovico Sforza, il Moro, duke of Milan, 1451-1508, Fiction, 8589
Ludvigh, Samuel Gottlieb, 1801-1869, 4315
Lugar del primer combate naval argentino, 18671
Lugenbell, James Washington, 1819?-1857, 24913
Luhr, Cary W., 14293, 14613, 14866-14868
Lujan Muñoz, Luis, 7686
Lukens, Mrs. Matilda Barns, 17064
Lull, Caspar Peter, 1189

Lulu, 11064
Lum, Dyer Daniel, 17065
Lumber, Seasoning of, 14804
Lumbering, California, 15937
Lumholtz, Karl Sofus, 1851-, 7340, 7341
Lumley, illustr., 4759
Lummi language, Glossaries, vocabularies, etc., 12232
Lummis, Charles Fletcher, 1859-, 7342
Lumpkin, C. P., 17838
Lunan, John, jr., 13406
Lundy, Benjamin, 1789-1839, 4316, 15859, 17017, 17066
The Luna papers, 4862
Luna y Arellano, Tristán de, d.1573, 4862
Lunacy, 11113
Lunan, John, 24914
Lund, Universitet, Student-sångförening, 2618
Lundy, Benjamin, 2969, 24915
Lundy, John Patterson, 1823-1892, 24916
Lunt, George, 1803-1885, 24917
Luquillo Mountains, Puerto Rico, Climate, 19492
The lure of fishing in Kentucky, 14561
Lusk, William Thompson, 1838-1897, 4317
Lussich, Antonio D., 1848-1928, 18931
Lutes, Ann, 14869
Luther, jr., pseud., 24918
Lutheran Church in California, 17667
Lutheran Church in Texas, 17691
Lutheran Church in the U.S., 1364, 4547, 23095; History, 24581
Lutheranism in America, 23095
Luttrell, Juanita Skaggs, 14870, 15376, 15647
Lutz, Bertha, 1894-, 19266
Luz de verdades católicas, 7427
Luzac, S., 7343
Lycoming Co., Pa., History, 23425
Lyddy, a tale of the Old South, 8634
Lydia Hersey, of East Bridgewater, 9578
Lydston, George Frank, 1858-1923, 17067
Lyell, Sir Charles, 1797-1875, 4318, 4319, 7344-7347, 13238
Lyford, C. P., 17068
Lyford, William G., 4320
The lying hero, 25011
Lyle family, 13791
Lyman, Albert, 17069, 17070
Lyman, Darius, 1821?-1892, 24919
Lyman, Horace Sumner, 1855-, 17071, 17072
Lyman, Jonathan, 1737-1766, 702
Lyman, Joseph, 1749-1800, 13407
Lyman, Theodore, 1792-1849, 23258, 24988
Lyman, Theodore, 1833-1897, 4321

Lynch, Benito, 19614
Lynch, James, 17073, 17074
Lynch, Jeremiah, 1849-, 17075
Lynch, Laurence K., 14871
Lynch, Sir Thomas, d.1684?, 13145
Lynchburg, Battle of 1864, 3324
Lynchburg, Va., Genealogy, 21824; History, 21824
Lynching, 13885
Lynd, Samuel W., 14872
Lynn, Mass., Biography, 10420; History, 10420
Lynx-hunting, 9216
Lyon, Mrs. Adelia Caroline Duncombe, 4323
Lyon, George Francis, 1795-1832, 7348, 7349
Lyon, James Adair, 1814-1882, 24920
Lyon, Mary, 1797-1849, 22505
Lyon, Matthew, 1750-1822, 14921; Fiction, 5003
Lyon, Nathaniel, 1818-1861, 22406
Lyon, Sidney S., 15107-15109
Lyon, William Franklin, 1842-, 4322
Lyon, William Penn, 1822-1913, 4323
The Lyon campaign in Missouri, 5610
Lyon Co., Ia. County board of supervisors, 16840; Description & travel, 16840; History, 16840
Lyons, John A., 14873
Lyons, T. L., 14874
Lyons, W. F., 22771
Lyra, Roberto, 19362
Lyra, and other poems, 2932
Lyra germanica, 14875
Lyric touches, 4714
Lyrics, 4604, 5332
Lyrics and idyls, 2952
Lyrics of a day, 11584
Lyrics of the war, 24921
Lysiphlebus testaceipes (Cresson), 19071
Lyttelton, George Lyttelton, 1st baron, 1709-1773, 2470, 13408

Mabel Clifton, 8844
Mabel Lee, 10971
Mably, Gabriel Bonnot de, 1709-1785, 22772, 22773
Mabry, John H., 14876
McAdam, J. T., 7350
McAdams, Mrs. H. K., 14635, 14877
McAdams, Mrs. W. K., 14829
MacAdoo, J. E., 14567
McAfee, Nelly (Nichol) Marshall, 1845-1895, 4325, 14879
McAfee, Robert Breckinridge, 1784-1849, 4326,

McAfee, Ky. New Providence Presbyterian Church, 14878
McAllister, Ward, 1827-1895, 4327
McAlpin, Robert, d.1852, 24212
McAlpine, William Jarvis, 1812-1890, 22774
McAnally, David Rice, 1810-1895, 22775
McArthur, John, 1755-1840, 22776
McArty, William, 22792
McBee, May Wilson, 14882
Macbeth, James, 24924
MacBrady, John E., 25124
McBride, James, 1788-1859, 14883
M'Bride, Robert Ekin, 1846-, 4328
MacBryde, Nancy, 14884
McCabe, James Dabney, 1842-1883, 4329, 4330, 22777-22779
MacCabe, Julius P. Bolivar, 22780
McCabe, William Gordon, 4331
McCaffery, Michael J. A., 22781
McCaffrey, John, 1806-1881, 22782
MacCain, Charles W., 17076
M'Caine, Alexander, 1768 (ca.)-1856), 22783
McCaleb, Walter Flavius, 1873-, 17453
McCall, Eli Robinson, 24925
McCall, George Archibald, 1802-1868, 4332, 4333, 5545
McCall, Hext, 22784
McCall, Hugh, 22785
McCall, Peter, 1809-1880, 22786
McCalla, William Latta, 1788-, 4334
McCallen, Robert Seth, 7351
M'Callum, Pierre Franc, 22787
McCamant, Wallace, 1867-, 7352, 7353
McCandless, Helen, 14885
MacCann, William, 22788
McCann, William Ray, 14886
McCann family, 14886
M'Carter, J. Mayland, 24926
McCarthy, Carlton, 1847-, 5575
MacCarthy, Jacques, 1785-1835, 22789
M'Cartney, Washington, 1812-1856, 22790
M'Carty, John Mason, 22791
McCarty, Joseph Hendrickson, 1830-1897, 7354
McCarty, W. C., 17077
McCarty, William, Philadelphia, pub., 22497
McCaslin, Mrs. Elbert, 14887
Macaulay, Catharine (Sawbridge), 1731-1791, 13409
Macaulay, Thomas, 1800-1859, 14881
Macaulay, Zachary, 1768-1838, 22793, 24922, 24923
MacCauley, Clay, 1843-1925, 4335
Macauley, James, 22794

McCauley, James Andrew, 1822-1896, 22795
McChesney, Harry V., 14018
M'Chesney, James, 22796
McChord, James, 1785-1820, 13670, 14316, 22797
McChord, John H., 14888
McChord family, 14888
McClellan, Ely, 14889
McClellan, George, 1796-1817, 21760, 22798
McClellan, George Brinton, 1826-1885, 84, 5537, 6560, 7067, 7286, 7355, 8138, 12014, 12017, 22487, 22763, 22799, 22800-22803, 22805, 23478, 23793
McClellan, Robert, 2528
M'Clellan, Rolander Guy, 17078, 22804
McClellan, Samuel, 1787-1855, 1415
McClellan's compaign, 22805
McClelland, Robert, 1807-1880, 940
McClenthen, Charles S., b.1827?, 22806
McClernand, John Alexander, 1812-1900, 17079
M'Clintock, Sir Francis Leopold, 1819-1907, 22807
McClintock, J., 4468
McClintock, John, 1814-1870, 22808
MacClintock, Samuel, 1732-1804, 22809, 22810
M'Clintock, James, 24927
McCloskey, Henry, 11540
McClung, John Alexander, 1804-1859, 4336-4338, 14890
McClung, John W., 22811
McClung, Zarah, 4339
McClure, Alexander Kelly, 1828-1909, 4340, 7356-7358, 17080
M'Clure, Alexander Wilson, 22812, 22813
McClure, David, 1748-1820, 22814, 22815
McClure, Dianna, 14891
McClure, Sir Robert John Le Mesurier, 1807-1873, 22816
Maclure, William, 1763-1840, 22817, 22819, 22820
McClure, William James, 1842-, 22818
McClurg, Virginia (Donaghe), 1858-1931, 17081
Maclurian lyceum, Philadelphia, 22821
McCoid, Moses Ayers, 1840-1904, 17082
M'Collum, William S., 22822
Macomb, Alexander, 1782-1841, 22823-22825
McConnell, H. H., 7359
M'Connell, Matthew, 22827
McConnell, William John, 1839-1925, 17083
McCord, John A., 1875-, 14892
McCord, Thomas, 22828
McCorkle, John, 1838-, 22829
MacCorkle, William Alexander, 1857-, 7338
McCormack, Mrs. Arthur Thomas, 14893
McCormack, Thomas Joseph, 1865-1932, 16962
M'Cormick, Charles, 1755?-1807, 22830
McCormick, Richard Cunningham, 1832-1901, 4341

279

McCoskry, Samuel Allen, bp., 1804-1886, 22831
McCoun, William T., 22832
McCowan, Archibald, 4342
McCoy, A. D., b.1813, 22833, 24928
McCoy, Amasa, 22834
McCoy, Isaac, 1784-1846, 4343, 4344, 17084, 17085
McCoy, Joseph Geiting, 1837-1915, 17086
McCoy, Terry L., 19914
McCoy family, 14844
McCrady, Edward, 1833-, 24929
McCrea, Jane, 1753-1777, 11688
McCrea, Robert Barlow, 22835
McCready, Benjamin William, 1813-1892, 22836
McCready, John Dudley, 14894
McCready, Richard Lightburne, 14895
McCreary, James Bennett, 1838-1918, 14896
McCreary, W. H., 13567
McCreary County, Ky., 14757
McCullock, Ben, 1811-1862, 4926
McCullock, Hugh, 1808-1895, 17087, 22837
McCullock, Hugh, 1869-1902, 4345
Maccullock, John, 1773-1835, 13756
McCullock, John Ramsay, 1789-1864, 22838, 22839
McCullok, James Haines, 1793?-1870, 22840
M'Cullok, James W., 12133
McCullock, Richard Sears, 22841
McCullough, Hiram, b.1813, 23220
McCurtin, Daniel, 698
McCutcheon, John T., illustr., 8479, 16753
McDaniel, Ernest, 14897
McDaniel, Samuel W., 22842
McDaniel, V. Rick, 18707
McDaniel family (Stephen McDaniel, 1793-1865), 14271
McDanield, H. F., 4346
McDermott, John Francis, 1902-, 16307
McDermott, William A., 1863-1913, 10675
M'Donald, Alexander, 22843
Macdonald, Augustin S., 17088
McDonald, Charles James, 1793-1860, 13127
MacDonald, Donald, 14668
Macdonald, Duncan George Forbes, 1823?-1884, 7360
Macdonald, Mrs. Flora (Macdonald) 1722-1790, 13309
McDonald, Frank Virgil, 1852-1897, 17089
Macdonald, James, 1852-1913, 17090
MacDonald, James Madison, 1812-1876, 22044, 22845, 24930
McDonald, John, 1775-1853, 4347
Macdonald, John Alexander, 1815-1891, 6845

McDonald, Richard Hayes, 1820-, 17089
McDonald family, 17089
The M'Donalds, 4736
M'Donnell, Alexander, 4348, 24931
McDougal, Henry Clay, 17091
McDougall, Mrs. Frances Harriet (Whipple) Greene, 1805-1878, 24932
M'Dougall, George Frederick, 22846
Macdougall, George Gordon, d.1885, 22259
McDougall, James Alexander, 1817-1867, 22847
McDougall, Marion Gleason, 24933
McDougall, William, 7361
McDougle, Ivan Eugene, 24934
McDowell, Ephraim, 1771-1830, 3708, 13605, 13620, 13965, 14066, 14371, 14893, 14898, 15041, 15209, 15554
McDowell, Irvin, 1818-1885, 22848
McDowell, James, 1796-1851, 13354, 22849, 24935, 24936
McDowell, Joseph Nashe, 1805-1868, 24937
McDowell, Mrs. Katherine Sherwood Bonner, 1849-, 14899
MacDowell, S. W., 17999
Macduff, John Ross, 1818-1895, 22850
M'Duffee, John, 4349
McDuffie, George, 1790-1851, 22851-22856
McDuffle, George, 1788-1851, 2422
McElhaney, Alan, 14227
M'Elhiney, Thomas, 22857
McElligott, James Napoleon, 1812-1866, 22858
McElrath, Thomson P., 17092
MacEl'rey, Joseph H., 22859
McElroy, Clarence L., 1903-, 7362
McElroy, John, 1846-1929, 4350, 24938
McElroy, Mrs. Lucy Cleaver, 1860-1901, 14900
McElroy, Robert McNutt, 1872-, 14901
McElroy family, 14888
McEwen, Abel, 1780-1860, 22860-22862
M'Ewen, John Alexander, 22864
M'Ewen, R. S., 22863
McFall, J. V., illustr., 15093
McFarlan, Arthur Crane, 1897-, 14902-14906
M'Farland, Asa, 1769-1827, 22865, 22866
Macfarland, William H., 14907, 22867
MacFarlane, Charles, 1799-1858, 22868
MacFarlane, Robert, 1734-1804, 22498, 22869
MacFarlane, Robert, 1815-1883, 22870
Macfie, Matthew, 7363
McGann, Agnes Geraldine, 14908
McGarrahan claim, 16783
McGarvey, John William, 1829-1911, 14909, 15035
McGary, Elizabeth Visere, 7364
McGavock, Randal William, 1826-1863, 22871
McGlachy, Edward, d.1851, 22872
McGee, Benjamin F., 1834-, 4351

McGee, L. N., 14910
McGee, L. R., 14911
McGee, Nora, 14280, 14912
McGee, Thomas D'Arcy, 1825-1868, 6549,
  22873-22879
McGeeney, Patrick Sylvester, 1873-, 17094
McGill, Alexander Taggart, 1807-1889,
  24939, 25304
McGill, Josephine, 14913
McGill, P. M., 22880
M'Gillivray, Duncan, d.1808, 17095
Macgillivray, William, 1796-1852, 7091
McGlynn, Edward, 8425
McGovern, John, 1850-, 4352
McGowan, D., 4353
Macgowan, Daniel Jerome, 1815-1893, 22881
McGowan, Edward, 1813-1893, 17097
MacGowan, Robert, 7365
McGowen, M., 7366
McGrain, Paul, 14839
McGrain, Preston, 14914-14916
McGrath, Price, 14043
McGreevy, W. H., 14781
M'Gregor, John, 1797-1857, 7367, 7368,
  22882-22885
MacGregor, John, 1825-1892, 17098
McGroarty, John Steven, 1862-, 17099
McGuier, Henry, 22886
M'Guire, Edward Charles, 22887
McGuire, J. A., 7369
McGuire, Judith White (Brockenbrough)
  "Mrs. John P. McGuire," 4354
McHatton-Ripley, Elizabeth, 7370
McHenry, George, 1794, 22888, 22889
M'Henry, James, 1753-1816, 22890
McIlhany, Edward Washington, 17100
McIlvain, Mrs. Clara (Lovell) 1836-1881,
  4355
McIlvaine, Charles Pettit, bp.1799-1873,
  22893, 22894
M'Ilvaine, William, jr., 7371
McIntire, James, 1846-, 17101
McIntosh, John, 22895, 22896
McIntosh, Maria Jane, 1803-1878, 22897,
  24941
M'Intyre, Archibald, 1772-1858, 22898
McJilton, John Nelson, 1805-1875, 10234,
  22899, 22900
Mack, Alonso W., 1822-1871, 24942
Mack, David, 1750-1845, 11836
Mack, Enoch, 1806-1881, 22496
Mack, Mrs. R. E., illustr., 12020
Mack, Ebenezer, 22901, 22902
Mack, Robert C., 22903, 22904
Mackall, Henry Co., comp., 23220
Mackay, Alexander, 1808-1852, 4356, 22905,

22906
Mackay, Charles, 1814-1889, 4357, 7372, 7373
McKay, F. E., 10283
Mackay, J., 22907
Mackay, James Aberigh, 10718
McKay, Neill, 22908
Mackay, Robert, 1772-, 4358
McKay, Robert Henderson, 1840-, 17102
MacKay, Robert W. Stuart, 22909
McKaye, James, 22910
Mackaye, Percy Wallace, 1875-1956, 14917
McKean, Joseph, 1776-1818, 12778, 22911, 22912
McKean, Thomas, 1734-1817, 23806
McKee, James Cooper, 17103
McKee, Lanier, 17104
McKee, Samuel, 1833-1898, 22913, 24943
McKee, William H., 22914
McKeehan, J. B., 22915
McKeen, Joseph, 1757-1807, 13410, 22916, 22917
McKeen, Silas, 24035
Mackellar, Patrick, 1717-1778, 22918
MacKellar, Thomas, 1812-1899, 22919, 22920
McKendree, William, bp. 1757-1835, 4679
McKenney, Samuel, 24944
McKenney, Thomas Lorraine, 1785-1859, 455,
  4359, 4360, 22921-22923
MacKenzie, Sir Alexander, 1763-1820, 4361,
  4362, 5457, 6221, 6748, 13411, 17104, 22924
Mackenzie, Alexander Slidell, 1803-1848,
  22925-22929
MacKenzie, Charles, F.R.S., 22793, 22930,
  24923
Mackenzie, Eneas, 1778-1832, 4363
Mackenzie, George Norbury, 1851-1919, 7374
Mackenzie, Henry, 1745-1831, 22931
Mackenzie, Robert, 1823-1881, 22932, 22933
Mackenzie, Ronald Slidell, 1840-1889, 16023
Mackenzie, William L., 13412
Mackenzie, William Lyon, 1795-1861, 22934,
  22935
Mackenzie district, Description & travel,
  8007, 8252, 17389
Mackenzie River, 6283
Mackenzie's last fight with Cheyennes, 16023
Mckeon, John, 1808-1883, 22936
Mackey, Albert Gallatin, 1807-1881, 22937
Mackey, John W., 4364
Mackey, Thomas Jefferson, 1830-1909, 22937
Mackie, John Milton, 1813-1894, 22938
McKim, Randolph Harrison, 1842-1920, 4365
Mackinac, History, Fiction, 8956
Mackinaw, Mich., 2080, 23101
McKinley, William, pres. U.S., 1843-1901,
  7375, 17105
McKinney, John, d.1825, 14971
McKinney, Mrs. Kate (Slaughter) 1857-, 4366

281

McKinney, Mordecai, 1796 (ca.)-1867, 22939
McKinnie, Robert, 6164
McKinnon, Daniel, 1767-1830, 22940
Mackinnon, Lauchlan Bellingham, 1815-1877, 22941, 22942
Mackinnon, William Alexander, 1789-1870, 22943, 22944
Mckinnon, William Charles, 22945
McKinstry, George, 16997
Mckinstry, Justus, b.1814, 22945
McKinstry, W., 25239
Mackintosh, Sir James, 1765-1832, 22947
McKitrick, Reuben, 17106
McKnight, Charles, 1826-1881, 4367
M'Knight, John, 1754-1823, 22948, 22949
McKnight, Martin Marshall, 14919
McKnight, Thomas, 1829-1899, 22950
MacKonochie, Alexander, 22951
Mackoy, Harry Brent, 7376, 14920
Mackoy, William Hardin, 1839-1923, 15758
Mackrill, Joseph, 22952
Maclachlan, May A., 8210
McLagan, John Campbell, 1838-, 7384
McLain, Raymond Francis, 1905-, 15346
M'Lain, William, 1806-1873, 22953
McLane, Louis, 1786-1857, 22954, 24945
McLane, Robert Milligan, 1815-1898, 22955
Maclaren, James, 22956
McLaughlin, Andrew Cunningham, 1861-1947, 24946
M'Laughlin, Charles, illustr, 3681
McLaughlin, James, 1842-1922, 17107
McLaughlin, James Fairfax, 1839-1903, 7338, 14921, 22957
McLaughlin, John, 16805, 24947
McLaughlin, Joseph R., 7377
Maclauries, Mr., 4361
M'Lean, Alexander, 22958
McLean, Archibald, 7378
M'Lean, James, 22959
McLean, John, 1799-, 4368
Maclean, John, 1800-1886, 22960
McLean County, Ky., 14220; Economic conditions, 14541; History, 15024
Macleane, Lauchlin, 22961
McLellan, Isaac, 1806-1899, 22962-22964
M'Lellans, Archibald, defendant, 8032
M'Lenan, John, illustr., 3004, 10922, 17336
McLennan County, Texas, marriage record, 16170
McLeod, Alexander, 12120, 22965
McLeod, Daniel, 22966
MacLeod, Donald, 11759, 14922, 22967
McLeod, Isabella, 22968

Macleod, Norman, 1812-1872, 22969
McLeod, Robert Randall, 7379
MacLeod, William, illustr., 12696
M'Mahon, Benjamin, 22970, 24948
MacMahon, Bernard, 1775-1816, 22971
McMahon, John Van Lear, 1800-1871, 13413
MacMahon, T. W., 13414
MacMaster, Erasmus Darwin, 1806-1866, 22972, 22973
McMaster, Gilbert, 1778-1854, 22974
McMaster, Guy Humphrey, 1829-1887, 22975
McMaster, S. W., b.1811, 17108
MacMechen, Edgar Carlisle, 1884-, 17109
McMechen, James H., 14923
McMeekin, Isabella (McLennan), 1895-, 13567, 14924
McMicken, Charles, 1782-1858, 22976
McMillan, John, 1752-1833, 1326
McMillan, Mary Lane, illustr., 14159
McMinnville, Tenn., History, 14237
McMorries, Edward Young, 4369
McMullen, Fayette, 1810-1880, 5270
McMurry, Kenneth Charles, 15327
MacMullen, John, 1818-1896, 22977, 22978
McMullen, John Mercier, 1820-1907, 22979
McMurray, William, 1783-1835, 22980, 24949
McMurtrie, Douglas Crawford, 1888-1944, 3994, 7029, 7380, 14925, 14926, 17110-17112
McMurtrie, Henry, 1793-1865, 4370, 14927, 14928
McMurtry, Robert Gerald, 1906-, 7381, 7382, 7383, 14291
McNair, John, 22981
McNally, William, 22982
Macnamara, Henry Tyrwhitt Jones, 1820-1877, 22983
McNamara, Mary C., 14929
Macnamara, Michael H., 4371
McNaughton, Margaret, 17113
MacNaul, Willard Carey, 1864-, 24950
McNeil, Samuel, 4372
McNeile, Hugh, 1795-1879, 22984
McNemar, Richard, 1770-1839, 4373, 4374, 14930
McPhail, Leonard C., d.1867, 22985
MacPherson, Charles, fl.1773-1790, 24953
Macpherson, David, 1746-1816, 22986
McPherson, Edward, 1830-1895, 22987, 22988
Macpherson, James, 1736-1796, 22161
M'Pherson, John, d.1806, 1667
Macpherson, the Confederate philosopher, 9876
McPhetres, Samuel A., 22989
McQuade, James, 4375
Macqueen, John Frazer, 1803-1881, 22990
Macrae, David, 1837-1907, 4376, 4377

McRae, John J., 1815-1863, 22991
McReady, John Dudley, 7385
McRee, Griffith John, 1819-1873, 22307, 22992
McReynolds, Robert, 17114
M'Robert, Patrick, 22993
McRoberts, Samuel, 1799-1843, 22994
McRoskey, Racine, 17115
McSherry, Richard, 1817-1885, 7386, 22995
MacSparran, James, 1693-1757, 22996
Mactaggart, John, 1791-1830, 22997
McTeague, 10428
McTyeire, Holland Nimmons, bp.1824-1889, 24954
McVean, Charles, 1802-1848, 22998
McVey, Frank LeRond, 1493
MacVickar, Archibald, 13385
McVickar, John, 1787-1868, 22839, 22999-23001
Macwhorter, Alexander, 1734-1807, 23002
McWhorter, Lucullus Virgil, 1860-, The border settlers of northwestern Virginia from 1768 to 1795, 13739
McWilliams, Carey, ed., 6278
Macaca, Cuba, History, 20548
The macadam trail, 5746
Macaria, 11185
Macario, 18207
Macedo, Joaquim Mamiel de, 1820-1882, 23003
The Macedonia Christian Church, 14325
Maceió, Brazil. Prémio Literário Guimarães Passos, 18658
Machado, Maria Clara. O boi e o burro no caminho de Belém, 18977
Machado de Assis, Joaquim Maria, 1839-1908, 19165
Machebeuf, Joseph Projectus, bp., 1812-1889, 16825
Machias, Me., 22892; Genealogy, 22892; History, 22892
Machpelah: a book for the cemetery, 23004
Macías, Juan Manuel, 24940
Mackau, Ange René, Armand, baron de, 1788-1855, 24428
Macomb, John N., 1810 or 11-1879, 17775
Macomb, Robert, 22826
Macon, Nathaniel, 1757-1837, 24951, 24952
Macon, Ga. Military prison, 3082
Macoun, John, 1831-1920, 6748, 7384
Macrobius, Ambrosius Aurelius Theodosius, 24421
Macumba: cultos afro-brasileiros, 20402
Macy, Jesse, 1842-1919, 24955
Macy, Obea, 23005
The mad penitent of Todi, 10675

Mad rush for gold in frozen North, 16390
Madame Butterfuly, 10238
Madame Clerc, 10283
Madame de Mauves, 10014
Madame Delphine, 8928
Madariaga, Salvador de, 1886-, 7387
Madden, John E., 14932, 14933
Madden, Richard Robert, 1798-1886, 23006, 23007, 24835, 24956, 24957, 24969
Madden, Samuel, 1686-1765, 23008
Maddox, Isaac, bp. of Worcester, 1697-1759, 23009
Madeira, Description & travel, 492, 24616; Description & travel, Guidebooks, 7653; Discovery & exploration, 129
Madelaine Darth, 9531
Madeleine, pseud., 7388
Madelin, Louis, 1871-, 7525
Madeline, 9898
Madelon, 9574; The story of, 3932
Mademoiselle Blanche, 8751
Mademoiselle Joan, 9355
Mademoiselle miss, 9741
Madigan, Mary Low S., 14934
Madison, Dorothy (Payne) Todd, 1768-1849, 7389
Madison, George, 1763-1816, 15387
Madison, James, Bp., 1749-1812, 23010, 23014
Madison, James, pres. U.S., 1751-1836, 77, 78, 822, 1379, 2364, 6002, 6833, 7389, 12140, 12348, 12603, 13209, 15650, 22172, 23011, 23013, 23015
Madison, James M., 23012
Madison, Wis., 2127; City council, 2127
Madison County, Ky., Bibliography, 14417; Biography, 14008; Economic conditions, 14536, 14544; History, 14008, 14935, 14970; Sesquicentennial celebration, 14935
Madison County historical society, Richmond, Ky., 14008, 14935
Madison Co., Mont., 16688
Madisonville, Ky., Economic conditions, 14542
The madmen's chronicle; exemplified in the conduct of George The Third, 23016
Madoc, fl.1170, 14035
Madog ab Owain Gwynedd, 1150-1180?, 1692
The madonna of the future, 10014
Una madre camino de los altares, 18102
Madre de Deus, Manuel da, b.1724, 23017
Madriga, Pedro de, Beschchryvinge van de regeringh van Peru, 21782
La madriguera, 19643
A Maecenas of the Pacific slope, 6973
Maffitt, John Newland, 1794-1850, 11607, 23018
Maga excursion papers, 23019

Maga stories, 10298
Magalhães, Domingos José Gonçalves de,
  visconde de Araguaya, 1811-1882, 23020
Magalhães, Fernão de, 1521, 7567
Magalhães de Gandavo, Pedro de, 23021
Magallón, M., 20051
Magaul, Michael, pseud., 24925
Magaw, Samuel, 1740-1812, 23022, 23023
Magdalena, Colombia (Dept.), 20304;
  Description & travel, 13350
Magdalena, Venezuela (Departmento),
  History, 18081
Magdaleno, Mauricio, El resplandor,
  19967
Maggie, a girl of the streets, 9212
Magic, 2431, 6376, 14155, 20068;
  Argentine Republic, Patagonia, 19891
The magic dice, 10693
The magic egg, 10896
Magical and sleight of hand performances,
  by Arikara, 17891
Magie, David, 1795-1865, 23024
Magie, James K., b.1827, 7390
Magill, John, 1759-1842, 7152, 14936
Um magistrado, 23895
Magna charta, 11660
Magnalia christi americana: or, The
  ecclesiastical history of New England,
  23305
Magnanini, Alceo, 20239
Magnetic instabilities in actinides,
  20447, 20448
The magnetic north, 4987
Magnetism, Terrestrial, 12239;
  Observations, 993
Magnificat, 20219
A magnificent plebeian, 10302
Magnificent scheme!, 14937
Magnolia leaves, 3849
Magnum Opus, 14938
Magnus Maharba, 8866, 8867
Magoffin, Beriah, 1815-1885, 15164
Magoffin County, Ky., 14259
Magoon, Charles Edward, 1861-1920, 20699
Magoon, Elias Lyman, 1810-1886, 23025,
  23026
Magoun, George Frederic, 23027
Magruder, Henry R., 7391
Magruder, Mary Lanier, 13567
Maguire, John Francis, 1815-1872, 23028
Maguire, Thomas, 1774-1854, 23029
Mahalinda, 10176
Mahaly Sawyer, 9426
Mahan, Alfred Thayer, 1840-1914, 14939
Mahan, Dennis Hart, 1802-1871, 23020,
  23031

Mahan, Milo, 1819-1870, 23032, 24958
Mahaska Co., Ia., History, 17384
Maher, John, 22730
Mahoney, Ann, 14940
Mahoney, William D., 8319
Mahony, Dennis A., 23033
Mahr, August C., 14941
Mai-jour, 23034
Maid Marian and other stories, 5118
The maid of Canal street, 10196
The maid of Maiden lane, 8733
The maid of the valley, 9855
The maid's revenge, 9846
Maidee, the alchemist, 8937
The maiden and negro, 9744
A maiden effort, 9331
The maiden's hand, 3997
Maierhauser, Fran, 14942, 14943
Mail steamers, U.S., 2271
Mailhe, Jean Baptiste, 1754-1839, 23035
Mailiard, N. Doran, 17117
Maillet, Benoit de, 1656-1738, 23036
Mailley, Édouard i.e. Nicolas Édouard, 1810-
  1891, 23037
Main, Thomas, 23038
La main-d'oeuvre à S. Thomé et à l'Île du
  Prince, 24966
La main d'oeuvre indigène à Angola, 23874
Main-travelled roads, 9606
Maine, 12409; Bibliography, 23040; Board of
  internal improvements, 12868; Boundaries,
  New Brunswick, 13463; Church history, 22273;
  Constitution, 23039; Description & travel,
  11194; Description & travel, Gazetteers,
  12766; Description & travel, Guide-books,
  1034; Fiction, 9657, 9946, 10035, 10038,
  10039, 10043; History, 23805; History,
  Colonial period, 972, 1803, 12514, 22164,
  23673; History, Colonial period, Sources,
  12930; Insane hospital, Augusta, 13018;
  Laws, statutes, etc., 745; Politics &
  government, 10822, 25892; State library,
  Augusta, 23040; Statistics, 12408; Surveys,
  12868
Maine artillery, 7th battery, 1863-1865, 4218
Maine cavalry, 1st regt., 1861-1865, 4458
Maine (District) Constitutional convention,
  1819, 23039
Maine historical society, 12515, 24959
Maine historical memorials, 24959
Maine infantry, 10th battalion, 1863-1864,
  3655; 1st regt., 1861, 3655; 5th regt. 1861-
  1864, 2709; 10th regt., 1861-1863, 3655;
  17th regt., 1862-1865, 12934, 20th regt.,
  1862-1865, 3592; 23d regt., 1862-1903, 4218;
  29th regt., 1863-1866, 3655

The Maine law, 11044
The Maine liquor law, 1916
Maine Union in Behalf of the Colored
  Race, 24960
Mains, George Preston, 1844-, 14944
Mair, Charles, 1838-, 7392
Mais, Charles, reporter, 23041
Majssin, Eugène, 2732
Maîtres et esclaves en Louisiane, 4451
Maize, 910, 11863; Varieties, 19513;
  West Indies, 19513
Maize in milk, 10776
Majó Framis, Ricardo, 7393
Major, Richard Henry, 1818-1891, 22252,
  23042, 23043
Major Jones' courtship, 5404
Major Jones' sketches of travel, 5405
Major Max, 10997
Majors, Alexander, 17118
Makemie, Francis, 1658-1708, 4378, 23044
Making an orator, 9216
Making haste to be rich, 10849
Making home happy, 8617
Making home peaceful, 8618
The making of a man, 8657
The making of Canada, 6149
Malan, César, 1787-1864, 23045
Malaria, 13757
Malarial fever, 13756; Law and legislation,
  Venezuela, 20637; Prevention, 13756
Malaspina, Alessandro, 1754-1809, 23046
Malcolm, Howard, 1799-1879, 23077
Malcolm, Mrs. Lydia M.(Shields) 1797-1833,
  23047
Malcolme, David, d.1748, 23048
Malden, Mass., 23049; History, 23049
Maldonado, Angel, bp., 1660-1728, 7860
Maldonado, Cristobal, 6677-6687
Malefijt, Annemarie de Waal, 20371
Malen, William Gunn, 23053
Malenfant, 23050
Das malerische Mexiko, 6155
Malespine, A., 7394
Malet, Sir Alexander, 2d. bart., 1800-
  1886, 23051
Malet, William Wyndham, 1804-1885, 4379
Malfatti, Anita, 18171
Malham, John, 1747-1821, 23052
Malheiro, Arthur, 19283
Mallard, Robert Q., 24961
Mallary, Rollen Carolus, 1784-1831, 23054,
  23055
Mallet, Alain Manesson, 1630?-1706?, 23056
Mallet, Edmond, 17120
Mallet, F., fl.1797, 23057
Mallet, John William, 1832-1912, 23058

Mallory, illustr., 10789
Malmiztic the Toltec, 9543
Malo de Molina y Espínola, Melchor, marqués
  de Monterrico, 6350
Malouet, Pierre-Victor, baron, 1740-1814,
  7395, 23059, 23060
Malpractice, 14677; Medical, 14676
Malte-Brun, Victor Adolphe, 1816-1889, 23061
Maltby, William J., 1829-, 17121
Malte-Brun, Conrad, originally Malthe Conrad
  Bruun, 1775-1826, 7396
Malthusianism, 2432
Malvar y Pintos, Sebastián, 7397
Mamamtavrishvili, D.G., 7398
Mamiani della Rovere, Ludovico Vincenzo,
  1652-1730, 23062
Mammals, 14694; Colombia, 20286; Cuba,
  Parasites, 20675; Fossil, 22514;
  Tamaulipas, 18212; North America, 174, 678,
  12684, 21764; Oregon, 17751; Paraguay, 590,
  597; Prehistoric, Kentucky, 14772
Mammoth, 494
Mammoth Cave, Ky., 3125, 3184, 3359, 3948,
  3949, 4242, 4324, 4403, 5006, 5401, 5486,
  13664, 13714, 13774, 13776, 13777, 14121,
  14204, 14354, 14448, 14481, 14839, 14860,
  14947, 15111, 15117, 15200, 15243, 15490,
  15728, 15729, 15779; Bibliography, 15243;
  Fiction, 2717
The Mammoth Cave and its inhabitants, 15111
Mammoth Cave National Park, 14947
Mammoth Cave National Park Association,
  14945-14947, 15200
Mammoth Veen Consolidated Coal Company, 23063,
  23064
Man, George Flagg, 23065
Man, Thomas, 23066, 23067
Man (Theology), 20634
Man, Influence of environment, 14328, 23804;
  Migrations, 22188; Origin, 11146, 13228;
  Prehistoric, 14151, 18664; Prehistoric,
  Argentine Republic, 18626; Prehistoric,
  California, 17622
The man and the mountain, 6975
The man at the semaphore, 6972
The man from Solano, 9779
The man machine, 10487
Man o'War, 15054, 15607, 15661
The man of enterprise, 10852
A man of her own faith, 15456
A man of honor, 3354
The man of sorrows, 6420
The man on the beach, 9779
Man proposes, 5498
A man story, 9933
The man that corrupted Hadleyburg, 9028

The man who "hadn't time", 8957
The man who likes Mexico, 6855
The man who worked for Collister, 9456
The man whose life was saved, 10899
The man whose yoke was not easy, 9779
The man with the branded hand, 24732
The man with the empty sleeves, 10808
The man with the hoe, 7412
The man without a country, 9684
Man's life considered under the similitude
   of a vapour, 21886
Man's wrongs, 10155
Manaos, Brazil, Harbor, Regulations,
   19342, 19343
Mañas, Uldarica, 7399
Manasseh ben Joseph ben Israel, 1604-1657,
   23068
Manatee Co., Fla., 5553
Manayunk, Pa., History, 12525
Manby, George William, 1765-1854, 23069
Mancera, Pedro de Toledo y Leiva,
   marqués de, 1585?-1654, 6851
Manchester (Ship), 12637
Manchester, Eng., Citizens, 24626, 25752
Manchester, N.H., City library, 23070;
   First Unitarian society, 2358; History,
   22904
Manchester and Abraham Lincoln; a side-
   light on an earlier fight for freedom,
   24626
Manchitas de color centroamericanas, 7343
Mancisidor, José, 1894-, 7400, 19967
Mandan Indians, 5374, 16168, 17458
The Mandan lodge at Bismarck, 17892
Mandar-Argeaut, pseud., 23071
Mandat-Grancey, Edmond, baron de, 1842-
   1911, 4381, 16261, 17122, 17123
Mandrillon, Joseph, 1743-1794, 6435, 23072
Mandry, Gustav von, 1832-1902, 24962
Manford, Erasmus, 4382, 23073
Manganese ores, 19508; Mexico, 18653
Mangino, Fernando Joseph, d.1806, 7401
The mangrove coast, 2707
Mangue Indians, 20080
Manhattan quartz mining company, 23074
The Manhattaner in New Orleans, 3732
El mani en su aspecto económico, 20546
Mania de grandeza, 19667
The maniac, 10310
A manifest destiny, 10303
The 'manifest destiny' of the American
   union, 24976
The manifesto, 14028
A manifesto of the lord protector of the
   Commonwealth of England, Scotland,
   Ireland, etc., 12368

Manigault, Gabriel, 1809-1888, 4383, 23075,
   24963
"Manin," 15089
Manitoba, 5234, 6769, 7384, 11353; Biography,
   6236; Description & travel, 3200, 3878,
   4361, 5674, 6233, 6299, 6531, 6941, 6943,
   7988, 8078, 8091, 8240, 8241, 13360, 15917;
   History, 6049, 6052, 6222, 6225, 6229, 6235,
   8128, 8411, 16438, 16552; History, Sources,
   7641
Manitoba and the Canadian northwest, 6621
Manitoba and the great North-west, 7384
Manitoba, and the North-west of the dominion,
   8091, 8387
Manitoba College, Winnipeg, 6217
Manley, James R., 1781-1851, 23076-23079
Manley, John, 23080
Manlius, 12318
Manly, William Lewis, 17124
Mann, Charles Wesley, 1862-1909, 24964
Mann, Cyrus, 1785-1859, 23081
Mann, Donald, 306
Mann, Edwin John, b.1812, comp., 23082
Mann, Herman, 1772-1833, 23085, 23229
Mann, Herman, 1795-1851, 23086
Mann, Horace, 1796-1859, 23083, 23084, 23087-
   23092
Mann, James, 23093
Mann, Joel, 1789-1884, 23094
Mann, William Julius, 1819-1892, 23095
Mannequin, Theodore, b.1819, 23096
Manners and customs in the West India Islands,
   25082
Manners and customs of several Indian tribes
   located west of the Mississippi, 3973
Mannheimer, Walter A., 18512
Manning, James, 1738-1791, 2425, 12492, 23097
Manning, John M., 14948
Manning, William Ray, 17125
Las manos de mama, 19967
Manpower supply, Costa Rica, 20589
Mansfeldt, Julius, 24965
Mansfield, Charles Finney, 1830-1865, 23110
Mansfield, Daniel, 1807-1847, 23098
Mansfield, Edward Deering, 1801-1880, 4384,
   14949, 23099, 23100-23108
Mansfield, Isaac, 1750-1826, 23109
Mansfield, Lewis W., 9727
Mansfield, Mrs. Lucy (Langdon), 23110
Mansfield, William Murray, 1st earl of, 1705-
   1793, 13389, 24833
Manship, Andrew, 1824-, 23111, 23112
Mansie, Alexander, 23113
Manstealers: will the Free church of Scotland
   hold Christian fellowship with them?, 25929
Mantegazza, Carlo, 23114

Mantegazza, Vico, 1856-, 4385
Mantero, Francisco, 24966-24968
Manti, Utah, Indians, 17470
Mantle and Cowan, firm, Louisville, Ky.,
 14950
Manton, Kate, pseud., 10155
Manual de historia y cronología de Mejico,
 482
Manual labour in S. Thomé and Principe,
 24967
A manual of American literature, 3803
Manuel, Cathy, 14951
Manuel Pereira, 46, 8459
Manufactures, Addresses, essays, lectures,
 300; Chile, Statistics, 20170
Manufacturing, Kentucky, 14245
Manufacturing, agricultural and industrial
 resources of Iowa, 16839
Manufacturing in the Concepción Region of
 Chile, 19597
Manufacturing interests of the city of
 Buffalo, 23115
Manumission and cases of contested
 freedom, 24589
Manumission Society of North Carolina,
 24970
Manuscripts, Greek (Papyri), 24344;
 Mexican, 6105; Mexican, Facsimiles,
 6438, 6644
Manwaring, Christopher, 1774-1832, 23116
Manzano, Juan Francisco, 1797-1854, 24969
Manzano Manzano, Juan, 5972
Manzini, Nicolás B.L., 1812-1896, 23117
Mão de mosa, 19166
Mãos vazias, 18040
Map and description of Texas, 4510
Map and directory of information, 14952
Map and guide to the Kansas gold region,
 4914
Map of Bureau county, Illinois, 17154
Map of Lexington and Fayette County,
 Kentucky, 14953
Map of Lexington and suburbs, 14954, 14955
Map of Lexington urban area, 14956
Map of the battle field of Fredericksburg,
 1446
Map of the Nez Percé and Salmon River gold
 mines, 4308
Map of the west coast of Africa, from
 Sierra Leone to Cape Palmas, 25943
A map of Virginia, 5204
Map projection, 19936
Mapes, James Jay, 1806-1866, 23118
Maple leaves from Canada, 23119
Mapleson, Thomas W. Gwilt, 23120
Mapleton, 9001

Maplewood Cemetery, Mayfield, Ky., 15422
Maps, Bibliography, Catalogs, 6296, 8210;
 Brazil, 19278
Mar del Plata, Argentine Republic, Instituto
 de Biología Marina, Boletín, 18712, 18714,
 19186, 19923, 20191, 20192
Maracaibo, Venezuela (Province), History,
 19483
Maracujá, Economic conditions, 20457
Marah, 4054
Maranhão, 5809; Brazil, Economic conditions,
 19453; (State), History, 11259
The Marbeau cousins, 3345
Marble, Manton, 1834-1917, 7402
Marble, Vermont, 12524
The marble faun, 9822
Marbourg, Dolores, jt. author, 9468
Marcandier, 23121
Marcellus, pseud., 23122, 23123
March, Alden, 1795-1869, 23124
March, Charles Wainwright, 1815-1864, 23125
March, Daniel, 1816-1909, 23126
March hares, 9568
Marchard, J.N., illustr., 13704
Marchese, Humberto G., 19675
Marching through Georgia, 3830
Marching with Sherman, 3887
Marchmont, Hugh Hume, 3d earl of, 1708-1794,
 23127
Marcia, 9355
Marckmann, Jørgen Wilhelm, 1804-1861, 23128
Marcou, Jules, 1824-1898, 4386, 17126, 23129
Marcus Aurelius, 5238
Marcy, Randolph Barnes, 1812-1887, 4387, 4388,
 4703, 5532, 5537, 5547, 5548, 17127, 17128
Mardi, 10344
Mardi gras, 11051
Marechal, Nicolas, b.1744?, 2466
Marest, Gabriel, 1662-1714, 16956
Margaret, 10075, 10076
Margaret Hall, Versailles, Ky., 15769
Margaret Smith's journal, 11154
Margaret's bridal, 10702
Margati, José, 1841-1887, 7403
Margret Howth, 9354
Margry, Pierre, 1818-1894, 7404, 17129
Marguerite, 9899
Maria, 23956
María Antonia de San Joseph, madre, 1708-1781,
 1797
María Cachucha, 19668
María de Jesús, mother, 1579-1637, 6717
Marian Elwood, 8887
Marian Grey, 3917
Marian Rooke, 10731
Mariátegui, Francisco Javier, 23130

287

Mariátegui, José Carlos, 1894-1930, 19815
Marie, 2658
Marie de Berniere, 10776
Marijuana: a pot of money for Kentucky, 14737
Marimba, 18542
Marin Co., Cal., Description & travel, 15979, 16596
Marin de Alfocea, Juan, 7405, 7406
Marine biology, 19187; Dictionaries, 19132
The marine climate of the Southern California coast, 17471
Marine fauna, Argentine Republic, Mar del Plata, 20191
Marine flora, 18713
Marine resources, Argentine Republic, 18428
El marinero instruido en el arte de navegar, 6007
Marines signalling under fire at Guantanamo, 9217
Mario Vargas Llosa y la literatura en el Peru de hoy, 19109
Marion, Francis, 1732-1795, 12729, 13157, 23770
Marion, Kentucky, 15686
Marion Co., Ia., History, 16411
Marion County, Ky., History, 14957
Marion Darche, 6498
Marion Graham, 10170
Marion National Bank, Lebanon, Ky., 14957
Marion-Sims, H., ed., 5170
Marion's faith, 10124
Marionelles, 9260
Mariotti, L., 3564
Mariposilla, 9306
Mariscal, Ignacio, 1829-1910, 7407
Mariscal, Mario, 18202
Maritime law, 812, 18200, 22009, 22882, 25676; Gt. Britain, 11713, 13478; Newfoundland, 385; Pennsylvania, 9918; Spanish America, History, 18858; U.S., 1494
Mariz, Pedro de, d.1615, 23131
Marjoribanks, Alexander, 4389
Marjorie Daw and other people, 8498
Mark Dunning's enemy, 8978
Mark Gildersleeve, 10706
Mark Heffron, 8640
Mark Rowland, 10788
Marke, Desdemona, 23132
Marked "personal", 10666
Markens, Edward Wasgate, 7408
Markens, Isaac, 7409, 7410
The market book, 2120

The market-place, 9569
Market surveys, Colombia, 18332; Santo André (São Paulo), 18971; São Paulo metropolitan area, 18971
Marketing research, 19921
Markets, Massachusetts, 22142
Markham, Sir Clements Robert, 1830-1916, 7411, 7964, 23133
Markham, Edwin, 1852, 7412, 17130
Markham, William, abp. of York, 1719-1807, 23134
Markland or Nova Scotia, 7379
Markoe, Peter, 1753?-1792, 23135
Marks, Alfred, 17131
Marks, David, 1805-1845, 23136
Marks, Elias, 1790-1886, 4390
Marks, James Junius, 1809-1899, 4391
Marks, Mrs. Marilla (Turner) ed., 23136
The marksmen of Monmouth, 9296
Marl, South Carolina, 12869
Marlborough, Mass., Genealogy, 22590; History, 22590
Marlow brothers gang, 17447
Marlowe, Judy, jt. author, 14227
Marly, 23137
Marmaduke, Meredith Miles, 1791-1864,
Marmaduke Wyvil, 9846
Marmier, Xavier, 1809-1892, 4392, 7413, 23138
Marmont, Auguste Frédéric Louis Viesse de, duc de Ragase, 1774-1852, 23139
Marmontel, Jean François, 1723-1799, 1544
The maroon, 10776
Marquand, Henri E., 24972
Marqués, José Frederico, 18126
La Marquesa de Yolombó, 19830
Marquette, Jacques, 1637-1675, 4393
Marquez, José Arnoldo, 23140, 23141
Marquez, Pedro [Jose] 1741-1820, 7414
Marr, Frances Harrison, 1835-, 4394, 4395
Marr, Janey Hope, 3933
Marr, Wilhelm, b.1819, 23142
Marrant, John, 1755-, 4396
Marraro, Howard Rosario, 1897-, 7415
Marriage, 301, 7032, 7033; U.S., 11663
Marriage brokerage, New York (City), 23349
Marriage customs and rites, 12607, 15525
Marriage law, Cambodia, 24804
Marriage of Marie Modeste, 10135
The marriages, 7122
Married against reason, 10290
Married by mistake, 10919
Married for a dinner, 10580
Married for both worlds, 10552
Married, not mated, 8949
"Married off", 1192
The married shrew, 10841

Marriott, Sir James, bart., 1730?-1803,
23144, 23145
Marriott, John, 1762-1797, 23146
Marriott, W. H., 14050
Marryat, Francis Samuel, 1826-1855, 17133
Marryat, Frederick, 1792-1848, 4397,
4398, 11685, 17134
Marryat, Joseph, 1757-1824, 23147, 23148
Marrying by lot, 10388
Marsden, Joshua, b.1777, 23149, 23150
Marse Chan, 10461
Marseille, Commerce, 11717
Marseille, Gotthold, 1852-, 3270
Marsena, 9567, 9570
Marsh, Catherine, 1818-1912, 23151, 23152
Marsh, Charles W., 1834-, 17135
Marsh, Edward Sprague, 1857-, 7416
Marsh, George Perkins, 1801-1882, 23153-
23156, 25151
Marsh, James, 1794-1842, 23156
Marsh, James B., 17136
Marsh, James W., 23157
Marsh, John, 15389
Marsh, John, 1743-1821, 23158-23160
Marsh, John, 1788-1868, 23161-23165
Marsh, Jonathan, 1689-1708, 21849
Marsh, Leonard, 1800-1870, 23166, 24973
Marsh, Othniel Charles, 1831-1899, 23167
Marsh, Ramona, 14958
Marsh, Roswell, 23168
Marsh, William, 1775-1864, 23152
A marsh island, 10039
Marshall, Mrs. A.J., 1813-, 17137
Marshall, Albert O., 4399
Marshall, Charles Henry, 1792-1865, 1774
Marshall, Christopher, 1709-1797, 23169
Marshall, Edward Chauncey, 1824-, 23170
Marshall, Humphrey, 1760-1841, 4400, 4878,
13415, 14587
Marshall, Humphrey, 1812-1872, 23974;
Port., 14378
Marshall, James, 1834-1896, 23171, 23172
Marshall, James V., 23173
Marshall, James Wilson, 1812-1885, 15808,
16790, 17358
Marshall, John, 1755-1835, 1311, 1625,
13416, 14078, 23174-23176
Marshall, John, 1783-1841, 1565
Marshall, John, 1784?-1837, 23177
Marshall, John A., 23178
Marshall, Josiah T., 23179
Marshall, Logan, 7417
Marshall, Thomas, 23975
Marshall, Thomas, 1730-1802, 14919
Marshall, Thomas Francis, 1801-1864, 4401,
15563

Marshall, Thomas Maitland, 17138
Marshall, Walter, 1628, 14959
Marshall, William Isaac, 1840-1906, 17139-
17141
Marshall College, Mercersburg, Pa.,
Diagnothian society, 1580
Marshall Co., Ia., History, 17560
Marshall Co., Ill., History, 2274
Marshall family, 14919
Marshall's gold discovery, 16790
The marshalship in North Carolina, 2439
Marshes, 18018
Marsillac, Jean, 23180
Marston, Mrs. Anna Lee, 1853-, 16657
Marsupials, 20527
Martens, Georg Friedrich von, 1756-1821,
23181
Martha Washingtonianism, 13249
Martha's lady, 10042
Marthas Vineyard, Mass., Description & travel,
2101; History, 23394
Martí, José, 1853-1895, 4402, 7664;
Bibliography, 19074
The Martial achievements of Great Britain
and her allies, 23182
Martial law, 1454, 13135; U.S., 6669, 13090,
23178, 25047
Martin, Archer Evans Stringer, 1865-, 6181
Martin, Asa Earl, 14960
Martin, Benjamin Ellis, d.1909, 23183
Martin, Charles I., 17142
Martin, Ella Rena, 14280
Martin, Ennalls, 1758-1834, 23184
Martin, Enrico, d.1632, 7418, 7419
Martin, Felix, 1804-1886, 1482
Martin, François Xavier, 1762?-1846, 23185,
23186
Martin, Franklin, 7420
Martin, Frederick, 1830-1883, 23187
Martin, George Madden, 1866-, 13553, 14961
Martin, George Washington, 1841-, 17143,
17144
Martin, Henri, 1810-1883, 2414
Martin, Henry, 23188
Martin, Horace, 4403
Martin, James W., 13717, 14962, 14963
Martin, John, 1741-1820, 23189
Martin, Jonah, 21928
Martin, Joseph, 4404
Martin, Leopold Charles, 1817-1889, 23190
Martin, Luther, 1748-1826, 13417
Martin, Michael, 1795-1821, 23191
Martin, Morgan Lewis, 1805-1887, 23192
Martin, Percy Falcke, 1861-, 7421, 7422
Martin, Robert Montgomery, 1803-1868, 6742,
7423, 23193, 23194

Martin, Robert Richard, 1910- , 14360
Martin, Stefan, illustr., 15001
Martin, William Charles Linnaeus, 1798-1864, 23195
Martin, William T., 1788-1866, 23196
Martin's Station, 13871
Martin-Chablis, illustr., 4381
Martin County, Ky., 14569, 15686
Martin Faber, 10777
Martin Fierro at the University of Texas, 18991
Martin Garatuza, 19968
Martin Mateo, Ranion, 20102
Martindale, Joseph C., 23197
The Martindale pastoral, 8987
Martineau, Harriet, 1802-1876, 7424, 7425, 23198, 24167, 24976
Martíney, Andres, of Anadarko, Ohio, 17186
Martínez, Gerardo Rubén, 20244
Martínez, José de Jesús. Aurora y el mestizo, 18052
Martínez, Juan J., 18947
Martínez Baez, Antonio, 19589
Martínez Caro, Ramón, 4405
Martínez de Amileta, Andrés, 6282
Martínez de Diego, Cayetano, 7426
Martínez de la Marcha, Hernando, 16th cent., 8168
Martínez de la Parra, Juan, 1655-1701, 7427
Martínez de la Puente, José, fl.1681, 23199
Martínez de la Torre, Rafael, 1828-1876, 7872
Martínez Tamayo, Francisco, 8027
Martinique, Description & travel, 4644, 7000, 11414; Eonomic conditions, 25564; Politics & government, Revolution, 8054
Martins, Antônio, 20015
Martins, J.B., 19869
Los mártires del Anahuac, 19968
Martirio de San Dionisio, 19782
Martius, Karl Friedrich Philipp von, 1794-1868, 23200, 23201
Martyn, Benjamin, 1699-1763, 4406, 23202
Martynov, Vladimir Alekseevich, 18077
The martyr, 8622
The martyr-president, 2184, 22515
The martyr prince, 699
Martyr's monument association, 23681
The martyrdom of Frederick, 13032
Martyria, 12621
The martyrs, 10076
The martyrs and heroes of Illinois in the great rebellion, 860

Martyrs to the revolution in the British prison-ships in the Wallabout Bay, 23681
Maruja, 9785
Marure, Alejandro, 1809-1851, 23203
Marvel, Ik, pseud., 10360, 10362
The marvellous country, 16287
Marvin, Abijah Perkins, 23204, 24977
Marvin, Donald Mitchell, 1893- , 7428
Marvin, Dudley, 1786-1856, 23205
Marvin, Henry, 23206
Marvin, Theophilus-Rogers, 1796-1882, 23207
Marvin, William F., 4407
Marvin, William Theophilus Rogers, 1832-1913, 1886
Marvin family (Matthew Marvin, 1600?-1678), 23207
Marvin family (Reinold, Marvin, 1593?-1662), 23207
Marxian economics, 19611
Marxism, 20027
Marxismo ortodoxo, 18391
Mary (Sloop), 22730
Mary, Virgin, 7318, 8766; Apparitions & miracles (modern), 6753, 6754, 7459; Art, 1786
Mary Barker, 9218
Mary Bunyan, 3506
Mary Crawford's chart, 15091
Mary Derwent, 10869
Mary Dyre, 10730
Mary Elmer, 11136
Mary Idyl's trials and triumphs, 8890
Mary Lyndon, 10422
Mary McIntire has arrived, 10953
Mary Morland, 8701
Mary Rice, 10760
Mary Staunton, 11142
Mary V.V., pseud., 2107
Maryland, Boundaries, 23733; Capital and capitol, 12652; Charters, 4929, 11748; Church history, 2088; Constitution, 1132, 23209, 23210, 23220, 25354; Constitutional convention, 1864, 23210; Description & travel, 2515, 2646, 2771, 2773, 2852, 2959, 3325, 3336, 3340, 3490, 3516, 3519, 3603, 3663, 3722, 3737, 4173, 4682, 4929, 4930, 4998, 5147, 5440, 5768, 14370, 14749, 15527, 23216; Economic conditions, 23216; General assembly, 1787, House of delegates, 23212; General assembly, House of delegates, Committee on federal relations, 23213-23215; General assembly, House of delegates, Committee on grievances and courts of justice, 24978; General assembly, House of delegates, Select Committee on the resources of Maryland, 23216; General assembly,

Senate, Committee on education, Report
with sundry resolutions, 23388; Governor,
1865-1869 (Thomas Swann), 23217;
History, 8051, 12435; History, Civil
war, 1849, 1850, 2479, 3635; History,
Colonial period, 170, 171, 769, 1603,
2088, 3221, 3764, 4929, 5305, 11472,
12526, 12627, 13413, 22782, 22995;
History, Colonial period, Fiction,
4156, 10096; History, Colonial period,
Sources, 2460, 4378; History, Fiction,
9003; History, Revolution, 3336, 12245,
21917; History, Revolution, Sources,
698, 23211; Laws, statutes, etc., 1686,
12210, 21908, 22428, 23218-23220, 25776;
Legislature, Senate, 8316; Maps, 22288;
Militia, 22448; Politics & government,
1510, 13413, 23220; Politics &
government, Civil war, 23213-23215,
24815; Politics & government, Colonial
period, 11560, 23208; Politics &
government, Revolution, 2423; Susquehanna
canal commissioners, 23221
Maryland (Colony), 23208; Convention, 1775,
23211; Governor, 1733-1742, (Samuel Ogle),
23208
Maryland artillery, 1st battery, 1861-
1864, 12264; 1st regt., 1793-, 13099
Maryland campaign, 1862, 22800, 22802
Maryland cavalry, 1st regt., Potomac home
brigade, 1861-1865, 4591
Maryland historical society, 171, 12245,
23381
Maryland infantry, 1st District of Columbia
and Maryland regt. 1847-1848, 13320
The Maryland resolutions, and the
objections to them considered, 23381
Maryland Society for Promoting the
Abolition of Slavery, 24049, 24979,
25232, 25491
Maryland State Colonization Society, 24980
Maryland toleration, 170
Marysville, Cal., Description, 21775
Marzio's crucifix, 6499, 9227
Maschke, Richard, 1862-1926, 24981
Maseres, Francis, 1731-1824, 23222-23225
Mashiaj, 18303
Mashpee Indians, 404
Masias, Felipe, 23226
The masked singer, 10304
Mäskōke hymns, 1648
Mason, Armistead Thomson, 1787-1819,
22791
Mason, Augustus Lynch, 7429
Mason, Benjamin, 23227
Mason, Charles, 1804-1882, 17145

Mason, Cyrus, 23228
Mason, Ebenezer, 23229
Mason, Emily Virginia, 1815-1909, 4408
Mason, Erskine, 1805-1851, 23230, 23231
Mason, Francis, 1799-1874, 23232
Mason, Frank Holcomb, 1840-1916, 4409
Mason, George, 428
Mason, George, 1725-1792, 7431
Mason, George Champlin, 1820-1894, 23233,
23234
Mason, John, 1586-1635, 13498, 23235
Mason, John, 1600-1672, 23236
Mason, John Mitchell, 1770-1829, 23237, 23238
Mason, John Young, 1799-1859, 23239
Mason, Jonathan, 1756-1831, 4410
Mason, Mrs. M.F.C., 24121
Mason, R. H., 7430
Mason, Richard Lee, d.1824, 14964
Mason, Richard R., 24983
Mason, Robert C., 7431
Mason, Samson, 23240
Mason, Stuart, pseud., 5704
Mason, Timothy B., 2776
Mason, Vroman, 24981
Mason, William, 1725-1797, 23241, 24985
Mason, William Powell, 1791-1867, 23242
Mason, Mass., History, 22467
Mason, N.H., Biography, 22476; History, 22476,
22477
Mason and Dixon's line, 23733
Mason Co., Ill., History, 23479
Mason Co., Ky., Biography, 14795; History,
13658, 13659, 13854, 14744, 14795
The masonic martyr, 4531
Masonic odes and poems, 4532
The Masonic union, 23243
Mass media, 14651
Mass transportation operations, Financing of,
15281
Massa's in de cold ground, 14123
Massabie, Armando C., 19675
Massachuset Indians, Missions, 12006, 13141,
23610, 23790
Massachusetts, pseud., 23244, 24986
Massachusetts, Ancient and honorable artillery
company, 1778; Astronomical and trigo-
nometrical survey, 23249; Biography, 2269,
11824; Board of Education, 23090; Board of
internal improvements, 23250, 23251;
Boundaries, 13051; Boundaries, Rhode Island,
505; Capital and capitol, 23260; Census,
1855, 23267; Charters, 11748, 13422, 22061;
Church history, 1886; Claims v. United
States, 11799; Commissioners on flats in
Boston harbor, 23252; Commissioners on
pauper system, 23253; Constitution, 21983;

Constitutional convention, 1779-1780, 23254; Constitutional convention, 1820-1821, 23255; Constitutional law, 1884; Description & travel, 783, 4222, 5147, 12279, 12542, 22547; Description & travel, Gazetters, 12764; Directories, 12768; Genealogy, 2448, 21801; General Court, 22075; General Court, 1809, 23256; General Court, 1832, 12358; General court, 1849, 23263; General Court, 1855, 12537; General Court, Committee to investigate convents, nunneries, etc., 12537; General Court, Committee to prepare a memorial to Congress on the subject of the prohibition of slavery in the United States, 24987; General Court, 1821, House of Representatives, 23257, 24459; General Court, 1849, House of Representatives, 25783; General Court, House of Representatives, Committee on admission into the state of free Negroes and mulattoes, 23258, 24988; General Court, House of Representatives, Committee on capital punishment, Report, 22150, 23259; General Court, House of Representatives, Committee on ventilation of the representatives' hall, 23260; General Court, House of Representatives, Privileges and immunities, 1883; General Court, Joint committee on anti-slavery societies, etc., 25000; General Court, Joint Committee on deliverance of citizens liable to be sold as slaves, 24989; General Court, Joint committee on ship canal to connect Barnstable Bay and Buzzard's Bay, 23261; General Court, Joint special committee on laws relating to registration of births, marriages, and deaths, 23262; General Court, Joint Special Committee on memorial of Oliver B. Morris and others, 24990; General Court, Joint special committee on petition of Asa Stoughton and others, 24951; General Court, Joint special committee on petition of Geo. R. M. Withington and others, 23263; General Court, Joint special committee on slavery, 24992, 24993; General Court, Joint special committee on so much of the governor's address as relates to slavery, 24994; General Court, Joint special committee on the treatment of Samuel Hoar by the state of South Carolina, 24995; General Court, Joint standing committee on towns, 558; General Court, 1814, Senate,

23264; General Court, 1836, Senate, 24996; Geological survey, 23265; Governor, 1800-1807 (Caleb Strong), 712; Governor, 1808-1809 (Levi Lincoln), 23257; Governor, 1812-1816 (Caleb Strong), 12109, 23266; Governor, 1861-1866 (John A. Andrew), 1785; Governors, 2247; History, 11493, 11672, 21771, 22460; History, 1775-1865, 586; History, To 1776, 21753; History, To 1776, poetry, 23502, 23703; History, Bibliography, Catalogs, 23273-23275; History, Civil war, 23204; History, Colonial period, 12052, 13422, 21754, 21755, 21806, 22106, 22250, 22588, 23277, 23433, 23783, 23809, 23810; History, Colonial period, Fiction, 8468, 8609, 8992, 10390, 10724, 11149; History, Colonial period (New Plymouth), 766, 922, 990, 991, 1513, 1755, 2018, 11824, 12806; History, Colonial period (New Plymouth), Sources, 23826; History, Colonial period, Poetry, 22762, 23450, 23683; History, Colonial period, Sources, 22627; History, Fiction, 10390; History, Revolution, 24364; History, Revolution, Addresses, sermons, etc., 22579; History, Societies, 23272; History, War of 1812, 11799; History, Local, 783; Manufactures, 1265; Manufactures, Statistics, 23268; Militia, 1328, 23257; Militia, Courts-martial, Goodale, 1812, 2438; Militia, regulations, 23248; Politics & government, 23256; Politics & government, 1775-1865, 11913, 12537, 21983, 22075, 22454, 22455, 24053, 24599, 25005, 25368; Politics & government, Civil war, 1785, 7592, 25236; Politics & government, Colonial period, 2175, 11258, 13422, 13493, 21931, 22203, 23667; Politics & government, Revolution, 181, 2012, 4873, 23246, 23247, 23430; Politics & government, War of 1812, 23264, 23266; Population, 1879; Sanit. Aff., 11921; Secretary of the commonwealth, 23267, 23268; Social life & customs, 10152; State prison, Charlestown, 12759; Statistics, 12764; Statistics, Vital, 23262; Supreme judicial court, 580, 856, 5997, 12681, 23229; Surveys, 23249; Zoological and botanical survey, 12329
Massachusetts (Colony), 22061; Charters, 23245; Council, 1712, 21904, 23667; General Court, 1773, 22628; General Court, 1725, House of representatives, 23245; Governor, 1760-1770 (Francis Bernard), 11258, 11385; Laws, statutes, etc., 23466; Provincial Congress, 23246; Provincial Congress, Oct.-Dec. 1774, 23247; Provincial Congress, Feb.-Apr. 1775, 13418, 23247, 23248

Massachusetts abolition society, 24997-24999
Massachusetts anti-slavery society, 1881, 11736, 24993, 24997, 24999, 25000-25003, 25211, 25263
Massachusetts artillery. 1st battery, 1861-1864, 2669; 10th battery, 1862-1865, 2715
Massachusetts Bay, History, 22071
Massachusetts cavalry. 1st regt., 1861-1865, 11430; 2d regt., 1862-1865, 3966
Massachusetts charitable fire society, 68
Massachusetts charitable mechanic association, 11604, 12874, 13201
Massachusetts emigrant aid company, 4411
A Massachusetts farmer, 25695
Massachusetts general hospital, Boston, 11433, 23269-23271
Massachusetts historical society, Boston, 505, 12052, 12054, 21747, 23272, 23277-23280; Library, 23273-23277
Massachusetts horticultural Society, 23281-23283
Massachusetts in mourning, 24600
Massachusetts Indians, Missions, 23299
Massachusetts infantry. 1st regt., 1861-1864, 3136; 2d regt., 1861-1865, 4537, 4874, 4876; 4th regt., 1861, 16402; 6th regt., 1861-, 3771; 9th regt., 1861-1864, 4371; 11th regt., 1861-1865, 1394; 12th regt., 1861-1864, 3076; 16th regt., 1861-1864, 2358; 18th regt., 1861-1864, 3186; 19th regt., 1861-1865, 2492; 20th regt., 1861-1865, 4757; 21st regt., 1861-1865, 5598; 23d regt., 1861-1865, 3381, 16402; 24th regt., 1861-1866, 2533; 25th regt., 1861-1865, 4870; 27th regt., 1861-1865, 3235; 29th regt., 1861-1865, 4661; 32d regt., 1862-1865, 4697; 33d regt., 1862-1865, 2751; 34th regt., 1862-1865, 1659; 36th regt., 1862-1865, 22842; 37th regt., 1862-1865, 5490; 38th regt., 1862-1865, 4842; 43d regt., 1862-1863, 5008; 44th regt., 1862-1863, 3729; 45th regt., 1862-1863, 3958; 49th regt., 1862-1863, 4062; 52d regt., 1862-1863, 3944; 55th regt. (colored) 1863-1865, 12154; 58th regt., 1863-1865, 22004
Massachusetts Junior, pseud., 25004
Massachusetts Medical Society, 23284, 23285; Library, 23286
Massachusetts missionary society, 4479
Massachusetts Peace Society (Founded
1815), 23287
Massachusetts Sabbath school society, 644, 12724, 13141, 22812; Committee of publication, 127, 23081
Massachusetts School of Agriculture, 23288
Massachusetts Society for Promoting Agriculture, 23289
Massachusetts State Disunion Convention, Worcester, 1857, 25005
Massachusetts State Texas Committee, 25006
Massachusetts Temperance Convention, Worcester, 1833, 23290
Massachusetts Temperance Society, 23291
Massacres of the mountains, 16440
Massay, Sheyla, 20225
Masse, Étienne Michel, b.1778, 23292
Masseras, E., 7432
Massey, Edmund, 23294
Massey, George Valentine, 1903-, 7433, 7434, 7435
Massey, Stephen L., 4412
Massie, I. N., 14965
Massie, James William, 1799-1869, 4413, 25007, 25008
Massie, Joseph, d.1784, 23293, 25009
Masson, Louis Francois Redrigve, 1833-1903, 17148
Master Ardick, buccaneer, 9176
Master of his fate, 8734
The master of magicians, 11074
The master of Rushen, 8723
The master of silence, 8628
Master William Mitten, 4295
The master's house, 10963, 25694
Mastigoproctus baracoensis Fraganillo, 18530
Mastin, Bettye Lee, 13868, 14966-14971
Mastronardi, Carlos, 18830
Masustegui, Pedro, 7436
Matabele war, 1896, 24564
Matagorda, Tex., History, 3833
Matanzas, Cuba (City), 153
Matanzas Bay, Cuba, Capture of the Spanish silver-fleet, 1628, 338
Match industry, Mexico, 19672
Mate (shrub), 11983
The mate of the daylight, 10040
The mate of the "Easter Bell", 8735
Mater Dolorosa, 9331
Mater Felix, 9331
Materia medica, 943; Spanish America, 23441
The material and the spiritual in our national life, 25816
Materiales para el estudio de la cuestión agraria en Venezuela, 19747
The materialist, 9530
Mateus e Mateusa de Qorpo-Santo, 19716

Mathematical statistics, 19824
Mathematics, Study and teaching
  (Secondary), 20092; Bibliography,
  18379; Curricula, 20604
Mather, Cotton, 1663-1728, 1073, 14972,
  23295-23318, 23364
Mather, Increase, 1639-1723, 1072,
  13419, 23306, 23308, 23319-23330
Mather, James, 4414
Mather, Joseph H., 23331
Mather, Moses, 1719-1806, 237, 23332
Mather, Nathaniel, 1631-1697, 23333,
  23335
Mather, Otis May, 1868-, 25010
Mather, Richard, 1596-1669, 23328, 23334
Mather, Samuel, b.1674, ed., 23306, 23335-
  23338
Mather, William Williams, 1804-1859,
  23339, 23340
Mather family (Richard Mather, 1596-1669),
  23330
Mathers, William, 23341
Matheson, James, 4912
Mathew, Theobald, 1790-1856, 23028, 24411
Mathews, Alfred E., 4415, 17150, 17151
Mathews, Mrs. Anne (Jackson) 1782?-1869,
  23342
Mathews, Charles, 13420, 23342
Mathews, Cornelius, 1817-1889, 435, 23343-
  23347
Mathews, Edward James, 1836-1901, 17152
Mathews, Janice, 14973
Mathews, Mrs. Mary McNair, 17153
Mathews, Samuel Augustus, 25011
Matilda Berkely, 9595
Matilda Douglas, 10258
Matlack, Lucius C., 1243, 25012
Matlack, Timothy, 1736-1829, 23348
Mato Grosso, fronteira Brazil-Bolivia
  e Rondônia, 19605
Matos, Mario C., 18881
Matrimonial brokerage in the metropolis,
  23349
Matrimonial infelicities, 9060
The Matrimonial Tontine Benefit Association,
  9639
Matson, Nehemiah, 1816-1883, 17154-17157,
  23350
A matter of friendship, 15264
A matter of honor, 13524
Matteson, Mrs. Frances F., 23351
Matteson, Orsamus B., 1805-1889, 23352
Matthes, Benno, 17158
Matthew Lyon, the Hampden of Congress,
  14921
Matthews, Alberta, 5216

Matthews, Brander, 1852-1929, 2695
Matthews, Mrs. Essie (Collins), 25014
Matthews, James Muscoe, b.1822, ed., 2061,
  2062, 2063
Matthews, John, 7437, 23353
Matthews, John W., d.1860, 13188
Matthews, Lyman, 1801-1866, 23354, 23355
Matthews, Sue Froman, 14974
Matthews, William Baynham, 1850-1914, 17159
Matthews, William L., 14689
Matthews' American armoury and blue book, 7437
Matthias, Benjamin, 23356
Mattingly, L. F., 14975
Mattison, Hiram, 1811-1868, 23357
Matto Grosso, Brazil (State), 11384
Mattson, Hans, 1832-1893, 17161
Maubert de Gouvest, Jean Henri, 1721-1767,
  23358
Maud Elbert's love match, 10427
Maud Evelyn, 10016
Maud Mansfield, 9908
Maud of the Mississippi, 2500
Maude, John, 7438
Maude and Miriam, 10285
Maudit passeport', 2908
Maudslay, Alfred Percival, 1850-, 7439
Maudslay, Anne Cary (Morris), 7439
Maudslay Collection of Maya sculptures, 19495
Mauduit, Israel, 1708-1787, 13421, 13422,
  23359-23362
Mauduit, Jasper, 23363
Maule, Joseph E., 23365
Maule, Thomas, 1645-1724, 23364
Maule (Province), Chile, 20163
Maull, D. W., 23366
Maumee Valley, History, 12920
Maunder, Samuel, 1785-1849, 23367
Maupertuis, Pierre Louis Moreau de, 1698-
  1759, 23368, 25015
Mauran, Joseph, 1796-1873, 23369, 23370
Maurice, Caesar, 8639
Maurice, Frederick Denison, 1805-1872, 23371
Maurice, Jacques, pseud., 10386
Mauricio, Jayme, 19154
Mauritania, Social conditions, 24535, 25153,
  25156
Maury, Abraham Poindexter, 1801-1848, 23372
Maury, Ann, 1803-1876, 2263, 3494
Maury, Dabney Herndon, 1822-1900, 4416
Maury, Matthew Fontaine, 1806-1873, 4417,
  4418, 23373-23377
Maury, Sarah Mytton (Hughes) "Mrs. William
  Maury", 1803-1849, 4419, 4420
Maury, Sarah Webb, 14976
Maury's wind and current charts, 23377
Maus, Marion Perry, 1850-1930, 17193

Maverick, Augustus, 11520
Maverick, George Madison, 1845-, 17162
Maverick, Mrs. Mary Ann (Adams) 1818-
1918, 17162
Maverick, Samuel, d.1770, 23477
Mavor, William Fordyce, 1758-1837, 23378,
23379
Mawe, John, 1764-1829, 23380
Max Keesler's horse-car, 9678
Maxey, Jonathan, 1768-1820, 23382-23385
Maxey, Virgil, 1785-1844, 23386-23388
Maxima and minima, 19030
Maximilian, emperor of Mexico, 1832-1867,
7188, 7205, 7206, 7872, 7944
Maximilien et le Mexique, 22422
Maxims, 793, 14484, 18169
Maximus, bp. of Saragossa, fl.599-619, 400
Maxson, Edwin R., 23389
Maxwell, Archibald Montgomery, 4421
Maxwell, Augustus Emmett, 1820-1903, 25016,
25017
Maxwell, William, 1784-1857, 4422, 4423
Maxwell, William Audley, d.1921, 17163
Maxwell, Wright & Co., Rio de Janeiro,
23390
May, Caroline, 1820(ca.)-, ed., 4424
May, Henry, 1816-1863, 25018
May, James, 1805-1863, 25019
May, John, 1748-1812, 4425
May, Mrs. Letitia, 11353, 15954
May, Samuel, 1810-1899, 25020
May, Samuel Joseph, 1797-1871, 25021,
25022
May, Sir Thomas Erskine, baron Farnborough,
1815-1886, 23391
May, William, d.1855, 16350
May-day in New York, 10820
May-flies, 23692
May Martin, 10959
Maya, Augustin, 7440-7442
Maya indians, 19495
Maya language, Dictionaries, English, 7590;
French, 7231; Grammar, 1136, 7231, 7590
Maya literature, Manuscripts, 20230
Mayall, Samuel, 23392
The Mayan calendar, 18887
Mayas, 20362; Antiquities, 6135, 6406-
6408, 7231, 7439, 7590, 8288, 23538;
History, 1440; Religion and mythology,
20229
Los mayas según el Códice Trocortesiano,
20229
Maycock, James Dottin, 23393
Mayer, Brantz, 1809-1879, 7443, 7444,
17164, 23381, 24187
Mayer, Joan P., 14977

Mayes, Daniel, 14978-14980
Mayes, Edward, 1846-, 4426
Mayfield, Eugene O., 17165
Mayfield, Ky. First Baptist Church, 14981
Mayflower (ship), 7374, 10904
Mayhew, Experience, 1673-1758, 23394
Mayhew, Jonathan, 1720-1766, 11495, 11788,
21955, 22235, 23395-23400
Mayhew, Thomas, 1621-1657, 23790
Mayhew family, 23394
Maynard, Mrs. Catherine Troutman (Simmons)
1816-1906, 17431
Maynard, Charles Johnson, 1845-, 23401
Maynard, David Swinson, 1808-1873, 17431
Maynard, Mrs. Henrietta Sturdevant (Colburn),
1841-1892, 7445, 7446
Maynard, Horace,1814-1882, 7447, 23402
Maynard, John W., 23403
Maynarde, Thomas, fl.1595, 23404
Mayne, Fanny, 23405
Mayne, Richard Charles, 1835-1892, 23406
Mayo, Amory Dwight, 1823-1907, 7448, 10335
Mayo, Robert, 1784-1864, 17166
Mayor des Planches, Edmondo, 1851-1920, 4427
The Maypole of Merry Mount, 9827
Maysville, Ky., History, 8010, 13854
Mazariegos, Cristobal, 6364
Maziel, Juan Baltasar, 1727-1788, 18931
Mazyck, Arthur, 1850-, 4428
Mazzei, Filippo, 1730-1816, 4429
Mazzuchelli, Samuel Charles, 1806-1864, 17167
Meacham, Alfred Benjamin, 1826-1882, 16000
Meacham, Henry H., 23407
Meacham, Joseph, 1742-1796, 12094
Mead, Asa, 1792-1831, 23408
Mead, Charles, 4430, 23409
Mead, Daniel M., 23410
Mead, John Mooney, 1826-1831, 23408
Mead, K.C. (Hurd), Dr., 9331
Mead, Samuel, 1764-1818, 23411
Meade, David, 1744-1838, 14449
Meade, George Gordon, 1815-1872, 4321
Meade, Richard Worsam, 1778-1828, 23412
Meade, Richard Worsam, 1807-1870, 23413
Meade, William, bp., 1789-1862, 4431, 7572,
22715, 23415
Meade, William, 14389, 23414
Meade's headquarters, 4321
Meade County, Ky., History, 15095, 15275;
Views, 15565
Meader, J.W., 23416
Meadow, Utah, 17682
Meadow-Brook, 9900
Meagher, Thomas Frances, 1823-1867, 22771
Means, Eldred Kurtz, 1878-1957, 25023
Means, Sterling M., 14982

Means and ends of education, 5241
Meares, John, 1756?-1809, 17168
Mears, W.E., 14900
Measures of adjustment, 24308
La mecanización agrícola en la Argentina, 18800
The mechanic, 10269
Mechanics and metals national bank, New York, 2182
Mechanics institutes, 12874
The Mechanics' magazine, 23417
Mecklenburg declaration of independence, 13309
Medals, 12875; Brazil, 18790; U.S., 1750
Medellín, Colombia, Economic conditions, 18599
Medellín and surrounding area, 18599
Medford, Macall, 23418
Medford, Mass., Genealogy, 1573; History, 1573; History, Civil war, 1572
The mediator between North and South, 23419
The Medical and agricultural register, 23420
Medical and physical memoirs, 13763, 13764
Medical and physical researches, 12685
Medical assistance in Kentucky, 13951
Medical care, Colombia, 20346; Cost of, 20279; Costs of, Kentucky, 15778; Cuba, 18958
Medical charities, Kentucky, 13951
Medical College of Ohio, Cincinnati, 14012
Medical delusions, 12884
Medical education, Colombia, 18593; U.S., 1923; Venezuela, 18969
Medical ethics, 14677
Medical geography, Barbados, 12791; Brazil, 12906; Canada, 2118; French Guiana, 680; Haiti, 22747; Jamaica, 13132; Louisiana, 938, 22431; North America, 14014; South America, 1434; South Carolina, 2960; U.S., 11908, 12149, 13768; Uruguay, 12906; West Indies, 12102
Medical jurisprudence, 14676, 14677, 21738
Medical literature of Kentucky, 5784
Medical records, Legal aspects, 14676
Medical society of the county of Cortland, Cortland, N.Y., 11503
Medical society of the state of New York, 1116, 00117, 00070, 00601
The medical student in Europe, 3631
Medicina y desarrollo social, 18593

Medicine, 13769; Addresses, essays, lectures, 1038, 1039, 3292, 11452, 13763, 21962, 23078, 23124; Anecdotes, facetiae, satire, etc., 8451; Bibliography, 18370, 18371; Bibliography, Catalogs, 23286; Bibliography, Colombia, 18960; Biography, 5170; Biography, Kentucky, 7737, 8010, 8203; Brazil, Pernambuco (State), 18276; Collected works, 12685; Early works to 1700, 6012; 15th-18th century, 6694, 6695; Formulae, receipts, prescriptions, 6694, 6695; History, 1623; History, Kentucky, 15772; History, Utah, 17370, 17524; Kentucky, 15209; Kentucky, Bibliography, 5784; Massachusetts, 132, 913, 11433; Period., 21760, 23420; Popular, 12123, 12647; Study and teaching, 3287, 3288, 3292, 3293, 13950, 14012, 15148, 15149, 20019; Study and teaching, Cincinnati, 11595; Study and teaching, Venezuela, 18601; U.S., 1029, 2659
Medicos jurídicos de impugnación en la Ley de vías generales de comunicación, 19888
Medicus romanus servus, 24693
Medidas administrativas de protección a la industria mexicana, 18330
Medill, William, 1805-1865, 23421
Medina, Baltasar de, d.1697, 23422, 23423
Medina, L.H., 10670, 14983
Medina Ávila, Juan de, 6851
Medina Madroñero, Edmundo, 1918-1964, 18004
Meditaciones sobre Beethoven, 20468
Meditemos, 19648
Mediterranean Sea, Commerce, 692
The Mediterranean shores of America, 17472
Medley, Julius George, 1829-1884, 4432
Medley, Mat., pseud., 2564
A medley of sketches and scraps, touching people and things, 10828
Medlinson, Ezra, 13833
Medoline Selwyn's work, 9080
Medora, N.D., 16426, 17457
Medranda y Vivanco, Pedro de, 8272
Medrano, Pedro de, 1649-1725, 7449
Medrano, Pedro Joaquín, 5807, 7013
Meears, George A., 17169
Meechan, Thomas Francis, 5045
Meek, Alexander Beaufort, 1814-1865, 4433-4437
Meek, Fielding Bradford, 1817-1876, 17775, 23424
Meeker, Ezra, 1830-, 17171, 17172
Meeker, Nathan Cook, 1817-1879, 4438
Meeker Massacre, 1879, 17452
Meekins' twinses, 2590
Meehan, Paddy, 1790-1866, 17170
Mooc, 11198
Mees, Walter, 4439

Meese, William Augustus, 1856-, 7450
Meg, 10163
Megalithic monuments, Gt. Britain, 13225
Megatherium, 22514
Meginness, John Franklin, 1827-1899, 23425
Meh Lady, 10462
Mehetable Roger's cranberry swamp, 10427
Meidinger and Associates, Louisville, Ky., 13570
Meigs, Charles Delucena, 1792-1869, 14984, 23426
Meigs, Henry, 1782-1861, 25025
Meigs, James Aitken, 1829-1879, 23427
Meigs, Josiah, 1757-1822, 23428
Meigs, Montgomery Cunningham, 1816-1892, 23429
Mein, John, 22738, 23430
Meine reise nach Nord-amerika im jahre 1842, 5067
Mejía, José Victor, 7452
Mejía Deras, Ismael, 7451
Mejía Valera, José, 19491
Mekeel, Scudder, 17174
Meksyk, 7213
Melanospora Cda., Argentine Republic, 19647
Melbourn, Julius, b.1790, 25026
Melee (woman in comand), 14401
Meléndez, Juan, 7453
Meline, James Florant, 1811-1873, 17175
Melish, John, 1771-1822, 4440-4445, 7454
Mellen, John, 1722-1807, 13423
Mellichampe, 10778
Mello, José Antonio Gonsalves de, 1916-, 19213
Mello, Zuleika, 18977
Melo, Mide, 20255
Melodies and mountaineers, 14924
A melodrame entitled "Treason, stratagems, and spoils", 15815
Melton Mowbray, 16558
Melville, Herman, 1819-1891, 6782, 25027
Melville letters, 25642
Memminger, Christopher Gustavus, 1803-1888, 2910, 4446, 25028
Memorial day addresses, 2266
Memphis, Tenn., Description, 3827; Directories, 1756
Memphis and Ohio Railroad, 14858
Men and events of forty years, 16649
Men and manners in America, 3761, 6945-6947, 14252
Men and memories of San Francisco, 15927
Men and things in America, 1086
Men and times of the revolution, 5636

Men of our day, 1546
Men, places and things, 4830
Men, women, and ghosts, 11075
Men with the bark on, 10608
Men's furnishing goods, 13996
Mena, Pedro de, 17th cent., 6470
Menageries, 2491
Menander, of Athens, 24766
Menard Co., Ill., History, 23479; Maps, 6169
Mendell, Miss, 4447
Mendell, Sarah, 13424
Mendieta, Alonso de, 6469
Mendinueta, Francisco de, 6386
Mendive y Doumy, Rafael María, 7850
Mendon association, Mendon, Mass., 1400
Mendoça Corte-Real, Diogo de, 25031
Mendoza, Antonio de, conde de Tendilla, 1480?-1552, 4631, 5969
Mendoza, Cristóbal, 6794
Mendoza, Cristobal L., 18846, 19077
Mendoza, Gumesindo, 6644
Mendoza, Jeremias, 18821
Mendoza, Juan de, fl.1656-1686, 7459
Mendoza, Argentine Republic, Constitution, 123; History, 17996
Mendoza, Argentine Republic (City) Universidad Nacional de Cuyo. Facultad de Ciencias de la Educación. Publicaciones de matemáticas y física, 18708
Menefee, Eugene L., 17179
Menefee, Richard Hickman, 1809-1841, 15581
Menegale, José Guimarães, 1898, 19348
Menegazzo, Lilia F. de, 19565
Menéndez, Francisco, 19909
Menéndez de Avilés, Pedro, 1519-1574, 5228
Meneses, Egas Moniz Barreto de Aragão Sousa e, 1870-1924, 19880
Menezes, Marion R., 19322
Menezes, Raimundo de, 18140
Menifee County, Ky., Bibliography, 14418
Meningitis, Cerebrospinal, 12540
Menken, Adah Isaacs, 1835-1868, 4448
Mennonites in Kentucky, 14223
Menominee Indians, 11358
Menomonie, Wis., 15848
Menor, Eldemar de A., 19950
Menores no meio rural, 19621
Mensagem ao Ceará, 20566
Mental hygiene, 20172
Mental illness, 14677; Kentucky, 15256
Mental tests, 14328, 18902
Mentally handicapped, 13954
Mentally handicapped children, Education, 18639
Mentally retarded offenders in adult and juvenile correctional institutions, 13954

Menton, Seymour, 19829
Mentoria, 10679
Menus, Kentucky, 14865
Menzel, Gottfried, b.1798, 4449
Menzies, Archibald, 1754-1842, 7460
Mera, Francisco de, 7461
Mercantile honor, 2105
Mercator [pseud.], 6668
Mercedarians. Provincia, de el santo
  evangelio de México, 6365
Mercedes, 9740
Mercer, Asa Shinn, 1839-1917, 17180-
  17182
Mercer, Charles Fenton, 1778-1858, 6826
Mercer County, Ky., History, 13817,
  14163, 14218, 15549; Maps, 14277;
  Views, 15168
Merchant marine, Signaling, 1207; U.S.,
  12787, 22982
A merchant of London, 24830
A merchant of Philadelphia, 22185
A merchant of the old school, 24875
The merchant's daughter, 10919
The merchant's widow, 10710
Merchants, American, 2480
The merchants' and tourists' guide to
  Mexico, 8437
Mercier, Alfred, 1816-1894, 4450-4452
Mercier, Honoré, 7462
Mercurio peruano, 7463, 7464
Mercury, 15947
Mercutio, The adventures of, 24067
Mère Pochett, 10037
Meredith, 10277
Meredith, Sir William, bart., d.1790,
  13425
Meredith, William Morris, 1799-1873, 1256
Mérida, Mexico, 7465
Mérida, Venezuela, Biography, 19787;
  History, 20035; Social life and customs,
  19787; Universidad de los Andes, 18735,
  21719; Universidad de Los Andes,
  Biblioteca Central "Tulio Febres Cordero",
  Publicaciones, 18181; Universidad de los
  Andes, Departmento de Extensión Cultural,
  Publicaciones, 18007
Meridionus, O.R., pseud., 25198
Merino sheep, 396
The merits of Thomas W. Dorr and George
  Bancroft, 11917
Meriwether, Lee, 1862-, 4453
Merkley, Christopher, 1808-, 17183
Merle d'Aubigné, Jean Henri, 1794-1872,
  25032
Merlin, María de las Mercedes (Jaruco) 1789-
  1852, 4454

Merluccidae, merluccius merluccius hubbsi,
  18298, 20190
The mermaid of Lighthouse Point, 6978
Merrell, William Howard, d.1897, 4455
Merriam, George Spring, 1843-1914, 25033
Merrick, George Byron, 1841-, 17184
Merrick, Richard Thomas, 1826-1885, 7466
Merrill, Abram D., 23909
Merrill, C.E., 14990
Merrill, D.D., 4456
Merrill, Frank T., illustr., 9592, 12629,
  13619, 16082
Merrill, George P., 14447
Merrill, Samuel, 1831-1924, 4457
Merrill, Samuel Hill, 1805-1873, 4458
Merrimac (Frigate), 22236
Merrimac Valley, 23416; History, Poetry,
  11701
Merrimack, 10177
Merrimack, N.H., History, 2297
Merriman family (Nathaniel Merriman, 1613-
  1693), 5835
Merry, J.F., 4459
The merry maid of Arcady, 9768
The merry monomaniacs, 10065
Merry Mount, 10390
Merry tales, 9029
The merry tales of the three wise men of
  Gotham, 10487
Merton, Thomas, 1915-1968, 14991, 14992
Mervine, William M., 23631
Merwin, James B., 7986
Merwin, Samuel, 1874-1936, 7467
Mesa Verde National Park, 16506, 16971
Mesas Redondas sobre Problemas de las Zonas
  Aridas de Mexico, Mexico, 1955, 7468
Mesas Redondas sobre Problemas del Tropico
  Mexicano, Mexico, 1955, 7469
Meserve, Arthur L., 4460, 4461
Meserve, Frederick Hill, 1865-, 7470, 7471
Mesocnus, 18566
Mesons, Decay, 17999
Mesons, Multiple production of, 20025
Messiter, Charles Alston, 17185
Metafísica del vino, 19957
Metacomet, 13470
Metallurgy, 5998; Early works to 1800, 773
Metals, 773, 5998
Metas, 19239
Métayer system, Argentine Republic, 18460
Metcalf, Samuel Lytler, 14993
Metcalf, Thomas, 1780-1855, 15379
Metcalf family (Michael Metcalf, 1586-1664),
  12706
Metcalfe, Grace, 5874
Metcalfe, Leonidas, 13872

Metcalfe County, Ky., 13610, 13613
Meteorites, Kentucky, 14048
Meteorological stations, Orcadas, 18503;
 Ushuaia, 18503
Meteorology, Arctic regions, 6302, 22807;
 Falkland islands, 11945; Mexico, 7969;
 Observations, 993; Observations,
 Antarctic regions, 18503; Rhode Island,
 11696; Virginia, 11621
The meteorology of Minnesota, 16013
Methodism, 1406, 22362, 22654; Biblio-
 graphy, 1847; Collected works, 4535
Methodism in Kentucky, 15677
Methodism in the Ohio Valley, 23073
Methodism in Wayne County, Kentucky,
 15445
Methodist Church (First United),
 Irvington, Ky., History, 13684
Methodist Church (United States)
 Conferences, Louisville, 14994
Methodist Church in Kentucky, 14050,
 14802, 14994, 15701
Methodist Church in Nova Scotia, 11794
Methodist Church of Canada, 13314
Methodist Church, Sermons, 2818
Methodist Episcopal Church, 3256, 4061,
 5672, 6387, 6423, 14995; Biography,
 23788; Clergy, 490, 750; Conferences,
 Missouri, 22775; Conferences,
 Philadelphia, 24926; Discipline,
 22958; Finance, 22958; General
 Conferences, Cincinnati, 25034;
 Government, 11337, 12321, 22783, 22958;
 History, 750, 12035, 12321; Kentucky,
 Music, 14996; Mexico, 6626; Missions,
 749, 4237, 4546, 13480, 16713;
 Missionary society, 749; Nebraska,
 16336; New York (State), 12241; Ohio,
 3554; Oregon, 15878, 16905; South,
 4679; South, History, 12035; Tennessee,
 2818; Texas, 15840, 16625; Virginia,
 3071, 3957
The Methodist Episcopal Church and
 slavery, 23970, 24283
Methodist Episcopal Church in the Old
 Northwest, 16794
Methodist Episcopal Church in the West,
 3453, 3636
Methodist pie, 14996
Methodist Protestant church, 13210
Methodists, Illinois, 13789; Kentucky,
 14119, 14323, 15260
Methods and means utilized in Cuba to
 eliminate illiteracy, 20688
Methow river and valley, Wash., 16547
Methvin, J. J., 17186

Método e interpretação, 19930
Metodología de la investigación histórica,
 19904
Métodos experimentais usados na determinação
 do compartamento de diodos de túnel, 18274
Métral, Antoine Marie Thérèse, 1778-1839,
 25035
Metropolitan areas, Argentine Republic, 21746;
 Brazil, 18385
Metropolitan sketches, 1331
The metropolites, 10694
The mettle of the pasture, 8515
Metzenbaum, Howard Morton, 1917-, 14997
Me-won-i-toc, 16039
Mexía, José Antonio, d.1839, 22197
A Mexican campaign, 10025
Mexican central railroad, 7403
Mexican central railway company, limited, 7901
Mexican exploration and trade northwest,
 16758
The Mexican guide, 7139
Mexican illustrations, 1018
Mexican Isthmus Land Co., Inc., Kansas City,
 Mo., 7472
A Mexican journeys, 6102, 7473
The Mexican, Kiowa captive, 17186
Mexican letters written during the progress
 of the late war between the United States
 and Mexico, 11477
Mexican literature, Periodicals, 7492, 7833,
 7834, 7854, 7855
Mexican National Railroad, 7474, 7475
The Mexican papers, 6636
The Mexican patriot, 3473
Mexican periodicals, 6612, 7836
Mexican poetry, 6692
Mexican railway company, limited, 6037, 6371,
 6372
Mexican Revolution Party, 7476
Mexican scenery and architecture, 7711
The Mexican spy, 9719
Mexican trails, 7198
Mexican typical view album, 7477
Mexican vignettes, 6448
Mexican vistas seen from highways and by-ways
 of travel, 8018
The Mexican war and its warriors, 12178
Mexican wit and humor, 6612
Mexicana (Schooner), 16477
Mexicanische zustände, 7208
Mexico, 3341, 4761, 6479, 6610, 6630, 6673,
 6841, 6857, 6875, 6898, 7097, 7103, 7315,
 7401, 7494, 7578, 7675, 7678, 7679, 7905,
 7914, 7958, 7994, 7998, 8025, 8233, 8295,
 8301, 8402, 8409, 13430, 15850;
 Administrative and political divisions,

20089; Antiquities, 5875, 5881, 6046, 6105, 6153, 6167, 6185, 6406, 6407, 6438, 6544, 6644, 6715, 6865, 6914, 7092, 7192, 7414, 7483, 7484, 7486, 7491, 7569, 7570, 7589, 8251, 8288, 18202, 18300, 18634, 18635, 19748, 20364, 20482, 23828; Antiquities, Bibliography, 19019; Bibliography, 17835, 20247; Biblioteca Nacional, Instituto Bibliográfico Mexicano, Publicaciones, 19589; Boundaries, 7480; Boundaries, British Honduras, 8433; Boundaries, Texas (Republic), 17138; Boundaries, U.S., 2624, 3658, 5064, 5513, 5546, 17125, 18886; Celebración del centenario de la independencia, 1910, 6585; Census, 7248; Church history, 17949; Climate, 7309; Comisión de limites, 7480; Comisión de minas, 6247; Comisión nacional de caminos, 7481; Commerce, 18764, 18806; Commerce, Missouri, 5528; Commerce, U.S., 5527, 11652; Congreso, 1822-1823, 18989; Congreso, Cámara de Diputados, 7482; Congreso, Camara de diputados, Gran jurado, 120; Consejo de Recursos Naturales no Renovables, Boletín, 18653, 19205, 19206; Constitution, 3341; Constitutional history, 17949, 18064, 18964, 20089; Departamento de Antropologia, 7483, 7484; Departamento de prensa y publicidad, 6811; Departamento de Turismo, 7485; Description & travel, 335, 336, 799, 1018, 1106, 1107, 1294, 1798, 2003, 2222, 2366, 2575, 2576, 2716, 3018, 3265, 3491, 3688, 3952, 4042, 4162, 4221, 4258, 4314, 4504, 4637, 4715, 4750, 4751, 4756, 4802, 4964, 4967, 4981, 5053, 5351, 5590, 5753, 5847, 5874, 5875, 5876, 5888, 5891, 5936, 5964, 5965, 5966, 5968, 5977, 5986, 5991, 6001, 6016, 6027, 5032, 6037, 6043-6046, 6057, 6065, 6067, 6068, 6073, 6074, 6084, 6085, 6087, 6088, 6099, 6102, 6117, 6121, 6122, 6139, 6144, 6165, 6185, 6208, 6246-6248, 6254, 6258, 6262, 6272, 6273, 6284, 6292, 6330, 6332, 6344, 6249, 6369, 6375, 6377, 6382, 6388, 6389, 6390, 6395, 6400, 6401, 6405-6410, 6441, 6444, 6452, 6453, 6456, 6460, 6475, 6490, 6617, 6629, 6535, 6544, 6557, 6561, 6606, 6607, 6603, 6594, 6603, 6606,6607, 6608, 6610, 6611, 6613-6615, 6624, 6636, 6642,

6661, 6672, 6673, 6689, 6692, 6693, 6697, 6708-6710, 6720, 6730, 6733, 6746, 6752, 6755, 6757, 6764-6767, 6776, 6777, 6784, 6787, 6791, 6795-6800, 6805, 6808, 6811, 6815-6817, 6819, 6834, 6835, 6838-6840, 6853, 6855-6857, 6861, 6862, 6867, 6872, 6883, 6889, 6893-6895, 6898, 6905, 6906, 6914, 6920, 6923, 6926, 6929, 6930, 6936, 6937, 6939, 6942-6944, 6950, 6953, 6955, 6961, 6984, 6986, 6990, 7004, 7018, 7020, 7041, 7047, 7050, 7056, 7057, 7064, 7080, 7082, 7084, 7085, 7087-7092, 7098, 7102, 7104, 7105, 7112, 7140, 7144, 7159, 7169, 7174, 7183, 7184, 7190, 7196, 7198, 7200, 7202, 7205-7208, 7213, 7228, 7232, 7235, 7236, 7248, 7249, 7255, 7256, 7262, 7265, 7304, 7309, 7310, 7320, 7334, 7340-7343, 7348, 7354, 7358, 7362, 7370, 7334, 7340-7343, 7348, 7354, 7358, 7362, 7370, 7371, 7386, 7388, 7391, 7396, 7398-7400, 7403, 7418, 7419, 7421, 7430, 7440, 7441, 7443, 7444, 7468, 7469, 7474, 7475, 7480, 7481, 7483-7486, 7489, 7493, 7508, 7512, 7514, 7518, 7529, 7532, 7533, 7536, 7540, 7541, 7543, 7508, 7512, 7514, 7518, 7529, 7532, 7533, 7536, 7540, 7541, 7543, 7548, 7549, 7559, 7581, 7584, 7588, 7589, 7609, 7610, 7619, 7624, 7643, 7648, 7649, 7654, 7655, 7658, 7659, 7684, 7698, 7705, 7706, 7710, 7711, 7716, 7724, 7735, 7736, 7740, 7741, 7754, 7756, 7759, 7763, 7772, 7777-7779, 7792, 7794, 7798, 7801, 7802, 7806, 7814, 7819, 7821, 7824, 7837, 7864, 7868, 7875, 7878, 7879, 7882, 7901, 7904, 7908, 7913, 7915, 7917, 7952, 7958, 7961, 7965, 7966, 7969, 7970, 7973, 7975, 7976, 7981, 7983, 7996, 7997, 8001, 8002, 8006, 8011, 8013-8015, 8018, 8020, 8033, 8035, 8036, 8038, 8041, 8043, 8062-8067, 8075, 8077, 8079, 8094, 8100, 8105, 8108, 8111, 8122, 8142, 8152, 8157, 8158, 8164, 8170, 8171, 8227, 8230, 8236, 8243, 8244, 8251, 8254, 8255, 8266, 8273, 8282, 8288, 8289, 8290, 8293, 8294, 9295, 8300, 8301, 8307, 8308, 8310, 8315, 8320, 8321, 8332, 8336, 8340, 8341, 8342, 8358, 8367, 8371, 8382, 8384, 8391, 8392, 8394, 8395, 8400, 8406-8408, 8422, 8424, 8439, 8440, 11834, 12256, 13003, 15192, 16404, 16797, 17056, 18075, 18185, 19050, 23061; Description & travel, Bibliography, 7488, 8049, 18901; Description & travel, Gazetteers, 6818; Description & travel, Guide-books, 5884, 5948, 5959, 5962, 5980, 6291, 6331, 6371, 6372, 6454, 6455, 6715, 6719, 6912, 7045, 7337, 7473, 7487, 7653, 7677, 7679, 7707, 7717, 7823, 7869,

7874, 7990, 8101, 8172, 8208, 8209, 8211, 8437; Description & travel, History, 7902; Description & travel, Poetry, 6448, 6646, 7233, 7234, 7237, 7238, 7323; Description & travel, Views, 5851, 6155, 6157, 6448, 6691, 6865, 6940, 7315, 7349, 7472, 7477, 7554, 7555, 7569, 7570, 7612, 7903, 8107, 8339, 8368; Dictionaries and encyclopedias, 6818; Dirección de antropología, 7486; Dirección general de correos, 7487; Dirección General de Geografía y Meteorología, 7448; Directories, 6733, 7896; Distances, etc., 6587, 7489; Economic conditions, 5994, 6072, 6585, 6917, 6944, 7476, 7494, 7512, 7736, 7983, 8110, 8236, 8244, 8315, 8367, 8423, 8439, 18028, 18150, 18805, 19018, 19069, 19940; Economic conditions, Bibliography, 18767, 18771, 18772; Economic policy, 18964, 19018; Estado mayor del ejército, 7489; Foreign relations, 1821-1861, 13328, 19185; Foreign relations, Argentine republic, 7792; Foreign relations, Belize, 18950; Foreign relations, Spain, 22748; Foreign relations, U.S., 6636, 7532, 15834, 17166, 17188, 19185, 19650; Historical geography, 19822; History, 482, 1863, 3497, 4980, 5531, 6249, 6332, 6427, 6444, 6490, 6689, 6692, 6756, 6785, 6817, 6927, 7021, 7273, 7418, 7441, 7444, 7549, 7581, 7649, 7736, 7794, 7801, 7823, 7873, 7877, 8025, 8214, 8255, 13430, 15907, 15916, 16278, 16538, 17486, 17898, 17949, 18061, 18079, 18208, 18224, 18561, 18646, 18811, 18928, 18989, 19081, 19596, 19729, 20007, 20223, 20364, 21724; History, To 1519, 5881, 6644, 7546, 11392, 11643, 18202, 22640; History, To 1519, Sources, 1443, 6150; History, 1540-1810, Sources, 6518, 6604; History, To 1810, 7419, 20006; History, To 1810, Sources, 6821; History, 1810, 996, 11791; History, 1810-1849, 7313; History, 1821-1861, 1104, 1758, 1760, 1761, 1825, 6043, 6045, 7568, 13111, 22748, 24611; History, 1910-1946, 7758; History, Addresses, essays, lectures, 7663; History, Colonial period, 7891; History, Colonial period, Fiction, 19968; History, Conquest, 1519-1540, 1440, 1864, 5969, 6478, 6644, 6863, 6864, 7111, 7387,

7546, 7774, 7775, 7931, 7932, 8004, 8057-8068, 8396, 11316, 11643, 12448, 16551, 20051, 20532, 21834, 22112, 23508; History, Conquest, 1519-1540, Fiction, 1332, 11053; History, Conquest, 1519-1540, Poetry, 13213; History, European intervention, 1861-1867, 1918, 6709, 6710, 7183, 7188, 7265, 7944, 8170, 12012, 12115, 16452, 16795, 19095, 22422, 22847, 22995; History, Periodicals, 7492, 7854; History, Republic, 1867-, 6767; History, Revolution, 6284, 6720, 7515, 8162, 19214, 19901; History, Revolution, Fiction, 19967; History, Sources, 6604, 7663; History, Spanish colony, 1540-1810, 5876, 5969, 16551, 18981, 23422, 23828; History, Spanish colony, 1540-1810, Sources, 7536, 7684; History, Wars of independence, 1810-1821, 1104, 1106, 1294, 1759, 7568, 7756, 8213, 8342, 8441, 13111, 13430, 18188, 18981; History, Wars of independence, 1810-1821, Biography, 1762; History, Wars of independence, 1810-1821, Fiction, 3473; History, Military, 1106; Industries, 6001, 20004; Industries, Bibliography, 18769, 18771; Industries, Directories, 18768; Inspección y conservación de monumentos arqueológicos de la República Mexicana, 7490, 7491; Instituto Nacional de Antropología e Historia, Memorias, 19019; Kings and rulers, 7546; Laws, statutes, etc., 7896; Maps, 7995, 8391, 8440; Ministerio de relaciones exteriores, 17188; Periodicals, 6462, 7844; Politics & government, 7476, 7549, 7779, 12509, 18561, 18568, 18989, 19577; Politics & government, 1540-1810, 1078; Politics & government, 1821-1861, 120, 6247, 7531; Politics & government, 1861-1867, 2368, 6608; Politics & government, 1867-1910, 6099; Politics & government, 1910-, 6268, 7482, 7682, 8300; Population, 7512, 18984; Public works, 19018; Registers, 7707, 8279; Religion, 8394, 8395; Secretaría de Comunicaciones y Transportes, 19843; Secretaría de relaciones exteriores, 22748; Social conditions, 6875, 7483, 7484, 7486, 19912; Social life & customs, 1105, 1236, 1798, 6036, 6065, 6272, 6273, 6819, 6940, 7205, 7206, 7364, 7430, 7842, 8033, 11261, 19901; Statistics, 7082, 7084, 7085, 7087, 7088, 7444, 7837, 7874, 7904, 7905, 8336, 13003
Mexico (City), 483, 6802, 7478, 7479; Antiquities, 7490; Ayuntamiento, 6802; Capilla de la Tercer orden de Santo Domingo, 8311; Cathedral, Archicofradía del Santísimo Sacramento, 6806, 7962, 7963;

Colegio de México, Centro de
Estudios Históricos, 18928; Concurso
Científico y Artístico del Centenario,
7902; Convento de Jesús María, 7220;
Description & travel, 6388, 6389, 6883,
7403, 7725; Description & travel,
Guide-books, 7769, 7869, 8279;
Directories, 6733, 7769, 8209, 8279;
Escuela Nacional Preparatoria, 22063;
History, 1787; Museo Nacional de Artes
Plásticas, 7555; Universidad, 5830;
Universidad Nacional, 18202, 19832;
Universidad Nacional, Instituto de
Derecho Comparado, 18858; Universidad
Nacional, Instituto de Geología, 19085,
19599; Universidad Nacional, Instituto
de Historia, 18634, 18635, 20647;
Universidad Nacional, Instituto de
Investigaciones Históricas, 18261, 20362-
20368
Mexico (Federal District), 5936
Mexico (Vice-royalty) Laws, statutes, etc.,
8085; Real audiencia, 1078, 8085
Mexico, Aztec, Spanish and republican, 7444
Mexico, Northeastern, History, Sources,
20005
México a través de los siglos, 7873
México al día, 6606
Mexico and her people, 6940
Mexico and the life of the conqueror, 7775
Mexico and the Mexicans, 6292
México arqueológico, 5875
Mexico as I saw it, 8248
Mexico as it is, 6883
México desde 1808 hasta 1867, 10561
México en conjunto, 8300
México en su primer siglo de independencia,
6585
Mexico from border to capital, 6730
México hacia el fin del fin del virreinato
español, 8214
Mexico im jahre 1827, 8341
Mexico in den ereignissvollen jahren 1832
und 1833, 6045
Mexico in revolution, 6284
Mexico in your own car, 7677
Mexico: its peasants and its priests, 8395
Mexico, its social evolution, 8025
Mexico, land und leute, 7041
México moderno, 7440, 7492
Mexico of today, 6905, 7342
México: our neighbor, 7864
Mexico pintoresco, 6156
Mexico prehispanico y colonial, 7441
El México que yo he visto, 6001
México? Si, Señor, 7901

México; síntesis geográfica y económica, 7493
Mexico thirty years ago, 6613
Mexico today and tomorrow, 8315
Mexico under Maximilian, 7183
Mexico versus Texas, 9598
México y sus capitales, 6332
Mexico's federal betterment boards, 18150
Mexico's treasure house, 7422
Mexico's western highways, 7717
Mexikanische briefe, 7976
Mexiko je v Americe, 6787
Mexiko, Skizzen und typen aus dem Italien der
neuen welt, 6067
Mexiko und die Mexikaner, 8196
Le Mexique, 6068, 6409, 7334, 7914
Le Mexique au début du xxe siecle, 7494
Le Mexique aujourd'hui, 6642
Le Mexique conquis, 11316
Le Mexique contemporain, 996
Le Mexique en 1823, 6247
Le Mexique et ses mines d'argent, 6117
Le Mexique tel qu'il est, 6608
Meyen, Franz Julius Ferdinand, 1804-1840,
13426
Meyer, Carl, of Basel, 17189
Meyer, Catherine B., illustr., 14885
Meyer, Eduard, 1855-1930, 25036, 25037
Meyer, Hugo Christoph Heinrich, 25038
Meyer, Leland Winfield, 14998, 14999
Meyer, Rudolf Hermann, 1839-1899, 4462
Meyers, Augustus, 1841-, 17190
Meynardie, Elias James, 25039
Mezières, Athanase de, d.1779, 16010
Miall, Charles S., 25040
Mi general! 19967
Mi viaje a México a propósito de la revolución,
6720
Miami Indians, 12920
Miami language, Glossaries, vocabularies, etc.,
5586, 13501
Miami University, Oxford, O., Eccritean
society, 22973; Erodelphian society, 3742,
22973; History, 25682
Miami woods, 3562
Michaux, André, 1746-1802, 4463, 4464
Michaux, François André, 1770-1855, 4465
Michelbacher, Maximilian J., 1811?-1879, 25041
Michigan, Description & travel, 3943, 5147,
8136, 12142, 13580, 22128; Description &
travel, Gazetteers, 11289; Finance, 17580;
History, 23609; Politics & government,
17587; Social life & customs, 10148;
University, William L. Clements Library,
15000
Michigan cavalry, 1st regt., 1861-1865, 4170;
2d regt., 1861-1864, 5373; 5th regt., 1862-

1865, 4170; 6th regt., 1863-1865,
4170; 7th regt., 1862-1865, 4170
Michigan infantry, 6th regt., 1861-1865,
2587; 24th regt., 1862-1865, 3145
Michler, Nathaniel H., 5547
Michoacán, Mexico, 7811; Manners and
customs, 19825
Micmac Indians, 7253, 22757
Micmac language and superstitions, 22053
Los microelementos como fertilizantes,
20521
Microfauna del Eoceno inferior de la
peninsula de Yucatán, 19599
Mid-summer convention assembled under the
auspices of the state immigration
association of Louisiana, 4305
The middle line, 23432
The middle period, 1817-1858, 24059
Middle states, Description & travel,
3399, 4695, 4844, 5341; Description &
travel, Guide-books, 2147; History,
Revolution, 12189
Middle West, Description & travel, 12566
Middleboro, Mass., First church, 804
Middlebury, Vt., 12571
Middlebury historical society, Middlebury,
Vt., 12301
Middlesex canal, 2177
Middlesex Co., Mass., tornado, 1851, 1574
Middlesex Co., Ont., 21819
Middleton, Charles Theodore, 4466
Middleton, Christopher, d.1770, 1924, 2112,
16394
Middleton, John W., 1808- , 17191
Middleton, Vt., History, 2341
Midgley, R. L., 13427
Midnight and noonday, 16548
A midnight fantasy, 8499
A midnight scene during the revolution,
10670
A midnight tramp in the Jerseys, 10670
Midway, Ky., 13521, 15769
Midway College, 15769
The midwest pioneer, his ills, cures, &
doctors, 15155
Midwives, Mormon, 17278
Mier, Gregorio, 7495
Mier Noriega y Guerra, José Servando Teresa
de, 1765-1827, 7496, 24095
Mier y Terán, Manuel de, 7480
Mier expedition, 1842, 8100
Miera y Pacheco, Bernardo, 15844, 15880,
15881, 17821
Miers, Earl Schenck, 15001
Miertsching, Johann August, 13428
Mifflin, Benjamin, 1718- , 4467

Mifflin, Warner, 1745-1798, 25042, 25043
Mighels, Ella Sterling (Clark) 1853-1934,
17192
The mighty destroyer displayed, 1152
A mighty hunter before the Lord, 10125
Migration, Internal, Mexico, 19517
Mijares, Augusto, 19077, 19577
Mike Fink, 2595, 2681, 2922, 2937, 3138, 3397,
3451, 3654, 3731, 3745, 3750, 3753, 3954,
3955, 4169, 4337, 4367, 4469, 4492, 4502,
4573, 4754, 4951, 5038, 5084, 5411, 5412,
5460, 5558, 5566, 5679
Mikhaĭlov, Sergeĭ Sergeevich, 18076
Mil doscientos grados de justicia, 19823
Mila, 3311
La milagrosa invención de un tesoro, 6753
Milam Co., Tex., Biography, 16780
Milburn, Page, 25044
Milburn, William Henry, 1823-1903, 4468,
4469, 13429, 15002
A mild barbarian, 9501
Mildred's dishes, 8663
Milena, 19584
Miles, Mrs. Emma (Bell) 1879-1919, 15003
Miles, James Warley, 1818-1875, 25045
Miles, Nelson Appleton, 1839-1925, 17193
Miles, Robert Whitfield, 1890-1952, 14807
Miles, Thomas Jefferson, 7497
Miles, William, of Carlisle, Pa., 4470
Miles, William Porcher, 1822-1899, 23635
Milfort, Louis, 1750(ca.)-1817, 17194
Militarism, 11333; Germany (Federal Republic,
1949-), 17990
Military art and science, 1706, 22153, 23139;
Addresses, essays, lectures, 12629; Early
works to 1800, 23817; Periodicals, 462, 463,
11228; U.S., 14029
Military bridges, 12743
Military collections and remarks, 22153
Military control, 2405
Military despotism, 25046, 25047
A military genius: life of Anna Ella Carroll,
6094
Military history, modern, 22011, 23182
Military incapacity, and what it costs the
country, 12017
Military journal of Major Ebenezer Denny, 3232
Military law, Colombia, 19151; Confederate
States of America, 12264, 24809; Kentucky,
14605; New York (State), 12912; U.S., 1805,
25046
The military laws of the United States, 1805
The military opinions of General Sir John Fox
Burgoyne, 1706
Military Order of the Loyal Legion of the U.S.
Indiana Commandery, 4471; Iowa Commandery,

7498; Maine Commandery, 6458;
Massachusetts Commandery, 7499, 7500;
Minnesota Commandery, 7501; Missouri
Commandery, 7502, 24614; New York
Commandery, 7503; Ohio Commandery,
7504, 8090; Pennsylvania Commandery,
7505
Military order of the medal of honor, 8055
Military posts, U.S., 8258
Military reminiscences of Gen. Wm. R.
Boggs, 2750
Military service, Compulsory, 12794; U.S.,
12167
Military telegraph, U.S., 4808
The military telegraph during the Civil
war in the U.S., 4808
Militia, Kentucky, 14105
Militia immaculatae conceptionis Virginis
Mariae, 5878
Militia laws, 14605
Milk, 18474
Mill, John Stuart, 1806-1873, 25048, 25848
Mill, Nicholas, 13430
Mill Springs, Wayne County, Kentucky,
Battle of, 13944
Millard, 16710
Millard County, Utah, 16591
Millbank, 9901
Miller, Andrew, 4472
Miller, Arthur McQuiston, 14562, 14565,
14904, 15004, 15005, 15512
Miller, Elvira Sydnor, 4473, 4474
Miller, Ernest C., 15414
Miller, George Funston, 1809-1888, 25049
Miller, George L., 17237
Miller, J. David, 15006
Miller, J. R., 13431
Miller, Jacob Welsh, 1800-1862, 1538
Miller, James Ira Deese, 4475
Miller, James Newton, 4476
Miller, Joaquin, 1841-1913, 17195
Miller, John, 7506
Miller, John, 1666-1724, 13432
Miller, Joseph, 6790
Miller, Marion Mills, 1864-, 25050
Miller, O. T., 10163
Miller, Samuel, 1769-1850, 13433, 22577,
25051
Miller, Stephen Franks, 1810?-1867, 13434
Miller, William, 1782-1849, 21788
Miller, William, 1795-1861, 7506
Miller, William H., 17196
Miller, William Harris, 15007
Miller family, 15007
Millesburg, Ky., Description, 14969
Millet, Thomas, 7507

Milligen, George, 4477
Milliken, James, 740, 7508
Milling-machines, 18117
A millionaire of rough-and-ready, 9786
A millionaire of tomorrow, 9521
The millionaire's daughter, 11033
Milliroux, J.F., 4478
Mills, Anson, 1834-1924, 17197, 17198
Mills, Enos Abijah, 1870-, 17199, 17200
Mills, Joseph C., 18819
Mills, Melbourne, 15008
Mills, Robert Curtis, 1819-1896, 25052
Mills, Samuel John, 1783-1818, 4479, 5090,
5254
Mills, William W., 17201
The mills of the gods, 11034
Millspaugh, Andrew Jackson, plaintiff, 1912
Millstones and stumbling blocks, 15091
Milner, Samuel, 14684
Milnor, James, 1773-1845, 25053
Milnor, William, jr., 1769-1848, 13435
Milton, John, 1608-1674, 12368
Milton, William Fitzwilliam, viscount, 1839-
1877, 4481, 17202
Milward, Burton, 13833, 15009-15012
Milward family, 14848
Milwaukee, Comm., 17203
Mimic life, 10623
Mims, Edwin, 1872-, 15413
Mims, Stewart L., 4518
A mina, 19696
Minas Geraes, Brazil, Economic conditions,
18748, 18749; History, 18835; Instituto de
Tecnologia Industrial, Boletim, 18117;
Serviço de Estudos Pedagogicos, 19219;
Social conditions, 18749, 19321
Mind and body, 13727
Miner, Charles, 1780-1865, 25054
Miner, James, 7509
Miner, Jessie S., 15013
Miner, T. B., 13436
Mineral industries, 18718
Mineral law, 14685
Mineral springs of North America, 15027
Mineral waters, 1089, 13079; Canada, 1088,
4514; New York (State), 13079; Queretaro,
Mexico (State), 6040; U.S., 1088, 4514,
15027; Virginia, 1714, 2858; West Virginia,
1714, 2858
The mineral waters of the U.S. and Canada,
4514
Minerales de manganeso en los Estados de
Sonora, Durango, Zacatecas y San Luis
Potosí, 18653
Mineralogy, 11955; California, 11282; Catalogs
and collections, 11282; Classification, 2185;

Connecticut, 23340; Massachusetts, 11956, 23265; Nova Scotia, 12221; Period, 270
The mineralogy of Nova Scotia, 12944
Minerals, Radioactive, Brazil, 19252
Miners, Argentine Republic, 18600; Chile, 19802
Miners and traveler's guide to Oregon, Washington, Idaho, Montana, Wyoming, and Colorado, 4549
Minerva, 7087
Mines, John Flavel, 1835-1891, 13437
Mines and mineral resources, 773, 5998, 18718; Argentine Republic, 18429; Bahia, Brazil, 18657, 18695, 18696; Brazil, Amazon region, 19445, 19446; British Columbia, 6174, 7072, 7822; California, 6913, 16701, 16768, 17572, 17745; Colombia, 20343; Colorado, 7868, 12859, 17301, 17632; Cuba, 17974; Government ownership, 17240; Kentucky, 14447, 15145, 15147, 15512, 15795; Laws and regulations, Colombia, 20342; Mexico, 5888, 6913, 6914, 7082, 7084, 7085, 7087, 7088, 7090, 7246, 7262, 7422, 7596, 7868, 8340, 8342, 19205, 19206; Minnesota, 13476; Nevada, 6913; New Mexico, 4665, 16624; Nova Scotia, 12944; Pennsylvania, 21811; Quebec (Province), 8393; South America, 22399; South Dakota, 16887; U.S., 387, 17525
Mines and mining, 16539; British Columbia, 11662; Mexico, 6139, 7348, 7904; Nevada, 15856; New Mexico, 22914; U.S., 17602
Mingo County, W. Va., History, 14844
Miniature of Dansville village, 11816
The miniature picture, 10921
Mining, camps, 17602; Laws and regulations, Kentucky, 15083
Mining industry and finance, 12063; Peru, 19719
Mining law, Bolivia, 19123; U.S., 4910
The mining laws of the state of Kentucky in effect June 17, 1918, 15083
A minister of the gospel, in Massachusetts, 24897
The minister's black veil, 9827
The minister's housekeeper, 10909
The minister's wooing, 10905
Ministers of grace, 2810
Minnesota, 11353, 17352, 22811; Climate, 16013; Constitution, 13438; Description & travel, 1352, 3359, 3955, 4609, 5354, 11352, 11681, 12142, 13069, 13360, 16012, 16026, 16227, 16405, 16678, 16748, 16914,

17049, 17303, 17610, 22248, 23476; Economic conditions, 7510; Finance, 17580; History, 1352, 4069, 15954, 16564, 16660, 17149, 17262, 17573, 17609, 17625, 17836, 23465; History, Societies, 17205; Legislature, 7510; Legislature, House of Representatives, Select Committee on the overland emigration route from Minnesota to British Oregon, 4482; Social life & customs, 17540; State teachers, college, Winona, 17261
Minnesota (Ter.) Constitutional Convention, 1857, 13438
Minnesota and its resources, 11352
Minnesota and the far West, 23566, 23476
Minnesota as it is in 1870, 22811
The Minnesota handbook, for 1856-7, 17352
Minnesota river, 13360
Minnie Herman, 8870
Minogue, Anna Catherine, 1874-, 25055
Minor, John D., et al., plantiffs, 13439
Minor place, 9564
Minority report of the Committee on ways and means, 2047
Minot, George Richards, 1758-1802, 23433, 23434
Minot, Lydia, d.1667, Poetry, 23730
The minstrel, 11998
Mint julep, recipe for, 13710, 14010
The mint julep, the very dream of drinks, 15395
Minthorn, Mangle, 22826
Minto, Walter, 1753-1796, 1632
Mints, Colombia, 18872
Minturn, Robert Bowne, 1836-1889, 13440
The minute men, a tale of '75, 9618
Mirabeau, Honoré-Gabriel de Riquetti, comte de, 1749-1791, 7511, 13441, 23435, 23436
Mirabeau, Jean Antoine Joseph Charles Elzear Riquetti, 1717-1794, 13441
Mirabeau, Marie (de Gonnorille) comtesse de, 2588
Mirabeau, Victor de Riquetti, marquis de, 1715-1789, 13441
Miramichi, 10708
Miranda, Francisco de, 1750-1816, 1713, 5858, 6042, 23614
Miranda Elliot, 10256
Miranda Fonseca, Mariano, 7512
Miranda y los origenes de la independencia americana, 5858
Miranda's expedition, 23614
Miriam, 9711
Miriam Coffin, 9775
Miriam Monfort, 5617
Mirick, Benjamin L., 13442

A mirror in America, 25065
Mirror of olden time border life...,
  15199
A mirrour or looking-glasse both for
  saints, and sinners, 11846
Mis' Elderkin's pitcher, 10909
Misantla, Relación de, 7730
Miscegenation, 206, 24230, 25265, 25510
Miscegenation endorsed by the Republican
  party, 6570
Miscellanea, 5249
Miscellaneous and patriotic poems, 12228
Miscellaneous sketches of occurrences
  during the late American war, 9086
Miscellaneous trifles in prose, 11661
The miscellaneous works of Colonel
  Humphreys, 22602
Miscellaneous works, prose and poetical,
  10210
Miscellanies, 2543
Miscellanies selected from the public
  journals, 11605
A miscellany, 1194
Misery Landing, 11205
The mishaps of Mr. Ezekiel Pelter, 9861
Misión cumplida, 19049
Misión de los capuchinos en Cumaná, 19527
Misión diplomática y militar, 7859
Misión mexicana a Sudamérica, 18806
Miskell, Tim, illustr., 13611
Miss Ayr of Virginia, 10304
Miss Bremer's visit to Cooper's Landing,
  9802
Miss Brooks, 11139
Miss Cherry-Blossom of Tokyo, 10239
Miss Claire's pupils, 15399
Miss Columbia's public school, 10579
Miss Debby's neighbors, 10040
Miss Eaton's romance, 8520
Miss Ellsabetha, 11207
Miss Esther's guest, 10041
Miss Frances Merley, 9277
Miss Gunton of Poughkeepsie, 10016
Miss Hurd, 10667
Miss Lou, 10649
Miss Ludington's sister, 8776
Miss Madam, 4903
Miss Maria, 9376
Miss Martha Brownlow, 10612
Miss Peck's promotion, 10037
Miss Rutherford's historical notes, 7926
Miss Slimmers' window, 11043
Miss Tempy's watchers, 10027
Miss Tiller's vegetable garden and the
  money she made by it, 11086
Miss Träumerei, 8638

Miss Van Kortland, 8778
The Miss Vanlears, 10197
Miss Washington, of Virginia, 10378
Missent, 8489
The missing chapter in the life of Abraham
  Lincoln, 6665
Mission de l'Immaculée Conception, 12353
Mission de la Colombie, 2753
Mission Indians of Southern California, 17865
The mission of death, 11065
The mission of South Carolina to Virginia,
  25028
A mission record of the California Indians,
  17207
A mission to the Indians of Orialla, South
  America, 11291
Missionaries, 4794, 22496
Missionary adventures in Texas and Mexico,
  16404
Missionary history of the Pacific Northwest,
  16766
Missionary Ridge, Battle of, 1863, 5362
The missionary sheriff, 9581
The missionary teacher, 4546
Missions, 6527, 7166; Africa, 8171, 11783;
  Africa, British East, 25137; Africa, West,
  11902; America, 2790, 19167, 21852; Arizona,
  6813; Bermuda Islands, 1195, 23149; Burma,
  23232; California, 16217, 16519, 16536,
  16829, 17115, 17344, 17345, 17423, 17549,
  17618, 17822, 17823; California, Lower,
  16217, 17822, 17823; Canada, 1025, 21818,
  23149, 23150; Chiloe, Chile (Province), 2436;
  Colorado, 16329; Cuba, 6907; Hawaiian Islands,
  1296, 1297, 22174; Idaho, 17843; Indian
  Territory, 4863; Jamaica, 23495, 25252;
  Japan, 1789; Kentucky, 651; Mexico, 6950,
  7802, 19901; Minnesota, 16800; Mississippi
  Valley, 4479, 5090; Negroes, 1556, 25867;
  New Mexico, 1145, 16713; North America,
  22601; Northwest, Canadian, 4542, 16552;
  Oceania, 13479; Ohio Valley, 4469; Oregon,
  2508, 4237, 4546, 15929, 16142, 16290,
  16517, 17242; Paraguay, 1789; Patagonia,
  12612; Peru, 18573; Pimeria Alta, 16951;
  Puerto Rico, 6907; Sermons, 654, 1007, 1196,
  11407, 11651, 13391, 22425, 22630, 23134,
  23492, 23710; Sonora, 6813; Southwest, Old,
  5254; Spanish, 19167; Spanish America, 2366,
  6796, 6799, 8171; Syria, 22551; Texas, 4742,
  6609, 17347; U.S., 22496; The West, 16035;
  West Indies, 1993, 1995, 11866; Western
  Reserve, 15894
Missions, Foreign, History, 22496
Missions, Home, 845
Missions, Medical, 22881

Missions of California, 17423
Missions of Nueva California, 16160
Missions of the North American people, 16602
Un missionnaire, 24358
Mississippi, 3741; Bibliography, 15014; Biography, 6093; Church history, 13305; Constitution, 25056, 25057; Convention, 1849, 25058; Description & travel, 3138, 3171, 3425, 3595, 4173, 4483, 4657, 4758, 4767, 11895, 13580, 14749, 15527; Description & travel, Guide-books, 13544; Fiction, 3135, 8782, 10913; Finance, 17580; History, 1772, 3003, 8287; Immigration and Agriculture Board, 4483; Legislature, Committee on State and Federal Relations, 25059; Mississippi Library Commission, 15014; Politics & government, 8344, 13205, 13402, 23577; Registers, 2699; Social life & customs, 707, 3037
Mississippi cavalry, 1st regt., 1861-1865, 4505
Mississippi et Indiana, 3314
Mississippi-fahrten, 3859
Mississippi Historical Society, 25623
Mississippi river, 337, 3029, 3517, 3654, 4632, 4824, 12018, 13476, 13683, 15278, 15749, 16173, 17108, 17184, 22600; Description & travel, 762, 2723, 2860, 2957, 3139, 3240, 3509, 3622, 3693, 4269, 5103, 11681, 13461, 14840, 16914, 17049, 17391, 22672, 24103; Description & travel, Poetry, 22225; Discovery & exploration, 1846, 2694, 3552, 3666, 4393, 5229, 5433, 7404, 16491, 16994, 17129, 22248, 22731; Fiction, 3474; History, Civil war, 16298; Levees, 22438; Navigation, 3139, 11895, 13990-13992, 21924; Sources, 1133, 1134, 22248
Mississippi scenes, 3037
Mississippi scheme, 3552
Mississippi Valley, 2784, 4320, 4728, 5100, 11506, 12151, 13957, 16315, 16526, 16567; Church history, 5090; Description & travel, 541, 542, 1133, 1206, 2561, 2594, 2758, 2760, 2831, 2871, 3081, 3103, 3117, 3138, 3147, 3163, 3169, 3248, 3360, 3380, 3397, 3468, 3479, 3647, 3859, 3988, 3990, 4065, 4126, 4258, 4472, 4479, 4653, 4696, 4717, 4729, 4755, 4919, 4951, 5090, 5099, 5112, 5773, 6271, 6403, 6404, 6529, 12024, 12573, 12678, 13143, 13580, 13956, 14264, 14840, 15344, 15698, 16135,

17360, 23493, 23579, 23950; History, 3067, 4502, 4752, 5038, 5229, 6737, 7008, 9585, 12184, 13074, 13482, 13750, 14181, 15002, 15655, 16173, 17356, 22411, 24227; History, To 1803, 3547, 3748, 3988, 8401, 12720, 13461, 16040; History, To 1803, Sources, 7404, 17129; History, 1803-1865, 17764; History, Civil war, 2033, 2068, 4192, 4415, 12953, 16452; Maps, 14471; Social life & customs, 10021, 10265
The Mississipp Valley, and prehistoric events, 15655
Mississippian scenery, 4430
Missouri (Frigate), 21799
Missouri, 970, 4698, 4728, 4761, 5100, 5633, 21778; Biography, 17091; Boundaries, Iowa, 16635; Commerce, Mexico, 5528; Constitution, 23437; Description & travel, 3302, 3468, 3479, 4173, 4598, 4653, 4729, 5062, 5098, 5263, 5680, 12142, 13580, 14749, 16204, 16798, 17297, 17574, 23558; Description & travel, Gazetteers, 21778; Description & travel, Guide-books, 4699; Fiction, 2634, 5476; General Assembly, 25060; General Assembly, 1840-1841, 17208; General Assembly, 1859, Senate, 22643; History, 4573, 6837, 14027, 16203; History, Civil War, 4192, 5610, 12170, 16263, 16451, 17219, 22458, 22829, 23484; History, Civil war, Fiction, 10092, 11190; History, Fiction, 9202; Politics & government, 23843, 25412; Politics & government, To 1865, 22954; Politics & government, Civil War, 24066, 24864; Social life and customs, 15693
Missouri as it is in 1867, 4698
Missouri cavalry, Frémont's body guard, 1861, 12170
Missouri Compromise, 11255, 23013, 23911, 24203, 24254, 24532, 24533, 24556, 24606, 24945, 24952, 25025, 25060, 25112, 25284, 25374, 25461, 25480, 25553, 25667, 25730, 25794, 25940
The Missouri harmony, 2911
Missouri infantry, 9th regt., 1861-1865, 4223
Missouri River, 2779, 2784, 3578, 4272, 4625, 16529, 16573, 17030, 17628, 17670, 22233
Missouri River Valley (Upper), an original culture in North Dakota, 17893
The Missouri trapper, 4262
Missouri Valley, Description & travel, 2779, 3092, 3137, 4134, 4262, 4755, 4802, 5098, 5374, 5425, 16307; Fiction, 3754
The mistake, 10310
Mr. Absalom Billingslea, 4081
Mr. Ambrose's letters on the rebellion, 4155
Mr. Beverley Lee, 10385

Mr. Billy Downs and his likes, 4082
Mr. Bilson's housekeeper, 6969
Mr. Bonaparte of Corsica, 8682
Mr. Buchanan's administration on the eve
  of the rebellion, 1634
Mr. Curran, 10310
Mr. Dide, his vacation in Colorado,
  16544
Mr. Dooley in peace and in war, 9438
Mr. Dooley's philosophy, 9439
Mr. Dunn Browne's experiences in the army,
  3457
Mr. Dunton's invention, 9817
Mr. Durant of Salt Lake City, 10613
Mr. Fity Foom in the country, 11043
Mr. Foley of Salmon, 16311
Mr. Fortner's marital claims, 4083
Mr. Frank, the underground mail-agent,
  11046
Mr. Grantley's idea, 9110
Mr. Greeley's letters from Texas and the
  lower Mississippi, 3675
Mr. Higginbotham's catastrophe, 9827
Mr. Hulme's journal, 3965
Mr. Isaacs, 9228
Mr. Isolate of Lonelyville, 9095
Mr. Jack Hamlin's mediation, 6972
Mr. Justice Brandeis and the University of
  Louisville, 14111
Mr. Lauren's true state of the case, 13374
Mr. MacGlowrie's widow, 6977
Mr. Opp, 15266
Mr. Philips' goneness, 8643
Mr. Rowan's motion, 14579
Mr. Smith, 10310
Mr. Singsly's yacht, 10916
Mr. Synick's anti-bad-break, 9533
Mr. Tangier's vacations, 9685
Mr. Tolman, 10892
Mr. Travers's first hunt, 9363
Mr. Vaughan's heir, 8779
Mistral, Gabriela, pseud., 6861
Mrs. Brayfield, 11198
Mrs. Beauchamp Brown, 8605
Mrs. Buckingham's revenge, 9460
Mrs. Bullfrog, 9823
Mrs. Cliff's yacht, 10894
Mrs. Délire's euchre party, 2614
Mrs. Ellerton's trials and reward, 9440
Mrs. Henry Ward Beecher, 2662
Mrs. Macsimum's bill, 10298
Mrs. May's private income, 11191
The mistress of Sydenham plantation, 10043
Mrs. Partington's carpet-bag of fun, 8616
Mrs. Peixada, 9742
Mrs. Piatt's select poems, 4785

Mrs. Ripley's trip, 9606
Mistress Rosamond Trevor, 10675
Mrs. Royall's southern tour, 5035
Mrs. Singleton, 8695
Mrs. Skagg's husbands, 9787
Mrs. Temperly, 7123
Mrs. Twitchell's inventions, 10088
Mrs. Washington Potts, 10197
Mrs. Wiggs of the Cabbage Patch, 14110
Mit dem Eselwagen durch U.S.A., 3586
La mitad de la luna, 19211
Mitchell, A. jr., 4484
Mitchell, Anne Mary, 1847-, 25061
Mitchell, David W., 4485
Mitchell, Donald Grant, 1822-1908, 13443
Mitchell, Elisha, 1793-1857, 4486
Mitchell, George Washington, 1865-, 25062
Mitchell, James, 7513
Mitchell, John, illustr, 15608
Mitchell, John, d.1768, 4487, 23438
Mitchell, John H., 17213
Mitchell, John L., 17214
Mitchell, Joseph, 23439
Mitchell, Ormsby MacKnight, 1800-1862, 22384
Mitchell, S. Mitchell, 15015
Mitchell, Samuel Augustus, 1792-1868, 4488-
  4491, 13067, 17215
Mitchell, Samuel Chiles, 1864-, 15413
Mitchell, Samuel Latham, 1764-1831, 12160,
  23041
Mitchell, W. H., 23440
Mitchell, William M., 15016
Mitchell family, 15544
A mite cast into the treasury, 24205
A mite into the treasury, 12563
Mitford, Mary Russell, 1787-1855, 4492
The mitherless bairn, 10415
Mitla, 8164
Mitla Zapotec grammar, 19490
Mitre, Bartolomé, 1821-1906, 18931
Mixson, Frank M., 1846-, 4493
Mneomi, 9164
Mob, under pretense of law, 25625
Moberly, Walter, 1832-1915, 6748
Mobile, Alabama, Description, 3755;
  Directories, 1756
MOBRAL-seminario interamericano de educacion
  de adultos, 19368
The MOBRAL system, 19369
The mock count of New York, 8831
Las modalidades de la reforma agraria, 19847
Model calculations for the density of states
  in actinide metals, 19065
A model murder, 9017
The model of the government of the province
  of East-New-Jersey in America, 23680

The model parish, 10747
Moderate better than rapid gains, 10987
Modern agitators, 901
Modern chivalry, 2782
Modern democracy; the extension of
  slavery in our own territory, 25084
A modern instance, 9948
A modern Mephistopheles, 8485
Modern pilgrims, 11200
The modern Psyche, 9678
A modern slavery, 25113
Modern vengeance, 10546
The modern warning, 7117
Modes of education, 10184
A modest proof of the order & government
  settled by Christ and his apostles in
  the church, 21891
Modificaciones a la legislación tributaria,
  20146
Modoc Indians, 10355; Wars, 1873, 17310
Modos con que podran los christianos
  desagraviar a Nuestro Señor Jesu Christo
  Sacramentado, 6809
Moehlman, Arthur Henry, 16012
Moelling, Peter August, 4494
Moeran's moose, 10125
Moffat, William David, 1863-, 10283
Moffett, Cleveland, 1863-, 17216
Moffette, Joseph F., 4495
Mogul empire, 2123
Mohave Indians, 5299, 5491
Mohawk, A romance of the, 3893
Mohawk Indians, 1183, 7429, 10744, 10745,
  13227
Mohawk language, 13169; Dictionaries,
  French, 11588
Mohawk Valley, New York, 1183, 11657,
  12928
Mohegan Indians, Language, 12004;
  Missions, 22391
The Mohocks, 12200
Moise, Abraham, 1799-1869, 12666
Mojica, Aguedo, 18195
The molding sands of Kentucky, 15272
Moler, Arthur Bass, 1866-, 7514
Molina Enríquez, Andrés, 7515, 20682
Molina y Saldivar, Gaspar de, marques de
  Urena, 1741-1806, 7516
Molinari, Gustave de, 1819-1912, 4496
Molleda y Clerque, Gregorio, abp., d.
  1756, 8027
Möller, Joachim van, 17217
Möllhausen, Balduin, 1825-1905, 4497-
  4501, 17218
Mollusks, 37; Argentine Republic, 19923;
  Catalogs and collections, 12328,

12533, 13182; fossil, Para, Brazil, 19792;
  North America, 1318, 5080; North America,
  Bibliography, 1317; Ohio river, 15230;
  Pacific coast, 11670; Pacific ocean,
  12328; Panama, 36; Periodicals, 259;
  Puerto Rico, 18038
Molly's Bible, 8979
The Moloch of decrees, 3159
Moloney, Martha A., 15017, 15018
Moluccas, 7567; History, 2467, 2468
Molybdenum mines and mining, Brazil, Rio
  Grande do Norte, 19293
Mom Bell, 9745
Momberger, illustr., 12554
Mommsen, Theodor, 1817-1903, 24632
Mona, the vestal, 9415
Monaldi, 2512
The monarchist, 4112
Monardes, Nicolas, 1493-1588, 23441
Monasteries, Mexico, 6819
Monasterio Camacho, Antonieta, 20504
Monasticism and religious orders, 584
Monckton-Dene, R., 10115, 10122
Mondría, Ramón, 6422
Mone, Franz Joseph, 1796-1871, 507
Monetary policy, Brazil, 18227
Monette, John Wesley, 4502
Money, Edward, 4503
Money, 1865, 2001, 11119, 16597, 18724, 19510;
  Bibliography, 19262; Canada, 11733;
  Connecticut, 11535; Massachusetts, 2245;
  Miscellanea, 22055; Tables, etc., 13154,
  22638, 23190; U.S., 23824; U.S., History,
  Colonial period, 11535, 11905
Money, and what came of it, 11125
The money diggers, 10959
Money don' make 'ristercrats, 8872
The moneyless man, 5260
Monge Alfaro, Carlos, 7517
Mongolism, 18454
The mongrelites, 25063
Monguagon, Michigan, Battle of, Aug. 9, 1812,
  11944
The monikins, 9138
Le moniteur haitien, 6924
A monitory, and hortatory letter, to those
  English, who debauch the Indians, by
  selling strong drink to them, 23307
Monja y casada, virgen y mártir, 19968
Monks, William, 17219
The monks of Monk-Hall, 10217
Monmouth County Historical Association, Red
  Bank, N.J., 24594
Monmouth's rebellion, 1685, Fiction, 9449
Monnette, Orra Eugene, 17220
Monod, Frederic Joël Jean Gerara, 1794-1863,

309

25629
Monod, Guillaume, 25064
Monody on the victims and sufferers by the late conflagration in the city of Richmond, Virginia, 12262
Monogenism and polygenism, 13019, 13773
A monograph of the fluviatile bivalve shells of the river Ohio, 14230
Monolciolophinae, Brazil, 19779
Monongahela river, Description, 2561
Monopolies, 19620; Bibliography, 18409
The monopoly and the people's line, 10385
Monroe, James, pres. U.S., 1758-1831, 73, 77, 78, 15801, 23011, 23442, 23443, 23708, 23738
Monroe Co., Indiana, History, 12899; Kentucky, 13610, 13613
Monroe doctrine, 7338, 11702, 12115, 25861
Monroy Padilla, Salvador, 7518
Monsalve, Miguel de, 7519
Monsieur Alcibiade, 9769
Monsieur Beaucaire, 10924
Monsieur du Miroir, 9823
Monsieur Matte, 10135
Monsipi Indians, 2620
Monson, Thomas, 15019
Monsters, 14741
The monster and other stories, 9213
Los monstruos sagrados, 19566
Montagnais Indians, 7216
Montagu, Irving, illustr., 3646
Montagu, Lord Robert, 1825-1902, 25065
Montague, E. J., 23444
Montaignes, François des [pseud.], 4504
Montana, 6140, 16419
Montana as it is, 5307
Montana, Description & travel, 2730, 3551, 4549, 5307, 5481, 16009, 17776, 17777; Description & travel, Guide-books, 3735; Description & travel, Views, 17151; History, 16070, 16530, 16910, 17014; History, Societies, 17221
The Montanas, 9730
Montanus, Arnoldus, 1625?-1683, 7629
Montcalm-Gozon, Louis Joseph de, marquis de Saint Véran, 1712-1759, 6397, 8414
Monte Carmelo, Fr. Juan del, 7520
Monteagudo, 18706
Montebelo, Antonio Felix Machado de Castro Silva e Orosco, Marquês de, 18276
Monteiro, Tobias do Rego, 1866-, 25066
Montemar, Diego Miguel Carrillo de Albornoz, conde de, 8277
Montemayor, Alonso de, 7096

Montemayor y Córdova de Cuenca, Juan Francisco de, 1620-1685, 1078, 8085
Montenegro, Joaquim Braga, 1907-, 18309, 18862, 19693
Monterde Garcia Icazbalceta, Francisco, 1894-, 17967
Monterey, Mexico, Archivo Municipal, 20005; History, Sources, 20005; Instituto Tecnologico y de Estudios Superiores, Publicaciones, 18607; Social life & customs, 7364
Monterey, Battle of, 1846, Poetry, 4407
Monterey, California, 17699
Monterey co., California, Biography, 16655; History, 16655
Monterroso, Thomas de, bp., d.1678, 5856
Montesinos, Fernando, 17th cent., 23445
Montesquieu, Charles Louis de Secondat, baron de La Brède et de, 1689-1755, 24669
Montesquieu et l'esclavage, 24669
Montevideo, Description, 12518; History, 18190; Instituto de Cultura Uruguaio-Brasileiro, Coleçao "Textos brasileiros", 19960; Junta Departamental, 20411; Universidad, Instituto de Investigaciones Históricas, Ensayos, estudios y monografias, 20045
Montezuma II, emperor of Mexico, ca.1480-1520, 7546; Fiction, 10331
Montezuma, the last of the Aztecs, 10331
Montezuma, the serf, 9982
Montezuma's castle, 9174
Montgomery, Cora, pseud., 2957, 8958
Montgomery, Elizabeth, 23446
Montgomery, Franklin Alexander, 1830-, 4505
Montgomery, George Washington, 1804-1841, 7521
Montgomery, James, 7522, 12848, 25285
Montgomery, John Teackle, b.1817, 25067
Montgomery, Richard, 1738-1775, 11482
Montgomery Co., Kansas, History, 16436; Biography, 15102; New York, 24692; Pennsylvania, Biography, 1637; Pennsylvania, History, 1637
A month in a country parish, 10383
The Monthly anthology, 23447
The Monthly magazine, 23448
The Monthly offering, 25067
Monti, Luigi, 1830-1914, 7523
Montlezun, baron de, 4506
Montluc, Leon-Pierre-Adrien de, 1847, tr., 25428
Montoto de Sedas, Santiago, 1890-, 7524
Montpelier, Vermont, History, 12429
Montpetit, Edouard, 1881-, 7525
Montreal, Description, 7070, 21007; Description, Guide books, 6551; History,

21807; Police court, 1167; Social
life & customs, 7526
Montreal after 250 years, 7278
Montreal Herald, 7526
Montresor, James Gabriel, 1709-1776, 5111
Montresor, John, 1736-1799, 5111
Montresor family, 5111
The Montresor journals, 5111
Montrol, François Mongin de, 1799-1862,
11522, 25069
Montt, Luis, 7848
Montufar, Manuel, 1791-1844, 23449
Montulé, Édouard de, 4507, 15020
Montvéran, Tournachon de, 25070
A monumental inscription of the fifth of
March, 23450
Moodie, Susannah (Strickland) 1803-1885,
7527, 7528, 13444
Moods, 8486
Moods and memories, 13802
Moody, Beulah C., 15132
Moody, Dan W., 1853-, 17224
Moody, Sid, 15021
Moody, Vernie Alton, 1888-, 25071
Moody, William Robert, bp., 1900-, 15022,
15346
Moon, 9551
Moon hoax, 10231
The moon in Kentucky and elsewhere, 15535
A moonlight boy, 9934
Moonshiners, 9246
Moor's Indian charity school, 23780
Moore, Bethuel, illustr., 14473
Moore, Charles J., 13706
Moore, Clement Clarke, 1779-1863, 23451
Moore, Daniel, fl. 1800, 13154
Moore, David N., 23452
Moore, Dorothy H., illustr., 14280
Moore, Edward Alexander, 1842-, 4508
Moore, Edwin Ward, 1811-1865, 17225,
17226
Moore, Elizabeth Fox, 14130, 15023
Moore, Ely, 1798-1861, 25072
Moore, Francis, fl.1744, 4509
Moore, Francis, jr., 4510
Moore, Frank, 1828-1904, 13232, 23453-
23455
Moore, George, 1806-1876, 4511
Moore, George Henry, 1823-1892, 25073
Moore, H. Judge, 7529
Moore, Henry D., 25074
Moore, Jacob Bailey, 1797-1853, 12138
Moore, James, 13833
Moore, John Bassett, 1860-1947, 24478
Moore, John Trotwood, 1858-1929, 25075
Moore, Joseph Hampton, 1864-, 7530

Moore, Langdon W., 1830-, 17227
Moore, Matilda B., 13621
Moore, McCabe, 23452
Moore, Mike, 1840-, 15024
Moore, Rebecca, 9331
Moore, Theophilus Wilson, 4512
Moore, Thomas Edward Laws, 1810-1872, 22556
Moore, Thomas Patrick, 1797-, 15025
Moore, W. J., 14494
Moore, Will Beno, pseud., 5706
Moore, William Cabell, 15026
Moore, William M., 14403, 14404
Moore, William V., 17228
Moore family (James Moore, b.1716), 23452
Moorhead, Isaac, 1828-1881, 4513
The Moorish bride, 3842
Moorman, John Jennings, 1802-1885, 1714, 4514,
4515, 15027
Mora, Emilio, 951
Mora-Osejo, Luis Eduardo, 19103
Moraes, Evaristo de, 25076
Moraes, Prudente de, 18236
Moragas, Jerónimo de, 18639
A moral blot, 8505
The moral character of the civil government,
22974
La moral de trabajo y su relación con las
funciones técnicas de personal, 19150
The moral significance of war, 661
Morale, 7719
Morales, Juan Bautista, 1788-1856, 7531
Morales, Vicente, 7532
Morales Benítez, Otto, 20328
The morality of the riot, 2347
The morals of freedom, 11720
Moran, Frank E., 3417
Morand, Paul, 1888-, 7533
A moratória, 18279
Moravian church, Catechisms and creeds,
German, 1027; History, 13467; Missions,
13467; North Carolina, 4615
The Moravian Indians, 10670; Missions, 13398,
22391
Moravians, 10388, 10389; Missions, 23517; A
tale of the primitive, 10388
Moravians in North Carolins, 23186
More, Charles Albert, chevalier de Pontgibaud,
comte de, 1758-1837, 4516
More, Gerard, 25077
More, Hannah, 1745-1833, 25078, 25079
More bed-time stories, 10392
More "short sixes", 8898
More than she could bear, 8543
More work for the Maine law, 9001
Moreau, F. Frederic, 4517
Moreau, Jacob Nicolas, 1717-1804, 23456, 23457

311

Moreau-Christophe, Louis Mathurin, 1799-1881, 25080
Moreau de Saint Méry, Médéric Louis Elie, 1750-1819, 4518, 25081
Morehead, Charles Slaughter, 1802-1868, 13363
Morehead, J. N., illustr., 24299
Morehead, James Turner, 1797-1854, 4519, 15424
Moreira de Pinto Freitas, Agnaldo, 19420
Moreland, Sinclair, 1885-, 17229
Moreland township, Pennsylvania, Genealogy, 23197; History, 23197
Morelet, Arthur, 1809-, 7534
Morelett, André, 6778
Morelia, Mexico, Description, 6311, 8277; Ordinances, etc., 7535; Universidad Michoacena de San Nicolás de Hidalgo, 5969
Morelli, Jacopo, 1745-1819, 1140
Morelli, Jorge R., 19675
Morelos y Pavon, José María, 1765-1815, 19081, 19589
Moreno Colmenares, José, 20240
Moreno de Montalvo, Jacinto, 7456
Moreno Mattos, Armando, 20276
Moreno Mora, Alfonso, 21720
Morès, Antoine Amédée Marie Vincent Manca de Vallombrasa, marquis de, 1858-1896, 16426, 17457
Moret, Nicolas d'Oxat, seigneur de, 1682-1738, 11742
Moret y Prendergast, Segismundo, 1838-1913, 23830
Moreton, J. B., 25011, 25082
Morfi, Juan Agustin, d.1783, 7536
Morfología castellana, 19970
Morford, Henry, 1823-1881, 4520, 4521
Morford's short-trip guide to America, 4520
Morgan, B. Q., 13577
Morgan, Dale L., 17230
Morgan, Daniel, 1736?-1802, 22263
Morgan, Edwin Vernon, 25083
Morgan, George, 13955
Morgan, Hazel Smith, 15030
Morgan, Sir Henry, 1635?-1688, 21765
Morgan, Henry James, 1842-1913, 1633, 4522
Morgan, Ike, illustr., 4902
Morgan, John, fl.1739, 24753
Morgan, John Hunt, 1825-1864, 2698, 3312, 4523, 13833, 13932, 14334, 15028, 15029; Fiction, 3507, 13980
Morgan, Julia, Mrs. Irby Morgan, 4523
Morgan, Kelly, 15030
Morgan, Louis, 1814-1852, 15197
Morgan, Margaret, 15031

Morgan, Mrs. Martha M., 4524
Morgan, Matthew Somerville, 1839-1890, 7537
Morgan, William, 1774-ca. 1826, 458, 4534, 10384, 11257, 11562, 12399
Morgan, William Ferdinand, 1817-1888, 7538
Morgan, William Henry, 1836-, 4525
Morgan, William Thomas, 17231
Morgan County, Ky., 14223, 15433, 15686; Description, 15432; Fourth of July celebrations, 14296; History, 14296
Morgan's cavalry division (C.S.A.), 3312
Morgan's escape, 14334
Morgan's raid, 1863, 3417, 4063, 4287, 14334; Fiction, 9251
Morgenstierne, Wilhelm, 5092
Mori, Samuel, 15032
Moria, Carlos, 16841
Moriah's mourning, 5314
Morice, Adrian Gabriel, 1859-1938, 7539
Morillas Osorio, Diego de, 6677-6679, 6687
Morillo y Morillo, Pablo, marques de la Puerta, 1778-1837, 7897
Morineau, Auguste de, 4526
Mormon Battalion, 16004, 16747, 16904
The Mormon country, 16221
Mormon midwives, 17278
The Mormon question in its economic aspects, 17065
The Mormon usurpation, 17275
Mormon way-bill, 2881
"Mormon" women's protest, 17551
The Mormon's wife, 10298
Mormonism, 17424
Mormonism exposed, 15910, 15965
Mormonism unvailed, 12950, 17011
Mormons and Mormonism, 1744, 2970, 2999, 3000, 3013, 3074, 3436, 3437, 3679, 3718, 4131, 4846, 4931, 5175, 5790, 11881, 12148, 12504, 12950, 15896, 15930, 15931, 15965, 16028, 16066, 16109, 16150, 16141, 16147, 16205, 16221, 16299, 16322, 16374, 16479, 16593, 16676, 16687, 16703, 16707, 16751, 16881, 16901, 16996, 17011, 17039, 17063, 17065, 17078, 17183, 17254, 17373, 17387, 17506, 17551, 17582, 17054, 17663, 17745, 17761, 17784, 17815, 17847, 22632, 23507; Fiction, 4948, 5748, 10613, 10990, 16485, 17906; Poetry, 16332; Satire, 17169
Mormons and Mormonism in Great Britain, 16945
Mormons and Mormonism in Illinois, 11695, 15965
Mormons and Mormonism in Iowa, 17501
Mormons and Mormonism in Missouri, 17208
Mormons and Mormonism in Utah, 17079, 17424, 17539
The Mormons and the Indians, 15845
The Mormons at home, 3437
Mörner, Magnus, 1924-, Bibliography, 18985

The morning chronicle, London, 24784
Morning mists, 9265
The morning road, 13803
Morning song, 14266
Morocco, Description & travel, 24690, 25185, 25217; Social life & customs, 25217
Morón, Guillermo, 20391
Morphis, J. M., 17232
Morrell, Z. N., 17233
Morrill, A. Reed, 17234
Morrill, Charles Henry, 1843-, 17235
Morrill, Gulian Lansing, 1857-, 7540, 7541
Morrill, Justin Smith, 1810-1898, 25084
Morrill, Lot Myrick, 1813-1883, 25085
Morrill family (Abraham Morrill, d.1662), 17235
Morris, Alexander, 7542
Morris, Benjamin Franklin, 1810-1867, 25086
Morris, Charles, fl.1749, 7764
Morris, Daniel, 1812-1889, 25088
Morris, E. Hugh, 15033
Morris, Earl H., 17236
Morris, Eastin, 4527
Morris, Edward Joy, 1815-1881, 25088
Morris, George W., 4528
Morris, Gouverneur, 1752-1861, 23650
Morris Graeme, 4001
Morris, Harrison Smith, 1856-, 10737
Morris, Ida Dorman, "Mrs. J.E. Morris", 7543
Morris, John, 15036
Morris, John, pseud., 4635
Morris, Maurice O'Connor, 4529
Morris, Oliver Bliss, 24990
Morris, Robert, 1818-1888, 4530, 13573
Morris, Robert Desha, 1814-1882, 25089
Morris, Thomas, 1776-1844, 25086
Morris, Thomas Asbury, bp., 1794-1874, 1178, 4535
Morris, William of Swindon, Eng., 4536
Morrison, James, 1755-1823, 14340
Morro, W. C., 15035
Morse, Charles Fessenden, 1839-, 4537
Morse, Charles W., 17846
Morse, Francis W., 4538
Morse, Horace Bassett, 1804-1825, 1740
Morse, Isaac Edwards, 1809-1866, 23459, 25090
Morse, Jedidiah, 1761-1826, 52, 1280, 4539, 15036, 23458
Morse, Samuel Finley Breese, 1791-1872, 25091
Morse, Sidney Edwards, 1794-1871, 25092, 25093
Morse, William Clifford, 15037

Morson, Henry, 25094
A morta, 18283
A mortal antipathy, 9906
Mortality, Law of, 938
A morte e a morte de Quincas Berro Dagua, 18233
The mortgage on Jeffy, 9582
Mortgages, 1254
Mortgages (Roman law), 25946
Mortier, Michel, 7544
Morton, Arthur S., 17095
Morton, J. R., 15038, 15181
Morton, Jeremiah, 25095
Morton, John P., & company, Louisville, Ky., 15691
Morton, John Watson, 4540
Morton, Julius Sterling, 1832-1902, 17237
Morton, Levi Parsons, 1824-1920, 7251
Morton, M. B., 15039
Morton, Samuel George, 1799-1851, 23426, 24427
Morton, Mrs. Sarah Wentworth (Apthorp) 1759-1846, Ouabi, 630
Morton, Thomas, 1575-1646, Fiction, 10390
Morton family (George Morton, 1585?-1624), 7251
Morton Montagu, 10389
Morton's artillery, C.S.A., 4540
Morton's Hope, 10391
Morton's manual, 15040
El Mosaico, 7545
Mosby, Charles Virgil, 1876-1942, 15041
Mosby, John Singleton, 1833-1916, 3114, 3417, 4365, 5107
Mosby and his men, 3114
Las moscas, 19967
Mose Evans, 8658
Mose Skinner's bridal tour, 8862
Mose Skinner's great world's jubilee and humstrum convulsion, 8863
Moseley, Henry Nottidge, 1844-1891, 17238
Moselle (Steamboat), 21925
Moser, James H., illustr.,8691, 24562
Moses and Joshua, 7805
Mosgrove, Dallas, 15042
Mosgrove, George Dallas, 4541
Mosher, Thomas Bird, 14343
Moshoquop, the avenger, 16592
Mosquitia, 2353; Description & travel, 7750, 7883, 8098
Mosquito Coast, 13485
Mosquito language, 22404
Moss, Frank Edward, 1911-, 15043
Moss family, 15640
Moss-side, 10942
Mosses from an old manse, 9823
Mossoró, Escola Superior de Agricultura, 20423

The most orderly of disorderly houses, 15585
Motezuma, Diego Luis de, 1619-1699, 7546
Moth and rust, 11214
Mothering on Perilous, 14169
The mother's question, 9540
The mother's rule, 8572
The motley book, 10325, 10326
Motor vehicles, 15336; Taxation, 15336
Mott, M. H., 23460
Mott, Valentine, 1785-1865, 2313, 12463
The moujik, 9265
Moulton, Augustus Freedom, 1848-, 24959
Moulton, Louise Chandler, 10163, 10899
Moultrie, William, 1730-1805, 12729
Moultrie, Fort, Battle of, 1776, 24397
The Moultrie Co. Lincolns, 6716
Mound-builders, 12184, 13457; Manitoba, 6215; Ohio, 4640
Mounds, 507, 11474; Georgia, 13290; Gt. Britain, 13225; North America, 933; Ohio, 23167
Mounds and mound builders of the United States, 16599
Mounds of Minnesota Valley, 17492
Mount Auburn, and other poems, 22963
Mount Auburn cemetery, 1269
Mount Holly, N.J., 527
Mount Holyoke, Mass., Description, Guide-books, 2181
Mount Hope, 12856
Mt. Pisgah's Christmas' possum, 24319
Mount Vernon, 13399, 21985
Mount Vernon Ladies Association of the Union, 5629, 22135
The Mount Vernon papers, 12116
Mountain, George Jehoshaphat, bp. of Quebec, 1789-1863, 4542
The mountain empire Utah, 15994
A mountain Europa, 9554
Mountain fiction from Abernethy to Zugsmith, 15135
Mountain fiction from Addington to Zugsmith, 13654
A mountain idyll, 15270
Mountain life, Southern states, Kentucky, 15261
Mountain Meadow massacre, 1857, 6335, 16593, 17009, 17010, 17011, 17945
Mountain Meadows, Utah, History, 5525
The mountain mourner, 10316
The mountain muse, 2844
The mountain of the two lovers, 10919
The mountain people of Kentucky, 3789
Mountain sheep, 8012
A mountain-white heroine, 14190

Mountain whites (Southern states), 2901, 3769, 14328, 15003, 15515
The mountaineer of the Atlas, 10336
Mountaineering, 6890, 8126, 8372, 16050, 16174, 16949; Periodicals, 6317
Mountains and molehills, 17133
The mountains of Oregon, 17665
Moura, Iraci Alfonso de, 19220
Mourão, Ronaldo Rogerio de Freitas, 18863
Mourelle, Francisco Antonio, 1755-1820, 23461
Mourik, Bernardus, 24690
A mournful Easter, 12561
A movimiento academicista no Brasil, 19926
El movimiento obrero en México, 20047
Moving pictures, 18642, 20633; Bibliography, 14704; Colombia, 20268
Moving-pictures actors and actresses, 20441
Moving pictures in education, 18031
Mowat, Henry, 1734-1798, 1803
Mowatt, Anna Cora Ritchie, 10622-10625
Mowris, James A., 4543
Mowry, William Augustus, 1829-1917, 17240, 17241
Moxon, Joseph, 7547
Moxoto (Vale), Brazil, Economic conditions, 20000; Social conditions, 20000
Moya, Rodrigo, 7440-7442
Mozambique, 18369
Mozambique Channel, Description & travel, 24604
Mudd, Samuel Alexander, 1833-1883, 1305, 6701
Mudge, Enoch, 1776-1850, 22496
Mudge, Zachariah Atwell, 1813-1888, 4546, 17242
Muerte de un ciclista (motion picture), 18842
Muerte de Virginia por la libertad de Roma, 19626
Muhlenberg, Henry Augustus, 1823-, 15044
Mühlenberg, Henry Melchior, 1711-1787, 4547
Muhlenberg, John Peter Gabriel, 1746-1807, 15044
Muhlenberg Co., Kentucky, 14220; History, 15300; Unity Baptist Church, 15302
Mühlenpfordt, Eduard, 7548
Muir, John, 1838-1914, 17243-17245
Muir John Wakefield, 1909-, 15045
Muirhead, James Fullarton, 1853-1934, 4548
La mujer del paraguas, 19823
Mulberry, 11840, 15218, 23797
Muleback, 15474
Mules, Santa Catarina, Brazil, Statistics, 19467
Mulgrave, Henry Phipps, 1st earl of, 1755-1831, 23011
Mullan, John, 1830-1909, 4549, 4560, 5540
Müller, Johann Wilhelm von, 1824-1866, 7549
Mulligan, James Hilary, 1844-1915, 8220

Mulloy, William P., 14667
Mulvaney, Charles Pelham, 7550
Mumford, Lewis, 1895-, 13577
Munchausen, Baron, jr., pseud., 10384
Mund, August, 5290
Mundo, hombre, historia, 20478
Mundo e contramundo, 20074
O mundo em números, 19277
Mundo pequeño, 20466
Munduruku Indians, 18554
Munford, Beverley Bland, 1856-, 25096
Munfordville, Ky., 13609
Municipal corporations, Uruguay, Congresses, 20411
Municipal finance, Brazil, 19282
Muñiz Vidarte, Luis, 19135
Munoff, Gerald J., 15046
Muñoz, Joaquín, 7551, 7552
Muñoz, Juan Bautista, Historia del Nuevo Mundo, 13112
Muñoz, Rafael F., Se llevaron el cañon para Bachimba, 19967
Muñoz Vernaza, Alberto, 18105
Munro-Fraser, J. P., 16770, 16772, 16777, 16778
Munroe, Kirk, 17246
Munsee Indians, 134
Munsell, Joel, 1808-1880, 13445; Publisher, Albany, N.Y., 15047
Munsell, Luke, 1790-1854, 15048
Munsell, Marion Ebenezer, 1862-, 17247
Münster, Sebastian, 1489-1552, 5920
Münsterberg, Hugo, 1863-1916, 4551
Mur, Pedro de, 13334
Murais da morte, 18118
Mural painting and decoration, Ixmiquilpan, Mexico, 19851
Murat, Achille, prince, 1801-1847, 4552, 25097
Murch, Abel B., joint author, 1624
Murchard, F., 17
Murchard, Friedrich Wilhelm August, 1779-1853, ed., 23181
Murder, 11963, 13241, 21979
The murder of Abraham Lincoln planned and executed by Jesuit priests, 7553
The murderer's doom!!, 16014
Murders and daring outrages, 21979
Murdock, William David Clark, 25098
Murfree, Mary Noailles, 1850-1922, 4553-4567
Murfreesboro, Battle of, 1862-63, 2708
Murqatroyd, Matthew, pseud., 10061
Muriel, Domingo, 1718-1795, 20084
Murillo, Gerardo, 1884-, 7554, 7555
Murillo, marqués de, 6386

Murphey, Claude Charles, 4568
Murphree, E. V., 14650
Murphy, Arthur, 1727-1805, tr., 23677
Murphy, D. F., 7566
Murphy, Henry Cruse, 1810-1882, 1568, 25099
Murphy, John M., 17248
Murphy, Lady Blanche Elizabeth Mary Annunciata (Noel) 1845?-1881, tr., 3618, 5032
Murphy, Thomas Dowler, 1866-, 17249, 17250
Murphy, Timothy, 1751-1818, 12334
Murray, Alexander Hunter, 1818-1874, 17251
Murray, Hon. Amelia Matilda, 1795-1884, 4569
Murray, Sir Charles Augustus, 1806-1895, 4570, 4571, 17252
Murray, David Christie, 1847-, 7556
Murray, Henry Anthony, 1810-1865, 7557, 7558
Murray, James, 1713-1781, 4572
Murray, James, 1732-1782, 23462
Murray, Mrs. Lois Levina (Abbott) 1826-, 17253
Murray, Orson S., 25100
Murray, Samuel, 1865-, 7559
Murray, William, 6666
Murray family, 4572
Murray, Kentucky, Woman's Club, 15049
Murray State University, Murray, Kentucky, 15050
Murrell, John A., 9931
Murriets, Joaquin, 1828 or 29-1853, 16841
Murton, John, fl. 1620, 23799
Murvale Eastman, Christian socialist, 10993
Muscatine, Iowa, History, 16867
Muscoma, 8588
Muscongus lands, 1817, 22164
The muse of Hesperia, 4741
Museo de Oro, Bogotá, 18761
Museo Municipal de Ciencias Naturales de Mar del Plata, Publicaciones, 20187
Los museos de historia natural en México y la Sociedad Mexicana de Historia Natural, 18962
Museu Goeldi, Belém, Brazil, 19323, 21737
Museum Americanum, 12994
Museums, Kentucky, 15692; Mexico, 18962
Musgrove, Charles Hamilton, 15051
Music, History and criticisms, 18812; New England, 12879; Study and teaching, Curricula, 20598, 20599; U.S., 274
Music, Latin American, 19820
Music, Spanish American, 20217; History and criticisms, 18633
Music on the march, 4899
Música e dança foldóricas, 18175
Musical prodigies, 15052
A musical reformation, 9091
Musicians, Fiction, 10307
Musick, John Roy, 1849-1901, 4573

Musings and pastels, 3448
Musings in life's evening, 14310
Muskets and medicine, 4064
Muskingum Co., Ohio, Maps, 1068
Musser, Amos Milton, 1830-1909, 17254
Mussey, Osgood, 25101
Musson, Eugène, 25102
Mustache, 21752
Mustang Gray, 9021
The mute singer, 10624
Mutis, José Alestino, 1732-1808, 7560
Mutterings and musings of an invalid, 11002
Myers, J. C., 4574
Myers, Leonard, 1827-1905, 7561
Mygatt, Mrs. Mary Stevens (Dickinson), 6592
Myrthe, A. T., pseud., 9598
Myrtis, 10760
Myrtle blossoms, 9869
Myrtle lawn, 2603
Mysteries, Religious, 2241
The mysteries and miseries of New York, 10080
Mysteries of city life, 10604
The mysteries of magic, 10693
The mysteries of Nashua, 10402
The mysteries of the back woods, 5411, 10964
The mysteries of the Catskills, 10458
The mysteries of the three cities, 9434
Mysteries of Washington city, during several months of session of the 28th Congress, 11229
The mysterious bell, 10693
A mysterious case, 10668
The mysterious chief, 11204
The mysterious companions of Old John Brown, 10007
The mystery, 9249
The mystery disclosed, 10673
Mystery Evans, 8648
A mystery explained, 10713
The mystery of a Christmas hunt, 10125
The mystery of choice, 8965
The mystery of Mahbin Mill, 10112
The mystery of the hacienda, 6963, 6971
The mystery of the locks, 9935
The mystery of the Meschianza, 10277
The mystery of the Westervelts, 9372
The mystery of Witch-Face mountain, 4561
The mystery reveal'd; or Truth brought to light, 23457
The mystery solved, 10846
The mystic number seven in the life of Abraham Lincoln, 7634
Mystical union, 22554
Mythology, Dictionaries, indexes, etc.,

22658; Aztec, 7491; Greek, 15364; Roman, 15364

Naaukeurige beschryving van Noord-America, 4575
Nabuco, Joaquim, 1840-1910, 25788
Nach Amerika im dienste Friedrich Schillers, 4765
Nach Amerika in einem auswandererschiffe, 5565
Nach dem Sacramento, 17189
Nachbin, Leopoldo, 18881
Nachricht von Suriname und seinen einwohnern; sonderlich den Arawacken, Warauen und Karaiben, 23517
Nacoochee, 2994
Nadal, Bernard Harrison, 1812-1870, 7562
Nadeshda (Ship), 16981, 22741
Nagy, Elemer, 20628
Nahant, 10404, 22546; Mass., Description, 22546
Nahum, Benjamin, 1937-, 18850
Nahuys, Joanna, 19178
The nail hit on the head, 25184
Nairne, Thomas, 4576
La naissance d'une nation, 6735
Nakam, a Menominee Indian, 11358
Nameless, 9428
The nameless hero and other poems, 13552
A nameless nobleman, 8606
Names, Geographical, Argentine Republic, Rio Negro (Province), 19890; Kentucky, 13787, 14086, 14089, 14359, 14734, 14941; México, Tlaxcala (State), 18261; New York (State), 1174; Quebec (Province), 7916; Texas, 16555; Utah, 17338, 17343; West Virginia, 14941
Names, Personal, Kentucky, 13546; Massachusetts, Suffolk Co., 11435; U.S., 13546
Names of people in title, 17380
Nan, 10163
Nancy Ward, 10134
Nancy Waterman, 8748
Nankivell, F.A., illustr., 10998
Nantucket, Mass., 6860, 21991; Description & travel, 8607; History, 23005; History, Sources, 12931
Nantucket scraps, 8607
Naomi, 10179, 10180, 15478
Napier, John, 1550-1617, 1632
Napier, John, 1915-1965, 15053
Napier, Robert, d.1766, 23456, 23457, 23924
Napier, Sue, 13521, 15054

The Napolead, 3587
Napoleon I, emperor of the French, 1769-
1821, 21964; Fiction, 11029; Poetry,
3587
Napoleon III, emperor of the French, 1808-
1873, 1125, 3617
Napoleon, Louis, respondent, 25129
Napoleon Jackson, the gentleman of the
plush rocker, 25639
Napoles recvperada por el rey don Alonso,
6118
Napoli, V. di, 19869
Narcotics, 14737; Brazil, 19410
Nariño, Antonio, 1765-1823, 17979
Narjot, Ernest, illus., 16482
Naron, L. H., Union scout, 5321
The Narraganset chief, 10503
Narragansett Bay, Description & travel,
Guide books, 764
Narragansett Indians, 23800
Narragansett language, 23800
Narragansett patent, 505
Narváez, José Ignacio, ed., 20317
Narváez, Pánfilo de, d.1528, 4631; Drama,
6328
Nasby, Petroleum V., pseud., 10226-10230
Nasby in exile, 10226
Nasby on inflation, 10228
The Nasby papers, 10227
Nash, Jeffrey, 25322
Nash, Wallis, 17255-17257
Nashua, N. H., History, 2297
Nashville, N. H., History, 2297
Nashville, Tenn., History, Civil war,
4523
Nashville, University, 22864; Medical dept.,
11453
Nashville, Chattanooga, and St. Louis
Railroad, 14748
Nason, Daniel, 4578
Nason, Elias, 1811-1887, 972, 7563
Nast, Thomas, 1840-1902, illustr., 5460,
6591, 10579, 11119
Nat Gregory, 10738
Natalie, 9712
Natchez, Miss., Description, 3424
Natick, Mass., Description, 645; History,
1285
Nation, Mrs. Carry (Moore) 1846-1911, 13687
La nation haitienne, 6064
The nation's grief: death of Abraham
Lincoln, 23171
The nation's prospects of peace, 23172
The nation's sin and punishment, 24615
The nation's success and gratitude, 1462
National Anti-slavery Bazaar, Boston, 25104

The National atlas and Tuesday morning mail,
23464
National banks, U.S., 12128
The national "barley cake", 556
National characteristics, 2268; American, 221,
1461, 5172, 5697, 12086; English, 21881;
Mexican, 8402
The national crisis, 25105
National editorial association of the U.S.,
8180
National equal suffrage association, 11376
National era, 24371
National income, Chile, 20162
National Institute for the promotion of
science, Washington, D.C., 21, 1475
National intelligencer, Washington, 395
National jewels: Washington, Lincoln, and the
fathers of the revolution, 23111
The national jubilee, 3384
National Lincoln monument association, 7564
The national nest-stirring, 1470
A national park in Kentucky, 14945, 14946
National parks and reserves, 18441; Argentine
Republic, 18442; Canada, 7173; Kentucky,
13917; U.S., 7173
The National party, 7870
National reconstruction, 7562
National Republican Party, Pennsylvania, An
address to the people of Pennsylvania, 24278
National Research Council, Publications, 19513,
20083; Revision of Earth Sciences, Foreign
field research program reports, 19597
National Research Institute of Amazonia, 19322
National ship-canal convention, Chicago, 1863,
2471, 13446
National Society of the Daughters of the
American Revolution, 13972
National songs, American, 12174, 12250, 22792
National songster, 13392
National Union Association of Ohio, 7565
National Union Convention, Baltimore, June 7-8,
1864, 7566, 7615
National virtue and national glory, 157
A national warning, 1216
Nationalism, Brazil, 18559
Nationality, 1955
"A native author called Roe", 10653
A native of Maryland, 24302, 24306
A native of Winby, 10041
Native races, 12965, 24567, 25663
Native trees of Kentucky, 14976
Nativism in Kentucky to 1860, 14908
The natural and civil history of the French
dominions in North and South America, 4051
Natural and statistical view, or picture of
Cincinnati and the Miami country, 3289

Natural Bridge, Ky., 14814, 14903
Natural gas in eastern Kentucky, 14439
Natural history, 12325, 15220, 15227,
  15233, 22041, 22322, 22323; Addresses,
  essays, lectures, 877; Alabama, 3650;
  Alaska, 5899; Amazon valley, 961;
  Amazon Valley, Periodicals, 18015;
  America, 16020; Arctic regions, 6058,
  7911; Atlantic states, 7172; Bahamas,
  2946; Barbados, 22592; Bermuda Islands,
  13306; Brazil, 19241; British Columbia,
  7324; Canada, 6768, 6954, 7170-7172;
  Canary Islands, 11381; Central America,
  7657; Collected works, 12685; Colombia,
  13451; Cuba, 7007, 18214; Dutch Guiana,
  24385; England, 7170; Florida, 5012;
  History, 11973; Jamaica, 11578, 22481,
  24884; Labrador, 6901; Louisiana, 5537;
  Mexico, 6400, 6401, 6862, 7932, 18075,
  19050; Nebraska, 15884; New England,
  22727; New York (State), 1907; North
  America, 6670, 22285; North Carolina,
  2799, 11515; Northwest, Canadian, 16731;
  Northwest, Old, 6768; Northwest
  Territories, Canada, 5899; Norway, 7170;
  Nova Scotia, 6575; Ohio, 540; Outdoor
  books, 5394, 5437, 17199, 17200, 22456;
  Panama, 13502; Paraguay, 598;
  Pennsylvania, 931; Pictorial works, 2946;
  Polynesia, 1172; Pre-Linnean works, 2946;
  Rocky Mountains, 17777; Societies, etc.,
  2472, 12049, 22821; South America, 7092,
  21853; South Carolina, 12049; Southern
  States, 2946; Spanish America, 5827;
  Study and teaching, Mexico, 18962;
  Superior, Lake, 108; Surinam, 733, 734;
  Tahiti, 3237; Texas, 5537; U.S., 4193,
  5700, 5701, 7170, 7171; Utah, 5255, 5501,
  17786; West Indies, 7657
The natural history of secession, 24502
Natural law, 13042, 22947
Natural resources, 14047, 19441; Amazon
  region, Brazil, 19447, 19451; Brazil,
  Northeast, 18277; Canada, 6436; Kentucky,
  13717, 14557, 14661, 14905, 15354;
  Northwest, Canadian, 6062; Texas, 17727;
  U.S., 4716; Venezuela, 20093
Natural theology, 2884
Naturaleza jurídica del arbitraje, 18355
A naturalist in Mexico, 5986
The naturalist on the river Amazon, 961
Naturalization, 1955; U.S., 1308, 1508,
  11580
Nature (Aesthetics), 11598
The nature and danger of heresy, 13056
Nature and human nature, 12546

Nature display'd, 5564
The nature of humiliation, fasting and prayer
  explained, 11501
A nature sketchbook, 13534
Un naufrage au Texas, 5076
Naufragio genuino, 20010
The naulahka, 10146
Nautical astronomy, 23823
The Nautilus, 9040
Nauvoo, Ill., 11695
Nava, Pedro José de, 7768
The Navajo and his blanket, 16804
Navajo country, Description & travel, 5167
Navajo Indians, 16804; Wars, 3962
Naval art and science, 462, 463, 7995, 19585;
  Dictionaries, 12722; History, 11424, 22928;
  Periodicals, 11228
Naval battles, 11424; Gt. Britain, 185, 1540,
  2187
The naval gazetteer; or, Seaman's complete
  guide, 23052
Naval history, 1690
Naval hygiene, 459, 11241
Naval stories, 18605
Navarrete, Martín Fernández de, 1765-1844,
  7567, 16477
Navarro, Nicolás Eugenio, abp., 1867-, 19738
Navarro, Tomás, 19726
Navarro de Patiño, Juana, 19570
Navarro y Rodrigo, Carlos, 1833-1903, 7568
Navies, 1218, 1757
Navigation, 5852, 6007, 6832; Dictionaries,
  20133; Early works to 1800, 23692, 23823;
  History, 311, 22928, 22986
Naylor, James Ball, 15648
Naylor, Robert Anderton, 4579
The Nazarene, 10214
Nazarene, Church of, 13650
Nazareth, R.A.M.A., 19868
Neal, John, 1793-1876, 192, 193
Neall, Rebecca B., 23920
Neapolitan captive, 23768
Near a whole city full, 10998
Near to nature's heart, 10650
Nebecker, John, 1813-, 17258
Nebel, Carl, 7569, 7570
Nebraska, 16746, 17596; Antiquities, 15957,
  17851; Bibliography, 17793; Biography,
  16361, 16450, 16785; Centennial celebrations,
  etc., 17793; Climate, 16216, 16633;
  Description & travel, 247, 2510, 2597, 2776,
  3063, 3551, 3938, 3955, 4411, 4495, 4651,
  4727, 5626, 5627, 5770, 12142, 15809, 15884,
  16096, 16097, 16098, 16111, 16112, 16216,
  16232, 16258, 16310, 16908, 16970, 16002,
  16785, 17259, 17351, 17845, 17915,

318

Description & travel, Guide-books, 3735; Directories, 17916; Economic conditions, 16785; Fiction, 5655; Geology, 15885; Gold discoveries, 2510, 4727; Governors, 17412; History, 15923, 16257, 16361, 16395, 16531, 16532, 16785, 17237, 17563, 17564, 17595, 17598, 17599, 17744, 17828, 17841, 17848, 24724, 25940; History, Societies, 17260; History, Sources, 17597; Legislature, 17917; Politics & government, 15923, 16262, 17804; State historical society, 17563, 17599
Nebraska and Kansas, 23966
Nebraska in 1857, 5770
Nebraska legends and poems, 11938
Necaxa, Mexico, 8273
Necesidad, apertura y constitución de la tutela ordinaria de menores en el derecho Venezolano, 18051
The necessity for that famous "Bible and revolver", 17068
Neck, S. Sanders, 4580
Necromancy in the wilderness, 2678
Ned Myers, 9139
Nederlandsche maatschappij ter bevorderine van de afschaffing der slavernij, The Hague, 25702
Nederlandsche Oost-Indische compagnie, 348
Nederlandsche West-Indische compagnie, 348, 1516, 22152, 25031
Nederst ved bordet, 3896
Needles, Edward, 25231
Neelmeyer-Vukassowitsch, Heinrich, 4581
Neerlands West-Indie in zijne belangen, 1126
Neese, George Michael, 1839-, 4582
Neff, S. E., 14358
De negerslaven in de kolonie Suriname en de uitbreiding van het Christendom onder de heidensche bevolking, 25675
The neglected period of anti-slavery in America (1808-1831), 23837
Negotiable instruments, Kentucky, 24715
The negotiation and breakdown of the Tripartile Convention of London of 31 October 1861, 19095
Nègre blanc, Dissertation physique à l'occasion du, 25015
Negro, English dialects, 3643
The negro and the nation; a history of American slavery and enfranchisement, 25033
The negro as there are few white men, 24778
Negro authors, 24895
Negro civilization in the south, 25398
The negro equalled by few Europeans, 24779
The negro in American history, 24231

The negro in Tennessee, 1790-1865, 25203
The negro in the new world, 4076
The negro labor question, 25106
"Negro law" (Kentucky), 24145
Negro literature, History & criticisms, 12421; U.S., 7165
The negro melodist, 4044
Negro myths from the Georgia coast told in the vernacular, 4106
Negro neighbors, bond and free, 25867
The "negro pew", 25107
The negro population of Kentucky, 13866
The negro population of Kentucky at mid-century, 13867
Negro race, 445, 2257, 13019, 24039, 24063, 24230, 24842
Negro-slavery, no evil, 25119
Negro slavery; or crime of the clergy, 25425
Negro songs, 4044, 24562, 24678
The negro: the southerner's problem, 25188
El negro uruguayo, 19884
The Negro's memorial; or, abolitionist's catechism, 24396
The negro's place in nature, 25109
Negroes, 116, 703, 1823, 1890, 1929, 2165, 3819, 3896, 12421, 12422, 13237, 23419, 23858, 24039, 24230, 24237, 24394, 24407, 24459, 24549, 24643, 24703, 24874, 24960, 24963, 25015, 25033, 25062, 25106, 25107, 25124, 25176, 25283, 25311, 25312, 25398, 25464, 25677, 25724, 25796, 25838, 25867; Antigua, 397; Baltimore, 13449; Barbados, 25264; Biography, 1890, 12421, 24039, 24231; Brazil, 18230, 18698, 19812, 24328; Civil rights, 960, 1304; Colombia, 18363; Colonization, 703, 1340, 1383, 2257, 24436, 24939; Colonization, Africa, 503, 639, 1340, 1459, 1699, 5039, 6429, 6486, 7513, 11563, 11565, 11783, 12506, 13508, 12618, 12692, 12827, 21930, 22980, 23858, 23960, 24074, 24126, 24127, 24170, 24171, 24200, 24232, 24422, 24434, 24455, 24457, 24537, 24544, 24549, 24612, 24716, 24772, 24773, 24832, 24944, 24949, 24980, 25053, 25192, 25211, 25514, 25523, 25669, 25712, 25748, 25767, 25798; Colonization, Central America, 23982; Colonization, Haiti, 24284; Colonization, South America, 23982; Colonization, Texas, 24761; Congresses, 24193; Cuba, 25179; Education, 357, 13292, 24001, 24428; Fiction, 25191; France, 5952; French Antilles, 6172, 6484, 6770, 6896, 6897, 7622, 7738; Georgia, 24402; Haiti, 12861, 25180, 25556; History, 24008, 24231; Illinois, 24568, 24643; Insanity, 22686; Jamaica, 11943, 13147, 23007, 24601, 24957; Kentucky, 13866, 13867,

13984, 14515, 14516, 15525, 15612, 24713;
Legal status, laws, etc., 13147, 24426,
25178; Lexington, Ky., 15607; Louisiana,
24130; Maryland, 25354; Massachusetts,
1328, 23258, 23954, 24459, 24988, 24989,
24995; Missouri, 24633; Moral & social
conditions, 4839, 23893, 23965; New
York (State), 12366, 25129; Ohio, 24220;
Orleans (Ter.), 25178; Pennsylvania,
23981, 25234, 25736; Philadelphia,
25456; Politics and suffrage, 11376,
24402, 25941; Puerto Rico, 18218, 25577;
Relgion, 646, 23931, 24112, 24676,
25107; South Carolina, 46, 2769, 8459;
Southern states, 4813, 24584, 25188;
Spanish America, 23856; Tennessee, 15612,
25203; Texas, 24130; U.S., 3260, 3827,
3975, 4076, 8047, 25456, 25917; U.S.,
Fiction, 2982; Uruguay, 19884; West
Indies, 1823, 11235, 25180; West Indies,
British, 6339, 22012, 24088, 24972,
25640; West Indies, French, 24426, 25739;
Wisconsin, 24984
Negroes and religion, 25108
Negroes who owned slaves, 25903
Negromonte, Alvaro, 19052
Los negros en sus diversos estados y
    condiciones, 24388
Los negros esclavos, 25179
Nehiro-iriniui aiamihe massinahigan, 7215
Neide, Charles A., 4583
A neighbor's landmark, 10038
Neighbours' prescriptions, 10841
Neill, Edward Duffield, 1823-1893, 17261-
    17264, 23465, 25110
Neill, John R., illustr, 14272
Neillsville, Wis., 15848
Neilson, Peter, 1795-1861, 4584, 25111
Nell'America del Nord, 5915
Nellie of Truro, 9922
Nelly Bracken, 10098
Nelly's silver mine, 16872
Nelse Hatton's vengeance, 24319
Nelson, Albert Hobart, 1812-1858, 23263
Nelson, David, 25707
Nelson, G. Patrick, illustr., 15092
Nelson, George E. W., 2054
Nelson, Helge Magnus Oskar, 4585
Nelson, Henry Addison, 1820-1906, 7571
Nelson, John, 1786-1871, 25112
Nelson, John P., 14496, 15056-15058
Nelson, Nels Christian, 17265
Nelson, Robert, 1656-1715, 1556
Nelson, Robert, missionary in China, 7572
Nelson, S., 8837
Nelson, Wilbur, 7573

Nelson, William, fl. 1720, 11660
Nelson Co., Kentucky, History, 14912; Maps,
    14224
Nelson Valley railway and transportation
    company, 7575
Nematodes, 18889-18891; Cuba, 19064
Nemesis, 10944
Nemos, William, 1848-, 5996, 15907
Neo-Scholasticism, 19694
Neogenyton, 15231
Neptune (Steamship), 6302
The Nereid, 9527
Nery Q., Victor, 20226
Nesbitt, C. R., 11457
Neshaminy, Pa., Log college, 141
Nesterowicz, S., 4586
Nestor, pseud., 94
The nests at Washington, 4774
The net in the bay, 2536
Netherlands, Colonies, Administration, 1127;
    Colonies, East Indies, 23974; Colonies,
    Guiana, 1516; Colonies, West Indies, 1127;
    Commerce, 12988, 22884; Commercial policy,
    12988; Economic conditions, 22884; Foreign
    relations, Gt. Britain, 2026, 23144, 23145;
    Foreign relations, Portugal, 104, 340;
    Foreign relations, U.S., 56; History, Naval,
    1435, 7827
Nettie (Yacht), 7012
Nettleroth, Henry, 15059
Neubreisuch, Germany (Alsatia), History, 22234
Die neue Welt, 6557
Neuf mois aux États-Unis d'Amérique, 13045
Neuman, Henry, 7243, 7244
"Die neuner," 5334
Neuquén, Argentine Republic (Province)
    Universidad, Facultad de Humanidades,
    Publicaciones, Mitología, 19828
Neuroptera, Cuba, 18086; North America, 12523;
    South America, 12523
The neutral French, 11171
Neutrality, 1141, 1143, 1204, 11808, 12222,
    12668, 13405, 22990
Neva (Ship), 16981, 17040, 22741
Nevada, 15856, 17420, 17794; Bibliography,
    Catalogs, 17794; Biography, 15855, 16334,
    16339, 16612, 17626, 17882, 17931;
    Boundaries, 16865; Centennial celebrations,
    etc., 17794; Description & travel, 3212,
    4931, 5152, 5685, 7057, 16222, 16797,
    17420, 17539, 17886, 17934, 17935;
    Directories, 16243, 16928; History, 15855,
    16334, 16339, 17153, 17230, 17870, 17884,
    17931; Missions, 17870
Nevada, Col., Description, 17914
Neverfail, 4992

"Never had no sleep", 10808
Nevers, Edmond de, 4587
Neves-Manta, I. de L., 20095
Neville, John H., 14881
Nevin, Afred, 1816-1890, 15062
Nevin, David Robert Bruce, 1828-, 15062
Nevin, John Williamson, 1803-1886, 2321
Nevinson, Henry Woodd, 1856-, 25113
Nevves from Virginia, 4947
The new Adam and Eve, 9823
The new age of gold, 10493
New Almaden quicksilver mines, California, 1166
New America, 3259
The new American atlas, 23678
The new American rational spelling-book, 5743
A new and compleat introduction to the grounds and rules of musick, 985
A new and comprehensive gazetteer of Virginia, 4404
A new and most exact account of the fertile and famous colony of Carolina, 3106
The new and the old, 17336
New approaches to legal research, 20001
The new assistant at Pine Clearing School, 6965
New Boston, N.H., Genealogy, 1987; History, 1952, 1987
New Britain, 12051
New Brunswick, 524, 6911, 12219, 23283; Boundaries, Maine, 13463; Description & travel, 524, 4078, 23150
The new cashier, 9463
A new constitutional convention, both necessary and expedient, 15748
The new doctrine, 10610
New education in California, 15820
The new empire, 17408
The new empire and her representative men, 16682
New England, 11286, 11336; Biography, 12007, 21813, 23305; Church history, 621, 13375, 22355, 22996, 23305; Commerce, 751, 2009, 22333, 23626; Description & travel, 2959, 3595, 3991, 4574, 4998, 6517, 13366, 13367, 21943, 21968, 22726, 25409; Description & travel, Guide-books, 2147, 12495; Description & travel, Maps, 7764; Fiction, 8971, 10563; Genealogy, 2219, 7971; History, 53, 10854, 13419; History, Bibliography, Catalogs, 23273-23275; History, Chronology, 11496; History, Colonial Period, 12, 34, 1148, 1456, 1513, 2306, 11865, 12747, 12970, 12976, 22006, 22007, 22588, 23305,

23320, 23325, 23626, 23810; History, Colonial period, Fiction, 767, 10958; Politics & government, 71, 22989; Politics & government, Colonial period, 1553, 13002, 13375; Religion, 11764, 23688; Sectional characteristics, 25151; Social life & customs, 10, 779, 2244, 9409, 9620, 10818, 10828, 11036, 12841, 23726
New England a degenerate plant, 23466
The New England anti-slavery almanac, 25114
New England Anti-slavery Convention, Boston, 1834, 25115, 25116
New England Anti-slavery Convention,3d, Boston, 1836, 25117
New England Anti-slavery Convention,4th, Boston, 1837, 25118
New England Anti-slavery Society, 25002
New England bride, Recollections of a, 3604
New England Emigrant Aid Company, Boston, 25119
The New-England farmer, 11957
The New-England farrier, 13224
New England historical and genealogical register, 2090, 12153
New England life in a village, 11773
New England Mississippi land company, 1346
New England Non-resistance Society, Boston, 23939
A New England nun, 9575
A New England prophet, 9578
New England society of San Francisco, 13021
New England society of the city of New York, 633, 1755, 11772, 12578, 12790
A New England tale, 10727
New England tears for old Englands feares, 12881
New England theology, 11896
New England's chattels, 9475
New England's Jonas cast up at London, 1886
New Englander and Yale review, 24892
New France, 6735; Bibliography, 2217, 7149, 12718; Description & travel, 22411; Description & travel, Maps, Bibliography, 12718; Discovery & exploration, 1289, 1481, 1482, 1827, 3666, 5433, 6396, 6403, 6404, 7008, 7149, 7197, 7268, 7404, 8401, 11715, 11762, 16956, 16995, 17129, 21874, 23520, 23473; Genealogy, Dictionaries, 8153
A new gazetteer of the U.S.A., 3173
A new geographical, historical, and commercial grammar, 3722
The new gold mines of western Kansas, 4708
The new gospel of peace, 8378, 11148
New Granada: twenty months in the Andes, 22540
New Hampshire, Biography, 11747; Constitution, 23467; Description & travel, 13336, 23416;

Description & travel, Gazetteers, 11747, 12138, 12765; Description & travel, Guide-books, 1034; Fiction, 11032; General court, 11419, 11504, 11792, 12361, 12551, 22866; History, 897, 1084, 11747, 11752; History, Colonial period, 1083; History, Colonial period, Sources, 11419; History, Revolution, 23468; Law, statutes, etc., 11755, 23468; Militia, Handbooks, 2220; Politics & government, 23467; Social life & customs, 9409; Statistics, 12765

New Hampshire Anti-slavery Convention, Concord, 1834, 25121

New Hampshire Anti-slavery Society, 25120, 25121

New Hampshire grants, 176, 13206, 21912

New Hampshire historical society, Concord, 11418

New Hampshire infantry, 2d regt., 1861-1865, 3824; 3d regt., 1861-1865, 3086; 18th regt., 1864-1865, 4285

New Hampshire patriot and state gazette, 936

New Harmony, Indiana, 4668; Tornado, 1852, 11739

The new Harry and Lucy, 9688

New Haven, 5760; Antiquities, 787; Common council, 22491; Description, Guide-books, 781, 12030; Description, Views, 792; First Church of Christ, 642; History, 787, 788

New Haven, Pa. Citizens, 24188

A new home - who'll follow?, 10149

New homes in the West, 5276

New Hope Church, 15730

New Indian sketches, 5182

A new invasion of the South, 3099

New Ipswich, N.H., History, 953

New Jersey, Biography, 475; Constitution, 12436; Description & travel, 784, 1651, 3446, 3568, 23580, 23694; Description & travel, Gazetteers, 12312; Description & travel, Guide-books, 12486; History, 784, 12313; History, Civil war, 22201; History, Colonial period, 1651, 7574, 13257, 22376, 23630, 23694; History, Revolution, 22344; History, Local, 784; Legislature, 7574; Militia, 22201; Politics & government, Colonial period, 23580; Supreme Court, 25617

New Jersey and the rebellion, 22201

New Jersey Colonization Society, 21613

New Jersey infantry, 9th regt., 1061 1866, 3294, 5043; 13th regt., 1862-1865, 5434

New Jersey Society for Promoting the Abolition of Slavery, 25122, 25123

New Liberty, Ky., History, 15295

The new life of Virginia, 4070

New London, Conn., 44; Biography, 1842; Burning by the British, 1781, 22306; History, 1842

New Madrid earthquake, 15280

The new man, Twenty-nine years a slave, 24044

A new map of Kentucky, 15015

New map of the mining regions of Oregon, 4249

New Mexican common life, 10863

New Mexico, 3688, 6893, 6895, 14896, 16003, 17266, 17392, 17494, 22914; Antiquities, 2915, 11474; Biography, 16849; Boundaries, Texas, 24503; Description & travel, 1145, 2488, 2555, 2624, 3197, 3268, 3343, 3415, 3955, 4150, 4333, 4500, 4715, 4799, 4922, 5060, 5167, 5512, 5545, 5546, 5753, 6139, 6165, 8108, 8408, 15811, 16158, 16180, 16287, 16371, 16730, 17126, 17175, 17391, 18886; Directories, 16243; Fiction, 4497, 4925; Historical society, 1150; History, 1150, 3068, 3343, 11474, 15922, 16272, 16341, 16342, 16538, 16849, 17430, 17451, 17798; History, Chronology, 17266; History, War with Mexico, 1845-1848, 3151, 3962; Politics & government, 17523, 23879, 24525, 24974; Public lands, 17669

The new military guide, 2220

The new mirror for travellers, 10488

The new moon, 4988, 14243

The new Munchausen, 10485

A new negro for a new century, 25124

The new Northwest, 16419

New Orleans, Description, 3424, 3425, 3597, 3647, 3732, 3755, 3828, 3947, 4178, 5212, 7159, 25125; Directories, 1756; Fiction, 4725, 5037, 5447; History, 3006, 3725, 4201, 16490; History, Civil war, 3091; Social conditions, 25125; Social life & customs, 3327, 3732; Ursuline convent, 3725, 5453

New Orleans, Battle of, 1815, 1862, 2072, 3079, 3625, 4810, 13995, 15402, 15738, 22474; Fiction, 3036

New Orleans as I found it, 3327

New Orleans as it is, 25125

New Orleans batture, 13393

The New Orleans sketch book, 11131

The new pantheon, 25126

A new parishioner, 10040

The new pastoral, 13465

New pictorial history of the life and times of the pioneer heroes and heroines of America, 5460

New pictures and old panels, 22156
The new Pilgrim's progress, 9027
New Plymouth colony, Laws, statutes, etc., 23466
New Providence Presbyterian Church, McAfee, Ky., 14878
The new purchase, 12554
The new regime, 1765-1767, 2523
New Rochelle, N.Y., Description, Guide-books, 11345
A new route from Europe to the interior of North America, 7575
New Salem, Ill., 14315; History, 5989, 7642; Poetry, 8039
New Salem as I knew it, 5989
The new settlement, 9967
The new slave laws of Jamaica and St. Christopher's examined, 25557
The new South, 3155, 3657
The new South and old Mexico, 7584
New South Wales, Description & travel, 13489; Exiles, 13489
New Spain, Commerce, 6161; History, 5854
The new states, 24986
A new survey of the West Indies, 6796, 6797
New Sweden, 1364, 11231, 11785; History, 30, 439, 21954; History, Fiction, 10486
New themes for the Protestant clergy, 1998
A new thing under the sun, 10304
The new Timothy, 8659
New Ulm, Minn., History, 15971
The new universal traveller, 2927
New views of penitentiary discipline, and moral education and reform, 13766
The new Virginians, 2505
A new voyage to Carolina, 4231
A new voyage to Georgia, 4588
New voyages to North America, 7223, 7224
A new way to pay debts of honour, 10310
The new west, 7576, 16003, 16032
New wine not to be put into old bottles, 12044
The new world, 6880
New Year in the little rough-cast house, 10841
New York (City), 7577; Biography, 2480; Birdewell, 22051; Church history, 2212, 12406; Church of the Puritans (Congregational), 24686; Churches, 12406; Citizens, 23001; College of Physicians and Surgeons, 23077, 23079, 23369; Collegiate Church, 22102; Committee of Safety, 1775, 1776, 22826; Description, 1076, 1077, 1893, 2704,
2773, 3602, 3827, 4222, 5147, 5263, 9545, 9546, 12388, 23334; Description, Guide-books, 6912, 12495, 12850; Directories, 1756, 2281; Eighteenth Ward Republican Association, 25127; Elgin Botanic Garden, 12916, 12918; Exhibition of the Industry of all Nations, 1853-1854, 12372; Fiction, 8540, 9505, 10308, 10327; Fire, 1835, 2281, 22100, 25899; Hahnemann Hospital, 9056; History, 1077, 7277, 12476, 21803, 22077; History, Civil War, 24903; History, Colonial period, 22051; History, Fiction, 8540; Markets, 2102; Mechanic Institute, 23118; Mercantile Library Association, 12339; National Academy of Design, 11901; Negro plot, 1741, 12911; Parks, Central Park, 22613, City Hall Park, 22051; Police, 852; Politics and government, 8378, 11145, 11148, 11769; Population, 12746; Public Library, 16560; Public works, 12338; Saint Mark's Church, 390; Saint Paul's Chapel, 22129; Sanitary affairs, 988; Social life and customs, 1893, 9547, 9932, 12025, 12086, 12158, 12159, 13330; State prison, 1965, 2180; Statistics, 12674; Suburbs, 12850; Trinity Church, 1209-1211, 12817, 13289; Union League Club, 13181, 24857; Union meeting, Dec. 19, 1859, 25128
New York (State), 22152; Antiquities, 1908; Biography, 1679, 22302, 22303; Boundaries, Massachusetts, 13051; Census, 1755; Chamber of commerce of the state of New York, 22412; Church history, 23044; Commerce, Canada, 22730; Commissioners for settling the titles to land in the county of Onondaga, Report, 1800, 12131; Comptroller's office, 22898; Constitution, 11985; Constitutional convention, 1821, 22258; Constitutional history, 11646, 22336; Court for the trial of impeachments and correction of errors, 1389; Court of Appeals, 25129; Court of chancery, 1389; Court of oyer and terminer (New York co.), 980; Description & travel, 785, 1907, 7203, 7438, 9652, 9727, 11242, 11292, 11948, 12670, 12963, 13117, 13227, 13337, 13432, 16313, 21968, 22794, 23150, 23331, 23674, 23818; Description & travel, Guide-books, 7748, 12696; Governors, 22706; Health officer, port of New York, 988; History, 785, 939, 2093, 11985, 11995, 12334, 21905, 22568, 22794, 23331, 23674; History, Colonial period, 546, 858, 1552,

9999, 10000, 11529, 13432, 21763, 22152, 22376, 23640; History, Colonial period, Fiction, 10074, 10401; History, Colonial period, Sources, 980; History, King William's war, 1689-1697, 981; History, Revolution, 1402, 11470, 12307, 12334, 12928; History, Revolution, Fiction, 9129, 9151, 10158, 10877; History, Local, 785; Imprints, 22486; Laws, statutes, etc., 1567, 1568, 1664, 1991, 11539, 11540, 25130; Legislature, 1552, 13242, 22303; Legislature, 1867, 22302; Legislature, Assembly, 24673, 25582; Legislature, Assembly, Select Committee on Slavery, 25346; Legislature, Senate, 22258; Militia, 12912; Politics & government, 12598, 13195, 13497, 24437; Politics & government, 1775-1865, 1011,1904, 6592, 12624, 21898, 21899, 22716, 22826, 22898, 24023, 25924; Politics & government, Colonial period, 546; Politics & government, Revolution, 23585-23587; Respondent, 25129; Secretary fo state, 12930; Social life & customs, 12241; University, Division of visual instruction, 7578

New York (Colony), 1552, 12931; Governor (Benjamin Fletcher, 1692-1695), 981; Provincial congress, 1775-1776, 7577; Supreme Court of Judicature, 23827

New York (County) Court of general sessions, 13188

New York above ground and under ground, 9544

New York academy of medicine, 23076

New York aristocracy, 13330

New York artillery, 4th independent battery, 1861-1865, 5201; 4th regt., 1862-1865, 2821; 9th regt., 1862-1865, 5002; 34th battery, 1861-1866, 5005; Varian's battery, 1861, 5201

New York, as it is, 1076

New York cavalry, 1st regt., 1861-1865, 47; 10th regt., 17403; 11th regt., 1861-1865, 2893

New York central railroad company (1853-1869), 11717

New York City Anti-slavery Society, 25131

The New-York conspiracy, 12911

New-York historical society, 74, 1148, 1553, 5900, 11529, 12112, 12158, 12917, 13227

New York in slices, 9546

New York infantry, 1st regt., 1846-1847, 16207; 2d regt., 1776-1783, 4589; 2d regt., 1846-1848, 22457; 5th regt., 1861-1863, 3177; 5th regt., 1861-1865 (Veteran), 5422; 9th regt., 1861-1863, 5691; 12th regt., 1861-1864, 5422; 16th regt., 1861-1865, 3144; 33 regt., 1861-1863, 13343; 48th regt., 1861-1865, 4602, 4687; 57th regt., 1861-1864, 3422, 3533; 60th regt., 1861-1865, 3337; 76th regt., 1862-1864, 5184; 79th regt., 1861-1865, 4317, 5430; 81st regt., 1861-1865, 3211; 83d regt., 1861-1864, 13162; 97th regt., 1862-1865, 12926; 104th regt., 1862-1865, 12926; 105th regt., 1862-1863, 12926; 112th regt., 1862-1865, 13060; 115th regt., 1862-1865, 3011; 117th regt., 1861-1865, 4543; 124th regt., 1862-1865, 5682; 125th regt., 1862-1865, 2469; 146th regt., 1862-1865, 3518; 173d regt., 1862-1865, 3518; 176th regt., 1862-1866, 4627

New York medical and surgical society, 22836

New York naked, 9547

New York, past, present, and future, 1077

The New-York review, 23469

New York Seventh regiment, 11194

New York Society for Promoting the Manumission of Slaves, 357, 25051, 25132, 25133, 24232, 25531, 25667

New York society for the information and assistance of persons emigrated from foreign countries, 2139

New York society library, 22977

New York Stock exchange, 12634

New York tribune, 25752

New York typographical society, 13223

New York university, 389, 2126, 13340, 22563

New York Young Men's Anti-slavery Society, 25134

New Zealand, Description & travel, 7556, 7858

Newark, Ohio, Antiquities, 23167

Newberry, John Strong, 1822-1891, 5524, 17775, 22636

Newbrough, J.B., 9493

Newbury, Mass., History, 1972

Newburyport, Mass., Citizens, 25844; History, 1972

Newcastle, Thomas Pelham-Holles, 1st duke of, 1693-1768, 2028, 16457

Newcomb, Mary A. "Mrs. H.A.W. Newcomb," 1817-1893?, 4590

Newcombe, C.F., 7460, 7579

Newcomer, Christopher Armour, 4591

Newell, Chester, 4592

Newell, Peter, illustr., 10889, 10896

Newell, William R., 6152

Newenham, Thomas, A view of the natural and commercial circumstances of Ireland, 13113

Newfoundland, 384, 1541, 11366, 13498, 23193; Description & travel, 383, 2902, 6550, 6954, 7784, 21872, 22251, 22835, 23235; Description & travel, Maps, 11707, 13498; History, 383, 7197, 7784

Newfoundland in 1842, 11366
Newfoundland to Manitoba through Canada's maritime mining, 17440
Newhall, Fales Henry, 1827-1883, 25135
Newhall, John R., 17268-17270
Newkirk, Mrs. Jane Bancker (Cathcart) d.1906, 24102
Newlin, William Henry, 4593
Newman, C.J., illustr., 8477
Newman, Clarence W., 15327
Newman, Francis William, 1805-1897, 7580, 25136
Newman, Fred Gus, 1893-1953, 15060, 15061
Newman, Henry Stanley, 25137
Newman, James A., 14390, 14804, 15063
Newman, John B., 7581
Newman, Louis C., 24317, 25138
Newmark, Harris, 1834-1916, 17271
Newmark, Marco Ross, 17271
Newport, R.I., 5840; Central Baptist church, 22646; Description, 16313, 23233; History, 1792, 23234; Old stone mill, 11543;
Newport illustrated, in a series of pen & pencil sketches, 23233
Newporte, Christopher, 4947
News from New England, by Thomas Lechford, 13375
News from the mines!, 4594
The newsboy, 10802
Newspapers, 6266, 14651; Argentina, 18240; Directories, 1983; Kentucky, 14211; Mexico, 19827; Mississippi, Bibliography, 15014; Poetry, 11584
Newspapers, Afro-American, 25220
Newsome, Edmund, 4595
Newson, Thomas McLean, 1827-1893, 17272
Newstead Abbey, 4027
Newton, Sir Isaac, 1642-1727, 1324, 4227
Newton, Joseph, of London, Eng., 4596
Newton, Mass., Genealogy, 22645; History, 22645
The next oil pool, 14440
The next room, 9581
The next time, 7118, 10012
Nez Percé and Salmon River gold mines, 4308
Nez Percé Indians, 17310; Missions, 17843; Wars, 1877, 16515, 16822
Nez Percé language, Glossaries, vocabularies, etc., 4690, 5018
Nezahualcóyotl, 19939
Niagara, and other poems, 22526
Niagara, Ont., History, 6532
Niagara Falls, 3092; Description, 796, 1694, 4636, 7008, 7438, 11242, 13117;

Description, Guide-books, 8246, 12995, 13238; Poetry, 1331, 1672, 22526
Niagara frontier, History, 939
Niblack, William Ellis, 1822-1893, 25139
Niblett, Mollie Glen, 8106
Nicaise, Auguste, 1828-, 4597
Nicanor Bolet Peraza, 19110
Nicaragua, Antiquities, Periodicals, 18730; Bibliography, 18730; Description & travel, 7750, 7883, 7917, 7974, 11461, 11655; History, 890, 19526, 20486; History, Filibuster war, 1855-1860, 7338, 11679, 16415; History, Periodicals, 18730; Periodicals, 18730; Politics & government, 20656
Nicaragua canal, 1124, 1125, 1897, 7338, 7751, 11654, 23203
Nicarao Indians, 20080
Niccolls, Samuel Jack, 1838-, 7582
Nicely, Wilson, 4598
Nicholas, Francis Child, 1862-, 7583
Nicholas, George, 1755?-1799, 4599, 14836, 15064
Nicholas, Samuel Smith, 1796-1869, 25140
Nicholas, Thomas, fl. 1560-1596, tr., 6863
Nicholas County, Ky., Biography, 13559; History, 15142
Nicholasville, Ky., 15066; History, 15066; Methodist Church, Annie Bryant Bible Class, 15065
Nichols, Beach, 1068
Nichols, George Ward, 1837-1885, 4600, 4601
Nichols, James Moses, 1835-1886, 4602
Nichols, James Thomas, 1865-, 7584
Nichols, Thomas Law, 1815-1901, 4603
Nicholson, Mrs. Eliza Jane (Poitevent) 1849-1896, 4604
Nicholson, John, d.1800, 22517
Nicholson, John, 1839-1909, 17273
Nick of the woods, 14983
Nick Whiffles, the trapper guide, 7887
Nickel, Cuba, 19560
Nickles, John M., 15067
Nicklin, Philip Holbrook, 1786-1842, 4605
Nicknames, 21988
Nicola, Lewis, 1717-1807, 23470
Nicolas, John, 1761-1819, 295
Nicolay, Charles G., 17274
Nicolet, Jean, d.1642, 16114
Nicolette and Aucassin, 9678
Nicollet, Joseph Nicolas, 1786-, 4606, 17611
Nieboer, H. J., 25141
A niece of Snapshot Harry's, 6969
Nielsen, Roger, 1888-, 4607
Nieremberg, Juan Eusebio, 1595-1658, 5907
Nietzsche, Friedrich, 1844-1900, 21720

Nieuwe wereld, 5487
The Nikkur Holl, 10693
Niles, Henry Edward, 1823-1900, 7585
Niles, John Milton, 1787-1856, 25142
Niles, Nathaniel, 1741-1828, 11688
Niles, Rena, 14339
Niles, Michigan, 17756
Nimmo, Joseph, 1837-1909, 17275
Nina, 9669
Niobrara River, 4246
Niox, Gustave Léon, 1840-1921, 7494
Nisbet, James Cooper, 4608
Nisbet, Richard, 25144, 25422
Nisi prius, 13720
Niterói, Brazil, Universidade Federal
  Fluminense, Faculdade de Educaçao, 19707
Nitrogen industries, 19685
Nitrous axide, 11911
Niveis de desenvolvimento de uma economia
  e sua abordagem politica, 19670
Nixon, Barnaby, 1752?-1807, 25143
Nixon, John Thompson, 1820-1889, 25145
Nixon, Oliver Woodson, 1825-, 17276, 17277
Nizza, Marco da, 1510 (ca.)-1570, 4631
No-fault divorce, 14667
No-fault insurance, 14614, 14663; Kentucky,
  14678
Noachidae, 9885
Noah, and his descendants, 9885
Noall, Claire, 17278
Noble, Mason, 1809-1881, 7587
Noble Co., Ind., History, 23460
A noble lord, 10840
A noble woman, 10870
The nobleman's son, 8541
Nobles, William H., 4609
Nobody, 11096
Nobody's husband, 9199
Nóbrega, Manoel de, 1517-1570, 19681
The No-din', 9283
Noe, James Thomas Cotton, 1864-1953,
  15068-15076
Noel, Baptist Wriothesley, 1798-1873, 25146
Noël, François Joseph Michel, 1755-1841,
  tr., 5894
Noel, Samuel Ayres, 1814-1842, 14479
Noel, Theophilus, 1840-, 4610
Noetica, 22718
Nöggerath, Johann Jakob, 1788-1877, 6254
Nogueira, Octaciano, 18271
Nojoque; a question for a continent, 24584
Nolden, Arnold, pseud., 7741
Noll, Arthur Howard, 1855-, 4877, 15077
Nolte, Vincent Otto, 1779-1856, 4011
Nome, Cape, 16556, 16647; Description &
  travel, 17104

The nomination of Abraham Lincoln, 6706
Non rex sed Caesar, 17991
Nona Vincent, 7126
Nonantum and Natich, 13141
Nonsense, 10536
Noon, and pain, and April, 15078
The nooning tree, 11162
Nootka Indians, 16477, 22713, 22714
Nootka language, Glossaries, vocabularies,
  etc., 16477
Nootka Sound, 22713, 22714
Nops ludovicorum Alayon, Cuba, 18088
Nops Mac Leay, Cuba, 18089
Nora Brady's vow, 9415
Norah, 9892
Nord-sud, 2649
Nordamerika, die Vereinigten Staaten nebst
  einem Ausflug nach Mexiko, 5980
Nordamerika, natur och kulturbygd, 4585
Nordamerika - Ohio, 12062
Der nordamerikanische freistaat Texas, 5021
Nordenskiöld, Gustaf Erik Adolf, 1868-1895,
  17279
Nordeste, espaço e tempo, 18282
Nordhoff, Charles, 1830-1901, 4612, 8597,
  17280, 17281, 25148
Norfolk, Thomas Howard, 4th duke of, 1536-
  1572, defendant, 22680
Norfolk, Va., 4966; Citizens, 25149
Norfolk district medical society, 132
Noriega, Eduardo, 7588
Noriega, José Esteban de, 7271
Nørlund, Poul, 1888-, 25150
Normal, Ill., History, 16100
Norman, Benjamin Moore, 1809-1860, 7589, 7590
Norman Leslie, 9505
Norman, Lucia, 17282
Normandy, History, 12082
Norridgewock, Me., History, 198, 12657
Norridgewock Indians, 198
Norris, John T., 1838-, 6164
Norris, Oliver, d.1825, 23415
Norris, Pauline, 15079
Norris' Chicago directory, 21911
A Norseman's pilgrimage, 8834
Norteamérica al dia, 3853
Norte América y los norteamericanos, 6422
North, Frederick North, baron, 1732-1792,
  11969, 13499
North, Thomas, 4616
North America, 8150, 12310, 22151; Antiquities,
  933; Biography, 201-203; Climate, 4039,
  5049; Description & travel, 1071, 1560,
  2520, 2519, 2541, 2549, 2667, 2701, 3647,
  4248, 4111, 4575, 4649, 4682, 5010, 5082,
  5480, 5568, 6073, 6167, 6797, 7225, 7266,

7368, 8228, 8229, 16416, 21881;
Description & travel, Gazetteers,
3178, 4613, 22042; Description &
travel, Guide-books, 6090; Discovery
& exploration, 7629; Entomology, 4684;
History, 17904, 22874; Maps, 14471
North America Fur Company, 2823
The North-American and West-Indian
gazetteer, 4613
North American pamphlet on South American
affairs, 11478
The North American tourist, 4614
The north and south, 10719, 24086, 25151,
25423
The North and South American review,
7757
North Carolina, 4615; Bibliography, 15140;
Biography, 1169, 5684; Boundaries,
Georgia, 22237; Boundaries, Virginia,
2878, 5188, 11656; Description & travel,
426, 491, 2553, 2568, 2745, 2773, 2779,
2959, 2997, 3261, 3340, 3403, 3425,
3516, 3519, 3568, 3603, 3626, 3678, 3720,
3766, 4713, 4217, 4231, 4236, 4486, 4588,
4682, 4790, 4998, 5040, 5087, 5109,
5147, 5444, 5768, 5798, 11515, 11656,
14370, 14749, 15527; Description &
travel, Gazetteers, 22166; Description &
travel, Guide-books, 4615, 13544;
Economic conditions, 15611; Fiction,
10543, 10903, 10922, 11133, 14754;
Finance, 17580; Governor, 1802-1805 (James
Turner), 22237; History, 1169, 3499, 5683,
5684, 14303, 14882, 23186; History,
Colonial period, 426, 2553, 23803; History,
Revolution, 3418, 12136, 13308, 14304;
Maps, 14183; Politics & government, 2439,
24548; Social conditions, 15611;
Statistics, 22166; Trustees of the public
libraries, 11515; University, History,
24548
The North Carolina guide and business office
companion, 3766
North Carolina historical society, 13116
North Carolina infantry, 30th regt., 1861-
1865, 2702
North Carolina (Province), Economic
conditions, 2765
A North Carolinian, 25573
North Central states, Population, 16144
North Chelsea, Mass., 11684
North Dakota, Antiquities, 17686, 17893;
Biography, 17058; Climate, 17619;
Description & travel, 16409, 16573, 17000,
17628, 17845; History, 16063, 16101, 16102,
16284, 16469, 16660, 16793, 16946, 17058,

17174, 17438, 17706, 17707, 17820; History,
Sources, 16876; Population, 16600; Social
life and customs, 16606, 17531; State
Historical Museum, 16063; State Historical
Society, 17894
The North Dakota state park system, 17462
The North Georgia gazette and winter chronicle,
7591
North Middletown, Bourbon County, Ky.,
History, 15080; Directories, 15080
North Middletown [Kentucky] Christian church,
Christian women's fellowship, 15080
North Pacific exploring expedition, 1853-1856,
12328
North Pacific history company of Portland, Or.,
16784
North Point, Battle of, 1814, 22448
North pole, 877, 878
North Platte, Neb., History, 15817
The north star: the poetry of freedom, 25876
Northampton, Mass., Description, Guide-books,
2181; Genealogy, 200; History, 200, 1504
Northborough, Mass., First Congregational
Unitarian church, 184; History, 22590
Northeast boundary of the U.S., 519, 1421,
2377, 6998, 10817, 12186, 12409, 12617,
13150, 13463
Northeast passage, 11623
Northend, William Dummer, 1823-1902, 7592
Northern and southern friends, 11951
Northern Bank of Kentucky, 1835-, 1898, 13833
Northern Bank of Kentucky, Lexington, 15081
Northern California, 16193, 16851
The northern invasion of October, 1780, 12928
Northern Pacific Railroad, 8261, 13103, 15876,
16921, 17327; Explorations and surveys,
4208; Fiction, 10225
Northern Pacific Railroad survey, 17528;
Northern presbyter, 24891
Northern railroad company (N.Y.), 12762
Northern rebellion and southern secession,
24367
The northern route to Idaho, 4456
The northern traveller, 2147
The northmen in Maine, 22071
Northrop, John Worrell, 4617
Northrup, Ansel Judd, 1833-, 25152
Northumberland County, Pa., History, 14453
Northup, Solomon, 1808-, 4618
Northwest, Canadian, 615, 2585, 3880, 4368,
4880, 5534, 5963, 6010, 6048, 6050, 6059,
6238, 6299, 6311, 6315, 6598, 6600, 6621,
6727, 6736, 6769, 6876, 7078, 7384, 7510,
7542, 7550, 7591, 7593, 7726, 7808, 7812,
8123, 8134, 8140, 8148, 8179, 8387, 12073,
16227, 16288, 17000, 17390, 17581;

Description & travel, 2536, 2604, 3200,
3528, 3529, 3784, 3877, 3878, 3879,
4037, 4130, 4362, 4481, 4482, 4685,
4955, 5057, 5169, 5354, 5674, 5925,
5941, 5990, 6055, 6192, 6237, 6263,
6264, 6283, 6295, 6314, 6321, 6531,
6549, 6605, 7009, 7046, 7209, 7676,
7595, 7830, 7886, 7922, 8030, 8091,
8252, 7256, 8322, 8428, 13411, 15917,
16394, 16474, 16508, 16685, 16731,
17148, 17185, 17389, 21871, 23543;
Discovery & exploration, 6221, 6886,
6887; History, 6052, 6221, 6228, 6235,
6316, 6283, 8000, 8106, 17558, 23543; History,
Sources, 7641; Religion, 5903; Social
life & customs, 6731
Northwest, Old, 3561, 16325; Biography,
12021; Commerce, 22333; Description &
travel, 1220, 1337, 3124, 3163, 3359,
3943, 4472, 4640, 5099, 5263, 5276,
6271, 6768, 10141, 13360, 17052,
23529, 23558, 23579, 23581; Description
& travel, Guide-books, 17367; Discovery
& exploration, 4144, 16114, 16995;
Fiction, 13542; History, 1723, 1878,
3869, 4092, 12184, 13750, 22967, 23465,
23483, 23609, 24322; History, Sources,
6297; History, War of 1812, 12741,
13129; Social life & customs, 4382
Northwest, Pacific, 6143, 6151, 6162,
8179, 17759; Description & travel,
2508, 2647, 3542, 3551, 4482, 4549,
4700, 16046, 16416; History, 5017,
5018, 6101, 15929, 16497, 17445;
Maps, 5506; Social life & customs,
16834
Northwest boundary of the U.S., 15925,
15929, 16064, 17202, 17759
Northwest British America and its relation
to the state of Minnesota, 5354, 7510
Northwest Coast of North America, 2647,
6891, 8283, 15876, 16394, 16432, 16477,
16638, 16639, 16640, 16981, 17168,
17759, 17943, 23461
Northwest Company of Canada, 4348, 6228,
6668, 7009, 7593, 8000, 16989, 17095,
17148
North-west Fox, 2301
Northwest passage, 434, 449, 489, 878,
1201, 1433, 1924, 2112, 2301, 5632,
6048, 6195, 6601, 6623, 6624, 6670,
7109, 7547, 7695, 7696, 7697, 7812,
7911, 7912, 7984, 8021, 8050, 8134,
8283, 12058, 16394, 16477, 16731, 17168,
22285, 22816, 23533
The Northwest rebellion, 6305

Northwest territories, Canada, 6140, 6995,
7641; Description & travel, 8240; History,
6129
Northwest Territory, 6450; History, 15678
Northwestern Association of Congregational
Ministers, 16455
Northwestern Conspiracy, 1864, 24100
The Northwestern Express and Transportation
Company, 16993
Northwestern historical association, Madison,
Wis., pub., 7455
Northwestern states, 11506, 13957, 16227,
16315, 16921; Biography, 16784; Description
& travel, 3163, 3455, 3862, 4026, 4250,
4686, 5181, 5183, 5269, 7009, 11681,
13236, 16784, 16989, 17325, 17541; Fiction,
7887; History, 12184, 16784, 16980, 17171
Northwood, 9700, 9701
Norton, Anthony Banning, 7594
Norton, Charles Ledyard, 1837-1909, 4619, 4620
Norton, Frank Henry, 1836-1921, 3449, 4621
Norton, Harry J., 17284
Norton, Henry Kittredge, 1884-, 17285
Norton, John, 1606-1663, 22813
Norton, John Nicholas, 1820-1881, 13822, 15082
Norton, John W., illustr., 16693
Norton, Lewis Adelbert, b.1819, 17286
Norton, Mary Aquinas, Sister, 17287
Norton, Oliver Willcox, 4622
Norton, Robert, fl.1865, 23119
Nortonville quadrangle, Kentucky, 13941
Norwalk, Conn., Genealogy, 12568; History,
21809; History, Sources, 12568
Norway, Description & travel, 7170
Norwegians in North Dakota, 17438
The Norwich cadets, 11141
Norwich, Conn., Biography, 1843; Description,
10761; History, 623, 1843, 12260; Second
Congregational church, 11351
Norwich university, Northfield, Vt., 13336;
Fiction, 11141
Norwood, 8768
Norwood, Charles J., 15083-15087
Norwood, Henry, fl.1649, 4623
Norwood, John Nelson, 1879-, 25154
Norwood, Joseph Granville, 1807-1895, 4664
Norwood, Thomas Manson, 1830-1913, 25155
Nossiter, Bernard D., 25153, 25156
Notaries, Argentine Republic, Congresses,
20415; Guatemala, 18046
Notman (William) & son, 7597
Nott, Benjamin, 25159, 25160
Nott, Charles Cooper, 1827-1916, 4627, 4628,
7283
Nott, Samuel, 1788-1869, 25161, 25162
Nottingham (Galley), 2089

Nourse, Charles Clinton, 1829-, 17288, 17289
Nouveau voyage dans les États-Unis de l'Amérique septentrionale, 2805
Nouveaux voyages de mr le baron de Lahontan, 4202
La nouvelle Atala, 5026
Nouvelle relation de la Caroline, 4629
Nouvelle relation de la France équinoxiale, 870
Les nouvelles Amériques, 5964
Nouvelles de Saint-Domingue, 7598
Nouvelles du Scioto, 2507
Nova Britannia, 4071
Nova-Caesaria, 23630
Nova Lusitania, 1542
Nova Scotia, 5872, 5873, 7379, 12853, 12854, 23193; Baronetage, 758; Boundaries, 11331; Commissioner of public records, 7599; Description & travel, 4920, 6111, 6487, 6575, 6882, 6954, 8343, 11794, 12777, 22993, 23150; Description & travel, Maps, 11707; Economic conditions, 12218, 12614; Executive Council, 7600; Genealogy, 7604; Governor, 1752-1756 (Hopson), 7601; Governor, 1756-1761 (Lawrence), 7602, 7603; History, 6575, 7197, 7379, 7601-7604, 7865, 7942, 13191; History, Fiction, 3218, 7881; History, Sources, 7599; History, To 1763, 6882, 6951, 8045, 22750; House of assembly, 7605, 7606; Laws, statutes, etc., 7607, 7608; Politics & government, 7600, 7605-7608, 22470
Nova Scotia historical society, Halifax, N.S., 7604
Novangius, pseud., 11246
Novario, Giovanni Maria, 17th cent., 5882
La novela de Benito Lynch, 19614
La novela del México colonial, 19968
Novellettes of a traveller, 10434
Novo, Salvador, 1904-, 7609
Novo orbe serafico brasilico ou chronica dos frades menores da provincia do Brasil, 22641
Novvis orbis, 7221
Now and forever, 8649
Now how, 14946
Now is the time to settle it, 1535
Nox, Owen, pseud., 3094, 3095
Noyes, Alva Josiah, 1855-, 17290, 17291
Noyes, George Freeman, 1824-1868, 4630
Noyes, John Humphrey, 1811-1886, 2159
Noyes, Nicholas, 1647-1717, 23471, 23472
Noyes, Theodore Williams, 1858-, 7610

Noyesism unveiled, 2159
Nuclear fission, 19867
Nuclear reactors, 19703
Nuclear reactions in molecular orbitals, 18936
Nuclear waste, Kentucky, 14629
Nuevo León, Mexico, Description & travel, 7837; History, Sources, 20005; Politics & government, 18149; Universidad, Monterrey, 16579
Nuevo Mundo, 19782
Nuevo Reino de León, Mexico, Description, 7219; History, 7219
Nugae, 4798, 8945
Nugae geórgicae, 13265
Nullification, 21844, 22367, 22369, 23662, 23759
Nullity, 25633
Numbers, Theory of, 18708
Numerical analysis, 18876
El número natural y sus generalizaciones, 18708
Nute, Benjamin H., 22523
Nutrition, 20095, 20096, 20124
The Nutshell, 25163
Nyassaland, 24488
Den Ny verden, 4058

Oaths, 24661
Ober, Benjamin, 25164
Oberbauer, Julius C., 25165
Oberlin College, 24065
Oberlin slave kidnapping case, 25376
Oberlin-Wellington rescue, 1858, 25496
Oberlin's part in the slavery conflict, 24065
Los obispos de Chile hablan, 19989
Objects of the rebellion, 25166
Obligado, Rafaelo, 1851-1920, 18931
Obra poética, 19938
El obrero industrial, 19491
O'Bryan, William, 1778-1868, 23473
O'Callaghan, Edmund Bailey, 1797-1880, 22152, 22730, 23818, 25167, 25168
Occupations, 18361
Ocean currents, 23374
Oceanica, 22115; Discovery & exploration, 22759, 23533
Oceanography, Atlantic Ocean, 19296
O'Connell, Daniel, 1775-1847, 23909, 25169-25171
Ocotlán, Mexico (Jalisco), Economic conditions, 19628
Odd-fellows, Independent order of, Fiction, 23012
Odes, and fugitive poetry, 22225

Odmann, Samuel Lorens, 1750-1829, 25603
Oeillet des Murs, Marc Athanase Parfait,
b.1804, 21853
The Office and Duty of Sheriffs, 21976
Ofidios da Amazônia, 21737
Ofrenda a una virgen loca, 20066
Ogg, Frederick Austin, 25172
Ogle, Sir Chaloner, 1681?-1750, 23735
Ohio, 23489, 23742; Description & travel,
Gazetteers, 22707; Economic condition,
24081; General assembly, 1865, 23985;
History, 21877; Penitentiary, Columbus,
22863; Politics & government, 24156,
25086, 25682; Social conditions, 539;
Social life & customs, 3745, 4382
Ohio Anti-slavery Society, 25034, 25309
Ohio artillery, Battery B, 1861-1865,
22019
The Ohio gazetteer, and traveler's guide,
22707
Ohio infantry, 42d regt., 1861-1864, 4409;
53d regt., 1861-1865, 3313; 55th regt.,
1861-1865, 4660; 58th regt., 1861-1865,
5317; 63d regt., 1861-1865, 4036; 73d
regt., 1861-1865, 3976; 78th regt.,
1861-1865, 5273; 101st regt., 1862-
1865, 2868, 3201; 105th regt., 1862-1865,
5439; 123d regt., 1862-1865, 4168
Ohio militia, Sherman brigade, 3882
Ohio River, 337, 4632, 12018, 13683,
14000, 14459, 14751, 15278, 15749,
21923; Description & travel, 1133, 1134,
2465, 3124, 3139, 3472, 3509, 5103,
11895, 14187, 14840, 15119, 22672;
Falls of the, 14057; Fiction, 2681,
5380; Navigation, 3139, 11895, 12015,
21924; Poetry, 5381
Ohio Valley, 2784, 4824, 13957, 23489;
Antiquities, 3797; Bibliography,
13825; Biography, 12021; Commerce,
23106; Description & travel, 1337,
2561, 2594, 3020, 3138, 3163, 3397,
3468, 3594, 3620, 3745, 3750, 3753,
3792, 3980, 3988, 4425, 4465, 4469,
4755, 5074, 5112, 5263, 5375, 6529,
13296, 13580, 13825, 13896, 13905,
13956, 14112, 14364, 14370, 14375,
14857, 14964, 15034, 15344, 22391,
23073, 23529; Fiction, 14243, 15316;
History, 3002, 3213, 3870, 4337,
4347, 4367, 5566, 13740, 13750,
13751, 13826, 13998, 14084, 14330,
15381, 15559, 16116, 17164, 22141,
23474; History, To 1795, 4338, 4711,
14890, 23485; History, 18 1795,
Sources, 23456, 23457; History, Fiction,

3545, 4364, 4461, 14477; History,
Periodicals, 287; Maps, 13597, 14471,
14927, 14928, 15015, 15311; Social life &
customs, 3745, 5679
Ohio Valley higher education in the nineteenth
century, 14233
The Ohio Valley in colonial days, 14084
Ohio Valley in fiction, 15534
Ohio's fugitive slave law, 24465
Oil and gas development in Warren County,
Ky., 14567
Oil and gas fields, the Kentucky, Appalachian
and lake states, 14432
Oil and gas in the bluegrass region of
Kentucky, 14441
Oil and gas pool and pipeline map of Kentucky,
14566
Oil and gas producing formations in the
Appalachian and adjacent fields, 14428
The oil and gas resources of Kentucky, 14442
Oil and gas sands of Kentucky, 14338
Oil without vinegar, and dignity without
pride, 23418
Oir con los ojos, 18918
Ojeda, Alonso de, ca.1466-1515, 7567
Ojer, Pablo, 19996
Ojerholm, John Melcher, 1858-, 17691
Ojetti, Ugo, 1871-1946, 4642
Los ojos de Aldo Coria, 19823
Okeechobee, Battle of, 1837, 232
Okeechobee, Lake, 4633
O-kee-pa, 16168
Okefenokee Swamp, 3517; Fiction, 4746
O'Kelly, Patrick, 4643
Oklahoma, 15900, 16186, 16885, 17160, 17293,
17300, 17331, 17433, 23591; Admission of,
16373; Bibliography, Catalogs, 17795;
Biography, 16868, 17414, 17731; Boundaries,
Texas, 17583; Centennial celebrations, etc.,
17795; Constitution, 17715; Description &
travel, 4029, 4173, 4632, 4799, 15527,
16088, 16868, 16885, 17210, 17299; History,
6824, 16143, 16203, 16280, 16314, 16439,
16605, 16759, 17509, 17688, 17731; Politics
& government, 17715
The Oklahoma bill, 17331
Oklahoma outlaws, 16626
Olabidocarpus Lawrence, 20674
O'Laughlin, Michael, d.1867, 1305
Olav, crown prince of Norway, 1908-, 5092
Olavarria, Diego Manuel de, 7910
Olavarria y Ferrari, Enrique de, 1844-1918,
7834, 7873
Olcott family (Thomas Olcott, 1609?-1654),
2440
Old, Robert Orchard, 17301

330

Old Abe's jokes, 7632
Old age, 2417
Old age pensions, 14679
The old agency, 11205
Old American company, 12828
The old and the new, 11746
Old anti-slavery days, 24253
The old apple dealer, 9823
Old army sketches, 16163
Old Bardstown Bourbon recipes, 15096
The old Bascom place, 9745
Old Block's sketch-book, 16357
The old boy in the omnibus, 9633
The old bureau, 9072
Old Californian days, 17662
Old capitol and Frankfort guide, 14081
Old Chester tales, 9376
Old churches, ministers and families of
   Virginia, 4431
The old Continental, 10489
Old Coon, pseud., 13569
The old corner cupboard, 4060
The old countess, 10871
Old Creole days, 8929
Old days in the old army, 16975
Old days in the Old Dominion, 9116
The old doctor's son, 8980
Old Dog Tray, 14125
The old Dominion, 22667
Old England and New England, 1681
The old farm and the new farm, 12901
The old farm house, 10197
Old Father Morris, 10904
Old Fort Duquesne, 10293, 10443
Old Fort Harrod, 14426, 15165
An old fox tarred and feathered, 23706
Old Gardiston, 11207
Old Gargoyle, 8957
The old gentleman of the black stock, 10463
Old Green river union meeting house, 14083
The old Hanging Fork, 3269
Old Hicks, the guide, 5651, 11115
The old history book, 5931
Old homes of the Bluegrass, 13901, 15097
Old Honesty, 10445
The old house by the river, 10573
The old Indian chronicle, 2125
The old inn, 8713
The old Jersey captive, 364
The old judge, 12547
An old Kansas Indian town on the Missouri,
   17473
Old Kaskaskia, 8954
The old Kentucky home, 13895
Old Kentucky watering places, 13882
The old log house, 13673

Old Madame, 10163
Old mahogany, 15091
The old maid's secret, 10738
Old maids, 10730
Old Man Henry, 13960
The old man's bridge, 8573
The old man's calendar, 2417
An old man's romance, 9070
The old manse, 9823
Old Mark Langston, 4085
The old merchants of New York city, 2480
Old Mexico and her lost provinces, 6088
Old neighborhoods and new settlements, 10841
Old New-England days, 9320
The old plantation, 9971
Old Quebec, 7687
The old red house among the mountains, 9896
The old revolutionary soldier, 8491
The old Romish mission in California, 17302
Old Rube, the hunter, 3908
The old sailor's protegé, 9050
Old Saint Augustine, 4939
Old school Presbyterianism vindicated, 11564
The old sergeant, 5733
Old settlers' society of Sangamon county,
   Illinois, 23505
Old song and new, 4855
The old south, 14247
The old south and the new, 4141
Old Southwest, Bibliography, 17835
The old stillhouse in the hollow, 3556
The old stone house, 10668
Old Stone Inn, Simpsonville, Ky., 13549,
   14063
The old stone mansion, 10512
Old Sue, 10465
Old Talbott Tavern, 15098
Old theories upset, 6023
The old things, 10017
Old Tildy, 10598
Old times and new, 10714
Old times in middle Georgia, 4086
Old times on the upper Mississippi, 17184
Old trail drivers association, 16835
The old windmill, 10580
The old woman who dried up and blew away,
   10298
Olden times in Colorado, 16333
The olden times, 23474
Olden times in New York, 22077
Older Kentuckians: their needs, 15722
The oldest abolition society, 25233
The oldest town in Kentucky, 1774, 13817
Oldfellow, Polywarp, pseud., 10799
Oldfield, 13590
Oldham, Kie, 15865

Oldham County, Ky., History, 14191, 15505
Oldmixon, John, 1673-1742, 4644
Oldmixon, John W., 4645
Oldroyd, Osborn Hamiline, 1842-1930, 7633, 7634, 8132, 23475
Oldtown folks, 10907
Ole mistes, and other songs and stories from Tennessee, 25075
The ole watch mill deserted by man and doomed to silence and decay, 24352
O'Leary, Daniel Florencio, 1800-1854, 7015, 7635-7637, 8127
O'Leary, Simón Bolívar, 7635
Olin, Stephen, 1797-1851, 4646
Olinda, Brazil, Capture, 1630, 653, 8323, 18681
Olinda conquistada, 18681
Oliphant, Laurence, 1829-1888, 4647, 7638, 23476
Olite, Fermín de, 18th cent., 18075
Olivares, José de, 7639
Olive Branch (Ship), 175, 178
The olive branch, 21846, 24392, 25173
Olive industry and trade, Mexico, 19575
Olive Logan's Christmas story, 10236
Olive, Pedro Maria de, tr., 7087
Oliveira Lima, Manuel de, 1865-1928, 7640
Oliver, Andrew, 1706-1774, 22628
Oliver, Edmund Henry, 1882-1935, ed., 7641
Oliver, Mordecai, 1819-1898, 5507
Oliver, Sir Sydney, 24563
Oliver, William, 4648
Olliffe, Charles, 4649
Ollivant, Joseph Earle, tr., 7205
Olmstead, Charles H., 4650
Olmstead, Samuel R., 4651
Olmstead, Victor Hugo, 1853-1925, 6524
Olmsted, Frederich Law, 1822-1903, 12280, 13447, 17304
Olmsted, John, 17305
Olney, George Washington, 1835-1916, 4652
Olney, Jeremiah, 1749-1812, 25390
Olshausen, Theodor, 1802-1869, 4653
Oltmanns, Jabbo, 1783-1833, 7092
Olympus, Mount, Washington, 17437
Omaha, History, 13481, 16663, 17641; Exhibition of industry & arts, 1899, 16571; Stock-yards, 17165
O'Malley, Charles J., 15099
O'Meara, James, 17306
Omicron, pseud., 15100
Omoo, 10345
Oña, Pedro de, b.ca. 1570, 6469
Onativia, Arturo, 18475
Onderdonk, Benjamin Tredwell, bp., 1791-1861, 979, 13179

Onderdonk, Henry Ustick, 1789-1858, 22893
Onderdonk, James Lawrence, 1854-1899, 17308
Onderzoek naar den toestand der land-ver-huizers in de Vereeingde Staten van Nord-America, 15451
One-electron propagators for actinide metals, 20446
Onea and Anyta, 10769
Oneida community, 2159
Oneida County, Id., 17762
Oneida Indians, 12929; Missions, 1414
Oneida Institute, 13744
Onesimus, 9173, 24363
Onesimus Secundus, pseud., 25175
Onkel Sam, 5801
Onkel Toms hytte efter hundrede aar, 13627
Onondaga Historical Association, Syracuse, N.Y., 25584
Onondaga language, 13169
Onondaga Co., N.Y., History, 11822
Onondaga Indians, 11822
Onstot, Thompson Gains, 1829-, 23479
Onstott, R.J., 7642
Ontañón, Eduardo de, 1904, 7485, 7643
Ontario, 6873, 8048, 21819; Biography, 12074; Description & travel, 1025, 1095, 2461, 2814, 3200, 3881, 5103, 6128, 6996, 7135, 7136, 7527, 7528, 8225, 11948, 12963, 22128; Directories, 8048; Economic conditions, 6873, 12337; History, Local, 8048; Politics & government, 6997; Politics & government, 6997; Statistics, 6873
Ontario, Lake, 12239
Ontwa, the son of the forest, 5692
Oonder hoofden, 11183
The open boat, 9214
An open-eyed conspiracy, 9949
Open market operations, Brazil, 18227
Opening a chestnut burr, 10651
Opening of the Mississippi, 3300
Opera House (theater), Lexington, Ky., 13520
Operas, Librettos, 1447
An operetta in profile, 9594
Ophiuroidea, South Atlantic, 19026; South Georgia Islands, 19025
Opie, John Newton, 4655
Opimius, pseud., 24074
La Opinión Nacional, Caracas, 18130
Opinions of the early presidents, 25176
Opinions on 'slavery' and 'reconstruction of the union' as expressed by President Lincoln, 7290
Opossums, 927, 929
The opponents, 15285
Opportunity, 10733
Opúsculo, 25177

Oquino, Juan, 7644
Ora, the lost wife, 10850
Oracion funebre, 1797
Oran, the outcast, 10449
Orange, 4512
Orange blossoms, fresh and faded, 8574
Orange county, California, 16850
Orange culture in Florida, 4512
Oranges and alligators, 3778
Orators, American, 3608, 23025
Oratory, 1596
Ord, Edward Otho Cresap, 1818-1883, 6510
Ord, George, 1781-1866, 5735, 15101
The ordeal, 9802
The ordeal at Mt. Hope, 24319
A Ordem, Rio de Janeiro, 18176
The order of exercises in the chapel of
  Transylvania university, 15595
Order of United American Mechanics, State
  Council of Pennsylvania, 7645
Order of United Americans, New York, 1583
Orderly book of Lieut. Gen. John
  Burgoyne, 1704
Orderly books of the Fourth New York
  regiment, 4589
Orders in council, 290, 537, 11548,
  11712, 12797, 13088
Orders of knighthood and chivalry, 584
The Orderville United Order of Zion, 17373
Orderville, Utah, History, 17373, 17582
Ordinances of the corporation of
  Georgetown, 12210
Ordinances of the village of Brooklyn,
  1570
Ordination, 12156, 21891, 23775;
  Anniversary sermons, 13064
Ordination sermons, 1072, 22578
Ordnance, Naval, 1219
Ordnance instructions for the Confederate
  States navy, 21977
Ordoñez de Ceballos, Pedro, b.1550?, 7646
Ordoñez y Aguiar, Ramón de, d.ca. 1840,
  1442
O'Rear, Edward Clay, 1863-1961, 14362,
  15102
Oregon, 4026, 5719, 5837, 6013, 15853,
  15869, 15925, 16916, 17238, 17256,
  17313, 17406, 17407, 17502, 17455,
  17768; Anthropology, 17716; Archives,
  17944; Biography, 15818, 16581, 16796,
  17410, 17415; Census, 1860, 17778;
  Census, 1870, 17779; Census, 1880,
  17780; Constitution, 16857; Description
  & travel, 1670, 2508, 2548, 2602, 3047,
  3322, 3350, 3515, 3551, 3955, 4068,
  4237, 4349, 4549, 4690, 5060, 5145,

5183, 5410, 5414, 5445, 7134, 15806, 15816,
  15832, 15869, 15876, 16027, 16222, 16285,
  16296, 16324, 16408, 16432, 16462, 16717,
  16764, 16824, 16896, 16917, 17972, 17215,
  17242, 17250, 17255, 17256, 17257, 17281,
  17307, 17314, 17319, 17320, 17322, 17407,
  17408, 17409, 17410, 17437, 17455, 17502,
  17529, 17546, 17589, 17593, 17665, 17668,
  17751, 17768, 17772, 17824, 17825, 17857;
  Description & travel, Guide-books, 3735;
  Directories, 17248; Economic conditions,
  16597; History, 4256, 5509, 5707, 11579,
  15877, 15878, 15970, 15999, 16021, 16072,
  16146, 16209, 16231, 16362, 16446, 16447,
  16581, 16585, 16597, 16638, 16639, 16689,
  16720, 16762, 16763, 16766, 16784, 16805,
  16895, 16933, 17020, 17045, 17071, 17072,
  17120, 17171, 17283, 17298, 17311, 17316,
  17348, 17445, 17566, 17568, 17569, 17570,
  17658, 17732, 17767, 17781, 17826; History,
  To 1859, 3323, 3524, 5017, 5018, 15925,
  15929, 16064, 16142, 16290, 16305, 16497,
  16517, 16629, 16671, 16690, 16717, 16761,
  16909, 16918, 16919, 17093, 17139, 17140,
  17141, 17144, 17241, 17276, 17277, 17321,
  17759, 17764, 17824, 17843, 17936, 17943;
  History, Periodicals, 17317; History,
  Pictorial works, Catalogs, 16769; History,
  Societies, 17318; History, Sources, 16640,
  17642; Industries & Resources, 17410, 17713,
  17912; Maps, 4249; Militia, Muster rolls,
  17826; Politics & government, 16064, 17213,
  17312, 17465, 17684; Politics & government,
  To 1859, 16418, 17929, 25845; Social life &
  customs, 17053; State penitentiary, Salem,
  16920; Statistics, 16433; University, Dept.
  of economics and history, 17642
Oregon and Eldorado, 1670
Oregon and the orient, 16027
The Oregon archives, 17309
Oregon as it is, 15816
Oregon branch of the Pacific railroad, 17374
The Oregon crisis, 4349
Oregon historical society, Portland, 17642
The Oregon missions, 15929
Oregon presidential electoral vote, 17213
Oregon question, 497, 521, 523, 1092, 1471,
  12475, 12989, 16255, 16497, 22994
Oregon territory, 4256
The Oregon Trial, 4705, 16345
O'Reilly, Alexander, 1725-1794, Poetry, 7516
O'Reilly, John Boyle, 1840-1890, 9641
O'Rell, Max, pseud., 2741
Orendain, Leopoldo I., 7647
Organic act of Montana territory, 17222
Organismo Internacional Regional de Sanidad

Agropecuaria, 18999
La organizaciŏn de los estudios en la Nueva España, 18935
La organizaciŏn de los tribunales y la implantaciŏn de la carrera judicial en Mexico, 18334
Organización Sindical, 20417
Organización y estadísticas electorales, 20350
Organization of American States, 18156, 19850
Organization of the Texas revolution, 15912
Oria y Senties, Enrique de, 7648
Orialla, Indians of, 11291
Oriana, 10762
Orient, N.Y., Genealogy, 12431
Orientación y educación, 18013
Orientación universitaria y profesional, 18361
Oriental harp, 1977
Oriental literature, Bibliography, 515
The oriental pearl, 9416
Oriental philology, Bibliography, 515
Origen, políticas y gestión, 18739
El origen de hombre americano, 20366
The origin and derivation of the names of towns and places in Clark County, 15488
Origin and fall of the Alamo, 16537
The origin and progress of despotism, 11406
The origin and progress of the United States, 22790
The origin of the baker's dozen, 10480
Origin of pestilential diseases, 13770
The origin of the Giddings resolutions, 25443
The origin of the late war, 24917
Original acrostics on all the states and presidents of the U.S., 6093
An original belle, 10652
An original, laughable and comical tale of Hughie Morrison, 8819
Original letters of Mozis Addums to Billy Ivvins, 2591
An original memoir, on the Floridas, 4656
Original memoirs in medicine, surgery, physiology, geology, 12685
Original papers relating to the expedition to Panama, 23735
Original revolutionary chronicle, 10215
Origine et progrès de la mission du Kentucky, 651
Orihuela, Augusto German, 19110
Orihuela y Miquel Hernández, 20625
Orion (ship), 16886
Orleans, Isle of, Quebec, History, 11449

Orleans (Ter.) Laws, statutes, etc., 16940, 25178
Ormond, 8860
Orozco y Berra, Manuel, 1816-1881, 5881, 7649, 7932
The orphan, 11223
The orphan bound-girl, 9495
Orphan Brigade, 14263, 15519, 15520
The orphan of Boston, 10642
An orphan of the Old Dominion, 10914
The orphan sisters, 9883
The orphan's trials, 8788
Orphanages, Lexington, Ky., 15653
Orphans and orphan asylums, 14192; Georgia, 23784
Orpheo, 18905
Orquestra Sinfŏnica de Brasília, 19226
Orr, J. W., illustr., 4403
Orr, James Lawrence, 1822-1873, 2051, 2053
Orr, Jehu Amaziah, 4657
Orr, N., illustr., 4403, 4903, 4924
Orrego Luco, Augusto, 1848?-, 7650
Orrego Luco, Luis, 1866-, 7651
Orrio, Francisco Xavier Alexo de, 1715-1763? 6160
Orser, John, 13288
Orta-undis, 4244
Ortega, Eulalio Maria, 7872
Ortega, José de, 1700-1768, 23480
Ortega Torres, Jorge, ed., 20316, 20319, 20321
Ortiz, Jorge Eugenio, 19076
Ortiz Fernández, Fernando, 1881-, 25179
Ortiz de Montellano, Bernardo, ed., 6462
Oruro, Bolivia (City), Carnival, 18967
Osage country, 1924
Osage County, Kan., History, 16634
Osage Indians, 3092, 5425, 12971, 16389, 21949
Osage language, Glossaries, vocabularies, etc., 2784
Osborn, Charles, 1775-1850, 4659, 24694
Osborn, Hartwell, 4660
Osborn, Samuel D., 15103
Osborn, Scott Compton, 1913-, 15104, 15693
Osborn, Sherard, 7652
Osborne, John, of the Royal mail steam packet co., 7653
Osborne, William H., 4661
Osborne of Arrochar, 9422
O'Shiell, B.B., 25180
Oskaloosa, Ia., History, 17384
Osman, bey, originally Frederick Millingen, 1839?-, 25181
Osŏrio, Beatriz, 19519
Osorio, Manuel Luiz, Marques de Herval, 1808-1879, 18993
Osŏrio de Moscoso Sarmiento de Valladares,

Ventura, marqués de Astorga, 7456
Osorio Mondragón, José Luis, ed., 8439, 8440
Ossorio y Florit, Manuel, 18472
Österreichischer touristen-klub, Vienna, Sektion für naturkunde, 7654
Ostraciidae, 18866
Osuna, Joaquín, 7789
Osvoboditel'noe dvizhenie v Latinskoi Amerike, 18076
Oswald, Felix Leopold, 1845-1906, 7655
Oswald, John W., 15105
Oswego (ship), 25185
Otey, James Hervey, bp.1800-1863, 22966
Otia conchologica, 12328
Otis, Amos, 13331
Otis, Belle, pseud., 11202
Otis, George Alexander, 1781-1863, 11390
Otis, Harrison Gray, 1765-1848, 24006, 25381
Otis, James, 1725-1783, 11385, 13492
Otis, Joseph, 1768-1854, 11350
Oto Indians, 3281
O'Toole's mallet, 6151
Otsego Co., N.Y., History, 1011
Ottawa Indians, 5343
Ottawa language, Texts, 21767
Otte, Elsie C., 13004
Otto, Adolf, 1842-, 4662
Otto, Fannie (St. Jean de Crèvecoeur), 9387
Otto, John, 4663
Otto the knight, 9582
Ottoni, Aureo, 19327
Ottoni, Teófilo, d.1869, 20073
Otuquis (Dept.),Bolivia, 606
Otuquis Indians, 606
Otzinachson; or, A history of the West Branch valley of the Susquehanna, 23425
Ould, Robert, 1820-1882, 2041
Ouray, chief of Ute Indians, 17452
Ouray (Unitah and) Indian Agency, Fort Duchesne, Utah, 17740
The outcast, 10837
The outcast redeemed, 9435
Outdoor life, 4216, 7240, 8380
An outing with the Queen of Hearts, 10995
The outlaw, 4101
The outlaw of the Bermudas, 3998
The outlaw's bride, 9441
The outlaw's crime, 14368
Outlaw's dream, 13115
Outlaws, 16323, 16819
Outlaws of the border, 16407
Outline history of the wilderness of Kentucky and the religious movements of the early settlers, 15390

An outline of the life of George Robertson, 4977
Outlines & sketches, 2514
Outlines of a general history of America, 15232
Outlines of character and manners, 10197
Outlines of history of the Territory of Dakota, 16541
Outlines of political economy, 22839
Outlines of their general history, ancient and modern, 15219
Outposts of Zion, 3636
Outram, Sir James, 1869-1925, 7656
Outre-mer, 2770, 10241
Outside the prison, 9363
Ovariotomy, 14898, 15554
Over the Alleghanies and across the prairies, 4764
Over the dead line, 3305
Over the purple hills, 16200
Over the wilds to California, 15940
Overarche, illustr., 10520
Overland, 9371
Overland express, 5336
Overland journey to California, 15964
Overland journey to Carson Valley, 2597
Overland journeys to the Pacific, 1744, 2486, 2498, 2508, 2528, 2575, 2597, 2700, 2711, 2784, 2825, 2846, 2926, 2936, 2970, 2989, 3005, 3047, 3105, 3220, 3437, 3676, 3730, 3784, 3862, 3936, 3992, 3994, 4026, 4049, 4125, 4139, 4147, 4213, 4339, 4372, 4470, 4482, 4501, 4524, 4597, 4690, 4700, 4931, 4963, 5078, 5086, 5091, 5125, 5145, 5175, 5331, 5336, 5445, 5491, 5492, 5538, 5639, 5719, 5966, 6751, 7358, 12721, 13001, 15804, 15861, 15897, 15919, 15964, 15976, 16007, 16286, 16295, 16296, 16308, 16388, 16501, 16560, 16594, 16623, 16631, 16717, 16723, 16744, 16866, 17004, 17019, 17020, 17063, 17080, 17096, 17152, 17163, 17171, 17175, 17218, 17286, 17292, 17346, 17394, 17405, 17522, 17571, 17751, 17756, 17936
Overland mail routes to the Pacific, 5757
The overland route to California, 2916, 2989
Overland routes to the Pacific, 2892, 2916, 3117, 3321, 3322, 3570, 3631, 3723, 3826, 3993, 4259, 4388, 4456, 4609, 5095, 5301, 5345, 5510, 5511, 5758, 6467
The overland stage to California, 17522
Overland to California in 1847, 3994
Overland to Cariboo, 17113
Overland to Oregon in the tracks of Lewis and Clarke, 17020
The overlanders of '62, 8322
Overstreet, Anne E., 15106

The overthrow of American slavery, 25333
Overton, John, 1766-1833, 23481
Oviatt, Henry, 22466
Oviedo y Valdés, Gonzalo Fernández de, 1478-1557, 7657, 8168
Ovies, D., 19064
Owen, David Dale, 1807-1860, 4664, 15107-15109, 22637
Owen, John, 1818-1889, 17325
Owen, Mary, 7279
Owen, Capt. Richard, 7917
Owen, Richard, 1810-1890, 4665
Owen, Robert, 1771-1858, 7658
Owen, Robert Dale, 1801-1877, 4666-4669, 17326, 22271, 25182
Owen, William, 1787-1837, 14435
Owen, William, 1802-, 4670
Owen, William Miller, 1832-, 4671
Owen County, Ky., History, 15295
Owen Wingrave, 10020
Owens, John Algernon, 4672
Owenton, Ky.,Beech Grove Baptist Church, 15110
Owls, 15525
Owsley County, Ky., 15730
Owyhee Co., Idaho, 16767; Direct, 16767
Owyhee reconnaissance, 3299
The ox team, 17171
Oxford, England, Earthquakes, 1693, 12208
Oxley, 9966
Oxmoor, Jefferson Co., Ky., 24055
Oxnaes, C. Berg, 25183
Ozanne, T.D., 4673
Ozark mountains, 5100, 17574

Pa-ha-sa-pah, 17525
Paasche, Hermann, 1851-1925, 4674
Pacheco, Antonia, 8276
Pacheco, José Ramón, 7659
Pachyschelomya Barretto, 20543
Pacific coast, 12256, 16682, 17193, 23533; Description & travel, 6853, 8014, 16432, 16508, 16871, 16898, 17822, 17823, 17849; History, 16070, 16432
Pacific coast Indians, Wars with, 1847-1865, 1070, 16608, 16834, 16942, 16953, 17826
Pacific Fur Company, 2784, 4026, 5017
Pacific history stories, 16070
Pacific Northwest, 15876, 17409; Description & travel, 17199; Economic conditions, 16597; History, 16597
Pacific ocean, 1066, 3117, 6238, 6256, 15908, 17168; Charts, maps, etc., 7109; Commerce, 22951
The Pacific railroad, 16029, 16205, 16602
Pacific railroad convention, Lacon, Ill., 1853, 23482
Pacific railroad surveys, 5370, 5523
Pacific railroads, 1586, 2079, 3615, 3630, 3667, 3723; Early projects, 1184, 2688, 2690, 16165, 16973, 17003, 17057, 17395, 23482; Explorations and surveys, 3540, 5514, 5518, 5519, 5521, 13236, 15961, 17337
Pacific states, 16293, 17078, 17928; Climate, 17037; Description & travel, 4068, 4951, 6117, 8878, 15811, 16071, 17244, 17717, 23461; Description & travel, Guide-books, 3899; Discovery & exploration, 12876; Economic conditions, 16073; History, 6891, 16638, 16639; Politics & government, Civil war, 16936; Social life & customs, 17602
Pacific trail camp-fires, 16933
Pacific wagon roads, 5511, 16854
Pacificator, pseud., 25184
Packard, Alpheus Spring, 1839-, 15111
Packard, Roy Dwight, 1889-, 7660, 7661
Paddock, Buckley B., 1844-, 17329, 17330
Paddock, Judah, 25185
Paddock, Wilbur Fisk, 1831-1903, 7662
Padial, C., 19639
Padial, Luis Ricardo, 24291
Padua, Fiction, 10898
Paducah, Ky., Churches, 14323; History, 15607
Paducah, University, 15112
Paducah lottery of Kentucky, 15112
Paéz, José Antonio, pres. Venezuela, 1790-1873, 7664
Paéz, Pedro, 1564-1622, 7665
Paéz Brotchie, Luis, 1893-, 7663
A pagan of the Alleghanies, 10688
Page, Frederic Benjamin, 4675
Page, Harlan, 1791-1834, 12591
Page, James Madison, 1839-, 4676
Page, Karl Gottfried, 4677
Page, Lawrence M., 15113
Page, Moses B., 25186
Page, Thomas Nelson, 1853-1922, 3643, 25187-25191
Page Co., Ia., Biography, 16941; History, 16941
A pageant to celebrate the founding of LaGrange, Oldham County, Kentucky, 1827-1927, 15505
Pageants, Lexington, Ky., 14812
Pagès, Pierre Marie François, vicomte de, 1748-1793, 4678
Páginas de filosofía, 19821

Pahute biscuits, 17020
The Pahute fire legend, 17339
Pahute Indian government and laws, 17340
Pahute Indian homelands, 17341
Pahute Indian medicine, 17342
Paige, Lucius R., 24475
Paine, Clarence Summer, 1867-1916, 17260
Paine, Elijah, 1757-1842, 25192
Paine, Lewis W., b.1819, 25193
Paine, Robert, 1799-1882, 4679, 14995
Paine, Thomas, 1737-1809, 1936, 7832,
    11709, 21897, 22205, 22931, 22301,
    23483
Paint Creek (Kentucky), 15432
The painted paleface, 4461
Painter, Charles C. C., 17331
Painter, Edward, 1812-1875, 17332
Painter, Henry M., 23484
Painter, Orrin Chalfant, 1884-, 17332
Painter, William, 1838-1906, 17332
Painters, 10186; Kentucky, 15197;
    Venezuela, 19651
Painting, Brazilian, 19365; Reproductions
    of, 22544; Uruguayan, Exhibitions,
    18762; Venezuelan, Exhibitions, 19740;
    Venezuelan, History, 19651
Paintsville, Ky., Description, 15432;
    History, 15687
Pairpoint, Alfred J., 4680, 4681
Pairpoint, Miss N. M., illustr., 4680
Paisagem do longe, 20510
El paisaje, 7554
Paiute Indians, 16814
Palabra de hombre, 18386
Palaces and prisons, 10872
Palacio, Diego García de, fl.1576-1587,
    8168
Palacio Itamaraty, Rio de Janeiro, 18880
Palacios, Lucila [pseud.], 19860
Palafox y Mendoza, Juan de, bp., 1600-1659,
    6158, 6380, 6558, 7666-7673, 8166
Palairet, Jean, 1697-1774, 4682
The Palais Royal, 10312
Palatines in New York (State), 1183
Palavicini, Felix F., 1881-, 6720
Palavra-levantamento no poesia de Cassiano
    Ricardo, 20077
Palenque, Mexico, 23628, 23538; Antiquities,
    1442; Description, 6788
Paleobotany, 18368
Paleontology, 22021; Addresses, essays,
    lectures, 12272; Argentine Republic, Mar
    del Plata region, 20187; California,
    1404, 11283; Carboniferous, 22054;
    Cretaceous, 2365; Eocene, 19599; Georgia,
    22514; Kansas, 23424; Kentucky, 14151;

Mississippi Valley, 4664, New England,
    22503; New Mexico, 17775; North
    America, 866, 11693; Nova Scotia,
    22053, 22054; Quaternary, 20187;
    Silurian, 866, 11693; U.S., 494,
    2365, 4386, 12685; Uruguay, 19917
Paleoyoic stratigraphy, Jackson Purchase
    Region, Ky., 15282
Palermo, 9508
Palestra historial de virtudes, 1702
Paletto's bride, 11183
Palfrey, Francis Winthrop, 1831-1889, 4683
Palfrey, John Gorham, 1796-1881, 25194
Palisot de Beauvois, Ambroise Marie François
    Joseph, 1752-1820, 4684
Palladino, Lawrence Benedict, 1837-1927, 17333
Pallio de seta, 727
Palliser, John, 1807-1887, 4685, 4686, 6885-
    6887
Palm oil, Pará, 20555
Palma y Freites, Luis de la, 7674
Palmblätter und Schneeflocken, 4499
Palmer, Abraham John, 1847-1922, 4687
Palmer, Benjamin Morgan, 1818-1902, 4688,
    25195
Palmer, Dr., 25806
Palmer, Donald McN., 4689
Palmer, Elva, 15114
Palmer, Frederick, 1873-, 7675, 17334
Palmer, Henry Spencer, 1838-1893, 6748
Palmer, James W., 14068, 14069, 14720, 15689
Palmer, Joel, 1810-1881, 4690, 17335
Palmer, John, of Lynn, Eng., 4691
Palmer, John McAuley, 1817-, 15115
Palmer, John S., 23643
Palmer, John Williamson, 1825-1906, 4692,
    17336
Palmer, Robert M., 1820-1862, 7676
Palmer, Mrs. Sarah A., 4693
Palmer, Sarah M., 23921
Palmer, Sutton, illustr., 15886
Palmer, Vivien M., 15116
Palmer, William Jackson, 1836-1909, 17337
Palmer, William R., 17338-17343
Palmetto leaves, 5295
Palmyra, N.Y., History, 12001
Palmyra, Syria, Fiction, 11084
Palos, Spain, Description, 13109
Palou, Francisco, 1723-1789, 17344, 17345,
    21953
Paltsits, Victor Hugo, 1867-, 4467, 6575,
    7008, 7224, 16560
Pam, 11198
Pambrun, Pierre Chrysologue, 7780
Pamphlets on the Constitution of the United
    States, 3502

337

Pan American Highway, 18629
Pan American tourist bureau, Laredo, Texas, 7677
Pan American Union, 7678; Travel division, 7679-7681
Pan-Americanism, 5848, 19755
Panama, 1250, 12454, 17067; Constitution, 18976; Description & travel, 4636, 5811, 5970, 6141, 6202, 6334, 6758, 6759, 6781, 6928, 6999, 7050, 7264, 7417, 7530, 7583, 7750, 7751, 8207, 8403, 9490, 11676, 13502, 16222, 16417, 21775; Description & travel, Guide-books, 6983, 7110, 7617, 7681; Description & travel, Poetry, 6849; Directories, 6983; Foreign relations, 19934; Foreign relations, U.S., 18912, 19933; History, Periodicals, 7856; Pacific international exposition, 16233; Relations (general) with the U.S., 19934
Panama (City),Universidad,Facultad de Derecho y Ciencias Políticas, Publicaciones, Serie D. Trabajos de graduación, 19022
Panama, l'oeuvre gigantesque, 6781
Panama and the canal today, 6758
Panama canal, 1250, 1323, 5811, 5970, 6202, 6758, 6759, 6781, 6928, 6999, 7110, 7417, 7751, 7858, 7859, 18912; Finance, 1323
Panama Canal Zone, 6258; Directories, 7110
Panama expedition, 1741, 23735
Panama patchwork, 6849
Panama railroad, 6999
Panama y los Estados Unidos, 19933
Panamanian literature, Bibliography, 18198; Biography, 18198; Periodicals, 7856
Panamanian spiders of the genus Tmartus, 20106
Pancho Villa's last hangout, 17634
Pancoast, Charles Edward, 1818-1906, 17346
Pandora (Frigate), 12609
Pangborn, Joseph Gladding, 1844-1914, 4694, 4695
Pani, Alberto J., 1878-, 7682
Panics, 13349; 1836-1837, 1511; 1857, 1511
The Panis; an historical outline of Canadian Indian slavery in the eighteenth century, 24546
Panola, 3274
Panorama agro-pecuario y socio-económico de Boyacá, 19971
Panorama da energía elétrica no Brasil e no Paraná, 18290
Panorama da história da filosofia no Brasil, 20680
Panorama de la nueva poesía colombiana, 18359
Panorama dos recursos naturais do Nordeste, 18277
Panoramas, 762
Pantaleon, Guillermo, jt. author, 20628
Pantano de Vargas, Battle of, 1819, 18909
Pantheon, The new, 25126
Panther Rock, 13745
Pantoja, Domingo de, pseud., 4872
Panton, J. Hoyes, 15117
Paolucci, Giuseppe, 1661-1730, 1873
Papel periódico ilustrado, 7683
Papeles de Nueva España, 7684
A paper city, 10229
Paper making and trade, Colombia, 20495
Paper money, Argentine Republic, 18727; Connecticut, 11535; New York (State), 22444; North Carolina, 2765; U.S., 754, 1457, 11342, 12327, 13487, 22300; U.S., Speeches in Congress, 11262, 11355
Papers from the Canadian archives, 6297
Papers of the California historical society, 16129
Papers relating to the appointment and proceedings of the Royal commission, 6183
Papin,Alexander, 5503
Pará, Brazil, History, 18678, 18820, 20666; Social life & customs, 18622; Universidade Federal, 18877
Parabola, 18119
Parade of progress, 14859
Paradise on earth, 16726
Paraguay, Boundaries, Brazil, 591, 596; Civilization, 18982; Civilization, History, 18650; Description & travel, 592, 598, 1380, 12518; Foreign relations, Uruguay, 19783; History, 1588, 6602, 18030, 19108, 19391; History, To 1811, 592, 20084, 21873; Intellectual life, 18982; Politics & government, 19163
Paraguayan War, 1865-1870, 18163, 18937, 22629
Paraíba, Conselho estadual de cultura, 7685
Paraíba, History, 7685; Social life and customs, 7685
Paramo de sueños, 20186
Paramo Pomaredo, Jorge, 19143, 19817, 20712
Paraná, History, 21742
The Parana; with incidents of the Paraguayan war, 22629
Parana River, 1028
Parasites, 18889-18893, 20527
Parati, Brazil, 19298
Os parceiros do Rio Bonito, 19723
Pardo, J. Joaquín, 7686
Pardo, Ricardo, 20710
Pardo, El, Treaty of, 1739, 13505
Paredes, Rómulo, 25772

Parentator, Memoirs of remarkables in the life and the death of the ever-memorable Dr. Increase Mather, 23308

O parentesco entre os indios Galibí do rio Oiapoque, 18555

Paris, Bibliothèque Nationale, 19632, 25196; Description, 10520; Exposition universelle, 1867, 15856, 22436; Exposition universelle, 1900, 24186; History, Commune, 1871, 3895; History, Commune, 1971, Fiction, 8966; Hospitals, 23389; Museum national d'histoire naturelle, 2472; Social life & customs, 13164; Treaty of, 1783, 2324, 12190, 13364, 22216

Paris, Ky. Christian Church, Ladies Bible Class, 15118; History, 14886

Parish, Elijah, 1762-1825, 22815

Parish, John Carl, 1881-, 16172

The parish-side, 9476

Parisian sights and French principles, seen through American spectacles, 13164

Parisot, Pierre Fourier, 17347

Park, Clyde William, 1880-, 15119

Park, Edwards Amasa, 1808-1900, 22548

Park, George S., 17147

Parke, Daniel, 1669-1710, 11272, 22209

Parke, John Grubb, 5522

Parke, Robert, fl.1588, 22252

Parker, Amos Andrew, 1792-, 4696

Parker, Cummings, 15783

Parker, Cynthia Ann, 1827?-1864, 16380

Parker, Francis Jewett, 1825-1909, 4697

Parker, Sir Gilbert, 1862-1932, 7687-7689

Parker, Henry Elijah, 1821-1896, 7690

Parker, Henry W., 17348

Parker, Henry Webster, 1822-1903, 16649

Parker, Isaac Charles, 1838-1896, 16700

Parker, James W., b.1797, 17349

Parker, Joel, 1795-1875, 25197, 25198

Parker, Joel, 1816-1888, 7691

Parker, Nathan Howe, 4698, 17350-17352

Parker, Quanah, 1854-1911, 16380

Parker, Samuel, 4700, 4701

Parker, Theodore, 1810-1860, 23908, 25199-25202

Parker, Theodoro, pseud, 23941

Parker, Thomas H., 4702

Parker, Thomas V., 13448

Parker, William B., 4703

Parker, William Belmont, 1871-, 24901

Parker, William Harwar, 1826-1896, 2066

Parker, William Thornton, 1849-, 17353

Parker & Huyett, St. Louis, pub., 3987

Parker's Fort, Tex., 16380; Massacre, 1836, 17349

Parker Co., Texas, Biography, 16781

Parkes, Mrs. G.R., see Elizabeth Robins

Parkhurst, Henry Martyn, 1825-, reporter, 24038

Parkinson, R. R., 17354

Parkinson, Richard, 1748-1815, 4704

Parkman, Francis, 1828-1893, 4705, 7692

Parkman, George, 1790-1849, 12872

Parks, Edd Winfield, 6960

Parks, 14434; Kentucky, 14638; North Dakota, 17459, 17461-17463; Utah, 17922

Parks and playgrounds (city and county facilities), 13611

The parks of Colorado, 16604

Parliamentary practice, 22002; Argentine Republic, 18418

Parnassus, 13115

Parodies, 1268, 1773

Une parole de paix sur le différend entre l'Angleterre et les Etats-Unis, 22232

Parra, Antonio, 7693

Parra, Jacinto de, 7694

Parra-Pérez, Caracciolo, 1883-, 17982

Parricide, 8070

Parrish, Randall, 1858-1923, 17356

Parry, Charles Christopher, 1823-1890, 4664, 17776

Parry, William, d.1585, defendant, 22680

Parry, William Edward, 7695-7697

Parson Beecher and his horse, 10797

Parson Ingram, 11101

Parsons, Charles Grandison, 1807-1864, 4706

Parsons, Eugene, 1855-, 17357

Parsons, George Frederic, 1840-1893, 17358

Parsons, Talcott, 1902-, 17952

Parsons, William Bostwick, 4707, 4708

The parted family, 5141

Parthenia, 10181

Partido Comunista de la Argentina, 18556, 20232

Partido del Pueblo (Peru), 19895

Partido Liberal (Paraguay), 19163

Partido Unión Revolucionaria Comunista (Cuba), 20701

A parting and a meeting, 9950

Partingtonian patchwork, 10755

The partisan, 10779

The partisan leader, 11019

Partisan life with Col. John S. Mosby, 5107

The partnership, 12293

Parts of a life else untold, 11181

Party leaders, 708

The party of Abraham Lincoln, 6707

Pascal, Blaise, 1623-1662, 19991

Paseo de la Habana a Acapulco, 6369

The Pasha papers, 9937

Paso y Troncoso, Francisco del, 1842-1916, 7684
Pasquall, the tailor of Venice, 11183
Passages from the correspondence and other papers of Rufus W. Griswold, 3700
Passages from the diary of an itinerant's wife, 9303
Passamaneck, Sidney B., 14997
The passing of Enriquez, 6975
The passing of Mammy Jane, 25282
The passing of New France, 8414
The passing of Sister Barsett, 10041
Passing of the Rees House, 15120
Passion and reality, 10876
Passion-flowers, 12955
A passionate pilgrim, 10014
The past, the present and the future of the Pacific, 16293
The past, present, and future of the United States, 447
Paste, 10016
Paste jewels, 8683
Pastime stories, 10465
Pastor, M.H., 7698
El pastor de noche buena, 7670, 7671
A pastoral letter, on the religious instruction of the slaves of members of the Protestant Episcopal Church in the State of South Carolina, 24001
Pastori, Luis, 19075
Pastorius, Francis Daniel, 1651-1720, 6713
Pastors versus poets, 14405
The Patagonia, 7123
Patagonia, Description & travel, 11409, 12498; History, 372
Patchwork, 9243
Patent laws and legislation, Mexico, 18710; U.S., 855, 12032
Patents, 4946; U.S., 12032
Paterson, Paul, pseud.? 4806
Paterson, William, 1745-1806, 11819
The path of the conquistadores, 6028
The pathbreakers from river to ocean, 16733
The Pathfinder, 9141
Pathology, 13920
Patience Strong's outings, 11153
O patinho torto, 20236
Patouillet, Louis, 1699-1779, 2466
The patriarch, 10762
The patriot preachers of the American revolution, 23455
A patriot's strategy, 14268
Patriotic poetry, American, 22792
Patrick Henry (school ship), 2066
The Patriot, 4709
A patriot, pseud., 6792

Patriotic poems, 13161
Patriotism, 1121, 12516
The patriots and guerillas of East Tennessee and Kentucky, 1478
The patrol of the mountain, 9297
Patron and client, 25452
A patron of art, 9363
El patronato disputado, 6071, 6269
Patten, Benjamin Adam, 1825-1877, 15927
Patten, Edmund, 4710
Patterson, A.W., 4711, 23485
Patterson, Adoniram Judson, 1827-1909, 7699
Patterson, Caleb Perry, 25203
Patterson, Catherine, 1793-1864, 13915
Patterson, Edwin Hamilton Norton, 4712
Patterson, J.B., 1366
Patterson, James Kennedy, 1833-1922, 13837, 14186, 14988, 15121
Patterson, James Willis, 1823-1893, 7700
Patterson, John, 4713
Patterson, Lawson B., 17359
Patterson, Richard S., 7701
Patterson, Robert, 1753-1827, 6457, 6459, 13915
Patterson, Robert Mayne, 1832-1911, 7702, 25204
The Patterson log cabin, 6459
Patti, Adelina, 1843-1919, 7544
Pattie, James Ohio, 1804?-, 4715
Patton, Jacob Harris, 1812-1903, 4716
Patton, William, 1798-1856, 22775
Patton, William Weston, 1821-1889, 25205, 25206
Patty Cannon's times, 11004
O pau-de-sebo, 19696
Paul, Almarin B., 7703
Paul, D., 25207
Paul, John, pseud., 11112
Paul, Nathaniel, 1775?-1839, 25208
Paul and Julia, 10532
Paul Ardenheim, the monk of Wissahikon, 10216
Paul Demarisi's mortgage, 9254
Paul Jones and Denis Duval, 9683
Paul Fane, 11181
Paul Lynde's sketch book, 8500
Paul Patoff, 6500
Paul Perril, the merchant's son, 9983
Paul Ralston, 9902
Paul Redding, 10599
Paul Ulric, 10330
Paul Wilhelm, duke of Württemberg, 1797-1860, 4717, 17360
Paul's orange grove, 9254
Paulding, James Kirke, 1778-1860, 4718-4721, 9355, 21021, 23486
Paulding, William Irving, 1825?-1890, 4721,

10483
Pauline of the Potomac, 2501
"Pauline's" (Bowling Green, Ky.), 15684
Pauline's trial, 9185
Pauling, John, 1753-1818, 1175-1177
Pauw, Cornelius, 1739-1799, Recherches
  philosophiques sur les Américains,
  11364
Pavía, Lázaro, 1844-, 7844
Pavie, Théodore-Marie, 1811-1896, 4722
Pawhuska, Okla., 16389
Pawlet, Vt., Genealogy, 12857; History,
  12857
The pawnbroker's heir, 2670
Pawnee Indians, 4025, 4571, 5503, 17851,
  24546; Fiction, 2570
Pawnshops, Peru, 8084; Spain, 8084
Pawtucket, R.I., History, 11285
Paxson, Frederic Logan, 1877-1948, 17361-
  17363
Paxton, John D., 1784-1868, 4723
Paxton, Philip, pseud., 3763
Paxton, W. M., 7704
Paxton boys, 2317; Fiction, 9840
Paxton family, 7704
Paybodie, Benjamin Frank, 22187
Payne, David L., 1838-1884, 16868
Payne, Edwin Waters, 1837-, 4724
Payne, Ruth, 15122
Payno, Manuel, 7705
Payno y Flores, Manuel, 1810-1894, 7706
Payson, Edward, 1783-1827, 21993
Payton Skah, 10827
Paz, Ireneo, 1836-1924, 7707
Paz, José María, 1791-1854, 7708, 19676
Paz-Castillo, Fernando, 18565
Paz Soldán, Carlos, 7857
Paz Soldán, Mariano Felipe, 1821-1886, 7709,
  7857
Paz Torres, Augusto, 19170
Pazos y Caballero, José H., 18550
Pea Ridge and Prairie Grove, 11244
Peabody, Alfred, 17364
Peabody, Ephraim, 1807-1856, 25209
Peabody, Henry Greenwood, 7710, 7711
Peabody, Mark, pseud., 11043
Peabody, William Bourn Oliver, 1799-1847,
  1419
Peabody family (Francis Peabody, 1614-1698?),
  22187
Peabody family (John Paybody, 1599?-1687?),
  22187
Peabody family (William Paybody, 1619?-1707),
  22187
Peabody, William Smith, 1818-1877, 22187
Peace, 1037, 1215, 1815, 8165, 9480, 11370,

12225, 13130, 13187, 22109, 22983
Peace Conference, Washington, D.C., February,
  1861, 24501
The peace-makers, 11311
The peace manual, 1037
Peace, not war, 12194
Peace River district, 6180, 6306
Peace River land recording division, 6180
The peace we need, and how to secure it, 11310
Peace with Mexico, 24467
The peaceable Americans of 1860-1861, 15342
A peaceable plea for the government of the
  Church of Scotland, 23560
Peach, 12181
Peach Melba, 20661
Peacock, Thomas Brower, 7712
Peak, Howard Wallace, 1856-, 4725
Peale, Franklin, 1795-1870, 22841
Peanuts, 7826, 8143; Argentine Republic, 20546
Pearce, Betsy, 15123
Pearce, John Ed, 15124-15126
Pearce, John J., d.1888, 25210
Pearce Amerson's will, 4087
Peareson, Philip E., d.1895, 17365
Pearl, Cyril, 1805-1865, 25211
Pearl-fisheries, Mexico, 6955
The pearl-shell necklace, 9814
Pearse, James, 1786-, 4726
Pearse, Mark Guy, 1842-, 8428
Peasantry, Germany, 24733; Spain, 7241
The peasant's fate, a rural poem, 22531
Pease, Edwin R., 4727
Pease, Theodore Calvin, 1887-, 24041
Pease, Verne Seth, 1856-, 25212
Peaslee, Stephen M., 13672
Peaslee family (Joseph Peasley, d.1660),
  22737
Peatfield, J.J., 15907
Peavyhouse, William W., 15127
Pebblebrook, and the Harding family, 11189
El pecado del siglo, 19968
Peck, Elisabeth S., 15130, 15131
Peck, George, 17366, 25213
Peck, George Record, 1843-1923, 7713, 7714
Peck, Henry Everard, 1821-1867, 24194, 25496
Peck, John Mason, 1789-1858, 4728, 4729,
  17367, 25214, 23487, 23488
Peck, Lucius B., 1802-1866, 25215
Peck, Nathaniel, 13449
Peck, Samuel Minturn, 1854-, 4730-4732
Peck, Simon Lewis, 1844-, 17368
Peck, Solomon, 1800-1874, 22496
Peck, William Henry, 1836-1921, 4733-4737
Peck's bad boy, 10502
Peckham, Howard H., 3205
Peckwell, Henry, 1747-1787, 12282

Pecos country, 16464
Peculiar, 10699
A peculiar people, 8662
Peculiarities of American cities, 3623, 6858
Peculio, Actio de, 25560, 25562
Peculio e 'in rem versio' nel diritto classico, 25561
Peculium, Über Begriff und Wesen des, 24962
Peddicord, Kelion Franklin, 1823-1905, 4287
A pedestrious tour, 3397
The pedlar, 15693
Pedro, João Rodriques, 19172
Pedro II, emperor of Brazil, 1825-1891, 18849, 19642
Pee Dee region, S.C., 12416
Peel, Bruce Braden, 7715
Peel, Sir Robert, bart., 1788-1850, 24485
Peele, John R., 4738
A peep at Mexico, 6834
A peep at "number five", 10515
A peep at realities, 11129
A peep at the Great west, 11507
A peep into Hymen's kingdom, 11143
Peeps at people, 8684
Peeps from a belfry, 10747
Peers, Benjamin Orrs, 1800-1842, 4739, 15128
Peet, Frederick Tomlinson, 4740
Pefia, David, 1865-, 5961
Peg, 10863
Peiramo Facio, J., 20636
Peirce, Bradford Kinney, 1819-, 15129
Peirce, Henry Augustus, 1808-, 15984
Peirce, Thomas, 1786-1850, 4741
Peixoto, Ernest C., illustr., 4565
Peixotto, Ernest Clifford, 1869-, 17369
Pelayo, a story of the Goth, 10780
Pelayo, King of Asturias, d.732, Fiction, 10780
Pelew Islands, 22523
Pelham, Henry, 1695?-1754, 2028, 16457
Pella, Ia., Description, 16801
Pellecery Pilares, Juan Antonio, 1738-1806, 399
Pelletan, Eugène i.e. Pierre Clément Eugène, 1813-1884, 25216
Pellow, Thomas, fl.1738, 25217
Pellowe, William Charles Smithson, 1890-, 7716
Pelotização de minério de manganês, 19508
Pelton, Louise, 15130, 15131
Pelzjäger, präricn und präsidenten, 8410
Pemaquid, 10563; Maine, 12930; Maine,

Description, Poetry, 12515
Pemba, 25137
Pember, Edward Henry, 1833-1911, 13104
Pemberton, 10513
Pemberton, John Clifford, 1814-1881, 2033
Pembina, N.D., Climate, 17619
Pembina County, N.D., 17737
Pembroke, 9576
Pemex travel club, Mexico, 7717
A pen-and-ink panorama of New-York city, 23344
Pen and ink portraits, 1679
Pen and powder, 5709
Pen knife sketches, 16358
Pen pictures of representative men of Oregon, 16796
Pen-pictures of the war, 11267
Peña, Domingo de la, 7108
Peña de Venegas, Nelly, 1946-, 20649
Peña Montenegro, Alonso de la, bp., d.1688, 7718
Peña y Reyes, Juan Antonio de la, 4742
Penaeidae, 19186
Peñafiel, Antonio, 947
Peñalosa, Diego Dionisio de, 1624-1687, 3547, 16503
Peñalosa y Zúñiga, Clemente, 7719
Penchansky de Zapata, Sandra, 20243
Pencil, Mark, pseud., 4743
Pencil sketches, 10197
Pencil sketches of Montana, 17151
Pencilled fly-leaves, 4776
Pencillings of scenes upon the Rio Grande, 190
Pendleton, Calvin Crane, 1811-1873, 17370
Pendleton, George Hunt, 1825-1889, 7720
Pendleton, James Madison, 1811-1891, 25218
Pendleton, John Strother, 1802-1868, 11686
Pendleton, Louis Beauregard, 1861-1939, 4744-4748, 25219
Pendleton, Mark A., 1868-, 17370-17373
Penelope's English experiences, 11157, 11159
Penelope's progress, 11158
Penet, Peter, d.1789, 12929
Pengra, P.J., 17374
Penguins, 18955
Peninsular campaign, 1862, 47, 838, 839, 3078, 4391, 13447, 16942, 22800, 22802
The penitential tyrant, 1428
Penitentiaries (U.S.), 3115
Penmanship, 6287
Penn, I. Garland, 25220
Penn, William, 1644-1718, 850, 2344, 3519, 8165, 11854, 11992, 12993, 13086, 23180
Pennacook Indians, 11417
Pennell, Orrin Henry, 7721
Penniman, Purcell, 25221

Pennington, Edgar Legare, 7722
Pennington, James W.C., 25222
Pennock, Abraham L., 25147
Pennsylvania, 7002; Boundaries, 23733;
  Charters, 11748; Constitution, 2355,
  21838; Council of censors, Address,
  21838; Court of admiralty, 9918;
  Description & travel, 1014, 1563, 1651,
  2170, 2771, 2986, 3472, 3595, 3792,
  4300, 4998, 5093, 5147, 7203, 11242,
  11785, 11992, 12486, 13163, 13233,
  13580, 13956, 14000, 14370, 23558,
  23694; Description & travel, Gazetteers,
  22253; General Assembly, House of
  Representatives, 7723, 12900, 22517,
  25223; General Assembly, Senate, 22517,
  25224; Historical society, 450, 2130,
  2248, 2410, 13093; History, 6822,
  11231, 23425, 23474; History, Colonial
  period, 444, 450, 1651, 2317, 2344, 6713,
  22254, 22376, 23631, 23694; History,
  Fiction, 1333, 14477; History, French
  and Indian war, 1755-1763, 23638;
  History, Revolution, 466, 467, 22049,
  23169; History, Revolution, Fiction,
  10066; Militia, 22049; Laws, statutes,
  etc., 21908; Politics & government,
  10317, 13101, 22939; Politics &
  government, 1775-1865, 2211; Politics
  & government, Colonial period, 2318,
  23638; Public works, 1458; Social life
  & customs, 9187, 10317; University,
  13174, 22688; University, Poetry, 694
Pennsylvania cavalry, 1st regt., 1861-
  1865, 4286; 4th regt., 1861-1865,
  22634; 6th regt., 1861-1865, 22260;
  7th regt., 1861-1865, 3271, 5171
Pennsylvania chronicle, 12293
Pennsylvania college, Gettysburg,
  Philomathean society, 1255; Phrenakosmian
  society, 1255
Pennsylvania German dialect, 7412
Pennsylvania Hall Association, Philadelphia,
  25225
Pennsylvania infantry, 1st regt., 1776-
  1783, 2248; 4th regt., 1776, 22049;
  37th regt., 1861-1864, 3871; 48th regt.,
  1861-1865, 2766; 51st regt., 1861-1865,
  4702; 63d regt., 1861-1864, 4391; 83d
  regt., 1861-1865, 4127, 4622; 85th regt.,
  1861-1865, 3648; 97th regt., 1861-1865,
  4857; 102d regt., 1861-1865, 5275; 106th
  regt., 1861-1865, 5608; 107th regt.,
  1862-1865, 12926; 114th regt., 1862-1865,
  4899; 141st regt., 1862-1865, 3107
Pennsylvania railroad company, 7724

Pennsylvania Society for Promoting the
  Abolition of Slavery, 25226-25233, 24460,
  24839, 25735
Pennsylvania society for the promotion of
  internal improvements in the commonwealth,
  24752
Pennsylvania State Anti-slavery Society,
  25234, 25235
The Pennsylvania state trials, 22517
A Pennsylvanian, pseud., 25420
Pennybacker, Mrs. Anna J. (Hardwicke), 17375
Pennyroyal region, Ky., 13611, 13613;
  Statistics, 13610; Weather, 13862
Penobscot expedition, 1779, 1803
Pensacola, Fla., History, 16441
Pensamento, código, informação, 18662
O pensamento juridico de Norberto Bobbio,
  19691
El pensamiento constitucional de Justo
  Arosemena, 18976
El pensamiento constitutional de Latinoamérica,
  17984
El pensamiento constitutional hispanoamericano
  hasta 1830, 17985
Pensamiento dominicano, 19182
The Pension Beaurepas, 10015
Pension Reform Act of 1974, 14679
Pensions, Cuba, 20693; Kentucky, 13570, 15716;
  Laws and regulations, 14686; Military, U.S.,
  7101
El pentagonismo, 19183
Peonage, Peru, 8193, 25772; Philippine Islands,
  25251
People I have met, 11182
The people and institutions of the U.S.A.,
  3490
The people of our neighborhood, 9577
The people's book of American history, 1598
The people's doctors, 3291
The people's keepsake, 7991
People's National Congress of Guyana, 19580
People's Party (Massachusetts), 25236
The people's presidential candidate; or The
  life of William Henry Harrison, of Ohio,
  22465
Peoria, Ill., 6653; Directories, 16427,
  16428; History, 16427, 16428, 17156
Peoria Co., Ill., History, 16428
Pepper, 1203
Pepper, George Whitfield, 1833-1899, 4749
Pepperell, Mass., Evangelical Congregational
  society, 599; First parish, 599; History,
  1766
Pepys' island, 371
Pequena bibliografía crítica da literatura
  brasileira, 19819

Pequeño libro de sonetos, 18817
Pequot Indians, 405
Pequot war, 1636-1638, 2398, 23236
Per eum hominem, qui serviat, quemamodum
  nobis acquiratur, 24493
Peraza Sarausa, Fermín, 6523
Percival, Charles G., 4750
Percival, Olive, 7725
Percival, Thomas, 1740-1804, 12757
Percival Mayberry, The life and adventures
  of, 4006
Percy, Algernon Heber, 7726
The Percy anecdotes, 13450
Percy, Mrs. Heber, 7726
Perdue, Frances D., 15132
Père Antoine's date palm, 8501
Père Jean, 10297
Pereda y Victoria, Victorino, 7727, 7728
Peregrinación de Philotea al santo templo,
  7672
Pereira, Cecilia Duprat de Britto, 19604
Pereira, Manuel, 46, 8459
Pereira Pinto, Antonio, 1819-1880, 19471
Pereyra, Carlos, tr., 7640
Perez, Felipe, 1834-, 13451
Pérez Amuchástegui, Antonio Jorge, 19904
Pérez Bayer, Francisco, 1711-1794, 400
Pérez Cabrera, José Manuel, 18968
Pérez de Amézaga, Juan, 7729
Pérez de Arteaga, Diego, 7730
Pérez de Guzmán, Juan, fl.1670, 21765
Pérez de Lara, Alfonso, fl.1608-1629, 7731,
  7732, 7733
Pérez de Lazcano, Diego, 7734
Pérez Vento, Rafael, 7779
Pérez Vila, Manuel, 19737, 20251
Pérez Winter de Tamburini, María J.,
  20087
Pérez y Hernández, José María, 7735
A perfect Adonis, 9755
The perfection of reason, 10487
The perfection of science, 10487
Perfil do mercado consumidor de Santo André
  e do "Grande São Paulo", 18971
Perforated stones from California, 16741
Perforations in the "Latter-day pamphlets",
  25925
El perfume de la mujer y el dandismo en la
  poesía de Baudelaire, 18921
Perigny, Maurice de, 1877-, 4751, 7736
The peril of our ship of state, 12315
Perils and pleasures of a hunter's life,
  3852
The perils of a Peruvian family amid the
  wilds of the Amazon, 23527
The perils of fast living, 8902

The perils of Pearl street, 9651
The perils of Peter Pliant, 9494
Perils of the border, 4460
Perils of the period, 9857
Periodicals, 18127; Bibliography, 19385,
  20442; Bibliography, Catalogs, 518;
  Classification and cataloging, 20198;
  Colombia, 20292; Cuba, 18913; Mexico,
  19827
Periodontics, 18168
Periwinkle, 9463
Perkins, Eli, pseud., 10162
Perkins, Frederic Beecher, 1828-1899, 9693
Perkins, James Handasyd, 1810-1849, 4752,
  23489
Perkins, Jared, 23909
Perkins, Thomas Handasyd, 1764-1854, 13037
La perla de la América, 13350
Perley, Jeremiah, 23039
Perley, Mae Clements, 4753, 15133
Perley, Moses Henry, 1804-1862, 6666
Permanent temperance documents, 307
Pernambuco, Brazil, Bibliography, 19111;
  Description & travel, 577; Economic
  conditions, 18784, 19274; Harbor, 19251;
  History, 1889-1920, 20567; History, Dutch
  period, 18992; History, Novembrada, 18281;
  History, Septembrizada, 18281; Universidad
  Federal, 19111, 19949
Perpetua heredad, 18966
Perreau, Jean André, 1749-1831, 23490
Perrin, Alfred H., 15134-15139, 15389
Perrin, Stephanie D.L., 15140
Perrin, William Henry, d.1892?, 4754, 13559,
  14380, 15141-15144
Perrin du Lac, François Marie, 1766-1824,
  4755
Perrine's new topographical war map of the
  southern states, 11277
Perrot, Nicholas, 1644-1718, 23491
Perry, Benjamin Franklin, 1805-1886, 25237
Perry, J.A., 4756
Perry, John Gardner, 1840-1926, 4757
Perry, Mrs. Martha Derby, 4757
Perry, N., 10163
Perry, Oliver Hazard, 1785-1819, 1697, 22687
Perry, William Stevens, bp., 1832-1898, 23492
Perry County, Kentucky, 14336, 15261; History,
  14454, 15162
Perry's saints, 4602
Perryman, James, d.ca.1882, 1648
Perryville, Ky., History, 14001; Hotels, inns,
  etc., 14058
Perryville, Battle of, 8 October 1862, 14222,
  14789, 15294, 15498, 15499, 15673; Fiction,
  13980

Persat, Maurice, 1788-1858, 4758
Persecution, 2298; Cuba, 18321
Perseverence of the saints, 4343
Pershing, John Joseph, 1860-1948, 19650
Persia, Fiction, 4923
Personal adventures in Upper and Lower
  California, in 1848-9, 23562
Personal experiences in the war of the
  great rebellion, 4538
Personal forgiveness and public justice,
  11375
Personal information and privacy, 14616
Personal liberty and martial law, 13090
Personal liberty laws, 1814, 25029,
  25197, 25499, 25582
Personal management, 19150, 20285
Personal memoirs and recollections of
  editorial life, 11606
Personal memories, social, political, and
  literary with sketches of many noted
  people, 4384
Personal memories of the United Order of
  Orderville, Utham, 17582
Personal narrative of travels in the U.S.
  and Canada in 1826, 6576
Personal recollections of Joan of Arc,
  9031
Personal recollections of John M. Palmer,
  15115
Personal recollections of the Civil War,
  3598
Personal reminiscences of a Maryland
  soldier, 2762
Personal reminiscences of early days in
  California with other sketches, 16510
Personals, 9857
Persons and pictures from the histories
  of France and England, 9847
Perspectivas que ofrece Bolivia al
  inversionista, 19117
Perth, Ontario, 1095
Peru, 7167; Antiquities, 11330, 19141,
  19587, 19748, 23566; Biography, 7770;
  Boundaries, Ecuador, 18196, 20652;
  Civilization, 19964; Commerce, 5855,
  19209; Culture, 18242; Description &
  travel, 6594, 6929, 6930, 7050, 7218,
  7411, 8193, 11403, 11654, 21853, 23133,
  23566; Economic conditions, 6732,
  18331, 18732, 18733, 18841, 19208;
  Economic policy, 17993, 19895; Fiction,
  23527; Foreign relations, Spain, 23140;
  History, 5937, 6732, 6794, 7964, 8029,
  8291, 19176, 19557, 20193; History, To
  1548, 11708, 20194, 21826, 23445; History,
  1548-1820, 6814; History, 1548-1820,

Periodicals, 7463; History, To 1820, 6468;
  History, Bibliography, 18894; History,
  Conquest, 1522-1548, 122, 408, 1015, 12448,
  23509; History, Periodicals, 5956, 7857;
  History, Spanish question, 1864, 23140;
  History, War of independence, 1820-1829,
  436, 6250, 6640, 6814, 7015, 7322, 7506,
  7709, 8112, 22278; Industries, 17968, 19209;
  Laws, statutes, etc., 2198, 18232, 18948,
  20458; Milicias disciplinadas, 5886;
  Periodicals, 6794, 7464, 7857; Politics &
  government, 5367, 18065, 18151, 18152,
  19965, 19966; Population, 19207; Social
  conditions, 18100, 18331; Social life &
  customs, 1245;
Peru (Viceroyalty) Laws, statutes, etc., 5886,
  6366, 6367, 6368, 6519
Peru, Ill., History, 15951
El Perú y la España moderna, 23140
Peru's Sinamos, governmental agency for
  coordinating reforms, 18151
Peruvian Amazon Company limited, 1921, 25772
Peruvian coast pilot, 2391
Peruvian literature, Periodicals, 7463; 20th
  century, History & criticisms, 19109
The Peruvian nun, 9721
Peruvian poetry, 20th century, 19848
Peruvian political perspective, 18152
Pervana de S. María, Rosa, 7694
La pesquería marítima peruana durante 1966,
  19170
Pesquisa sobre a consumo de produtos
  industriais, 18692
Pesquisas e depoimentos para a historia,
  25066
Pesquisas relativas à incubação artificial
  e natural dos ovos do Bombyx mori L, 17965
Pessoa, Dirceu Murillo, 20000
The pest house, 10310
Pesticides, 19315
The pestilence, God's messenger and teacher,
  11903
Pétalos yertos, 19646
Petals plucked from sunny climes, 2817
Pete Featherton, 3754, 14242
Peter, Alfred M., 15145
Peter, Johanna, 15150
Peter, Robert, 1805-1894, 7737, 13605, 15107-
  15109, 15145-15150
Peter, Saint, apostle, 7449
Peter I, the Great, emperor of Russia, 1672-
  1725, 1611, 1612
Peter Carradine, 8987
Peter Pilgrim, 2717
Peter Rugg, the missing man, 10693
Peter Stuyvesant's voyage up the Hudson, 9995

Peter the parson, 11205
Peter Tütt, 23950
Peter Weaver, 11191
Peters, Absalom, 1793-1869, 261
Peters, Charles, b.1825, 17376
Peters, De Witt Clinton, d.1876, 4759
Peters, Jeremy, pseud., 10824
Peters, Phillis, see Wheatley, Phillis
Peters, Richard, 1744-1828, 1455
Peters, Richard, 1780-1848, 25313
Peters, Theodore Curtis, 4760
Petersburg, Va., Siege, 1864-1865, 4331
Peterson, T.B., & brothers, Philadelphia,
    pub., 22763
Pethion de Vilar, pseud. of Egas Moniz
    Barreto de Aragão Sousa e Meneses, 19880
Petigru, Thomas, 22068
Petit, Emilien, b.1713, 24238
Petit Muñoz, Eugenio, 20045
Petit-Thouars, Abel du, 7858
Petition, Right of, 76, 13268, 23888,
    24243, 24990, 25348, 25381, 25391, 25749
Petition nouvelle des citoyens de couleur
    des îles françoises, 7738
Petitions of sundry inhabitants of the
    state of Missouri, 4761
Petitions of the early inhabitants of
    Kentucky to the General Assembly of
    Virginia, 15288
Peto, Sir Samuel Morton, bart., 1809-1889,
    4762
Petrarca, Francesco, 1304-1374, 7739
Petrelli, Ralph S., 14667
Petroff Rojas, Ivan, 1956, 20649
Petroglifos prehistóricos de Colón del
    Tachira, 19627
Petroglyphs, Colón, Venezuela (City), 19627;
    Patagonia, 19891
The petrography of certain igneous dikes
    of Kentucky, 14771
El petróleo y el desarrollo económico de
    México, 19940
Petroleum, 11444, 12075, 12220, 13939,
    14447, 15512, 20343; Appalachia, 14432;
    Chile, 20122; Geology, 14338, 14441,
    14442, 14565; Kentucky, 14428, 14432,
    14440, 14566; Laws and regulations,
    Colombia, 20342; Lake states, 14432;
    Pennsylvania, 2030, 12699; Pennsylvania,
    Venango Co., 2171, 12699; U.S., 11359;
    Warren County, Ky., 14567
Petroleum industry and trade, 18799; Mexico,
    19940; Venezuela, Congresses, 20418
Petrology, 2030
Petrology, Brazil, Salvador, 19949
Pettengill, Amos, 1780-1830, 12724

Pettigrew, James Johnston, 1828-1863, 25566
Pettis, George Henry, 1834-, 17377-17379
Pettis, George William, 1874
Pettit, Charles, 1736-1806, 13071
Pettit, Eber M.. b.1800 or 1801, 25239
Le peuple de xxe siècle aux Etats-Unis, 3633
"Pew 89", Lincoln and Beecher, 7039
Peyton, Jim, 15151
Peyton, John Howe, 1778-1847, 23493
Peyton, John Lewis, 1824-1896, 4763, 4764,
    11298, 13452, 23493
Peyton, John Rowzée, 1752-1798, 23493
Peyton, William Madison, 1805-1868, 13452,
    25466
Peyton family, 13452
Peytraud, Lucien Pierre, 1858-, 25240
Pfaff, Ivo, 1864-, 25241
Pfeiffer, G. Simon Friedrich, 25242
Pfeiffer, Ida (Reyer) 1797-1858, 13453, 13454
Pfeiffer, Peter W., 14785
Pferdekamp, Wilhelm, 1901-, 7740, 7741
Pfister, Albert von, 1839-1907, 4765
Pfleiderer, Joh. Gottlob, 4766
Phalen, W.C., 15152
The phantom of the forest, 2682
The phantoms of the foot-bridge, 4562
Pharaon, Florian, 1827-1887, 24117
Pharmacy, Early works to 1800, 22331; Laws
    and legislation, Chile, 21725; Societies,
    etc., 281; Study and teaching, 14655
Pharmacy, medicine and the Battle of
    Perryville, Kentucky, 14222
Phases of an inferior planet, 9625
Phases of life in town, 10692
Phelps, Amos Augustus, 1805-1847, 25364
Phelps, Frank T., 15153
Phelps, Humphrey, 4768
Phelps, Matthew, 1748(ca.)-1817, 4767
Phelps, Nicholas, 23466
Phelps, Samuel Shethar, 1793-1855, 25243
Phelps, William D., 23494
Phelps's travellers' guide through the U.S.,
    4768
Phemie Frost's experiences, 10873
Phemie's temptation, 10945
Phi beta kappa addresses, 1222, 2400, 21885,
    22865
Phi beta kappa, New York Alpha, Union
    university, 2078
Phials of amber full of the tears of love,
    2993
Phil-Ellena, Germantown, Pa., 11667
Phil Scott, 9715
Philadelphia (Frigate), 11965, 25345
Philadelphia; Anti-slavery convention, 1833,
    25244; Bank street church, 12425; Chamber

of commerce, 12080, 13322; Christ church, 21936; Commerce, 23106; Committee of arrangement for the Jackson obsequies, 1845, 22030; Councils, 207; Description, 2773, 4928, 11056, 11992, 13086; Description, Guide-books, 21820; Directories, 1756, 12676; First African Presbyterian church, 1840; History, 22272; History, Colonial period, Fiction, 8809; Mayor's court, 12834; Pennsylvania Hall, 2363, 25225; Pennsylvania Hospital, 23053; Politics & government, Civil war, 10925; Riot, 1849, 10204; St. Peter's church, 11977; Southwark Presbyterian church, 24935; Statistics, Vital, 22180; Union league, 7742, 7743, 25245; Wharves, 1033
Philadelphia Anti-slavery Society, 25246, 25247
Philadelphia County medical society, President, Addresses, 13218
The Philadelphia dun, 14242
Philadelphia female anti-slavery society, 534, 25248
Philadelphia Ladies' Anti-slavery Society, 25359
Philadelphia medical society, 1923, 2021
Philadelphian, pseud., 25158
Philaenus, Junius, pseud., A letter to Thomas Jefferson, 1807
Philalethes, pseud., 8816, 23511
The philanthropic results of the war in America, 1548
A philanthropist, 10600, 23772
Philanthropos, pseud., 25249
Philbrook, Horace W., 17380
Philip, 9304
Philip, King (Metacomet) sachem of the Wampanoags, d.1676, 12, 403, 12856; Drama, 2157; Fiction, 12856
Philip and his wife, 9377
Philip IV, 1605-1665, King of Spain, 6277
Philip V, 1683-1746, King of Spain, 6451
Philip Kearney, Fort, Massacre at, 1866, 16151-16153
Philip Nolan's friends, 9691
Philip Seymour, 10273
Philip Vernon, 10368
Philip Vickers Fithian, journal and letters, 3458
Philip Winwood, 10879
Philippine Islands, 7994; Commerce, 6161; Dept. of the Interior, 25251; Description & travel, 7639, 22252; History, 2467, 2468; Human slavery in the, 25782
Philips, George, 5456, 8228, 8229
Phillipia, a woman's question, 9302

Phillippo, James Mursell, 1798-1879, 4769, 23495, 25252
Phillips, A. & Co., 17381, 17382
Phillips, D. L., 17383
Phillips, Mrs. Horatio G., 1793-1864, 6457
Phillips, John, 25253
Phillips, John M., illustr., 7063
Phillips, Mount Vernon, 1902-, 15154
Phillips, Paul Chrisler, 1883-, 17325
Phillips, Samuel, 1752-1802, 714
Phillips, Semira Ann (Hobbs) "Mrs. T.G. Phillips," 17384
Phillips, Stephen C., 25534
Phillips, Stephen Clarendon, 1801-1857, 17385
Phillips, Ulrich Bonnell, 1877-1934, 25254-25259
Phillips, Wendell, 1811-1884, 7107, 7744, 25260-25263, 25690
Phillips, William Allison, 17386
Phillips family, 15640
Phillis, 23496
Philly and Kit, 8988
Philo, pseud., 25806
Philo Africanus, pseud., 24833
Philo-Bentham, pseud., 1180
Philo-Jackson, pseud., 13455
Philo-Xylon, 25264
Philology, Comparative, 22699
The philosophical & political history of the thirteen United States of America, 3527
Philosophical anthropology, 18041, 18382
Philosophical apparatus at Transylvania College, 13724
Philosophy, 18114; Addresses, essays, lectures, 18377, 18610, 18616, 19821; Collections, 19769; Periodicals, 21747
Philosophy, Argentine, 19821, 19992-19994, 20413, 20414, 21747; Brazilian, 18865, 19558, 20680; Brazilian, History, 19694; Greek, Pre-Socratic, 19734; Mexican, 18895; Modern, History, 20478; Spanish, 18344
The philosophy of human nature, 13730
The philosophy of mind according to Thomas Brown, M.D., 13727
Philothea, 8993
Philpot, Francis, 25265
Phinney, Jerry, see Finney, Jerry
Phips, Sir William, 1651-1695, 23309
Phoenicians, History, 23570
Phoenix Hotel, Lexington, 15582
Phoenixiana, 9392
Phosphate industry, Brazil, Jacupiranga region, 18269
Phosphate rocks of South Carolina and the "great Carolina marl bed," 12869

Phosphates, Kentucky, 15152; South Carolina, 12869
Photofission cross sections of ^{209}Bi, ^{232}Th and ^{238}U at intermediate energies, 19869
Photographs, Catalogs, 16769
Phrenology, 931, 3061, 13754, 13755, 13766, 25542
Phyle, Francis Adam Joseph, 1720(ca.)-1778, 527
A Phyllis of the Sierras, 9789
Physical education, Kentucky, 13848; Study and teaching, Curricula, 20597
Physical education and training, Audio-visual aids, 18346
Physical geography, 5586, 13004; Brazil, 22320; Canada, 7979; Chile, 18358; Costa Rica, 7620; Mexico, 6611, 8439; Mississippi valley, 12015, 12151; Nebraska, 15884; U.S., 3615, 8003, 13016, 13501, 16602; Venezuela, 19767
Physical survey of Virginia, 4417
A physician, 23835
Physician, patient privilege, 14676
Physician man power in Kentucky, 14373
Physicians, 2021; Biography, 3705, 3706, 13617, 14456; Cincinnati, 3286; Directories, Kentucky, 13557; Kentucky, 13616, 14373, 15209, 15778; Kentucky, Biography, 15561; Massachusetts, 23285; Norfolk Co., Mass., 132; Rome, 24693; Utah, 17524; U.S., 12462
The physician's wife, 10848
Physicienne (Corvette), 421, 422
Physics, 13724; Bibliography, 20023; Congresses and conventions, 20475
Physiognomy, 911
Physiology, 13730
Phytogeography, 13426
Phytoplankton, 18713
Pi, Juan, 18685
Pia opera pel riscatto delle fanciulle more, Genoa, 25266
Pianists, 3856
Piatt, John James, 1835-1917, 4770-4779, 4848
Piazza, Walter F., 19108
The piazza, 10346
The piazza tales, 10346
Pica, Chile, History, 19014
Pica en el siglo XVIII, 19014
Picard, Alfred, 1844-, 7494
Picaresque novels, Spanish, 18143
Pickard, Madge E.; 10166
Pickard, Samuel, b.1020, 23497
Pickens, Andrew, 1739-1817, 12729

Pickens, Francis Wilkinson, 1805-1869, 25267-25269
The picker and piler, 11183
Pickering, Joseph, 4789
Pickering, Timothy, 1745-1829, 75, 13495
The picket line and campfire stories, 7745
Pickett, Albert James, 1810-1858, 13456
Pickett, John T., 15156
Pickett, Joseph Worthy, 1832-1870, 17553
Pickett, LaSalle Corbell, "Mrs. G.E. Pickett," 1848-1931, 7746
Pickett, Thomas E., 15157
Pickett's infantry division (C.S.A.), 22310
Pickett's men; a fragment of war history, 22310
Pickings from the portfolio of the reporter of the New Orleans "Picayune", 9167
Pickle, Peregrine, pseud., 11040
A pic-nic at the sea-shore, 10197
Picó, Rafael, 7747
Picón Febres, Gonzalo, 1860-1918, 20428
Picton, Sir Thomas, 1758-1815, 2354, 11966
A pictorial description of the U.S., 5113
The pictorial field-book of the revolution, 13400
Pictorial guide to the Mammoth Cave, Ky., 4403, 13664
A pictorial history of Texas, 5413
Pictorial history of the civil war in the U.S.A., 4302
Pictorial life of George Washington, 22214
Pictorial Oregon, 17410
The pictorial sketch-book of Pennsylvania, 21811
A picture journey through tropical Mexico, 7472
Picture of a factory village, to which are annexed, remarks on lotteries, 23066
A picture of a picturesque country, 4790
Picture of Boston, 11442
A picture of pioneer times in California, 17872
The picture of Quebec and its vicinity, 11411
A picture of slavery, 25270, 25818
A picture of Woonsocket; or, The truth in its nudity, 23067
Picture-writing, Mexican, 6105, 6153, 6438
Pictures from Italy, 6588, 6589, 6591
Pictures from prison life, 12759
Pictures of an unland sea, 16968
Pictures of society and people of mark, 11182
Pictures of southern life, social, political, and military, 23559
Pictures of the patriarchs, 4094
Pictures of the Virgin and her Son, 8766

Picturesque America, 6214, 7173
Picturesque B. and Q., 4695
Picturesque California and the region
  west of the Rocky Mountains, 17244
Picturesque "Cheyenne and Arrapahoe(!)
  army life", 16448
Picturesque Mexico, 8422
Picturesque Panama, 6999
Picturesque sketches of American progress,
  2655
The picturesque tourist, 7748, 12852
Picturesque Utah, 17081
Pidgeon, William, 13457
A piece of red Calico, 10892
Pieces in prose and verse, 8945
Pierce, Franklin, pres. U.S., 1804-1869,
  11678, 25271
Pierce, George Foster, 1811-1884, 4791
Pierce, Henry Niles, bp., 1820-1899, 4792
Pierce, John, 1814-1840, 22321
Pierce, Lovick (port.), 14995
Pierce, William Leigh, 4793
Piercy, Frederick, illustr., 4281, 17387
Pierian Club, Lawrenceburg, Ky., 13686
Pierre, 10347; the partisan, 9848
Pierrepont, Edwards, 1817-1892, 7749
Pierson, Hamilton Wilcox, 1817-1888, 4794-
  4796
Pierson, Roscoe Mitchell, 15158, 15159,
  15447
Pietas in patriam, the life of His
  Excellency Sir William Phips, Knt.,
  23309
Pietro Ghisleri, 6501
Piett, Sam, 15160
Pike, Albert, 1809-1891, 3065, 4797-4800,
  17388
Pike, James, 1834-, 4801
Pike, Warburton Mayer, 1861-1915, 17389,
  17390
Pike, Zebulon Montgomery, 1779-1813, 4802,
  17391
Pike County, Ky., Economic conditions,
  14543; History, 14844; Maps, 14592
Pike county ahead!, 16356
Pike's Peak, Colorado, 3008, 3297, 3616,
  3987, 4803, 5573, 16674; Poetry, 12407;
  Views, 16049
The Pike's Peak region, 16245
Pikeville, Ky., Economic conditions, 14543;
  First Christian Church, Gleaners' Class,
  15161
Pikeville College, 14543
Pilaski, Alphonsus, 25272
Pilate and Herod, 10859
Pilcher, Louis, 15162, 15163

The Pilgrim, 5382
The pilgrim and the pioneer, 15959
Pilgrim fathers, 922, 11824, 12806, 13026,
  13027, 22106, 22005, 22143, 23826; Addresses,
  commemorations, etc., 4, 80, 219, 633, 711,
  1060, 1061, 1641, 1755, 1853, 1925, 2150,
  11731, 11925, 12306, 12386, 12578, 12790,
  12811, 12865, 13021
Pilgrim's letters, 5031
A pilgrimage over the prairies, 5055
The Pilgrims of Boston and their descendants,
  1506
A pill for Porcupine, 1945
The pillar of fire, 9984
Pills for the delegates, 12468
Pillsbury, Parker, 1809-1898, 25273-25275
The pilot, 9142
Pilot guides, 23052, 23823; Atlantic coast
  (North America), 2526, 2527; Atlantic ocean,
  530; Antarctic regions, 20121; Bahamas,
  1109; Caribbean sea, 362; Chile, 20120,
  20121; Haiti, 1109, 13464; Magellan, Strait
  of, 20155; Massachusetts, 11431; Mexico,
  Gulf of, 362, 5012; Pacific coast, 23549;
  Peru, 2391; Río de la Plata, 11393; Sandy
  Hook, 23376; West Indies, 1110, 5012, 7950
Pilots and pilotage, 6007
Pilsen, John, 13458
Pima Indians, 16951
Pim, Bedford Clapperton Trevelyan, 1826-1886,
  7750, 7751
Pimentel, Francisco, conde de Heras, 1832-,
  947
Pimentel, Maria Josefa Alfonso, duquesa de
  Benavente, 7321
Pimeria, Alta, 16951
Pinchon, 10827
Pinckard, George, 1768-1835, 25276
Pinckney, Charles, 1758?-1824, 295, 13459
Pinckney, Mrs. Eliza (Lucas) 1723-1793, 4804
Pinckney, Henry Laurens, 1794-1863, 12666,
  25277, 25765, 25766
Pinckney, Thomas, 1750-1828, 25278
Pine, 16416
The pine and the palm greeting, 5634
Pine knot, 2629
Pine Knot, a story of Kentucky life, 13619
Pinerolo, Italy, Battle of, 1630, 8323
Pinetum del Instituto Nacional de Investiga-
  ciones forestales, 19602
Piney Woods travern, 3762
Pingree, Enoch M., 1816-1849, 4059
Pinilla, Sabino, 1851-1909, 7752
Pink and black, 11191
Pink Marsh, 8479
The pink typhoon, 15286

Pinkerton, Elizabeth W., 15164
Pinkerton, John, 1758-1826, 23498
Pinkney, William, 1764-1822, 2364, 25279
Pinnacle Mountain, Ky., 15380
Pino, Pedro Bautista, 17392
Pinto-Escobar, P., 19103
Pintores venezolanos, 19651
Pintura venezolana, 19740
Pinzón, Leopoldo, 18620
Pinzón, Martín Alonso, 1440?-1493, 7305
Pioneer, 12241, 14243, 17181, 22261
Pioneer (ship), 7652
Pioneer biography, 14883
The pioneer bishop, 5302
The pioneer campfire, 16937
The pioneer church, 10716
Pioneer days in California, 16149
Pioneer days of Oregon history, 16209
Pioneer days on Puget Sound, 16363
A pioneer emancipator, 25280
Pioneer families of Clay County, Kentucky,
  15030
A pioneer from Kentucky, 14381
Pioneer history, 3870, 12307
The pioneer history of Illinois, 23528
Pioneer Kentucky, 13925, 14443
Pioneer life, Iowa, 17495; Texas, 17561
Pioneer life in and around Cedar Rapids,
  Iowa, from 1839 to 1849, 16154
Pioneer life in Kentucky, 14013
Pioneer life in Richland county, Ohio,
  10273
Pioneer life in the west, 3450
Pioneer Memorial State Park, Harrodsburg,
  Ky., 15165
The pioneer preacher, 16047
The pioneer press of Kentucky, 15144
A pioneer railway of the west, 14782
Pioneer record and reminiscences of the
  early settlement of Ross County, Ohio,
  14096
Pioneer tales of the Oregon trail and of
  Jefferson county, 16345
The pioneer to the Kentucky emigrant,
  14936
A pioneer voyage to California and round
  the world, 16228
Pioneer Weapons Hunting Area, 13917
Pioneering in the Far East, 16735
Pioneering in the San Juan, 16329
The pioneers, 9143
Pioneers, Arizona, 16874; Colorado, 16755,
  17591; Illinois, 23528, 23554; Kentucky,
  13969; Oregon, 17685; U.S., 14498
Pioneers and prominent men of Utah,
  16479

Pioneers of El Dorado, 17806
The pioneers of '49, 15903
The pioneers of Kentucky [New York] 1862,
  15166
Pioneers of Scioto County, 4169
The pioneers of the Klondyke, 16727
The pioneers of the west, 15453
Pioneers of Illinois, 17156
Les pionniers de Oregon, 16021
The pious constancy of Inez de Mencia Mont-Roy,
  10338
Pious memorials, 1732
The pirate, 10310
The pirate of the Roanoke, 8699
Pirates, 2123, 9962, 10074, 11363, 21765,
  22190, 22280, 23304, 23317, 24476;
  Caribbean, Fiction, 11195
The pirates of Cape Ann, 8614
The pirates of the prairies, 15825
El piropo, 20648
Pirotto, Armando D., 1907-, 18017
Pirtle, Alfred, 15167
The Pisgah book, 15362
Pisgah Church, Woodford County, Ky., 15769
Pitcairn island, 884, 1554, 10698, 23615
Pitcher, Nathaniel, 1685-1723, 23499
Pithole, Pa., History, 22760
A pitiful surrender, 10122
Pitman, Joseph S., 12403
Pitney, A. de F., illustr., 13704
Pitt, William, 1st earl of Chatham, 1708-1778,
  222, 11227, 13460
Pittenger, William, 1840-1905, 3417, 4805
Pittier, Henri, 1857-1950, 20392
Pittman, Hannah (Daviess) 1840-, 7753, 15168
Pittman, Phillip, 13461
Pitts, F. E., 15169
Pittsburgh, Description, 4320; Directories,
  13315; Fiction, 11224; History, 13315;
  University, Foster Hall collection, 14126
Pius IX, pope, 1792-1878, 23130
Pixley, Frank, 4904
Pizarro, Francisco, marqués, 1470-1541,
  Drama, 1544
A place in thy memory, 22081
Placer county, Calif., History, 16774
Plada Suárez, Washington, 18774
Plague, 13752, 21848
A plain and friendly persuasive to the
  inhabitants of Virginia and Maryland for
  promoting towns and cohabitation, 4378
A plain and seasonable address to the free-
  holders of Great Britain, 23500
Plain dealing, 13375
Plain facts, 13508
A plain state of the argument between Great-

Britain and her colonies, 13462
A plain statement addressed to all honest
  Democrats, 25281
Plain truth, 2318
The plain truth about California, 17417
The plains, being a collection of veracious
  memoranda, 4504
A plan for abolishing the American Anti-
  Slavery Society and its auxiliaries, 23835
Plan nacional de desarrollo, 1965-1969,
  18430
El plan nacional de desarrollo y la
  integración de la industria estañifera,
  18944
Plan nacional de vivienda, 18810
Plan of an improved system of the money
  concerns of the Union, 11342
The plan of reform in Transylvania
  University, 15100
Plan of the Danville Theological Seminary,
  15170
Planktological dictionary, 19132
Plankton, Argentine Republic, Mar del
  Plata, 18714; South Atlantic, 18711
Planning, Kentucky, 14868; Venezuela,
  20102
Planning machines, 1008
Plano de valorização econômica do vale de
  Sao Francisco, 19256
Plano orientador da Universidade de
  Brasília, 19222
Plano trienal de investimentos, 20013
Plantain, John, pirate, 2123
Plantation agriculture in Yucatan, 20083
Plantation life, 25014, 25254, 25410,
  25506
Plantation life before emancipation, 24961
Plantation life before the war, 25829
A planter, pseud., 25697
The planter, 2822
The planter's daughter, a tale of
  Louisiana, 24326
The planter's northern bride, 3846
The planter's plea, 23783
Plants, Diseases, Bolivia, 19129;
  Cultivated, 13426
Plaschke, Paul A., illustr., 15051
Plasencia Mord, Aleida, 18569
P'laski's tunament, 10460
El Plata Científico y Literario, 18632
Platería virreynal, 18745
Plato, 19728
Platon, Jean Georges, 1859-1917, 24129
Platón, Servillano, 1877-, 25251
Platonic love, 9249
Platte County, Neb., History, 17547

Platte County Self-defensive Association,
  Platte Co., Mo., 25282
Platte River, 5421
Plautus, Titus Maccius, 25852
Player-Frowd, J.G., 17393
Playfair, Hugo, R.N., pseud.?, 4806
Playfair, Robert, 4807
Playfair, William, 1759-1823, 22154
The Playfair papers, 4806
A plea for a miserable world, 328
A plea for Africa, 24434
A plea for the Indians, 1070
A plea for the South, 25004
Pleas for progress, 3819
Pleasant Hill, Ky., 14218, 14958
Pleasant Waters, 9017
Pleasants, Mary Minta, 1853-, 25283
Pleasants, William James, 1834-, 17394
Pledges (Roman law), 25946
Pleton, Sir Thomas, 1758-1815, 22787
El pleyto de Hernán Cortés con Panfilo de
  Narváez, 6328
Plinius, Caecilius Secundus, C., 24421
Plodder's promotion, 10112
The plough and the sword, 10760
Plover (Ship), 22556
Plum Grove, Kentucky, 15461
Plum, William Rattle, 4808
Plumb, Ralph, 1816-1903, 25496
The plumb idiod, 9582
A plumb pudding for the humane, chaste,
  valiant, enlightened Peter Porcupine, 21847
Plumbe, John, 17395, 23501
Plumero the Good, 9254
Plummer, Mrs. Clarissa, 4577, 12698
Plummer, Henry, d.1864, 16392
Plummer, Mary Wright, 1856-, 7754
Plummer, Mrs. Rachel, d.1839, 17349
Plummer, W. Kirtman, illustr., 15476
Plummer, William, 1789-1854, 25284
Plymouth, Mass. Cushman monument, 22005
Plymouth Co., Mass., 24413; Description
  & travel, 9602
Pneumatic-tube transportation,13068
Poa pratensis, 14024, 14723
Población y desarrollo económico, 19846
Pocahontas, d.1617, 3190, 4667, 11187,
  11735, 22489, 24607; Drama, 1447, 4667;
  Fiction, 9111, 11187; Poetry, 22489
Pocket gazetteer of United States, 15036
The pocket guide to the West Indies, 5950
The pocket piece, 8633
Poçohda Cruz (Açude), 20000
Poda de lavid, 18458
Podolampacea, 18712
Poe, Edgar Allan, 1809-1849, 4809

351

Poe, John William, 1850-1923, 7755
A poem, 816
The Poem which the Committee of the town
of Boston had voted unanimously to be
published with the late oration, 179
El poema de la creación, 18608
Poema del retorno, 19772
Poemas ao outro, 20623
Poemas de la vida simple, 18082
Poemas de Mexico, 6646
Poemas desde la cárcel, 18253
Poems, 3470, 3821, 4306, 4423, 4848, 5048,
5395, 5470, 5667, 5669, 5738
Poems, national and patriotic, 3150
Poems, original and translated, 3152
Poems and essays, 3960
Poems and parodies, 2933
Poems and tales, 8790
Poems by a slave in the island of Cuba,
recently liberated, translated from the
Spanish, 24969
Poems by Eleanora May Bell, 13651
Poems by Ellis, 3374
Poems by Samuel Browning, 1604
Poems of America, 4294
The poems of Duval Porter, 4831
The poems of Frank O. Ticknor, 5416
Poems of house and home, 4777
Poems of Orelia Key Bell, 2666
Poems of the Confederacy, 5261
Poems of the Mohawk valley, 11657
Poems of the prairies, 11569
Poems of the Rt. Rev. George Burgess, 1701
Poems of the war, 11325
Poems of two friends, 4778
Poems on man in the republic, 10326
Poems on several occasions, 3713
Poems on the abolition of the slave
trade, 25285
A poesia, 20657
The poet, 14094
The poet and nature, 13803
The poet soldier, 1659
A poet's message, 6227
The poet's praise, 5242
El poeta, 20638
Poetas guayaneses, 18538
A poetess, 9575
Poética, 19192
Poetical pen-pictures of the war, selected
from our union poets, 22371
A poetical picture of America, 4966
A poetical rhapsody on the times, 1945
The poetical works of Elizabeth Margaret
Chandler, 2969
Poetry, Collections, 4692; Early works to

1800, 24421; History & criticisms, 19192,
20657
Poetry for the times, 25286
Poetry of places, Canada, Quebec, 22907;
Colorado, Pike's Peak, 12407; Guatemala,
7233, 7234, 7237, 7238; Honduras, Comayagua,
18520; Iowa, 11569; Italy, Pompeii, 9492;
Kentucky, 14431; Maine, Pemaquid, 12515;
Mexico, 6448, 6646, 7233, 7234, 7237, 7238,
7323; Mississippi River, 22225; Niagara
Falls, 1331, 1672, 22526; Panama, 6849;
Rhode Island, 1575; Sucre, Bolivia (City),
18383; Venezuela, 18534
The poetry of travelling in the U.S., 3603
Poets, Colombian, 19195; Canadian, 6549;
Ecuadorian, 19569
The poets and poetry of America, 3701
The poets and poetry of Texas, 3258
The poets and poetry of the West, 3043
Poets of Appalachia, 1813-1975, 15136
Poets of Ohio, 15644
Poeyana, serie A, 18018
Poezdka v Meksiku, 8011
Poganuc people, 10908
Pohlkamp, Diomede, 15171
Poindexter, George, 1779-1853, 4810, 12972
Poinsett, Joel Roberts, 1779-1851, 7756
The point of view, 10015
Point Pleasant Battle of (Dunmore's War),
15424
Pointon, Mair, 2980
Poisons, 13660
Pokeguma, Battle of, 15939
Pokonchi language, Grammar, 2366, 6769, 6799
Poland, Luke Potter, 1815-1887, 25768
Poland and liberty, 10197
The polar world, 22322
Polenz, Wilhelm von, 1861-1903, 4811
Poles in the U.S., 4586
Policarpo Bonilla, 7451
Police, Argentine Republic, 18495; Barbados,
18823; Brazil, 20424; Louisiana, St.
Landry Parish, 25431; Uruguay, Pensions,
18774
Police, Traite de la, 11884
The police control of the slave in South
Carolina, 24588
Police power, Quebec, 11884
Policy, as well as honesty, forbids the use of
secular force in religious affairs, 622
A policy for the economic development of
the Northeast, 19273
Política científica y organización de la
investigación científica en la Argentina,
18436
Política de desarrollo nacional, 20165

Política de desenvolvimento do Nordeste, 19801
Una política de transportes para Chile, 19512
Política dos negocios, 19671
Política educacional de Guatemala, 20088
Política exterior de Panamá, 19934
Política fiscal en la Argentina, 18426
Política indiana, 8073
Política industrial, 19672
Política lusitana en el Río de la Plata, 18397
La política minera desde el punto de vista sindical, 18600
Política y huelga bancaria, 19966
Political abolition exposed, 25332
A political account of the island of Trinidad, 11966
Political action against slavery, 25287
Political annals of the present united colonies, from their settlement to the peace of 1763, 21863
Political ballads and songs, American, 13050
The political beginnings of Kentucky, 13721
The Political Club, Danville, Kentucky, 15426
Political conventions, 16343
A political creed, 15172
Political division, British Columbia, 6175
Political economy, founded in justice and humanity, 25693
The political economy of slavery, 5041
The political effects of the paper system considered, 13487
Political essay on the kingdom of New Spain, 7088, 7089
Political essays, 12191
Political ethics, 1999, 6779, 9098, 12642, 13151
The political family, 13017
The political green-house, for the year 1798, 229
Political history of secession, to the beginning of the American civil war, 24628
The political manual, 23107
Political parties, 16939; Great Britain, 22126; Kentucky, 14169; New York (State), 13195; U.S., 1746, 6888, 8888, 6938, 12866, 13487, 21846, 22989
Political philosophy, 11547
A political primer for the new voter, 15944
The political record of Senator F.A. Sawyer and Congressman C.C. Bowen, of South Carolina, 22937

Political science, 59, 60, 1181, 1606, 6579, 11547, 11781, 12077, 12443, 13042, 22082, 22089, 22439, 23341; Addresses, essays, lectures, 13084, 23075, 23116, 23387, 24470; Periodicals, 19750
The political sermons of the period of 1776, 23699
Political tracts, 13258
Political transactions in and concerning Kentucky, 14835, 14836
The politician, 10492
The politician's register, 23356
The politicians, 10326, 23345
Politico-economic considerations in the Western Reserve's early slave controversy, 25358
Politics, Fiction, 9889; Poetry, 5218
Politics and pen pictures at home and abroad, 3874
Politics and the pulpit, 25288
Politics for American Christians, 1999
Politics in Ohio, 2978
Poliuto, pseud., 5709
Polk, J.M., 1838-, 7757
Polk, James Knox, pres. U.S., 1795-1849, 13197, 21875, 22644
Polk, Jefferson J., 1802-, 4812
Polk, R. ↓., pub., 17397, 17398
Polk family, 7757
Polk Station, Ky., 15674
Pollard, Edward Albert, 1828-1872, 4813-4822, 5144, 25289, 25290
Pollard, Hugh Bertie Campbell, 1888-, 7758
Pollard, The romance of, 8955
Pollen, A.H., illustr., 8074
Polley, Joseph Benjamin, 1840-, 4823, 17399
Pollock, J. M., 17400
Pollution, Environmental, 20561
Polly, 10466
Polly Oliver's problem, 11160
Polvo y espanto, 18509
Polygamy, 12887
Polynesia, 8406, 8407; Description & travel, 1172, 10345, 16981
Polytechnic society of Kentucky, Louisville, 13818
Pombo, Rafael, 20711
Pomeroy, Samuel Clarke, 1816-1891, 25291
Pomeroy, Swan Lyman, 1799-1869, 24625
Pomfret, Conn., History, 13015
Pomfrey, J. W., 15173
Pompeii, Poetry, 9492
The Ponca removal, 16728
Ponce, Alonso, 16th cent., 5874, 18185, 20205
Ponce de León, Juan, 1460?-1521, 18717
Ponce, Puerto Rico (City) Feria-exposición,

1882, 17946
Pond, Fred E., 3758
Pond, Gideon Hollister, 1810-1878, 17401, 23535
Pond, Samuel William, 1850-1916, 17401
Pond Creek, Ky., Maps, 14592
Pondon, Samuel William, 1806-1891, 17401
Pons, François Raymond Joseph de, 1751-1812, 2473
Pons, Jacques Samuel, 1035
Ponte, Miguelina, 18913
Ponteach: or, The savages of America, 23548
Pontiac: or, The siege of Detroit, 22823
Pontiac's conspiracy, 1763-1765, 22571, 23548; Drama, 22823
Pony tracks, 17469
Pool, Maria Louise, 1841-1898, 8969
Poole, Mrs. Annie Sampson, 7759
Poole, De Witt Clinton, 1828-, 17402
Poole, T. W., 4304
Poole, William Frederick, 1821-1894, 13053
Poor, Peabody, 15174
Poor, Great Britain, 686; Massachusetts, 23253
Poor Caroline, the Indiaman's daughter, 10882
A poor fellow, 10547
Poor laws, 5882; Great Britain, 12337
Poor Mr. Ponsonby, 10546
The poor old slave, 25292, 25829
The poor rich man, and the rich poor man, 10728
The poor scholar, 9702
The poor unhappy transported felon's sorrowful account of his fourteen years transportation in Virginia, 4934
Poor whites in the South, 3902
Poosey Ridge, Madison County, Ky., Description, 14970
Pope, Alexander, 1688-1744, 2917, 13782
Pope, Dunbar H., 4825
Pope, John, 4824, 5520, 15175
Pope, Nancy, 13954
Pope, Richard M., 15176
Pope, Samuel, 1826-, 25293
Pope, William F., 1814-1895, 4825
Popes, Temporal power, 24788
Popham colony, 12748
Poplars, 18636
Popocatepetl, 2186
Popoluca language (Vera Cruz), Dictionaries, Spanish, 20208
Popp, Stephan, 1755-, 4820
Popp's journal, 1777-1783, 4820
Poppaea, 9261
População e desenvolvimento, 18816

Popular actions, Cuba, 18221
Popular essays on naval subjects, 22928
Popular excitements, 780
Popular fallacies relating to the American question, 25722
Popular resorts, 2583
Population, 18816, 19562, 20215, 20560, 21861, 21950; Chile, 19230; Kentucky, 15789
Population growth in Kentucky, 1820-1960, 14327
The population of the Valley of Teotihuacan, 7483, 7484
Population policy, 18716
Populism and national awareness in Latin America, 18092
Por las rutas del sureste, 8290
Por las tres Américas, 6561
Por los campos de México, 7235, 7236
Porcher, Francis Peyre, 1825-1895, 4827
Porcupine-Chiltat districts, 6181
Porcupine, Peter, pseud., 5841
Porcupine's works, 1940
Port Hudson, La., Siege, 2587
Port Royal (S.C.) expedition, 1861, 22765
Port Royal, Jamaica, Description, 22481
Port Talbot, Ont., 12074
The portal of dreams, 13733
Portalis, Albert Edouard, 1845-, 4828
Porter, Albert Gallatin, 1824-1897, 25294
Porter, Barton B., 1832-, 17403
Porter, David Dixon, 1813-1891, 4829
Porter, Duval, 1844-, 4830, 4831
Porter, Ebenezer, 1772-1834, 23355
Porter, Edward Clarke, 1836-1876, 12521
Porter, Fitz-John, 1822-1901, 7157, 7312, 7325, 8373
Porter, Kenneth W., 17404
Porter, Mrs. Lavinia Honeyman, 17405
Porter, Peter Augustus, 1827-1864, 11704
Porter, Valentine Mott, 1870-1915, ed., 16914
Porter, William Trotter, 1809-1858, 4832, 4833, 22356
The Port-folio, 4879
Pórtico al Quijote, 20679
A portion of life's voyage, 22219
Portland, Me., Commerce, 13103; First parish, defendant, 856
Portland, Ore., Description, 4350, 17408, 17409
Portland family, Leaves from the life of a, 8508
Porto Alegre, Brazil, Instituto Tecnológico do Rio Grande do Sul, Boletim, 19178
The portrait, 10510
Portrait and biographical album of Henry county, Iowa, 7760

A portrait of a girl, 13530
The portrait of a lady, 7124
A portrait of the times, 2904
Portraits of Kentuckians, 14154
Portraits of my married friends, 11143
A portraiture of Quakerism, 21951
Portraitures of Hebrew character, 10616
Portsmouth, N.H., 137; Churches, 135;
  Description, 1488; History, 1488;
  North Church, 22538; Social life &
  customs, 10182
Portsmouth anti-slavery society, 11798
Les Portugais d'Amérique: souvenirs
  historiques de la guerre du Brésil en
  1635, 22083
Portugal, 696, 1551; Armada, History,
  1543; Bibliography, 82; Biography, 23131;
  Colonies, 1551, 19375; Colonies, Africa,
  West, 23870, 23874, 24966, 24967, 24968;
  Colonies, Period.,379; Commerce, Africa,
  25031; Description & travel, 3228, 5087,
  7223, 7224, 22751; Foreign relations,
  Netherlands, 104, 340; History, 11397,
  23131; History, Modern, 1580-, 1543;
  History, Period of discoveries, 1385-
  1580, 882, 23199; Kings and rulers,
  23131; Ministerio das colonias, 23870;
  Treaties, etc. 1834-1853 (Maria II),
  24519
Portuguese in India, 882
Portuguese language, Brazil, 19662, 20003;
  Dialects, 19568; Dictionaries, 18995;
  Grammar, 17963, 19497; Study and
  teaching, 17963
Portuguese literature, Bibliography, 82;
  Early to 1500, 19530; Magnetic
  recordings, 18054
Portuguese philology, Addresses, essays,
  lectures, 21733
Portuguese planters and British
  humanitarians; the case for S. Thomé,
  24968
Portuguese slavery, Britain's dilemma,
  24566
Portus Novi-Archangelisensis, 16001
Posada Gutiérrez, Joaquín, 1797?-1881, 7761
Posadas, Gervasio Antonio de, 1757-1832,
  7762
Posie, 9053
The position and course of the South,
  23709, 25720
The position of Christianity in the United
  States, 2000
Posselt, Louis, 7763
The possessed, 8555
Possession (Roman law), 24495, 24962,

25272, 25562
Possibilidades da utilização de carga pré-
  reduzida nos altos-fornos para o caso
  brasileiro, 19509
Post, Mrs. Amy (Kirby) b.1802, 24169
Post, Christian Frederick, 1710-1785, 23503
Post, Truman Augustus, 17416
Post, Truman Marcellus, 1810-1886, 17416
The post-mistress of Laurel Run, 6965
Postage stamps, 6555; Central America,
  History, 19060; Cuba, 18958; Mexico, 20081
Postal service, 6555; Brazil, 19374;
  Confederate States of America, 11873;
  Guatemala, 18853; Mexico, 19843, 20081;
  Mexico, Laws and regulations, 18047; Rates,
  959; U.S., 894, 22519; U.S., Charlestown,
  Mass., 552; U.S., History, 2801, 3449, 5336;
  U.S., Rates, 23352; The West, 16993
Postl, Karl Anton, 10717-10719, 15344
Poston, Charles Dibrell, 1825-1902, 4834
A pot of gold, 9575
Potatoes, Sweet, 14010
Pote, William, 1718-1755, 7764
The Potiphar papers, 9289
The Potomac and the Rapidan, 4875
Potomac company, 21908
Potomac River, 4136, 4232
Potomac Valley, Description & travel, 8051;
  Historic houses, etc., 8051
El potro adulterio, 19990
Potter, Albert W., 17417
Potter, Alonzo, 1800-1865, bp., 2321
Potter, Andrew Jackson, 1830-1895, 16625
Potter, Eliza, 4835
Potter, Israel Ralph, 1744-1826?, 23504
Potter, Theodore Edgar, 1832-1910, 17418
Potter, William James, 1830-1893, 7765
Potter, Woodburne, 4836
Potter Creek Cave, Cal., 17621
Pottery, Venezuela, 18007
Potthast, Edward, illustr., 25639
Potts, Benjamin Franklin, 1836-1889, 16921
Potts, Daniel T., 4837
Potts, Mrs. Eugenia Dunlap, 4838, 15177,
  25295
Pouchot, Pierre, 1712-1767, 7766
Poultry, 1731
Poultry industry, Maceió, Brazil, 18786;
  Parnaíba, Brazil, 18787
Pouponne et Balthazar, 3218
Le pour et le contre, 1495
Pousa, Horacio, 19980
Poussielgue, Achille, 25296
Poussin, Guillaume Tell, 1794-1876, 7767
Poverty, Kentucky, 13743, 14891
O povo no poder, 18559

Powder maker, Hortense, 4839
Powell, Aaron Macy, 1832-1899, 25297
Powell, Anna D., 15178
Powell, Edward Lindsay, 1860-1933, 15178
Powell, Harriet, fl.1839, 25584
Powell, James Augustus, 1808-1828, 12996
Powell, John J., 17419-17421
Powell, John Wesley, 1834-1902, 17422
Powell, Lazarus Whitehead, 1812-1867, 14578, 25298
Powell, Lewis Thornton, called Lewis Payne, 1845-1865, defendant, 1305
Powell County, Ky., 14259
Powell family, 12996
Power, Frederick Dunglison, 1851-1911, 15179
Power, John Carroll, 1819-1894, 23505
Power, John Hamilton, 1798-1873, 25299
Power, Mrs. Sarah A. (Harris 1824-, 24505
Power, Tyrone, 1797-1841, 4840
The power of Christian benevolence, 22505
The power of religion upon the mind, 1732
The power of the commander-in-chief to declare martial law, 6669
The power of the "S.F.", 9482
Power to sell land for the non-payment of taxes, 1377, 1378
Power's guide to Mexico for the motorist, 7677
Powers, Caleb, 14355, 15038, 15180, 15181
Powers, Elvira J., 4841
Powers, Frederick William, 14182
Powers, George Whitefield, 1833 or 4-1903, 4842
Powers, Laura Bride, 17423
Powers, Stephen, 4843, 23506
Powers, William, 1765-1856, 5754
Powhatan Indians, 429
Pownall, Thomas, 1722-1805, 4844, 12432
Pozo y Honesto, José del, 7768
The practicability of the abolition of slavery, 25475
Practical considerations founded on the Scriptures, 25300
Practical essays on medical education, 3292
Practical lessons under the code duello, 9910
Practical notes made during a tour in Canada, 6718
Practical views of Catholicity, 9881
The practice of duelling in view of human and divine law, 2807
Prado, Caio, 18036
Prado, Pedro, pseud., 0000
The prairie, 9144

Prairie and mountain life, 3443
Prairie and Rocky mountain adventures, 5561
The prairie-bird, 4570
Prairie du Chien, Wis., 1613; Description, 3894; History, 16443
Prairie farming in America, 6271
The prairie flower, 2683
A prairie infanta, 2812
Prairie Grove, 11244
The prairie province, 6941
The prairie schooner, 16810
Prairie sketches, 16473
The prairie traveler, 4388
Prairiedom, 4675
Prairies, 4027
Prantl, Adolfo, 7769
Prat de Saba, Onogre, 1733?-1810, 7770
Pratt, Harry Edward, 1901-, 7771
Pratt, John F., 16274
Pratt, John J., 4845
Pratt, Minot, 25301
Pratt, Orson, 1811-1881, 4846, 17424
Pratt, Parley Parker, 1807-1857, 17425, 23507
Pratt G., Rodrigo, 20182
Pratt family, 21870
Pratt family (John Pratt, d.1655), 21870
Pratt family (William Pratt, d.1678?), 21870
Pratter, Henry, 4664
Prayer for the oppressed, 25691
The prayer of the presidents, 6257
A preacher and a shrine, 13884
Preaching, 617, 7954, 22894
Preamble and resolutions of the legislature of Kentucky, 14580
Preble, William Pitt, 1783-1857, 13463
Precaution, 9145, 9146
Prece ao vento, 20511
Los precios del acero, 19943
Precious metals, 1866, 6702, 17676, 22657
Precious stones, Brazil, 18751
Precipitación diaria en milimetros, 20493, 20494
Précis de deux lettres avec une réflexion générale sur l'état présent de la colonie de Surinam, 25435
El predicador, 7954
Predpriiatle (ship), 22740
Pre-emption law, U.S., 4910
Preemption rights to Kentucky not possessed by the Indians, 15489
Preface, 10338
Prehistoria de la región pampeana sur, 18626
The prehistoric men of Kentucky, 15791
Prejudice, 8630
Prejudices, 9702
Preliminary studies of the Texas Catholic

356

historical society, 5368
Premio Blanes, 18762
The premises of Dorothea, 9376
La prensa en Mexico, 19827
Prentice, Archibald, 1792-, 4847
Prentice, George Denison, 1802-1870, 4848,
  4849, 14309, 15183, 15676
Prenticeana, 4849
Prentis, Noble Lovely, 1839-1900, 4850,
  7772
Prentiss, A., 17426
Prentiss, Charles, 1774-1820, pub., 246
Prentiss, Samuel, 1782-1857, 25302
Prepost, Istvén, 5783
Presas y paisajes del agro mexicano, 6122
Presbrey, O.F., 7773
Presbury family, 6286
Presbyterian church, 13433, 14322;
  Doctrinal and controversial works, 4893;
  First, Lexington, Ky., 15184, 15185;
  First, Lexington, Ky., History, 15320;
  Hymns, 464; Sermons, 848, 1063, 1065,
  1216, 11317, 12507, 22264, 23785, 23786,
  25525
Presbyterian church in America, 15793
Presbyterian church in Delaware, 2264
Presbyterian church in Kentucky, 13806,
  13974, 14457, 15191, 15545
Presbyterian church in New Hampshire,
  Clergy, 11416
Presbyterian church in New York, 22568
Presbyterian church in North Carolina,
  22908
Presbyterian church in the U.S.A., 674,
  853, 16838; Biography, 141; Board of
  foreign missions, 2375; Board of
  publication, 674, 22678; Catechisms and
  creeds, Chippewa, 2375; Clergy, 23775;
  Directories, 15062; Executive committee
  of publication, 464, 25303; General
  assembly, 1326, 24510, 25305, 25594;
  History, 22484; History, Civil war,
  25791; History, Schism, 1837-1870,
  11564, 25541; Kentucky, 4866, 14064,
  14097, 15322; New School, Presbytery
  of Philadelphia, Third, 13357;
  Ohio Valley, 15186; Old school,
  11564; Old School, Board of
  Publications, 25304; Periodicals,
  3167; Presbytery of Cincinnati, 15186;
  Presbytery of Ebenezer, 15321;
  Presbytery of Lexington, Ebenezer, 15321;
  Presbytery of Ohio, 1326; Presbytery of
  West Lexington, 15321; Synod of Kentucky,
  4851, 4852, 15187-15190; Synod of
  Kentucky (South), 13806; Synods, South

Carolina, 25306
Presbyterian church in Wisconsin, 11857
Presbyterian church (U.S.), Bowling Green,
  Ky., 16191
Presbyterianism, 16074
Presbyterians in Kentucky, 13918, 14852,
  14878, 15323
Prescience, 5477
Prescott, George F., 17009
Prescott, William Hickling, 1796-1859, 7774,
  7775, 23278, 23508, 23509
La prescripción extintiva y la caducidad, 19854
Presencia de Francia en la cultura colombiana,
  20242
Presencia de humo, 20453
Present and extinct lakes of Nevada, 17539
The present and future productions of Florida,
  4580
The present condition and future prospects
  of the country, 24882
The present crisis, 2143
A present for the Whigs of '76 & '37, 13353
The present problem, 8818
The present state of Algiers, 1425
The present state of Great Britain and North
  America, 4487
The present state of North America, 13046
The present state of Nova Scotia, 12854
The present state of the British empire in
  Europe, 4853
The present state of the country and
  inhabitants, 2966, 23510
The present state of Virginia, 3805, 4108
Presente y futuro de la filosofía en la
  Argentina, 19994
Presente y futuro de la lengua española, 20407
The preservation of Land Office records, 15306
The preservation of the state united, 12056
Preserve Indian Peoples' Environment (PIPE),
  14162
President (Steamship), 1619
President Lincoln, 15384
The President's death and its lessons, 21858
The President's policy; speech on the policy of
  the President for the restoration of the
  Union, 23981
Presidential candidates, 902
Presidential control of the extended state,
  18704
Presidential document, 25307
The presidential election, 13455
Presidential succession, Argentine Republic,
  18417
Presidents, U.S., 6257; Biography, 280;
  Election, 431, 1817, 8099, 22854; Election,
  1825, 22855; Election, 1840, 7594; Election,

1860, 6938; Election, 1868, 22989;
Powers and duties, 937, 6669, 11361,
11914, 13083, 22397, 22402
Press, Charles, jt. author, 14312
Press, Great Britain, 226; History, 1983;
U.S., 1983, 11356; Venezuela, 19753
Press congress of the world, Regional
convention, Mexico, 1931, 6673
Press law, Colombia, 20333
Pressa Carrillo, Isabel de la, 8277
Preston, George C., 1875
Preston, Henry C., 22661
Preston, Mrs. Margaret (Junkin) 1820-1897,
4854, 4855
Preston, Walter, 2046
Preston, William, 1816-1887, 15192
Preston, William Campbell, 1794-1860,
4856, 25308
Preston, William Thomas Rochester, 1851-,
7776
Preston family (John Preston, d.1753),
13452
El presupuesto del estado, 19502
Presupuestos familiares en el area metro-
politana de Caracas, 18736
Prêto, Manuel, 18666
Prétrel, Louis Nicolas, 1705-1765, 11742
Pretty Mrs. Gaston, 9113
The pretty sister of José, 8909
A pretty story written in the year of our
Lord 2774, 9919
Previdéncia social no Estado de Rio de
Janeiro, 19326
Prevost, Antoine François, called Prévost
d'Exiles, 1697-1763, 211
Prevost, Sir George, 1st bart., 1707-1816,
21918
Prewitt family, 15193
Price, George Frederic, d.1888, 17428
Price, Isaiah, 1822-, 4857
Price, James Franklin, 15194
Price, Morgan Philips, 1885-, 4858
Price, Paul P., 15195
Price, Richard, 1723-1791, 12304, 13390,
23189, 23436, 23776
Price, Robert, 25309
Price, Sir Rose Lambart, bart., 1837-1899,
7777, 17429
Price, Samuel Woodson, 15196, 15197
Price, Thomas, 4275, 25414
Price, Thomas W., 7778
Price, William Newton, 1831-1905, 4859
Price, William Thompson, 1845-1920, 4860
Price's Missouri expedition, 1864, 12796
The price of gold and the presidency, 25310
The price of liberty, 10489

The price of peace, 8454, 9916
The price of the harness, 9217
Prices, 3084, 11684, 19564, 19620; Bibliography,
18409; Confederate States of America, 11871;
History, 17676; Kentucky, 14911
Prichard, Walt, illustr., 15053
Prichard, William, fl.1782-1809, 10317
Pricilla, 9463
Prida y Arteaga, Francisco de la, 1850-, 7779
Priddy, Dottie, 14615
Pride o' the jug, 13830
The pride of Britannia humbled, 1941
The pride of the Mercers, 3225
Priest, Mrs. Deborah (Beach) b.1768, 10569
Priest, Josiah, 1788-1851, 11573, 25311, 25312
Priest, William, 4861
The priest of El Paso, 10863
The priest of the black cross, 9615
The priest's turf-cutting day, 10282
Priestley, Herbert Ingram, 1875-1944, 4862,
6863
Priestley, Joseph, 1733-1824, 7270
Prieto, Julio, illustr., 5969
Prigg, Edward, 25313
Primavera triunfante, 20460
Prime, Nathaniel Scudder, 1785-1856, 25314
Primer centenario de los primeros sellos
postales de Centro America, 19060
El primer llanto, 19823
Primeros ensayos constitucionales del Mexico
independiente, 18064
Primeros sueños, primeros espejismos, 19649
Los primeros 25 años de industrializacion en
Puebla, 19913
The Primes and their neighbors, 4088
Primitive Baptists, North Carolina, Kehukee
primitive Baptist association, 11619
Prince, Benjamin F., 1840-, 25315
Prince, Frederick Octavius, 1818-1899, 6869,
23988
Prince, Le Baron Bradford, 1840-1922, 17430
Prince, Thomas, 1687-1758, 23236, 23394, 23511
Prince Albert (Ship), 1116, 1117, 8050
Prince Edward Island, 23193; Description &
travel, 13279, 22482; History, 8337
The prince of darkness, 10842
A prince of good fellows, 10021
The prince of India, 11054
The prince of Parthia, 2427
The prince of the House of David, 4008
The Prince of Wales in Canada and the U.S.,
8418
Prince Saroni's wife, 9814
Princess, 10262
The princess Aline, 9361
The Princess Casamassima, 7125

Princess I-would-I-wot-not, 9916
The princess of the moon, 10576
The Princess Sonia, 10305
Princeton (Frigate), 1768, 11648, 12057
Princeton, Ky., First Baptist Church, 14887, 15198
Princeton, Mass., Congregational church, Mutual council, 732; History, 12636
Princeton university, 8712, 12376, 22272; Alumni association of Nassau hall, 1257, 22849; Class of 1763, 22109
A Princetonian, 8712
Principe (Island) West Africa, 25113
Principia queda ex quibus procedendum, 6362
Principios de derecho de jentes, 18956
Principios de economía minera 18718
Principios de ética, 19531
Principios físicos del transistor de juntura, 19180
The principles of civil union and happiness considered and recommended, 12303
The principles of naval staff rank, 1919
Principles of the revolution, 1412
Pringle, Edward J., 25316
Prinsep, Charles Robert, 1789-1864, 23578
Printing, 1693; Cuba, 18913; Dictionaries, 23537; Exhibitions, Rio de Janeiro, 19289-19291; History, Brazil, 18702, 19289; History, California, 16282; History, Cuba, 611; History, Fiction, 10497; History, Kentucky, 6445, 7380, 7885, 15144, 15537, 15746; History, Louisiana, 7885; History, New York (state), 22198, 22486; History, North Dakota, 17112; History, Spanish America, 8187; History, Utah, 17111; Kentucky, 13855, 15011; Periodicals, 23513; Utah, 17110; Practical, 18250; Public, Confederate States of America, 2054
Printing and collections of printing in Kentucky, 15537
Printing guide, 14693
Printing the old ways, 14223
Prinz Heinrichs Amerika-fahrt, 4228
Priscilla, 767
Prismatics, 9196
The "Prison journal" of Stephen F. Austin, 5968
Prison life in the Old Capitol, 5728
Prison life in the South, 2487
Prison-life in the tobacco warehouse at Richmond, 3793
Prison prose and poetry, 10057
The prisoner of Perote, 11023

The prisoner of war, and how treated, 4970
A prisoner of war in Virginia, 4867
Prisoners, Personal narratives, 18970
Prisoners of conscience, 8737
The prisoners of Niagara, 9890, 14342
The prisoners of Perote, 8100
Prisoners of war and military prisons, 4031
The prisoners' memoirs, 356
Prisons, 608, 12675, 12957, 13766, 18970, 23948; Columbia, 20277; Kansas, 17480; Kentucky, 13953; Mexico, 18025; Michigan, 24463; Missouri, 17480; New York (State), 2279; Pennsylvania, 2289; Peru, Laws and regulations, 20458; U.S., 3115, 3229, 4129, 11988
Prisons of air, 9101
Prisons without walls, 10825
Pritchard, John, 7780
Pritchett, John Perry, 16660
Prittie, Edwin J., illus., 16467
Pritts, Joseph, 15199
Privacy, Personal, 14616
Private enterprise, 18598
Private Jones of the Eighth, 10122
Private presses, Kentucky, 15537; Lexington, Ky., 15523
The Privateer of '76, 9051
Privateering, 411, 1143, 1204, 1221, 1980, 11950, 23549
The privateers of the revolution, 10880
A privilege, a duty, an opportunity for Kentucky, 15200
The privilege and dignity, 25317
The privilege of the writ of habeas corpus under the Constitution, 6082, 11272
Privileged statements (legal), 20462
The prize essay, 10415
A prize essay on fairs, 22142
Prize law, 12222; France, 12298
Pro-slavery convention of the state of Missouri, Lexington, Mo., 1855, 25488
Pro-slavery overthrown; and the true principles of abolitionism declared, 24896
Probability, 19157
Probate law and practice, New Hampshire, 11755
The probe, 13348
The problem solved, 9883, 24484
Problemas de las zonas áridas de México, 7468
Problemas del trópico mexicano, 7469
Proceedings of a board of general officers, 354
The proceedings of a Court of enquiry, 12687
Proceedings of a general court martial for the trial of Major General Arnold, 466
Proceedings of a general court martial of the line, 467
Proceedings of the general court martial

convened for the trial of Commodore
James Barron, 880
Proceedings of the Grand Lodge of
Kentucky, 14139
Proceedings of the High court of
impeachment, 2323
Proceedings of the impeachment of
William Blount, 11296
Proceres, 1810, en el sesquicentenario de
la independencia, 18756
El proceso creador, 19954
El proceso didáctico de la lección, 19236
Proceso político de Francisco Isnardy,
17986
A process in the Transilvania presbytery,
4893
The procession of life, 9823
Proclamation of emancipation, 7781
The proclamation of freedom, 25898
Procter, Addison Gilbert, 1838-, 7782
Proctor, Edna Dean, 1829-1923, ed., 1058,
10163
Proctor Knott on Duluth, 14767
The prodigal father, 9741
La producción rural argentina en 1968,
18794
Produce trade, 18819; Colombia, 20335
Production functions for the industrial
sector of Peru, 19209
The production of I-131 in IPR-R1 reactor,
19703
Productividad, 19980
Products liability, 14664
The profane swearer, 10580
Professional licensing in Kentucky, 15333
Professional responsibility, Report of
seminar on, 14680
Professions, Licensing of, Kentucky,
14221
Professions, Regulation of, 15333
Professor Phantillo, 10298
Professor Pressensee, materialist and
inventor, 9114
Professor Rafinesque, 15201
The professor's daughter, 8793
The professor's skylarking, 9330
The professor's story, 9905
The professor's wife, 10275
Profit sharing and pension plans, 14668
Profits on manufactures at Lowell, 11686
Program of exercise in commemoration of
the centennial anniversary of the visit
to Lexington of the Marquis de Lafayette,
15202
Programa pedra preciosas, 18751
Programación de obras y proyectos por el

método P.E.R.T., 20542
Programas de estabilización en América Latina,
20619
Programas especiais na área do Ministério dos
Transportes, 18288
The programme of peace, 25926
The progress of America, 7368
The progress of the age, and The danger of the
age, 22441
Progressive petticoats, 10672
Prohibition, 1534, 1916, 11603
Project Mackau (Du), 23979
Projeto de constituição, 19270
O projeto do código civil, 19658
Projeto Gráfica da UnB, 19225
Projeto Orquestra Sinfônica de Brasília, 19226
Projeto Tungstenio/Molibdênio, 19293
Prólogo y epílogo de la batalla de Maipú, 20519
Promendade à travers l'Amérique du sud,
Nouvelle-Grenade, Équateur, Pérou, Brézil,
22223
Promenade en Amérique, 5891
Promenades et chasses dans l'Amerique du Nord,
5568
Prometheus, a meditation, 14992
The prominent families of the U.S.A., 6255
Promissory notes, Kentucky, 24715
Promotion of medical science, 2081
Prontuario geográfico de la República
Mexicana, 7518
La pronunciación del español en América, 19726
Properties of plants and flowers, 23281
Property (Roman law), 25434
Property, Mexico, 18875
The prophet of the Great Smoky mountains, 4563
The prophet of the West, 3545
The prophetic pictures, 9827
Proportional representation, 12273
A proposal for altering the eastern front of
the city of Philadelphia, 1033
A proposal for establishing by act of
Parliament the duties upon stampt paper,
13494
Proposals for a subscription to form colonies
in Canada, 12350
Proposals relating to the Education of Youth
in Pensilvania, 2319
The proposed slave empire, its antecedents,
constitution, and policy, 25040
Proposicion, y manifiesto, 7734
Propositions for amending the Constitution of
the United States, 12793
A proprietor, 25524
Prosapia Fennah, 20212
Prösch, Thomas Wickham, 1850-1915, 17431
Prose and verse, 10500

Prose sketches and poems, 4799
The prose writers of America, 3702
The prosecution of Mrs. Dullet, 10465
A prospect from the Congress-gallery, 1942
The prospect of peace, 817
The prospects of art in the United States, 1227
Prosper's "old mother", 6977
Prostitution, 2642, 14074; Kentucky, 15585; Lexington, Ky., 13718, 13833, 14164, 14352, 15597; Los Angeles, Cal., 17507; Louisville, Ky., 14164; New Orleans, 25125
The protective policy in literature, 1984
The protégé, 11024
A protégée of Jack Hamlin's, 6971, 9790
Protest of the state of Louisiana to the Senate of the United States, 25318
Protestant Episcopal Church in Kentucky, 13814
Protestant Episcopal Church in Mexico, 6883
Protestant Episcopal Church in the U.S.A., 2943, 2944, 3015, 5643, 12818, 14389, 15454; Board of Missions, 3267, 3790; Board of Missions, Domestic committee, 4863; California, 16955; Clergy, 167; Doctrinal and controversial works, 22577; Eastern diocese, 12453; Government, 11337; History, 11694, 13510; Lexington (Diocese), 13748, 15203; New York, Diocese of, 22690; Pastoral letters and charges, 13166; Sermons, 979, 1211, 1740, 12453, 22134, 22715, 23492; Virginia (Diocese), 23010
Protestant Episcopal Society for the Advancement of Christianity in South-Carolina, 24435
Protestant Episcopal Society for the promotion of evangelical knowledge, New York, 358
Protestantism, 1998, 4937
Protestants in Mexico, 19901
Protestants in Mississippi, 13305
El protocolo de Rio de Janeiro, 18196
Proud Mahaska, 17384
Provence, Description & travel, 4227
Providence (ship), 6192
Providence, R.I., Citizens, 25319; City Council, 7783, 11832; First Baptist Church, 12528; First Congretional Church (Unitaria⁻), 12565; History, 23653
Providence and government of God, 13063
Providence Anti-slavery Society, 25320
Providence Society for Abolishing the Slave Trade, 25231, 25232

Providential escape, 11173
The province of law in distinction from that of truth, 11806
A provincia de Santa-Catarina nas guerras do Uruguai e do Paraguai, 19108
Provincial papers, 11419
The provisional government of Nebraska territory, 16262
Provost, Etienne, 1782-183-?, 15882
The prowess of the Whig Club, 2423
Prowse, Daniel Woodley, 7784
Proyecciones de la población de México, 1960-1980, 18984
Proyecto de ley sobre abolición de la esclavitud en la isla de Puerto-Rico, 24592
Proyecto para el establecimiento en México, 7401
Prthibī parikramā, 6413
Prudence Palfrey, 8502
Prud'homme, Louis Arthur, 7785
Prue and I, 9290
La prueba en el proceso civil guatemalteco, 18067
Pruett, Rebecca K., 15204
Prussia, Description & travel, 11974
Prussing, Eugene Ernest, 1855-, 25322
Prutsman, Christian Miller, 4864
Pryor, Albert C., 13867
Pseudacanthocera Lutz, 20543
Psicoanálisis y Argentina en una novela, 19047
Psicometría escolar, 18902
Psicopatología de Bolivar, 19761
La psique o personalidad del delincuente, 19721
Psychiatry, Argentine Republic, 19011; Ecuador, 21721
A psycho-physical study, 9331
Psychology, 13730; Religious, 1406; Study and teaching, 19573
Psychometrics, 19959
Public administration, 15638, 15639, 18353, 19349, 19886; Argentine Republic, 18426; Brazil, 18654; Chile, 20151
Public drama and common values in two Caribbean islands, 17955
Public education in Kentucky, 14575
Public employee labor relations, 14688
Public health, 20094; Brazil, 19377, 19401, 20379, 20382; Colombia, 20279; Cuba, 18366; Kentucky, 13557, 13951, 14633; Pennroyal region, Ky., 13608; Venezuela, 20419
The public land system of Texas, 1823-1910, 17106
Public lands, Laws and regulations, 18243
Public lands of Wyoming, 16175
Public libraries, 19534
Public Library of Kentucky, 14100

The Public library paper, 15205
Public library services, 14625
Public morals, 157
Public opinion, 22944
Public relations, 20098
Public school finance in Jefferson
  County, 15057
Public schools, California, 17696;
  Massachusetts, 23087; South Carolina,
  218; U.S., 795
Public service commissions, 14689
Public utilities, Laws and regulations,
  14689; Rates, Kentucky, 14776
Public utility, 15206
Public welfare, Argentine Republic,
  Bibliography, 18456; Brazil, 19406;
  Brazil, Laws and regulations, 19359;
  Costa Rica, 20612; Kentucky, 13648;
  Latin America, Bibliography, 20400
Public works, Brazil, 19406
Publishers and publishing, Brazil, 18702;
  Colombia, 20270; U.S., 3234
Publishers and stationers trade list
  directory, 1867-1869, 21859
Publishers' uniform trade list directory,
  21859
El puchero, 7386
Puckett, Ellen, 17433
Puckett, Garrett E., 15207
Puckett, James Louis, 1863-, 17433
Puddleford, and its people, 10620
The Puddleford papers, 10621
Puebla, Mexico, 6077-6079, 6270;
  (Archdiocese), 7669; Description,
  6159, 744?; History, 6158
Pueblo Indians, 8673, 17175, 17488
Puelles, José María de Jesús, 17434
El puente maldito, 19200
Puerto Jimenez, Costa Rica, 19005
Puerto Montt, 20134
Puerto Quepos, Costa Rica, 19006
The Puerto Rican economy and United States
  economic fluctuations, 18679
Puerto Rican literature, Bibliography,
  18315
Puerto Rico, 8264, 17946, 25734;
  Bibliography, 7305, 18315; Description
  & travel, 3, 2252, 6595, 6907, 6948, 7049,
  7639, 7747, 16031, 19944; Description &
  travel, Guide-books, 8264; Economic
  conditions, 18674, 18679; History, 7305,
  19227; History, To 1898, 3; History,
  Periodicals, 6107; Laws, statutes, etc.,
  24592, 25323, Politics & government,
  11340, 23013, 24079, 24291, 24592, 25509,
  25787; Politics & government, To 1898,

18717; Politics & government, 1898-1952,
  20250; University, Mayaguez, College of
  Agriculture and Mechanic Arts, 18311;
  University, Rio Piedras, 18128; University,
  Rio Piedras, Institute of Caribbean Studies,
  18604; University, Rio Piedras, Library,
  18315
Puerto y Salgado, Nicolas del, bp., d.1681,
  5856
Puertos en el territorio antárctico de Chile,
  20135
Puertos en la costa de Arauco, 20136
Los puertos libres mexicanos, 18068
Puffer Hopkins, 10326
Puget Sound, 6151, 16363
Pugh, George Ellis, 1822-1876, 25324
Pulaski, Kazimierz, 1748-1779, 13266; Fiction,
  13403
Pulaski County, Ky., Description, 15409
Pullen, William H., 25325
Pullen-Burry, Bessie, 1858-, 7786
The pulpit of the American revolution, 23699
Pulpit sketches, 23018
Pulszky, Ferencz Aurelius, 1814-1897, 4865
Pulszky, Terezia (Walder), 4865
Pumarino Valenzuela, Mario, 18676
Pumpelly, Raphael, 1837-1923, 17435
Pumping machinery, Early works to 1800, 806
Punch, 8334
Punch, brothers, punch!, 9032
Punderson, Lemuel S., 788
Punishment, 7242, 12300; Pennsylvania, 2289
Punnebaker, C.D., 14631
The pupil, 7122
A pupil of Chestnut Ridge, 6977
The pupils of Marvel hall, 1114?
The puppet, 10674
Puppets and puppet plays, 20046
Purdom, Billy Joe, 15208
The purification and reconstruction of the
  American union, 2250
The Puritan and his daughter, 10490
A Puritan pagan, 9262
The Puritan's daughter, 9384
Puritans, 1654, 2150, 11536, 11865, 22097
Purnell, Linda B., 15494
Puros cuentos, 18049
Purple eyes, 10238
The pursuit of the house-boat, 8685
Purviance, David, 1766-1847, 4866, 15292
Purviance, Levi, 4866
Purviance, Samuel A., b.1809, 25326
Pusey, William Allen, 1865-1940, 15209
Pustule, Malignant, 1085
Put to the test, 8960
Putnam, Alfred Porter, 1027 1906, ed., 24253

Putnam, Frederic Ward, 1839-1915, 15111, 15210
Putnam, Israel, 1718-1790, 22065, 22602
Putnam, Mary Burham, 25327
Putnam, Mrs. Mary (Lowell) 1810-1898, 25328, 25329
Putnam, George, 1807-1878, 7787, 11437
Putnam, George Haven, 1844-1930, 4867, 7788
Putnam, George Palmer, 1887-1950, 17437
Putnam, George W., 4868
Putnam, Israel, 1718-1790, 1882, 11930, 13011
Putnam, Joseph Duncan, 1855-1881, 17776
Putnam, Rufus, of Chillicothe, Ohio, 15096
Putnam, Sallie A. (Brock) "Mrs. Richard Putnam," 1845?-, 4869
Putnam, Samuel Henry, 4870
Putnam's magazine, 1853-1870, 10298, 23019
Putnam County, Ill., History, 2274
Putnam County, N.Y., History, 1402
"Putting yourself in her place," 9426
Putumayo River, 8193, 25772
Puységur, Antoine Hyacinte Anne de Chastenet comte de, 1752-1807, 13564
Pyatt, Charles Lynn, 1886-, 15556
Pye, S., 25330
Pyle, Howard, 1853-1911, illustr., 9376
Pynnshurst, 10296
Python, pseud., 25360
Pythonomorpha, 22239

Qarra, N.M., 2915
Quackenbos, George Payn, 23512
Quacks and quackery, 3291
The Quadrat, 23513
The quadroon's triumph, 4283
The quadroone, 4009
Quadros, Janio, Pres, Brazil, 1917-, 19800
Quaife, Milo Milton, 1860-, 3696, 25331
The Quaker City, 10217
A Quaker forty-niner, 17346
Quaker marriages, births, deaths, slaves, 24451
The Quaker soldier, 10066
The Quaker vindicated, 23514
The Quakers Farewel to England, 23515
Quakers in Pennsylvania, 14453
The Quakers in the old Northwest, 24868
Qualey, Carlton C., 17438
The quality of mercy, 9951
Quandary, Christopher, pseud., 23516

Quandt, Christlieb, 1740, 23517
Quantrill, William Clarke, 1837-1865, 15862, 16263, 16323, 16407, 22829
Quantrill and the border wars, 16263
Quarantine, 13771; Pennsylvania, 13218
The quare women, 14158
Quark-parton fragmentation functions, 20222
Quarré, Jean Hugues, 1580-1656, 22749
Quarry slaves, a drama, 24069
The quarter loaf, 9916
A quarter past six, 10283
A quarter race in Kentucky, 4833
Quarterly Christian spectator, 23518
Quatorze mois dans l'Amérique du Nord, 5484
Quaw, James E., 25332
Que ceux qui ont une âme lisent ceci, 7790
¿Que es la archivistica? 18260
¿Que es la reforma agraria? 20028
Qué publicó la prensa venezolana durante la dictadura, 19753
¿Que representa Ecopetrol para Colombia? 19096
¿Qué sabe usted de víboras? 17948
Queal, William G., 25333
Quebec (City), Description, 25, 22357; Description & travel, Guide-books, 11411; History, 7008, 7687, 22357; Religious institutions and affairs, 11254; St. Louis theatre, 5863; Siege, 1775-1776, Drama, 11482; Université Laval, 6307
Quebec (Province), 899; Description & travel, 4204, 4691, 6128, 6214, 8393, 13117, 25690; Description & travel, Guide-books, 1034; Description & travel, Poetry, 22907; History, 1441; Laws, statutes, etc., 7791, 22828; Legislature, Legislative assembly, 12426; Politics & government, 7791, 11782, 12426, 21918; Superior court, 1167
Quebec, The harp, and other poems, 22361
Quebec campaign, 1750, 21984, 22729, 23817
Quebec campaign, 1759, 8412, 12474; Fiction, 10060; Poetry, 12771, 12948
Quebec Hill; or, Canadian scenery, 22907
Queechy, 11097
Queen Charlotte (ship), 6600
Queen City, Tales and sketches from the, 3284
Queen Krinaleen's plagues, 9075
The queen of bedlam, 10123
The queen of islands, 2957
Queen of spades, 10653
The queen of the coral cave, 8702
Queen of the woods, 15316
The queen's garden, 9350
Queen's rangers, 5153
The queen's sailors, 9663
The queen's twin, 10042

Queenie Hetherton, 9903
The queens of American society, 12022
Queensland, Description & travel, 12165
Queiroz, Jerônimo Geraldo de, Homens de palha, 18170
Quellenburg, Henrik van, 6798
Quélus, D. de, 23519
Quen, Jean de, 1603-1659, 23520
Quentin, Karl, 4871
Quer durch Mexiko vom Atlantischen zum Stillen Ocean, 7975
Querbeuf, Yves Mathurin Marie Treaudet de, 1726-1797, 2466
Queretaro, Mexico, Description, Bibliography, 18648; History, Bibliography, 18648
The querist, 23521, 23522
Quesada, Ana de, 20060
Quesada, Vicente Gregorio, 1830-1913, 4872, 7792
Quesne, J. S., 4209
The quest for fortune, 10731
The quest of Heracles and other poems, 4345
The quest of Mr. Teaby, 10043
The question, "How far is slavery prohibited by the Christian religion and the Holy Scriptures?" impartially examined, 24404
The question before Congress, various phases of the race question, 25062
The question before us, 12493
Question cubaine, 25334
A question in slavery, 25335
A question of honor, 10972
La question Riel, 7793, 8155
A question unanswered, 14394
Questions and answers, Periodicals, 5889
Questions and expositions of slavery, obtained from those who have experienced it, 25221
Quevedo y Zubieta, Salvador, 1859-, 7794
Quick, Thomas, 1734-1796, 6822
The quick or the dead?, 11013
A quiet road, 4918
Quijano Otero, José María, 1836-1883, 7322
Quijano Quesado, Alberto, 7795
Quill Lake history, 7796
Quill Lake, Sask. School, 7796
Quilmes, Description, 18142; History, 18142, 20645
Quilmes a través de los años, 20645
The quilt, a pageant of Kentucky's Jewry, 15133
Quincy, Edmund, 1681-1738, 12644
Quincy, Edmund, 1808-1877, 7797, 25336

Quincy, Josiah, 1772-1864, 4873, 7797, 23280
Quincy, Samuel Miller, 1833-1887, 4874
Quincy, Ill., Anti-slavery Concert for Prayer, 1842, 25337; Biography, 23526; Bridges, 11849; History, 15873, 23526
Quincy, Mass., First church of Christ, 22296
Quindio, Colombia (Dept.), Description & travel, 18339
Quindio, Colombia (Province), Social conditions, 20352
Quiner, Edwin Bentlee, d.1868, 23523
Quinine, 227, 7560
Quint, Alonzo Hall, 1828-1896, 4875, 4876
Quintana, Jorge, 8109
Quintana, Juan Nepomuceno, La intolerancia politico-religiosa vindicada, 19780
Quintard, Charles Todd, bp., 1824-1898, 4877
Quirk's Scouts, 4287
Quiroga Méndez de Sotomayor, Vicente, 6657, 8278
Quiroz, Manuel de, bp., d.1699, 5856
The quirt and the spur, 17543
Quisenberry, Anderson Chenault, 1850-1921, 4878, 15211-15215
Quisenberry, Joel T., 14106
Quitman, John Anthony, 1799-1858, 3003, 24533
Quito, Colegio real de San Fernando, 7461; Colegio seminario de San Luis, 7461; Description, 19232; Museo de Arte e Historia, Publicaciones, 18124
Quito monumental y pintoresco, 19232
Qorpo-Santo, pseud., 19716, 19717
A quiver of arrows, 9330
Quivira, 3547, 16503, 17564
Quodlibet, 10095
Quozziana, 10100
Qvattro orationi di M. Bartolomeo Spathaphora di Moncata, 25578

RA-3 reactor nuclear de experimentación y producción, Informe sobre el, 18406
Rabe, Johann E., 7798
Rabstvo v drevnosti, 25037
"Raccoon John" Smith, 13861
Raccoons, 15208
A race for a wife, 9976
A race for liberty, 2864
The race for life, 3373
The race of the swift, 14032
Race problems, 1823, 22100, 24021, 24878
Race question, 24237

Races of maize in the West Indies, 19513
Races of mankind, 9613
Rachel, 9562
Rachel and the New world, 1024
Rachel Dyer, 10410
Rachel's lovers, 10465
The Raciad, 3108
Racine, Jean, 1639-1699, 19156
Rack, Edmund, 1735?-1787, 11992
Radical Political Abolitionists, 25338
Radical rule, 25339
Radio, History, 15675
Radio addresses, debates, etc., 14156
Radio broadcasting, 14651, 19955, 20355;
  Argentine Republic, 18497; Colomiba,
  19955
Radisson, Peter Esprit, 1656-1685(?), 7785,
  7799
Radius 100 years, 14071
Rae, John, illustr., 15397
Rae, John, 1813-1893, 434, 4880, 17439
Rae, William Fraser, 17440
Rafinesque, Constantine Samuel, 1783-1840,
  4881-4883, 6153, 13775, 14030, 14152,
  14449 , 15201, 15216-15234, 15405, 15589,
  15774
Rafn, Carl Christian, 1795-1864, 1005
The raftsman of the Susquehannah, 9985
Ragged lady, 9952
Ragland, Thomas, 12135
The rag-man and the rag-woman, 9683
Rahman, Abdul, 13819
Raht, Carlysle Graham, 17441
Raids and romance of Morgan and his men,
  3507
Railey, William Edward, 15235-15237
Railroad engineering, 17324
Railroad routes to the Pacific, 5499
Railroads, 3035, 4219, 14504; America,
  22872; Brazil, 12519, 18347, 19344;
  Canada, 6319, 5323, 6552, 6704, 7331;
  Cuba, 12141; Early works to 1850, 12762;
  Employees, 10930; Georgia, 709; Kansas,
  4995; Kentucky, 14006, 14549, 14637,
  14859, 15066, 15707; Laws and regulations,
  Brazil, 19344; Laws and regulations,
  Kentucky, 14858; Laws and regulations,
  Tennessee, 14858; Latin America, 20416;
  Management, 10930; Massachusetts, 1420,
  23250, 23251; Mexico, 8079, 8315;
  Nebraska, 17915; New England, 12762;
  New Jersey, 2407; Oregon, 17374;
  Pennsylvania, 21842; U.S., 1860, 3596,
  5370, 11862, 17324, 23106, 23779; U.S.,
  Directories, 292; U.S., History, 14840,
  16398; Wisconsin, 22743

Railroads and state, 2407
Railway economy, 4219
Raimond, C.E., pseud. of Elizabeth Robins,
  4983-4988
Rain and rainfall, 806; Sao Paulo, 20445
The rainbow of gold, 2520
Raines, Caldwell Walton, 1839-1906, 16799,
  17442, 17939
Raines, Jeffrey, 15722
Rainier, Mount, 17437
Rainier, Peter William, 4884
Rains, George Washington, 1817-1898, 4885
Raisin river, Battle of, 1813, 15875
Raising the wind, 10736
Raking straws, 9265
Raleigh, Sir Walter, 1552?-1612, 7800, 22680
Raleigh's Roanoke colonies, 1584-1590, 768,
  13309
Ralph, Julian, 1853-1903, 4886
Ralphton, 8848
Ralston, Robert, 1761-1836, 11932
The Ralstons, 6502
Ramage, James A., 15238
Ramberg, Carl August, 1873-1915, 4887
A ramble of six thousand miles through the
  U.S.A., 4639
A ramble through the U.S., 3719
A ramble through the U.S., Canada, and the
  West Indies, 5132
The Rambler, 4888
"Rambler," pseud., 4889
The rambler in Mexico, 7249
The rambler in North America, 4225
A rambler in the West, 13067
Rambles about Portsmouth, 1488
Rambles about the country, 3358
Rambles and reveries, 11022
Rambles and scrambles in North and South
  America, 5319
Rambles by land and water, 7589
Rambles in America, past and present, 4680
Rambles in Chile, 10574
Rambles in Mammoth Cave, 3125
Rambles in the path of the steamhorse, 2771
Rambles in the Rocky mountains, 4529
Rambles in the U.S. and Canada during the
  year 1845, 4043, 7134
Rambles in Yucatan, 7590
The rambles of Fudge Fumble, 8923
Ramblings in California, 17592
Ramel, Jean Pierre, 1768-1815, 366
Ramírez, José Fernando, 1804-1871, 6644,
  7802
Ramírez Báez, Carmen Celeste, 17443
Ramírez de Aguilar, Fernando, 1887-, 7801
Ramírez de Mendoza, Francisco, 6677, 6678, 6687

365

Ramirez Lavoignet, David, 7730
Ramirez Olarte, David, 1952-, 20649
Ramirez S., Alvaro, 20335
Ramiz Galvão, Benjamin Franklin, 1846-1938,
  18160
Ramon, the rover of Cuba, 10586
Ramón y Rivera, Luis Felipe, 1913-, 18392
Ramona, 10005
Ramp, A.T., pseud., 3261
Ramsay, Allan, 8480
Ramsay, David, 1749-1815, 4890
Ramsay, James, 1733-1789, 25340
Ramsay, John, 23646
Ramsey, Hugh, 6790
Ramsey, William, 1013
Ramsing, H. U., 7803
Ranch life, 15831, 16092; North Dakota,
  16426, 16469, 16793, 17586
Ranch notes in Kansas, Colorado, the
  Indian territory and Northern Texas,
  15831
The rancheros of the poisoned lance, 10069
Ranchers and sovereignty, 17497
Ranches in the Great American Desert, 16092
Ranching, sport and travel, 16158
Ranching as I found it, 17400
Ranching with lords and commons, 16288
A ranchman's recollections, 16716
Rancho del Muerto, 10125
Ranck, George Washington, 1841-1900, 4891,
  14031, 15239-15242
Ranck, Glenn N., 17445
Rand, Asa, 1783-1871, 24780
Randal, Thomas, 2987
Randall, James Garfield, 1881-, 24041
Randall, P. K., 4892, 17446
Randall, Samuel Sidwell, 1809-1881, 261
Randel, Jesse F., 3970
Randolph, 10411
Randolph, Anson Davies Fitz, 1820-1896,
  pub., 23004
Randolph, Helen Fitz, 15243
Randolph, Innis, 7804
Randolph, John, 1773-1833, 708, 3572, 6428,
  8232, 10952, 10953, 23656
Randolph, Peter, 25341
Randolph, Peyton, 1721-1775, 12468
Randolph, Thornton, pseud., 10509
Randolph Co., Ill, Citizens, 25342;
  Directories, 23444; History, 23444
Randolph Co., W.Va., Description &
  travel, 4157
The Randolph epistles, 23946
Random recollections of a long life, 1806
  to 1876, 17579
Random shots and southern breezes, 5349

Rangel, Leyla Castello Franco, 19336
A ranger of commerce, 4725
The ranger of Ravenstream, 9298
The ranger of the Gulf, 9720
The rangers and regulators of the Tanaha,
  481
Rankin, Adam, 1755-1827, 4893-4895,
  13833
Rankin, Arthur, 25498
Rankin, Frank, 15244
Rankin, Jeremiah Eames, 1828-1904, 7805
Ranschoff, Joseph, 15245
Ransom, H.C., illustr., 9553
Ransom, John L., 4896
Rantoul, Robert, 1805-1852, 22150, 23259,
  25343
Raousset-Bourbon, Gaston Raoul, comte de,
  1817-1854, 8308
Rape, Chile, 18342
Rape of the gamp, 10320
Raphael Inglesse, 9390
Raphaelis Landivar Rusticatio mexicana, 7237
Raphall, Morris Jacob, 1798-1868, 24031,
  24342, 25344
Rappaccini's daughter, 9823
Rapport van den Gouverneur van Suriname
  omtrent de ontworpen Nederlandsche West-
  Indische ontginningen handelmaatschappij,
  25811
Rapport sur les missions du diocèse de
  Québec, 5227
The rapture of Hetly, 9529
A rare and new discovery, 12734
Rare books, 14702, 15363, 19240
Rare books and very special collections at
  Berea College, 15137
Rascoe, Burton, 15249
Rasgo épico, 5803
Rasgos biográficos para la historia de la
  vida pública del general Guzmán Blanco,
  18130
Rasles, Sebastien, 1657-1724, 16956
"Rasmus", 10465
Rasmussen, Vilhelm, 1869-, 4897
Raster, Hermann, 1827-1891, 7806
Der rathgeber und wegweiser für auswanderer
  nach den Vereinigten Staaten von
  Nordamerika und Texas, 5755
Rathmoll, William, 17447
Rationalism, 18378
Ratliff, Beulah Amidon, 17448
Rattlehead's chronicles, 8924
Rattles and rhymes, 5583
Rats, Parasites, 20675
Ratzel, Friedrich, 1844-1904, 7807
Raumer, Friedrich Ludwig George von, 1781-

1873, 4898
Rauscher, Frank, 4899
Ravellings from the web of life, 8936
Ravenia, 9435
Ravens Creek, 15246
Ravines, Rogger, 19141
Ravoux, Augustin, bp. 1815-1906, 17449
Raw materials, Brazil, Statistics, 19429
Rawlings, Thomas, 7808, 7809
Rawlins, Joseph L., 17450
Raxworthy's treasure, 9817
Ray, William, 1771-1827, 25345
Ray's recruit, 10126
Raymond, Daniel, 1786-1849, 24483
Raymond, Grace, pseud. of Annie Raymond
    Stillman, 5283
Raymond, Henry Jarvis, 1820-1869, 25346
Raymond, James, 1796-1858, 25347
Raymond, Jill, 14410
Raymond, Samuel, 7810
Raymond family, 7810
Raynal, Guillaume Thomas François, 1713-
    1796, 4900
Rayner, Kenneth, 1808-1884, 25348
Raynolds, William Franklin, 3816, 4901
Razón de la vigilia, 18514
Rea, Alonso de la, 7811
Read, Benjamin Maurice, 1853-, 17451, 25349
Read, Jesse, 11619
Read, John Meredith, 1797-1874, 25350
Read, Oliver, d.1803, 11173
Read, Opie Percival, 1852-1939, 4902-4907,
    15247-15249
Read, William George, 24356
Readers, Elementary, Spanish, 18222
Readers and speakers, 1800-1870, 12936,
    13667, 21883, 22733; Geography, 6776
Reading, 19236
Reading (Elementary), 18673
The reading parties, 10197
Ready-reckoners, 23511
Reagan, Albert B., 17452
Reagan, John Henninger, 1818-1905, 17453,
    25351
Real estate, 13592, 14214; Costa Rica,
    20182; Hardin County, Ky., 14262
El Real Hospital Nuestra Señora del Pilar
    en el siglo XVIII, 18366
Real life in the backwoods, 16523
The real North America pocket guide book,
    6090
A real pirate, 10338
Real property, 1254; Arkansas, 2739;
    Babylonia, 24248; Florida, 13503;
    Menard Co., Ill., Maps, 6169;
    Muskingum Co., Ohio, Maps, 1068;

Paraíba, Brazil (State), 20377;
    Sacramento, Cal., 12838; San Francisco,
    16445, 17867; U.S., 12555, 12556, 24879;
    Virginia, 24879; West Indies, 22013
The real thing, 7126
The real United States and Canada pocket
    guide-book, 6091
La realidad del derecho, 18567
Realities of life, 10600
Reality, 9731, 11033
Reality in romance, 8662
Realizaciones y proyectos para la reforma
    carcelaria y penitenciaria, 20277
A realized ideal, 10306
Rear Admiral Goldsborough, 13202
Reavis, Logan Uriah, 1831-1889, 7813, 17454
Rebecca, 10680
A rebel cavalryman with Lee, Stuart, and
    Jackson, 4655
The rebel general's loyal bride, 8615
The Rebel invasion of Maryland, 13140
Rebel invasion of Missouri and Kansas, 12796
The rebel of Dorchester, 10774
Rebel private, front and rear, 3471
A rebel war clerk's diary at the Confederate
    states capital, 4113
A rebel's recollections, 3355
A rebelião dos jovens, 18122
La rebelión de 1767 en el Tucumán, 17997
The rebellion: its origin and mainspring,
    25651
A rebellious heroine, 8686
Rebello, Carlos, 20692
The rebels, 8994
Rebels and tories, 10158
The rebuke of secession doctrines, 23525
Rebullosa, Jaime, 7814
Receipts, 13128
Receitas mágicas, 20068
Recent carnival of crime, 9035
Recent exploring expeditions to the Pacific,
    13200
The recent mammals of Tamaulipas, 18212
The recent past from a southern standpoint,
    5734
Reception of George Thompson in Great
    Britain, 24062
Recherches sur la législation cambodgienne
    (droit privé), 24804
Recherches sur leurs [nègres] facultées
    intellectuelles, 12421
Recinos, Adrián, 1886-, 18916
Reciprocity, 12738, 12954
The reciprocity treaty, 12738
Récit d'aventures dans le nord-ouest, 6010
Récits de voyages, 5059

Reck, Philipp Georg Friedrich von, 1710-1798, 4908
Réclamations pour les colonies des Antilles, 7815
Reclus, Elisée, 1830-1905, 7494
The recluse of Jamestown, 2923
The recluse of the Conewaga, 8715
Recognition (International law), 1142, 12231
Recollects, Missions, 6511, 6512, 23563
Reconciliation, 10919
La reconquista española de Chile en 1814, 5893
Reconstruction, 361, 1585, 2250, 3155, 3546, 4818, 7290, 7562, 11868, 12265, 12958, 13329, 16542, 22913, 22987,23934, 23944, 23953, 24130, 24233, 24334, 24478, 24596, 24658, 24704, 24727, 24729, 24787, 24802, 24843, 24943, 25027, 25612, 25673, 25768, 25887; Fiction, 9383, 10467, 10992, 24275, 24298, 24300, 25212, 25529, 25713; Georgia, 2124, 2227, 4796, 25339; Louisiana, 11928, 25318; Mississippi, 8344, 25056, 25059; Poetry, 25063; Speeches in Congress, 472, 1004, 22147, 24702, 24763, 24878, 25049; Tennessee, 2323; Texas, 17921; Virginia, 12265
Reconstruction and amendments of the Constitution, 24763
Reconstruction in America, 24727
Reconstruction on "my policy", 11868
The Record of news, history and literture, 25352
Recording and registration, Costa Rica, 20591
Records management and state archives, 14626
Recreation, Kentucky, 13611, 13848, 13917
Recreations of long vacation, 1025
A recruit at Christmas, 9363
Recruiting and enlistment, 12230
The rector of St. Bardolph's, 10748
The rectory of Moreland, 10956
El recurso de inconstitucionalidad, 18221
La red, 19630
The red-blooded, 16053
The red box, 10197
The Red Coats, 10881
Red Cross, 11451
The Red Eagle, 4434
The red men of Iowa, 16566
The Red Mile, 1875-1977, 15250
The Red Mile, 13522, 14820
The red republic, 8966
Red River, 4626, 6311
Red River Colony, 16135

The Red River country, 7922
Red River Gorge, land of arches, 15628, 15629
Red River Gorge Legal Defense Fund, Lexington, Ky., 15251
The Red River insurrection, 5813
Red River of Canada, Description, 7922
Red River of Kentucky, 14814, 15251, 15536, 15629, 15630
Red River of Louisiana, 5537
Red River of Texas, 17583
Red River of the North, 1133, 1134, 3200, 3881, 6941, 15978, 16012, 16227, 17303
Red River rebellion, 1869-1870, 6049, 6129, 6212, 6467, 6635, 7831, 16438, 16552
Red River settlement, 334, 3880, 4348, 5674, 5904, 6029, 6041, 6224, 6229, 6300, 6301, 6304, 6305, 6313, 6316, 6398, 6399, 6467, 6542, 6668, 6845, 7361, 7457, 7522, 7641, 7780, 7793, 7999, 8000, 8120, 8141, 8146, 8147, 8155, 8185, 8231, 8411, 17404, 17527; (Canada), History, 7462
Red River Valley, Minnesota, 17750
Red Rock, 10467
The Red Rover, 9147
Red Rupert, the American bucanier, 8671
Red Sulphur Spring, W.Va., 13037
Red-tape and pigeon-hole generals, 4521
Red Wood and blue, 15287
Redburn, 10348
Rede, Leman Thomas, d.1810, 2476
Redemption by the blood of Christ, 15798
The Redemption of David Corson, 9631
The redemptioner, 9463
Reden gehalten bei der Berliner todtenfeier für den präsidenten Lincoln, 8125
Redfield, 9593
The rediscovery of Kentucky, 15538
Redmond, Patrick H., 23526
Redondo y Godino, Juan, 1859-1921, 4909
Redpath, James, 1833-1891, 4910, 4911
The redskins, 9148
Redwood, 10729
Redwood Library and Athenaeum, Newport, R.I., 1575; History, 23234
Reed, Andrew, 1787-1862, 861, 4912
Reed, H.B., 7816
Reed, Henry E., 17455
Reed, Isaac, 4913
Reed, J.W., 4914
Reed, James Armstrong, b.1830, 7029
Reed, John Calvin, 1836-1910, 25353
Reed, Joseph, 1741-1785, 739, 1790, 13245
Reed, Mrs. Margaret Allison (Ross) 1787-1895, 24716
Reed, Seth, 1823-, 7817

Reed, William Bradford, 1806-1876, 7818, 13245
Reed, William Howell, 1837-, 4915
Reed-Hudson, Deborah, 15252
Reeder, Robert S., 25354
Reedsburg, Wis., 15848
Reelfoot Lake, 14167, 15280
Reemelin, Charles, b.1814, 23168
Rees, Thomas, 1777-1864, 17030, 17391
Rees, Thomas, 1850-1933, 7819
Rees, William, 17456
Rees House, Winchester, Ky., 15120
Reese, Lizette Woodworth, 1856-1935, 4916-4918
Reese, Mary E., 7820
Reese family, 7820
Reese River, 5685
Reeve, Henry, 1813-1895, 5429
Reeves, John Estill, 13717, 15253
Reference books, Bibliography, Catalogs, 19540; Periodicals, Bibliography, Catalogs, 19541
The refined poetry of the South, 1325
Reflections and tales, 10606
Reforestation, Brazil, Minas Gerais, 19680
Reforma agraria, 19027, 19234, 19361, 19644, 19768, 19861, 20112, 20210, 20211
La reforma judicial, 20329
La reforma social agraria, 20330, 20331
La reforma tributaria, 20147, 20332
The reformation of James Reddy, 6971, 9790
The reformation of lawsuits, 22453
A reformation of morals practicable and indispensable, 1062
Reformed church in America, Sermons, 21833, 22101
Reformed church in the United States, 12660
The reformed common wealth of bees, 12733
The reformed Virginian silkworm, 12734
Reformers, 901
Refraction, 4227
The refugee, 10061
The refugees, 6622
Refugees, Southern, 313, 2840, 3969, 11328
Refuse and refuse disposal, 14137; Kentucky, 15056; Pennroyal region, Ky., 13612
Refutación de varios artículos concernientes a ese país, 24441
A refutation of Andrew Stewart's fabrication against General Lewis Cass, 22085
A refutation of the calumnies circulated against the southern and western states, respecting the institution and existence of slavery among them, 24618
Regan, John, 4919

Regeneration (Theology), 22104
Regester, Seeley, 10899
The regicides, 8632, 9064, 23663
Regicides, Fiction, 9064
El régimen de propiedad intelectual y de prensa, 20333
El régimen jurídico de los capitales extranjeros, 19594
Régimen legal de baldíos en Colombia, 18243
Régimen legal del comercio exterior chileno, 18329
El régimen y personalidad de la sociedad conyugal, 18145
Regina Coeli (Emigrant ship), 24773
Reginald Archer, 10734
Regional planning, Amazon Valley, 19435; Brazil, Northeast, 19455, 19456; Chile, 20165; Choco, Colombia, 20259; Magdalena River Valley, 20490; São Francisco Valley, Brazil, 19256; Sinú Valley, 20490
Regionalism (International organization), 19755; Brazil, Northeast, 19708
Register of the commissioned and warrant officers of the navy of the Confederate States, 2065
Register of the National Society of the Colonial Dames of America in the Commonwealth of Kentucky, 13897
Register of the officers and graduates of the U.S. military academy, 11889
A register of the weather, 214
Registers of births, etc., Dutchess Co., N.Y., 24451; Mason, N.H., 22476; Portland, Me., 21973; Shelby Co., Ky., 15723; Stamford, Conn., 22619; Venezuela, 18178; Worcester, Vt., 15
Registro bibliográfico de publicaciones de catedráticos de la Facultad de Humanidades, 19629
Registro de estrangeiros, 19242
Reglamento, sobre estableces una casa, 6482
Reglamento de la Cámara de Diputados y Constitución política de la República de Chile, 20113
Reglamento y aranceles reales para el comercio libre de España a Indias, 23649
Reglas comunes al procedimiento civil, 19022
Regnard, Jean-René, 20082
Regulamentação de Zona Franca de Manaus, 19343
Regulamento para arredação do taxa dos escravos a que se refere o decreto n.7536 de 15 novembro de 1879, 24011
Regulating the Indian department, 5504
The regulations lately made concerning the colonies, 13509

The regulators, 5662
Regulus, pseud., 11968
Rehabilitation, Rural, Colombia, 20287
Rehoboth, Mass., History, 11285
Reich, Emil, 1854-1910, 25355
Reiche, Karl Friedrich, 1860-, 7821
Reichert, Rolf, 18691
Reid, Christian, pseud., 10966-10970,
 10972- 10973
Reid, Hugo, 1809-1872, 4920
Reid, James, 25356
Reid, Jesse Walton, b.1824, 4921
Reid, John, d.1816, 22165
Reid, John Coleman, b.1824, 4922
Reid, John S., 4923
Reid, R. L., 7822
Reid, Russell, 17457-17463, 17820
Reid, Samuel Chester, 1818-1897, 4926
Reid, Thomas Mayne, 1818-1883, 4924, 4925,
 23527
Reid, Whitelaw, 1837-1912, 4927, 9510,
 25547
Reid's tramp, 4922
Reider, J. H., 7823
The reign of law, 8516
The reign of reform, 8824
A reign of terror, 23866
The reign of terror in Kansas, 25357
The reign of terror in Missouri, 10092
The reign of the demagogue, 3664
The reign of the Messiah, 3110
The reigning king, 11118
Reilley, Edward C., 25358
A re-incarnation, 9740
Reiner, John, d.1676, 22752
Reinhard, Charles de, 8032
Reinhart, Charles Stanley, 1844-1896,
 illustr., 10809, 11090
Reis, Mônica de Santa Luzia, 19220
Reisado da borboleta, 18977
Reise-berichte über Amerika, 2593
Reise durch die Felsengebirge und die
 Humboldtgebirge nach dem Stillen Ocean,
 5091
Reise durch die mexikanischen provinzen
 Tamaulipas, Coahuila und Texas im jahre
 1834, 4314
Reise durch einige der mittlern und
 südlichen Vereinigten nord-amerikanischen
 Staaten nach Ost-Florida und den Bahama-
 Inseln unternommen in den jahren 1783
 und 1784, 5101
Reise in das innere Nord-America in
 den jahren 1832 bis 1834,
 5700
Reise in das moderne Mexiko, 6593

Reise in den Vereinigten Staaten und Canada
 im jahr 1837, 5681
Reise-skizzen in poesie und prosa, 4494
Reise sr. hoheit des herzogs Bernhard zu
 Sachsen-Weimar-Eisenach, 2696
Reise- und kulturbilder aus den Vereinigten
 Staaten von America, 3379
Eine reise vom Mittelrhein, 14061
Reise von Hamburg nach Philadelphia, 4928
Reisebilder und studien aus dem norden der
 Vereinigten Staaten von Amerika, 4871
Reisen in den Vereinigten Staaten, 7549
Reisen in die Felsengebirge Nord-Amerikas,
 4500
Reisen in Mexiko in den jahren 1845-1848,
 7004
Reisen in Nordamerika in den jahren 1852
 und 1853, 5595
Reiseskizzen aus West-Indien, Mexico und
 Nord-Amerika, 6208
Reister, J.T., 17464
Reize naar Surinamen, en door de binnenste
 gedeelten van Guiana, 25604
O reitor Antônio Martinas Filho, 20015
Rejano, Juan, 1903-, 7824
The relation between the races at the South,
 25045
The relation of the individual to the
 republic, 21868
Relations between the U.S. and northwest
 British America, 5534
The relations of the business men of the
 United States to the national legislation,
 22472
The relations of the federal government to
 Slavery, 24336
The relative territorial status of the North
 and the South, 25360
Relativity (Physics), 19636
A relic of the revolution, 22419
The relief of the Franklin expedition, 8123
As religiões africanas no Brasil, 18903
Religion, 5243, 23166; Addresses, essays,
 lectures, 9596; Appalachia, 13691;
 Dictionaries, 50, 54; Kentucky, 14203;
 Periodicals, 23518; U.S., 4766
Religion, agnosticism and education, 5243
Religion and art, 5244
Religion and education in America, 4211
Religion and science, 1800-1859, 23451
Religion at home, 11172
The religion of politics, 22226
The religion of the revolution, 1576
Religion to be minded, under the greatest
 perils of life, 11825
Religión y magia entre los indios de Costa

Rica de origen sureño, 18042
Las religiones de Perú, 8296
Religions, 1075, 1147, 7658, 22370, 23371;
   African, 18903
Les religions africaines au Brésil, 18903
The religions of the world and their
   relations to Christianity, 23371
The religious denominations in the United
   States, 1075
Religious education, 12703; U.S., 2000,
   13292
Religious education of adolescents, 18617
Religious freedom, 7145, 23015
Religious liberty, 2327, 3503, 19197,
   22122, 23744; Haiti, 12420; Massachusetts,
   620; New York (State), 22427; Venezuela,
   19780
Religious life, Brazil, 18903
The religious opinions and character of
   Washington, 22887
Religious principle, a source of public
   prosperity, 22652
A religious retreat sounded to a religious
   army, 23743
Religious tract society, London, 1541,
   5924, 7829
Religious views of Abraham Lincoln, 7721
El reloj, 18917
Relox astronómico de temblores de la
   tierra, 6008
The remains of Rev. James Marsh, D.D., late
   president and professor of moral and
   intellectual philosophy in the University
   of Vermont, 23156
Remains of William S. Graham, With a
   memoir, 22267
The remarkable adventures of Jackson
   Johonnot, 4096
The remarkable financial fortunes and
   misfortunes of a remote island community,
   11119
The remarkable history of the Hudson's bay
   company, 6228
Remarkable providences illustrative of the
   earlier days, 13419
Remedios, Nuestra Señora de los, 6753
The remedy for duelling, 1063
A remedy for the "irrepressible conflict";
   or, Constitutional ethics, 25160
Remember the Alamo, 8738
A remembrance of beloved companions, and
   years bygone, 10444
Remick, William, b.1804, 17466
Remington, Frederic, illustr., 10608,
   14350, 17467-17469
A reminiscence of federalism, 10730

Reminiscences, 3015, 16838, 17897
Reminiscent ramblings, 8366
Remodino, Peter C., 17471, 17472
Remonstrance against the treaty with the
   Great and Little Osage Indians, 21949
Remonstrance of New Netherland, and the
   occurrences there, 22152
Remorse, 14094
Removal of ancient landmarks, 1673
Remove Indians westward, 5505
Remsburg, George J., 17473
Remsburg, John Eleazer, 1848-, 7832, 17474
Rémusat, Charles François Marie, comte de,
   1797-1875, 22529
Remy, Jules, 1826-, 4931
El Renacimiento, 7833, 7834; (Indexes),
   18910
El renacimiento de la danza guatemalteca y
   el origen de la marimba, 18542
Renard, Jules, 1864-1919, Poil de carotte,
   19818
Renault, Abgar, 18673
The rending of the solid south, 3226
René, 20087
The renegade, 9163
Rengifo, Cesar, illustr., 18534
Renick, William, b.1804, 17475
Rensselaerswyck, N.Y., 821
Rensselaerville, N.Y. Trinity church, 22218
Renny, Robert, 25369
Renville, Joseph, 17625
Renz, Hugo, 4932
Reparos que propone al exc.^{mo} s.^{or} conde de
   Alva de Aliste virrey deste reyno, 8312
Repaso final, 18581
Repentance, 23398
Repertorio americana, 7835
El Repertorio pintoresco, 7836
Replevin and endorsement laws, Kentucky,
   14580
Replication by the House of representatives,
   11757
A reporter of the New York press, 23349
Reporters and reporting, 12234
Reportorio de los tiempos e historia
   natural de Nueva España, 7418, 7419
Representación del reyno de Chile, 8309
Representation and petition of the
   representatives, 13402
Representations of groups, 20621
Representative government and representation,
   23223, 23603
Reptiles, Cuba, 18892, 19563; Kentucky,
   13706; U.S., 12683
Reptiles, Fossil, 22239
Reptiles de la peninsula Hicacos, 19563

371

The republic, a little book of homespun verse, 13804
The republic of Mexico in 1882, 6377
La república de Méjico, 6479
La República Mexicana, 7837
The Republican, 13173
Republican Association, Washington, D.C., 25481
Republican Congressional Committee, 1859-1861, 24263, 24878; 1863-1865, 24134, 25729
Republican Convention, Richmond, Va., 18 March 1839, 7838
The republican court: or, American society in the days of Washington, 22275
Republican homes, 22563
The republican judge, 1943
Republican opinions about Lincoln, 6572
Republican party, 210, 6483, 12369, 22137, 23833, 24324, 25652; History, 6134, 6707, 12557, 23867; Illinois, Convention, 1858, 7839; Illinois, State Central Committee, 25371; Kentucky, Executive Committee, 15254; National Convention, 2d, Chicago, 1860, 2477, 7180, 7782, 7840; National Convention, 15th Chicago, 1912, 16487
The Republican-party vindicated - the demands of the South explained, 24866
The Republican pocket pistol, 1717
The Republican Rush-light, 2478
The Republican scrap book, 25372
Republican songster, 13050
Republicanism in America, 22804
Republics, 1264, 13173, 23773
Requited Labor Convention, Philadelphia, 1838, 25373
Rerum hispaniscarum scriptores aliquot, 1094
Resa till Montevideo och Buenos Ayres, 1380
The rescue case of 1857, 25315
The rescued maiden, 8837
Research, Argentine Republic, 18435
Research Institute for the Study of Man, 20371
Researches on America; being an attempt to settle some points relative to the aborigines of America, etc., 22840
Reseña de la tarea realizada por el Departamento de Metalurgía de la Comisión Nacional de Energía Atómica, 18407
Reseña histórico, descriptiva de la Ciudad de México, 8883
Reservoirs, 6121; Kentucky, 15495
Resin, Fossil, Brazil, 19950

Resistance to slavery every man's duty, 172
Resolute (Ship), 22846
Resolutions of a meeting of the citizens of Connellsville, Newhaven, etc., Fayette County, Pennsylvania, with the subject of slavery in the District of Columbia, 24188
Resolutions of the committee on federal relations of the House of delegates of Maryland, with Senate amendments, 23215
Resolutions of Virginia and Kentucky, 15650
Resorts, Southern states, 4958
Resources and attractions of Colorado for the home seeker, 17476
The resources and attractions of the Texas Panhandle for the home seeker, capitalist and tourist, 5500
The resources and attractions of Utah, 16803
The resources and condition of the Commonwealth of Kentucky, 14511
The resources and prospects of America, 4762
The resources of California, 16791
The resources of Missouri, 5633
Resources of the southern fields and forests, 4827
Resources of the state of Arkansas, 16739
The resources of the United States of America, 2806
The resources of Utah, 16486
Resources of West Virg;nia, 4418
The respective pleas and arguments of the mother country, 23723
El resplandor, 19967
The responsibilities of rulers, 11420
A responsibility, 9740
Restituta, 1631
Restivo, Paulo, 1658-1741, 7921
Resultados provisionales para la Provincia de Córdoba del censo minero, 20472
Resumen de la historia de Venezuela desde el año de 1797 hasta el de 1830, 772
Resumen de la investigación sobre esclavitud y peonaje en las Islas Felipinas, por el comté que investigó el asunto, 25251
Resumen de reales cedulas, para las Indias, 8085
Retail Merchants Association, Louisville, Ky., 15255
Retirement and benefit plans for Kentucky state employees, 13570
Retirement for non-certified school board employees, 14499, 14742
El retorno, 18614
Retratos do Brasil, 19812
Retribution at the court-house, 13885
The retrospect, 2638
Retrospect of western travel, 7424

Retrospection, political and personal, 15909
Retrospections of America, 2695
Return, 10274, 12083
The return of a private, 9606
A returned prisoner of war, 5585
Re-union Convention of the Old Abolitionists of Eastern Ohio and Western Pennsylvania, Alliance, O., 1879, 24005
The reunion of the ghost, 10863
Re-union of the sons and daughters of Newport, R.I., August 23, 1859, 23234
Reuthebuck, George L., 13954, 15256
La revancha, 19967
Réveillaud, Eugène, 1851-, 7841
Revel, Gabriel Joachim du Perron, comte de, 1756-1814, 4933
Revel, James, 4934
Revelação de homem, 19168
Revelations of a life, 10422
·Revenge, 10209
The revenge of Saint Nicholas, 10480
The revenge of the Adolphus, 9217
Revenge punished and constancy rewarded, 10402
Revenue laws and custom house regulations, comp. by P.P.F. Degrand, 22079
The reverberator, 7127
Revere, Joseph Warren, 1812-1880, 7842, 17477
Rev. Calvin Fairbank during slavery times, 3412
The Reverend Washington Ham's triumph, 9460
Reverente satisfacción, 7843
Reveries of a bachelor, 10362
The reverse, 10760
The reverses of fortune, 10332
A review of all that hath pass'd between the courts of Great Britain and Spain, relating to our trade and navigation from the year 1721, to the present convention, 21776
Review of Bishop Hopkin's Bible view of slavery, 25916
A review of Captain Basil Hall's Travels in North America, 1262
The review of contemporary poetry, 15257
A review of Father O'Daniel's estimate of early secular missionaries of Kentucky, 14357
A review of Garrisonian fanaticism and its influence, 25024
Review of government, 15258
Review of pamphlets on slavery and colonization, 639

A review of the decision of the Supreme Court of the United States in the Dred Scott case, 25374
A review of the noted revival in Kentucky, 4895
Review of the Remarks on Dr. Channing's Slavery, by a citizen of Massachusetts, 25504
A review of the Rev. Dr. Junkin's synodical speech, 25375
Review of the slave question, 24572
The reviewers reviewed, 25612
Reviews of Jefferson Davis, constitutionalist, 15259
Revilla Gigedo, Juan Francisco Guemes y Horcasitas, conde de, 1682?-1766, 7479
Revilla Gigedo, Juan Vicent Güemez Pacheco de Padilla Horcasitas y Aguayo, conde de, 1740-1799, Poetry, 7626
Revilliod, Gustave, 1817-1890, 16587
Revision of the United States statutes, 25775
Revista azul, 7844
Revista cubana, 7845
Revista de bibliografía chilena y extranjera, 7846
Revista de Bogotá, 7847
Revista de Chile, 7848
Revista de Cuba, 7849
Revista de educación (La Plata) Suplemento, 20624
Revista de La Habana, 7850
Revista de las Fuerzas Armadas, Supplement, 19946
Revista de Santiago, 7851, 7852
Revista del Rio de la Plata, 7853
Revista moderna, 7854, 7855
Revista nueva, 7856
Revista peruana, 7857
Revistas agricolas bolivianas, 19788
Revivals, 1660, 11246, 21975; Boston, 22008; U.S., 13634, 15518; Vermont, 1687
Revocet, Samuel, 25376
Révoil, Bénédict Henry, 1816-1888, 4935, 4936
The revolt of "Mother", 9575
Revolution in Greenup County, 15481
Revolution or Reform, 25474
The revolt of the Mexitili, 9982
A revolução brasileira, 18667
La revolución cubana, 20707
La revolución en el campo laboral, 20698
La revolución industrial en el mundo, 18987
Revolution the only remedy for slavery, 25377
The revolutionary officer, 10197
Revolutionary soldiers in Clark County, 15215

Revolutionary war pensioners of Clark
  County, Ky., 14829
Revolutions, 6005, 24406
Les révolutions du Mexique, 1104
The reward of virtue, 9740
Rex Macarthy, 8723
Rey, José del, 19905
Rey, William, 4937
Reybaud, Louis, 7858
Reyes, Alfonso, 7496, 18896
Reyes, Rafael, pres. Colombia, 1851-1931,
  7859
Reyes Baena, Juan Francisco, 1909-, 20537
Reyna, Francisco de, d.1708, 7860
Reynal, Rafael, 4938
Reynolds, Charles, 1844-1876, 17474, 17709
Reynolds, Charles Bingham, 1856-1940, 4939
Reynolds, Elhanan Winchester, 1827-1867,
  25378
Reynolds, J. Owen, 15260
Reynolds, John, 1788-1865, 4940, 15261,
  23528, 23529
Reynolds, John Hugh, 17478, 17479
Reynolds, John N., 17480
Reynolds, Lewis Gardner, 7861
Reynolds, Noah M., 15261
Reynolds, Sharon M., 15361
Reynolds, Thurston Howard, 15056
Rhapsodies of restless hours, 12717
Rhetoric, 11723
Rhett, Robert Barnwell, 1800-1876, 25379
Rhoades, Nelson Osgood, 1869-, 7374
Rhoads, Samuel, 25147, 25380
Rhoda of the underground, 24706
Rhode Island, 11168; Bibliography, 906;
  Biography, 909; Boundaries, Massachusetts,
  505; Charters, 11748; Church history,
  100, 1812, 13126; Constitutional history,
  2424; Description & travel, 3663, 5147;
  Description & travel, Guide-books, 764;
  General assembly, Committee appointed to
  inquire into the charges against masonry
  and masons in Rhode Island, 12587, 22372;
  General Assembly, House of Representatives,
  Select Committee to Whom were Referred the
  Resolutions of Mr. Wells, on slavery,
  25381; History, 477, 13126; History,
  Colonial period, 478, 1812, 12193, 12322,
  23809; History, Colonial Period, Sources,
  2167; History, Revolution, 25390;
  Politics & government, 12798; Politics
  & government, 1775-1865, 2339, 2340;
  Social life & customs, Colonial period,
  24580; Supreme court, 12311
Rhode Island (Colony) Commissioners to the
  Albany congress, 1754, 12898

Rhode Island, Battle of, 1778, 25390
Rhode Island historical society, 478, 12393
Rhode Island infantry, 1st regt.,1777-1783,
  25390; 2d regt., 1861-1865, 1802; 12th
  regt., 1862-1863, 12351
Rhodes, Harrison Garfield, 1871-, 4941
Rhodesia, 24564
Rhopalosiphum maidis (Fitch), 19071
Rhymes and roses, 4731
Rhymes of the Rockies, 16369
Rhys, Horton, 7862
Riachuelo, Battle of, 1865, 20552
Rialto series, 10688
Ribas, José Félix, 1775-1815, 6866
Ribas, Manuel José de la, 7863
Ribas family, 6866
Ribault, 1520(ca.)-1565, 22285
Ribeiro Fernandes, João, 1860-1934, 18160
Rica's eyes, 9330
Ricardo, Cassiano, 1895-, 20077, 20515
The Ricaree Indian fight, 4942
Ricaud, J.A., 4943
Ricci, Angelo, 20657
Ricci, Elvira Rina Malerbi, 19046
Rice, Alice Caldwell Hegan, 1870-1942, 14110,
  15262-15267
Rice, Cale Young, 1872-1943, 4944, 15265
Rice, David, 1733-1816, 1359, 4945, 15268,
  15269, 25382
Rice, Harvey, 1800-1891, 17481
Rice, John Asaph, 1829-1888, 23530
Rice, John H., 7864
Rice, John Holt, 1777-1831, 4422
Rice, Laban Lacy, 1870-, 15270
Rice, Martin, b.1814, 17482
Rice, Nathan Lewis, 1807-1877, 25383
Rice Corner, 9896
Rich, Elihu, 1819-1875, 23566
Rich, Isaac B., 12201
Rich, Obadiah, 1783?-1850, 4393, 4946
Rich, R., 4947
The rich merchant of Cairo, 10298
Richard and Robin, 9639
Richard Carvel, 9003
Richard Edney and the governor's family,
  10077
Richard, Edouard, 1844-1904, 7865
Richard, Louis Claude Marie, 1754-1821,
  7092
Richards, Adolphus E., 3417
Richards, Augustus Long, 7866
Richards, C.A.L., 13148
Richards, Franklin Dewey, 1821-1899, 17483
Richards, Jarrett Thomas, 17484
Richards, Robert, pseud., 4948
Richards, Thomas Addison, 1820-1900, 4949,

5918
Richards, William Carey, 1818-1892, ed..,
4950
Richardson, Mrs. Abby (Sage), 1839-1900,
7867
Richardson, Albert Deane, 1833-1869,
4951, 4952, 7867, 17485
Richardson, Amanda Cranwill, 15271
Richardson, Anna H., 25384
Richardson, Charles Henry, 15272
Richardson, Ebenezer, 23450
Richardson, Frank Herbert, 1867-, 4953
Richardson, John, 1667-1753, 4954
Richardson, Sir John, 1787-1865, 4955,
4956
Richardson, John G., 25385
Richardson, Margaret S., 14263
Richardson, Nathaniel Smith, 1810-1883,
25386
Richardson, Paul D., 15273
Richardson, R., 15274
Richardson, William Alexander, 1811-1875,
87, 25387
Richardson, William H., 4957
Richardson's southern guide, 4953
Richardville, Jean Baptiste, ca.1761-1841,
7880
Richelet, Pierre, 1631-1698 tr., 12195
Richers, Raimar, 19303
The riches of Mexico, 6630
Riches without wings, 10803
Richman, Irving Berdine, 16534, 17486
Richmond, C.W., 23531
Richmond, Ky., Biography, 14008; Chamber
of commerce, 14008; Economic conditions,
14544; History, 14008
Richmond, Legh, 1772-1827, 23532, 25388
Richmond, Va., Description, 3015, 3401,
3755, 4128, 5794; Description,
Guidebooks, 2984; Directories, 1756;
History, Civil war, 4113, 4869; Siege,
1864-1865, 6206, 7871, 11647, 21812;
Theater disaster, 1811, 142, 21757;
Theater disaster, 1811, Poetry, 12262
The Richmond age, a southern eclectic
magazine, 23849
Richmond and Danville Railroad, 4958
Richmond during the war, 4869
Richmond Examiner, 2589
Richmond: her glory and her graves, 13326
Rickard, Thomas Arthur, 1864-, 7868
Rickman, John, 23533
Rickman, Thomas M., 4959
Riddell, William Renwick, 7243, 25389
Riddle, George W., 1839-, 17487
The riddle of Lincoln's religion, 7661

A ride across a continent, 11461
The ride of Saint Nicholas on New Year's eve,
10480
A ride over the Rocky mountains, 3047
A ride with Kit Carson through the Great
American Desert and the Rocky mountains,
2796
Rideing, William Henry, 1853-1918, 17488
Ridenour, George L., 15275
Rideout, Mrs. J. B., 17489
Rider, Sidney Smith, 1833-1917, 25390
The riders of the plains, 6995
Ridge, John, Cherokee chief, d.1839, 17490
Ridge, John Rollin, 1827-1867, 17490
Ridgely, Frederick, 15365
Ridgely, James Lott, 1807-1881, 14987
Ridgeway, Florence Holmes, 15276
Riding and driving, 13551
Riedel, Emil, 7869
Riedesel, Friedrich Adolf, freiherr von,
1738-1800, 2960, 23534
Riedesel, Friederike Charlotte Luise (von
Massow) freifrau von, 1746-1808, 4960,
23534
Riegling, George L., 15778
Riel, Louis, 1844-1885, 6212, 6300, 5301,
6304, 6398, 6399, 6845, 7462, 7793, 8155,
8185, 8231, 16438
Riel rebellion, 1885, 6129, 6298
Ries, Julius, 4961
The rifle, axe, and saddle-bags, 4468
Rifle practice, 4242, 6353
Rifles, 11989; Muzzle-loading, 13917
Le riforme cinesi, costituzione cinese,
assemblea nazionale, abolizione della
schiavitu, 24538
Rigby, T.C., 4962
Riggs, Stephen Return, 1812-1883, 17491,
17492, 23535
The right and the wrong, 10156
Right and wrong in Massachusetts, 11736
Right flanker, 2277
The right of petition, 25391
The right of recognition, 25392
The right of way, 9358
The right real thing, 10016
Right side of the car, 10225
Right thoughts in sad hours, 23310
The right way and the wrong way, 8572
The right way to shake off a viper, 23311
The rightful remedy, 24046
The rights of colonies examined, 12897
The rights of Parliament vindicated, 23536
The rights of the Congregational churches of
Massachusetts, 12469
Riker, Carroll L., 7870

375

Riker, John F., 4963
Riland, John, 1778-1863, 25393
Riley, Franklin Lafayette, 1868-1929, 15413
Riley, Herbert Parks, 15277
Riley, James, 1777-1840, 25394, 25395
Riley, James Whitcomb, 1849-1916, 10436
Riley, Ralph, pseud., 16067
Riley, William Willshire, 25395
A rill from the town pump, 9827
Rimas, 18093
Rinaldi, Carlos A., 19675
Rincones mexicanos, 6544
Ringold Griffitt, 9985
Rings and love-knots, 4732
Ringwalt, John Luther, 23537
Rintelen, Fritz J. von, 18895
Rio, Antonio del, 23538
Rio de Janeiro, 20002; Biblioteca de Itamaraty, 19385; Commerce, 691, 23390; (State), Description & travel, 18317 (State), History, 19243, 19244, 19956, 20550; Observatorio Nacional, Serviço Astronomico, Publicações, 18863; Universidade Católica, 19660
O Rio de Janeiro verso e reverso, 18141
Rio de la Plata, 13335, 21761, 23046
Rio de la Plata region, History, Sources, 18397; Relations (general) with Brazil, 18397
Rio Grande, 5513, 5549, 8255, 17031, 17441
Rio Grande del Norte, 190, 8199
Rio Grande do Sul, Brazil (State), Description & travel, 578; Description & travel, Gazetteers, 425; History, Addresses, essays, lectures, 17961; History, Bibliography, 20531; History, Colonial period, 20057; History, Sources, 20058; Literature, 20056; Statistics, 19405
Rio Grande river, 8110, 17105
Rio Negro, Argentine Republic (Province) Dirección de Energía, 19062
Los ríos profundos, 18505
Rip Van Winkle, 9995
Riparian rights, Chile, 20138; Massachusetts, 11436
Ripley, Edward H., 7871
Ripley, Mrs. Eliza Moore (Chinn) McHatton, 1832-1912, 4964
Ripley, Henry, 1847-, 17493
Ripley, Mrs. Martha (Pedley) 1856-, 17493
Ripley, William Putnam, 1776-1842, 1517
Ripples on the stream of poesy, 13587
Risdon, F. Ray, 8354
The rise, progress and downfall of aristocracy, 23341
The rise and progress of civilization in the Hairy nation, 16481
Rising electricity rates, 14776
Rising in the world, 8576
The rising son; or, The antecedents and advancement of the colored race, 24039
The rising village, 2434
Riske, Mrs. Charlotte (Chambers) Ludlow, d.1821, 16576
Ritch, William Gillet, 1830-1904, 17494
Ritchie, Anna Cora (Ogden) Mowatt, 1870-1819, 4965
Ritchie, Martha C., 14876
Ritmos e legendas, 18211
Ritos y costumbres de nuestros pueblos primitivos, 20678
Ritson, Mrs. Anne, 4966
Rittenhouse, David, 1732-1796, 21773, 21848
Rittenhouse, Rufus, 1825-, 17495
Ritter, Federica de, tr., 18325
Ritter, George, 25396
Riva Agüero, José de la, pres. Peru, 1783-1858, 22278
Riva Palacio, Mariano, 1803-1880, 7872
Riva Palacio, Vicente, 1832-1896, 7873, 19968, 21766
Rivail, Hippolyte Leon Denizard, 1803-1869, 19664
The rival belles, 4114, 10063
The rival sisters, 9842
The rival volunteers, 9936
The rivals, 9022
The rivals of Acadia, 8984
Rivascacho, marqués de, 7405, 7406
River drift, 15278
River Plate Publishing Company, 7874
River transportation in Dakota, 16045
Rivera, Luis Manuel del, 7875
Rivera y Sanromán, Agustín, 1824-1916, 7876, 7877
Rivera y Villalón, Pedron de, fl.1740, 4967, 7878
Rivero, Nicolás, 1849-, 7879
Rivers, Pearl, pseud., 4604
Rivers, William James, 1822-, 23539
Rivers, Argentine Republic, 19916; Kentucky, 14547, 14549, 15123, 15354, 15646; Spain, 25710
Rives, Amélie, see Troubetzkoy, Amélie (Rives) Chanler
Rives, Hallie Erminie, 1876-, 4968, 15279
Rives, William Cabell, 1825-1889, 5601
La Rivière Rouge, 4626
Rivington, Alan., 4060
Rivington, Harris, 4969

Rivolba, pseud., 2754
Rix, Samuel Wilton, 11321
Rizzo, Henrique Perotta, 19507, 19509
Roach, Alva C., 4970
Roach, Philip A., 17496
The road back, 15499
The road to Dream Acre, 13653
The road to Frontenac, 7467
The road to ruin, 11275
Roads, 11293, 18629, 19001
Roads, Argentine Republic, 19549, 19550,
  19551; Bibliography, 19308, 19552;
  Brazil, 19528; Central America, 20022;
  Colombia, 19233, 20344, 20487, 21731;
  Colombia, Finance, 20455; Construction,
  14038; Costa Rica, 20611; Illinois,
  5820; Information services, 19308;
  Kentucky, 13833, 14601, 14637, 15602;
  Maintenance and repair, Handbooks,
  manuals, etc., 19294; Mexico, 7481;
  Military, 4550; Oregon. 16972; U.S., 3163,
  3861, 4440, 4761, 5127; Venezuela, 19766;
  Virginia, 756; The West, 1184
Roah, Sidney, 4971
Roanoke island, N.C., Capture, 1862, 2049
Rob of the Bowl, 4156, 10096
Robb, Charles, 6666
Robb, John S., 4972
Robbe-Grillet, Alain, 1922-, La jalousie,
  20074
The robber, 10568
The robber baron, 14832
The robber of Guatemala, 10209
Robbers and outlaws, 6164, 6958; Kentucky,
  14460
The robbers of Adullam, 24900
Robbins, A., 15280
Robbins, Archibald, 1792-1865, 25397
Robbins, Chandler, 1810-1882, 23275, 23540
Robert, Charles Edwin, 25398
Robert, the hermit of Massachusetts, 23715
Robert and Harold, 3656
Robert Fulton, an historical novel, 22341
Robert Graham, 3847
Robert Greathouse, 10917
Robert Morton, 10683
Robert Severne, his friends and his
  enemies, 9728
Robert Toombs, 5294
Robert Warren, the Texas refugee, 14004
Roberts, fl. 1692-1696, 22280
Roberts, Bernie K., 7880
Roberts, Sir Charles George Douglas, 1860-
  1943, 6318, 7881, 10448
Roberts, Daniel Webster, 1841-, 17497
Roberts, Edwards, 7882

Roberts, Edwin F., 1819-1864, 8798
Roberts, Ingham S., 16697
Roberts, James R., 15281
Roberts, Joseph Jenkins, pres. Liberia, 1809-
  1876, 24773
Roberts, Joseph K., 15282
Roberts, Lou (Conway) "Mrs. D.W. Roberts",
  17498
Roberts, Louis A., illustr., 10862
Roberts, Morley, 1857-, 4973, 17499
Roberts, Nathan S., 21909
Roberts, Oran Milo, 1815-1898, 4974, 17500
Roberts, Orlando W., 7883
Roberts, Robert, 15504, 25399
Roberts, Robert Richford, 1778-1843, 12036,
  12180
Roberts, Sidney, 4975, 17501
Roberts, William, fl.1763, 4976
Robertson, Alexander Hamilton, 4977
Robertson, Daniel A., 1813-1895, 25400
Robertson, David, reporter, 11628
Robertson, Douglas Sinclair, 1877-, 6922
Robertson, George, 1790-1874, 4977, 4978,
  15283, 15284
Robertson, Harrison, 1856-, 15285-15287
Robertson, James, of Manchester, Eng., 4979
Robertson, James Alexander, 1873-, 5469
Robertson, James Road, 15288
Robertson, John, jr., 1787-1873, 25401
Robertson, John Blount, 4980
Robertson, John Ross, 1841-1918, 8210
Robertson, Joseph Clinton, 1788-1852, 13450
Robertson, Mabel D., 15289
Robertson, Thomas William, 8876
Robertson, William Parish, 4981
Robertson, Wyndham, 1803-1888, 17502
Robidoux, Antoine, 1794-1860, 16922
Robidoux, Michelle, 5503
Robidoux, Fort, 17234
Robin, Claude C., 1750-, 4982
Robins, Elizabeth "Mrs. G.R. Parkes," 1862-,
  4983-4988
Robinson, Alfred, 1806-1895, 17503
Robinson, Asa P., 17324
Robinson, C.H., 25402
Robinson, Charles Seymour, 1829-1899, 7884
Robinson, Conway, 1805-1884, 23541, 25403
Robinson, D., 10122
Robinson, Edgar E., 17504
Robinson, Elrie, 7885
Robinson, Fayette, d.1859, 1864
Robinson, Henry M., 7886
Robinson, Henry S., 15574
Robinson, Jacob S., 4989
Robinson, John Hovey, 1825-, 4990-4994, 7887
Robinson, Joseph W., 4995

Robinson, Lee Lamar, 15290
Robinson, Lewis, d.1810, 13241
Robinson, Luther Emerson, 1867-, 7888
Robinson, Philip Stewart, 1847-1902, 17506
Robinson, Rachel Sargent, 1891-, 25404
Robinson, Reuben D., 6423
Robinson, Richard P., 11165
Robinson, Sophie Michau, 5074
Robinson, Stuart, 1814-1881, 7889
Robinson, Thomas Hastings, 1828-1906, 7890
Robinson, William Davis, 4996, 23542
Robinson, W. W., 17507
Robinson, William Henry, 1867-, 17508
Robinson Crusoe's money, 11119
Robinsoniads, American literature, 2664
Robles, Antonio de, 1645?-17--, 7891
Robson, Joseph, 23543
Robson, W., 25405
Rochambeau, Jean Baptiste Donatien de
    Vimeur, comte de, 1725-1807, 4997
Roche, Emily Langdon, illustr., 25406
Roche, Henry Philip, 22379
Roche, James Maurice, 1858-1942, 15584
Roche, Richard W., 23544
Rochefort, Charles, 1605-, 4998
Rochester Anti-slavery Society, 24619
Rochester ladies' anti-slavery society,
    9666
Rock, James L., 4999, 16094
Rock, Marion Tuttle, 17509
The Rock or the Rye, 9385
Rockefeller, John Davison, 1839-1937, 6196
Rockford, 8812
Rockford parish, 10431
The Rockies of Canada, 8383
Rockingham, Charles Watson-Wentworth, 2d
    marquis of, 1730-1782, 11969
Rockingham Bible Society, 24033
Rockport, Ind., 6662, 6664; Biography,
    6663; History, 6665
Rockport, Mass., History, 605
Rockwell, John Arnold, 1803-1861, 7892,
    25407
Rockwell, William S., 5000
Rocky mountain historical company, 16666
Rocky Mountain Indians, 4701
Rocky Mountain national park, 17512
Rocky Mountains, 2730, 2823, 3047, 3438,
    4028, 4529, 5752, 6317, 6324, 7063,
    7656, 8126, 8383, 15832, 15945,
    15997, 16369, 16853, 16893, 17122,
    17150, 17199, 17200, 17335, 17429,
    17801, 17914; Description & travel,
    4155, 4500, 4705, 4837, 4951, 5007,
    5018, 5053, 5060, 5098, 5180, 5183,
    5561, 5772, 6342, 7196, 16285, 16348,

16366, 16723, 16852, 17080, 17123, 17126;
    Fiction, 5748; Views, 7597, 16049, 16480
Rocky Mountains, A lady's life in the, 6086
Rod and gun on the west coast of Florida,
    5001
A rod for the backs of the critics, 1932
Rod's salvation, 11018
Rode, Charles R., 1825-1865, 265
Rodenberg, Rudolf, 20222
Rodgers, G. B., 25408
Rodgers, John, 1727-1811, 23545
Rodgers, John Kearny, 1793-1851, 11975, 12915
Rodman the keeper, 11207
Rodman, Hugh, 15291
Rodney, George Brydges Rodney, baron, 1719-
    1792, 4654
Rodrigues, Carlos, 20422
Rodríguez, Carlos César, 21719
Rodríguez, Gabriel, 1830-1901, 25555
Rodríguez Cerna, José, 7892
Rodríguez de Almogabar, Mateo, 6348
Rodríguez de Leon Pinelo, Antonio, d.1660,
    7894
Rodríguez de Rivas y Velasco, Diego, bp.,
    d.1771, 7895
Rodríguez de San Miguel, Juan, 7896
Rodríguez Demorizi, Emilio, 18683
Rodríguez Léal, Edgard, 18006
Rodríguez Ruiz, José Napoleon, 18547, 18548
Rodríguez V., Joel, 18544
Rodríguez Villa, Antonio, 1843-1912, 7897
Rodway, James, 7898
Roe, Alfred Seelye, 1844-1917, 5002
Roe, Mrs. Frances Marie Antoinette (Mack),
    5004
Roe, Sir Thomas, 1581?-1644, 12067
Roebuck, 10685
Roebuck, John, 1718-1794, 23546
Roehrig, Frederic Louis Otto, 1819-1908, 515
Roemer, Ferdinand, 17516
Roemer, Jacob, 1818-1896, 5005
Roger Catron's friends, 9779
Roger Irving's ward, 9901
Roger Malvin's burial, 9823
Rogerenes, 623
Rogers, Artemas, 2218
Rogers, Carlton H., 5006
Rogers, Cornelius, 5007
Rogers, Edward H., 5008
Rogers, George, fl.1838, 5009
Rogers, Howard S., 23547
Rogers, James Richard, 1840-, 15292
Rogers, John, 1800-1867, 5288
Rogers, John, 1812-1882, 11347
Rogers, John C., 15293
Rogers, John Davenport, 1857-1914, 7899

Rogers, Joseph Morgan, 1861-, 7900
Rogers, Justus H., 17517
Rogers, Nathaniel Peabody, 1794-1846, 25409
Rogers, Robert, 1731-1795, 5010, 5011, 22571, 23548
Rogers, Robert M., 15294
Rogers, Thomas L., 7901
Rogers, W. A., illustr., 9553
Rogers, William, 1784-1862, 15292
Rogers, Woodes, d.1732, 23549
Rogers' rangers, 5011
Rojas, Fernando de, d.1541, Celestina, 18059
Rojas, Isidro, 7902
Rojas Cardoso, Amador, 20504
Rojo, T., 19639
Rokeby, Matthew Robinson-Morris, 2d baron, 1713-1800, 23550-23552
Roland, Clayton, 15295
Roland and Wilfred, 9200
Roles, John, 25410
Roll, William H., 15297
A roll of the officers in the Virginia line, 15296
Rolling Ridge, 9477
Rollins, Edward Henry, 1824-1889, 25411
Rollins, James Sidney, 1812-1888, 25412
Rollins, John R., 17518
Romaine, Dexter, pseud., 10492
Roman law, 24589, 24689, 25355
A Roman singer, 6503, 9227
Romance, no fiction, 2887
Romance and humor of the road, 10823
Romance dust from the historic placer, 10338
Romance in real life, 10730
The romance in the life of Hefty Burke, 9358
The romance of a Spanish nun, 8665
Romance of a tin roof and a fire-escape, 10448
The romance of a western trip, 10899
Romance of American history, 768
The romance of American landscape, 13469
The romance of Beauseincourt, 5618
The romance of certain old clothes, 10014
The romance of Davis mountains and Big Bend country, 17441
The romance of Dollard, 6379, 8955
The romance of forest and prairie life, 15682
The romance of Guardamonte, 9336
The romance of hunting, 3852
The romance of Monte Beni, 9822
The romance of natural history, 12325

Romance of student life abroad, 10104
A romance of summer seas, 9364
The romance of the age, 16435
The romance of the green seal, 5619
Romance of the history of Louisiana, 3584
A romance of the line, 6978
Romance of the ocean, 2260
A romance of the republic, 8995
The romance of the revolution, 11611
A romance of the sea serpent, 8756
The romance of the table, 9959
Romance of travel, 11183
The romance of Uncle Bill and Aunt Sis, 15114
The romance of yachting, 12722
Romance on El camino real, 17484
Romance without fiction, 11025
Romanceiro goiano, 19158
El romancero chileno, 18878
Romancero de Bolivar, 20467
Romances of New Orleans, 8598
Romanism in the United States, 8770
Romans, Bernard, 1720(ca.)-1784(ca.), 5012
Romantic adventures in Northern Mexico, 4925
Romantic California, 17369
The Romantic historian, 10670
Romantic passages in southwestern history, 4435
The romantic settlement of Lord Selkirk's colonists, 6229
A romantic tale of high American life, 10912
A romantic young lady, 9644
Romanticism, 19931; Brazil, 18172; Ecuador, 19569
Romapert, George W., 17519
Román, fray, fl.1496, 20356
Rome, Economic condition, 24894; History, 16038; History, Aurelian, 270-275, Fiction, 11082; History, Civil war, 49-48 B.C., Fiction, 9366; History, Empire, B.C. 30-A.D. 284, 23677; Schola Xantha, 24632; Social conditions, 25080; Social life & customs, 10191
Romero, Carlos A., 5937
Romero, José Rubén, 19967
Romero, Mario Germán, 20718
Romero, Matias, 1837-1898, 7904, 7905
Romero de Terreros y Vinent, Manuel, marqués de San Francisco, 1880-, 7903
Romero Rojas, José, 18314
Romero Valdes, Isidro, 7321
Romero y Cordero, Remigio, 1895-1967, 21722
Romig, Mrs. Edna (Davis) 1889-, 7906
Romilly, Sir Samuel, 1757-1818, 23435
Romo Celis, Guillermo, 7907
Romo de Vivar y Torres, Joaquín, 1841-1899, 7907

Romsa, Gerald, 13613
La ronda de los nietos, 18682
Rondônia, Brazil, Economic conditions,
18744, 20554
Roney, Donald F., 15336
Rood, Anson, 1802-1857, 25198
Rooker, Alfred, 1814-1875, 25413
Roosevelt, Robert Barnwell, 1829-1906,
23553
Roosevelt, Theodore, pres., U.S., 1858-
1919, 16426, 17520, 17521
Root, Elihu, 1845-, 7532
Root, Frank Albert, 1857-, 17522
Root, Joseph Mosley, 1807-1879, -7523
Roper, Moses, 25414
Ropes of sand, 10023
Roraima, Brazil, Economic conditions,
18744
Rosa, Luis de la, d.1856, 7908
Rosa e Silva, Francisco de Assis, 1857-
1929, 20567
Uma rosa no tempo, 20512
Rosales de Velasco, José Maximiliano, 7955
Rosanna, 10187
Rosario, Argentine Republic (Sante Fé)
Universidad Nacional del Litoral,
Departamento de Extensión Universitaria,
Extensión universitaria, 18523; Facultad
de Ciencias Matemáticas, Físico-Químicas
y Naturales Aplicadas a la Industria,
Publicaciones, 19919; Instituto de
Fisiografía y Geología, Publicaciones,
19917
Roscio, Juan Germán, Patriotismo de Nirgua
y abuso de los reyes, 19780
Rose, Aquila, 11314
Rose, Blanche E., 17524
Rose, David B. G., 15298
Rose, Edward, 3919
Rose, George, 1817-1882, 5013
Rose, George B., 1860-, 15871
Rose, Isaac P., 1815-1899, 17136
Rose, Robert Hutchinson, 1776-1842, 13233
Rose, Victor M., d.1893, 5014
Rose and Elza, 9301
The rose-bower, 4923
Rose Bradshaw, 10921
Rose Brake, 3165
Rose Clark, 10478
Rose Mather, 3918
A rose of a hundred leaves, 8739
A rose of Glenbogie, 6963
The Rose of Quisconsin, 5061
The Rose of Winnebikon, 10218
A rose of yesterday, 9230
Rosecrans' campaign with the fourteenth army

corps, 2708
Rosen, Maud, grevinna von, 1802-, 5015
Rosen, Peter, 1850-, 17525
Rosenberg, Charles G., 5016, 10508
Rosenberg, Georgeann, 14816
Rosengarten, Joseph G., 4826
Roses and thorns, 10468
Rosillo de Lara, Juan, 7909, 7910
Rosina Meadows, the village maid, 9483
Rosine Laval, 10233
Ross, Albert, pseud., 10551
Ross, Alexander, 1783-1856, 5017, 5018,
17526, 17527
Ross, Alexander Milton, 1832-1897, 25415,
25416
Ross, Clinton, 1861-1920, 8969
Ross, Fitzgerald, 5019
Ross, George M. von, 5020, 5021, 8408
Ross, Harvey Lee, 23554
Ross, Isaac, 1765-1836, 24716
Ross, J., 7930
Ross, Sir James Clark, 1800-1862, 7911
Ross, Sir John, 1777-1856, 7911, 7912
Ross, Lawrence Sullivan, 1833-1898, 16380
Ross, Ralph Colin, 1923-1941, 5022
Ross, Thomas, d.1865, 25417
Ross' Texas brigade, 5014
Ross Brigade, C.S.A., 16894
Ross County, Ohio, History, 14096
Rosser, Thomas L., 17528
Rossi, L. abbé, 17529
Rothert, Otto Arthur, 1871-1956, 15299-15304
Rothery, Agnes Edwards, 1888-, 5023
Rothschild, Edward A., 14668
Rotten republics, 7541
Roubaud, Pierre Joseph Antoine, b.1724, 16956
The rough diamond, 9201
Roughing it around Paris, 10133
Roughing it in the bush, 7527, 7528
Rouhaud, Hippolyte, 7913
Round Anvil Rock, 13591
Round the block, 8826
Round the world in a hack, 9683
The round trip by way of Panama through
California, 16222
The round trip from the Hub to the Golden
gate, 16208
A round trip in North America, 3712
The roundup, 17674
Rouquette, Adrien Emmanuel, 1813-1887, 5024-
5027
Rous, John, 23466
Rousiers, Paul de, 1857-, 5028
Route across the Rocky mountains, 4068
Route and distances to Oregon and California,
5145

380

Route from the Gulf of Mexico and the lower Mississippi valley to California and the Pacific ocean, 3117
Routier, Gaston, 1868-, 7914
Routledge's American handbook and tourist's guide through the U.S., 5029
Roux de Rochelle, Jean Baptiste Gaspard, 1762-1849, 23555
Rovella, Maria Angelica, 19150
The rover of the reef, 9722
The rover's oath of blood, 8798
Rowan, James H., 6748
Rowan, John, 1773-1843, 13538, 13886, 14579, 15305
The Rowan-Chambers duel, 13886
Rowan County, Ky., Maps, 14597
Rowbotham, Francis Jameson, 17531
Rowland, Kate Mason, d.1916, 5030
Rowlandson, Mrs. Mary (White), 23556
Rowson, Susanna (Haswell) 1762-1824, 1935, 25418
Roxbury, Mass., 22269; Biography, 22113; City council, 7787; Roxbury Latin school, 22113
Roxy, 9467
Roy, Joseph Edwin, 1827-1908, 5031
Roy, Just Jean Étienne, 1794-1870, 5032, 7915
Roy, Pierre Georges, 7916
Royal African company of England, 2097, 25419
The royal ape, 5220
Royal bank of Canada, 7428
Royal descent, Families of, 6203-6205
Royal empire society, London, 6903
Royal geographical society, London, 7917
Royal naval biography, 23177
The royal police, 10632
The royal road to Mexico, 7716
Royal society of Canada, Ottawa, 16474
Royall, Mrs. Anne (Newport) 1769-1854, 5033-5037
Royalty in the New world, 3090
Royce, Charles C., 1845-, 15975, 17533
Royce, Jack F., 15306
Royce, Josiah, 1855-1916, 17534
Rozier, Firmin A., b.1820, 5038, 17535, 25420
Rozier's history of the early settlement of the Mississippi valley, 5038
Rúa, Hernando de la, 7918; Carta pastoral, 6374
Rube Burrows, king of outlaws, 15821
Rube Burrows, the famous outlaw, murderer and train robber, 21769
Rubek, Sennoia [pseud.], 1710

Rubin, Simon, 25421
Rubin de la Borbolla, Daniel Fernando, 1907-, 18584
Rubio, pseud., 4043, 7134
Rubio, Alfonso, 20219
Ruby Dana, 8651
Ruby Duke, 10558
Ruby's husband, 5360
Rudd, Robert W., 15307
Ruddell's Station, 13871
Rudeen, E. F., 7919
Ruder, Friedrich August, 1762-1856, 8340
Ruffin, Edmund, 1794-1865, 5039-5041, 23643
Ruffner, Ernest Howard, 17536
Rugendas, Johann Moritz, 1802-1858, illustr., 7965, 7966
Rühl, Karl, 17537
Ruidiaz y Caravia, Eugenio, La Florida, su conquista y colonización, 5228
Ruins of innocence, 10949
Ruiz, Juan de Dios, 1731-1799, 6160
Ruiz Canduelas, Francisco, d.1696, 8292
Ruiz de la Peñuela, Francisco, 7920
Ruiz de Montoya, Antonio, 1585-1652, 7921
Ruiz de Torres, Juan Manuel, 20495
Rujub, the juggler, 7010
Rule, Lucien V., 1871-, 5042
Rule and misrule of the English in America, 12548
Rulers should be benefactors, 12642
Rules and regulations of the House of Representatives, 14585
Rules of practice under the sequestration act, 2056
Rules of the Board of education, 1875
The ruling and ordaining power of congregational bishops, 12156
Rum, 24189
Rumford, Sir Benjamin Thompson, count, 1753-1814, 1270
The run for the roses, 15308
"Run to seed", 10460
Rund um die Erde, 3409
Rundle, Thomas, 1688?-1743, 23557
Runyan, Morris C., 5043
Runyon, Keith, 15309
Rupert's land, 5903, 6311, 6436, 7641; Description & travel, 4955; Northern dept. Council, 7641
Rupp, Adolph Frederick, 1901-1977, 15310
Rupp, Israel Daniel, 1803-1878, tr., 25242, 23558
The Rupp legacy, 15310
Rural life in Texas, 17873
Rural manpower in eastern Kentucky, 14171
Rural rhymes, 1748?

Rural schools, Brazil, 19621; Mexico, 20483; U.S., 795
Rural sketches of Minnesota, 16678
Rural sports, 4115
Rural youth, Brazil, 19621
Rurality, 10918
Ruscelli, Girolamo, d.1556, 25578
Rüse, M. J., tr., 2938
Rush, Benjamin, 1745-1813, 2478, 13245, 25144, 25422
Rush, Caroline E., 25423
Rush, Richard, 1780-1859, 22447
The Rush-light, 2478
Rushton, Edward, 1756-1814, 25424
Rushville, Ill., History, 6652
Rusk, Thomas Jefferson, 1802-1856, 22403
Rusling, James Fowler, 1834-1918, 5044
Russell, Alex J., 7922
Russell, Benjamin, 1761-1845, 989
Russell, Charles Russell, baron, 1832-1900, 5045
Russell, David E., 5046
Russell, George G., 5047
Russell, Ike, 17538
Russell, Irwin, 1853-1879, 5048
Russell, Israel Cook, 17539
Russell, J., 15311
Russell, John, 1773?-1795, 11460
Russell, John Dale, 14624
Russell, John Lewis, 23282
Russell, John Russell, 1st earl, 1792-1878, 1040, 11348
Russell, Matthew, 5045
Russell, Morris Craw, 1840-, 17540
Russell, Osborne, b.1814, 17541
Russell, Robert, d.1871, 5049
Russell, Robert W., 5050
Russell, Thomas C., 16206, 23461
Russell, William H., 16923
Russell, Sir William Howard, 1820-1907, 5051, 5052, 7923, 23559
Russellville, Ky., History, 13865, 14095
Russia, 11466, 11467; Description & travel, 5409; Foreign relations, U.S., 547
Russia to Abraham Lincoln, 5947
Russian language, Dictionaries, 19132
Russo, Pasquale, 25425
Rust, Francis Marion, ed., 8330
The rustic financiers, 10957
Rustic rhymes, 13812
Rusticación méjicana, 7238
Rusticus [pseud.], 6531
la ruta de occidente, 6811
Rutaceae, Brazil, Taxonomy, 10113
Ruth Bergen's limitations, 10946

Ruth Emsley, the betrothed maiden, 8943
Ruth Hall, 10479
Ruth Whalley, 9849
Ruth's sacrifice, 10496
Rutherford, Mildred Lewis, 1852-1928, 7924-7928
Rutherford, Samuel, 1600?-1661, 23560, 23561
Rutherford, Susan B., 15312
Rutledge, 9756
Rutledge, Ann, 1813-1835, 5912, 5960, 5974, 6830, 7022, 8369, 14313, 14314; Poetry, 8039
Rutledge, John, 1739-1800, 12729
Rutledge, S. H., 13911
Rutt, John Towill, 1760-1841, 1796
Ruxton, George Frederick Augustus, 1820-1848, 5053, 5054, 17542
Ruy Díaz, Petronila, 7495
Ruy Díaz, Simón, 7495, 8306
Ruysdale, Philip, 5055
Ruyter, Michiel Adriaanszoon, 1607-1676, 1435
Ruzicka, Z., 19071
Rvbi (Ship), 7929
Ryan, Abram Joseph, 1838-1886, 5056
Rycraft, John, 25911
Rye, Edgar, 17543
Ryerson, John, 1799-1878, 5057
Ryland, Robert, 1805-1899, 25426
Ryus, William Henry, 1839-, 17544
Ryves, Elizabeth, 1750-1797, 22082

Saad, Eduardo Gabriel, 19328
Saavedra, Alvaro, 16th cent., 7567
Sabanera, 18925
Sabato, Ernesto, 19047
Sabbath, 2990, 10904
The Sabbath breakers, 10580
Sabin, Edwin Legrand, 1870-, 7930, 17545
Sabin, Joseph, 1821-1881, 23530, 23544
The sable cloud, 8472
Sabre, Gilbert E., 5058
Sac Indians, 16108
Sacajawea festival, 15313
Un sacerdote del obispado de Puebla, 2011
Sachot, Octave Louis Marie, 1824-, 5059
Sack and destruction of the city of Columbia, S.C., 5163
A sack of gold, 10048
The sack of Unquowa, 10881
Sackett, William Augustus, 1812-1895, 25427
Sackhouse, John, 1797-1819, 12803
Saco, José Antonio, 10000 1070, 111 25428
Saco, Me., Citizens, 8164; First church of

Christ, 2144
Sacramento, Cal., 15969
Sacramento River, Cal., 16442
Sacraments, Catholic church, Addresses, essays, lectures, 19674
Sacred dirges, hymns and anthems, 7058
Sacred vocal music, 7058
The sacrifice of Irene, 11062
A saddle in the wild West, 17488
Saddle mountain, 16088
Sadlier, Anna Theresa, 1854-, 10675
Sadlier, Mary Ann (Madden) "Mrs. James Sadlier," 1820-1903, 10675, 22877
Saenz, Rodrigo, jt. author, 22097
Saenz Peña, Roque, Pres. Argentine Republic, 1851-1914, 19765
A safe deposit, 9692
Safe in purgatory, 10283
Safeguarding Kentucky's natural resources, 13717
Saffarans, Ada Meade, 13833
Safford, Clarindo (Bascom) 1804-, 12701
Safford, William Harrison, 1821-, 15314
The saga of Shitty Smith, 14256
Sagard-Théodat, Gabriel, 17th cent., 23563
Sage, Rufus B., 1817-, 5060
Sage, Russell, 1816-1906, 25429
Sagittarius's letters and political speculations, extracted from the Public ledger, 23430
Sagra, Ramón de la, 1798-1871, 23564
Sagua la Grande, Cuba, History, 5857
Sahagún, Bernardino de, c.1499-1590, 7931, 7932
Sahara, 24408; Description and travel, 23839, 25394, 25397
A sail in sight, 11010
The sailing of King Olaf, 2820
Sailors' life and sailors' yarns, 9055
St. Albans Confederate raid, 1864, 1167, 13973
St. Aloysius College, Louisville, Ky., 15315
Saint-Amant, Pierre C. de, 17546
Saint Augustine, Fla., 4298, 23598; Description, 3219; History, 4939
St. Augustine expedition, 1740, 2879, 3989, 23644
St. Augustine expedition, 1742; 4172
St. Bo, Theodore, 25430
St. Catharine's eve, 10730
Saint Cecilia, 10314
St. Christopher, History, 22234
St. Clair, 11024
St. Clari, Arthur, 1734-1818, 4096, 23565;

Fiction, 13542
St. Clair, Stuart, 14447
St. Clair County, Ill. Citizens, 25342
St. Clair flats, 11205
St. Clair's campaign, 1791, 23565
St. Clare's Church, Hardin County, Ky., 14873
Saint-Cricq, Laurent, 23566
St. Croix, Virgin Islands of the U.S., 5747
St. David's benevolent society, New York, 13286
Saint-Domingue, Assemblée Provinciale du Sud, 7933; Chambre d'agriculture du Cap, 7934; Comité colonial à Paris, 7935; Commissaires, 7936, 7937; Conseil supérieur, 7938, 7939; Députés a l'Assemblée nationale, 7940; Gouverneur-général, 7941
Saint Dominigue à la vielle de la révolution, 8399, 19107
St. Elias, Mount, 16050
St. Elmo, 11186
St. Frances of Rome Church, Louisville, Ky., 15450
St. Francisville, La., Description, 2578
St. Francois Co., Mo., History, 22458
St. François de Sales, Missions, 1288, 1290
Ste. Genevieve, Mo., History, 17535
St. George, 22945
St. George De Lisle, 10695
St. George's Hundred, Del., First Presbyterian church, 2264
Saint-Hilaire, Augustin François Cesar Prouvençal de, 1779-1853, 7092
St. John (Ship), 25168
St. John, Percy Bolingbroke, 1821-1889, 5061, 15316, 15825, 15827
St. John, Peter, 1720-1811, 23567
St. John, Samuel, 3515
St. John's River, 4298
St. John's River society, 7942
St. John's wooing, 10261
St. Joseph Hospital, Lexington, Ky., 14811
St. Joseph's convent, Emmitsburg, Md., 8896
St. Joseph's Paris, Bowling Green, Ky., 15317
St. Laudry Parish, La., 25431
St. Lawrence, Gulf of, 6575
St. Lawrence Co., N.Y., History, 22573
St. Lawrence river, 22730; Description & travel, 22128
Saint Leger, 10105
St. Louis, 12832, 23568; Biography, 16328; Description, 3158, 3755, 4932; History, 5084, 16197, 16328, 23568; Iron Mountain & Southern Railway Company, 5062
St. Louis, Louisiana purchase exposition, 1904, 2740, 4187, 5581, 5981, 16414;

Kentucky, 14514
St. Louis River, 16564
St. Louis' isle, 3927
St. Lucia, 11509, 11742
St. Mark's Parish, Va., 3680
St. Martin, Alexis, 1797?-1880, 15946
St. Martin, Dutch West Indies, 23959
St. Martin's Brotherhood, 1872-1947, 15171
St. Michael's day, 4009
St. Nicholas society of Nassau island,
  Brooklyn, 13262
St. Paul, Henry, 23569
St. Paul, Minneapolis & Manitoba
  railway, 16409
St. Paul's Church, Louisville, Ky., 14033
St. Paul's college, Bermuda Island, 1195
St. Peter Clover Church, Louisville,
  Kentucky, 15318
St. Peter's at Rosendale, 10747
St. Philip's, 9757
St. Pierre (Island), 6401
Saint-Quantin, Adolphe de, 24176
St. Simon's niece, 8781
St. Twel'mo, 11114
St. Vincent, John Jervis, earl, 1735-1823,
  1476
Saint Vincent, Description & travel, 6339;
  Governor, 1809-1829 (Brisbane), 25433;
  History, 574; House of Assembly, 25433;
  Legislative Council (1763-1867), 25433
Sainte-Croix, Guillaume Emmanuel Joseph
  Quilhem de Clermont-Lodève, baron de,
  1746-1809, 23570
Ste. Foye, Battle of, 1760, 21889
Ste. Foye monument, Quebec, 21889
Sala, George Augustus Henry, 1828-1895,
  5063, 11455
Salado river, Sauta Fé (Province) Argentine
  republic, 13054, 13144
The salamander, 10804
Salander and the dragon, 10749
El salariado minero en Chile colonial, 19802
Salazar Ylarregui, José, 5064
Salcedo, Gaspar de, 6348
Salcedo, José de, 6348
Saldias, Adolfo, 1850-1914, 7943
Salem, Mass., Biography, 24601; City
  council, 1518; History, 2243, 22186
Salem, N.J., History, 13257
Salem female charitable society, Salem,
  Mass., 11340
Sales, José Hipólito, Bp., 18336
Sales, Luis, 1745-1807, 17549
Sales, Brazil, 19220
Sales, conditional, Brazil, 19338
Sales tax, Mexico, 19493

Salesbury, Conn., History, 21919
Salina, N.Y., 1030
Salinas Martinez, Arturo, 20218
Salinas y Cabrera, Diego de, 1691-1764, 8056
Saline toxicity in poplar and white willow,
  18636
Salisbury, N.C., Military prison, 2761
El salitre, 19685
Salkowski, Karl, 1838-1899, 25434
Sally, 9376
Sally Ann's experience, 15092
Sally Dows, 9791
Salm-Salm, Felix Constantin Alexander Johann
  Nepomuk, prince du, 1828-1870, 7944
Salmon, Thomas, 1679-1767, 5065, 5066
Salmon River, 4250
The Salmon River Mission, 17608
Los salmos, 19023
Salomy Jane's kiss, 6975
Salontha, de, 25435
Salt, 1030
Salt Desert Trail, 16924, 16926
Salt Lake City, 16229, 16546, 17763;
  Biography, 15983, 17760; Description, 1744,
  2510, 2970, 16009, 16378; Direct, 16583;
  History, 17760
Salt of the earth, 9916
Salt River, 14358
Salt water bubbles, 10789
O salteào, 19080
Salted with fire, 8933
Salter, William, 1821-1910, 7945, 17552,
  17553
Saltonstall, Leverett, 1783-1845, 1451
Saltpeter, Chile, 19685
La salud mental y la asistencia psiquiátrica
  en la Argentina, 19011
Saludo lírico a Comayagua, 18520
Salut au Kentucky, 14234
Salvaalegre, Juan Pio de Montufar y Frasco,
  marques de, 7946
El Salvador, 1129, 13484, 20642; Agricultural
  policies, 20640; Commerce, 20642;
  Description & travel, 7521, 8164; History,
  18829, 19909; History, To 1838, 18847;
  Politics & government, 21749; Population,
  20640
Salvador, Brazil, Universidade, Publicações,
  III, 19212
Salvage, 18703
El salvamento marítimo y su diferencia con
  otras figuras jurídicas, 18703
Salvatierra, García Sarmiento de Sotomayor
  Enriquez de Luna, conde de, d.1659, 7920
Salvatierra, Sara M., 19970
Salvation, 23303, 23666

384

Salzbacher, Joseph, 1790-1867, 5067
The Salzburgers and their descendants, 13486
Salzburgers in Georgia, 4908
"Sam," 5652
Sam Houston and the war of independence in Texas, 17899
Sam Johnson, 9044
Sam Lawson's Oldtown fireside stories, 10909
Sam Shirk, 9395
Sam Slick in Texas, 3762
Sam Squab, the Boston boy, 8467
Samantha at Saratoga, 9888
Sambrano Urbaneta, Oscar, 1929-, 18001, 18565
Samford, William Flewellen, 1818-1894, 24417
Sampey, John R., 15418
Sampitch Indians, 17470
Sampleton, Samuel, pseud., 7523
Sampson, Flem D., 7947
Sampson, Francis Asbury, 1842-, 17132
Sampson, Marmaduke Blake, d.1876, 25436
Sampson, Susan Steele, 13663
Sampson, William, 1764-1836, 13241, 22453
Sampson against the Philistines, or The reformation of lawsuits, 22453
Samson, George Whitefield, 1819-1896, 25437
Samson, William Holland, 1860-1917, 16105
San Alberto, José Antonio de, abp., 1727-1804, 7948
San Antonio, Description, Guidebooks, 16275; History, 15918, 16275, 17932
San Benito Co., Calif., Biography, 16655; History, 16655
San Bernardino County, California, 16850
San Diego, Calif., Description, 17554; Direct, 17554
San Diego county, California, 16850
San Fernando de Bexar, 16283
San Fernando, Argentina, History, 20463
San Francisco, 15969, 17699; Committee of vigilance, 17047, 17097, 17534, 22191; Description, 7306, 16358, 16374, 17666, 21775; Direct., 16944; Fiction, 9067; History, 15927, 16068, 16445, 16789, 17097; Journal of a voyage to, 16886; Politics & government, 16445
San Francisco bay, 16421, 16534; Antiquities, 17265
San Isidro, 9253
San Jacinto (Ship), 23413
San Jacinto, Battle of, 1836, 4405
San Joaquin River, Cal., 16442
San Joaquin Valley, Cal., Biography, 16656
San Jose, Calif., History, 16667

San Juan, P.R., History, Addresses, essays, lectures, 18590; Social life & customs, 18590
San Juan Baptista (Frigate), 8272
San Juan County, Utah, 17070; History, 16902
San Juan del Norte, Nicaragua, History, 890
San Juan exploring expedition, 17775
San Juan mountains, 16329
San Juan region, Col., Description & travel, 16589
San Luis Obispo Co., Calif., 16775; Biography, 16655; History, 16655
San Luis Park, Col., 16604; Description & travel, 15993
San Luis Potosí, Mexico (City), 6690
San Martin (ship), 6352
San Martín, José de, 1778-1850, 7949, 8112, 18399, 19586, 19844; Poetry, 20465
San Martín Suárez, José de, 7950
San Miguel (Costa Rica) formation, 19760
San Nicolas, Argentine Republic, History, 18671
San Pablo, Costa Rica, Maps, 20572
San Rafael, Calif., Description, 16596
San Salvador, Agustín Pomposo Fernández de, 17556; Museo Nacional "David J. Guzman", 7951; Universidad Nacional, 23873
Sanabria Martínez, Victor, abp., 1899-1952, 19082
The sanative influence of climate, 11815
Sanborn, Charles Henry, 1822-1899, 11754
Sanborn, Franklin Benjamin, 1831-1917, 25438
Sanborn, Helen Josephine, 1857-1917, 7952
Sanborn, Kate, 17557
Sánchez, Manuel Segundo, 7637
Sánchez, Tomás Antonio, 1725-1802, 399
Sánchez Espinosa, José, 7406
Sánchez Fontáns, J., 20636
Sánchez Pascual, Diego, 17th cent., 8305
Sánchez Reulet, Aníbal, ed., 20409
Sánchez Santos, Trinidad, 1864-, 6332
Sánchez Somoano, José, 5068
Sánchez Sorondo, Matías Guillermo, 1880-, 7953
Sánchez Valverde, Antonio, d.1790, 7954
Sancho Dávila y Bermúdez, Antonio, 7611
Sanctification, 13779, 14959
The sanctuary, 10421
Sand, 14173, 15272
Sand Cave, Ky., 13857
Sand Creek, Battle of, 1864, 16823
Sand Creek investigation, 2995
Sand, George, pseud. of Mme. Dudevant, 1804-1876, 1104
Sand 'n' bushes, 10545
La sandalia de madera, 18980

Sandborn, Ruth Ellen, 17558
Sandburg, Carl, 1878-1967, 7471
Sanders, Daniel Clarke, 1768-1850, 23571
Sanders, Harlan, 1890-, 15319
Sanders, Robert Stuart, 15184, 15185,
  15320-15325
Sanders, Mrs. Sue A. (Pike) 1842-1931,
  17559
Sanderson, James M., 23572
Sandhum, Henry, illus., 16870
Sandiel y Palacios, Mariano Buenaventura,
  7955
Sandoval, Jeronimo de, 7827
The Sandown victory, 9863
Sands, Frances M., 1065
Sands, Robert Charles, 1799-1832, 2157,
  21821, 23469, 23573
Sandwich, Edward Montagu, 1st earl of,
  1625-1672, 773
Sandwich Islands to lower Oregon, 16324
Sandy, 15267
Sandys, Ed. W., 10125
Sanford, David, 998
Sanford, Ezekiel, 1796-1822, 23574
Sanford, Mrs. Nettie, 17560
Sanford, Washington L., 1825, 15326
Sangamon Co., Ill., Biography, 23505;
  Description & travel, Maps, 6168;
  Genealogy, 23505; History, 6847
Sanger, George Partridge, 1819-1890, 239
Sangre de Cristo, Slopes of the, 16370
Sangre de mestizos, 20059
Sangster, M. E., 10163
Sangston, Lawrence, 2479
Sanillac, 5693
Sanitation, Brazil, 20379, 20382
Sanpete Co, Utah, 16776
Sanromá, Joaquín María, 1828-1895, 24291,
  25439
Sanson, Nicolas, 1600-1667, 23575
Sant' Ilario, 6504
Santa, Eduardo, 1928-, 20333
Santa Anna, Antonio López de, pres. Mexico,
  1795-1876, 1758, 12256
Santa Catalina, 8291
Santa Catarina, Brazil, 11525, 19420;
  History, 19108
Santa Clara Co., Cal, History, 16777
Santa Cruz, Andrés, Pres. Bolivia, 1794-
  1865, 18897; Poetry, 951
Santa Cruz, Bolivia (Dept.), 606
Santa Cruz Co., Cal., Biography, 16655,
  16777; History, 16055
Santa Cruz de Mompox, 20508
Santa Fé, N.M., 3111, 5531; Description,
  5739

Santa Fé and the far west, 5069
Santa Fé, Conquest of, 3068
Santa Fé Expedition, 3491, 4989
The Santa Fé trade, 16636
Santa Fé Trail, 3688, 5739, 6894, 6895, 7080
  16636, 16725, 17041, 17132, 17544
Santa Fé y Bogotá, 7956
Santa María, José de, 7957
Santa Marta, 13350
Santa Marta, Colombia, History, Sources,
  20018; Maps, 20307
"Santa Marta Fabril Sociedade Anônima,"
  18161
Santana, Maria Celina, 18605
Santander, Juan de, 1145
Santangelo, Francesco Orazio Giuseppe de
  Attellis, 1807?-1826, 13328
Santangelo, Orazio Donato Gideon de Attellis,
  b.1774, 13328
Santee dialect, Texts, 23535
Santee River, 3358
Santiago de Chile, Biblioteca Nacional, 7275,
  20166, 20522; Cathedral, 18335
Santiago de Chile, Universidad, Facultad de
  Ciencias Jurídicas y Sociales, 20399,
  20401; Colección de estudios jurídicos y
  sociales, 18337; Instituto de economía,
  19230, 19512; Instituto de Geografía,
  18358; Instituto de historia, 18341;
  Instituto Histórico y Bibliográfico de
  Ciencias Jurídicas y Sociales, Cartillas,
  19024
Santiago León Garabita, Juan de, bp., 6754
Santibáñez, Enrique, 1869-, 7958
Santleben, August, 1845-, 17561
Santo Domingo, History, 18683
Santo Domingo, Costa Rica, Maps, 20571
Santo Domingo (District), Colombia, Economic
  conditions, 20258
Santo Domingo (French colony), 19; Laws,
  statutes, etc., 24425
Santos, Eurico, 19420
Santos, Brazil, 19805
Sanz de Monroy, Miguel Elias, 7959
São Francisco river, Brazil, 11636
São Francisco Valley, Brazil, Economic
  policy, 19256
São João del Rei, Brazil, Churches, 18204
São Luis (Brazil) Departmento de Cultura do
  Estado, 19055
São Paulo, Brazil (City), Commerce, 17958;
  Description, 20358; Museo de Arte Moderna,
  18171; Social life & customs, 19664;
  Universidade, Biblioteca Central, 20198;
  Universidade, Escola de Comunicações e
  Artes, 19665; Universidade, Escola de
  Comunicações e Artes, Departamento de

Journalismo e Editoração, Serie
Jornalismo, 19730; Universidade, Escola
Politécnica, Instituto de Pesquisas
Tecnológicas, Publicação, 19506-
19509; Universidade, Faculdade de
Ciencias Economicas e Administrativas,
Boletim, 19670; Universidade,
Faculdade de Direito, Coleção
"Direito e cultural", 19691
São Paulo, Brazil (State), Economic
conditions, 20564; History, 19529,
22231; Serviço de Serici-cultura,
17965
São Thome e Principe (Province), 24967;
Economic conditions, 25935
São Thome Island (West Africa), 24966,
24968, 25113
Sapia Martino, Raúl, 7874, 7960
Sapper, Carl, 7961
A Sappho of Green Springs, 6973
Saracinesca, 6505, 9231
Saratoga, 9299, 10751
Saratoga, N.Y., Fiction, 9949
Saratoga campaign, 1777, Fiction, 10510
Saratoga in 1901, 10162
Saratoga Springs, N.Y., 23414; Description,
Guide-books, 195; High Rock Spring,
22886
Saravia, Manuel de, 7962, 7963
Sarfatti, Margherita Grassini, 5070
Sarg, Tony, illustr., 13859
Sargent, Angelina M., 5071
Sargent, Fitzwilliam, 1820-1889, 25440,
25441
Sargent, John Osborne, 1811-1891, 12663
Sargent, Winthrop, 1825-1870, 5072, 23576,
23577
Sarinana y Cuenca,Isidro, 1630?-1696, 5856
Sarmiento, Domingo Faustino, pres. Argentine
republic, 1811-1888, 5073, 7708, 19793,
19797
Sarmiento de Gamboa, Pedro, 7964
Sarmiento de Mendoza, Diego, 7920
Sarria, Vicente Francisco, 1767-1835, 17207
Sartine, Antoine Raymond Jean Gualbert
Gabriel de, comte d'Alby, 1729-1801,
23701
Sartorius, Christian, i.e. Carl Christian
Wilhelm, 1796-1872, 7965, 7966
Sartorius von Waltershausen, August,
freiherr, 1852-, 25442
Saskatchewan, Description & travel, 3877,
3879; History, 7715, 7796
Saskatchewan and the Rocky Mountains, 6342,
8080
The Saskatchewan country of the north-west

of the dominion of Canada, 8092
Saskatchewan river, 3878
The Saskatoon story, 7715
Satanstoe, 9149
Satin, Mark Ivor, 1946-, 7967
Satire, English, 7591
Satire, Uruguayan, 20045
Saturday-night musings and thoughtful papers,
10538
The Saturniad, 694
Sauce for the goose, 9538
Saucier, John Baptiste, b.1726, 5226
Saude e sistemas, 20094
Sauer, Carl Ortwin, 1889-, 15327
Saugrain de Vigni, Antoine François, 1763-
1820, 5074
Sauk Indians, 16634
Saunders, Charles Francis, 17562
Saunders, George Washington, 1854-, 16835
Saunders, Rolfe S., 7968
Saunders, William, 1823-1895, 5075
Saussure, Henri Louis Frédéric de, 1829-1905,
7969
Sauvage, Henry, 24176
Sauvalle, Paul Marc, 1857-, 7970
Savage, Charles R., illus., 17081
Savage, James, 1784-1873, 7971
Savage, James Woodruff, 1826-, 17563, 17564
Savage, William Sherman, 25443
The savage beauty, 10857
Les savanes, 5027
Savannah, Ga., City council, 22521;
Directories, 1756; History, 6419, 24810;
Libraries, 12045; Siege, 1779, 12933
Savardan, Augustin, 5076
Savery, William, 1750-1804, 5077
Savine, Albert, 8399
Sawyer, Frederick Adolphus, 1822-1891, 22937
Sawyer, George S., 25444
Sawyer, Lorenzo, 5078
Sawyier, Paul, 1865-1917, 15350
Saxton, Charles, 17566
Say, Jean Baptiste, 1767-1832, 23578
Say, Thomas, 1787-1834, 2465, 5079, 5080,
5081, 13360
Say and seal, 11098
Sayer, Robert, 1725-, 5082
Sayre School, Lexington, Ky., 13873
Sayings and doings at the Tremont House,
10791
The sayings of Dr. Bushwhacker, and other
learned men, 9197
Sayre, James V., 17410
Scadding, Henry, 1813-1901, 7972
Scale insects, Cuba, 18087
Scales, Thomas, 1786-1860, 25445

The scalp hunters, 4925
Scalzo, Nilo, 18272, 19147
Scammell, Alexander, 1746?-1781, 21971
Scammon, Jonathan Young, 1812-1890,
  reporter, 22635
Scandinavian travellers in the South, 15539
Scandinavians in the U.S., 6387
Scarce Kentuckiana, 13887
The scare-crow, 1944
Scarlet Feather, 9986
The scarlet letter, 9824
Scarritt, Winthrop Eugene, 1857-, 7973
Scattered leaves, 15271
Scattered leaves from a physician's diary,
  8451
Scattergood, David, Philadelphia, pub.,
  24921
Scenery, science and art, 387
Scenery of the plains, mountains and
  mines, 4213
The scenery-shower, 1745
Scènes américaines, 4649
Scenic and historic Garrard, 15328
The scenic attractions and summer resorts
  along the railways of the Virginia,
  Tennessee, and Georgia air line, 5576
Scenic Utah, 16969
The scent of the roses, 9575
Schade, Louis, 1829-1903, 5083
Schafer, Joseph, 17568-17570, 17684
Schaff, Philip, 1819-1893, 25446
Schaghticoke, N.Y., History, 8814
Schaller, Frank, tr., 23139
Schalk, Emil, 1834-, 13458
Scharf, John Thomas, 1843-1898, 5084, 5085
Scharmann, Hermann B., 5086, 17571
Schatten über Mexiko, 8358
Schaub, Friedrich,
Schaw, Janet, 1731(ca.)-1801(ca.), 5087
Scheeps-togt van Anthony Chester, 2983
Scheibert, Justus, 1831-1904, 5088
Schell, Fred B., illustr., 9006
Schelling, Felix Emmanuel, 1858-, 10737
Scherer, Marie Luise, illustr., 3586
Scherff, Julius, 5089
Scherger, Carl, 7974
Schermerhorn, John Freeman, 1786-1851, 5090
Scherzer, Carl, 1821-1903, 5595, 8324
Scheuerle, Joe, illustr., 5583
Schevichaven, Herman Diederik Johan van,
  1827-1918, 25448
La schiavitù e la guerra negli Stati
  Uniti d'America, 25449
Schiel, James, 5091
Schiess, Wilhelm, 7975
Schieve, Jens, 1900-, 5092

Schilderungen des treibens im leben und
  handel in den Vereinigten Staaten und
  Havana, 4961
Schiller, Johann Christoph Friedrich von,
  1759-1805, 4765
Schilling, John L., 25450, 25451
Schizomus, Cuba, 18526
Schlagintweit, Robert von, 1833-1885, 17572
Schlatter, Michael, 1716-1790, 5093, 12660
Schlett, A., ed., 25502
Schlözer, Karl von, ed., 7976
Schlözer, Kurd von, 1822-1894, 7976
Schlumberger, Gustav León, 1844-, 4758
Schmidel, Ulrich, 7977
Schmidt, Friedrich, of Stuttgart, 5094
Schmidt, Karl Adolf, 1815-1903, 25452
Schmölder, B., 5095
Schoelcher, Victor, 1804-1893, 25196, 25453,
  25454
Schofield, John McAllister, 1831-1906, 24864
Schoharie Co., N.Y., History, 11567
A scholar's adventures in the country, 10910
Scholl, John, 14020
Scholl, Joseph, 14021
Scholl's Station, 13614
Schönauer, Georg, 5096
School buildings, Kentucky, 13523
School census, Canada, Statistics, 19031
School children, Food, Brazil, 18228
School discipline, 13217, 15636
School employees, Non-certified, Kentucky,
  14499, 14742
The school for politics, 9610
School government, 13217
School-houses, 2329, 11750
School lands, Maryland, 23388
The school lands of Colorado, 16642
Schoolcraft, Henry Rowe, 1793-1864, 5097-5100,
  5693, 15329, 17573, 17574, 23579
Schoolcraft, Mary (Howard) "Mrs. H.R.
  Schoolcraft", 25455, 25456
Schoolings, Sir William, 1860-, 7978
Schoonover, Thomas J., 17575, 17576
Schöpf, Johann David, 1752-1800, 5101
Schott, Carl, 7979
Schott, Charles Anthony, 1826-1901, 22807
Schrader, Floyd F., 15330
Schrieke, Bertram Johannes Otto- 1890-, 5102
Schriver, Lester Osborne, 1891-, 7980
Schroeder, Osw., 7981
Schten, Edward V., 15331-15333
Schuchardt, Hugo, 20713
Schuhmann, Ellen B., 14997
Schüller, Donaldo, 20091
Schultz, Christian, 5103
Schulz, Fritz, 1826-1905, 25457

Schurz, Carl, 1829-1906, 6288, 25458
Schütz, Günther, 20716
Schütze, Albert, 5104
Schütze's jahrbuch für Texas und emigranten-
  führer für 1883, 5104
Schuyler, Montgomery, 1843-1914, 17577
Schuyler Co., Ill., History, 16794
Schuylkill Co., Pa., History, 6620
Schuylkill County and some of its people,
  6619
Schuylkill fishing company, 13435
Schwab, Edith C., 15334, 15335
Schwab, Edith M., 15336
Schwabe, Johann Joachim, 211
Schwalbe, J.F.G., 6808
Schwartz, Stephan, 5105, 17578
Schwartyweller, Harry K., 15337
Schwatka, Frederick, 1849-1892, 7982
Schweinitz, Lewis David von, 1780-1834,
  13360
Schwendeman, Gerald, 15338
Science, 12902, 19263, 20215, 20643;
  Addresses, essays, lectures, 1324, 13004;
  Argentine Republic, 18436; Bibliography,
  19553; Early works to 1800, 11463,
  23036; History, U.S., 11973; Methodology,
  18154; Societies, etc., 285, 286, 509,
  22821; Study and teaching (Elementary),
  19033; Study and teaching, Curricula,
  20596
Science, History of, 13626
Science and civilization, 20353
Science and state, Colombia, 20353
Science fiction, 19804; American, 20213
Scientific expeditions, 615, 1324, 2585,
  7007, 7091, 7092, 7170-7172, 7218, 21853;
  Handbooks, 11463
Scientists, 1324
Scioto County, Ohio, Biography, 4169;
  History, 4169
Scioto Valley, Ohio, 2507
Scituate, Mass., Genealogy, 22063; History,
  22063
Scobel, Albert, 1851-, 7983
Scoble, John, 146, 25460
Scollard, Clinton, 1860-, 10283
Scoperta dell' America fatta nel secolo x da
  alcuni Scandinavi, 1322
Scoresby, William, 1789-1857, 7984, 22651
Scorpions, 18527; Cuba, 18524, 18528, 18529,
  18531-18533
Scot, George, d.1685, 23580
Scotch in North Carolina, 22908
Scotch-Irish in the U.S., 853
Scotland, Description & travel, 5927, 11158;
  High court of justiciary, 13013

Scott, Alfred L., 1862-, 17691
Scott, Charles, 1749-, 14104, 15339
Scott, Dred, 11255, 11538, 23922, 24366,
  25197, 25374
Scott, Mrs. Elizabeth Slaughter Bassett,
  14031
Scott, James Leander, 23581
Scott, Job, 1751-1793, 5106
Scott, John, 1785-1861, 25461
Scott, John, 1820-1907, 5107
Scott, John, 1824-1896, 25768
Scott, John, of Centreville, Ind., 23582
Scott, Joseph, 5108
Scott, Orange, 1800-1847, 25462
Scott, Otho, 23220
Scott, R.E., 7985
Scott, R.H., 15340
Scott, Robert Eden, 1808-1862, 25463
Scott, Thomas, 1580?-1626, 23583
Scott, Sir Walter, bart., 1771-1832, 4027,
  23001
Scott, William, 1840?-1862, 7138
Scott, William A., 17580
Scott, Winfield, 1786-1866, 7986, 13121,
  16942, 22382, 23104, 23584
Scott Countian chess master, 13693
Scott Co., Ia., 16106
Scott County, Ky., Biography, 13559; History,
  14166, 15142, 15373; Maps, 14591
Scott's pond thirty years ago, 11173
Scottish songs, ballads, and poems, 2397
Scotus Americanus, pseud., 5109
The scourge of the ocean, 8920
The scourge of the river, 4461
The scout, 9977
The scout and ranger, 4801
The scout's mistake, 10863
The scout's revenge, 5663
The scouting expeditions of McCulloch's
  Texas rangers, 4926
Scouts and scouting, 15941, 17224
Scoville, Joseph Alfred, 1815-1864, 2480,
  25464
Scrap book on law and politics, 4978
Scraps, 10260
Scraps of California history, 16844
Scraps of early Texas history, 3833
Scraps of poetry and prose, 22446
Scraps of song and Southern scenes, 3492
Scribblers' club, Lexington, Ky., 15341
Scribblings and sketches, 11109
Scribblings by the Scribblers' club, 15341
Scribner, Benjamin Franklin, 1825-1900, 5110
Scribner, Isaac W., d.1864, 25465
Scripps, John Locke, 1818-1866, 7987, 17581
A scriptural view of the character, causes

The secret witness, 8860
El secreto profesional del abogado, 19838
Secrets of the convert and confessional, 11217
Secrets of the priesthood, 11017
Section 558, 9815
Sects, 1075, 11510, 22370; U.S., 1075, 12320
Los secuestros en la guerra de independencia, 19521
Secularization, Mexico, 18928
Securities, 12634, 21972
Security Trust Company, Lexington, Ky., 13902
Seddon, James Alexander, 1815-1880, 24182-24184
Sedgwick, Chatharine Maria, 1789-1867, 21821
Sedgwick, Theodore, 1780-1839, 25475
Sedgwick & co., 1809
Sedimentos neógenos del S.W. del Uruguay, 19919
See exotic Mexico, 7267
See-saw, 9038
See Yup, 6975
Seebohm, Frederick, 1833-1912, 25476
Seed by the wayside, 8723
Seedlings, 18351
The seeds and fruits of crime, 9335
Seeds and shells, 2348
Seegmiller, Emma Carroll ("Emma S. Higbee"), 17582
Seekers after God, 4095
Seeking fortune in America, 16643
Seeking the golden fleece, 17675
Seekonk, Mass., History, 11285
Seemann, Berthold Carl, 1825-1871, jt. author, 7750
Seemingly experimental religion, 1326
Seems Southern to we, 15345
Segar, Joseph E., 1804-1885, 25477
Segura, Diego de, 8272
Segura, P. Nicolás de, 7994
La seguridad social del trabajador rural en el Uruguay, 20050
El seguro de crédito de exportación, 19567
El seguro social en América Latina, 20031
Seilhamer, George Overcash, 1839-, 5122
Seixas y Lovera, Francisco de, 7995
Selden, Henry M., 25545
The Seldens in Chicago, 9334
Selecciones de la tribuna y de la prensa, 8442
Select and fugitive poetry, 22118
Select antiquities, curiosities, beauties, and varieties, of nature and art, in

America, 12994
Select committee on charges against Benjamin Sebastian, 14586
Select committee on charges against Humphrey Marshall, 14587
The select letters of Major Jack Downing, 10822
A select party, 9823
Selected speech rhymes, 14406
A selection of hymns and poems, 4374
Selections from the poetical literature of the West, 2376, 3563
Selections from the religious and literary writings of John H. Bocock, 2746
Selections from the writings of Mrs. Sarah C. Edgarton Mayo, 10335
Selections from the writings of the late Thomas Hedges Genin, 3588
A selection of the patriotic addresses, to the President of the United States, 23590
Seler, Eduard, 1849-1922, 7932, 7998
Seler, Frau Caecilie (Sachs) 1855-, 7996, 7997
Self-convicted violators of principle, 25930
Self-giving, 8646
Self-made, 11121
A self-made woman, 8890
Self-raised, 10843
Selkirk, Alexander, 1676-1721, 23549
Selkirk, Thomas Douglas, 5th earl of, 1771-1820, 6221, 6668, 7999, 8000, 8120, 17404
Selkirk Range, 6890, 8372
Selkirk Settlement, Canada, 11352
Sellers, Matthew B., 14943
Sellier, L. M., 14562, 14590, 14591, 14593, 14594, 14597
Selma the soprano, 10448
Selskabet for trykkefrihedens rette brug, Copenhagen, 23128
Selter, H. Foure, 5074
Selwyn, Alfred Richard Cecily, 1824-1902, 6748
Sem lei nem rei, 19702
Semalle, René de, 23591
Semblanza de Honduras, 8286
As sementes da independência, 19695
A semi-centenary discourse, 1840
Semi Rosa, 20206
Semi-tropical California, 17757
Seminario de Integración Social Guatemalteca, 20403
Seminario Ibero-americano de Comunicaçao e Mobilidade, 19364
Seminole war, 1st, 1817-1818, 12238, 22165, 23481; 2d., 1835-1842, 1990, 2617, 3046, 4332, 4836, 12238, 16458, 23463; 2d, 1835-

391

1842, Fiction, 9410, 10589
Semmes, John Edward, 1851-, 23592
Semmes, Raphael, 1809-1877, 5123, 8001,
8002, 23593
Semmes, Thomas Jenkins, 1824-1899, 2052
Semple, Ellen Churchill, 1863-1932, 8003
Semple, Robert, fl.1848, 16717
The sempstress, 10904
O Senai em São Paulo, 19422
Señan, José Francisco de Paula, 1760-1823,
17207
The senator's son, 11044
El sendero y los dias, 20200
Seneca, Lucius Annaeus, 24421
Seneca Co., O., History, 11653
Seneca Indians, 22138, 23589; Missions, 134
Seneca language, Glossaries, vocabularies,
etc., 13125
Senex, John, d.1740, 22288
Senior, Bernard Martin, 25478
Senior, Nassau William, 1790-1864, 25479
El Señor Root en Mexico, 7532
Señora, Cavsas ay que obligan à romper el
silencio, 6421
El Señorio de los Incas, 20194
Sens et usage du terme structure dans les
sciences humaines et sociales, 18904
Sense, 10538
The sense of the past, 7128
Sensors, Remote, 19010
The sentiments of a British American, 23689
Sentinon, G., 8025
Separatism in Utah, 1847-1870, 16322
The Septameron, 10737
A September scamper, 16112
September the eleventh, 1777, 10212
Septic tanks, 14256
Septimus Felton, 9825
Sepúlveda, Juan Ginés de, 1490-1573, 6355,
8004, 19894
Sepúlveda Lozano, Rubén, 20310
The sequel to Rolling Ridge, 9478
Sequestration act, Rules of practice under
the, 2056
The serenades, 10197
Serfdom, 24648, 25448, 25521; France, 23864,
23968; Germany, 24733
Sergeant, John, 1710-1739, 12895, 24278,
25480
Sergeant, John, 1779-1852, 1314
Sergeant Atkins, 9410
Sergeant Barnacle, 10783
Sergeant Croesus, 10114
The sergeant's private madhouse, 9017
Sergio Visca, Arturo, 10071
Sergipe, Brazil (State), Description, 18345

Sericulture, 19172, 23797
A series of answers to certain popular
objections against separating from the
rebellious colonies, 23724
A series of essays on the principles and
policy of free states, 13173
A series of wisdom and policy, 23594
A serious address to the rulers of America,
on the inconsistency of their conduct
respecting slavery, 24206
Serious considerations on important subjects;
observations on slavery, 23963
A serious review, affectionately recommended
to the careful examination of Friends,
23365
Serle, Ambrose, 1742-1812, 23595
Sermon de honras funerais, 8005
A sermon occasioned by the destruction of
Pennsylvania hall, 2363
A sermon on American slavery, 3303
Sermon on the life and character of Abraham
Lincoln, 12622
Sermon on the Mount, Sermons, 1384
A sermon on the operations of Divine
Providence, 24346
Sermones inéditos, 20534
Sermons, Fast days, 22917
Sermons, American, 632, 841, 1062, 1073, 1211,
1216, 1384, 1687, 1778, 2259, 11746, 12046,
12507, 22006, 22007, 22093, 22264, 22321,
22450, 22548, 22810, 23018, 23238, 23323,
23338; American (Selections: Extracts,
etc.), 1058; English, 23785, 23786;
Spanish, 6809, 7013, 8434; Spanish,
Colombia, 20534; Spanish, Peru, 7031
Serpent, worship, 16025
The serpent's sting, 10695
Serpents, New York, 679; North America, 677
Serra, Girolamo Francesco Luciano, marchese,
1761-1837, 727
Serra, Junipero, father, 1713-1784, 17115,
21953
Serrano A., Luis F., 20329, 20330
Serrano Montaner, Ramón, 20155
Serrano y Sanz, Manuel, 1868-, 20356
Serrote prêto, 19875
Os sertanejos que eu conheci, 18622
The servant-girl of the period the greatest
plague of life, 8961
Service afloat, Memoirs of, 5123
Service industries, Brazil, Statistics, 19430,
19431
Service with the Sixth Wisconsin volunteers,
3198
La servicia civil, 20334
Servicio social, 19978

Servicio Técnico Agrícola Colombiano Americano, 18640
Do Serviço de Estudos Pedagógicos, 19219
O Serviço de Pesquisas Tecnológicas do Departamento de Estradas de Rodagem da Bahia, 18693
El seseo en el Nuevo Reino de Granada, 20227
The sesquicentennial addresses given at Christ Church, Lexington, Kentucky, 15346
Sesquicentennial celebration of the battle of the Blue Licks at Blue Licks Battle-field Park, 14641
Sesquicentennial of Kentucky, 1792-1942, 14261
Sesquicentennial stories..., 14783
Sesto, Julio, 8006
The set of china, 10197
Setenta y cinco años de vida económica del Perú, 1889-1964, 18841
O sétimo dia, 20101
Seton, Ernest Thompson, 1860-1946, 8007
Settle, Evan Evans, 1848-1899, 15618
The settlement and early history of Albany 857
Settlement institutions in Appalachia, 13715
The settler's new home, 5210
The settlers, 9977
Seven (the number), 7634
Seven and nine years among the Camanches and Apaches, 16449
The seven brothers of Wyoming, 10739
Seven dreamers, 10790
Seven Mexican cities, 7184
Seven months a prisoner, 3726
Seven months in prison, 5046
"Seven Oaks," 6230
Seven Oaks, Manitoba, Battle of, 1816, 6230
The seven sleepers, 10747
Seven stories, 10363
Seven wives and seven prisons, 8448
Seven years a soldier, 17046
Seven years in America, 3641
Seven years on the Pacific slope, 16547
Seven years' residence in the great deserts of North America, 3266
Seven years' war (French-English) 1755-1763, 13073, 22389, 22869
Seven years with the Indians, 9305
Seventeen days in the Mexican jungle, 7362
Seventeen years in the Canadian northwest, 6055
Seventh-day Baptists, Missions, 23581
A seventh essay on free trade and finance, 23764
Seventy-five years in the Bluegrass, 1865-1949, 15347
The Seventy-ninth Highlanders, 5430
Seventy-six, 10412
Seventy-six association, Charleston, S.C., 1870
The several acts relative to the stamp duties, 15632
Severance, Luther, 1797-1855, 1382
Severim de Faria, Manuel, 1583-1655, 882
Severin, Ernest, 1871-, 17691
Sevier, John, 1744-1815, 8163
Sevilla, Feliciano de, d.1722, 8008
Sevilla, Pedro José de, 8008
Sevilla, Rafael, d.1856, 8009
Sevilla, Universidad, Escuela de Estudios Hispano-Americanos, Publicaciones, 19689
Sewage, Jefferson County, Ky., 15058, 15371
Sewall, Hannah Hull, 1657/8-1717, 22040, 23316
Sewall, Jonathan, 1729-1796, 23596, 23597
Sewall, Rebekah, 1704-1710, 23705
Sewall, Rufus King, 1814-1903, 23598
Sewall, Samuel Edmund, 1799-1888, 25701
Sewanee, Tenn. University of the South, 2110
Seward, Anna, 1747-1809, 8526, 23628, 23599
Seward, William Henry, 1801-1872, 683, 5124, 6288, 11778, 17584, 22185, 24354, 25391, 25481-25485
Seward's land of gold, 16556
Sewing machine patent, Application for an extension of, 7076
Sewing machines, Patents, 7076
Sex, 20095
Sexo, nutrição e vida, 20095
Sexto censo jeneral de la población de Chile, 20159
Sexuality in drama, 15532
Seybold, Christian Friedrich, 1859-1921, 7921
Seyd, Ernest, 1833-1881, 17585
Seymour, E. Sandford, 5125
Seymour, Horatio, 1810-1886, 7286, 22779
Seymour, Silas, 23600
Seymour, William, 5126
Sforza, a story of Milan, 8589
Shackleford, John, 1801-1885, 8010
Shackleford, John, Jr., 8010
Shackelford, Nevyle, 15348
The shadow of Moloch mountain, 8608
Shadows, 2897
Shadows and realities, 10207
The shadows of the trees, 5741
Shadows on the wall, 5659, 14094
Shaeffer, Luther Melanchthon, 17567
Shafer, Charles E., 1851-1930, 16179

Shafer, George F., 17586
Shaffner, Taliaferro Preston, 1819-1881, 14987, 25486
Shahmah in pursuit of freedom, 10270
Shakerism unmasked, 5766
Shakers, 3009, 4373, 5766, 12013, 12093, 12094, 13916, 14028, 14149, 14218, 14930, 15349, 15709; Biography, 12094; Hymns, 4374
Shakers in Kentucky, 14958, 15603
Shakertown, Ky., 14218, 15603
Shakertown at Pleasant Hill, Ky., Inc., 15350
Shakertown offers special retreat to another way of life, 14958
Shakespeare, William, 1564-1616, 18918; Authorship, 12722; Criticism and interpretation, 3691
Shaking dispensations, An essay upon the mighty shakes, which the hand of heaven, hath given, and is giving, to the world, 23313
Shaler, Nathaniel Southgate, 1841-1906, 5127, 14369, 14595, 15351, 15352
Shall the free men of Kentucky secure their rights?, 15353
Shall we have a convention?, 14206
Shall we save our country, 2131
Shall we wed her?, 10668
Shame, 9216
Shamir, Asher, 19051
Shan Dempsey's story, 10675
Shanafelt, J.R., 25487
Shane, John D., 13729
Shanks, John P.C., 3044
Shannon, James, 1799-1859, 25488
Shannon, Jasper B., 15354
Shannon, Peter C., 17587
Shantyboat, 13683
Shapes and shadows, 2953
Shapleigh, Frank H., 1842?-1906, 3958
Sharan, James, 1762-, 5128
Sharland, George, 23602
Sharp, Mrs. Abigail (Gardner) 1843-, 17012
Sharp, Granville, 1735-1813, 23603, 25489-25492
Sharp, Leander J., 5129
Sharp, Solomon Porcius, 1787-1825, 5129, 13635, 13636, 13870, 13907
Sharpe, Bartholomew, fl.1679-1682, 21765, 22280
The shattered violin, 9764
Shattuck, George Burbank, 1869-, 25932
Shattuck, Joseph C., 16240
Shattuck, Samuel, 1620?-1689, 23466
Shaver, Lewellyn Adolphus, 1842-, 5130

Shaw, D. A., 17590
Shaw, James, 5131
Shaw, John, M.D., 5132
Shaw, Joshua, 5133
Shaw, Luella, 1886-, 17591
Shaw, Norton, d.1868, 11714
Shaw, Pringle, 17592
Shaw, Thomas, 1843-1918, 17593
Shaw, William, 17594
Shaw, William H., 1833-, 5134
The Shawnee captives, 15316
Shawnee Indians, 12739, 13296, 14707, 16345, 23503, 23697
Shawnee names and migrations in Kentucky and West Virginia, 14941
Shawnee Prophet, 15167
Shawnee Prophet, 1775?-1837?, Poetry, 5603
The Shawnee scout, 11166
The Shawnee witch, 4364
Shay's rebellion, 1786-1787, 23434; Fiction, 8774, 10232
Shcherbakov, Dmitriĭ Ivanovich, 8011
She had on her geranium leaves, 10465
She waited patiently, 9349
Shea, John Dawson Gilmary, 3547, 4654, 11588, 13227, 13432
Sheahan, James Washington, d.1883, 5933
Shebbeare, James, 1709-1788, 23604-23608
Shebbeare, John, 1709-1788, Answer to the queries contained in a letter to Dr. Shebear, 663
The Sheep Eaters, 15839
Sheffey, Daniel, 1770-, 15355
Sheffield, John Baker Holroyd, 1st earl of, 1735-1821, 11713, 13327
Shehekeh, Mandan chief, 5374
Shelby, Isaac, 1750-1826, 13515, 13615, 13970, 14304, 15357, 15358, 15424, 15720, 15753, 22316
Shelby, John Todd, 1851-1920, 14379
Shelby, Joseph Orville, 1830-1897, 16451, 16452
Shelby, Lucy Goodloe, 1862-1957, 15359
Shelby, Mrs. Susan Goodloe (Hart) 1839-1923, 15753
Shelby, William Kinkead, 1861-1900, 15753
Shelby family, 15753
Shelby College, Shelbyville, Ky., 14287, 15356
Shelby College lottery of the state of Kentucky, 15356
Shelby co., Kentucky, History, 6199, 15723
Shelby County History Genealogical Society, 15723
Shelby County (Texas) War, 1841-1842, 17131
Sheldon, Addison Erwin, 1861-, 17200, 17505

394

17599
Sheldon, Charles, 1867-1928, 8012
Sheldon, Mrs. Electa M. (Bronson) d.1902,
   23609
Sheldon, George, 1818-1916, 25493
Sheldon, Lionel Allen, 1831-, 8013
Sheldon, Winthrop Dudley, 1839-1931, 5135
Shells, 12328, 13022, 15201
Shelton, William Henry, 1840-, 3417
Shelton family (Daniel Shelton, 1668-1728),
   22131
Shelvocke, George, fl.1690-1728, 1221, 8014
Shely, Forest Wyatt, 15360
Shenandoah (Confederate cruiser), 22608
Shenandoah, The valley of the, 5474
Shenandoah Valley, Description & travel,
   2646, 5630; History, 22735
Shepard, Ashbel K., 8015
Shepard, Charles Upham, 1804-1886, 23643
Shepard, Cyrus, 1798-1840, 4546
Shepard, Josiah, 1782-1814, 22167
Shepard, Tomas, 1605-1649, 127, 23610
Sheperd, John D., 13672
Shepherd, Nathaniel, 1712-1752, 617
Shepherd, William Robert, 1871-, 8016
Sheppard, John H., 8017
Sheppard, Moses, 25494
Sheppard, W.L., illustr., 4795, 5419, 9006
Sheppard Lee, 8805
Sherborn, Mass., History, 1284
Sherbrooke, Sir John Coape, 1764-1830, 11782
Sherburne, Andrew, 1765-1831, 23611
Sherburne, John Henry, 1794-1850?, 23612,
   23613
Sheridan, Emma V., 10283
Sheridan, Louis, 25669
Sheridan, Philip Henry, 1831-1888, 1547,
   5136, 17777, 25708
Sheridan, Richard Brinsley Butler, 1751-
   1816, 1544
Sheridan's ride, 13466
Sheridan and Kotzebue, 1544
The sheriff of Siskyou, 6963
Sheriffs, 21976; Kentucky, 24715
Sherley, Douglas, 4473, 15361
Sherman, Edwin Allen, 1829-, 17600
Sherman, Ernest Anderson, 1868-, 5137
Sherman, John, 1823-1900, 25495
Sherman, John H., 23614
Sherman, William Tecumseh, 1820-1891, 1547,
   3075, 6419, 11454
Sherman's march through the Carolinas,
   3887, 4601
Sherman's march to the sea, 2787, 3075,
   3546, 3830, 3887, 4601, 4749, 16116,
   16884, 23602; Fiction, 4736

Sherman brigade, 3882
Sherratt, Harriott Wight, 8018
Sherwood, Adiel, 1791-1879, 5138
Sherwood, J. Ely, 17601
Shewmake, Oscar Lane, 8019
Shewmaker, William Orpheus, 1869-, 15362
Shiftless folks, 10806
Shillibeer, John, 23615
Shillitoe, Thomas, 1754-1836, 5139
Shiloh, Battle of, 1862, 12125
Shindler, Mrs. Mary Stanley Bunce (Palmer)
   Dana, 1810-1883, 5140-5143
Shine, Frances Smith Dugan, 15363
Shine, Lee, 15364
Shinn, Charles Howard, 1924
Shinn, Earl, 1837-1886, 5144
Shinn, Josiah Hazen, 1849-1917, 17603, 17604
Ship canal from the Mississippi to Lake
   Michigan, 473
The ship-carpenter's family, 11150
Shipherd, Jacob R., 25496
Shipley, Jonathan, bp. of St. Asaph, 1714-
   1788, 2012, 23616
Shipley family, 15544
Shippen, William, 1736?-1808, 13761
Shipping, Great Lakes, 12577; Kentucky River,
   13888; Mexico, 11652; Pacific coast, 1913
Shipping bounties and subsidies, U.S., 11379
Shipton, Quebec, 21961
Ships, 22928
The shipwreck, 10434
The shipwrecked gold seekers, 9650
Shipwrecks, 199, 586, 2308, 6511, 6512, 7657,
   12577, 18703
Shirley, Myra Bell, 1846-1889, correct name
   of Belle Starr, 6958
Shirley, William, 1694-1771, 11991, 17176,
   21758, 23431
Shirley, Mass., History, 1766
Shively, J. M., 5145, 17605
Shober, Charles, illustr., 12721
A shock to Shakerism, 3009
Shoemaker, Michael Myers, 1853-, 8020
Shoemaker, W.B., 5146
The shoemaker's daughter, 8569
Shook, Martha Caroline (Dial) 1838-, 17606
Shooting, 3924, 12257, 22356
Shooting Niagara, and after?, 11665
Shooting stars as observed from the "sixth
   column" of the Times, 8493
Shopping with a country cousin, 10549
Shoreham, Vt., History, 12301
Shores of Vespucci, 11025
Shorey, Laurence, 1488
Short, Charles Wilkins, 15365
Short, Rich, 5147

Short, Mrs. Thompson, 10139, 10140,
14752-14754
Short stories, 8223, 10448; American,
8969, 9769, 10122; Argentine, 18932;
Brazilian, Ceará (State), 18309; Peruvian,
19849
Short stories and reminiscences of the last
fifty years, 10310
Short story masterpieces, 10757
Shorter, Eli Sims, 1823-1879, 25499
Shortfield, Luke, pseud., 4116
Shortt, Adam, 1859-1931, ed., 8023
Shoshoni Indians, 4398, 17678, 17134, 17901
Shot-guns, 23553
Shotwell, Randolph Abbott, 1844-1885, 5148
The shoulder-knot, 10931
Shouse, Frances Johnson Taylor, illustr.,
14258
Showalter, Jackson Whipps, 1859-1935, 13693
"Showin' off", 9216
Shreve, Thomas H., 1808-1853, 3067, 5149
Shrimp, 20224
Shrimps, Atlantic coast (South America),
19186, 19811
The shrine of love, 5042
Shriver, John Schultz, 1857-1915, 3795
Shuck, Oscar Tully, 17607
Shuck, Richard H., 1851-, 15366
Shuck family, 14888
Shuffett, D. Milton, 15307
Shumard, Benjamin Franklin, 1820-1869,
4664
Shurtleff, Nathaniel Bradstreet, 1810-
1874, 22005
Shurtliff, Lewis W., 1835-1922, 17608
Shute, Daniel, 1722-1802, 23617
Sial, Alcides Nóbrega, 19949
Siballa the sorceress, 4737
Siberia, Description & travel, 6237, 7091
The Siberian sable hunter, 9629
Sibley, Guy C., 25500
Sibley, Henry Hastings, 1811-1891, 16660,
17607-17612
A Sicilian romance, 9591
Sicily, 11020; Description & travel, 3092,
11020; Fiction, 4450
The sick mother, 9486
Side trips in Jamaica, 6145
Sidney, Henry, 8024
Sidney Elliott, 10636
Sieben monate in den rebellenstaaten
während des nordamerikanischen krieges
1863, 5088
Siebert, F. T., 16681
Siebert, Wilbur Henry, 1866-, 15367,
15368, 25501

The siege of Baltimore, 5494
The siege of Charleston, 5493, 12932
The siege of Cuautla, 7313
The siege of London, 10015
The siege of Richmond, 3078
The siege of Savannah, 12933
The siege of Spoleto, 22781
The signs of the times, 23075
The siege of Vicksburg, 10054
Siege of Washington, D.C., 8461
The sieges, 3999
Sierra, Justo, 1848-1912, 5150, 8025
Sierra Nevada, 2892, 3631
Sierra Nevada mountains, 16949, 17029, 17421,
17437
Sierra O'Reilly, Justo, 1814-1861, 8109,
19968
Siesta y amarillo, 19823
Siete capítulos en la vida del gran mariscal
Andrés Santa Cruz, 18897
The sights and secrets of the national
capitol, 12059
Sights from a steeple, 9827
Sights in Boston and suburbs, 13427
Sights in the gold region, 16897
Siglo de oro en las selvas de Erifile, 8271
The sign of the cross, 10173
The signet of King Solomon, 8551
Significado de la revolución de noviembre,
18869
Sigüenza y Góngora, Carlos de, 1645-1700,
19968
Sihler, Wilhelm, 1801-1885, 25502
Sikes, William Wirt, 10899
Siksika Indians, 3112, 16291, 16807; Legends,
17036
Siksika language, Conversation and phrase
books, 16984; Grammer, 16984
Silence, 9578
The silent partner, 11077
Silhouette, 10259
Silhouettes of American life, 9355
Silica, 14916
Silk manufacture and trade, 11840; Water-
supply, 19171
Silkworms, 11840, 12734, 17965
Silliman, Augustus Ely, 1807-1884, 5151
Sills, Kenneth Charles Morton, 1879-, 24959
The Silurian, Devonian and Irvine formations
of east central Kentucky, 14115
Silva, Antonio Camilo da, 20013
Silva, Ivan de Hugo, 19363
Silva, J. Francisco V., 1893-, 8026
Silva, Leonor, 18341
Silva, Medardo Angel, 21720
Silva, Pedro Cyriaco da, 1790(ca.) 1856, 21777

Silva Mafra, Manuel da, b.1831, 25503
Silva y la Vanda, Manuel de, 8027-8029
Silver, 7734
Silver and pewter, 9964
The silver buckle, 9268
The silver country, 15850
The silver cup of sparkling drops, 10548
The silver districts of Nevada, 5152
Silver-Knife, 4993
Silver lake, 9579
The silver lining, 9674
The silver mine, 14243
Silver mines and mining, California,
  17702; Nevada, 2837, 3212, 5152, 17934;
  North America, 17239; The Northwest,
  862; Southwest, New, 15850
Silver mining, 17755
Silver mining regions of Colorado, 5695
Silver question, 7610
Silver Reef, Utah, History, 17371, 17372
The silver ship of Mexico, 4010
The silver trumpets of the sanctuary,
  12047
Silversmithing, Brazil, 18229
Silverware, Peru, Colonial period, 18745
Silverwood, Francis B., 17613
Silvo, Jayro, 18384
Simcoe, John Graves, 1752-1806, 5153,
  23618
Siméon, Remi, 7931
Simmons, Franklin, 1839-1913, 24959
Simmons, George Frederick, 1814-1855,
  25504, 25505
Simmons, James Fowler, 1795-1864, 25381
Simmons, Louis A., 5154
Simms, Thomas, 25199
Simms, William Gilmore, 1806-1870, 5155-
  5165, 5459, 15369, 23619
Simon Girty, the outlaw, 4122, 14480
Simon Kenton, 5663, 10953
Simon Suggs, 3925
Simoncini, Aldo, illustr., 19154
Simonde de Sismondi, Jean Charles
  Leonard, 1773-1842, 24922
Simonds, Frederic William, 1853-, 17614
Simonin, Louis Laurent, 1830-1886,
  17615, 17616
Simons, M. Laird, 3332
The simple cobler of Aggavvam in America,
  23744
A simple heart, 3368
Simple settings, 2623
Um simple afeto recíproco, 18882
Simplicity's defence against seven-
  headed policy, 12322
Simpson, Alexander, b.1811, 5169, 8030

Simpson, Benjamin, pseud., 4830
Simpson, Sir George, 1792-1860, 5166, 6221,
  17618, 23620
Simpson, Howard E., 17619
Simpson, James Hervey, 1813-1883, 5167, 5168,
  5501, 5542, 5543, 5547, 5548, 17620
Simpson, Rev. John, of Leeds, Eng., 15940
Simpson, John Hawkins, 25506
Simpson, Louisiana (Wood), 15370
Simpson, Matthew, bp., 1811-1884, 8031
Simpson, Sidrach, 1600?-1655, 12308
Simpson, Thomas, 1808-1840, 5169, 8030
Simpson, William S., 8032
Simpson County, Ky., 13610, 13613
Simpson of the Slashers, 9460
Simpsonville, Ky., Christian Church, 14803;
  Inns and taverns, 14063
Sims, J.C., 15038, 15181
Sims, James Marion, 1813-1883, 5170
Sims, Richard, 15371
Sin, 14959
The sin and danger of self-love, described
  in a sermon preached at Plymouth, in New
  England, 1621, 22007
Sin and redemption, 3968
The sin of reviling, 12317
Sinai, Ky. Friendship Baptist Church, 15360
Sinaloa, Mexico (State), Politics &
  government, 12509
Since the beginning of time, 18311
A sincere friend to America, 12600
Sincerus, pseud., 1516
Sinclair, John, 16997
Sinclair, Sir John, 1754-1835, 23753
Sinclair, John Frederick, 1733-1811, 13241
Sinclair, Peter, 25507
Sinclair, Ward, 15372
Sinclair, William J., 17621, 17622
Sinclair family in Bottineau County, 16104
El sindicalismo en América Latina, 18376
Sindicato dos Bancos do Estado da Guanabara,
  18227
Sinding, Paul Christian, 1812-1887, tr.,
  22341
Sinfire, 9816
Sinfonia en negro, 18557
Sinfonia tropical, 18641
Sinfulness of American slavery, 14052
The sinfulness of slaveholding, 1342
Singer, James W., 15373
A singer from the sea, 8740
The singing wire, 4968
A single gentleman, 9481
Single lessons, five dollars, 9802
Single tax, 6581, 8425
Singleton, Arthur, pseud., 4188

Singraduara, 19784
A singular life, 11076
Sinking-funds, Gt. Britain, 12008; U.S.,
    12008
Sinners and saints, 17506
Sinnett, Jane, "Mrs. Percy Sinnett," 7203,
    17218
The sins of society, 10334
Síntesis de estadística vitivinícola, 18459
Síntesis de historia mexicana, 18224
Sioux Expedition of 1863, 16660
Sioussat, St. George Leakin, 1878-, 5188
Sioux Indians, 17705-17708, 17710
Sipes, Georgia, 15374
Sipes, William B., d.1905, 5171
Sipkins, Henry, 25508
Sir Dominick Ferrand, 7126
Sir Edmund Orme, 7122
Sir Rohan's ghost, 10855
The siren of Three-mile bend, 10122
Siringo, Charles A., 1855-1928, 17623,
    17624
Sisal hemp, 18789, 20083
Sisk, Morgan E., 15375
Sist' Chaney's black silk, 9582
O sistema brasileiro cooperativo de extensao
    rural, 18603
El sistema educativa en Costa Rica, 20440
El sistema educativo en Guatemala, 20436
El sistema educativo en Honduras, 20437
El sistema educativo en Nicaragua, 20438
Sister Carrie, 9430
Sister Jane, her friends and acquaintances,
    9750
Sister Liddy, 9575
Sister St. Luke, 11207
Sister Tabea, 9463
A sister to Esau, 8741
A sister to Evangeline, 7881
Sitgreaves, Lorenzo, 5517
Sitka, Alaska, 16001
Situação social da America Latina, 20038,
    20039
La situación de Puerto Rico, 25509
Six cent Sam's, 9817
The size of the slave population at Athens
    during the fifth and fourth centuries
    before Christ, 25404
Skaggs family, 14870, 15376, 15647
Skaggs quarterly, 15376
Skal, Georg von, 5172
Skean, Marion Holcomb, 15377
The skeleton at the banquet, 10899
The skeptic, 9628
Skepticism, Controversial literature, 8886
The sketch book of Geoffrey Crayon, 10001

Sketchley, Arthur, pseud., 5013
Skill in trials, 16413
Skillman, Isaac, 1740-1799, 181
Skinner, Ichabod Lord, d.1852, ed., 262
Skinner, John Edwin Hilary, 5174
Skinner, Mark, 1813-1887, 22417
Skinner Klee, José, 18023
The skipper's daughter, 10580
Skisser från en Kaliforniafärd, 3772
Skitt, pseud., 10922
Skizzen aus Amerika, 4195
Skizzen aus den Vereinigten Staaten von
    Nordamerika, 4181
Ein sklavenkauf aus der zeit des Antonius
    Pius, 24344
Das Sklavenwesen in den Vereinigten Staaten
    von Nordamerika, 25512
Die Sklaverei, ihre biologische Begründung
    und sittliche Rechfertigung, 24541
Die Sklaverei im Altertum, 25036
Skowhegan, Me., History, 12657
The Sky Land Company, Middlesboro, Ky., 15380
Slack, John, 14276
Slade, Frederick J., 22436
Slade, William, 1786-1859, 25513
Slang, 12558
Slanker, Barbara O., 15698
Slashes at life with a free broad-axe, 10072
Slater, Med, b.1830?, 580
Slater, Nelson, 5175
Slaughter, B.R., 9331
Slaughter, Benjamin Franklin, 1842-1896,
    17628
Slaughter, Gabriel, 1767-1830, 14140
Slaughter, Philip, 3680, 25514
Slaughter, Robert, 25819
The slave, 9865
The slave-auction, 24739
The slave colonies of Great Britain, 25558
Slave-hiring in the upper south: a step
    toward freedom, 24331
The slave holder abroad, 10861
The slave holder tested, 24484
A slave holder's daughter, 4133, 8460
Slave holding piety illustrated, 25515
The slave in Canada, 25389
Slave insurrection in Virginia (1830-1865),
    24316
Slave insurrections in the United States,
    1800-1865, 24093
Slave labor, 2019, 22833, 24032, 24051,
    24432, 24928, 25254, 25347, 25373
Slave life in Virginia and Kentucky, 3426
Slave market of America, 25516
The slave power! Its heresies and injuries
    to the American people, 24547

A slave rescue in Niagara sixty years
  ago, 24090
Slave ships, 24015
The slave states of America, 2850
Slave trade, 145, 522, 1153, 1403, 1512,
  6643, 8052, 11563, 23852, 23929, 24015,
  24050, 24187, 24196, 24207, 24221,
  24318, 24339, 24356, 24472, 24516,
  24517, 24560, 24604, 24646, 24652,
  24653, 24654, 24655, 24726, 24833,
  24920, 24956, 25031, 25168, 25179,
  25238, 25285, 25340, 25369, 25454,
  25491, 25572, 25734, 25756, 25767,
  25774, 25778, 25779, 25832; Africa,
  1114, 2209, 11852, 23241, 24829, 24985,
  25077, 25587, 25711; Africa, West,
  12147; Brazil, 24013; Cuba, 24835,
  24969, 25334; Gt. Britain, 11851;
  Jamaica, 24914, 25082; Law, 24785;
  Liberia, 24773; Nyassaland, 24488;
  Portuguese, Africa, 24091; Santo
  Domingo, 24425; U.S., 98, 1794, 9429,
  24019, 24266, 24267, 24739, 25130,
  25271, 25406, 25490, 25508, 25566,
  25689, 25775, 25819, 25878; United
  States, History, 25579; West Indies,
  British, 2209
The slave trade between Kentucky and
  the cotton kingdom, 24137
The slave trade in the West African
  hinterland, 25402
Slaverispörgsmaalet, 25183
Slavernij en dienstbaarheid,
  hoofdzakelijk in de vroege
  middeleeuwen, 25448
Slavery, 106, 145, 443, 846, 1403,
  1888, 1894, 4046, 4389, 15269, 22690,
  23844, 23929, 23948, 24018, 24099,
  24129, 24198, 24215, 24249, 24265,
  24327, 24333, 24356, 24374, 24387,
  24388, 24396, 24403, 24434, 24442,
  24472, 24489, 24508, 24516, 24541,
  24567, 24593, 24621, 24648, 24700,
  24734, 24736, 24790-24800, 24812,
  24826, 24833, 25038, 25081, 25089,
  25097, 25141, 25238, 25370, 25444,
  25445, 25448, 25449, 25454, 25467,
  25517, 25518, 25521, 25519, 25537,
  25538, 25578, 25616, 25624, 25660,
  25663, 25685, 25686, 25698, 25710,
  25716, 25755, 25756, 25757, 25832,
  25867, 25886, 25925; Africa, West,
  25402; Bibliography, 25196; Congresses,
  23897, 24186, 24197, 24199, 24652;
  Controversial literature, 1878, 25182;
  Emancipation, 146, 23830, 23831, 23836,
  23852, 23979, 23980, 24207, 24381,
  24922, 25453, 25908; Emancipation,
  Societies, 25120; Fiction, 8803;
  Fugitive slaves, 24823; Greece, 24981;
  History, 11852, 24051, 24612, 24671,
  24893, 25036, 25037, 25609, 25825;
  Justification, 299, 451, 1212, 1926,
  2474, 2475, 2735, 3671, 11100, 11357,
  12343, 12625, 12839, 12843, 13019,
  23834, 24003, 24022, 24046, 24052,
  24401, 24456, 24457, 24504, 24510,
  24551, 24555, 24617, 24670, 24717,
  24728, 24828, 24886, 24899, 24944,
  25091, 25175, 25195, 25265, 25282,
  25306, 25311, 25312, 25444, 25517,
  25518, 25573, 25632, 25692, 25714,
  25724, 25784, 25796, 25868, 25883;
  Mauritania, 24535, 25153, 25156;
  Morocco, 25217; Orange Free State,
  24045; Orleans (Ter.), 25178;
  Periodicals, 23831, 23974, 24371;
  Poetry, 24666, 25079, 25890 Societies,
  24650, 24876, 25266
Slavery (International law), 24196,
  24653, 24654, 24655
Slavery (Jewish law), 25421
Slavery (Mohammendan law), 25399
Slavery (Roman law), 23855, 24256, 25355,
  24493, 24495, 24766, 24962, 24981, 25457,
  25559-25562, 25676, 25851, 25946;
  Emancipation, 24271, 24496, 25291, 25452,
  25563, 25633
Slavery, a poem, 25079
Slavery, Indian, 17638
Slavery, secession and the constitution, 24887
Slavery a divine institution, 25699
Slavery among the Puritans, 23894
Slavery and abolitionism, 24060
Slavery and conversion in the American
  colonies, 24676
Slavery and famine, 13489
Slavery and four years of war, 24699
Slavery and infidelity, 25206
Slavery and its prospects in the United
  States, 25520
Slavery and its results, 23965
Slavery and peonage in the Philippine
  Islands, 25250
Slavery and secession in America, historical
  and economical, 22175, 24347
Slavery and serfdom considered, 25521
Slavery and slaves in literature, 25852
Slavery and the Bible, 25446, 25624
Slavery and the Boston riot, 24531
Slavery and the church, 1915, 11784, 24035,
  24084, 24124, 24141, 24246, 24283, 24301,

24362, 24382, 24404, 24420, 24486,
24528, 24720, 24725, 24788, 24839,
24856, 24916, 24924, 25288, 25378,
25425, 25629, 25670, 25786, 25929;
Baptist church, 25327; Catholic
church, 24356, 24909; Congregational
church, 23889, 24625, 25856; Free
church of Scotland, 25684, 25929;
Free Will Baptists (Founded in N.H.),
24433; Friends, Society of, 4659,
23901, 23920, 23921, 24337, 24432,
24444, 24786, 24868, 25735; Lutheran
church, 24581; Methodist Episcopal
church, 948, 23909, 24075, 24926,
25012, 25154, 25213, 25325, 25864;
Methodist Episcopal church, South,
24043; New Jerusalem church, 12843,
24269; Presbyterian church, 1341,
4851, 15187, 24185, 24430, 24510,
25303, 25304, 25305, 25306, 25541,
25594, 25682, 25791; Protestant
Episcopal church, 1214, 13180,
23032, 24001, 24672, 24958, 25108;
Unitarian church, 23891, 23892,
24656; United Presbyterian church,
Synods, Ohio, 25207
Slavery and the domestic slave trade,
2545
Slavery and the race problem in the
South, 24402
Slavery and the remedy, 25162
Slavery as a divine trust, 25195
Slavery as an industrial system, 25141
Slavery as seen in its punishment,
25624
The slavery code of the District of
Columbia, 25776
The slavery convention of Geneva,
September 25, 1926, 25832
Slavery conventions, 24198
Slavery doomed: or, The contest between
free and slave labour in the United
States, 24335
Slavery illustrated in its effects
upon woman and domestic society,
23996
Slavery in Abyssinia, 24213
Slavery in Africa, 23964, 24488, 24514,
24519, 24563, 24650, 25587
Slavery in Africa, East, 25850
Slavery in Africa, Portuguese, 24566,
25659
Slavery in Africa, Portuguese West,
23870, 23874, 24214, 24450, 24500,
24967, 24968, 25935
Slavery in Africa, West, 24565, 24622,

24113
Slavery in Algiers, Drama, 25418
Slavery in America, 6636, 24085, 25349
Slavery in Angola, 25113 •
Slavery in Babylonia, 24248
Slavery in Barbados, 23940, 24261, 25264
Slavery in Brazil, 23895, 23941, 24009-24013,
24063, 24101, 24125, 24328, 24440, 24737,
24738, 24749, 24965, 25066, 25076, 25788,
25826, 25884; Emancipation, 25503;
Kindnapping, 19080
Slavery in British colonies, 25558
Slavery in British Guiana, 22739, 24735,
24881, 25459, 25697; Insurrections, 24048
Slavery in British Honduras, 24020
Slavery in Burma, 24515
Slavery in California after 1848, 24321
Slavery in Cambodia, 24804
Slavery in Canada, 24546, 24757, 25389,
25805, 25916; New Brunswick, 24659
Slavery in Central America, 23873
Slavery in Chile, 24381
Slavery in China, 24159, 24538, 24742
Slavery in Cuba, 7083, 7086, 7137, 23830,
23853, 23854, 23871, 23913, 23914, 24099,
24234, 24235, 24236, 24325, 24359, 24386,
24441, 24509, 24539, 24578, 24657, 24747,
24940, 24956, 24969, 25177, 25179, 25334,
25428, 25439, 25454, 25576, 25734, 25787;
Emancipation, 25771
Slavery in Dutch Guiana, 24348, 24385, 24583,
24741, 24862, 25435, 25603, 25604, 25675,
25811; Drama, 25575
Slavery in Egypt, 24344, 24520
Slavery in Europe; a letter to neutral
governments from the Anti-slavery Society,
23906; Middle ages, 25447
Slavery in France, 23864, 23968; Anti-slavery
movements, 24669
Slavery in French Guiana, 1831, 24176, 24743,
24803
Slavery in Greece, 24490, 24766, 25080,
25404, 25944
Slavery in Guadeloupe, 24315
Slavery in Guiana, 25564
Slavery in Guinea, 24092
Slavery in Haiti, 24339, 25556
Slavery in Iceland, 25893
Slavery in Islam, 24329
Slavery in its national aspects as related
to peace and war, 24027
Slavery in its relation to God, 24897
Slavery in its relation to God, 1035, 1499, 8386, 22970,
23405, 23955, 23957, 24082, 24142, 24211,
24339, 24841, 24884, 24948, 24957, 25082,
25252, 25256, 25369, 25478, 25494, 25497,

25524, 25619, 25629, 25871; Condition
of slaves, 25082; Fiction, 23137, 24971;
Law, 13147, 24914, 25011, 25557
Slavery in Kentucky, 1792-1865, 13833,
14770, 24934
Slavery in Mississippi, 25662
Slavery in North Africa, 24690
Slavery in Orleans (Ter.), 25178
Slavery in Pemba, 25137
Slavery in Peru, 25772
Slavery in Puerto Rico, 2252, 23830, 23871,
23913, 24079, 24099, 24291, 24325, 24359,
24406, 24509, 24592, 24747, 25323, 25509,
25555, 25577, 25734, 25787
Slavery in Rome, 23863, 24421, 24543,
24589, 24632, 24689, 24693, 24894, 25080,
25150, 25272, 25355, 25434; Emancipation,
24343
Slavery in St. Christofer, 25557
Slavery in St. Vincent, 25433
Slavery in Santo Domingo, 24425, 24751,
25608
Slavery in Sicily, Drama, 24069
Slavery in Sierra Leone, 24512
Slavery in Spanish America, 23856, 24094,
24095, 24585, 25077, 25789
Slavery in Sudan, 24513, 25643
Slavery in Surinam, 24767
Slavery in Texas: illegal aliens, 24224
Slavery in the Bahamas, 25932
Slavery in the Barbary States, 2133, 11036,
24102, 24281, 24408, 24419, 24691, 24752,
24753, 24768, 25185, 25242, 25345, 25394,
25395, 25397; Poetry, 23862
Slavery in the British colonies, 23972;
Law, 25492
Slavery in the Cape Verde Islands, 24092
Slavery in the church ensures infidelity
in the world, 25206
Slavery in the Dutch East Indies, 23974;
Emancipation, 25665
Slavery in the French colonies, 24534;
Reunion, 24770
Slavery in the Philippine Islands, 24329,
25251, 25782
Slavery in the Sahara, 23839
Slavery in the southern states, 25316
Slavery in the territories, 24782, 25900
Slavery in the U.S., 18, 89, 470, 641, 799,
1527, 1584, 1888, 1894, 1926, 1929, 2133,
2691, 2822, 2850, 2968, 2978, 3022, 3185,
3361, 3526, 3689, 3721, 3755, 4413, 4673,
4706, 4920, 5285, 5308, 5318, 5442, 5452,
5658, 6089, 7557, 7558, 8958, 9666,
11324, 12779, 13168, 13186, 14011, 14770,
15557, 16383, 16580, 18968, 23838, 23840,

23850, 23859, 23899, 23904, 23910, 23923,
23932, 23965, 23987, 24008, 24017, 24019,
24039, 24070, 24126, 24160, 24165, 24179,
24180, 24181, 24191, 24202, 24221, 24231,
24237, 24264, 24282, 24288, 24311, 24318,
24330, 24334, 24335, 24346, 24351, 24358,
24361, 24366, 24367, 24368, 24387, 24388,
24446, 24447, 24450, 24463, 24466, 24470,
24473, 24479, 24480, 24502, 24505, 24522,
24540, 24554, 24576, 24579, 24614, 24615,
24628, 24631, 24660, 24661, 24664, 24682,
24699, 24731, 24745, 24750, 24774, 24811,
24847, 24877, 24880, 24883, 24888, 24925,
24932, 24961, 24987, 24989, 24990, 24991,
24996, 25001, 25030, 25033, 25050, 25062,
25105, 25110, 25119, 25124, 25136, 25146,
25165, 25172, 25209-25216, 25254, 25255,
25257, 25258, 25267, 25274, 25283, 25291,
25293, 25295, 25305, 25307, 25312, 25353,
25360, 25372, 25388, 25398, 25425, 25436,
25440, 25441, 25443, 25464, 25451, 25470,
25471, 25512, 25522, 25544, 25547, 25565,
25568, 25593, 25610, 25622, 25651, 25657,
25658, 25672, 25674, 25683, 25695, 25699,
25704, 25706, 25707, 25712, 25722, 25723,
25725, 25741, 25746, 25759, 25760, 25778,
25779, 25780, 25795, 25797, 25807, 25818,
25824, 25836, 25837, 25867, 25883, 25902,
25903, 25904, 25916, 25922, 25927, 25930,
25941; Addresses, essays, lectures, 25089,
25510; Alabama, 5717, 10521, 23925, 24506,
25061, 25406; Anti-slavery movements, 1043,
1339, 2094, 3412, 5330, 5831, 13184, 15714,
23833, 23837, 23893, 23930, 23977, 24000,
24005, 24065, 24108, 24138, 24157, 24169,
24194, 24201, 24253, 24312, 24373, 24413,
24422, 24599, 24609, 24620, 24637, 24649,
24680, 24686, 24694, 24757, 24781, 24849,
24955, 24964, 25012, 25022, 25086, 25114,
25117, 25118, 25232, 25260, 25262, 25273,
25275, 25297, 25309, 25358, 25384, 25415,
25416, 25438, 25585, 25601, 25625, 25671,
25682, 25701, 25732, 25769, 25858, 25874,
25892, 25924; Bibliography, 908, 23945,
24559, 25020, 25912; California, 24321,
24332; Colonial period, 5768; Colonization,
1429, 23842; Condition of slaves, 48, 325,
429, 551, 646, 1491, 1881, 2658, 3426,
4821, 4911, 11439, 23924, 23931, 23956,
23996, 24044, 24112, 24363, 24435, 24590,
24634, 24651, 24665, 24861, 24954, 25014,
25102, 25410, 25456, 25505, 25642, 25662,
25681, 25801, 25838, 25878, 25938;
Connecticut, 24605, 25545, 25605;
Controversial literature, 3026, 7290, 15859,
17017, 23832, 23911, 24007, 24251, 24711,

24780, 25032, 25109, 25630, 25718,
25859; 1737, 24786; 1740, 25870; 1753-
1770, 5769; 1762, 1158; 1764, 24808;
1766, 1158; 1767, 24807; 1772, 25205;
1773, 24290, 25422, 25489; 1776, 24624,
24777; 1778, 23963; 1783, 24206; 1791,
25661; 1792, 4945, 25382; 1793, 24049,
25043, 25490, 25491; 1796, 25042; 1797,
256, 25051, 25424; 1799, 24448; 1802,
25396; 1803, 24636; 1804, 25122, 25693;
1805, 1429; 1806, 23857, 25143; 1807,
1428; 1809, 25508; 1813, 23244, 24986;
1809, 25508; 1816, 23995; 1817, 23712;
1819, 23990, 24266, 24834; 1820, 24227,
24471, 24606, 24607, 24801, 24945, 25730,
25933; 1822, 24569, 24618, 25278, 25712;
1823, 15989, 24459, 25300; 1824, 24320,
24646; 1825, 25469; 1826, 23963, 25806;
1827, 24074, 25347; 1828, 24293, 24357,
24728; 1829, 23847; 1830, 24384, 24970,
25814; 1831, 24645, 24839, 25475; 1832,
23912, 24223, 24536, 24975, 25021, 25330;
1833, 639, 1881, 3132, 4723, 12783, 24232,
24270, 24840, 24846, 25131, 24211, 25244,
25365, 25875; 1834, 534, 1341, 1915,
2720, 4851, 15187, 23842, 24598, 24764,
25115, 25116, 25681; 1835, 563, 2257,
2719, 3131, 23973, 24111, 24531, 24831,
24960, 25364, 25366, 25644, 25808; 1836,
888, 1887, 17066, 17145, 23888, 23926,
24006, 24062, 24338, 24397, 24992, 24993,
25034, 25277, 25301, 25359, 25363, 25462,
25504, 25528, 25790, 25899; 1837, 325,
451, 1043, 2165, 11357, 23791, 23898,
23933, 23996, 24114, 24398, 24444, 24449,
24619, 24915, 25234, 25535, 25785, 25828,
25877; 1838, 21935, 23835, 24058, 24132,
24360, 24407, 24484, 24561, 24662, 24725,
24845, 25164, 25225, 25287, 25373, 25379,
25523, 25536, 25570, 25696, 25882; 1838-
1846, 25409; 1839, 11798, 23939, 24123,
24171, 24362, 24400, 24429, 24436, 24474,
25265, 25367, 25381, 25641, 25909; 1840,
3303, 5699, 6919, 24107, 24200, 24416,
24574, 24717, 24730, 24927, 25403, 25505,
25589, 25743, 25827; 1841, 11853, 24167,
24487, 24918, 25632; 1842, 17, 2718,
12344, 22693, 23921, 23984, 24363, 24674,
25222, 25581; 1843, 721, 1722, 23920,
24420, 25171; 1844, 13186, 24122, 24143,
24144, 24151, 24185, 24443, 24898, 25356,
25375, 25436, 25465, 25517, 25574, 25626,
25914; 1845, 948, 3884, 12625, 13280,
17366, 00001, 24195, 24289, 24456, 24528,
24551, 24555, 24827, 24848, 24854, 24800,
24900, 25006, 25151, 25213, 25332, 25380,

25383, 25538, 25571, 25614, 25617, 25929;
1845-1850, 24901; 1846, 846, 1342, 23992,
24430, 24475, 24656, 25194, 25534, 25684,
25928; 1847, 172, 11437, 13122, 24038,
24087, 24667, 24896, 25004, 25169, 25532;
1848, 1214, 23841, 24177, 24353, 25098,
25174, 25569, 25670, 25815; 1849, 11439,
14098, 23879, 23967, 24052, 24391, 24549,
24553, 24855, 25058, 25101, 25463, 25599,
25667, 25783; 1849-1860, 25690; 1850,
1490, 5282, 14052, 21940, 23709, 23880,
24000, 24022, 24035, 24046, 24103, 24119,
24168, 24173, 24269, 24305, 24401, 24460,
24663, 24675, 24754, 24850, 24924, 25158,
25346, 25720, 25754, 25844; 1851, 2104,
2282, 2963, 3023, 12522, 23892, 24002,
24021, 24136, 24280, 24302, 24306, 24414,
24455, 24457, 24461, 24477, 24570, 24587,
24623, 24718, 24772, 24897, 24935, 25209,
25214, 25268, 25288, 25530, 25583, 25862;
1852, 2474, 2475, 11740, 23878, 24016,
24105, 24390, 24403, 24851, 25024, 25198,
25263, 25306, 25311, 25316, 25336, 25385,
25842; 1853, 443, 23915, 24941, 24983,
25262, 25361, 25607, 25709, 25880, 25919,
25942; 1854, 387, 1381, 11918, 13260, 22020,
22734, 24086, 24140, 24174, 24891, 24973,
25112, 25200, 25282, 25466, 25647; 1855,
42, 1049, 6095, 24023, 24113, 24120, 24371,
24545, 24844, 24892, 24944, 25092, 25338,
25377, 25412, 25488, 25533, 25869; 1856,
2735, 12772, 13176, 13216, 23866, 23876,
24060, 24254, 24337, 24511, 24548, 24627,
24647, 24656a, 24695, 25696, 25919, 25054,
25202, 25206, 25221, 25281, 25474, 25481,
25499, 25613, 25621, 25792, 25841, 25945;
1857, 154, 155, 4797, 5041, 24043, 24241,
24283, 24510, 24856, 24976, 25005, 25159,
25223, 25374, 25400, 25426, 25482, 25515,
25520, 25525, 25742, 25751, 25866; 1858,
98, 5281, 24032, 24324, 24389, 24560,
24617, 25106, 25405, 25444, 25519, 25600,
25629, 25858; 1859, 1383, 7297, 23861,
23970, 24061, 24072, 24147, 24175, 24382,
24673, 24692, 24863, 24899, 25135, 25261,
25299, 25354, 25572, 25582, 25595, 25691,
25733, 25798, 25816, 25863, 25864; 1859-
1863, 1057; 1859-1867, 21810, 23998, 25128;
1860, 14, 106, 689, 1895, 3025, 6888, 10861,
12122, 12839, 22185, 22642, 23890, 23922,
23958, 23961, 23993, 24003, 24042, 24089,
24121, 24135, 24286, 24354, 24376, 24393,
24394, 24439, 24462, 24504, 24679, 24784,
24836, 24838, 24930, 24937, 24951, 25093,
25107, 25160, 25162, 25325, 25371, 25458,
25518, 25591, 25652, 25714, 25713, 25716,

25727, 25753, 25860, 25865, 25858,
25920, 25923; 1861, 110, 637, 1212, 1885,
11372, 12315, 12843, 13490, 24031, 24342,
24369, 24454, 24501, 24872, 25029, 25045,
25074, 25100, 25161, 25195, 25296, 25344,
25378, 25446, 25477, 25526, 25573, 25645,
25724, 25737, 25804, 25854, 25883; 1862,
116, 291, 1794, 11280, 13351, 13414,
24131, 24279, 24314, 24395, 24431, 24458,
24626, 24672, 24939, 25102, 25163, 25184,
25392, 25479, 25507, 25542, 25598, 25615,
25700, 25809, 25888, 25889, 25891, 25926;
1863, 889, 12985, 23935, 24073, 24215,
24226, 24238, 24317, 24709, 24710, 24828,
24858, 24859, 24909, 24916, 25007, 25019,
25040, 25091, 25108, 25138, 25166, 25170,
25175, 25176, 25270, 25502, 25537, 25540,
25784, 25821; 1864, 471, 1354, 2149,
11100, 24547, 24871, 24912, 24947, 25386,
25487, 25653, 25657, 25680, 25881; 1865,
23985, 24942, 25148; 1866, 23834; 1870,
25796; Delaware, 24274, 25249; District
of Columbia, 997, 1393, 23917, 24047,
24097, 24150, 24188, 24243, 24244,
24287, 24293, 24542, 24603, 24630,
24642, 24708, 24719, 24816, 25044,
25072, 25121, 25142, 25269, 25302,
25348, 25401, 25411, 25483, 25513,
25516, 25650, 25719, 25761, 25765,
25766, 25776, 25781, 25820, 25846,
25907; Drama, 25328, 24329, 25430, 24829;
Emancipation, 393, 4669, 6934, 8046,
12288, 12493, 23846, 23978, 23981, 23987,
23988, 23997, 24029, 24208, 24209, 24210,
24220, 24229, 24277, 24380, 24392, 24431,
24469, 24485, 24491, 24499, 24521, 24557,
24610, 24643, 24761, 24857, 24864, 24865,
24887, 24970, 25044, 25064, 25069, 25140,
25182, 25186, 25192, 25204, 25205, 25236,
25294, 25317, 25330, 25364, 25367, 25396,
25450, 25472, 25473, 25476, 25483, 25495,
25500, 25527, 25602, 25648, 25654, 25702,
25702, 25717, 25728, 25887, 25898, 25908,
25918; Extension to the territories,
11255, 11916, 23843, 23936, 23967, 23990,
24014, 24071, 24098, 24153, 24216, 24242,
24259, 24260, 24304, 24345, 24410, 24417,
24418, 24497, 24526, 24644, 24762, 24782,
24801, 24974, 24982, 25084, 25099, 25197,
25210, 25237, 25319, 25324, 25331, 25346,
25350, 25407, 25463, 25678, 25762, 25783,
25800, 25830, 25853, 25921, 25945;
Fiction, 2974, 4283, 4451, 5363, 8634,
8849, 9202, 9457, 9494, 9866, 10270,
11100, 12237, 16219, 23868, 23950, 24037,
24067, 24068, 24117, 24326, 24352, 24558,

24602, 24608, 24706, 24778, 25111, 25423,
25455, 25596, 25668, 25726, 25745, 25938;
Foreign public opinion, 2805; Fugitive
slaves, 1814, 3042, 9665, 12366, 23946,
23954, 23989, 23991, 24061, 24090, 24096,
24097, 24156, 24157, 24158, 24178, 24182,
24183, 24184, 24250, 24251, 24310, 24445,
24461, 24465, 24529, 24530, 24600, 24629,
24677, 24740, 24756, 24758, 24959, 24977,
24978, 24984, 25149, 25193, 25201, 25222,
25239, 25313, 25315, 25335, 25337, 25415,
25416, 25496, 25498, 25546, 25638, 25666,
25770, 25810, 25839, 25896, 25911;
Fugitive slaves, Bibliography, 24933;
Georgia, 719, 24034, 25193, 25689; History,
1403, 2963, 11751, 11784, 12295, 23601,
23867, 23908, 23960, 23994, 24115, 24192,
24302, 24306, 24336, 24347, 24478, 24613,
24647, 24697, 24938, 25155, 25245, 25413,
25442, 25486, 25579, 25584, 25849; History,
Colonial period, 24676; Illinois, 15989,
23875, 24036, 24568, 24950, 25322, 25835;
Indian Territory, 23829; Indiana, 24322,
24323, 24644, 25342; Insurrections, 23999,
24093, 24601, 24618, 24832, 25831;
Insurrections, Charleston, S.C., 24110;
Kansas, 24217, 25357, 25803; Kentucky,
1243, 1341, 2793, 3014, 3532, 3782, 4852,
5196, 10521, 13726, 14960, 15188, 15189,
24021, 24040, 24055, 24137, 24143, 24145,
24146, 24162, 24163, 24331, 24683, 24873,
24934, 25173, 25315, 25335, 25382, 25551,
25554, 25664, 25748, 25843; Kentucky,
Fiction, 24352; Kidnapping, 24412, 24636;
Law, 1885, 13038, 24057, 24164, 24192,
24641, 24668, 24776, 24785, 24827, 25130,
25197, 25228, 25229, 25248, 25403, 25437,
25623, 25634, 25635, 25761, 25773-25776,
25819, 25905; Law, Kentucky, 24715; Legal
status of slaves in free states, 580,
24080, 24568, 25103, 25129, 25897;
Louisiana, 24212, 25071, 25125, 25431;
Maryland, 719, 23846, 23931, 24096, 24527,
24926, 24979, 24980, 25192, 25279, 25354,
25614, 25823, 25839, 25931; Massachusetts,
24267, 24268, 25073, 25493, 25690, 25731,
25834; Mississippi, 24590, 24716, 25623,
25662, 25819; Missouri, 12288, 23942,
24028, 24044, 24066, 24405, 24633, 24817,
24844, 24864, 25337, 25488, 25648, 25721,
25821; New England, 23894, 24321; New
Jersey, 24204, 24594, 25123, 25617; New
York (State), 24451, 24550, 24822, 25083,
25130, 25152, 25167, 25168, 25208; North
Carolina, 23925, 23949, 24001, 25026;
Northwest, Old, 24323, 24950; Northwest

Territory, 25543; Ohio, 3042, 24158, 24465, 25546; Ohio, Columbiana County, 24464; Pennsylvania, 23971, 25224, 25228-25230, 25736; Pennsylvania, Lancaster County, 23951; Periodicals, 23877, 23905, 24849, 25068, 25114, 25147; Personal narratives Virginia, 25894; Poetry, 1428, 1710, 1711, 3960, 11737, 23791, 23916, 24166, 24255, 24292, 24577, 24582, 24867, 24885, 24902, 24932, 25126, 25285, 25286, 25333, 25356, 25408, 25586, 25720, 25872, 25873, 25876, 25877; Pro-slavery arguments, 4446; Rhode Island, 24580, 24685, 25321, 25390; Sermons, 24262, 24452, 24523, 24898, 25201, 25816; Slave narratives, 3818; Societies, 23881-23888, 23900, 23901, 23907, 25128, 24432, 24433, 24960, 24979, 24997-25000, 25002, 25003, 25104, 25116, 25123, 25132-25134, 25173, 25226-25233, 25235, 25246, 25247, 25320, 25321, 25735; Songs and music, 24166, 24577, 25292; South Carolina, 98, 719, 3370, 24110-24112, 24118, 24154, 24588, 24776, 24929, 24995, 25039, 25253, 25259, 25300, 25368, 25414, 25468, 25566, 25636; Southern states, 24500, 25747; Speeches in Congress, 23860, 24030, 24294, 24698, 25391, 25879; 1819, 25667; 1820, 23942, 24203, 24532, 24556, 24952, 25025, 25284, 25461, 25480, 25533, 25794; 1835, 24287, 25513; 1836, 23838, 24243, 24603, 24630, 24816, 25142, 25269, 25308, 25401, 25820; 1837, 76; 1838, 25302, 25846; 1839, 24148; 1840, 13268, 25590; 1841, 25348; 1842, 25749; 1843, 24077; 1847, 25915; 1848, 23919, 24216, 25225, 25099, 25800, 25845, 25921; 1849, 24411, 25688; 1850, 1091, 23872, 23936, 23952, 23976, 24026, 25076, 24098, 24106, 24260, 24285, 24410, 24503, 24525, 24640, 24721, 24974, 25090, 25095, 25215, 25243, 25387, 25417, 25427, 25484, 25761, 25793, 25822, 25847, 25900; 1852, 24313; 1854, 23966, 25940; 1855, 24081, 24825, 25485, 25646; 1856, 23869, 23943, 23975, 24053, 24071, 24222, 24364, 24482, 24533, 24571, 24635, 24639, 24707, 24818, 25017, 25210, 25326, 25429, 25618, 25762, 25763, 25812, 25830; 1857, 11890, 24365, 25016, 25744; 1858, 1162, 1422, 2121, 23982, 23983, 24133, 24228, 24307, 24498, 24552, 24700, 24789, 25679; 1859, 24240, 24375, 24507; 1860, 499, 23918, 24025, 24162, 24239, 24258, 24263, 24304, 24309, 24526, 24638, 24759, 24771, 25084, 25139, 25324, 25351, 25549, 25813, 25833;

1861, 24149, 24273, 25548, 25799; 1862, 1393, 24220, 24245, 24642, 24708, 25411, 25495, 25605, 25650, 25891, 25907; 1864, 24024, 24029, 24134, 25298, 25649, 25729; 1865, 24468, 25552; 1882, 23917; Tennessee, 25203; Territories, 25861, 25900; Texas, 24054, 25460; Vermont, 25840; Virginia, 1213, 3153, 23937, 23938, 23986, 24223, 24316, 24331, 24378, 24483, 24494, 24572, 24820, 24832, 24936, 24975, 25013, 25096, 25188, 25189, 25341, 25419, 25506, 25514, 25539, 25855; Virginia, Fiction, 24608; Wisconsin, 24257
Slavery in the Virgin Islands, 24415
Slavery in the West Indies, 1126, 1246, 1895, 6919, 7898, 8181, 24250, 24431, 25070, 25180; Emancipation, 24922; Fiction, 9833
Slavery in the West Indies, British, 23845, 24083, 24088, 24155, 24189, 24190, 24339, 24349, 24350, 24396, 24509, 24518, 24595, 24597, 24616, 24813, 24860, 24931, 24953, 24972, 25094, 25136, 25144, 25157, 25276, 25362, 25422, 25511, 25608, 25609, 25637, 25656, 25857, 25885, 25901; Emancipation, 23903, 24056, 24372, 24485, 24837, 25340, 25393, 25454, 25640, 25857, 25910; Poetry, 25285
Slavery in the West Indies, Danish, 24415, 24509, 25454
Slavery in the West Indies, Dutch, 23959
Slavery in the West Indies, French, 23979, 24424, 24426, 24509, 24748, 24803, 24869, 24953, 25081, 25240, 25739; Laws, 25238
Slavery in Turkey, 25181
Slavery in Ubang Shari, 25705
Slavery in Venezuela, 25802
Slavery in Zanzibar, 25137
Slavery inconsistent with justice and good policy, 15269
Slavery indispensable to the civilization of Africa, 24944
The slavery issue in federal politics, 25258
Slavery justified; by a southerner, 24401
Slavery not forbidden by Scripture, 25144
The slavery of to-day: or The present position of the open sore of Africa, 25659
Slavery on Louisiana sugar plantations, 25071
Slavery or "sacred trust"? 24567
Slavery petitions and papers, 24323
The slavery question, 24052, 25522
The slavery question in New-York, 25346
Slavery the mere pretext for the rebellion; not its cause; Andrew Jackson's prophecy in 1833, 24710
Slavery unmasked, 5442
Slaves, value of, 24361

Slaves and masters, 10509
Slaves and slavery: now affected by the war, 25495
Slaves in Algiers, 25418
Sledd, Benjamin, 1864-, 5167
The sleep-rider, 9633
A sleeping-car experience, 9779
The sleeping sentinel, 7138
A sleeveless errand, 9741
Sleigh, William Wellcocks, b.1796, 23835, 25523
Sligo, Howe Peter Browne, 2d Marquess of, 1788-1845, 25524
Sloan, Edward L., 16583
Sloan, Robert W., 15994, 17170
Sloane, James Renwick Wilson, 1823-1886, 25525
Sloane, William Milligan, 1850-1928, 25525
Sloat, John Drake, 1781-1867, 17600
Sloat Monument Association of California, 17600
Slocum, Charles Elihu, 15381
Slocum, George Mertz, 1889-, 8036
Slocum, William Neill, 1828-, 25527
Slopes of the Sangre de Cristo, 16370
Slosson, Annie (Trumbull) 1838-1926, 9769
Slums, Guanabara, Brazil, Statistics, 19427
Small, Frank O., illustr., 10896
Small, George, 8037
Small, Jonathan, 25528
Small, Samuel, 8037
Small family, 8037
A "small fisted farmer", 24369
A small testimony of that great honour due to that honourable servant of God and his generation John Alden, 23623
Small town tales, 14231
Smallpox, Inoculation of, 11465, 22961, 23009, 23294
Smallwood, Robert, 15382
Smallwood, William, d.1792, 698
Smedley, Charles, 1836-1864, 5177
Smedley, W.T., illustr., 3365, 9694, 9916, 10896, 11088, 14132
Smet, Pierre Jean de, 1801-1873, 5178-5183, 17525, 17629
Smiles and frowns, 11123
Smiles and tears from the Klondyke, 16292
Smiley, Jerome Constant, 17630
Smilodan neogaeus, 20187
Smirke, R., illustr., 25285
Smith, Abram P., 5184
Smith, Adam, 1723-1790, 24808
Smith, Adelaide W., 1831-, 5185
Smith, Ann Eliza (Brainerd) "Mrs. J.G. Smith" 1818-1905, 8038

Smith, Arthur G., 8039
Smith, Ashbel, 1805-1886, 17531
Smith, Benjamin B., 13833
Smith, Buckingham, 1810-1871, 12345, 23642
Smith, Charles Henry, 1826-1903, 5186, 5187, 25529
Smith, Charles W., 1636, 8040
Smith, Charles Wesley, 1877-, 15989
Smith, Daniel, 1748-1818, 5188, 23624
Smith, Daniel, 1789-1823, 4479
Smith, David, 1753-1835, 14382
Smith, Delazon, 1816-1860, 5189
Smith, E. Quincy, 5190
Smith, Earl Hobson, 15383-15386, 15766
Smith, Edward, 1818?-1874, 5191
Smith, Edward Dunlap, 1802-1883, 25530
Smith, Edward Payson, 1840-1892, 24668
Smith, Eli, 1787-, 15387
Smith, Elihu Hubbard, 1771-1798, 25531
Smith, Emily Ann, 15131
Smith, Francis, 6624
Smith, Francis Hopkinson, 1838-1915, 5192-5194, 8041, 13438
Smith, Mrs. Frank A., 15313
Smith, George Charles, 1782-1863, 23532
Smith, George D., 1870-1920, 7001
Smith, George Gilbert, 1825-, 5195
Smith, George Gilman, 1836-, 15388
Smith, Gerrit, 1797-1874, 23840, 24143, 24474, 24484, 25532-25536
Smith, Goldwin, 1832-1910, 2276, 8042, 25537
Smith, Hal, 15389
Smith, Harry, 1815-, 5196
Smith, Henry, 1784-1851, 2328
Smith, Henry Clay, 15390
Smith, Henry Erskine, 8043
Smith, Horace Wemyss, 1825-1891, 355
Smith, Hormond Dunlap, 1900-, 3205
Smith, Hubbard Madison, 1820-1907, 5197, 15391
Smith, Hugh, 1795-1849, 391
Smith, Israel, 11628
Smith, J. Alden, 17632
Smith, J. Allan, 15392
Smith, J. Calvin, 3806
Smith, J. Gray, 5198
Smith, J. R., 5200
Smith, J. Soule, 13710, 15393-15395
Smith, James, 25538
Smith, James, 1737-1812, 5199, 15396
Smith, James, 1791? 5200
Smith, James E., b.1831 or 1832, 5201
Smith, Sir James Edward, 1759-1828, 5202
Smith, James F., 23625
Smith, James Lindsay, 25539

Smith, James McCune, 24469
Smith, Jedediah Strong, 1790-1831, 5203, 16924, 16926, 27923
Smith, Jeremiah, 1805-1874, 25540
Smith, John, 1580-1631, 3190, 5204, 5205, 9917, 22469, 23626, 23627
Smith, John, 1790-1824, 24881
Smith, John, fl.1854, 24292
Smith, John ("Raccoon John"), 13861
Smith, John Augustine, 1782-1865, 23077, 23079
Smith, John Calvin, 5206
Smith, John Talbot, 1855-1923, 10675
Smith, Joseph, 1805-1844, 8044, 15965, 17208
Smith, Joseph, 1815-1875, 8203, 15561
Smith, Joseph Tate, 25541
Smith, Joseph Warren, 1831-, 5207
Smith, Joshua Hett, 1736-1818, 23628
Smith, Julie P., d.1883, 10805
Smith, Justin Harvey, 1857-, 17633
Smith, L.M., 25542
Smith, Mrs. Lilla May (Hall) 1860-, 15397
Smith, Lyman B., 20685
Smith, Marcus, b.1815, 6748
Smith, Margarete C., 15398
Smith, Mrs. Mary Ettie V., 3679
Smith, Matthew Hale, 1810-1879, 23091
Smith, Mattie S., 15399
Smith, Melancthon, 1744-1798, 23629
Smith, Milton Hannibal, 1836-1921, 14006
Smith, Nathan, 1762-1829, 21760
Smith, Nathan Ryno, 1797-1877, 21760
Smith, Paul L., 15375
Smith, Philip Henry, 1842-, 8045
Smith, Phillip S., 15400
Smith, R. F., pub., 5208
Smith, Robert, 1757-1842, 1041
Smith, Samuel, 1720-1776, 23630, 23631
Smith, Samuel, 1752-1839, 23632, 23633
Smith, Samuel, 1759-1854, 5209, 23634
Smith, Samuel, lecturer of St. Albans, 23635
Smith, Samuel, vicar of Lois Weedon, 23636
Smith, Samuel Stanhope, 1750-1819, 23995
Smith, Sarah Lanman (Huntington) 1802-1836, 22551
Smith, Sidney, 5210
Smith, Sidney, 1771-1845, 23637
Smith, Solomon Franklin, 1801-1869, 5211, 5212
Smith, Mrs. Susan E. D., 1817-, 5213
Smith, Theodore Clarke, 1870-, 25543, 25544
Smith, Truman, 1791-1884, 8046
Smith, Venture, 25545
Smith, W.F., 5547

Smith, W.F., & co, New York, 6912
Smith, W.I., 4999
Smith, William, 5214
Smith, William, 1727-1803, 267, 12099, 23638, 23639
Smith, William, 1728-1793, 23640
Smith, William, 1769-1847, 23029
Smith, William A., 14995
Smith, William Andrew, 1802-1870, 25299
Smith, William B., 5215
Smith, William Benjamin, 8047
Smith, William H., 11541
Smith, William Henry, 8048
Smith, William Henry, 1833-1896, 25546, 25547
Smith, William Loughton, 1758(ca.)-1812, 5216
Smith, William Nathan Harrell, 1812-1889, 25548, 25549
Smith, William Russell, 1815-1896, 5217-5222, 25550
Smith, William Townsend, 15401, 24715
Smith, Winton S., 13863
Smith, Zachariah Frederick, 1827-1911, 15402-15404, 25551
Smith College stories, 8635
Smith of Bear City, 16083
Smith's guide to the southwest, 5208
Smithers, Nathaniel Barratt, 1818-1896, 25552
Smithers, Wilfred Dudley, 1895-, 17634
Smithsonian Institution, 675, 676, 1475, 8049, 11287, 19325; History, 12064
Smithwick, Noah, 1808-1899, 5223
Smoked glass, 10418
The smoked Yank, 3695
The Smoky City, 11224
Smoky Hill Expedition, 3677
Smyth, Alexander, 1765-1830, 25553
Smyth, Clement, bp., 1810-1865, 16932
Smyth, Sir David William, bart., 1764-1837, 7243
Smyth, John Ferdinand Dalziel, 5224
Smyth, Samuel Gordon, 1859-, 15405
Smyth, Thomas Alfred, 1822-1865, 23366
Snake-dance, 16025
Snake Indians, 3257, 17629; Language, 5307
Snake lore, 15540
The snake of the cabin, 10783
Snake River Indians, 5509
Snakes, 14153, 15525, 21737; South American, 17948
Snapp, Frank, illustr., 13733
The snare broken, 23400
Sneed, W. II., 15406

Sneed, William C., 25554
Snelling, William Joseph, 1804-1848, 404
Snook, James E., 17635
Snow, W. Parker, 8050
Snow, William J., 17636-17638
Snow-bound at Eagle's, 6974
The snow-image, 9826
Snowden, Clinton A., 16459
Snowden, William H., 8051
Snyder, Adam Wilson, 1790-1842, 5225
Snyder, John Francis, 1830-, 5225, 5226
So many calls, 10904
Sobrinho, Mansel Duarte Ferreira Porto, 18322
Sociable visiting, 10197
Social destiny of man, 1530
Social fetters, 5262
Social history, 22944; 20th cent., 18987
A social history of the American negro, 24008
Social life in old Virginia before the war, 25189
The social monitor; or, A series of poems, on some of the most important and interesting subjects, 22501
Social problems, 6981, 12374
Social problems of to-day, 17065
Social relations in our southern states, 3967, 22606
Social science research, 18104
Social sciences, Addresses, essays, lectures, 12374; Bibliography, 18877; Costa Rica, 19715; History, Colombia, 18362; Miscellanea, 22880; Societies, etc., 20037; Study and teaching, 2287, 19727, 20037; Venezuela, Bibliography, 19744
Social security and the farmer in Kentucky, 13823
Social security and the teacher, 15018
Social service and race problems, 18230
The social significance of our institutions, 22669
Social silhouettes, 9502
Social studies, Study and teaching, Curricula, 20601
The social war of the year 1900, 10161
Social work, 19978
Social work with youth, Costa Rica, 21744
Social workers, Costa Rica, Handbooks, manuals, etc., 21744
Socialism, 7658, 8775, 18638, 25797; Addresses, essays, lectures, 19231; Brazil 20049; Christian, 24720; Fiction, 10660
Socialism and labor and other arguments, 5245

Socialismo, marxismo y bolcnevismo, 20027
Socialismo premarxista, 19231
Sociedad abolicionista española, Madrid, 23831, 25509, 25550
Sociedad Académia de Amantes de Lima, 7463
La sociedad anonima, 20245
Sociedad de amigos del pais, Panama, 1250
Sociedad de Entomologia Mexicana, 20485
Sociedad de geografia e historia, Guatemala, 8182
Sociedad de Ingenieros Agronomos de Bolivia, . Boletin bibliografico, 19788
Sociedad económica de amigos del pais, Havana, 11343
Sociedad mexicana de geografía y estadística, 17392
Sociedad Mexicana de Historia Natural, 18962
Sociedad Venezolana de Ingenieros de Petroleo, 20418
Sociedade Botânica do Brasil, 20423
Sociedade de geographia de Lisboa, 24214
Sociedade dos Cem Bibliofilos do Brasil, 18233
Las sociedades financieras privadas en Mexico, 19713
La société américaine, 3305
Société américaine de France, Paris, 1100
Société de colonisation européo-americaine au Texas, Brussels, 3072
Société de géographie de Lillie, 19944
Société des amis des noirs, Paris, 6172, 8052, 8053, 8054, 25556
Société pour l'aboliton de l'esclavage, Paris, 23836
Societies, Bibliography, Catalogs, 518
Society, manners and politics in the United States, 1867
Society as I have found it, 4327
Society for Mitigating and Gradually Abolishing the State of Slavery throughout the British Dominions, 25557, 25558
Society for propagating the gospel among the Indians and others in North America, 840, 964, 2174, 22210
Society for the commemoration of the landing of William Penn, Philadelphia, 13086
Society for the Diffusion of Political Knowledge, New York, 25030
Society for the encouragement of the British troops in Germany and North America, 12659
Society for the Propagation of the Faith, Quebec (Diocese), 5227
Society for the propagation of the gospel

in foreign parts, London, 419, 654, 1007, 11407, 11651, 12124, 13391, 21941, 22601, 23397, 23492; Proceedings, 1732, 1196; Proceedings, 1738, 22425; Proceedings, 1746, 22630; Proceedings, 1750, 23710; Proceedings, 1777, 23134
Society for the relief of the destitute sick, 23238
A society for the special study of political economy, 2287
Society in America, 7425
Society, in New York, for Promoting the Manumission of Slaves and Protecting Such of Them as Have Been, or May Be Liberated, 24624
Society of California Pioneers, San Francisco, 16790
Society of Colonial Wars in the Commonwealth of Kentucky, 15407
Society of the Army of the Potomac, 8055
Society of the Cincinnati, 23435; Connecticut, 2146, 2148, 22604; New Jersey, 11401; Pennsylvania, 1259, 1822; Rhode Island, 12808; South Carolina, 11448, 12391, 12445, 12611
Society of the Diffusion of Useful Knowledge, London, 11547
Society of the friendly sons of St. Patrick of Philadelphia for the relief of emigrants from Ireland, 12880
Society of the sons of New England of the city and county of Philadelphia, 1456
Society of United Irishmen of Dublin, Proceedings, 1931
Society silhouettes, 8703
Society's stepchildren: the mentally retarded, 15256
The Socini-Arian detected, 3028
Socinianism, 3028
Sociocultural origins and migration patterns of young men from eastern Kentucky, 15337
Socio-economic bibliography of Lexington and Fayette County, 15116
La sociología en Venezuela, 18104
Sociology, 18231, 18904, 20075; Addresses, essays, lectures, 18103; History, Venezuela, 18104; Study and teaching, 17952, 17953, 18104
Sociology, Christian, 1998, 18098; France, 23968; Middle Ages, 23968
Sociology, Christian (Catholic), 18516
Sociology, Rural, 19988, 20349
Socorro Island, Mexico, 18026
Socrates, 469-399 B.C., 19663

Soft drinks, Brazil, 20504
The soft side, 10016
Los sogadores, 18843
Soil conservation, Argentine Republic, 18440; Venezuela, Mérida (State), 18044; Venezuela, Tachira, 18044
Soil surveys, Colombia, 20302
Soils, 15145, 18587, 20281; Brazil, Ceará (State), 20012; Brazil, Parana Valley, 19683; Brazil, Uruguay River Valley, 19683; Colombia, Mercaderes, 20301; Costa Rica, 19475, 19476; Cuba, 17975, 18705
Sojo, José Raimundo, 18620
A sojourn in the Old Dominion, 10097
Sokolova, Elena A., 18094
Sol sobre o pecado, 18572
Sol veritatis, 5879
Solano, Francisco, Saint, 1549-1610, 6469, 6470
Solano, Vicente, 21720
Solano Co., California, Biography, 16778; History, 16778
Solar system, 1696
Solazzi, Siro, 1875-, 25559-25563
The soldier God's minister, 2419
A soldier of Manhattan, 2521
A soldier of the empire, 10460
The soldier of the revolution, 9702
The soldier's aid society, 10122
The soldier's bride and other tales, 3749, 14242
The soldier's friend, 5213, 9460
The soldier's orphans, 10874
A soldier's recollections, 4365
A soldier's reminiscences in peace and war, 4069
The soldier's revenge, 9200
The soldier's story of his captivity at Andersonville, 3649
A soldier's story of the war, 2625
The soldier's text-book; or, Confidence in time of war, 22850
Soldiering in Dakota Territory in the seventies, 16284
Soldiers, 7719; Prayer-books and devotions, English, 22850; Suffrage, Michigan, 16542; United States, Biography, 23085
Soldiers of fortune, 9362
Soleau, Alexandre, b.1804?, 25564
A solemn appeal to the church, 13289
Solid waste: the third pollutant, 14107
A solid waste inventory for the Barren River Area Development District,

13612
Solis de Meras, Gonzalo, 5228
Solis Folch de Cardona, José, duque de
    Montellano, d.1770, 7946
Solis Vango, Juan Prospero de, 8056
Solis y Rivadeneyra, Antonio de, 1610-
    1686, 8057-8068
El solitario de la habitación 5 Guión 3,
    20011
Solitary, 9575, 10434
Solitary places made glad, 16336
Solitary rambles and adventures of a
    hunter in the prairies, 4686
La solitude avec Dieu, 5024
Solomon, 11205
Solomon, William (known as King Solomon)
    ca. 1775-1854, 15577
Solorzano Pereira, Juan de, 1575-1655,
    8069-8073
Solos da Bacia Paraná-Uruguai, 19683
The solution, 7122
Somatology, 20365
Somatometria de los indios triques de
    Oaxaca, Mexico, 20368
La sombra del caudillo, 19967
Somebody's neighbors, 9121
Somebody's stocking, 10236
Somers (brig), 22926, 22929
Somers, Robert, 1822-1891, 23641
Somerset, Henry Charles Somers Augustus,
    8074
Somerset, Ky., 15409; Presbyterian
    Church, 15408
Somerset, Lake Cumberland, Daniel Boone
    National Forest, Burnside, Kentucky,
    15409
Somerset Co., Me., History, 12657
The Somerset cook book, 15408
Something about California, 16596
Something for every body, 9706
Something to do, 10024
Sommer, Johann Gottfried, 1792 or 3-1848,
    8075
A son of temperance, 2290
A son of the forest, 405
A son of the middle border, 16575
A son of the Old Dominion, 9770
A son of the South, 24745
The song of higher water, 5607
The song of Lancaster, Ky., 4838
A song of reason, 3159
Song of the rivers, 1171
Songs, California, 17436
Songs, American, 13420; English, 274;
    Religious, 14374
Songs, odes, and other poems, on national

subjects, 22792
Songs and poems of the South, 4436
Songs and satires, 14450
Songs chiefly from the German, 5246
Songs of a day, 5257
Songs of fair weather, 5396
Songs of the free, 11737
Songs of the heart, 4473
Songs of the Sierras, 17195
Songs of the soil, 5257
Um sonho! Impressões de uma viagem aos
    Estados Unidos, 3716
Sonneck, Oscar G., 1873-1928, 25705
Sonol, A., 19614
Sonora (ship), 23461
Sonora, Mexico, 17239; Description & travel,
    2624, 2837, 4398, 4544, 4922, 6955, 7837,
    17134, 18886; History, 8308, 23480
La Sonora et ses mines, 23061
La sonrisa y la via, 18959
Sons and daughters of pioneer rivermen,
    Cincinnati, Ohio, 13825
Sons and fathers, 3346
Sons of Colorado, 17640
The sons of Ham, 4748
Sons of Liberty, 21755
Sons of Temperance of North America, 22103,
    22173
Sons of the American Revolution, 8076;
    Kentucky Society, 15410; Empire State
    Society, 6700; Kentucky chapter, 15751
Sons of the Revolution in the State of
    Kentucky, 15411
The sons of the border, 10863
Sophonisba Preston Breckinridge, 1866-1948,
    15412
The soprano, 8709
Sorarte, Francisco, 8272
Sorbic acid, 18457
Sorenson, Alfred Rasmus, 1850-, 17641
Sorghum, 13059, 22395
Sorondo, Xavier, 1883-, 8077
Sorrows of Don Tomas Pidal, reconcentrado,
    10608
The sorrows of Nancy, 13700
Sosa, Francisco, 1848-1925, 21766
Soto, Hernando de, 1500 (ca.)-1542, 5469,
    7825, 12195, 13108, 15749, 17905, 23642
Soublette, Carlos, 1789-1869, 19486
The soul of Ann Rutledge, 5974
The soul-sisters, 11198
The soul winner, 14228
Soule, Don M., 14141
Soule, Joshua (port.), 14995
The soules exaltation, 22554
Soulsby, Lucy Helen Muriel, 5230

The sources of the Susquehanna, 9143
The Souris country, 6234
Sous les tropiques; souvenir de voyage, 22107
The South, 23934; Description & travel, 12217; Description & travel, Bibliography, 15529; Fiction, 4748
The South: a tour of its battle fields and ruined cities, 5468
The south after the war, 4152
The south alone, should govern the South, 25715
The south and its people, 2834
South and North, 14
The South as it is, 4673
The South in the building of the nation, 15413
The South: its industrial, financial, and political condition, 4340
The South must have her rightful place in history, 7927
South songs, 3227
The South without the shadow, 10992
South Africa, Description & travel, 3991
South America, 2213, 11479, 13272; Antiquities, 21853; Climate, 4039; Commerce, 492, 23373; Commerce, Gt. Britain, 196; Description & travel, 359, 1431, 2003, 4636, 6057, 6141, 6440, 6939, 7042, 7091, 7092, 7306, 7368, 7624, 7648, 7777, 8014, 8075, 8171, 8178, 8243, 8254, 8307, 11934, 11964, 13004, 13200, 13335, 15942, 16253, 16520, 17854, 19852, 21853, 22223, 22358, 22399, 23615; Description & travel, Guide-books, 7473, 7653; Discovery & exploration, 7629; History, 3406, 6734, 11479; History, Sources, 19375; History, To 1806, Sources, 18010; History, Wars of independence, 1806-1830, 6028, 7245, 7506, 7625, 7635, 7637, 7664, 8112, 11478; History, Wars of independence, 1806-1830, Foreign participation, 12517; History, Wars of Independence, 1806-1830, Poetry, 18302; History, Wars of independence, 1806-1830, Sources, 6108, 6109, 6110, 7636, 8127, 8319; Politics, 1806-1830, 1713, 19783; Politics & government, 11479
South Carolina, 3298; Agricultural survey, 23643; Bibliography, 15140; Biography, 12729; Climate, 2960; Commission to negotiate with the government of the U.S., 1860-1861, 23645; Convention, 1860-1862, 25566; Description & travel, 426, 491, 2553, 2560, 2919, 3425, 3568, 3627, 3720, 3722, 3737, 3876, 4173, 4222, 4477, 4576,

4588, 4646, 4682, 4890, 4949, 4998, 5159, 5427, 5597, 5712, 5742, 11515, 14749, 15527; Description & travel, Guide-books, 13544; Economic conditions,3724, 5562, 5563, 5788, 15611; Fiction, 25455; Finance, 17580; General Assembly, Committee to whom was referred the message of Gov. James H. Adams, relating to slavery and the slave trade, Reports, 98; General Assembly, House of Representatives, Special Committee on Slavery and the Slave-trade, 25566; General Assembly, Senate, 23646, 25567; Governor, 1834-1836 (George McDuffie), 25568; History, 5161, 12416, 24272, 25779; History, Civil war, 23645; History, Colonial period, 426, 2553, 3106, 3860, 4075, 5787, 23539; History, Colonial period, Fiction, 10784; History, Colonial period, Sources, 4804, 23539; History, Revolution, 3418, 5164, 13157, 13246, 21864, 23647, 24364; History, Revolution, Fiction, 9433, 10775, 10778, 10779; Industries, 22295; Maps, 14183; Politics & government, 3370, 12446, 12635, 23647; Politics & government, 1775-1865, 23237; Politics & government, 1865-, 22937; Politics & government, Colonial period, 13383, 24852; Politics & government, Revolution, 11614; Social conditions,15611; Social life & customs, 2530, 10446, 10715, 25111, 25455; State Agricultural Society, 218
South Carolina (Colony) Assembly, Committee to enquire into the causes of the disappointment of success, in the expedition against St. Augustine, 23644;
South Carolina (Colony) Court of vice admiralty, 11363
South Carolina (Colony) Provincial Congress, Feb.1-April 11, 1776, 23647
South Carolina (Province) General Assembly, 3989
South Carolina bar association, 12695
South Carolina historical society, 12639
South Carolina in the Revolutionary war, 5164
South Carolina nfantry, Edisto rifles, 1851-, 4033; 1st regt., 1862-1865, 4493; 4th regt., 1861-1865, 4921; Gregg's brigade, 1862, 2889; Hagood's, 1861-1862, 4493; Kershaw's brigade, 3244; McGowan's brigade, 1863-1865, 2889
South Carolina Institute, 22295
A South-Carolinian, 25300, 25468
South Dakota, Description & travel, 16707, 17525, 17045, 17071; History, 16402, 16779

The South Devil, 11207
South Frankfort Kentucky, 13967
South Fulton, Tenn., History, 14150
South Hadley, Mass., Genealogy, 21800
South Meadows, 9402
South Middlesex Conference of Churches, 25569
South Sea Company, 119, 2228, 2470, 12129, 25077
South Union, Ky., 4019
South Windsor, Conn., History, 23664
Southampton, Henry Wriothesley, 3d earl of, 1573-1624, defendant, 22680
Southampton, N.Y., Genealogy, 12961; History, 12961
Southampton insurrection, 1831, 23999, 24316, 25738, 25831; Fiction, 22667
Southard, Mary Young, 15414
Southard, Nathaniel, 25570
Southbridge, Mass., History, 22046
Southeastern Kentucky Regional Library Cooperative, 15415, 15416
Southern and south-western sketches, 2600
Southern and western liberty convention, Cincinnati, 1845, 24151, 25571
Southern and western Texas guide for 1878, 4999
Southern Appalachian mountain lore, 15138
Southern Association of Colleges and Secondary Schools, 14648
Southern attitude toward slavery, 25795
A Southern auntie's war tale, 2774
Southern Baptist Convention, 15417; Sunday school board, 14144
Southern Baptist publication society, 24954
Southern Baptist Theological Seminary, 15418
The Southern bivouac, 5231
Southern boundary of the U.S., 3360, 12024
The Southern business directory and general commercial advertiser, 13780
Southern California, 16915, 17643, 17644
Southern Commercial Convention, Knoxville, Tenn., 1857, 24043
Southern Commercial Convention, Vicksburg, Miss., 1859, 25572
The Southern Confederacy and the African slave trade, 1794
Southern convention, Nashville, 1850, 23648
The Southern cross, 13959
Southern excursionists' guide-book to cheap and pleasant summer homes in the mountains of Virginia, 5232
Southern hearts, 11191
The Southern highlander and his homeland, 2901

Southern historical publication society, Richmond, pub., 15413
Southern history of the war, 4820
A Southern lady, 25456
Southern letters, 4850
Southern life as it is, 9457
Southern Manitoba and Turtle Mountain country, 8078
Southern matron, Recollections of a, 3604
The Southern orator, 22733
Southern Pacific company, 8079, 8173, 23927; Explorations and surveys, 3667, 5520, 5522
The Southern poems of the war, 4408
Southern poets, 15073
Southern prisons, 3279
Southern Railway System, 4790, 15419; Bridges, 13938
Southern rambles, 3095
A Southern record, 5482
Southern sidelights, 3995
Southern slavery and the Bible, 11100
Southern slavery and the Christian religion, 25635
Southern slavery considered on general principles, 25573
Southern soldier stories, 9469
The Southern South, 3800
The Southern spy, 4821
Southern state rights, 25574
Southern states, 3657, 7927, 14098, 14749, 24391, 24553, 25101; Agriculture, 4459, 11368; Biography, 15413; Church history, 16838; Description & travel, 14, 361, 946, 2631, 2850, 2870, 2958, 3031, 3052, 3091, 3098, 3099, 3202, 3222, 3277, 3278, 3315, 3358, 3360, 3407, 3425, 3428, 3441, 3490, 3619, 3630, 3669, 3734, 3779, 3795, 3818, 3934, 3975, 3986, 4066, 4135, 4152, 4173, 4188, 4217, 4242, 4340, 4379, 4465, 4706, 4738, 4760, 4813, 4824, 4839, 4843, 4850, 4888, 4911, 4927, 4958, 5006, 5035, 5052, 5077, 5116, 5126, 5285, 5318, 5349, 5442, 5468, 5558, 5587, 5578, 5691, 5712, 5730, 5755, 7584, 12024, 12139, 12781, 13513, 13563, 14749, 15539, 15725, 16523, 17245, 22938, 23073, 23506, 24238, 25801; Description & travel, Guide-books, 2552, 3603, 4953; Description & travel, Poetry, 4294; Directories, 1756; Economic conditions, 1997, 3902, 4141, 4475, 4611, 4673, 15413, 23643, 24500, 25254; Fiction, 10782; History, 6000, 15259, 15413, 15578, 24596, 25406; History, 1865-1877, 25768; History, Colonial period, 12754; History, Periodicals, 4231; History, Revolution, 2392, 2393, 4238, 5347, 13246, 13380;

History, Revolution, Fiction, 4336;
History, War of 1812, 4224, 22165,
23732; Manners and customs, 14247;
Politics & government, 6483, 23619;
Politics & government, 1775-1865, 23244,
23648, 24986, 25155; Politics &
government, 1865-1900, 2124, 3226;
Population, 15504; Sectional
characteristics, 25151; Social conditions,
2579, 3425, 3800, 5734, 23641, 25440;
Social life and customs, 2834, 3262,
3967, 3995, 4013, 4133, 4719, 4835,
4886, 4888, 5320, 5349, 5558, 5641,
5799, 8634, 8926, 12841, 22606, 23619,
24055, 25014
The Southern states hardened until ruined,
25052
Southern statesmen of the old regime, 8232
A Southern story, 5320
A Southern view of the invasion of the
Southern states, 5943
A Southern view of the Negro problem, 8047
Southern war songs, 3411
The Southern women of the second American
revolution, 4035
Southern writers, 2632
Southerne, Thomas, 25575
Southerner, 2214, 24299
A Southerner among the spirits, 5142
Southesk, James Carnegie, earl of, 1827-
1905, 8080
Southold, N.Y., Genealogy, 12431
Southward ho! 3783, 10781
The South-west, 4012, 9987
The Southwest: its history, character, and
prospects, 4437
Southwest, New, 3688, 5064, 5292, 6893,
6894, 6895, 15850, 16640, 17337;
Bibliography, 15850; Biography, 17427;
Description & travel, 2411, 2575, 2837,
4500, 4715, 4922, 5516, 5524, 5541, 5542,
5548, 6784, 6813, 6937, 7080, 7140, 7174,
7772, 7882, 8122, 15961, 16273, 16795,
16960, 17031, 17488, 17787, 17875, 23506;
Description & travel, Bibliography, 7488;
Discovery & exploration, 16503; History,
15992, 16334; History, Civil War, 17377,
17378; History, Sources, 7080; Social
life & customs, 15887
Southwest, Old, 3497, 4435, 14303, 16567;
Description & travel, 3163, 3594, 3867,
3979, 4012, 4162, 4332, 4470, 5411, 9987,
10964, 16960, 17247, 23506; History,
4437, 8016, 15682; History, Civil War,
2808, 3895, 17900; History, Revolution,
4767; History, Sources, 16010; Social

life & customs, 4012, 4795, 9987
Southwest on the turquoise trail, 7080
Southwestern Indiana Historical Society,
Evansville, Ind., 6665
South-western letters, 7772
Southwestern states, Cattle, History, 17086;
Cattle trade, 17086
Southwick, Josiah, 23466
Southworth, Edward, 1804-1869, 12471
Souto, Paulo Ganem, 18657
Souto Maior, Mario, 19710
Souvenir book of historic Springfield, Ill.,
8081
Souvenir de mon voyage aux États-Unis et au
Canada, 6578
Souvenir of a tour in the U.S.A. and Canada,
5637
A souvenir of Wilmore, 15420
Souvenirs atlantiques, 4722
Souvenirs d'outre-mer, 6609
Souvenirs d'un diplomate, 2588
Souza, João da Oniz e, 1861-1898, 20514
Souza, José Antonio Soares de, 18271, 19391
Souza, Roberto Pimentel de, 19508
The sovereign rule of South Carolina, 8459
Sovereignty, 15752
The sovereignty of the people, 12402
The Soviet penetration of Cuba, 18888
Sowell, Andrew Jackson, 17647
Spaeth, Adolph, i.e. Philip Friedrich
Adolph Theodore, 1839-1910, 8082
Spain, Bibliography, 18839; Bio-bibliography,
399, 400; Colonies, 2437, 7274; Colonies,
Administration, 6432, 8073, 8085, 8342,
24079, 24291, 24441, 24657, 25787; Colonies,
America, 6355-6363, 6432, 7657, 8073,
12145, 19893, 19894, 20484, 23680, 24094,
24095; Colonies, America, Fiction, 4010;
Colonies, History, 7034, 7035, 8235;
Colonies, Law, 8073, 8085; Colonies, North
America, 4502, 15992; Colonies, South
America, 2473; Commerce, 6329; Commerce,
Spanish America, 402, 23649; Commercial
policy, 402, 2473, 23680; Consejo de las
Indias, 23649; Cortes, 24291; Cortes, 1879-
1880, 25576; Cortes, Congreso de las
diputados, 24079; Description & travel,
3228, 3555, 7842, 8212, 11811, 12722,
25710; Economic conditions, 1918-, 20417;
Exploring expeditions, 16477, 23461; For.
rel., 5854; For. rel., Gt. Britain, 12129,
12368, 13408, 21776, 23127, 23583, 23594,
23740; For. rel., Haiti, 22480; For. rel.,
Mexico, 22748; For. rel., Peru, 23140;
For. rel., U.S., 8087, 19893, 21890,
History, 8253; History, Charles II, 1665-

1700, 7729; History, Civil war, 1936-1939, Personal narratives, 7176; History, Ferdinand and Isabella, 1479-1516, 1200; History, Gothic period, 414-711, Fiction, 10780; History, Historiography, 16038; History, Sources, 1094, 19632; History, Naval, 7827; Imprints, 18839; Junta directiva del cuarto centenario del descubrimiento de America, 8083; Junta informativa de ultramar, 1866-1867, 25577, 25787; Laws, statutes, etc., 402, 5972, 8084-8086; Laws, statutes, etc., 1759-1788 (Charles III), 23649; Laws, statutes, etc. 1874-1885 (Alfonso XII), 24234; Ministerio de estado, 22748; Officials and employees, 8071; Politics & government, 1819, 5864, 8069; Relations (general) with Central America, 20484; Sovereigns, etc., 1700-1746 (Phillip V) Manifeste de Sa Majesté Catholique, 12129; Sovereigns, etc., 1788-1808 (Charles IV), 8087
Spain's lost jewels, 7819
Spalding, Alva, 1773-1796, 12862
Spalding, Charles C., 5233
Spalding, Henry Harmon, 1803-1874, 4690, 5234, 17843
Spalding, John Lancaster, abp., 1840-1916, 5235-5248
Spalding, Martin John, abp., 1810-1872, 5240, 5249, 5250, 5251
Spangler, Edward, defendant, 1305
The Spanglers and Tingles, 10063
Spaniards in America, 19204
Spaniards in California, 15905
Spaniards in Chile, Poetry, 6680, 6681, 6685, 6686
Spaniards in the U.S., 16441
Spanish America, 432, 5827, 21830, 25796; Bibliography, 18295, 18839; Bibliography, Catalogs, 19511; Commerce, 11383; Commerce, Spain, 402, 23649; Constitutional history, 17984, 17985, 18976; Description & travel, 1, 26, 950, 5703, 5964, 6073, 6186, 6760, 6798, 7248, 8171, 8289, 8307, 11367, 11714, 13192, 22035, 22041, 22252, 23493, 23549; Description & travel, Gazetteers, 128; Description & travel, Maps, 13192; Economic integration, 20032; Economic policy, 20443; For. rel., Gt. Britain, 1713, 22769; For. rel., U.S., 8269, 23542; History, 1, 1186, 1187, 8073, 11367, 11523, 18994, 21782, 21783, 24585; History, To 1830, 7393;; History, Chronology, 6430; History, Revolution,

1810-1824, 19115; History, Sources, 7524, 7567, 8168, 8169; History, Wars of independence, 1806-1830, 8269; Imprints, 18839; Periodicals, 7853; Politics & government, 1713, 2437, 12145, 20048, 20238, 22885, 23542; Rural conditions, 20520; Social conditions, 20238
Spanish American literature, Addresses, essays, lectures, 18813, 19795, 19954; Collections, 19872; History and criticism, 18515, 18576, 18633, 18720, 19796; Magnetic recording, 18054
Spanish American poetry (Collections), 18996
Spanish and Mexican exploration and trade northwest from New Mexico into the Great Basin, 16758
The Spanish archives of California, 16460
Spanish colonization in the Southwest, 15-92
The Spanish conspiracy, 3682
The Spanish conquest of New Mexico, 16342
The Spanish empire in America, 21830
Spanish fiction, 18143; Translations from foreign literatures, 8223
Spanish language, Addresses, essays, lectures, 20407; Chrestomathies and readers, 6699, 6861; Consonants, 20227; Dialects, Chile, 18357; Dialects, Costa Rica, 18580; Dialects, Cuenca, Ecuador, 20476; Dialects, Guanajuato, Mexico (State), 19203; Dictionaries, 18083, 18255, 18541, 19132; Dictionaries, Aztec, 19479; Dictionaries, Guarani, 7921; Dictionaries, Popoluca (Vera Cruz), 20208; ; Dictionaries, Totonac, 18588; Etymology, 17998, 20713; Foreign words and phrases, Indian, 18192; Grammar, 18182, 19488, 19872; Orthography and spelling, 18181; Pronunciation, 19726, 20227; Provincialisms, Boca del Toro, Panama (Province), 20016; Provincialisms, Central America, 20618; Provincialisms, Colombia, 18083; Provincialisms, La Rioja, Argentine Republic (Province), 19609; Provincialisms, Puerto Rico, 18218; Provincialisms, Spanish America, 19726; Societies, 20405; Spelling, 17976; Study and teaching, 18268; Study and teaching, Argentine Republic, 18492; Study and teaching, Curricula, 20600; Word formation, 19970
Spanish literature, 19184; Addresses, essays, lectures, 17966, 19947, 19954; Bibliography, 18191; Bibliography, Early, 399, 400; Classical period, 1500-1700, Bibliography, 399; Collections, 19872; Early to 1550, Bibliography, 400; History, 21750, 21751; Magnetic recordings, 18054

Spanish Main, 362, 7075, 7898, 8239, 13192, 21765, 22190; Description & travel, 7095; Fiction, 4010
Spanish mission in California, 16155
Spanish mission of California, 16668, 17207, 17662
Spanish philology, Addresses, essays, lectures, 19947; Congresses, 18586
Spanish poetry (Collections), 18996
The Spanish press of California, 1833-1844, 16282
The Spanish pretentions confuted, 11523
Spanish Succession, War of, 1701-1714, 1357, 22299
Spanish Trail, The Old, 16758
Spanning the centuries, 15421
Sparing the spend, 8578
Sparks, Jared, 1789-1866, 239, 2490, 23381, 23650
Sparks from my Christmas tree, 14750
Sparrow, Edward, 2044
Sparrow, William, 1801-1874, 22715
The Sparrowgrass papers, 9198
Sparrows, 15525
Sparrows in Bluegrass tradition, 15541
Sparta, Wis., 15848
Spatafora, Bartolomeo, fl.1554, 25578
Spaulding, Elbridge Gerry, 1809-1897, 8088
Spaulding, Pam, photographer, 15309
A speakin' ghost, 9769, 10790
Speaking of operations, 13859
Speaking the truth for a day, 10832
Spear, Samuel Thayer, 1812-1891, 8089
Spears, James E., 15422
Spears, John Randolph, 1850-1936, 17648, 25579
Spears, John R., 11994
Spears, Woodridge, 15423
Special Education, Kentucky, 13927
Special interest organizations in Kentucky, 13622
Special souvenir programme of the presentation of a portrait bust of Governor Isaac Shelby, 15424
Specimens of newspaper literature, 1640
Specimens of the garbling of letters by the majority of the trustees of Dudley Observatory, 12332
Le spectateur américain, 23072
Spectator, pseud., 25753
The spectral mortgage, 10892
The spectre lover, 10844
The spectre of the cathedral, 9716
The spectre steamer, 4011
The spectre's voyage, 10919
Speculation, 461, 10849
Speculum justit

Speech disorders, 19092
Speech rhymes, 14406
Speed, James, 1812-1887, 8090, 8262, 25580
Speed, John, 1772-1840, 14319
Speed, Joseph J., 25581
Speed, Joshua, 6831
Speed, Joshua F., 15685
Speed, Thomas, 1841-, 15426-15428
A speedy end to slavery, 25910
Speleology, Kentucky, 14595
Spellers, 5743, 11761
Spelman, Henry, 1595-1623, 5252
Spelman, John A., 15429
Spence, Thomas, b.1832, 8091, 8092
Spencer, Ambrose, 1765-1848, 820
Spencer, Mrs. Burrilla B., 15430
Spencer, Charles S., 25582
Spencer, John H., 15430, 15431
Spencer, Oliver M., 1781?, 5253
Spencer, Philip, 22929
Spencer Co., Ind., 6662, 6664; Biography, 6663; History, 6665
Spencer Co., Ky., Maps, 14224
The spendthrift, 10172
Spermaceti for inward bruises, 25583
Sperry, Earl Evelyn, 1875-, 25584
Sphecidae, 18084
The sphinx's children and other people's, 9122
Spicy, 10160
Spiders, 20106; Cuba, 18090, 20673; Kentucky, 13707
Spiders and rice pudding, 8694
Spikerman, Juan P., 19675
Spin polarization, 19066
Spindler, Adeline B., 25585
Spindler, Charles, 9546
Spindletop Research, Inc., 14227, 14734
Spinelli, E. Osvaldo, 18796
A spinster's story, 9518
The spinster's ward, 10860
A spirit in exile, 8688
Spirit Lake, Ia., Massacre, 1857, 17012
Spirit of adventure, 2684, 17252
"The spirit of 1861," 3670
The spirit of military institutions, 23139
The spirit of old Kentucky, 15521
The spirit of Rhode Island history, 478
The spirit of Roger Williams, 13251
The spirit of Sweetwater, 9607
The spirit of the mountains, 15003
The spirit-rapper, 1607
Spirit rapping unveiled!, 23357
"A spirit, yet a woman too", 9487
Spiritual manifestations, 1050
Spiritual vampirism, 5657
Spiritual visitors, 11003

The spiritual voyage, 8823
Spiritualism, 1050, 1406, 1985, 5142, 7445, 7446, 9325, 9920, 10587, 11986, 19664, 19814, 23357
The spiritualists and the detectives, 10530
Spirituals, 24678
Spittle (The Rev. Solomon), Diary of, 10701
Spittlebugs, 20212
Spivey, Herman E., 14650
The spleen, 12384
Spofford, H. P., 10163
The spoiler of the folds, 14832
The spoils of Poynton, 10017
The spoils of the strong, 14754
Spoleto, Italy, History, 22781
Spoon bread and other deep south delights, 15444
Spooner, Lysander, 1808-1887, supposed author, 89
Sport and adventures among the North-American Indians, 17185
Sporting excursions in the Rocky mountains, 17751
Sporting scenes and sundry sketches, 9803
Sports, Brazil, 20395; Texas, 3465
Spot tail darter, 15113
Spotorno, Giovanni Battista, 1788-1844, 727
Spotswood, Alexander, 1676-1740, 6761
Spotswood family (Alexander Spotswood, 1676-1740), 1820
Spottsylvania, Battle of, 1864, 5490
The spouse of Christ coming out of affliction, 213
Sprague, Amasa, 1798-1843, 12311
Sprague, Isaac, 1811-1895, illustr., 12355
Sprague, John T., 17650
Sprague, Peleg, 24006
Sprague, William Buell, 1795-1876, 8093
The sprightly romance of Marsac, 10721
Spring, Arthur L., 8094
Spring, Gardiner, 1785-1873, 5254
Spring, Leverett Wilson, 1840-, 8095
Spring notes from Tennessee, 5436
Spring winds, 9802
Springfield, Ill., Court House, 6847; History, 7771; Views, 8081
Springfield, Mass., History, 1418; Springfield cemetery, 1419
Springfield Presbyterian Church, Bath County, Kentucky, 15322
Springs, 806, 9702; Virginia, 4605; W. Va., 4743
Springs and mountains of Virginia, 4822
Spurr, Josiah Edward, 17651
The spy, 9151, 14243
The spy of Osawatomie, 10007

The spy unmasked, 863
The square pew, 10747
The squarer, 9533
Squatter life and border warfare in the far West, 12281
Squatter sovereignty, 1368, 11916
Les squatters, 1108
Squibb, Robert, 23651
The Squibob papers, 9393
Squier, Ephraim George, 1821-1888, 8096-8098
The squire of Sandal-Side, 8742
The squirrel inn, 10895
Der Staat Kentucky und die Stadt Louisville, 15441
The stability of Christ's church, 804
Stabler, Edward, 1794-1883, 11585
Stacy, George W., 25586
Stacy, Helen Price, 15432, 15433
Staden, Hans, 16th cent., 23652
Stadnichenko, T., 15512
The stage-coach, 10704
The stage in romance, and the stage in reality, 10603
Stage lines in Dakota, 16043
The stage of life, 14275
Stagecoaches, Kentucky, 13833; the West, 16993
Stairs of sand, 2608
Stallings, S.J., 14667
Stallons, Malcolm, 13744, 15434
Stamford, Conn., History, 233, 22619; History, Civil war, 22620
Stamford soldiers' memorial, 22620
Stamp act, 1765, 572, 2288, 11763, 11789, 13091, 13368, 13474, 21992, 22250, 22762, 23363, 23400, 23536, 23666
Stamp act congress, New York, 1765, 572
Stamp duties, Peru, 6368; U.S., 15632
Stamping Ground, Ky. Baptist Church, 15373
Stanbrook Abbey Press, 14696
Standing, Joseph, 17273
Standish, 9736
Standisn of Standish, 8609
Standish the Puritan, 9737
Stanford University, Fiction, 9509
Stanhope, Philip Henry Stanhope, 5th earl, History of England from the peace of Utrecht to the peace of Versailles, v.6, 2272
Stanley, 11052
Stanley, Sir Henry Morton, 1841-1904, 17653, 25587
Stanley, Jacob, 25588
Stanley, M.D., 10206
Stanly, Edward, 1810-1872, 25589, 25590
Stansbury, Howard, 1806-1863, 5255, 17654
Stanton, Benjamin, 1809-1872, 12125

Stanton, Daniel, 1708-1770, 5256
Stanton, Edwin McMasters, 1814-1869, 6586, 13278
Stanton, Elizabeth Cady, 1815-1902, 25533, 25591
Stanton, Frank Lebby, 1857-, 5257
Stanton, Frederick P., 25592
Stanton, Henry B., 24764
Stanton, Henry Thompson, 1834-1898, 5258-5262, 14031
Stanton, Robert Livingstone, 1810-1885, 25593, 25594
Stanwood, Edward, 1841-1923, 8099
Stanzas to Queen Victoria, 1711
Staples, Charles Richard, 1875-1954, 15435
Staples, John Summerfield, 1844-1888, 6338
Staples, Nabor Augustus, 1830-1864, 25595
Staples, William Read, 1798-1868, 12322, 23653
Stapp, William Preston, 8100
The star brethren, 10769
The star corps, 2787
Star forty-six, Oklahoma, 16143
Star-Hunt, Jack, 8101
The star in the West, 2977, 11402
The star of freedom, 25596
Starboard and port, 7012
Stark, James Henry, 8102
Starke, Peter B., 25597
Starks, Rick, 13611
Stark's illustrated Bermuda guide, 8102
Starks, Me., History, 12657
Starley, James, 1817-1914, 17655
Starley family, 17655
Starling, Edmund L., 15436, 15437
Starr, Belle, 1846-1889, 6958
Starr, Frank Farnsworth, 8103
Starr, Frederick, jr., 1826-1867, 25598
Starr, Nathan, 1731-1752, 22170
Starring, William Sylvanus, d.1889, jt. comp., 16842
The stars and bars; or, The reign of terror in Missouri, 10092
Stars and stripes, 2435
Stars and stripes en maple leaves, 4439
The startled sewing society, 9208
Startling incidents of the War between the States, 13952
The starving settlers, 10957
State, The, 13151, 18907, 19032
State and prospects of religion in America, 673
State Bar Association of Kentucky, 14527
State governments, 23356
The state of country, 849, 1466
The state of Ohio vs. Forbes and Armitage, 24412
A state of the province of Georgia, 5266
A state of the rise and progress of our disputes with Spain, and the conduct of our ministers relating thereto, 23127
The state of the trade and manufactory of iron in Great Britain considered, 23654
State or province?, 4800
The state parks of Kentucky, 14639, 14640
State rights, 320, 11878, 12153, 12402, 12445, 12635, 12639, 13028, 13082, 22368, 22692, 22851, 23646, 23662, 24505, 24628, 25050, 25155, 25268, 25470, 25567, 25760, 25824
State, territorial, and ocean guide book of the Pacific, 3899
Statehood bill, 16373
Statement and appeal in behalf of Centre College, 15190
Statement of Major General Buell, 1658
A statement of the receipts and disbursements for the support of the missions, 1995
The states of Central America, 8097
States vs. territories, A true solution of the territorial question, 25407
The statesman and the man, 188
Statesmen, American, 869, 902, 4420, 7091, 22550, 23757
Statesmen, British, 223, 11741, 12802
The statesmen of America in 1846, 4420
A statewide movement to make a record of Kentucky's part in the World war, 14530
Statewide survey of historic sites in Kentucky, 14734
Gli Stati Uniti, 3571
Statistical abstract of the Republic of Chile, 20160
A statistical account of the U.S., 4443
A statistical and commercial history, 13342
Statistical gazetteer of the state of Virginia, 3351
Statistical survey of the economy of Colombia, 20260
A statistical view of the district of Maine, 12408
Statistics, 19697, 20528; Bibliography, 14704; Societies, 303
Statistics and information concerning the state of Texas, 17211
Statistics of the West, 3750
The statute law of Kentucky; with notes praelections, and observations on the public acts, 24715
The statutes at large of the provisional government of the Confederate States of America, 2063

Staughton, William, 1770-1829, 14872
Staunton, Sir George Thomas, bart., 1781-1859, 22252
The staying power of Sir Rohan, 10896
Steam-boilers, Incrustations, 11717
Steam navigation, History, 854, 22870; Mississippi River, 12573, 17184; Mississippi Valley, 14840; Ohio River, 12573
Steamboat days, 15119
Steamboat disasters, 14840
Steamboating on the Red River, 15978
Steamboats, 4320, 15278; Kansas, 4995
Steamboats on the Kentucky River, 13888
Stearns, Charles, 25599
Stearns, Edward Josiah, 1810-1890, 25600
Stearns, Frank Preston, 1846-1917, 25601
Stearns, George Luther, 1809-1867, 25601
Stearns, Isaac, 25602
Stearns, William Augustus, 1805-1876, 327
Stearns, Ky., 14757
Stecher, W.F., illustr., 2635
Stedman, John Gabriel, 1744-1797, 25603, 25604
Steedman, I.G.W., 5628
Steel, Metallurgy, 12905, 19509; Prices, Argentine Republic, 19943
Steel industry and trade, 22436; Argentine Republic, 19943; Dictionaries, English, 20385; Dictionaries, Spanish, 20385
Steele, Allen, 11337
Steele, Mrs. Eliza R., 5263
Steele, James William, 1840-1905, 8104, 8105, 17659-17662
Steele, John, 1821-, 17663
Steele, John, 1832-1905, 17664
Steele, John Benedict, 1814-1866, 25605
Steele, Joshua, 1700-1791, 23655
Steele, Robert Wilbur, 1857-1910, 17888
Steele, Samuel Benfield, 1849-, 8106
Steele, William G., 17665
Steele, Zadock, 1758-1845, 13078
Steen, Enoch, 3257
Steenis, Hendrik Cornelis, 24690
Steevens, John, 7060
Steevens family, 7060
Stehney, A.F., 19868
Steight's expedition, 1863, 4970
Steinby, Torsten, 14300
Steiner, Bernard Christian, 1867-1926, 3077, 5264, 25606
Steinthal, S. Alfred, 25607
Stella Delorme, 10081
Stella Lea, 10580
Stellmann, Edith Kinney, 17666
Stembal, Laura McBride, 14883

Stellmann, Louis J., illustr., 17666
Sten, Maria, 8107
Stensrud, Edward Martinus, 17667
Stephen, James, 1758-1832, 23656, 24349, 25608, 25609
Stephen, a soldier of the cross, 10137
Stephen, son of Douglas, pseud., 6115
Stephen Dane, 9423
Stephen Foster, 15385
Stephen Skarridge's Christmas, 10896
Stephens, Alexander, 1757-1821, 13352
Stephens, Alexander Hamilton, 1812-1883, 3030, 4080, 8232, 25612, 25762, 25610-25612
Stephens, Charles Asbury, 1845-1931, 8108
Stephens, Henry Louis, 1824-1882, illustr., 9910, 10537
Stephens, John Lloyd, 1805-1852, 8109
Stephens, Louise G., 1843-, 17668
Stephens, Thomas, 5265, 23657
Stephens, William, 1671-1753, 5266, 23658, 23659
Stephenson Co., Ill., History, 4092
The step-mother, 10683
The step-mother's recompense, 9440
Stepping heavenward, 10564
Steps to the kingdom, 11050
Sterling, James, 1701?-1763, 23660
Sterne, Simon, 1839-1901, 17669
Sterns, C.P., 16700
Sterope: the veiled Pleiad, 8455
Sterret, James, 25613
Stetson, Grace Ellery (Channing) 1862-1937, 8969
Stetson, Isaac, 1796-1718, 23499
Stetson family, 891
Stetson family (Robert Stetson, 1613-1703?), 891
Steuart, Richard Sprigg, 1797-1876, 25614
Steuben, Friedrich Wilhelm Rudolf Gerhard Augustus von, 1730-1794, 6714, 7866, 23729
Steuben, N.Y., 7866
Steuben Co., N.Y., History, 22975
Stevens, Benjamin, 1720-1791, 23661
Stevens, Charles, 23662
Stevens, Charles Augustus, b.1835, 5267
Stevens, George Thomas, 1832-1921, 5268
Stevens, Harry R., 15438
Stevens, Isaac Ingalls, 1818-1862, 5269, 5270, 5518, 16041
Stevens, John, d.1726, 2468
Stevens, John Austin, 8110
Stevens, O. A., 17670
Stevens, Rayfred Lionel, 8111
Stevens, Thaddeus, 1792-1868, 1393, 7353, 17671, 23923, 25615, 25918
Stevens, Walter Barlow, 1848-, 5271, 17672

Stevens, William, 25616
Stevenson, Benjamin Franklin, 5272
Stevenson, Carter Littlepage, 1817-1888, 2073
Stevenson, Charles L., 704
Stevenson, Dwight E., 15439, 15440
Stevenson, Edward Irenaeus Prime, 10283
Stevenson, John White, 1812-1886, 13318
Stevenson, Robert Louis, 1850-1894, 8220
Stevenson, Thomas M., b.1825 or 26, 5273
Stevenson, William Bennet, b.1787? 8112
Stevenson, William G., 5274
Stevin, Simon, 1548-1620, 23823
Stewart, Alexander Morrison, 1814-1875, 5275
Stewart, Alvan, 1790-1849, 25617
Stewart, Andrew, 1792-1872, 22085
Stewart, Catherine, 5276
Stewart, Mrs. Elinore (Pruitt) 1878-, 17673
Stewart, Ella Vonnegut, 13567
Stewart, James Augustus, 1808-1879, 25618
Stewart, John, of Jamaica, 25619, 25620
Stewart, John, 1786-1823, 23439
Stewart, Judd, 7288
Stewart, Richard, 22700
Stewart, Robert A.M., 5277
Stewart, Thomas R., 1198
Stewart, Virgil Adam, b.1809, 9931
Stewart, Sir William George Drummond, 7th bart., 1796-, 5278, 5279
Stickney, V. H., 17674
Stickney, William, 1827-1882, 14502
Stierlin, L., 15441
Stiff, Edward, 5280
Stifter, Adalbert, 1805-1868, 19612
Stiles, Ezra, 1727-1795, 22532, 23663
Stiles, Henry Reed, 23664
Stiles, Joseph Clay, 1795-1875, 5281, 5282, 15442
Stiles, William Henry, 1808-1865, 25621
Still, Lavinia, 10521
Still, Peter, 10521
Still, William, 1821-1902, 25622
Stille, Moreton, 1822-1855, 12855
Stillman, Annie Raymond, 5283
Stillman, J.D.B., 17675
Stillman, Samuel, 1738-1807, 23665-23667
Stillwell, Leander, 1843-, 5284
Stillwell, Lucille, 15443
Stimson, Frederic Jesup, 1855-1943, 9641
Stintans Amerikafärd, 2744
Stirling, Earl of, 13013
Stirling, James, 1906-1982, 5285
Stirling, Patrick James, 1809-1891, 17676
Stitzel-Weller Co., Louisville, Ky., 15444

Stobo, Robert, b.1727, 23668
Stock and stock-breeding, Venezuela, History, 20477
Stock and stock-breeding, The West, 15920
Stock exchange, Argentine Republic, 18137; Buenos Aires, Law, 19536
Stock-ranges, 15920, 16107, 16288
Stock ranges of northwestern California, 16107, 16344
Stockard, Henry Jerome, 1858-1914, 5286
Stockbridge, Mass., History, 12895, 13297
Stockbridge Indians, 13297; Missions, 12895
Stocking, Charles Henry Wright, 8113
Stocks and stock-jobbing in Wall-street, 461
Stockton, Richard, 1764-1828, 23669
Stockton, Robert Field, 1795-1866, 5406, 25158
Stoddard, Amos, 1762-1813, 5287
Stoddard, Charles Warren, 1843-1909, 10675, 17677
Stoddard, Elizabeth Drew (Barstow) 1823-1902, 9769
Stoddard, John Lawson, 1850-1931, 8114
Stoddard, Richard Henry, 1825-1903, 3701, 8115
Stokes, Anthony, 1736-1799, 23670
Stokes, Bess D., 15445
Stokes, Frances K. Wister, 8116
The stolen child, 3849
A stolen Christmas, 9575
The stolen jewel, 11220
The stolen Stradivarius, 9762
The stolen white elephant, 9033
The stolen will, 9480
Stolty, Charles, 1864-1931, 15446
Stone, Alfred Holt, 1870-, 25623
Stone, Andrew Leete, 1815-1892, 8117
Stone, Barton Warren, 1772-1844, 3028, 5288, 13833, 14940, 15292, 15447, 15448
Stone, Elizabeth Arnold, 17678
Stone, James W., 25343
Stone, Jacob L., 25624
Stone, Ross Conway, 5289
Stone, Wilbur Fiske, 1833-1920, ed., 17679
Stone, William Hale, 1875-, 17680
Stone, William Leete, 1792-1844, 15449, 23671, 23672
Stone, William Leete, 1835-1908, 5290, 23534
Stone houses, 14968
Stoneham, Mass., History, 22059
Stoneholt, 13797
Storer, David Humphreys, 1804-1891, defendant, 2221
Storey, Samuel, 17001
The stork, 10310

Stork, William, 5291
Storm, Theodor, 1817-1888, 19612
The storm at sea, 9977
Stormcliff, 11066
Stormont, Gilbert R., 3866
Storrs, Augustus, 5292
Storrs, George, 23909, 25625
Storrs, Richard Salter, 1821-1900, 8118, 25626
Story, Joseph, 1779-1845, 8119, 12410, 25759
Story, Thomas, 1662-1742, 5293
Story, William Wetmore, 1819-1895, 8119
The story reader's garland ; a cluster of tales, 10295
A story-teller's pack, 10896
Stott, Edwin, 1836-1928, 17682
Stott family, 17682
Stoughton, Asa, 24991
The stout Miss Hopkins' bicycle, 9580
Stovall, Pleasant A., 5294
The stove, 9216
Stow, Kesiah, d.1822, 12464
Stowe, Charles Edward, 1850-, 25628
Stowe, Mrs. Harriet Elizabeth (Beecher) 1811-1896, 5295, 8766, 9693, 10163, 15572, 21934, 24591, 25627-25631, 25848; Uncle Tom's cabin, 48, 1527, 13627, 23908, 24163, 24212, 25316, 25479, 25600, 25919
Stowe, Timothy, 24194
Strachan, John, bp. of Toronto, 1778-1867, 8120, 8121
Strachey, William, 5296
Strade d'America, 5333
Strahan, Edward, pseud., 5144
Strahorn, Robert E., 17683
A strange affair, 7291
A strange bird in New-Amsterdam, 10480
A strange career, 7144
The strange case of Esther Atkins, 10448
The strange experience of Alkali Dick, 9793
Strange news from Virginia, 5297
A strange, sad comedy, 5119
A strange story, 9255
Strange visitors, 9920
A strange voyage, 8510
A stranger in America, 3920
The stranger in Baltimore, 5666
Stranger, traveller, and merchant's guide through the U.S., 5298
"The stranger within thy gate," 9768
The stranger's gift, 11327
Strangers and wayfarers, 10043
Strangled liberty, 7351

Straten-Ponthoy, Gabriel Auguste Van der, comte, 15452
Stratford-on-Avon, 11183
Strathcona and Mount Royal, Donald Alexander Smith, 1st baron, 1820-1914, 7776
Stratton, Royal B., 1875-, 5299
Strauss, Louis, 1844-, 5300
Stawberries, 8706
Stray leaves from an Arctic journal, 7652
Stray leaves from the world's book, 10604
Stray subjects, arrested and bound over, 9453
A stray Yankee in Texas, 3763
Streaks of squatter life, and far-West scenes, 10629
Strebor, Eiggam, pseud., 10630
Street, Franklin, 5301
Street, George G., 8122
Street thoughts, 9396
Strickland, William Peter, 1809-1884, ed., 2922, 3450, 3453, 5302, 11783, 15453
Strictures addressed to James Madison, 11879
Strictures on a pamphlet, 13379
Strictures on African slavery, 3132
Strictures on some of the defects and infirmities of intellectual and moral character, in students of medicine, 3293
Strictures on the necessity of inviolably maintaining navigation, 13478
Strictures on the Philadelphia mischianza or triumphs upon leaving America unconquered, 23361
Strictures upon the Declaration of the Congress at Philadelphia, 13052
Strikes, 14675; Kentucky, 13556, 14005, 14269
Strikes and lockouts, Buneos Aires, 18494; Colorado, 16549; Harlan County, Ky., 13719; Mexico, 18906; Peru, 19966
Striking facts about Kentucky, 15127
Stringfellow, Benjamin, d.1891, 25119, 25282
Stringfellow, Thornton, 25632
Strip mining, 14016
Strobel, Phillip A., 13486
Strode's Station, Ky., 14210
Stroehlin, Ernest, 1844-, 5303
Ströftåg och irrfärder hos min vän Yankee Doodle, 4183
Strohal, Emil, 1844-1914, 25633
Strohm, Isaac, 3093
Strong, Anna Louise, 1885-1970, 5304
Strong, Beulah, illustr., 15090A
Strong, Frank, 1859-1934, 17684
Strong, George Crockett, 1832-1863, 2481
Strong, Leonard, fl.1655, 5305
Strong, T., 15454

Strong, T.W., pub., 12987
Strong, Thomas Nelson, 1853-, 17685
Strong, William Duncan, 17686
Strong hearts, 8930
Stroud, George McDowell, 1795-1875, 25634, 25635
Stroup, Thomas Bradley, 1903-, 13657
Strosberg, Don, 15454, 15455
Stroyer, Jacob, 1849-, 25636
Struan, 10307
Strubberg, Friedrich Armand, 1808-1889, 5306, 17687; Amerikanische Jagd- und Reiseabenteuer, 5772
Struble, Isaac S., 17688
Structural sociology, 18904
The structure of the visible heavens with hints on their celestial religion, and theory of futurity, 15224
The structures on The friendly address examined, and a refutation of its principles attempted, 11239
Struggle for life, 9698, 10427
The struggle of the hour; a discourse delivered at the Paine celebration in Cincinnati, 25100
The struggles for life and home in the North-west, 16543
Struthers, and The comedy of the masked musicians, 9408
Struve, Gustav, 1805-1870, 6186
Stryker, James, 1792-1864, 2482
Stuart, C., 25498
Stuart, Charles, 1783?-1865, 24232, 25637
Stuart, Granville, 1834-1918, 5307
Stuart, James, 1775-1849, 5308
Stuart, James Ewell Brown, 1833-1864, 2034
Stuart, Jane, 15456, 15482; Bibliography, 15765
Stuart, Jesse Hilton, 1905-, 13545, 14176, 14359, 15050, 15160, 15457-15486; Album of destiny, 14796, 15486; Bibliography, 15764-15767
Stuart, John, 8123
Stuart, Martinus Cohen, 5309
Stuart, Moses, 1780-1852, 25638, 25828; Conscience and the Constitution, 21940, 23894
Stuart, Robert, 2528, 3971
Stuart, Mrs. Ruth (McEnery) 1856-1917, 5310-5314, 25639
Stuart, T. G., 15487-15489
Stuart, Villiers, 1827-, 5315
Stuart-Wortley, Emmeline Charlotte Elizabeth (Manners) 1806-1855, 5816, 0104
Stuart Robinson School and its work, 13922
Stub Toe the champion, 13830

Stubblefield, Nathan B., 15675
Stubbs, Robert, 14727-14730
Stuber, Johann, 1838?-1895? 5317
Student cooperatives, Colombia, 18934
Students, 18374; Brazil, 19249; Buenos Aires, Health and hygiene, Yearbooks, 19546; Language (new words, slang etc.), 12558; U.S., 12558
Studien zum Besitzrecht, 24495
Studien zur römischen Rechtsgeschichte, 24343
Studies, literary and social, 4089
Studies in literature, 3691
Studies in the South and West, 5624
Studies of the town, 13061
Studies on slavery, in easy lessons, 24403
Study and use of ancient and modern history, 11266
A study of Mexico, 8367
Sturbridge, Mass., History, 21939, 22046
Sturge, Edmund, 1808-1893, 25640
Sturge, Joseph, 1793-1859, 5318, 24880, 25370
Sturges, Joseph, 25641
Sturgis, C. F., 25642
Sturgis, O. F., 24954
Sturgis, Mich., 17756
Sturm, William P., 14668
Sturz, Johann Jakob, 1800-1877, ed., 8125
Stutfield, Hugh Edward Millington, 1858-1929, 8126
Stuyvesant pear tree, 2141
Style, Literary, 17967
Suassuna, Ariano, 19702, 19712
A subaltern's furlough, 1992
La sublevación de Maracaibo en 1799, 19483
Subsidies, Mexico, 18330, 20454
Los subsidios federales en México, 20454
Substance of the debates on a resolution for abolishing the slave trade, 24516
Subterranean wonders, 14860, 15490
Suburban homes, 9695
Subways, New York (City), 13068
Success (ship), 1221
A successful man, 9263, 10356
Succession and descent, Gt. Britain, 21976
A succinct abridgment of a voyage made within the inland parts of South America, 7218
A succinct view of the origin of our colonies, with their civil state, founded by Queen Elizabeth, 21798
Sucinto noticia del ramo de la cera en la isla de Cuba, 11343
The sucker's visit to the Mammoth Cave, 8101
Sucre, Antonio José de, pres. Bolivia,

420

1795-1830, 7106, 8127
Sucre, Bolivia (City), Description, Poetry, 18383
Sudak, Leo, 20369
Sudan, Governor-general, 1927-1933 (Maffey), 25643
Sudbury, Mass, History, Colonial period, 11421
Sudene dos anos, 19461
Los suelos y su utilización agrícola en el Valle de la Juventud, 18587
The sufferings of William Green, 3683
Suffolk surnames, 11435
Suffrage, 25925; Gt. Britain, 11334; Rhode Island, 2339, 2340; U.S., 12645
Sugar, 12078, 19216, 23519; Argentine Republic, 18091; Cuba, 20690; Economic aspects, 20299; History, 19316; Manufacture and refining, 12103, 13345; Manufacture and refining, Colombia, 20299
Sugar cane, 12103, 20214; Brazil, Minas Geraes, 20556; Colombia, 20299; Cuba, 18235
Sugar growing, 576, 1080, 25564; Brazil, 18291; Cuba, Statistics, 20692; Jamaica, 1035, 23957, 24142, 25082; Louisiana, 13276; West Indies, British, 24252
Sugar industry and trade, Argentine Republic, 18091; Bolivia, 19116; Brazil, 20556; France, 11970; Gt. Britain, 23292, 23845, 24189, 25009; Puerto Rico, 19722; West Indies, 500, 501, 2009, 13471; West Indies, British, 25857; West Indies, French, 25070
Sulgrave Manor, 5930
Sulla "condicio emancipationis", 25563
Sullivan, Sir Edward Robert, bart., 1826-1899, 5319
Sullivan, George, 1771-1838, 88
Sullivan, James, 1744-1805, 333, 1646, 23673
Sullivan, M.A., illustr., 5186, 25529
Sullivan, Mrs. Margaret Frances (Buchanan), jt. author, 6099
Sullivan, Thomas Russell, 1799-1862, 25644, 25645
Sullivan, William, 1774-1839, 25644
Sullivan Co., N.H., Biography, 7094; History, 7094
The Sullivan looking-glass, 10909
Sullivan's Indian campaign, 1779, 1417, 12096, 21905
Sullivan's Island, 3108
Sulphur (ship), 6059
Sulphur industry, Mexico, 19654
Sulphur-springs, 13079
Sulte, Benjamin, 1841-1923, 8128, 8129

Sulzer, Elmer Griffith, 15491
Suma de geographia, 6674
Sumichrast, Frederick Caesar John Martin Samuel Roussy de, 1845-, 10283
Summa triunfal da nova, e grande celebridade do glorioso, e invicto martyr s. Gonçalo Garcia, 23017
A summary view of America, 2906
A summary view of the rights of British America, 22695
Summer drift-wood for the winter fire, 10555
Summer etchings in Colorado, 16632
Summer gleanings, 10984
A summer in Alaska, 7982
Summer in Arcady, 8517
Summer in the winter time, 2557
The summer-land, 5320
The summer of 1882 among the health resorts of northeast Georgia, 4958
The summer of the pestilence, 452
A summer on the borders of the Caribbean Sea, 12704
A summer on the Rockies, 17429
Summer rambles in the West, 3359
Summer resorts, Canada, 3253; U.S., 12567
Summer-savory, gleaned from rural nooks in pleasant weather, 17701
A summer story, 13466
The summer tourist's pocket guide to American watering places, 12567
Summer tours, 6322
A summer's romance at Newport, 10201
Summerfield, John, 1770-1825, 12848
Summering in Colorado, 16702
Summerland sketches, 7655
Summers, Thomas O., 4791
Summit Co., O., History, 1263, 16976
Sumner, Charles, 1811-1874, 6288, 8130, 24235, 25646-25655, 25770; The crime against Kansas, 1856, 23908, 25479
Sumner, Charles Allen, 1835-1903, 1166
Sumner, Helen L., 17690
Sumner, William, d.1855, 1951
Sumner, William Graham, 1840-1910, 8131
Sumter (Confederate cruiser) 5123, 23593; Fiction, 4733
Sumter, Fort, 11243, 12712, 23545, 24906, 24908
The Sumter anniversary, 1863, 24908
The Sun, New York, 8132
The sun of Saratoga, 2522
Sun pictures of Rock Mountain scenery, 16723
Sunday, 23161
Sunday at home, 9827
Sunday-school Union of the Methodist Episcopal church, 4546

Sunday schools, 13606
Sunderland, LeRoy, 1802-1885, 23909, 24651, 25528
The sunny land, 10057
The sunny South, 4013
Sunnybank, 5361
The sunset trail, 17028
The sunshine and shadow of seventy years, 14837
Sunshine and shadow of slave life, 24494, 25894
Sunshine and sport in Florida and the West Indies, 2495
Sunshine and storm, 8812
Sunshine in storm, 8795
Sunshine in the palace and cottage, 11041
Superannuated, 10748
Superintendência da Zona Franca de Manaus, 19342, 19343
Superintendência do Desenvolvimento da Amazônia, Documento GASPLAM, 20554
Superior, Lake, 108, 984, 9619, 23476
Supernatural, 12037; Fiction, 10693
Superstition, 15513, 15525, 19663; Kentucky, 15543
Supervisors, New York (State), 12323
Supplement to an Address to the members of the new Parliament, 25656
A supplement to the Selection of all the laws of the United States, 1494
Supply and demand, Bibliography, 18409
The supply at Saint Agatha's, 11079
The suppressed book about slavery! 25657
The suppression of slavery, memorandum submitted by the Secretary General, 25755
Supreme Court, 25313
Sur les hauts-plateaux mexicains, 8424
Surby, Richard W., 1832-, 5321
Surcos y chimeneas, 18131
The surf skiff, 9988
Surface water pollution of the inner Bluegrass region, 15006
The surface waters of Kentucky, 14751
Surgeons, Kentucky, 13605, 15209; New York (City), 2312
Surgery, 6801; Congresses, 7398; Early works to 1800, 13304
Surinam, Description & travel, 733, 734; Economic conditions, 24767; Politics & government, 2026
Surly Tim, 8910
Surnames in the United States census of 1970, 13543
The surprising case of Rachel Baker, who prays and preaches in her sleep, 23041

Surratt, John Harrison, 1844-1916, 7749, 8133
Surratt, Mary E. (Jenkins) d.1865, defendant, 1305, 22439
Surry Co., N.C., Social life & customs, 10922
Surtees, William Edward, 5322
A survey of the survey of that summe of church-discipline, 23561
Surveying, History, 6676; Public lands, U.S., 22353
Les survivances françaises au Canada, 7525
Susan's escort, 9694
Susie Rolliff'e Christmas, 10653
The suspending power and the writ of habeas corpus, 13273
Susquehanna company, 12183
Susquehanna Co., Pa., Description & travel, 13233
Susquehanna Indians, 2515
Susquehanna River, 23221
Susquehanna Valley, History, 23425
Susy, a story of the plains, 9792
Sut Lovingood, 3787
Sut Lovingood travels with old Abe Lincoln, 6960
Sutcliff, Robert, 5323
Suther, Evelyn Greenleaf, 10127
Sutherland, Patrick, 5324
Sutherland, Peter C., 8134
Sutil (schooner), 16477
Sutphen, Morris Crater, 1837-1875, 8135
Sutten's death-bed confession, 10932
Sutter, Archibald, 5325
Sutter, John Augustus, 1803-1880, 12838, 17575, 17576
Sutterlin, Violet C., 13972
Sutton, Carol, 15492
Sutton, Richard, 24714
Sutton, William Loftus, 1797-1862, 15493
The Sutton-Dudleys of England, 101
Sutton family, 101
Suwanee River, On the, 4905
Suzette, 10976
Svmarios de las cedvlas, ordenes y provisiones reales, 8085
Swain, B., 25658
Swain, D.L., 3418
Swainson, William, 4956
Swallow, G.C., 4698
Swallow barn, 10097
Swalue, Edelhardus Bernardus, 1806-1865, 670, 4098
The swamp outlaws, 5444
The swamp state of Conelachita, 10773
Swan, Charles Albert, 25659
Swan, Lansing D., 1809 , 8136

Swanannoa camp-meeting, 14302
Swansea, Henry Hussey Vivian, 1st baron, 1821-1894, 5326
Swanton, John R., 17692
Swanwick, John, 22931
Swasey, William F., 17693
Swearing, 2990
Swedes in Delaware, 21954
Swedes in the U.S., 1364, 4585, 17691
Sweeney, Mary E., 15494
Sweet, Alexander Edwin, 1841-1901, 5327, 17694
Sweet, George H., 17695
Sweet, O.P., 5328
Sweet's amusement directory and travelers' guide, 5328
Sweet bells out of tune, 9771
Sweet Cicely, 9889
Sweet Lake, 4837
Sweet revenge, 10358
Sweetbrier and thistledown, 2635
Sweethearts and wives, 8580
Sweets and meats and other good things to eat, 15118
Sweetser, Seth, 1807-1878, 8137
Swell life at sea, 10916
Swem, Earl Gregg, 1870-1965, 4264
Swett, John, 1830-, 17696
Swett, John Appleton, 1808-1854, 22836
Swett, Samuel, 1782-1866, 1882, 2349, 13011
Swift, Jonathan, 1667-1745, The conduct of the allies, 22299
Swift, Morrison Isaac, 25660
Swift, Zephaniah, 1759-1823, 25661
Swiggett, Samuel A., 1834-, 5329
Swimming pool reactors, 18406
Swindlers and swindling, 10736
Swinford, Mac, 1899-1975, 13709
"Swingin'round the cirkle", 10230
Swinton, Archibald Campbell, 1812-1890, reporter, 13013
Swinton, William, 1833-1892, 8138
Swisher, Mrs. Bella French, 1837-1894, ed., 15848
The Swiss peasant, 23045
Swisshelm, Mrs. Jane Grey [Cannon] 1815-1884, 5330
Switzerland, Militärdepartement, 24806
The Switzerland of America, 16030
The sword and gun, 3338
Sword and pen, 4672
The sword and the distaff, 10782
Swords, Thomas, 5331
Sybaris and other homes, 9695
Sybil Knox, 9696
Sycamore Bend, 14055

Sydenham, A.H., 10115
Sydenham, Alvin, 10122
Sydney Clifton, 9506
Sydnie Adriance, 9424
Sydnor, Charles Sackett, 1898-, 25662
The sylphs of the seasons, 2514
Sylva telluriana, 15234
Sylvain, Benito, 25663
Sylvan lyrics and other verses, 3822
Sylvan secrets, 5398
Sylvester, Nathaniel Bartlett, 1825-1894, 8139, 23674
Sylvestris, pseud., 5479
Sylvia Seabury, 10071
Sylvia's world, 8829
Symmes, Elmore, 25664
Symmes, William, 1731-1807, 23675
Symonds, William, 1556-1616? 5204, 23676
The Symposium, 9817
A symposium of tributes to Lexington on the occasion of the sesquicentennial of its birth, 15754
Syndicalism, Brazil, 19866, 19873
Synge, Millington Henry, 8140, 8141
Synopsis of debates, in the Massachusetts legislature, 23264
Synopsis of the changes in the law affected by the civil code of Lower Canada, 22828
Sypesteyn, Cornelis Ascanius Van, 1823-1892, 25665
Syracuse, N.Y., History, 21906; Manners and customs, 8189
"The system of colonial law" compared with the eternal laws of God, 25492
A system of exchange, 13154
A systematic treatise, historical, etiological, and practical on the principal diseases of the interior valley of North America, 14014
Szyszlo, Vitold de, 8142

Los tábanos de Cuba, 20676
Tabares de Ulloa, Francisco, 8143
Tabb, John Bannister, 1845-1909, 5332
Taber, I.W., illustr., 5004
Tabla chronológica de los descvbrimientos, 6431
A table for critics, 14473
Table of distances of the Overland daily stage line, 3901
Tableau de la situation actuelle des colonies, 8144
Tableau de l'universe et des corps

organisés, 15220
Taboada e Irarrázabal, Manuel Gervasio
    de, 8145
Tabor, Ia., 17746
El tabu bolivarista, 1825-1828, 18963
Tabular history of the Kentucky derby
    from Aristides to Tim Tam, 13716
Taché, Alexandre Antonin, abp., 1823-
    1894, 8146-8148, 16552
Tache, Joseph Charles, 1820-1894, 8194
Tacitus, Cornelius, 23677
Tacking up the Hudson, 10798
Tacna-Arica question, 7650
Tactics, 1638, 9664, 23030
Taddei, Mario, 5333
Tadeuskund, the last king of the Lenape,
    9840
Tafel, Gustav, 5334
Taft, William Howard, 1857-1930, 6483
Tage in Mexico, 7388
Tagebuch einer Reise vom Mississippi nach
    den Küsten der Südsee, 4501
Tagebuch eines Bayreuther soldaten, 3264
Tagebuchblätter eines hessischen offiziers
    aus der zeit des nord-amerikanischen
    unabhängigkeits-krieges, 3270
Taggart, Charles Manson, 1821-1853, 11746
Taggart, Tom, 14983
Tagliaferro, José A., 21728
Tahan, out of savagery into civilizaton,
    16644
Tahiti, Description & travel, 3977, 7858
Tah-koo wah-kan, 17491
Tailfer, Patrick, 5335
The tailor of Gotham, 5654
Tainted souls, 15386
Taken alive, 10653
Taking chances, 9270
The taking of the Captain Ball, 10043
Talamanca Cordillera, Costa Rica, 19008
Talbot, Ethelbert, bp. 1848-, 17697
Talbot, John, 8150
Talbot, Thomas, 1771-1853, 12074
Talbot, Thomas Hammond, 1823-1907, 25666
Talbot, William, 4236
Talbot Co., Md., History, 4017
Talbott, G.M., and Bro., Bardstown, Ky.,
    14865
Talbott, J. Dan, 1883-, 13628
Talbott, John H., 15145
Talboys, David Alphonso, 1700?-1840, 22396
Talboys, William P., 8151
Talca (Province), 20163
A tale for the rich and poor, 8576
A tale of a lonely parish, 6506, 9232
Tale of a physician, 9335

A tale of our own times, 10723
A tale of Poland, 10760
A tale of St. Domingo, 10670
A tale of the Old Dominion, 11860
A tale of three truants, 9793
A tale of two oceans, 15921
The talent in the napkins, 9533
Tales, 10188, 11173; Ecuadorian, 19881;
    French-Canadian, 13048
Tales and ballads, 3606
Tales and sketches, 10172, 10730
Tales and sketches from the Queen City, 3284
Tales and souvenirs of a residence in
    Europe, 10627
Tales by the way, 9195
Tales for you, 10919
Tales of a garrison town, 9460
Tales of a traveller, 10002
Tales of California life, 16357
Tales of city and country life, 8934
Tales of Glauber-Spa, 21821
Tales of masonic life, 4533
Tales of old Bardstown, 14912
Tales of terror, 10693
Tales of the backwoods, 4903
Tales of the border, 3751, 14243
Tales of the Caddo, 10985
Tales of the Colorado pioneers, 16756
Tales of the dark and bloody ground, 14451
Tales of the devils, 8836
Tales of the Emerald isle, 10920
Tales of the ex-tanks, 9271
Tales of the fireside, 10921
Tales of the garden of Kosciusko, 10153
Tales of the good woman, 10492
Tales of the home folks in peace and war,
    9751
Tales of the Indians, 15511
Tales of the North American Indians, 12750
Tales of the Northwest, 10827
Tales of the Puritans, 8632
Tales of the southern border, 5653
Tales of the Spanish seas, 9850
Tales of the trail, 16856
Tales of three cities, 7129
Tales of trail and town, 9793
Talking for life, 9463
Talks of a tourist about Oregon and
    Washington, 17825
Tallack, William, 1831-1908, 5336, 5337
A Tallahassee girl, 5399
Talley, Brooks, 14227, 15495
Tallmadge, James, 1778-1853, 25667
Tallmadge, Samuel, 4589
The Tallow family in America, 11043
Tallulah, 4034

Tallulah and Jocasse, 4949
Tallulah Falls, 3358
Das talmudische Recht auf den verschiedenen
  Stufen seiner Entwicklung mit dem
  römischen verglichen und dargestellt,
  25421
Talvi's history of the colonization of
  America, 13472
Tam-tam y margaritas, 19990
Tam's fortnight ramble, and other poems,
  22920
Tama Co., Ia., Direct, 16177; History,
  16177
Tamandaré, Joaquím Marques Lisboa, marques
  de, 1807-1897, 20553
Tamaulipas, Mexico, 7589; Description &
  travel, 4314, 7837
Tamayo, Antonio, 5803
Tamayo, Jorge L., 1912-, 8152
Tamayo, Pío, 18039
The tame seal, 10310
Tammany society, or Columbian order, 13244
Tampico expedition, 1835, 22197
Tamworth, N.H., History, 1988
Taney, Mary Florence, 15496
Taney, Roger Brooks, 1777-1864, 8250
The Tangletown letters, 10611
Tangorra-Milano, Angelo, illustr., 25668
Tanguay, Cyprien, 1819-1902, 8153
Tanis, Norman E., 16886, 17315
Tanis, the sand-digger, 5466
Tannehill, Wilkins, 1787-, 5338
Tanner, Henry, 15497
Tanner, Henry Schenck, 1786-1858, 5339-
  5342, 23678
Tanner, James, 1844-, 5201
Tanner, John, 1780?-1847, 5343, 6233
Tannstetter Collimitius, Georg, 126
Tansill, Robert, 5344
Tans'ur, William, d.1783, The royal melody
  compleat, 985
Taos, N.M., 2411
The taper, 10448
Tapley, Rufus Preston, 1823-1893, 8154
Tapp, Hambleton, 13751, 15498, 15499
Tapp, Jesse Washington, 14650
Tappan, Arthur, 1786-1865, 25671
Tappan, Benjamin, 1788-1863, 25192
Tappan, David, 1762-1803, 11501, 23679,
  23795
Tappan, Lewis, 1788-1873, 23880, 25336,
  25669-25671, 25842
Taquisara, 9233
A tar heel Confederate soldier, 4254
Tarahumare Indians, 7310,18582
Tarascan Indians, 7341, 8266, 19825

Tarascan language, 947
Tarascon, Berthoud and co., firm,
  merchants, Philadelphia, 15500
Tarbell, J., 5345
Tardes nubladas, 7706
Tardy, Mrs. Mary T., 5346
La tarea de hemeroteca, 18127
Tarentola americana, 20673
Tariff, 22882; Colombia, 20283; Confederate
  States of America, 2060; Confederate
  States of America, Law, 2064; Gt. Britain,
  22121, 23148, 23293, 25009; Mexico, 7707;
  Mexico, Law, 8209, 18330; Spain, 23649;
  U.S., 291, 687, 688, 1266, 1608, 2031,
  2111, 2338, 2453, 4946, 11226, 11505,
  11618, 11716, 12446, 12595, 21843, 21845,
  21982, 22545, 23100, 23103, 23132, 23188,
  24165, 25574; U.S., Law, 1494, 22079,
  22080; U.S., Speeches in Congress, 430,
  876, 22853, 23055, 23155, 23760, 24705
Tariff (of 1857) made of force by act of
  Congress of the Confederate States of
  America, 2064
Tariff of duties, on importations into the
  United States, 22080
Tarleton, Sir Banastre, bart., 1754-1833,
  5347
Tarnished angels, 17507
Tarrant, Eastham, 5348
Tarrant Co., Tex., Biography, 16781
Tasistro, Louis Fitzgerald, 5349
Tasmania, Description & travel, 12784
Tasse, Joseph, 8155
Tassin, Algernon, 10283
The taste of the age, 2564
Tatham, William, 1752-1819, 5350, 23680
Tattle-tales of Cupid, 9538
Taughannock Falls, N.Y., 12593
Taunton, Mass.,Church of Christ, 22183;
  Religious institutions and affairs, 22183
Tauste, Francisco, 1626-1685, 19855
Tavares, José Edvaldo, ed., 19355
Tavares, O.A.P., 19869
La tavola di bronzo, 727
Tax administration and procedure, Chile,
  20144
Tax aspects of dissolution of marriage,
  14667
Tax counts, Brazil, 19309
Tax exempt bonds of the Commonwealth of
  Puerto Rico, 18674
The tax-payer's manual, 11422
Tax-sales, U.S., 1377, 1378
Taxation, 6712, 13425; Addresses, essays,
  lectures, 18215; Argentine Republic, 18429;
  Argentine Republic, Laws, statutes, etc.,

18473; Brazil, 19352, 19373, 24011;
Brazil, Law, 19357; Brazil, Law, Addresses,
essays, lectures, 19309; Chile, 19887,
20161; Chile, Cases, 18951; Chile, Law,
20146, 20147; Colombia, Law, 20326;
Confederate States of America, 2047,
11871; Gt. Britain, 6712, 23194; Kentucky,
14141, 14963, 15336, 15803; Mexico, 19493;
Mexico, Law, 8209; Pernambuco, Brazil
(State), Law, 19357; Peru, Colonial period,
6282; U.S., Speeches in Congress, 1393;
Venezuela, 18294
Taxation, Exemption from, Mexico, 18330
Taxation of U.S. bonds, 1616
Taxidermy, 23401
Taylor, Benjamin Franklin, 1819-1887, 5352,
5739, 17700, 17701
Taylor, Bert Leston, 1866-1921, 6921
Taylor, Burrell B., 17702
Taylor, Edward Burnett, 8159
Taylor, Eli F., 17703
Taylor, Frank Hamilton, 5353
Taylor, George, 1820-1894, 23681
Taylor, George W., 1803-1891, 25147
Taylor, H. West, 16727
Taylor, Hannis, 25672
Taylor, Henry Ryder, 1850-, 17704
Taylor, Henry W., 7473
Taylor, Isaac, 1759-1829, 8160
Taylor, James, 13841
Taylor, James W., 7510
Taylor, James Wickes, 1819-1893, 5534
Taylor, John, 1753-1824, 5355, 13487,
13488, 15503, 23682
Taylor, John, 1779-1863, 7090
Taylor, John Glanville, 1823-1851, 8161
Taylor, Joseph Henry, 17705-17710
Taylor, M. Lee, 15504
Taylor, Oliver Alden, 1801-1851, 350
Taylor, Reuben Thornton, 15505
Taylor, Richard, 25673
Taylor, Robert Belt, 15673
Taylor, Samuel, jr., 4210
Taylor, Mrs. Sarah Louisa (Foote) 1809-1836,
13310
Taylor, Mrs. Susie King, 1848-, 5356
Taylor, T.U., 17711
Taylor, William, 1821-, 17712
Taylor, William S., 1855-1928, 15254
Taylor, William Septimus, 14661
Taylor, Zachary, pres. U.S., 1784-1850, 215,
1093, 2374, 13092, 14146, 15502, 22215,
23231
Taylor and his campaigns, 15502
Taylor Manor, Versailles, Ky., 14100
Taylor meeting, 14806

Tazewell, Littleton Waller, 1774-1860,
12439
Tazewell Co., Va., History, 1249
Te Deum laudamus, 22345
Tea, 11368
Tea destroyed by Indians, 23683
The tea-rose, 10904
Teacher education and certification, 13927
Teachers colleges, 20149; Kentucky, 14572
Teachings and tendencies, 10610
Teachings of patriots and statesmen; 11751
The teachings of the crisis, 22229
Teal, Joseph N., 17713
The tear in the cup, 4906
The tears of the foot guards, 23684
Tears on the diadem, 9417
El teatro como fenómeno colectivo, 18523
El teatro de Roberto Arlt, 19906
Teatro espacial, 20539
Teatro francés, 19029
Teatro grego e teatro romano, 18954
Teatro integrado, 18348
El teatro y su ámbito cultural, 18125
Tebicuary river, Paraguay, 593
Tecajic, Mexico, Nuestra Señora de los
Angeles (Shrine), 7459
Technical assistance, American, Argentine
Republic, 18404
Technical education, 18381; Brazil, Espirito
Santo (State), Curricula, 19423; U.S.,
12261
Technology, 19263; Bibliography, 19742;
Latin America, 18021; Period, 262, 269,
23417
Technology and civilization, 20353
Técnica gráfica, 18250
Técnicas audiovisuais nas escolas de
educação física, 18346
Las técnicas del trabajo gubernamental en el
estado moderno, 19032
Tecnologia moderna para a agricultra, 19315
Tecumseh, Shawnee chief, 1768-1813, 2197,
3283, 12741, 15167, 15790, 16346; Drama,
2197
Tee-total anti-slavery pledge, 25674
Teenstra, Marten Douwes, 1795-1864, 25675
Tefft, B. F., 14052
Teggart, Frederick John, 16533
Tehuantepec canal, 2390
Tehuantepec, Isthmus of, 1444, 1748, 2390
Tehuantepec railroad company of New Orleans,
1748
Teissier, Georges, 1862-, 25676
Teixeira Junior, Jeronymo José, 24009
Teja Zabre, Alfonso, 1888-, 8162
Tekel, 8840

Telecommunication, 18853; Laws and regulations, 19333; Law and legislation, Mexico, Criminal provisions, 18047, 18860
Telegraph, 4808, 9044, 15579; Brazil, 19374; History, 11520, 13287; Period, 306; The West, 16205
O telescópio, 18280
Television, 19712, 20355; Educational, Kentucky, 15331
Television broadcasting, 14651; Argentine Republic, 18497
Television in education, 13728
Os telhados, 20070
Telie, the renegade's daughter, 14983
The tell-tale, 10516
Telliamed; or The world explain'd, 23036
Telltruth, Timothy, pseud., 23685
Temas da atualidade na literatura de cordel, 19730
Temas de amor, 18249
Temas de filosofía contemporánea, 20414
Temas de folklore venezolano, 19770
Temas de historia social y de las ideas, 19842
Temas de sociología política mexicana, 19912
El témpano de Kanasaka, 20256
Un temperamento, 18004
Temperance, 1152, 2990, 7715, 9973, 10548, 13687, 15796, 20172, 21867, 23028, 23092, 23164, 23963, 24413, 25674; Addresses, essays, lectures, 11247, 13219, 22096, 23162, 23163, 23165, 24692, 25143; Exercises, recitations, etc., 10156; Fiction, 2290, 8871, 8892, 8892, 9077, 9405, 10702, 10703, 13599, 23081; History, 457, 668, 11603, 22313; Societies, 307, 2077, 13249
Temperance Congresses, 23290
The temperance doctor, 8982
Temperance recollections, 23164
Temperance tales, 8581
Temperance versus intemperance, 8892
Tempest and sunshine, 9904
Tempest-tossed, 10979
The Templar's daughter, 8551
Temple, Oliver Perry, 8163
Temple, Wayne C., 1924-, 6197, 15506-15508, 15662
Temple, N.H., Genealogy, 11290; History, 11290
The temple of liberty, 3382
O tempo e o modo, 18577
Tempo reverso, 19139
Os tempos de Rosa e Silva, 20567
Tempsky, Gustav Ferdinand von, 8164

The temptation, 10841
Ten chapters in the life of John Hancock, 22454
Ten days on the plains, 16331
Ten millions, 8650
Ten months in Brazil, 20231, 21967
Ten months in Libby prison, 11706
Ten nights in a bar-room, and what I saw there, 8582
The ten-share horse, 25023
Ten thousand miles in a yacht round the West Indies and up the Amazon, 5939
Ten thousand miles of travel, 5449
Ten thousand miles on a bicycle, 2592
Ten years among the mail bags: or, Notes from the diary of a special agent of the Post-office department, 22519
Ten years in Oregon, 2508, 4237, 15832
Ten years in Nevada, 17153
Ten years in Texas, 3686
Ten years in the ranks, U.S. army, 17190
Ten years in the U.S., 4485
Ten years in Washington, 2532
Ten years in Winnipeg, 6056
Ten years of a lifetime, 9927
Ten years of preacher-life, 4469, 13429
Ten years of torture, 10932
Ten years on a Georgia plantation since the war, 4247
The tenant of Woodfell, 5721
The tenants of a lord bishop, 10339
Tendéncia da urbanização, 20014
Tennant, Charles, 1796-1873, 2483
Tennent, Gilbert, 1703-1764, 23522
Tennent, William, 1705-1777, 11400
The Tennessean, 5037
The Tennessean's story, 5156
A Tennessean abroad; or Letters from Europe, Africa, and Asia, 22871
Tennessee, 23624; Antiquities, 12770; Bibliography, 15140; Boundaries, Kentucky, 14469; Bureau of agriculture, statistics and mines, 5357; Conservation Department, Parks Division, 14167; Description & travel, 2745, 2752, 3089, 3261, 3342, 3425, 3739, 4173, 4217, 4559, 4646, 4758, 4791, 5382, 5436, 5601, 5706, 5723, 12770, 13580, 14748, 14749, 15344, 15527; Description & travel, Gazetteers, 4527; Description & travel, Guide-books, 3798, 4160, 13544; Economic conditions, 2745, 5357, 15611; Fiction, 3366, 4553-4558, 4560-4567, 4907, 10592, 17580, 25726; General assembly, 1867, Senate, 2323; Historical geography, 14087, 14088; History, 4527, 11508, 12769, 13555, 14027,

14303, 14882, 15613, 15756; History,
Civil war, 1658, 2050, 2156, 3371, 3611,
4523, 11328, 11329; History, Civil war,
Fiction, 8755; History, Fiction, 10134;
History, Sources, 5723; Maps, 14183,
15311; Names, Geographical, 14087, 14088;
Politics & government, Civil war, 2840,
22966; Social conditions, 15611; Social
life & customs, 25075; Views, 15419
Tennessee, East, Description & travel, 5198;
History, Civil war, 1478; Social life &
customs, 5402
Tennessee, Middle, History, 11674; Social
life & customs, 25075
Tennessee; its agricultural & mineral
wealth, 5357
Tennessee cavalry, 1st battalion, 1861-1862,
3767; 7th battalion, 1861-1862, 3767;
1st regt., 1846-1847, 6791; 2d regt.,
1862-1865, 3767; 7th regt., Co.E., 1861-
1865, 3959
The Tennessee gazetteer, 4527
The Tennessee hand-book and immigrant's
guide, 2752
Tennessee Historical Society, 2110
Tennessee infantry, 1st regt., Co.H., 1861-
1865, 5635
Tennessee River, 14280
Tennessee River valley, Antiquities, 15681
Tennessee Skaggs, 14870
A Tennessean, 23835
Tennet, William, 1740-1777, 23686
Tenney, Edward Payson, 1835-1916, 17714
The tent, 10172
The tenth of January, 11075
Teotihuacán, Mexico, 7483, 7484, 7486, 19020
Terán, Luis de, 8112, 8319
Terasaki, Taro, 8165
The tercentenary history of Canada, 8224
Tercentenary of the Westminster Assembly,
15755
Tercera iglesia de Terceros dominicos, 8311
Terentius Afer, Publius, 25852
Teresa, Saint, 1518-1582, 8166
Tereza Cristina Maria, empress of Brazil,
1822-1899, 18849
Terhune, Albert Payson, 1872-1942, 10937
Terhune, Mrs. Mary Virginia (Hawes) 1830-
1922, 5358-5361, 8167, 10163
Termer, Franz, El valor histórico, geográfico
y etnológico de los apuntes de Cockburn,
8303
Ternaux-Compans, Henri, 1807-1864, 8168,
8169, 23687
Terra patrum, 20513
Terranova, M.L., 19869

La terre chaude, 11261
Terrell, Alexander Watkins, 1827-1912, 8170
Terrell, Robert Heberton, 1857-1925, 25677
Terres mexicaines, 7262
Terrien, Ferdinand, 8171
Territorial government, and the admission
of new states into the union, 25913
The territorial question, 24640, 25678
Territorial waters, 18201
The territories of Kansas and Nebraska, 4495
Territories of the U.S., 25853
Terror (ship), 614
Terry, James, 15509, 17716
Terry, Thomas Philip, 1864-, 8172, 8173
Terry rangers, 2726
Terwecoren, Ed., 5178
Tesis de nacionalización de los bienes de la
empresa Bolivian Gulf Oil Co., 19725
Tesis existentes en la Biblioteca de la
Facultad de Medicina, 18960
Los tesoros del Perú, 19893
The test of loyalty, 9860
Tested, 9601
Los testigos de oidas, 18254
Testimonios de la época emancipadora, 17987
The testimony of a number of New-England-
ministers met at Boston Sept. 25, 1745,
23688
The testimony of an escaped novice from the
Sisterhood of St. Joseph, 8896
Testut, Charles, 5362, 5363
Teton dialect, Dictionaries, English, 16842
Teton Indians, 17174
Têtu, David, 13973
Teverbuagh, Solomon, 3940
Tevis, A.H., 17717
Tevis, John, 1792-1861, 5364
Tevis, Julia Ann (Hieronymus) 1799-, 5364
Tevis, Lloyd, 17718
Texada Island, 6183
The Texan captain and the female smuggler,
10252
The Texan declaration of causes for taking
up arms against Mexico, 15916
Texas Declaration of Independence, 15914
The Texan emigrant, 5280
Texan Emigration and Land Company, 5365
Texan ranch life, 7140
The Texan ranger, 16523
Texas Santa Fé expedition, 3414, 4150
The Texan virago, 5654
The Texarkana gateway to Texas and the
Southwest, 17212
Texas, 2292, 2732, 2942, 3341, 3903, 4999,
15962, 16037, 16352, 16353, 16578, 16938,
17516, 17014, 17016, 17010, 17939;

Annexation, 41, 12191, 12623, 13280, 13371, 13835, 15814, 15833, 15834, 15859, 16211, 16695, 16738, 17017, 17146, 17187, 17326, 17385, 17396, 17631, 17633, 17671, 22644, 22681, 23781, 24122, 25006, 25194, 25302; Bibliography; Bibliography, Catalogs, 17796; Biography, 2827, 15990, 16057, 16327, 16352, 16697, 16875, 16892, 16894, 17229, 17329, 17330, 17647, 17691, 17838, 17939, 17940; Boundaries, 17125; Boundaries, Louisiana, 17434; Boundaries, Mexico, 17138; Boundaries, Oklahoma, 17583; Boundaries, New Mexico, 24503; Bureau of immigration, 5367; Capitol, 16967; Centennial celebrations, etc., 17796; Constitution, 15901, 17361; Description & travel, 2575, 2624, 2759, 2777, 2789, 2942, 3117, 3209, 3241, 3265, 3362, 3414, 3415, 3442, 3464, 3465, 3491, 3510, 3566, 3573, 3675, 3686, 3763, 3789, 3833, 3886, 3903, 3927, 3947, 3955, 3963, 3985, 4041, 4150, 4158, 4173, 4314, 4316, 4334, 4346, 4398, 4494, 4504, 4510, 4586, 4657, 4675, 4696, 4703, 4791, 4868, 4922, 4973, 5060, 5076, 5104, 5191, 5223, 5271, 5280, 5306, 5327, 5365, 5366, 5367, 5369, 5500, 5532, 5549, 5579, 5590, 5648, 5755, 5763, 5772, 6607, 6609, 7140, 7159, 7219, 7489, 7536, 7581, 7798, 8174, 8180, 10717, 14749, 15527, 15831, 16158, 16265, 16300, 16352, 16387, 16404, 16509, 16522, 16523, 16572, 16938, 16964, 16978, 17033, 17077, 17116, 17134, 17138, 17211, 17212, 17233, 17267, 17304, 17349, 17516, 17617, 17646, 17672, 17687, 17694, 17695, 17719, 17721, 17723, 17725, 17726, 17728, 17770, 17787, 17802, 17829, 17861, 17873, 17876, 18886; Description & travel, Guide-books, 3970, 4021, 16557; Economic conditions, 3072, 3886, 4974, 5021, 15962, 16265, 16352, 17727; Emigration & immigration, 5365; Executive departments, 16502; Fiction, 4991, 8958, 9256, 10717; Foreign relations, Gt. Britain, 16630; History, 2559, 2596, 2826, 3762, 4069, 4150, 4282, 5368, 5413, 5775, 6249, 7219, 7581, 14285, 15813, 15836, 15852, 15860, 15901, 15907, 15912, 15913, 15914, 15915, 15916, 15918, 15950, 15970, 15990, 16011, 16084, 16283, 15294, 16314, 16337, 16379, 16383, 16444, 16509, 16511, 16538, 16565, 16578, 16619, 16694, 16697, 16710, 16780, 16781, 16821, 16892, 17023, 17024, 17044, 17117, 17178, 17191, 17201, 17226, 17232, 17323, 17329, 17330, 17375, 17441, 17561, 17634, 17647, 17650, 17657, 17704, 17720, 17724, 17725, 17741,
17866, 17899, 17904, 17911, 17921, 17924, 17930, 17932, 24172; History, 1810-1821, Fiction, 8543; History, To 1846, 3241, 3341, 3497, 3947, 4158, 5280, 5786, 5968, 8255, 15888, 16441, 16491, 17093, 17166, 17365, 17807, 20223; History, To 1846, Sources, 4742, 16010; History, Annexation, 22721; History, Civil war, 4616, 5105, 16351, 15724, 16894, 17500, 17578, 17940; History, Fiction, 10372, 17606; History, Republic, 1836-1846, Sources, 16630; History, Revolution, 1835-1836, 568, 3122, 3356, 3442, 3669, 4233, 4282, 4405, 4592, 4696, 13639, 16034, 16056, 16514, 16537, 17066, 17188, 24915; History, Revolution, 1835-1836, Fiction, 8738, 9020, 9597, 9598, 10372; History, Societies, 5368; History, Sources, 16170; History, Local, 16565; Imprints, 17909; Laws, statutes, etc., 22317; Legislature, Senate, 16502; Marriage bonds, 16170; Navy, 17225; Politics & government, 16220, 16487, 16698, 17361, 22403; Politics & government, 1805-, 16799; Politics & government, 1865-, 3010; Politics & government, Civil war, 12605; Politics & government, Republic, 1836-1846, 17722; Politics & government, Revolution, 1835-1836, 15888; Public lands, 17106; Social life & customs, 4616, 4725, 8958, 15840, 16830, 16869, 17347, 17543
Texas, University, 16502, 16974
Texas, before, and on the eve of the rebellion, 15852
Texas: its history, topography, agriculture, commerce and general statistics, 3985
Texas: the home for the emigrant from every-where, 5367
Texas, the marvellous, the state of the six flags, 17910
Texas and Mexico in 1846, 7581
Texas and Pacific railway company, 5366
Texas and the Massachusetts resolutions, 41
Texas and the Texans, 3497
Texas artillery, 1st battery, 1861-1865, 16830
The Texas bravo, 4991
Texas brigade, 1861-1865, 4823, 17399
Texas Catholic Historical Society, 5368
Texas cavalry, 13th battalion, 1862-1865, 4610; 3d regt., 1861-1865, 2619; 4th regt., 1861-1865, 4610; 5th regt., 1861-1865, 4610; 7th regt., 1861-1865, 4610; 8th regt., 1861-1865, 3600, 16396; 26th regt., 1861-1865, 16625; 32d regt., 1861-1865, 16625
Texas cavalry, McCulloch independent company,

1845-1848, 4926; Morgan's battalion, 1861-1865, 3828; Ross's brigade, 1861-1865, 5014; Sibley's brigade, 1861-1865, 4610
Texas centennial exhibition, 17796
A Texas cow-boy, 17624
Le Texas et sa révolution, 4233
Texas governors' wives, 16875
Texas im jahre 1848, 2777
The Texas immigrant and traveller's guide book, 16353
Texas in 1840, 5369
Texas Indian troubles, 15950
Texas infantry, 1st regt., 1861-1865, 4823; 4th regt., 1861-1865, 3195, 4823, 7757, 17399; 5th regt., 1861-1865, 3471, 4823
Texas literature, 3258
Texas o Nuevas Filipinas, 8174
Texas Panhandle, 17770
Texas rangers, 4057, 17497, 17498
The Texas rifle-hunter, 3465
A Texas scrap-book, 2596
Texas und seine revolution, 3356
Texas Vol. Cav., 26th Reg., 1811-1865, 16351
Texas Western Railroad Company, 5370
The Texas women's hall of fame, 17229
A Texian, 9598
Textbooks, U.S., 7070
Textile industry and fabrics, Puebla, Mexico (City), 19913; South Carolina, 5563; U.S., 22193
Textos que interessam à histórica do romanticismo, 19931
Textor, Lucy Elizabeth, 17730
Teza, Emilio, 1831-1912, 20712
Thacher, James, 1754-1844, 5371
Thacher, Oxenbridge, 1720-1765, 23689
Thacher, Peter, 1752-1802, 23690
Thacher, Samuel Cooper, 1785-1818, 23447
Thackeray, William Makepeace, 1811-1863, 3133
Thaddeus Stevens and slavery, 23923
Thames, Battle of the, 15424, 15790; Drama, 2197; Poetry, 5494
Thanet, Octave, pseud., 9581
Thankful blossom, 9794
Thanksgiving Day addresses, 447, 1190, 1300, 1445, 2131, 11305, 11308, 11317, 11972, 11982, 12725, 22717, 22862, 23109, 24587, 25222
Thanksgiving Day sermons, 24667, 24890, 25195, 25530, 25595
The Thanksgiving party and its consequences, 9896
Tharin, Robert Seymour Symmes, 1830, 6372
Tharp, B.C., 17503
That fortune, 11089

That gentleman, 10197
That Island, 9247
That lass o' Lowrie's, 8911
That new world, 4786
That old-time child, Roberta, 15343
That same old 'coon, 10892
Thatcher, Benjamin Bussey, 1809-1840, 15510, 15511, 23691
Thatcher, Marshall P., 5373
Thatcher, Maurice Hudson, 1871-1973, 15622
Thayer, Eli, 1819-1899, 24680, 25679
Thayer, James Bradley, 1821-1902, 8175
Thayer, William Makepeace, 1820-1898, 8176, 8177, 22385
Thayer & Eldridge, Boston, pub., 22764
Thayer expedition, 1865-1866, 22320
Thaxter, C.A., 10163
Thaxter, Samuel, d.1842, 13036
Theater, 18523; Boston, 12549; Córdoba, Argentina, 19068; Greece, 18954; History, 18125, 19159; Moral and religious aspects, 6918, 21757; New Orleans, 5212; Period., 11933; Philadelphia, Period., 11933; Study and teaching, 18348; U.S., 2695, 5211, 5212; U.S., History, 5122, 12828
Theaters, Colombia, 20268; Fires and fire prevention, 5863; Lexington, Ky., 13520, 13788, 13833
The theatrical journey - work and anecdotical recollections of Sol. Smith, 5211
Theatrical management in the West and South for thirty years, 5212
A theatrical trip for a wager! 7862
Theatro americano, 8310
Theatro naval hydrográphico, 7995
"Their children," 9014
Their pilgrimage, 11090
Their shadows before; a story of the Southampton insurrection, 23999
Their silver wedding journey, 9954
Their uncle from California, 9791
Thekla, 8549
Theodora, 10284
Theodore and Matilda, 10950
Theodosia Ernest, 9367
Theognis, 10986
Theological education, 15556
Theology, Bibliography, 349; Bibliography, Catalogs, 350; Collected works, 17th century, 7733; Collected works, 18th century, 1098, 2959; Collected works, 19th century, 4535; Pastoral, Anecdotes, facetiae, satire, etc., 11110, 13450;
A theoretical and practical grammar of the Otchipwe language, 771
Therapeutics, 943

There shall not be left here one stone upon another, 15483
Theriaca, 22331
Thesavrvs, 18191
These hills, 14161
Thévenot, Melchisedech, 1620?-1692, 23692
They bore a hand, 10608
They met by chance, 10237
The thief in the night, 10856
Thiel, Johannes, illustr., 2693
Thielmann, Max Franz Guido, freiherr von, 1846-, 8178
Thierman, Sue McClelland, 15185
Thiessen, Reinhardt, 15512
Things as they are in America, 2964, 11710
Things of the mind, 5247
Things seen and heard, 9854
The thinking bayonet, 9925
A third letter to the people of England, on liberty, taxes, and the application of public money, 23605
The third person, 10016
The third troublesome voyage, 6989
The third violet, 9215
The thirst and the draught, 10304
Thirteen, 16734
Thirteen at table, 9768
Thirteen months in the Rebel army, 5274
Thirteen years' experence in the itinerancy, 23112
Thirteen years in Mexico, 6626
Thirteen years in the Oregon penitentiary, 16920
Thirty years a slave, from bondage to freedom, 24634
Thirty years in the wilderness, 3034
Thirty years of Army life on the border, 17128
Thirty years on the frontier, 17114
Thirty years' view, 1185
Thirty Years War, 1618-1648, 8323
Thirty years with the Mexicans, 19901
Thirty-one years on the plains and in the mountains, 16424
Thirty-five years of detective life in the mountains and on the plains, 16270
Thirty-six years in Texas and two winters in Honduras, 17233
Thirty-six years of a seafaring life, 8179
This fine pretty world, 14917
This is the story of Mexico, 8173
This majestic lie, 9217
This tilting dust, 14015
This was Montreal in 1814-1817, 7526
Thistle, Timothy, pseud., 9481
Thoburn, James M., 10333

Thoburn, Joseph Bradfield, 1866-, 17731
Thom, Adam, 17732
Thomas, Abel, 23693
Thomas, Abel Charles, 1807-1880, 25680
Thomas, Alfred Addison, 25682
Thomas, Daniel Lindsey, 15513
Thomas, David, 1732-, 15514
Thomas, David, 1776-1859, 5375
Thomas, Dr., 5374
Thomas, E., 25681
Thomas, Ebenezer Smith, 1775-1845, 5376
Thomas, Frederick William, 1806-1866, 5377-5381
Thomas, Gabriel, 17th cent., 23694
Thomas, George Henry, 1816-1870, 1547
Thomas, Isaiah, 1749-1831, 244
Thomas, Mrs. Jeannette (Bell) 1881-, 15515
Thomas, John, 1724-1776, 21971
Thomas, Joseph, 1791-1835, 5382, 5383, 14826
Thomas, Lucy Blayney, 15513
Thomas, Robert Horatio, 1861-1916, 8180
Thomas, Thomas Ebenezer, 1812-1875, 25682
Thomas, William, d.1836?, 25683
Thomas, William Augustus, d.1951, 13578
Thomas, William R., 17733
Thomas Aquinas, Saint, 1225?-1274, 19694
Thomassy, Marie-Joseph-Raymond, 1810-1863, 5384
Thome, James Armstrong, 5385, 8181, 24764
Thomes, William H., 17734, 17735
Thompson, Algernon Smith Dickson, 1922-1962, 15516, 15517, 15530
Thompson, Almon Harris, 1839-1906, 17736
Thompson, Charles Lemuel, 1839-, 15518
Thompson, David, 1770-1857, 7009
Thompson, David, of Niagara, Ont., 23695
Thompson, Ed Porter, 15519, 15520
Thompson, Francis M., 5386
Thompson, Frank B., 15521
Thompson, George, gunner, 13489
Thompson, George, 1804-1878, 24062, 24338, 25337, 25684-25686
Thompson, George Alexander, 128, 8182, 8183
Thompson, George B., 14878
Thompson, J. J., 15522
Thompson, James F., 13743
Thompson, James Maurice, 1844-1901, 5387-5400
Thompson, John Caldwell, 1831-1904, 8184
Thompson, John Sparrow David, 8185
Thompson, Joseph Parrish, 1819-1879, 313, 13957, 16316, 25519, 25687
Thompson, Kenneth H., 15802
Thompson, L., 13490
Thompson, Lawrence Sidney, 1916-, 8186-8190, 13535, 13719, 14410, 14701, 14897, 15523-

15543, 15728
Thompson, Ralph Seymour, 5401
Thompson, Richard Wigginton, 1809-1900,
  25688
Thompson, Robert Blatsell, 1811?-1841,
  16945
Thompson, Samuel Hunter, 1876-, 5402
Thompson, Stith, 15544
Thompson, Thomas, 1708?-1773, 25489
Thompson, Waddy, 1798-1868, 8191
Thompson, William Tappan, 1812-1882, 5403-
  5405, 10861
Thompson, Zadock, 1796-1856, 23696
Thompson & West, pub., 16774
Thompson family (Shipley, Mitchell, and
  Thompson families), 15193, 15544
Thompson family (Anthony Thompson, d.
  1648), 22552
Thompson family (Augustus Thompson,
  1770-1851), 22252
Thompson family (James Thompson, 1741-
  1817), 22552
Thomson, C.T., 8192, 15545
Thomson, Charles, 1729-1824, 23697
Thomson, George N., pub., 21979
Thomson, James, 1700-1748, 12368
Thomson, John, of New York, 23698
Thomson, John, 1777-1799, 295
Thomson, John Lewis, 15546
Thomson, John Renshaw, 1800-1862, 5406
Thomson, Mortimer, 1832-1875, 11038, 25689
Thomson, Norman, 8193
Thomson, Peter Gibson, 5407
Thomson, William, 5408
Thoreau, Henry David, 1817-1862, 25690
Thorlaksson, Paul, 1849-1882, 17737
Thornbury, George Walter, 1828-1876, 5409
Thorne, James A., 25691
Thorne, Robert, d.1527, 22285
Thornton, Anthony, 6391
Thornton, Jessy Quinn, 5410, 16923
Thornton, John Wingate, 1818-1878, 23673,
  23699
Thornton, Kitty ("Mrs. James W. Thornton"),
  15547
Thornton, Thomas C., 1794-1860, 25692
Thornton, William, 1761-1828, 25693
Thornton, a Kentucky story, 15719
Thornwell, James Henley, 1812-1862, 4688,
  25306
Thoroughbred Record marks its 100th
  anniversary, 15548
Thoroughbreds, 15308
Thorpe, 10305
Thorpe, Thomas Bangs, 1815-1878, 5411, 5412,
  25694
Thorston, Samuel R., 16896

Those old lunes, 10783
Those orphans, 9158
Thoughts about the city of St. Louis, 12832
Thoughts and theories of life and education,
  5248
Thoughts and things at home and abroad,
  11632
Thoughts for the times, 320
Thoughts in a series of letters, in answer
  to a question respecting the division of
  the states, 25695
Thoughts on American slavery, 25696
Thoughts on British Guiana, 25697
Thoughts on education in its connexion with
  morals, 1618
Thoughts on emigration, 15568
Thoughts on popular and liberal education,
  2888
Thoughts on quarantine and other sanitary
  systems, 13771
Thoughts on schools of medicine, 13772
Thoughts on "the excitement" in reply to a
  letter to Hon. Edward Everett, 173
Thoughts on the increasing wealth and
  national economy of the United States
  of America, 11288
Thoughts on the late transactions respecting
  Falkland's islands, 13259
Thoughts on the nature of war, 1157
Thoughts on the original unity of the human
  race, 13773
Thoughts on the slavery of the negroes,
  25698
Thoughts upon the political situation of the
  United States of America, 13131
A thousand a year, 8888
Thraldom in ancient Iceland, 25893
Thrall, Homer S., 5413
Thrall, Stephen Chipman, 1825?-1892, 8194
Thrasher, John B., 25699
Thrasher, John S., 1817-1879, 7086
The threads of life, 10105
The three Bernices, 8847
Three brave men, 14490
The three brides, 9454
Three cases of extirpation of diseased
  ovaria, 14898
Three chapters in a life, 10556
Three cups of tea, 10546
Three days, 9161
Three days at Nauvoo, in 1842, 11695
The three day's battle of Chattanooga, 23d,
  24th, 25th November, 1864, 23429
Three days on the White Mountains, 718
Three decades of progress, 14574
Three experiments of living, 10189
The three fates, 6507

The three golden balls, 11216
Three gringos in Venezuela and Central America, 6545
Three Kentucky gentlemen of the old order, 15584
Three letters to a member of Parliament, 23700
Three letters to Dr. Price, 13390
Three letters to Lieut.-General Sir William Howe, 23362
The three Misses Benedict at Yale, 9762
Three months in Canada and the United States, 2763
Three months in the southern states, 3539
The three orphans, 10677
Three partners, 6976
Three per cent a month, 8902
Three rivers, the James, the Potomac, the Hudson, 3419
Three successful girls, 9252
Three Thanksgiving kisses, 10653
Three unlike speeches, 25700
Three vagabonds of Trinidad, 6978
Three visits to America, 3413
Three weeks in politics, 8687
Three weeks on the wing, 11507
The three widows, 11010
Three years among the Comanches, 4240
Three years among the Indians and Mexicans, 4042
Three years among the Indians in Dakota, 16425
Three years and a half in the army, 17900
Three years' campaign of the Ninth, 13162
Three years in a mad house, 13018
Three years in a man-trap, 8582
Three years in Arizona and New Mexico, 16287
Three years in California [1851-54], 16018
Three years in camp and hospital, 13396
Three years in Canada; an account of the actual state of the country in 1826-7-8, 22997
Three years in North America, 5308
Three years in Texas, 3442
Three years in the army, 3186
Three years in the Army of the Potomac, 1394
Three years in the Confederate horse artillery, 4582
Three years in the federal cavalry, 3624
Three years in the Holy City, 4008
Three years in the Rocky mountains, 2823
Three years in the Sixth corps, 5268
Three years' slavery among the Patagonians, 12497
Three years' wanderings of a Connecticut Yankee, 17854

Three years with Quantrell; a true story, 22829
Three years with the armies of the Ohio, 5592
The threefold destiny, 10919
Thrilling adventures among the early settlers, 15715
Thrilling adventures among the Indians, 16562
Thrilling adventures by land and sea, 1450
Thrilling adventures of a pioneer boy, 2586
Thrilling adventures, travels and explorations of Doctor Elijah White, 15832
The thrilling and romantic story of Sarah Smith and the Hessian, 10965
Thrilling events in the life of Mira Dana, 11035
Thrilling incidents of Indian warfare, 14923
A thrilling narrative of the adventures, perils and suffering endured by John Dixon and his companions, 16291
Thrilling narrative of the adventures, sufferings and starvation of Pike's Peak gold seekers, 2743
A thrilling narrative of the Minnesota massacre and the Sioux war of 1863-63, 16264
Thrilling scenes among the Indians, 17272
Thrilling stories of the forest and frontier, 15549
Throckmorton, 5120
Throckmorton, Sir Nicholas, 1515-1571, 22680
The throne of David, 9989
Through cities and prairie lands, 3780
Through Evangeline's country, 6882
Through one administration, 8912
Through shadow to sunshine, 9520
Through southern Mexico, 6795
Through storyland to sunset seas, 16960
Through Texas, 5271, 17672
Through the American landscape, 4186
Through the land of the Aztecs, 8195
Through the light continent, 5075
Through the Mackenzie Basin, 7392
Through the Santa Clara wheat, 6973
Through the South and West with the President, 3795
Through the subarctic forest, 17390
Through the years, 15550
Through two administrations, character sketches of Kentucky, 15761
Thruston, Rogers Clark Ballard, 15551
Thulstrup, T. de, illustr., 5116, 6622, 9352
Thumb, Thomas, pseud., Monster of monsters, 1754, 22203
Thümmel, A. R., 8196

The thunderbolt to the hearth, 10841, 10842
Thunderstorms, 44
Thurman, Mary Elizabeth (Mrs. Alexander
  Pericles Farnsley) 1836-1906, 14073
Thurston, Richard Bowers, 1819-1895, 24856
Thurston, Samuel Royal, 5414
The Thurstons of the old Palmetto state,
  8932
Thwaites, Reuben Gold, 1853-1913, 5754,
  7008, 7149, 7224, 8197, 14077, 14112,
  14364, 17739
Thyfault, I. M., 5415
Tia Gemma, 20648
Tickell, Richard, 1751-1793, 23701
"Ticket 1939?," 9743
Ticknor, Francis Orray, 1822-1874, 5416
Ticknor, George, 1791-1871, 7316, 22348
Ticknor, firm, publishers, Boston, (1866,
  Ticknor & Fields, 22144
Ticks, Cuba, 20669-20671
Ticonderoga, or The Black Eagle; a romance
  of days not for distant, 22668
Ticonderoga, N.Y., 23206; History, French
  and Indian war, 1755-1763, Fiction,
  22668
Tides, 806, 22035; Louisiana, 607
Tidwell, H. M., 17740
Tiempo de escalpelo, 20054
Tiempo de morir, 18546
Tienhoven, Cornells van, 22152
Tiernam, Mrs. Frances Christine (Fisher)
  1846-1920, 5417-5420, 8198, 10675
Tierney, Luke, 5421
Tierra, 19967
Tierra de promisión, 7648
Tierra de sol y de montaña, 7893
Tierra del Fuego, 12637
La tierra y el hombre, 18545
Tiffany, Mrs. Nina (Moore), 25701
Tiger-lilies, 10164
The tiger-slayer, 15826
The tiger's cave, 10693
The tiger's daughter, 4474
Tijdschrift (anti-slavery), 25702
Tilden, Bryant Parrot, 1817?-1859, 8199
Tilden, Daniel R., 25703
Tilden, Samuel Jones, 1814-1886, 8200
Tilghman, Edward, 1750-1815, 1312, 11271
Tilghman, Oswald, 3796
Tilghman, Tench, 1744-1786, 3796
Tilghman, William, 1756-1827, 1310, 12296
Tiling, Moritz Philipp Georg, 1851-, 17741
Tillers of the Andes, 18899
Tillotson, John, abp. of Canterbury, 1630-
  1694, 25870
Tillotson, Romanta, 22315

Tilmon, Levin, 1807-1863, 25704
Tilney, Robert, 5422
Tilting at windmills, 9093, 13913
Tilton, George F., 17742
Tilton, James, 15552
The Tim Bunker papers, 9041
Timbered tunnel talk, 15553
Timberlake, Henry, 1730-1765, 5423
Timberlands taxation in Kentucky, 15803
Timbuktu, Description, 23839
Time and chance, 9960
The times; a poem, 23138
Times of refreshing, 15518
Times of the first settlers, 8999
The times of the rebellion in the West, 12953
Times-review, Port Erie, Ont., 8201
The times we live in, 10758
Timothy's quest, 11161
Tin industry, 18942, 18944
Tin mines and mining, Mexico, 19205, 19206
"Tincter ov iron," 10808
Tinieblas elegidas, 18045
Tinkham, George Henry, 1849-, 17743
Tinkling cymbals, 9503
Tip Sams again, 15075
Tip Sams of Kentucky and other peoems and
  dramas, 15074
Tippecanoe, Battle of, 1811, 5745, 15167;
  Poetry, 5603
Tipton, Ida, 15554
Tipton, L. H., 15555
Tipton, Thomas Weston, 1817-1899, 17260,
  17744
Tirar y Soult, 9355, 10163
Tiriyó Indians. 19998, 20540
Tissandier, Albert, 1839-, 5424
Tisserant, Charles, 25705
Tit for tat, 1945
Titan Agonistes, 10982
El titán de bronce, 20020
Tithes, 23324, Peru, 6828
Titicaca (Lake) region, Bolivia, Social
  conditions, 19576
Un título para trabajo en la Constitución de
  1917, 18974
Titus, Frances W., 24481
Titus, a comrade of the cross, 10138
Tiverton tales, 8858
Tixier, Victor, 1815-1885, 5425
Tlaloc, 7491
Un tlamanalli encontrado en Tlatelolco, 18300
Tobacco, 1555, 2208, 3628, 5350, 11656,
  11682, 13207, 15525, 15558, 22070; Brazil,
  18291; Early works to 1800, 11691;
  Kentucky, 15607; Pests, 20010; Taxation,
  Peru, 7426

Tobacco and the Civil war, 15558
Tobacco manufacture & trade, Córdoba,
  Mexico, 6481; Orizaba, Mexico, 6481;
  Virginia, 11691
Tobey, Samuel Boyd, 1805-1807, 23370
Tobias Wilson, 9023
Tobie, Edward Parsons, 1838-, 25708
Tobler, Johannes, 5427
Toby, 14273
Toca Velasco, Jose Ignacio de, 5428
Tocqueville, Alexis Charles Henri Clerel
  de, 1805-1859, 5429, 24423
To-day, 10106
Today in America, 3809
Todd, Albert, 1854-, 8202
Todd, Charles Stewart, 1791-1871, 3690
Todd, John, 1750-1782, 15559
Todd, John, 1800-1873, 17743
Todd, John, 1818-1894, 17746
Todd, Lyman Beecher, 8203, 15560, 15561
Todd, Robert S., 15562
Todd, William, b.1839 or 1840, 5430
Todd family, 14045
Todd family (Adam Todd, d.1765?), 12398
Todo el códice (Códice liberado), 20009
Tohill, Louis Arthur, 17747
Toil and travel in further North America,
  4973, 17499
Toiling and hoping, 10318
Toinette, 10996
A token for children, 13159
Tokens, New York (City), 1752; U.S., 1750,
  11756
Told between the acts, 11198
Told by the colonel, 8994
Told in the coffee house, 8480
Told in the hills, 10689
Toledano, Francisco de Paula, 8204
Toledo, Antonio Sebastian de, marqués de
  Mancera, d.1715, 7918
Toleration, 7574
Toll bridges, Kentucky, 15154
Tolliver, Arthur S., 8205, 8206
Tolliwotte's ghost, 10298
Tolmer, J., 5431
Tolstoy, L., 10448
Toluca, Mexico, Description, 6811
Tom and Joe, 9074
The Tom-cod catcher, 23703
Tom Foster's wife, 10163
Tom Grogan, 10809
Tom Hanson, the avenger, 11225
Tom Marshall of Kentucky, 15563
Tom o' the Blueb'ry Plains, 11162
Tom Sawyer abroad, 9034
Tom's husband, 10040

Tomas Barrera, The cruise of the, 7007
Tomb, Samuel, 1766-1832, 23702
Tombos das cartas das sesmarias do Rio de
  Janeiro, 19244
Tombs, Ohio, 23167
Tomes, Robert, 1817-1882, 8207, 24063
Tomismo e neotomismo no Brasil, 19694
Tomlinson, William S., 17748
Tomo-chi-chi, Creek chief, d.1739, 4104
Tompkins, Daniel D., 1774-1825, 22898
Tompkins, Hamilton Bullock, 15564
Tompson, Benjamin, 1642-1714, 23704, 23705
Tonelli's marriage, 9943
Toner, Joseph Meredith, 1825-1896, 5432
Tonge, Thomas, 17749
Tonti, Henry de, d.1704, 5433, 16491
Tony, the maid, 10948
Too soon to be early, 15463
Too truthful spirits, 9460
Tooke, John Horne, 1736-1812, 13352
Tools, 14950
Toombs, Robert Augustus, 1810-1885, 5294,
  8232, 25709
Toombs, Samuel, 1844-1889, 5434
Toor, Frances, 8208
Topankalon, 5495
Topics of jurisprudence connected with
  conditions of freedom and bondage, 13038
Toplady, Augustus Montague, 1740-1778,
  23706
Topographia media, 16001
A topographical description of such parts of
  North America as are contained in the map
  of the middle British colonies, 4844
Topographical description of Texas, 2759
A topographical description of the state of
  Ohio, Indiana Territory, and Louisiana,
  3147
A topographical description of Virginia,
  Pennsylvania, Maryland and North Carolina,
  3980, 14370
A topographical description of the western
  territory of North America, 14375
Topographical memoir of the command against
  the Snake Indians, 3257
The topography of Kentucky, 14452
Topography of Mexico, 8391
La toponimía indígena en la historia y la
  cultura de Tlaxcala, 18261
Toppan family (Abraham Toppan, 1606?-1672),
  1973
Toppleton's client, 8688
Tories, English, 22126
Tornado!!!, 15565
The tornado of 1851, 1574
Tornel, Manuel, 7707, 8209

435

Toronto, Description, 7972; History, 7972; Public Library, 8210
Toronto Anti-draft Programme, 7967
Torpedoes, 2362, 19585
Torrance, Tablot, 10125
Torre, Juan de la, 8211
Torre, Tomás de la, d.1567, 8212
Torre Barrio y Lima, Lorenzo Felipe de la, 8275
Torre Revello, José de, 1893-, 18940
Torre y Caso, Toribio de la, 8272
Torre y Franco Romero, Lucas de, 1878-, ed., 7546
Torrens, Robert, 1780-1864, 23707
Torrente, Mariano, 1792-1856, 8213
Torreon, Mexico, History, 6910
Torres, Sergio, 20520
Torres Asensio, Joaquin, 5909, 18299
Torres Campos, Raphael, 1853-1904, 25710
Torres Quintero, Gregorio, 8214
Torres Texugo, F., 25711
Torres-Varela, Hilda, ed., 20087, 20243
Torres y Morales, Rodrigo, marqués de Matallana, 1687 (ca.)-1755, 6536, 7929
Torres y Vergara, José de, 1661-1727, 7405, 7406
Torrey, Bradford, 1843-1912, 5435-5437
Torrey, Jesse, fl.1787-1834, 25712
Torrey, Jesse, jr., 24047
Torrey, John, 1796-1873, 235, 5255
Torrey, Joseph, 1797-1867, 23156
Torrey, Rodney Webster, b.1836, 5438
Torriano, Nathanael, the elder, 501
Torrie, Hiram D., 8215
Torrijos, José María, 1791-1831, 7506
Torrison, Alfred, 17750
Tortillo y tiros al aire, 19990
The Tory of Carolina, 9433
The Tory proprietors of Kentucky lands, 15367
Toscanelli, Paolo del Pozzo, 1397-1482, 1081
A toss-up for a husband, 10298
Totemwell, 10494
Totman family (Henry Tottenham, d.1728), 2372
Totonac language, Dictionaries, Spanish, 18588
Totten, Joseph Gilbert, 1788-1864, 835, 23183
Touch not, taste not, handle not, 9877
Touched with the tar-brush, 9460
A touchstone, 11130
Toulmin, Harry, 1767-1824, 15566-15568, 21756
Tour book, Southeastern, 13544
Tour in America, 6241

A tour in Mexico, 7543
A tour in the states and Canada, 3687
Tour in Virginia, Tennessee, etc., 3089
A tour of duty in California, 17477
The tour of H.R.H. the Prince of Wales through British America and the U.S., 4522
A tour of historic Louisville and surrounding areas, 15569, 15570
A tour of St. Louis, 3158
A tour of the prairies, 4029
A tour of the U.S.A., 5224
Tour through part of the north provinces of America, 23083, 22993
A tour through part of Virginia, 2890
A tour through the island of Jamaica, 8386
A tour through the western country, 1818-1819, 14264
A tour through Upper and Lower Canada, 7628
Tourgée, Aimée, illustr., 10994, 10995
Tourgée, Albion Winegar, 1838-1905, 3073, 5439, 25713
Tourism, Amazon region, Brazil, 19444; Brazil, 20379, 20383; Kentucky, 13923, 14652; Venezuela, 20505
Tourist trade, West Indies, 6333
The tourist's California, 17919
The tourist's guide of Florida, 4239
Tourist's guide to Colorado and the carbonate fields, 16148
Tourists' and settlers' guide to Florida, 4018
Tourists' guide for pleasure trips to the summer resorts, 5440
Touro, Judah, 1775-1854, 5840
Tousey, Sinclair, 1818-1887, 8216
Toussaint Louverture, Pierre Dominique, 1746-1803, 3237, 23114
Toutain, Paul, 1848-, 5441
Tovar Mozo, Wenceslao, jt. author, 18243
Tower, Philo, 5442
Towering pines, 14216
Towgood, Micaiah, 1700-1792, 23097
Towle, George Makepeace, 1841-, 5443
Towles, Susan Starling, 8217
Town, Ithiel, 1784-1844, 2096
Town-country relations in special interest organizations, four selected Kentucky counties, 14259
Town House, Danville, Ky., 15571
The town poor, 10043
Towne, Benjamin, d.1793, 12293
Townsend, Charles, 1857-, 15572
Townsend, Charles Wesley, 15584
Townsend, Dorothy Edwards (Mrs. John Wilson Townsend) 1915-, 15573

Townsend, George Alfred, 5444, 8218
Townsend, Howard, 1823-1867, 11827
Townsend, John, fl.1860, 25714, 25715
Townsend, John Kirk, 1809-1851, 5445, 17751
Townsend, John Wilson, 1885-1868, 8219-8222, 14746, 15573-15584
Townsend, Mrs. Mary Ashley (Van Voorhis) 1832-1901, 5447, 5448
Townsend, Peter S., 11779
Townsend, William Henry, 1890-1964, 14724, 15585, 15586
Townshend, Frederick Trench, 1838-1924, 5449, 5450
Townshend, Samuel Nugent, 1844-1924, 5451, 17752
Toxar, Francisco de, ed. and tr., 8223
Toxicidad salina en álamo y sauce álamo, 18636
Toynbee, Arnold Joseph, 1889-. A study of history, 19044
El trabajo libre, 23914
Trachurus picturatus australis, 20626
Tracie, Theodore C., 1836-, 15587
Tracked by blood-hounds, 3305
A tract descriptive of Montana Territory, 5481
Tracy, Ebenezer Carter, 1796-1862, 5452
Tracy, Frank Basil, 1866-, 8224
Tracy, Harry, 1870-1902, 16903
Tracy, Joseph, 1793-1874, 22496
Tracy, Susan, 15588
Tracy, Uriah, 1755-1807, 23708
Tracy and brothers, Claremont, N.H., pub., 13078
Trade and currency in early Oregon, 16597
Trade schools, Brazil, São Paulo (State), 19422
Trade unions, Argentine Republic, 18600; Chile, 19094; Mexico, 20047; San Francisco, 24332; Spain, Congresses, 20417
Tradescant, John, d.1637?, 12192
A tradesman's travels, in the U.S. and Canada, 5408
The Tradewater River region, 14193
El Tradicionista, 19816
Traditions of De-Coo-Dah, 13457
Traditions of the earliest visits of foreigners to North America, 14035
Traduções de autores brasileiros, 19390
Tragedies of the wilderness, 14017
The tragedy of Abraham Lincoln, 8215
Tragedy of errors, 25328
Tragedy of success, 25329
A tragedy of the mountains, 9867
The tragic career of Mary Todd Lincoln,

15446
The tragic muse, 7130, 10018
Tragic scenes in the history of Maryland and the old French war, 769
The trail drivers of Texas, 16835
The trail hunter, 2496
The trail of the "Bull-dog", 4750
The trail of the lonesome pine, 9558, 14133
The trail of the Loup, 16531
Trailings, 15013
Traill, Mrs. Catherine Parr (Strickland) 1802-1899, 8225, 8226
Trails through romantic Colorado, 16241
Train, George Francis, 1829-1904, 15966, 25716, 25717
Traite des noirs, see Slave trade.
Traité sur le gouvernement des esclaves, 25238
Traité théorique et pratique de droit public et administratif, 952
The Traitor; a story of the fall of the invisible empire, 24300
Traits of American humor, 3731
Traits of American Indian life and character, 4641
Traits of American life, 2458
The tramp at home, 4453
Tramp and farmer in USA, 5096
The tramp's wedding, 10546
Tramps, 4738
Tramps and triumphs of the Second Iowa infantry, 2665
Tranchepain de St. Augustine, Marie, d.1733, 3725, 5453
Trans-Pacific sketches, 3416
Transactions of the Antiseptic club, 8452
A transatlantic holiday, 3461
Transatlantic rambles, 5454
Translantic sketches, 1852, 2502, 4138
Transatlantic tracings, 3254
Transatlantic wanderings, 4645
Transatlantisches skizzenbuch, 3935
Transcendental wild oats, 10163
The transferred ghost, 10892
Transferencia de bancos y empresas industriales nacionales a similares extranjeros, 20397
Transferencias de fondos de comercio, 20241
La transfiguración 6726
La transformación agraria, 18675
Transformación en el mundo rural latino-americano, 20520
The transformation, 8861
The transformation of Buckeye Camp, 9791
Transfusion, 13975
Transplantation of organs, Legal aspects,

437

14676

Transport properties of LI-compensated
gallium antimonide, 21741

Transportation, Bibliography, 19552
Brazil, 18288, 18289, 18663,
20373; Canada, History, 6638;
Chile, 19512; Dakota Territory, 16043;
Great Lakes, 13235; Kentucky, 14533,
14549, 14620, 15281; Mexico, Laws and
regulations, 19888; Mexico, Laws and
regulations, Criminal provision, 18860;
Rates, 12016; Southwest, New, 3113;
U.S., 4768; U.S., History, 6638; The
West, 16349

Transportation by steam from Missouri
river to the Rocky Mountains, 17324

Transportation Consultants, Inc.,
Washington, D.C., 20022

Transportations systems, 14637

Os transportes no Brasil, 18289

Transportes sem rumo, 18663

Transunion and Tehuantepec route (railroad),
1748

Transvestites in fiction, 4199

Transylvania, pioneer university of the
west, 14393

Transylvania College, Lexington, Ky.,
15100, 15589, 15590; History, 13724

The Transylvania colony, 14306, 14798,
14799

Transylvania Company, 14305, 14306

The Transylvania library, 15590

Transylvania Printing Company, Lexington,
Kentucky, 15011

Transylvania University, 5785, 13694,
13772, 13794, 14367, 14393, 14743,
14978-14980, 15150, 15202, 15209, 15591-
15596; Medical Department, 2887, 13616,
15148, 15596

Trapp, Joseph, 24778

The trapper's bride, 2684, 3142, 5061,
17252

Trapping, 16164, 22615

Trappists, 7858, 13543, 13828

Trash, John Broadman, 1824-1879, 17133

El Tratado antártico y nuestras fuerzas
armadas, 19724

Tratado coprobatorio del imperio soberano,
6363

Tratado del folklore ecuatoriano, 19885

Tratamento de publicações periódicas numa
biblioteca, 20198

The trauailes of Iob Hortop, 7065

Trautz, Margurete, 0007

Le travail dans la Grèce ancienne, 24490

Le travail en Amérique avant et après

Colomb, 24085

Travaux publics des États-Unis d'Amérique en
1870, 4380

Travel, Anecdotes, facetiae, satire, etc.,
10930

Travel and talk, 3811

A travel study tour through Mexico, 7098

The traveled spider, 10046

A traveler from Altruria, 9955

The traveler's and tourist's guide through
the U.S. and Canada, 5726

Traveler's companion and guide westward,
4892

The traveler's directory through the U.S.,
4444

The traveler's dream, 12773

The traveler's guide, 2616, 15036

The traveler's guide through the middle and
northern states, 6547, 6548

Traveler's guide through the U.S., 4768

Traveler's guide to the new gold mines in
Kansas and Nebraska, 5455

A traveler's mail bag, 15899

The traveler's own book, 12721

Travelers and outlaws; episodes in American
history, 24601

Travelers five along life's highway, 14466

The travelers' entertainment, 8713

Travelers' handbook to southern California,
16880

Traveling about over new and old ground,
2819

The traveling tin-man, 10197

Travels across the plains in 1852, 4339

Travels and adventures in Mexico, 6344

The travels and researches of Alexander von
Humboldt, 7091

The travels and romantic adventures of
Monsieur Violet, 17134

Travels at home and abroad, 5190

Travels by sea and land of Alethitheras, 10453

Travels: comprising a journey from England
to Ohio, 3408

Travels from ocean to ocean, 3652

Travels from ocean to ocean, and from the
lakes to the gulf, 14204

Travels in America, 2561, 2917, 9652

Travels in Canada, and in the United States,
in 1816 and 1817, 3738

Travels in Central America, 7534

Travels in Europe and America, 2755

Travels in India a hundred years ago, 5488

Travels in Mexico and California, 3018

Travels in North America, 4319, 5456, 7346,
7347, 8228, 8229

Travels in North America in the years 1827

and 1828, 3734
Travels in Peru and Mexico, 7050
Travels in search of a settler's guide book of America and Canada, 3921
Travels in some parts of North America, 5323
Travels in South America from the Pacific Ocean to the Atlantic Ocean, 23566
Travels in South and North America, 4389
Travels in the Californias, 3420
Travels in the central portions of the Mississippi valley, 5099
Travels in the great western prairies, 3421
Travels in the interior inhabited parts of North America, 6290
Travels in the interior of Mexico, 6955
Travels in the two hemispheres, 3304
Travels in the U.S.A., 4445, 5147
Travels in the U.S. and Canada in 1826, 6577
Travels in the West, Cuba; with notices of Porto Rico, and the slave trade, 25734
Travels in Trinidad during the months of February, March & April, 1803, 22787
Travels of an American owl, 10049
Travels of Anna Bishop in Mexico, 8230
The travels of Capts. Lewis and Clarke, 5457
Travels through America, 3508, 3511
Travels through Lower Canada, and the U.S.A., 4204
Travels through North America, during the years 1825 and 1826, 23969
Travels through North and South Carolina, 2631
Travels through part of the U.S. and Canada, 6639
Travels through the Canadas, 7016
Travels through the interior parts of America, 345, 346
Travels through the middle settlements in North America, 2861
Travels through the states of North America, 8363
Travels through the states of North America, and the provinces of Upper and lower Canada, 5671
Travels through the United States and Canada, 2734
Travels through the western interior of the U.S., 4162
Travels to the source of the Missouri river, 17030
Travesi, Gonzalo G., 6585
Travis Co., Texas, Biography, 16780

Travis family, 15194
Trayectoria histórica y cultural de la Universidad de Guayaquil, 18651
Trayectoria y ritmo del crédito agrícola en Mexico, 18106
Treachery in Texas, 17650
Treadmill, 12675
Treason, stratagems, and spoils, 15815
Treason and law, 12662
Treason in the camp, 8785
A treasure of the galleon, 6965
A treasure of the redwoods, 6969
Treat, Selah B., 17491
Treaties, 7913, 11371, 23181
A treatise of church discipline, 4120
A treatise of military exercise, calculated for the use of the Americans, 23470
A treatise on expatriation, 22363
A treatise on slavery, 25718
A treatise on the patriarchal, or co-operative, systems of society... in America... under the name of slavery, 24728
A treatise showing the best way to California, 4975
Treaty-making power; Slavery and the race problem in the South, 24402
Treaty with the Cherokees, October 7th, 1861, 21978
The tree and its fruits, 8869
The tree of knowledge, 10016
Trees, Argentina, 18636; Cuba, 7693; Kentucky, 13534, 14244, 14550, 14976; North America, 1828, 15216, 15234
Treiman, Jane, comp., 19641
Tremain, Mary, 25719
Trembley, Ernest, 8231
Tremenheere, Hugh Seymour, 1804-1893, 5458
Trends in the size and distribution of the southern population, 15504
Trent (ship) 1818, 1067
Trent, Paul, 15597
Trent, William Peterfield, 1862-1934, 5459, 8232, 24668
Trent affair, Nov. 8, 1861, 22232
Trent's trust, 6977
Trentini, Francisco, 8233
Trenton, First Presbyterian church, 12575
Trenton, History, 22343
Trenton, Battle of, 1776, 12945, 22344
Tres acciones tácticas de la Guerra del Chaco, 19909
Tres almas, 18873
Tres conferencias, 7399
Três critérios, 19619
Tres domingos, 19137

Tres siglos de teatro en Córdoba, 19068
Tres tiempos de poesia en Venezuela, 18296
Las tres vertientes de la historia de la
   cultura, 21727
Trescot, William Henry, 1822-1898, 23709,
   25720
Tressilian and his friends, 10292
Trevisano, Marco Antonio, doge of Venice,
   d.1554, 25578
Trevitanus, pseud., 24871
Trevor, Richard, bp. of Durham, 1707-1771,
   23710
Trexler, Harrison Anthony, 1883-, 25721
Triaca producida de un veneno, 5428
Trial: Commonwealth vs. J.T. Buckingham,
   11607
The trial, execution, and burial of Homer
   Phelps, 9216
Trial and defence of First Lieutenant James
   Hall, 3752
Trial of Abraham Lincoln by the great
   statesmen of the republic, 8234
The trial of Amos Broad and his wife, 11526
The trial of Beryl, 10163
Trial of Brig. Gen. William Hull, for neglect
   of duty and un-officerlike conduct, 22594
Trial of Charles M. Jefferds for murder,
   13188
The trial of genius, 10580
The trial of Henry Joseph and Amos Otis,
   13331
Trial of John Y. Beall, 1002
The trial of Rev. Albert Barnes, 13357
The trial of spirits, both in teachers and
   hearers, 11980
Trial of the assassins and conspirators for
   the murder of Abraham Lincoln, 8235
Trial of the conspirators, 1305
The trial of the constitution, 24395
Trial of the eleven disciples of Christ,
   9858
The trial of the Rev. William Hogan, 12834
The trial sermons on Bull-Skin, 24319
Trials, 1256; Canada, 334; Gt. Britain,
   22680; New York (City), 12342; Quebec,
   6596; U.S., 11719
The trials and sufferings of a pioneer,
   9159
Trials and their uses, 10514
Trials and triumph, 9448
Trials of a housekeeper, 10904
The trials of a seamstress, 8571
The trials of a stepmother, 9158
Trials of Holen More, 10159
Trials of the heart, 8846
A triangular society, 8508

Tribuna liberal, Asunción, 19163
The tribute book, 2440
A tribute for the Negro, 445
A tribute to the memory of Peter Collinson,
   22114
A tribute to the memory of the Pilgrims,
   22355
A tribute to the memory of the Rev. George
   G. Cookman, 1619
Tributes of the bar and of the Supreme
   judicial court, 5997
Tricentenario de Parati, 19298
Tried and true, 10851
Tried for her life, 10845
Trifleton papers, 10980
Trigg Co., Ky., Economic conditions, 14537
Triggs, J. H., 17754
Trigo, Jose M., 8236
Trimble, Ernest Greene, 15598
Trimble, Robert, 25722
Trimble Co., Ky., 15273
Trinidad, 22787, 23057; Description &
   travel, 6028, 6339, 7194, 7195;
   Emigration & immigration, 13449, 25608;
   Politics & government, 2354, 11966, 22787
Trinidad, Cuba, 7399
Trinitarians, 24691, 24752, 24753
Trinity, 5140, 5853
Trinity bells, 8744
Trinity Co., Cal., Biography, 16149
A trip across the Pacific, 2486
A trip across the plains, and life in
   California, 4139
A trip from Houston to Jackson, 4657
A trip from the Sandwich Islands to lower
   Oregon, 16324
The trip of the Porgie, 10798
The trip of the steamer Oceanus to Fort
   Sumter and Charleston, S.C., 8237
A trip to America, 3776
A trip to Florida, 2841
A trip to Manitoba, 6743, 8241
A trip to Mexico, 6046, 6757
A trip to Pike's Peak, 3008
A trip to prairie-land, 17531
A trip to the tropics and home through
   America, 5928
A trip to the United States in 1887, 2650
A triple entanglement, 9772
Triplett, Frank, 5460, 15599
Triplett, Robert, 15600
Triplett, Thomas, 15601
Triplette, Ralph R., 15602
Tripp & Morrill, pub., 12406
Trippings in author-land, 10001
Trique Indians, 20300

Trist, Nicholas Philip, 1800-1874, 21938
The triumph of music, 2954
Triumphal pompa, 7479
Triumphs of science, 5603
Trivnfo del agva bendita, 7957
Trobriand, Philippe Regis Denis de
  Keredern, comte de, 1816-1897, 5461
Trois ans d'esclavage chez les Patagons,
  12498
Trollope, Anthony, 1815-1882, 5462, 8237,
  8239
Trollope, Mrs. Frances (Milton) 1780-1863,
  5463, 23711, 25723
A trooper Galahad, 10128
Trooper tales, 9087
Tropa vieja, 19967
Tropical America, 6760
Tropical tours to Toltec towns in Mexico,
  7474, 7475
The tropical world: a popular scientific
  account of the natural history of the
  animal and vegetable kingdoms in the
  equatorial regions, 22323
Trópico e nutrição, 20096
Tropics, 7569, 20096, 22323; Agriculture,
  11368; Diseases and hygiene, 11578,
  12791, 13132, 13240, 22747
Tropisuridae Yamaguti, 18889
Tropisurus confusus, Cuba, 19064
Tross, Edwin, 1822-1875, ed., 7268
Trotter, Isabella (Strange) 1816-1878, 5464
Trotter, William B., 25724
The troubadour, 14758
Troubetzkoy, Amelie (Rives) Chanler, 1863-
  1945, 5465-5467, 11011, 11014
The trouble brothers, 10608
A troubled heart, and how it was comforted
  at last, 10897
The troubles of Martin Coy, 9749
The troublesome trio, 21829
Troup, George Michael, 1780-1856, 22297
Trout fishery in Lake Cumberland, 13574
Trout fishing, 9981
Trow, James, 1827-, 8240, 8241
Trow, John Fowler, 1810-1886, pub., 25725
Trowbridge, John Townsend, 1827-1916,
  5468, 25726
Trowbridge, Mrs. Mary Elizabeth (Day),
  17756
Troy, Drama, 15383; Romances, legends,
  etc., 8783
Troy, N.H., Genealogy, 11700; History,
  11700
Troy, New York, Citizens, 8242; History,
  1656
Troy for fifty years, 1656

Trübner, Karl J., 1846-1907, 23190
The truce of God, 10351
A true account of the most considerable
  occurrences that have happened in the
  warre between the English and the Indians
  in New England, 23712
The True American, 3021, 3884, 21969
True and authentic narratives of captives
  who have been carried away by Indians,
  14017
A true and faithful account of the four
  chiefest plantations of the English in
  America, 21943
A true and historical narrative of the colony
  of Georgia, 5335
A true and minute history of the assassin-
  ation of James King, 22191
A true copy of three judgements, 1652
A true declaration of the troublesome voyage,
  6990
True Democrat, Cleveland, 11487
True detective stories from the archives
  of the Pinkertons, 17216
A true disclosure and explosition of the
  Knights of the Golden Circle, 15173
A true discourse of the present estate of
  Virginia, 3765
A true history of a late short administration,
  13395
The true interpretation of the American Civil
  War, and of England's cotton difficulty,
  25175
The true means of establishing public
  happiness, 2148
The true patriot, 23773
A true picture of emigration, 2859
True relation of the hardships suffered by
  Governor Fernando de Soto, 5469
A true relation of Virginia, 5205
The true remedy for the wrongs of woman,
  1046
A true representation of the plan formed
  at Albany, 12898
The true state of the case, 11855
A true state of the proceedings in the
  Parliament of Great Britain, 22758
A true story, 9035
True story of the lost shackle, 9305
The true story of the surrender of the
  Marquis Cornwallis, 10465
True to him ever, 10588
A true vindication of the South, 25155
True womanhood, 10413
Trueblood, Felicity M., 19914
El trueque, 20648
Truesdell, Mrs. Helen, 5470

Trujillo Molina, Rafael Leonidas, pres.
   Dominican Republic, 1891-, 6726
Truman, Benjamin Cummings, 17757, 17758
Trumbull, Benjamin, 1735-1820, 23714
Trumbull, Henry, 13078, 23504, 23715
Trumbull, Henry Clay, 1830-1903, 5471
Trumbull, James Hammond, 1821-1897, 13375
Trumbull, John, 1750-1831, 23716
Trumbull, John, 1756-1843, 6645
Trumbull, Jonathan, 1710-1785, 22178
Trumbull, Lymna, 1813-1896, 25727-25729
Trumpeter Fred, 10129
Trumps, 9291
Trust in God the strength of a nation,
   22831
Trusta, H., pseud., 10515
Trustees' House: Shakertown at Pleasant
   Hill, 15603
Trusts, 14668, 14669
Trusty, no.49, 9582
Truth, Sojourner, d.1883, 24481
Truth, 14484
The truth about America, 4503
Truth and fancy, 11188
Truth and righteousness triumphant, 6991
Truth at home, 8390
Truth exalted in the writings of...John
   Burnyeat, 1735
Truth stranger than fiction, 1047
Truth triumphant, 8806, 9414
A truthful woman in southern California,
   17557
Truths from the West Indies, 24616
Truths of history, 7928
A trve declaration of the estate of the
   colonie in Virginia, 23713
Tryals of Major Stede Bonnet, 11363
Trying the world, 9424
Trying to be a patron of husbandry, 10794
Tryon, George Washington, 1838-1888, 259,
   1318
Trzy barwy Meksyku, 8107
Tschiffely, Aimé Felix, 1895-, 8243
Tuberculosis, 17471; Preventive inoculation,
   Congresses, 18922
Tuchnin, Ruslan Aleksandrovich, 8244
Tucker, Ephraim W., 17759
Tucker, George, 1775-1861, 5472-5475, 25730
Tucker, John, 1719-1792, 11718, 23717
Tucker, Joshua Thomas, 1812-1897, 8245
Tucker, Josiah, 1712-1799, 23718-23725
Tucker, Nathaniel, 13491
Tucker, Nathaniel Beverley, 1784-1851, 5476,
   5477
Tucker, St. George, 1020-1063, 5478, 5479
Tucker family, 16828

Tuckerman, Bayard, 1855-1923, 25732
Tuckerman, Henry Theodore, 1813-1871, 15604
Tucuman, Battle of, 1812, 7708
Tucupido, Venezuela, 18539
Tudor, Henry, 5480
Tudor, William, 1779-1830, 13492, 23726
Tuesday morning mail, 23464
Tufts, Henry, 1748-1831, 24601
Tufts, James, 1829-1865, 5481
Tufts, Samuel N., 25733
Tug River, Maps, 15626
Tukuarika Indians, 15839
Tulare Co., Cal., 17689; Biography, 17179;
   History, 17179
Tulare valley, California, Description &
   travel, 16157
Tulip Female Seminary, Tulip Ark., 17388
Tullidge, Edward Wheelock, 17760, 17762
Tully, William, 1785-1859, 11534
Tungsten mines and mining, Brazil, Rio Grande
   do Norte, 19293
Tunis, W.E., pub., 8246
Tunis's topographical and pictorial guide to
   Niagara Falls, 8246
Tunnard, William H., 5482
Tunnel diodes, 18274
Tunneling, 13068
Tupac Amaru, 7964
Tupi language, 7339; Texts, 1228
Tupinamba Indians, 23652
Turbines, 2311
Turchin, John Basil, 1822-1901, 5483
Turcios, Froylan, 1875-, 5955
Turenne d'Aynac, Gabriel Louis, comte de,
   1843-1907, 5484
Turismo a dois, 18247
Turistskizzer från andra sidan atlanten,
   5590
Turget, Guy Jean Baptiste, 1783-1818, 23435
Turgot, Anne Robert Jacques, baron de Aulne,
   1727-1781, 23435
Turkeys, Wild, 13917
The Turkish spies, 8672
Turks and Caicos Islands, 12704
The turn of the screw, 7131
Turn the sausages, 10310
Turnball, Marion, 5485
Turnbull, David, 25734
Turnbull, Jane M. E., 5485
Turned from the door, 10381
Turner, Charles, 1732-1813, 13493
Turner, Edward Raymond, 1881-, 25735, 25736
Turner, Frederick Jackson, 1861-1932, 16478,
   17594, 17764
Turner, James William, 1848-, 5486
Turner, Jonathan Baldwin, 1805-1898, 25737

Turner, Justin G., 15605
Turner, Nat, 1800?-1831, 25738
Turner, William Wadden, 4898
Turner's Lane hospital, Philadelphia, 11329
Turning all to gold, 8937
Turning points in successful careers, 8177
Turnover, 11032
Turpin family, 7146
Turrill, Charles B., 17765
Turtle Mountain Country, Description, 8078
Turtle River State Park, N.D., 16966, 17463
Tuscaloosa, Ala., History, 5219
Tussac, Fr. Richard de, 25739
Tutein Nolthenius, R.P.J., 5487
La tutela penal del secreto, 18923
Tuthill, Franklin, 17766
Tutoría en educación, 19932
Tutors and tutoring, 19932
Tuttle, Charles Richard, 1848-, 15606
Tuttle, Joseph Farrand, 1818-1901, 8247
Tuttle, Samuel W., 10899
Tuxpan, Mexico (Vera Cruz), 6959
Tweedie, Ethel Brilliana (Harley) "Mrs. Alec Tweedie", 8248
The twelfth guest, 9575
The twelfth juror, 14790
Twelve months in Andersonville, 4293
Twelve months in Klondike, 16958
A twelve month's residence in the West Indies, 23007, 24957
The twelve months volunteer, 6791
Twelve nights in the hunters' camp, 15924
Twelve years a slave, 4618
Twelve years in America, 5131
Twelve years of my life, 10394
Twelvetrees, Harper, 1823-1881, 25740
Twentieth century, Forecasts, 23008
Twenty eventful years of the Oregon Woman's Christian temperance union, 15818
Twenty years ago, and now, 8584
Twenty years among our hostile Indians, 16831
Twenty years in a newspaper office, 15842
Twenty years of detective life in the mountains and on the plains, 16269
Twenty years on the range, 16288
Twenty-one plans, with explanations, of different actions in the West Indies, during the late ware, 23353
Twenty-two months a prisoner of war, 5105
Twenty-four years a cowboy and ranchman in southern Texas and old Mexico, 17680
Twenty-five years a parson in the Wild

West, 16067
Twenty-five years in the secret service, 6038
Twenty-five years in the West, 4382
Twenty—seven years of autobiography, 4668
The Twenty-seventh Indiana volunteer infantry in the war of the rebellion, 2824
Twice crowned, 10286
Twice taken, 9707
Twice-told tales, 9827
Twilight hours, 11485
The twin hells, 17480
Twin roses, 10625
The twin sisters, 10093
Twining, Thomas, 1776-1861, 5488
Twining, William H. G., 5488
Twining of Twickenham, Thomas, 5488
Twiss, Sir Travers, 17767
Twisted threads, 10637
Twitchell, Amos, 1781-1850, 11429
The two admirals, 9152
The two altars, 10524
Two Americans, 9793
The two Americas, 7777
The two Bibles, 10910
Two bites at a cherry, 8503
The two camps, 10783
The two circuits, 9207
Two coronets, 10981
Two countries, 7117
The two cousins, 10176
Two cypresses, 15463
The two epistles, 13153
The two friends, 10342
The two fruitfull sisters Virginia and Mary-land, 12627
The two ghosts of New London turnpike, 10899
Two gentlemen of Gotham, 8931
Two gentlemen of Kentucky, 8518
Two gray tourists, 4090
Two hundred years, 15607
Two hundred years ago, 10958
Two lectures, delivered at Newcastle-upon-Tyne, 4414
Two lectures on a short visit to America, 4267
Two lttle Confederates, 25190
Two lives, 10280
The two lost daughters, 4735
The two magics, 7131
Two memorable relations, 8323
Two men in the West, 6937
Two months in the Confederate States, 3091
The two neighbors, 10747
Two noes make one yes, 9981
Two of a trade, 5722
Two papers on the subject of taxing the

British colonies in America, 13494
Two presidents, 6848
The two proposals, 10871
The two roads, 10156
Two runaways, and other stories, 3347
Two saints of the foot-hills, 9779
The two schools, 9968
The two sister republics, 3582
The two sisters, 10528
Two soldiers, 2945
Two summers among the Musquakies, 16108
$2,500 reward, 25741
Two thousand miles on horsebacks, 17175
Two thousand miles' ride through the
  Argentine provinces, 22788
Two thousand miles through the heart of
  Mexico, 7354
Two wars: an autobiography of Gen. Samuel
  G. French, 3546
Two ways of living in the world, 8562
Two women and a fool, 8974
Two women in the Klondike, 16787
Two years before the mast, 16326
Two years campaigning in Virginia and
  Maryland, 13343
Two years in California, 16259
Two years in Oregon, 17257
Two years in the French West Indies, 7000
Two years on the farm of Uncle Sam, 2934
Two years' residence in the settlement on
  the English prairie, 5765
Tyler, Daniel F., 5489
Tyler, John, pres. U.S., 1790-1862, 2043,
  6137, 8249, 11897
Tyler, Lyon Gardiner, 1853-1935, 8249
Tyler, Mason Whiting, 1840-1907, 5490
Tyler, Samuel, 1809-1877, 8250
Tyler, William Seymour, 1873-, 5490
Tyler family, 8249
Tylor, Sir Edward Burnett, 1832-1917, 8251
Tyng, Dudley Atkins, 1825-1858, 25742
Tyngsborough, Mass., History, 2297
Types of the Old Testament, 23335
Typhoid fever, Georgetown, Ky., 15493
Typhus, 13919
Typhus fever, Boston, 2389
Typology (Theology), 23335
Tyranny stripped of the garb of patriotism,
  12143
Tyrrell, James William, 1863-, 8252
Tyson, Elisha, 1750-1824, 24840
Tyson, J. Washington, 25743
Tyson, Job Roberts, 1803-1858, 25744
Tyson, John Shoemaker, 1797-1864, 11480
Tyson, Mrs. Martha (Ellicott) 1795-1873,
  12889

Über relative Unwirksamkeit, 25633
Ubilla y Medina, Antonio Cristobal, marques
  de Rivas, 1645-1726, 8253
Ubique [pseud], 12257, 16601
Ucedo, Sebastian de, 17th cent., 8254
Udall & Hopkins' Chicago city directory, also,
  Hall & Smith's Chicago city directory, 21911
Udell, John, 1795-, 5491, 5492
Uhde, Adolf, 8255
Uhlendorf, Bernard Alexander, 1893-, 5493
Uhler, Philip Reese, 1835-1913, 12523
Uit het land van Benjamin Franklin, 3045
Ulises criollo, 19967
Ulloa, Antonio de, 1716-1795, 7167
Ulster Co., New York, Biography, 8139;
  History, 8139
Ultimo año de residencia en México, 5847
Uma vez, em Olduvai, 18138
Umfreville, Edward, 8256
Umphraville, Angus, 5494
Unadilla, N.Y., 16673
Unamuno y Jugo, Miguel de, 1864-1936,
  18194
Unchanging Amish stick to old ways, 15434
Uncle Bernard's story, 10298
Uncle Dudley's odd hours, 17540
Uncle Duke's "b'ar" story, 10125
Uncle Ethan Ripley, 9606
Uncle Jack's views of geography, 10465
Uncle Jacob's legacy, 8650
Uncle Jim and Uncle Billy, 6975
Uncle Johnny Furlong, café owner, 15608
Uncle Lot, 10163
Uncle Nathan's farm, 9168
Uncle Ned's cabin, 25745
The uncle of an angel, 10027
Uncle Phil, 9016, 13847
Uncle Phillip, 10197
Uncle Remus, his songs and his sayings,
  24562
Uncle Remus in Syracuse, 8189
Uncle Sam and his country, 4681
Uncle Sam in pontifical robes, 5848
Uncle Sam married an angel, 15484
Uncle Sam's Bible, 9098
Uncle Sam's emancipation, 10910
Uncle Sam's legacy of slaves, 24329
Uncle Sam's palace, 11118
Uncle Tim, 10904
Uncle Tom at home, 48
Uncle Tom's cabin, 15572, 25627, 25631
The Uncle Tom's cabin almanack, 25746
"Uncle Tom's cabin" contrasted with
  Buckingham hall, the planter's home, 9245
Uncle Tom's cabin in ruins! 1527
Unconstitutionality of the fugitive slave

act, 25911
Under a cloud, 10899
Under a fool's cap, 14343
Under-currents of Wall-street, 10107
Under fire, 10130
Under friendly eaves, 9323
Under golden skies, 10454
Under silken skies, 13977
Under six flags, 16337
Under the black flag, 16323
Under the cedars, 9797
Under the convent wall, 9764
Under the eaves, 6978
Under the empire, 3932
Under the gridiron, 3179
Under the lion's paw, 9606
Under the man-fig, 3193
Under the palmetto in peace and war, 8625
Under the prophet in Utah, 16141
Under the redwoods, 6978
Under the sky in California, 17562
Under the Southern Cross, 7095
Under the stars, 9730
Under the stars and bars, 3016, 4099
Under the surface, 9094
Under the turquoise sky in Colorado, 17511
Under the yoke, 11218
Underdeveloped areas, 18028, 18077, 18778;
    Congresses, 20398
Underground railroad, 3042, 3412, 14288,
    15016, 15727, 24158, 24373, 24676, 25239,
    25501, 25622, 25896; Fiction, 24706;
    Indiana, 24157
The under-ground railroad from slavery to
    freedom, 15016
Underhill, Updike, pseud., 11036
Undertones, 2955
Underwood, Francis Henry, 1825-1894, 5495
Underwood, John Cox, 1840-, 25747
Underwood, Joseph Rogers, 1791-1876, 25748,
    25749
Underwood, T. H., 25750
The undeveloped west, 2651
The undiscovered country, 9956
The undivided household, 9005
Uneffectual fire, 11018
Unemployed, Kentucky, 14520; Mexico, 20535
The unequal marriage, 10710
An unexpected result, 10653, 10654
The unexpectedness of Mr. Horace Shields,
    9376
The unfathomable mystery, 10957
An unfinished story, 9363
The unfortunate Englishmen, 1958
The unfortunate shipwright, 805
Ungaretti, Giuseppe, 19601

The ungrateful god, 15609
Uniform laws in Kentucky, 15008
Uniform trade list circular, 21859
The union, 13945, 25386, 25751
The Union almanac for 1866, 8257
Union and disunion, 24060
Union and emancipation society, Manchester,
    2276, 25752
Union Co., Ky., 14845; Description, 14193,
    15782; History, 15099, 15782
Union Co., N.J., History, 22337
Union Co., Pa., History, 23425
L'union des provinces de l'Amérique
    britannique du Nord, 1841
Union down, 9343
Union foundations, 13016
Union League, Philadelphia, 7743
The union must be preserved! 15753
Union Nacional de Estudiantes Católicos,
    19633
Union Pacific Railroad, 247, 3255, 5168,
    5499, 5500, 16398, 17019, 17337, 17476,
    23600
Union safety committee, 24890, 25754
Union University, Schnectady, N.Y. Delphian
    Institute, 12996
Unique life portraits portrayed in simple
    verse, 14407
Unitah and Ouray Indian agency, 17740
Unitarian church, Sermons, 2176, 11746
Unitarian church in England, 23892
Unitarian churches in the U.S., 23891
Unitarianism, 2176, 11252, 11845, 12053,
    14060, 15448
Unitarianism unmasked, 13850
Unitarians in Kentucky, 13679
United brothers of temperance, 12937
United Confederate Veterans, Georgia
    Division, Confederate Survivors'
    Association, Camp no. 435, 4885
United Daughters of the Confederacy, 7924;
    Lexington, Ky., Chapter, 15610, 25295
United Fruit Company, 20469
United Mine Workers of America, 13556, 13719,
    14005, 14269
United Nations, 18885, 19265, 25756;
    Economic and Social Council, 23929, 25755;
    Secretary-General, 1946-1953 (Lie), 25755,
    25756; Secretary-General, 1953-1961
    (Hammarskjöld), 25757
United Nations publications, 25755
United Press Association, 2129
United Society of Christian Endeavor, 15179
United States, 263, 322, 1086, 1166, 1536,
    2315, 2742, 2806, 3064, 3909, 4363, 5094,
    7767, 11263, 11281, 11754, 16526, 16813,

21791, 22890, 23072, 23555
U.S. Adjutant-general's office, 8258
U.S. Agency for International Development,
20398
U.S. American Freedman's Inquiry Commission,
24629, 25758
U.S., Annexations, 17187; Antiquities, 12746
U.S., Armed Forces, Period, 462, 11228
U.S. Army, 3757, 10601, 16448; Ambulances,
11427; Appropriations and expenditures,
12940; Army of the Potomac, 22799, 22800,
22802; Continental Army, 23727; Continental
Army, Bibliography, 23085; Cavalry, History,
2783; Chaplains, 3087, 12628, 12775, 13247;
Commissariat, 12907; Corps of engineers,
5501; Corps of Topographical Engineers,
11283; Courts-martial, Arnold, 1779, 466,
467; Courts-martial, Byrne, 1859, 1782;
Courts martial, Fremont, 1848, 22208;
Courts-martial, Gardner, 1815, 2401; Courts-
martial, Henley, 1778, 22410; Courts-
martial, Hull, 1814, 13000, 22594; Courts
of inquiry, Harmar, 1791, 12687; Dept. of
the Platte, 17197; East sub-district of
Nebraska, 5502; Fiction, 10109, 10112-10115,
10117, 10118, 10129; Fourth Kentucky
Volunteer Infantry, 15192; Guard duty,
23030; History, 16942; Infantry, Drill and
tactics, 23729; Military commission, Beall,
1865, 1002; Military life, 3081, 4069, 4332,
5004, 7359, 15868, 16151, 16163, 16317,
16473, 16608, 16786, 16948, 16975, 17031,
17060, 17102, 17127, 17128, 17190, 17198,
17829, 17847; Ohio Valley, 3752;
Organization, 2405; Recruiting, enlistment,
etc., Civil war, 6338, 11649, 12167, 12794;
Registers, 2273, 2402, 7003, 8263;
Regulations, 23729; 2d cavalry (Colored),
16402
U.S. Army Engineer Corps, 5501, 14459, 15123
U.S. Army Field Detachment R., 18888
U.S. artillery, 3d regt., 1821-1901, 16953
U.S., Biography, 201, 202, 203, 869, 901, 902,
1546, 1678, 4420, 6188, 8177, 10952, 11318,
12023, 12171, 12455, 17091, 22275, 22550,
23173; Bio-bibliography, 212; Biography,
Dictionaries, 7227, 22570; Board of
commissioners for the adjustment of French
spoliation claims, 22820; Boundaries,
13016, 16491, 16811; Boundaries, Canada,
1334; Boundaries, Mexico, 2624, 3658,
5064, 5513, 5546, 17125, 18886; Bureau of
Agricultural Economics, 15611; Bureau of
Labor Statistics, BLS Reports, 19228,
19229, 20479; Bureau of Refugees,
Freedmen, and Abandoned Lands, 11750,

15612; Capital, 22318, 25775; Cavalry,
1st regt., dragoons, 1833-1861, 3081,
17060; Cavalry, 2d regt., 1836, 4069;
Cavalry, 3d regt., 1846-1875, 4416;
Cavalry, 5th regt., 1855-, 16947, 17428;
Cavalry, 6th regt., 1861-, 16162; Church
history, 512, 670-673, 24668, 25593;
Church history, Colonial period, 1007;
Circuit court (1st circuit) 12403, 13331,
25759; Circuit court (3d. circuit), 21986;
Circuit court (4th circuit), 11627, 11628;
Circuit court (8th circuit), 16770;
Civilization, 1461, 2556, 2925, 3061, 3663,
4129, 4279, 4587, 4811, 5565, 12118, 12818,
13085, 13087, 21793, 23141, 23726; Claims
vs. France, 12111; Claims vs. Mexico, 19234;
Claims vs. Naples, 12111; Claims vs.
Netherlands, 12111; Climate, 4585, 11287,
11908, 12149, 13768; Coast and Geodetic
Survey, 245, 1920; Commerce, 692, 1019,
1020, 1424, 2007, 2008, 11796, 12016,
12079, 24540, 24888; Commerce, Brazil,
691; Commerce, Canada, 893, 2007, 5534,
12738, 12954; Commerce, Directories, 13780;
Commerce, East (Far East), 1913; Commerce,
France, 2805, 22184, 24784; Commerce,
Gt. Britain, 1329, 11713, 13477, 21817,
22184, 23147, 23418, 23632, 23656; Commerce,
History, 6260, 6261; Commerce, Ireland,
11248; Commerce, Mexico, 5527, 11652;
Commerce, Spain, 23680; Commerce, West
Indies, British, 13327; Commissioner on
the boundary between the United States
and the prossessions of His Catholic
Majesty in America, 12024; Commissioners
on revision of the United States statutes,
25775; Congress, 15613, 15614, 22472;
Congress, Chaplains, 13247; Congress,
Districting, 14692; Congress, House, 15622,
15623; Congress, House, Committee appointed
to investigate the state of the Treasury,
23816; Congress, House, Committee on
commerce, 940; Congress, House, Committee
on Indian Affairs, 5503-5505; Congress,
House, Committee on Military Affairs,
5506, 25764; Congress, House, Committee
on naval affairs, 13202; Congress, House,
Committee to investigate the troubles in
Kansas, 5507; Congress, House, Select
Committee on Slavery in the District of
Columbia, Report... May,18,1836, 25401, 25765,
25766; Congress, House, Select Committee to
Whom Were Referred to the Memorial
of the American Society for Colonizing the
Free People of Color of the United States,
25767; Congress, Joint Select Committee on

the Condition of Affairs in the Late Insurrectionary States, 25768; Congress, Memorial addresses, 187; Congress, Senate, 15624; Congress, Senate, Committee on Indian affairs, 5508; Congress, Senate, Expulsion, 13231; Congress, Senate, Select Committee on Circulation of Abolition Literature, 25769; Congress, Senate, Select Committee on Slavery and the Treatment of Freedmen, 25770; Congress, Senate, Select ommittee on the Oregon territory, 16640; 4th Congress, 1st sess., 1795-1796, 1942; 5th Congress, 3d sess., 1798-1799, Senate, 11296; 8th Congress, 2d sess., 1804-1805, House, 11757, 13402; 8th Congress, 2d sess., 1804-1805, Senate, 11757, 21878; 12th Congress, 1st sess., 1811-1812, House, 88; 16th Congress, 2d sess., 1820-1821, House, 23437; 20th Congress, 2d sess., 1828-1829, House, 25760; 21st Congress, 1st sess., 1829-1830, 23728; 24th Congress, 1st sess., 1835-1836, House, 25765; 25th Congress, 3d sess., 1838-1839, House, 25381; 28th Congress, 1st sess., 1843-1844, 11229; 29th Congress, 1st sess., 1828, House, 24293; 31st Congress, 1st sess., 1849-1850, House, 24285; 31st Congress, 1st sess., 1849-1850, Senate, 24285, 25761; 34th Congress, 1st sess., 1855-56, House, 5507, 24219, 24533, 25762; 34th Congress, 1st sess., 1855-1856, House, 24219, 24533; 34th Congress, 1st sess., 1855-1856, Senate, 25763; 36th Congress, 1859-1861, House, 601, 11389, 24240, 25068; 38th Congress, 1863-1865, 2076; 38th Congress, 2d sess., 1864-1865, House, 24468; 39th Congress, 1st sess., 1865-1866, 742, 5995, 11233; 40th Congress, 2d sess., 1867-1868, House, 22436; 40th Congress, 2d sess., 1867-1868, Senate, 13230; 42d Congress, 3d sess., 1872-1873, 15615; 51st Congress, 2d sess., 1890-1891, 15616; 53d Congress, 3d sess., 1894-1895, 15617; 56th Congress, 1st sess., 1899-1900, 15617; 68th Congress, 2d sess., 1924-1925, House, 15619; 82d Congress, 1st sess., 1951, 15620; 84th Congress, 2d sess., 1956, 15621; Constitution, 74, 280, 705, 973, 1737, 3084, 3502, 7432, 11919, 12140, 12198, 12534, 12653, 13382, 13417, 14745, 21989, 22172, 22689, 23111, 23629, 23763, 23806, 24120, 24135, 24192, 25260, 25783, 25889; Constitution,

Amendments, 12793; Constitution, 13th Amendment, 24134, 24468, 24942, 25298, 25552, 25649, 25729; Constitutional convention, 1787, 12204, 13382, 13417, 13459, 22172; Constitutional history, 1736, 1960, 24668, 25470, 25611; Constitutional history, Sources, 11445; Constitutional law, 11361, 15305, 23176; The United States constitutional manual, 22939; Consulate, Iquitos, Peru, 25772; Continental congress, 1774, 572, 2107, 12468, 11722, 12600, 23586, 23587; Continental congress, 1775, The twelve United Colonies... To the inhabitants of Great Britain, 13388; Continental congress, 1780, 467; Corps of Engineers, Louisville District, 14459; Custom-house, 7061; Custom-house, Boston, 2441; Declaration of independence, 280, 2272, 2320, 11967, 13052, 13387, 23111; Declaration of independence, Signers, 280, 475, 1590, 13347; Defense Department, 15625; Defenses, 2142, 2370, 12677; Dept. of Agriculture, 22565; Dept. of Agriculture, Economic Research Service, 18618, 18619; Department of Justice, 8262; Dept. of State, 11844, 16640, 17188, 25771, 25772; Dept. of the Interior, 5509-5513; Department of the Interior, Archives, 16876; Dept. of the Interior, Engineer Office, 5168; Description & travel, 18, 28, 230, 298, 335, 336, 344, 346, 440, 441, 541, 587, 628, 669, 950, 1108, 1134, 1197, 1233, 1337, 1373, 1495, 1665, 1681, 1777, 1788, 1852, 1933, 1992, 1994, 2129, 2200, 2234, 2293, 2316, 2357, 2435, 2485, 2489, 2493, 2502, 2504, 2539, 2543, 2562, 2563, 2570, 2571, 2573, 2578, 2584, 2588, 2593, 2618, 2626, 2639, 2640, 2642, 2643, 2644, 2645, 2649, 2650, 2655, 2661, 2691, 2693, 2696, 2697, 2704, 2705, 2706, 2713, 2716, 2721, 2722, 2734, 2744, 2747, 2754, 2755, 2763, 2767, 2770, 2804, 2805, 2809, 2813, 2814, 2831, 2842, 2851, 2854, 2861, 2862, 2863, 2866, 2873, 2894, 2902, 2906, 2912, 2914, 2917, 2918, 2927, 2934, 2938, 2939, 2940, 2941, 2944, 2947, 2964, 2967, 2973, 2979, 2988, 2998, 3001, 3013, 3031, 3032, 3035, 3039, 3045, 3048, 3049, 3052, 3061, 3062, 3083, 3090, 3109, 3116, 3118, 3121, 3133, 3143, 3174, 3175, 3176, 3179, 3185, 3190, 3196, 3203, 3210, 3228, 3238, 3242, 3243, 3248, 3249, 3254, 3256, 3277, 3278, 3302, 3304, 3308, 3319, 3326, 3331, 3340, 3358, 3379, 3385, 3392, 3394, 3396, 3400, 3406, 3407, 3409, 3416, 3423, 3431, 3433, 3434,

2580, 3084, 3424, 3634, 3641, 3855, 4176, 4260, 4261, 4383, 4442, 4462, 4487, 4677, 4691, 4716, 4762, 4883, 4961, 4979, 5028, 7425, 11288, 12292, 12378, 12447, 12964, 13070, 14098, 14847, 18679, 21802, 21989, 22087, 22154, 22333, 23228, 24351, 24379, 24391, 24553, 24882, 24963, 25101; Economic conditions, Bibliography, 14284; Economic policy, 11446, 22472; Emigration & immigration, 337, 1933, 2139, 2194, 3214, 3559, 4442, 4847, 5083, 11319, 11533, 11639, 12112, 15452, 17387, 23473; Emigration & immigration, History, 7158; Emigration, Internal, 3630; Engineer dept., 1404, 2238, 2239, 5514-5524, 13322, 15626; Exploring conditions, 5255, 5516; Exploring expeditions, 2465, 2920, 3541, 3542, 5099, 5501, 5513, 5524, 5537, 7982, 12560, 13360, 16273, 16554, 16914, 17218, 17391, 17422, 17620, 17776, 17777, 17786, 17787; Exploring expeditions, 1838-1842, 21, 11820, 11867, 12328, 13200; Executive departments, 25668; Federal Bureau of Investigation, Lexington, Ky., 14410; Foreign Agricultural Service, Foreign agriculture report, 19575; Foreign relations, 1141, 6259, 6766, 11702, 19183, 24492; Foreign relations, 1789-1797, 12603, 13495, 21965; Foreign relations, 1797-1801, 1934, 11927, 12251, 13410, 23459; Foreign relations, 1801-1809, 75, 974, 1019, 1020, 2364, 13088, 13102, 23443; Foreign relations, 1809-1812, 13404; Foreign relations, 1815-1861, 12478; Foreign relations, 1849-1853, 11309, 24411; Foreign relations, 1851-1865, 11466; Foreign relations, 1853-1857, 12098; Foreign relations, 1861-1865, 547, 1142, 11467, 22691; Foreign relations, 1913-1921, 7689; Foreign relations, Colombia, 7859, 12716; Foreign relations, Constitutional period, 1789-1809, 92, 295, 812, 818, 12230; Foreign relations, France, 1868, 1917, 1934, 2364, 5841, 6773, 6774, 11712, 11927, 12251, 12298, 12801, 13410, 13495, 23459, 23701, 23708, 23919; Foreign relations, Gt. Britain, 295, 519, 520, 1142, 1948, 2183, 2416, 12199, 12231, 12378, 12797, 13405, 21817, 23418, 23443, 25440; Foreign relations, Japan, 7701; Foreign relations, Mexico, 6636, 7532, 15834, 17166, 17188, 19185, 19650; Foreign relations, Netherlands, 56; Foreign relations, Panama, 18912, 19933; Foreign relations, Revolution, 58, 11959, 11960, 13118; Foreign relations, Russia,

547, 5947; Foreign relations, Spain, 5531, 16962, 19595, 21896; Foreign relations, Spanish America, 8269, 20238, 23542; Foreign relations, Treaties, 12026, 12027, 24402; Forest Service, 15627-15630; Genealogy, 6203, 6204, 6205, 6255, 6286, 7374, 7433, 7434, 7435, 7437, 7753, 8365, 12847; Genealogy, Sources, 7971; General land office, 4664, 11273; Historical geography, 8003; History, 9, 512, 775, 786, 790, 791, 1188, 1598, 2010, 2456, 3406, 3642, 4502, 4946, 5647, 8150, 11494, 12176, 12482, 12541, 13472, 13626, 15968, 17904, 21793, 22274, 22459, 22583, 22790, 22804, 22933, 23173, 23367, 23512, 24334, 24601, 25050; History, 1755-1809, 22204; History, 1783-1809, Fiction, 2782; History, 1783-1865, 1960, 5276, 10952, 23198, 24628; History, 1809-1817, 294; History, 1815-1861, 241, 321, 1634, 3496, 11679, 12446, 13672, 14465, 22041, 23579, 24059, 25565, 25597, 25760, 25913, 25940; History, 1815-1861, Fiction, 4117; History, 1816-1869, 21772; History, Addresses, essays, lectures, 137, 447, 6393, 11264, 12538, 12725, 15712, 16578, 22605, 23014, 23116; History, Bibliography, 14704, 19514; History, Civil war, 381, 465, 693, 725, 2116, 2598, 2900, 3187, 3202, 3498, 4311, 4808, 4814, 4815, 4820, 4869, 5052, 5759, 5988, 6094, 6419, 6915, 7239, 7989, 11244, 11597, 12913, 13128, 13735, 13881, 13928, 13944, 14219, 14465, 14512, 14513, 14770, 14843, 15010, 15028, 15042, 15558, 15605, 15800, 15852, 16483, 22212, 22499, 23599, 23859, 24272, 24277, 24491, 24805, 24806, 25289, 25290, 25550, 25936, 25937; History, Civil war, Addresses, sermons, etc., 65, 157, 308, 447, 453, 498, 538, 661, 844, 889, 898, 1053, 1057, 1137, 1138, 1299, 1300, 1438, 1460, 1462, 1468, 1469, 1470, 1582, 1802, 1872, 1880, 2140, 2178, 2230, 2419, 2791, 2792, 6047, 6063, 6934, 7565, 7890, 7924, 8089, 8357, 11264, 11301, 11306, 11310-11313, 11375, 11559, 11640, 11645, 11830, 11922, 11982, 12042, 12044, 12164, 12266, 12316, 12493, 12505, 12572, 12584, 12679, 12814, 12831, 12836, 13063, 13152, 14827, 21810, 21920, 22148, 22319, 22393, 22398, 22508, 22537, 22650, 22717, 22831, 23024, 23172, 23998, 24027, 24377, 24614, 25041, 25052, 25295; History, Civil war, Anecdotes, 1726, 4035, 6025, 7745, 10057, 11267, 12390, 12516, 13075, 15088; History, Civil war, Bibliography, 908, 23945, 24559, 25912; History, Civil war, Biography, 909,

1546, 6560, 11528, 16483; History,
Civil war, Blockade, 3890; History,
Civil war, Campaigns and battles, 828,
968, 1591, 1658, 1849, 1850, 2034, 2035,
2036, 2040, 2050, 2068-2071, 2073, 2153,
2764, 2808, 2984, 3041, 3075, 3078, 3085,
3162, 3195, 3324, 3395, 3546, 3661, 3922,
4079, 4610, 4630, 4749, 5088, 5136, 5321,
5461, 6651, 7067, 8138, 11267, 11454,
11826, 11864, 12017, 13458, 13827,
14147, 15115, 16397, 22310, 22805,
22806, 22848, 23793; History, Civil war,
Campaigns and battles, 24399, 24699,
25673, 25708; History, Civil war,
Cartoons, 7537; History, Civil war,
Causes, 378, 1930, 2149, 2214, 2223,
5943, 6096, 6848, 7447, 7928, 11590,
11727, 12649, 15342, 22240; 24395, 24540,
24670, 24917, 25028, 25593, 25651;
History, Civil war, Cavalry operations,
2654; History, Civil war, Chronology,
1741, 11277, 22111; History, Civil war,
Drama, 13959; History, Civil war,
Fiction, 2500, 2501, 2516, 2565, 2774,
3097, 3192, 3507, 3610, 3918, 4199,
4329, 4733, 4736, 4746, 5186, 5187,
5715, 8524, 8603, 8615, 8752, 8791,
8882, 8970, 9023, 9073, 9074, 9211,
9269, 9288, 9399, 9469, 9493, 9565,
9567, 9570, 9621, 9623, 9736, 9749,
9860, 10057, 10110, 10121, 10130,
10131, 10132, 10208, 10300, 10358, 10380,
10421, 10462, 10500, 10612, 10630, 10657,
10682, 10685, 10686, 10699, 10793, 10851,
10913, 10975, 11133, 11141, 11156, 11190,
11197, 11471, 13618, 13952, 13980, 14004,
14190, 14268, 16219, 22781, 22968, 23953,
25529, 25726; History, Civil war,
Finance, commerce, confiscation, etc.,
602, 2056, 2064, 7432, 8564, 11297,
21866, 22837, 24184, 25085, 25087, 25310,
25464, 25728; History, Civil war, Foreign
public opinion, 291, 367, 368, 875, 994,
1055, 1522, 1584, 1929, 1946, 2204, 2276,
2414, 2421, 2483, 7580, 11324, 12580,
12822, 12992, 21934, 22878, 24131, 24626,
24744, 24746, 24821, 25008, 25040, 25048,
25065, 25175, 25293, 25392, 25449, 25507,
25630, 25752; History, Civil war,
Guerrillas, 1478, 12953, 15862, 16271,
15323, 22458; History, Civil war,
Hospitals, charities, etc., 130, 313,
1548, 2002, 2156, 2275, 2440, 3140, 3737,
4284, 4693, 4757, 4841, 4915, 5185, 5213,
10433, 11528, 12835, 13447, 22518, 22932,
24781; History, Civil war, Humor,

caricatures, etc., 8461, 8693, 8866, 8867,
9714, 10482; History, Civil war, Indian
troops, 15854, 23829; History, Civil war,
Italian troops, 7415; History, Civil war,
Kentucky, 15800; History, Civil war, Maps,
13829; History, Civil war, Medical and
sanitary affairs, 2803, 2865, 4064, 11295,
12633; History, Civil war, Naval operations,
4829, 5085, 5123, 11469, 12003, 12597,
12744, 14939, 23413; History, Civil war,
Naval operations, Confederate States,
16085; History, Civil war, Nebraska, 5502;
History, Civil war, Negro troops, 1251,
12223, 24115, 24615, 25615; History, Civil
war, Period., 463, 24755, 25352; History,
Civil war, Personal narratives, 47, 130,
551, 1394, 1765, 2358, 2469, 2492, 2533,
2542, 2587, 2611, 2657, 2725, 2727, 2733,
2787, 2803, 2821, 2830, 2839, 2864, 2865,
2868, 2893, 2945, 3007, 3012, 3041, 3050,
3086, 3087, 3091, 3126, 3144, 3162, 3168,
3211, 3242, 3307, 3335, 3339, 3353, 3371,
3375, 3393, 3417, 3422, 3428, 3440, 3454,
3457, 3518, 3520, 3525, 3538, 3580, 3585,
3592, 3598, 3611, 3624, 3648, 3695, 3726,
3757, 3807, 3812, 3830, 3864, 3871, 3887,
3895, 3939, 3944, 3956, 3966, 3983, 4036,
4064, 4067, 4077, 4113, 4142, 4159, 4163,
4170, 4192, 4212, 4218, 4245, 4285, 4317,
4321, 4323, 4328, 4335, 4342, 4379, 4391,
4399, 4415, 4416, 4521, 4537, 4538, 4590,
4593, 4595, 4616, 4622, 4628, 4630, 4672,
4673, 4683, 4689, 4740, 4757, 4801, 4829,
4874, 4875, 4952, 4960, 5005, 5110, 5134,
5177, 5195, 5215, 5275, 5284, 5317, 5329,
5371, 5372, 5422, 5438, 5490, 5554, 5555,
5592, 5708, 5709, 5714, 5732, 6953, 7303,
11993, 12351, 12781, 12986, 14483, 14784,
15868, 15941, 16116, 16188, 16298, 16402,
16458, 16525, 16679, 16884, 17046, 17137,
17190, 17193, 17219, 17403, 21854, 23407,
23572, 23602, 23924; History, Civil war,
Personal narratives, Confederate side,
968, 1002, 2153, 2537, 2577, 2619, 2625,
2654, 2663, 2698, 2702, 2703, 2750, 2762,
2764, 2875, 2907, 2921, 2935, 2945, 2961,
2962, 2971, 3010, 3016, 3054, 3056, 3161,
3222, 3320, 3333, 3355, 3395, 3444, 3471,
3546, 3581, 3601, 3609, 3640, 3696, 3697,
3728, 3791, 3851, 3951, 3959, 4033, 4063,
4099, 4230, 4254, 4271, 4287, 4297, 4354,
4365, 4493, 4505, 4508, 4525, 4540, 4541,
4582, 4608, 4655, 4877, 4921, 4964, 5019,
5107, 5148, 5274, 5628, 5635, 5638, 5675,
5728, 5764, 5800, 6744, 7757, 9117, 10092,
11194, 13306, 13607, 14777, 15799, 15943,

16396, 16594, 16625, 16830, 17399, 17453
17902, 22310, 22829, 23484, 24100, 25673;
History, Civil war, Personal narratives,
Southern, 21779; History, Civil war,
Personal narratives, Union side, 3306,
3645, 17377; History, Civil war,
Pictorial works, 4302; History, Civil
war, Poetry, 1358, 1600, 2314, 2836,
11267, 11276, 11325, 11326, 11413,
12201, 14506, 15369, 21836, 22016,
22371, 22432, 24819, 24921, 25027,
25333, 25872; History, Civil war, Poetry,
Confederate, 2775, 3227, 3280, 3411,
4854, 10057, 13120, 13326, 22957; History,
Civil war, Portraits, 7470; History, Civil
war, Prison life, 2761, 2876, 3130, 3204,
3275, 3279, 3335, 3387, 3432, 3501, 3513,
3520, 4067, 4212, 4278, 4476, 4874, 5215,
5728, 17578, 22211, 22572; History, Civil
war, Prisoners and prisons, 2277, 2463,
2479, 2487, 2538, 2586, 2725, 2749,
2839, 2864, 3082, 3088, 3168, 3181,
3294, 3305, 3307, 3585, 3621, 3649,
3684, 3695, 3726, 3799, 3807, 3966,
3983, 4031, 4077, 4140, 4142, 4145,
4230, 4255, 4350, 4455, 4595, 4617,
4627, 4819, 4864, 4867, 4952, 4970,
5046, 5047, 5058, 5105, 5177, 5329,
5585, 5665, 6063, 10057, 11706, 12404,
13507, 16116, 23178; History, Civil war,
Prisoners, Exchange of, 2041; History,
Civil war, Regimental histories, Ala.
inf., 1st, 4369; History, Civil war,
Regimental histories, Ala. inf., 60th,
5130; History, Civil war, Regimental
histories, Arkansas infantry, 1st,
Company G, 2703; History, Civil war,
Regimental histories, Army of Northern
Virginia, 4119; History, Civil war,
Regimental histories, Army of the
Cumberland, 2708; History, Civil war,
Regimental histories, Army of the
Potomac, 839, 1394, 3050, 4097, 4521,
5461, 8055, 12014, 21854, 22799, 22800,
22802; History, Civil war, Regimental
histories, Army of the Potomac, 5th
corps, 5422; History, Civil war,
Regimental histories, Army of the
Potomac, 6th corps, 5268; History,
Civil war, Regimental histories, Army
of the Tennessee, 3140, 3922; History,
Civil war, Regimental histories, Cal.
inf., 1st, 17378; History, Civil war,
Regimental histories, Coburn's brigade,
2787; History, Civil war, Regimental
histories, Colorado cav., 2d., 17900;

History, Civil war, Regimental histories,
Col. Inf. Volunteers, 1st, 3904; History,
Civil war, Regimental histories, Conn. inf.,
6th, 2880; History, Civil war, Regimental
histories, Conn. inf., 16th, 2729; History,
Civil war, Regimental histories, Conn. inf.,
27th, 5135; History, Civil war, Regimental
histories, Conn. inf., 29th, 3873; History,
Civil war, Regimental histories, D.C. cav.,
1st, 4458; History, Civil war, Regimental
histories, 11th corps, 966; History,
Civil war, Regimental histories, Duryee's
brigade, 12926; History, Civil war,
Regimental histories, First Kentucky
Brigade, C.S.A. ("Orphan Brigade"), 14263;
History, Civil war, Regimental histories,
Forrest's cavalry, 4540; History, Civil
war, Regimental histories, Ga., 2262, 24688;
History, Civil war, Regimental histories,
Ga. art, Chatham art, 4103; History, Civil
war, Regimental histories, Ga. inf., 1st,
4650; History, Civil war, Regimental
histories, Ga. inf., 6th, 3127; History,
Civil war, Regimental histories, Ga. inf.,
30th, 2494; History, Civil war, Regimental
histories, Ga. inf., 61st, 4600; History,
Civil war, Regimental histories, Ga. inf.,
Oglethorpe inf., 3016; History, Civil war,
Regimental histories, Ill. art., 1st,
Battery A, 4171; History, Civil war,
Regimental histories, Illinois cav.,
14th, 15326; History, Civil war, Regimental
histories, Ill. cav., 8th, 3775; History,
Civil war, Regimental histories, Ill. inf.,
7th, 2524; History, Civil war, Regimental
histories, Ill. inf., 14th, 3306; History,
Civil war, Regimental histories, Ill. inf.,
15th, 2611; History, Civil war, Regimental
histories, Ill. inf., 33d, 4399; History,
Civil war, Regimental histories, Ill. inf.,
34th, 4724; History, Civil war, Regimental
histories, Ill. inf., 40th, 3801; History,
Civil war, Regimental histories, Ill. inf.,
47th, 2847; History, Civil war, Regimental
histories, Ill. inf., 59th, 4223; History,
Civil war, Regimental histories, Ill. inf.,
75th, 3263; History, Civil war, Regimental
histories, Ill. inf., 77th, 2687; History,
Civil war, Regimental histories, Ill. inf.,
81st, 4595; History, Civil war, Regimental
histories, Ill. inf., 84th, 5154; History,
Civil war, Regimental histories, Ill. inf.,
85th, 2567; History, Civil war, Regimental
histories, Ill. inf., 86th, 4179; History,
Civil war, Regimental histories, Ill. inf.,
88th, 3525; History, Civil war, Regimental

histories, Ill. inf., 102d, 3439; History, Civil war, Regimental histories, Ill. inf., 113th, 4143; History, Civil war, Regimental histories, Ill. inf., 124th, 3953; History, Civil war, Regimental histories, Illinois volunteer infantry, 125th, 15294; History, Civil war, Regimental histories, Ind. art., 11th battery, 4663; History, Civil war, Regimental histories, Ind. cav., 7th, 3044; History, Civil war, Regimental histories, Ind. inf., 6th, 2798, 3670; History, Civil war, Regimental histories, Ind. inf., 12th, 3557; History, Civil war, Regimental histories, Ind. inf., 21st, 6953; History, Civil war, Regimental histories, Ind. inf., 27th, 2824; History, Civil war, Regimental histories, Ind. inf., 36th, 3704; History, Civil war, Regimental histories, Ind. inf., 42d, 3939; History, Civil war, Regimental histories, Ind. inf., 51st, 3804; History, Civil war, Regimental histories, Ind. inf., 57th, 4164; History, Civil war, Regimental histories, Ind. inf., 58th, 3866; History, Civil war, Regimental histories, Ind. inf., 68th, 3865; History, Civil war, Regimental histories, Ind. inf., 70th, 4457; History, Civil war, Regimental histories, Ind. inf., 72d, 4351; History, Civil war, Regimental histories, Ind. inf., 75th, 3489; History, Civil war, Regimental histories, Ind. inf., 81st, 4528; History, Civil war, Regimental histories, Ind. inf., 82d, 3972; History, Civil war, Regimental histories, Ind. inf., 99th, 4313; History, Civil war, Regimental histories, Ia., 13096; History, Civil war, Regimental histories, Ia. cav., 1st, 4303, 17294; History, Civil war, Regimental histories, Ia. inf., 1st, 5610; History, Civil war, Regimental histories, Ia. inf., 2d, 2665; History, Civil war, Regimental histories, Ia. inf., 6th, 5774; History, Civil war, Regimental histories, Ia. inf., 20th, 2615; History, Civil war, Regimental histories, Ia. inf., 22d, 4121; History, Civil war, Regimental histories, Ia. inf., 36th, 5329; History, Civil war, Regimental histories, Irish brigade, 3087; History, Civil war, Regimental histories, Iron brigade, 3145; History, Civil war, Regimental histories, Kan. cav., 7th, 3523; History, Civil war, Regimental histories, Ky. cav., 1st, 5348; History, Civil war, Regimental histories, Ky. cav. (Confederate), Partisan rangers, 4063;

History, Civil war, Regimental histories, Ky. inf., 8th, 5777; History, Civil war, Regimental histories, Ky. infantry (C.S.A.), 1st brigade, 15799; History, Civil war, Regimental histories, La., 2625; History, Civil war, Regimental histories, La. art., Washington art., 2625, 4671; History, Civil war, Regimental histories, La. cav. (Confederate), 1st, 2921; History, Civil war, Regimental histories, La. inf., 3d, 5482; History, Civil war, Regimental histories, La. inf., 26th, 3756; History, Civil war, Regimental histories, Me. art., 7th battery, 4218; History, Civil war, Regimental histories, Me. cav., 1st, 4458; History, Civil war, Regimental histories, Me. inf., 1st, 3655; History, Civil war, Regimental histories, Me. inf., 5th, 2709; History, Civil war, Regimental histories, Me. inf., 10th, 3655; History, Civil war, Regimental histories, Me. inf., 17th, 12934; History, Civil war, Regimental histories, Me. inf., 20th, 3592; History, Civil war, Regimental histories, Me. inf., 23d, 4218; History, Civil war, Regimental histories, Me. inf., 29th, 3655; History, Civil war, Regimental histories, Md. (C.S.A), 3635; History, Civil war, Regimental histories, Md. cav., 1st, Potomac home brigade, 4591; History, Civil war, Regimental histories, Mass. art., 1st battery, 2669; History, Civil war, Regimental histories, Mass. art., 10th battery, 2715; History, Civil war, Regimental histories, Mass. cav., 1st, 11430; History, Civil war, Regimental histories, Mass. inf., 1st, 3136; History, Civil war, Regimental histories, Mass.inf., 2d, 4537, 4876; History, Civil war, Regimental histories, Mass. inf., 6th, 3771; History, Civil war, Regimental histories, Mass. inf., 9th, 4371; History, Civil war, Regimental histories, Mass. inf., 12th, 3076; History, Civil war, Regimental histories, Mass. inf., 18th, 3186; History, Civil war, Regimental histories, Mass. inf., 19th, 2492; History, Civil war, Regimental histories, Mass. inf., 21st, 5598; History, Civil war, Regimental histories, Mass. inf., 23d, 3381; History, Civil war, Regimental histories, Mass. inf., 25th, 4870; History, Civil war, Regimental histories, Mass. inf., 27th, 3235; History, Civil war, Regimental histories, Mass. inf., 29th, 4661; History, Civil war, Regimental histories, Mass. inf., 32d, 4697; History,

Civil war, Regimental histories, Mass. inf., 33d, 2751; History, Civil war, Regimental histories, Mass. inf., 38th, 4842; History, Civil war, Regimental histories, Mass. inf., 43d, 5008; History, Civil war, Regimental histories, Mass. inf., 44th, 3729; History, Civil war, Regimental histories, Mass. inf., 45th, 3958; History, Civil war, Regimental histories, Mass. inf., 49th, 4062; History, Civil war, Regimental histories, Mass. inf., 52d, 3944; History, Civil war, Regimental histories, Mass. inf., 55th (colored), 12154; History, Civil war, Regimental histories, Mass. inf. 58th, 22004; History, Civil war, Regimental histories, Mich. cav., 2d, 5373; History, Civil war, Regimental histories, Mich. cav. brigade, 4170; History, Civil war, Regimental histories, Mich. inf., 24th, 3145; History, Civil war, Regimental histories, Minnesota infantry, 2d, 13668; History, Civil war, Regimental histories, Mo. (C.S.A.), 1st brigade, 2537; History, Civil war, Regimental histories, Mo. cav., Frémont's body guard, 12170; History, Civil war, Regimental histories, Mo. inf., 9th, 4223; History, Civil war, Regimental histories, Morgan's cavalry division (C.S.A) 3312; History, Civil war, Regimental histories, Morton's artillery, C.S.A., 4540; History, Civil war, Regimental histories, N.H. inf., 2d, 3824; History, Civil war, Regimental histories, N.J. inf., 9th, 5043; History, Civil war, Regimental histories, N.J., 22201; History, Civil war, Regimental histories, N.J. inf., 13th, 5434; History, Civil war, Regimental histories, New York, 12926; History, Civil war, Regimental histories, N.Y. art., 9th, 5002; History, Civil war, Regimental histories, N.Y. art., 34th battery, 5005; History, Civil war, Regimental histories, N.Y. art., Independent battery, 4th, 5201; History, Civil war, Regimental histories, N.Y. inf., 5th, 3177; History, Civil war, Regimental histories, N.Y. inf., 9th, 5694; History, Civil war, Regimental histories, N.Y. inf., 16th, 3144; History, Civil war, Regimental histories, N.Y. inf., 33d, 13343; History, Civil war, Regimental histories, N.Y. inf., 40th, 16525; History, Civil war, Regimental histories, N.Y. inf.,

48th, 4602, 4687; History, Civil war, Regimental histories, N.Y. inf., 57th, 3533; History, Civil war, Regimental histories, N.Y. inf., 60th, 3337; History, Civil war, Regimental histories, N.Y. inf., 76th, 5184; History, Civil war, Regimental histories, N.Y. inf., 79th, 5430; History, Civil war, Regimental histories, N.Y. inf., 81st, 3211; History, Civil war, Regimental histories, N.Y. inf., 83d, 13162; History, Civil war, Regimental histories, N.Y. inf., 113th, 13060; History, Civil war, Regimental histories, N.Y. inf., 115th, 3011; History, Civil war, Regimental histories, N.Y. inf., 117th, 4543; History, Civil war, Regimental histories, N.Y. inf., 124th, 5682; History, Civil war, Regimental histories, N.C. inf., 7th, 3488; History, Civil war, Regimental histories, O., 3882; History, Civil war, Regimental histories, O. art., Battery B., 22019; History, Civil war, Regimental histories, Ohio artillery, 19th independent battery, 15587; History, Civil war, Regimental histories, O. inf., 3d, 2657; History, Civil war, Regimental histories, O. inf., 6th, 3770; History, Civil war, Regimental histories, O. inf., 7th, 5756; History, Civil war, Regimental histories, O. inf., 9th, 5334; History, Civil war, Regimental histories, O. inf., 11th, 3940; History, Civil war, Regimental histories, O. inf., 29th, 5121; History, Civil war, Regimental histories, O. inf., 39th, 1880; History, Civil war, Regimental histories, O. inf., 42d, 4409; History, Civil war, Regimental histories, O. inf., 53d, 3313; History, Civil war, Regimental histories, O. inf., 55th, 4660; History, Civil war, Regimental histories, O. inf., 58th, 5317; History, Civil war, Regimental histories, O. inf., 63d, 4036; History, Civil war, Regimental histories, O. inf., 73d, 3976; History, Civil war, Regimental histories, O. inf., 78th, 5273; History, Civil war, Regimental histories, O. inf., 101st, 2868, 3201; History, Civil war, Regimental histories, O. inf., 105th, 5439; History, Civil war, Regimental histories, O. inf., 123d, 4168; History, Civil war, Regimental histories, Pa. cav., 1st, 4286; History, Civil war, Regimental histories, Pa. cav., 4th, 22634; History, Civil war, Regimental histories, Pa. cav. 6th, 22260; History, Civil war, Regimental histories, Pa. cav., 7th, 3271, 5171; History, Civil war, Regimental

histories, Pa. inf., 31st, 5767; History, Civil war, Regimental histories, Pa. inf., 37th, 3871; History, Civil war, Regimental histories, Pa. inf., 48th, 2766; History, Civil war, Regimental histories, Pa. inf., 51st, 4702; History, Civil war, Regimental histories, Pa. inf., 83d, 4127; History, Civil war, Regimental histories, Pa. inf., 97th, 4857; History, Civil war, Regimental histories, Pa. inf., 102d, 5275; History, Civil war, Regimental histories, Pa. inf, 106th, 5608; History, Civil war, Regimental histories, Pa. inf., 107th, 12926; History, Civil war, Regimental histories, Pa. inf., 114th, 4899; History, Civil war, Regimental histories, Pa. inf., 141st, 3107; History, Civil war, Regimental histories, Pickett's division (C.S.A.), 22310; History, Civil war, Regimental histories, R.I. inf., 1st, 5761; History, Civil war, Regimental histories, R.I. inf., 12th, 12351; History, Civil war, Regimental histories, Sibley's brigade, 4610; History, Civil war, Regimental histories, S.C.inf., 2889; History, Civil war, Regimental histories, S.C. inf., Edisto rifles, 4033; History, Civil war, Regimental histories, S.C. inf., 4th, 4921; History, Civil war, Regimental histories, S.C. inf., Kershaw's brigade, 3244; History, Civil war, Regimental histories, Stonewall brigade, 2935; History, Civil war, Regimental histories, Tenn. cav., 1st battalion, 3767; History, Civil war, Regimental histories, Tenn. cav, 2d, 3767; History, Civil war, Regimental histories, Tenn. cav., 7th battalion, 3767; History, Civil war, Regimental histories, Tenn. inf., 1st, Co.H., 5635; History, Civil war, Regimental histories, Texas brigade, 4823; History, Civil war, Regimental histories, Texas cav., 3d, 2619; History, Civil war, Regimental histories, Texas cav., 8th, 2726, 3600, 16396; History, Civil war, Regimental histories, Texas cav., Morgan's battalion, 1861-1865, 3828; History, Civil war, Regimental histories, Tex. cav., Ross's brigade, 5014; History, Civil war, Regimental histories, Texas cav., Sibley's brigade, 4610; History, Civil war, Regimental histories, Texas cavalry, 26th rgt., 1861-1865, 16351; History, Civil war, Regimental histories,

Texas inf., 4th, 3195; History, Civil war, Regimental histories, U.S. cav., 6th, 16162; History, Civil war, Regimental histories, U.S. inf., 8th, 5105, 17578; History, Civil war, Regimental histories, U.S. inf., 33d, 3864, 5356; History, Civil war, Regimental histories, U.S. inf., 1st sharpshooters, 5267; History, Civil war, Regimental histories, U.S. inf., 2nd sharpshooters, 5267; History, Civil war, Regimental histories, Vt., 1149, 5600; History, Civil war, Regimental histories, Vt. inf., 10th, 3823; History, Civil war, Regimental histories, Va., Richmond howitzers, 3166; History, Civil war, Regimental histories, Va. art., Carpenter's battery, 3493; History, Civil war, Regimental histories, Va. art., Parker battery, 3444; History, Civil war, Regimental histories, Va. art., Richmond howitzers, 5575; History, Civil war, Regimental histories, Va. art., Surry light artillery, 1861-1865, 4099; History, Civil war, Regimental histories, Va. cav., 9th, 2656; History, Civil war, Regimental histories, Va. cav., 43d battalion, 3114; History, Civil war, Regimental histories, Va. cav. (Union), Loudoun rangers, 3637; History, Civil war, Regimental histories, Va. inf., 11th, 4525; History, Civil war, Regimental histories, Va. inf., 17th, 5751; History, Civil war, Regimental histories, Va. inf., 21st, 5771; History, Civil war, Regimental histories, Va. inf., 33d, 2935; History, Civil war, Regimental histories, Walker's Texas division (C.S.A.), 2737; History, Civil war, Regimental histories, West Va., inf., 4th, 2627; History, Civil war, Regimental histories, Wis. inf., 6th, 2980; History, Civil war, Regimental histories, Wis. inf., 8th, 3198, 3300; History, Civil war, Regimental histories, Wis. inf., 12th, 4323; History, Civil war, Regimental histories, Wis. inf., 37th, 3338; History, Civil war, Registers, lists, etc., 3621, 3882, 8263, 17940; History, Civil war, Registers of dead, 4896; History, Civil war, Religious aspects, 1776, 24581; History, Civil war, Religious life, 2002, 2686, 2702, 4119, 12516; History, Civil war, Secret service, Confederate states, 1002, 12404, 16085; History, Civil war, Societies, 312, 4471, 15012; History, Civil war, Songs and music, 7498, 7501, 7502, 7745, 7804; History, Civil war, Sources, 14703; History, Civil war, Statistics, 15127; History, Civil war, Unit historics, Kentucky

(C.S.A.), 15519, 15520; History, Civil war, Women, 7370; History, Civil war, Women's work, 11528; History, Colonial period, 230, 468, 512, 737, 738, 769, 2018, 2117, 2867, 3276, 3404, 5010, 5781, 6260, 6261, 6843, 7054, 11299, 12173, 12548, 13046, 21862, 21863, 21950, 22288, 22564, 23174, 23186, 23574; History, Colonial period, Biography, 21780; History, Colonial period, Drama, 23596; History, Colonial period, Fiction, 8600, 8602, 9389, 10483, 10484, 10977; History, Constitutional period, 1789-1809, 293, 1806, 1809, 1811, 1940, 23820, 23016; History, Constitutional period, 1789-1809, Period.,322; History, Drama, 5931; History, Fiction, 5652, 10033; History, French and Indian war, 1755-1763, 575, 769, 2027, 5243, 6148, 6261, 6397, 7766, 8414, 8814, 12474, 13333, 16658, 21758, 22349, 23457, 23503; History, French and Indian war, 1755-1763, Addresses, sermons, etc., 35, 3015, 2305, 11626, 11825, 13423, 21865, 21895, 21984, 23660; History, French and Indian war, 1755-1763, Fiction, 7688, 8841, 10293, 10443, 11225, 22668; History, French and Indian war, 1755-1763, Naval operations, 8413; History, French and Indian war, 1755-1763, Personal narratives, 2158, 5011, 5072, 5111, 5199, 23668; History, French and Indian war, 1755-1763, Poetry, 22151; History, French and Indian war, 1755-1763, Sources, 23456; History, Humor, caricatures, etc., 1914, 6115, 10753; History, King George's war, 1744-1748, 25, 11991, 17176, 21931, 23431; History, King George's war, 1745-1748, Personal narratives, 7764; History, King William's war, 1689-1697, 981, 12514; History, King William's war, 1689-1697, Addresses, sermons, etc., 23314; History, Period., 254, 287; History, Poetry, 786, 13012, 22603; History, Reconstruction, 6582, 6616; History, Reconstruction, Fiction, 8525, 8927; History, Revolution, 62, 192, 193, 354, 468, 738, 1012, 1398, 1751, 2535, 3418, 3614, 3659, 4200, 4203, 4572, 6714, 7077, 7101, 7247, 7250, 11390, 11483, 11741, 12394, 13281, 13400, 13499, 13515, 14642, 14829, 15244, 15296, 15381, 15449, 22031, 22090, 22149, 22756, 23035, 23458, 23462, 23723, 23749; History, Revolution, Addresses, sermons, etc., 296, 579, 969, 1550, 1576, 1771, 1821,

11894, 12096, 12282, 12314, 12775, 12808, 13029, 13044, 13295, 13344, 21983, 22123, 23109, 23158, 23455, 23545, 23699, 23778, 23792; History, Revolution, Anecdotes, 662, 2392, 2393, 9978, 10219, 10570, 11611, 13246, 22153; History, Revolution, Biography, 662, 1407, 1408, 2392, 2393, 5371, 11923, 12023, 12729, 12775, 12789, 13199, 21971, 23455; History, Revolution, British forces, 12799, 12960, 23362; History, Revolution, Campaigns and battles, 2731, 4238, 4982, 5126, 5347, 12189, 22388, 23727; History, Revolution, Causes, 223, 237, 380, 1071, 11333, 11395, 11617, 11721, 11790, 12379, 12437, 13390, 13474, 21759, 21992, 22695, 22738, 23550, 23616, 23723, 23776; History, Revolution, Claims, 160, 755, 12190; History, Revolution, Drama, 1707; History, Revolution, Fiction, 1639, 2521, 2522, 3893, 4112, 8604, 8631, 8670, 8700, 8715, 8749, 8922, 9003, 9022, 9043, 9058, 9129, 9151, 9268, 9294, 9296, 9297, 9298, 9299, 9536, 9612, 9737, 9852, 9855, 9919, 9928, 10061, 10094, 10103, 10220, 10277, 10311, 10412, 10489, 10513, 10739, 10765, 10774, 10775, 10778, 10779, 10814, 10879, 10880, 11175, 12901; History, Revolution, Finance, commerce, confiscations, etc., 1457; History, Revolution, Foreign public opinion, 13359; History, Revolution, French participation, 2731, 3239, 4124, 4654, 4933, 4982, 4997; History, Revolution, German mercenaries, 3270, 3328, 4826, 4960, 5290, 23534; History, Revolution, Humor, caricatures, etc., 2107; History, Revolution, Loyalists, 23468; History, Revolution, Naval operations, 2096, 2384, 3405, 4654, 12352, 22419, 23353, 23611, 23613; History, Revolution, Negro troops, 24874; History, Revolution, Period.,105; History, Revolution, Personal narratives, 346, 779, 863, 1754, 2248, 2832, 2872, 3205, 3239, 3264, 3270, 3315, 4516, 4767, 4879, 5636, 5702, 11537, 11680, 12155, 12334, 12367, 12943, 22273, 22388, 22626, 23504, 23611; History, Revolution, Personal narratives, British, 344, 345, 347, 4203, 5111, 5209, 5894, 5895, 12136, 21864, 23169, 23534, 23634, 23670; History, Revolution, Poetry, 152, 236, 256, 351, 352, 809, 817, 819, 2107, 6911, 11386, 11688, 12070, 13009, 22656, 22891, 23684; History, Revolution, Prison life, 1753, 1754, 1966; History, Revolution, Prisoners, Exchange of, 571, 23279; History, Revolution, Prisoners and

prisons, 161, 163-166, 364, 2128, 2367, 11284, 12070, 12753, 22410, 22419, 23504, 23681; History, Revolution, Regimental histories, American loyalist, 5153; History, Revolution, Regimental histories, Md., 698; History, Revolution, Regimental histories, R.I., 25390; History, Revolution, Regimental histories, U.S. artillery, Harrison's regt., 11537; History, Revolution, Registers, lists, etc., 1370, 7003, 15723; History, Revolution, Societies, 8076, 15411; History, Revolution, Sources, 250, 698, 4589, 13369, 13473, 22268, 22294, 23246, 23453, 23454, 23700, 23727, 23755; History, Revolution, Welsh participation, 13286; History, Seminole war, Fiction, 10589; History, Societies, 255; History, Spanish American war, Fiction, 14131; History, Study and teaching, 2117; History, Tripolitan war, 1801-1805, 256, 2172, 11965, 25345; History, War of 1812, 548, 665, 1937, 1941, 1978, 6617, 7613, 8804, 9507, 11475, 11574, 12248, 13129, 14465, 15213, 15340, 15355, 15358, 15402, 15790, 21918, 22497, 22611, 23622, 23695; History, War of 1812, Addresses, sermons, etc., 114, 363, 416, 562, 566, 11249, 11557, 11810, 11911, 12870, 13099, 22965; History, War of 1812, American forces, 23669; History, War of 1812, Biography, 656, 22704; History, War of 1812, Campaigns and battles, 1436, 2236, 3625, 4224, 4326, 11458, 11574, 11575, 12741, 12999, 13100, 13119, 22165, 23584, 23732; History, War of 1812, Causes, 57, 11771, 13404, 21846, 22028, 22184; History, War of 1812, Claims, 11799; History, War of 1812, Fiction, 2517, 3397, 9636, 10432, 11204; History, War of 1812, Naval operations, 1980, 2325, 12841, 13155, 22673; History, War of 1812, Naval operations, Fiction, 9388; History, War of 1812, Period., 316; History, War of 1812, Personal narratives, 15875; History, War of 1812, Personal narratives, 1682, 11575; History, War of 1812, Poetry, 1379, 2136, 3188, 3383, 12250, 15770; History, War of 1812, Prisoners and prisons, 11107, 15875; History, War of 1812, Regimental histories, Kentucky, 14507; History, War of 1812, Regimental histories, Md., 22448; History, War of 1812, Regimental histories, Pa., 22440; History, War of 1812, Registers, lists, etc., 14507; History, War of 1812,

Songs and music, 12250; History, War of 1812, Sources, 316, 1436, 2236, 13119; History, War of 1898, 20253; History, War of 1898, Campaigns and battles, 8265, 8379; History, War of 1898, Negro troops, 25124; History, War of 1898, Regimental histories, U.S. cav., 6th, 16162; History, War with Algeria, 1815, 12841, 22611; History, War with France, 1798-1800, 182; History, War with Mexico, 1845-1848, 992, 1579, 1763, 3546, 4980, 6785, 6791, 8002, 12178, 13185, 13196, 14101, 16034, 16458, 17093, 17187, 17895, 20223, 21875, 22955, 23105, 24467; History, War with Mexico, 1845-1848, Addresses, sermons, etc., 1688, 12194, 22314; History, War with Mexico, 1845-1848, Campaigns and battles, 1666, 4151, 4926, 6144, 7386, 7529, 8001, 8035, 16272, 22413, 23584; History, War with Mexico, 1845-1848, Causes, 1215; History, War with Mexico, 1845-1848, Fiction, 9020, 9295, 9649, 9718, 9719, 10069, 10213; History, War with Mexico, 1845-1848, Naval operations, 17477; History, War with Mexico, 1845-1848, Personal narratives, 190, 2605, 3661, 4332, 4416, 4957, 6344, 6614, 6615, 6791, 6906, 13158, 15192, 16335, 16625, 16795, 17286, 22092, 22457, 22995; History, War with Mexico, 1845-1848, Poetry, 24902; History, War with Mexico, 1845-1848, Prisoners and prisons, 6614, 6615; History, War with Mexico, 1845-1848, Regimental histories, Army of Chihuahua, 1666; History, War with Mexico, 1845-1848, Regimental histories, Lane's brigade, 6144; History, War with Mexico, 1845-1848, Regimental histories, N.Y. inf., 1st, 16207; History, War with Mexico, 1845-1848, Regimental histories, N.Y. inf., 2d., 22457; History, War with Mexico, 1845-1848, Regimental histories, O. inf., 5th, Co.C., 13158; History, War with Mexico, 1845-1848, Regimental histories, Tex. cav., McCulloch's independent company, 4926; History, World War II, 13604; History, Comic, satirical, etc., 9507; History, Juvenile, 11362; History, Military, 17428; History, Naval, 275, 276; History, Hydrographic office, 23376; Indus., History, 1356; Infantry, 1st regt., 17829; Infantry, 1st regt. sharpshooters, 1861-1865, 5267; Infantry, 2d regt. sharpshooters, 1861-1865, 5267; Infantry, 6th regt., 3081; Infantry, 8th regt., 17578; Infantry, 8th regt., 1838-, 5105; Infantry, 8th regt., Colored, 1863-1866, 4822; Infantry, 18th regt., 1861-,

16151, 16153; Infantry, 33d Colored regt., 1862-1866, 3864, 5356; Insular possessions, 7639; Intellectual life, 12502, 19793; Laws, statutes, etc., 1494, 1686, 1805, 11422, 12085, 12210, 13302, 15631, 17222, 22079, 22080, 22179, 22428, 22666, 25130, 25773-25776; Laws, statutes, etc., 1797-1799, (5th Cong., 1st-3d sess.), 15632; Laws, statutes, etc., 1849-1850 (31st Cong., 1st sess.), 25777; Library of Congress, Archive of Hispanic Literature on Tape, 18054; Life & customs, 2588; Mail, 5757; Manners and customs, 4478; Manufacturing, History, 1356; Maps, 2913, 3399, 5082; Marine corps, Biography, 12597; Marine corps, History, 22092; Marine corps, Registers, 2402; Military Academy, West Point, 557, 836, 2481, 11470, 12135, 22801, 23108; Military Academy, West Point, Fiction, 9664, 10111; Military Academy, West Point, Registers, 11889; Military secretary's dept., 8263; Militia, 2402, 25775, 23669; Mint, 2173; Moral cond., 4129, 11308; National Park Service, 14734; Nationality, 13016; Naval academy, Annapolis, 23170; Naval observatory, 2160, 23374; Naval shipyard, Boston, 12997; Naval station, New London, Conn., 1432; Navy, 2142, 6576, 6577, 7842, 13264, 15291, 22982; Navy, Appointments and retirements, 13202; Navy, Appropriations and expenditures, 13167; Navy, Biography, 656, 12597, 21981; Navy, Chaplain corps, 13247; Navy, Courts-martial, Barron, 1808, 880; Navy, Courts-martial, Mackenzie, 1843, 22929; Navy, Courts-martial, Meade, 1806, 23413; Navy, Courts of inquiry, Hull, 1822, 12997; Navy, History, 182, 11831, 12174, 12297; Navy, History, Civil war, 11469; Navy, History, War with Mexico, 1845-1848, 8002; Navy, officers, 1919; Navy, Registers, 2273, 2402; Navy Dept., 25778; Office commissioner for exchange, 2041; Office of Education, Division of Higher Education, 14624, 15633; Office of Indian affairs, The Cherokee question, 1866, 11775; Office of Internal Revenue, 11422, 12085, 22179; Officials and employees, 12871; Officials and employees, Appointment, qualifications, tenure, etc., 937, 11489; Officials and employees, Salaries, allowances, etc., 2106, 21960; Patent office, 1032; Politics & government, 113, 133, 280, 705, 776, 859, 1020, 1021, 1022, 1244, 1606, 1630, 1867, 1914, 1999, 2149, 2326, 2404, 2525, 2988,

3051, 3664, 3872, 4261, 4526, 4551, 4898, 5050, 5355, 5429, 5462, 5609, 7425, 7913, 8099, 8238, 8329, 9098, 11324, 11494, 11759, 12029, 12077, 12101, 12253, 12254, 12290, 12447, 12557, 12866, 12951, 13173, 13208, 13325, 13924, 13949, 14650, 15040, 15744, 15773, 15944, 16962, 17785, 21862, 21879, 22206, 22536, 22790, 22804, 22906, 22939, 22974, 23107, 23619, 23708, 23867, 24334, 24478, 24877, 25050, 25470, 25547; Politics & government, 1780-1797, 21966; Politics & government, 1783-1789, 74, 332, 10317, 13131, 22490; Politics & government, 1783-1800, 7141; Politics & government, 1783-1805, Sources, 21969; Politics & government, 1783-1809, 2780, 4599, 11299, 11671, 12367, 13381, 22405, 23756; Politics & government, 1783-1865, 63, 279, 1403, 7005, 8249, 11751, 11878, 14806, 15649, 22716, 23198, 24628, 24697, 25892; Politics & government, 1789-1797, 1931, 1932, 1942, 1945, 5890, 11500, 11501, 12318, 12603, 13244, 21965, 22890, 22948, 23123; Politics & government, 1789-1815, 21837; Politics & government, 1797-1801, 57, 58, 229, 556, 1344, 1345, 1387, 1808, 1910, 2478, 11768, 11770, 12068, 12693, 21847, 21988, 22890, 23772; Politics & government, 1801-1809, 94, 519, 712, 1019, 1347, 1348, 1996, 2192, 12204, 12289, 12348, 12349, 12599, 12654, 12844, 13506, 21817, 22075, 23773; Politics & government, 1801-1815, 21964, 22461; Politics & government, 1809-1817, 78, 9552, 12243, 21846, 23244, 24986; Politics & government, 1811-1841, 23781; Politics & government, 1811-1860, 13840; Politics & government, 1815-1861, 1185, 2963, 3093, 3301, 3663, 3874, 4384, 4401, 7186, 11391, 11447, 12592, 12624, 12871, 14502, 16463, 17087, 17764, 22240, 22885, 23838, 23850, 23904, 24059, 24335, 24437, 24502, 25026, 25409, 25543, 25732, 25799, 25913, 25927; Politics & government, 1817-1821, 23757; Politics & government, 1817-1825, 78; Politics & government, 1825-1829, 935, 24483; Politics & government, 1829-1837, 1592, 8824, 12002, 12106, 12444, 12479, 12677, 13845, 14502, 17166, 22369, 23759, 25790; Politics & government, 1837-1841, 1592, 7594, 13353, 13846, 15713, 22378, 22662, 25086, 25590; Politics & government, 1841-1845, 41, 67, 1605, 8249, 11897, 12623, 13280, 15833, 17799, 24898, 25574; Politics & government, 1845-1849, 1647, 4296, 13197, 21875, 22029, 23841, 24294, 24698, 25901, 25098, 25463, 25569,

25571, 25879; Politics & government,
1845-1861, 3875, 6592, 11740; Politics
& government, 1848-1861, 5831, 12144,
25530; Politics & government, 1849-1853,
1655, 5477, 6711, 11303, 12191, 23648,
23843, 23952, 24285, 24663, 25058;
Politics & government, 1849-1861, 2643,
6888, 24086, 25438, 25544, 25583;
Politics & government, 1849-1877, 3022,
7945, 16649, 24041, 25601; Politics &
government, 1853-1857, 895, 1161, 2430,
11678, 11890, 11931, 12772, 13216, 23392,
23866, 23943, 23975, 24023, 24219, 24241,
24365, 24545, 24571, 24707, 24919, 25016,
25372, 25412, 25488, 25647; Politics &
government, 1854-1872, 16230; Politics
& government, 1857-1861, 412, 601, 682,
1160, 1163, 1165, 1282, 1438, 1463, 1718,
1727, 1953, 1997, 2233, 3898, 4154, 4920,
6586, 6938, 7283, 7284, 11313, 11389,
12010, 12056, 12315, 12650, 13065, 13212,
15342, 22097, 22576, 22766, 22915, 23168,
23848, 24078, 24089, 24149, 24152, 24153,
24160, 24241, 24258, 24259, 24273, 24309,
24345, 24375, 24383, 24389, 24393, 24498,
24638, 24762, 24889, 24937, 24951, 24976,
25028, 25088, 25127, 25128, 25159, 25162,
25360, 25426, 25482, 25548, 25645, 25715,
25753, 25813, 25854, 25860; Politics &
government, 1865-1869, 849, 1409, 2032,
2129, 2188, 4647, 7592, 8216, 8378, 11669,
11793, 11868, 13181, 13254, 13255, 21829,
24233, 24729, 24843, 25291; Politics &
government, 1865-1969, Fiction, 10418;
Politics & government, 1865-1870, 22987;
Politics & government, 1865-1973, 11233;
Politics & government, 1865-1898, 4830,
17087, 24165; Politics & government, 1865-
1900, 14483; Politics & government, 1869-
1877, 9798, 10228, 10579; Politics &
government, 1885-1889, 4402, 5848, 6433;
Politics & government, 1893-1897, 6981,
7870; Politics & government, 1897-1901,
7351, 7377; Politics & government, 1909-
1913, 16487; Politics & government,
Addresses, essays, lectures, 1412, 4414,
5587, 11622, 22973, 23865, 24251, 24907;
Politics & government, Bibliography,
14312; Politics & government, Civil war,
87, 121, 209, 248, 299, 320, 381, 469,
470, 471, 551, 602, 638, 706, 801, 827,
999, 1003, 1053, 1055, 1057, 1121, 1122,
1251, 1281, 1302, 1303, 1313, 1354, 1355,
1369, 1386, 1410, 1454, 1535, 1676, 1685,
1728, 1785, 1946, 1961, 2076, 2082, 2223,
2414, 2483, 2840, 3242, 3969, 4155, 4302,

4413, 4816, 4819, 6082, 6096, 6097, 6115,
6189, 6351, 6416, 6515, 6539, 6586, 6592,
6597, 6792, 7185, 7214, 7286, 7288, 7289,
7355, 7394, 7402, 7497, 7566, 7580, 7592,
7691, 7743, 7928, 8216, 8234, 8378, 8693,
11148, 11272, 11297, 11373, 11391, 11577,
11644, 11649, 11727, 11758, 11861, 11999,
12199, 12461, 12613, 12649, 12873, 12891,
12913, 12980, 12985, 12992, 13094, 13095,
13134, 13153, 13203, 13231, 13232, 13273,
13329, 13351, 13350, 13414, 15605, 16542,
16580, 16942, 17087, 17145, 21810, 21959,
22056, 22189, 22309, 22397, 22423, 22520,
22609, 22691, 22801, 22803, 22910, 22936,
22966, 22988, 23033, 23157, 23168, 23403,
23419, 23601, 23833, 23924, 23935, 23978,
23998, 24070, 24124, 24208, 24210, 24226,
24245, 24274, 24279, 24282, 24314, 24330,
24367, 24395, 24473, 24499, 24502, 24505,
24522, 24573, 24710, 24727, 24744, 24745,
24746, 24760, 24775, 24819, 24857, 24866,
24871, 24887, 24904, 24905, 24906, 24908,
24910, 24911, 24912, 24917, 24925, 24947,
24963, 25007, 25018, 25046, 25047, 25048,
25067, 25096, 25145, 25161, 25166, 25184,
25294, 25296, 25310, 25353, 25386, 25477,
25486, 25527, 25542, 25605, 25611, 25653,
25700, 25717, 25722, 25737, 25809, 25881,
25883, 25895, 25905, 25918, 25926, 25934;
Politics & government, Colonial period,
1373, 7767, 12132, 12437, 13361, 21759,
21798, 21863; Politics & government,
Constitutional period, 1789-1809, 69, 71,
553, 812, 815, 818, 962, 1349, 1807, 1809,
1940, 12143, 12298, 12348, 12598, 12694,
12801, 13071, 13087, 13497, 21898, 21899;
Politics & government, French and Indian
war, 1755-1763, 12894, 13046, 13191, 21950,
22389, 23438, 24830; Politics & government,
Handbooks, manuals, etc., 264, 1715, 12640,
17684, 22559, 23356; Politics & government,
Miscellanea, 2120; Politics & government,
Revolution, 22, 28, 63, 74, 93, 181, 224,
250, 572, 625, 663, 1179, 1509, 1708, 1709,
2012, 2288, 2320, 2382, 3392, 4429, 4487,
7005, 7141, 9919, 11239, 11258, 11395,
11617, 11690, 11705, 11722, 11796, 11947,
11960, 11967, 11968, 12089, 12126, 12134,
12207, 12287, 12304, 12379, 12468, 12600,
12731, 12842, 12896, 12897, 12901, 13017,
13052, 13076, 13160, 13211, 13370, 13376,
13377, 13378, 13379, 13387, 13388, 13389,
13390, 13394, 13409, 13425, 13460, 13462,
13493, 13509, 21798, 21860, 22110, 22161,
22433, 22443, 22663, 22738, 22758, 22767,
22772, 22773, 23189, 23223, 23225, 23247,

23336, 23337, 23343, 23430, 23432, 23436, 23500, 23546, 23551, 23552, 23585, 23586, 23587, 23588, 23595, 23655, 23686, 23689, 23706, 23718, 23720, 23721, 23722, 23724, 23725, 23776; Politics & government, War of 1812, 71, 88, 395, 975, 1275, 1941, 2017, 11373, 11771, 12109, 22125, 22911, 23264; Politics & government, War with France, 1798-1800, 23590; Politics & government, War with Mexico, 1845-1848, 502, 887, 1215, 1472, 11477, 12867, 13185, 23154, 25703; Population, 23792; Post-office dept., 894, 16196; Posts and forts, 17008; President, 14249, 21969; President, 1798-1801 (John Adams), 23590; President, 1801-1809 (Jefferson), 5457, 5529, 5530, 11627, 12599; President, 1817-1825 (Monroe), 5531; President, 1829-1837 (Jackson), 5526-5528, 25779; President, 1841-1845 (Tyler) Message returning bank bill, Sept. 9, 1841, 23240; President, 1845-1849 (Polk), 5533; President, 1853-1857 (Pierce), 1844, 5532; President, 1857-1861 (Buchanan), 5525, 23645; President, 1861-1865 (Lincoln), 24024, 25780; President, 1865-1869 (Johnson), 5168; President, 1885-1889 (Cleveland), 6433; Provost-marshal-general's bureau, 2084; Public lands, 2240, 11273, 11299, 13267, 17159, 17788, 22353, 23483; Public lands, Speeches in Congress, 12479, 22052, 25050; Public works, 4380, 5342, 12016; Puerto Rico reconstruction administration, 8264; Quartermaster's dept., 4245, 22946; Race questions, 1823, 5102, 6485, 24008, 24402, 25062, 25257, 25353; Race questions, Fiction, 10785; Registers, 263; Relations (general) with Gt. Britain, 22133; Relations (general) with Ireland, 22874; Relations (general) with Panama, 19934; Religion, 4098, 4268, 4288, 4937, 12124, 13098, 21902, 22044, 25146; Santiago battlefield commission, 8265; Seal, 25775; Secret Service, 1775-1783, 863; Secret Service, 1861-1865, 2598; Social conditions, 1592, 1630, 1867, 2606, 2988, 3326, 3558, 3721, 4194, 5304, 5429, 8410, 12892, 23956, 25146; Social life & customs, 221, 1473, 1681, 1788, 1914, 2005, 2357, 2660, 2695, 2713, 2722, 2741, 2800, 2866, 3039, 3053, 3058, 3083, 3160, 3259, 3260, 3413, 3458, 3565, 3646, 3689, 3711, 3761, 3809, 3811, 3858, 4045, 4046, 4098, 4181, 4190, 4261, 4381, 4397, 4492, 4552, 4753, 4769, 4806, 4835, 4865, 4920, 5112, 5411, 5443, 5460, 5463, 5928, 6157, 6188, 6880, 6922, 6945, 6946, 6947, 7424, 7425, 9552, 9652, 10488, 11685, 11759, 12477, 13087, 13303, 14300, 21879, 23619, 23950, 25097, 25785; Social life & customs, Colonial period, 22275; Statistics, 918, 11754, 12520, 15773, 22154; Supreme court, 11459, 22414, 24366, 25819; Surveys, 2239, 5342; Territorial expansion, 17093; Territories, 24497, 25350; Treasury Department, 2848, 5534, 23816, 25781; Treaties, etc., 2183, 12026, 12027; Treaties, etc., 1789-1797 (Washington), 22270; Utah Commission, 17079, 17815; War Dept., 463, 3658, 4333, 5370, 5535-5550, 5604, 23729, 25782; Yearbooks, 5679;

U.S.A., Amerikas forenede stater, 4897
The U.S.A.: their climate, soil, productions, population, manufactures, religion, arts, government, etc., 5277
USA-nackt!, 2692
The United States and Canada, as seen by two brothers in 1858 and 1861, 8259
The United States and the British Northwest, 1865-1870, 17558
The United States biographical dictionary and portrait gallery of eminent and self-made men, 8260
United States Christian commission, 1776, 12949, 12661
The United States consulate in California, 16931
The United States gazetteer, 5108
U.S. general directory, 5298
United States labor greenback song book, 5143
United States lessons, 12936
The United States manual of biography and history, 23173
The United States marshalship in North Carolina, 2439
The United States' naval chronicle, 12297
The United States of yesterday and of tomorrow, 15926
United States sanitary commission, 1548, 4284, 11295, 13447, 22417, 22518
The United States unmasked, 4383, 24963
U.S.S.R., Foreign relations, Brazil, 19387
The unity of God, 2176
A universal biographical dictionary, 700
The universal masonic record, 13061
A universal pronouncing gazetteer, 715
The universal traveller, 5066
Universalist church, Sermons, 22321
Universalist church in the U.S., Northwest, Old, 4382
La universidad colonial, 20708
La universidad latinoamericana, 18064

Universities and colleges, 18374;
Argentine Republic, 18434, 20203;
Bolivia, 20654; Brazil, 18615, 19189,
19190, 19221, 19249, 19707; Brazil,
History, 19808; Caribbean area, 18604;
Central America, 20434, 20439; Chile,
20390; Colombia, 19104, 19859, 20293,
20295; Colombia, Statistics, 20296;
Colorado, 17021; Costa Rica, 20617;
Indonesia, 13810, 15699; Latin America,
19557, 20203; Nebraska, 16120; Peru,
20431; U.S., 826
Universities, Latin American, and the
church, 20430
University extension, 14656
The unknown, 9635
Unknown Mexico, 7341, 8266
Unleavened bread, 9645
An unofficial patriot, 9599
The unrevealed secret, 10640
Unruh, Conrad Max von, 1842-, 5551
Unseen hand, 10585
Unser Karl, 6975
Unsere Bischöfe, 14255
An unsophisticated exposition of
Calvinism, 16074
The unsummoned witness, 10953
Until the day break, 15736
Untold tales of California, 16513
The untold word, 10283
The unvarnished West, 17400
The unveiled heart, 11039
The unwelcome visitor, 14094
An unwritten chapter of Salt Lake, 1851-
1901, 16707
Up Broadway, 8530
Up-country letters, 10315
Up in the Blue Ridge, 11207
Up Primrose Hill, 9575
Up Terrapin River, 10598
Up the Coule, 9606
Upham, Charles Wentworth, 1802-1875, 77,
5552, 25783
Upham, Samuel Curtis, 1819-1885, 5553,
17805
Uplands and lowlands, 10556
Upon the death of the virtuous and
religious Mrs. Lydia Minot, 23730
The upper Ordovician rocks of Kentucky
and their bryozoa, 15067
Upper Sandusky, Ohio, 3451
The upper ten thousand, 8851
The uprising of a great people, 16580
Ups and downs in business, 10812
Ups and downs of a country cutter, 3410
Ups and downs of an army officer, 15868

Upshur, Abel Parker, 1790-1844, 11648
Upson, Theodore Frelinghuysen, 1845-1919,
5554
Upton, Charles Elmer, 17806
Upton, Emory, 14470
Uranie (corvette), 421, 422
Uranium, 19252, 19867; Brazil, 19379, 19380
Urban, John W., 5555
Urban dialogues, 10756
Urban education, Kentucky style, 14299
Urbanization, 20403; Guatemala, 20403;
Latin America, 18929, 20036
Urdaneta, Alberto, 1845-1887, 7683
Urdaneta, Rafael, 1788-1845, 8267
Urgência para conclusão da Brasília - Acre,
19528
Uribe Castejón, José Joaquín de, 7108
Uribe Echevarria, Juan, 18157
Urinary calculi, 15146
Uring, Nathaniel, 5556
Uroderma bilobatum, 18707
Urquizo, Francisco L., Tropa vieja, 19967
Urquhart, David, 1805-1877, 17807
Urquinaona y Pardo, Pedro de, fl.1820, 8268
Urrea, Blas [pseud.], 6268
Urrutia, Carlos de, 6756
Urrutia de Vergara y Estrada, Manuel, 5807
Urrutia, Francisco José, 1872-, 8269, 8270
Ursachen der amerikanischen concurrenz, 4462
Ursula, Saint, 22749
Ursulines, 5453, 22749
Urteaga, Horacio H., 5937
Uruguay, Description & travel, 1380, 2308,
12906, 22629; Economic conditions, 18850;
Foreign relations, Argentine republic,
1764; Foreign relations, Paraguay, 19783;
History, 1588, 19108, 20620; History,
1810-1930, 18850; History, 1830-, 1764,
22788; History, Comic, satirical, etc.,
20045; Politics & government, 19686;
Population, 19982; Religion, 18378
Uruguayan literature, 18071
Uruguayan poetry (collections), 18931
The useful man, 14242
The uses of solitude, 5521
Usina piloto de breu e terebintina, 18605
Uslar Pietri, Arturo, 1906-, 17987
Uso do microscópio electrônico de varredura
na observação de pelotas de minério de ferro,
18512
Usos e sentidos do têrmo "estrutura" nas
ciências humanas e sociais, 18904
Usseliux, Willem, 1567-1647?, 348
Usufruct (Roman law), 25946
Usurpation of the Senate, Two speeches of
Hon. Charles Sumner, 25655

Utah, 15994, 16410, 16881, 17550, 17771;
Admission of, 17907; Antiquities, 17636;
Bibliography, 17110; Bibliography,
Catalogs, 17791; Biography, 15983, 16299,
16334, 16429, 16479, 17626, 17761, 17762,
17846, 17856; Board of trade, 16803;
Centennial celebrations, etc., 17791;
Church history, 16189; Constitution,
16429, 17809; Description & travel,
1744, 2597, 2926, 2999, 3436, 3551, 3718,
3955, 4281, 4931, 5543, 5544, 15809,
15847, 15896, 15910, 16198, 16221, 16222,
16229, 16371, 16374, 16378, 16410, 16687,
16803, 16996, 17081, 17170, 17173, 17387,
17424, 17506, 17620, 17771, 17786, 17801,
17847; Description & travel, Guide-books,
3735; Description & travel, Views, 15872,
16969; Description & travel, Yearbooks,
17810; Directories, 16243, 17811, 17812,
17814; Economic conditions, 16486, 17065;
Geneal., 16479; History, 3074, 5175, 5525,
15809, 15847, 15882, 15930, 15931, 15932,
16140, 16147, 16304, 16312, 16322, 16332,
16334, 16350, 16592, 16659, 16675, 16703,
16707, 16708, 16714, 16751, 16864, 16889,
16904, 16913, 16922-16926, 17039, 17042,
17068, 17110, 17173, 17230, 17234, 17254,
17258, 17450, 17637, 17638, 17655, 17663,
17682, 17736, 17761, 17762, 17782, 17821,
17840, 17846, 17855, 17880, 17907, 17923,
17945; History, Period., 17813; History,
Sources, 15846, 16004, 16590, 16747,
17608, 17942; Maps, 15844, 15880, 15881,
17821; Militia, 17426; Politics &
government, 11881, 12887, 15991, 16141,
16811, 16913, 16939, 17079, 17275,
17483, 17538, 17548, 17551, 17784,
17809, 17815, 17816; Politics &
government, Handbooks, manuals, etc.,
16429; Politics & government, Satire,
17169; State prison, Salt Lake City,
17273; Statistics, 17808; Surveys, 5501
Utah Indian slavery, 17638
Utah Indians, 17343
Utah State Association of County Officials,
17810
Utah State Historical Society, 17813
Ute Indians, 16891, 17340, 17452, 17470,
17638
Utica, N.Y., Riots, 25683
Utilizaçåo e custo da energia elétrica,
19212
Utley, H.T., 25784
Utopias, 8775, 9247, 9695
Utterly wrecked, 10382
Uxmal, Mexico, 7655

V., Mary V., pseud., 2107
Vacaciones, 20648
A vacation tour in the U.S. and Canada,
5670
The vade mecum for America: or, A companion
for traders and travellers, 23511
Vadillo y Medina, Francisco, 8028, 8274
The vagabond, 8636
Vagaries of Vandyke Browne, 1437
Vague, Lexington, Xi Chapter of Chi Delta
Phi, University of Kentucky, 1946-1951,
15634
Vahl, S., 7803
Vail, Eugene A., 23731, 25785
Vail, Stephen Montford, 1818-1880, 25786
Val, Chagas, 18310
Val-Maria, 11029
Vala, 9628
Valbuena, Bernardo de, 1568-1627, 8271
Valcarce Velasco, Manuel Antonio, 8272
Valcarcel Esparza, Carlos Daniel, Biblio-
graphy, 19054
Valdano Morejón, Juan, 1939-, 20649
Valderrama Andrade, Carlos, 19816
Valdés, A., 19064
Valdés, Maximino, 8273
Valdés, Octaviano, 7235
Valdés Flores Banzán y Peón, Cayetano, 1767-
1835, 16477
Valdivia, Aniceto, 6720
Valdivia Altamirano, Juan, 19124
Valdivielso, José de, 1560-1638, 18060
Valdivieso y Torrejon, Miguel de, 8274-8277
Vale do Moxoto, 20000
The vale of Tempe, 13805
The vale of Yumuri, 8853
A valedictory discourse, delivered before the
Cincinnati of Connecticut, 22604
Valedictory letter to the trustees of
Dartmouth college, 12535
Valenciennes, Achille, 1794-1865, 7092
Valentino, 8590
Valenzuela, Francisco Ramirez de, d.1739,
8073
Valenzuela D., José, 6279
Valerie Aylmer, 10973
Valerius, Victor, 19340
Valette, Henry F., joint author, 23531
Valiente, Porfirio, 25787
Valladão, Alfredo, 1873-, 25788
Valladares de Sotomayor, Antonio, 3
Vallandingham, Clement Laird, 1820-1871,
7565
Vallandre, Leonel, 20213
Vallarna, Francisco Maria de, 8072, 8278
Valle, Juan N. del, 8279

Valle, Maria Teresa del, 18893
Valle, Rafael Heliodoro, 1891-, 7233, 7451, 8280
Valle, Vera Beltrão do, 19154
Valle Moré, José G. del, 1892-, 25789
Valle de la Juventud, Cuba, 18587
El valle de las hamacas, 18506
Vallejo, Antonio R., 8281
Vallejo, César Abraham, 1892-1938, 18297
Los valles interandinos, 18637
Valles y montañas de México, 7555
Vallette Laudun, de, 5557
The valley of Baca, 23316
The valley of peace, 10710
Valley of the Ohio, 13751
The valley of the Shenandoah, 5474
The valleys of Parnassus, 15076
Valli, Virginia, 18234
Vallmitjana, A., 19833
Valois, Alfred de, 8282
Valparaiso (City), History, 11347
Valuation of real estate, 15335
The value of a banana leaf, 9254
¡Vamonos con Pancho Villa!, 19967
Vampires, 9264
Van Arman H.M., 17817
Van Bibber, 9363
Van Bibber at the races, 9363
Van Bibber's man-servant, 9357, 9363
Van Buren, A. De Puy, 5558
Van Buren, John, 6568
Van Buren, Martin, pres., U.S., 1782-1862, 3123, 5559, 5906, 5914, 12849, 22462, 22857, 22934
Van Buren Co., Ia., 16375
Van Buskirk, Jacob Edwin, 1901-, 7428
Van Cleave, Horace W., 20212
Van Cleve, Benjamin, 1773-1821, 15635
Van Dorn, Earl, 1820-1863, 2068
Van Dyke, Henry Jackson, 1822-1891, 110, 11372, 12315, 25526, 25791
Van Dyke, John, 1807-1878, 24627, 25792, 25793
Van Dyke, Nicholas, 1769-1826, 25794
Van Dyke, Theodore Strong, 1842-, 17818, 17819
Van Evrie, John H., 1814-1896, 25796
Van Fleet, Donald, 13728, 15636, 15637
Van Horne, John Douglass, 8287, 25795
Van Meter family, 15640
Van Meter, Benjamin Franklin, 1834-, 15640, 25797
Van Ness, William Peter, 1778-1826, 21898, 23732
Van Ostrand, Ferdinand A., 1840-1877, 17820
Van Rensselaer, Cortlandt, 1808-1860, 25798

Van Rensselaer, Stephen, 1765-1839, 821
Van Sinderen, Adrian, 1887-, 8288
Van Texas naar Florida, 5589
Van Tramp, John C., 5561
Van Voorhis, J.S., 24223
Van Vorst, Bessie (McGinnis) "Mrs. John Van Vorst," 1873-1928, 5562, 5563
Van Vorst, Marie, 5563
Van Wart, Isaac, 1760-1828, 1175-1177
Van Wert Co., O., Biography, 6854; History, 6854
Van Wyck, Charles Henry, 1824-1895, 25799
Vancouver, George, 1758-1798, 6748, 7460, 8283
Vancouver, John, 8283
Vancouver Island, 6143, 6742, 7363, 7423, 16477, 17168, 23406; Council, 8284; Description, 6173, 6555, 7324, 7360, 7579, 8285, 8286, 8420; History, 12774; House of Assembly, 8285, 8286; Politics & government, 8284-8286
Vandalia, Ill., History, 7980
Vandenbosch, Amry, 14650
Vandenhoff, George, 1820-1885, 5560
The Vanderheyde manor-house, 9267
Vangrifter, Zachary Philemon, pseud., 10791
Vanlandingham, Kenneth E., 15638, 15639
Vannini de Gerulewicz, Maria, tr. and ed., 18994
Vanover, Frederic D., 15641
Vanquished, 9870
The vanquished life-dream, 9752
Vans, William, b.1763, 1884
Vaquero, pseud., 8289
Varela, Alfredo, 20625
Varela, Enriqueta, 20243
Varela Florencio, 1807-1848, 21761
Varela, James, 20301
Vargas, Elvira, 8290
Vargas Llosa, Mario, 1936-, 19109
Vargas Nariño, Enrique, 20308
Variações estacionais de preços, 19310
Varias relaciones del Perú y Chile y conquista de la isla de Santa Catalina, 8291
The varieties of love, 9795
The variety book containing life sketches and reminiscenses, 24413
Varios desnudos y dos docenas de naturalezas muertas, 18625
Varlo, Charles, 1725-1796?, 5564
Varnhagen, Francisco Adolpho de, visconde de Porto Seguro, 1816-1878, 582
Varon de deseos, 7673
Varona y Pera, Enrique José, 1849-, 7845
Varones ilustres en santidad, 5907

462

Varzea, Virgilio, 1865-, 20514
Vasconcelos, Jose, Ulises criollo, 19967
Vasek, Stephen J., 14667
Vasquez Aguirre, Isaac, 19170
Vasquez de Velasco, Pedro, 8292
Vassal, William, d.1655, 1886
Vassall family, 12702
Vassall family (William Vassall, 1590?-
  1655), 12702
Vassall Morton, 10475
Vater, Johann Severin, 1771-1826, 97
Vaughan, Benjamin, 8017
Vaughan, C. M., 14911
Vaughan, John Champion, 11487
Vaughan, Mary C., 11528
Vaughan family, 8017
Vaughn, C.R., 2746
Vaughn, Laurence Meredith, 15642
Vaughn, Neil, 15643
Vay, Péter, gróf, 1864-, 5565
Vázquez, Jesús María, 7872
Vázquez, Pedro Tomás, 1923-, 18019
Vázquez de Coronado, Francisco, 1510-1549,
  8293, 8294, 17563
Vázquez de Coronado, Juan, 1523-1565, 18852
Vázquez Santa Ana, Higinio, 1889-1962,
  18034
Veech, James, 1808-1879, 23733
Veer, Theo de, 8295
Vega, Alonso de la, 17th cent., 8296
Vega Bazán, Juan de, 7827
Vega y Mendoza, Francisco José de la, 8297
Vegetable gardening, 8705, 8706, 11086;
  Southern states, 23651; U.S., 11629;
  Varieties, 11629
The veiled doctor, 9365
Veinte canciones chilenas en versiones
  corales de diversos autores, 18686
Vela, David, 8298
Velarde Maass, Mario, 18768
Velas contra el viento, 18132
Velasco, Diego del, d.1648, 8299
Velasco, Juan de, 1727-1819, 8168, 23734
Velasco y Pérez, Carlos de, 1884-1923, 6522
Velásquez, César Vicente, 8300
Velázquez, Gonzalo, 18315
Velez de Escalante, Silvestre, fl.1708-1779,
  15844, 15846, 15880, 15881, 17821
O velho e a moça, 18384
Vellozo, José Mariano da Conceição, 1742-
  1811, 1128, 19241
Venable, Abraham Watkins, 1799-1876, 25800
Venable, Emerson, 1875-, 15644
Venable, William Henry, 1831-1920, 5566,
  5567, 25801
Vendors and purchasers, 1254

Venegas, Miguel, 1680-1764?, 17822, 17823
Venereal diseases, 726
A Venetian June, 9588
The Venetian marriage, 13213
A Venetian study in black and white, 8718
Venezuela, 2473, 19996, 21728; Archivo
  General de la Nación, 19485; Antiquities,
  19748; Bibliography, 17979, 19744, 19745;
  Church history, 20251; Commerce, 19845;
  Description & travel, 5319, 6028, 6471,
  6545, 7204, 7530, 8299, 8319, 12744, 18325,
  18389, 18537, 18543, 19169, 19635, 19639,
  19767, 22162; Description & travel, Poetry,
  18534; Dirección de Economía y Estadística
  Agropecuaria, 19113; Dirección de
  Planificación Agropecuaria, 11913; División
  de Estadística Vital, Informe especial,
  18178; Economic conditions, 18003, 18589,
  18734, 18775, 19499, 19502, 19846, 20102,
  20240, 20499-20501, 20646; Economic
  conditions, Sources, 18388; Foreign
  relations, 17982; Geography, 18537;
  Historical geography, 19822; History, 772,
  17981, 18535, 19537, 19589, 18846, 19169,
  19489, 19577, 19842, 20523; History, 1556-
  1772, 18036; History, To 1810, 6229,
  19905, 22195; History, To 1810, Sources,
  6793, 17980, 17988, 18536, 19855; History,
  1830-, 18130; History, Discovery
  and German occupation to 1556, 18036;
  History, Historiography, 19840, 19841;
  History, Miranda's expedition, 1806, 1278,
  1279, 1713, 6042, 23614; History, Period.,
  19751; History, Sources, 17978, 18389,
  19484; History, War of Independence, 1810-
  1813, 2396, 6629, 7014, 7635, 7637, 7664,
  7897, 8009, 8268, 12517, 18627, 19079,
  20251; History, War of Independence, 1810-
  1823, Confiscations and contributions,
  19521; History, War of Independence, 1810-
  1823, Sources, 6476, 6793, 17982, 17983,
  17987, 19738; Industries, 20503; Laws,
  statutes, etc., 19845, 25802; Ministerio
  de relaciones exteriores, 11514; Politics
  & government, 11514, 12088, 18540, 19035-
  19043, 19577, 19622, 19623; Politics &
  government, Addresses, essays, lectures,
  19075; Politics & government, Period.,
  6476; Politics & government, Sources, 6793;
  Population, 18571, 19846
Venezuela en los cronistas generales de
  Indias, 17988
Venezuela's agrarian reform at mid-1977,
  20639
Venezuelan drama, 19754
Venezuelan fiction, Bibliography, 19741

Venezuelan letters, 17983
Venezuelan literature, 19754; Bibliography, 18838, 19785; Collections, 18307, 20523; History & criticism, 18966, 19915, 20513
Venezuelan periodicals, Indexes, 18838
Venezuelan poetry, Bolívar (State), 18538; History & criticism, 18296, 19787
La venganza (motion picture), 18843
Venice, History, 697-1508, 1139, 1140; History, 1508-1797, Fiction, 11028; History, Fiction, 11028
Veniero, Francesco, doge of Venice, d. 1556, 25578
Ventilation, 23260
O vento solar, 20213
Venus (planet), Transit of, 1769, 6400, 6401
Vera, pseud., 4277
Vera, Agustín, La revancha, 19967
Vera Cruz, Description & travel, 6171
Vera Cruz (City), Mexico, Hospitals, 6482
Vera Cruz (State), Mexico, 7589; Description & travel, 6959
Verbrugghe, Georges, 5568
Verbrugghe, Louis, 5568
La verdad, y la justicia, 6584
Verdadera idea de la primera campaña de Tejas, 4405
Verdadera medicina, cirurgía, y astrología, 6012
Verdadera relacion: de lo sussedido en los Reynos e provincias del Peru, 122
Verdades del barquero, 19163
Verdugo, Pomposo, 12509
Verdugo Marinkovic, Mario, 20140
Die Vereinigten Staaten von Amerika, 4581
Die Vereinigten Staaten von Nordamerika, 2873
Die Vereinigten Staaten von Nordamerika im Jahre 1852, 4653
Verhoeff, Mary, 15645, 15646
Veríssimo, Erico, 1905-, 8301
La vérité sur la révolution actuelle au Mexique, 1825
Vermejo River, 437
Vermilion Co., Ill., 16226
Vermont, 162, 23801; Biography, 22290; Constitution, 25840; Description and travel, 12341; Description & travel, Gazetteers, 12767; General assembly, 23153, 25803; History, 1036, 1770, 11673, 11752, 12919, 23696, 23801; History, To 1791, 162, 175-178, 12559, 21912, 22290; History, Civil war, 1149, 12472
Vermont Colonization Society, 24200

Vermont Historical Society, 1770
Vermont infantry, 10th regt., 1862-1865, 3823; Vt. brigade, 1861-1865, 5600
Vernon, Edward, 1684-1757, 573, 1829, 23735
Vernon, Francis V., 23736
Vernon, Ruth, pseud., 10585
Vernon in the value, 9842
Verot, Augustine, bp., 1804-1876, 25804
Verplanck, Gulian Crommelin, 1786-1870, 1904, 10697, 23573, 25535
Verrazzano, Giovanni da, 1485?-1527, 22285
Verrill, Alpheus Hyatt, 1871-, 5569, 8302
Vers le coeur de l'Amérique, 5594
Versailles, Ky., 15769; History, Fiction, 9904
Verse with news significance, 14408
Verses of a life time, 3607
Versoïdes, 20235
Versuch einer getreuen schilderung der republik Mejico, 7548
Versuch über den politischen zustand der Vereinigten Staaten von Nord-Amerika, 5094
Vertebrates, Fossil, 4246
Verzura, Jose Abel, 19547
Vespucci, Amerigo, 1451-1512, 582, 7567; Bibliography, 17951
O vestibulo, 19696
Vesty of the basins, 9657
The veteran of the Grand Army, 9049
Veterans, 14618
Veterinary colleges, U.S., 1622
Veterinary medicine, 19603; Early works to 1800, 13224
Vethake, Henry, 1792-1866, 23737
Veto, 23240
Vi titta på Amerika, 5015
Via crucis, 9235
Via media, 25891
Viage a Méjico, 6765
Viagem ao Mexico, 6475
Viaggio negli Stati Uniti dell' America Settentrionale, 2940
Viaje a Yucatán, 8109
Viaje argentino, 18957
Viaje de indios y diario del Nuevo México, 7536
Viaje por los Estados Unidos del Norte, 4938
El viajero en México, 8279
Los viajes de Cockburn y Lièvre por Costa Rica, 8303
Viajes de fray Alonso Ponce al occidente de México, 18185
Viajes de vacaciones, 5949
Viajes en Europa, Africa i America, 5073
Viajes y estancias en América del Sur, 7264
The vial poured out upon the sea, 22717

Vianzone, Thérèse, 5570
Viaud, Julien, 1850-1923, 7119
The vice president's daughter, 11048
Vicich, Mollie, 14870, 15647
Vicissitudes exemplified, 3278
Vicissitudes in both hemispheres, 9506
The vicissitudes of life, 8891
Vickers, William B., 1838-, 16782
Vickery, Oliver, 15648
Vicksburg, Siege, 1863, 2033, 4143; Fiction, 10054
Vicksburg, Miss., History, 24590
The victim of excitement, 3848
The victim of intrigue, 10929
As victimas-algozes, quadros da escravidão, 23003
The victims of gaming, 11042
The victims of revenge, 10670
Victor, Benjamin, d.1778, 2986, 21910
Victor, Mrs. Frances (Fuller) 1826-1902, 17824-17827
Victor, Orville James, 1827-1910, 8304, 17828
Victor, William B., 15649
Victor La Tourette, 11102
Victoria, Paulo de, 8305
The victorious, 6083
A victorious defeat, 8666
Victory (ship), 7911
Victory turned into mourning, 13114
Vicuña Cifuentes, Julio, 1865-1936, 5967
Vicuña Mackenna, Benjamin, 1831-1836, 5892
A vida de D. Pedro II, 19642
La vida económica de Mexico de 1824 a 1867 y sus proyecciones, 19069
La vida en México, 6273
La vida es sueño (versión moderna), 18002
Vida politica de Caracas en el siglo XIX, 18540
Vida salobra, 19876
Vidal Ladrón de Guevara, Juan José, 8306
Vidart, Daniel D., 18606
Vidart, Luis, 1833?-1897, 7306
Vidrio soplado, 18210
La vie aux États-Unis, 3407
La vie du R.P. Pierre Joseph Marie, 11762
Vieira Neto, Manoel Augusto, 19335
Los viejos olivos, 18101
Viele, Teresa (Griffin) "Mrs. E.L. Viele", 1832-, 17829
El viento en la pared, 21748
Viento sobre las aguas, 19237
Vier wege durch Amerika, 8178
Viermund, Alvera von, 1617-1649, 1189
Le vieux Salomon, 5363
A view of religions, 54

A view of South Carolina, 3298
A view of the American slavery question, 888
A view of the controversy between Great Britain and her colonies, 23588
A view of the Dutch trade in all the states, empires, and kingdoms in the world, 12988
A view of the past and present state of the island of Jamaica, 25620
A view of the political conduct of Aaron Burr, esq., vice-president of the United States, 21899
A view of the relative situation of Great Britain and the United States, 1329
A view of the trade of South Carolina, 5788
View of the U.S., historical, geographical, and statistical, 3174, 3825
View of the valley of the Mississippi, 2595
A view of the whole ground, 22791
A view of West Florida, 23798
Views and descriptions of Burlington & Missouri river railroad lands, 16098
Views and reviews in American literature, history and fiction, 5165
Views around Ithaca, 11838
Views in New Haven and its vicinity, 792
Views of American slavery, 1158
Views of Louisiana, 2779
Views of society and manners in America, 3175
Views of the public debt, 12188
Vieyra, Antonio, 881
Viger, Jacques, 25805
Vigil, José Maria, 1829-1909, 7873
The vigil of Fenton Barlowe, 10283
Vigilance committees, 16392, 16980; Indiana, 23460; Louisiana, 15911
Vigilante days and ways, 16980
Vigilia en pie de muerte, 18669
Vigne, Godfrey Thomas, 1801-1863, 5571, 8307
Vigneaux, Ernest, 8308
Vignettes of American history, 22583
Vignoles, Charles Blacker, 1793-1875, 5572
Vigornius, pseud., 25806
Villa, Francisco, 1877-1923, 17634, 19650
Villa y Hano, Antonio de, 7108, 7909
Village choir, Memoirs of a, with occasional reflections, 9620
The village doctors, 8585
A village Lear, 9575
Village life in New England, 8768, 11949
The village musician, 14242
A village Ophelia, 8496
The village school mistress, 9702
A village shop, 10037
A village singer, 9575
A village Stradivarius, 11162

The village watch-tower, 11162
Villalba-Villalba, Luis, 20708
Villar y Andrade, José del, conde del
  Villar de Fuentes, 6657, 8278
Villar y Zubiaur, Pedro de, 7495, 8306
Villard, Henry, 1835-1900, 5573
Villarreal, Francisco Joaquín de, b.1691,
  8309
Villareal, Jaime A., 20244
Villasenor y Sánchez, José Antonio de,
  8310
Villaverde, Juana, 7495, 8306
Villebois, Pierre, 22749
Villegagnon, Nicolas Durand de, 1510-1571,
  7268
Villegas, Antonio Claudio de, b.1700,
  8311
Villegas, Francisco de, 8312
Villettes, William Anne, 1754-1808, 11440
Villiot, Jean de, pseud., 25807
La viña estéril, 18511
Vince, Samuel, 1749-1821, 23498
Vincennes, Ind., History, 4229, 15391,
  17001; History, Fiction, 10961; History,
  Revolution, 21938
Vincennes Historical and Antiquarian
  Society, Vincennes, Ind., 17001
Vincent, Mrs. Elizabeth Kipp, 8313
Vincent, Marvin Richardson, 1834-1922, 8314
Vincent, Ralph Waterman, 8315
Vincenzi, Atilio, 20590
Vinde, Victor, 5574
Vindex, pseud., 25808
Vindex on the liability of the abolitionists
  to criminal punishment, 25808
Vindicación del juez circuito de Sonora,
  12509
The vindication of John Banks, 13589
The vindication of N. Jekyll, esq., late
  captain of the 43d (or Monmouthshire)
  regiment, 22700
A vindication of the address, to the
  inhabitants of the British settlements,
  on the slavery of Negroes in America,
  25422
A vindication of the Bishop of Landoff's
  sermons, 13098
Vindication of the captors of Major
  André, 1175-1177
Vindication of the character of the late
  Col. Solomon P. Sharp, 5129
Vindication of the General Assembly of the
  Presbyterian Church (O.S.), of 1866,
  25594
A vindication of the government of New-
  England churches, 23813

A vindication of the measures of the present
  administration, 12349
A vindication of the measures of the President
  and his commanding generals, in the
  commencement and termination of the
  Seminole war, 23481
A vindication of the negotiators of the
  treaty of 1783, 12617
A vindication of the Protestant Episcopal
  church, in a series of letters addressed
  to the Rev. Samuel Miller, D.D., 22577
A vindication of the result of the late
  Mutual Council convened in Princeton, 732
A vindication of the validity and divine
  right of Presbyterian ordination, 23775
Viñetas, 8077
Vingt années de la vie d'un négrier, 24187
Vingut, Mrs. Gertrude (Fairfield), 25809
Vinson, Frederick Moore, 1890-1953, 13571
Viola, 10741
Violación de correspondencia, 18047
Violación de los derechos humanos por la
  legislación comunista de Castro, 18184
Violanta Cesarina, 11183
The violet, 10308, 10758
Violets, 8764
Viollet-le-Duc, Eugène Emmanuel, 1814-1879,
  6408
Virgin Islands of the U.S., Bibliography,
  18672
Virginia, 1231, 1232, 4050, 4395, 24607;
  Bibliography, 15140; Biography, 12440,
  12441, 15296; Boundaries, 23483, 23733;
  Boundaries, North Carolina, 2878, 5188,
  11656; Charters, 11748; Church history,
  4431, 24820; Circuit Court (Jefferson Co.),
  13386; Constitution, 11985; Constitutional
  convention, 1829-1830, 12441; Court of
  Appeals, 7101; Description & travel, 1198,
  2646, 2771, 2773, 2852, 2890, 2959, 2983,
  2985, 3071, 3089, 3325, 3340, 3342, 3404,
  3425, 3426, 3446, 3490, 3516, 3519, 3568,
  3603, 3614, 3628, 3663, 3720, 3722, 3737,
  4071, 4108, 4719, 4822, 4998, 5147, 5173,
  5204, 5232, 5473, 5601, 5623, 5630, 5632,
  5688, 5712, 5749, 5768, 6463, 8360, 8363,
  11656, 13301, 14370, 14749, 14845, 15527,
  17902, 21943, 22580, 23774; Description &
  travel, Gazetteers, 3351, 4404, 22166;
  Description & travel, Maps, 5204; Economic
  conditions, 2852, 14098, 15611, 24391;
  Fiction, 5476, 8758, 8759, 9766, 9770,
  9894, 10686, 10807, 24341, 24608, 25191;
  Finance, 17580; General Assembly, 1798-1799,
  15650; General Assembly, House of Delegates,
  23912, 25810; Governor, 8316; History, 486,

2601, 3500, 7146, 7247, 8019, 8051,
11985, 13739, 13809, 14303, 15640,
15678, 16218, 22580, 23555, 25597;
History, Bibliography, 14292; History,
Civil war, 1849, 1850, 2727, 3969;
History, Colonial period, 768, 1198,
1231, 1232, 2242, 3221, 3494, 3727,
3765, 4070, 4623, 4934, 4947, 5204,
5205, 5252, 5296, 5632, 6761, 9917,
11613, 12627, 22288, 22677, 23676,
23713; History, Colonial period,
Fiction, 2923, 3189, 8943, 9111, 9630;
History, Colonial period, Registers,
list, etc., 15651; History, Colonial
period, Sources, 4378; History,
Fiction, 8903, 9571; History, Local,
22580; History, Revolution, 3659, 11613;
History, Revolution, Fiction, 9104;
History, Sources, 14168; Laws, statutes,
etc., 1686, 21908, 24715, 25776; Maps,
14183, 22288; Politics & government,
5906, 5913, 5914, 7838, 12441;
Politics & government, 1775-1865,
12596, 13452, 23015, 24483; Politics &
government, Civil war, 25096; Politics
& government, Colonial period, 3805;
Politics & government, Revolution, 1955,
12440; Public lands, 7985; Social
conditions, 15611; Social life &
customs, 660, 2785, 3957, 4658, 5023,
23493, 25189; Social life & customs,
Colonial period, 4966; Social life &
customs, Fiction, 9116; State Library,
14292; State library, Dept.
of archives and history, 15651;
Statistics, 3351, 22166; University,
Society of Alumni, 11638, 24470
Virginia, daughter of Virginia, Drama,
19626
Virginia, daughter of Virginius, 24981
Virginia, her past and her future, 2601
Virginia, Tennessee and Georgia air line,
5576
Virginia, the new dominion, 5023
Virginia after the war, 3071
Virginia artillery, Carpenter's battery,
1861-1865, 3493; Chew's battery, 1861-
1865, 4582; Parker battery, 1862-1865,
3444; Richmond howitzers, 1859-1865,
3166, 5575; Rockbridge battery, 1861-
1865, 4508; Surry light artillery, 1861-
1865, 4099
The Virginia Bohemians, 9115
Virginia cavalry, 43d battalion, 1863-1865,
3114, 5107; 6th regt., 1861-1865, 4655;
9th regt., 1861-1865, 2656

Virginia cavalry (Union) Loudoun rangers,
1862-1865, 3637
The Virginia chronicle: with judicious and
critical remarks, 24820
Virginia (Colony) Commissioners on North
Carolina boundary, 1728-1729, 11656
Virginia (Colony) Commissioners to lay out
the bounds of the northern neck, 1736,
11656
Virginia (Colony) General assembly, 11691
The Virginia comedians, 9116
The Virginia convention of 1776, 12440
The Virginia convention of 1829-30, 12441
A Virginia cousin, 9773
Virginia Historical Society, Richmond, 12441,
23541
Virginia History in Documents, 1621-1788,
14168
Virginia impartially examined, 2852
Virginia infantry, 5th regt., 1861-1865,
4655; 6th regt., 1861-1865, 2961; 8th
regt., 1861-1865, 5148; 11th regt., 1861-
1865, 4525; 12th regt., 1861-1865, 2830;
33d regt., 1861-1865, 2935; 56th regt.,
1861-1865, 12837
Virginia of Virginia, 5467
A Virginia raid in 1906, 5988
Virginia Society for Promoting the
Abolition of Slavery, 25232
Virginia State Agricultural Society, 24617
The Virginia tourist, 4822
Virginia White Sulphur Springs, 4515
Virginia's discovery of silke-wormes, 23797
A Virginian, 24572
A Virginian, pseud., 315
A Virginian, now a citizen of New York,
12366
The Virginian orator, 13667
The Virginians in Texas, 8660
Virginie: a tale of the slave-trade: and
other poems, 24666
Virginius (steamer), 8328
Virgo triumphans, 5713
Viriato, Santos Gaspar, 1952-, 18310
Virtue and vice contrasted, 10068
Virtue in war, 9217
A virtuoso's collection, 9823
Visão panoramica dos Estados Unidos, 2918
Viscardo y Guzman, Juan Pablo, 1713
Vischer, Edward, 17830, 17831
Visconti-Venosta, Enrico, marchese, 1883-,
5577
The visible church, in covenant with God:
or, An inquiry into the constitution of
the visible Church of Christ, 23332
The vision, and other poems, 11457

The vision of All Souls' Hospital, 10810
The vision of Columbus, 819
The vision of judgment, 13353, 25408
The vision of Randalthus, 9551
A vision of the fountain, 6978, 9827
Visit Honduras, 7680
The visit of the merchants and manufacturers
  of Philadelphia to "The World's exposition"
  at New Orleans, 5578
Visit Old Fort Harrod, 15165
Visit Panama, 7681
A visit to Canada and the U.S.A., 3555
A visit to Cincinnati, 10310
A visit to Louisville, 10310
A visit to Mexico, 4981
A visit to Mount Vernon, 10310
A visit to New-Orleans and the battle
  ground, 10310
A visit to North America and the English
  settlements in Illinois, 5668, 23774
A visit to St. Louis, 10310
A visit to Texas, 5579
A visit to the States, 5580
A visit to the U.S. in 1841, 5318
Visit to the vineyard, 10310
A visit to Uncle Tom's cabin, 24212
A visit to the wounded English officers,
  10310
Visitations, Ecclesiastical, Maryland, 1448
Visiting the sin, 10592
Visits and sketches at home and abroad,
  22675
Visits of state, Mexico, 19389; U.S., 19389
Visits to Brunswick, Georgia, and travels
  south, 5207
Vísperas de la luz, 20183
Visscher, William Lightfoot, 1842-1924,
  5581-5583, 15652, 17832
Viticulture, 23797; Argentine Republic,
  18458; Bourbon Co., Ky., 15771
Vitória, São Paulo, Brazil, 18352
Viva Mexico! 6746
Vive l'empereur, 2547
Vivian of Virginia, 9592
Vivian, Sir Arthur Pendarves, 1834-, 5584
Vivien, Louis, 1714-1756, 16956
Vivienda, 18413
La vivienda rural en Paraguana y en
  Margarita, 18009
Vivisection, 6031, 24812
Vizcaino, Sebastian, 1550?-1615, 17823
Vizcarrondo Coronado, Julio L. de, 1830-
  1889, ed., 23831
Vizetelly, Henry, 1820-1894, 17833
Vliet, Leonard van, 25911
Vocabulario jurídico, 20636

Vocabulario mexicano de Tetelcingo, 19479
Vocal music, Guatemala, History & criticism,
  18914
Vocal music, History & criticism, 18914
Vocational education, Argentine Republic,
  19538; Brazil, 18273, 19421, 20043;
  Kentucky, 13927
Las voces, 19823
As voces do morto, 19698
Voeu patriotique d'un américain, 8317
Vogt, Karl, 1817-1895, 23153
A voice from Kentucky, 412
A voice from Rebel prisons, 5585
A voice from the motherland, answering
  Mrs. H. Beecher Stowe's appeal, 21934
A voice from the past, 10740
A voice from the South, 4296
The voice of gratitude, 11317
Voice of nature, 1629
The voice of the people, 9626
The voice of the rod, 6918
The voice of the spirit, 10256
A voice of warning, and instruction to all
  people, or, an introduction to the faith
  and doctine of the Church of Jesus
  Christ of Latter Day Saints, 23507
A voice to the United States of America,
  from the metropolis of Scotland, 24338
Voina za nezavisimost' Meksiki, 18188
The volcano diggings, 10145
Volcanoes, Costa Rica, 19007; Mexico, 18187
Volck, Adalbert, John, 1828-1912, illus.,
  22957
Volksverband der bücherfreunde, Berlin, 7740
Vollmer, Carl Gottfried Wilhelm, d.1864,
  17834
Volney, Constantin François Chasseboeuf,
  comte de, 1757-1820, 5586
A Volunteer, pseud., 256/8
Volver de si misma, 20354
Vom Atlantischen zum Stillen Ocean, 2747
Vom Rhein zum Mississippi, 3981
Von Chicago nach Chungking, 5022
The Von Toodleburgs, 8462
Voorhees, Daniel Wolsey, 1827-1897, 5587
Voorhees, Harriet Cecilia, 5587
Voorhees, Luke, 8318, 16997
Voorhis, Robert, b.1769-70, 23715
Voting by proxy in charitable societies,
  24673
Vow fulfilled, 5664
Vowell, Richard Longeville, 8319
Voyage à la Louisiane, 2641
Voyage au Chile, 6930
Voyage au pays des mines d'or, 15889
Voyage au pays des Osages, 3092

Voyage aux Antilles, françaises, anglaises, danoises, espagnoles, 24509
Voyage aux prairies osages, 5425
Voyage d'Amérique, 11408
Voyage dans l'Amérique Septentrionale, 13896
Voyage dans l'intérieur des États-Unis, 2646
Voyage dans les Etats-Unis d'Amérique, 4220
Voyage dans les parties sud de l'Amérique septentrionale, 946
Voyage dans les solitudes américaines, 16405
Voyage des capitaines Lewis et Clarke, 22233
Voyage en Amérique, en Italie, en Sicile et en Egypte, 4507
Voyage fait dans les années 1816 et 1817, 4506
Voyage in a six-oared skiff to the Falls of Saint Anthony in 1817, 17049
Voyage of George Clark, 3019
Voyage of the paper canoe, 2724
Voyage pittoresque et archéologique dans la partie la plus intéressante du Mexique, 7570
A voyage to California, 6401
A voyage to Georgia, 4509
A voyage to Mexico and Havana, 799
A voyage to South America, 2308
A voyage to the moon, 5475
A voyage to Virginia, 4623
A voyager's letters from Mexico, 7508
The voyages, dangerous adventures and imminent escapes of Captain Richard Falconer, 2987
Voyages, relations et mémoirs originaux pour servir à l'histoire de la découverte de l'Amérique, 21826, 22640, 23445, 23652
Voyages, travels and discoveries of Tilly Buttrick, jr., 2874
The voyages and adventures of Capt. Barth. Sharp, 21765
The voyages and adventures of Captain Robert Boyle, 2986
The voyages and adventures of the Chevalier Dupont, 8320
Voyages and discoveries of the companions of Columbus, 13109
Voyages and travels, 2, 211, 387, 420, 582, 1589, 1611, 1612, 1682, 1777, 1979, 1981, 2301, 2819, 2874, 2927, 3019, 4146, 4198, 4209, 4227, 4637, 4678, 4751, 4887, 5128, 5556, 5920, 6154, 6162, 6256, 6390, 7556, 7646, 7842, 8179, 8212, 9488, 9829, 11424, 11576, 11624, 11749, 11820, 11867, 11945, 12067, 12137, 12841, 13142, 13440, 16158, 16326, 16567, 16886, 17653, 21963,

22035, 22280, 22285, 22358, 22421, 22639, 22421, 22639, 22651, 22789, 22941, 23232, 23378, 23494, 23627, 23736, 24726; Bibliography, 11749; Collections, 64, 23019; Collections, Bibliography, 495
Voyages and travels of a sea officer, 23736
Voyages around the world, 421, 422, 423, 1221, 1967, 2838, 3249, 4678, 5166, 6059, 6527, 6600, 8014, 8283, 12609, 13453, 13454, 15973, 16228, 16981, 17040, 22035, 22041, 22280, 22516, 22740, 22741, 22759, 23533, 23549, 23620
Voyages chez différentes nations sauvages de l'Amérique Septentrionale, 13397
Voyages dans les parties intérieures l'Amérique, 347, 5895
Voyages du baron de Lahontan dans l'Amérique Septentrionale, 7225
Voyages du Capitaine Robert Lade, 4198
Voyages du r.p. Emanuel Crespel, 6512
Voyages d'un François, 3325
Voyages en California et dans l'Orégon, 17546
Les voyages et aventures du capitaine Robert Boyle, 21910
Voyages et aventures du chevalier de, 8321
Voyages from Montreal, 4362
Voyages made in the years 1788 and 1789, 17168
Voyages of the slavers St. John and Arms of Amsterdam, 1659, 1663, 25168
Voyages to the Pacific coast, 4524, 5125, 5351, 8157, 8158, 8406, 8407, 15921, 16145, 16253, 16657, 16709, 16736, 16886, 17007, 17477, 21775
Voyages, Imaginary, 2986, 9551, 10735, 21910
Le voyageur américain, 6435
Vries, Hugo de, 1848-1935, 5588, 5589
Vucko de Goy, Matilde, 20243
Vue de la colonie espagnole du Mississippi, 1206
El vuelo de las horas, 18216
Vues d'Amerique, 2489
Vues et souvenirs de l'Amerique du Nord, 2939
Vues pittoresques de la Jamaïque, 1035

Waage, Chris M., 16417
The Wabash, 1220
Wabash Valley, 16470; History, 3102, 5687
Wabshutt, Robert, fl.1754-1758, 805
Wachtmeister, Hans, greve, 1828-1905, 5590
Wachusetts (U.S. steamer), 2051

Waco Baptist Association, Texas, 17838
Wacousta, 10670
Waddel, John Newton, 1812-1895, 5591
Waddle, Angus L., 1826?-, 5591
Wade, Benjamin Franklin, 1800-1878, 6288
Wade, Charles T., illustr., 14897, 15533
Wade, Edward, 1803-1862, 25812
Wade, Mark Sweeten, 8322
Wade, Mrs. May A. (Thompson), 10962
Wadsworth, James Samuel, 1807-1864, 11704
Wadsworth, Samuel, 1630?-1676, 11421
Wadsworth's map of Cariboo, Saskatchewan,
  Nez Percés and Salmon River gold fields,
  5593
Waechter, Carl Georg von, 1797-1880, 24962
Waerdenburgh, Dirk van, 8323
Wage-hour laws, 14675
Wager of battle, 9851
Wages, U.S., 2338
Wages or the whip, 2019
Waggeries and vagaries, 1747
Wagnalls, M., 10448
Wagner, Charles, 1852-1918, 5594
Wagner, Henry Raup, 5739, 17835
Wagner, Moritz, 1813-1887, 5595, 8324
Wagner-Bousquet, Elvira, baroness, Fiction,
  19482
Wagon road, 2652
Wagon road from Fort Defiance to the Colorado
  River, 2653
The Wagonauts abroad, 3261
Wah-to-yah and the Taos trail, 2411
Wahlgren, Sue F., 15653
A waif of the plains, 6979
A waif of the war, 3263
Waifwood, 10883
Waiilatpu, its rise and fall, 1836-1847,
  16142
Waikna, 8098, 13485
Wait and see, 10469
Wait, Frona Eunice, pseud., 9067
Wait, Marvin, 1843-1862, 2169
Wakefield, 9827
Wakefield, Edward Gibbon, 1796-1862, 6648
Wakefield, John Allen, 1797-1873, 5596
Wakefield, Mrs. Priscilla (Bell) 1751-1832,
  8325
Wakefield Anti-slavery Association,
  Wakefield, Eng., 24625
Wakefield Standley, a story of the flag,
  25872
Wakeman, George, 24230
Wakona-Kariri-Yukuru, 18313
Wakondak, 10326, 23346
Walcot, James, 5597
Walcott, Charles Folsom, 5598

Walcutt, illustr., 10520
Walden, P.E., 2060
Walden, Treadwell, 1830-, 8326
Waldenfels, W., Freiherr von, 3264
Waldenses, 11188
Waldimar, 657
Der waldläufer, 1103
Waldo, Samuel Putnam, 1780-1826, 5599, 12761,
  23738
Waldo family, 13311
Waldron, Henry, b.1819, 25813
Wales, History, 7820
Walhalla, 9355
Walk in the still nights, 15654
Walker, Aldace F., 5600
Walker, C. B., 15655
Walker, Courtenay J., 15656
Walker, David, 17837
Walker, David, 1785-1830, 25814, 25815
Walker, Edwin C., 8327
Walker, Francis Amasa, 1840-1897, 23739
Walker, Frank H., 14906
Walker, G. A., Dr., 9331
Walker, George Leon, 1830-1900, 25816
Walker, Henry Augustus, d.1839, 2101
Walker, James, 25817
Walker, James Lafayette, 1851-, 17838
Walker, Jeanie Mort, 8328
Walker, Jonathan, 1799-1878, 24007, 24651,
  24732, 25818
Walker, Joseph R., 16926
Walker, Robert James, 1801-1869, 8329, 17119,
  25819
Walker, Mrs. Rosa (Kershaw), 7753
Walker, Thomas, 1715-1794, 5601, 8330, 13747,
  13955, 14467, 15642, 15763
Walker, Timothy, 1806-1856, 5602
Walker, Tom I., 15658
Walker, William, 23439, 24463
Walker, Wilma J., 15659
Walker (Yawheraw), Chief of Utes, 17470,
  17855
The Walker Foxhound, 15657
Walker's Texas division (C.S.A), 2737
The walking doll, 10419
Wall, Bennett H., 15660
Wall, Garret Dorset, 1783-1850, 25820
Wall, James Walter, 1820-1872, 25821
Wall, Maryjean, 15661
Wall, Moses, 23068
Wall street, 461, 2295, 10004
Wall-street to Cashmere, 22639
Wallace, Caleb, 1742-1814, 15703
Wallace, Daniel, d.1859, 8331, 25822
Wallace, Dillon, 1863-, 8332
Wallace, Frances Jane (Todd), 1817-1899, 15662

Wallace, Frederick T., 16501
Wallace, Jack C., 15663
Wallace, Lewis, 1827-1905, 17839
Wallace, Susan Elston, 2582
Wallace, William Alexander Anderson, 1816-1899, 3330
Wallace, William Ross, 1819-1881, 5603
Wallace, William Ross, 1865-, 17840
Wallace, William Stewart, 1884-, 8333
Wallen, Henry Davies, 5544, 5604
Wallen, S., illustr., 4403
Waller, Edwin, 1800-1883, 17365
Waller, James Breckinridge, 1817-, 25824
Wallin, Ruth, 18815
Wallingford, Conn., History, 11952
Wallis, Severn Teackle, 1816-1894, 23214
Wallon, Henri Alexandre, 1812-1904, 25825
Walpole, Horatio Walpole, baron, 1678-1757, 23740
Walls, David, 15664
Walls: res sanctae/res sacrae, 13577
The Walltown, Kentucky, meteorite, 14048
Walnut, Seedlings (Weed control for), 14804
Walnut Hill Presbyterian Church, Fayette, Co., Ky., 14457, 15325
Walsh, Robert, 1784-1859, 293, 294
Walsh, Thomas, 1875-1928, 5605
Walsh, William Shepard, 1854-1919, 8334
Walter, John, 1818-1894, 5606
Walter, Thomas, 1696-1725, 985, 21890
Walter, Thomas Ustick, 1804-1887, 12276
Walter, William, 1737-1800, 912
Walter Colebrooke, 9492
Walter Warren, 9432
Walter Wilson, 9702
Walters, Charles, 17954
Waltham, Mass., Geneal., 21801
Walton, Blaine C., 15665
Walton, John, 1816?-1860, 13188
Walton, William, d.1668, 12006
Walton, William, 1784-1857, 1020
Walton Co., Ga., 22237
Walworth, Reuben H., 8335
Walty, Mrs. Elizabeth (Cherry) 1866-1903, 15666, 15667
Wamesit Indians, 197
Wampanong Indians, Missions, 23394, 23790
The wanderer in America, 8390
Wandering Jew, 11054
The wandering Jew in America, 9071
The wandering philanthropist: or, Letters [!] from a Chinese, 9552
Wanderings in Mexico, 6856
Wanderings in the western land, 5584
Wanderings north and south, 11329

Wanderings of a vagabond, 4635, 15034
Wanderings of an artist among the Indians of North America, 4130
Wanderjahre in Mexiko, 7232
Wanderley, João Mauricio, barão de Cotegipe, 1815-1889, 25826
Wanderungen durch die mittelamerikenischen Freistaaten Nicaragua, Honduras und San Salvador, 7974
Wanderungen durch die prairien und das nordliche Mexiko, 6895
Wanderungen eines jungen norddeutschen durch Portugal, Spanien und Nord-Amerika, 3228
Wanderungen in Mexico, 7169
Wanderungen zwischen Hudson und Mississippi, 2866
Wansey, Henry, 1751-1827, 23741
Wanted: a chaperon, 9762
Wanted, a match maker, 9539
Wanton, Mrs. Abigail, 1735?-1771, 1360
Wappäus, Johann Eduard, 1812-1879, 8336
Wappinger Indians, Wars, 1655-1660, 11518
War, 1037, 1277, 2151, 11370, 12072, 13130, 13187, 22292, 23963, 24661; Cost of, 1949, 21861; Maritime (International law), 941, 12744, 22009, 22342, 22379, 22990, 23011, 23144, 23145
War and peace: the evils of the first, and a plan for preserving the last, 13187
The war and slavery and their relations to each other, 889
The war between the U.S. and Mexico, 4151
War cook book, 15494
A war correspondent's field notebook, 6750
A war debt, 10038
War diary of Rodney W. Torrey, 5438
The war dreams, 10608
War experiences and the story of the Vicksburg Campaign, 4143
The war in Florida, 4836
The war in Kansas, 11512
The war in Texas, 17066, 24915
War letters of a disbanded volunteer, 8693
War letters of William Thompson Lusk, 4317
War memories, 9217
War of races, 12265
The war of slavery upon the constitution, 24314
War of the metals, 7610
War of the rebellion, 3498
War-path and bivouac, 16515
War pictures from the South, 3395
War poems, 22017
War power of the President, summary imprisonment, habeas corpus, 22397
The war revenue bill, 13604

War-ships, 1218
War stories and school-day incidents for the children, 5800
War the work of the Lord, 14317
The war-time journal of a Georgia girl, 1864-1865, 2544
A war-time wooing, 10131
The war widow, 9567, 9570
Warbler, Forest, pseud., 10267
Warburton, Alexander Bannerman, 1852-1929, 8337
Warburton, George Drought, 1816-1857, 8338
Ward, Anna Bell, 1897-, 7551
Ward, Charles James, 7114
Ward, Emily Elizabeth (Swinburne) lady, 8339
Ward, George Atkinson, 11923
Ward, Henry, 14044
Ward, Sir Henry George, 1797-1860, 8340, 8341, 8342
Ward, Herbert Dickinson, 1861-, 11069, 11074
Ward, J.H.H., 8381
Ward, James Warner, 1817?-1897, 5607
Ward, Jonathan, 1769-1860, 25827, 25828
Ward, Joseph Ripley Chandler, 1845-, 5608
Ward, Mary Augusta ("Mrs. Humphry Ward") 1851-1920, 7119
Ward, Nahum, 1785-1860, 23742
Ward, Nathaniel, 1578-1652, 22057, 23743, 23744
Ward, S. D., 25368
Ward, Sally, 1827-189-, 13661
Ward family, 14363, 22057
A ward of Colonel Starbottle's, 6977
A ward of the Golden Gate, 6980
Warden, David Baillie, 1772-1845, 5609, 12422, 13156, 23745, 23746
Warden refuted, 13156
Wardlaw, Ralph, 1779-1853, 25928
The wardman's wooing, 9533
The wards of Mount Vernon, 10814
Ware, Eugene Fitch, 1841-1911, 5610, 17841
Ware, Mrs. Mary Lovell (Pickard) 1798-1840, 22286
Ware, Norman, 13567
Ware, Mass., History, 22633
Warehouses, 1608; Law and legislation, Confederate States of America, 2060; U.S., 12080
Warfel, Harry R., 15702
Warfield, Mrs. Catherine Ann (Ware) 1816-1877, 5611-5621
Warfield, Ethelbert Dudley, 1861-1936, 5622
Warhaffte Nachricht 3727
Warhafttige Historien einer Wunderbaren

Schiffart; vierte Schiffart von Ulrich Schmidel, 7977
Waring's peril, 10132
Warland, J.B., 15668
Warner, Anna Bartlett, 1820-1915, 11098, 11099
Warner, Charles Dudley, 1829-1900, 5623, 5624, 8343, 17842
Warner, Edward, 17324
Warner, Harry B., 25828
Warner, Helen Garnie, 1846, 5625
Warner, Hiram, 1802-1881, 25830
Warner, Oliver, 1818-1885, 23268
Warner, Samuel, 25831
Warner, Seth, 1743-1784, 21912
Warner, Wareham, 24223
A warning to lovers, 9538
The warnings of an Old Kentuckian to his fellow citizens on the danger of electing partisans of the old Court of appelas, 14822
Warnshuis, Abbe Livingston, 1877-1958, 25832
Warrau Indians, 23517
Warren, Edward, 5279
Warren, Edward L., 15669
Warren, Eliza (Spalding) 1837-1919, 17843
Warren, F. K., 17844
Warren, Gouverneur Kemble, 1830-1882, 4246, 5514, 5515, 5626, 5627, 17845, 23747
Warren, Henry Waterman, 1838-, 8344
Warren, Jack R., 15670
Warren, John, 1753-1815, 915
Warren, John C., 14011
Warren, John Collins, 1778-1856, 23991
Warren, Joseph, 1741-1775, 11571, 23748; Drama, 1707
Warren, Louis Austin, 1885-, 8345-8351, 15671
Warren, Mrs. Mercy (Otis) 1728-1814, 1423, 23749
Warren, Owen Grenliffe, 23750, 23751
Warren, Robert, 23752
Warren, Fort, 2479
Warren, Me., Geneal., 22164; History, 22164
Warren Co., Ky., 13592, 12610, 13613, 14214, 14220; Description, 13697; History, 14083; Maps, 14567
Warren Co., Tenn., History, 14237
Warrick Co. Lincoln route association, 8352
Warrum, Noble, 17846
Wars of the nineteenth century, 22011
Warwick, 11067
Warwick, R.I., History, 12322
Warwick of the Knobs, 14841
Was Abraham Lincoln a Christian?, 5922
Was he guilty?, 9450

Was he successful?, 10108
Was it a ghost?, 1474
Was it a postil?, 5222
Was it right to forgive? A domestic
  romance, 8745
Was she engaged?, 9076
Wasco Co., Or., 17053
Wash, W. A., 5628
Wash-A-Kie, chief of the Shoshones, 17678,
  17901
Washburn, Cadwallader Colden, 1818-1882,
  25833
Washburn, Emory, 1800-1877, 1500, 25834
Washburn, John Davis, 1833-1903, 16421
Washubrn, Robert Morris, 8353
Washburne, Elihu, Benjamin, 1816-1887,
  3487, 25835
Washington, Booker Taliaferro, 1859?-1915,
  25124, 25836, 25837
Washington, Bushrod, 1762-1829, 12903
Washington George, pres. U.S., 1732-1799,
  9, 43, 74, 476, 728, 730, 2367, 2885, 5629,
  5630, 5631, 5930, 6762, 6842, 6994, 7230,
  7432, 7577, 7832, 8232, 11818, 12116,
  12501, 13008, 13057, 13347, 13416, 15756,
  23753-23756, 25424; Addresses, sermons,
  etc., 5, 138, 143, 183, 216, 555, 713,
  729, 842, 851, 916, 949, 962, 982, 1069,
  1275, 1276, 1385, 1391, 1405, 1578, 1583,
  1643, 1734, 1739, 1769, 1968, 2020, 2330,
  7676, 11279, 11300, 11315, 11492, 11608,
  11633, 11835, 11891, 11898, 11906, 11971,
  12252, 12285, 12358, 12438, 12499, 12594,
  12708, 12710, 12723, 12809, 13030, 13242,
  13473, 21884, 21985, 22015, 22037, 22135,
  22176, 22213, 22214, 22249, 22276, 22385,
  22402, 22521, 22533, 22558, 22562, 22569,
  22616, 22655, 22809, 22814, 23002, 23022,
  23237, 23411, 23597, 23702, 23777, 23795;
  Anecdotes, 22430; Anniversaries, etc.,
  15751; Bibliography, 12925; Drama, 1293;
  Farewell address, 11270; Funeral and
  memorial services, 12413; Last illness
  and death, 22648; Music, 7058;
  Personality, 22887; Poetry, 228, 649,
  1799, 5868, 23702; Portraits, 2296;
  Religion, 12661, 22887
Washington, John, 13452
Washington, John M., 5167
Washington, Martha (Dandridge) Custis,
  1732-1802, 2083, 22430
Washington, Mary (Ball) 1708-1789, 2083,
  8167, 22430
Washington family, 1857, 13452
Washington Vita, Luiz, 19694
Washington, our example, 25471

Washington, D.C., 1475, 7610, 7867, 11229,
  12059, 15485; Capture by the British, 1814,
  12095, 13100; Churches, 13248; Daily
  morning chronicle, 8354; Description &
  travel, 2532, 2588, 3180, 4232, 5147,
  13087, 14847, 22580; Description & travel,
  Gazetteers, 4404; Description, Guide-books,
  12033; History, 6514, 16072; History, Civil
  war, 8461; Lincoln Memorial, 7299; Lincoln
  statue (Lincoln park), 6618; Maps, 4249;
  Old capitol, 5728; Ordinances, etc., 1686,
  25776; Public buildings, 25775; Public
  life, 1120, 12020, 12059, 12290, 23757;
  Social life & customs, 6188, 7389, 12020
Washington, Ky., History, 13658, 13659,
  14744
Washington (State), 5837, 6013, 16484, 17172;
  Description & travel, 2408, 3551, 3955,
  4549, 5270, 8403, 15869, 15876, 16408,
  17182, 17408, 17409, 17824, 17825;
  Description & travel, Guide-books, 3735;
  History, 15552, 16041, 16363, 17032, 17431;
  Politics & government, 16834, 16970
Washington (Ter.) Legislative Assembly,
  16484
Washington, Mt., N.H., 718
Washington, Treaty of, 1842, 1595, 2265,
  6259
Washington-Virginia Railway, 8051
Washington and the union, 7676
Washington as a camp, 11194
Washington benevolent society, Worcester,
  Mass., 1390, 1734, 12708
Washington benevolent society in the city
  of New York, 392, 22562
Washington benevolent society of Exeter,
  N.H., 22461
Washington benevolent society of Massachusetts,
  1275
Washington benevolent society of the county
  of Hampshire, Northampton, Mass., 962
Washington College, Lexington, Va., 23737
Washington Co., Idaho, History, 16705
Washington Co., Md. Committee of arrangement
  for the Elliot celebration, 1843, 12039
Washington Co., Neb., History, 15960
Washington Co., O., Description, 11976
Washington Co., Va., History, 16218
The Washington guide, 12033
Washington is a swell place!, 15485
The Washington Manor House, 5930
Washington society, Charleston, S.C., 13014
Washington Square, 7132
Washington territory, 17182
A Washington winter, 9313
Washington's birthday addresses, 13767

Washington's Expedition to the Ohio, 1st, 1753-1754, 5631, 16658
Washington's first battle, or Braddock's defeat, 10338
Washington's words to intending emigrants to America, 2863
Washoe Co., Nev., 8878, 16071
Washoe silver mines, Sketches of the, 3212
Wasserburg, Philipp, 1827-, 6074
Wastelands, Gt. Britain, 6789
Watanabe, S., 19134
The watchman, 9529
Water, 15330; Pollution, Kentucky, 15006
Water buffalo, 20286
Water conservation, Colombia, 20309
Water-drops, 10763
The water ghost and others, 8689
A water-logged town, 10808
Water power, 14114, 14741; Argentine Republic, Calchaqui Valley, 19981; Kentucky, 14751
Water-power electric plants, Paraiba do Sul watershed, 18164
Water quality, Brazil, Campinas, 19171; Lago de Maracaibo, 19179
Water resources, Kentucky, 15330
Water resources development, Paraiba do Sul watershed, 18164
Water-rights (international law), 19768
Water rights, Chile, 20138; Mexicali Valley, 19768
The water-spirit's bride and other poems, 2648
Water supply, Colombia, 20309; Kentucky, 14227, 15123, 15495; Mendoza, Argentine Republic, 19979; Mexico, Bibliography, 19085
Water, Underground, Mexico, Bibliography, 19085
Waterbury, Conn., 12724
Watergate scandal, 14666
Waterhouse, Edward, fl.1622, 5632
Waterhouse, Sylvester, 1830-1902, 5633
Watering places, etc., America, 4039
Waterloo, 10310
Waterman, Arba Nelson, 1836-1917, 25838
Waterman pamphlets, 23291
Waters, Mrs. Abigail (Dawes) 1721-1816, 13034
Waters, Thomas H., 3884
Waters, Wilburn, 1812-, 3033, 16218
Waters, William Elkanah, 1833-, 17847
The waters of Caney Fork, 4907
Watertown, Mass., Geneal, 21801; History, 2309, 21021
Watertown, Wis., City council, 23523;

Description, 23523
Waterways, Kentucky, 14549
Wates, Thomas Hill, 1819-1892, 24182
Watie, Stand, 1806-1871, 15854
Watkins, Albert, 1848-, 17237, 17260, 17848
Watkins, Arthur Vivian, 1886-, 17791
Watkins, Floyd C., 8355
Watkins, James, b.1821? 25839
Watkins, N. J., 5634
Watkins, Samuel R., 5635
Watkins, Tobias, 1780-1855, 192, 193
Watmough, Edward Coxe, 1821-1848, supposed author, 11109
Watrous, John Charles, 1806-1874, 12939, 21994
Watson, Edmund Henry Lacon, 1865-, 8356
Watson, Elkanah, 1758-1842, 5636, 11961
Watson, Henry Clay, 1831-, 15672
Watson, John, of Glasgow, 5637
Watson, John Henry, 1851-, 25840
Watson, Thomas Edward, 1856-1922, 15413
Watson, Thomas S., 15673-15675
Watson, William of Skelmorlie, Scotland, 5638
Watson, William J., 5639
Watson, Winston Cossoul, 1803-, ed., 5636
Watson family (George Watson, 1603?-1689), 11961
Watterson, George, 1783-1854, 23754
Watterson, Henry, 1840-1921, 5640, 5641, 15676
Watts, E. C., 15677
Watts, John C., 15066
Watts, William Courtney, 1830-1897, 5642
Wau-bun, the "early day" in the Northwest, 10141
Wauna, the witch-maiden, 10122
The Waverlian formations of east central Kentucky and their economic values, 15037
Way, Frederick, 13825
The way it all ended, 10030
The way it came, 7118, 10012
The way of the world and other ways, 9100
The way out, 14351
Way sketches, 5078
The way to the West, 14350
A wayfaring couple, 9575
Wayland, Francis, 1796-1865, 24456
Wayland, John W., 15678
Waylen, Edward, 5643
Wayman, James, 5644
Wayne, Anthony, 1745-1796, 6464; Fiction, 13542
Wayne Co., Ky., History, 15445
Ways and means, 10609
The ways of the hour, 9153
Wayside courtships, 9608

474

A wayside episode, 9355
Way-side glimpses, north and south, 2286
Way-side violets, 10584
We and our neighbors, 10911
We four villagers, 9541
Wealth, Ethics of, 23822
Wealth and wine, 8983
Wearing of the gray, 9117
Wearing out the carpet, 10598
Wearithorne, 10605
Weather and climate of the Barren River
  Area Development district, 13862
Weather in the Luquillo Mountains of
  Puerto Rico, 19492
The Weatherford, Hammond Collection of
  Berea College, 15139
Weaver, Rufus, 15679
Webb, Ben J., 15680
Webb, Charles Henry, 1834-1905, 9026
Webb, Edwin Bonaparte, 1820-1901, 8357
Webb, James Watson, 1802-1884, 5278,
  5645, 25841
Webb, Richard Davis, 25842
Webb, Samuel, 25225
Webb, Thomas Hopkins, 1801-1866, 5646,
  23370
Webb, William, 25843
Webb, William Bensing, 1825-1896, 6514
Webb, William Seward, 1851-, 17849
Webb, William Snyder, 1882-1964, 14151,
  15861
Webber, Charles Henry, 5647
Webber, Charles Wilkins, 1819-1856, 5648-
  5657, 15682
Webber, Horace Hervey, 11344
Weber, Max, 1864-1920, 17952
Webster, Daniel, 1782-1852, 207, 763, 925,
  1680, 8202, 11304, 12745, 12813, 13193,
  22367, 22369, 22693, 22834, 23125,
  23402, 23758-23760, 23990, 24076, 24674,
  24987, 25574, 25844-25847; Speech, on
  Mr. Clay's resolutions, March 7, 1850,
  24675; Speech on the subject of the
  northeastern boundary, April 15, 1843,
  12186
Webster, Kimball, 1828-1916, 17850
Webster, Noah, 1758-1843, 266, 328, 5658,
  15683, 23761, 23762
Webster, Pauline Tabor, 15684
Webster, Pelatiah, 1725-1795, 23763, 23764
Webster, Samuel, 1719-1796, 23765
Webster Co., Ky., 14220; Description,
  14193
Wedded bliss, 9533
Weddell, Hugues Algernon, 21853
Wedderburn, John Walter, 13306

A wedding, 9265
The wedding and the funeral, 9702
The wedding days of former times, 9973
The wedding guest: a friend of the bride and
  bridegroom, 8586
The wedding knell, 9827
Wedel, Waldo Rudolph, 1908-, 17851
The wedge of gold, 16614
Wee Davie, 22969
Weed, Thurlow, 1797-1882, 360
Weeden, Miss Howard, 1847-1905, 5659
Weeden, Howard, illustr., 25075
Weedon, George, 1730?-1790, 698
A week at Port-Royal, 22481
A week in Wall street, 10004
Weeks, Stephen Beauregard, 1865-, 25848,
  25849
Weems, Mason Locke, 1759-1825, 23766-23773
Weenoknenchak Wandeeteekah, 10827
Weep no more my lady, 15385
Weke, Trude (Petersen) 1888-, 8358
Weichardt, Karl, 5660
Weichmann, Herbert, 5661
Weidner, Fritz, 25850
Weik, Jesse W., 1857-1930, 15685, 16745
Wein, Paul, 2018
Weinberg, Felix, 18302
Weinman, Adolph Alexander, 1870-, 7296
Weir, Harrison William, 1824-1906, illustr.,
  3594, 16588
Weir, James, 1821-1906, 5662-5664
Weise, Arthur James, 17852
Weisenberger Flour Mill, Midway, Ky., 14143
Weiser, George, 5665
Weishampel, John F., 5666
Weiss, Oscar, 25851
Weiss, Mrs. Susan Archer (Talley), 5667
Weissmann, Konrad Maximilian Heinrich, 1888-,
  25852
Welby, Adlard, 5668, 14077, 23774
Welby, Amelia Ball (Coppuck) 1819-1852, 5669
Welch, Andrew, 23463
Welch, S. L., 17853
Welch [!] Indians, 1692
Weld, Charles Richard, 1813-1869, 5670
Weld, Isaac, 1794-1856, 5671, 8359, 8360-8364
Weld, Theodore Dwight, 1803-1895, The Bible
  against slavery, 25914
Well! Well!, 11055
The well-spent life, 13573
Well-spring in the wilderness, 13986
Weller, Stuart, 14447, 15686
Welles, Albert, 8365
Welles, Alonzo Merritt, 8366
Welles, C. M., 17854
Welles, Noah, 1718-1776, 23775

Welling, James Clarke, 25853
Wells, Alfred, 25854
Wells, Daniel H., fl.1848, 17855
Wells, David Ames, 1828-1898, 8367
Wells, Emmeline Blanche (Woodward),
  1828-1921, 17856
Wells, J. K., 15687
Wells, John Doane, d.1830, 1896
Wells, William, d.1812, 6617
Wells, William Charles, 1757-1817, 2622,
  13617
Wells, William V., 17857
Welsh, Joseph S., 15688
Welsh in Ohio, 16190
Welsh in the U.S., 13286
Welsh Indians, 1692, 14035
Welshmen and their descendants of the
  American revolution, 13286
Wemett, W. M., 17858
Wender, Ernesto J., 8324
Wenham, Mass.,Congregational church, 23098;
  History, 191
Wensley, 10583
Went to Kansas, 3059
Wentworth, Thomas, fl.1741, 573
Wentworth, Thomas P., 15870
Wenzell, A. B., illustr., 15279
The wept of Wish-ton-wish, 9154, 9155
Wernli, Humberto A., 18460
Wesley, Charles, 1707-1788, 5672, 22654,
  25078
Wesley, Edgar B., 17859, 17860
Wesley, John, 1703-1791, 5673, 22783, 23776;
  A calm address to our American colonies,
  23706; Free Grace, 23789
Wesleyan Methodist church, Missions, 1995,
  23149, 23150
Wesleyan Methodist church in West Indies,
  1993
Wesleyan Methodist Church Mission, 4037
The Wesleyan student, 12845
Wesleyan University, 4646
West, Benjamin, 1738-1820, 2387
West, Gerald Montgomery, 25855
West, Henry Byrd, 9429
West, John, chaplain to the Hudson's Bay
  Company, 5674
West, John Camden, 1834-, 5675
West, Mary Eliza, 5682
West, Samuel, 1731-1807, 23777, 23778
West, Stephen, 1735-1819, 22561
The West, 3753; Biography, 16169; Commerce,
  16740; Description & travel, 2465, 2486,
  2490, 2498, 2499, 2528, 2572, 2581, 2597,
  2607, 2616, 2621, 2651, 2652, 2653, 2668,
  2688, 2689, 2710, 2766, 2772, 2783, 2796,

2823, 2845, 2846, 2881, 2891, 2892, 2916,
2926, 2936, 3005, 3017, 3047, 3081, 3100,
3105, 3111, 3117, 3129, 3169, 3179, 3220,
3257, 3266, 3268, 3299, 3321, 3349, 3380,
3414, 3421, 3438, 3444, 3462, 3521, 3524,
3540, 3543, 3551, 3570, 3578, 3630, 3651,
3658, 3676, 3723, 3790, 3795, 3826, 3837,
3862, 3888, 3901, 3923, 3955, 3982, 3992,
3993, 4026, 4027, 4028, 4020, 4032, 4042,
4068, 4118, 4125, 4134, 4139, 4147, 4177,
4208, 4213, 4235, 4257, 4259, 4272, 4281,
4339, 4386, 4387, 4388, 4398, 4456, 4501,
4529, 4550, 4597, 4606, 4609, 4625, 4696,
4700, 4705, 4712, 4791, 4802, 4837, 4846,
4892, 4951, 4963, 4973, 4975, 5007, 5044,
5054, 5055, 5060, 5069, 5078, 5086, 5095,
5145, 5178, 5180, 5181, 5203, 5208, 5233,
5255, 5278, 5301, 5306, 5345, 5274, 5386,
5445, 5449, 5451, 5457, 5502, 5504, 5506,
5510, 5511, 5515, 5523, 5526, 5528, 5529,
5530, 5533, 5535, 5536, 5540, 5547, 5561,
5579, 5584, 5604, 5686, 5752, 5757, 5773,
5779, 5983, 6065, 6330, 7196, 7638, 7777,
7867, 8043, 8175, 8178, 8318, 8322, 8366,
11507, 12217, 12678, 13001, 13192, 13236,
13335, 13982, 15806, 15809, 15810, 15830,
15832, 15853, 15891, 15917, 15919, 15926,
15940, 15977, 15996, 15997, 16007, 16009,
16028, 16029, 16035, 16066, 16099, 16195,
16202, 16205, 16235, 16261, 16286, 16295,
16318, 16325, 16331, 16338, 16388, 16398,
16401, 16406, 16422, 16434, 16437, 16448,
16501, 16508, 16527, 16529, 16546, 16554,
16588, 16601, 16631, 16679, 16717, 16722,
16723, 16729, 16733, 16742, 16744, 16747,
16753, 16758, 16806, 16854, 16866, 16896,
16904, 16925, 17019, 17022, 17025, 17030,
17043, 17060, 17063, 17080, 17128, 17134,
17175, 17185, 17193, 17218, 17244, 17335,
17337, 17346, 17368, 17391, 17394, 17400,
17405, 17446, 17460, 17481, 17485, 17499,
17506, 17510, 17519, 17522, 17528, 17542,
17577, 17605, 17615, 17626, 17649, 17663,
17697, 17729, 17736, 17751, 17834, 17875,
17914, 17923; Description & travel,
Fictional accounts, 4809; Description &
travel, Guide books, 2510, 3027, 3673,
3736, 3936, 4699, 4803, 12721; Description
& travel, Views, 17468; Distances, 3027,
3343, 3677, 3901; Economic conditions,
1586, 16349; History, 13074, 14498, 15578,
16099, 16195, 16205, 16385, 16933, 16980,
17093, 17144, 17356, 17764, 17860; History,
Bibliography, 16281; History, Sources,
7404, 17129; Maps, 4353, 15844, 15880,
15881; Posts and forts, 17008; Public

works, 16740; Social life & customs, 15959, 15987, 16053, 16054, 16818, 17041; Statistics, 5233
West Bridgewater, Mass. First Congregational Society, 24414
West Brookfield, Mass., First Church, 25856
West Brookfield Anti-slavery Society, 25856
The west coast of Florida, 2707
West Fincastle, now Kentucky, 15757
West Florida, Description & travel, 1206; History, 13404
The West from a car window, 16338
West India affairs, 24252
West India Association, Glasgow, 25857
West India "compensation" to owners of slaves, 25640
West India pickles, diary of a cruise through the West Indies, 8151
The West India question, 25637
West Indian incumbered estates acts, (a treatise on the), 22013
West Indies, 7049, 12589, 25285; Bibliography, 18672; Commerce, 196, 576, 23418; Description & travel, 362, 522, 669, 1246, 1852, 2851, 3047, 3048, 3947, 4506, 4636, 4900, 4981, 5087, 5132, 5319, 5556, 5730, 5747, 5928, 5939, 6074, 6333, 6404, 6471, 6655, 6739, 6786, 6911, 6919, 6939, 6961, 6984, 6989, 6990, 7006, 7064, 7075, 7095, 7305, 7343, 7530, 7533, 7583, 7618, 8151, 8160, 8228, 8229, 9839, 8320, 8321, 13110, 15020, 15725, 18075, 18375, 22233, 22938, 23600, 24082, 24509, 25497, Description & travel, Gazetteers, 3178, 4613, 22042; Description & travel, Guide-books, 5940, 5951, 7616, 7653; Description & travel, Maps, 13192; Emigration & immigration, 24869; History, 1993, 4051, 6739, 6956, 7898, 18375, 21765, 22190, 23353, 24339
West Indies, British, 24339, 24518, 24931; Commerce, 12287, 24349; Commerce, U.S., 13327; Description & travel, 669, 986, 1110, 2502, 6154, 6786, 8239, 12589, 21789, 22940, 23007, 24616, 24957, 24972, 25276, 25511; Economic conditions, 24349, 25094, 25857; History, 986, 1993, 24339; History, Chronology, 986; Politics & government, 22012, 24518, 24616, 25362, 25817; Social life & customs, 24953
West Indies, Dutch, 1126; Description & travel, 11382; Politics & government, 1127
West Indies, French, Description & travel, 4227, 22234, 22697, 24509; Economic conditions, 24748, 25070; History, 12209,

22234; Social life & customs, 24953
The West Indies as they are, 1246
West Liberty, Ky., 15433
West Newbury, Mass., History, 1972
West Point, N.Y., History, 11470
West Randolph, Vt. Anti-slavery convention, 1858, 25858
West Roxbury, Mass., Directories, 1566
The West vs. Harriman, 17538
West Virginia, Bibliography, 15140; Biography, 17091; Description & travel, 3104, 3206, 3613, 3977, 4173, 4418, 5173, 13580, 14370, 14749, 14845; Economic conditions, 15611; History, 3213, 5754, 14084, 14235; History, Civil war, 3670, 22802; Maps, 15626; Social conditions, 15611
The West Virginia hand-book and immigrant's guide, 3206
West Virginia infantry, 4th regt., 1861-1864, 2627; 6th regt., 1861-1865, 17091
West Woods, Jefferson County, Kentucky, 25664
Westbrook parsonage, 10287
Westchester Co., N.Y., Geneal., 11346; History, 11346
Westerberg, Thor Julius, 1874-, 17691
Westerman, Albert G., illustr., 13576
The western address directory, 4320
The western Avernus, 4973, 17499
Western Baptist educational association, 13139
Western border life, 11126
Western characters, 10265
Western clearings, 10150
Western country, Sketches of a tour to the, 3138
The Western farmer's almanac, 15689-15691
The western gazetteer, 2831
The western Ginevra, 9678
Western grazing grounds and forest ranges, 15920
A western journey with Mr. Emerson, 8175
Western Kentucky, above ground and below, 4324
Western Kentucky University, 15692
Western lands and western waters, 12217
The western merchant, 4116
The Western monthly review, 5677
Western museum society, Cincinnati, 3285
The western navigator, 6529
Western North Carolina as a health resort, 3626
The western pilot, 11895
A western pioneer, 16077
Western portraiture, and emigrants guide,

13957
Western, pseud., 5676
Western railroad, 12494
The Western railroad corporation, 1420
Western Reserve, Description & travel,
  16645; Economic conditions, 25358;
  History, 24156; Religion, 15894
The Western Reserve and the fugitive
  slave law, 24156
The Western review and miscellaneous
  magazine, 5678, 15517
The Western sanitary commission, 2275
Western scenes and reminiscences, 15329
The western sketch-book, 9596
The Western souvenir, 5679
Western state historical society, 17884
The Western traveler's pocket directory
  and stranger's guide, 23779
Western windows, 4779
The western world, 4356
Westfield, Mass., History, 22045
Westman, Georgius A., 2484
Westminster, Mass.,Anti-slavery picnic,
  1843, 721; History, 12983
Westminster Assembly of Divines, 15755
Weston, Theodore, 1571
Weston, William, 17862
Weston, Mass., Geneal., 21801
The Westover manuscripts, 2878
Westport, 14191
Westward empire, 23026
Westward Ho!, 4720
Westward the course of empire, 17577
Wet days at Edgewood: with old farmers,
  old gardeners, and old pastorals, 13443
Wetherbee, F.l., illustr., 16493
Wetherbee, John, jr., 17864
Wetherby, Lawrence W., 14558
The Wetherel affair, 9373
Wetherell, Elizabeth, pseud., 11097
Wethersfield, Conn.,First Church of Christ,
  23158
Wetmore, Alexander, 1793-1849, 15693
Wetmore, Alphonso, 1793-1849, 4761, 5680
Wetmore, Charles A., 17865
Wetmore, Prosper Montgomery, 1798-1876,
  10403
Wette, Ludwig de, 5681
Wetzel, Lewis, 1764?-1808, 22316
Weyer's Cave, Va., 4100
Weygant, Charles H., 1839-1909, 5682
Weymouth, Mass.,North church, 2193
Whale, Theophilus, ca.1616-ca.1719, 23663
The whale fishermen, 9775
Whales, 21903
Whaling, 2838, 11570, 21903, 23009

Whalley, Edward, d.1675?, 23663
Wharf property, 11436
Wharton, Charles Henry, 1748-1833, 12438
Wharton, Edward Clifton, 1827-1891, 6880
Wharton, Joseph, 8368
Wharton, Thomas, 1731-1783?, 12293
Wharton, William M., 17866
What a farmer can do, 9042
What answer?, 9399
What are you going to do about it?, 8534
What can she do?, 10655
What constitutes the state?,13151
What dreams may come, 8594
What Fanny Hunter saw and heard in Kansas
  and Missouri, 11126
What happened at the fonda, 6969
What I did in "The long", 2626
What I did with my fifty millions, 8639
What I saw and suffered in rebel prisons,
  4140
What I saw in California, 2846
What I saw in Dixie, 2876
What I saw in Texas, 3510
What I saw on the old Santa Fé trail, 17041
What I saw on the west coast of South and
  North America, 15942
What I think of you, 9471
What is best?,10427
What is gentility, 10813
What "Jeems Pipes, of Pipesville" saw and
  did, 10321
What Maisie knew, 7133, 10019
What may have been, 9304
What not, 9391
What shall be done?,25859
What shall be done with the confiscated
  negroes?, 25464
What shall we do with the Hudson's Bay
  territory?, 7809
What the North said to the South, 25860
What the poets have found to say of the
  beautiful scenery on the Denver & Rio
  Grande, 16369
What the world made them, 10050
What the years brought, 9797
What think ye of the Congress now?, 11722
What was the matter?,11075
What was thought of Amberglow, 8369
What would the world think, 9045
What's cooking in Frankfort, 13972
Whately, Thomas, d.1772, 22738
Whates, Harry Richmond, d.1923, 8370
Wheat, Marvin T., 8371, 25861
Wheat, 1032, 1615, 23636; Argentine Republic,
  20547
Wheat and tares, 9018

Wheatley, Phillis, afterwards Phillis Peters, 1753-1784, 24779
Wheatley, Ky.,Dallasburg Baptist Church, 15694
Wheaton, Nathaniel Sheldon, 1792-1862, 25862
Wheaton and the panther, 10570
Whedon, Daniel Denison, 1808-1885, 25012
The wheel of time, 10020
Wheeler, Alfred, 1822-1903, 17867
Wheeler, Arthur O., 8372
Wheeler, Christine Gordon, 16277
Wheeler, Esther W., 17868
Wheeler, George Bomford, 1805-1877, 1794
Wheeler, George C., 17868
Wheeler, John H., 3418
Wheeler, John Hill, 1806-1882, 5683, 5684, 25897
Wheeler, Joseph, 1836-1906, 3224, 6651, 8373
Wheeler, Patton Galloway, 15695
Wheeler, Peter, b.1789, 24822
Wheeling, Bridges, 12019
Wheelock, Eleazar, 1711-1779, 22815, 23780
Wheelock, Harrison, 5685
Wheelock, Mrs. Irene (Grosvenor), 17869
Wheelock, John, 1754-1817, 2134
Wheelock, Mrs. Julia Susan, 3537
Wheelock, Thompson B., 5686
Wheelwright, John T., 9641
Whelpley, James Davenport, 1817-1872, 317, 8597
When a document is official, 10608
When I am king, 9740
When I was a boarder, 10088
When knighthood was in flower, 10309
When little Mordecai was at the bar, 10465
When love enslaves, 11191
When love is done, 9341
When the century was new, 8447
When the colonel was a duellist, 10465
When the waters were up at "Jules'", 6972
Where Avon into Severn flows, 9565
Where I saw Lincoln, 5905
Where men only dare to go, 3444
Where Tex meets Mex, 8036
Where the battle was fought, 4566
Where the laborers are few, 9376
Where the souls of men are calling, 14272
Where the trade-wind blows, 9254
Where to emigrate and why, 3630, 12292
Where to go in Florida, 5489
Where's Duncan? 9745
Where's Nora, 10042
Whether it paid, 11007
Whether white or black, a man, 9338

Which, the right or the left, 11135
Which of three? 9254
Whicker, John Wesley, 1863-, 5687
Whiffles, Nick, fictional character, 7887
The Whig chief, 15668
Whig party, 1605, 7594, 11929; (Gt. Britain), 22126; Maryland, 1510; Massachusetts, 11931
Whigs and Tories, 9460
Whilomville stories, 9216
The whims of Captain McCarthy, 9749
The whip, hoe, and sword, 12781
Le Whip-poor-will, 16021
Whipple, Amiel Weeks, 1818-1863, 5521, 17218
Whipple, Charles King, 1808-1900, 24625, 25863-25866
Whipple, Henry Benjamin, bp., 1822-1901, 12776
Whipple, John, 1784-1866, 25381
Whipple, Phila M., 25867
A whirl asunder, 8595
Whiskey, 14056, 15096, 15125, 15521, 15543
Whiskey frauds, 14483
Whiskey in Kentucky folk belief, 15543
Whiskey insurrection, 1794, 11476, 11484; Fiction, 10266
Whiskey running still thrives throughout state, 13655
Whiskey tax, 13655
Whispering pines, 2757
Whiston, William, 1667-1752, 13332
Whitaker, Alexander, 1585-1617? 5688
Whitaker, Daniel Kimball, 1801-1881, 23781
Whitaker, Fess, 1880-, 15696
Whitaker, Nathaniel, 1732-1795, 23782
Whitaker, Ozi W., 17870
Whitaker, Robert, 1863-, 17020
Whitcher, Mrs. M. L. Ward, 11136
White, illustr., 11046
White, Addison, 25315
White, Andrew, 1579-1656, 4929
White, Charles Thomas, 1863-, 8374
White, David, 15512
White, E. P., 15697
White, Elijah, d.1879, 2508
White, Elijah, 15832
White, Erskine Norman, 1833-1911, 8375
White, G.G., illustr., 12729, 12730
White, George, 1802-1887, 7722
White, George W., 15698
White, Hugh Lawson, 1773-1840, 23372
White, J. M., 17871
White, James, 1863-, 16474
White, John, 1575-1648, 23783
White, Jonah H., 5689
White, Joseph W., 5690
White, Josiah, 1781-1850, 8376

White, Lucy, d.1894, 25868
White, Martin Marshall, 1904-, 15699
White, Matthew, jr., 10283
White, Mrs. Peter A., 15700
White, Pliny Holton, 1822-1869, 8377
White, Richard Grant, 1821-1885, 8378
White, Samuel, of Adams Co., Pa., 8379
White, Stewart Edward, 1873-, 8380
White, William Francis, 1829-1891?, 17872
White family (John White, b.1683), 5835
White's guide to Florida and her famous
  resorts, 5690
White, red, black, 4865
White acre vs. Black acre, 1749
White and black, 2899
White conquest, 3260
The white flame, 9169
The white forest, 10608
White Hall, Madison County, Ky., 13715
A white hand, 10559
The white islander, 8956
White-jacket, 10349
White Marie, 3774
The white mask, 11061
White Mountains, 718, 1271; Description
  & travel, Guide-books, 1034, 12485,
  12495
White Pass and Yukon railway, 16627
White Plains, N.Y. Bloomingdale hospital,
  2152
The White Rocks, 9867
The white rose road, 10043
The white rover, 4994
The white side of a black subject, 25917
The white slave, 9866
White slavery, 1/46
White slavery in the United States, 25869
The white snake, 2956
White Sulphur papers, 4743
White Sulphur Springs, W.Va., 4515, 4743;
  Fiction, 11187; Social life & customs,
  11187
White supremacy and negro subordination,
  25796
A white umbrella in Mexico, 8041
Whitefield, George, 1714-1770, 1074, 5124,
  5691, 11764, 12821, 22244, 23496, 23784-
  23789, 25870
Whitehill, John, 1729-1815, 25585
Whiteley, Henry, 25871
Whitely, Ike, 17873
Whiteman, Susan Godfred (Hooker), 1838-
  1928, 25872
Whiteside, Frederick W., 14686
Whitefield, Henry, 1597-1660?, 00700
Whitefield, James M., 13237

Whitford, William C., 17874
Whither curiosity led, 11198
Whiting, Henry, 1788-1851, 5692, 5693
Whiting, Lilian, 1859-, 17875
Whiting, Samuel, pub., 3892
Whiting, William Henry Chase, 1825-1865,
  5547, 17876
Whitlaw, Jonathan Jefferson, 25723
Whitley, Mrs. Wade Hampton, 13695, 15701
Whitley, William, 1749-1813, 14208, 14951
Whitman, Albert Allson, 1851-1901, 25873
Whitman, Elizabeth, 1752-1788, Fiction, 9549,
  9550
Whitman, Marcus, 1802-1847, 16062, 16142,
  16290, 16355, 16671, 16690, 17139, 17141,
  17241, 17276, 17277
Whitman, Mrs. Narissa (Prentiss) 1808-1847,
  16142
Whitman, Walt, 1819-1892, 14796, 15702
Whitney, Adeline Dutton (Train) 1824-1906,
  9693
Whitney, Asa, 1797-1872, 17395
Whitney, Ernest, 17877
Whitney, J. H. E., 5694
Whitney, Joel Parker, 1835-1913, 5695, 17878
Whitney, John Prescott, 5696
Whitney, Josiah D., 17879
Whitney, Orson F., 13932, 17880
Whitney, William Dwight, 1899-, 5697
Whitney's Florida pathfinder, 5696
Whitsitt, William H., 15703
Whitson, Thomas, 25874
Whittaker, Frederick, 15704
Whittaker, James, 1751-1787, 12094
Whittelsev Charles, 1723 or 4-1764, 11953
Whittier, John Greenleaf, 1807-1892, 76,
  13442, 23791, 23908, 23988, 24681,
  25875-25877
Whittlesey, Charles, 1808-1886, 4664
Whittlesey, Walter R., 15705
Whitworth, Miles, 2089
Who are the Americans, 5697
Who conquered California?, 16845
Who did it?, 10442
Who fought the battle? Strength of the Union
  and Confederate forces compared, 15427
Who goes there?, 8791, 11318
Who is free?, 10207
Who is the captain?, 9981
Who is to blame?, 12344
Who was he?, 11045
Who was my quite friend?, 9779
Who was the first governor of Massachusetts?,
  2247
Who was who in Hardin county, 6952
Who were the early settlers of Maryland, 171

480

Who would have thought it?, 8918
Who's who in Kentucky, 14156, 15706
Who's who in Pacific southwest, 17883
The whole story in few words, 12995
Whose wife was she?, 10006
Why a rich Yankee did not settle in
  California, 15890
Why and what am I? 10029
Why are we still at war? 2017
Why Constantinople fell, 11054
Why I am a Republican, 6134
Why I am a temperance man, 8871
Why I have not gone to the South, 25405
Why I married Eleanor, 10546
Why Mrs. Radnor fainted, 10899
Why our flag floats over Oregon, 16671
Why the Confederacy failed, 9749
Why we went gypsying in the Sierras, 17029
Why work for the slave? 25658, 25878
Wible, Benjamin M., 1814-1877, 15561
Wick, William W., 1796-1868, 25879
The wicked man's portion, 23329
Wickliffe, Robert, 1775-1859, 1465,
  1467, 2794, 5698, 5699, 15707-15713,
  24145
Wickliffe family, 14888
Wicksteed, Charles, 25880
Wide Awake Central committee, 8381
Widney, Joseph Pomeroy, 1841-, 17037
Widow Guthrie, 4091
A widow of the Santa Ana Valley, 6978
The widow Rugby's husband, 3926
Widow Spriggins, 11136
The widow's bandbox, 10909
The widow's cruise, 10896
The widow's offering: an authentic
  narrative of the parentage, life, trails
  and travels of Mrs. Elizabeth Hill,
  22468
Wie lebt und arbeitet man in den Vereinigten
  Staaten? 3883
Wieczorek, Rudolph, 25881
Wied-Neuwied, Maximilian Alexander Philipp,
  prinz von, 1782-1867, 5700, 5701
Wieland, 8861
Wieliczka salt-mines, 8877
Wier, Jeanne Elizabeth, 17884
Wiesse, Maria, 1894-, 8382
The wife of his youth, 2982
The wife of Leon, 5621
The wife of Lothario, 11191
The wife of two husbands, 11048
The wife's messengers, 9923
The wife's secret, 10875
Wiggins, John H., 25882
Wigglesworth, Edward, 1693-1765, 21890,

23792
Wigglesworth, Michael, 1631-1705, 22058
Wigham, Eliza, 15714
Wight, Samuel F., 17885
Wightman, Elias R., 3833
The wigwam and the cabin, 10783
Wikoff, Henry, 1813-1884, 25883
Wilber, Charles D., 17886
Wilberforce, Edward, 1834-, 25884
Wilberforce, Robert Isaac, 1802-1857, 25886
Wilberforce, Samuel, successively bp. of
  Oxford and of Winchester, 1805-1873,
  1214, 25886
Wilberforce, William, 1759-1833, 24350,
  25885, 25886
Wilbour, Charles Edwin, 1833-1896, 13188
Wilbur, Henry Watson, 1851-1914, 25887
Wilbur Smith Associates, New Haven,
  Connecticut, 20022
Wilcox, Andrew Jackson, 1835-1870, 25888,
  25889
Wilcox, E. W., 10163
Wilcox, Walter Dwight, 1869-, 8383
Wilcox, the counterfeiter, 10310
Wild, Ebenezer, 1758-1794, 5702
Wild bats sowings, 16316
Wild flowers, 3961, 15246; Kentucky, 14339,
  15348
The wild girl of the Nebraska, 5655
Wild Jack, 3849
Wild Nell, the White Mountain girl, 10375
The wild north land, 6264, 6265
Wild oats sowings, 3146
The wild riders of the First Kentucky
  cavalry, 5348
The wild rose of Cherokee, 10134
Wild scenes and wild hunters, 5650
Wild scenes and wild hunters of the world,
  5656
Wild scenes on the frontiers, 2685
Wild shrubs of Alabama, 12717
Wild southern scenes, 4117
Wild sports in the far West, 3594, 16588
Wild western scenes, 10064
Wilda, Johannes, 1852-, 5703
Wildash, 4014
Wildcat stalked Lexington teacher, 14971
Wilde, Oscar Fingall O'Flahertie Wills, 1856-
  1900, 5704, 21720
Wilde, Richard Henry, 1789-1847, 5705
Wilder, Marshall P., 17887
Wilder, Walter Lawson, 17888
The wilderness and the war path, 3754
The wilderness hunter, 17521
The wilderness of the upper Yukon, 8012
The Wilderness Road, 13542, 13715, 13809,

14133, 15428
Wildfire, Walter, pseud., 21974
Wildfire the wanderer, 9718
Wildlife, Conservation, 14047; Kentucky, 13534, 13917, 15784
Wild life in Florida, 5450
Wild life in Kentucky, 14157
Wild life in Oregon, 16764, 17857
Wild life in the far West, 16795
Wild life in the interior of Central America, 11655
Wildmoor, 8900
Wildwood, Warren, pseud., 15715
Wildwood, Will, pseud., 3758
Wile, Benjamin F., 25882
Wiley, Allen, 1789-1848, 14341
Wiley, Thomas, 25540
Wiley, William, 15716
Wilfrid and Mary, 25430
Wilhelm, Honor Lupfer, 1870-, 5706
Wilhelmina, 11205
Wilkes, George, 1820-1885, 5707, 23793
Wilkes, John, 1727-1797, 11406, 12424
Wilkeson, Frank, 1845-, 5708
Wilkie, Franc Bangs, 1832-1892, 5709, 23794
Wilkins, Isaac, 1742-1830, 23585-23588
Wilkins, James, 16701
Wilkins, James Hepburn, 8384
Wilkins Wylder, 10356
Wilkinson, Ann Biddle, 15717
Wilkinson, James, 1757-1825, 3682, 8016, 14449, 14836, 16490, 21970
Wilkinson, Jemima, 1752-1819, 12984
Wilkinson, R. A., 5710
Wilkinson, Thomas, d.1836, 25890
Wilkinson, Thomas Read, 5711
Will, George Francis, 1884-, 17889-17894
The will, 10085
A will and a way, 10580
Will it blow over? 10579
Will she succeed, 9447
Willamette University, 16752
Willamette Valley, Ore., 4690; Frontier and pioneer life, 16977
Willard, Archibald M., illustr., 2630
Willard, Conrad Brown, 1775-1826, 4715
Willard, Mrs. Emma (Hart) 1787-1870, 17895, 25891
Willard, James Field, 17896
Willard, Joseph, 1738-1804, 23795
Willard, Solomon, 1783-1861, 23251
Willcox, Giles Buckingham, 1826-1922, 8385
Willcox, Orlando Bolwar, 1823-, 3417
Willett, P. N., 17897
Willett, Edward, 1830-, 10115
Willett, F.C., pub., 10686

Willett, Herbert L., 14207
Willey, Austin, 1806-1896, 25892
Willey, Samuel H., 17898
William III, king of Great Britain, 1650-1702, 663
William Augustus, duke of Cumberland, 1721-1765, 23456, 23457, 23524
William (brigantine), 11281
William, Father, pseud., 5712
William and Mary College, Williamsburg, Va., 4124; Fiction, 9118; Licivyronean society, 1959
William Forbes, 9702
William Gilmore Simms, 5459
William Morgan, 458, 4534
William Penn et la paix, 8165
William Russell, autobiography of, 5377
William Wirt, 10953
Williams, Abraham, 1726-1784, 23796
Williams, Alfred M., 17899
Williams, Anna Vernon (Dorsey), 8969
Williams, C.D., illustr., 10924, 24298, 24300, 24341
Williams, C. Scott, 17344
Williams, Carl O., 25893
Williams, Cynric R., 8386
Williams, Daniel, 1752-1823, 14497
Williams, David, 1754-1831, 1175-1177
Williams, Edward, fl.1650, 5713, 23797
Williams, Edward Peet, 5714
Williams, Ellen, 17900
Williams, Ezekiel, fl.1807-1827, 3105, 16286
Williams, Mrs. Fannie Barrier, 25124
Williams, Francis Howard, 1844-1922, 10737
Williams, George Forrester, 1837-, 5715
Williams, George W., 5716
Williams, Herbert Deland, illustr., 14474
Williams, Isaac D., b.1821? 24494, 25894
Williams (J.D. & M.),Boston, 2441
Williams, James, 1796-1869, 25895
Williams, James, 1805-, 5717
Williams, James, b.1825, 25896
Williams, John, 1664-1729, 23802
Williams, John Aug., 1824-1903, 4366, 15718, 15719
Williams, John Lee, 5718, 23798
Williams, John N., jt. author, 15056
Williams, John S., 287
Williams, John Sharp, 7263
Williams, Joseph, 5719
Williams, Les, 14800
Williams, Mrs. Martha McCulloch, 5720-5722
Williams, Mary Ida, 15720
Williams, Oliver P., 14312
Williams, Parley L., 17901
Williams, Richard, 1815-1851, 12612

Williams, Robert Hamilton, b.1831, 17902
Williams, Roger, 1604?-1683, 12193, 13251,
  23799, 23800; Bibliography, 12489
Williams, Roger P., Kentucky general,
  14977
Williams, Roy L., illustr., 13704
Williams, Sally, American slave, 23925
Williams, Samuel, 1743-1817, 23622, 23801
Williams, Samuel Cole, 1864-, 5723
Williams, Samuel L., 1782?-1872, 15718
Williams, Stephen West, 1790-1855, 23802
Williams, Thomas, 50
Williams, Thomas, 1815-1862, 2587
Williams, U.V., 15721
Williams, W.H., 8387
Williams, Wellington, 5724-5726, 8388, 8389
Williams, William, 1763-, 5727
Williams, William R., 1804-1885, 23232
Williams family, 14497
Williamsburg, Battle of, 1862, 11625
Williamson, Caleb, 8103
Williamson, Hugh, 1735-1819, 23803, 23804
Williamson, James Joseph, 1834-1915, 5728
Williamson, John, 1822-, 17082
Williamson, Judith, 15722
Williamson, Mary Cobb, 8103
Williamson, Passmore, 24080, 25103, 25897
Williamson, William Durkee, 1779-1846, 23805
Williamson family, 8103
Williamson Co., Ill., History, 3389
Williamson Co., Tex., Biography, 16780
Willie Baker's good sense, 9254
Willis, George Lee, 1862-, 15723, 15724
Willis, Nathaniel Parker, 1806-1867, 5729,
  5730, 15725
Willis, Richard D., 14615
Willis, Simeon, 1879-, 7153
Williston, Timothy, d.1893, 24856
Willoughby, Sir Hugh, d.1554, 12192
Willoughby, Hugh Laussat, 1856-, 5731
Willows, 18636
Wills, Charles Wright, 1840-1883, 5732
Wills, Mrs. Mary H., 17903
Wills, Kentucky, 24715
Willson, Augustus E., 1846-, 15726
Willson, Edmund Burke, 1820-1895, 25898
Willson, Forceythe, 1837-1867, 5733
Willson, James Renwick, 1780-1853, 25899
Willson, Marcius, 1813-1905, 17904
Willson, Shipley Wells, 23909
Wilmer, Lambert A., 1805?-1863, 17905
Wilmer, Richard Hooker, bp., 1816-1910,
  5734
Wilmere, Alice, 11714
Wilmington, Del., Biography, 23446; History,
  23446; Maps, 14424

Wilmore, Ky., Description, 15420
Wilmot, David, 1814-1868, 25900
Wilmot, Franklin A., 15727
Wilmot-Horton, Sir Robert John, bart., 1784-
  1841, 25901
Wilmot proviso, 1846, 1214, 4296, 24087,
  25915
Wilson,_____, commissary of General
  Amherst's army, 1759, 331
Wilson, A. E., 10163
Wilson, Alexander, 1766-1812, 5735, 15101
Wilson, Calvin Dill, 1857-, 25902, 25903
Wilson, Charles Henry, of Northallerton, 8390
Wilson, Daniel Love, 1849-1902, 24824
Wilson, Frazer E., 13702
Wilson, Gordon, 15728, 15729
Wilson, Grady, 15021
Wilson, Harry Leon, 1867-, 17906
Wilson, Henry, 1812-1875, 6288, 25904, 25907
Wilson, Herbert Michael, 8391
Wilson, Hiero Tennant, 1806-1892, 16609
Wilson, James, 1759 or 60-1814, 12433
Wilson, James, 1742-1798, 23806
Wilson, James A., 8392
Wilson, James Grant, 14824
Wilson, Jane Adeline, 5736
Wilson, Jeremiah M., 17907
Wilson, John, 1588-1667, 22813, 23807
Wilson, John Alfred, 1832-, 5737
Wilson, John Lyde, 1784-1849, 9910
Wilson, Joseph Thomas, 25908
Wilson, Joshua Lacy, 1774-1846, 14317, 14322
Wilson, Joyce, 15730
Wilson, Lawrence Maurice, 1896-1963, 7526,
  8393
Wilson, Leonard Seltzer, 1909-, 15731
Wilson, Lizzie, 1835-1858, 5738
Wilson, Mrs. Mary Bullock (Shelby), 1876-,
  15753
Wilson, Mary Helen, 15732-15734
Wilson, Obed Gray, 1836-, 17908
Wilson, Richard Lush, 5739
Wilson, Robert Anderson, 1812-1872, 8394,
  8395, 8396
Wilson, Robert Burns, 1850-1916, 5740, 5741,
  15735, 15736
Wilson, Samuel, fl.1678-1682, 5742
Wilson, Samuel (of Kentucky) 5743
Wilson, Samuel (writer on temperance) 8397
Wilson, Samuel Mackay, 1871-1946, 13583,
  13642, 13680, 13681, 13737, 13993, 14018,
  14532, 15737-15758, 15762
Wilson, Thomas, 1655?-1725, 5744
Wilson, William, the whistling shoemaker,
  10849
Wilson, William Dexter, 1816-1900, 25909

Wilson, William Thomas, 1834-1890, 8398
Wilson, Woodrow, pres. U.S., 1865-1924,
  15121
The Wilson House, 10197
Wilstach, John Augustine, 1824-1897, 5745
Wimpffen, François Alexandre Stanislaus,
  baron de, 8399
Winans, William (port.), 14995
Winchendon, Mass., History, 13058
Winchester, Carroll, pseud., 9284, 9285
Winchester, Elhanan, 1751-1797, 23808
Winchester, Ky., 15759; Buildings, 15120;
  Commissioner, 15760; Description, 13644;
  Epidemics, 14102; History, 13638, 13643,
  13926, 14102, 14108, 14965, 15120, 15487;
  Newspapers, 15211; Postal service, 13808;
  Public utilities, 15759
Winchester in 1812-14, 13926
Wind and whirlwind, 9479
The wind from the sun, 20213
Winder, William Henry, 1775-1824, 13100
Windham, N.H., History, 22904
Winds, 806, 1969, 22035, 23374
Windsor, Conn., Geneal., 23664; History,
  23664
Windsor Locks, Conn., 23664
Wine and wine making, 14933, 18457, 23797;
  Argentine Republic, 19570; Argentine
  Republic, Statistics, 18459; Bourbon
  County, Kentucky, 15771; France, 14932;
  Germany, 14932
Wineburgh, Michael, 8400
The Wing-and-wing, 9156
The Wing of the Wind, 4015
The winged chariot, 8817
Winkler, Ernest William, 1875-1960, 16892,
  17722, 17909
The Winkles, 10065
Winn, Mary Day, 5746
Winn, T.S., 25910
Winnebago, Fort, Wis., 10141
Winning his spurs, 10117
The winning of the far West, 17093
Winnipeg, History, 6056, 6216
Winnipeg board of trade, 6062
Winnipeg country, 6235, 7988
Winnipesaukee Lake, 2454, 12485
Winny, 10841, 10842
Winslow, Edward, 1595-1655, 1886, 23809
Winslow, Richard H., d.1861, 16983
Winsor, Justin, 1831-1897, 8401
Winston, Michael, 14668
Winter, John, 12664
Winter, John F., 10088
Winter, Nevin Otto, 1869-, 8402, 17910
Winter, William H., 1819-1879, 4008

A winter courtship, 10043
Winter evening tales, 8746
The winter fire, 10557
A winter from home, 3031
A winter holiday in summer lands, 7112
A winter in California, 17903
A winter in Central America and Mexico, 7952
A winter in Florida, 2714
A winter in the country, 9702
A winter in the West Indies and Florida, 5747
The winter lodge, 5664
Winter resorts, Florida, 2557
Winter sketches from the saddle, by a
  septuagenarian, John Codman, 21968
Winter studies and summer rambles in Canada,
  7135, 7136
Winterborough, 11140
Winther, Oscar Osborn, 5554
Winthrop, John, 1588-1649, 23810; Poetry,
  22770
Winthrop, John, 1606-1676, 22221
Winthrop, Robert C., 17911
Winthrop, Theodore, 1828-1861, 5748, 8403
Winwood, 4016
The wire cutters, 3194
Wirt, William, 1772-1834, 5749, 5750, 8404,
  10952, 10953, 13362, 23811
Wirth, Conrad Louis, 1899-, 8405
Wirz, Henry, 1823?-1865, 4676, 5728
Wisconsin, 12423, 16985; Church history,
  11857; Description & travel, 11524, 11738,
  12142, 12169, 16012, 16648, 16678, 17268,
  22755; Description & travel, Gazetteers,
  13020; History, 16648, 22967, 23192;
  History, To 1848, 23812; History, Period.,
  15848; History, Sources, 6297; State
  Historical Society, 23812, 24984; State
  Historical Society, Library, 25912;
  Supreme Court, 25911; (Territory), 17612
Wisconsin, University, Madison, Land Tenure
  Center, LTC, 18032, 20079; Lincoln statue,
  7296
Wisconsin infantry, 6th regt., 1861-1865,
  Co.A., 2980; 8th regt., 1861-1865, 3198,
  3300; 12th regt., 1861-1865, 4323; 37th
  regt., 1864-1865, 3338
Wisdom, M.D., 17912
The wisdom of fools, 9378
The wisdom of preserving moderation in our
  wishes, 9486
Wise, George, 5751
Wise, Henry Alexander, 1806-1876, 12596,
  24121, 25913
Wise, Henry Augustus, 1819-1869, 8406, 8407,
  17913
Wise, John, 1652-1725, 23813

The wise woman, 8915
Wishart, George, 1703?-1785, 11764
Wislizenus, Adolphus, 1810-1889, 5752, 5753, 8408
Wisner, William Carpenter, 1808-1880, 25914
Wisser, J.P., 10122
Wistar, Caspar, 1761-1818, 12296, 13758
Wister, Owen, 1860-1938, 8116
Wiswell, Ichabod ca.1637-1700, 23814
Wit and humor, 10101, 14391
Wit and humor in paragraphs, 4849
The witch in the glass, 4787
The witch of Prague, 6508
Witchcraft, 2431, 10549, 13049, 17173, 23347; New England, 13053, 23315, 23318, 23322, 23326; New England, Fiction, 9402, 10410; Salem, 12037
The witchery of archery, 5400
With brains, sir, 8705
With fire and sword, 16116
With gyves of gold, 8596
With John Brun in old Mexico, 6950
With Omar, 4944
With rod and line in Colorado waters, 16545
With sack and stock in Alaska, 16050
With Sherman to the sea, 5554
With Speaker Cannon through the tropics, 7530
With Stevenson to California, 1846, 17073
With Sully into the Sioux land, 16693
With Thackeray in America, 3133
With the border ruffians, 17902
With the entrées, 9779
With the fifth corps, 10608
With the immortals, 9236
With the light guns in '61-'65, 5764
Withers, Alexander Scott, 1792-1865, 5754
Witherspoon, James Franklin, 1840-1921, 6472
Witherspoon, John, 1723-1794, 23815
Witherspoon, Pattie French, 15761
Within a shadow, 5262
Without my gloves, 4753
Without scrip or purse, 4860
Withycombe, James, 17437
Witlenborger, J., 5755
The witness of the sun, 11014
Witnesses, New York (State), 22427
Witter, Marina (Krebs) 1838-, 8409
The wizard of the sea, 4000, 9979
Woeikof, A. Die klimate der erde, 4039
Woelmont, Arnold de, baron, 17914
Wolcott, Oliver, 1760-1833, 23816
Wolcott, Richmond, 10899
Wolcott, Vt., History, 12978
Woleben, Sally V., 14864

The wolf detected, 25332
Wolfe, James, 1727-1759, 23817
Wolfe, J.M., & comp. publisher, 17915-17917
Wolfe family (Christian Wolff, 1762-1841), 2203
Wolfe family (George Michael Wolff, 1696?-1746), 2203
Wolfert Webber, 9995
Wolff, Emil Theodor von, 1818-1896, 7344
Wolley, Charles, 23818
Wollschläger, Alfred, 1901-, 8410
Woman, Biography, 1891, 2459, 6188, 12021, 16057, 16299, 16875, 17229, 21823; Employment, 11939, 19266; Employment, Brazil, 19266; Employment, Lowell, Mass., 905; History and condition of women, 23102; Legal status, laws, etc., 11939, 15944, 19266, 23102; Rights of women, 22649; Social and moral questions, 1044, 1102, 10902, 11545, 22897; Societies and clubs, 14487; Suffrage, 2207, 11642, 11783, 24413
Woman an enigma, 10281
Woman and the war, 11276
A woman in armor, 8957
A woman in the case, 11030
A woman of war, 8482
Woman on a horse, 6057
Woman under difficulties, 10863
A woman with a record, 8535
A woman who toils, 5563
The woman Zoe, 10499
Woman's Christian Temperance Union, Oregon, 15818
Woman's Club, Louisville, Ky., 15762
Woman's faith triumphant, 8748
Woman's foibles, 10155
A woman's inheritance, 9425
A woman's journey round the world, 13454
A woman's life work, 14288
Woman's medical college of Pennsylvania, Philadelphia, 9331
A woman's poems, 4788
A woman's reason, 9957
Woman's record, 2459
Woman's relation to education, labor, and law, 11939
A woman's reminiscences of six years in camp with the Texas rangers, 17498
A woman's right, 8531
The woman's story, 10163
A woman's wanderings in the western world, 1557
A woman's way through unknown Labrador, 6671
Woman's work in the civil war, 11528
Woman's wrongs, 9970
Women, 10300; Biography, 12023, 13851;

Fiction, 13976
Women as authors, 2334
Women as physicians, 17856
Women in America. 1102, 11545
Women in Fayette County history, 15547
Women in Kentucky, 13986
Women in New York (City), 9732, 12025
Women in the Confederate States of
America, 4035, 17774
Women in the U.S., 1044, 11663, 22649,
22897; Biography, 12022
Women in Turkey, 25181
Women of the South distinguished in
literature, 3536
Women's rights, 13711
Women's studies, Bibliography, 14704
Won by a bicycle, 9976
Wonder tales of early American history,
2870
Wonder-land illustrated; or, Horse-
back rides through the Yellowstone
National Park, 17284
The wonder-worker of Padua, 10898
The wonderful adventures of a Pullman,
9680
The wonderful adventures of Captain
Priest, 9724
Wonderful curiosity, 14481
The wonderful preservation of Mrs. Moore,
when a prisoner among the Indians,
10570
The wonderlands of the wild West, 16147
Wonderley, Anthony Wayne, 1913-1975,
14875
Wonders and curiosities of the railway,
14504
Wonders of the great Mammoth Cave of
Kentucky, 5486
Wonders of the Sierra Nevado, 17421
Wontus, 10682
Wood, Bradford, Ripley, 1800-1889, 25915
Wood, Edith, 13549, 15763
Wood, F.T., illustr., 16083
Wood, Fernando, 1812-1881, 7286
Wood, Frank Hoyt, 25916
Wood, George L., 1837 or 8-, 5756
Wood, J.C., 5757
Wood, John, 5758
Wood, John, fl.1670, 22280
Wood, John, 1775?-1822, 11768, 23819, 23820
Wood, John Taylor, 3417
Wood, Linda B., 15058
Wood, Louis Aubrey, 1883-, 8411
Wood, Myron W., 16770
Wood, Norman Barton, 1857-, 25124, 25917
Wood, Robert Crooke, 9755

Wood, Ruth Kedzie, 17919
Wood, S., 5760
Wood, Stanley, 17920
Wood, William Charles Henry, 1864-, 8412-
8414
Wood, William D., 1828-, 17921
The wood demon, 10919
Wood notes wild, 2582
Woodbridge, Benjamin Ruggles, 1775-1845,
22578
Woodbridge, Hensley C., 13545, 15764-15767
Woodburn, James Albert, 1856-, 25918
Woodburn, 4055
Woodbury, Angus M., 1886-, 17922, 17923
Woodbury, Augustus, 1825-1895, 5761, 8415,
8416
Woodbury, John H., 5762
Woodbury, Mrs. John L., 13993
Woodbury, Levi, 1789-1851, 17924, 22644
Woodcliff, 10288
Woodcraft, 10782
Woodfill, Samuel, 14260
Woodford Bank and Trust Company, Versailles,
Ky., 15768
Woodford Co., Ill., Politics & government,
24570
Woodford Co., Ky., 15769; Description,
15512; History, 14997, 15235, 15768;
Maps, 13646
Woodland lays, legends and charades, 12536
Woodlawn Cementery, Malden, Mass., 2356
Woodley, William J., 8417
Woodman, David, jr., 5763
Woodman family (Edward Woodman, fl.1635),
1971
Woodmancy, John, d.1684(?), 23704
Woodreve manor, 9418
Woodruff, George H., 17925
Woodruff, William Edward, 1831-, 5764
Woods, Daniel B., 17926
Woods, James, 17927
Woods, John, 5765, 5766, 14364
Woods, Nicholas Augustus, 8418
Woods, Samuel D., 17928
Woodstock, Conn. First Congregational church,
12467
Woodville, 10983
Woodward, A., 25919
Woodward, Augustus Brevoort, d.1827, 23821
Woodward, Bernard Bolingbroke, 21772
Woodward, Elsie McLennan, 13567
Woodward, Evan Morrison, 5767
Woodward, George Washington, 1809-1875,
25270, 25920
Woodward, Joseph Addison, 1806-1885, 25921
Woodward, Walter Carleton, 17929

Woodward, William H., 2226
Woodworth, Samuel, 1785-1842, 9649, 15770
Wooing and warring in the wildness, 4180, 14760
Wool, John Ellis, 1784-1869, 992
Wool, Kentucky, 15206
Wool-gathering, 3262
Wooldridge, Henry C., d.1899, 15422
Wooldridge, John, 6514
Wooldridge family, 15422
The Wooldridge monuments, 15422
Woolen and worsted manufacture, 4019
Woolf, Virginia (Stephen) 1882-1941, 20216
Woolman, John, 1720-1772, 5768, 5769, 23822, 25922
Woolsey, F. W., 15771
Woolson, A. G., 10163
Woolworth, Aaron, 1763-1821, 1661
Woolworth, James, 5770
Woon, Basil Dillon, 1893-, 16119
Woonsocket, R.I., 23067
Wooten, Dudley C., 17930
Worcester, Dean Conant, 1866-, 25250
Worcester, Joseph Emerson, 1784-1865, 239
Worcester, Samuel Austin, 1798-1859, 16183
Worcester, Mass., Cemeteries, 945; First church, 636; First Unitarian church, 731; History, 12966; History, Civil war, 23204
Worcester as it is, 12966
Worcester central conference of Congregational churches, 172
Word for word and letter for letter, 8800
A word in season, 23636
A word of remembrance and caution to the rich, 23822
Worden, A.T., 8546
Words in affliction, 8419
Words that burn, 8881
Work, Alanson, 25337
Work, John, 8420
Work: a story of experience, 8487
The work of preaching Christ, 22894
Work projects administration, Kentucky, 15772
The work shall praise the master, 13708
The working men of Manchester and President Lincoln, 25752
The workingman's paradise, 3613
Workmen's Compensation, Kentucky, 14681, 14690
The works of God declared by one generation to another, 2283
The works of Jeremy Peters, 10824
The world, 15774

The World, New York, 7402
The World almanac, 1868, 15773
World Health Organization, Monograph series, 19524
World history, 12175
The world in a man-of-war, 10349
The world of chance, 9958
A world of green hills, 5437
World politics, 1947; Period., 7275, 20522
World statistics, 19277
The world to blame, 10518
World War, 1939-1945, 19929; Brazil, 19929
World's fair ecclesiastical history of Utah, 16189
World's masonic register, 13062
The world's progress, 12396
Worm, A.W. van den, 670
Wormeley, Elizabeth, see Latimer, Elizabeth Wormeley, 10167, 10168
Wormsloe quartos, 3208
Worrosquoyacke, 9768
Worsham, John H., 5771
Worsley and Smith, Lexington, Ky., 15775
Worsley's & Smith's Kentucky almanac, 15776
The worst enemy conquered, 1073
Worth, 19728
Worthies of old Red river, 6236
Worthington, William G.D., 11480
Wounded in the house of a friend, 8561
Wounds, Treatment, 13304
Wounds in the rain, 9217
Wraxall, Sir Frederick Charles Lascelles, 3d bart., 1828-1865, tr., 2496, 5772, 15777, 15824, 15826, 17687
The wreath of Eglantine, 4312
A wreath of Virginia bay leaves, 3933
The wreck on the Indian Ocean, 8669
Wrecked, but not lost, 8692
The wrecker's daughter, 9977
The wreckers of St. Agnes, 10693
Wrede, Friedrich W. von, 5773
Wren, Thomas, 1824-1904, 17931
Wright, Benjamin, 1770-1842, 21909
Wright, Charles L., 15778
Wright, Charles W., 15779
Wright, Edward, 1558?-1615, 23823
Wright, Elizur, 1804-1885, 25923-25926
Wright, Elsie Southwood, 15780
Wright, G.F., 14082
Wright, George, illustr., 15249
Wright, Henry Clarke, 1797-1870, 25684, 25927-25930
Wright, Henry H., 1840-1905, 5774
Wright, Ione William (Tanner) "Mrs. S.J. Wright", 1861-, 17932
Wright, Irene A., 7274, 8421

Wright, Sir James, 1st bart., 1716-1785, 23784
Wright, James Martin, 1879-, 25931, 25932
Wright, John, 5775, 25933
Wright, John, M.D., 22163
Wright, John, fl.1761-1765, 23824
Wright, John W., 5776
Wright, John Stephen, 1815-1874, 25934
Wright, Lucy, 1760-1821, 12094
Wright, Mrs. Marie (Robinson) 1866-1914, 8422
Wright, Quincy, 1890-, 25832
Wright, Ray Herbert, 15780
Wright, Robert Marr, 1840-, 17933
Wright, Silas, 1795-1847, 12269, 12624, 13198
Wright, Thomas J., captain 8th Kentucky infantry, 5777
Wright, William, 1829-1898, 17934, 17935
Wrightstown township, Pa., Geneal., 1636; History, 1636
Writers' Program, Kentucky, 15781, 15782; Puerto Rico, 8264
Writers' Project, Kentucky, 15783
Writing, 13792; History, 2351
The writing on the wall, 9358
Writings, 3026, 4243
The writings of Laco, as published in the Massachusetts Centinel, 22455
Writs, Illinois, 13302
Written in red, 10371
The wrong of slavery, 4669
Wrottesley, George, 1827-1909, 1706
Wunnissoo, 204
Wuny, Gerald A., 15784
Wurty, George B., 15785
The Wyandot's story, 9618, 10919
Wyandott Mission, 3451
Wyandotte, 9157
Wyatt, J.B., 15648
Wych Hazel, 11099
Wyeth, John Allan, 1845-1922, 5778
Wyeth, John B., 5779
Wyeth, Nathaniel Jarvis, 1802-1856, 17936
Wyeth, Newell Convers, 1882-1945, illustr., 16223
Wylie, Andrew, 1789-1851, 5780
Wyllie, John Alfred, 24967, 24968
Wyllie, Robert Crichton, 1798-1865, 8423
Wynne, John Huddlestone, 1743-1788, 5781
Wynne, Thomas Hicks, d.1875, 11656, 12136
Wyoming, pseud., 23825
Wyoming, 16468, 17366, 17769; Bibliography, 17797; Biography, 15928; Capitol, 17937; Description & travel, 2877, 4549, 15809, 16852, 17683, 17754, 17769, 17770,

17777, 17871, 17941; Directories, 16243; History, 8318, 15928, 16153, 16175, 16475, 16732, 16826, 17180, 17197, 17783, 17797, 17841, 17937; Land, 16175; Libraries, 17432; Politics & government, 16475, 16732
Wyoming massacre, 1778, 10569
Wyoming Valley, Pa., History, 1824, 11734, 17366, 23672
Wyse, Francis, 5782
Wyse, Sir Thomas, 1791-1862, Education reform, 2280
Wyss-Dunant, Edouard, 8424
Wythe, George, 1726-1806, 8019

The XY company, 6228
Xántus, János, 1825-, 5783
Xariffa's poems, 5448
Xavier de Brito, José Joaquin, 25935
Xilografias de Maria Bonomi, 19155
Ximénez, Andrés, fl.1643, 6469, 6470
Ximénez de Cisneros, Francisco, cardinal, 1436?-1517, 25789
Xuares, Fernan, 122
Xyclo of Argos, 23751

The yacht "Alice", 3950
Yachts and yachting, 7012, 12722
Yacimientos de estano, 19205, 19206
Yale University, 2371, 11800-11802, 12819; Amasa Stone Mather memorial publication fund, 3887; History, 701
Yamoyden, 2157
Yanacocha, Battle of, 1835, Poetry, 951
Yanamarca Valley, Peru, Social conditions, 18100
Yancey, William Lowndes, 1814-1863, 3301, 25936, 25937
Yandell, David Wendell, 1826-1898, 15786
Yandell, Lunsford Pitts, 1805-1878, 5784, 5785, 15787
Yanger, Samuel, 25376
The Yankee, 10760
A Yankee among the nullifiers, 9653, 9654
Yankee chronology, 2136
The Yankee conscript, 3454
Yankee doddle court, 8824
Yankee doodle Dixie, 10686
Yankee farming, 9041
A Yankee in Canada, with Anti-slavery papers, 25690

The Yankee in London, 11221
Yankee land and the Yankees, 23126
Yankee notions, 10101
The Yankee roué, 10492
The Yankee slave-dealer, 25938
The Yankee traveller, 11222
The Yankee's story, 9618
Yankees in Japan, 10071
The Yankey in London, 11037
Yaradee, 24434
Yardley, Edmund, 8425
The Yares of the Black mountains, 9355
Yarico to Inkle, an epistle, 22709
Yarmouth, N.S., History, 21832
Yarmouth Co., N.S., Geneal., 6194;
  History, 6194
Yarns of a Kentucky admiral, 15291
Yates, Andrew, 1772-1844, 21833
Yates, Edward, 1829-1864, 25939
Yates, John Van Ness, 1779-1839, 23640
Yates, Lorenzo Gordin, 17938
Yates, Richard, 1818-1873, 7813, 25940
Yates, Robert, 1738-1801, 12204
Yates, William, 25941
Yazoo land companies, 1346
Ye book of copperheads, 24819
Ye olde Shaker bells, 14218
Yeadon, Richard, 25942
Yeaman, George Helm, 1829-1908, 8426
The year, with other poems, 22964
A year book of Kentucky woods and
  fields, 13948
A year in the great republic, 2639
A year of American travel, 16553
A year of breakthrough, 19582
The year of the Cats, 15788
A year of wreck, 8782
A year with the Franklins, 8952
A year worth living, 8661
A year's residence in the United States
  of America, 3039
Yeary, Mamie, 1876-, 17940
A yellow dog, 6971
Yellow fever, 735, 11572, 11779, 11910,
  12914, 13752, 13763; Brazil, 19501;
  British Guiana, 25276; Havana, 1128;
  History, 22952; Jamaica, 459; Moultrie,
  Fort, 1782; New York (City), 86, 988,
  12449, 12672; Norfolk, Va., 1855, 452,
  11903; Philadelphia, 1792, 1820, 11910,
  13284, 13133, 21848, 22091; Philadelphia,
  1798, 2022, 11909; Portsmouth, Va.,
  1855, 11903; Prevention, 12757;
  Preventive inoculation, 23117
Yellow fever, and deer hunt, 10310
Yellow poplar, 14804; Kentucky's state

  tree, 15063
Yellowstone Expedition, 1819, 4625, 4901,
  17860
Yellowstone highway, 17941
Yellowstone National Park, 16722, 16979,
  17284, 17429, 17776; Description & travel,
  17092; Guide-books, 17941
Yellowstone River, 2572, 4901
Yellowstone valley, Description & travel,
  17092
The Yemassee, 10784
Yepes Trujillo, Rafael, 18818
Yermah the Dorado, 9067
Yerrinton, James M.W., d.1893, 25202
Yesterday and today in Arkansas, 15893
Yet one warning more, 681
Yieger's cabinet, 5657
The yield of sugar cane in Barbabos in 1968,
  20214
Yoakum, Henderson K., 1810-1856, 5786
Yohn, F.C., illustr., 2547, 9553, 9555, 9557,
  9558, 10961
The yoke and burden, 8813
Yonge, Francis, 5787, 5788
Yonkers, N.Y., History, 21763
York, Lem A., 17541
York, Pa., 22318
York Factory express journal, 16474
Yorktown, 9300
Yorktown, Va., Siege, 1781, 2248, 3796, 4124,
  12097, 12352, 13473, 23428; Siege, 1781,
  Fiction, 9300; Siege, 1781, Poetry, 3928
The Yosemite, 16087
Yosemite Valley, 16200, 17572; Description &
  travel, Views, 12815, 16650; Guide-books,
  22625
You and me, 8832
Youma, 9833
Youmans, E. Grant, 15789
Youmans, Edward Livingston, 1821-1887, 6740
Young, Alexander, 1800-1854, 23826
Young, Arthur, 5789
Young, Arthur, 1741-1820, 23754
Young, Bennett Henderson, 1843-1919, 1167,
  13973, 14031, 15790-15794
Young, Brigham, 1801-1877, 3679, 5790, 10613,
  17011, 17068, 17761, 17943, 17945
Young, Charles, 1865-1922, 14973
Young, David M., 15795
Young, Edward, 1814-1909, 1356
Young, Edward James, 1829-1906, 8427
Young, Egerton Ryerson, 1840-1909, 8428
Young, Frederick George, 1858-, 17072, 17642,
  17936, 17943, 17944
Young, J.H., 25943
Young, Jacob, 1776-1859, 5791

Young, James Lewis, 1837-1878, 13712
Young Jo., assumed author, 12087
Young, John Clarke, 1803-1857, 4851, 15187, 15796-15798
Young, John R., 17945
Young, Lot D., 1842-, 17599
Young, Milton, 14043
Young, Thomas M., 5792
Young, W.A., 5793
Young, William Henry, 5794
Young Lopez, Norton, 20300
The young abolitionists, 10059
Young Abraham Lincoln and Log College, 7070
A young American in England, 10310
The young captive prince, 9459
The young Carolinian of 1776, 8848
The young chief of the Abenaquies, 9986
A young Christian's choice, 10389
The young citizen's catechism, 12951
Young County (Texas) war, 1857, 17191
The young disciple, 9008
The young emigrants, 8226
The young franctireurs and their adventures in the Franco-Prussian War, 7011
A young girl's wooing, 10656
Young Goodman Brown, 9823
Young Greer of Kentucky, 10140
Young knighthood, 10471
A young lady of the state of New York, 9542
The young lady's friend, 10679
The young marooners on the Florida Coast, 3656
Young men, 957
Young Men's Association of the City of Lockport, 24623
Young Men's Christian Association, Chicago, 8429
Young Men's Democratic Club, Philadelphia, 12269
Young Men's Republican Union, New York, 8430, 25651
The young mill-wright & miller's guide, 12100
Young Miss Giddy, 10551
The young mountaineers, 4567
The young pilot of the Belle Creole, 3843
Young Robin Gray, 6963
Young Women's Christian Association, Louisville, Ky, 14885
Younger, Cole, 1844-1916, 15862, 16079, 16407
Younger, Henry Washington, d.1862, 15862
Younger, James Henry, 1848-, 15862, 16079
Younger, John, 1850-1874, 15862
Younger, Robert Ewing, 15862, 16079
The Younger brothers, 16052

The Youngers' fight for freedom, 16052
The youngest prospector in Calaveras, 9793
Yount, Charles Allen, 8431
Your Kentucky Historical Society, 14934
Yourtree, Samuel L., d.1880, 8432
Youth, 18122; Religious life, 18617; Rural, Costa Rica, 21744
Youth and manhood, 10264
Youth and other things, 15061
The youth of Jefferson, 9118
A youth's history of the great Civil War in the United States from 1861 to 1865, 15800
Yucatan, 6612, 7836, 7998, 8433; Antiquities, 1830, 5932, 6406, 6407, 7590, 19495; Description & travel, 3491, 5932, 5986, 7590, 8109; History, 2215, 5825, 7231, 7465, 21766; Politics & government, 7465
Yukon river and valley, Description & travel, 7982, 16727; History, 7630
Yukon Territory, 7630, 17251; Bibliography, 7328; Description & travel, 7369, 8012, 16727
Yurami, Antonio Miguel, 8434
Yusef, 8880

Zabel, Eugene, 1851-, 5795
Zaborowski-Moindron, Sigismond, 1851-, 25944
Zabriskie, Andrew Christian, 1853-, 8435
Zabriskie, James C., 25945
Zacatecas, Mexico, Festivals, etc., 6160
Zacatecas, Mexico, Santo Domingo (Church), 5803
Zadoc Pine, 8899
Zamora Castellanos, Pedro, jt. author, 7686
Zamorano, Rodrigo, b.ca.1542, 8436, 23823
Zannini, Alessandro, conte, 5796
Zanzibar, 25137; Description & travel, 11576
Zapapan, Mexico, Santuario de Nuestra Señora, 6754
Zapata, Ciénaga de, 20687
Zapotec language, Dialects, Mitla (Oaxaca), 19490
Zaragoza, Ignacio, 1829-1862, 18579
Zaragoza, Justo, d.1896, 6789
Zaragoza, Lorenzo de, 19855
Zárate, Julio, 1844-1917, 7873
Zarco, João Gonçalves, ca.1400-ca.1465, 129
Zaremba, Charles W., 8437
Zavala, Lorenzo de, 1788-1836, 5797
Zayas Montero, Lorenzo, 18085
Zehntausend meilen im sattel vom kreuz des südens zum polarstern, 8243

Zeigler, Wilbur Gleason, 5798
Zeitlin and Ver Brugge, booksellers, Los Angeles, 15801
Zelayeta, Martin de, d.1756, 8145
Zelotes, pseud., 5799
Zenaida, 8536
Zenana missions, 8852
Zenger, John Peter, 1680?-1746, defendant, 23827
Zenkovich, Vsevolod Pavlovich, 1910-, 8438
Zeno, Antonio, d. ca. 1405, 22285
Zeno, Niccolo, d. ca. 1395, 22285
Zeolitic rocks, Cuba, 20627
Zepeda Rincón, Tomás, 8439, 8440
Zerecero, Anastasio, 1799-1875, 8441
Zes maanden in Amerika, 5309
Zetina Infante, Juan Pablo, 6269
Zettlemayer, Charles, 14618, 15802, 15803
Zettler, Berrien McPherson, 1842-, 5800
De zevende haven, 7159
Ziegler, Eustace Paul, illustr., 4568
Zigzag, Zelotes, pseud., 5799
A zigzag journey in the sunny South, 2870
Zigzag journeys on the Mississippi, 2871
Zimmermann, Erich Walter, 1888-, 17571
Zimmermann, Karl, 5801
Zimmermann, Margaret Hoff, 17571
Zinc, 14173; Kentucky, 15005
Zincke, Foster Barham, 1817-1893, 5802
Zinzendorf, Nicolaus Ludwig, graf von, 1700-1760, 1027
Zion's harp, 15169
Zipaquira, Colombia, Historical houses, etc., 20507

Zoë, 4283
Zollicoffer, Felix Kirk, 1812-1862, 25762
Zoltowski, Joseph Johann Maria von, 1847-, 25946
Zoological specimens, Collection and preservation, 23401
Zoology, 22660, 22740; Arctic regions, 4956; Argentine republic, 1719; Classification, 107; French Guiana, 680; Kentucky, 13576, 14156, 14694; Massachusetts, 12329, 22502, 23265; Mexico, 7549; New York, 22660; North America, 12150, 16164; Oregon, 5445; Pará, 18116; South America, 7092; Southwest, New, 5513; U.S., 107; Subterranean, 15111
Zoroaster, 6509, 9237
Zulia, Venezuela (State), History, 19483
Zuloaga, Joaquin de, 6386
Zuni River, 5517
Zúñiga Montúfar, Tobías, 8442
Zur Lehre vom Sklavenerwerb, Ein Beitrag zur Dogmatik des römischen privatrechts, 25434
Zur strafrechtlichen Stellung der Sklaven bei Deutschen und Angelsachsen, 24671
Zürich, Comité zur unterstützung der befreitein farbigen, 12295
Zurita, Alonso de, 1511 or 12, 23828
Zurita, Fernando, 8443
Zustände in Amerika, 23950
Zuvekas, Clarence, 19084
Zwei briefe aus Amerika, 15032
Zyx and his fairy, 8868

Adamson, Sydney, 13824
Almeida, Nicholas, 18138
Anderson, Alexander, 1775-1870, 12851
Andrade, 7955
Andrew, John, 4403, 17687
Anthony, A.V.S., 17336
Asche, E.M., 2546
Bache, René, 10253
Ballinger, H.R., 15091
Bame, H.D., 8630
Barry, Etheldred B., 2613
Bauerle, Charles, 4283
Bayliss, Lilian, 13824
Beard, Daniel Carter, 1850-1941, 13618
Bedford, Cornelia E., 9268
Bellorin, José Francisco, 19952
Berger, W.M., 15265
Bessau, Oscar, 4215
Betts, Louis, 13704
Bewick, Thomas, 1753-1828, 82
Bianco, Enrico, 20073
Bowen, William Clayton, 13696, 15447
Brock, Charles E., 11159
Brown, Virginia Stuart, 5816
Burr, Helen M., 13745
Caddy, Alice, 2860
Carleton, Clifford, 9581
Castaigne, A., 6492
Cavalcanti, Emiliano di, 1894-, 2002, 18233
Champney, J. Wells, 4173, 14749
Chao, Villar, 18546
Chapman, J. Linton, 11196
Cheney, J., 2513
Cheney, S.W., 2513
Christy, Howard Chandler, 3639, 9360
Church, Frederick C., 24562
Clark, Walter Appleton, 22579
Clinedienst, V. West, 9637, 25191
Coffin, Frederick M., 10476
Cowles, The Misses, 25189
Crafty, 4381
Crockett, Ingram, 1856-, 13947, 13948
Croome, William, 12174
Cruikshank, George, 1792-1878, 24594
Cruikshank, Isaac Robert, 1789-1850, 4806
Darley, Felix Octavius Carr, 1822-1888, 1747, 3840, 4832, 4833, 5403, 5405, 5411, 5460, 9453, 10000, 10361, 10964, 11101, 22157
Day, Francis, 9534

Deland, Clyde O., 2982, 6520
Dickey, Robert, 25075
Dillard, Ruth, 14167
Doré, Gustave, 1832-1883, 7396
Duer, Douglas, 13731, 13732
Earl, J.C., 8516
Eastman, Seth, 1808-1875, 2163, 11996
Eaton, H.M., 5392
Eytinge, Sol, 8156, 11113, 11114
Fenn, Harry, 8516, 13704
Fisher, Harrison, 9569
Flameng, Leopold, 1831-, 1123
Forestier, A., 10894
Forrest, Archibald Stevenson, 7006
Fortuna, J., 18204
Fraser, Malcolm, 4567, 5192
Fredericks, Alfred, 9805
Garnsey, John Henderson, 9817
Garrett, Edmund H., 14466
Gasche, Charles, 7886
Gascon, Elvira, 19898
Gibson, Charles Dana, 1867-1944, 8674, 9361, 9362, 9637
Gilbert, A., 4048
Giles, Howard, 13704
Gordon, J.S., 8252
Grau, Ricardo, 18975
Greatorex, Eleanor, 15805
Green, Jasper, 10049
Groome, W., 6785
Gruger, F.R., 13541, 14159, 14961, 15262
Guard, Louis, 17687
Guerrero, Miguel, 6754
Guipon, Leon, 15266
Hall, Sydney, 5926
Hapgood, Theodore, 15092
Harlow, Louis K., 3219
Hartman, 13947
Hassam, F. Childe, 1859-1935, 17735
Healy, 10520
Heming, Arthur Henry Howard, 1870-, 8252
Henry, J., 14351
Herndon, Robert, 14897
Heustis, Louise L., 10429
Hill, Paul T., 3316
Holloway, Edward, 8800
Hoppin, Augustus, 1828-1896, 1775, 9289, 9291, 10049
Howard, J.H., 10536, 10538
Hows, Iohn A., 11592, 12742
Huntington, Charles S., 13481, 17641

Hyde, W.H., 9637
Jacobs, W.L., 25187
Johnson, D. Vertner, 4053
Johnston, David Claypoole, 1797-1865,
    10414
Justice, Martin, 13977
Keller, Arthur I., 5192, 9553, 24296
Kemble, E.W., 2741, 3192, 4091, 10896
Kern, Edward M., 5167
Kilburn, 10789
Knapp, J. Augustus, 10224
Lau, Persy, 20073
Ledyard, Addie, 10392
Lees, James Arthur, 7259
Lincoln, A.W.B., 9533
Lloyd, James T., 14840
Lovie, Henry, 4283
Lowell, Orson, 4087, 10886
Lumley, 4759
McCutcheon, John T., 8479, 16753
McFall, J.V., 15093
Mack, Mrs. R.E., 12020
M'Laughlin, Charles, 3681
M'Lenan, John, 3004, 10922, 17336
MacLeod, William, 12696
McMillan, Mary Lane, 14159
Mallory, 10789
Marchard, J.N., 13704
Martin-Chablis, 4381
Martin, Stefan, 15001
Merrill, Frank T., 9592, 12629, 13619,
    16082
Meyer, Catherine B., 14885
Miskell, Tim, 13611
Mitchell, John, 15608
Momberger, 12554
Montagu, Irving, 3646
Montgomery, Riley B., 15447
Moore, Bethuel, 14473
Moore, Dorthy H., 14280
Morehead, J.N., 24299
Morgan, Ike, 4902
Moser, James H., 24562
Nankivell, F.A., 10998
Narjot, Ernest, 16482
Neill, John R., 14272
Nelson, A. Patrick, 15092
Newell, Peter, 10889, 10896
Newman, C.J., 8477
Norton, John W., 16693
Orr, J.W., 4403
Orr, N., 4403, 4903, 4924
Overache, 10520
Pairpoint, Miss N.M., 4680
Palmer, Sutton, 15886
Peixoto, Ernest, 4565

Phillips, John M., 7063
Piercy, Frederick, 4281,
    17387
Pitney, A. de F., 13704
Plaschke, Paul A., 15051
Plummer, W. Kirtman, 15476
Pollen, A.H., 8074
Potthast, Edward, 25639
Prichard, Walt, 15053
Prieto, Julio, 5969
Prittie, Edwin J., 16467
Pyle, Howard, 1853-1911, 9376
Rae, John, 15397
Ransom, H.C., 9553
Reinhart, Charles Stanley, 1844-1896,
    10809, 11090
Remington, Frederic, 10608, 14350, 17467,
    17468, 17469
Rengifo, César, 18534
Roberts, Louis A., 10862
Roche, Emily Langdon, 25406
Rogers, W.A., 9553
Rugendas, Johann Moritz, 1802-1858, 7965,
    7966
Sandhum, Henry, 16870
Sary, Tony, 13859
Savage, Charles R., 17081
Schell, Fred B., 9006
Scherer, Marie Luise, 3586
Scheuerle, Joe, 5583
Sheppard, W.L., 4795, 5419, 9006
Shober, Charles, 12721
Shouse, Frances Johnson Taylor, 14258
Simoncini, Aldo, 19154
Small, Frank O., 10896
Smedley, W.T., 3365, 9694, 9916, 10896,
    11088, 14132
Smirke, R., 25285
Snapp, Frank, 13733
Sprague, Isaac, 1811-1895, 12355
Stecher, W.F., 2635
Stellman, Louis J., 17666
Stephens, Alice Barber, 9577, 10896
Stephens, Henry Louis, 1824-1882, 9910,
    10537
Strong, Beulah, 15090A
Sullivan, M.A., 5186, 25529
Taber, I.W., 5004
Tangorra-Mitano, Angelo, 25688
Thiel, Johannes, 2693
Tourgée, Aimée, 10994, 10995
Wade, Charles T., 14897, 15533
Walcutt, 10520
Wallen, S., 4403
Weeden, Howard, 25075
Weir, Harrison William, 1824-1906, 3594,

Aba, B., 4195
Achates, 25278
Addums, Moses, 2590, 2591
Adeler, Max, 9006
Alvarez, Alonzo, 25861
Amaru, Severino, 7516
Ambrose, Paul, 24710
Amelia, 5669
An American soldier, 10601
Americanus, 11879
Americus, 23894
Amicus republicae, 332
Ana, Marcos, 18253
Anglo-Californian, 378
Appomattox, 23912
Arimand, 5306
Aristides, 12652, 12653
Aristodemus, 1516
Bard, Samuel A., 13485
Barton, Andrew, 926
Biblicus, 25138
Boisgilbert, Edmund, 9412
Bonner, Sherwood, 14899
Boylston, Peter, 9268
Bradford, Annie Chambers, 10098
Bramantip, Bocardo, 6243
Brent, Linda, 10008
Bricktop, 10792, 19793, 10794,
   10795, 19796, 10797, 10798
Brimblecomb, Nicholas, 1527
Broaderick, Cephas, 9613
Browne, Dunn, 3457
Brutus, Lucius Junius, 11587
Brydges, Harold, 2800
Bull-us, Hector, 10482
Buntline, Ned, 10078, 10079,
   10080, 10081
Caius Gracchus, 24074
Camillus, 12801
Campbell, Scott, 9343
Candidus, 24833
Canot, Capitaine, 21487
Caxton, Laura, 9088
Cecil, E., 11703
Cher, Henry W.B., 11773
Cincinnatus, L. Quincius, 21931
Civis, 11797
Civis Anglicus, 21934
Clarice, 20206
Clark, Henry Scott, 13932
Columbus, 17323, 24172
Colvil, Edward, 10581
Comitatus, Zedekiah, 11868
Conciliator, 2017

Concolorcorvo, 19852
Conyngham, Dave, 9278
Cornelison, J.H., 13715
Corporal, 3729
Cosmopolite, 10172
Crambe, 4887
Crayon, Geoffrey, 9996, 10001, 10002
Crowfield, Christopher, 10902
Curtuis, 5355
Cymon, 10828
Czeika, 5594
Dale, J.S., 964
Decino, 11966
Declaves, Alonso, 13982
Democratus, 24279
Denslow, W.W., 4902
Depuson, 25682
Dulac, George, 10507
Eaves, Catherine, 6656
Elivas, Knarf, 10709
Ellington, George, 12025
Epaminondas, 12068
Escritor, 9068
Etheridge, Kelsic, 10825
Evangelicus, 24363
Falcon, 15394
Fern, Fanny, 10476-10479
Ferry, Gabriel, 6065
Fischer, Grete, 10713
Foley, Fanny, 2260
Forester, Fanny, 10084
Franklin, 3526
Free Suffrage, 3534, 14140
Freeport, Andrew, 6783
Garretson, Hans van, 10714
Gerard, Just, 1794-1870, 3618
Goldsmith, Christabel, 10805, 10806
Gordon, Julien, 9257, 9258, 9259, 9260,
   9261, 9262, 9263, 9264, 9265
Goussencourt, Chevalier de, 4654
Gracchus, 14206
Gray, Barry, 9060
Green-back, 12387
Greenwood, Grace, 16632
Grile, Dod, 8802
Grotius, 12468
Gruff, Growler, 11933
Haco, Dion, 8133, 22282
Hall, Eliza Calvert, 15091, 15092, 15093
Hambden, 12595
Hamilton, Gail, 3262
Hamilton, Henry, 5236, 5242
Hampden, 12635
Hannibal, Julius Caesar, 10198

Harlan, Marion, 8167, 10163, 10934,
  10935, 10936, 10937, 10938, 10939,
  10940, 10941, 10942, 10943, 10944,
  10945, 10946
Hazel, Harry, 10068, 10069, 10070,
  10071
Helfenstein, Ernest, 10804
Henry, Patrick, 13588
Hibernian, 9991
Historicus, 12668, 12669
Hold-fast, Simon, 12844
Hood, Fred, 3981
Hope, Anthony, 9804
Huber, 8458
Humanitas, 24636
Hyder Ali, 14746
Impartial, 572
Iron Gray, 25680
Jahnsenykes, Rev. Williamson, 10033
Janus, 13160
Japheth, 24670
Jenkins, Geoffrey, 22703
Johnson, S.M., 24458
Johnson, Tom, 14217
Jonathan, 4098
Jones, Pleasant, 10861
Joseph, 13330
Junius, 12277, 12432, 13352, 14488
Junius, jr., 13353
Junius redivivus, 25097
Juvenis, 23862
Keckley, Betsy, 7177
Kirk, Edmund, 3610, 3611, 3612, 3613,
  9621, 9622, 9623, 14190
Lacon, 24750
Lafayette, 14778
Laicus, Philipp, 6074
Lambert Lilly, 12754
Landas, K., 6535
Lander, Meta, 10169
Legion, 24813
Lennox, Mary, 9103
Libertas, 6669, 11570
Luther, jr., 24918
Madeleine, 7388
Magaul, Michael, 24925
Mandar-Argeaut, 23071
Manton, Kate, 10155
Marcellus, 23122
Martingale, Hawser, 10788
Marvel, Ik, 10360, 10362
Mary V.V., 2107
Mason, Stuart, 5704
Massachusetts Junior, 25004
Maurier, Jacques, 10386

Medico, 25024
Medley, Mat, 2564
Mercator, 6668
Meridionus, O.R., 25198
Mistral, Gabriela, 6861
Montaignes, François des, 4504
Montgomery, Cora, 2957, 8958
Moore, Will Beno, 5706
Morris, John, 4635
Munchausen, Baron, jr., 10384
Murgatroyd, Matthew, 10061
Myrthe, A.T., 9598
Nasby, Petroleum V., 10226, 10227, 10228,
  10229, 10230
Nestor, 94
Nolden, Arnold, 7741
Novangius, 11246
Nox, Owen, 3094, 3095
Old Coon, 13569
Oldfellow, Polywarp, 10799
Omicron, 15100
Onesimus Secundus, 25175
Opimius, 24074
O'Rell, Max, 2741
Otis, Belle, 11202
Pacificator
Palacios, Lucila, 19860
Pantoja, Domingo de, 4872
Parker, Theodoro, 23941
Paterson, Paul, 4806
A patriot, 6792
Paxton, Philip, 3763
Peabody, Mark, 11043
Pencil, Mark, 4743
Pennsylvanian, 25420
Perkins, Eli, 10162
Peters, 10824
Philalethes, 23511
Philanthropos, 25249
Philo, 25806
Philo Africanus, 24833
Philo-Bentham, 1180
Philo-Jackson, 13455
Philo-Xylon, 25264
Pickle, Peregrine, 11040
A planter, 25697
Playfair, Hugo R.N., 4806
Poliuto, 5709
Porcupine, Peter, 5841
Prado, Pedro, 9000
Python, 25360
Qorpo-Santo, 19716, 19717
Quandary, Christopher, 23516
Rambler, 4889
Ramp, A.T., 3261

Randolph, Thornton, 10509
Raymond, Grace, 5283
Regulus, 11968
Reid, Christian, 10966, 10967, 10968,
    10969, 10970, 10972, 10973
Richards, Robert, 4948
Riley, Ralph, 16067
Rivers, Pearl, 4604
Rivolba, 2754
Romaine, Dexter, 10492
Ross, Albert, 10551
Rubek, Sennoia, 1710
Rubio, 4043, 7134
Rusticus, 6531
Sampleton, Samuel, 7523
Sand, George, 1804-1876, 1104
Scotus, Americanus, 5109
Shortfield, Luke, 4116
Simpson, Benjamin, 4830
Sincerus, 1516
Singleton, Arthur, 4188
Sketchley, Arthur, 5013
Skitt, 10922
Spectator, 25753
Steven, son of Douglas, 6115
Strahan, Edward, 5144
Strebor, Eiggam, 10630
Sylvestrus, 5479
Thanet, Octave, 9581
Thistle, Timothy, 9481
Thulstrup, Thule de, 5116, 6622, 9352
Trevitanus, 24871
Trusta, 10515
Ubique, 12257, 16601
Underhill, Updike, 11036
Urrea, Blas, 6268
V., Mary V., 2107
Vaquero, 8289
Vera, 4277
Vernon, Ruth, 10585
Villiot, Jean de, 25807
A Virginian, 315
A volunteer, 25678
Wait, Frona Eunice, 9067
Warbler, Forest, 10267
Western, 5676
Wetherell, Elizabeth, 11097
Wildfire, Walter, 21974
Wildwood, Warren, 15715
Wildwood, Will, 3758
Winchester, Carroll, 9284, 9285
Zelotes, 5799
Zigzag, Zelotes, 5799

T